The Handbook of
SOCIAL PSYCHOLOGY

SECOND EDITION

Edited by GARDNER LINDZEY and ELLIOT ARONSON
University of Texas

VOLUME FIVE
APPLIED SOCIAL PSYCHOLOGY

ADDISON-WESLEY PUBLISHING COMPANY
Reading, Massachusetts
Menlo Park, California · London · Amsterdam · Don Mills, Ontario · Sydney

ISBN 0-201-04266-5
EFGHIJKLMN-HA-79876

Preface to the First Edition

The accelerating expansion of social psychology in the past two decades has led to an acute need for a source book more advanced than the ordinary textbook in the field but yet more focused than scattered periodical literature. Murchison's *Handbook of Social Psychology* (1935), the only previous attempt to meet this need, is out of date and out of print. It was this state of affairs that led us to assemble a book that would represent the major areas of social psychology at a level of difficulty appropriate for graduate students. In addition to serving the needs of graduate instruction, we anticipate that the volumes will be useful in advanced undergraduate courses and as a reference book for professional psychologists.

We first considered the possibility of preparing a *Handbook* three years ago. However, a final decision to proceed with the plan was not reached until the fall of 1951. During the interval we arranged an outline of topics that represented our convictions concerning the present state of social psychology. We then wrote to a large number of distinguished social psychologists asking them whether they felt our venture was likely to be professionally valuable and asking for criticisms of the outline we had prepared. The response to these letters was immensely gratifying—social psychologists as a group appear sufficiently altruistic to spend large amounts of time criticizing and commenting on a project of which they approve even though they may be unable to participate in it themselves. We also asked for specific recommendations of people who seemed best qualified to prepare the various chapters. After receiving answers we drastically revised our outline and proceeded to invite authors to prepare the various chapters. It was not until the spring of 1952 that we completed our list of contributors and even this list later underwent change. We first suggested (tongue in cheek) that the manuscripts be submitted by September 15, 1952. However, as we secretly expected, we were forced to change this due date to January 1, 1953. This "deadline" we tried hard to meet. But of course we failed and shifted our aspiration to June 15, 1953. Again we failed, although by now we were making substantial progress. By early in the fall of 1953 we had all the chapters excepting two, and the first volume was completed and in the hands of the publishers. The last two chapters were not received until early in 1954, when the second volume went to press.

Something should be said concerning the basis for the organization of the subject matter of these volumes. It became apparent early that there are many ways to subdivide social psychology but very little agreement concerning just which is best. Although we sought the advice of others, we found for almost every compelling suggestion an equally compelling countersuggestion. Thus, in the end, it was necessary to make many arbitrary decisions. So much for our knowledge that the *Handbook* could have been organized in many different ways. There is no single scheme that would satisfy all readers.

We early discovered that the subject matter was too voluminous to be contained in a single volume. Given this decision it seemed quite natural to present in one volume the chapters that dealt primarily with theoretical convictions or systematic positions, and also the methods and procedures commonly employed in social psychology. Likewise it seemed wise to present in one volume those chapters that focus upon the substantive findings and applications of social psychology. The decision to place the historical introduction, theory, and method chapters in the first volume reflects a bias in favor of investigation that begins with an awareness of the message of the past, an attempt at theoretical relevance, and finally with a full knowledge of the procedural or measurement alternatives. All of the content of the first volume is seen, at least by the editor, as a necessary preparation for good investigation. These are the things the social psychologist should know before he lifts a single empirical finger. The second volume, then, can be seen as a justification of the contents of the first volume. Here are the empirical fruits stemming from the theories and methods summarized in the first volume.

But does this ideal scheme mirror common practice? Are the major empirical advances summarized in the second volume in reality a legitimate by-product of theoretical conceptions and sophisticated method? In fairness to science in action (as opposed to science on the books) we are afraid the answer is No. Social psychology has made its advances largely on the shoulders of random empiricists and naive realists. Inability to distinguish between analytic and synthetic and a tendency toward reification of concepts has accompanied many of the most significant advances in this field. Who would say that those who view an attitude as a "construct" created by the investigator have made more of a contribution to this area of psychology than those who naively view attitudes as real and concrete entities? Thus we sorrowfully admit the organization we have imposed upon the *Handbook* may bear little relation to the path thus far trod in the development of social psychology. Nevertheless, it stands as a suggestion of the manner in which future development may well take place and as a reminder that the powerful weapon of systematic theory is now more nearly within the grasp of the wise psychologist than formerly. Where yesterday the theoretically oriented investigator and the random realist may have been on even terms, recent developments within the field may well have destroyed this equality. An approach efficient in the wilderness may be foolish in a more carefully mapped region. In summary, the precedence we give to theoretical positions reflects our conviction of the importance of theories as spurs to research, but may also represent a program for the future rather than a reflection of the past.

It must be conceded that not all areas of social psychology are covered in these volumes with equal thoroughness. Some gaps are due to the blind spots of the editor while others are the result of contributors failing to cover an area they originally agreed to cover and, in a few cases, to contributors who withdrew altogether. In spite of these shortcomings, the volumes in their present state provide the most comprehensive picture of social psychology that exists in one place today.

While deficiencies of the final product are my own responsibility, they exist in spite of a number of advisors who gave their time and energy generously throughout the venture. Of these collaborators none was nearly so important as Gordon Allport. In fairness he should be co-editor of the volume, as he contributed immeasurably both in matters of policy and in matters of detail. I owe a very special debt of gratitude to my wife Andrea for her tolerance, encouragement, and detailed assistance. Likewise of great importance is the contribution of Shirley H. Heinemann, who has been of constant help throughout the editorial process and in preparing the Index. Crucial to the success of this work were various additional colleagues who served as referees, reading individual chapters and suggesting changes and deletions. On this score I express my gratitude to Raymond Bauer, Anthony Davids, Edward E. Jones, Kaspar Naegele, David Schneider, and Walter Weiss. In addition, many of the contributors served as referees for chapters other than their own. I am indebted to E. G. Boring, S. S. Stevens, and Geraldine Stone for many helpful suggestions based on their experience in arranging the *Handbook of Experimental Psychology*. Mrs. Olga Crawford of Addison-Wesley played an indispensable role in final preparation of the manuscripts.

April 1954   G. L.

Preface to the Second Edition

In the fourteen years that have elapsed since the last edition of this *Handbook*, the field of social psychology has evolved at a rapid rate. The present volumes are intended to represent these changes as faithfully as possible and at a level appropriate for the beginning graduate student as well as the fully trained psychologist.

The reader familiar with the previous *Handbook* will realize that we have employed the same general outline in the present volumes. The many new chapters reflect the increased quantitative and methodological sophistication of social psychologists, the development of certain specialized areas of research, and the increased activity in a variety of applied areas. In some instances we have attempted to compensate for known deficiencies in the coverage of the previous edition.

One can never be certain of portraying adequately the changes in a large and diverse area of scholarship, but we can be certain that this *Handbook* is very different from its predecessor. It is substantially larger—instead of one million words, two volumes, and 30 chapters, there are now approximately two and one-half million words, five volumes, and 45 chapters. We are convinced that our decision to present this material in five volumes will increase its utility for those who have specialized interests linked to either teaching or research activities. But the difference goes beyond mere size. The list of contributors has a decidedly new flavor—of the 45 authors in the previous edition, only 22 have contributed to this volume. Viewed from another vantage, of the 68 authors contributing to the current volume, 46 are represented in the *Handbook* for the first time. Only one chapter is reprinted without a thorough revision, and this, an essay (Hebb and Thompson) presenting a point of view that seems little affected by recent research and formulation. There are 15 chapters that are completely new and, in addition, a number of the replacements bear little resemblance to the chapter of the same, or similar, title that appeared earlier.

Plans for the current revision were begun in January of 1963. By July of that year a tentative chapter outline had been prepared and distributed to an array of distinguished social scientists, including the previous contributors to the *Handbook*. We benefited materially from the advice of dozens of persons in regard to both the chapter outline and the nomination of potential authors; we are grateful for their efforts on behalf of the *Handbook*. By fall of 1963 we had succeeded in constructing a final outline and a list of contributors. Our initial letters of invitation asked that completed manuscripts be submitted by January 1, 1965. We managed to obtain the bulk of the chapters eighteen months and several deadlines later, and the first two volumes were sent to the publishers early in 1967. The final chapters were secured the following July, when the remaining volumes went to press.

In selecting contributors we made every effort, within the general constraints of technical competence and availability, to obtain scholars of diverse professional and institutional backgrounds. Thus, we take special pleasure in the fact that almost all areas of the country are well represented, that six of the contributors are affiliated with institutions outside the United States, and that the authors include political scientists, sociologists, and anthropologists as well as psychologists.

We consider it extremely fortunate that of the chapters listed in our working out-line, all of those that we regarded as "key" or central chapters are included here. Indeed, there are only three chapters from that list that are not a part of the present volumes; this includes one (attitude change) that was deliberately incorporated within another chapter because such an arrangement seemed to offer a greater likelihood of satisfactory integration and coverage. It should be noted that this success is in marked contrast to the previous *Handbook,* where such essential areas as attitudes and social perception were omitted because of last-minute delinquencies. Although a few invited contributors did withdraw from the present *Handbook* after initially having agreed to prepare a chapter, in all cases we were fortunate in being able to find equally qualified replacements who were willing to take on this assignment on relatively short notice. To these individuals we owe a special debt of gratitude.

We wish to acknowledge the indispensable assistance of Judith Hilton, Shirley Cearley, and Leslie Segner in connection with the final preparation of the manuscript. Finally, we would like to express our gratitude to Mary Jane Whiteside for her tireless efforts in the final indexing of all volumes of the *Handbook.*

February 1968   G. L.
Austin, Texas   E. A.

Acknowledgments

The Editors wish to thank a number of publishers and copyright holders for permission to reproduce tables, figures, and excerpts from the following sources:

Abingdon Press: P. E. Johnson, *Psychology of Religion* (rev. ed., 1959).

Aldine Publishing Company: R. D. Hess and J. V. Torney, *The Development of Political Attitudes in Children* (1967).

Allyn & Bacon, Inc.: W. W. Charters, Jr., and N. L. Gage (Eds.), *Readings in the Social Psychology of Education* (1963).

American Association for the Advancement of Science: J. P. Scott, "On the Evolution of Fighting Behavior," in *Science*, Vol. 148 (1965).

The American Political Science Association: A. Campbell and W. E. Miller, "The Motivational Basis of Straight and Split Ticket Voting," in *American Political Science Review*, Vol. 51 (1957); P. E. Converse, A. Campbell, W. E. Miller, and D. E. Stokes, "Stability and Change in 1960: A Reinstating Election," in *American Political Science Review*, Vol. 55 (1961); J. Dennis, "Support for the Party System by the Mass Public," in *American Political Science Review*, Vol. 60 (1966); A. S. Goldberg, "Discerning a Causal Pattern among Data on Voting Behavior," in *American Political Science Review*, Vol. 60 (1966); M. K. Jennings and R. G. Niemi, "The Transmission of Political Values from Parent to Child," in *American Political Science Review*, Vol. 62 (1968); H. McClosky, "Consensus and Ideology in American Politics," in *American Political Science Review*, Vol. 58 (1964); R. E. Wolfinger and F. I. Greenstein, "The Repeal of Fair Housing in California: An Analysis of Referendum Voting," in *American Political Science Review*, Vol. 62 (1968).

Association for Education in Journalism: R. J. Hill and C. M. Bonjean, "News Diffusion: A Test of the Regularity Hypothesis," in *Journalism Quarterly*, Vol. 41 (1964).

Columbia University Press: P. F. Lazarsfeld, B. Berelson, and H. Gaudet, *The People's Choice* (2nd ed., 1948).

Doubleday & Company, Inc.: S. A. Stouffer, *Communism, Conformity, and Civil Liberties* (1955).

Harper & Row, Publishers, Inc.: B. Bettelheim and M. Janowitz, *Dynamics of Prejudice* (1950); S. Lubell, *The Future of American Politics* (3rd ed., 1965); A. Campbell, G. Gurin, and W. E. Miller, *The Voter Decides* (published by Row, Peterson, 1954).

Harvard University Press: A. Davis, *Social Class Influences Upon Learning* (1948); V. O. Key, Jr., *The Responsible Electorate* (published by The Belknap Press of Harvard University Press, 1966).

Holt, Rinehart and Winston, Inc.: E. E. Maccoby, T. M. Newcomb, and E. L. Hartley (Eds.), *Readings in Social Psychology* (1958).

The Journal of Conflict Resolution: M. Deutsch, "Trust and Suspicion," in *Journal of Conflict Resolution*, Vol. 11 (1958).

Alfred A. Knopf, Inc.: V. O. Key, Jr., *Public Opinion and American Democracy* (1961).

Macmillan Company: E. Burdick and A. J. Brodbeck (Eds.), *American Voting Behavior* (published by The Free Press, 1959); J. Gould and W. L. Kolb (Eds.), *A Dictionary of the Social Sciences* (published by The Free Press, 1964); M. Greenblatt, D. J. Levinson, and R. H. Williams (Eds.), *The Patient and the Mental Hospital* (published by The Free Press, 1957); R. E. Lane, *Political Ideology: Why the American Common Man Believes What he Does* (published by The Free Press, 1962); J. Rosenau (Ed.), *Domestic Sources of Foreign Policy* (published by The Free Press, 1967).

Princeton University Press: G. A. Almond and S. Verba, *Civic Culture: Political Attitudes and Democracy in Five Nations* (published by Princeton University Press for the Center for International Studies, 1963).

The Public Opinion Quarterly: P. E. Converse, "Information Flow and the Stability of Partisan Attitudes," in *Public Opinion Quarterly*, Vol. 26 (1962); W. A. Gamson and A. Modigliani, "Knowledge and Foreign Policy Opinions: Some Models for Consideration," in *Public Opinion Quarterly*, Vol. 30 (1966); E. J. Rosi, "Mass and Attentive Opinion on Nuclear Weapons Tests and Fallout, 1954–1963," in *Public Opinion Quarterly*, Vol. 29 (1965); P. B. Sheatsley and J. J. Feldman, "The Assassination of President Kennedy: A Preliminary Report on Public Reactions and Behavior," in *Public Opinion Quarterly*, Vol. 28 (1964).

Rand McNally & Co.: L. W. Milbrath, *Political Participation* (1965).

Random House, Inc.: R. Ellison, *Invisible Man* (published by The New American Library, 1952).

Stanford University Press: W. Schramm, J. Lyle, and E. B. Parker, *Television in the Lives of Our Children* (1961).

University of Chicago, Midwest Administration Center: A. W. Halpin (Ed.), *Administrative Theory in Education* (1958).

University of Illinois Press: C. E. Osgood, *An Alternative to War or Surrender* (1962).

University of Michigan, Survey Research Center: S. B. Withey, *The U.S. and the U.S.S.R.* (1962).

University of Minnesota Press: M. Deutsch and M. E. Collins, *Interracial Housing: A Psychological Evaluation of a Social Experiment* (1951).

University of North Carolina Press: J. Dollard, "Hostility and Fear in Social Life," in *Social Forces,* Vol. 17 (1938).

D. Van Nostrand Company, Inc.: R. K. Goldsen, M. Rosenberg, R. M. Williams, Jr., and E. A. Suchman, *What College Students Think* (1960).

War/Peace Report: C. E. Osgood, "Escalation as a Strategy," in *War/Peace Report,* Vol. 5 (1965).

John Wiley & Sons, Inc.: A. Campbell, P. E. Converse, W. E. Miller, and D. E. Stokes, *The American Voter* (1960) and *Elections and the Political Order* (1966); R. D. Luce and H. Raiffa, *Games and Decisions: Introduction and Critical Survey* (1957); W. W. Waller, *The Sociology of Teaching* (1965).

Yale University Press: F. I. Greenstein, *Children and Politics* (1965).

Contents

Prejudice and Ethnic Relations

JOHN HARDING, *Cornell University*

HAROLD PROSHANSKY, *Brooklyn College*

BERNARD KUTNER, *Albert Einstein College of Medicine*

ISIDOR CHEIN, *New York University*

This field of study is sometimes designated "ethnic relations," sometimes "intergroup relations," and sometimes "race and minority group relations." The last title is the one used in the UNESCO *Dictionary of the Social Sciences* (Rose, 1964). Major writers in the field have usually taken one or another of three quite different approaches. The first may be called the "ethnic group" approach. Here the focus is on a single racial, religious, linguistic, or nationality group, usually one that is a clearly identifiable minority in some modern national state. An attempt is made to describe the group's historical development, cultural traditions, distinctive values, relations with neighboring groups, and changing political and economic fortunes. The classic example of this approach is the five-volume work of Thomas and Znaniecki, *The Polish Peasant in Europe and America* (1918).

The second major point of view may be called the "social interaction" approach. Here the focus is not on a single ethnic group, but on the interrelationships of two or more such groups, frequently on the relationships of all the major ethnic groups in a particular geographical area. Very commonly the analysis is in terms of the major forms of social interaction distinguished by Park and Burgess (1921): competition, conflict, accommodation, and assimilation. One of the best-known examples of this approach is Thompson's *Race Relations and the Race Problem* (1939).

The third major point of view is more recent; Rose calls it the "social problems" approach. Here the focus is on "the behavior of discrimination, the attitude of prejudice, and the consequences for the minority and majority groups of both of these" (Rose, 1964, p. 571). This point of view was first fully elaborated in Myrdal's great and controversial work, *An American Dilemma: The Negro Problem and Modern Democracy* (1944). What makes this approach controversial is the fact that the values of the social scientist are inextricably involved in the key concepts of his analysis:

"prejudice" and "discrimination" are pejorative terms in a way that "competition" and "conflict" are not.

The study of intergroup relations has expanded greatly since World War II, especially in the United States; and many new investigators with a social-problems approach have entered the field. The most widely used textbook at present is probably Simpson and Yinger's *Racial and Cultural Minorities: An Analysis of Prejudice and Discrimination* (3rd ed., 1965). This comprehensive work is written partly from the "social interaction" and partly from the "social problems" point of view; however, the latter approach has become more and more prominent in successive editions of the book.

All the writers mentioned so far have been sociologists in their professional identification. Psychologists have also been active in the field, investigating mainly the attitudes of one ethnic group toward another, or the attitudes toward various "minority groups" of a not very clearly defined population often referred to as "white majority group members." There have been two major points of view among the psychologists. More common has been the social-problems approach already described; here the key concept is that of "prejudice." Less common, especially since World War II, has been an approach that attempts to maintain ethical neutrality and to speak simply of "positive and negative intergroup attitudes."

The social-problems approach dominates both the most widely known textbook by a psychologist, Allport's *The Nature of Prejudice* (1954), and the most influential empirical study, *The Authoritarian Personality* (Adorno et al., 1950). It is characteristic of the social-problems approach that the values of the author are explicit in his treatment of his subject. Textbooks written from this approach usually end with a discussion of possible remedial social action; in Allport (1954) this section is called "Reducing Group Tensions," while in Simpson and Yinger (1965) it is called "Prejudice, Discrimination, and Democratic Values."

The present chapter is written from the social-problems point of view. The authors belong to the generation of American psychologists who became interested in the study of ethnic relations during or at the end of World War II. Our concern with this field has continued precisely because we feel that prejudice and discrimination are "social problems" in the sense defined by Louis Wirth; that is, they represent "an existing situation [that] diverges from a situation which is preferred in accordance with certain values" (Wirth, 1939, p. 4). Like most authors who write from this point of view, we feel that our values do not impair our capacity for objective description and scientific analysis. Our position is essentially that of Myrdal and Rose as stated in their "Methodological Note on Facts and Valuations in Social Science" (Myrdal, 1944, pp. 1035–1064).

Limitations of space and time prevent our attempting a comprehensive discussion of ethnic relations as a social problem. We shall focus mainly on *attitudes* rather than *actions* (that is, on "prejudice" rather than "discrimination"). We shall limit our discussion mainly to prejudice in the United States. We shall discuss primarily attitudes of the so-called "majority group" toward various ethnic minorities, and only secondarily attitudes of these groups toward one another. And we shall barely touch on the question of the identification of ethnic group members with their own groups. These emphases do not represent an arbitrary selection of topics on our part; they reflect rather the major preoccupations of social-psychological research in this area during the past two decades.

DEFINITIONS

The problem of definition is difficult in any field of social science; it is unusually difficult in the field of prejudice and ethnic relations. Although there are a few very widely used key terms, most of these terms are used in somewhat different senses by different authors. Most of the major writers have tried hard to be consistent in their own usage, but they have shown little interest in distinguishing their particular usage of a term like "prejudice" from that of other authors. By far the most serious problem is the lack of correspondence between the conceptual definitions of prejudice advanced by theoretical writers and authors of textbooks and the operational definitions embodied in the measurement procedures used in empirical studies. This lack of correspondence is the main reason why a few major "theories of prejudice" survive unmodified decade after decade while unrelated measurement procedures go on proliferating without any apparent limit.

Definitions in this chapter have been chosen with three major purposes in mind. The first is to conform as well as possible to the usage of a substantial number of writers in the field; the second is to emphasize concepts that are clear and unambiguous; and the third is to provide as much articulation as possible between these concepts and other concepts in psychological and sociological theory. These objectives have led us to depart radically at several points from the definitions proposed in the previous version of this chapter (Harding *et al.*, 1954). So far as possible we have tried to make our new definitions consistent with those in *A Dictionary of the Social Sciences* (Gould and Kolb, 1964).

The basic concept in our field is that contained in one major usage of the term "ethnic group" (Tumin, 1964). An *ethnic group* is a collection of people considered both by themselves and by other people to have in common one or more of the following characteristics: (1) religion, (2) racial origin (as indicated by readily identifiable physical features), (3) national origin, or (4) language and cultural traditions. In primitive and traditional societies these criteria of classification usually vary together, so that it is often possible to find ethnic groups that differ sharply from their neighbors in a number of respects. In complex industrial societies, by contrast, ethnic characteristics are more likely to vary independently; and we find individuals who are simultaneously members of two or more different ethnic groups. In the United States we find Irish Catholics and Italian Catholics; in Lebanon we find Arab Christians and Arab Moslems; and in India we encounter within Hinduism a variety of caste and linguistic divisions that baffles Western understanding.

In industrialized societies ethnic group membership is, on the whole, less important than it is in traditional societies. The group membership that is most important for a particular individual at any given time depends partly on his own attitudes and partly on those of other people. Every ethnic group has on its fringes individuals who are considered by some to belong, and by others not to belong, to the group in question. It becomes a hopeless task to attempt to specify exactly the boundaries of any particular ethnic group.

An ethnic attitude is an attitude which a person has toward some or all members of an ethnic group, provided that the attitude is influenced to some degree by knowledge (or presumed knowledge) of the other individuals' group membership. Ethnic attitudes are frequently referred to as "intergroup attitudes," though they include the attitudes of individuals toward the groups of which they themselves are members.

We shall follow Smith (1947), Kramer (1949), and Chein (1951) in distinguishing *cognitive, affective,* and *conative* components of ethnic or intergroup attitudes. The cognitive components are the perceptions, beliefs, and expectations that the individual holds with regard to various ethnic groups. The beliefs and expectations of an individual with regard to the members of a particular ethnic group—for example, Catholics or Negroes—may vary along a number of dimensions. Probably the most important of these are the following: (1) simple (or undifferentiated) versus complex (or differentiated), (2) central (or salient) in consciousness versus peripheral (or embedded), (3) believed tentatively versus believed with assurance, (4) inadequately grounded versus grounded on appropriate evidence, (5) accurate versus inaccurate, and (6) tenacious versus readily modified. A belief that is simple, inadequately grounded, at least partially inaccurate, and held with considerable assurance by many people is called a *stereotype* (*cf.* Lippmann, 1922).

The affective components of an ethnic attitude include both a general friendliness or unfriendliness toward the object of the attitude and the various specific feelings that give the attitude its affective coloring. On the positive side they include such feelings as admiration, sympathy, and "closeness" or identification; on the negative side they include feelings like contempt, fear, envy, and "distance" or alienation.

The conative components of an ethnic attitude include beliefs about "what should be done" with regard to the group in question, and action orientations of the individual toward specific members of the group. The former type of component is sometimes called a "policy orientation" (Smith, 1947) and is typically investigated by means of "third person" questions in attitude surveys (for example, "Should Negroes be allowed to . . . ?"). The latter type of component includes both general action orientations toward "typical" members of an ethnic group (for example, "How would you feel about working under a Negro supervisor?") and specific action orientations toward particular members of the group in question (for example, "How would you feel about working under Jones?" or "Do you know any Negro well enough that you might invite him to your home?").

Our usage of the term "conative" is rather unorthodox, since "ought" and "should" propositions represent a class of beliefs, though not beliefs about "matters of fact." Similarly an "I would" proposition is a belief, though a belief that can be verified only in action. In the traditional meaning of the term "conative," only desires or impulses toward representatives of the class of objects of an attitude could be regarded as conative components—for example, an impulse to break off contact, regardless of whether the impulse is acted out. We have broadened the traditional meaning of the term for the sake of having a single convenient label for the class of attitudinal components that are directly concerned with action.

American social scientists during the past 30 years have rarely been willing simply to describe the ethnic attitudes of an individual; they have wanted also to evaluate these attitudes. Thus arises the concept of *prejudice.* As we noted before, this concept is a central one for the whole social-problems approach to ethnic relations. We feel that none of the many definitions advanced by previous writers expresses adequately the range of meanings of the term "prejudice" or of the underlying concept. Consequently, we shall try to develop a broader definition that will be more adequate (we hope) to the actual usage of social scientists, especially American social scientists, during the past 30 years.

A starting point for definition can be found in the fact that it is always considered "bad" to be prejudiced. This implies that the essential characteristic of an attitude that makes it prejudiced is that the attitude departs in some way from some kind of norm. The norm or norms involved are evidently ones that are subscribed to quite generally by social scientists and perhaps by other educated members of our society, but are not universally followed in practice. All writers on prejudice agree that there are individual differences in degree of prejudice. Thus the norms involved must be what Williams (1960) calls "ideal norms": standards of conduct that everyone is felt to have some obligation to follow, but that are not actually followed by everyone.

Careful examination of writings on prejudice discloses three different ideal norms from which a prejudiced attitude may be said to depart. Each of these has been emphasized by a different group of writers. We shall refer to them as the *norm of rationality*, the *norm of justice*, and the *norm of human-heartedness*.

The norm of rationality is basic for the definitions of prejudice proposed by Powdermaker (1944), Lippitt and Radke (1946), Allport (1954), Kelman and Pettigrew (1959), and Simpson and Yinger (1965). This norm enjoins a persistent attempt to secure accurate information, to correct misinformation, to make appropriate differentiations and qualifications, to be logical in deduction and cautious in inference. Prejudice in the sense of deviation from the norm of rationality may occur in the form of hasty judgment or prejudgment, overgeneralization, thinking in stereotypes, refusal to modify an opinion in the face of new evidence, and refusal to admit or take account of individual differences.

The norm of justice is crucial for the definitions of prejudice advanced by Myrdal (1944), Williams (1947), and Merton (1949). The standard of justice here is one of equal treatment. It was included in what Myrdal called "the American Creed" and was later embodied in the report on discrimination by the United Nations Commission on Human Rights (1949). The norm of justice requires that in all areas of public concern individuals be treated equally except insofar as unequal treatment is based on abilities or achievements functionally relevant to the requirements of the situation. Action which violates this norm is called discrimination. The norm of justice enjoins an individual to avoid discrimination himself and to recognize and oppose it when he sees it directed by others against a third party.

The third ideal norm involved in definitions of prejudice is less easy to explicate than the other two. We call it "human-heartedness," following a suggestion of Gordon Allport's; the term comes from Confucian ethics (Smith, 1958), but its equivalent is found in many other religious and ethical systems, often as the norm of brotherly love. It is the major norm involved in the definition of prejudice offered by Hartley (1946) and in the opposed concept of "tolerance for nations and races" studied by Murphy and Likert (1938). A somewhat different concept involving the same norm is that of "sympathetic identification with the underdog" (Schuman and Harding, 1963). The norm of human-heartedness enjoins the acceptance of other individuals in terms of their common humanity, no matter how different they may be from oneself. This acceptance is a direct personal response, in either feeling or action, and includes the area of "private" as well as "public" relationships. Prejudice in the sense of deviation from the norm of human-heartedness ranges from indifference through rejection to active hostility. This form of prejudice is often called "intolerance."

It seems to us impossible to make sense of the voluminous social-science literature on prejudice without recognizing that the term is widely used to designate departures from *each one* of these three ideal norms. The attitude scales available for empirical study of prejudice have been based for the most part on a conception of prejudice as simply an "unfavorable ethnic attitude"; however, there are at least one or two carefully constructed measures oriented toward each of the ideal norms we have distinguished. Consequently, it seems most useful to us to define prejudice as a failure of rationality *or* a failure of justice *or* a failure of human-heartedness in an individual's attitude toward members of another ethnic group.

Although the three ideal norms we have distinguished are analytically separable and may often make conflicting demands on an individual in a concrete situation, there are a number of reasons why a person who internalizes one of these norms to a considerable extent is likely to internalize the others as well. All three are embedded in our "official" value system, and it is easy to find innumerable appeals to them in the statements of political, religious, and educational leaders. To the extent that an individual is exposed to and is receptive to such influences, he is likely to accept rationality *and* justice *and* human-heartedness as appropriate standards of thought and behavior. Conversely, if he is prejudiced in the sense of deviating from one of these norms, he is likely to be prejudiced also from the perspective of the other two. We should expect to find very sizable correlations among different measures of prejudice, regardless of the norm toward which they are oriented. As we shall see later, this is actually the case for almost every pair of prejudice measures that has been studied. This is one reason why empirical investigators of prejudice have for the most part shown little interest in conceptual definitions, and have usually made their selection of measuring instruments on the basis of practical considerations, such as convenience and split-half reliability. The lack of perfect correlation among prejudice measures results partly from defects in the measures, and partly from inconsistency in the presentation and assimilation of the three ideal norms.

The last major concept we shall attempt to define is that of *intergroup behavior*. The most prevalent usage (which we shall follow) applies the term "intergroup behavior" to the behavior of a person toward some member or members of an ethnic group other than his own, *whether or not this behavior is influenced by the person's ethnic attitudes*. With this definition the relationship between ethnic attitudes and intergroup behavior becomes a problem for empirical study. There seem to be some individuals whose ethnic attitudes are continually being expressed in intergroup behavior of various sorts, whereas the intergroup behavior of other individuals is virtually independent of whatever ethnic attitudes they have. Also, behavioral situations vary tremendously in the extent to which they allow ethnic attitudes to be expressed.

Intergroup behavior is usually studied from the perspective of two questions: (1) Is it discriminatory (according to the standards specified by the norm of justice)? (2) Where does it lie along the friendly-hostile continuum? Some attention has also been given to different forms of accommodation between one ethnic group and another (*cf.* Hughes and Hughes, 1952).

THE MEASUREMENT OF INTERGROUP ATTITUDES

Systematic work on the measurement of intergroup attitudes was first carried out by Bogardus (1925a, 1925b, 1925c, 1927). His basic method was a paper-and-pencil questionnaire, with the following directions: "According to my first feeling reactions I would willingly admit members of each race (as a class, and not the best I have known, nor the worst members) to one or more of the classifications which I have circled." There were seven classifications, intended to represent gradually increasing degrees of "social distance": "To close kinship by marriage," "To my club as personal chums," "To my street as neighbors," "To employment in my occupation in my country," "To citizenship in my country," "As visitors only to my country," and finally "Would exclude from my country." Bogardus included as "races" ethnic and nationality groups of many sorts, such as Canadians, Chinese, English, Scotch, Scotch-Irish, Serbo-Croats, Hindus, German Jews, etc.

Since Bogardus' investigations many, many other methods of attitude measurement have been devised, and scores of articles and even books have been written about their respective merits. Major approaches to the measurement of ethnic attitudes were reviewed by Deri *et al.* (1948) and by Cook and Selltiz (1964). Campbell (1950) has published a useful review of disguised and indirect approaches. It is probably safe to say that the field has been dominated at all times by the direct approach and the paper-and-pencil questionnaire. There has been a very lively interest in indirect approaches, especially since ethnic prejudice became a topic of national concern in the United States during the course of World War II. But there has been unceasing controversy about the validity of these methods, and no single one has gained anything like the wide acceptance of the Bogardus scale and the other major direct techniques (*cf.* Cook and Selltiz, 1964).

The bulk of our information about ethnic attitudes has come from the direct approaches, and it is on them that we shall rely mainly in the following discussion. We shall discuss first some of the major findings regarding the cognitive, affective, and conative components of intergroup attitudes as determined from investigations in which no attempt was made to assess the "legitimacy" of the attitude—that is, whether or not the attitude was "prejudiced" in any of the three senses we have distinguished. Then we shall discuss findings from investigations oriented toward the measurement of *prejudice.*

COGNITIVE COMPONENTS

Katz and Braly (1933) developed a simple procedure for studying cognitive aspects of intergroup attitudes that has completely dominated the field since its introduction. One hundred American college students were asked to select from a list of 84 traits those they considered most characteristic of each of the following 10 groups: Americans, Chinese, English, Germans, Irish, Italians, Japanese, Jews, Negroes, and Turks. Following this initial selection, they were asked to choose the five "most typical" traits for each group. The list of 84 traits available for choice was extremely diverse, including characteristics such as "intelligent," "industrious," "lazy," "artistic," "scientifically minded," "very religious," "superstitious," "happy-go-lucky," etc. Katz and Braly constructed for each ethnic group an index of "definiteness of stereotype" by counting the fewest number of traits required to include 50 percent of the 500 choices by all subjects. This index ranged from a minimum of 4.6 for Negroes to a maximum of 15.9 for Turks.

Katz and Braly felt that the degree of consensus shown by their college student subjects went far beyond anything justified by the objective characteristics of these various ethnic groups, so they described their research as a study of "racial stereotypes." Actually they made no attempt to ascertain whether or not any particular set of judgments by an individual student did or did not result from stereotyped thinking of the sort described by Lippmann (1922). In effect, Katz and Braly were using the term "stereotype" simply as a pejorative designation for "group concept."

The simplicity of the Katz and Braly procedure led to its adoption (with minor variations) in dozens of other investigations. These were typically described as studies of "ethnic stereotypes," though we have not been able to find any instance in these studies of a serious attempt to determine the actual basis of the judgments recorded or the extent to which they involved a failure of rationality. There has been, however, a great deal of discussion of the "kernel of truth" hypothesis (Klineberg, 1950), which asserts that if we could determine objectively and accurately the characteristics of a defined social group, and if we ascertained the beliefs of some other social group about the first, we would find a more than random correspondence between the two sets of characteristics. This modest claim is probably correct for most sets of beliefs about most ethnic groups; however, in at least one intensive study of attitudes toward an ethnic group (Armenians in California), a negative relationship was found between the actual characteristics of the group and the stereotype of it held by nonmembers (LaPiere, 1936).

It seems to be true that most individuals feel able to make at least a guess about the characteristics of almost any defined ethnic group on the basis of information that to the social scientist appears quite inadequate. Opinions are picked up from other individuals, from the mass media, and to some extent from direct personal contact. Some ethnic groups now enjoy an international reputation for certain characteristics, whether well deserved or not. Prothro and Melikian (1954) used the Katz and Braly procedure with a group of 100 Arab college students in Beirut, Lebanon, and a newly derived list of 99 traits. For some ethnic groups (for example, Turks) the characterizations of these Arab students showed scarcely more than a random resemblance to the characterizations by the American students 20 years earlier, but for other ethnic groups (for example, American Negroes) there was a high degree of similarity between the two sets of judgments. There were also some highly revealing differences; for example, the 10 traits most frequently ascribed to Negroes by the Arab students included "downtrodden" and "enslaved"—terms that had almost never been applied to Negroes by Katz and Braly's subjects (all of whom were white).

When members of two different ethnic groups are asked to rate both themselves and each other in the Katz and Braly manner, two things usually happen. The first is that the array of characteristics selected by group X as most typical of itself is similar to the array selected by group Y as most typical of group X. The second is that socially desirable characteristics are more likely to be emphasized in a group's description of itself, while undesirable characteristics are more likely to be stressed in descriptions of the group by members of another group—especially if there has been a recent history of conflict between the two groups (Rath and Sircar, 1960; Reigrotski and Anderson, 1959; Vinacke, 1949). Sometimes the low status of a group in a particular society is so firmly established that even the traits used by group members to characterize themselves are predominantly unfavorable (Bayton, 1941; Rath and Sircar, 1960).

During the past 30 years there have been a vast number of studies devoted to assessing the attitudes of some defined population toward members of some particular ethnic group. Nearly all these studies have asked (in one way or another) for judgments of "typical characteristics" or "outstanding characteristics" of the group in question. Taken together, this research seems to us to have demonstrated that the cognitive components of an ethnic attitude are strongly influenced by at least three major classes of determinants: (1) the objective characteristics of the group which is the target of the attitude; (2) the relationships (friendly or hostile) of this group to the group whose attitudes are being investigated; and (3) psychological characteristics of individual members of the group whose attitudes are being investigated. There has been no systematic investigation of the relative importance of these three classes of determinants.

AFFECTIVE COMPONENTS

Empirical study of the affective components of intergroup attitudes has focused almost exclusively on the general favorability-unfavorability or "friendly-hostile" dimension. One basic approach was established by Thurstone and several collaborators, who developed a series of attitude scales intended to tap this dimension and (so far as possible) only this dimension (Hinckley, 1932; Peterson and Thurstone, 1932; Thurstone, 1931a, 1931b, 1931c). The method of scale construction consists of assembling a large number of emotionally toned statements about the ethnic group in question and asking judges to sort these statements into 11 categories according to the degree of favorable or unfavorable affect that each statement seems to express. The final scale consists of statements ranging from maximally favorable through neutral to maximally unfavorable. Statements are included in the final scale only if a large proportion of the judges agree on their affective value. Subjects are asked to check each statement with which they agree, and they are assigned scores on the basis of the median scale value of the statements they endorse.

Methodological research in this area since 1932 has been devoted mainly to showing that the friendly-hostile dimension of an ethnic attitude can be measured just about as well by other types of attitude scales that are a good deal simpler to construct than the Thurstone scales. Murphy and Likert (1938) showed this for the "Likert type" of attitude scale (*cf.* Chapter 11 of this *Handbook*). In a similar manner Riker (1944) compared self-ratings of intensity of feeling toward Negroes and Germans with scores on the corresponding Thurstone scales. The correlation for affect toward Negroes was 0.69, and for affect toward Germans 0.61. These values are lower than the correlation reported by Murphy and Likert between their scale of attitude toward Negroes and the corresponding Thurstone scale, and the difference is probably attributable to the higher repeat reliability of Likert-type scales. Since 1950 the Likert type of scale has largely replaced the Thurstone type of scale as a measure of degree of friendliness or unfriendliness toward members of a particular ethnic group.

There has been very little research on the specific feelings involved in attitudes toward various ethnic groups. In his analysis of questions used in public opinion polls and other empirical surveys of ethnic attitudes, Kramer (1949) found only 28 items concerned with specific emotional orientations. Some additional information has come from free-response questions in interviews. For example, Deutsch and Collins (1951) report the following remarks made by a white woman living in an integrated Negro-white housing project, whose general attitude toward Negroes had become more negative (in contrast to the favorable changes in attitudes reported by the majority of their respondents) (p. 100):

> They are drunk and they follow you at night. I was walking down the street and one of them followed me for two blocks making remarks . . . . I won't go out alone when it is dark now.

The affect involved in this statement seems to be primarily fear. The specific emotional response of an individual toward members of a particular minority group is probably strongly influenced by the individual's general temperament (sanguine, apprehensive, choleric, or phlegmatic) and also by the social situation in which he finds himself. An individual whose general orientation toward Negroes is unfriendly may feel primarily contempt or indifference if he is living in an all-white suburb far removed from the nearest Negro neighborhood; if a Negro "invasion" occurs on the next block, these feelings are likely to be replaced by hostility and fear.

While there is very little direct research evidence to go by, it is probably true also that there are characteristic differences from ethnic group to ethnic group in the specific emotional responses they tend to evoke. Such differences are to be expected whenever there are persisting differences in the stereotypes held regarding various ethnic groups, whether or not these stereotypes contain any "kernel of truth." Bettelheim and Janowitz (1950a), for example, report marked differences in the emotional reactions of prejudiced war veterans toward Jews and toward Negroes (p. 42):

> In the United States, where two or more ethnic minorities are available, a tendency has emerged to separate the stereotypes into two sets and to assign each of them to one minority group. One of these two sets indicates feelings of anxiety over the first minority's power or control (Jews exercising control, having power). The other set of stereotypes indicates anxieties aroused by the second minority's assumed ability to permit itself the enjoyment of primitive, socially unacceptable forms of indulgence or gratification (the Negroes'—and one might add the Mexicans'—dirtiness and immorality).

The authors contrast this situation with that prevailing in Nazi Germany, where the whole list of unfavorable stereotypes was applied to Jews.

CONATIVE COMPONENTS

In this category Kramer (1949) includes acceptance of individual members of an ethnic group in various personal and social relationships (social distance), succorance versus nonsuccorance, withdrawal versus nonwithdrawal, aggression versus non-aggression, and enforcement of status differentials versus acceptance of status equality. The greatest amount of empirical research has been devoted to the first of these components, where the tradition begins with Bogardus (1925a, 1925b, 1925c), and to the last. Probably the main reason for the heavy emphasis on the last category is the fact that such a high proportion of the research on ethnic attitudes has been carried out in the United States, and that such a high proportion of American research has been concerned with Negro-white relations.

A typical questionnaire dealing with conative components of attitude toward a particular ethnic group consists of a series of discrete items to which the subject is asked to respond. The response may be (1) dichotomous (as in circling or not circling a category on the Bogardus scale), (2) multiple-choice, or (3) a graduated expression of agreement-disagreement (the Likert method). The responses to almost any such item can be readily classified in terms of favorability toward the ethnic group in question, so it is easy to construct a total score based on the number of favorable responses. Thus for each respondent the questionnaire provides information about his opinions on a variety of specific policy questions or his predicted reactions in a variety of specific situations; it also yields an overall score on favorability of conative orientation to members of that ethnic group.

Much attention has been given to the question of the extent to which responses to specific items can be predicted from knowledge of a subject's overall favorability score. One extreme situation would be that in which predictability is perfect, provided we know the "order of difficulty" of the items—that is, the item on which a favorable response is most likely for the population to which the given subject belongs, the item on which a favorable response is next most likely, etc. This is the situation in which the items form what Guttman (1950) calls a unidimensional scale; it is implied by the metaphor of "social distance" which inspired construction of the original Bogardus scale. Bogardus (1925b, 1925c) hypothesized that each individual would respond to the seven items for a particular ethnic group as if he were saying, in effect, "You may come this close to me, but no closer."

Extensive study with the original Bogardus items has shown that for most American populations they come close to the "ideal type" of the unidimensional Guttman scale (Bogardus, 1928; Hartley, 1946). However, when additional types of social relationship are included, discrepancies between empirical results and those predicted by the unidimensional model become marked; and there has been a tendency in recent research to reject the unidimensional model entirely in analyzing the results of social-distance questionnaires (Triandis, 1964).

The extreme opposite of the unidimensional scale is a set of items that are completely uncorrelated, so that information about an individual's response to one item, or group of items, adds nothing to our ability to predict his response to any other item. This situation is virtually unknown for items measuring any aspect of an ethnic attitude. It is not difficult to find *two* policy-oriented questions regarding a particular ethnic group which have a correlation of zero, or two questions about "typical characteristics" of group members that are uncorrelated. But when a series of policy-oriented questions is asked, or a series of questions dealing with ethnic stereotypes, it is almost impossible to find any item that does not show at least small positive correlations with a majority of the other items. Thus complete heterogeneity of ethnic attitude items is as rare as complete homogeneity.

Investigators using conatively oriented ethnic questionnaires have most commonly had one or the other of two very different purposes. The first is to gather information that will be helpful in predicting public reaction to some situation in which members of a particular ethnic group may be involved—that is, in predicting intergroup behavior; the second is to derive a score on overall favorability of attitude for each member of some sample or population and then study possible determinants of individual differences in this score. Investigators with the first purpose typically make a separate analysis of responses to each item on their questionnaire (for example, Bogardus, 1928; Hyman and Sheatsley, 1956; LaPiere, 1934). Researchers for whom the second purpose is dominant treat the overall favorability score as their dependent variable and try to determine why some people score higher than others, or whether the average score of a group will be increased or decreased by some particular kind of experience (Harlan, 1942; MacKenzie, 1948; Minard, 1931).

ATTEMPTS TO MEASURE ETHNIC PREJUDICE

One of the outstanding characteristics of American research on intergroup attitudes is the lack of correspondence between "prejudice" as defined conceptually by theorists and writers of textbooks and "prejudice" as defined operationally by the busy constructors of attitude scales. We have spelled this out in the cognitive area by contrasting the characteristics of an ethnic "stereotype" as described by Lippmann (1922) and two subsequent generations of textbook writers with the characteristics of the ethnic group concepts studied by Katz and Braly (1933), which they casually referred to as "racial stereotypes." The story is much the same in the affective and conative area: the usual practice of constructors and users of attitude scales since World War II has been to refer to any unfavorable ethnic attitude as a "prejudice."

In 1954 it seemed to us best to follow the blurred terminology of the empirical investigators; however, our present judgment is that it is not only possible but desirable to distinguish, among the multitude of empirical measures of ethnic attitudes, a small group that can lay serious claim to being considered measures of *prejudice* according to one or more of the three major types of definition discussed on pp. 5–6. It seems to us that distinctions of this sort are essential if there is to be any real increase in theoretical sophistication in the intergroup relations research of the next decade.

There is actually quite a long tradition of attempts to measure prejudice in the sense of failure of rationality, though no single measurement procedure seems to have been used in serious research by anyone except its originator. The tradition begins with Watson's monograph, *The Measurement of Fair-Mindedness* (1925). Watson provided several different procedures for assessing irrational bias in 12 different directions, including prejudice in favor of economic radicals, economic liberals, economic conservatives, religious radicals, religious liberals, fundamentalists, Roman Catholics, and Protestants. Watson was primarily interested in assessing the general level of an individual's rationality or irrationality about social issues, rather than in attempting to measure the extent of bias for or against specific ethnic groups. Consequently, he later collaborated with Glaser in revising his test into a measure of capacity for critical thinking, without regard to the direction of irrational bias.

Thistlethwaite (1950) and Prentice (1957) developed measures of irrational bias based on valid and invalid formal syllogisms dealing with Negroes and Jews. These measures seemed reasonably satisfactory for assessing prejudice in college students, but could not be used with subjects lacking a firm grasp of the general concept of deductive reasoning. More recently, Schuman and Harding (1964) have developed a measure of prejudice in the sense of failure of rationality which can be used with subjects having no more than six years of formal schooling. The kinds of irrationality tapped by their measure are primarily overgeneralization, thinking in stereotypes, and refusal to take adequate account of individual differences.

All these investigators have recognized that irrationality in thinking about members of an ethnic group can take the form of favorable as well as unfavorable bias—what Allport (1954) has called "love prejudice." Prentice (1957) and Schuman and Harding (1964) report considerably higher proportions of "love prejudice" than "hate prejudice" in three samples of college students and one general sample of adults in the Boston metropolitan area. These studies demonstrate that any adequate conceptualization of intergroup attitudes must include some strong psychological (or sociological) forces working in the direction of *more favorable* attitudes as well as forces tending toward *less favorable* attitudes.

It was not until the 1930's that American social psychologists really became sensitized to discrimination as a social problem and began looking at ethnic attitudes in terms of the extent to which they embodied a failure of justice. The first investigator to develop an attitude scale from this general point of view seems to have been

Minard (1931). Revisions of Minard's scale have been used in unpublished research by Julian Pathman and Isidor Chein. Meanwhile, several psychologists had realized that high rejection scores on the Bogardus social-distance scale necessarily implied both a failure of adherence to the norm of justice (in the sense of the American Creed) and a failure of human-heartedness. Murphy and Likert (1938) were the first to sum up the number of social relationships to which an individual would willingly admit members of a variety of ethnic groups and to use this score as a measure of "tolerance for nations and races." Hartley (1946) appears to have been the first to refer to such a score as a measure of ethnic prejudice. It seems to us that this usage is eminently sound, but it requires a recognition that prejudice may take the form of departure from the norms of justice and human-heartedness as well as (or instead of) the norm of rationality.

The authors of *The Authoritarian Personality* (Adorno *et al.*, 1950) reject the term "prejudice" in favor of something they call "ethnocentrism," but their concept of ethnocentrism is very different from the traditional meaning of this term (*cf.* Williams, 1964, Chapter 3) and is virtually equivalent to a combination of failure of rationality and failure of human-heartedness (with perhaps some failure of justice thrown in). These authors took far more pains than most investigators have done to construct an empirical measure with characteristics appropriate to their conceptual definition, and we would unhesitatingly describe the California E scale as a measure of ethnic prejudice.

A questionnaire intended to measure a special kind of failure of human-heartedness was constructed by Schuman and Harding (1963). It differs from the Bogardus scale in being oriented to the cognitive aspect of human-heartedness rather than the conative, and it is described by the authors as a measure of "sympathetic identification with the underdog."

Among the measures described in this section, the only ones that have been widely used are the Bogardus scale and the California E scale. This would present a grave problem for our attempt to review scientific knowledge concerning prejudice except for one ameliorating fact: most measures of ethnic attitudes are so strongly saturated with the general favorability-unfavorability dimension that their intercorrelations are not greatly below their split-half reliabilities. The correlations between attitude scales designed explicitly as measures of prejudice according to some conceptual definition and other attitude scales thrown together intuitively are sufficiently high that either type of scale can be treated for most practical purposes as a measure of prejudice.

The major exception is prejudice considered as failure of rationality. The only measures of prejudice in this sense that correlate highly with other measures of prejudice and other types of ethnic attitude scale are measures of irrational bias *against* members of a particular ethnic group. Irrational bias in favor of one or more ethnic groups can be assessed only by measures specifically designed for this purpose (Schuman and Harding, 1964).

RELATIONSHIPS AMONG INTERGROUP ATTITUDINAL COMPONENTS

Our analysis of ethnic attitudes so far has been entirely *a priori*. We have distinguished between cognitive, affective, and conative components, and we have discussed what it means for an attitude to be "prejudiced" in terms of its departure from three different ideal norms. It is also possible, however, to take an empirical approach to the analysis of ethnic attitudes. One can assemble a battery of attitude measures, administer them to a large sample of respondents, intercorrelate the resulting scores (or treat them by scale analysis), and then attempt to determine from the intercorrelations relatively independent, or at least usefully distinguishable, item clusters or dimensions of attitudinal variation. Two major efforts in this direction have been made during the past 20 years, using as subjects members of the American "white majority group" (D. T. Campbell, 1947; Woodmansee and Cook, 1967).

Campbell set himself the task of determining the extent to which "prejudice" could be regarded as a psychological unity. Specifically, his investigation was designed to reveal whether "intraethnic" or "interethnic" generality characterized the organization of intergroup attitudes. For the former, the problem is one of the degree of relationship among attitudinal components for particular ethnic attitudes, whereas the latter involves the question of whether or not attitudinal components operate as separate and independent response tendencies which are uniformly applied to any and all minorities. For his investigation Campbell selected the following five attitudinal components or, as he prefers to designate them, "specific subtopics": social distance; blaming minorities; beliefs about their capability or intelligence; beliefs about their morality; and finally, "affection" for the group, that is, liking or disliking it.

For each of the five ethnic groups (Negro, Jewish, Japanese, Mexican, English), five-item scales were prepared for the attitudinal areas indicated above. Thus, there were 25 such scales, each involving five items. The resulting 125 items were then presented in a mixed order as an anonymous questionnaire to 150 college students and 239 high school students. Intercorrelations of the sets of scores for the 25 scales with one another plus systematic scale analysis led Campbell to conclude that "attitudes have greater generality as organized around individual minority groups rather than as topically discrete modes of response applied to any and all outgroups" (D. T. Campbell, 1947, p. 98). The average intercorrelation of the five attitude scales dealing with a particular ethnic group was 0.52 for the college students and 0.58 for the high school students.

Woodmansee and Cook (1967) took as their goal the delineation of a number of different dimensions of variation in attitudes of white Americans toward Negroes. They set up the requirement that each dimension be represented by at least 10 items that would "cluster" empirically, and they went through a long process of item selection and revision in order to develop subscales with maximum internal consistency and minimum interscale correlations. An additional requirement was that each subscale differentiate clearly among groups that were known (on other grounds) to differ in their attitudes toward Negroes. Subjects in pro-Negro criterion groups were members of prointegration organizations such as CORE or NAACP; subjects in anti-Negro criterion groups were members of right-wing political clubs or racially exclusive fraternities or sororities. The research went on for several years in different parts of the United States and involved a total of 1832 college students as subjects.

Woodmansee and Cook succeeded in identifying 12 different item clusters that met their criterion of internal consistency. Ten or 11 of these also met the criterion of systematic differentiation among the criterion groups. The nature of their item clusters can be illustrated by citing the six clusters which turned out to be most differentiating between members of pro-Negro and anti-Negro organizations.

1. *Private rights: for example, "A hotel owner ought to have the right to decide for himself whether he is going to rent rooms to Negro guests."*

2. *Derogatory beliefs: for example, "Although social equality of the races may be the democratic way, a good many Negroes are not yet ready to practice the self-control that goes with it."*

3. *Local autonomy: for example, "Even though we all adopt racial integration sooner or later, the people of each community should be allowed to decide when they are ready for it."*

4. *Gradualism: for example, "Gradual desegregation is a mistake because it just gives people a chance to cause further delay."*

5. *Acceptance in close personal relationships: for example, "I would not take a Negro to eat with me in a restaurant where I was well known."*

6. *Ease in interracial contacts: for example, "I would probably feel somewhat self-conscious dancing with a Negro in a public place."*

The findings of Woodmansee and Cook do *not* contradict those of Campbell and other investigators who argue for the importance of a general factor of favorability-unfavorability toward members of a particular ethnic group. The intercorrelations of their different subscales are not markedly lower than the intercorrelations of Campbell's five subscales dealing with Negroes. Actually, this work demonstrates a conclusion very similar to the one that emerged from the controversy between Spearman and Thurstone over the nature of intelligence: It is possible to analyze the same set of intercorrelations in terms of a single general factor (with subordinate group factors and specifics) or in terms of multiple group factors (plus specifics). Since both types of analysis are mathematically legitimate and theoretically meaningful, the decision between them in a particular substantive area must be made in terms of empirical usefulness. It seems to us that the usefulness of the Woodmansee and Cook analysis will be tested mainly by the ability of their subscales to make differential predictions about different types of intergroup behavior.

We have described in some detail the studies of D. T. Campbell (1947) and Woodmansee and Cook (1967) because these investigations were systematic assaults on the problem of generality-specificity and patterning in attitudes toward a particular ethnic group. Other studies, less systematic, have also provided much evidence on the question. Major sources of information are the reports of MacKenzie (1948), Bettelheim and Janowitz (1950a), Adorno *et al.* (1950), Stember (1961), and Williams (1964). Possibly some day there will emerge from this empirical work a classification of attitudinal components superior to the cognitive-affective-conative scheme we have adopted; however, our present judgment is that this taxonomy is both the clearest and most widely applicable of the various ones proposed.

RELATIONSHIPS AMONG ATTITUDES TOWARD DIFFERENT ETHNIC GROUPS

Many investigators believe there is a general factor of prejudice or tolerance which tends to unify the reactions of an individual toward members of all minority groups. According to this view, the individual who is favorably disposed toward the Negro will respond in like manner toward Jews, Chinese, and outgroups in general. On the other hand, the anti-Negro individual will also be bigoted with respect to other minorities. A number of investigations support this thesis.

Murphy and Likert (1938) administered a form of the Bogardus social-distance scale involving judgments of 21 ethnic groups. A generalized social-distance score was constructed by giving each individual one point for each relationship to which he was willing to admit members of the first ethnic group, similar points for each relationship to which he was willing to admit members of the second ethnic group, and so on. Scores based on responses to 10 of the ethnic groups, chosen at random, correlated 0.88 and 0.90 with scores based on the other 11 groups when the test was administered to 25 students at Columbia and 60 at the University of Michigan. These high correlations provide clear evidence of the generalized nature of the students' responses toward various ethnic groups. However, their attitudes could not be interpreted solely in terms of a factor of general tolerance toward outgroups, since social-distance scores based on responses to all 21 ethnic groups correlated only 0.68 with scores on a separate test of attitudes toward Negroes at Columbia and 0.33 with the same test at Michigan. These correlations are well below the split-half reliability coefficients of the two tests.

Essentially the same results were found by Hartley (1946) in a similar study, using the Bogardus technique. Hartley included in an alphabetical list of 35 ethnic groups three which were nonexistent: Danireans, Pireneans, and Wallonians. For the college and university groups studied, he found a consistently high correlation between average social distance for the real ethnic groups and average social distance for the three fictitious groups; the correlation coefficients ranged from 0.78 to 0.85. Correlations between social-distance scores for the Jews and for the three fictitious groups ranged from 0.55 to 0.73 for the same student groups.

From their extensive study of personality and prejudice Adorno *et al.* (1950) were led to the conclusion that ethnocentrism is a general response tendency manifested by hostility indiscriminately expressed toward Negroes, Jews, and outgroups in general. Subscales dealing with Negro-white relations, minorities other than Negroes and Jews, and America as an ingroup in relation to foreign nations were combined into a general ethnocentrism scale. Intercorrelations of the three subscales ranged from 0.74 to 0.83, and the scale as a whole correlated 0.80 with the anti-Semitism scale described later in this chapter.

Similar findings indicating the existence of a general tolerance factor have been reported by Bolton (1937), Kerr (1944), Prothro and Jensen (1950), Prothro and Miles (1952), and Williams (1964). These studies included a great variety of subjects drawn from many different ethnic groups.

D. T. Campbell (1947), in an investigation we have already cited, showed that general tolerance or ethnocentrism is not the *only* factor operating in intergroup attitudes. His 25 scales (covering five specific areas of prejudice for each of five different ethnic groups) were not sufficiently related that all of them could be regarded as measures of a single underlying variable. A considerable number of his subjects were significantly more favorable or less favorable toward some particular group than could have been predicted from their scores on the test as a whole. Campbell found much more evidence for unidimensionality of attitude toward a specific ethnic group than for unidimensionality of attitude toward outgroups in general.

Bettelheim and Janowitz (1950a, 1964) report findings similar to those of Campbell. In their study, anti-Semitism and anti-Negro attitudes seemed to operate as separate, though closely related, variables.

It seems to us essential for the understanding of intergroup attitudes to keep firmly in mind the existence and importance of a general factor (tolerance versus ethnocentrism) *and* group factors (degree of favorability or unfavorability toward Negroes, Jews, Turks, etc.) *and* a variety of specific factors (for example, beliefs about Jewish power and influence, acceptance of Negroes in close personal relationships, and so on). At times we need to focus on the fine details, and at other times we need to stand back to see the big picture.

THE DEVELOPMENT OF INTERGROUP ATTITUDES

Social scientists agree that ethnic attitudes are learned and that their acquisition is a gradual and complex process (Horowitz, 1944; Metraux, 1950; and others). Although the development of such attitudes is a continuous process throughout childhood, Goodman (1964) suggests that, roughly approximated, at least three overlapping stages are indicated by existing research findings: a stage of ethnic awareness; a stage of ethnic orientation or "incipient" ethnic attitudes; and finally, the emergence of "true" or adult-like ethnic attitudes. The discussion that follows is organized in terms of these stages. However, it should be emphasized that most of our conclusions are derived from comparisons of samples of children at different age levels rather than from long-range longitudinal investigations.

STAGES IN THE DEVELOPMENT OF INTERGROUP ATTITUDES

Ethnic attitudes begin to take shape during the nursery school years (age three or four) in the form of an emerging *ethnic awareness.* During this period and as part of the larger process of establishing a sense of self, the child develops an awareness of his own ethnic identity by virtue of the reciprocal and simultaneous process of taking cognizance of the ethnic identities of others. Thus, at the very beginning, the child becomes aware that ethnic group distinctions are made, and that he and others are clustered into such groups.

Goodman (1952) studied 57 Negro and 46 white children between the ages of three and five-and-a-half in three nursery schools. All these children lived in or near a mixed Negro-white area of a large Northeastern metropolis. One of the nursery schools contained an approximately equal number of Negro and white children, one was all Negro, and one was approximately 80 percent white.

Employing a variety of observational procedures and play-interview techniques (pictures, dolls, etc.), Goodman found that for *both* Negro and white children, 85 percent had either high or medium awareness of racial characteristics and of the favorable or unfavorable social implications of racial membership. However, even among the remaining 15 percent of the Negro and white children with low awareness, there was usually some idea of color distinctions as applied to people, and some differential valuing of people in terms of color.

Of special importance, but not unexpected, is Goodman's finding that racial awareness *increased with age.* High awareness did not appear before the age of four years and three months, and low awareness did not occur in this sample after four years, eleven months.

In a far more extensive study involving 253 Negro children between the ages of three and seven attending either interracial schools in Massachusetts or segregated schools in Arkansas, Clark and Clark (1947) not only found that racial awareness occurred early and increased with age, but that the kind of school attended by the Negro child had no appreciable effect on the extent to which he was racially aware. Goodman (1952) also reported no significant differences in racial awareness among the children in the different nursery schools, that is, racially segregated versus racially mixed nurseries. Findings for both Negro and white children consistent with Goodman's have been reported with considerable frequency (Ammons, 1950; Horowitz and Horowitz, 1938; Landreth and Johnson, 1953, Morland, 1958; Stevenson and Stevenson, 1960; Stevenson and Stewart, 1958; Vaughan, 1964).

The development of racial awareness in white and Negro nursery school children undoubtedly is aided by the visibility factor inherent in skin color distinctions. Although little research has been done on awareness of other types of ethnic distinctions among children in this age range, there is evidence that the development of such awareness roughly parallels that found for racial distinctions. Thus Hartley, Rosenbaum, and Schwartz (1948) studied racial, religious, and national group identifications among 86 New York City schoolchildren between the ages of three and ten by means of an extended interview ("What are you?" "What is daddy?" "Are you Catholic?" etc.). It was found that "with increasing age children shift from describing themselves . . . and the people who surround them by reference to their own names or the names of specific individuals to the use of ethnic designations" (p. 374). Similar findings are reported by Radke, Trager, and Davis (1949).

Hartley and his associates (1948) reported that membership in an ethnic minority was a predisposing factor in the early development of ethnic awareness. Not unrelated is the finding by Radke, Trager, and Davis (1949) that Jewish children between the ages of five and nine were more aware of their group membership and were more strongly identified with their own ethnic group than were Catholic or Protestant children. Consistent with both of these results is Goodman's finding (1952) that, in the North, Negro children are, by and large, "racially" aware at a slightly earlier age than are white children. Although Porter's (1963) observations of Negro and white children in a Northern community confirm this finding, those reported by Morland (1958) and Stevenson and Stewart (1958) suggest that white rather than Negro children achieve racial awareness earlier.

However, the last two investigations were carried out in Southern communities. It may well be that white children in these settings, as compared to those in the North, are more sensitive to racial differences by virtue of the explicitly normative character of Negro-white relationships; or it may be that Negro children in the South are less willing to verbalize their racial awareness than are Northern Negro children. Perhaps a better answer lies, as Goodman (1964) suggests, in the fact that, in contrast to her approach, the two Southern studies employed a far less probing method for assessing the level of racial awareness in their preschool subjects.

An *ethnic orientation*, as distinguished from an adult-like ethnic attitude, refers to the rudimentary ethnic attitudes which characterize the child roughly between the ages of four and seven or eight (Goodman, 1964). Early in this period the child is not only ethnically aware, but he has already learned some of his ethnic ABC's, that is, the words, concepts, and phrases used to describe members of other groups. Yet he is still confronted with the critical task of matching his level of understanding with his verbal facility. What eludes him is not only the full meaning of these ethnic terms and, therefore, their consistently correct use, but more important, the *conceptual* nature of the ethnic labels he has at his command. Only with increasing age does he gradually learn to generalize the concepts of "Negro," "Jew," and "Italian" appropriately, that is, to all the members of these groups rather than to specific people in familiar contexts (Allport, 1954).

In what sense, then, can we speak of an ethnic attitude, inchoate or otherwise, in the very young child? The fact is that his ethnic awareness is by no means affectively neutral. He reveals clear preferences for some groups, while others are rejected. Thus, a fundamental ingredient of an intergroup attitude is present: an evaluative orientation that is expressed in ingroup-versus-outgroup terms. As we suggested above, however, it is only when the child can grasp the categorical or class character of the ethnic labels he uses that his ethnic preferences and rejections assume the essential nature of the ethnic attitudes of the adult.

Goodman (1952) found that very large proportions of Negro as well as white nursery school children preferred *white* dolls and storybook characters; and, as the comments of these subjects indicated, their preferences applied to real people as well. In addition, 84 percent of the Negro children expressed some positive friendliness toward persons of the opposite color, whereas this was true for only 56 percent of the white children. In a more recent study by Morland (1962) of 407 very young Southern children, it was found that, for measures of racial acceptance-rejection and racial preference using a picture technique, a greater proportion of Negro children were attracted to whites than of whites to Negroes. In the case of the preference measure, approximately 60 percent of the Negro children and only about 10 percent of the white children preferred to play with children of the other race; the corresponding figures for preference for one's own racial group were 18 and 72 percent respectively. Studies by Clark and Clark (1947), Radke, Trager, and Davis (1949), Landreth and Johnson (1953), Morland (1958), and Stevenson and Stewart (1958) reveal similar findings.

Other data suggest that the young Negro child does more than simply identify with the white society which surrounds him. He is ambivalent about, if not outright hostile toward, his own racial group. In the study by Goodman (1952) only nine percent of the Negro children expressed hostility toward whites, compared to 24 percent who directed it at members of their own racial group. Of the white children, 33 percent showed hostility toward Negroes, whereas none of them were antagonistic toward their own racial group. Among the three- to seven-year-old Texan children investigated by Stevenson and Stewart (1958), the Negroes often exhibited not only preference for the white group but disparagement or rejection of members of their own racial group. The investigations by the Clarks (1947), Radke and Trager (1950), Landreth and Johnson (1953), and Morland (1958) provide additional evidence for the tendency of the Negro child to reject his own racial group. These same studies as well as others also demonstrate quite clearly that the young white child not only identifies with his own racial group but tends to withdraw from, if not reject, individuals from the other racial group.

The position of the young Negro child is difficult, to say the least. That he identifies with the white majority and rejects his own racial group carries with it the implications of self-doubt, if not self-rejection. It is understandable, therefore, that in the studies by the Clarks (1947) and Goodman (1952) some of the Negro children were disturbed by the investigation, especially when they were required to make self-identifications. And Morland (1958) found that many of his preschool

Negro subjects who identified with their own racial group did so with reluctance and emotional strain.

Rejection of one's own ethnic group is likely to be accompanied not only by self-rejection but also by insecurity, anxiety, and a sense of helplessness. In this respect Goodman (1952) observed that greater racial awareness and outgroup orientation in the Negro child (moving toward whites and away from Negroes) typically carried with it increased emotionality, a sense of personal threat, and insecurity with respect to racial status. Some of the other studies of preschool children noted above reveal very similar findings (for example, Clark and Clark, 1947; Morland, 1958; Stevenson and Stewart, 1958). And among older Negro schoolchildren the picture is by no means different. In comparison to white children at the grammar school level, they tend to experience greater anxiety (Palermo, 1959); to perceive the world as more hostile and threatening (Mussen, 1953); to exhibit greater defensiveness by aspiring to higher-level occupations (Boyd, 1952); and to be more passive, morose, and fearful as a consequence of their more negative self-conceptions (Deutsch, 1960).

The studies by the Clarks (1947), Radke and Trager (1950), and Morland (1962) provide suggestive evidence that the preference of Negro children for the white group decreases with age. More certain is the change which occurs with age in the own-group preference of the white preschool child. Morland (1962) found that for white children between the ages of three and five there was a clear-cut and steady increase in preference for a white playmate. Similar findings are reported by Landreth and Johnson (1953) and by Stevenson and Stewart (1958). Finally, a positive relationship between increasing age and extent of rejection or hostility toward Negroes among young white children is indicated in studies by Horowitz (1936), Radke, Trager, and Davis (1949), and Morland (1962). That a similar relationship may hold for the attitudes of Negro children toward their white peers is indicated in the study by the Clarks (1947). A majority of their Negro subjects at all age levels selected the white doll as "nice" and the colored doll as "looking bad." However, the first attribute was decreasingly applied and the second increasingly applied to the white doll with an increase in age from four to seven years.

Of the various studies considered above, only one (Radke, Trager, and Davis, 1949) sheds any light on the acceptance or rejection by very young children of members of other kinds of ethnic groups (religious, nationality, etc.). Three equivalent groups of white Catholic, Jewish, and white and Negro Protestant children between the ages of five and eight were interviewed with respect to a picture (among others) in which a child obviously isolated from other children was identified respectively as Catholic, Protestant, and Jewish. It was found that in general the tendency to perceive the isolated boy as rejected or excluded from the group was slightly greater when he was identified as Jewish than when he was described as Catholic or Protestant. Other findings in the study also suggest that very young non-Jewish children may already exhibit ingroup-outgroup orientations toward Jews.

Earlier we pointed out that many children in the ethnic-orientation stage had the "verbal fluency" but not the conceptual grasp of ethnic labels, stereotypes, and values. Thus, in Goodman's low- and medium-awareness groups, both Negro and white children used racial terms to describe and label others, but not always accurately. Her high-awareness or older subjects were apparently able to generalize race distinctions, but whether they fully grasped the class nature of the racial concepts in the sense of extending beyond the nursery school itself is unclear. In a study by Vaughan (1963) of the development of racial concepts (ability to categorize or generalize in abstract terms) in white New Zealand children, he found that the actual attainment of racial concepts (categorization) first appears at seven years of age and only after the child has learned to first identify and then discriminate among members of different racial groups.

Ostensibly, to grasp and apply nationality and religious-group concepts should be an even more difficult task for the child than to apply racial concepts. Thus, in the study by Hartley, Rosenbaum, and Schwartz (1948), their young subjects were asked what it means and what it takes to be "American," "Jewish," "Catholic," and so on. It was found for their six- to ten-year-old subjects as well as the younger ones that the definitions given were "so 'inaccurate' and 'insufficient' to make impossible their classification in terms of an adult logical system." To many of the children at all levels it appeared possible to be simultaneously "Jewish and Catholic" or "American and German," but not "Jewish and American" or "Negro and Protestant." The lack of clarity of religious-group concepts in children between the ages of five and eight was similarly revealed in the study by Radke and her associates (1949).

If *ethnic attitudes* (in contrast to ethnic orientations) finally emerge during the early grammar school years, it must then be asked what is involved in their development from this point on. Allport (1954) cogently points out that "A bigoted personality may be well under way by the age of six, but by no means fully fashioned" (p. 297). In general, investigators assume that such attitudes become fully fashioned by the addition and organization of new details, that is, through the *differentiation* and *integration* of beliefs, feelings, and behavioral tendencies regarding the members of various ethnic groups. While our concern here is with the differentiation and integration of these attitudinal components during the grammar and high school years, it should be stressed that such processes are probably involved in ethnic attitude formation from the very beginning of the nursery school years. Even at this early period the child—whether he fully comprehends or not—is beginning to learn what groups are like, how you should treat them, and indeed how one ought to feel about them.

Most, if not all, investigators are ready to assume that the three types of attitudinal components become increasingly differentiated with age. Support for this assumption, however, is restricted to a few studies of cognitive and conative components. In a study of the development of stereotypes in Southern white children in grades four through eleven, Blake and Dennis (1943) found that the children at all levels were strongly anti-Negro; those in the lower grades, however, attributed only negative traits to the Negro, whereas the upper-grade children attributed some favorable traits to him as well as many unfavorable ones. Radke and Sutherland (1949) also found an increasing differentiation of stereotypes of the Negro (also the Jew), but the direction of attitude change was reversed; rather than changing from primarily negative to (some) positive traits, as Blake and Dennis found, their subjects changed from primarily positive to a mixture of positive and negative stereotypes.

However, Radke and Sutherland's study involved 275 white children in grades five to twelve in a small Midwestern community in which there were no Negroes. On this basis it is not unlikely that Negro prejudice was not a salient normative event in the community, and therefore that learning negative stereotypes of the Negro was considerably delayed compared to the Southern child's experience. Of course, in the case of a highly valued group one would expect the evaluations of younger children to be uncritically favorable and then to become somewhat less favorable and more realistic with increasing age. This indeed is what Radke and Sutherland (1949) found when "Americans" were described by their young subjects. Similar findings are reported by Greenstein (1960) in the evaluations of political leaders by fourth- to eighth-grade children.

In a previous discussion we considered the integration of the three different types of attitudinal components in terms of the relationships among them—that is, the extent of their evaluative consistency. Only the study by Horowitz (1936) sheds any light on the development of such integration or consistency as the child matures. He found that while the intercorrelations among his three tests, computed separately for each age group in the five- to 14-year-old range were low, they did increase with advancing age. Other studies of adults, high school, and college youth have reported moderate to high consistency in this respect (Bettelheim and Janowitz, 1950a; Katz and Braly, 1933; Langner, 1953; MacKenzie, 1948; M. B. Smith, 1947).

Still another question concerns relationships within a particular type of attitudinal component. In other words, are the individual's potential actions *or* beliefs primarily unfavorable or are they both favorable and unfavorable? The studies by Blake and Dennis (1943) and Radke and Sutherland (1949) both indicate that some mixture of positive and negative beliefs is likely to occur as the child grows older. We have already interpreted this as indicating increasing differentiation; it is reasonable also to interpret it as indicating increasing commitment to the norm of rationality.

There is some evidence that behavioral components of intergroup attitudes tend to become more consistent—and more prejudiced—as the child grows older. Radke, Sutherland, and Rosenberg (1950) studied the racial attitudes of Negro and white elementary school children by means of their sociometric choices of actual children in the school and neighborhood, and of unknown children in a series of photographs. They found that both the younger and older Negro and white children tended to prefer members of their own racial group as friends when they had to choose them from children in the school who were not their classmates. On the other hand, when they had to make friendship choices from among their classmates, such ethnocentrism was far more evident among the older children than among the younger ones. In effect, there was an increase with age in the racial consistency of the friendship choices—their behavioral orientations—made by the Negro and white children across the two choice settings.

ETHNIC ATTITUDES IN YOUTH

The most extensive and perhaps earliest study of prejudice during the high school years was reported by Minard (1931). Approximately 1300 Iowa schoolchildren were given a questionnaire describing 32 behavioral situations involving a variety of ethnic groups. The child was asked a great many questions about what was the right thing to do and also how he himself would feel or what he would be likely to do in most situations. By the first criterion there was a small decrease in prejudice from the seventh to the tenth grade, and no change from the tenth to the twelfth grade. By the second criterion there was a steady *increase* in prejudice from the seventh through the twelfth grade. This second criterion, of course, more closely approximates the student's actual behavioral tendencies in contrast to his verbalizing the espoused ideals of American society, which is most likely what was involved in the first criterion.

Horowitz (1936) also reports an increase in ethnic prejudice during the grammar school years of the kind we have called a failure of human-heartedness. He found an average increase in prejudice against Negroes among white New York City boys from age five to 12 on his Show Me and Social Situations tests, both of which focus on the behavioral tendencies of the child. His third measure, the Ranks test, which measures affective orientations toward Negroes without any reference to any behavioral situation, showed no relationship to age in the groups studied. Generalized preference for whites as compared with Negroes was well established by age five and continued thereafter without any noticeable alteration. This finding for a generalized-preference measure is consistent with those found for white nursery school children. The preference of the white child for his own group increases with age during this period; however, by the time the child begins grade school this preference is practically at a maximum (Goodman, 1952; Morland, 1962).

Radke and her associates (1950) also employed a technique focused on the behavior orientations of the white child (sociometric choices) toward the Negro, and like Horowitz found increasing prejudice with age in children between the ages of seven and 13. Similar findings are reported for Tennessee by Boynton and Mayo (1942) and by Mayo and Kinzer (1950).

Of interest is a recent study of the relationship between ethnic attitudes and age in another cultural setting. Vaughan and Thompson (1961) studied the attitudes of 120 New Zealand children of 8, 12, and 16 years of age toward the Maori (a Polynesian native group) by means of two sets of 10 TAT pictures depicting themes of play, school, etc. The two sets of pictures were identical except that in one the crucial figure was a Maori, and in the other a white person. An increase in unfavorable attitudes occurred between the ages of 8 and 12, but no difference in this respect was found between the 12- and 16-year-old groups. The first finding is consistent with those reported by Radke and her associates (1950), Horowitz (1936), and Radke and Sutherland (1949) for American children in this age range.

A very recent study by Wilson (1963) tested the hypothesis that the average level of an ethnic attitude becomes stabilized only in late adolescence. He studied male pupils in the Boston area between the ages of 13 and 18 with a behavioral and evaluative opinion questionnaire relevant to Negroes, Jews, and Southerners. Wilson's findings only partially confirmed his hypothesis. On a social-distance measure of attitude toward the Negro, the level of prejudice was stabilized in later adolescence. However, generalized scales in which Negroes and Jews were evaluated directly revealed attitude stability much earlier.

Some studies of the ethnic attitudes of youth who are members of American minority groups have also been reported. Unfortunately, comparable data on the relationship of age to degree of prejudice are not readily available. Of some importance, however, is a comparison of the *order of preference* for different ethnic groups by majority and minority group youth. By age 11 these preferences have become fairly well stabilized; and the rank ordering for different ethnic groups is essentially the same as that found among adults. In the studies by Zeligs and Hendrickson (1933, 1934) in Cincinnati, it was found that when 39 ethnic groups were ranked in order of preference, the correlations between the ranking by Jewish and non-Jewish children were quite high. Other investigations have consistently found high correlations between the rankings of minority- and majority-group high school and college youth (Gray and Thompson, 1953; Horowitz, 1944; Katz and Braly, 1935;

Meltzer, 1939a, 1939b). The only notable exception to the pattern of agreement in rankings among different groups occurs when group members rank their own group. In this instance a difference arises because each group ranks itself as the most preferable.

A final word is in order concerning the development of integration or evaluative consistency among different ethnic attitudes. Frenkel-Brunswik and Havel (1953) interviewed 81 white American Gentile children between the ages of 10 and 15 about their attitudes toward Negroes, Jews, and other minority groups. Correlations between attitude toward different minority groups were large and positive. Prejudice toward Negroes, however, was greater than toward Jews, Mexicans, Japanese, and Chinese. The generalized nature of ethnic prejudice and its greater intensity for Negroes as compared to other minority groups (for example, Jews and Catholics) are also evident in the study by Galtung (1960) of high school youth in 21 communities and in Trager and Yarrow's (1952) investigation of young children in kindergarten through second grade.

THE DEVELOPMENT OF INTERGROUP BEHAVIOR

Developmental studies of interethnic behavior are rare; even more so are attempts to measure both ethnic attitudes and behavior so that one can compare the relationships between them. While some research has included incidental observation of actual interethnic behavior, such behavior has not been systematically investigated except with reference to studies of the voluntary self-segregation or self-selection of actual classmates among children. Even here the data are generally of a quasi-behavioral sort, that is, sociometric preferences.

Studies of very young children clearly suggest that there is little relationship between their ethnic behavior and their ethnic orientation, that is, between what they say and do publicly with other children or adults and what they indicate in private or reveal on doll and picture tests. Goodman (1952) found that nursery school children who gave evidence in private of racial awareness and racial preferences were quite free of racialism in their public behavior. Stevenson and Stevenson (1960) found that, while most of their Negro and white nursery school children were very much racially aware and to a lesser degree racially oriented, there were no differences between them "in the frequency or types of intra-racial and interracial behavior."

It is also of importance to note that Goodman (1952) found that racial and religious epithets were often coupled with friendly interaction between her white and Negro nursery school subjects. Of course this may not be an inconsistency in behavior at all if the child who uses such epithets does not perceive them as capable of hurting the other child; or if he regards using them as a form of play because of their strong affective and taboo nature. The emotionally laden character of such terms as "nigger," "goy," "dago," and "kike" for the child is well illustrated in the observations of very young children reported by Lasker (1929) and Radke and Trager (1950) as well as Goodman. As "powerful" words, racial epithets are able to express the inner excitement experienced by the child.

Many of the studies discussed earlier establish that prejudice in very young children (in the sense of negative ethnic orientation) begins to manifest itself by the third or fourth year. Some studies of intergroup behavior, however, reveal that racial or religious cleavage begins to occur only at a much later age. In his study of New York City public school children from the first to the eighth grade, Moreno (1934) found by means of the sociometric technique that racial cleavage between white and Negro children does not occur to any great extent before the third grade, and by the fifth grade, or around the age of 10, the cleavage has reached its height.

Support for this finding was provided in later studies by Criswell (1937, 1939) and by Radke, Sutherland, and Rosenberg (1950). One interpretation of these results is that, while at first the child selects playmates and school chums on the basis of personal experiences and specific pleasant or unpleasant situations, as he grows older his attraction or repulsion with respect to members of a given group is dependent on the formation of generalized attitudes toward that group. There is, in other words, an increasing integration of ethnic attitudes and behavior.

Lambert and Taguchi (1956), however, challenge the generalization that racial cleavage begins to appear only between the ages of 8 and 10 years. They suggest that such cleavage exists in preschool children, but is not revealed in the kinds of choices required by the standard sociometric techniques. In their own study, therefore, of six Oriental and seven Occidental children in a Montreal preschool, the subjects were asked to make choices believed to be more meaningful to them, for example, choosing a child to receive candy from them. It was found that the measure elicited ethnocentric choices among the Oriental children, but that a similar trend among the Occidental children was not statistically significant.

McCandless and Hoyt (1961) made time-sampling observations of 33 Oriental children and 25 Caucasian children at the University of Hawaii preschools over a three-and-a-half-month period. Clear evidence of ethnic cleavage was obtained. Oriental children played more with other Oriental children, and Caucasian children more with other Caucasian children, despite the fact that the mixing of races was commonplace in the broader social setting. Just when racial cleavage begins—that is, in preschool or only after the child reaches the third or fourth grade—still remains an open question. There are simultaneous differences in measurement techniques, social settings, and racial groups between the early and later investigations; thus no firm conclusion on the issue is possible.

Ethnic cleavage among high school youth has also been investigated. Loomis (1943) employed a modified sociometric technique to study cleavages in two high schools in the Southwest. It was found that Spanish-American and Anglo-American students reported much greater association with members of their own group. In each school the minority group, whether Anglo- or Spanish-American, showed a greater tendency toward ingroup selection and exclusion of the outgroup than was manifested by the majority group. This pattern tends to be reversed with respect to religious ethnocentrism, at least insofar as children from upper-class homes are concerned. Goodnow and Tagiuri (1952) studied the sociometric preferences of Jewish, Catholic, and Protestant students in a private high school and found evidence of ethnocentrism among all three groups. However, Jews chose Catholics and Protestants more than the members of those groups chose Jews. Greater ethnocentrism among non-Jewish school students between the ages of 8 and 12 from upper-class homes has also been reported by Harris and Watson (1946). In an extensive study involving over 1000 high school students, Lundberg and Dickson (1952) found that, in general, every ethnic group in the sample showed a preference for its own members in four sociometric choice situations: selecting a leader, work partner, friend, and dating companion. Among non-Jewish white students, ethnocentrism was found to increase with age.

DETERMINANTS OF INTERGROUP ATTITUDES

Notwithstanding the differences among investigators in the determinants they emphasize to explain ethnic attitudes, there are three broad assumptions on which most if not all authorities are agreed: first, that intergroup attitudes are learned; second, that they are multicausally determined; and finally, that they are functional or need-satisfying in character for the individual.

As Allport notes (1954), most theories of prejudice "are advanced by their authors to call attention to some important causal factor, without implying that no other factors are operating" (p. 207). The various theoretical conceptions are complementary and overlapping rather than mutually exclusive. And it is generally recognized that intergroup attitudes are rooted in both the social environment that defines the person's existence and in those psychological processes which initiate and direct his behavior in this environment. Accordingly, in the discussion that follows, we shall begin with influences external to the individual (such as cultural norms), continue with situations in which the individual may be involved (such as contact with minority-group members), and finally move to a consideration of selected psychological determinants of prejudice (such as frustration, cognitive factors, and individual personality factors).

CULTURAL AND GROUP NORMS

The powerful influence of the broader sociocultural properties of our society (social structure, economic and political traditions, etc.) on the development of intergroup attitudes is reflected in the normative character of such attitudes among Americans. For some theorists, therefore, ethnic prejudice is a problem rooted in the social organization and practices of a society and not in the unique problems or pathologies of the individual (Clark, 1955; Sherif *et al.*, 1961). In the previous section we cited investigations which have demonstrated a relatively enduring and uniform hierarchy of preferences for ethnic groups in America.

Perhaps the best evidence for the regularity of ethnic attitudes in the United States is to be found in the previously considered studies of the development of racial prejudice. In 1936, Horowitz found that white children in New York City, urban Tennessee, and urban and rural Georgia developed essentially similar attitudes toward the Negro. Some two decades later approximately the same attitudes (or ethnic orientations) were revealed in young children in two Northeastern urban communities (Goodman, 1952; Trager and Yarrow, 1952), in a Texas community (Stevenson and Stewart, 1958), and in a Virginia community (Morland, 1958, 1962). These findings support Horowitz' (1936) conclusions that emerging attitudes toward Negroes are "now chiefly determined not by contact with Negroes but by contact with the prevalent attitude toward Negroes" (p. 35).

We do not have a full understanding of the normative determination of ethnic attitudes until we see that for most people conflicting norms are involved. This insight is the great achievement of Myrdal's *An American Dilemma* (1944). Myrdal showed that in situation after situation the attitudes of white Americans could be understood as compromises between the universalistic demands of what he called "The American Creed" and the particularistic requirements of solidarity with one's class, kin, and color. Subsequent experience with desegregation has demonstrated the correctness of Myrdal's analysis.

The normative character of ethnic prejudice involves far more than the fact that attitudes are shared by members of a majority or minority group. Each member is *expected* to hold such attitudes, and on those who fail to conform in this regard, pressures in a variety of forms are brought to bear (for example, loss of status, verbal condemnation, group rejection). These pressures toward conformity are often subtle, but they are very real. They become far less subtle in the experience of the individual when he deviates in what he says or does from the established ethnic norms of his own group. The fact that so many individuals do risk group ostracism by persistent deviation testifies to the power—for them—of counternorms. This is the key to the psychology of the ethnic revolutionary and the ethnic martyr.

The importance of social norms in the development of ethnic prejudice is well illustrated in two studies reported by Pettigrew (1958). In an investigation of 600 white South African university students, he obtained measures of the degree to which they were anti-Negro, authoritarian in personality, and tended to exhibit conformity to social norms independently of prejudice. It was found that more prejudiced students, as compared with those of greater tolerance, not only tended to conform more generally but were also more authoritarian in personality. Though this suggested that the conformers were more anti-Negro because they were more authoritarian, Pettigrew was able to demonstrate clearly that the individual's tendencies toward social conformity independently influenced the extent to which he was prejudiced. For example, though native-born South African students were more anti-Negro than those who were not born there, they did not differ in authoritarianism. These findings are consistent with those in a parallel study of adults from four Southern and four Northern communities in the United States. Here too, despite the difference in anti-Negro prejudice, the two populations did not differ in authoritarianism.

PARENTAL INFLUENCES

Parents are the primary agents of socialization. On their shoulders falls the major responsibility for the transmission of cultural norms for intergroup attitudes. In many instances, however, the attitudes of parents deviate to some extent from the norms of their group. In such instances it is appropriate to speak of "family norms" for intergroup attitudes, and it is these norms to which the child must conform in order to avoid parental disapproval.

Many studies reveal and emphasize the crucial role parents play in the formation of ethnic attitudes. Horowitz and Horowitz (1938), in a study of Southern grade school children, found that parents were the primary source from which racial attitudes were learned. Younger children were aware that their own attitudes stemmed from those of their parents, but older children were likely to forget the source and rationalize their attitudes in various ways. Notwithstanding the latter finding, 69 percent of a large group of college students studied by Allport and Kramer (1946) declared themselves to have been influenced to some degree by their parents' ethnic attitudes. A higher proportion of prejudiced than of unprejudiced students reported taking over their parents' attitudes directly. These findings are consistent with others reported by Frenkel-Brunswik and Sanford (1945), Rosenblith (1949), and Bird, Monachesi, and Burdick (1952).

Granted that parents are a significant influence in the development of the child's ethnic attitudes, it is important to ask how this influence is exerted. In the study by Horowitz and Horowitz (1938), which involved interviewing rural Tennessee children, it was found that the white child is taught Negro prejudice by a method both direct and harsh ("I play with colored children sometimes and Mama whips me"). In other cultural settings, the learning of ethnic prejudice may be just as direct but far more "refined" in its approach. The child may be told that Negroes or Jews are "not nice," or "not to be seen with," and the actual or threatened punishment may be psychological rather than physical (for example, loss of love).

It is evident, however, from the studies of Goodman (1952) and Radke-Yarrow and her associates (1952) that children may learn similar attitudes in an *indirect* fashion. In the Radke-Yarrow study, about one-half of the Negro families and three-quarters of the white ones believed that their own children should be taught to recognize differences between groups, but only about four percent *obviously* attempted to instill prejudice. Nevertheless, about one-third of the Protestant and Catholic parents made use of hostile descriptions and stereotypes in explaining racial and religious differences to their children. It is equally possible for favorable ethnic attitudes to be learned in the home since, as Trager and Yarrow (1952) point out, "Parents' teaching of intergroup attitudes is frequently unconscious and is rarely direct or planned" (p. 349).

On the other hand, it should be emphasized that the effects of parental influence are by no means unlimited. In the study by Bird and his associates (1952), the correlations obtained were not only low (+0.21), but parents resembled each other more than they did their children in attitudes toward the Negro. Frenkel-Brunswik and Havel (1953) also report only low positive correlations between children's ethnic attitudes and those of their parents.

In an unpublished paper Kenneth B. Clark warns against weighting too heavily the role of parents in the transmission of interracial attitudes. He contends that symbols of racial discrimination, such as residential segregation and segregated schools and churches (implying the inferiority of Negroes), act as more powerful educators in interracial ways; and furthermore, that children often develop hostile ethnic attitudes in the face of parental as well as clerical admonitions of tolerance and brotherhood. The reverse pattern also frequently occurs, in which children develop democratic attitudes in the face of ethnic hostility in the home. Not only is there a subtle interplay between general cultural as well as family influences impinging on the child, but particular children for a variety of reasons may develop specific attitudes contrary to the prevailing sentiments surrounding them.

EDUCATION, SOCIOECONOMIC STATUS, AND RELIGIOUS INFLUENCES

Most of the studies in this area have been correlational in method, and few, if any, have succeeded in disentangling the effects of numerous factors varying simultaneously in an uncontrolled fashion. Rose (1948b) has ably summarized studies reported up to the mid-1940's, and a review of recent studies of anti-Semitism is provided by Tumin (1961). The most dependable finding in this area is the negative correlation between prejudice of most kinds and amount of formal education (Allport, 1954; Rose, 1948b; Williams, 1964). Of course, education correlates highly with socioeconomic position, and therefore its negative relationship to intolerance might be a function of the selective processes that determine who will receive a higher education as well as of the educational experience itself. However, Bettelheim and Janowitz (1964) point out that "on the basis of some 25 national sample surveys since 1945, the positive effect seems to be real, not spurious. The lower levels of prejudice among the better educated seem to involve the social experience of education specifically and not merely the sociological origins of the educated" (p. 18).

On the other hand, it should be emphasized that the influence of education on ethnic attitudes is far from being a simple process. Thus Stember (1961) carefully reviews the impact of schooling on ethnic attitudes and notes that in most respects the better educated are less likely to be prejudiced. Yet they are also more likely to avoid intimate contacts with minority groups; to hold highly affective, derogatory stereotypes; and to favor discrimination in some areas of behavior on an informal basis. In part, this may explain why at least one investigation (A. A. Campbell, 1947) reports a positive correlation between education and anti-Semitism in a national sample of respondents. Later surveys have supported this finding, at least in terms of specific questions relevant to stereotyping Jews in highly affective and derogatory terms (Stember, 1961).

When education is controlled, socioeconomic status usually shows a positive correlation with anti-Semitism (Fortune Survey, 1946; Harlan, 1942; Levinson and Sanford, 1944; Williams, 1964). Its relationship with attitude toward Negroes is not so clear, because it varies with the type of question asked and the attitudinal components being investigated. The most common finding is that individuals of low economic status are most likely to have unfavorable attitudes toward Negroes (Bettelheim and Janowitz, 1964; Williams, 1964). These correlations suggest that upper-class white Gentiles are most likely to feel threatened by competition with Jews, while lower-class individuals are most likely to feel threatened by competition with Negroes (Williams, 1964).

Taken together, the findings on the role of religious background in the development of ethnic attitudes do not provide any consistent picture. Several investigators have reported Catholics to be most hostile toward the Negro; Protestants next most prejudiced; and Jews and those with no religious affiliation least prejudiced (Allport and Kramer, 1946; Bettelheim and Janowitz, 1950a; Merton, 1940). On the other hand, two other studies only partially confirm or do not confirm these findings at all (MacKenzie, 1948; Rosenblith, 1949). Most investigators have found little or no difference between Catholics and Protestants in the extent of prejudice toward Jews. In a recent study by Triandis and Triandis (1960), overall ethnic prejudice based on a total social-distance score of 16 stimulus groups was highest for Catholics, next for Protestants, and lowest for Jews.

Attempts to determine the relationship between prejudice and measures of the strength of religious influences (such as frequency of church attendance) have also produced conflicting results. Some of the apparent conflict in findings may perhaps be resolved by taking into account the differing churchgoing habits of the various religious groups, the relative degree of prejudice characterizing each group, and the religious-group composition of the populations studied. A good discussion of the major findings is provided by Williams (1964, pp. 57–61).

It may well be—other things being equal—that what is significant in the influence of religion on ethnic prejudice is not the particular church affiliation or the degree of participation in church activities, but rather the extent to which the individual is committed to the values and precepts of his chosen religion (Allport, 1954). Thus, in a study by O'Reilly and O'Reilly (1954), it was found that among Catholic students attending college in a Southern city, those who agreed with the Catholic Church on certain social, moral, and religious issues were more favorable to Negroes and Jews and opposed to segregation.

INTERGROUP CONTACT

What is the role of personal contact in the formation of ethnic attitudes? In the first place, it seems reasonable to believe that frequent contacts with members of other groups increase the *salience* of attitudes toward these groups. Horowitz (1944) reports the results of a *Fortune* survey made in 1939 in which respondents were asked, "Is there any one group—racial, religious, economic, or social—in your city (county) who represents an important problem?" There was a definite correlation between the number of members of a particular minority group in a geographical region and the frequency with which the group was described as a "problem" by residents of that region. Thus Negroes were most frequently mentioned in the South and the East, Jews in the Northeast and Middle West, Mexicans in the West, and Japanese on the Pacific Coast.

It also seems reasonable to believe that direct observation of ethnic group members over a period of time plays some role in the formation of stereotypes concerning them. This is the "kernel of truth" hypothesis (Klineberg, 1950) to which we have previously referred. Zawadzki (1948) argues for this hypothesis as a substitute for the "well-earned reputation" theory, which he rejects.

Finally, it seems probable that personal contact between members of different ethnic groups may play a decisive role in the formation of intergroup attitudes if the contact takes place under conditions of genuine cooperation or serious competition or conflict. Under these conditions it is not primarily the objective characteristics of the group members which are important, but the relationship of the two groups to each other. Evidence for the importance of cooperative contact comes almost entirely from experimental studies of attitude change, which will be reviewed later in this chapter. The general principle has been formulated by Williams (1947) in the following terms: "Lessened hostility will result from arranging intergroup collaboration, on the basis of personal association of individuals as functional equals, on a common task jointly accepted as worthwhile" (p. 69). Evidence for competition and conflict as determinants of ethnic attitudes comes mainly from nonexperimental studies, to some of which we shall now turn.

CONFLICT, COMPETITION, AND STATUS MOBILITY

Conflict among members of different ethnic groups reaches its peak in open warfare. It seems almost a truism to say that such conditions exert an extremely powerful force toward the development of unfavorable intergroup attitudes. The hatred of warring nations for each other is proverbial, and much of the hatred remains after the war is over. One example of the influence of open conflict on intergroup attitudes is to be found in the studies of changes in attitude toward Japanese and Germans during World War II on the part of American respondents (Dudycha, 1942; Meenes, 1943, 1950; Seago, 1947). Another example is the investigation by Sinha and Upadhyaya (1960) of the dispute between India and China concerning the borderline between their countries. Stereotypes of the Chinese held by Indian college students were measured in February 1959, before the state of conflict had occurred, and again in December when tensions had increased. Whereas before the conflict Chinese had been looked upon as friendly, progressive, brave, cultured, and the like, following it they were perceived as aggressive, selfish, cruel, shrewd, warmongering, cheating, and stupid. Stereotypes of other countries showed only minor changes during the same period. Other studies by Dodd (1935) and Buchanan (1951) have also shown changes in national stereotypes as a result of recent group conflict.

Economic competition, either actual or potential, is a powerful source of intergroup conflict, although within the boundaries of a single country efforts to restrict competition do not usually take the form of open warfare. The history of American immigration is full of riots directed against immigrant groups. The most active agents in these riots were usually people who felt economically threatened by the immigrants.

Dollard (1938, pp. 25–26) has provided a simple and instructive example of the influence of economic competition on ethnic attitudes:

> A final case will be that of a group of Germans who invaded a small American industrial town in the early twentieth century. Local whites largely drawn from the surrounding farms manifested considerable direct aggression toward the newcomers. Scornful and derogatory opinions were expressed about these Germans, and the native whites had a satisfying sense of superiority toward them. . . . The chief element in the permission to be aggressive against the Germans was rivalry for jobs and status in the local woodenware plants. The native whites felt definitely crowded for their jobs by the entering German groups and in case of bad times had a chance to blame the Germans who by their presence provided more competitors for the scarcer jobs. There seemed to be no traditional pattern of prejudice against Germans unless the skeletal suspicion of all out-groupers (always present) be invoked in this place.

An ethnic group may engage in economic competition with other groups through upward social mobility as well as by geographical migration. It seems fairly clear that there was more hostility—and certainly more violence—toward Negroes on the part of Southern white workers following the American Civil War than there had been during the slavery period. Similarly, in the North there has typically been a hostile reaction on the part of white workers whenever Negroes were introduced into what had been considered "white men's jobs."

Throughout history there have been many opportunities for the economic exploitation of one ethnic group by another. In these situations the attitudes of the dominant group toward the subordinate one have usually been friendly so long as the system of economic relations was not challenged, but the attitudes have become hostile whenever the subordinate group attempted to improve its position. The attitudes of Southern white plantation owners toward Negroes before and after the Civil War illustrate this phenomenon, as do the attitudes of ruling minorities in colonial countries.

Agitation for the expulsion of ethnic groups from certain areas has often been initiated by people who hoped to take over the property of the group in question or to eliminate them as economic competitors. McWilliams (1944) has shown that the evacuation of Japanese-Americans from the American West Coast in 1942 occurred in a context of such agitation, and there is good reason to believe that similar motives played a large part in the persecution of German Jews by the Nazis. Perhaps the clearest example of this phenomenon is the demand for the expulsion of dominant European minorities which has been widespread in colonial areas since the end of World War II.

A widespread form of competition in American society that is not strictly economic in nature is competition for prestige and social status. In the United States, status depends primarily on economic success, and status mobility is high. But there is also a hierarchical ranking of ethnic groups on the status scale, and this fact provides an element of stability in the social position of each group member. In these circumstances each individual member of a group not at the bottom of the prestige scale has a vested interest in maintaining the belief that individuals in lower-ranking groups are intrinsically inferior. The strength of this vested interest is greatest for those individuals whose own status position is most insecure.

Dollard (1937) concluded that the desire of white individuals to maintain their status was one of the major factors responsible for the persistence of anti-Negro prejudice in the Deep South. He also found that this motive seemed to be most important in the poor white group. More recently, a study made in a Southern county in the United States to determine the varying attitudes of male Southerners toward desegregation identified one group of men who would resort to violence if necessary to halt desegregation (Tumin, Barton, and Burrus, 1958). As a group, these men are at the bottom of the status hierarchy in terms of education, occupation, and income, and therefore they not only have little chance of improving their own position, but they are most threatened by the rise of Negro status.

A. A. Campbell (1947) found anti-Semitism most common among people who were dissatisfied with their own economic situation. Bettelheim and Janowitz (1950a), in their study of Chicago war veterans, found both anti-Semitism and anti-Negro attitudes most frequent among those whose economic status had declined from its prewar position. Those who had improved their economic status were more friendly toward both Jews and Negroes than those whose status had remained the same, except for a samall group whose income had increased markedly and who were more anti-Semitic than the general average.

In a reconsideration of their original findings on the effects of downward social mobility on ethnic prejudice, Bettelheim and Janowitz (1964) reviewed seven studies subsequent to their own which were relevant to this question. In general, the finding of greater ethnic prejudice among those individuals whose economic status had declined was confirmed, despite the variations in the methods and populations employed in these later investigations.

An experimental study of the role of competition and conflict in the development of intergroup attitudes has been reported by Sherif *et al.* (1961). The two groups in question were formed artificially at a boy's camp, but became strongly knit and very important for their members through a succession of group activities. After the groups were well established, a program of intergroup competition was begun, which quickly led to the development of hostile feelings between the groups. Not only did the social distance between the groups increase, but in addition, the members of one group developed and applied highly negative stereotypes to the members of the other group. How this intergroup hostility was reduced is a problem which we shall consider later.

FRUSTRATION AND THE DISPLACEMENT OF HOSTILITY

The general process of displacement of hostility, first described by Freud, has been examined in great detail by Dollard *et al.* (1939). Williams (1947) describes the conditions necessary for its occurrence in the following terms (p. 52):

a) Frustrations or deprivations are imposed by sources which are either:
1) difficult to define or locate, or
2) persons or organizations in a position of power or authority over the individual, or
3) persons to whom the individual is closely tied by affectional bonds.

b) Aroused hostilities are blocked from direct expression against the sources of frustration.

c) Substitute objects of aggression are available and are:
1) highly *visible*, and
2) *vulnerable*, i.e., not in a position to retaliate.

This formulation expresses very well the displacement of hostility from one *object* to another, but it does not mention alternative transformations that sometimes qualify displacement, as in the change from one *form of expression* to another. Both processes are well illustrated in the recent history of attitudes of American Negroes toward American whites. Under conditions of intense repression, as in the Deep South before World War II, hostility was rarely expressed except in fantasy or in conversation and jokes with other Negroes (Wright, 1945). In subsequent years more direct forms of expression became possible, especially for Negroes who migrated to the Northern cities. In the race riots of the 1960's direct attacks by Negroes against whites were fairly common. They were occasionally directed against the white policemen and landlords who were the objects of greatest Negro resentment, but they were more commonly focused on neighborhood storekeepers, or on passing motorists or pedestrians (*cf.* Cohen and Murphy, 1966).

The role of displaced hostility in ethnic prejudice has been emphasized particularly by psychoanalytically oriented writers (Ackerman and Jahoda, 1950; Bettelheim and Janowitz, 1950a, 1964; Brown, 1942; Dollard *et al.*, 1939). Probably the most compelling evidence for its importance comes from case studies and intensive observations, such as those of Wright (1945) and Cohen and Murphy (1966). But there have been a number of quantitative investigations as well. Much of the research already cited on the effects of economic competition on prejudice illustrates displaced hostility as well as hostility directly expressed. The same is true of a series of investigations in the American South showing a positive relationship between economic deprivation and various forms of hostility expressed by whites toward Negroes (Cantril, 1941; Hovland and Sears, 1940; Pettigrew and Cramer, 1959; Raper, 1933).

The earliest *experimental* demonstration of displaced hostility was reported by Miller and Bugelski (1948) in a study of boys 18 to 20 years of age attending a summer camp. The attitudes of the boys toward Japanese and Mexicans were measured before and after a severe frustration imposed by the camp management: they were prevented from attending the very attractive bank night at the local movie house by the requirement that they take a series of long, difficult, and boring tests. It was found that after frustration they attributed a smaller number of positive traits to Japanese and Mexicans, and to a lesser extent they also attributed more undesirable qualities to the two nationalities. The Miller and Bugelski findings were replicated by Cowen, Landes, and Schaet (1959), although Stagner and Congdon (1955) failed to find any change in ethnic attitudes after frustration by the experimenters.

Some writers have hypothesized that more prejudiced individuals have a greater tendency to displace hostility (in general, but especially toward minority groups) following frustration than have those who are relatively unprejudiced. The earliest test of this hypothesis was reported by Lindzey (1950). Twenty college students, half of whom were known to be high in minority-group prejudice and the other half low in prejudice, were individually subjected to severe frustration in a small-group cooperative task situation. No difference in displaced hostility as revealed in two projective tests (TAT and Rosenzweig Picture Frustration Test) was found between the two groups—notwithstanding the fact that there was clear evidence that the prejudiced subjects were more intensely frustrated by the experimental manipulation than were the more tolerant ones.

Employing another student (experimental confederate) as the "innocent victim," Berkowitz (1959) found that highly anti-Semitic college girls, subjected to annoyance and frustration at the hands of the experimenter, tended to increase in hostility toward their peer. Given the same frustration, the more tolerant subjects became somewhat friendlier to the other girl. Weatherley (1961) carried out a similar study, except that his high and low anti-Semitic college groups responded to a fantasy test involving Jewish and non-Jewish figures. It was found, first, that after frustration the more anti-Semitic subjects directed more aggressive responses toward the Jewish characters in their stories than did those who were low in anti-Semitism; and second, that there was no difference in this respect between these two groups when non-Jewish characters were involved. In this instance, then, what was established was a specific rather than a generalized tendency to aggression in the prejudiced person. Other studies by Berkowitz (1961) and Berkowitz and Green (1962) provide additional evidence that prejudiced subjects are more prone to display aggression of some sort following frustration.

A fairly well-established finding is that prejudiced individuals are more susceptible to frustration than are individuals who are more tolerant toward other ethnic groups. As we have already noted, Lindzey (1950) found that his highly prejudiced subjects experienced significantly more frustration than did his less prejudiced subjects when experimentally aroused. However, Berkowitz (1959), in the study of anti-Semitic women described above, found no evidence of such a relationship. On the other hand, there are a number of correlational studies that support Lindzey's original finding. Of particular interest is the observation by Bettelheim and Janowitz (1950a) that prejudiced war veterans experienced more frustration during their army service than did tolerant ones, although there were no significant differences in the objective conditions to which the two groups were exposed. In a study of 271 high school students in a Midwest community, Gough (1951) reports that the subjects were "less able to overlook and ignore minor irritations." Similar relationships between prejudice and feelings of frustration are suggested by the findings of Morse (1947), Allport and Kramer (1946), and Rosenblith (1949).

Worthy of particular note is Lesser's (1958) study of the relationship between anti-Semitism and extrapunitiveness as measured by Rosenzweig's Picture Frustration Test in Jewish and non-Jewish boys between 10 and 13 years of age. In both groups of boys, greater anti-Semitism was strongly correlated with more extrapunitive reactions to frustration (0.60 and 0.48 respectively). Thus, it may well be that displacement of hostility occurs in the more prejudiced individual because, along with other factors already noted, he cannot assume responsibility for the frustrations he experiences and thus must condemn others. Some support for this interpretation is revealed in the study by Berkowitz (1959) described earlier.

A crucial problem for any psychological theory in which displaced hostility plays a role is that of explaining the selection of a target for the hostile impulses. Two essential requirements for the target are described by Williams (1947) in the passage quoted at the beginning of this section: the target must be visible, and it must have little power to retaliate. Many ethnic groups have both of these characteristics. To explain why some particular group becomes the object of especially intense hostility on the part of certain people, it is necessary to invoke additional hypotheses; we shall examine only a few of the large number which have been proposed.

Dollard (1938) argues that any group with which an individual is in direct competition or conflict is likely to become the object of displaced hostility as well. Another very general possibility is that an ethnic group may *symbolize* certain things which an individual detests. Thus it has been argued that hostility is frequently directed against Jews because they symbolize fraud (Ichheiser, 1944), or paternal authority (Levinger, 1936), or successful nonconformity (Tarachow, 1946), or urbanism (Rose, 1948b), or capitalism (Beard, 1942), or both capitalism and communism (Riesman, 1942), or the devil (Trachtenberg, 1943), or Christ and Christian morality (Maritain, 1939). Each of these theories probably has some validity in explaining the attitudes of certain individuals; the difficulty with them is that little or nothing is known of the conditions under which an ethnic group such as the Jews will be accepted as a symbol of some disliked practice or institution, and the conditions under which the symbolic equation cannot be made.

In a recent discussion Berkowitz and Green (1962) have considered in detail the problem of why particualr groups are selected as scapegoats. While they recognize the importance of the *visibility* and *strangeness* of the group, these factors in themselves are not the determinants of the displaced aggression. What is important is the meaning these characteristics have for the frustrated person. And in this respect the strange group receives displaced hostility to the degree that it is *disliked* by the individual for its differences. Psychoanalytic writers argue that the differences most disliked by the prejudiced individual are those he unconsciously recognizes and rejects as potential characteristics in himself (Ackerman and Jahoda, 1950; Fenichel, 1946). Berkowitz and Green (1962) recognize this possibility, but do not really take any position on the factors responsible for initial dislike of an ethnic group.

BELIEF CONGRUENCE

In recent years Rokeach and his associates have argued vigorously for the importance of "belief congruence" as a determinant of ethnic attitudes (Rokeach, 1960; Rokeach and Rothman, 1965). This claim has been challenged by Triandis (1961), and has led to a good deal of additional experimental work (Byrne and Wong, 1962; Rokeach, 1966; Stein, Hardyck, and Smith, 1965). In discussing this subject, one must distinguish between a narrower claim made by Rokeach and a much broader claim advanced at the same time (see especially the chapter by Rokeach, Smith, and Evans entitled "Two Kinds of Prejudice or One?" in Rokeach, 1960).

The narrower claim is that for certain types of individuals perceived similarity or dissimilarity of beliefs is more important than ethnic differences in willingness to associate with other individuals on friendly terms (social distance). This claim can be tested, provided one is willing to specify a respondent population, the ethnic groups involved, and the nature of the belief differences. It has been clearly established that, for white American college and high school students in the 1960's, perceived belief congruence on subjects with a high emotional charge (such as communism, atheism, etc.) *is* a more important determinant of social distance than ethnic differences, even Negro-white differences (Smith, Williams, and Willis, 1967; Stein, Hardyck, and Smith, 1965).   Thus Rokeach's narrower claim is basically correct.

It is Rokeach's broader claim, however, that is responsible for most of the current interest in belief congruence. This claim begins with the proposition described in the previous paragraph and continues with two additional assertions: (1) members of a particular ethnic group typically believe that most members of groups toward whom they feel great social distance hold beliefs on topics of fundamental importance that are greatly divergent from their own; and (2) this perceived dissimilarity of beliefs is a major determinant (or *the* major determinant) of the actual degree of social distance expressed by members of one ethnic group toward another. In its extreme form the broader claim asserts that ethnic attitudes can be accounted for *entirely* on the basis of assumed belief congruence; hence the question, "Two Kinds of Prejudice or One?" (Rokeach, 1960).

Actually Rokeach has never maintained the broader claim in its extreme form, and it is doubtful that anyone could take it seriously. The actual importance of assumed belief congruence as a determinant of social distance is a matter for detailed investigation and specification. So far, the major relevant study (in addition to the ones already cited) is that of Byrne and Wong (1962), who showed that white subjects with strongly anti-Negro attitudes are indeed more likely than subjects with pro-Negro attitudes to assume that the majority of Negroes hold beliefs different from their own on issues of fundamental importance. There remains the question of the extent to which the assumed belief dissimilarity determined, or was determined by, the affective and conative orientation toward Negroes.

It is difficult to read reports of these studies without feeling acutely the gulf between the world of the college student and his questionnaire or laboratory responses and the world of race relationships *in vivo*. Perhaps the ethnic attitudes so vividly described by Goodman in *Race Awareness in Young Children* (1952) and by Wright in *Black Boy* (1945) are mainly the result of assumed belief dissimilarity, but it seems scarcely possible that this is really true. The area in which it seems to us that assumed belief congruence may be of real importance is as a determinant of the attitudes of one religious group toward another. The reasons for this assertion are that the basis for membership in a religious group is to a large extent defined by assent to certain beliefs, and that differences in these beliefs and the value orientations associated with them frequently lead to sharply divergent positions on many social issues, even though there is likely to be a common core of agreement on major value premises among the established religious groups of any particular society. This whole subject is discussed by Hager, Glock, and Chein (1956).

OTHER COGNITIVE FACTORS

Many investigators have observed differences in "cognitive style" between individuals who are highly tolerant and those who generally reject members of other ethnic groups, and they have argued that such differences play an important role as determinants of individual differences in overall level of prejudice. To the extent that prejudice is defined as a failure of rationality, it follows necessarily that there will be some differences in the characteristic modes of thinking of prejudiced and unprejudiced individuals. However, the nature and extent of the differences remain matters for investigation.

Frenkel-Brunswik (1948) studied 120 children between the ages of 11 and 16 who were either very high or very low in prejudice as measured by the California *E* scale. Children high in prejudice tended to be intolerant of ambiguity (becoming anxious about or resisting situations that were not clearly structured), dichotomous in their thinking about sex roles, and inclined to define position in the family in terms of hierarchical roles. Those low in prejudice were found to be tolerant of ambiguity, to have egalitarian views toward the opposite sex, and to think in terms of individualized and equal-treatment roles in the family.

We might expect that intolerance of ambiguity would lead intolerant individuals to *create* situational or stimulus structure where little or none exists. Various investigations have tested this hypothesis but have failed to produce consistent results (Block and Block, 1951; Davids, 1955; Fisher, 1951; Millon, 1957).

Rokeach (1951a, 1951b, 1951c) found that highly ethnocentric individuals exhibit concreteness and "narrow-mindedness" in their thinking, whereas the low in prejudice usually show a more abstract and less narrow-minded cognitive orientation. However, in one study (1951b) his low-prejudice subjects tended to show a greater tendency to personify or concretize abstract ideas in their thinking, a finding which Rokeach related to the dogmatism often ascribed to the extremely unprejudiced (Dombrose and Levinson, 1950).

Kutner (1958) undertook a comprehensive investigation of cognitive processes in 60 seven-year-old children rated high or low in ethnic prejudice. These children were administered abstract-reasoning, concept-formation, and deductive-logic tests, and it was found that the ethnocentric children were more intolerant of ambiguity (in this case, an inability to face uncertainty in solving problems) than were the less prejudiced children. The more prejudiced children, in comparison with their more tolerant classmates, also exhibited a lower level of abstract reasoning, though the two groups did not differ in intelligence. Similar findings are reported by O'Connor (1952) in a study of tolerant and intolerant undergraduate students. Finally, ethnocentric attitudes were found to be related to the child's ability in concept formation and deductive logic, where intelligence was not a significant variable. These two relationships were confirmed in a more recent study by Klein (1961), though, unlike Kutner, he did not find any relationship between ethnocentrism and abstract reasoning.

Kutner and Gordon (1964) were able to restudy 33 of the original 60 seven year-old children first studied by Kutner (1958) some nine years earlier. Again the tolerant subjects generally exhibited greater ability to reason logically than did those high in prejudice, and on this occasion levels of prejudice and general intelligence were found to be negatively related.

PERSONALITY AND PREJUDICE

Often research workers have viewed intergroup attitudes as but one facet of the many manifestations of individual personality organization, and have studied the role of social attitudes in the economy of the total individual (Ackerman and Jahoda, 1950; Adorno *et al.*, 1950; Bettelheim and Janowitz, 1950a; Gough, 1951; Hartley, 1946; Rokeach, 1960). Thus, the tendency to displace hostility which we considered earlier is conceived of as only one of many characteristic response tendencies embedded

in personality structures that are particularly susceptible to the development of
ethnic prejudice or extreme social attitudes in general.

In a major investigation, *The Authoritarian Personality,* Adorno and his associates
(1950) studied both college students and groups of noncollege adults and demonstrated the generality of the individual's ethnic attitudes. High correlations were
obtained between scores on an anti-Semitism scale (*A* scale) and a more general
ethnocentrism scale (*E* scale); and the latter, in turn, correlated highly with the *F*
(fascism) scale, which was designed to measure the ways of thinking and feeling assumed to characterize those with a readiness to accept an antidemocratic ideology.
The critical part of the study, however, involved an intensive clinical interview with
45 subjects who were highly anti-Semitic and another 35 subjects who were low in
anti-Semitism.

It was found that highly prejudiced subjects, in contrast to those who were
tolerant, showed a more rigid personality organization, greater conventionality in
their values, more difficulty in accepting socially deviant impulses as part of the self
(for example, fear, weakness, aggression, and sex), a greater tendency to externalize
these impulses by means of projection, and more inclination to be status- and power-
oriented in their personal relationships. These personality attributes as well as
others (for example, idolizing one's parents, impersonal and punitive aggression,
dichotomous thinking) represented the defining features of the authoritarian personality. These attributes in turn were found to be related to early childhood experiences in a family setting characterized by harsh and threatening parental discipline, conditional parental love, a hierarchical family structure, and a concern for
family status. The unconscious conflict involving fear of and dependency on parents,
on the one hand, and strong hatred and suspicion of them, on the other, seemed to
be contained by an authoritarian personality structure tuned to expressing this
repressed hostility toward members of socially sanctioned outgroups.

Because of the scope and dramatic nature of its findings, *The Authoritarian
Personality* has had immense repercussions in generating both heated controversy
and new research (Christie and Jahoda, 1954; Titus and Hollander, 1957). Within
the limits of the present discussion we can consider only some of the more significant
studies and issues.

Smith and Rosen (1958) compared relatively matched groups of college students
who were at opposite extremes in "world-mindedness" (nationalist versus internationalist) in terms of variables similar to those of the California study. World-mindedness turned out to be closely and inversely related to authoritarianism as measured
by the *F* scale, and more important, many of the same differences in personality traits
and parent-child variables reported in the earlier study were found here. For example, internationally oriented students—or those low in authoritarianism—were
significantly more independent and less obedient in their relations with their parents
than the "nationalist" students.

It should be noted that much research, beginning with Murphy and Likert
(1938), has revealed medium to high correlations between attitudes toward ethnic
groups and such other factors as political and economic conservatism, a traditional
(authoritarian) family ideology, nationalistic political attitudes, tendencies toward
conformity, alienation or "anomie," and concern with social status (Christiansen,
1965; Kaufman, 1957; Kerr, 1944; Lentz, 1939; Levinson and Huffman, 1955;
Levinson and Sanford, 1944; McClosky, 1958; McDill, 1961; Pettigrew, 1958; Roberts

and Rokeach, 1956; Srole, 1956). We have already provided some evidence in the previous section that a *consistent* ethnic orientation begins to take shape only during adolescence. On the basis of his review of studies in political development, Hyman (1959) comes to the same conclusion regarding the emergence of a consistent political orientation. It is clear that by late adolescence both of these orientations become integrated or consistent with each other and with the individual's outlook on international affairs, family life, and child-rearing methods.

Authoritarianism is not confined to members of majority groups. Jews who score high on the *F* scale not only exhibit prejudice toward other groups, but they are also more anti-Semitic (Radke-Yarrow and Lande, 1953). Like other authoritarians, they were less analytical and gave more categorical reactions on group issues. Negro authoritarians are similar in their attitudes. They are more likely to defend segregation, dislike the NAACP, and display more ethnocentric group pride while being more susceptible to self- and own-group hatred (Grossack, 1957).

Are prejudiced children the product of a disciplined, status-oriented, and harsh family setting, as indicated by the California study (Adorno *et al.*, 1950)? If this question is assumed to ask simply whether prejudice in children is correlated with the harsh, disciplined, and status-oriented family setting, then the answer is certainly "Yes." Gough and his associates (1950), in a questionnaire study of 240 fourth-, fifth-, and sixth-grade children employing variants of the California techniques, arrived at generally similar findings. They then sent questionnaires to the mothers of these children eliciting their views on specific practices in child training (Harris, Gough, and Martin, 1950). In contrast to the mothers of the tolerant children, the mothers of highly prejudiced children believed, among other things, that obedience is the most important thing a child can learn; that a child should never be allowed to set his will against that of his parents; that a quiet child is preferable to one that is noisy; and that sex play by the child should be punished. Studies by Kates and Diab (1955), Lyle and Levitt (1955), Hart, (1957), Siegman (1957), and Weatherley (1963) confirm or partially confirm these findings.

Although the correlational findings relating personality and prejudice are quite consistent, two major problems of interpretation remain. The first is the extent to which the correlations reflect simply the influence of differing amounts of education on both sets of variables. This problem has been attacked by studies in which level of education was controlled, and the general finding is that most correlations remain significantly high (Allport and Kramer, 1946; Gough, 1951; Kaufman, 1957; McClosky, 1958; Roberts and Rokeach, 1956; Smith and Rosen, 1958). The second problem concerns the extent to which the demonstrated correlations between the ethnic attitudes of parents and children are determined in the manner assumed in *The Authoritarian Personality*—that is, one in which authoritarian child-rearing practices produce children with low frustration tolerance, high repressed hostility, and other personality factors that later generate hostile ethnic attitudes—or are determined instead by a direct process of identification in which the ethnic attitudes of parents are taken over by their children as part of the general process of socialization. No study of which we are aware has tackled this problem. What is necessary is an investigation focused on the ethnic attitudes of children of two uncommon types of parents: those with a combination of high ethnic prejudice and permissive or democratic child-rearing practices, and those with low prejudice but authoritarian child-rearing practices.

DETERMINANTS OF INTERGROUP BEHAVIOR

It is impossible for several reasons for us to present a systematic discussion of the determinants of intergroup behavior. There is as yet no really satisfactory classification of types of intergroup behavior, and—partly as a result of this fact—the great majority of discussions of interethnic behavior have been organized in terms of the relations of two or more specific ethnic groups with one another. We have an enormous amount of information about Arab-Jewish relations in Palestine, Anglo-French relations in Canada, Negro-white relations in the United States, and Hindu-Moslem relations in the Indian subcontinent, but there have been surprisingly few efforts to derive from this mass of information any general propositions about determinants of intergroup behavior. Williams (1947) assembled an impressive set of propositions on intergroup hostility and conflict, and Rose (1960) attempted to test some of these propositions using published materials on 40 literate societies. More recently, Campbell and LeVine (1961) have begun a large-scale program of research on attitudes toward and relationships with neighboring peoples in primitive and traditional societies. Wright (1965) has made a monumental study of war, the most destructive and highly institutionalized form of intergroup conflict. A question that has not been adequately faced in these cross-national and cross-cultural surveys concerns the extent to which intergroup behavior *within* complex societies in which multiple ethnic group membership is the rule follows the same principles as does intergroup behavior between members of two different primitive societies. Williams (1964, pp. 369–372) has made a strong case for the proposition that multiple ethnic group membership reduces the likelihood of intergroup conflict in complex societies, especially when the lines of ethnic cleavage also cut across differences of social class, region, and political party.

About all we can do in this section is outline some of the major forms of inter-ethnic behavior and indicate some major determinants on an impressionistic basis. A useful beginning is to distinguish between selective and unselective interethnic behavior. By *unselective* interethnic behavior we mean behavior directed toward other individuals without any awareness of their ethnic group membership or (if there is awareness) without any intention of selective treatment on an ethnic basis. An example would be a highway engineer who marks several blocks of a residential neighborhood for condemnation without any knowledge of the ethnic composition of the residents, or a sales clerk who sells articles at a fixed price to anyone who wants to buy them. *Selective* interethnic behavior is behavior toward other individuals that is shaped to some extent by knowledge of their ethnic group membership. This includes both discriminatory behavior and behavior that does not involve discrimination in the sense of departure from the standards of the American Creed. Examples of this latter type of behavior might be a political candidate who learns a few words of greeting in the native language of an ethnic group whose votes he is seeking, or a tourist who goes to visit an Indian reservation.

It is evident immediately that the determinants of unselective interethnic behavior are exactly the same as those of social behavior generally. No special analysis is called for. If there are any special determinants of interethnic behavior, their sphere of operation must be limited to their influence on *selective* interethnic behavior. Four main types of selective intergroup behavior have been distinguished in the social science literature: (1) competition and rivalry, (2) conflict and aggression, (3) segregation and discrimination, (4) cooperation and friendly association. Each of these merits a brief discussion.

COMPETITION AND RIVALRY

Competition is best defined as "that form of interaction which involves a struggle for goals which are scarce or are believed to be scarce; the interaction is normatively regulated, may be direct or indirect, personal or impersonal, and tends to exclude the use of force and violence" (Friedsam, 1964). Rivalry is conscious competition. In the field of intergroup relations, unconscious competition is an example of unselective interethnic behavior, while rivalry is selective interethnic behavior. When white settlers arrived on the North American continent they began a prolonged competition with the Indians for control of the continent's natural resources, even though it was a long time before very many Indians became conscious of this fact. Many of the Indian tribes had mutual treaties regulating the use of hunting grounds and other land areas; to the extent that these were honored, the tribes lived in a state of mutual economic competition. When they were not honored, conflict resulted. There was no mutually recognized set of normative principles that could provide a basis for stable treaties between whites and Indians; consequently, the conscious recognition of competition usually led directly to conflict.

CONFLICT AND AGGRESSION

Conflict is probably best defined as "a struggle over values and claims to scarce status, power, and resources in which the aims of the opponents are to neutralize, injure, or eliminate their rivals" (Coser, 1964). This definition focuses on group conflict and assumes it to be instrumental in nature. It is possible to have interindividual conflict as well, and we would include this under the category of selective interethnic behavior if it is shaped to some extent by the opponents' knowledge of each other's ethnic membership. A businessman may refrain from attacks on competitors who belong to his own ethnic group but attempt to destroy a rival who is a member of another ethnic group.

Closely related to the notion of conflict is aggression, which Williams (1947) defines as "an act whose end is the belief that injury to or destruction of a person or his values and symbols has been achieved." Direct acts of aggression are typical occurrences in the course of intergroup conflict; they may be primarily *instrumental* (that is, intended to help one party achieve the ends for which the struggle is being waged), or they may be primarily *expressive*, serving mainly to relieve the feelings of the aggressors. Most of the aggression in warfare is instrumental; most of the aggression in a race riot is expressive.

SEGREGATION AND DISCRIMINATION

The typical resolution of a territorial conflict is some form of boundary agreement. Occasionally one party to a conflict becomes so much more powerful than the other that he is able to draw boundaries that leave the other party only enclaves within a larger territory; this has been the typical outcome of group conflict between whites and Indians in North America. If the weaker party is required to stay in prescribed

areas, we refer to the arrangement as segregation. A less complete form of segregation does not isolate members of the weaker group geographically but requires them
to use separate facilities (railroad cars, schools, restaurants, waiting rooms, etc.).
The basic social function of all forms of segregation is to reduce the ability of the
weaker ethnic group to compete with the stronger.

Discrimination attempts to limit interethnic competition in a somewhat different
fashion. In its strongest form, members of a particular ethnic group are completely
excluded from certain types of employment, certain educational institutions, certain
fraternal organizations, etc. Weaker forms of discrimination are the imposition of
quotas limiting the number of members of a particular ethnic group in various
situations, or the requirement of different and higher standards of qualification for
the minority group members. Both segregation and discrimination aim at stabilizing
a particular set of power and status relationships; conflict ensues only when these
relationships are challenged by members of the disadvantaged group.

COOPERATION AND FRIENDLY ASSOCIATION

Cooperation is defined as "common action toward shared goals which may be corporate or distributive" (Dahlke, 1964). It is typical for ethnic groups (as well as other
social groups) to be simultaneously engaged in competition as well as cooperation with
one another. The cooperation may involve unlike efforts, as in interethnic trading
or in voluntary ethnic specialization in occupational roles (for example, the Jewish
physician or the Chinese laundryman); it may equally well involve similar efforts,
such as political alliances on the national scene or collaborative action at the local
level. Much rivalry may accompany this cooperation without damaging the interethnic relationship. It is conflict and cooperation that are incompatible (Davis, 1949,
pp. 166–167).

"Friendly association" is a somewhat broader and vaguer term than cooperation;
we use it to include not only common action toward some specific goal or goals but
also personal relationships in which the interaction is an end in itself. Interethnic
cooperation and friendly association are not always shaped by knowledge of the ethnic
membership of the interacting parties, but they are likely to be influenced by this
knowledge.

ETHNIC ATTITUDES AS DETERMINANTS OF INTERGROUP BEHAVIOR

A little reflection should make clear to anyone the complexity of determination of each
of the major forms of intergroup behavior just described. Williams (1947) illustrates
this complexity with a hypothetical case (pp. 43–44):

> Suppose that the causal factors in an urban race riot can be shown to include
> at least the following: (1) a high level of frustration arising from poor housing,
> low incomes, excessive crowding of transportation systems and other public
> facilities, lack of satisfying recreation, disruption of family life and community
> membership; (2) patterns of prejudice of complex origin established prior to
> the immediate situation; (3) a rapid change in relative numbers of the two con-
> tending groups; (4) a lack of intergroup familiarity because of segregation and
> other factors; (5) a rapid differential change in incomes of the two groups; (6)
> the presence of "hoodlum" elements emerging from prior social disorganization;

(7) the presence of opportunistic leaders who can advance their private interests through encouraging conflict; (8) absence of adequate, well trained, well organized, and relatively impartial law-enforcement forces . . . . This hypothetical case shows how a comparatively few variables may be combined in a most complex system of interrelations.

It is noteworthy that of the eight different determinants indicated by Williams in this example, only (2) and, possibly, (4) can be considered ethnic attitudes. It seems to us that Williams' hypothetical example reflects pretty well the kinds of factors that determine the actual occurrence of race riots in the United States, although it does not mention the role of precipitating incidents and rumors concerning them (*cf.* Chicago Commission on Race Relations, 1922; Cohen and Murphy, 1966; Dahlke, 1952; Grimshaw, 1960; Lee and Humphrey, 1943; Rudwick, 1966). And the role of ethnic attitudes in the determination of riots and other forms of intergroup conflict provides a fair indication of their general importance as determinants of intergroup behavior: they are usually relevant but not crucial.

Considerable research effort has been devoted to identifying forms of intergroup behavior in which ethnic attitudes play a maximum role and forms in which they play a minimum role. One major generalization is that their role is minimal as determinants of short-lived and segmental relationships and maximal as determinants of intimate and long-lasting relationships. Studies showing no correlation between ethnic attitudes and intergroup behavior have nearly always involved either (1) behavior that was so stongly determined by other factors that it did not vary from individual to individual in the situation studied (for example, white landlords bound by a restrictive covenant not to sell to Negroes, or white workers required by union and company policy to work under Negro supervisors); or else (2) relationships of very brief duration, such as renting a room to a couple for the night or buying from one sales clerk rather than another (Kutner, Wilkins, and Yarrow, 1952; LaPiere, 1934; Minard, 1952; Saenger and Gilbert, 1950). One exception to this generalization is a study by Wolf (1957) in which there appeared to be no relationship between attitude toward Negroes among white homeowners and the speed with which they moved out of a neighborhood changing from white to Negro occupancy.

The major area in which ethnic attitudes have been shown to affect intergroup behavior is that of friendly association (Williams, 1964; Wilner, Walkley, and Cook, 1952). We emphasize these two studies because their design made it possible to demonstrate *both* a significant influence of association on attitudes *and* a significant influence of attitudes on frequency of friendly association. It seems almost self-evident that ethnic attitudes play a crucial role in the willingness of individuals to marry across ethnic lines, but we cannot point to any studies demonstrating this relationship.

There is a good deal of informal research that indicates the importance of ethnic attitudes, along with many other factors, in behavior toward employees and coworkers in industrial situations (Hughes and Hughes, 1952; Southall, 1950). The situation is rather similar for voting and other forms of political behavior. We do not refer here to studies showing differential patterns of voting by members of different ethnic groups, though such differences have been clearly demonstrated. Instead we have in mind more qualitative investigations which seem to indicate that many voters are influenced in their choice of candidates by the candidate's ethnic group membership (Lubell, 1965; Wilson, 1960).

There is only one more thing we feel able to say about the determinants of inter-group behavior: an adequate analysis of these determinants in any particular society will have to include most if not all of the structural features of the society (*cf.* Williams, 1964, Chapter 10).

CHANGING INTERGROUP ATTITUDES

Intergroup attitudes are neither simple nor ephemeral response tendencies. Their persistence is rooted in their complexity, their instrumental importance for the individual, and, of no less importance, their normative significance for a society. By far the greater portion of investigations to be considered below are concerned with the effects of specific change-inducing procedures on the *direction* of the attitude, that is, on its favorable-unfavorable dimension. Far less frequent are investigations of attitude change in which the effects of such procedures on different types of atti-tudinal components are examined separately; or in which such change is considered in terms of specific psychological processes (for example, underlying needs) rather than in terms of a particular stimulus setting. Of course, all the above approaches will be represented to some extent in the discussion that follows. We turn first to those concerned with psychological processes.

PSYCHOLOGICAL PROCESSES IN ATTITUDE CHANGE

One type of attitude-change study focuses on relationships among attitudinal compo-nents and the extent to which changes in one kind of component have consequences for changes in the others. Rosenberg (1960a, 1960b), for example, presents a theory of attitude change based on the assumption that affective-cognitive *consistency* repre-sents a stable psychological state in the individual; if either kind of component shifts markedly, inconsistency arises and induces a drive or force toward changing the other component until consistency is restored. Employing hypnosis in a laboratory setting to shift affect in college students, Rosenberg (1956) has demonstrated striking changes in associated cognitions, though not with respect to ethnic attitudes *per se*.

A study by Mann (1960) investigated whether changes in one kind of ethnic attitudinal component induced changes in the others. He measured the cognitive, affective, and behavioral components of racial attitudes in six-person interracial groups formed as part of a graduate course in education. These measures were obtained twice—after the third and eleventh sessions—and it was found that the beliefs of the students became more favorable but that corresponding changes did not occur for the other kinds of components. A study by Merz and Pearlin (1957) and findings by Deutsch and Collins (1951) also suggest that the cognitive components of intergroup attitudes may change without inducing a change in the individual's feelings.

These findings would seem to contradict Rosenberg's cognitive-affective consis-tency conception of attitude change. It should be pointed out, however, that Rosenberg specifies particular conditions under which such change would be expected to occur (for example, the discrepancy between feelings and beliefs must exceed the person's tolerance level for such inconsistency), and there is no way of knowing whether or not these conditions were met in the studies cited above. Perhaps the most reasonable conclusion that can be drawn at this point is that different ethnic attitudinal components may require different methods for inducing changes in them (Katz and Stotland, 1959).

FUNCTIONAL BASIS OF ATTITUDE CHANGE

Katz and his associates have stressed the functional character of social attitudes as a basic approach to the problem of attitude change (Katz, 1960; Katz and Stotland, 1959). According to this view, four major functions can be performed by attitudes for the person: they can (1) provide an understanding of his external world, (2) maximize his rewards and minimize punishments, (3) express his underlying values and self concepts, and (4) protect him from unconscious impulses that threaten his psychological integrity while allowing partial expression of these same impulses.

In one study Katz, Sarnoff, and McClintock (1956) compared the effectiveness, in an attempt to modify the racial attitudes of 243 white college students, of presenting relevant factual information about Negroes with a self-insight approach or an interpretive approach. The latter method involved use of a case history to highlight and explain the self-defensive nature of ethnic prejudice. It was found that unfavorable attitudes toward the Negro were modified to a significantly greater extent by the self-insight procedure than by the informational approach. However, the insight method was least effective with subjects who were high in self-defensiveness. This result was interpreted as due to resistance; that is, the highly defensive person is threatened by and, therefore, will reject any appeal that might eliminate his ethnic prejudices. Prejudices in these persons are sorely needed to bolster a faltering self-esteem.

Katz and his associates interpreted the positive effects of their self-insight method as resulting from an actual personality change (a reduction in self-defensiveness). For example, it was found that the effects of the self-insight method took longer to occur than those of other approaches, in line with the assumption that "deeper" personality changes would require more time to be realized. However, subsequent studies by Stotland, Katz, and Patchen (1959) suggested that the change was more a function of the person's realization that he lacked self-consistency—the specific prejudice did not fit in with his conception of himself—than of any change in or realization of the ego-defensive character of his bias.

If the value satisfaction provided by ethnic prejudice is seen as less than that achieved by a more tolerant attitude, then attitude change should occur. Carlson (1956) tested this hypothesis by having college students provide arguments favoring Negro-white integration in housing as a means of attaining *wider* value satisfactions. In comparison with a control group, a significant proportion of the experimental subjects changed toward seeing the instrumental value of Negro housing integration for the realization of such values; and their attitudes toward racially integrated housing became significantly more favorable. Subjects whose initial attitudes were moderate changed more than those at either extreme. Of particular interest is the fact that attitude change appeared to generalize toward other ethnic groups.

Other research has focused on the person's position on an ethnic issue (for example, desegregated housing) and his acceptance of new information. Peak and Morrison (1958) had college students present arguments for and against segregated housing, after their attitudes toward the issue had been measured. Following their presentation of arguments (the change procedure), the subjects were required to

take the attitude measure again, to list the good and bad consequences of desegregation in housing, and to indicate their own positions on this list. It was found that
new information compatible with one's own attitude on desegregation was more
readily accepted than information that contradicted it. However, consistency between
attitude and content of the communication did not influence the amount of knowledge or information the subject gained. Similar findings are reported by Ford (1956).

Some of the research cited above suggests that self-consistency may be an important ingredient in any attempt to change ethnic attitudes. Culbertson's research
(1957) points not only to the significance of this factor in attitude change, but to the
factor of personal involvement as well. She measured the attitudes of Junior College
students toward Negroes generally and toward Negro-white housing integration
specifically, both before and after role-playing sessions. The subjects had to advocate
a theme favorable to residential integration in situations in which there was a new
influx of Negroes into a community. The role playing was conducted in groups of
six each, with half the subjects as performers and the other half observers of respective role players. In comparison with control subjects, far greater proportions of
both the observers and the participants became more favorable toward Negroes and
toward racial integration in housing; however, the role players shifted more than
the observers.

EFFECTS OF KNOWLEDGE

Most investigations reveal that Americans with a high level of formal education are
less prejudiced than those who have little such education (Bettelheim and Janowitz,
1964; Samelson, 1945). It is true, however, that the differences in prejudice typically
found among differentially educated adults cannot be attributed to the effects of
education *per se*, since these individuals also differ in intelligence, intellectual interest,
social environment, etc.

Frequent attempts have been made to determine the effects of education on
intergroup attitudes by evaluating the same students at various points in their careers
(Barkley, unpublished study cited in Chase, 1940; Eddy, 1964; Jones, 1938; McNeill,
1960; Murphy and Likert, 1938). Control groups have not been used in these studies,
and the results have been quite inconsistent. Some of the major sources of inconsistency in findings are probably variation in age of students tested, variation in educational programs, variation in attitudes measured, and variation in the type of social
and economic change occurring in the larger society during the period of the study.

Research on the effects of specific school courses has more frequently employed
control groups and has produced somewhat more consistent findings. In these
studies, significant favorable changes in attitudes are reported about twice as often
as no change. There is still a great deal of variation in results from study to study,
however, and the methods of the different investigators have been so diverse that it
is difficult to determine what factors are of major importance in producing the variation in findings. Good interpretive summaries of the relevant literature are provided
by Rose (1948b) and Stember (1961).

School courses attempt to reduce intergroup prejudice by modifying the individual's ethnic beliefs, and this objective, of course, depends primarily on the transmission of information about specific groups. Of importance, therefore, is the fact
that most correlational investigations have reported that persons with considerable
information about a specific group tend to have more favorable attitudes toward that

group. However, there is no way of learning from such studies whether changes in attitude resulted from increased information, or increased information from favorable attitudes, or to what extent both resulted from other personality or situational factors. The probable importance of these "other factors" is revealed in the finding by Closson (1930) of a correlation of 0.59 between general tolerance toward ethnic groups and general information (of all sorts) among 840 Iowa high school students.

School courses involve not only the presentation of information but a relationship between students and teacher. It is reasonable to suppose that a course in intergroup relations will produce favorable changes in the ethnic attitudes of students if (1) a favorable balance of information about an ethnic group is presented, (2) the instructor communicates to the students that his own attitude toward the ethnic group is more favorable than theirs, and (3) a positive relationship between instructor and students exists to the point that they will accept his feelings and action orientations toward the group as well as the information he presents. It is not unlikely that, if any one of these conditions is missing, a school course on intergroup relations will not produce any significant changes in ethnic attitudes. Thus, in a study by Greenberg, Pierson, and Sherman (1957), neither a formal debate on the desegregation decision of 1954, nor a lecture on the dynamics of prejudice, nor a single class discussion of the latter led to changes in the ethnocentrism scores of Texas college students upon retesting in the *next* class period.

In sharp contrast are the findings of Levinson and Schermerhorn (1951) and Levinson (1954), who studied the effects of a six-week intergroup-relations workshop on the attitudes of schoolteachers. Notwithstanding the low level of prejudice in the group to begin with, there was a significant decrease in the average level of prejudice by the time the workshop was over. How much change in ethnic attitudes will occur depends also on the specific approach taken. Hayes and Conklin (1953) used one of three methods with eighth-grade students: (1) direct experience with minority group members, (2) academic instruction on the problem of prejudice, and (3) a "vicarious experience" approach in which the subjects read, acted, and listened to the experiences of minority group members. The last approach proved most effective. Working with Christian high school students in church-sponsored seminars on the Psalms presented in three different ways, Kagan (1952) found significant reductions in prejudice only when anti-Semitism was directly discussed either in class or in private meetings after class. When the experimenter adhered closely to the announced subject matter of the course, no changes in the students' attitudes toward Jews occurred, despite the fact that the contribution of the Jews to the development of Christianity was stressed.

PROPAGANDA AND ATTITUDE CHANGE

The use of motion pictures as a propaganda technique for altering ethnic attitudes has received most attention from investigators, beginning with a study by Peterson and Thurstone (1933). By the use of films they were able to produce large pro-German, anti-Negro, and pro-Chinese shifts in attitude among high school students; and some of these attitude changes tended to persist over time, for example, 19 months for the pro-Chinese attitude. An anti-Chinese film resulted in a small average change in the expected direction. Hovland, Lumsdaine, and Sheffield (1949) studied the effects of the film *The Battle of Britain* on the attitudes of American soldiers toward the British during World War II; in this case the amount of change in attitudes was small. The results may indicate a lack of persuasive power in the film or a greater sophistication and resistance to propaganda of soldiers as compared with high school students. Rose (1948b) reports that another World War II film on the Chinese was more effective in changing soldiers' attitudes than either of two different types of lectures covering the same material.

Subsequent research on the effects of motion pictures on ethnic attitudes has been sporadic, but a number of important findings have emerged. Rosen (1948) found a large and significant reduction in anti-Semitism among a group of 50 Gentile college students who saw the film *Gentleman's Agreement.* Employing an army film (*Don't Be A Sucker*), Cooper and Dinerman (1951) reported success in altering the beliefs of New York City Catholic and Protestant high school students regarding the influence of the Nazi regime on their own religious groups; a second theme in the movie, that Americans should be on their guard against Nazism in the United States, had no demonstrable effect. Goldberg (1956) compared the effects of two types of films dealing with prejudice shown to Detroit fraternal groups. Before-and-after measures on the California *E* scale revealed that a "general" or abstract film on prejudice had no effect on the groups who saw it, whereas the second film, involving realistic enactment of a social situation, produced a significant reduction in prejudice in four of the seven groups tested.

And finally, Kraus (1960) compared various racial versions of a movie in an attempt to change attitudes of eleventh-grade white children toward the Negro. The films dealt with the efforts of two high school teachers to get a Negro student into college; the versions differed only in having the teachers both white, both Negro, or white and Negro. Significantly more favorable attitudes toward Negroes occurred only after the biracial version of the film.

The effects of other propaganda techniques—lecture, broadcasts, stories, etc.—on attitude change have been studied but not in recent years, and far less often than the effects of films have been studied with reference to ethnic groups. For this reason we need only summarize some of these findings for the present discussion. There is some evidence that the propaganda lecture is effective in changing ethnic attitudes but with much less durability than Peterson and Thurstone (1933) reported for motion pictures (Chen, 1933, 1936). Face-to-face speeches are usually found to be more effective than radio presentation of the same material, and the latter usually more effective than written or pictorial presentations (Cantril and Allport, 1935; Elliott, 1936; Knower, 1935, 1936; Wilke, 1934). Comparisons of television with the other media have not been reported. Studies of the effects of stories and mail propaganda on ethnic attitudes are very small in number, and no firm conclusions can be drawn (Bettelheim and Janowitz, 1950b; Hall, 1938; Peregrine, 1936; Remmers and Morgan, 1936).

INTERGROUP CONTACT AND ATTITUDE CHANGE

Contact between ethnic groups may lead to an increase or decrease in intergroup prejudice. As we noted earlier, attaining more favorable ethnic attitudes depends on conditions of interaction in which the members of different groups are cooperatively engaged in the pursuit of common objectives under equal-status conditions or as functional equals. Sherif (1958) found that intense conflict between two groups of boys at a summer camp was most successfully reduced when they were confronted with a common and compelling problem which could be solved only by cooperative action on the part of members of both groups. On the other hand, it is also true that studies of interethnic contact in the same kind of setting do not always demonstrate a reduction in prejudice. A key factor is probably the relative balance of competitive and cooperative elements in the specific contact relationship.

Contact in school settings

In his original study, Horowitz (1936) compared the attitudes toward Negroes of 11 white sixth-grade boys in a mixed New York City school with those of a much larger group of New York City boys of the same age attending two all-white schools. On the Ranks and Show Me tests, the two groups of boys displayed the same attitude, but the boys from the mixed school showed a slight preference for interracial social situations as compared with all-white ones, while the boys from all-white schools showed a substantial preference for all-white situations.

In the earlier-cited study by Vaughan and Thompson (1961) of the attitudes of white New Zealand school youth toward their Maori classmates, it was found that among the 16-year-olds greater interethnic contact was associated with more favorable attitudes toward the Maori. This relationship, however, was not evident among the 8- and 12-year-old students.

Dorothy Singer (1964) compared the racial attitudes of white children in two fifth-grade classes, each from a neighboring suburb of New York City. One class attended a school in a community that had ended segregation 13 years earlier, and in which school integration was established in the very best sense of the word (that is, proper ratio of Negro to white students in class, directed emphasis on interracial cooperation, etc.). The second group of fifth-graders attended an all-white school in a community that was comparable except for the fact that it had no "Negro problem," since Negro families were almost nonexistent.

Children in the integrated school showed significantly more positive and fewer negative stereotypes about Negroes than did those in the all-white school; indicated a greater desire for personal contact with Negroes; and finally, exhibited more familiarity with and greater positive affect toward Negro celebrities.

Whitmore (1957) measured the attitudes toward Negroes of comparable groups of white eighth-, tenth-, and twelfth-graders before their school was desegregated and five months afterward. He found that the eighth-grade students and two tenth-grade groups became significantly less prejudiced, but that this change was unrelated to opportunity for classroom contact. The latter finding, plus the fact that the positive shift in attitude was more characteristic of the younger students than the older ones, suggests that the change was more a response to the new adult norms for Negro-white relations in the school and less to changing conceptions and feelings engendered by the equal-status contacts.

Campbell (1958) gave a Negro attitude questionnaire to the same 746 white high school students just before and six months after school integration, and he found that a change toward more favorable Negro attitudes was a function of classroom contact and friendship with Negroes. Some white students became less prejudiced, while others became more prejudiced. Perhaps of greater significance is Campbell's finding that the direction of attitude change (less prejudiced or more prejudiced) was related to how his subjects perceived the racial attitudes of their parents and friends. Lombardi (1962) also reports no general change in Negro attitudes among ninth- and tenth-grade students in a Maryland high school when they were tested before and seven months after integration. More favorable attitudes toward Negroes were found to be related only to the educational level of the student's mother.

Quite rare is Webster's (1961) study of attitude change among *both* white and Negro students in an integrated junior high school in California. Both groups were tested by means of a social-acceptance scale and a sociometric test, first in their separate schools and then in the integrated school some six months later. It was found that white students accepted Negroes less following integration, and that Negro attitudes moved toward the extremes but with more changing in the favorable than in the unfavorable direction.

We do not know how to explain the divergent results of these different studies. Part of the explanation may lie in characteristics of the white and Negro children who were interacting in the various schools, part in the organization of classes and extracurricular activities, part in the attitudes of teachers and school administrators, and part in factors external to the school (community atmosphere, parental attitudes, etc.).

Contact in educational settings outside the school

Studies in this area have typically involved noncompetitive contact situations and have typically shown favorable attitude change. Smith (1943) found a very substantial increase in favorable attitudes toward Negroes among Columbia Teachers College students who spent two weekends on guided tours of Harlem. The tours included a number of social gatherings arranged so as to be enjoyable for the students and to emphasize the high cultural level of their Negro hosts. Young (1932) arranged a similar program of contacts with Negroes, in addition to a course in American race relations, for 16 graduate students in sociology. Course and contacts together produced a small and statistically unreliable average increase in favorable attitudes toward Negroes.

Williams (1934) found results similar to those of Smith for 15 white high school girls participating in an interracial project conducted by the New York City YWCA. However, an educational tour of Japan produced no significant changes in favorableness of attitude toward the Japanese among a group of California high school students, even though it resulted in a very large increase in information (National Education Association, 1932).

Contact in recreational settings

Studies of the effects of interracial contact in recreational settings have not produced consistent evidence of a reduction in prejudice. Mussen (1950) and Hogrefe, Evans, and Chein (1947) report no change in the overall direction of attitudes toward Negroes among white boys in an interracial camp and an interracial play center respectively. In the camp study, in which white and Negro boys spent four weeks living and playing together, it was found that there were significant changes in attitude in many of the boys, but unfavorable changes were as frequent as favorable ones. Yarrow and a team of associates (1958) studied 8- to 13-year-old white and Negro boys and girls from low-income homes during a two-week stay at summer camp under conditions of racial integration and racial segregation. Detailed observations, sociometric choices, interviews, and other techniques were employed to get at both attitudinal components and overt behavior in each camp setting. Although radical shifts in long-standing interracial orientations did not occur, it was found that, in general, the social distance between the two groups was reduced under integrated conditions, and race as a criterion of friendship exerted less influence at the end of the two-week period. As in the Singer study (1964), a major factor which determined the new standards of conduct and feeling was the consistent expectation of equality that characterized the behavior of the counselors toward the children and that was reflected in the integrated culture of Negro and white counselors.

Yarrow and her associates (1958) indicate that cross-racial friendships in the integrated camp developed primarily with cabinmates, and these positive interactions were largely confined to the cabin setting. In broader settings (swimming, games, etc.), small segregated groups appeared more frequently. What this suggests is a role-specific attitude change, that is, a positive attitude of the white child toward the Negro child as a cabinmate but not as a recreation participant in general. As we shall see later, role-specific attitude changes are frequent results of equal-status contacts among adults in residential and occupational settings.

Contact in residential and occupational settings

The most dramatic changes in attitude as a result of intergroup contact have been observed in situations in which two different ethnic groups both lived and worked together in circumstances requiring a high degree of mutual cooperation. The general policy of the U.S. Army during World War II was to keep Negro troops out of combat assignments; however, in the spring of 1945, platoons of Negro riflemen were assigned to some of the infantry companies in eleven combat divisions operating in Europe. A survey several months later (Star, Williams, and Stouffer, 1965) showed that 64 percent of the white enlisted men in companies to which Negro platoons had been assigned thought that this procedure was a good general policy for the Army to follow; in contrast, only 18 percent of the enlisted men in divisions that contained no Negro combat platoons thought that Negro platoons would be a good idea.

Brophy (1946) found a similarly striking reduction in anti-Negro prejudice among white merchant seamen who had shipped one or more times with Negro sailors; however, his results were probably influenced by the fact that nearly all the seamen who had shipped more than once with Negroes were members of a union with a militant antidiscrimination policy.

Servicewide desegregation of Army units was not carried out until nearly a decade after World War II. Foreman (1955) reports that white soldiers who had fought with Negroes in combat were more favorable toward integration than those who had not, while white soldiers serving *near* large Negro units were least favorable.

Changes in Negro attitudes toward whites were studied by Roberts (1953). The author drew on autobiographical material supplied by 219 Negro veterans after World War II. About 75 percent of the group reported they had had negative attitudes toward whites prior to military service. Following the war 51 percent reported they felt less hostile to whites, 29 percent were unchanged, and 20 percent were more antagonistic. Roberts suggests that reversals of attitude are likely to have been the result of novel experiences, including exposure of Southern Negroes to unsegregated facilities, formation of friendships, and contact with European whites.

Studies of residential contact between different ethnic groups in noncompetitive, equal-status situations have typically shown substantial favorable changes in attitude following such contact. Deutsch and Collins (1951) found that 53 percent of the white housewives in two integrated interracial public housing projects favored a policy of interracial integration for city housing projects in general, while only 5 percent of the white housewives in two segregated projects favored such a policy. The experience of interracial living also made these housewives more willing to accept Negroes as fellow workers on a job, as fellow members in an informal social club, as schoolmates for their children, and more ready to accept a Negro as mayor of their city.

Deutsch and Collins found that the experience of living in integrated housing projects produced changes in beliefs about Negroes and changes in feelings toward Negroes, as well as changes in policy orientation toward them. The changes seem to have been greater for attitudes toward Negroes in the projects than for attitudes toward Negroes in general.

Deutsch and Collins (1951) also provide some data on a related problem: the extent to which changes in attitude toward one ethnic group tend to be accompanied by similar changes in attitude toward other groups. Their interview schedule included five social-distance questions asked with regard to Negroes, Chinese, and Puerto Ricans, though the latter two groups were almost entirely absent from the projects.

The authors found large differences in attitudes toward Negroes on all five social-distance questions, with the largest difference occurring in willingness to have Negroes as tenants in the same building. Attitudes toward Puerto Ricans were slightly more favorable in the integrated projects, but no more so than would be expected from the differences in education and political liberalism in the two types of project. Attitudes toward Chinese were substantially more favorable in the integrated projects, especially with respect to willingness to have Chinese as tenants in the same building.

At least two other studies have reported findings similar to those of Deutsch and Collins. Wilner, Walkley, and Cook (1952) compared white housewives living near Negro families and those living far from Negro families in four public housing projects in four different cities. The differences between "near" and "far" respondents were of the same nature as the differences found by Deutsch and Collins for respondents in integrated as compared with segregated projects, but considerably smaller in size. Wilner, Walkley, and Cook attribute the smaller differences to the reduced range of variation in opportunities for contact with Negroes among their subjects, as compared with those of Deutsch and Collins. Irish (1952) found that Caucasian residents of Boulder, Colorado who had had Japanese-American neighbors during the war were significantly more favorable toward Japanese-Americans several years later than were similar residents who had not had Japanese-American neighbors.

The results of intergroup contact are quite different, however, in residential areas which are being "invaded" by Negroes. In this situation the white residents typically perceive the presence of Negro families as a serious threat to their own social status, and their attitudes become more unfavorable (Kramer, 1951; Winder, 1952).

That equal-status contact may not yield simultaneous and identical reactions of Negroes and whites is seen in a study by Hunt (1959), who interviewed 46 Negro families and 133 white families having a 10-year history of biracial housing in a Kalamazoo, Michigan neighborhood. Although 65 percent of both racial groups "liked" the neighborhood in general, only 20 percent of the whites and 46 percent of the Negroes favored the mixed-race character of the area. Only 3 percent of the whites but 65 percent of the Negroes regarded the movement of Negroes into the area as "friendly." On the other hand, Rose, Atelsek, and McDonald (1953) report general acceptance by white neighbors of isolated Negro families in formerly all-white areas. Their research was carried out in Minneapolis, a Northern city with a very small percentage of Negroes in its population. On the basis of his research in still another city, in the Northeastern United States, Fishman (1961) suggests that the typical initial reaction of white residents to Negro immigration is a pattern of withdrawal behavior and negative attitude change; however, continuous experience in the interracial neighborhood leads eventually to a limitation of this withdrawal.

Enough research has been done to demonstrate that the effects of intergroup contact on racial attitudes are likely to follow one course of development in situations such as schools and public housing projects, in which the interracial character of the situation can be established and maintained by administrative decision; and an entirely different course in situations such as private housing, in which continuation of the contact depends to a large extent on the attitudes of the participants. A hypothesis that seems to us extremely plausible is that entry of substantial numbers of minority group members into an "open situation" (for example, movement of Negro families into a formerly all-white neighborhood) results in a polarization of attitudes on the part of the majority group. Some majority group members leave the situation, and their attitudes toward the invading minority remain the same or become less favorable; other majority group members stay, and their attitudes toward the minority remain the same or gradually improve. The proportion of majority group members who stay or leave is determined by a host of factors having little or nothing to do with their attitudes toward the invading minority (Wolf, 1957). This formulation has at least the virtue of being applicable *both* to open situations such as employment, in which American experience shows that introduction of Negroes rarely leads to an exodus of white workers, *and* to situations such as private housing, in which white residents typically move out of a neighborhood as soon as substantial numbers of Negroes move in.

A special kind of intergroup contact occurs in the experience of college students who go to foreign countries for periods of residence and study. Selltiz *et al.* (1963) report the results of an elaborate study of changes in attitude on the part of 542 foreign students during their first year of residence in the United States. Early in the year their characterizations of people in the United States tended to be extremely favorable and to emphasize qualities that previous research has shown are generally considered "typical American characteristics"—for example, friendliness, interest in improving physical conditions, practicality, energy. Six months later there was a significant trend toward somewhat less favorable (and more realistic?) characterizations. The authors devoted a great deal of care to the construction of an overall index of the extent of friendly interaction with Americans, and found no significant differences in direction of attitude change among students high and low in amount of interaction.

Studies of the effects of intergroup contact in work situations fall into two groups: those focused on a particular type of work situation, and those in which a question on interethnic work experience was asked as part of a general survey dealing mainly with other topics. In the first category is a study by Harding and Hogrefe (1952) of the attitudes of white department-store employees toward Negro coworkers. The authors found that employees who had worked with Negroes on an equal-status basis were more willing to continue such a relationship in the future than were those who had never worked with Negroes; however, there was no evidence of any other change in attitudes as a result of the work experience. Similar results are reported by Palmore (1955) in a study of the reactions of white packing-house employees to the introduction of Negro workers. Initial hostility was followed by gradually increasing acceptance, but this acceptance was limited to the work situation.

Evidence from the survey studies is considerably more diverse. Merton, West, and Jahoda (1949) report more favorable attitudes toward Negroes among white respondents who had worked with Negroes on an equal-status basis. Irish (1952) found no significant differences in attitudes toward Japanese-Americans among Caucasian respondents who had and those who had not worked with them; and Deutsch and Collins found a comparable lack of effect of work experience on the attitudes of white housewives toward Negroes (cited in Harding and Hogrefe, 1952, pp. 27–28).

Williams (1964) has presented evidence that interethnic contact in work situations does lead in many cases to the development of friendships across ethnic lines. In Elmira, New York, 423 white, non-Jewish adults were asked in 1949 and again in 1951 about their contacts with Jews and Negroes at work, in organizations, and in the neighborhoods in which they lived. Most of the reported contacts were maintained over the two-year period. There was a strong tendency for work contacts to become closer and more intimate, while neighborhood contacts usually remained on a casual basis. Contacts with Jews in organizations tended to develop into friendships, while contacts with Negroes in organizations tended to remain on a casual basis.

CHANGES IN GROUP MEMBERSHIP

Among the most powerful influences on the original development of ethnic attitudes are those exerted by the various social groups in which an individual finds membership. It is consequently to be expected that, when an individual finds himself in a new group whose standards vary markedly from his previous ones with regard to ethnic relations, there will be a strong tendency for his own attitudes to change. This process was studied directly in the case of Northern students attending a Southern college (Sims and Patrick, 1936). These authors found, to begin with, that white students from Northern homes attending a Northern college had much more favorable attitudes toward Negroes than did white students from Southern homes attending a Southern college. White students from Northern homes attending the same Southern college occupied an intermediate position, and the degree of favorableness of their attitudes was strongly influenced by the number of years they had been in residence at the Southern college. Freshmen in this group held attitudes only slightly less favorable to the Negro than those of Northern college freshmen, but juniors and seniors had moved nearly all the way to the position of their Southern classmates. Eddy (1964) found that attitudes toward Negroes among Southern-born white students on a Northern campus shifted positively from freshman to senior year, but primarily with regard to the integrated use of public facilities. Border-state students shifted positively according to the degree of interracial extracurricular contact and the regional origin of close friends.

A change in group membership does not always result in a change in attitudes. Pearlin (1954) found that the presence of white Southern students on an integrated campus does not in itself lead to changes in attitude toward Negroes, but that change of this kind depends on a strong identification with college values and a parallel reduction in identification with home values. Horowitz (1936) found a complete lack of anti-Negro prejudice among a group of white children living in a New York City housing project run under Communist Party auspices. Gundlach (1950) found a very low degree of prejudice against Negroes among a group of white female factory workers in New York City who belonged to a left-wing union with a militant anti-discrimination policy. Gundlach's factory workers were significantly less prejudiced than white housewives in nonsegregated New York City housing projects (Deutsch and Collins, 1951), though the latter came from the same social class and had as great or greater opportunities for personal contacts with Negroes. Gundlach's subjects had had no option about joining the union, or about which union to join.

Evidence of a quite different sort is presented in a study of 45 New York City residents who reported that at some time in their lives there had been a marked change in their attitudes toward Negroes or Jews (Watson, 1950). These people were intensively interviewed about the circumstances associated with their changes in attitudes, and half of them reported that the change had been preceded by their entry into a new institutionalized group whose standards were different from their previous ones. The experiences most commonly reported under this heading were taking one's first job, going to college, and entering the armed services. A considerable additional number of respondents associated their changes in attitude with a change in geographical residence which, of course, resulted in a variety of new group memberships.

Watson also found that, for four-fifths of her respondents, attitude change was associated with some new personal contact with members of the group toward whom the revision of attitudes occurred. Of 23 respondents who had had new contacts with Negroes or Jews of status at least equal to their own, 21 had changed their attitudes in a favorable direction. Of 14 respondents who had had new contacts with Negroes or Jews in lower-status positions, only four had become more favorable toward them, while ten had become less favorable. Though the number of cases involved is small, this evidence is probably the best available on the differential effects of equal- and unequal-status contact between members of different ethnic groups.

CHANGING INTERGROUP BEHAVIOR

Throughout history, massive changes in interethnic behavior have been produced by the application of military force. English became the national language of what is now the United States of America through a long series of wars in which the military forces of several European nations and scores of Indian tribes were successively defeated. Military force in Africa made people from certain tribal groups available for export as slaves to the United States. The vast majority of the descendants of these people remained in slavery until they were freed by military force during the American Civil War.

In the twentieth century the most common use of military force to change interethnic behavior has been in struggles for ethnic independence. One type of struggle has been the effort of an ethnic minority to win independence as a national state separate from a larger political unit in which it was submerged. Good examples are the successful struggles for independence of the Irish in what is now Eire and the Jews in what is now Israel. Another type of military struggle has been the revolt of a native majority to win control of a territorial unit from a European minority. Good examples are the wars for independence in Indonesia and Algeria.

Often a combination of military and legal or political force is used in an effort to keep an ethnic group in subjection within the boundaries of a national state, or even to exterminate it entirely. One extreme instance was the treatment of Armenians in Turkey at the end of World War I. Less extreme, perhaps, have been the treatment of Indians in the United States in the nineteenth century and the treatment of Negroes in the American South following the withdrawal of federal troops in 1876.

We have cited these examples to illustrate three points: (1) the strong and durable nature of ethnic identifications, (2) a frequent and perhaps perennial tendency of members of one ethnic group to exploit members of another, and (3) a persistent and probably perennial tendency of members of a submerged ethnic group to attempt to improve their status by collective action. The use of force to maintain or change intergroup behavior is often effective from the point of view of the group using it. To attempt to explain the circumstances under which it will or will not be used would require an examination of the whole theory of social control and the nature and functioning of the modern political state (*cf.* Davis, 1949, Chapter 18). All we can do in this chapter is point out that organized force, whether in the form of military expeditions, police action, guerilla warfare, or terrorist activity, is a common method of attempting to change interethnic behavior. Fortunately it is not the only method, especially within the confines of a modern national state.

LEGAL AND POLITICAL APPROACHES

It is well known that in the latter part of the nineteenth century state legislatures in the American South enacted a whole series of laws designed to control the behavior of Negroes toward whites and vice versa. The laws were vigorously enforced, and their provisions became established custom. When they were declared unconstitutional in a series of twentieth-century decisions by the United States Supreme Court, it took a long series of administrative actions by the federal government, combined with legal and political initiative at the local level, to chip away at behavior patterns that were established as folkways. Much of the local political action took the form of mass protest—demonstrations, "sit-ins," selective boycotts, etc. Frequently, district court orders were sought and obtained requiring a bus station to desegregate its facilities or a school board to prepare a plan for gradual or speedy desegregation. Local and state police were often used to oppose desegregation efforts; state militia and federal troops were sometimes used to support them. It is important to recognize, however, that the decisive factors in every situation were political and legal, not military.

The overall result of these struggles has been an upheaval and partial reorganization of patterns of interracial behavior in the American South. One of the most visible indices of change has been school desegregation: the presence of Negro children in formerly all-white classrooms. American social scientists have devoted a good deal of attention to the study of this particular type of intergroup behavior since the crucial Supreme Court decision of 1954. One of the results of this study is a basic distinction between *de jure* and *de facto* segregation. *De jure* segregation is imposed by law or by school-board regulations; this type of segregation was declared unconstitutional in 1954. *De facto* school segregation occurs as a result of residential segregation combined with a policy of requiring students to attend school in the district in which they reside. By 1954 *de jure* segregation was almost unknown in the United States outside the South, but *de facto* segregation was extremely common in the great cities of both North and South. *De facto* segregation does not violate the American Constitution, and it has probably been increasing gradually during the 1950's and 1960's as a result of steady out-migration from the cities on the part of the white population and in-migration by Negroes. The studies of desegregation to be described are all studies of the reduction or elimination of *de jure* segregation.

Pettigrew and Cramer (1959) studied demographic factors related to the speed of desegregation and concluded that the major factor was the proportion of Negroes in the population. The smaller the proportion of Negroes in the population, the sooner the school district was likely to desegregate. It is reasonable to interpret this as resulting from realistic expectations on the part of the white authorities concerning the extent to which admission of Negroes would change the existing pattern of social relations in the schools and (over a longer period of time) the balance of political and economic power in the community. (Perhaps we should explain that at the time of the study public schools in the South were entirely controlled by white school boards, and that Negroes were generally excluded from political participation by being denied the vote. Thus they had no direct voice in the selection of school-board members.)

Dwyer (1958) studied school desegregation in seven Southern communities through interview, observation, and questionnaires administered to teachers and pupils. He found that opposition to school integration is minimized when administrative policies and actions are clear, definite, and firm. Vacillation leads to opposition and possible conflict. Favorable administrator attitudes lead to greater intergroup contact within the schools. Administrator hostility leads to minimum contact, with limited involvement of Negro children in school activities. Dwyer also found that the younger children tend to a greater degree to involve themselves in informal relationships and more readily adjust to the integration process than do the older children.

Williams and Ryan (1954) made a series of case studies of desegregated communities. They found that, in the presence of weak opposition or nonpolarized attitudes, the local school board and local officials have the most significant role in desegregation. They also found that prior discussion of the issue of desegregation leads either to the facilitation of the transition or to the mobilization of opposing groups. The reaction of a particular community may be diagnosed by taking into account such factors as the number and proportion of Negroes, the presence of other minority groups, the extent and nature of segregation, the activity of related organizations; the organization and financing of the school system, the level of communication between school board and citizens, the status and qualifications of Negro and white teachers, the local attitudes toward schools, the practices of state agencies, and the role of local groups. Following desegregation, there have usually appeared good interpersonal relations in the school but racial cleavage outside the school. It is interesting to note that the Williams and Ryan report did not anticipate the significant incidence of violence associated with desegregation during the 1950's and 1960's.

Clark (1953) reviewed experiences with desegregation up to that time and concluded that desegregation resulting from litigation was as effective as desegregation resulting from other methods. However, he felt that immediate rather than gradual desegregation reduced obstacles to peaceful transition and decreased the likelihood of resistance. Resistance he found to be associated with ambiguous or inconsistent policies, ineffective action, and conflict between competing authorities. Efficient desegregation is dependent on the unequivocality of prestige leaders, the firm enforcement of changed policy, the willingness to deal with violations, the refusal of those in authority to tolerate subterfuges, and the readiness to appeal to morality and justice.

Tumin, Barton, and Burrus (1958) found that actions taken by white Southern males to deter or prevent desegregation showed little if any relationship to stated attitudes. The best predictor of action was number of years of formal education—the more education, the less the likelihood of action designed to block desegregation.

In the Northern United States, changes in interethnic relations during the past century have taken a much less dramatic course than they have in the South. In many ways the pieces of legislation with the most profound impact on intergroup relations were the Immigration Acts of 1921 and 1924, which reduced to a trickle the flow of immigrants from abroad. By restricting the competition for unskilled and semiskilled jobs, this legislation provided a basis for continuation of the "Great Migration" of American Negroes from the rural South to the industrial North that began during World War I.

A legal device that had a profound influence on interethnic behavior in the North for about 30 years was the *restrictive covenant*. This device was a clause written into land deeds forbidding the owner to rent or sell to members of a particular ethnic group—usually Negroes, but sometimes Jews and "Orientals" as well. These clauses became extremely popular in many cities after a 1917 Supreme Court decision declared residential segregation laws unconstitutional. Their effect has been most clearly documented in Chicago, where they were used to create a pattern of almost complete residential segregation (Drake and Cayton, 1945; Duncan and Duncan, 1957). Restrictive covenants became virtually obsolete in 1948, when they were declared unconstitutional and unenforceable by the U.S. Supreme Court.

Very important in the Northern and Western United States is antidiscrimination legislation of various types. Shortly after the Civil War, many states passed laws forbidding discrimination in various types of public accommodation, especially hotels and restaurants. These laws had little effect on interethnic behavior because a person who had been refused service could not obtain redress except by instituting legal action in a state court. The maximum result that could be expected from a successful legal action was payment of a small fine by the offending businessman, so court cases were rare.

At the end of World War II a new type of antidiscrimination legislation was developed that placed responsibility for enforcement in the hands of a state commission with a paid staff. The major purpose of this type of legislation has been to combat discrimination in employment, but in many states it has been extended to include the area of public accommodations and, in some states, housing of certain types. Ordinances of a similar nature have been enacted in many of the larger cities.

In considering antidiscrimination legislation as an approach to changing interethnic behavior, one must realize that the process only begins with passage of the legislation. Whether or not change will occur, and how fast it will occur, depends on three major types of variable: (1) the skill and energy of the enforcing body; (2) the strength of opposition by employers, businessmen, and landlords; and (3) the strength of support by groups opposed to discrimination. The process of enforcement, or attempted enforcement, is as much educational and political as it is legal and administrative. Probably the major impact of antidiscrimination legislation and associated enforcement efforts has been the opening up of new job opportunities for Negroes; but there have undoubtedly been many other effects as well in other areas of intergroup behavior. The whole subject has been discussed by Berger (1952), Maslow (1955), and Konvitz and Leskes (1961).

Part of an overall political approach to changing interethnic behavior is the activity popularly known as "lobbying." In the United States every ethnic group of any size is represented by at least one organization devoted to furthering the perceived interests of the group in a variety of ways, including representation of the group's point of view on pending legislation. Major ethnic groups usually have a number of different organizations with somewhat different points of view competing for the support of the ethnic group members and attempting to influence in various ways the behavior of the rest of the American population toward them. Sometimes it is possible for the great majority of these groups to enhance their effectiveness by combining in an overall "civil rights movement"; sometimes effectiveness is lost through interethnic and intraethnic disagreements over political goals and political means.

The overall political impact of an ethnic group depends not only on the number of registered voters who identify themselves with the group, but also on their political sophistication and the energy and skill of their leaders. The best general discussion of ethnic relationships in American political life is Lubell's *The Future of American Politics* (1965), which demonstrates the importance of ethnic identification even unto the tenth generation. Among his most valuable contributions is his analysis of ethnic factors in the development of leadership within the two major political parties (pp. 85–86):

> Patronage is peculiarly important for minority groups, involving much more than the mere spoils of office . . . . In most northern cities, the Democrats have actually developed a ladderlike succession of posts, through which the political progress of various minority elements is recognized . . . . The earliest stirrings of any group usually are appeased by an appointment as assistant district attorney, which entails little more than that some members of the group be educated as lawyers. A county judgeship, on the other hand, requires a candidate who has succeeded in a lower post, a large enough vote to withstand the competing claims of other minority blocs, and the economic backing to finance a campaign . . . . Largely through this system of seniority and by playing off one ethnic element against the others the Irish have been able to cling to a much larger representation among officeholders than their voting strength would warrant.

EDUCATIONAL AND INFORMATIONAL APPROACHES

We have already mentioned the educational activities of state and local agencies striving to enforce antidiscrimination legislation. A tremendous amount of additional educational work goes on in the United States in an effort to change patterns of intergroup behavior. The most active agencies tend to be the schools, the churches, and the various organizations representing specific ethnic groups. It is impossible to make any general statement about the effect of all this activity, or any differential statement about what types of educational strategy are most likely to have an influence on some particular form of intergroup behavior. We shall confine ourselves to describing two particular educational programs that have been devised by social scientists for special purposes and that seem to be moderately effective in furthering these purposes.

The first of these programs is the community self-survey technique developed by Charles S. Johnson and his associates at Fisk University (Selltiz and Wormser, 1949; Wormser and Selltiz, 1951). The goal of this procedure is to focus community attention on areas of discrimination in such a way as to mobilize support for ending, or at least reducing, the discrimination. The essential part of the procedure is a reasonably detailed survey of community practices in each of a number of areas of suspected discrimination, carried out by volunteers under the supervision of a broadly based committee representing both the "power structure" and the major ethnic groups of the community. Usually such a survey requires the cooperation of at least one professional social scientist. The procedure has been carried out in a number of Northern and Western cities during the past 20 years, and there is good reason to believe it has played a useful role in helping to bring about a reduction of certain forms of discrimination in these cities.

A very different procedure is the workshop intended to increase the effectiveness of people who are already committed, at least in principle, to trying to bring about some changes in interethnic behavior in their communities. Usually these workshops are staffed by professionals; they may last anywhere from a day to a month. Lippitt (1949) has described in great detail a two-week workshop for community leaders sponsored by the Connecticut State Interracial Commission, and has attempted to evaluate its effectiveness in changing the behavior of these community leaders.

Thirty-two participants were interviewed before and after the workshop experience, and for nearly all of these individuals two additional informants made independent reports both before the workshop and several months afterward. The most striking change following the workshop was the increased level of activity of the participants. Two-thirds reported that they were spending more time on intergroup-relations activities than before the workshop, and three-fourths were reported by their associates to be spending more time. The increase in activity was greatest for individuals who attended the workshop in teams of six or seven members from a single community. Lippitt attributes this primarily to the effects of mutual reinforcement among team members after the close of the workshop.

One particularly important kind of workshop is the one organized to train policemen in dealing with members of ethnic groups other than their own. These training programs are intended partly to reduce the likelihood that the behavior of policemen will be influenced by their own prejudices, and partly to develop skill in handling investigations, arrests, and control of crowds in an effective but noninflammatory manner. The development of such training programs has been spurred in both the North and the South by recognition of the tremendous importance of the police in either promoting or reducing interracial violence (*cf.* Kephart, 1957; Lohman, 1947; McEntire and Weckler, 1946; Weisberg, 1951).

A theoretical question of great interest is that of the relationship between changes in intergroup attitudes and changes in intergroup behavior. We do not have very much evidence on this point, but we can venture some broad generalizations. The first is that substantial changes in ethnic attitudes may occur without being accompanied or followed by any discernible changes in intergroup behavior. The second is that substantial changes in ethnic attitudes may occur and be followed by changes in intergroup behavior that seem to be attributable largely to the change in attitudes. A good example is the college student whose attitudes on race relations become more liberal during a particular academic year, and who spends the following summer working on a civil rights project. It seems reasonable to assume that the likelihood that a change in ethnic attitudes will be followed by a corresponding change in ethnic behavior is directly proportional to the size of the change in attitude, and inversely proportional to the extent to which the possibilities for interethnic behavior are constrained by other factors (for example, the individual is bedridden, or lives in an ethnically homogeneous community, or is a professional diplomat or an army officer).

We do not feel able to venture any generalizations about the circumstances in which a change in intergroup behavior is likely to be followed by a corresponding change in ethnic attitudes, and those in which it is likely to lead to a contrasting change or no change at all. Clearly the outcome is determined in part by the way in which the change in behavior was brought about—external force, external persuasion, acquisition of new information, increase or decrease in ability, change in internal motivational state, etc. The problem has been discussed in general terms by Festinger (1957) and Kelman (1961). Clark (1953) has contributed a discussion of the probable effects on racial attitudes of participation in school desegregation.

REFERENCES

Ackerman, N. W., and Marie Jahoda (1950). *Anti-Semitism and emotional disorder*. New York: Harper.

Adorno, T. W., Else Frenkel-Brunswik, D. J. Levinson, and R. N. Sanford (1950). *The authoritarian personality*. New York: Harper.

Allport, G. W. (1954). *The nature of prejudice*. Cambridge, Mass.: Addison-Wesley.

Allport, G. W., and B. M. Kramer (1946). Some roots of prejudice. *J. Psychol.*, 22, 9–39.

Ammons, R. (1950). Reactions in a projective doll-play interview of white males, 2–6, to differences in skin color and facial features. *J. genet. Psychol.*, 76, 323–341.

Bayton, J. A. (1941). The racial stereotypes of Negro college students. *J. abnorm. soc. Psychol.*, 36, 97–102.

Beard, Mirian (1942). Anti-Semitism: product of economic myths. In I. Graeber and S. H. Britt (Eds.), *Jews in a gentile world*. New York: Macmillan. Pp. 362–401.

Berger, M. (1952). *Equality by statute*. New York: Columbia Univ. Press.

Berkowitz, L. (1959). Anti-Semitism and the displacement of aggression. *J. abnorm. soc. Psychol.*, 59, 182–188.

———— (1961). Anti-Semitism, judgmental processes and the displacement of hostility. *J. abnorm. soc. Psychol.*, 62, 210–215.

Berkowitz, L., and J. A. Green (1962). The stimulus qualities of the scapegoat. *J. abnorm. soc. Psychol.*, 64, 293–301.

Bettelheim, B., and M. Janowitz (1950a). *Dynamics of prejudice.* New York: Harper.

———— (1950b). Reactions to fascist propaganda: a pilot study. *Publ. Opin. Quart., 14,* 53–60.

———— (1964). *Social change and prejudice, including dynamics of prejudice.* New York: Free Press.

Bird, C., E. D. Monachesi, and H. Burdick (1952). Infiltration and the attitudes of white and Negro parents and children. *J. abnorm. soc. Psychol., 47,* 688–699.

Blake, R., and W. Dennis (1943). The development of stereotypes concerning the Negro. *J. abnorm. soc. Psychol., 38,* 525–531.

Block, J., and Jeanne Block (1951). An investigation of the relationship between intolerance of ambiguity and ethnocentrism. *J. Pers., 19,* 303–311.

Bogardus, E. S. (1925a). Analyzing changes in public opinion. *J. appl. Sociol., 9,* 372–381.

———— (1925b). Measuring social distance. *J. appl. Sociol., 9,* 299–308.

———— (1925c). Social distance and its origins. *J. appl. Sociol., 9,* 216–226.

———— (1927). Race friendliness and social distance. *J. appl. Sociol., 11,* 272–287.

———— (1928). *Immigration and race attitudes.* Boston: Heath.

Bolton, Euri B. (1937). Measuring specific attitudes toward the social rights of the Negro. *J. abnorm. soc. Psychol., 31,* 384–397.

Boyd, G. F. (1952). The levels of aspiration of white and Negro children in a non-segregated elementary school. *J. soc. Psychol., 36,* 191–196.

Boynton, P. L., and G. D. Mayo (1942). A comparison of certain attitudinal responses of white and Negro high school students. *J. Negro Educ., 11,* 487–494.

Brophy, I. N. (1946). The luxury of anti-Negro prejudice. *Publ. Opin. Quart., 9,* 456–466.

Brown, J. F. (1942). The origin of the anti-Semitic attitude. In I. Graeber and S. H. Britt (Eds.), *Jews in a gentile world.* New York: Macmillan. Pp. 124–148.

Buchanan, W. (1951). Stereotypes and tensions as revealed by the UNESCO international poll. *Int. soc. Sci. Bull., 3,* 515–528.

Byrne, D., and T. J. Wong (1962). Racial prejudice, interpersonal attraction, and assumed dissimilarity of attitudes. *J. abnorm. soc. Psychol., 65,* 246–253.

Campbell, A. A. (1947). Factors associated with attitudes toward Jews. In T. M. Newcomb and E. L. Hartley (Eds.), *Readings in social psychology.* New York: Holt. Pp. 518–527.

Campbell, D. T. (1947). The generality of a social attitude. Unpublished doctoral dissertation, University of California, Berkeley.

———— (1950). The indirect assessment of social attitudes. *Psychol. Bull., 47,* 15–38.

Campbell, D. T., and R. A. LeVine (1961). A proposal for cooperative cross-cultural research on ethnocentrism. *J. Confl. Resol., 5,* 82–108.

Campbell, E. Q. (1958). Some social psychological correlates of direction in attitude change. *Soc. Forces, 36,* 335–340.

Cantril, H. (1941). *The psychology of social movements.* New York: Wiley.

Cantril, H., and G. W. Allport (1935). *The psychology of radio.* New York: Harper.

Carlson, E. R. (1956). Attitude change through modification of attitude structure. *J. abnorm. soc. Psychol., 52,* 254–261.

Chase, W. P. (1940). Attitudes of North Carolina college students (women) toward the Negro. *J. soc. Psychol., 12,* 367–378.

Chein, I. (1951). Notes on a framework for the measurement of discrimination and prejudice. In Marie Jahoda, M. Deutsch, and S. W. Cook, *Research methods in social relations.* Vol. 1. New York: Dryden. Pp. 382–390.

Chen, W. K.-C. (1933). The influence of oral propaganda upon students' attitudes. *Arch. Psychol., N.Y.,* No. 150.

———— (1936). Retention of the effect of oral propaganda. *J. soc. Psychol., 7,* 479–483.

Chicago Commission on Race Relations (1922). *The Negro in Chicago: a study of race relations and a race riot.* Chicago: Univ. of Chicago Press.

Christiansen, B. (1965). Attitudes towards foreign affairs as a function of personality. In H. Proshansky and B. Seidenberg (Eds.), *Basic studies in social psychology.* New York: Holt, Rinehart, and Winston. Pp. 706–716.

Christie, R., and Marie Jahoda, Eds. (1954). *Studies in the scope and method of "The Authoritarian Personality."* Glencoe, Ill.: Free Press.

Clark, K. B. (1953). Desegregation: an appraisal of the evidence. *J. soc. Issues, 9,* No. 4.

———— (1955). *Prejudice and your child.* Boston: Beacon Press.

Clark, K. B., and Mamie P. Clark (1947). Racial identification and preference in Negro children. In T. M. Newcomb and E. L. Hartley (Eds.), *Readings in social psychology.* New York: Holt. Pp. 169–178.

Closson, E. E. (1930). A study of the factor of information in race prejudice. Unpublished Master's dissertation, Iowa State University.

Cohen, J., and W. S. Murphy (1966). *Burn, baby, burn!* New York: Dutton.

Cook, S. W., and Claire Selltiz (1964). A multiple-indicator approach to attitude measurement. *Psychol. Bull., 62,* 36–55.

Cooper, Eunice, and Helen Dinerman (1951). Analysis of the film "Don't Be a Sucker": a study in communication. *Publ. Opin. Quart., 15,* 243–264.

Coser, L. A. (1964). Conflict. In J. Gould and W. L. Kolb (Eds.), *A dictionary of the social sciences.* New York: Free Press. Pp. 123–124.

Cowen, E. L., J. Landes, and D. E. Schaet (1959). The effects of mild frustration on the expression of prejudiced attitudes. *J. abnorm. soc. Psychol., 58,* 33–38.

Criswell, Joan H. (1937). Racial cleavage in Negro-white groups. *Sociometry, 1,* 81–89.

———— (1939). Social structure revealed in a sociometric re-test. *Sociometry, 2,* 69–75.

Culbertson, F. M. (1957). Modifications of an emotionally-held attitude through role playing. *J. abnorm. soc. Psychol., 54,* 230–233.

Dahlke, H. O. (1952). Race and minority riots: a study in the typology of violence. *Soc. Forces, 30,* 419–425.

_____ (1964). Co-operation (sociology). In J. Gould and W. L. Kolb (Eds.), *A dictionary of the social sciences.* New York: Free Press. Pp. 140–141.

Davids, A. (1955). Some personality and intellectual correlates of intolerance of ambiguity. *J. abnorm. soc. Psychol., 51,* 415–420.

Davis, K. (1949). *Human society.* New York: Macmillan.

Deri, Susan, Dorothy Dinnerstein, J. Harding, and A. D. Pepitone (1948). Techniques for the diagnosis and measurement of intergroup attitudes and behavior. *Psychol. Bull., 45,* 248–271.

Deutsch, M. (1960). Minority group and class status as related to social and personality factors in scholastic achievement. *Soc. Appl. Anthropol. Monogr.,* No. 2.

Deutsch, M., and Mary E. Collins (1951). *Interracial housing: a psychological evaluation of a social experiment.* Minneapolis: Univ. of Minnesota Press.

Dodd, S. C. (1935). A social distance test in the Near East. *Amer. J. Sociol., 41,* 194–204.

Dollard, J. (1937). *Caste and class in a southern town.* New Haven: Yale Univ. Press.

_____ (1938). Hostility and fear in social life. *Soc. Forces, 17,* 15–26.

Dollard, J., L. W. Doob, N. E. Miller, O. H. Mowrer, and R. R. Sears (1939). *Frustration and aggression.* New Haven: Yale Univ. Press.

Dombrose, L. A., and D. J. Levinson (1950). Ideological 'militancy' and 'pacifism' in democratic individuals. *J. soc. Psychol., 32,* 101–113.

Drake, St. C., and H. R. Cayton (1945). *Black metropolis.* New York: Harcourt, Brace, and World.

Dudycha, G. J. (1942). The attitudes of college students toward war and the Germans before and during the second world war. *J. soc. Psychol., 15,* 317–324.

Duncan, O. D., and Beverly Duncan (1957). *The Negro population of Chicago: a study of residential succession.* Chicago: Univ. of Chicago Press.

Dwyer, R. J. (1958). A report on patterns of interaction in desegregated schools. *J. educ. Sociol., 31,* 253–256.

Eddy, E. M. (1964). Attitudes towards desegregation among Southern students on a Northern campus. *J. soc. Psychol., 62,* 285–301.

Elliott, F. R. (1936). Eye vs. ear in moulding opinion. *Publ. Opin. Quart., 1,* 83–87.

Fenichel, O. (1946). Elements of a psychoanalytic theory of anti-Semitism. In E. Simmel (Ed.), *Anti-Semitism: a social disease.* New York: International Univ. Press. Pp. 11–32.

Festinger, L. (1957). *A theory of cognitive dissonance.* New York: Row, Peterson.

Fisher, J. (1951). The memory process and certain psychosocial attitudes, with special reference to the law of Prägnanz. *J. Pers., 19,* 406–420.

Fishman, J. A. (1961). Some social and psychological determinants of intergroup relations in changing neighborhoods: an introduction to the Bridgeview study. *Soc. Forces, 40,* 42–51.

Ford, L. I. (1956). The relationship between prejudice and dogmatism in opinion change. *Diss. Abs., 16,* 2522.

Foreman, P. B. (1955). The implications of Project Clear. *Phylon, 16,* 263–274.

Fortune Survey (1946). *Fortune, 33*, No. 2, 257–260.

Frenkel-Brunswik, Else (1948). A study of prejudice in children. *Hum. Relat., 1*, 295–306.

Frenkel-Brunswik, Else, and Joan Havel (1953). Prejudice in the interviews of children: attitudes toward minority groups. *J. genet. Psychol., 82*, 91–136.

Frenkel-Brunswik, Else, and R. N. Sanford (1945). Some personality correlates of anti-Semitism. *J. Psychol., 20*, 271–291.

Friedsam, H. J. (1964). Competition. In J. Gould and W. L. Kolb (Eds.), *A dictionary of the social sciences.* New York: Free Press. Pp. 118–119.

Galtung, J. (1960). *Anti-Semitism in the making: a study of American high school students.* Oslo: Institute for Social Research.

Goldberg, A. L. (1956). The effects of two types of sound motion pictures on the attitudes of adults toward minorities. *J. educ. Sociol., 29*, 386–391.

Goodman, Mary E. (1952). *Race awareness in young children.* Cambridge, Mass.: Addison-Wesley. (2nd ed. New York: Crowell-Collier, 1964.)

Goodnow, R. E., and R. Tagiuri (1952). Religious ethnocentrism and its recognition among adolescent boys. *J. abnorm. soc. Psychol., 47*, 316–320.

Gough, H. G. (1951). Studies of social intolerance: I. Some psychological and sociological correlates of anti-Semitism. *J. soc. Psychol., 33*, 237–246.

Gough, H. G., D. B. Harris, D. B. Martin, and M. Edwards (1950). Children's ethnic attitudes: I. Relationship to certain personality factors. *Child Develpmt., 21*, 83–91.

Gould, J., and W. L. Kolb, Eds. (1964). *A dictionary of the social sciences.* New York: Free Press.

Gray, J. S., and A. H. Thompson (1953). The ethnic prejudices of white and Negro college students. *J. abnorm. soc. Psychol., 48*, 311–313.

Greenberg, H., J. Pierson, and S. Sherman (1957). The effects of single-session education techniques on prejudice attitudes. *J. educ. Sociol., 31*, 82–86.

Greenstein, F. I. (1960). The benevolent leader: children's images of political authority. *Amer. polit. Sci. Rev., 54*, 934–943.

Grimshaw, A. D. (1960). Urban racial violence in the United States: changing ecological considerations. *Amer. J. Sociol., 66*, 109–119.

Grossack, M. M. (1957). Group belongingness and authoritarianism in Southern Negroes: a research note. *Phylon, 18*, 261–266.

Gundlach, R. H. (1950). Effects of on-the-job experience with Negroes upon the racial attitudes of white workers in union shops. *Amer. Psychologist, 5*, 300. (Abstract)

Guttman, L. (1950). The basis for scalogram analysis. In S. A. Stouffer *et al., Measurement and prediction.* Princeton: Princeton Univ. Press. Pp. 60–90.

Hager, D. J., C. Y. Glock, and I. Chein, Eds. (1956). Religious conflict in the United States. *J. soc. Issues, 12*, No. 3.

Hall, W. (1938). The effect of defined social stimulus material upon the stability of attitudes toward labor unions, capital punishment, social insurance, and Negroes. *Purdue Univ. Stud. higher Educ., 34*, 7–19.

Harding, J., and R. Hogrefe (1952). Attitudes of white department store employees toward Negro co-workers. *J. soc. Issues, 8,* No. 1, 18–28.

Harding, J., B. Kutner, H. Proshansky, and I. Chein (1954). Prejudice and ethnic relations. In G. Lindzey (Ed.), *Handbook of social psychology.* Vol. 2. Cambridge, Mass.: Addison-Wesley. Pp. 1021–1061.

Harlan, H. H. (1942). Some factors affecting attitude toward Jews. *Amer. sociol. Rev., 7,* 816–827.

Harris, A., and G. Watson (1946). Are Jewish or gentile children more clannish? *J. soc. Psychol., 24,* 71–76.

Harris, D., H. Gough, and W. E. Martin (1950). Children's ethnic attitudes: II. Relationships to parental beliefs concerning child training. *Child Develpmt., 21,* 169–181.

Hart, I. (1957). Maternal child-rearing practices and authoritarian ideology. *J. abnorm. soc. Psychol., 55,* 232–237.

Hartley, E. L. (1946). *Problems in prejudice.* New York: King's Crown Press.

Hartley, E. L., M. Rosenbaum, and S. Schwartz (1948). Children's use of ethnic frames of reference: an exploratory study of children's conceptualizations of multiple ethnic group membership. *J. Psychol., 26,* 367–386.

Hayes, M. L., and M. E. Conklin (1953). Intergroup attitudes and experimental change. *J. exp. Educ., 22,* 19–36.

Hinckley, E. D. (1932). The influence of individual opinion on construction of an attitude scale. *J. soc. Psychol., 3,* 283–295.

Hogrefe, R., Mary C. Evans, and I. Chein (1947). The effects on intergroup attitudes of participation in an interracial play center. *Amer. Psychologist, 2,* 324. (Abstract)

Horowitz, E. L. (1936). The development of attitude toward the Negro. *Arch. Psychol., N.Y.,* No. 194.

———— (1944). 'Race' attitudes. In O. Klineberg (Ed.), *Characteristics of the American Negro.* New York: Harper. Pp. 139–247.

Horowitz, E. L., and Ruth E. Horowitz (1938). Development of social attitudes in children. *Sociometry, 1,* 301–338.

Hovland, C. I., A. A. Lumsdaine, and F. D. Sheffield (1949). *Experiments on mass communication.* Princeton: Princeton Univ. Press.

Hovland, C. I., and R. Sears (1940). Minor studies in aggression: VI. Correlation of lynchings with economic indices. *J. Psychol., 9,* 301–310.

Hughes, E. C., and Helen M. Hughes (1952). *Where peoples meet: racial and ethnic frontiers.* Glencoe, Ill.: Free Press.

Hunt, C. L. (1959). Negro-white perceptions of interracial housing. *J. soc. Issues, 15,* No. 4, 24–29.

Hyman, H. H. (1959). *Political socialization.* Glencoe, Ill.: Free Press.

Hyman, H. H., and P. B. Sheatsley (1956). Attitudes toward desegregation. *Sci. Amer., 195,* No. 6, 35–39.

Ichheiser, G. (1944). Fear of violence and fear of fraud, with some remarks on the social psychology of anti-Semitism. *Sociometry, 7,* 376–383.

Irish, D. P. (1952). Reactions of Caucasian residents to Japanese-American neighbors. *J. soc. Issues, 8*, No. 1, 10–17.

Jones, V. (1938). Attitudes of college students and the changes in such attitudes during four years in college. *J. educ. Psychol., 29*, 14–25, 114–134.

Kagan, H. E. (1952). *Changing the attitude of Christian toward Jew: a psychological approach through religion.* New York: Columbia Univ. Press.

Kates, S. L., and L. N. Diab (1955). Authoritarian ideology and attitudes on parent-child relationships. *J. abnorm. soc. Psychol., 51*, 13–16.

Katz, D. (1960). The functional approach to the study of attitude change. *Publ. Opin. Quart., 24*, 163–204.

Katz, D., and K. W. Braly (1933). Racial stereotypes of 100 college students. *J. abnorm. soc. Psychol., 28*, 280–290.

———— (1935). Racial prejudice and racial stereotypes. *J. abnorm. soc. Psychol., 30*, 175–193.

Katz, D., I. Sarnoff, and C. McClintock (1956). Ego-defense and attitude change. *Hum. Relat., 9*, 27–45.

Katz, D., and E. Stotland (1959). A preliminary statement to a theory of attitude structure and change. In S. Koch (Ed.), *Psychology: a study of a science.* Vol. 3: Formulations of the person and the social context. New York: McGraw-Hill. Pp. 423–475.

Kaufman, W. C. (1957). Status, authoritarianism, and anti-Semitism. *Amer. J. Sociol., 62*, 379–382.

Kelman, H. C. (1961). Processes of opinion change. *Publ. Opin. Quart., 25*, 57–78.

Kelman, H. C., and T. F. Pettigrew (1959). How to understand prejudice. *Commentary, 28*, 436–441.

Kephart, W. M. (1957). *Racial factors and urban law enforcement.* Philadelphia: Univ. of Pennsylvania Press.

Kerr, W. A. (1944). Correlates of politico-economic liberalism-conservatism. *J. soc. Psychol., 20*, 61–77.

Klein, M. (1961). Cognitive functions related to authoritarianism and dogmatism. Unpublished doctoral dissertation, Yeshiva University.

Klineberg, O. (1950). *Tensions affecting international understanding.* New York: Social Science Research Council, Bull. 62.

Knower, F. H. (1935). Experimental studies of changes in attitudes: I. A study of the effect of oral argument on changes of attitude. *J. soc. Psychol., 6*, 315–347.

———— (1936). Experimental studies of changes in attitudes: II. A study of the effect of printed argument on changes in attitude. *J. abnorm. soc. Psychol., 30*, 522–532.

Konvitz, M. R., and T. Leskes (1961). *A century of civil rights.* New York: Columbia Univ. Press.

Kramer, B. M. (1949). Dimensions of prejudice. *J. Psychol., 27*, 389–451.

———— (1951). Residential contact as a determinant of attitudes toward Negroes. Unpublished doctoral dissertation, Harvard University.

Kraus, S. (1960). Modifying prejudice: attitude change as a function of the race of the communicator. *Audiovisual Communic. Rev., 10*, No. 1, 14–22.

Kutner, B. (1958). Patterns of mental functioning associated with prejudice in children. *Psychol. Monogr., 72*, No. 7 (whole No. 460).

Kutner, B., and N. B. Gordon (1964). Cognitive functioning and prejudice: a nine-year follow-up study. *Sociometry, 27*, 66–74.

Kutner, B., Carol Wilkins, and Penny R. Yarrow (1952). Verbal attitudes and overt behavior involving racial prejudice. *J. abnorm. soc. Psychol., 47*, 649–652.

Lambert, W. E., and Y. Taguchi (1956). Ethnic cleavage among young children. *J. abnorm. soc. Psychol., 53*, 380–382.

Landreth, Catherine, and B. C. Johnson (1953). Young children's responses to a picture and inset test designed to reveal reactions to persons of different skin color. *Child Develpmt., 24*, 63–79.

Langner, T. S. (1953). A test of intergroup prejudice which takes account of individual and group differences in values. *J. abnorm. soc. Psychol., 48*, 548–554.

LaPiere, R. T. (1934). Attitudes vs. actions. *Soc. Forces, 13*, 230–237.

_____ (1936). Type-rationalizations of group antipathy. *Soc. Forces, 15*, 232–237.

Lasker, B. (1929). *Race attitudes in children.* New York: Holt.

Lee, A. M., and N. D. Humphrey (1943). *Race riot.* New York: Dryden.

Lentz, T. F. (1939). Personage admiration and other correlates of conservatism-radicalism. *J. soc. Psychol., 10*, 81–93.

Lesser, G. S. (1958). Extrapunitiveness and ethnic attitudes. *J. abnorm. soc. Psychol., 56*, 211–282.

Levinger, L. J. (1936). *Anti-Semitism, yesterday and tomorrow.* New York: Macmillan.

Levinson, D. J. (1954). The intergroup relations workshop: its psychological aims and effects. *J. Psychol., 38*, 103–126.

Levinson, D. J., and Phyllis E. Huffman (1955). Traditional family ideology and its relation to personality. *J. Pers., 23*, 251–273.

Levinson, D. J., and R. N. Sanford (1944). A scale for the measurement of anti-Semitism. *J. Psychol., 17*, 339–370.

Levinson, D. J., and R. A. Schermerhorn (1951). Emotional-attitudinal effects of an intergroup relations workshop on its members. *J. Psychol., 31*, 243–256.

Lindzey, G. (1950). An experimental examination of the scapegoat theory of prejudice. *J. abnorm. soc. Psychol., 45*, 296–309.

Lippitt, R. (1949). *Training in community relations: a research exploration toward new group skills.* New York: Harper.

Lippitt, R., and Marian Radke (1946). New trends in the investigation of prejudice. *Ann. Amer. Acad. Polit. Soc. Sci., 244*, 167–176.

Lippmann, W. (1922). *Public opinion.* New York: Harcourt, Brace.

Lohman, J. D. (1947). *The police and minority groups.* Chicago: Chicago Park District.

Lombardi, D. N. (1962). Factors affecting changes in attitudes toward Negroes among high school students. *Diss. Abs., 23*, 1413–1414.

Loomis, C. P. (1943). Ethnic cleavages in the Southwest as reflected in two high schools. *Sociometry, 6,* 7–26.

Lubell, S. (1965). *The future of American politics* (3rd ed.). New York: Harper.

Lundberg, A., and L. Dickson (1952). Selective association among ethnic groups in a high school population. *Amer. sociol. Rev., 17,* 23–34.

Lyle, W. H., Jr., and E. E. Levitt (1955). Punitiveness, authoritarianism, and parental discipline of grade school children. *J. abnorm. soc. Psychol., 51,* 42–46.

McCandless, B. R., and J. M. Hoyt (1961). Sex, ethnicity, and play preferences of preschool children. *J. abnorm. soc. Psychol., 62,* 683–685.

McClosky, H. (1958). Conservatism and personality. *Amer. polit. Sci. Rev., 42,* 27–45.

McDill, E. L. (1961). Anomie, authoritarianism, prejudice, and socio-economic status: an attempt at clarification. *Soc. Forces, 39,* 239–245.

McEntire, D., and J. E. Weckler (1946). The role of police. *Ann. Amer. Acad. Polit. Soc. Sci., 244,* 82–89.

MacKenzie, Barbara K. (1948). The importance of contact in determining attitudes toward Negroes. *J. abnorm. soc. Psychol., 43,* 417–441.

McNeill, J. D. (1960). Changes in ethnic reaction tendencies during high school. *J. educ. Res., 53,* 199–200.

McWilliams, C. (1944). *Prejudice: Japanese-Americans, symbol of racial intolerance.* Boston: Little, Brown.

Mann, J. H. (1960). The differential nature of prejudice reduction. *J. soc. Psychol., 52,* 339–343.

Maritain, J. (1939). *A Christian looks at the Jewish question.* New York: Longmans, Green.

Maslow, W. (1955). The uses of law in the struggle for equality. *Soc. Res., 22,* 297–314.

Mayo, G. D., and J. R. Kinzer (1950). A comparison of the 'racial' attitudes of white and Negro high school students in 1940 and 1948. *J. Psychol., 29,* 397–405.

Meenes, M. (1943). A comparison of racial stereotypes of 1935 and 1942. *J. soc. Psychol., 17,* 327–336.

———— (1950). Racial stereotypes among Negro college students since 1935. Paper read at Eastern Psychological Association, Worcester, Mass., April, 1950.

Meltzer, H. (1939a). Group differences in nationality and race preferences of children. *Sociometry, 2,* 86–105.

———— (1939b). Nationality preferences and stereotypes of colored children. *J. genet. Psychol., 54,* 403–424.

Merton, R. K. (1940). Fact and factitiousness in ethnic opinionnaires. *Amer. sociol. Rev., 5,* 13–28.

———— (1949). Discrimination and the American creed. In R. M. MacIver (Ed.), *Discrimination and national welfare.* New York: Institute for Religious and Social Studies. Pp. 99–126.

Merton, R. K., Patricia S. West, and Marie Jahoda (1949). *Social fictions and social facts: the dynamics of race relations in Hilltown.* New York: Columbia Univ. Bureau of Applied Social Research. (Mimeo)

Merz, L. E., and L. I. Pearlin (1957). The influence of information on three dimensions of prejudice toward Negroes. *Soc. Forces, 35,* 344–351.

Metraux, A. (1950). *Race and civilization.* Paris: UNESCO.

Miller, N. E., and R. Bugelski (1948). Minor studies in aggression: the influence of frustrations imposed by the in-group on attitudes expressed toward out-groups. *J. Psychol., 25,* 437–442.

Millon, T. (1957). Authoritarianism, intolerance of ambiguity, and rigidity under ego- and task-involving conditions. *J. abnorm. soc. Psychol., 55,* 29–33.

Minard, R. D. (1931). Race attitudes of Iowa children. *Univ. Iowa Stud. Char., 4,* No. 2.

—————— (1952). Race relationships in the Pocahontas coal field. *J. soc. Issues, 8,* No. 1, 29–44.

Moreno, J. L. (1934). *Who shall survive?* Washington: Nervous and Mental Disease Publ. Co.

Morland, J. K. (1958). Racial recognition by nursery school children in Lynchberg, Virginia. *Soc. Forces, 37,* 132–137.

—————— (1962). Racial acceptance and preference of nursery school children in a Southern city. *Merrill-Palmer Quart., 8,* 271–280.

Morse, Nancy C. (1947). Anti-Semitism: a study of its causal factors and other associated variables. Unpublished doctoral dissertation, Syracuse University.

Murphy, G., and R. Likert (1938). *Public opinion and the individual.* New York: Harper.

Mussen, P. H. (1950). Some personality and social factors related to changes in children's attitudes toward Negroes. *J. abnorm. soc. Psychol., 45,* 423–441.

—————— (1953). Differences between the TAT responses of Negro and white boys. *J. consult. Psychol., 17,* 373–376.

Myrdal, G. (1944). *An American dilemma: the Negro problem and modern democracy.* New York: Harper.

National Education Association, Department of Superintendence (1932). *Character education: tenth yearbook.* Washington: National Education Association.

O'Connor, Patricia (1952). Ethnocentrism, 'intolerance of ambiguity,' and abstract reasoning ability. *J. abnorm. soc. Psychol., 47,* 526–530.

O'Reilly, C. T., and E. J. O'Reilly (1954). Religious beliefs of Catholic college students and their attitudes toward minorities. *J. abnorm. soc. Psychol., 49,* 378–380.

Palermo, D. S. (1959). Racial comparisons and additional normative data on the Children's Manifest Anxiety Scale. *Child Develpmt., 30,* 53–57.

Palmore, E. B. (1955). The introduction of Negroes into white departments. *Hum. Organizat., 14,* No. 1, 27–28.

Park, R. E., and E. W. Burgess (1921). *Introduction to the science of sociology.* Chicago: Univ. of Chicago Press.

Peak, Helen, and H. W. Morrison (1958). The acceptance of information into attitude structure. *J. abnorm. soc. Psychol., 57,* 127–135.

Pearlin, L. I. (1954). Shifting group attachments and attitudes toward Negroes. *Soc. Forces, 33,* 47–50.

Peregrine, D. (1936).   The effect of printed social stimulus material upon the attitudes of high school pupils toward the Negro.   *Purdue Univ. Stud. higher Educ., 31*, 55–69.

Peterson, Ruth C., and L. L. Thurstone (1932).   The effect of a motion picture film on children's attitudes toward Germans.   *J. educ. Psychol., 23*, 241–246.

———— (1933).   *Motion pictures and the social attitudes of children.*   New York: Macmillan.

Pettigrew, T. F. (1958).   Personality and sociocultural factors in intergroup attitudes: a cross-national comparison.   *J. Confl. Resol., 2*, 29–42.

Pettigrew, T. F., and M. R. Cramer (1959).   The demography of desegregation. *J. soc. Issues, 15*, No. 4, 61–71.

Porter, Judith D. (1963).   Racial concept formation in preschool age children.   Unpublished Master's dissertation, Cornell University.

Powdermaker, Hortense (1944).   *Probing our prejudices.*   New York: Harper.

Prentice, N. M. (1957).   The influence of ethnic attitudes on reasoning about ethnic groups.   *J. abnorm. soc. Psychol., 55*, 270–272.

Prothro, E. T., and J. A. Jensen (1950).   Interrelations of religious and ethnic attitudes in selected Southern populations.   *J. soc. Psychol., 32*, 45–49.

Prothro, E. T., and L. H. Melikian (1954).   Studies in stereotypes: III. Arab students in the Near East.   *J. soc. Psychol., 40*, 237–243.

Prothro, E. T., and O. K. Miles (1952).   A comparison of ethnic attitudes of college students and middle class adults from the same state.   *J. soc. Psychol., 36*, 53–58.

Radke, Marian, and Jean Sutherland (1949).   Children's concepts and attitudes about minority and majority American groups.   *J. educ. Psychol., 40*, 449–468.

Radke, Marian, Jean Sutherland, and P. Rosenberg (1950).   Racial attitudes of children.   *Sociometry, 13*, 154–171.

Radke, Marian, and Helen G. Trager (1950).   Children's perceptions of the social roles of Negroes and whites.   *J. Psychol., 29*, 3–33.

Radke, Marian, Helen G. Trager, and Hadassah Davis (1949).   Social perceptions and attitudes of children.   *Genet. Psychol. Monogr., 40*, 327–447.

Radke-Yarrow, Marian, and B. Lande (1953).   Personality correlates of differential reactions to minority group belonging.   *J. soc. Psychol., 38*, 253–272.

Radke-Yarrow, Marian, Helen Trager, and J. Miller (1952).   The role of parents in the development of children's ethnic attitudes.   *Child Develpmt., 23*, 13–53.

Raper, A. F. (1933).   *The tragedy of lynching.*   Chapel Hill: Univ. of North Carolina Press.

Rath, R., and N. C. Sircar (1960).   The mental pictures of six Hindu caste groups about each other as reflected in verbal stereotypes.   *J. soc. Psychol., 51*, 277–293.

Reigrotski, E., and N. Anderson (1959).   National stereotypes and foreign contacts. *Publ. Opin. Quart., 23*, 515–528.

Remmers, H. H., and C. L. Morgan (1936).   Changing attitudes toward a racial group.   *Purdue Univ. Stud. higher Educ., 31*, 109–114.

Riesman, D. (1942).   The politics of persecution.   *Publ. Opin. Quart., 6*, 41–56.

Riker, B. L. (1944). A comparison of methods used in attitude research. *J. abnorm. soc. Psychol., 39*, 24–42.

Roberts, A. H., and M. Rokeach (1956). Anomie, authoritarianism, and prejudice: a replication. *Amer. J. Sociol., 61*, 355–358.

Roberts, H. W. (1953). The impact of military service upon the racial attitudes of Negro servicemen in World War II. *Soc. Problems, 1*, 65–69.

Rokeach, M. (1951a). A method for studying individual differences in narrow-mindedness. *J. Pers., 20*, 219–233.

―――― (1951b). Prejudice, concreteness of thinking, and reification of thinking. *J. abnorm. soc. Psychol., 46*, 83–91.

―――― (1951c). 'Narrow-mindedness' and personality. *J. Pers., 20*, 234–251.

―――― (1960). *The open and closed mind.* New York: Basic Books.

―――― (1966). Race and shared belief as factors in social choice. *Science, 151*, 167–172.

Rokeach, M., and G. Rothman (1965). The principle of belief congruence and the congruity principle as models of cognitive interaction. *Psychol. Rev., 72*, 128–142.

Rose, A. M. (1948a). Anti-Semitism's root in city-hatred. *Commentary, 6*, 374–378.

―――― (1948b). *Studies in reduction of prejudice* (2nd ed.). Chicago: American Council on Race Relations.

―――― (1960). The comparative study of intergroup conflict. *Sociol. Quart., 1*, 57–66.

―――― (1964). Race and minority group relations. In J. Gould and W. L. Kolb (Eds.), *A dictionary of the social sciences.* New York: Free Press. Pp. 570–571.

Rose, A. M., F. J. Atelsek, and L. R. McDonald (1953). Neighborhood reactions to isolated Negro residents: an alternative to invasion and succession. *Amer. sociol. Rev., 18*, 497–507.

Rosen, I. C. (1948). The effect of the motion picture "Gentleman's Agreement" on attitudes toward Jews. *J. Psychol., 26*, 525–536.

Rosenberg, M. J. (1956). Cognitive structure and attitudinal affect. *J. abnorm. soc. Psychol., 53*, 367–372.

―――― (1960a). An analysis of affective-cognitive consistency. In C. I. Hovland and M. J. Rosenberg (Eds.), *Attitude organization and change.* New Haven: Yale Univ. Press. Pp. 15–64.

―――― (1960b). A structural theory of attitude dynamics. *Publ. Opin. Quart., 24*, 319–340.

Rosenblith, Judy F. (1949). A replication of "Some roots of prejudice." *J. abnorm. soc. Psychol., 44*, 470–489.

Rudwick, E. M. (1966). *Race riot at East St. Louis: July 2, 1917.* Cleveland: World.

Saenger, G., and Emily Gilbert (1950). Customer reactions to the integration of Negro sales personnel. *Int. J. Opin. Attitude Res., 4*, No. 1, 57–76.

Samelson, Babette (1945). Does education diminish prejudice? *J. soc. Issues, 1*, No. 3, 11–13.

Schuman, H., and J. Harding (1963). Sympathetic identification with the underdog. *Publ. Opin. Quart., 27*, 230–241.

_____ (1964). Prejudice and the norm of rationality. *Sociometry, 27*, 353–371.

Seago, Dorothy W. (1947). Stereotypes: before Pearl Harbor and after. *J. Psychol., 23*, 55–63.

Selltiz, Claire, June R. Christ, Joan Havel, and S. W. Cook (1963). *Attitudes and social relations of foreign students in the United States.* Minneapolis: Univ. of Minnesota Press.

Selltiz, Claire, and Margot H. Wormser, Eds. (1949). Community self-surveys: an approach to social change. *J. soc. Issues, 5*, No. 2.

Sherif, M. (1958). Superordinate goals in the reduction of intergroup conflicts. *Amer. J. Sociol., 63*, 349–356.

Sherif, M., *et al.* (1961). *Intergroup conflict and cooperation: the robbers cave experiment.* Norman, Okla.: Univ. of Oklahoma, Institute of Group Relations.

Siegman, A. W. (1957). Authoritarian attitudes in children: I. The effect of age, IQ, anxiety, and parental religious attitudes. *J. clin. Psychol., 13*, 338–340.

Simpson, G. E., and J. M. Yinger (1965). *Racial and cultural minorities: an analysis of prejudice and discrimination* (3rd ed.). New York: Harper.

Sims, V. M., and J. R. Patrick (1936). Attitude toward the Negro of northern and southern college students. *J. soc. Psychol., 7*, 192–204.

Singer, Dorothy (1964). The impact of interracial classroom exposure on the social attitudes of fifth grade children. Unpublished study.

Sinha, A. K. P., and O. P. Upadhyaya (1960). Change and persistence in the stereotypes of university students toward different ethnic groups during the Sino-Indian border dispute. *J. soc. Psychol., 52*, 31–39.

Smith, Carole R., L. Williams, and R. H. Willis (1967). Race, sex, and belief as determinants of friendship acceptance. *J. Pers. soc. Psychol., 5*, 127–137.

Smith, F. T. (1943). *An experiment in modifying attitudes toward the Negro.* New York: Teachers College, Columbia Univ.

Smith, H. (1958). *The religions of man.* New York: Harper.

Smith, H. P., and E. W. Rosen (1958). Some psychological correlates of world mindedness and authoritarianism. *J. Pers., 26*, 170–183.

Smith, M. B. (1947). The personal setting of public opinions: a study of attitudes toward Russia. *Publ. Opin. Quart., 11*, 507–523.

Southall, Sara E. (1950). *Industry's unfinished business.* New York: Harper.

Srole, L. (1956). Social integration and certain corollaries: an exploratory study. *Amer. sociol. Rev., 21*, 709–716.

Stagner, R., and C. S. Congdon (1955). Another failure to demonstrate displacement of aggression. *J. abnorm. soc. Psychol., 51*, 695–696.

Star, Shirley A., R. M. Williams, Jr., and S. A. Stouffer (1965). Negro infantry platoons in white companies. In H. Proshansky and B. Seidenberg (Eds.), *Basic studies in social psychology.* New York: Holt, Rinehart, and Winston. Pp. 680–685.

Stein, D. D., Jane A. Hardyck, and M. B. Smith (1965). Race *and* belief: an open and shut case. *J. Pers. soc. Psychol., 1*, 281–290.

Stember, C. H. (1961). *Education and attitude change: the effects of schooling on prejudice against minority groups.* New York: Institute of Human Relations Press.

Stevenson, H. W., and N. G. Stevenson (1960). Social interaction in an interracial nursery school. *Genet. Psychol. Monogr., 61,* 37–75.

Stevenson, H. W., and E. C. Stewart (1958). A developmental study of race awareness in young children. *Child Develpmt., 29,* 399–410.

Stotland, E., D. Katz, and M. Patchen (1959). The reduction of prejudice through the arousal of self-insight. *J. Pers., 27,* 507–531.

Tarachow, S. (1946). A note on anti-Semitism. *Psychiatry, 9,* 131–132.

Thistlethwaite, D. (1950). Attitude and structure as factors in the distortion of reasoning. *J. abnorm. soc. Psychol., 45,* 442–458.

Thomas, W. I., and F. Znaniecki (1918). *The Polish peasant in Europe and America* (5 vols.). Boston: Richard Badger.

Thompson, E. T., Ed. (1939). *Race relations and the race problem.* Durham, N.C.: Duke Univ. Press.

Thurstone, L. L. (1931a). Influence of motion pictures on children's attitudes. *J. soc. Psychol., 2,* 291–305.

―――― (1931b). The measurement of change in social attitudes. *J. soc. Psychol., 2,* 230–235.

―――― (1931c). The measurement of social attitudes. *J. abnorm. soc. Psychol., 36,* 249–269.

Titus, H. E., and E. P. Hollander (1957). The California F scale in psychological research: 1950–1955. *Psychol. Bull., 54,* 47–64.

Trachtenberg, J. (1943). *The devil and the Jews.* New Haven: Yale Univ. Press.

Trager, Helen G., and Marian R. Yarrow (1952). *They learn what they live: prejudice in young children.* New York: Harper.

Triandis, H. C. (1961). A note on Rokeach's theory of prejudice. *J. abnorm. soc. Psychol., 62,* 184–186.

―――― (1964). Exploratory factor analyses of the behavioral components of social attitudes. *J. abnorm. soc. Psychol., 68,* 420–430.

Triandis, H. C., and Leigh M. Triandis (1960). Race, social class, religion, and nationality as determinants of social distance. *J. abnorm. soc. Psychol., 61,* 110–118.

Tumin, M. M. (1961). *Inventory and appraisal of research on American anti-Semitism.* New York: Freedom Books.

―――― (1964). Ethnic group. In J. Gould and W. L. Kolb (Eds.), *A dictionary of the social sciences.* New York: Free Press. Pp. 243–244.

Tumin, M. M., P. Barton, and B. Burrus (1958). Education, prejudice and discrimination: a study in readiness for desegregation. *Amer. sociol. Rev., 23,* 41–49.

United Nations Commission on Human Rights, Subcommission on Prevention of Discrimination and Protection of Minorities (1949). *The main types and causes of discrimination.* Lake Success, N.Y.: United Nations.

Vaughan, G. M. (1963). Concept formation and the development of ethnic awareness. *J. genet. Psychol., 103,* 93–103.

_____ (1964). Ethnic awareness in relation to minority group membership. *J. genet. Psychol., 105*, 119–130.

Vaughan, G. M., and R. H. T. Thompson (1961). New Zealand children's attitudes towards Maoris. *J. abnorm. soc. Psychol., 62*, 701–704.

Vinacke, W. E. (1949). Stereotyping among national-racial groups in Hawaii: a study in ethnocentrism. *J. soc. Psychol., 30*, 265–291.

Watson, G. B. (1925). *The measurement of fair-mindedness.* New York: Teachers College, Columbia Univ.

Watson, Jeanne (1950). Some social and psychological situations related to change in attitude. *Hum. Relat., 3*, 15–56.

Weatherly, D. (1961). Anti-Semitism and the expression of fantasy aggression. *J. abnorm. soc. Psychol., 62*, 454–457.

_____ (1963). Maternal response to childhood aggression and subsequent anti-Semitism. *J. abnorm. soc. Psychol., 66*, 183–185.

Webster, S. W. (1961). The influence of interracial contact on social acceptance in a newly integrated school. *J. educ. Psychol., 52*, 292–296.

Weisberg, B. (1951). Racial violence and civil rights law enforcement. *Univ. Chicago Law Rev., 18*, 769–783.

Whitmore, P. S., Jr. (1957). A study of school desegregation: attitude change and scale validation. *Diss. Abs., 17*, 891–892.

Wilke, W. H. (1934). An experimental comparison of the speech, the radio, and the printed page as propaganda devices. *Arch. Psychol., N.Y.,* No. 169.

Williams, D. H. (1934). The effects of an interracial project upon the attitudes of Negro and white girls within the Young Women's Christian Association. Unpublished Master's dissertation, Columbia University.

Williams, R. M., Jr. (1947). *The reduction of intergroup tensions: a survey of research on problems of ethnic, racial, and religious group relations.* New York: Social Science Research Council, Bull. 57.

_____ (1960). *American society: a sociological interpretation* (2nd ed.). New York: Knopf.

_____ (1964). *Strangers next door.* Englewood Cliffs, N.J.: Prentice-Hall.

Williams, R. M., Jr., and Margaret W. Ryan, Eds. (1954). *Schools in transition: community experiences in desegregation.* Chapel Hill: Univ of North Carolina Press.

Wilner, D. M., Rosabelle P. Walkley, and S. W. Cook (1952). Residential proximity and intergroup relations in public housing projects. *J. soc. Issues, 8*, No. 1, 45–69.

Wilson, J. Q. (1960). *Negro politics: the search for leadership.* New York: Free Press.

Wilson, W. C. (1963). Development of ethnic attitudes in adolescence. *Child Develpmt., 34*, 247–256.

Winder, A. E. (1952). White attitudes towards Negro-white interaction in an area of changing racial composition. *Amer. Psychologist, 7*, 330–331. (Abstract)

Wirth, L. (1939). *Contemporary social problems.* Chicago: Univ. of Chicago Press.

Wolf, Eleanor P. (1957). The invasion-succession sequence as a self-fulfilling prophecy. *J. soc. Issues, 13*, No. 4, 7–20.

Woodmansee, J. J., and S. W. Cook (1967). Dimensions of verbal racial attitudes: their identification and measurement. *J. Pers. soc. Psychol.,* 7, 240–250.

Wormser, Margot H., and Claire Selltiz (1951). *How to conduct a community self-survey of civil rights.* New York: Association Press.

Wright, Q. (1965). *A study of war* (2nd ed.). Chicago: Univ. of Chicago Press.

Wright, R. (1945). *Black boy: a record of childhood and youth.* New York: Harper.

Yarrow, Marian R., Ed. (1958). Interpersonal dynamics in a desegregation process. *J. soc. Issues, 14,* No. 1.

Young, D. (1932). *American minority peoples.* New York: Harper.

Zawadski, B. (1948). Limitations of the scapegoat theory of prejudice. *J. abnorm. soc. Psychol., 43,* 127–141.

Zeligs, Rose, and G. Hendrickson (1933). Racial attitudes of two hundred sixth-grade children. *Sociol. soc. Res., 18,* 26–36.

———— (1934). Checking the social distance technique through the personal interview. *Sociol. soc. Res., 18,* 420–430.

38

Effects of the Mass Media of Communication

WALTER WEISS, Hunter College of the City University of New York

Part of the meaning of modern society, and one of its essential characteristics, is the ubiquitous presence of mass media. To people born into the urban centers of the world, the rich diversity of formal media is a natural element of the environment. Like current modes of transportation, kinds of occupations, and styles of dwellings, the mass media compose one of the characterizing features of the modern scene. Obviously, they contribute to the carrying out of daily routines, to relaxation and respite, to an informed understanding of the world, to action, to personal education and intellectual stimulation. However, their larger significance for societies and nations extends beyond their contributions to individual lives; for modern society not only uses mass media, but requires and is fostered by them (Davison, 1965; Lerner, 1958; Pye, 1963; Schramm, 1964; Wirth, 1956). In this perspective, no large society can meet current requirements of viability and growth without efficient, rapid, varied, and repeatable means of communicating to multitudes of people.

The political significance of the media is evident in the tight control exercised by dictatorships over all means of communication. Seizure of the media is one of the first acts of modern revolutionaries. And, in developing countries, official policy of the government tends to control the rates of growth of the various media (Fagen, 1964; Pool, 1963).

To the extent that a relatively homogeneous symbolic environment is provided by the media, either through governmental direction or through common actions of private controllers, uniformity of political and social behavior is fostered. Since the contents of the media not only refer to topical events but may also reflect societal values, norms of behavior, and traditional perspectives for interpreting the environment, the media may be said to contribute to the transmission of culture to the native-born and to the acculturation of immigrants and long-term residents (Lasswell, 1949).

Preparation of the chapter was aided by funds from the Office of Naval Research under Contract Nonr-4309(00). Grateful acknowledgment is made for the varied aid provided by Sandra Steenbock, Henry Solomon, Irene Spalter, Marjorie Kunc, and, most of all, Edith Weiss. For his pervasive professional contributions and continuing though stilled personal influence, the greatest debt is owed the late Carl I. Hovland.

Only a little imaginative effort is needed to appreciate the dependence of an already industrialized society on the mass media. It is sufficient merely to think about the consequences of a sudden elimination of all mass media in the United States! Even the temporary unavailability of but one of them, the New York City newspapers, as the result of a labor strike, produced marked personal discomfort (Berelson, 1949b; Kimball, 1959) and had adverse economic effects. But it is in the examination of the role of the mass media in the transition of traditional societies or developing nations to a modern form that the media's contributions can best be seen (Doob, 1961).

Both Lerner (1958) and Schramm (1964) have espoused the view that, to a considerable extent, mass media prepare, instigate, and undergird the development of a modern society. They present static evidence bearing on this contention in the form of sizable positive associations between the magnitude of media development in a country and indices of urbanization, industrialization, per capita income, and literacy. Of course, such correlations do not lead univocally to any causal interpretation of the effects of mass media. But, in the context of their conceptions of the central role of the media, the data are suggestive. Furthermore, both Lerner and Schramm acknowledge the interlocking and mutually interactive relationship between mass media and other characteristics of modern society, whether these are a certain economic development necessary to support the media or a certain level of social and geographic mobility. Also, Lerner holds that increasing urbanization leads to increased literacy which increases media exposure; the outcome is wider economic opportunity and development and wider participation in the political process, for instance, through voting. The interrelated but also independent significance of literacy and exposure to the mass media is evidenced in research among Colombian peasants by Rogers (1965) and Rogers and Herzog (1966).

In Lerner's (1958) thinking, the psychological key to the transition from a traditional to a modern society is a characteristic of personality which he labels "empathic capacity" or the ability to "see oneself in the other fellow's situation." In simplified terms, his argument is that the media present new objects and ideas which engage and activate this capacity and stimulate its development. In a sense, a person's horizons are expanded and new incentives generated by the act of imaginatively possessing a new and possible way of life. For he can conceive of himself as a proprietor of a bigger grocery in a city or as having nice clothes and living in a nice house or as being rid of stifling drudgeries or crippling disabilities. In the past, this kind of "psychic mobility" occurred through direct experiences, as when new roads and routes brought new goods of trade and new concepts of life, or travel put people in contact with new opportunities. But the effects of such occurrences were limited to relatively few matters and impinged on relatively few people and diffused slowly to a wider group. Now, according to Lerner, the media relate the multitudes to the "infinite vicarious universe" and, as a consequence, function as a "mobility multiplier."

Of course, such effects occur in highly industrialized societies; in fact, both critics and interpreters of advertising's societal function acknowledge the role of advertising in the development of new wants (Galbraith, 1958; Taplin, 1960). But, in this regard, the mass media are likely to have a far stronger if not socially revolutionary impact in countries, localities, and peoples just beginning their modernization. For, as Schramm (1964) writes: "The mass media come to the traditional villages of the world with a freshness they have long ceased to carry in highly developed cultures" (p. 105).

From a perspective similar to Lerner's, Schramm (1964) suggests that the media redefine the meaning of "localness" by making personally relevant distant happenings and even such esoteric occurrences as scientific discoveries. His general perspective on the media is that they serve three traditional societal functions of communication: as "watchman," as an aid to social decision making, and as a teacher. As "watchman," a function akin to Lasswell's (1949) notion of "surveillance," the media report on events in the near and far-off environment which are of actual or potential significance to a society; such reporting embraces information about threats and opportunities and is designed to produce an informed understanding of relevant parts of the environment. Included in this function is the widening of horizons and raising of aspirations, which are so central to Lerner's (1958) conceptualization. As a contributor to social decision processes, the media make available to relevant groups the material necessary for a "dialogue" on issues; by so doing, they can modify attitudes, preferences, and actions, particularly lightly supported ones. The shaping of the discussion and of a perspective on the issue are also media effects which influence decisions on matters of social concern. These two functions were evident in the striking role the media played in giving orientation, allaying anxieties, providing catharsis for the dominant feeling of grief, and arousing integrative national norms during the period of uncertainty and national mourning following the assassination of President Kennedy (Schramm, 1965). As teacher, the media help substantially in all types of education and training. In fact, Schramm sees the media as an educational multiplier which can speed and facilitate the necessary growth of literate and educated people and can contribute to educational economies and the quality of educational practice —for example, by replacing or supporting the poorly trained teacher.

THE MEANING OF "MASS MEDIA"

Though the term "mass media" has been used a number of times, its meaning has not yet been specified. At the least, mass media are organized means of reaching large numbers of diverse kinds of people quickly and efficiently. However, even this seemingly obvious criterion contains ambiguity; for speed, efficiency, and the size and heterogeneity of the audience are relative matters. For instance, books, which are customarily considered a means of mass communication, may reach small numbers of people, and the dissemination of a book may take considerable time. Also, mail, which is not often thought of as a mass medium, can be counted as one in the context of direct-mail advertising and when employed systematically for political purposes. However, nothing is gained theoretically at this time by fussiness in characterizing the criterial attributes of mass media.

For the specific purposes of this chapter, a denotative interpretation is probably more suitable. Mass media may be said to include the print media of newspapers, magazines, and books; the broadcast media of radio and television; and the movies. The effects of these media are what this chapter is about.

However, certain exclusions and limitations must be mentioned. To a great extent, the experimental literature on communication effects will be omitted. A survey of such research can be found in Chapter 21. Instead, primary emphasis will be placed on nonexperimental studies of the effects of the mass media as they are normally used in their customary environments. A major exception will be made in respect to certain experimental studies which have been given unusual weight in public discussions of the effects of media portrayals of violence. These will be critically examined. Of course, selected references to other pertinent experimental research will be made in appropriate places. Special uses of the media, as in formal education, will not be considered. Neither will the relationship between media effects and the economic and organizational structure of the media (for example, private versus public ownership) be examined (see Lazarsfeld, 1942; Waples, Berelson, and Bradshaw, 1940). Finally, rather than a separate medium-by-medium analysis, emphasis will be placed on common effects and uses and general characteristics of the media. However, as necessary, effects specific to a medium will be noted. In a sense, assertions of effects will be supported by research without regard to the medium, whenever this seems justifiable and the evidence permits.

MEDIA EFFECTS: CATEGORIZATION AND SUBSTANCE

Over a decade ago, Hovland (1954) wrote that no satisfactory or theoretically derived schema was available for categorizing media effects. Not only was it true then, but unfortunately it still is, despite the considerable heuristic value that a sound "accounting" system has. For it not only reveals gaps in research but imposes a rational order on diverse kinds of research. By so doing, salient differences and similarities are more sharply illuminated and restraint is placed on loose discussion of what the mass media can and cannot do. Furthermore, the resulting collation can be of use in testing theory and suggesting theory.

No attempt will be made here to present a formal classificatory system. But it is worthwhile to consider a number of relevant dimensions that can provide a framework for an empirical organization of effects. These are the nature or "size" of the effective stimuli, the social unit affected, the temporal extent of the effect, and the types of effects (*cf.* Lazarsfeld, 1948, 1963b).

THE NATURE OR "SIZE" OF THE STIMULUS

For any assertion about effects to be empirically or theoretically useful, the nature of the presumed agent of the effects must be specified with reasonable precision. If this is not done, the meaning of the assertion is open to faulty or partial understanding and the assertion itself to misapplication. While this is a constant requirement of all statements of relationships, it is of particular relevance when the asserted stimulus is a conglomerate event amenable to different levels of analysis. The danger of ignoring this requirement is particularly acute in respect to assertions about the mass media. For what is to be understood as the effective agent when it is said that the media or a particular medium has certain effects? Among several possibilities, this can mean that the effects are due to the mere existence of one or more media, to the special characteristics of the media, to certain kinds of contents or programs provided by the media, to a single program or communication, to a specific factor in a communication. Any of these and other meanings is conceivable, since the unit of analysis can vary from the global to the refined. When overlooked, such variation across studies may yield apparent discrepancies in effects. For instance, in the laboratory, some degree of attitude change is often induced by communication stimuli, while survey research suggests that, in the normal communications environment, attitudes are quite stable.   Hovland (1959) has conjectured that one reason for this difference lies in the nature of the communication stimuli: refined and precise in the laboratory, global and diffuse in the normal environment.

Also to be kept in mind is that each unit of analysis contains the more refined ones; hence, an effect attributed to a complex stimulus may be due to one or more of its components.   If these vary from one occurrence of the stimulus to another, as do the contents of media, the effects may also vary.   This will make for crude relationships between stimulus and effects and for relatively poor predictability, if not inaccuracy.   On similar reasoning, Blumer (1959) has questioned the meaning of attributing effects of a political campaign to a particular medium, for the contents of a medium vary from day to day and are usually not unique to any one medium. The same may be said about the campaign as a whole.   This problem of units of analysis is of the same kind as occurs when effects are attributed to such conglomerate entities as the home, the church, the school.

There is no implication in what has been said that a particular unit of analysis is the proper one or the most informative.   Theory and empirical generalizations can be developed for each level, from statements about the persuasive effects of fear-arousing communications to the societal functions of media.   The unit chosen will depend on the purposes of the investigator, but it should be one that is most suitable for interpreting the effects and permitting prediction of repetitions of the effects. In a sense, the size of stimulus employed in research ought to be chosen in terms of the kinds of effects to which it is most suitably related and to the assumptions and theoretical or interpretive risks involved in using it as an explanation of the particular effect.   To exemplify this perspective, it is worthwhile mentioning some effects which can be attributed to a medium as a whole and examining the problem of attributing effects to categories of media content.

Effects of a medium as a whole

A type of effect which is properly related to a mass medium as an entity is one which derives from its mere existence and availability.   That is, the primary characteristics of mass media as means of communicating information and viewpoints and providing vicarious experiences are the basis for the attributed effects.   Some of these have been taken up in the previous discussion of the role of the mass media in developing countries and of the consequences of their advent where they did not exist previously. In a society where mass media are already present, effects associated with their sheer presence are not often considered.   It takes the unavailability of an existent one or the appearance of a new one to make the obvious point that attention to mass media takes time away from other pursuits.   For instance, television has been charged with such an effect; some of the pertinent evidence on this will be discussed later.   In respect of this kind of effect, it is well to keep in mind that the media are no different basically from any other kind of innovation which invites continued attention.

The intrinsic characteristics of a medium may relate to other kinds of effects and be the basis for intermedia differences in effects.   If the manner by which a medium conveys its content is more appealing, then more time will be spent with it by more people and, hence, its effect on allocation of time will be greater.   If it is a new medium, this consequence will be quite dramatic.   Besides differences in reach, distribution, and efficiency of transmission, the personal skills required to use a medium effectively are also of consequence. At least two kinds of effects can result from such differences: the fewer the skills or the less training needed, the greater will be the audience attracted and the greater the time devoted to the medium; and the generic appeal of the medium may act as an incentive to learning the skills needed to use it efficiently, as reading may be fostered and improved by the desire to participate in the use of print media.

Differences between media in the manner in which their content is conveyed also constitute a basis for differences in effects. For instance, it is tritely obvious that television and the movies have a marked advantage over print and radio when a visual demonstration will increase learning, interest, and persuasion. Also, there is some evidence from experimental research that a delivered speech is more effective than a written one in changing opinion (Knower, 1935, 1936; Wilke, 1934). Many people have suggested that the audiovisual media can induce a sense of personal contact with what is being seen. To the extent that this involvement affects belief (for example, "seeing is believing") or encourages an empathic experience, these media should be better able to produce that psychic mobility which Lerner (1958) has emphasized. In this regard, although certain content may not be exclusive to a medium and hence its effects cannot be simply attributed to the medium, the ability of the medium to make the content more vivid and "real" may heighten its impact. To an acceptance of this possibility can be traced some of the public concern about the effects of the movies and television on moral, sexual, and social behavior.

If the degree of trust people place in a medium influences its effectiveness in gaining belief for the information, opinions, and interpretations it conveys, then, to the extent that media vary in this regard, intermedia differences in effectiveness would be expected (see Chapter 21 for relevant experimental research on communicator credibility). In some areas of the world, the newspaper is trusted more than the radio, and in some the reverse obtains (Carter and Sepúlveda, 1964; Schramm, 1954). To some extent, this is due to public belief that one or the other medium is extremely partial to certain views or is controlled by special interests or is simply venal. In developing countries, radio and film are the primary formal media for many people, being more widely distributed than print; hence, their greater use in a weak-print environment with a long-standing oral tradition will enhance their importance relative to print, more so than in other areas where print was highly developed before the appearance of the audiovisual media (Schramm, 1964). In the United States, surveys have sought evidence on the relative trust accorded the media, by asking people which medium they would be most likely to believe if different ones carried conflicting reports of an event or by asking people to evaluate the general reliability of a medium as a news source. By and large, the primary broadcast medium of the day (radio in the past, television now) has been viewed more favorably in this regard than have the newspapers, even among young people and children, a difference which to some extent reflects the frequency of use of a medium in general or as a news source (Carter and Greenberg, 1965; Lazarsfeld and Field, 1946; Lyness, 1952; Roper and associates, 1965; Schramm, Lyle, and Parker, 1961; Westley and Severin, 1964b). But also involved are the attractiveness and compellingness of the visual dimension provided by television, as well as the temporal priority and continuous up-to-dateness of broadcast media with respect to news, and the perception of newspapers as more clearly partisan or biased on issues (Carter and Greenberg, 1965). However, caution must be exercised in taking the public's response to a hypothetical query as evidence of the differential effectiveness of the media.

Attempts to assess nonobvious intermedia differences in effects by examining their normal impact in ordinary use face serious methodological difficulties. For instance, differences in the audiences naturally attracted to the media will make for a difficult-to-separate contribution to the effects. In this regard, Lazarsfeld (1940) argues that only after it is known whom each medium reaches and why people are attracted to it does it make sense to compare the effects of the media.

Media content as stimulus or incentive

A stimulus unit smaller than that of the entire medium is a category of media content, such as news, entertainment, drama, Westerns. Such categories may range from the broad and diffuse to the narrow and specific. Some, like entertainment, are applicable to all media; others, like Westerns, are associated with certain media rather than others. Though such categories designate smaller and more refined slices of mass communication than that represented by the whole medium, they are still quite gross and comprise a variety of constituent factors. To attribute effects to a category of content is not to specify with any great precision the nature of the stimulus. For instance, there are many ingredients that make up entertainment fare or drama programs and what their relative contributions are is not known. Furthermore, the different instances of the category vary in numerous ways, having as a common feature only the general characteristic which is the category name. This makes for relative crudeness of principles and low predictability in respect to the likely effect of a new example of the same category. As television producers are well aware, the success of one type of program or format does not guarantee the success of another of the same kind, even leaving aside such considerations as placement, competition, and audience satiation.

The general principles and problems of content analysis can be found in Chapter 16. Only selected comments are needed here.

A content analysis may be performed merely to describe what the media are making available to people. To accomplish this, major categories or themes may be noted by impressionistic analysis, for example, as Wolfenstein and Leites (1950) did for the movies or Arnheim (1944) for daytime radio serials; or they may be specified quantitatively, for example, as Lowenthal (1944) did for biographies in two national magazines or Dale (1933) for the movies. The result may be quite useful and informative, for instance, providing evidence of correspondence between native-fascist and Nazi propaganda (Lasswell, 1949) or revealing changes over time in the content characteristics of a medium (Lowenthal, 1944; U.S. Senate, 1964).

At a minimum, the justifiability of the analysis depends on the reliability of the assignment of content to particular categories and on the suitability of the categories themselves. Different descriptive purposes will give rise to different descriptive categories. But any meaningful unit of content possesses sufficient complexity and a variety of characteristics that, depending on the descriptive system used, it could be assigned to different categories. That is, if all conceivable descriptive categories for mass media content could be listed, any unit of content could be assigned to more than one category. Which category it is assigned to depends in large part on which category was included in the descriptive system that is employed. The larger the content unit chosen for analysis (for example, a newspaper versus an editorial, or an entire movie versus a scene, or an entire speech versus a paragraph), the more varied and numerous its content characteristics and, hence, the more likely is multiple categorization to be possible. For instance, a film which depicts a true story of a murder that occurs on a cattle drive could be categorized as a Western, a drama, a murder story, history, and so on. When a multiplicity of categories or themes are available, the apparently dominant theme is often taken as the basis for the assignment. In respect to the hypothetical example, if the murder was the main focus of the film, then the film would be assigned to this category. It is easy to see the difficulties that follow when descriptive categories reflect ethical, social, moral qualities, or the style of relations between people, as in Emery's (1959b) categorization of themes in Western movies.

However, it is not often that analyses of media content have description as their sole purpose. More frequently, the intent is to make statements about some relationship between content and audience. To accomplish this, an implicit assumption is made that the relevant public perceives the material in terms of the same descriptive system and initially categorizes the content in the same way. But without empirical evidence of this, there can be no firm assurance that the analysis reflects the public's perceptions. This is particularly so when the name of the category is taken as the presumed incentive for exposure to the content, as Carter (1957) critically notes, or as the reality depicted by a medium (DeFleur, 1964; Jones, 1942; Smythe, 1954). Of interest is the assertion by Lazarsfeld and Kendall (1948) that the answers to questions on radio program preferences depended on the wording of the questions, for there was no standard way of describing program types.

The problems considered in respect to descriptive content analyses of single media are obviously present when intermedia comparisons are attempted. Evidence is needed that the material is perceived the same way across media, particularly when the categories are presumed to reflect the appeals of the content. Maclean (1954) provided people with two lists of categories, one appropriate to the content of radio and the other to newspapers. The respondents indicated which of the radio categories they would like to listen to and which of the newspaper categories they had read something about that day. Based on scale analysis of the responses, clusters of content types were obtained for each medium. Radio yielded such cluster names as "serious" (news; classical music), "entertainment" (serial dramas; sports), "nostalgic" (children's programs; old, familiar music); and newspapers, "public affairs" (war-related; economic), "entertainment" (comics; pictures), and "social" (leisure-time; religion and church). There was relatively little correlation between radio and newspaper categories that might be expected to intercorrelate or might be thought to be media counterparts of each other, such as "serious" and "public affairs," and the entertainment categories.

Of course, in terms of actual behavior, there may be correlated attention to types of content within a medium or across media. For example, Lazarsfeld (1940) reported that serious print reading and serious radio listening were associated and that the type of radio program most sensitive to differences in serious reading was classical music, even among members of the Book of the Month Club. Similarly, Himmelweit (1962) claims that children's television preferences not only fall into five categories (excitement, social empathy, artistic, intellectual, and mixed social empathy and intellectual), but relate to corresponding categories of preferences in the media. The existence of a correlation between exposure to similarly labeled media content is customarily *assumed* to signify that they serve the same psychological function. Relevant research will be considered later, when effects and uses of the mass media are discussed. But direct and independent evidence is needed in support of such an assumption; and, since the content so categorized is complex enough to serve a variety of uses, evidence should be provided that the designated function is the dominant and controlling one.

The danger of assuming that the category name constitutes the likely *effect* of such content is particularly evident in discussions of the behavioral consequences of media portrayals of violence. Not only is the display of violence singled out as either the most prominent characteristic of a story or program or the one which the descriptive system focuses on, but it is presumed that the person perceives the content in this way and with this emphasis and that the presentation has its effects in terms of how people react to depicted violence—aroused aggressiveness, fear, etc. Obviously, what is required is evidence concerning the actual effects produced by the experience.

THE SOCIAL DIMENSION OF EFFECTS

Another dimension along which effects can be categorized is the size and nature of the social unit involved. Obviously, communication influence may be limited to a few individuals or may extend to large groups of people or societies. However, the nature of the desired effect may itself require that a certain social unit be influenced. For instance, as Katz, Levin, and Hamilton (1963) have pointed out, certain innovations such as fluoridation require a group as the adopting unit and, hence, as the target of influence; whereas others, such as agricultural practices, can be adopted by the individual. Of course, a rigid distinction is not implied, for individuals have to be persuaded even when group decision is required, and personal or social influence is involved even when individual decision suffices.

Also contributing to this dimension of categorization is the social context of exposure. That is, an individual can be alone or with others when exposed to media stimuli. It is not the adventitious occurrence of a particular social context which is relevant, but the possible relation of social context to normal media use. For instance, Freidson (1953) reports that boys in grade school classes from kindergarten to sixth grade said that they usually watched television with family members, attended the movies with family or peers, and read comic books alone. Related data on moviegoing are provided by Handel (1950) and Dale (1933), and on television by Maccoby (1951).

Differences between the media, at least in their short-term effectiveness, may be a result of differences in their social contexts of reception, to the extent that these contribute to communication effects. If this is so, such effects could be assigned to the medium as a whole. Of relevance is Knower's (1935) report that a speech was less effective when people heard it as members of an audience than when exposed to it alone. However, Cantril and Allport (1935) conjectured that radio may have an advantage over print precisely because people listening to radio imagine themselves to be members of a wider audience of simultaneous listeners.

THE TEMPORAL DIMENSION OF EFFECTS

Time is considered a coordinate in that some types of effects can be brought about within a relatively short period, while others need time to develop. Obviously, effects which can be defined in terms of the responses of individuals take less time than those which involve a society. An increment in knowledge or some change in weakly supported attitudes or behavior may follow on exposure to a communication, whereas effects on deeply held views or those with wide social significance, if they occur at all, require considerable time.   While the differences in time for such effects are still arranged in the same order, it is quite likely that modern mass media have reduced the amount of time required for widespread social effects or for the extension of effects throughout a society.   Schramm's (1964) assertion of the social revolutionary influence of the media in developing countries takes cognizance of this.

Time is also involved in media effects in a partly methodological sense. The kind and extent of effects that will be observed depend partly on how long after a communication experience the measurements are made. For instance, though the effects of a single communication are usually greatest shortly after exposure and decline as time passes, this is not always so, as research on delayed effects demonstrates (see Chapter 21).   But a complication arises when the long-term effects of a communication event are sought: the more time that has elapsed, the more likely it is that the supposed residual or continuing effects are a resultant of other contributing influences as well.   As Waples, Bradshaw, and Berelson (1940) point out in respect to books, the more remote effects are modulated by the influence of discussion and comment and by other communications on the topic.   Furthermore, if the effects of an experience are assessed some time afterwards, no evidence of residual effects may be obtained even though there were some immediately after exposure.   The erroneous implication might then be drawn that the experience had no effect at all.

THE NATURE OF THE EFFECTS

We shall discuss the nature of the effects of the mass media under the following headings: (1) cognition, (2) comprehension, (3) emotional arousal, (4) identification, (5) attitude, (6) overt behavior, (7) interests and interest-related behavior, (8) public taste, (9) outlook and values, and (10) family life.

COGNITION

The simplest effect of the media is to make people aware of events, persons, and possibilities beyond their direct experience. This effect refers to cognition in its broadest sense, encompassing mere awareness as well as extensive knowledge.   That even awareness alone is related to wider effects is evidenced by the considerable emphasis in advertising strategy on fostering brand awareness, and in politics on the value to a candidate of being familiar as a name and person to the public.

The advantage of being first with the news obviously lies with the broadcast media over the slower and more rigid schedules of newspapers and magazines. In fact, one of the effects attributed to radio was the elimination of the newspaper extra (Levin, 1954).   But the print media are sources of first awareness for many special-interest topics that the other media do not or cannot present.

Of course, experimental research based on "captive" audiences has demonstrated over and over again the ability of communications to increase the audience's knowledge on some matter (Hovland, Janis, and Kelley, 1953; Hovland, Lumsdaine, and Sheffield, 1949).   Many studies have been concerned with the improvement of communications techniques for just this purpose, particularly those designed to foster the acquisition of skills and technical knowledge (Hoban and van Ormer, 1950; Lumsdaine, 1961).

To say that mass media contribute to awareness of events is not to say that awareness is affected in any simple or direct fashion by media content. For many events beyond direct experience, the media's role is limited to establishing the external precondition of awareness, that is, making available a supply of pertinent information. But the closing of the communication system requires, at the minimum, the response of attention. To be sure, the media can use devices such as bold headlines, color, placement in a prominent location, and so on, to engage perceptual or motivational factors which can entice attention (Doob, 1948); nevertheless, the distinction between supply and awareness is still fundamental. Errors of interpretation and erroneous expectations can occur if what the media emphasize is taken as what is in the actual focus of public attention.

During the height of Senator McCarthy's widely publicized actions and charges concerning Communist influence in the United States, nearly one-third of a national sample could not name any Senator or Congressman who had been playing a leading role in the investigation of Communism (Stouffer, 1955). An examination of the content of the media during this time would have suggested that the internal Communist threat was a salient concern of the American public. Yet Stouffer reports that less than one percent of the sample mentioned this threat as a matter they worried about most; rather, personal and family problems were mentioned by the great majority. Using poll data, Kriesberg (1949b) reported that, on the average, about 30 percent of the American people were unaware of almost any matter of foreign affairs, and an additional 45 percent were aware of important occurrences only but were uninformed about them. In respect to domestic matters, the percentage unaware was about the same as for foreign affairs, but more people were both aware and informed. Similar evidence of what Kriesberg called "dark areas of ignorance" was reported by Hyman and Sheatsley (1947). Furthermore, even at the height of past presidential campaigns, approximately half the electorate could not name either vice presidential candidate (Stouffer, 1955).

Noelle-Neuman (1959) reported that for two years, every time the "Bundesrat" was mentioned in a news broadcast, Radio Stuttgart explained to its German listeners what this unit of the German Federal Republic is. Nevertheless, surveys turned up no evidence that radio listeners had learned the information. Swanson, Jenkins, and Jones (1950) claimed that what people recalled of a speech by Truman in 1949 bore little relationship to the themes emphasized in newspaper and radio reports of the speech. Also, research (Cutlip, 1954) suggests that the average newspaper reader examines only 20 to 25 percent of the stories printed in the average paper. And Lazarsfeld (1940) reported that Gallup surveys conducted in 1932 and 1938 showed that less than half the newspaper readers examined the news stories under the front-page banner headline. In general, more people give more attention to the comics, news pictures, human interest articles, and immediately gratifying stories than to information on public affairs or "hard" news (Lazarsfeld, 1940; Schramm and White, 1949; Swanson, 1954).

Selective exposure

In addition to the role played by nonpsychological factors (Waples, Berelson, and Bradshaw, 1940), discrepancy between media supply and cognition is to be sought in the psychological characteristics of human beings. Probably the most significant and prominent one is interest in the subject matter of the communication. Obviously, except when an unusual event occurs, attention to a topic is motivated by its personal or social relevance; for example, those attentive to one aspect of foreign affairs, for whatever reasons, are likely to be attentive to others (Hyman and Sheatsley, 1947). Also, Lazarsfeld (1940) reported that a radio series devoted to the contributions of minority groups to American life attracted to each program an audience dominated by members of the minority being featured.

Such a conception carries the implication that, on any matter, the uninterested and uninformed are harder to reach than are others. That is, even with equal accessibility to information, prior interest will influence exposure. This is clearly evidenced in a study which also underscores the need to separate media supply and cognition (Star and Hughes, 1950). Beginning in September 1947, a six-month information campaign was undertaken to make the people of Cincinnati more knowledgeable about and conscious of the United Nations. Over this time, all kinds of media were used repeatedly to provide pertinent information and to publicize the campaign slogan: "Peace begins with the United Nations—the United Nations begins with you." Analyses of survey data uncovered no evidence that the campaign increased information about the United Nations or its activities; both before and after the campaign, approximately one out of three had no idea what the main purpose of the organization was. A little more than half of the people were unable to recall the slogan, even though it had been broadcast about 150 times a week at the end of one-minute "spot" announcements. Also, the people reached by the campaign were those already interested in international problems and most likely to be better informed.

In discussions of communication effects, the more customary use of the term "selective exposure" is in relation to an active screening-out of influences that would run counter to existing views and attitudes. In this sense, it connotes a defensive maneuver designed to protect a current perspective or keep it unchallenged (see Chapter 21 for relevant experimental research). The operation of such exposure bias requires awareness of the availability of a contrary viewpoint and a choice not to expose oneself to it. The awareness may be of a specific communication or event, or represent knowledge that a disturbing view is likely to be presented by a particular source, as by a commentator or newspaper of known partiality. In respect to the previously mentioned study by Lazarsfeld (1940), selective exposure in this sense would mean that people were aware of a program and did not listen, not merely for lack of time or interest, but because of hostility toward the minority group to be featured, coupled with the expectation that the program would be complimentary to the group. Since exposure is being motivated by the consonance or discrepancy between the person's attitude and the viewpoint being presented, the concept should also include exposure that seeks reinforcement or confirmation of an existing view. That is, selective exposure may defend a current position by avoiding countering information and assertions or by seeking out reinforcing material.

Cartwright (1949) reported that most of the people who accepted free tickets to a documentary movie already showed the behavior the movie was designed to encourage. In the study by Star and Hughes, those who were more favorably disposed to the United Nations, even before the campaign, were the most attentive to information about the organization. A similar finding was reported by Bogart (1957b) in respect to the effects of an information campaign in Greece. Greenberg and Parker (1965) report that, even in respect to the events surrounding Kennedy's assassination and funeral, exposure to the media and evaluation of the partiality of the presentations were related to partisan political preferences. (Data from studies of voting behavior will be considered later).

Selectivity of attention may also result from differential attitude toward and use of the media or of a particular vehicle such as a specific newspaper, a given magazine, etc. To the extent that media or vehicles differ in the scope and content of their coverage of matters of public concern, an audience will be put in the way of certain information or views and not others. In addition, those who use a medium frequently are more likely to expose themselves to material of interest presented by that medium than are those who are infrequent users or regard it less well. For example, radio-minded women were more likely to begin listening and to continue to listen to a well-publicized radio series on child care than were women who were less frequent radio users, despite comparable interest in such material (McCandless, 1944). Lazarsfeld (1940) reported that, if people have a choice between radio and print for fairly comparable subject matter, the higher their cultural level, the more likely they will be to read than to listen.

Though selective attention has been referred to as the basis of the above results, a partly methodological caution must be raised. In general, research on simple cognitive effects of campaigns have not provided precise evidence on the specific material people have exposed themselves to. In addition, measures of the information learned from information campaigns or news reports have been taken some time after exposure occurred, if it occurred at all. as a consequence, an unknown part of the data is probably due to selectivity of *retention* rather than of attention. For instance, it would be difficult to attribute the inability of many people to recall the name of either vice-presidential candidate during an election campaign, or the high percentage unaware of the frequently repeated slogan about the United Nations, entirely to a lack of exposure to these items. Experimental research provides some evidence concerning the selective forgetting of communication content that is inconsistent with people's attitudes (see Chapter 21).

Though a distinction must be kept in mind between what the media make available and what people are aware of, media emphasis has been found to bear a positive relationship to simple awareness. Confirming evidence of this is provided by Berelson (1942) and Trenaman and McQuail (1961) in respect to awareness of issues employed in political communications during an election campaign, and by Stewart (1964) in regard to repetition of newspaper advertising for new consumer products. In general, however, there has been little systematic research on these or other effects of media emphasis. Plausible conjecture is what is most often found.

Secondhand reality

In making people aware of a world beyond their own direct experiences, mass communications do more than merely mediate the environment; they shape it into the secondhand reality which characterizes much of the "known" world (Lippmann, 1922). To the extent that the media are unfettered and independent, the depiction of the environment, though selective, need not be controlling. But when output is uniform, for whatever reason, then the known world comes closer to being the symbolic environment portrayed by the media. This is particularly so for events and people removed from ordinary experience. The inability to use direct experience as a check makes such conceptions vulnerable to influence by mass media (Speier, 1939).

Even when deliberate bias is not involved, unwitting bias necessarily occurs. This results from the need to select from the multitude of events only those few which are newsworthy or which meet the requirements of the medium. For instance, Cutlip (1954) found that only about ten percent of the news copy that entered the Associated Press agency home office appeared on the pages of four Wisconsin dailies published in nonmetropolitan areas.

A similar selective bias is to be found even in televised presentations of newsworthy events. Lang and Lang (1960) compared the reports by eyewitnesses of General MacArthur's homecoming parade through Chicago in 1952, with the impressions of people who watched the proceedings on live television. Through commentary and crowd shots of cheering people, television tried to maintain the official version of the occasion as a day of public welcome and honor for MacArthur. This attempt led to discrepancies between actual observations and the sense of the occasion given by television. In another study, Lang and Lang (1955) showed that different networks' telecasts of the 1952 Democratic National Convention provided differing perspectives on some of the confusing and dramatic events that were occurring. The particular facts reported were the same and the scenes shown were not markedly different. But differences were generated by the way in which any given event was linked by camera and commentary to prior events and backstage occurrences. One network emphasized the "action" of the convention; another's commentator admitted personal confusion over the events and hinted at backstage pressures; and the third tried to make political sense of what was going on.

Anecdotal evidence and conjecture have suggested that American movies and television can influence foreign people's views of life in the United States. Though much has been said on this matter, systematic research is lacking. In 1961, at least half of the screen time throughout the world, and as much as 90 percent in some areas, was devoted to showing American films; and in 11 countries at that time movies were credited with being a major source of information about the United States by 28 percent of the people, on the average (U.S. Information Agency, 1961). In 1962, an average of close to 40 percent of the people in four NATO countries believed that American television programs gave a true picture of American life (U.S. Information Agency, 1962). Carter and Sepúlveda (1964) reported that 56 percent of moviegoers in Santiago, Chile believed that commercial films from the United States and Mexico, the two most popular sources of movies, depicted faithfully everyday life in these countries. Most of the sample had little information about life in the United States and Mexico apart from what the movies showed. In respect to Americans' views of life in foreign countries, Holaday and Stoddard (1933) found that children accepted Hollywood movies as true representations and used the information in the stories to answer fact questions concerning these countries; the effects of the films persisted over the two- to three-month testing period.

The mere characteristic of having been singled out from the multitude of daily happenings suffices to establish an occurrence or person as newsworthy and meriting attention. Hence, such matters gain in public significance as they gain public attention. As a consequence, the media through their effect on awareness tend to confer status, prestige, and legitimacy on people and events (Lazarsfeld and Merton, 1948). For instance, some of the civil rights episodes in the South might very well have been construed as of local and not of national significance, if not for the attention given to them by the mass media. Similarly, relatively unknown and unimportant religious or political movements or self-appointed leaders of protest movements seem to loom larger in significance when given attention by the media. Lazarsfeld and Merton (1948) have also suggested that news reports can expose a discrepancy between private attitudes and behavior and public morality, thereby forcing the public to a decision on the matter. However, such news can also create symbolic social support for the discrepant practice by revealing to those who exhibited it covertly that others feel or act the same way (Williams, 1947).

Besides having an effect on the audience, publicity can foster a sense of prestige and importance in the members of a group singled out by media (Waples, Berelson, and Bradshaw, 1940; Davison, 1956). And in an action situation, the knowledge that relevant others are "watching" can fortify a group's determination to struggle for their goals or to resist an enemy (Davison, 1956).

COMPREHENSION

How people interpret the contents of communications is obviously an important aspect of cognitive effects and is involved in other kinds of media effects. The extreme of sheer inability to make sense of the material, for whatever reason, needs no comment. But subtler aspects of comprehension deserve some mention. Briefly, difficulty of comprehension or miscomprehension may reside in the manner of presentation or in the relation between the content and people's significant attitudes and values. A demonstration of the former is contained in Lazarsfeld's (1948) report that a number of people who listened to a radio broadcast designed to warn the public of the dangers of having X-ray pictures taken by unlicensed operators interpreted the program as a "plug" for the medical profession. Analysis of the script revealed that more than half the program had been devoted inadvertently to attempts to impress the listener with the importance of trained X-ray specialists. Belson (1956) found that British women interpreted a television program, designed to reduce concern about taking a trip to France, as demonstrating unthought of difficulties attendant on such a trip; the result was increased apprehension, rather than the desired opposite effect. Bogart (1957b) reported that many people in Greece interpreted the message of an advertising campaign, whose purpose was to project the concept of Greek–U.S. unity in support of universal human rights, in terms of the rights of children, which were featured in the advertisements. Other instances of miscomprehension and misinterpretation are recorded by Cooper and Dinerman (1951).

Lazarsfeld (1948) cited an unpublished study by Goodwin Watson concerned with people's interpretations of a series of cartoons called "There Are No Master Races." The change in the Mexican people from aggressive warriors to peaceful peasants was used to illustrate the thesis that characteristics of national groups are neither unchanging nor inherited. Interviews with people who were shown the cartoons revealed that many had misconstrued the main point; interpretations ranged from assertions that the pictures confirmed the natural superiority of some groups to assertions of the adverse effects of racial (Spanish-Mexican) intermarriage. Some of the misinterpretations may have been motivated by attitudes on the issue.

A clearer demonstration of the effect of attitude on comprehension is provided by the research reported by Cooper and Jahoda (1947) and Kendall and Wolf (1949) in which cartoons subtly ridiculed the prejudiced views of a cartoon figure called

Mr. Biggott. It was hoped that the prejudiced person would identify with the cartoon figure and, then, recognizing the foolishness of Mr. Biggott's views, would see the idiocy of his own bigotry. Even nonprejudiced people misinterpreted the meaning and purpose of the cartoons at times; but, more important, the prejudiced showed a subtle kind of miscomprehension. The ridiculousness of the cartoon figure was appreciated, but initial identification was not sustained. In a number of instances, the cartoon figure was roundly criticized by the respondent in a way that protected the person's own prejudice. Surprisingly, there is little published research on people's comprehension of the contents of mass communications.

EMOTIONAL AROUSAL

The emotional provocativeness of communication stimuli does not inhere in their physical qualities but depends on the way in which they are perceived and interpreted. As a result, perceptual and cognitive processes and their bases in learning, motivation, and personality must be considered in any analysis of the emotional effects of mass media. Since these processes are continuously active during a communication experience, emotion can be elicited by the parts of any complex communication. Emotional response to such a part may be due to the way in which the content of the unit is ordinarily perceived and interpreted. A creeping approach by a person with a knife in hand is generally taken to mean harm or danger to the unsuspecting target. Gross acts of this kind are unlikely to be misinterpreted or to produce divergent perceptions; and relatively little past experience or learning is required to arouse common expectations and interpretations. But more subtle behavior is open to variant meanings and depends on an understanding of its symbolic significance. On such matters, cultural and age differences can lead to differing perceptions and, consequently, differing emotional reactions. Not surprisingly, Dysinger and Ruckmick (1933) found that children may interpret an innocuous occurrence as a sign of danger for a movie character but be unaware of the erotic significance of other actions.

However, the total meaning of a particular portion of a communication is not given by its content alone, but is affected by the context in which it is placed. Of particular relevance is the interpretive contribution made by the cognitive implications of the preceding parts. This has been amply demonstrated by research on the effects of prior scenes on people's judgments of the emotions in posed photographs (Bruner and Tagiuri, 1954; Goldberg, 1951). In the example previously given, the meaning of and reactions to the knife attack would differ depending on such matters, among others, as whether it were seen as an act of vengeance, a deliberate murder, or the act of a crazed person.

Mood

Besides having cognitive implications, preceding parts may generate a mood which can affect emotional responsiveness to a particular segment of the communication. The sadness aroused by the knowledge that a love affair will end tragically is likely to color emotional reactions to sexual-affectional behavior, as well as impart special meaning to it. Support for such plausible expectations comes from research on the effects of prior mood-instigating experiences on affective responses to stimuli. Murray (1933) found that children in a game-induced mood of fearfulness perceived more malevolence in photographs of faces than they otherwise did. Leuba and Lucas (1945) demonstrated that hypnotically induced moods influenced people's descriptions of photographs taken from current magazines. Schachter and Wheeler (1962) reported that people who had been given a drug which stimulates the sympathetic nervous system found a slapstick sequence from a comedy film funnier than did placebo-treated controls, while those treated with a depressant drug were less responsive. It is interesting that the drugs reduced the influence of past attitude toward such movies.

Cognitive schema

A portion of the total meaning of a unit is also given by the *perceived* pattern and theme of the entire communication or of its major parts. That is, the significance of a unit depends not only on its content but also on its contribution to and place within the whole communication. Hence, when the main features of a communication are familiar or can be anticipated, an interpretive cognitive schema may be generated and used implicitly to give meaning to the individual parts and to bring them into a sensible relationship with each other. Such a schema may be moderately detailed and complex or be no more than an awareness that a particular story is a love triangle comprising a good man, a bad man, and the female object of their attentions, or is of the boy-meets-girl, loses-girl, wins-girl variety; even knowledge of the required way of treating illicit love or crime constitutes the basis of a schema. The interpretive function of schemas is clearly evidenced when people try to make sense of communications that deviate greatly from previous patterns of experience. Studies of remembering (for example, Bartlett, 1932; Mandler, 1962), of the learning of complex skills from audiovisual presentations (Sheffield, 1961), and of expectancies about personal relations or cognitive connections (for example, Abelson and Rosenberg, 1958; DeSoto, 1960; DeSoto and Kuethe, 1958, 1959; Heider, 1958) suggest that schemas have general significance for responses to the elements of a larger pattern.

To the extent that expectancies generated by a schema are borne out repeatedly, the amount of "information" (Attneave, 1959) contained in a type of communication will be reduced. This will weaken people's inclination to expose themselves to repetitions of the same or similar communications, if the story line is the main feature attracting and holding attention (*cf.* Berlyne, 1960). Some of the changes in mass media taste shown by children as they grow older may be due to this effect, for example, the change in types of comic books read (Wolfe and Fiske, 1949), and not only to a change in interests and needs. A slackening of interest among adults in television programs and movies with a recurring pattern of events or relationships also has some of its roots in this effect of schemas.

Since a schema confers meaning on the parts of a communication, emotional responsiveness to the individual units will be determined less by their content than would otherwise be true. Awareness that the hero in most stories, and always in a series, will be alive at the end should tend to moderate emotional disturbance when the hero is placed in dangerous or threatening situations. But the development of a cognitive schema requires a certain conceptual ability and, even in respect to a particular type of communication, repetition of experiences with different examples. On these counts, young children are likely to be deficient in the variety and salience of their schemas in comparison with older children and adults. This inference is consistent with the finding that children below the ages of 10 to 11 tend to respond to isolated scenes and particular incidents rather than to the story as a whole (Dysinger and Ruckmick, 1933; Himmelweit, Oppenheim, and Vince, 1958). They seem to perceive a movie as a series of disparate incidents and are less likely to react to or comprehend the psychological motivations of the characters. Also, Wolfe and Fiske (1949) found that, up to the age of 12, approximately one-third of the children claimed they did not know how the story in a comic book would turn out; but from age 13 on, only one out of 20 said they did not know.

When the structure is simple and the sequence of units follows a regular and easily discernible pattern, less conceptual effort or active thinking about the pattern is required, and more people will arrive at one and the same schema. An obvious example is the simplicity and recognizability of the pattern in a stereotyped Western. Himmelweit, Oppenheim, and Vince (1958) found that the stylized violence of such Westerns does not particularly disturb children who are familiar with the format. However, the less patterned or, perhaps, less familiar violence in horror or crime programs did elicit unpleasant emotions, and so did a televised dramatization of Jane Eyre.

The schema can also function as an aid and basis for recalling the substance of a story. Particularly discriminating details may be remembered as the means for distinguishing one instance of the type from another. But variations around the main outline that are not distinctive are likely to be assimilated to the schema (Bailyn, 1959; Bartlett, 1932; Emery, 1959b).

A cognitive schema also constitutes a basis for perceiving similarity in communication experiences that differ in details. This would mean similarity of reactions and the decline of emotional responsiveness as experience with the same type of communication accumulates, even though exactly the same communication is not repeated. The greater the variation around a common theme or the greater the time between exposures, the more slowly should a schema develop and emotional reactivity decline. The opposite extreme would be the rapid repetition of the same simple pattern. Dysinger and Ruckmick (1933) found a decline in reactivity to danger scenes when the same movie was shown several times. Himmelweit, Oppenheim, and Vince (1958) reported that, when the nature of the story varied, children's emotional responsiveness to television programs was not affected by their frequency of viewing or the number of years they had a television set; under this condition, even age and intelligence were not related to emotional responsiveness to televised material, within the sample studied. They also found that children who are selective viewers, seeking out specific television programs rather than watching indiscriminately, report more emotional arousal than do the nonselective viewers. They acknowledge that the selective viewers could be the more imaginative children and, hence, the more responsive; choice of programs might also be a contributing difference.

This discussion should not be taken to imply that only if a conceptual schema is generated can emotional adaptation occur when different communications are experienced. In terms of the concept of adaptation level (Helson, 1964), such experiences would center the point of neutral or average provocativeness at a kind of central tendency of provocativeness of the entire set. This would mean that, to elicit emotions, a media presentation would have to exceed the existing central tendency in provocativeness. An obvious instance of this effect is the dulling of concern and fright as a consequence of repeated warnings about the dangers of war or frequent occurrences of international crises (*cf.* Janis, 1962).

Cognitive schemas may not only develop naturally as a result of experiences with communications, but can be induced by verbal influence. No matter how established, they should still function as an interpretive framework, guiding perceptions of communication experiences and, as a result, emotional responses. Such an effect should occur so long as the communication or relevant incidents are open to different interpretations. Interpretive commentary can influence perceptions, as Lang and Lang (1955, 1960) found in respect to televised events. More relevant is research by Lazarus and associates (Lazarus and Alfert, 1964; Speisman *et al.*, 1964), who studied the effects of commentaries on the emotional provocativeness of a movie that detailed a crude surgical rite performed on adolescent boys of an aboriginal Australian tribe. College students, informed that the boy undergoing the subincision operation felt little pain and was thinking expectantly about the new status he would achieve, exhibited less physiologically evidenced disturbance while watching the film than did those who viewed the original silent version of the film. A later study (Lazarus *et al.*, 1965) employed a work-safety film that depicted several bloody accidents resulting from negligent behavior. Prefilm information designed to establish an intellectualized approach to the accidents reduced physiological arousal below the level elicited by a control orientation; orienting material which emphasized the make-believe quality of the filmed accidents was not as effective as the intellectualized approach with these college students.

A cognitive schema is not the only kind of interpretive framework that influences perception of communications and emotional responsiveness. Another kind of overarching perspective is whether the stimuli refer to real events or to occurrences that are fictional, if not sheer fantasy. The importance of discriminating between real and unreal events and reacting to them differently is a matter of learning and an aspect of socialization; and the ability to make correct discriminations is likely to depend on the background of relevant knowledge and experiences. Awareness that events conveyed by a communication are not real or have a low probability of occurrence might be expected to reduce emotional reactivity. Since this interpretive perspective is likely to be more continuously salient among adults during a communication experience than among children, it has been referred to as "adult discount" (Dysinger and Ruckmick, 1933). The analytic significance of the concept can be increased if it encompasses a wider range of levels of reality-irreality; even within a communication there are shifts from one level to another, as when a pure fantasy or dream sequence is included in a fictional setting. Himmelweit, Oppenheim, and Vince (1958) suggest that one way to reduce the emotional disturbance of children resulting from exposure to fictional material is to assure them of its make-believe character.

When conditions are such that the protection of adult discount does not occur, perhaps because of the style of presentation of the communication, then even adults become hyperresponsive. The panic and hysteria produced by the 1938 radio dramatization of H. G. Wells's *The War of the Worlds* is a remarkable example of such an occurrence (Cantril, 1940). This story of a Martian invasion of Earth was presented with consummate skill as a factual, excited, on-the-scenes account of events that were purportedly taking place at that moment. As a result, many listeners, particularly among the less well-educated, were convinced that they were hearing a real news broadcast, and their reactions ranged from fear to panic-driven flight.

Brodbeck (1961) suggests that, even among adults 20 years and older, positive covariation between age and judgments of how close to reality a movie is can lead to increasing emotional responsiveness with increasing age. Also relevant, though bearing primarily on learning and the potential behavioral effect of a communication, is Schramm's (1964) report that a primitive people was unaffected by a health film because the "giant" lice shown on the screen were not like any lice the villagers had seen.

Considerably more research guided by theory is needed on these matters. Assessing general reactivity to emotion-provoking media stimuli in relation to age is unlikely to be particularly informative, since an analytic view of the role of perceptual factors must be taken and since the emotions which are responsive to media stimuli change with age; for example, fear may be less evocable, while sexual-affectional feelings are more readily stimulated. Without such an approach, discrepant findings will be difficult to interpret and the development of systematic knowledge impeded.

Setting of exposure

It would be expected that the social and physical setting in which media exposure occurs can influence the extent of emotional arousal. A stereotypical example of this is the frightened reader of a horror story who is alone in a creaky house during a violent storm. Self-reports by children indicate that they are more frightened when viewing television alone or in the dark than under other conditions (Himmelweit, Oppenheim, and Vince, 1958). Social and physical characteristics of the setting may relate to emotional arousal, by influencing psychological involvement in the program or by influencing the salience of the make-believe quality of a presentation. In addition, the emotional behavior of one or more people in an audience can have a contagious effect on others. Cantril (1940) provided evidence that families or friends hearing *The War of the Worlds* together often stimulated and supported each other's fearfulness. However, emotions may be held in check by others' restraint or by the increased salience of a social norm of restraint (Blumer, 1933). Of general relevance are the findings of research that the "normal" effects of certain drugs on self-descriptions of mood or on behavior can be modified by the actions of others who have been medicated with other drugs or instructed to behave in a particular way (Nowlis and Nowlis, 1956; Schachter and Singer, 1962).

Arousal of specific emotions

Anecdotal and casual evidence based on self-reports constitutes the basis for most assertions about the effects of mass media stimuli on *specific* emotions. In addition to ethical and methodological difficulties, the seeming obviousness of gross demonstrations of specific emotional effects may account for the limited interest in conducting such research. (The effects of media-portrayed violence will be considered later.) Yet systematic and precise analyses of the effects on specific emotions of the relationship between media stimuli, the setting of exposure, perception, temporary or characteristic predispositions, and past experience would be most informative. In view of the interacting influence of these factors, a simple one-to-one relationship is unlikely to be found. For instance, it might be thought that a televised drama featuring loving parents and a warm family life would not upset children. Yet Redl (cited in Schramm, Lyle, and Parker, 1961) reported that such shows were quite disturbing to institutionalized children whose lives were empty of affiliative support. The preceding discussion on the role of perceptual and cognitive factors in emotional responsiveness to media stimuli is also germane to this point.

Using the GSR as a measure of general reactivity, Dysinger and Ruckmick (1933) found a peak of responsiveness among 16-year-olds to scenes of conflict or to scenes with sexual connotations. In a study of sex differences in the reported emotional effects of self-chosen movies, Wall and Simonson (1950) found that the arousal of affectional or love-making feelings was reported more often by boys than girls (average over movies: boys, 33 percent versus girls, 17 percent), with boys reporting such arousal to a wider range of movies. The girls approached the boys in percentage claiming the arousal of such feelings when the film was clearly a romantic one. In contrast to the results on affectional responses, crying or near-crying and fear were reported more often by girls than by boys. Altruistic feelings were noted by one out of four of the boys and girls in response to an appropriate film. However, it is difficult to determine how much of these results is due to the selection of films to see by boys and girls who are differentially susceptible to particular emotions, to inhibitions against admitting certain feelings, and to the fallibility of memory. Dysinger and Ruckmick (1933) did not find sex differences in responsiveness to movie scenes of love or suggestiveness. This could be due to the obvious romantic quality of the episodes, hence supporting Wall and Simonson, or represent a more general result which will be found when a measure is used which does not depend on verbal report.

There has been no systematic study by communications researchers of the persistence of emotional effects resulting from specific media presentations. Renshaw, Miller, and Marquis (1933) found that the effects of some movies, seen before bedtime, on gross physical movements during sleep lasted for several nights. But what characteristics differentiated these movies from others was not determined; nor can sleep motility be taken as valid evidence of persisting emotional responsiveness.

Some information of relevance to the general issue of specific emotional arousal is provided by research on moods, particularly when films are used as instigating stimuli. Nowlis (1965) had 450 male college students respond to a mood-adjective check list before and after six weekly one-hour sessions that were held in a large auditorium. Factor analyses revealed that mood adjectives commonly believed to be opposites and therefore unlikely to be present simultaneously were often checked together. For example, hostility and social affection, or a feeling of vigor and also of fatigue, were found to coexist. Haefner (1956) found that different movie soundtracks which were designed to incite fear or guilt produced changes on other mood factors as well as on these. Using films portraying violence, such as *The Ox-Bow Incident, High Noon,* and *A Walk in the Sun,* Handlon (1962) found an increase in the checking of adjectives descriptive of aggression, depression, and anxiety. Scores on these mood factors were lowered by presumably unprovocative films, such as Disney nature studies. One inference to be drawn from the research of these and other investigators is that, without independent empirical evidence, considerable caution should surround an assumption that a particular mood or feeling is the dominant or sole one induced by a communication and is the controlling affective determinant of behavior, or that a particular communication had no relevant affective consequences.

In contrast to the preceding investigators, Tannenbaum and Gaer (1965) composed a single measure of felt "stress" from the responses of college students to a mood-adjective checklist. The students rated themselves before viewing an abridged version of *The Ox-Bow Incident,* after seeing the major portion of the film, and again at the conclusion of the film. The sequence of events in the final section of the film was varied to establish a sad, a happy, or an ambiguous ending. Stress was significantly increased by the common, tension-provoking portion of the film; a further rise occurred with the sad ending, a marked decline with the happy ending, and a smaller decrease with the ambiguous one or when no ending was shown. However, the reduction in stress under the latter two conditions was not sufficient to compensate for the rise induced by the first portion of the film; hence, even after the happy ending, the students exhibited some degree of residual stress.

IDENTIFICATION

"Identification" or a term like it, for example, Lerner's (1948) "empathy," is a key concept in discussions of the general effects of mass communications or of the uses made of mass media. It is particularly central to any interpretation which is based on the media's role as a contributor of vicarious experiences. The great attractiveness and appeal of heroes and personalities also suggest its significance in communication experiences. Basically, "identification" refers to a person's involvement in the depicted events through a psychological relationship with one or another of the participants. In a sense, a person is pulled into the world of the communication by his sentiments toward a "story" character. As a result, he participates vicariously in the events, feelings, and behavior that relate to the object of identification, and experiences the communication more personally and deeply. The particular character whose perspective is taken may change during the communication experience, but it is likely that one identificand predominates throughout.

In the previously mentioned study by Tannenbaum and Gaer (1965), those who rated themselves relatively similar in qualities to the main protagonist, whose life was in danger, exhibited greater stress arousal and greater stress change in accord with the film endings than did those who rated themselves less similar to the protagonist. As the authors noted, the results provide only circumstantial evidence of the effect of identification on vicarious experiencing of the events involving the protagonist. For a more cogent test of the theory, experimental manipulation of identification is required.

Often, "identification" is taken to include or imply a kind of "as if" experience in which the person assumes in imagination the personality and role of one of the participants. This extension is particularly relevant to the use of the term in analyses of the imitative or modeling effects of media-portrayed behavior. If a person perceives that his own behavior and personality are exhibited by an identificand who is successful, the "match" can serve as a confirmation or reinforcement. However, if there is a perceived discrepancy, then the person may seek to model his behavior on the style of the identificand's. As in actual role playing (Sarbin, 1954), the extent of personal involvement in the role may range from an abnormal loss of self-identity during the experience to a superficial or intellectually detached commitment.

"Identification" emphasizes positive attachment to a suitable object. But psychological involvement can also be induced by negative sentiment toward a participant, such as a disliked political candidate engaged in a televised debate. The desired consequences of events impinging on such a character would tend toward the reverse of those wished for an identificand, as would the feelings aroused by the consequences (Berger, 1962). Negative consequences would induce satisfaction; and positive ones, dissatisfaction. This kind of involvement may be termed "disidentification." A person would tend to reject the behavior of such a character or, perhaps, behave in the opposite manner. However, this may happen even when identification occurs, if the identificand's behavior did not achieve desired ends.

As with other complex psychological processes, identification cannot be observed directly. Hence, evidence concerning it is obtained by measuring overt behavior which *on supposition* is linked to the unobservable aspects of the phenomenon. But to make the concept predictive, it is necessary to determine what conditions lead to the occurrence and depth of identification or the choice of an identificand. In other words, to increase the concept's theoretical value, the kind of involvement it points to must be linked to instigating conditions as well as to resultant behavior. Since a sentiment toward a character is at the root of identification, the attractiveness of the character's qualities should be a determinant of identification. Attractiveness may result from the identifier's perception of the desirability of one or more of the identificand's salient characteristics. These the person may already possess or, if not, would like to possess. This line of reasoning implies that the attributes, motives, and values of the perceiver determine the characteristics which will form the basis of identification.

Sex as a characteristic

In view of the significance of sex typing in society, similarity of sex should afford a basis for identification. This is suggested by popularity polls which show that men nominate male stars as their favorites and women name female stars; this tendency to prefer stars of their own sex is stronger for men than for women (Handel, 1950). Arnheim (1944) and Warner and Henry (1948) suggested that women listeners identified with the heroines in the daytime radio serials.

Wall and Simonson (1951) found that, although almost every one of the boys in their sample of 13- to 17-year-old children chose a male lead in a recently seen movie as the character they wanted to be like and none selected a female player, approximately one out of five of the girls did choose a male character. The two reasons mentioned most frequently by the boys for their choices were the abilities exhibited by the star in playing the movie role (for example, being a smart detective) and the prestige of the part itself; relatively few mentioned the material possessions associated with the role or the sex of the star. No boy mentioned physical characteristics as a reason for his choice, whereas these qualities constituted the most popular reason named by the girls, who gave second choice to attributes of personality (for example, bravery, pleasant disposition). Preference for a same-sex movie character by seventh-grade children was also found by Maccoby and Wilson (1957).

In a rare attempt to obtain evidence of identification *during* the communication experience, Maccoby, Wilson, and Burton (1958) measured the relative amount of time male and female college students watched a male and female movie star who acted together in several movie scenes. The researchers assumed that a viewer's attention would be directed more often to the identificand than to the other person in the scene and that similarity of sex would be a basis of identification. However, as they noted, identification could lead to orientation toward the source of actions directed at the identificand; hence, attention might be turned instead to the other person. Eye movements and visual fixations of the individually tested viewers were noted by observers who watched the students through unnoticed holes in the movie screen, on which the film was projected. The results indicated that the males gave more attention to the hero and less to the heroine than did the females, though both watched the heroine more than the hero.

Though not utilizing a communication situation, Kagan and Phillips (1964) also sought evidence of ongoing identification by young children, during a con- trived contest between a same-sex parent and a stranger. Based on behavioral and autonomic measures, the data suggest that the children were vicariously sharing in the positive experiences of their parents. However, as the authors noted, the results do not unequivocally implicate identification as the determinant, in view of the difficulty of distinguishing between differential identification, empathy, and famili- arity with the contestants.

Behavior

Kagan (1958) presumed that one incentive for identification is the perception that the model commands or attains a rewarding and satisfying state. Psycho-logic may lead the identifier to conclude that, if he possessed the characteristics of the identifi- cand, he too would achieve desired goals. Some relevant data are obtained from a study by Zajonc (1954), who exposed children 9 to 13 years of age to one of two supposed radio programs about a trip to Mars. Both programs focused on the dif- ferent leadership styles of the two captains of the spaceship. One leader empha- sized supportive personal relations in his dealings with the crew, while the other coped with problems through the use of his authority and power. The versions differed in respect to which of the two leaders was more successful in handling the problems that arose during the trip, including an attempted mutiny. The children were more likely to choose the successful leader, regardless of his leadership style, as the one they would rather be like. However, only half of the children who had selected the successful authoritarian leader mentioned power-oriented attributes as the reason, whereas the choice of the other leader was justified primarily in terms of affiliative characteristics of leadership. Also, cultural values which favor an emphasis on personal relations were evident in the greater preference for the affiliative leader and his characteristics. Zajonc conjectured that, if the power-oriented leader had deviated too far from accepted or desired standards of behavior, his success would not have saved him from rejection. Also, it may very well be that in critical situations, involving the success of a group effort and the safety of the members, leadership style may not matter so much as success. However, in a study by Albert (1957), children chose the hero as the person they would want to grow up to be like, no matter whether they saw a version doctored so as to make the villain appear to win over the well-known cowboy hero, or whether they saw the customary version with the hero triumphing. The children's familiarity with this type of story and with the cowboy hero probably influenced their choice of identificand. Also, following Zajonc's sug- gestion, the villain's behavior may have deviated too far from what is considered acceptable.

Other characteristics

Wolfe and Fiske (1949) suggested that children's preferences for types of comic books may reflect the close relationship between identification with a type of hero and the psychological gratifications sought from the content. They asserted that the young child selects the free, rule-breaking animal, for this purpose; the somewhat older child chooses the fantastic Superman and then moves on to the human with extraordinary abilities, such as Batman; and, finally, because real or realistic heroes are sought as identificands, comics depicting true stories or classic fiction are chosen.

Emery (1959b) proposed that, when the possible identificands are of the same sex, the age of the viewer relative to the ages of the characters may determine the choice. He found that boys around the age of 11 were more likely to identify with the boy hero in a Western movie, while the older boys were more likely to choose the adult hero. There was also some evidence that boys who scored high on extrapunitiveness and low on a group-conformity measure tended to choose the adult hero over the boy hero in the film.

Maccoby and Wilson (1957) found that, when two same-sex characters were prominent in the story, seventh-graders were more likely to identify with the one representing the viewer's aspired social class (based on viewer's desired occupation) rather than with the character closer to his own objective status (based on father's occupation). This kind of upward-looking choice is also suggested in research on daytime radio serials, where the socioeconomic status of the leading characters was often somewhat higher than that of most of the women listeners (Arnheim, 1944).

Scollon (1956) found that soldiers were more influenced by an Army veteran than by a scientist in regard to their attitude toward unusual foods, particularly C-rations, presumably because of a greater sense of personal relationship to the veteran. The relevance of identification to the persuasive influence of communications has been incorporated by Kelman (1958) into a theoretical analysis of bases of opinion change. Rosen (1948) has some, but by no means unequivocal, evidence that the film *Gentleman's Agreement* had greater influence on those who said that what they learned from the film was "how it felt to be a Jew."

Considerably more research of a systematic nature is needed to determine the types of characteristics which produce the fullest identification. Also, greater attention should be given to the perceiver's motives and values as determinants of the choice of identificand. And more attempts should be made to obtain behavioral evidence of identification *during* the communication experience.

ATTITUDE

Much of the research customarily cited in discussions of the effects of mass communications on opinions and attitudes has been conducted under experimental procedures which involve compulsory exposure of selected audiences to single communications. Chapter 21 contains a survey of the relevant literature. Other frequently mentioned studies derive from research on the influence of political campaigns on voting intentions; such research will be taken up later, in a general discussion of the effects of mass communications on voting behavior.

Of course, the previous sections of this chapter are relevant, since cognition, comprehension, selective exposure, and retention are intimately connected with effects on opinions and attitudes. For instance, lack of awareness resulting from selective exposure or a failure of comprehension will preclude any direct and desired influence on opinions. In fact, research pertaining to such intermediary processes and responses quite often forms the basis for the generalization that the media are relatively limited in their ability to produce a change from one viewpoint to another (Klapper, 1960). However, more than grudging acknowledgment must be given to the media's role in conserving or reinforcing existing views by providing justifying or supporting reasons for a preference, whether for a particular brand or a candidate, or in transforming uncertainty or unawareness into a definite opinion. These occurrences do constitute significant attitudinal effects, even though they are not so dramatic as a "change of heart."

In mass communications research, there has been a near-exclusive emphasis on the effects of campaigns, whether short or long, or of single, special events. What is most lacking and particularly needed are studies which focus on the continuous impact of the media over an extended period of time, to trace out the slow cumulative changes that may be occurring as the media carry out their functions and convey their contents from day to day (Emmett, 1966; Goto, 1966). Even the experimental literature lacks adequate research on the attitudinal effects of exposure to the same communication more than once or to an interrelated set of communications that project a common viewpoint. Peterson and Thurstone (1933) reported that, while a single motion picture may have only a limited effect on opinions, two or three which are related in a general way to the same theme can produce a significant impact. Other reports (Hovland, Lumsdaine, and Sheffield, 1949; McGinnies, Lana, and Smith, 1958), suggesting that several congruent communications on a topic may have greater influence than a single one, are based on comparisons between different samples tested at different times. In respect to the effects of newspaper advertisements for two new consumer products, the data from Stewart's (1964) field experiment suggest that repetition produced little change in brand "image." More research, particularly of a theory-directed kind, is needed on this important question.

There seems little doubt that the ability of the media to influence and shape attitudes varies directly with the extent to which they convey the same information and perspectives, as when there is central governmental control over their contents. In addition, effects should be inversely related to the intensity of feeling or certainty of opinion on the topic, characteristics which often reflect knowledge on the issue or the extent to which the communication content engages a general attitude or personal or social factors. The magnitude of attitudinal effects of the media should be dependent in part on the joint influence of these general variables, with the maximum being approached as conditions approximate the extreme of complete homogeneity of information and opinions in the media and the presence of facilitating personal or social factors. This perspective on the effects of mass communications has been expressed in part or in full by many people; the most organized and systematic exposition is Klapper's (1960).

It has often been averred that a movie, a play, a television program, or a novel which portrays a member of a minority group unfavorably is likely to have an adverse effect on people's attitude toward that group. On empirical and theoretical grounds, this is unlikely to occur with any great magnitude unless the same kind of portrayal is consistently and uniformly presented and personal, social, and attitudinal factors are neutral or sympathetic to the viewpoint presented. In addition, of course, the audience must extrapolate and generalize from a fictional representation to the real environment. Of relevance to this matter is research by Peterson and Thurstone (1933) on the attitudinal effects of Hollywood films. In one study, children who resided in a town where there were no Negroes and who were unlikely to have had more than minimal contact, if even that, with Negroes changed from a slightly favorable attitude to an anti-Negro one as a result of viewing *Birth of a Nation*. A film, *Welcome Danger*, which had been criticized as unfavorable to Chinese people, was found to produce only a slight and insignificant change in attitude. And a film, *Alibi*, which depicted criminals as incorrigible and which had been barred as anti-social by the censorship board of a large city, had no effect on children's attitude toward the punishment of criminals. Rosen (1948) reported that *Gentleman's Agreement* produced a favorable change in attitude toward Jews, but principally among those who were only slightly anti-Semitic beforehand.

In carrying out their news functions, the media convey not only opinions of editorialists, columnists, and public figures who are quoted in the news stories but also the sheer events that make up the significant happenings meriting publication. The latter are often presumed to have potent effects on the public's orientations toward issues, policies, and personalities. Although, even when presented objectively, news events are not "raw facts" devoid of wider meaning or implications, they are oftentimes and for many people neutral or ambiguous in significance, capable of diverse and even contradictory interpretations. Their import accrues, not from their cognitive quality by itself, but from the interpretive links that connect them with attitudes and perspectives (Berelson, 1949a). The attitudinal significance or interpretations given to events may be influenced by predispositional factors, by the language used to convey them (Sargent, 1939), or by assertions of inference by news sources and public figures. For example, Sheatsley and Feldman (1964) reported that the assassination of President Kennedy had no effect on people's judgments about the trustworthiness of other people, the strength of their religious beliefs, or their attitudes toward school integration. They suggested that other opinions, such as the need for greater protection of the President, would have been influenced because of the more evident connection between the event and such an evaluation. But there might even have been changes in views on the queries used, if well-regarded persons had publicly linked the assassination with, for example, the need for a return to religion. They also supposed that in 1940, following the air blitz on British cities, the increase in popular approval of the need to help Great Britain, even at the risk of American involvement in the war, resulted primarily from the wider significance placed on the raids by the President's public statements.

Of relevance to this perspective concerning the significance of the interpretive context in which news events are placed is evidence suggesting an increase in communication effectiveness when the desired conclusion is explicitly stated (Fine, 1957; Hovland and Mandell, 1952). Also supportive is research which finds that opinions specifically referred to in communications are affected more than are related, but unmentioned ones (Belson, 1957; Hovland, Lumsdaine, and Sheffield, 1949).

OVERT BEHAVIOR

Allocation of time

Discussions of the effects of mass media on behavior have customarily focused on the media's influence on specific kinds of actions. The question has been: What contributions do mass communications make to the development, maintenance, or change of particular behavior? Yet one of the most general effects of the media lacks that kind of specificity but nevertheless has considerable impact on the patterning of behavior. This is its influence on the allocation of discretionary time to various activities. Time that is not taken up by required activities, such as household responsibilities, school, business, or sleep, is filled with "free" behavior. Within the constraints set by the total amount of discretionary time available, interests, motivations, etc., will be the primary determinants of what activities are chosen and how much time is devoted to each. But the more time absorbed by attention to the media, the less there is for other activities. This kind of effect was touched on briefly in the earlier discussion of effects of a medium as an entity. It can hardly be said to be a particularly illuminating observation. Yet, when it is realized that attention to all media consumes a number of hours of free time each day (Schramm, 1957), the importance of the media in this regard becomes obvious.

Though available research has dwelt on television, many of the same types of effects probably occurred with the advent of radio and the movies or with the mass circulation of print. This is particularly likely to be so in developing countries that are first experiencing modern mass media. However, the great attraction that home television has for people of all ages and the limited demands it makes on personal skills and abilities has made it a prime consumer of time. For example, a number of studies have found that, *in general*, American children watch television an average of two to three hours per day over the week (Maccoby, 1951; Merrill, 1961; Schramm, Lyle, and Parker, 1961; Witty, Kinsella, and Coomer, 1963). Schramm (1962) estimated that television fills approximately one-sixth of the waking hours of an American child three years of age or older. In pretelevision days, children spent approximately the same number of hours per day listening to the radio as they now spend in front of the television set (Lyness, 1952).

Of course, once the novelty of any medium has worn off, the continuing long-term changes wrought in the allocation and budgeting of time may be reduced somewhat. The new pattern of distribution of time becomes stable and an accepted feature of social life. Those growing up in an environment that has already absorbed these changes have no awareness of the prior rearrangements and effects produced by the medium (Himmelweit, Oppenheim, and Vince, 1958).

Though television reduced the time spent on most other media, the reduction was not sufficient to compensate for the amount of attention given to television. Hence, the total time devoted to the mass media increased (Crile, 1953; Maccoby, 1951; Schramm, Lyle, and Parker, 1961). This increase was made up, in part, by a reduction in other activities, but also by a coordination of viewing with ordinary household routines (Bogart, 1962; Coffin, 1955; Maccoby, 1951; Okabe, 1963; Schramm, Lyle, and Parker, 1961). The latter method of accommodation suggests that the ways in which the media fit into the daily lives of people are affected by the extent to which they require exclusive attention and the kinds of activities with which they are compatible. Clearly, the media differ in this regard (Kumagai and Takashima, 1966). Kojima (summarized in Fujinama, 1964) gave attention to this matter in his analysis of the role of radio listening in Japan; he suggested that the exploitation of the possibilities of radio requires an emphasis on a compatible type of listening, in which radio is used as more than a mere background, even though other activities are being carried on. Of relevance is the finding of Lazarsfeld and Dinerman (1949) that over half of the women who said they never listened to morning radio on weekdays claimed that this was because they were "psychologically incapable of listening and working at the same time" and concentrated instead on their household chores.

It is of little theoretical value merely to catalog television's effects on the allocation of time to different activities. What is wanted are generalizations which will impose an order, even though a postdictive one, on the changes that have occurred and provide a basis for predictions of other changes. The most general principle would be that the amount of time given to any experience varies directly with its attractiveness or satisfyingness relative to that of other available alternatives. Hence, the appearance of a new, attractive activity or an increase in attractiveness of an existing one will reduce the time devoted to others, especially to the least attractive ones. In a sense, the allocation of time may be viewed as the outcome of a decision process which takes account of the need to engage in certain required activities and of the relative utilities of available alternatives. For instance, the lure of outdoor activities will draw attention away from the media, as is indicated by the seasonal variation in television viewing, with the major trough occurring in the summer and the peak embracing the winter season (Bogart, 1962).

Similarly, the amount of time devoted to the media should vary inversely with the number and variety of alternative activities that are actually available. This is supported by evidence that, in pretelevision days, the extent of listening to morning radio was negatively associated with diversity of general interests among women (Herzog, 1944; Lazarsfeld and Dinerman, 1949), and having something else to do distinguished heavy from light moviegoers among children (Shuttleworth and May, 1933); that the amount of television viewing by children was greater in a Rocky Mountain community than in the San Francisco area (Schramm, Lyle, and Parker, 1961); and that, in general, the more diversified the child's leisure pattern before the advent of television, including involvement in outdoor play and social activities, the less use was made of television when it became available (Himmelweit, 1962). The dependence of elderly people on television is well known (Steiner, 1963). Also, people whose incomes exceed $8000 per year are less positive to television and less dependent on it than are those with smaller incomes, a finding which Steiner attributed largely to differential availability of other recreational activities and interests. Lazarsfeld (1940) made a similar suggestion concerning a negative relation between extent of radio listening and the cultural level of the respondent. And Schramm, Lyle, and Parker (1961) suggested that national, as well as regional, differences in the amount of time devoted to television, though small, may reflect differences in alternative availabilities in the environment rather than differences in the cultural value placed on television.

Based on their extensive research with British schoolchildren, Himmelweit, Oppenheim, and Vince (1958) have enunciated three organizing generalizations for interpreting the impact of television on the use of other media and the continuance of other activities and interests. Each of these generalizations can be viewed as a special instance or corollary of the basic principle stated above.

1. If some activities have to be reduced or eliminated in order to make room for television, then the ones curtailed are likely to be fringe or marginal activities. Himmelweit, Oppenheim, and Vince cited as supporting evidence the fact that television reduced the time spent on unstructured activities which merely serve to pass time, that is, which fill the periods of doing "nothing special," either alone or with casual companions, but had little effect on outdoor play, social activities, and hobbies. Furu (1962) confirmed the latter but did not find that television adversely affected the time devoted to resting or idle talk. However, Maccoby (1951) and Mahoney (1953), using mothers' assertions and children's own appraisals, respectively, reported that television reduced children's play time, though no information was obtained on

the type of play affected. For the principle to have predictive utility, the necessary problem to be solved is to determine in advance which activities are marginal and therefore expendable.

2. A marked reduction will occur in the time given to media that are not as satisfying as television but are functionally similar or equivalent to it, in the sense that they serve the same needs. Any medium serves a number of purposes and contributes in a variety of ways to the lives of those who use it, and different media can make similar contributions. What has to be established are the purposes a given medium serves and the ones that control its use. Without an independent determination of this information, the principle will be difficult to apply or test precisely.

In a general way, and often implicitly, the basis of functional similarity is taken to reside in such gratifications as entertainment, escape fantasy, and relaxation. That is, these characteristics are presumed to reflect the major uses to which commercial television is put. Both Schramm, Lyle, and Parker (1961) and Steiner (1963) have noted that children and adults approach television primarily as a source of entertainment. (As Schramm, 1957, has noted, this also holds true of movies and radio, both of which began as mass media, whereas print established itself initially as a more private purveyor of information and serious thought to relatively small groups of people.) Hence, attention to media that emphasized these same gratifications would be reduced, while those which are principally reality-oriented or which serve other functions should be less affected. Attention to the latter may be reduced at the outset because of the considerable amount of time devoted to television and because television may initially seem to satisfy a wider range of needs than is confirmed with experience (*cf*. Himmelweit, 1962; Seldes, 1962).

On this line of reasoning, the advent of television should curtail radio listening, moviegoing, and the reading of comic books and "pulp" magazines (detective, adventure, confession), whereas it should have less or no adverse effect on the reading of newspapers, books, and quality magazines. The former group of activities are presumed to gratify a desire for entertainment or fantasy and the latter to serve reality-seeking needs. A large number of studies have reported confirming results (for example, Coffin, 1955; Furu, 1962; Himmelweit, Oppenheim, and Vince, 1958; Schramm, Lyle, and Parker, 1961). The principal exception is Belson's (1961) report of a television-induced decline in the buying and reading of "quality" newspapers and magazines but an increase in the use of "popular" ones. In general, the effects were not large and varied from one paper or magazine to another. In part, Belson attributed these effects to the tendency of many British people to indulge in light reading which can be interrupted while the television set is on; this supposition is consistent with his assertion of reduced attention to serious material and increased attention to items permitting piecemeal concentration, such as comic strips and cartoons. The methodology of the research has been sharply criticized by Parker (1963a) and defended by Belson (1963). Of interest is Okabe's (1963) report that, in Japan, where radio still presents a variety of types of programs, listening to educational programs on radio declined more than listening to entertainment programs. He conjectured that perhaps Japanese television is better at presenting educational-cultural fare than entertainment. However, Furu (1962) found that television reduced children's attention to radio programs of adventure, action, and other kinds of fiction.

To the extent that a medium in its normal use possesses salient appeals left unsatisfied by television, attention to that medium will tend to recover; also, those who prize the nonoverlapping appeals of a medium should be less affected by television even at the outset. These inferences receive support from evidence that reading of fiction and nonfiction books, as evidenced by withdrawals from public libraries, recovers after being initially depressed by television (Parker, 1963b; Spain and Scoggin, 1962). Also, Himmelweit, Oppenheim, and Vince (1958), but not Furu (1962), found that the adverse effect of television on frequency of moviegoing was less among 13- to 14-year-olds than among 10- to 11-year-olds. They supposed, as others have (for example, Lazarsfeld and Kendall, 1948), that attendance at movies has a social value for young people, and home television does not satisfy this interest. In respect to radio listening in television households, Merrill (1961) reported that prior to age 13, children are almost exclusively a television-only audience (*cf.* Witty, Kinsella, and Coomer, 1963); but at 13, radio listening rises sharply and increases through age 18. This is probably due to the increased attractiveness of popular music.

3. To continue to attract attention, media which are adversely affected by television will be transformed so as to satisfy needs they did not formerly satisfy or so as to maximize their satisfaction of needs that television does not. For example, in the United States, commercial radio has become essentially a purveyor of popular music and brief news reports and is used extensively as background diversion (Schramm, Lyle, and Parker, 1961). Even before television, these characteristics were in evidence (Baker, 1949). In a Canadian community which had not yet been reached by television, even though it was available in not too distant areas, Schramm, Lyle, and Parker (1961) found that children still used local radio for a wide variety of programs. Of course, transistors have increased radio's portability and ready availability, thereby permitting listening at times previously less popular (Bogart, 1962) and making listening at home more an individual matter than it once was. Movies are fewer but have become lavish and spectacular vehicles of increased length, detail, variety of incident, and authenticity of scenery. And magazines have reduced the space devoted to entertainment content, an obviously dominant feature of television (Bogart, 1962).

Consumer purchases

Within the context and limits of this chapter, there is little to be said about the role of the media in consumer behavior. Much of the effect is due to paid sales messages—commercials and advertisements—carried by the media. To a considerable extent, the efforts of advertisers are directed toward canalizing current values and motives in the service of a particular product purchase or holding current brand users and attracting product users away from other brands (Flowerman, 1947; Lazarsfeld and Merton, 1948). Except for dramatic and unpredictable successes, the effectiveness of particular advertising campaigns, involving the repeated use of a "mix" of media over an extended period of time, remains a commercial secret. However, sales are not often considered a suitable criterion for evaluating the effectiveness of a campaign, because of the difficulty of determining the contributions of advertising to the manifold of factors that influence consumer purchases (Colley, 1961). Instead, such mediate responses or communication goals have been used as salient awareness of a brand, recall of the sales message, evaluations of the characteristics of a brand, stated interest in purchasing a brand, and so on.

Bauer (1964) has sought to put the sales effectiveness of advertising into a sounder perspective, by noting that promotions which on practical grounds of dollar increment in sales are highly successful may mean no more than an increase of one percent in a current brand's share of a high-turnover product market, such as cigarettes; in terms of the total population, this increment may represent the successful influencing of no more than 0.5 percent of all adults. Even the outstanding financial success of a new brand or a variant of a product category may constitute the capture of only a small percentage of a highly competitive market. These facts led Bauer to the inference that a promotion can be profitable, even if it wins over fewer people than it alienates.

Nothing that has been said should be taken to mean that the contents of the media, whether in terms of commercials and advertisements, news (for example, about fashions), or the incidental effects of entertainment content, are less than potent influences on consumer behavior. Given the fertile conditions that exist in many developing countries, the considerable influence of the media on buying appetites can be readily discerned (Bogart, 1959; Schramm, 1964).

INTERESTS AND INTEREST-RELATED BEHAVIOR

How effective are the mass media in stimulating people's interests in various activities, and what are the differences between such media-stimulated interests and those developed on other grounds? For instance, does a televised dressmaking lesson or a movie based on a novel stimulate or slake interest in making a dress or reading the book? These questions can best be answered through experimental research, but the use of such an approach has been scarce indeed.

Himmelweit (1962) suggested that television stimulates passive interest in some activity, if any interest is aroused, rather than direct, interest-related behavior. This assertion is based on reports that no more than 2 percent of the audience watching a model-making demonstration on television sent in a model in response to a request for entries in a competition, and most were hobby-oriented already; only one out of over 100 women who watched a dressmaking lesson attempted to make the skirt demonstrated; and less than 5 percent of those who watched a cooking lesson tried the recipe. Crile (1953) cited somewhat similar findings, particularly in respect to the importance of the existence of prior interest and related skills as determinants of the behavioral effects of televised demonstrations. Also, Himmelweit, Oppenheim, and Vince (1958) found that a program which displayed a portion of a new exhibit of Cretan objects at a British museum had no discernible effect on children's attendance at the museum; actually, only 10 percent of the children who came to the museum had seen the program and few of them went to the gallery containing the Cretan collection.

It has often been asserted that movies or television programs based on novels stimulate an interest in reading the novel or related material. In support of this contention, Spain and Scoggin (1962) cited the many requests received by the New York Public Library for books on Davy Crockett, trappers, folktales, and histories of the Old West that were set off by a television series on Davy Crockett. Similar effects were reported by Thorp (1939) for the movies. However, an experiment by Lumsdaine (1958) did not find that seeing a movie increased the reading of the novel on which it was based. Groups of high school students were shown an edited version of the movie *David Copperfield;* though abbreviated, it presented most of the first part of the original and dealt with the hero's boyhood years. The exposed students were no more likely than those not shown the movie to request the book from the school library, even though they were more than twice as likely (77 percent versus 37 percent) to *say* on a questionnaire that they would be quite or very anxious to read the book. Yet in 1936, when the full-length version of the movie had been shown, the Cleveland Public Library reported that all available 450 copies in its main building and branches went into circulation and that five months later only 67 copies were on the shelves.

Lazarsfeld (1940) reported that a radio program can stimulate people to read related material if, as a result of prior training (for example, formal education) and experiences, they were already prepared for and favorably disposed toward reading.

May and Jenkinson (1958) conjectured that a novel-based movie may stimulate the reading of the book if it is specially designed to accomplish this purpose. High school students were shown one of two versions of *Kidnapped*, a movie based on the novel by Robert Louis Stevenson. One group saw only a few exciting scenes and heard a narrator suggest that they might like to read the book to enjoy other interesting parts and to find out how the story ends. The other group watched an abbreviated version which covered the entire story. A significantly higher percentage of those shown the "teaser" version than of the other group requested the book from the school library (27 percent versus 20 percent).

In a study of the influence of radio in arousing interest in serious music, Suchman (1941) found that those who claimed that radio initiated their interest exhibited a lower level of taste (for example, preferred Dvorak to Bach) than did those who asserted that radio essentially supplemented their preexisting interest in good music. The radio-initiated people listened with a "romantic" attitude, using the music as a stimulus and background for daydreaming; or reacted in a more physical and emotional way; or considered the listening to be an entertaining and pleasant pastime. Rarely did they develop a serious understanding and appreciation of classical music.

Riley, Cantwell, and Ruttiger (1949) reported that television seemed to have increased the family's interest in sports, though it decreased attendance at sports events; other research also suggests a decrease in attendance (Bogart, 1962). However, Belson (1959a) found a rise not only in interest but also in attendance, in respect to such sports as soccer, horse racing, and show jumping.

Of course, the earlier comments on the role of the mass media in developing countries or backward areas clearly imply that the media can awaken interests and stimulate related behavior. Confirming instances of this appear in reports of UNESCO-sponsored projects on the effects of organized listening to radio or viewing of television followed by group discussion (for example, Louis and Rovan, 1955; Mathur and Neurath, 1959; UNESCO, 1960).

PUBLIC TASTE

In respect to public taste, the media have often been charged with one or more of the following adverse effects: degrading public taste or pandering to its commonest level; reinforcing low cultural interests; precluding the development of a proper appreciation and understanding of high culture; or failing to act as an educator of public taste. Much has been written on these matters in criticism and in defense of the media's cultural role; a sampling may be had by examining Rosenberg and White (1957), Jacobs (1961), and Berelson (1961), and a critical analysis of differing views may be found in Bauer and Bauer (1960). It would serve no value to restate the various contentions here, for much of the controversy revolves around varying standards of judgment and expectations and differing interpretations of the evaluative significance of the same data or the singling out of different data to support the critic's position. Perhaps the question should be: What role *can* the media play in developing public taste for a culturally more varied range of programs and more serious or demanding offerings?

The basic assumption underlying much of the critical commentary is that public taste is responsive to the quality of materials made available by the mass media. However, there is little doubt that the influence of the media will be constrained by the far greater role played by social, personal, educational, and family determinants of taste. For instance, Suchman (1941) found that most of those who claimed that radio stimulated their interest in classical music had previously had some musical training or were friendly with people who were interested in serious music. But, within such constraints, what effects can the media have on public taste?

Over 20 years ago and from time to time since then, Lazarsfeld (1963a) has recommended that an experimental study be conducted to determine whether public taste can be upgraded by the media. Though research of the specific kind he suggested has not been carried out yet, there are some data that are germane to its purposes.

Crile (1953) reported that, in an area in Iowa which in the early days of television received only one channel, audiences for educational programs were as large as those for preceding or following entertainment shows. Similarly, Himmelweit, Oppenheim, and Vince (1958) found that, when only the BBC operated a television network in Great Britain, children watched educational and informational programs rather than choose the alternative of not watching television at all. However, when a commercial network was permitted to operate and the more customary entertainment fare made available, most deserted the serious programs on the BBC channel for the competing offerings of the commercial station. The availability of a second channel did not increase total viewing time (see also Bogart, 1962). Himmelweit (1962, 1963) suggested that, when television channels offer competing programs of different quality, taste crystallizes or "freezes" at its own level rather than develops. As a consequence, interest in the more "demanding" informational and cultural programs suffers.

Essentially what this suggests is that people do not ordinarily use the media to seek out new experiences beyond the level of their customary interests, tastes, and backgrounds. Hence, given the availability of diverse types of programs, people will avoid those which exceed the bounds of their current tastes. Lazarsfeld (1940) noted that, when one of two competing variety-music shows went off the air, the other one increased its audience, while the interview program broadcast at the same time did not gain.

Not only may serious programs be turned to when nothing else is available, but less stimulating fare may be accepted if alternatives are limited. Lazarsfeld and Field (1946) pointed out that even women, who were contemptuous of daytime radio serials, became involved in them, if some circumstance, such as illness, induced listening for want of something else to do (*cf.* Dunn's data, 1952, on college-educated, rural women). They suggested that people become accustomed to what they get, for they lack the ability to conceive of alternatives markedly different from what is available. In substantiation, Lazarsfeld and Field noted that many songs become popular through deliberate repetition ("plugging") and that, when asked what kind of programs they would like to hear more of, people choose more of what they already enjoy.   The latter finding has also been reported in respect to television (Himmelweit, Oppenheim, and Vince, 1958; Schramm, Lyle, and Parker, 1961; Steiner, 1963).

Schramm, Lyle, and Pool (1963) reported that, a year after 28 people had been asked to watch and had watched a program on the educational television station in Boston, half claimed still to be viewers of the station; only five persons in a control group had become educational television viewers in this time.   Since only a small number of those who were originally nonviewers and had promised to watch the special program actually did so, those who did watch constitute a self-selected group. These people may very well have been more receptive than others to such programming.   Besides acknowledging this possibility and noting the difficulty of motivating people to watch educational television, the authors suggested that, if people can be induced to view by means of suitable incentives, there is a good chance that many will be influenced to continue.

When the introduction and use of the broadcast media involve organized listening or viewing followed by group discussion, even people in rural areas, including illiterates, can come to view radio and television as instruments of personal and popular enlightenment and not merely as sources of diverting entertainment (Louis and Rovan, 1955; Mathur and Neurath, 1959; Mathur and Saksena, 1963; UNESCO, 1960, 1965).   A lively appreciation is engendered for thought-provoking programs that are pertinent to the viewers' needs and interests and that contain authentic touches rather than make-believe and exaggeration.   Similarly, experiences in a variety of countries reveal that systematic cultural broadcasting can evoke an interest in demanding literature, theater, and music; in fact, in India, it stimulated the revival of classical music and musicianship (UNESCO, 1956).

OUTLOOK AND VALUES

Despite "silent" assumptions or frequently expressed expectations, there is scant research on the purported influence of the mass media on personal or social values, ethical or moral views, or attitudes toward life.   Conjecture and self-reports of influence (for example, Blumer and Hauser, 1933) are in far greater abundance than "hard" data.   For instance, because children tend to respond strongly to individual scenes, it has been supposed that they are less likely to be influenced by the final consequences or the terminal judgment that, from a maturer perspective, gives the movie its unity and purpose and transforming moral (Himmelweit, Oppenheim, and Vince, 1958).   Also, it has been supposed that the exposure of children to experiences and content beyond their years may conduce to a "premature sophistication" or an "immature maturity" about life (Blumer, 1933; Klapper, 1960).   However, in view of the weightiness of stable family, social, and environmental influences, of personal experiences, and of preexisting views, it is unlikely that the media alone can have a decisive or marked effect.

In their study of the effects of movies on the attitudes and values of elementary and junior high school students, Shuttleworth and May (1933) compared the questionnaire responses of a group of heavy and light moviegoers (three to four times per week versus one to two times per month) who had been matched on a number of characteristics related to frequency of movie attendance and to the attitudes to be studied. They found little evidence of differences between these groups in ethical-moral judgments and values, and none of a systematic nature.

Based on comparisons between viewers and nonviewers of television, Himmel-weit, Oppenheim, and Vince (1958) reported a modicum of evidence that adolescent girl viewers were more concerned about growing up and marrying, presumably because of the troubled lives women were shown to lead. In general, viewers up-graded the jobs they wished they could have but chose realistically when asked which ones they were likely to have. (This is in contrast to the concern expressed by DeFleur, 1964, on the basis of a content analysis of television programs.) Similarly, except in fantasy, they did not seek to model themselves after television performers. Also, viewers were more likely than nonviewers to select "drive," "self-confidence," "brains," and "not being afraid" as qualities needed for success in the world. In general, the reported differences are not particularly striking and their magnitudes are hardly sufficient to constitute socially significant effects.

Similarly, Bailyn (1959) found little evidence of a relationship between degree of exposure to entertainment and fantasy media by fifth- and sixth-grade schoolchildren and perceptions of threat or a sense of powerlessness in the face of environmental pressures.

As previously noted, there is danger in assuming gratuitously that the outcomes of content analyses constitute the likely effects of the contents of the media. This danger is particularly to be guarded against when the analyst "sees" in the content a very abstract value or conception of life and assumes without evidence that most people will perceive and absorb this view. The difficulty of resisting such an assump-tion is manifested in the volume by Himmelweit, Oppenheim, and Vince (1958). Though stating a comparable warning, they asserted that violence in television programs can teach that violence is inevitable or manly, or that life is cheap and conflict is to be solved by violence. Similarly, Arnheim (1944), in his qualitative analysis of the themes of radio serial dramas, averred that listeners can gain wrong or harmful impressions of what life is about. Purportedly, if they identify with the character who instigates conflicts or makes problems for others in the episodes, they will learn that people are imperfect and all are sinners, whereas identification with the character who is undeservedly faced with trouble will lead to the conception that decency and virtue do not bring their just rewards. Also, Dale (1933) suggested that children may acquire the wrong conception of criminality from the roughly one out of four films, among the large number examined, which permitted the crimi-nal to "get away with it." However, Shuttleworth and May (1933) found that children who were heavy moviegoers believed that few criminals escape their proper punish-ment.

Unless a general view of life or a moral is made explicit, the audience must ex-tract the inference from the media experience. And, as previously noted, experi-mental research suggests that, when this is required, the effectiveness of a message in achieving acceptance of a desired conclusion is likely to be less than when the conclusion is explicitly stated. Hence, since a moral is not explicitly drawn in many presentations, the impact of such offerings is likely to be less than would be assumed or expected. Also, since a moral is itself a schema for organizing the events of a program or story, its development in the context of media experience is likely to be gradual and to be open to influences that affect schemas generally. In addition, the active sensitivity to and salience of such moralistic schemas, and their engagement by communication content, may very well be a dispositional and preexisting characteristic of the individual.

FAMILY LIFE

In general, television has not had any marked or sweeping effects on family life. Belson (1959b) found that, while at-homeness may increase at certain times, a compensatory decrease occurs at other times; the major effect seems to be a redistribution of time spent at home by children and young people. He also found that the effects vary with local, seasonal, and personal factors and from family to family. In time, the effects wear off and the pattern of home-centered and joint activities returns to pretelevision levels. Though the family may be in each other's presence while watching television, it is a moot point whether this physical togetherness binds them more strongly. Conversation is usually inhibited and interaction is minimized (Fine and Maccoby, 1952; Maccoby, 1951; Steiner, 1963). Television is more likely to reinforce or bring to the surface existing family relations than to create new ones (Bogart, 1962; Forsey, 1963). Some pertinent evidence of this comes from a study by Robinson (1941) of the uses of radio by farm families. Apparently, radio had a beneficial effect on the cohesiveness of integrated families by stimulating group listening and discussion, but had the opposite effect on families whose members were poorly adjusted to each other.

Passivity

Though fears have been expressed and charges made that television will encourage social isolation and passivity, particularly among young people (Glynn, 1956), there is little cogent evidence to support these contentions. Unfortunately, neither critics nor investigators of media effects have provided a precise explication of "passivity." Consequently, what is meant by such a concept and how it is to be tested as a dependent variable often constitute personal and implicit value judgments.

As already noted, play activities were not curtailed by television; in fact, Himmelweit, Oppenheim, and Vince (1958) found that viewers, even before they obtained television, were more sociable and interested in play with others than were nonviewers. Though Maccoby (1951) claimed that television reduced creative or productive activities, such as playing a musical instrument, neither Himmelweit, Oppenheim, and Vince (1958) nor Furu (1962) found this to be true in their studies. On the basis of an analysis of children's favorite activities, Okabe (1963) reported no evidence of television-induced passivity. Furu (1962) also reported that children living in television households were no more likely than those without television to choose passive, "onlooker" responses to questionnaire items. Bailyn (1959) considered that only about 3 percent of the boys in her sample of schoolchildren possessed the combination of psychological characteristics (extrapunitiveness, unsatisfactory relationship with parents or others, significant personal problems) which disposed them to heavy use of television, movies, and comic books as a means of withdrawing or maintaining isolation from the environment. Similarly, Schramm, Lyle, and Parker (1961) suggested that television may reinforce withdrawal and passivity when these preexisted or are latent, but does not create them.

As regards adults, there is no evidence of anything more than a minor and temporary effect on their pattern of social and leisure activities (Belson, 1958; Marx, 1953). The more general charge by Lazarsfeld and Merton (1948), that the media "narcotize" people by overwhelming them with great quantities of attention-attracting material, by inducing them to substitute knowing for doing, and by leaving little time for organized action, remains unsupported by available data.

Schoolwork

Despite fears that television would take time from homework and make school seem pallid by comparison, there is little evidence of any adverse effects on schoolwork (Coffin, 1955; Furu, 1962; Himmelweit, Oppenheim, and Vince, 1958). Since there are so many influences bearing upon the quality of schoolwork, some of which also affect the amount of time devoted to television, it is unlikely that television would be found to be a significant determinant for the great majority of children (Bogart, 1962). In respect to the same concern about the effects of the movies, Shuttleworth and May (1933) found that light moviegoers were scholastically superior to heavy moviegoers; but rather than degree of moviegoing being a causal factor, other differentiating characteristics seemed implicated. Heisler (1947, 1948) found no relationship between educational achievement and comic book reading or movie-going.

Schramm, Lyle, and Parker (1961) have suggested that television may contribute to a faster start in learning, leading to an enriched and more extensive vocabulary and a wider store of symbolic and vicarious experiences. In time, television's supplementing contribution to general knowledge declines, though the brighter 10-year-old and the duller 13-year-old may still benefit. Somewhat similar sentiments have been voiced by Himmelweit, Oppenheim, and Vince (1958).

Bedtime

Subjective impression has led to the assertion that children stay up much later than was the custom before television and, thereby, are deprived of needed rest and sleep. However, both Himmelweit, Oppenheim, and Vince (1958) and Furu (1962) found that, despite slightly delayed average bedtimes, which Maccoby (1951) also recorded but Merrill (1961) did not, children in television households reported as much actual sleeping time as did those in radio-only homes, for they played or read less in bed than did the other children. While the problem of getting youngsters away from the television set and to bed is mentioned with some frequency by parents, (Maccoby, 1951), Himmelweit, Oppenheim, and Vince (1958) pointed out that really late bedtimes derive from the general home atmosphere and from parental attitudes rather than from television; in fact, they found that, even before television became available, children who were among the first to have sets already had later bedtimes.

FUNCTIONAL ORIENTATION

In experimental communications research, effects can usually be attributed to known and prearranged stimulus conditions, for the occurrence of a given communication experience is determined by the experimenter and not by the audience, and provision is made for necessary and valid comparison groups. Preexisting differences between those who receive a communication and those who do not are eliminated by the design of the experiment, unless they themselves are under study. Under such circumstances, it is justifiable to phrase the outcomes in terms of the effects of communication stimuli. However, this way of stating results does not assume that the recipient is passive in the situation or lacks initiative in determining the nature of the effects. Interpretations of research and theoretical formulations do take into account such contributing influences as the recipients' perceptions or interpretations of the stimuli and the psychological processes or personality-based predispositions aroused by the stimuli (see Chapter 21). A full theory of communication effects requires the introduction of these linking concepts.

However, in the natural communications environment, exposure is voluntary and, hence, is a matter of individual choice. This means that not only the initial contact with a communication derives from the initiative of the audience, but also continuation of exposure and reexposure to the same or similar materials. Furthermore, to the extent that the medium permits it, a person may choose to attend only to parts of a communication and in a self-determined order. This characteristic of self-determination of exposure raises some obvious interpretive problems, including the need to establish that behavior presumed to represent effects did not exist prior to the communication experience or would not have occurred without it.

But from a broader theoretical perspective, self-exposure compels consideration of the perceived incentives which attract and hold an audience. Since incentives relate to motives, an obvious assumption is that continuous attention is given to material which is congruent with or satisfies predispositions. Put in another way, those who choose to expose themselves frequently to certain types of communications or to a medium do so because they seek certain gratifications from the experiences or desire to use the medium in personally satisfying ways. If this is so, then, to some extent a given effect may be said to be determined by the audience itself. The usual way of phrasing this is to insist that media effects must be viewed from the perspective of what people *use* the media for rather than what the media *do* to people (Fearing, 1954; Klapper, 1960; Mendelsohn, 1964; Schramm, Lyle, and Parker, 1961). This emphasis on the role of the audience in determining effects is strengthened when to self-exposure is added the influence of such psychological processes as motivated perception, interpretation, and recall; all of these contribute to the outcomes of communication experiences, even the unintended ones or those which the recipient is not conscious of. Also, an emphasis on the initiative of the audience brings into central focus the importance of considering the social, psychological, and attitudinal attributes of media users, if the natural effects of the media are to be understood.

This perspective does not deny that media content can be a determining influence and, under the special circumstances of minimal arousal of predispositions, even have a direct effect on attitudes, values, and behavior. What is rejected is any conception that construes media experiences as alone sufficient for a wide variety of effects. The transactional nature of communication is clearly implied by this orientation, for to have a chance at an effect, the communicator must seek to satisfy some expectations and desires of people (Bauer, 1964; Davison, 1959). This necessity is implicit in Doob's (1948) distinction between auxiliary and related attitudes—between the functions of the lovely model in the automobile commercial and of the copy lauding characteristics of the car.

Since there is need to attract and hold an audience, the media cannot vary too much from the audience's expectations or values or desires. Hence, the media tend to reflect current characteristics of people and, by reinforcing them, act as a conservative influence (Berelson, 1942; Lazarsfeld, 1942; Wirth, 1948). In other words, a significant portion of the total outcome of communication experiences is the reinforcement or intensification or elicitation of preexisting responses. To the extent that such responses do not constitute the total consequences of communications, the media can function as more dominant influences in other effects. In a proper description and interpretation of the outcomes of a communication experience, it would make little difference whether the media are said to have effects, even of the reinforcing or satisfying kind, or the effects are said to be determined by the recipients.

In pursuing this orientation, care must be taken against interpreting outcomes of media experiences as reflecting nothing more than what the audience brought to the situation. It is easy to reduce the role of media content to elicitors of predispositions, and to focus exclusively on the interplay between media and predispositions to the neglect of an analysis of the distinctive contributions of the media themselves (Klapper, 1960). That is, the media may be denied both influence and any qualities separate from those of any other stimulator of predispositions. This prejudgment and narrowing of analysis may stultify research and theory or preclude the development of a conceptual framework more suitable to the complexities of the communication experience. A second and particularly evident danger is the tendency toward *post hoc* interpretations of the influence of media content. Since a multitude of predispositions can contribute to any exposure, it is most difficult to *predict* which predispositions are most relevant and will be engaged by the communication stimuli. Too often, the consequence may be plausible but *postdictive* explanations that should be construed as hypotheses for further test, but instead, are taken as confirmations of hypotheses. Also, it should be kept in mind that the same content can satisfy more than one need and different content can satisfy the same need (Emery, 1959a; Schramm, Lyle, and Parker, 1961; Smythe, 1954). Hence, more is required to establish that a particular need is being satisfied than the mere examination of the content of the media or respondents' assertions concerning their reasons for using the media.

In capsule form, what has been argued as a required orientation toward the analysis of mass media effects is consideration of the crucial role played by audience dispositions. These function in two ways: to determine exposure to communications and to modulate the results of exposure. Since experimental research eliminates the first (unless information seeking is itself under study) and *may* ignore the second, its utility has been questioned by those more concerned with the natural communications environment (for example, Lazarsfeld, 1963a; Mendelsohn, 1964; Okabe, 1964). It is not that such criticism holds laboratory findings to be invalid; rather it views them as of less value than they might otherwise be, in consideration of the fact of voluntary exposure and the significance of factors of greater weight than those inhering in much of experimental research. Hovland (1959) has proposed that the utility of controlled research might be increased if experimental samples contained people whose characteristics reflected those which would be related to self-exposure to such communications in the normal environment.

GRATIFICATIONS OR USES

This orientation leads directly to an interest in the gratifications people seek or obtain from the media or in the uses they make of the media. It would serve no value to list the innumerable specific ones asserted by media viewers or program audiences themselves. However, most of the reasons can be grouped into a few general categories, without doing particular injustice to their specific qualities. Brief consideration will be given to these categories, even though they have appeared explicitly or implicitly in material presented earlier.

Time filling

This use is obvious and has been mentioned in respect to every one of the media (Berelson, 1949a; Himmelweit, Oppenheim, and Vince, 1958; Shuttleworth and May, 1933). When this use is associated with particular periods during the day and has become part of the daily routine, people show considerable disturbance if a relevant medium is unavailable. For instance, studies of people's reactions to the absence of newspapers during a labor dispute (Berelson, 1949a; Kimball, 1959) have made clear the almost ritualistic use of the newspaper for this purpose, for instance, during the periods of commuting to and from work. In fact, Passin (1959) has suggested that the long commuting times which are common in Japan are in part responsible for the greater bulk of Japanese than of American magazines.

Relaxation or diversion

Where the time-filling use is nonselective as to content or in respect to psychological responses, this use requires suitable content and represents a type of experience. But since what is relaxing or diverting is a function of interests, motives, etc., people will differ in respect to the kinds of material and media selected for this purpose. This general category of use is represented by a variety of terms designating specific appeals or functions of media, such as "escape," entertainment, fantasy, respite.

Most of the comments on this category of use have focused on the nature or content of the media. In general, content which is relaxing or diverting is said to relate to something other than real problems of life or ordinary concerns and routines, and is not anxiety provoking (Waples, Berelson, and Bradshaw, 1940). Clearly, the customary content of entertainment, fantasy, and fiction abounds in such characteristics. Of relevance is the listing by Schramm, Lyle, and Parker (1961) of the characteristics differentiating fantasy and reality content. These are presented in Table 1. These authors also pointed out that the media are originally presented to children as entertainment, even in respect to the stories read to them; this implies that the initial stage of socialization to the media contributes to the ways in which they are later used. Of some relevance to this viewpoint is Schramm, Lyle, and Parker's finding that children admit to a preference for having their learning from the media incidental to their being entertained.

Almost by definition, diversion represents a form of escape from the real environment or a turning away to a fantasy world or, at the least, to content of little use in the real world of most people. The readiness of people to seek diversion, coupled with the excellence of certain media in providing content deemed to be "otherworldly,"

TABLE 1

"IDEAL" CHARACTERISTICS OF FANTASY AND REALITY CONTENT
(FROM SCHRAMM, LYLE, AND PARKER, 1961)

Fantasy content	*Reality content*
Invites the viewer to take leave of his problems in the real world	Constantly refers the viewer to the problems of the real world
Invites surrender, relaxation, passivity	Invites alertness, effort, activity
Invites emotion	Invites cognition
Works chiefly through abrogating the rules of the real world	Works chiefly through realistic materials and situations
Acts to remove, at least temporarily, threat and anxiety, and often offers wish-fulfillment	Tends to make viewer even more aware of threat, perhaps more anxious, in return for better view of problem
Offers pleasure	Offers enlightenment

has led to charges that a dysfunctional or narcotizing escapism may be engendered (Lazarsfeld and Merton, 1948). The concern is that the abundance of material removed from the real environments of people will divert attention too much from real problems and their realistic solutions. The vagueness of the concept "escape" was explored by Katz and Foulkes (1962), who argued that diverting material can have a realistic use and that to establish the escapist dysfunction requires establishing the lack of any social or personal value in the content of entertainment programs. The problem of determining this is evident in analyses of the informational utility of the contents of daytime radio serials (Herzog, 1944; Warner and Henry, 1948); for a sensible interpretation of such data, see Klapper (1960). Also to be considered is the suggestion that fantasy content feeds a normal need for imaginative material, particularly among children (Schramm, Lyle, and Parker, 1961).

Social

The utilization of material in the media as conversational currency has been remarked on by a number of investigators (for example, Berelson, 1949a; Mendelsohn, 1964; Okabe, 1963; Schramm, Lyle, and Parker, 1961). This is not the deliberate seeking of information on special topics of interest, but the use of media content as the ingredient of casual conversation. Put in another way, ordinary social conversation requires topics to feed and keep it going and the media help to supply these. Schramm, Lyle, and Pool (1963) reported that conversations often included references to programs televised the previous evening and that this sharing of recollections is relevant to the continued watching of an educational television program.

Attention to a particular medium may also serve a social reference function, in that it gratifies a desire for social prestige or reflects a person's self-image or enables a person to relate himself to relevant others. For instance, in intellectual and educated circles, print carries high prestige and the reading of books or selected magazines or particular newspapers may represent what is expected of an intelligent, cultured person. In fact, it has been suggested that the purchase of a newspaper is an attribute of social class and reflects the social prestige value of the medium (Berelson, 1949a; Westley and Severin, 1964a). Merton (1949), noting the different types of magazines and newspapers taken by different kinds of community leaders, said: "Gratifications derived from mass communications . . . are not merely psychological in nature; they are also a product of the distinctive social roles of those who make use of these communications" (p. 205). This use of the media can obviously be generalized to all social levels and groups.

Of interest in this regard is research by Riley and Riley (1951). They suggested that children who are related to others in friendship groups tend to conceive of the fantasy content of media in terms of its social utility for play activities, while nonpeer-group members respond in terms of personal reactions and uses. However, Klapper (1960) has suggested that personality differences between the two types of children may also be involved.

Mention has already been made of the utilization of theater movies in the context of dating (Lazarsfeld and Kendall, 1948). Also, one reason some children gave for watching television was that it provided an opportunity for boys and girls to sit close together (Schramm, Lyle, and Parker, 1961).

Personal

There are innumerable personal uses to which the media have been put, particularly when the personality dynamics and tensions generated by personal relationships are considered (*cf.* Emery, 1959b; Forsey, 1963). Certain children are said to react to a frustrating home environment with greater use of television (Maccoby, 1954) or to satisfy their need for ego enhancement by using suitable comic books (Wolf and Fiske, 1949); women are presumed to have listened to daytime radio serials for such gratifications as emotional release, vicarious enjoyment of the happy marital relationship they lacked, support for their conceptions of the "good" wife and mother, and contemplation of their own problems through the happenings in the story (Herzog, 1944; Ono, 1959; Warner and Henry, 1948); people are supposed to be attracted to television because it affords them a pseudo-interaction with featured personalities or other program participants (Himmelweit, Oppenheim, and Vince, 1958; Horton and Wohl, 1956); lower-class adult males are said to seek a break in the monotony of the ordinary day and fantasy satisfactions by reading newspaper comic strips (Bogart, 1957a). Obviously, the listing of such uses could be expanded, but an exhaustive categorizing would serve no useful purpose.

That people say they use the media in order to obtain wanted information or to be informed about significant daily happenings has often been reported. The educational value of commercial television has been asserted as a reason for watching, but adults and children often couple this use with its acclaimed entertainment value (Schramm, Lyle, and Parker, 1961; Steiner, 1963). Even radio quiz programs, to a greater extent than news programs (Lazarsfeld, 1940), and daytime radio serials (Herzog, 1944) have supposedly been listened to for their informational utility. The same has been claimed for movies, in regard to dress, love techniques, and social behavior (Blumer, 1933). Of course, this use is the dominant reason given for reading a newspaper.   But careful analysis of people's statements during a newspaper strike suggests that, for many, this reason had the characteristic of a nominal or normative response (Berelson, 1949a; Kimball, 1959).   "Educational value" is often claimed for educational television, as might be expected (Schramm, Lyle, and Pool, 1963).

Though not often given its due, the sheer "consummatory" pleasure of reading or hearing or watching has also been reported in some studies (Himmelweit, Oppenheim, and Vince, 1958; Kimball, 1959).

SOME FACTORS RELATED TO USE OF THE MEDIA

Media behavior of others

As previously noted, media enter a primary group by active choice, have social utility, and may meet their audiences within social contexts of exposure.   In view of these considerations, it is likely that the extent of use of selected media would be affected by the use patterns and attitudes toward the media of significant others.   A number of studies have indicated that the frequency of children's use of a particular medium, and to some extent their choice of content, is positively related to the media and content preferences of members of their family (Bogart, 1962; Himmelweit, Oppenheim, and Vince, 1958; Schramm, Lyle, and Parker, 1961; Shuttleworth and May, 1933; Wolfe and Fiske, 1949).

Age and intelligence

As might be expected, age and intelligence of children affect their use of the media. While the significance of each has been considered separately in some research, their interrelation yields a more fruitful understanding of the place of the media in the lives of children.   For adults, education would replace intelligence as a correlate of media use.

In their early years, approximately to the age of 10, brighter children are heavy users of entertainment media; but at about 10 to 13 years of age, they reduce their attention to such media to a moderate level (Furu, 1962; Schramm, Lyle, and Parker, 1961; but *cf.* Himmelweit, Oppenheim, and Vince, 1961).   In addition, as they move from the childhood years toward the early teens, their content preferences turn increasingly toward serious or reality-oriented material, whereas light or fantasy content continues to dominate the preferences of the less intelligent children (Furu, 1962; Lyle, 1962; Meine, 1941; Schramm, Lyle, and Parker, 1961; Wolfe and Fiske, 1949).

In view of the change in use of the media by age and intelligence, Schramm, Lyle, and Parker (1961) suggested that the bright child seeks a wide range of experiences and knowledge.   In the early years, this leads to relatively heavy use of all media, which, by the sixth grade, is at or near a maximum for all children.   But as the satisfactoriness of this method of exploring the environment and gaining experiences vicariously wanes, the bright child turns to reality-oriented modes and to print media more and more, though maintaining some contact with a wide range of material.   The child who lacks such intellectual curiosity and is less demanding in what will satisfy him continues his heavy and restricted use of the fantasy media. This general pattern of development in children's use of the media is formulated as "the principle of maturation."

This perspective suggests that the significance of media use as a characteristic differentiating the more and the less intelligent will increase with age. As already noted, the data give some support to this conception. Also consistent is the finding by Shuttleworth and May (1933) that differences between heavy and light moviegoers in their responses to a paper-and-pencil measure of social and moral characteristics increase with age; the age groupings were: under $11\frac{1}{2}$, $11\frac{1}{2}$ to 13, and 13 or older. Himmelweit, Oppenheim, and Vince (1958) found that, even before television was available, the differences in preference for intellectual, creative, and social activities of children who later acquired television sets versus those who did not was most prominent among young people of 13 to 14 years of age. Though boys and girls differed in their program preferences at both age ranges included in the study, there was a tendency for the differences to be greater among the older than the younger children. A similar pattern is noted by Furu (1965). Lyle (1962) reported that, among tenth-grade children, but not particularly among sixth-graders, attention to types of newspaper content (entertainment only, "hard" news only, both) was clearly related to frequency of use of newspapers and television and to conflicts with parents over goals. Also, Schramm, Lyle, and Parker (1961) found that there were no marked differences between sixth-grade children, whether high or low users of television and print, on a social-aggression measure, but that among tenth-grade children of high socioeconomic background those who were high print and low television users ("reality-oriented") scored higher on aggression anxiety and lower on antisocial aggression than did the low print and high television users ("fantasy-oriented"). There were no differences among the children of low socioeconomic background.

The nature of the developmental changes in children's use of the media, earlier for some than for others but falling close to the beginning of the teens for most, is relevant to the suggestion of Himmelweit, Oppenheim, and Vince (1958) that their findings based on 13- to 14-year-olds can be generalized to adults. They noted that the viewing habits and reactions of this age group are similar to those of adults. Of interest in this regard are the findings of Becker and Wolfe (1960) that adults predicted more accurately the interest reactions of 11- to 12-year-olds than of 4- to 5-year-olds to educational television programs; however, their predictive accuracy even for the older children was not very high ($r=0.30$), and neither educational specialists nor mothers of preschoolers were able to achieve reliable accuracy in respect to the younger children. Also, Greenberg (1964b, 1965a) reported that the pattern of evaluative judgments of two programs by television personnel matched more closely, though still with significant discrepancies, the reactions of seventh-grade children than of third-grade children.

Data concerning the attention range of adults to media content bear a similarity to those for the older children, when education or its correlates replace intelligence as the differentiating characteristic. Schramm, Lyle, and Pool (1963) found that people who occasionally watched educational television were as knowledgeable about popular heroes as those who watched only commercial television, but more knowledgeable about public affairs figures. Also, though watching commercial television less, they did look at a wider range of programs. Similarly, Steiner (1963) reported that well-educated adults differ primarily from the less educated in giving attention to a greater variety of types of programs, including the most popular ones. Related is the finding reported by Swanson (1954), that heavy readers of public affairs material in newspapers, who are generally of higher educational and economic status, are also heavy readers of human interest articles. Also consistent are the data of Schramm and White (1949), implying a wider spread of attention over types of newspaper content at the upper economic and educational levels.

The earlier remarks concerning the use of the media to fill discretionary time suggests that media use should be evaluated *relative* to the number of "free" hours that people have available. Samuelson, Carter, and Ruggels (1963) provided some evidence that, when differences in the amount of time devoted to required or role-related activities are controlled statistically, the slightly negative association between education and extent of use of television is eliminated. Also, Schramm, Lyle, and Parker (1961) reported data indicating that, among children, intelligence is less strongly related to the number of hours spent watching television on Sundays than on weekdays.

Middle-class values

In respect to children's use of television, social class does not seem to be strongly related, within the samples studied, to time spent viewing or choice of preferred programs (Himmelweit, Oppenheim, and Vince, 1958; Schramm, Lyle, and Parker, 1961). Of greater significance, according to Schramm, Lyle, and Parker (1961), is acceptance of middle-class norms or values regarding the importance of schoolwork and education, aspirations for high occupational status, and willingness to defer gratifications rather than to emphasize immediate rewards. Schramm, Lyle, and Parker found that, among middle-class children, those with high educational and occupational aspirations spent less time with television than did those with low aspirations; among working-class children, the relationship was not so clear. To assess acceptance of deferred versus immediate impulse gratification, the investigators employed a three-item questionnaire. On the basis of a dichotomization of de-

TABLE 2

MEDIA USE AND ORIENTATION TOWARD IMMEDIATE VERSUS DELAYED
IMPULSE GRATIFICATION (FROM SCHRAMM, LYLE, AND PARLER, 1961)

Orientation of viewers	"The best way to live is to enjoy today and not think about tomorrow"	"The best way to be happy is to plan ahead"	"It's a good idea to work harder today so you can enjoy tomorrow more"
	Disagreeing	*Agreeing*	*Agreeing*
Fantasy-oriented (high TV, low print)	43%	36%	40%
Low users (low TV, low print)	57	43	39
High users (high TV, high print)	59	59	50
Reality-oriented (low TV, high print)	83	58	56

gree of use of television and, separately, of books and serious magazines, four categories of media users were formed: those who were either high users of both media or
low users of both media, those who were low users of television but high users of
print ("reality" group), and those who were high users of television and low users of
print ("fantasy" group). They assumed that reality seeking is characteristic of those
accepting middle-class values and fantasy seeking, of those holding to working-
class values. If the delayed- versus immediate-gratification orientation is one of these
two types of values, then children differing in this orientation should also differ in
their use of the media. As shown in Table 2, this expectation receives some support:
children in the "reality" group tend to be most likely to give delayed-gratification
responses to the questionnaire, those in the "fantasy" group least likely, and those
in the other groups tend to fall in between. Schramm, Lyle, and Pool (1963) found
that viewers of educational television were more likely than nonviewers to accept a
delayed-gratification orientation, to be future-oriented, and to value learning and
self-improvement—all characteristic of a middle-class value system. And, as might
be expected, education and socioeconomic status were positively related to viewing
educational television (see also Schramm, 1960). Fujitake (summarized in Fujinama,
1964) stated that Japanese who find television indispensable exhibit an immediate-
reward orientation and lack social awareness or a broad perspective on life.

PERSONALITY

It has often been suggested that personality characteristics are related to the use
of the media. This can be taken to mean that content or media preferences relate to
stable characteristics of the individual or are chosen for the vicarious satisfactions
they provide for persistent needs and motives. As previously noted, this kind of
interpretation has been given to the results of many studies of the effects of the media
on outlook, values, and other personal characteristics. The previously presented
data on the relationship between intelligence and media use are also relevant. A
number of other studies and findings will now be mentioned. However, as will be
evident, much systematic and theory-guided research remains to be done before a
confident understanding of the relationship between personality characteristics and
media use is attained.

   Herzog (1944) attempted to determine whether women who listened to daytime
radio serials differed in personality characteristics from those who did not follow
such programs. No reliable personality differences were found; the most prominent
difference was that the serial fan listened more to radio in general than did other
women. A similar finding of no differences in personality characteristics was reported
in a later, unpublished study by CBS radio (Lazarsfeld, 1940). Katz and Lazarsfeld
(1955) found that women who admitted to worrying at least to the same extent as
others or to feeling depression on occasion were more likely than other women to
give their attention to "popular" fiction, comprising magazines of the "true story"
type, movie magazines, and daytime radio serials. A composite index based on these
three constituents was used in the research.

   Scott (1957) found few significant relationships, and of unimpressive magnitudes,
between personality characteristics measured by the MMPI scales and preference
for types of movies.

   Wolfe and Fiske (1949) reported a modicum of data suggesting that the avid
reader of comic books was more likely than the nonfan to be insecure in his life or

to be nonnormal physically in some regard. Himmelweit, Oppenheim, and Vince (1958) found that children who were in the top 30 percent in viewing time were emotionally insecure and socially ill at ease; also, they preferred family-type programs and adventure or mystery dramas. Bailyn (1959) found no relationship between the number of personal problems in the everyday lives of children and degree of combined exposure to television, movies, and comic books, but a negative relationship with respect to exposure to radio and serious books.

Maccoby (1954) suggested that middle-class children subjected to restrictions and frustrations watch television more than do those who are less frustrated by their parents, but that, among children of a lower socioeconomic level, degree of parental frustration is not a differentiating factor. She interpreted this to mean that frustrated children turned to television; but since lower-class parents and children are heavy users themselves (Bogart, 1958), the lower-class frustrated children cannot increase viewing time, though this is possible for upper-class children. Results consistent with Maccoby's were obtained by Schramm, Lyle, and Parker (1961). Among upper-class children, the greatest amount of television use was exhibited by those who had high scores on a measure of antisocial aggression and reported the greatest discrepancy between their own educational and occupational aspirations and those held for them by their parents. However, among children from lower-class homes, the greatest television use was found among those of low parent-child discrepancy who had low scores on the aggression scale.

EFFECTS OF MEDIA PORTRAYALS OF VIOLENCE

No effects of the mass media have been the subject of more persistent controversy than their presumed contribution to antisocial conduct, such as aggressive or delinquent behavior. Regardless of which of the modern media is considered, hopes that it would uplift and instruct yielded to concern that it created or abetted some of the ill conduct of the day. The penny press, dime novels, radio, comic books, movies, and now television have all been charged in their time as instigators of socially undesirable behavior. However, the bulk of such claims, as well as defending assertions, have been based on tenuous grounds of moot evidence. In numerous instances, the evidence is little more than the assertion itself; or case histories are presented as the ground for claims of ill effects (for example, see Wertham, 1954, 1962; see Thrasher, 1949, and Pittman, 1958, for a critique of this approach).

The social significance of the effects of media-portrayed violence on conduct and values is of such moment these days that a disinterested analysis of the available evidence is not often made. Any suspicion that so attractive a medium as television may be contributing to aggression or violent behavior, particularly in children, produces public alarm. Under such circumstances, the canon of scientific doubt is easily breached. The danger of this is that needed research checking on the soundness of the evidence will be inhibited as many people proclaim the supposed implications of early investigations. However, social policy can be adopted regardless of the uncertainties of research findings. As Schramm has pointed out (U.S. Senate, 1964), the mere *possibility* of harmful effects, even in the absence of firm scientific proof, may be taken as sufficient ground for stern action against the frequent display of violence in the media. Society may not wish to gamble on a matter of such importance. But action taken on such grounds must not preclude continued research on the very question of effects, nor be taken as evidence that certain effects have been demonstrated. This perspective has actually been put into practice in Japan, where the Japan Broadcasting Corporation has maintained a policy of minimizing the display of violence on television and the National Association of Commercial Broadcasters has supported research on the effects of television on children (Furu, 1965).

Data concerning the frequency of acts of violence portrayed on television (U.S. Senate, 1964) cannot be taken as evidence of likely effects. The error of assuming effects from a content analysis has been noted earlier. At the least, what must be known is how children perceive or interpret these acts, for example, what they mean to the children. In this connection, Himmelweit, Oppenheim, and Vince (1958) reported that adults did not predict well the kinds of programs that disturb children. They found that more important than sheer violence as a basis for disturbance was identification or involvement with a character who was in a dangerous situation. Of interest is the experience of one television station which found that giving an educational guise to a series of Western films, by presenting them as stories that conveyed the flavor and record of the Old West, drew compliments from adult viewers on the suitability of the films for a juvenile audience; previously, without this facade, the same series had elicited criticism (Bogart, 1958).

Also to be considered as a caution against a simple assumption of direct effects is the general lack of evidence concerning any serious influence of the media on other kinds of conduct or on values. Furthermore, a proper evaluation of the social significance of televised violence requires consideration of the nature of the influences and activities being replaced. In this regard, Schramm, Lyle, and Parker (1961) remarked that television is substituting for such conveyors of violence as crime comics, detective magazines, and radio programs of crime and violence.

In respect to the movies, the results of relevant Payne Fund Studies summarized by Charters (1933) can best be interpreted as yielding the pallid and useless conclusion that some movies have some effects considered to be adverse on some viewers. Evidence of degrading effects on moral values or the incitement of antisocial conduct is very weak (*cf.* Shuttleworth and May, 1933), and assertions implicating the movies as a contributor to delinquency receive little valid support (*cf.* Blumer and Hauser, 1933).

Concerning the effects of television on aggressive behavior, the medium currently under sustained criticism in this regard, there is little relevant evidence from non-experimental studies. On the basis of parents' assertions about the favorite television programs of their children, Eron (1963) found that the degree of violence depicted in the favorites was positively related to rated classroom aggressiveness of third-grade boys but not of third-grade girls. However, total reported viewing time was negatively related to aggressiveness. In view of the correlational basis of the evidence, there is no warrant for Eron's assertion that aggressiveness was the result of the modeling effect of television violence. In Bailyn's (1959) study, aggressive hero content in radio, television, and comic books was preferred much more by those children who were highly exposed to these media *and* were "rebelliously independent," or had many personal problems, or scored high on a measure of extrapunitiveness, than by the highly exposed who lacked these characteristics. Also, among boys who were well-behaved in school, those who were high in extrapunitive tendencies preferred aggressive-hero content more than did the other boys; there was no relation between extrapunitiveness and content preference among the less well-behaved boys. Bailyn suggested that the well-behaved but extrapunitive boy may be using such content as a fantasy expression of antisocial behavior. Okabe (1963) reported that normal Japanese children and children with strong latent delinquency tendencies did not differ in their television viewing habits or in their program preferences, including their preference for programs of violence.

EXPERIMENTAL RESEARCH

There is little doubt that, by displaying forms of aggression or modes of criminal and violent behavior, the media are "teaching" and people are learning. But whether such symbolically acquired information is ever used depends on a number of factors, as is the case with any kind of learning (Lumsdaine, 1961; Miller *et al.*, 1957). Relevant motivation to exhibit the learning in actual behavior, ability to do so, and a proper opportunity and the necessary materials for doing so must all occur. Knowledge of a method for committing a crime or some sadistic act will not issue in behavior if there is no motive for stealing or being sadistic, if the method is beyond the person's capabilities and skills, if the situation in which the behavior could be exhibited does not occur and the material means for carrying out the behavior are unobtainable. Furthermore, if the information is to be used, it must come to mind in the relevant situation. Whether it does or not will depend on the similarity between aspects of the person's actual environment and the media setting in which the behavior was exhibited, the frequency with which the learned information has been thought about or put into use in imagination, and the lapse of time between the original learning and the opportunity to use it. Finally, whether the behavior will be exhibited depends also on the strength of restraints against doing so; these restraints may derive from within the person (for example, values opposing any form of violence) or from the environment (for example, fear of punishment).

Of a number of inferences that can be drawn from this listing of preconditions for behavior, only three will be mentioned. First, the variety of factors involved in putting perceptual learning into practice can be expected to reduce the likelihood that exposure to violence in the media will lead to violent behavior. Second, much depends on the person, since motivation, personality, and ability will affect his receptivity to the information and the likelihood of his using it. This point has often stood as a general statement of conclusion concerning effects of the media (Himmelweit, Oppenheim, and Vince, 1958; Schramm, Lyle, and Parker, 1961). Third, the nature of the social and physical characteristics of a person's normal environment will play a significant role, since they will determine the availability of suitable opportunities for the behavior and whether the behavior will be rewarded or punished.

Also relevant is the question of what is learned from media violence and, therefore, what the behavioral effects may be. The implication in many discussions is that specific acts of aggression or violence are learned and imitated: for example, how to carry out a crime, should one want to. An alternative is that a role is learned or a style of behavior exhibited by an identificand is adopted. For instance, when a child plays with a toy gun, he may not be merely imitating what he saw concerning how a gun should be worn, drawn, and fired, but rather acting out the attractive guise of a gunfighter who defends law and order and uses his gun when necessary (Emery, 1959a; Warshow, 1954). Obviously, these alternatives are not mutually exclusive; the specifics of behavior and the role containing the behavior can both be learned. But where the emphasis lies in the learning may affect the meaning of the behavior and the circumstances under which it may actually be exhibited.

COGNITIVE EFFECTS

Though what can be recalled from media portrayals of aggression need not be shown in behavior, it might be expected that those who, for reasons of personality or motivation, are disposed toward aggressive behavior would retain aggressive content better than would others. Two studies were conducted by Maccoby, Levin, and Selya (1955, 1956) to test the more specific expectation that the prior arousal of aggressive tendencies through frustration would induce greater retention of the aggressive material in a movie. In the first study conducted in suburban Boston schools, children frustrated by failure in a spelling contest showed greater retention of the aggressive content of a film than did nonfrustrated children when recall was measured a week later. But when the study was replicated in a semirural area in upper New York State, no difference in recall was found between the frustrated and nonfrustrated children.

Another kind of cognitive effect is a change in perspective concerning the frequency of violence in the environment and where its social or physical loci may be. For instance, without an actual change in the crime rate, an increase in the frequency of stories about crimes can induce the impression of a crime wave (Bauer and Bauer, 1960). Emery (1959b) suggested that a Western movie led some Australian boys to view the environment as more hostile and threatening.

Also, acts and styles of aggression may become associated with a category of people or a social group. It has often been averred that fictional media portrayals of Italians as gangsters or Negroes as knife wielders sustain or contribute to stereotypical expectations of violence by these groups. Though there is no direct evidence on this, it is unlikely that media portrayals *alone* can markedly influence or change the attribution of aggressiveness to known groups. But what effect can stories have on conceptions of relatively unknown groups?

In a relevant experiment, Siegel (1958) sought to determine whether a radio serial that depicted taxi drivers as people who respond to frustration with aggression would lead children to believe that taxi drivers generally behaved this way. The children were drawn from a semirural area and had unclear expectations about taxi drivers. On three consecutive occasions, they heard a purported radio drama about taxi drivers; for half of the children, the taxi driver in each story reacted with aggression to frustrating situations, and for half with nonaggressive behavior. On a story-completion test, the former group indicated greater expectation of aggressive behavior when the story was similar to one in the series but *not* when it was dissimilar. Hence, the research gives little evidence of the generalization of expectations to the point of incorporating them into the ascribed role behavior of taxi drivers. Besides offering a number of other reasons for the results, Siegel suggested that three stories may be insufficient to establish a role expectation. This is obviously an important issue in respect to the effects of media, and deserves further research.

THEORETICAL CONSIDERATIONS

Before considering the results of experimental studies on the effects of filmed aggression on behavior, some attention should be given to the meaning of the terms "aggression" and "behavior" and to the theoretical bases suggested for the effects.

Though there may be differences in wording or emphasis, many theorists have interpreted aggression as behavior whose goal is the injury of some person or object (Berkowitz, 1962; Kaufmann, 1965; *cf.* Buss, 1961). Such behavior has two defining characteristics: it is directed against an object, and its (primary or subsidiary) intent or purpose is to injure. Obviously, the latter characteristic is the key one distinguishing aggressive behavior from other kinds of directed acts. Though this characteristic is difficult at times to assess and may be underemphasized by some theorists, it seems to be called for in order to exclude from "aggressive behavior" acts which are ordinarily taken to be nonaggressive, though injurious (Feshbach, 1964; Kaufmann, 1965). The punch that is thrown but misses its mark is aggressive behavior, but the accidental collision that knocks someone down or the hard slap to stop hysterical outburst are not ordinarily considered to be.

Of course, the criteria used to determine intent and to define injury have a silent framework of social consensus. That is, what is considered aggressive varies in some respects from one social group to another. Perhaps of greater importance is that not all aggressive behavior is considered socially significant and that social concern varies along an implicit scale of degree of aggressive behavior. However, the concept of aggression in its scientific use is cast so broadly as to encompass a multitude of aggressive acts, even though only some of these, for example, physical aggression against another person, may represent behavior of concern to society. Hence, care must be taken in extrapolating the results of experimental research to the wider, normal social environment and in utilizing them as the basis of social policy.

The general and vague term "behavior" requires some comment. Gross motor acts that can injure physically and which are directed openly at an object are obvious kinds of aggressive behavior. Others that are verbal but which are directed at the intended object and can produce injury in a broad psychological sense, encompassing loss of self-esteem, hurt feelings, etc., may also be counted as aggressive. But beyond these are the wide variety of symbolic acts, for example, drawings of aggressive behavior, that are not directed at the presumed target. To take account of such behavior and also vigorous but nondamaging play with toys, such as hitting a rubber doll, the definition of aggression may require extension to include acts which, if they *were* directed at a person, would be injurious (*cf.* Bandura and Walters, 1963). However, as evidenced by Kaufmann's (1965) argument against including in the concept all acts which cannot conceivably affect the object of the attack, the problem of arriving at an accepted conceptualization is still unresolved.

Without becoming involved in the issue of whether frustration, however defined, inevitably leads to an instigation to aggression, we may note that some instigating condition has been postulated in all explanations. Current thinking (see Berkowitz, 1962; Buss, 1961) has interposed the emotion of anger between the antecedent condition interpreted as some kind of frustration and the instigation toward aggression. If anger is not aroused, then aggressive tendencies need not be evoked. Of course, aggression may be elicited as an answer to aggression, even in the absence of anger; and aggression may be used instrumentally as a means of attaining some desired object. But the important point is that some motivation instigates a tendency toward aggression. Whether this tendency will be realized in actual aggressive behavior, and what kind of aggressive behavior it will be realized in, depend on a number of factors. Among these are the strength of the instigating motivation, the strength of the forces opposing the expression of aggression, the place of aggression in the behavior repertoire associated with frustration or anger, the presence of stimuli associated with the frustrator, and knowledge of suitable aggressive behavior.

In respect to the effects of filmed violence, these factors have received differential emphasis by different researchers. The learning of new aggressive responses or the shaping of new patterns of aggressive behavior by the observation of media-portrayed violence has been proposed by Bandura (1962) as an effect that is greater than the media's direct influence on an instigation toward aggression. Others (for example, Berkowitz, 1964a; Walters, 1966) have given greater weight to the effects of the media on forces inhibiting aggression. These inhibitors may stem from inner restraints or from environmental forces. If in socialization the child is punished for aggression or is taught, by withdrawal of rewards, to control his aggressive tendencies, then the arousal of an instigation to aggression may elicit anxiety or concern and thereby inhibit the expression of aggression. Similarly, anticipation of punishment or of the loss of desired satisfactions may evoke restraints against aggressive behavior. Hence, the extent to which media-portrayed aggression influences these restraining forces, by suggesting that aggression is permissible or desirable or the opposite, will modulate the likelihood that aggressive behavior will be shown (Walters, 1966). The importance of the restraining forces is a theme that runs through much of the experimental work on the effects of filmed violence. However, the carry-over effect of the media experience is also presumed to depend on the associated similarity between the justified target of the vicariously realized aggression and the actual object of the observer's own aggressive inclinations (Berkowitz, 1964a, 1964b, 1965b; Berkowitz and Geen, 1966).

In the original formulation of the frustration-aggression hypothesis (Dollard *et al.*, 1939), it was proposed that not only may an instigation to aggression issue in a variety of aggressive responses each of which may satisfy the instigation, but the occurrence of aggressive behavior will reduce the likelihood of additional acts of aggression. This is the hypothesis of the equivalence of forms of aggression. Its application to the effects of filmed violence requires the assumption that viewing such behavior has the same psychological function as the active production of fantasy aggression. For this to occur, the viewer must become vicariously involved in the aggression through identification with the aggressor or by virtue of the similarity between the victim and the person's actual object of aggression. In addition, fantasy aggression must constitute for the viewer a satisfactory substitute or equivalent for the aggressive behavior he would prefer to exhibit. This latter requirement is contained in Berkowitz' (1964a) proposal that an instigation to aggression sets up a "completion" tendency, involving a suitable response directed at the desired object of aggression. On the assumption that fantasy aggression does not "complete" aggressive motivation, Berkowitz proposed that catharsis is not likely to occur through vicarious participation in aggression. In his view, evidence of purported catharsis through media experience may represent the effects of temporary distraction or diversion from thinking about aggression against an instigator, the induction of a pleasant mood by an entertaining presentation, or an induced increase in inhibitions against the expression of aggression (*cf.* Kaufmann, 1965).

CATHARSIS

Evidence for a cathartic effect of fantasy aggression was obtained by Feshbach (1955) in a study using college students but not employing filmed violence. To instigate anger and a tendency to aggression, the experimenter insulted one group of students by degrading their intellectual capabilities; other students were not insulted. Then half the students wrote stories to TAT cards and half did not. Toward the end of the session, all the students gave evaluative ratings of the experimenter. The comparisons suggested that the insulted students given an opportunity to write TAT stories showed greater aggressiveness in their themes than did their noninsulted counterparts, but less hostility in their evaluations of the insulting experimenter than did the students who were insulted but did not have the opportunity to express aggression in stories.

A later study (Feshbach, 1961) repeated the procedure in its essential outline, but instead of using TAT stories as the mode of fantasy aggression the college students watched a vicious ten-minute prizefight sequence from the movie *Body and Soul*. A neutral film was used in the control condition. Half of each of the film groups had been insulted and half had not. One measure of aggression comprised evaluative ratings of the experimenter. The other was a word-association technique in which a list of intermixed neutral and five aggressive words (for example, "choke," "massacre," "murder") were read to the students, who were asked to write down their associations to each. Feshbach assumed that the perseveration of aroused aggressive motivation would raise the normal frequency of aggressive associations by activating all relevant aggressive response systems. The insulted students who saw the fight film gave fewer hostile responses on both measures than did those who were insulted but saw the neutral film. In respect to the noninsulted students, the films had no differential effect on their ratings of the experimenter or production of aggressive associates.

The possibility of a cathartic effect of filmed violence was also investigated by Siegel (1956), who hypothesized that fantasy aggression would reduce the normal level of instigation to acts of aggression. Pairs of nursery school children four to five years old were shown a ten-minute Woody Woodpecker cartoon which displayed "raw aggression and unrelenting hostility" in almost every scene, or a nonaggressive cartoon for the same period of time. Then each pair was taken *together* into another room and permitted to play for 14 minutes with no adult present. The room contained a variety of toys, including two rubber daggers and a large child-size punching toy. An observer watching through a one-way mirror recorded the children's behavior. The children exposed to the aggressive cartoon exhibited slightly but not significantly less rated anxiety/guilt in play than did the group which saw the nonaggressive cartoon. But no evidence was found of either a cathartic or a stimulating effect of watching fantasy aggression.

In research with five- to eight-year-old children, Feshbach (1956) also found no evidence of a cathartic effect. Children who on four occasions listened to a record and a story and then played with "aggressive" toys, all of which pertained to a given theme (for example, soldiers or cowboys), did not show less theme-unrelated aggressive behavior in play or in the classroom than did children whose themes and toys were nonaggressive. In fact, boys who were rated initially as less aggressive in the classroom than other boys exhibited a slight increase in aggressive behavior as a result of play with the aggressive toys. This was not true for the girls. Feshbach conjectured that, for a vicarious or fantasy experience to reduce relevant motivations, a necessary condition is that the related motives be previously aroused and be active during the experience.

Though Gordon and his associates (Gordon and Cohn, 1963; Gordon and Smith, 1965) have not been concerned with a possible cathartic effect of vicarious participation in aggression, their research bears on the effects of stories emphasizing affiliative themes on the subsequent expression of aggressive behavior. They found that children aged three to five showed less aggressive responses in a special doll-play situation after they had been read a story of a lonely dog seeking but not finding any friends to play with, than when they had been read a story of a dog looking for a ball. This differential effect was not exhibited by six- to seven-year-olds, whom the authors conjectured may not have found such stories convincing.

STIMULATION OF AGGRESSION

In an attempt to establish that acceptable aggressive fantasy can produce an increase in aggressive play if the play situation is permissive, Mussen and Rutherford (1961) conducted a study involving the individual testing of six- to seven-year-old children. Half were frustrated by their teacher by being made to work on a monotonous task and by being criticized for their performance; half were not frustrated. Then one-third of each group saw an "aggressive" film, a nonaggressive film, or no film. The aggressive film was an eight-minute cartoon in which an animated weed tried to choke a flower while a panda bear attempted to destroy the weed. After viewing the film, the child was given the following test of "aggression": an inflated balloon was held by the tester, who asked the child a set of five questions concerning whether or not the child would want to see the tester "pop" the balloon. The child's "popping" score, which was taken as the index of aggressive inclinations, was the number of times a "yes" answer was given. The data indicated that the frustrating procedure had no significant effect on the "popping" score, though the frustrated children were adjudged by the tester to be more "tense" than the nonfrustrated children. Regardless of whether they were frustrated or not, the children who had seen the aggressive cartoon had a significantly higher "popping" score than did the other children. Mussen and Rutherford attributed the heightened "popping" score to a film-induced reduction in inhibition of expression of aggression.

Berkowitz and Rawlings (1963) conjectured that Feshbach's (1961) results may have been due to the arousal of aggression anxiety by the film itself. That is, the punishing fight shown in the movie scene may have produced anxiety which inhibited the free expression of aggression, thus leading to what appeared to be a cathartic effect of the film experience. (Such a possibility does not seem particularly relevant to the data based on aggressive response associates.) On this line of reasoning, the investigators supposed that filmed violence would stimulate aggressive behavior if the depicted aggression were presented as justified. Justification should prevent the development of aggression anxiety by implying that it is acceptable to be hostile to a person who deserves such treatment, though not actually condoning such behavior (Walters, 1966). This would free the viewer to aggress against his own tormentor. In a test of these suppositions, half of a group of college students were insulted by an experimenter, and half were not; then half of each group were given a questionnaire on their attitude toward the insulting experimenter. Following this, all were shown a brief scene from the movie *Champion* in which the champion takes a fearful, unrelenting beating from the challenger during the fight. Immediately prior to seeing the scene, a brief synopsis of the story up to the point of the scene was read to the students. Half were led to believe that the champion was an incorrigible, remorseless scoundrel; and half, that he had recognized the injustice of his past behavior and was turning over a new leaf. The former condition is referred to as the "justified" aggression treatment, and the latter as the "less justified" one. After viewing the film, all the students responded to a questionnaire containing two items testing their attitude toward the insulting experimenter; this was the measure of aggression. The justification manipulation had no effect on the responses of the students who had not been insulted. Only among those insulted students who did not state their appraisal of the insulting experimenter before seeing the film, and only on one of the two post-movie attitude items, did the justified-aggression synopsis lead to a less favorable response than did the less-justified-aggression synopsis. Less sympathy for the champion was evidenced by those who had been given the justified-aggression synopsis than by the other students, but this difference was exhibited primarily by the insulted students.

A study by Berkowitz, Corwin, and Hieronymous (1963) was essentially a replication of the previous one, with the addition of a neutral film group. It yielded a similar pattern of results. Only among the insulted students and only on one attitude item (the same one that yielded the difference in the previous study) did the students given the justified-aggression synopsis respond less favorably toward the insulting experimenter than did the other students.

In further research, Berkowitz (1964b, 1965a) changed the measure of aggression to the number and duration of electric shocks given another person. College students were tested in pairs, only one of whom was a naive or true subject, the other being a confederate of the experimenter. Half the students were insulted by the confederate during the early part of the session, and half were not. Shortly after seeing either the fight scene from *Champion* or a neutral film on canal boats, the real subject was asked to rate the quality of the confederate's solution to a problem concerning the design of the floor plan of an apartment; all students were given the same floor plan as the purported work of the other person. Instead of a verbal or written rating, the student was to give electric shocks to the other person: one shock for the most favorable rating, and increasing numbers of shocks for less and less favorable ratings. Essentially, then, the student was not merely permitted to shock the other person but *required* to do so in order to indicate his rating of the floor plan. All students tested during one college semester were given the justified-aggression synopsis before the fight scene, and all tested during the following semester were read the less-justified-aggression synopsis. Comparing across semesters, Berkowitz reported that, as in the previous research, the synopses had no differential effect on the shocks given by the noninsulted students; but, among the insulted students, more shock aggression (approximately one shock more) was delivered by the students who had the justified-aggression synopsis than by those given the less-justified-aggression synopsis.

In none of the prior investigations was there any similarity or connection between the insulter and the fighter who received a beating. If they could be linked, then, catharsis theory might lead one to expect a reduction in postfilm aggression against the insulter. However, Berkowitz conjectured that the result would be, not catharsis, but an increase in aggression against the insulter; this prediction is based on the assumptions that catharsis is unlikely to be produced by fantasy aggression and that witnessing a beating to a person who resembles one's own tormentor may reduce aggression anxiety, thereby permitting a freer expression of aggression. In research to test these expectations (Berkowitz, 1964b, 1965a), students were told that the coworker was a "college boxer" or a "speech major." Half of them were insulted by the coworker and half were not insulted; half were shown the fight scene, and half the neutral film on canal boats. By itself, type of film had no differential effect on aggressive behavior. When the students were not insulted, the "boxer" received more shock aggression than did the "speech major"; but when they were insulted, there was no difference in aggressive behavior due merely to the labeling of the confederate. However, among the insulted students, greater aggression was shown when the confederate was identified as a "boxer" *and* the fight film was viewed than when the neutral film was seen or, regardless of the film watched, the confederate was identified as a "speech major." In a sense, the first-named group was the "odd" one among the four receiving the insulting treatment. The data offer no support for any expectation of a catharsis effect.

Essentially comparable results were obtained when the justified-aggression synopsis was used *and* when the tormenting confederate was given the same first name as the well-known movie star who played the role of the champion (Berkowitz and Geen, 1966) or the same last name as the champion in the film (Berkowitz, 1965b). However, when the confederate's name was different, exposure to the fight film, even when the justified-aggression synopsis was used, did not produce an increase in shock aggression beyond that exhibited by angered subjects exposed to an exciting but nonaggressive film; nor was there a difference between the subjects given the "justified" versus the "less justified" film synopsis, when the confederate's name was different. These results are not comparable to those obtained previously by Berkowitz and Rawlings (1963), Berkowitz, Corwin, and Hieronymous (1963), or Berkowitz (1964b, 1965a). In sum, a slight but significant increase in shock aggression is found when a particular conjunction of conditions occurs: an angered subject witnesses a justified beating given to someone who bears some role- or name-mediated resemblance to his own tormentor. However, the experimental arousal of anger alone produces a greater increase in shock aggression against the tormenting confederate than did exposure to the fight film or the symbolically mediated resemblance between the champion in the film and the confederate.

Only in the study by Mussen and Rutherford (1961) is there any presumed evidence (the "popping" score) that the mere viewing of filmed aggression stimulated aggressive behavior. Yet social concern regarding the effects of filmed violence does indicate a belief that such effects can occur.

Research by Walters and his associates (Walters, Thomas, and Acker, 1962; Walters and Thomas, 1963) provides some indication of a stimulating effect of observing filmed violence, even though there are no evident differences reflecting *theoretically* based expectations between their research and the noninsult conditions of the previous studies. People were told that they were participating in a learning study concerned with the effects of punishment by electric shock for errors. On a series of 30 trials, the "learner," who was in reality a confederate of the experimenter, made 15 errors and received 15 shocks at levels determined by the real subject, who acted as the "teacher." Then, during a recess period, the "learner" and "teacher" watched a scene from the movie *West Side Story*, which depicted a knife fight between two adolescents, or watched a neutral film showing adolescents engaged in a cooperative activity. Immediately afterwards, 30 more learning trials were completed, on 15 of which an error was made by the "learner." The difference between the levels of shock used before and after viewing the film was taken as evidence of the effects of the film. The results of both studies are comparable: compared to the people who saw the neutral film, those exposed to the knife fight scene showed a significant increase in the level of shock delivered to the learner when errors were made; on the average, the difference was half a setting higher. Hence, the pattern of data is consistent with the interpretation that the filmed violence stimulated aggressive motivations or aggressive response tendencies and that this aroused aggressiveness was manifested in permissive aggression against another person. If this is so, then the sheer display of violence does not have an inhibiting effect, as Berkowitz (1964b) suggested in his interpretation of Feshbach's (1961) data. Also, it is a moot question whether the subjects in the research by Walters and his associates supposed that the knife fight involved justified aggression.

Other research purporting to demonstrate the aggression-stimulating effect of exposure to filmed aggression is reported by Lovaas (1961). Preschool children four to six years old were used in a series of three experiments. In all the studies, the putative measure of aggressiveness was the frequency with which the child operated a toy that caused one doll figure to strike another with a stick every time a lever was depressed. The children saw either a cartoon in which one humanlike figure aggressed almost continuously against another, or a cartoon depicting pleasant play between bear cubs and a mother bear. In the first study, the sequence of film followed by doll play was repeated three times, once on each of three days; in the second, the sequence occurred only once. But in both studies, the children were permitted to play with the toy for a maximum of two minutes. In neither study did the aggressive cartoon produce a higher frequency of aggressive play than did the nonaggressive cartoon. The third study employed the same children used in the second experiment, with each child exposed to the film not seen previously. But now two toys were available: the doll toy and a ball toy. The children could play with both toys for a maximum of four minutes. However, they *had* to begin with the doll toy; and if they had not shifted to the ball toy at the end of two minutes, they were reminded that they could play with the other toy. The children who saw the aggressive cartoon played approximately equally long with each of the two toys, while the other group played less with the doll toy than with the ball toy. Since a four-minute play limit had been set, the former group must have played more with the "aggressive" toy and less with the "nonaggressive" one than did the latter group. The author and others have interpreted the data of the third experiment as indicating that aggressive behavior was stimulated by the aggressive cartoon.

In what was essentially a replication of Lovaas' third experiment, Larder (1962) found that an "aggressive" story increased the relative frequency of responding to the doll.

IMITATION OF AGGRESSIVE BEHAVIOR

In the research considered so far, the behavior taken as the measure of effect was in no instance similar in form to that displayed in the films or the story. Yet the learning of specific acts of aggression is often suggested as an effect of exposure to media violence. Bandura and his associates (Bandura and Huston, 1961; Bandura, Ross, and Ross, 1961, 1963) have focused their research on this behavioral consequence of observed violence. In order to establish that the exhibited acts were modeled after those displayed by another, they utilized novel responses, that is, behavior which is not in the repertoire of the observer or not likely to be exhibited without a demonstration by a model. Since the learning of such behavior does not itself lead to and is not aroused by exposure to displayed aggressiveness, it is referred to as incidental learning. Within the context of the research, no distinction is made between the concepts of identification and imitation. Since the evidence for both would be matching behavior or the degree of similarity between the model's acts and those exhibited afterwards by the observer, Bandura (1962) accepted the equivalence of the two concepts. This avoids the problems of the motivation of the behavior and of obtaining evidence concerning the occurrence of any special psychological relationship or process considered to be a necessary discriminator between identification behavior and mere imitative behavior.

Bandura and Huston (1961) demonstrated that preschoolers will imitate the nonfunctional behavior of an adult model in addition to matching the model's discrimination choice. The nonfunctional responses comprised the style of marching to the discrimination boxes, verbalizations made while marching, and striking a doll set on the lid of the discrimination box. The latter behavior was designated "aggressive" by the authors. When the model displayed these behaviors, so did the children. Whether the children did or did not have a nurturant experience with the model prior to the discrimination phase of the session had no influence on imitation of aggressive behavior toward the doll. But the prior nurturant experience increased the imitation of all nonfunctional acts. Since the doll was physically associated with the discrimination box and striking the doll occurred just before the discrimination choice, the children may have associated that act with the choice itself. The nurturant experience might have had a differential effect on the imitation of the aggressive behavior if a doll had been struck during the march of the model toward the discrimination box.

Later published studies by Bandura and his associates used the following paradigm: preschool children observed an adult model aggress against a large, standing, rubber toy (Bobo doll) which rebounded after being struck; then the children were frustrated by not being permitted to play with some interesting toys; and finally, children and frustraters went into another room containing a variety of toys including a Bobo doll, where observations were made of the children's play behavior during a 20-minute period. Bandura, Ross, and Ross (1961) compared the effects of a live model who struck the doll, hit it with a mallet, threw it up in the air, sat upon it, and accompanied some of the behavior with suitable aggressive verbalizations, with a model who worked constructively and quietly with another toy in the child's presence. A control group of children who were not exposed to any model was also included. The major effect of the aggressive model was to increase significantly imitation of aggressive behavior toward the Bobo toy; other kinds of aggressive acts which were not imitations of the model's behavior were also increased, but not significantly; hence, it appears that these children were less inhibited in general. The children exposed to the nonaggressive model showed less aggressive behavior than did the children who had not observed any model. Also, boys were more aggressive than girls when the aggressive model was male, particularly in regard to such sex-typed behavior as attacking the Bobo toy; the girls were more likely than the boys to sit on the toy rather than pummel it. (The latter data bear a similarity to those reported by Maccoby and Wilson, 1957, concerning the differential retention of film content by seventh-grade boys and girls.)

A further study by Bandura, Ross, and Ross (1963) tested the supposition that the likelihood or extent of imitation of aggressive behavior would be positively related to the degree of reality inherent in the demonstration of the behavior. The order of effectiveness of models should be: live adult > filmed adult model > filmed fantasy character. The data concerning the effects of the live model were taken from the previous study by the authors. A film of the behavior of the live aggressive model was made and shown to some of the children used in this study. The filmed fantasy character was the female model dressed as a black cat, who exhibited the same aggressive behavior and made appropriate catlike sounds while she did so. All the experimental groups showed more aggressive behavior than did the controls, particularly in regard to attacks against the Bobo toy. The groups exposed to a model, whether live, filmed, or fantasy, were not particularly different from each other; however, in opposition to the authors' preresearch expectations, the children who observed the filmed adult model displayed more aggressive behavior than did the others. Play with a gun, which was included among the toys in the playroom, was somewhat greater among the children who had seen film models than among those who had watched the live model. (Since the live-model condition was drawn from the earlier study, Hartley, 1964, suggested that this difference may reflect a change in "play culture" occurring during the period between the two studies.) As in the previous study, the style of aggressive play was affected by the relation between the sex of the child and the sex of the model. For instance, though the boys exhibited more aggressive behavior than did the girls, the girls were more likely than the boys to sit on the Bobo toy; and the greatest difference in gun play occurred between boys exposed to a male model and girls exposed to a female model. Degree of characteristic aggression anxiety, as evidenced by ratings of the children's behavior in the nursery school, was not related to aggressiveness in the experimental test situation. Bandura, Ross, and Ross interpreted these two studies as evidence that observing aggressive behavior can stimulate and also shape the form of aggressive behavior, even in normal children.

Imitation of a model's behavior is likely to be affected by whether the model is rewarded or punished for the actions. While learning of the behavior may not be affected, in the sense of knowing and remembering what was done and being able to carry out the behavior if required or motivated to do so, performance of the behavior is likely to be influenced by anticipated reinforcements or incentives. This should be true so long as the learner expects that imitation in a given situation will attract a reinforcement similar to that experienced by the model. In the previous research on imitation of aggressive models, the model's behavior was not rewarded or punished. At best, the absence of explicit reinforcement may have suggested that the model's behavior was not disapproved or inappropriate, or even that it was acceptable.

The effect of explicit reinforcement was examined in an unpublished study by Bandura, Ross, and Ross (cited in Bandura, 1962). Preschool children saw a film in which two *adult* male models played with children's toys. In one version, the models played vigorously but not aggressively. In another, one model broke up the other's toys and games, aggressed against the other, and at the end, walked out of the room with the toys in a sack—a commentator's voice designated him as the victor. In a third version, the aggressive model was spanked for his aggressive actions by the other model and cowered in apparent fear after the punishment, while the other model took the toys—the commentator remarked on the aggressive model's punishment. A fourth group did not see any film. The play behavior of the children was observed while each was alone in another room which contained many toys, including the aggressive ones used in the film. Significantly more imitative aggressive behavior was exhibited by the children who saw the aggressive model rewarded than by the children in the other conditions. The latter groups did not differ from each other. In posttest interviews, the aggressive model was chosen as the one the children would prefer to emulate by 60 percent of those who had seen him rewarded, by 20 percent of those who had seen him punished, and by no one who had seen the non-aggressive version. The other model was chosen by 5, 20, and 30 percent of these groups, respectively. Evidence that the choice of model was related to the satisfactory, rewarding consequences of his behavior rather than to the intrinsic attractiveness of his behavior was obtained through further questioning of the children, and was manifested in their critical and negative comments about the aggressive model, even though he was their choice as an object of imitation.

The outcomes of this research bear a similarity to Zajonc's (1954) finding that children will select the spaceship leader whose style of leadership is successful, even though a coercive, power-oriented style is used. However, as in that study, a sizable minority of the children do not identify with the character whose behavior, though rewarded, is not ordinarily acceptable. But, in contradistinction, identification with the nonaggressive model was not increased by his success in acquiring the toys.

That learning without performance can occur is manifested in research by Bandura (1965). Punishment of an adult film model for aggression against a Bobo doll reduced children's imitation of the model's aggressive responses; however, unlike the previous research, rewarding the model did not increase imitation of aggressiveness. When the children were offered an incentive to demonstrate the model's responses, the differences between the groups were eliminated, and the usual disparity between boys and girls in their imitation of aggressive behavior was markedly reduced.

That children can recall more of the model's aggressive behavior *vis-à-vis* a Bobo doll than they themselves exhibit is also suggested by data provided by Hicks (1965). In addition, when the film model was a peer, children imitated a boy model more than a girl model; but when the model was an adult, girls were unaffected by the sex of the model, whereas boys tended to imitate the female more than the male. In fact, boys imitated the adult male model least and the male peer most.

It would be expected that the consequences of a model's behavior would affect imitation of other kinds of undesirable acts besides aggressive ones. Walters, Leat, and Mezei (1963) sought to test this expectation in respect to the violation of a warning against playing with certain toys. Kindergartners watched a film in which a child of their age played with the same toys that they themselves had been forbidden to play with. In one version, the child's mother accepts and rewards his play with encouragement and smiles; in the other version, she acts disapprovingly, shaking her finger at the child who drops the toys and shows signs of upset at the rebuke. The only difference between the children who saw the rewarded model play with the toys and a no-film control group was in the latency of the first deviation; the former touched one of the forbidden toys sooner than did the latter. The model-punished group deviated fewer times than did the control group, revealing inhibition of deviant behavior. The two film groups differed on all measures of deviant behavior in the expected direction. Evidence that seeing a model rewarded facilitated transgression of a prohibition is meager at best, being limited only to latency of first deviation.

It is worth noting that the children had the choice of touching and handling the toys which were set in front of them or doing nothing, until the experimenter returned, for the room was bare of nonforbidden playthings. Hartley (1964) suggested that the data support more strongly an assumption that the display of negative consequences of violating the prohibition increased the force of the prohibition.

In further research with young children, Walters, Parke, and Cane (1965) turned up relatively comparable results. Essentially, children watched a film in which a child model was forbidden by his mother to play during her absence with toys that were on a table, but instead was told to read a book which she gave him. However, the model disobeyed, and the mother, on her return, either approved (in one version), reproved (in another), or made no comment concerning his disobedient behavior (in the third). Afterwards, all the children in the study, whether they had or had not seen one of the three film versions, were placed in a situation similar to that of the film model; that is, the female experimenter gave them a dictionary to read during her absence from the room and warned them not to play with toys placed on a table. The children exposed to the model-punished version waited longer than the other film groups before disobeying, and played less with the toys. The latter two groups were not different from the no-film group. Consequently, the results support Hartley's conjecture, noted above, rather than any interpretation that approval of the model's disobedience produced more ready disobedience on the part of the children in the research, even though the filmed and the actual setting and circumstances were very similar.

SUMMARY AND COMMENTARY

In view of the implications for public policy and the wider generalizations that have been drawn from the research on the effects of media violence, it seems desirable to sum up the outcomes of the studies and to suggest research gaps and controversial points of interpretation.

Catharsis. Evidence for the cathartic reduction of aggressive motivation through vicarious participation in aggression is meager, at best. Only the study by Feshbach (1961) offers any support to such an expectation, but the results of Berkowitz' research (1964a, 1964b) are inconsistent with it. The hypothesis of the equivalence of forms of aggression is the primary theoretical basis for predicting catharsis. But this hypothesis says little about the effect of witnessed aggression on a viewer's inclination to aggress. If the other person functions as a surrogate, in the sense that the viewer identifies with him and psychologically experiences the aggression as a proper expression of his own motivation, then the hypothesis should predict a cathartic reduction in inclination to aggress. But none of the studies purporting to test the cathartic hypothesis, or for that matter any of the research discussed, has established evidence of such an identifying involvement with the aggressor.

Also, for the hypothesis to apply, the object of the fantasy aggression should bear some similarity to the desired object of aggression. Again, only in the research by Berkowitz (1964a, 1964b, 1965b) and Berkowitz and Geen (1966), in which symbolic mediation is the basis for the similarity, can this requirement be said to have even been approached, and in these studies catharsis was not found. However, it would be expected that, if both the object and the response are substitutes, the cathartic effect of the fantasy aggression should be minimal, if it occurs at all.

Finally, none of the research has obtained independent evidence concerning the degree to which various kinds of aggressive responses are deemed to be similar to each other. Lack of such knowledge prevents a more precise test of a catharsis hypothesis, even if other requirements are met. Knowing what kind of aggressive response, *if any*, would be the natural or desirable one for the aroused person to make would be helpful in devising or interpreting relevant research. For instance, a person who is angry enough to want to physically attack his tormentor may consider a vicious boxing match an equivalent and satisfying substitute, if the tormentor is seen as the beaten participant in the match, and be cathartically relieved by it; on the other hand, one whose anger would lead only to strong verbal aggression may consider a physical beating a nonequivalent substitute psychologically.

Stimulation of aggression. At best, most of the research suggests that, under certain circumstances, observation of filmed violence may lead to *what the researchers call aggressive behavior*. For instance, prior instigation to aggression is associated with greater aggressiveness toward a frustrater when (1) the intervening fantasy aggression is presented as deserving *and* (2) an associative connection exists between the *victim* of the witnessed aggression and the frustrater *and* (3) some magnitude of a noxious stimulus must be given (Berkowitz, 1965b; Berkowitz and Geen, 1966). Or the imitation of *novel* aggressive responses is greater when (1) the witnessing of aggression is followed by a frustrating experience and (2) the behavior is "normal" for the sex of the model or the viewer (Bandura, Ross, and Ross, 1961, 1963), or the model's behavior is not punished (Bandura, 1962, 1965).

In addition, external as well as internal barriers to expressing aggression should be minimal. Even those researchers (for example, Berkowitz, 1964a) who interpret their results as evidence of a potentially dangerous social effect of witnessing violence acknowledge that the absence of aggressive outbursts following exposure to media violence in the natural environment is due to the inhibiting controls emanating from the environment or from within the individual. In all the studies, the testing situation is designed to give the impression that aggression is permissible if not encouraged; in the shock studies, aggression is required and only the degree of aggression can vary. And it is only under this circumstance that there are any data suggesting that the mere viewing of filmed violence alone may increase the self-expressed display of aggressive behavior (Walters, Thomas, and Acker, 1962; Walters and Thomas, 1963). Yet Lovaas (1961) found that requiring play solely with an "aggressive" toy was insufficient to reveal a significant effect of viewing fantasy aggression; for a difference to be demonstrated, it was necessary to compel children to play with "aggressive" *and* "nonaggressive" toys. However, in view of Siegel's (1956) data, it would seem that, when the requiredness of play with designated toys is eliminated, the prior viewing of filmed aggression need not have an aggression-stimulating effect.

Meaning of the behavior. A central question to be considered is the propriety of referring to the responses used in the research as aggressive behavior. It has already been pointed out that injury is taken as the goal of a response which is labeled "aggressive," but that some writers (for example, Bandura, 1962) extend the concept to include responses which, *if* directed at an object, would injure. Since goal implies purpose or motivation and in this context it refers to *intent* to hurt, there should be reasonable evidence of such intent. Epstein (1962) has criticized Bandura for failing to consider the motivation for the imitation and for focusing exclusively on the mere fact of imitation. Even data revealing the arousal of anger or an instigation to aggress would be of value in this regard. But rarely have the studies sought or provided any valid evidence of such motivation. This lack applies not only to the research in which arousal, if it were to occur, would be due solely to the stimulating effect of the media violence, but also to the research in which an insult or a frustration experience was part of the procedure.

Implicit in the foregoing is the importance of determining the meaning of the responses to the subjects. This potentially illuminating information, which could aid in distinguishing between alternative interpretations, has not been obtained in any of the studies. Even an increase in shock need not be evidence of an increase in aggression nor signify the freer expression of aggression. In the studies by Walters and his associates (Walters, Thomas, and Acker, 1962; Walters and Thomas, 1963), there is no information about what the people thought was the function of shock as a "teaching" device, or about why any given level was used or why the level was changed within the prefilm or postfilm trials.

In respect to the research with children, Hartley (1964) suggested that "aggression" may mean a way of handling toys designed for that kind of handling. Also, the children exposed to the aggressive adult model who attacked the Bobo toy may have assumed that they were being shown the play behavior appropriate to this kind of toy and perhaps required in the situation.

More generally, there is a total lack of information concerning the subjects' definitions of the experimental situations and the meanings or interpretations they gave to the movie or the behavior of the models, or concerning their reactions during the observation of the model or the movie. In the absence of such knowledge, and in view of the fact that the fight scenes are out of their normal context and the disordered behavior of the adult model was given no rationale, any facile assumption about the viewers' reactions and interpretations should be viewed with considerable caution.

Subjects. Much of the research is based on college students and preschool children. In only one study have teenagers been used (Walters and Thomas, 1963). Yet inferences are drawn which are said to apply to exposure to media violence in ordinary settings and to children between the preschool and adult years. Discussions of the adverse effects of media violence usually focus on just this neglected range of years. Concern is not so often expressed about effects on preschoolers or on normal adults.

Bandura, Ross, and Ross (1963) have asserted that their research reveals that even normal children can be stimulated to aggression by observing aggressive behavior. To establish a more useful form of such an assertion, comparisons would be required among children who vary in some attribute relevant to what is meant by normality. Within the theoretical framework accepted by most researchers, an important characteristic of people which would be related to their responsiveness to such stimuli is the degree of their normal aggressiveness, or the ease of arousal of aggressive motivation, or the likelihood of a display of aggression when aggressively aroused. Comparisons among people differing in these attributes would not only be informative but would provide evidence relevant to interpretations of the effect of observing media violence. None of the research employing filmed aggression has any data on such factors, except for Siegel's (1956) finding that aggressive behavior in the test situation following exposure to an aggressive cartoon was associated positively with rated aggression in nursery school (rho = 0.68 for attacking others physically, rho = 0.56 for destroying others' property). However, in the study by Bandura, Ross, and Ross (1963), rated aggression anxiety in the nursery school was not related to aggressive play in the test situation.

Control group. Except for some of the research on imitation of a model's behavior, most of the studies lacked a control group which did not see a film. The putative aggressive behavior of such people would have established a baseline for assessing the directions of the effects of the films, as well as their significance. For example, in Feshbach's (1961) study, the "neutral" film might have moved the level of normal aggressive behavior either up or down, with a consequent change in the meaning of the difference between the two film groups; and in Siegel's (1956), both films may have reduced or increased or had no effect on aggressive play behavior. In the research by Walters, Thomas, and Acker (1962) and Walters and Thomas (1963), the neutral movie, by emphasizing cooperativeness, may have restrained a normal increase in shock level from the first 30 trials to the second 30; in fact, these investigators had suggested that Feshbach's (1961) results might be due to the heightening of aggression by the "neutral" film about rumor mongering, on the assumption that rumor mongering represents socially aggressive behavior. Without a suitable no-film control group, such useful and theoretically significant information cannot be obtained.

Cumulative effects. Except for Siegel's (1956) research, none of the experimental studies has examined the cumulative or long-term effects of repeated exposure to displays of aggression. While a single program or movie may have an effect on aggressive behavior, it is likely to be short-lived and of little magnitude. It is in the slow cumulation of effects brought about by voluntary exposure in the normal environment to a variety of programs depicting violence that the media are likely to have an influence on aggressive motivations and behavior. This has been suggested by many investigators (for example, Himmelweit, Oppenheim, and Vince, 1958). In an appearance before a U.S. Senate subcommittee in 1954, Lazarsfeld (1955) pointed out that lack of knowledge concerning the extended effects of media violence is a serious shortcoming in our understanding of media effects and is one of the reasons why so little was known then about the effects of depicted violence on children. The same comment can still be made today, as Lazarsfeld himself implies (1963a).

THE ROLE OF INTERPERSONAL COMMUNICATION

In all of the preceding, whether the analysis has been from the perspective of the media or of the audience, only the formal and impersonal part of the communications environment has been considered. While personal relations have been touched on from time to time, as in the discussion of the social context of exposure or the social uses of the media, the significance of the flow of informal communications and the role of personal influence in the uses and effects of the mass media have not been examined. Yet it is obvious on momentary reflection that a considerable portion of the total communications environment comprises person-to-person messages. These may represent the ingredients of ordinary conversation, the deliberate attempts of one person to influence another, the giving of requested information, advice, or interpretations, the exchange of comments concerning a common communications experience, and so on. Consideration of the significance of such influences will add further complexity to the increasingly complex view of mass media effects.

Literature relevant to the circumscribed treatment to be given here to the contributions of person-to-person communications and their interrelations with formal communications may be found in the many studies by sociologists, anthropologists, and others concerning the adoption of new agricultural, cultural, and educational practices and concepts. For convenient surveys and extensive lists of references, consult Lionberger (1960), Rogers (1962), Rogers and Smith (1965), and Katz, Levin, and Hamilton (1963). See Katz and Lazarsfeld (1955) for an examination of the relevance of research findings on small groups to the role of personal influence in the natural communications environment. Relevant research on vote decisions will be mentioned here only briefly; a fuller discussion will be presented later in the context of an examination of the role of the media in voting behavior.

OPINION LEADERSHIP

In their study of the 1940 Presidential campaign, Lazarsfeld, Berelson, and Gaudet (1948) reported that candidate preferences and vote decisions, particularly among the late deciders, were dominated more by active personal influence and face-to-face communications than by the mass media. Coupled with this was the finding that, on an average day, 10 percent more people claimed to have engaged in conversations than reported exposure to political communications through the mass media. Primarily as a result of such evidence, the authors conjectured that ideas and information conveyed by the mass media, instead of impinging directly on the general public, or at least on those who would normally become aware of them, often reach the attentive and concerned segment of the public first and are then transmitted by these "opinion leaders" to others who are less actively interested. This conception, formulated as a hypothesis of a two-step flow of communications, brought to prominence the role of opinion leaders in the total process and effects of mass communications.

What the concept essentially points to is that people are often influenced by others explicitly or implicitly, rather than directly or simply by the mass media; hence, as Katz and Lazarsfeld (1955, p. 133) put it, "knowledge of an individual's interpersonal environment is basic to an understanding of his exposure and reactions to the mass media." These investigators also made clear that the type of personal influence referred to by the concept is one which derives naturally from the informal personal relations that exist in ordinary living. They wrote (p. 138): "What we shall call opinion leadership, if we may call it leadership at all, is leadership at its simplest: it is casually exercised, sometimes unwitting and unbeknown, within the smallest grouping of friends, family members, and neighbors. It is not leadership on the high level of a Churchill, nor of a local politico; it is the almost invisible, certainly inconspicuous form of leadership at the person-to-person level of ordinary, intimate, informal, everyday contact."

The particular effectiveness that informal communications may have lies in the personal relationship binding the participants and in the face-to-face quality of the interaction. A number of specific characteristics have been noted by Lazarsfeld, Berelson, and Gaudet (1948) and by Hovland (1948). The communication process can be timed for propitious occasions and repeated, if necessary; attention is assured and miscomprehension can be minimized; appeals can be developed to fit the salient motivations and characteristics of the recipient; objections can be countered and arguments elaborated or strengthened; regard for the communicator deriving from the personal relationship will lend weight to his words; the benefits of social conformity and maintaining a satisfactory personal relationship may act as incentives to acceptance of the communication. In many instances, the process is initiated by a desire for information or advice; under such circumstances, the initiator is motivated to be influenced and is likely to be influenced.

Some of these characteristics are not inherently unattainable by the mass media. For instance, attempts have been made to increase the flexibility of the broadcast media and to give them a person-to-person quality, for example, by permitting telephone conversations between members of home audiences and participants in a political broadcast or discussion program. Schramm (1964) mentioned that, in Jordan, radio is used to answer farmers' questions on the specific everyday problems they face; thereby the contents of programs are knowingly fitted to the salient interests of the audience. Many have speculated that televised presentations invite a sense of intimacy and establish a more personal relationship with the performers.

ASSESSMENT OF OPINION LEADERSHIP

Since none of the studies of opinion leaders has been concerned with an examination of acts of opinion leadership at the time they occur, the methods of assessment have depended on techniques of nomination or self-designation. People have been asked whom they go to for advice and information about some matter or whom they discuss certain topics with; or informants may be asked to designate the influential persons in a group. Self-designation may take the form of inquiring whether a respondent has been asked for advice recently on some topic, or how the respondent feels he compares with his friends in regard to the relative frequency with which his advice is sought. Some degree of overlap appears between the names turned up as opinion leaders by different methods of assessment (Coleman, Katz, and Menzel, 1957; Rogers and Cartano, 1962; Troldahl and Van Dam, 1965); also, Katz and Lazarsfeld (1955) found that respondents' assertions about instances of influence were quite often confirmed by the person named as a participant in the influence relation.

OPINION LEADERS' SOURCES OF INFORMATION AND INFLUENCE

In the context of the two-step hypothesis, the opinion leader would be expected to be more highly exposed to the mass media and to other formal sources of information. Katz and Lazarsfeld (1955) found that women who were opinion leaders in one of the four areas they studied (marketing, fashion, public affairs, and movies) read more magazines or books than did the nonleaders. In addition, they were more likely to read a type of magazine relevant to their area of leadership (for example, a movie or fashion magazine for these areas, or a national news weekly for public affairs) than were the nonleaders. However, in comparison with nonleaders, only the fashion leaders were more likely to mention the media as a source of influence in respect to a recent change or decision. Other studies have turned up similar evidence that those taken to be opinion leaders are more exposed to relevant media content, to technical or formal professional communications, or to commercial sources of information

(Emery and Oeser, 1958; Katz, 1961; Lionberger, 1960; Menzel and Katz, 1955; Rogers, 1962).

Stycos (1965) has suggested using this characteristic of opinion leaders in the service of a government program on family planning. In the villages of Turkey, the political leader is more likely to own and use a radio than is the religious leader, and is more favorable than the religious leader to the concept and practice of family planning. For both of these reasons, but particularly because of his greater accessibility to formal communications via radio, Stycos recommended that the political leader rather than the religious leader be made the channel of influence for winning popular acceptance of family planning.

Though opinion leaders attend more to the mass media, they are also more in contact with other opinion leaders or "experts." Katz and Lazarsfeld (1955) reported that, in comparison with nonleaders, public affairs opinion leaders were less likely to mention the media as the source of a recent change in opinion and more likely to name personal influence. Also, women who knew someone who was generally knowledgeable about public affairs were more likely to be influential themselves than were those who could not furnish the name of a well-informed person. Furthermore, in comparison with the original sample of women, more than twice as many of the people named as generally knowledgeable knew someone who was also very knowledgeable (50 percent versus 22 percent). When the nominees of these knowledgeable women were interviewed, the percentage who could name other like persons increased to 66; and when this third set of nominees was interviewed, the percentage rose to 80. Similarly, studies of the adoptions of innovations by farmers and doctors have shown that people who are earlier than most others in adopting the new item are more likely than the others to be in contact with technically competent or knowledgeable professionals (Coleman, Katz, and Menzel, 1957; Menzel and Katz, 1955; Rogers, 1962). Troldahl and Van Dam (1965) reported that people who claimed that their views had been sought on recent public affairs topics were more likely than nonclaimants to report having also asked others for their opinions on such topics.

SOME SOCIAL CHARACTERISTICS OF OPINION LEADERS

Opinion leaders are found on all social levels, with some variation depending on the area of leadership. Katz and Lazarsfeld (1955) found little variation in the percentages of opinion leaders on each of three social status levels in respect to women's decisions on moviegoing and marketing; the averages over the levels were close to 25 percent. On matters relating to fashion, 16 percent of the low-status women were designated as opinion leaders, compared to 26 percent on the middle and high levels. Public affairs yielded the smallest percentages of women who were opinion leaders, with a steady decline from the highest to the lowest level (19 to 12 to 6 percent). The reduced percentages in respect to public affairs coincides with the reduced interest and involvement of most women in such matters, with men being named as influencing opinions on public affairs by approximately two-thirds of the sample. In a study conducted in Chile, Carter and Sepúlveda (1964) found public affairs opinion leaders to be distributed equally in all walks of life and predominantly male. The latter finding was attributed to the cultural emphasis that men should have opinions on matters of public concern.

Katz and Lazarsfeld (1955) also found that most of those designated as influential were of the same social status as the persons who acknowledged being influenced by them. However, in public affairs there is a stronger tendency than in other areas for the low and middle status levels to be influenced by the high-status group. In studies of the adoption of agricultural innovations (Rogers, 1962), opinion leaders tended to be of somewhat higher socioeconomic status than were nonleaders. A similar finding is reported in research on drug adoption leaders among doctors (Coleman, Katz and Menzel, 1957).

Since opinion influence travels through networks of personal relations, opinion leaders are more likely than nonleaders to be linked sociometrically to others (Coleman, Katz, and Menzel, 1957; Menzel and Katz, 1955) or to be involved in a variety of groups and social activities (Abelson and Rugg, 1958; Katz, 1961; Katz and Lazarsfeld, 1955; Rogers, 1962).

GENERALIZATION OF LEADERSHIP

Katz and Lazarsfeld (1955) found that opinion leadership was limited to a particular area of decision making; the actual percentages of women who were designated as leaders in any two of the three areas of marketing, fashion, and public affairs (movie leadership was excluded) did not exceed what might be expected by chance alone, though chance expectation was exceeded by the percentage of women who were leaders in all three areas. On the basis of a recomputation of the estimates of chance percentages, Marcus and Bauer (1964) suggested that the data of Katz and Lazarsfeld do reveal evidence of generalization of opinion leadership. However, the actual percentages of two-area and three-area leaders were quite small, ranging from 2.4 to 5.1.

Merton (1949) suggested that, in a community which he studied, the opinion leadership of those who were oriented toward the local scene in their commitments seemed to extend over a number of areas, whereas opinion leaders who were more cosmopolitan in orientation were more restricted in their range of influence. He conjectured that the wider latitude of the "local" leaders may be related to the greater heterogeneity of their personal contacts throughout the community.

It is likely that generalization of opinion leadership, as is the case with other kinds of leadership (Carter, 1953), will vary with the extent that there is an intrinsic connection between the knowledge and skills required for leadership in different areas. Emery and Oeser (1958) observed that persons who were influential on agricultural matters were not opinion leaders on local political or community affairs. Wilkening, Tully, and Presser (1962) reported little generalization of leadership in respect to different agricultural innovations, unless the practices were closely interrelated.

There is little to be gained by the pursuit of the gross question of whether leadership is general or specific, or of what kinds of characteristics conduce to the generalization of opinion leadership. The voluminous literature on general studies of leadership (see Gibb, 1954, and Chapter 31 of this *Handbook*) makes it clear that, except for a few characteristics, such as small-group leaders being somewhat more intelligent or more self-confident than nonleaders, the search for generalized traits of leadership without regard for the social situation in which leadership is expressed has been fruitless. This approach has been supplanted by an orientation that emphasizes analyses of situational and social determinants, acts of leadership, and the social definition of roles as a means of illuminating the behavioral meaning and requirements of leadership.

INTEREST AS A CHANNEL FOR INFLUENCE

Katz and Lazarsfeld (1955) noted that, although opinion leaders were quite interested in matters pertaining to their area of leadership, the people whose decisions they influenced were also reasonably interested in the same area. In fact, Katz and Lazarsfeld suggested that access to others who are also interested is a precondition for the realization of opinion leadership. This led them to propose that the flow of influence is from the highly interested to those with somewhat less interest, not to the uninterested. However, in the research on voting by Lazarsfeld, Berelson, and Gaudet (1948), the late deciders who were most susceptible to personal influence were relatively uninterested in the campaign.

Greenberg (1963) reported that conversations between citizens on a local tax bond issue were primarily between those who had children in the public schools or between those who had preschool children. Such people rarely discussed the issue with those without children or with those who no longer had children in the local schools, even though the latter were potential voters. In addition, though both school personnel and lay people were interested in the issue, conversations tended to take place within each group rather than between them; when citizen-educator conversations did occur, they were likely to be motivated by a desire for information by the citizen.

TRANSMISSION OF INFORMATION OR "NEWS"

Katz and Lazarsfeld (1955) and Katz (1957) suggested a distinction between the transmission of information and of influence. Since information can influence, this differentiation relates to whether or not the mediator between the mass media and the general public merely acts as a relay or, in addition, offers judgments and opinions selectively taken from the media or presented as his own views. The former may be designated an "information transmitter," the latter an "influential." Opinion leaders, in the sense in which they have been examined in studies of personal influence, have been considered to be influentials.

However, other research, particularly on the diffusion of news events, has focused on the transmitter. In isolated or backward areas of the world, a person who regularly travels from one locality to another, for example, a salesman or a bus driver, often functions in this way, as does a literate person who reads or reports the news to the illiterates in a village. Such people may act merely to permit others to come into contact with the contents of a mass medium, in the same way that the person who owns the only radio in a village does; or they may be selective in respect to the content or programs they transmit to others (Stycos, 1952). Of relevance to the broader concept of the "gatekeeping" function of information transmitters are studies, for example, of the role of news reporters, editors, and others in determining what appears in newspapers (Carter, 1958; Gieber, 1956; Rosten, 1937; White, 1950).

For a number of years, Dodd and his associates studied the diffusion of messages on civil defense contained in leaflets dropped on American communities from airplanes. Some of the main results and a bibliography of published and unpublished papers are presented in a summary report by Dodd (1958). Along the same lines, DeFleur and Larsen (1958) detailed the outcomes of a major study in which the main variables were the number of leaflets dropped per capita of population and the number of drops made. One general finding was that the spread of information declines from the area of distribution to outlying regions as a function of the distance from the region of the leaflet drop. Also, friendship and familial relations constitute the main channels for diffusion. Passing on the leaflet itself was the primary means by which the message was distributed, but young people under sixteen were more likely to transfer the information by word of mouth than were older people. In research of this kind, the transmitter plays an active role in conveying the information to another person and must be motivated to do so.

The role of motivation in transmitting news is brought out in a study by Festinger, Cartwright, *et al.* (1948) of the spread of a rumor in a housing project. The rumor had it that the initiators and principal supporters of the idea of a project nursery school were Communists. Interviews conducted some six months later with residents of the project revealed that reported awareness of the rumor was directly associated with having friends in the project, having children of nursery school age, and participating in project affairs. However, only the latter characteristic distinguished those who passed on the rumor to someone else from those who did not. The authors supposed that residents who were actively caught up in project affairs were keenly interested in matters relating to the project and not only would be informed of the rumor by others who were aware of their involvement, but would themselves be motivated to pass it along. Somewhat similar findings were reported by Swank (1961), who studied the diffusion of information presented through a sound filmstrip to a selected subgroup of a church congregation.

Other research has been concerned with the spread of information about special news events, for example, Eisenhower's mild stroke in 1957 (Deutschmann and Danielson, 1960), Roosevelt's death (Miller, 1945), Taft's death (Larsen and Hill, 1954), Kennedy's assassination (Greenberg, 1964a; Hill and Bonjean, 1964; Sheatsley and Feldman, 1964), and an event of local interest (Bogart, 1950). Extraordinary occurrences such as Roosevelt's death and Kennedy's assassination were known by more than two out of three people within the first 15 to 30 minutes after they were made public through the media; and 95 percent or more were knowledgeable within the first hour-and-a-half. In respect to the Kennedy assassination, geographical proximity seemed to have played a role in the first half-hour in the diffusion of knowledge of the event; in Dallas, 84 percent had heard the news by this time (Bonjean, Hill, and Martin, 1965), while nationally only 68 percent had (Sheatsley and Feldman, 1965). On the basis of their own and others' research on the spread of awareness of six news items in the first hour-and-a-half after each was announced, Hill and Bonjean (1964) suggested that, in general, the greater the public significance or "news value" of an event, the more rapid the diffusion of knowledge of its occurrence. However, they had no independent measure of news value other than the diffusion rates themselves; and these lead to the questionable implication that the launching of Explorer I, which was not completely unanticipated, was of greater significance to the public than was Eisenhower's stroke.

In respect to Roosevelt's death, 87 percent of a sample of college students learned of it through personal communication (Miller, 1945). But approximately half the general public were first made aware of Kennedy's death through radio or television, and the other half through personal sources (Hill and Bonjean, 1964; Sheatsley and Feldman, 1964). The latter means of communication was much more likely to characterize those who learned relatively late about the occurrence, that is, after the death announcement itself (Greenberg, 1964a). Many who were made aware via personal

TABLE 3

SOURCE OF FIRST EXPOSURE TO A NEWS EVENT (FROM HILL AND BONJEAN, 1964)

News event	Source of first exposure				
	Radio	Tele-vision	News-paper	Inter-personal	Total
Kennedy's assassination	17.0%	25.9%	0.0%	57.1%	100.0%
Roosevelt's death	11.2	0.0	1.4	87.4	100.0
Launching of Explorer I	23.0	41.0	18.0	18.0	100.0
Eisenhower's stroke	32.0	38.0	12.0	18.0	100.0
Alaskan statehood	27.0	29.0	38.0	6.0	100.0
Eisenhower's decision to seek a second term	39.0	14.0	27.0	20.0	100.0
Taft's death	48.8	14.6	10.6	26.0	100.0

sources turned to the broadcast media for further news. Greenberg (1964a) remarked that, since formal and informal sources were operating efficiently, the news of the assassination diffused very rapidly.

Obviously, the more diverse and numerous the channels of communication, the more rapidly and completely will news spread through a population. In contrast to the rates of diffusion of major news events in the United States, Schramm (1964) reported that several months after the Chinese-Indian clash in the Himalayas only 83 percent of Indian villagers were aware of the fighting; approximately 60 percent of them had been informed by word of mouth. In addition, Schramm noted that, in comparison with a developing country such as Brazil, knowledge of ordinary news items is not markedly different in populous and in rural areas in a country like the United States, with its variety of efficient and widely used news channels.

On the basis of the data presented in Table 3, Hill and Bonjean (1964) suggested that the significance of personal communication as the initial source of awareness increases with the news value of the information, while that of the formal media tends to decline. Furthermore, they suggested that the two-step hypothesis is of greater relevance for news of high than of low value. Deutschmann and Danielson (1960) implied a similar interpretation when they asserted that talking about a news story varies with its significance to people; on this basis, and in contrast to the afore-mentioned judgment of Hill and Bonjean, they set Eisenhower's stroke ahead of Explorer I in news value.

However, Greenberg (1964c) proposed that the frequency of personal commu-nication as the first source of information is greater when news events are of over-whelming importance or, when of little importance to most people, are particularly significant for those who are aware of them and are motivated to transmit them to others. Telephone interviews with people, concerning how they first learned of each of 18 news stories, confirmed a U-shaped relationship between the percentage who claimed awareness of the events and the percentage who said that personal communi-cation was the first source. (The former percentage constituted the measure of personal significance.) However, except for the assassination of Kennedy, a personal source was named by no more than an average of approximately 10 percent for events with similar percentages of awareness; also, the mass media comprised the overwhelming means of first knowledge of 17 of the news stories.

COMPARATIVE EFFECTIVENESS OF PERSONAL INFLUENCE AND MASS MEDIA

In the voting studies, Lazarsfeld, Berelson, and Gaudet (1948) and Berelson, Lazarsfeld, and McPhee (1954) emphasized the role of personal influence in producing the relatively infrequent changes in candidate preferences. But it was in the research by Katz and Lazarsfeld (1955) that an attempt was made to determine the comparative influence of the mass media and opinion leadership on recent decisions concerning marketing, fashion, and moviegoing. On the basis of responses to a series of probing questions, the authors sought to determine what influences impinged on those who admitted to recent changes or decisions in these areas; and in respect to each influence, whether the respondent merely acknowledged exposure to it ("ineffective exposure") or admitted that the source of influence played some part in the decision ("contributory exposure") or claimed that it was the decisive factor in the decision ("effective exposure"). Since these were mutually exclusive categories, the total percentage of women mentioning a particular source as having had something to do with a decision was the sum of the percentages in the three categories. In respect to marketing and fashion changes, a higher percentage of the women (in the neighborhood of a 10-percent difference) mentioned some person as having played some role in the decision that mentioned any single mass medium. (The aggregate percentage for the media combined was not reported; many women did mention more than one type of source.) But as for the choice of movie, almost twice as many people admitted obtaining relevant information from newspapers as named other people as sources of information or influence.

To show the relative influence of a particular source in determining the decision, Katz and Lazarsfeld calculated the percentage of women mentioning a given source who named it as the decisive factor. In each area, this "effectiveness index" was higher for personal contacts than for the media. Principally on this evidence, the authors suggested that personal influence was more effective than exposure to media content.

On the basis of the government's wartime experiences with bond drives, Cartwright (1949) suggested that appeals through the media are not as effective as direct personal solicitation in producing sales. Also, Merton (1946) contended that the seemingly personal relationship Kate Smith established with her radio audience contributed significantly to the effectiveness of her marathon attempt to induce purchases of war bonds.

Katz (1961) reported that approximately 60 percent of a sample of doctors named personal sources as having had decisive influence on their adoption of a new drug, with salesmen being mentioned nearly twice as often as medical colleagues; formal commercial and technical communications were cited by the remaining 40 percent. However, as the last source they were exposed to before deciding to prescribe the drug, colleagues and medical meetings were mentioned by 36 percent of the doctors, commercial and professional publications by 56 percent, and drug salesmen by a bare 5 percent. In regard to the adoption of hybrid seed corn (Ryan and Gross, 1943), half the farmers mentioned neighbors or relatives as the most influential source and 32 percent cited salesmen, while 14 percent named formal media.

The adoption process

Since a decision about some matter is not a discrete event but involves several phases or steps, it might seem that a more sophisticated view of the contributions of formal and informal communications would require an examination of the uses and effectiveness of types of sources in relation to each phase in the decision process. This has been the orientation of rural sociologists who have been concerned with the adoption of agricultural innovations, such as a new type of corn or a new method of farming, whose acceptance and use are spread out in time. In general, five separable though overlapping stages in the total adoption process have been discriminated (Rogers, 1962): (1) awareness concerning the innovation; (2) interest in the innovation, leading to effects on further information seeking or, at least, on the likelihood of self-exposure to additional information; (3) evaluation of the learned information; (4) trial or test of the innovation in the person's own situation; and (5) adoption or a decision on continued and full use of the innovation. As finally adopted, the innovation may be accepted without change, or may be modified to meet local or personal requirements, or may be used in form only rather than being integrated into the life of the individual or group. The length of time required for the total adoption process to run its course or for individual stages to be completed is influenced by many factors (Katz, Levin, and Hamilton, 1963; Rogers, 1962), among which are (1) the nature of the adoption unit required by the innovation, that is, whether it is a single individual (for example, for the purchase of a consumer product) or a group (for example, for the acceptance of a dance), and whether there is individual option after group decision (for example, for group insurance versus fluoridation); (2) the nature of the item, including its "riskiness," cost, and benefits (and the ease with which they can be demonstrated) relative to those of the current practices or conceptions; (3) the ramifications of the innovation in the life of the individual or the group, to the degree that these can be determined in advance; (4) the degree of departure from current practice; and (5) the cultural or personal compatibility of the innovation with respect to the values, attitudes, and motives of the potential adopting unit.

By implication, the stages of the total adoption process, from first awareness to a decision concerning adoption, presumably follow the order in which they have been presented. This arrangement would constitute the sequence expected when a "rational" decision-making process is operating. But there are circumstances involving such conditions as coercion, unusual trust in a change agent, or despair with current practice, where some stages might be omitted or rearranged. Schramm (1964) cited a report which found that in India a decision to adopt an agricultural innovation preceded a proper information-seeking phase, while reassurance concerning the practice and even learning how to put the innovation into effect also took place following adoption.

Research by rural sociologists (Lionberger, 1960; Rogers, 1962) suggests that the importance of impersonal or nonlocal sources of information, including specialized and technical media, technical personnel, salesmen, and governmental personnel, is greatest at the awareness stage of the adoption process. But at the crucial stage of evaluation, face-to-face interchanges involving local sources are most important.

At the other stages there is a mixture or complex interrelationship of sources. Professional change agents have their influence at the trial stage, but principally for early adopters, with whom they tend to communicate.

In respect to drug adoptions, doctors' first awareness of new drugs is also due to nonlocal or impersonal sources, including salesmen, commercial media, and technical communications (Caplow and Raymond, 1954; Katz, 1961). But as previously noted, most doctors name some personal source as being most influential in leading to their use of a drug (Katz, 1961). In addition, Coleman, Katz, and Menzel (1957) found that doctors who are sociometrically integrated within the local medical community, in that they are chosen by several others as friends or as drug advisors or drug discussants, not only adopt a new drug earlier than the nonchosen, but appear to be influenced by other chosen doctors who are already prescribing the drug. These investigators also found that the early spread of adoption depends more on personal relations that involve professional connections and bring into play technical competence than on friendship relations, whereas, after a time, friendship relations become more significant as the channel for the flow of influence. Those who are reached by neither channel and still have not adopted may be influenced to adopt by commercial sources or technical communications, if they do so at all. In general, sociometric networks seem to be influential primarily during the first five months after the drug's release.

Katz (1961) noted that the role of personal influence by "peers" in early and late adoptions of agricultural innovations differs from that for the adoption of drugs. In regard to farming practices, the contribution of formal or less intimate sources is of particular importance for those who adopt early or at least by the time the majority does; the laggards are more likely to gain awareness and be influenced through personal contact or informal communication, as the two-step hypothesis would suggest. In contrast, early drug adopters are apparently affected by peer influence, while late adopters do not prescribe the drug close to the time their personally chosen colleagues do more often than would be expected by chance. Nevertheless, as Katz noted, both lines of research indicate that commercial and impersonal sources appear to play an informational role in the adoption process, while local, personal ones seem to be salient at the point of decision and to legitimize the use of the innovation.

The nature of the innovation

Rogers (1962) reported that peer influence was of particular importance in the spread of acceptance of "miracle fabrics," while commercial representatives were more important than peers in the adoption of an antibiotic swine supplement. This suggests that the pattern of effective influences conducing to adoption may vary with the nature of the innovation (*cf.* Copp, Sill, and Brown, 1958).

In view of the significant contribution of sociometric relations to use of a drug during the first few months after its release, at a time when its efficacy is in question, Coleman, Katz, and Menzel (1957) conjectured that personal influence may be more influential in uncertain situations than in clear-cut ones. Menzel and Katz (1955) expressed a similar thought, since they found that medical colleagues are implicated three times as often (22 percent versus 7 percent) in the adoption of drugs for chronic diseases (where there are alternative methods of treatment and effectiveness is not readily determined) as in the adoption of drugs used in acute conditions (where the circumstances tend toward the opposite).

Bauer (1961) reported that, when a drug has been on the market for less than a year, a doctor is more likely to try it because of his regard for the company's reliability and scientific competence than when a drug has been available for a longer period of time. Presumably, during the early period of uncertainty concerning the drug's direct and side effects, there is greater dependence on the assumed technical quality of the source of influence (the pharmaceutical house) then when information concerning its efficacy becomes available from doctors' actual experiences with the drug. Bauer also reported that regard for a drug concern is of greater weight than preference for the company's sales representative in the decision to try a "risky" drug, whereas these two sources of influence are equally relevant when the drug is a relatively "safe" one. Bursk (cited by Bauer, 1961) found that, in response to queries on hypothetical situations, doctors were more likely to emphasize professional and commercial sources of information as the diseases increased in severity. Also, Rogers (1962) reported that an unpublished study by Wilkening obtained evidence that personal influence from other farmers increased in significance when the innovations involved greater economic risk.

Media and personal influence

The suggestion that mass media and personal relations can supplement each other is supported by results of the deliberate linking of the two through group listening and discussion. A number of UNESCO-sponsored projects (for example, Louis and Rovan, 1955; Mathur and Neurath, 1959; UNESCO, 1960) have demonstrated the particular effectiveness of radio and television broadcasts of information and advice, when groups of people in rural localities came together to listen or watch and afterwards discussed the material as a prelude to possible action. Presumably, group norms involving attitudes and behavior were more amenable to change under such circumstances (*cf.* Bennett, 1955; Cartwright, 1949; Lewin, 1953; Lewin and Grabbe, 1945).

Mitnick and McGinnies (1958) conducted a study with high school students to determine whether group discussion following an antiprejudice film would influence the attitude-change effectiveness of the film. Even though the film was successful in lowering scores on an ethnocentrism scale, discussion did not generally modify its effectiveness. However, the authors presented data suggesting that students who were initially most ethnocentric (the groups had been classified as low, middle, and high in ethnocentrism) were less favorably affected by the film when they were permitted to discuss it than when they merely viewed it. Though the highly ethnocentric students who discussed the film changed as much as did those who were initially less ethnocentric, it is possible that mutually supporting discussion lowered the full impact of the film on these students. However, the only information given on the substance of the discussions was that the least ethnocentric groups focused on the material presented in the film, while the most ethnocentric groups devoted little attention to the content of the film. On the average, the discussion groups seemed to retain better the effects of the film over a period of a month than did the film-only groups. A later report (McGinnies and Altman, 1959) based on additional analyses of the data from this research indicated that the least ethnocentric groups talked more, were more likely to keep the discussion going on their own initiative, and had a higher average rate of participation by their members than did the most ethnocentric groups, which were higher on these characteristics than were the moderately ethnocentric ones. It is not clear whether these differences were due to attitude toward the message of the film (presumably, favorableness would be inversely related to degree of ethnocentrism) or to preexisting and correlated differences in normal willingness to engage in discussions. In another study, McGinnies, Lana, and Smith (1958) found no significant effects of group discussions by adults following the viewing of one or three films on mental illness.

Lazarsfeld (1942) and Lazarsfeld and Field (1946) claimed that radio became more effective when it was linked to preexisting personal relations, as when some organization urged people to listen and organized listening groups. Robinson (1941) reported that more than half of his sample of farm women stated that book reviews, home demonstration talks, and farm-related information heard on the radio were often discussed at club meetings, and that women were assigned to listen to such programs. McCandless (1944) found that almost two-thirds of the women who were still listening to a long-term radio series on child guidance said they had begun to listen because an organization of which they were a member was a sponsor of the program; membership in such an organization was reported by only approximately one-third of the ex-listeners or by those who knew of the program but had never listened.

COMMENTARY

Clearly, the original two-step notion is too simplified a conception of the relationship between the mass media, opinion leaders, and the wider public. Shortly after the publication of *Personal Influence* (Katz and Lazarsfeld, 1955), Menzel and Katz (1955) suggested that, in view of the evidence that drug-adoption leaders turned to other leaders, the two-step sequence should be extended to a multistep one; that is, several levels of personal relationships may have to be passed through, rather than just one, before dependence on personal contacts is markedly reduced. In addition, they noted that the class of formal communications is not restricted to those conveyed by the mass media; for example, professional meetings constitute a source of significant information for drug opinion leaders. Furthermore, even isolates or nonleaders draw information from certain channels of ready access, such as communications from pharmaceutical companies and from drug salesmen who may bring both awareness and influence. Rogers (1962) criticized the simplicity and grossness of the two-step hypothesis in neglecting to consider the relationship between types of sources of information and influence and the stages of the adoption process. Also, though one source may be most prominent at a given stage, other sources are also influential. Other qualifications come from research suggesting that characteristics of the innovation or of the behavior to be changed modify the patterning of effective influences and information sources, and from evidence that the public significance of unanticipated news events affects the contribution of person-to-person communications to the spread of awareness of the events. Katz (1961) and Katz, Levin, and Hamilton (1963) acknowledged that the simple question of which is more effective, personal contacts and informal communications or the mass media, has given way to a more sophisticated conception which recognizes their supplementing and complementary contributions and their flexible use for different information tasks.

The intertwining of informal and formal modes of communication is also evidenced by the frequency with which people who were first informed by others of the assassination of Kennedy turned to the mass media for confirmation and further information (Greenberg, 1964a). In general, it would seem that any hypothesis that the flow of information or opinions ends simply with informal or even formal communications is an inadequate representation of the reverberating relationship between both types of communication channels.

Except for some anecdotal material in Lazarsfeld, Berelson, and Gaudet (1948), and leaving aside the activities of governmental and commercial change agents, there is little *direct* evidence from research that the people designated as opinion leaders *actively* sought to convince others to accept a point of view or to adopt an innovation. Assumptions about the basis for the shapes of adoption curves do not constitute sufficient evidence in this regard (*cf.* Coleman, Katz, and Menzel, 1957; Katz, 1961). In view of the methods used to assess opinion leadership, opinion leaders in most studies could be said to have functioned more as resource persons or passive influentials than as active influentials, though in some instances farm neighbors or medical colleagues were named as sources of first knowledge of innovations (Katz, 1961). In a sense, the question addressed by research on the role of opinion leaders was: Whom do people turn to when they want additional information or advice, or whom do they look to as exemplars of desirable behavior? In contrast, in research on the diffusion of news events, active transmission of information is involved; however, opinion leadership was not examined in such research. The distinction between active and passive channels for communications relates to the locus of the motivation for the initiation of the flow of information and influence. An active mediator is moved to communicate, whereas a passive mediator responds to the initiative of the information seeker. For example, in the Katz and Lazarsfeld study (1954), flow of influence should connect the very interested and involved opinion leader with the somewhat less interested nonleader rather than with the uninterested; the latter is simply not motivated to seek advice on or to give much attention to the topic. However, in the voting study, to the extent that the opinion leader is actively proselytizing, he should seek out those who are undecided and amenable to personal influence; and these are generally people with much less interest in the campaign. In the transmission studies, motivation to transmit information and, hence, the contribution of person-to-person communication would depend on the general significance of the information; the more newsworthy it is generally or the more relevant it is to a potential recipient, the greater is the motivation to transmit it or use it as conversational currency. Also, it would be expected that the more generally significant an item of news is, the more will "weak" friendship channels or channels involving less intimate personal relations contribute to diffusion. For example, Banta (1964) reported that almost half of his Denver sample claimed to have heard the news of Kennedy's assassination from a casual acquaintance or a complete stranger.

Not keeping the active-passive distinction in mind can lead to unwarranted assertions about opinion leaders actively influencing others or to conceptual unclarity about what is meant by the term "opinion leader." The problem is exemplified by the following two consecutive sentences by Rogers (1962, p. 208): "Those individuals who have a greater share of influence are called 'opinion leaders' because they take the lead in influencing the opinions of others. Opinion leaders are defined as those individuals from whom others seek advice and information." Information is needed on the details of the actual behavior of opinion leaders *vis-à-vis* those whom they are presumed to influence.

MASS MEDIA AND VOTING BEHAVIOR

Consideration of the role of mass media in voting behavior does not imply that mass media have novel or markedly different effects in this area than in regard to other kinds of attitudes and behavior. General principles of mass communication apply here as well. Many of the points touched on previously will reappear in analyses and investigations of political effects. Nevertheless, it is worthwhile to draw together such research in one place, since this content area is a focus of continuous study and was the original locus of the development of significant communications principles.

INTEREST

Interest in a campaign (or its correlate, the felt importance of an election) has been taken to reflect a complex aggregation of motives that orient a person toward political affairs. On this motivational perspective, the greater the interest (indexing the strength of relevant motivation to orient), the greater should be the attention to campaign matters. This the data show, for the most consistent finding in all studies of the role of the media in political campaigns has been a positive association between interest in the campaign and the extent of exposure to political communications. In fact, Lazarsfeld, Berelson, and Gaudet (1948) claimed that, in the 1940 election, interest was an even more important contributor to exposure than were other correlates, such as education, socioeconomic status, age, rural-urban residence, or whether or not a vote decision had been reached. However, in any campaign, relatively few individuals are extremely interested and heavily exposed; most are characterized by moderate interest and, largely because of their ordinary attention to the media, by moderate exposure to political material. Speculating on this pattern, Berelson, Lazarsfeld, and McPhee (1954), who also found positive covariation between interest and degree of exposure, suggested that, up to a point, the volume of political material in the media modulates the degree of attention to and interest in a campaign of those who are ordinarily only moderately attentive and interested. In contrast, the degree of interest and attentiveness of the strongly involved is due to personal and social factors and is largely independent of and prior to exposure to political material in the media.

Since the evidence linking interest to exposure is correlational, care must be taken in imputing a directional relationship between the two. However, it is likely that each affects the other, once exposure becomes continuous. That is, preexisting interest may lead to exposure and thereby be sustained or even strengthened; and continued or increased exposure may be induced by the stimulated interest (Berelson, Lazarsfeld, and McPhee, 1954; Lazarsfeld, Berelson, and Gaudet, 1948).

Since the highly interested are motivated to attend to political news, they should actively seek out or put themselves in the way of such information. In support of this assumption, Trenaman and McQuail (1961) reported that people who watched political broadcasts on television tended to be the ones who read election speeches in newspapers. Furthermore, the same overlap of audiences held for other means of receiving election material, such as radio and political meetings. Deutschmann (1962) found that more viewers than nonviewers of the Kennedy-Nixon debates exposed themselves to additional material on the debates in other media, particularly in newspapers. Indirect evidence may also be inferred from the finding by Lazarsfeld,

Berelson, and Gaudet (1948) and Berelson, Lazarsfeld, and McPhee (1954) that people reached through one medium tended to be the ones who reported exposure to political communications through another medium. In a sense, the availability of diverse media of information does not lead to an extension and evening-out of exposure over the population; rather, exposure tends to concentrate among the same people. Further support for this judgment is found in the positive associations between degree of exposure in the early periods of the 1940 and 1948 election campaigns and in the later months.

FLUCTUATION OF ATTENTION

It has traditionally been assumed by politicians and others that the American public is relatively inattentive to political material in a national election until October at the earliest. Surprisingly, there are very few published data on this assumption, despite the tendency of political parties to devote the bulk of their advertising efforts to the final period of the campaign (for example, Mullen, 1963). Of course, single, dramatic events may attract huge audiences regardless of when they occur. But contrary to the assumption of high attentiveness at the end of the campaign is the finding by Lazarsfeld, Berelson, and Gaudet (1948) that, at the height of the 1940 contest during the last 12 days, relatively little attention was being given to political communications. Siebert *et al.* (1954) reported that, during the 1952 campaign, the percentages of their panel members who viewed televised political programs were generally highest during the conventions (ranging from 30 to 59 percent), lowest during the bulk of the campaign in September and October (in the teens or less)—except for selected events such as Nixon's defense of his personal integrity—and rose during the last 10 days (into the twenties mainly), with roughly one out of three persons viewing the election eve broadcasts of each party. More information is needed on the changes in public attention to party propaganda during the course of a campaign.

SELECTIVE EXPOSURE

Earlier in the chapter, some evidence was presented which suggested that information congenial to attitudes is given attention, while counterattitudinal material is avoided. This is the phenomenon of selective exposure. Before considering the data from voting studies, which have been the source of much of the relevant evidence, it is worth noting that other motives or attractions may induce exposure to a disagreeable message or a communicator. For example, Robinson (1941) reported that, although farmers would avoid radio programs by New Deal proponents, they would listen to speeches by President Roosevelt in order to learn about governmental planning that might affect their livelihood. Also, general exposure to preferred media may bring attention to contrary material that would not otherwise be sought out. Hence, it is not to be expected that selective exposure would produce a complete separation of audiences. At best, people would be exposed *more* to political communications by a favored party or candidate than to those from less esteemed sources.

Evidence consistent with an assumption of selective exposure was presented by Lazarsfeld, Berelson, and Gaudet (1948). More Republicans than Democrats were found to have listened to Willkie's addresses, while more Democrats than Republicans had exposed themselves to Roosevelt's. Not only did undecided people tend to expose themselves more to political material consonant with the political direction of their predispositions than to nonconsonant material, but a somewhat higher percentage of the decided who remained constant showed consonant bias, and a lower percentage showed nonconsonant bias. (However, roughly one out of five of the latter group did expose themselves predominantly to opposing communications.) Also, among those who remained constant in their vote decisions, the greater the interest, the greater the biased exposure.

Additional data from the same study are also taken by the authors to support the selective-exposure hypothesis. The newspapers read by the sample were presumed to favor Willkie, while Roosevelt's remarkable speaking ability was thought to make him more effective than Willkie on radio. Hence, the media were expected to be differentially attractive to Republicans and Democrats. The data support this assumption. Republicans exposed themselves more to newspapers than to radio, while the reverse imbalance held for Democrats. Consistent with this is the judged impartiality of the two media; Republicans rated newspapers more imparual than radio to a greater extent than did the Democrats. Also, Republicans claimed that the newspapers presented more congenial ideas, while the Democrats favored radio in this regard.

In their study of voting behavior in the 1948 national election, Berelson, Lazarsfeld, and McPhee (1954) also found a tendency for people to see and hear their own side more than that of the other. However, each group of partisans paid considerable attention to the opposition's communications. The data are derived from a survey question asking people to indicate which of a group of items they had read or heard. Approximately 55 percent of the Republicans and Democrats claimed knowledge of more items favorable to their own Presidential candidate, while approximately 45 percent of both groups showed a greater awareness of items favorable to the opposition candidate than to their own. This occurred despite the disproportion of pro-Dewey material in this strongly Republican community. However, people who followed the Republican convention more closely also gave more attention than did others to the later Democratic one.

Siebert *et al.* (1954) found that, in a predominantly Republican area, nationally televised speeches by Eisenhower and Nixon were watched more often than were those by Stevenson during the 1952 campaign, an outcome which implies that selective exposure was operating. However, although Democratic voters were more likely to be in the television audience for Stevenson's speeches than were Republican voters, candidate preference was only weakly related to exposure to the speeches of the Republican candidates.

Of interest is a study by Schramm and Carter (1959) of the effectiveness of a 20-hour telethon by Senator Knowland in his unsuccessful bid to win the California governorship in 1958. Interviews were conducted four days after the telethon. Only a little more than 10 percent of the sample watched any of the program, perhaps in part because it was not well-publicized. Though Republicans composed only 25 percent of the sample, they made up almost half of the group which watched at least part of the telethon. Democrats were represented among the viewers in nearly the same percentage they constituted of the sample, whereas the percentage of "independents" among the viewers was approximately one-third of their percentage in the sample. Republicans not only watched almost twice as long as did Democrats, but they were also more likely to contribute to the audience during the nonprime hours of daytime and late night. In addition, Republicans were less likely than were Democrats (48 percent versus 67 percent) to assert that they tuned in by accident. That is, deliberate tuning in was more a characteristic of Republican watchers, while accidental exposure typified the Democrats.

A study by Greenberg (1965b) of people's exposure to information concerning a local school bond issue suggests that exposure was affected by expectations concerning the likelihood of a desirable outcome in the referendum. Those who were favorable to the proposal and expected it to pass claimed more media exposure on the issue than did those whose views and expectations were at variance; this was particularly true among people whose personal characteristics and attitudes disposed them ordinarily to less interest or involvement in school affairs. The main difference resided in the degree of asserted exposure to print media, namely, to pamphlets and bulletins which supported the proposal and, to some extent, to the local newspapers. This factor of consistency between desired and expected outcome should be examined in the context of a political campaign.

Of particular interest is an attempt by Stempel (1961) to conduct an experimental test of the selective-exposure hypothesis. Taking advantage of an impending campus election, he arranged to have two stories, one for each of the two candidates, printed on the front page of the college newspaper. Approximately 31 percent of the students read more about their own candidate than about the opposing one, while 49 percent read equal amounts concerning each. Essentially, when there was a difference in the amounts read, the direction was in favor of the student's preferred candidate. Nevertheless, approximately 54 percent read something about the nonpreferred candidate.

Milne and Mackenzie (1958) reported that in 1955 the exposure behavior of British voters was only slightly imbalanced in favor of their own party's propaganda. This held for the broadcast media, for mailed literature, and for news of political significance in the newspapers. In respect to the latter, they suggested that, while party preference leads to the reading of newspapers expressing a politically congruent viewpoint, voters expose themselves in a nonpartisan way to news articles conveying the opponents' campaign activities. Furthermore, in regard to the broadcast media, extent of exposure to one major party's programs was found to be positively associated with extent of exposure to the other's; this relationship may reflect a correlated connection with interest in the election. In a sense, and as was noted earlier in respect to general exposure to campaign communications, there was a concentration of viewing or seeing among a relatively small number of voters.

In their study of the 1959 election in Great Britain, Trenaman and McQuail (1961) found little evidence of selective exposure to the general mass media. Approximately half of the audiences attentive to at least one of the programs sponsored by a major party on television or radio was composed of people who voted for the other major party. That is, as many supporters as opponents were in the audience of a broadcast. Also, there was considerable overlap between the audiences viewing one or more Labour Party programs and one or more Conservative programs. Though political partisanship was a determinant of choice of a newspaper to read, approximately one out of five people read a paper whose editorial policy opposed their political preference. The authors asserted that the electorate did expose themselves and were exposed to all political viewpoints, noting that the broadcast media were impartial in their presentations and the evening newspapers gave wide coverage to all types of political communications and events.

An unpublished study by the British Broadcasting Corporation (1964) on the 1964 election confirms the main findings of Trenaman and McQuail. The sizes of television audiences were not affected by the party (Conservative, Labour, or Liberal) sponsoring the program, even despite the relatively small percentage of Liberal voters in the electorate. The minor differences that appeared were attributed to variations in the numbers of people watching the preceding program or to the strength of the counterattractions, rather than to political allegiance. Comparable results were found in regard to the radio audiences of political broadcasts.

Even without the essentially negative British results, the data from the American studies do not support a strong form of the selective-exposure hypothesis. Political partisanship and predispositions are associated with imbalanced exposure to party propaganda, but the degree of such partiality is not overly strong. People are exposed to and aware of arguments supporting an opposition viewpoint or candidate, though frequency of exposure to such may be considerably less than to congenial material. However, a precise determination of frequency of exposure has not been made.

Factors countering a more marked bias in exposure are likely to be operating. The British data could signify a cultural difference in attention to political communications, perhaps related to the shorter time devoted to an election campaign in Britain or to a different tradition concerning the value of equal exposure to differing political viewpoints (Milne and Mackenzie, 1958). Besides culture, the very diversity of the mass media, their need to reach politically heterogeneous audiences (for example, Schramm, 1957), and traditions of journalistic integrity in respect to the news combine to facilitate exposure to differing political viewpoints.

Also to be considered are the attractiveness of a medium and the pleasure obtained from using it. Such factors are probably involved to some extent in the finding of Trenaman and McQuail (1961) that people were more likely to watch a political broadcast by an opposing party than to read a newspaper whose editorial policy opposed their political allegiance.

A political event can be set in a dramatic or entertaining context and thereby attract people of opposing persuasion. The shift from the simple use of television as a means of presenting a speech by a political candidate to a more flexible, inviting format for campaign activities and to five-minute trailers and spots suggests awareness of its potentiality for overcoming indifference and bias in exposure and for attracting a large and politically diverse audience (Kelley, 1956). A remarkable event, such as a convention or Nixon's fund defense, will reduce considerably the influence of selective exposure. In 1960, the Kennedy-Nixon debates were touted not only as a means of producing a true dialogue and confrontation of political viewpoints, but also as an opportunity to expose people to the perspectives of both major Presidential candidates on a variety of salient issues. Presumably, people desirous of watching their own candidate would also be induced to attend to his debate opponent. The evidence suggests that party preference had little effect on exposure to the debates (Deutschmann, 1962; Carter, 1962). However, watching the debates is not the same as equal exposure to both candidates, for people may attend closely when their preferred candidate is speaking, and talk or engage in other activities when the opposition candidate makes his comments (see Maccoby, cited in Krech, Crutchfield, and Ballachey, 1962).

Though selective exposure has been construed as an active screening-out and seeking-out by people, in order to avoid contrary information and to obtain reinforcement for their views, there may also be selective exposure without motivated intent. To the extent that media vehicles, such as individual newspapers or magazines, differ in the viewpoints favored and emphasized, choice of a vehicle will affect the scope and partiality of the person's information environment. This kind of passive bias in attention will contribute to the apparent selectivity of exposure to political communications during campaigns and to presumed evidence of such selectivity at those times. This possibility is suggested by Lazarsfeld, Berelson, and Gaudet (1948) in regard to their finding that approximately 60 percent of the people who were initially undecided in the 1940 election were exposed more to propaganda consonant with their political predispositions than to nonconsonant material. That is, these data may be due in part to no more than normal, preexisting exposure to media vehicles that reflect a consonant partiality. Obviously, if this interpretation is applicable to the exposure patterns of the undecided, it should also be relevant to those of the already decided.

From this perspective, relating customary habits of media use to the contents of the media between and during campaigns can provide useful information. Studies of the effects of media on political behavior have neglected to do this and have, in fact, omitted consideration of normal media use except in a very gross and crude way.

CROSS PRESSURES AND EXPOSURE

In voting studies, the term "cross pressures" refers to dispositional conflicts involving voting preferences that pull in opposite directions. These contesting preferences derive from conflicting motives which are aroused by the relationship between campaign stimuli, personal and attitudinal factors, and social influences. It is assumed that the magnitude of cross-pressuring will be inversely related to the degree of imbalance between the net attractiveness of the different parties and candidates. Since cross pressures involve internal conflict, it would be expected that their magnitude would relate to exposure to campaign material.

Janowitz and Marvick (1956) reported data suggesting an inverse relationship between cross pressures and media use in the 1952 election. Mehling, Kraus, and Yoakam (1962) suggested that, in 1960, cross pressures led Catholic Republicans to use television less than Catholic Democrats; party preference was not related to the extent to which Protestants used television. On the basis of evidence of exposure to the first Kennedy-Nixon debate, Deutschmann (1962) confirmed the data of Mehling, Kraus, and Yoakam in regard to Catholics, but found some evidence that Protestant Republicans were more likely to have watched than were Protestant Democrats, a result also attributed to the avoidance-inducing effect of cross pressures.

Trenaman and McQuail (1961) found a curvilinear relation between degree of total exposure to campaign material and the difference between the expressed favorableness of attitude toward the party for which the respondent had actually voted and his attitude toward the other major party. In general, higher exposure was associated with a slight or a marked difference in attitudes.

The relation between cross pressures, interest, and degree of exposure is not likely to be a simple one. According to Lazarsfeld, Berelson, and Gaudet (1948), when cross pressures are strong but interest low, people give little attention to the campaign and tend to belittle the importance of the election. Such people are little motivated to attend and strongly moved to avoid having to aggravate their conflict. In contradistinction, strong cross pressures coupled with high interest lead to continued attention and even discussion or argument with others, until some event triggers a decision.

Though the term "cross pressures" signifies that people are caught in a conflict of motivations, there is little evidence from election research that people designated as being under cross pressures are aware of the divergent tendencies or experience conflict. That people may differ in their awareness of such conflicts is brought out in a nonvoting study by Kriesberg (1949a). The sample comprised union members most of whom were Catholics but whose union contained admitted Communists among the officers and among the general membership. Local newspapers supported the Church view on American-Soviet relations, whereas the weekly union news-paper, as well as some of the vocal members, supplied the Communist line on this matter. Those union members who were unconcerned and uninformed about American-Soviet relations were unaware of the cross pressures and, though moderate in their views, were inconsistent or uncertain. In contrast, the interested and informed were aware of the cross pressures and, though relatively moderate in position, tended to favor a particular viewpoint.

SELECTIVE RETENTION

Over time, what was originally learned from a political communication may be for-gotten in whole or in part or undergo change in memory. Simple forgetting of specific content is to be expected. But selectivity in retention may also occur, in that knowledge discordant with voting preference and predispositions may be more readily forgotten than knowledge which is congruent.

Using a true-false test, Carter (1962) found that those who claimed to have been interested in and attentive to the first Kennedy-Nixon debate remembered both candidates' arguments equally well; however, among the less interested and attentive, correct recall was higher for the arguments of their own candidate than of the other one. Biased recall was not related to strength of party allegiance or to an index based on degree of liking the debate or talking about it. Total correct recall was greatest for those who said that both candidates presented effective arguments, next for those who said only their preferred candidate did, and least for those who said neither did. In fact, the latter group, not the preceding two, showed biased recall in favor of their own candidate's arguments. The value of these interesting results would have been strengthened if knowledge of the candidates' stands could have been assessed before the debate or after it among a suitable control group of nonviewers.

Berelson, Lazarsfeld, and McPhee (1954) found that people who are objectively in disagreement with the stand of their own candidate on an issue are more likely than those in actual agreement to claim that they do not know what their candidate's posi-tion is. Furthermore, though the evidence is not strong, there is the suggestion that, when both candidates' views on an issue are unclear, people tend to see their preferred candidate as similar and the nonpreferred one as dissimilar to themselves. This effect increases with strength of partisanship.

Sebald (cited in Katz and Feldman, 1962) found that college students were more likely to attribute political statements they disagreed with to their nonpreferred candidate, whereas statements they agreed with were more accurately assigned to the candidate who made them. When spontaneous recall was asked for, the students tended to remember their own candidate's statements with which they agreed and the opposing candidate's with which they disagreed.

COGNITION

From the perspective of the political parties and candidates, one function of campaign activities is to make the electorate knowledgeable about party and candidate stands on major issues and to convey to the public a politically advantageous conception of which issues are the salient ones. Though beliefs and voting preferences need not be affected by such information, and though selective exposure and retention may be operating, it is important to know what changes in knowledge are brought about by the campaign.

Berelson, Lazarsfeld, and McPhee (1954) found that the greater the degree of exposure to campaign material, the greater was the accuracy in perceiving both Presidential candidates' positions on issues. Furthermore, accuracy was more strongly related to exposure than it was to education or to interest in the campaign. On this evidence, the authors averred that campaign messages may act to correct selective awareness or clarify understanding of political policies. Similarly, Katz and Feldman (1962) suggested that the Kennedy-Nixon debates made people more aware of the candidates' views. Ben-Zeev and White (1962) found that, as the 1960 campaign progressed, there was a decline in the percentage of people who said they did not know where Kennedy stood on issues; but there was no marked change in people's awareness of Nixon's positions. The latter is not surprising, since many of Nixon's views were well-known or could be assumed to be those of the Eisenhower administration.

In support of Milne and Mackenzie (1958), Trenaman and McQuail (1961) reported that, regardless of party preference, awareness of what the parties stood for increased as a result of the campaign. They also found a slight positive correlation (0.11) between the number of political programs viewed on television and the before-after increase in knowledge of the policies of the parties during the 1959 election in Britain. When only those who changed parties were considered, the correlation rose to 0.32. However, increment in knowledge was not related to the degree of exposure to political material on the radio, in the newspapers, or through local participation in the campaign. Even in households without television, degree of radio exposure was not related to increased knowledge. Trenaman and McQuail attributed the difference between television and the other media to a number of factors: television's greater impartiality coupled with the newspapers' greater partisanship and, hence, likelihood of attracting politically congruent audiences; and radio's greater use by the older, the poorer, and the less well-educated, who are also less motivated to learn or less capable of learning.

Even if knowledge of party position is not markedly affected by the campaign, it might be expected that awareness that certain issues are being raised would influence people's conceptions about their importance. Of course, there are often national or local issues that exist prior to a campaign and produce voting tendencies for or against a party or candidate. But one function of partisan political communications may be to crystallize and emphasize vague feelings, turning them into major political issues and connecting them with a particular party (*cf.* Dexter, 1955).

Lang and Lang (1959) suggested that in 1952 the media helped make salient the Republican issues of the Korean War and of national security. Kelley (1956) reported that Roper surveys found only one out of four people mentioning the Korean War as a political issue in January, 1952; but by late October of 1952, after considerable emphasis on this matter in the national campaign, approximately one out of two so considered it. As he noted, it was the verbal environment, not the objective environment, that had changed. Similarly, according to Kelley, the activities of a public relations firm transformed the concept of "socialized medicine" from a peripheral issue into a politically significant one in a number of local and state elections. Katz and Feldman (1962) suggested that the Kennedy-Nixon debates made some issues of foreign and domestic affairs more salient.

However, Trenaman and McQuail (1961) found that the 1959 British campaign had little or no effect on which general issues the electorate considered important. In general, the political parties agreed on what the important issues were, and the ones emphasized had been considered important by the public even before the campaign. Nevertheless, issues not mentioned in the campaign declined in the degree of importance attached to them by the electorate. Differential emphasis on an issue by a party did not increase the number of supporters who considered it more important after than before the campaign. But supporters of each party attached differing importance to selected issues; and this relativity of rating was not affected by the campaign. Trenaman and McQuail found some evidence, though equivocal, that the campaign may have served to connect the importance of issues more closely to party preferences, reducing the influence of personal characteristics and experiences. In a sense, greater party homogeneity of views on the relative importance of issues was achieved.

Relevant to the question of the cognitive effects of exposure to political communications is how the experiences are perceived or evaluated by people. That is, even if exposure occurs, predispositions may affect the evaluation of the communication. Evidence from the British election studies of 1959 (Trenaman and McQuail, 1961) and 1964 (British Broadcasting Corporation, 1964) suggests that the supporters of the party sponsoring a political program judged it more favorably than did those who preferred a different party. The uncommitted to any party were intermediate in the favorableness of their evaluations. In their study of viewers' reactions to Knowland's 1958 political telethon, Schramm and Carter (1959) found that party affiliation did not affect the percentage of viewers who commented negatively about the program. However, Republicans were more than twice as likely to make favorable comments (62 percent versus 29 percent), while the Democrats were three times as likely to say they learned nothing new (45 percent versus 14 percent).

Deutschmann (1962) found that approximately the same percentage of Republicans and Democrats chose Kennedy as the winner of the first debate, but a higher percentage of the Republicans claimed Nixon had won. Among Nixon's supporters, the greater the strength of their preference for him, the less frequently was Kennedy selected as the winner; but among pro-Kennedy viewers, choice of Kennedy as winner did not vary with the strength of their support for him. Independents were more likely than the partisans to assert that a winner could not be chosen. Lang and Lang (1962) reported that an overwhelming majority of those who were either undecided or pro-Kennedy before the first debate judged Kennedy to have been superior to Nixon; Nixon supporters also picked Kennedy, but by a much smaller majority.

VOTE PREFERENCE

The payoff in political campaigns is the actual voting behavior of the electorate. From a pragmatic point of view, attention, knowledge, motivation are all of interest only as they influence votes, though theoretically they are significant in their own

right. The purpose of the campaign is to induce preferential voting, and any conceptualization of the role of media in voting behavior must consider the influence of
political communications on vote intentions and voting turnout.

Time of vote decision

It is obvious that the magnitude of campaign effects is constrained by the open-
mindedness of the electorate concerning a choice between candidates. Hence, it is
important to know how long before election day people arrive at a firm decision on a
voting preference. In general, the data indicate that, in national elections, a considerable majority of the electorate, ranging from two-thirds to three-fourths or more,
make up their minds prior to the formal beginning of the campaign (for example,
Berelson, Lazarsfeld, and McPhee, 1954; Campbell *et al.*, 1960; Katz and Feldman,
1962; Lazarsfeld, Berelson, and Gaudet, 1948; Milne and Mackenzie, 1958; Siebert
et al., 1954). Those who decide later are usually less interested, under cross pressures,
and more unstable in their vote intentions. Of course, variations have been found
over elections and between parties, perhaps due to heightened conflicts concerning
one or another candidate. For instance, Katz and Feldman (1962) noted that, in
1960, 60 percent knew whom they would support at the time of the conventions,
whereas in 1956 the figure was 76 percent; and Berelson, Lazarsfeld, and McPhee
(1954) reported that in 1948 only 63 percent of the Democrats, compared to 87
percent of the Republicans, in their sample had come to a stable decision by August
(*cf.* Campbell and Kahn, 1952).

Activation

Since motivations play so strong a role in behavior, it would be expected that the
effects of political communications relate to their ability to engage relevant motivational predispositions. However, only a few of the many values, motives, and attitudes
of an individual are stirred up and connected to the issues. In this selection process,
the contents of mass communication can play a decisive role (Berelson, Lazarsfeld, and
McPhee, 1954). Noting that final vote decision was strongly associated with political
predispositions, Lazarsfeld, Berelson, and Gaudet (1948) asserted that campaigns
are important because they activate latent dispositions and suggest the vote which is
consonant with those dispositions that are aroused.

    The 1948 election is a particularly dramatic occurrence of such an effect. The
data gathered by Berelson, Lazarsfeld, and McPhee (1954) suggest that the trend toward Truman from August to October was a "rally" to Truman of Democratic defectors and potential Democrats (independents who had voted Democratic previously),
rather than a conversion of vote intentions. Analyses of the candidates' radio speeches
revealed that Truman emphasized "position issues" related to domestic concerns and
party differences, while Dewey focused on "style issues" of the unity of the American
people and other noncontroversial topics. The rally toward Truman during the later
months of the campaign was coincident with the increasing prominence he gave to
position issues likely to engage Democratic predispositions. Supporting this interpretation of one of the main reasons for Truman's success is evidence that, even in the
early period of the campaign, Democrats who considered position issues preeminent

were more favorable toward Truman than were those who did not consider them so important.

Reinforcement

Besides the activation of loyalties and latent preferences, a significant effect of campaign stimuli is the reinforcement of a decision that is consistent with politically relevant predispositions. Some information concerning this kind of influence can be obtained by examining the relationship between stability of vote preference and exposure to the media. However, since relevant data are based on self-exposure to the media, it is very likely that the evidence represents, not the effects of media exposure, but the way in which people differing in partisanship or stability of preference use the media.

Lazarsfeld, Berelson, and Gaudet (1948) reported that a stable preference was associated with an early choice of candidate coupled with partisan exposure and supporting social influences. But those exposed primarily to information concerning the party opposing their political predispositions were more likely to vote for that party's candidate than were those whose exposure bias and predispositions coincided.

In respect to general exposure to campaign material, Berelson, Lazarsfeld, and McPhee (1954) found a positive relationship between degree of attention to the media and stability of vote intention at each level of interest in the election.

Converse (1962) has suggested that those with *very little* interest or involvement in a campaign show high vote stability but, from that point on, stability increases with involvement and possession of political information. This supposition is supported by data from the 1952 campaign, showing that stability (the relation between party identification and the vote cast or between intended and actual vote) was greater among the relatively few who used no formal media to obtain campaign information than among those who used one or two media, with an increase again for those using three or four media. Additional support is reported by Converse in that the correlation between intended and actual vote was higher among those who did not watch *any* Kennedy-Nixon debates in 1960 than among those who watched at least one; this was particularly so for people who said they were too uninterested in politics to watch the debates or offered no reasons for not watching. However, Katz and Feldman (1962) reported that watching the Kennedy-Nixon debates was positively related to strength of commitment to a candidate or a party; so-called "independents" were less likely to watch or hear the debates.

Trenaman and McQuail (1961) reported that women showed less evidence of a swing toward the Conservative Party than did men and were less likely to change from one part to another. They suggested that this may be due to the fact that women, particularly those whose allegiance was with the Labour Party, had less access than men to political communications. These same investigators found that, even though about 27 percent of the electorate made some change from the voting intention they had in September, no formal medium nor any combination of them had any discernible effect on such changes. As was found by others (for example, Lazarsfeld, Berelson, and Gaudet, 1948), the voter whose vote intention was unchanged exhibited the greatest degree of exposure to formal communications, and the nonvoter the least degree; but those who changed from one party to another were more exposed than were those who started out undecided and selected a party during the campaign.

Effects of specific campaign events

Studies of voting behavior indicate that activation and reinforcement are the major contributions of the mass media (Berelson, Lazarsfeld, and McPhee, 1954; Lazarsfeld, Berelson, and Gaudet, 1948). Nevertheless, it is worth noting that the relationship between vote stability or change and a general index of exposure to political communications is at most a gross one. What is needed is an assessment of the effects of a specific stimulus or series of related communications by a candidate or party. Also, the determination of effects should occur shortly after the experience, rather than some unknown time after. Otherwise, too many other kinds of stimuli, countering and supporting, will impinge upon people to permit any clear evidence of the effects of particular ones; for an open, contested election involves communication and countercommunication and a plethora of other kinds of campaign and extracampaign events.

A number of reports have implicated the Presidential nominating conventions as events which help to crystallize and set the vote decisions of sizable percentages of voters (Berelson, Lazarsfeld, and McPhee, 1954; Campbell and Kahn, 1952; Campbell *et al.*, 1960; Siebert *et al.*, 1954; Thomson, 1956). Schramm and Carter (1959) found that Knowland's telethon had little effect on the expressed vote intentions of viewers. In general, viewers' comments indicated that preexisting impressions were reinforced and vote intentions rationalized.

Many people have asserted that the dramatic Kennedy-Nixon debates were a key factor in Kennedy's narrow victory. some have even claimed that his victory was due to them, particularly to the first debate (Burdick, 1962; Evans, 1962). However, no available data can cogently establish this. A more reasonable appraisal was given by Lang and Lang (1962), who remarked simply that the election was too close and that too many influences and events contributed to the victory for any one factor, such as the debates, to be the sole determinant. In fact, Katz and Feldman (1962) reported that Gallup polls indicated that from August on, even before the debates, Kennedy was gaining on Nixon. Nevertheless, the question of the effects of the debates on vote intentions and candidate preferences can still be raised.

Enormous numbers of people watched the debates. The Neilson Index reported that the first debate was viewed in approximately 27 million homes, the second in 24 million, the third in 25 million, and the fourth in 24 million (Evans, 1962). The debates drew larger audiences than the average of the displaced commercial programs. Approximately one out of four people watched all the debates, and more than half watched three of them. On the basis of people's own assertions of influence, Roper found that approximately half claimed that the debates influenced their voting decisions (Evans, 1962; Salant, 1962). Lang and Lang (1962) reported that there were few conversions of candidate preferences following the first debate. A sharp increase for Kennedy came mainly from the initially undecided whose allegiance to the Democratic party was weak.

Before and after the first debate, Deutschmann (1962) assessed the voting intentions of a panel of viewers residing in a predominantly Republican community. Those who had been leaning only to one or the other candidate were more likely to change by at least one point on a voting-intention scale than were the "independents" (50 percent versus 37 percent); the latter were more likely to change than were the viewers who had been somewhat positive about their vote intention (37 percent versus

20 percent); those who were positive beforehand were the least likely to change (6 percent). However, there was no difference in the percentage changing at least one scale unit between those who watched versus those who did not watch the debate, or between those who reported having been exposed to some kind of communication about it versus those who reported none. In general, the Democrats showed a strong shift to Kennedy, the Republicans a very slight shift toward Nixon. There were very few conversions; the increase in the numbers preferring a candidate came mainly from the initially undecided.

Carter (1962) reported that, of a panel of respondents who were tested before and after the first debate and after the fourth, more than half said that their attitudes toward the candidates had not changed. Of those who said their attitudes were affected, more Republicans reported increased favorableness to Nixon than to Kennedy, whereas the reverse held for the Democrats; but as Deutschmann (1962) found, the net gain in favorableness of attitude for Kennedy was greater among the Democrats than was the net gain for Nixon among the Republicans.

Using successive surveys of different people, Ben-Zeev and White (1962) obtained voting intentions before and after the second, third, and fourth debates. They reported that Kennedy gained continuously while Nixon showed a sharp decline from the second to the third debate and no change thereafter. Their data indicate that marked changes occurred between the debates rather than from before to after a debate. However, when comparisons were made between viewers and nonviewers, viewers showed slight changes from before to after the debates for Kennedy but not for Nixon.

As Katz and Feldman (1962) implied, apart from differentially strengthening or activating Democratic convictions, particularly among those initially undecided or weakly predisposed toward Kennedy, it is difficult to determine what effects the debates had. Of course, this result alone, if it can be truly attributed to the debates, would stand as a contribution to so narrow a victory.

Election night coverage

Some concern has been voiced that televised reports of Presidential returns from earlier time zones, coupled with computer-determined projections, would influence the voting behavior of people in later time zones who had not yet cast their ballots. Presumably, such communications might induce them to vote for the apparent winner ("bandwagon effect") or to support the trailing candidate ("underdog effect") or not to vote at all. Research based on voting behavior in the 1964 election found no evidence of any significant effects of such broadcasts (Lang and Lang, 1965; Mendelsohn, 1965; Miller, 1965).

VOTING TURNOUT

There have been few studies of the effects of the media on voting turnout. Gosnell (1927) found that, in comparison with a control sample, a higher percentage of people who were sent mailed appeals to register for the forthcoming 1924 Presidential election actually did register. A later mailing had little effect on the percentage voting, probably because of the considerable publicity already being given the election. In a less provocative, local campaign, mailed notices concerning the election did increase voting turnout. These results accord with the outcomes of a more recent experiment by Eldersveld (1956), which will be discussed later.

As might be expected, nonvoters have been found to be less exposed to the formal media during a campaign than are voters (Berelson, Lazarsfeld, and McPhee, 1954; Campbell, Gurin, and Miller, 1954; Glaser, 1965; Janowitz and Marvick, 1956; Lazarsfeld, Berelson, and Gaudet, 1948; Milne and Mackenzie, 1958). However, since the data are correlational, differences in interest, normal media use, and a variety of other relevant characteristics are likely to be involved. Nevertheless, to the extent that exposure to political communications and interest interact with each other, as has been suggested previously, and interest relates to casting a vote, the media can be said to contribute to turnout. From this point of view, the amount of campaign material carried by the media should be associated in some degree with the percentage of the electorate who vote.

Though a systematic study of the relationship has not been carried out, it is relevant that an attempt by Converse (1962) to study the newspaper content devoted to a Congressional election, which normally produces a considerably smaller vote than is cast in a Presidential year, had to be terminated for lack of sufficient and continuous news concerning the campaign. Referring to such elections as "low-stimulus" ones, he linked the stimulus intensity of elections to the type of people who vote and to the partisan constituents of the two-party vote. Essentially, low-stimulus elections tend to bring out the loyal two-party vote, while high-stimulus ones tap the normally less interested segment who are more open to vote change as a result of short-term influences. A direct implication of this line of reasoning is that an off-year election is likely to produce a return toward the basic two-party division of loyalties.

It has been claimed that television, by bringing some campaign activities more vividly to people, would increase public interest in an election and, thereby, voting (Evans, 1962). Such assertions were made very often in respect to the 1952 election, in which a higher percentage of the electorate voted than in the past and television was widely available and extensively used by both parties. However, a careful study by Simon and Stern (1955), based on voting statistics from counties in Iowa with a high density of television sets and those with a low density, found no evidence to support these claims. Neither voting turnout nor the party division of the vote in 1952 was affected by television. Voting differences between these types of counties could be accounted for by other factors. Also, as the authors demonstrated, there had been increases in voting from one election to another in pretelevision days. A similar appraisal was offered by Campbell (1962), based on an examination of national voting statistics from 1922 to 1960.

PERSONAL INFLUENCE

Extensive consideration has already been given to the supplementing and interactive relationship between the media and person-to-person communications. However, only scant reference was made at that time to pertinent findings from voting studies. Such evidence will now be examined at length, with repetition of previously presented material held to a bare minimum.

Lazarsfeld, Berelson, and Gaudet (1948) began their investigation of the effects of the 1940 national campaign on voting behavior with the expectation that political information conveyed by the mass media would be influential in affecting the nature of the vote. However, the relative infrequency of change in party preference attributable to formal campaign messages, coupled with anecdotal evidence contained in the comments of some respondents, led these researchers to consider explicitly the role of informal communications. Support for the significance of person-to-person interchanges came from data indicating that political attitudes and candidate preferences tended toward uniformity within the family and among friends, and that attitudinal homogeneity within the family was positively associated with stability of vote intention. Of particular importance to the authors was the finding that 10 percent more people claimed to be involved in conversations about the election on an average day than claimed to have listened to a major speech or to have read about the campaign on such a day. They took this to imply that informal communications through networks of personal relations achieve wider coverage, particularly among the undecided and uninterested, than do formal communications through the media. This led them to assert, without particular elaboration or emphasis, the hypothesis of a two-step flow of communications. Presumably, ideas made available by the mass media flow to "opinion leaders," who then convey them to less active individuals with whom they are in personal contact.

In this study, political opinion leadership was determined by self-designation; that is, those who said that they had tried to convince someone of their political views *and* that they had been asked for advice on politics were called "opinion leaders." Approximately one out of five (21 percent) of the sample met the requirements of opinion leadership. Opinion leaders were found at all socioeconomic levels and without much variation over occupational levels, except for a decrease among farmers, housewives, and the unemployed.

In the context of the two-step hypothesis, opinion leaders should exhibit greater exposure to the mass media. The data confirmed this. Opinion leaders not only exhibited greater interest in the campaign than did others—a characteristic which is strongly associated with exposure to the media—but, at each level of interest, they claimed greater exposure to campaign material in the media. In fact, opinion leaders with mild interest asserted greater exposure to the formal media than did nonleaders with high interest. In addition, the hypothesis implies that opinion leaders should engage in discussions about the campaign more frequently than do nonleaders; the data confirmed this too. (However, one of the defining characteristics of opinion leadership is persuasive conversation; hence, this finding may be intrinsically correlated with the criteria for determining opinion leadership.)

In their study of the 1948 election, Berelson, Lazarsfeld, and McPhee (1954) again used the self-designation technique for determining opinion leadership. Those who said that, compared to others whom they knew, they were at least as likely to be asked their views about politics *and* said that they had talked politics with someone recently were designated "opinion leaders." As in the previous study, approximately one out of five (23 percent of the sample) were so categorized. Again, their characteristics fit the requirements of the two-step hypothesis. As compared to nonleaders, they were more interested in the election and more exposed to the media at each level of interest, and were better informed on political matters. And they were found at all socioeconomic levels, with some, but not marked, variation from level to level. They also showed greater allegiance to their party in terms of support for their party's position on central issues.

Milne and Mackenzie (1958) increased the stringency of the criteria used by Berelson Lazarsfeld, and McPhee by requiring that political discussion be with someone outside the family. Drawing on postelection responses to survey questions, they designated only approximately one-eighth of their 1955 sample as opinion leaders. But such people were found roughly equally at all socioeconomic and educational levels and possessed similar characteristics to those reported by the American researchers. Also, they named discussions, which often appeared to be held with other opinion leaders, as the prime source of their political information.

A nomination technique was used by Anderson (1962) in research conducted in Sweden. He reported that general influentials, many of whom were not personally known by those who named them, were more likely than others to claim an active role in alerting people to politically relevant information and to attempting to influence the vote intentions of other people.

Personal influence is brought into the two-step hypothesis via the link between opinion leaders and those who are the recipients of their communications. The key dynamic element of the model lies in the discussions or conversations opinion leaders are supposed to have with others. Hence, an analysis of the contents and frequency of conversations, of the relationship between the discussants, and of the effects of the discussions would seem to be of central importance.

However, few data have been gathered on the *contents* of political discussions. Berelson, Lazarsfeld, and McPhee (1954) found that, at the height of the 1948 campaign, conversations about the campaign were primarily an exchange of mutually agreeable rather than controversial remarks. Most comments tended to reinforce common positions, with a considerable minority centering on topics that did not seek to affect candidate preferences directly, for example, comments on the likely winner, neutral comments on the conduct of the campaign, and exchanges of information. Similar results were found for June discussions before the campaign had begun and when involvement was not so great.

While this pattern does not seem to make discussion the key element supposed in the hypothesis, it is one that might be expected if most of the conversations occurred between individuals of like political views and vote intentions. Consistent with this conjecture is the finding by Berelson, Lazarsfeld, and McPhee that, outside the family, people talked politics primarily with those of like views; for example, the greater the number of Republican friends a person had, the more likely was his most recent political discussion to have been with a Republican.

However, these investigators also reported that, at each level of interest in the campaign, the more frequently people claimed to have talked politics, the less likely they were to say that their vote intention was the same as that of the majority of their friends. In view of this finding, and since having a political discussion recently was one of the two conjunctive criteria used to determine opinion leadership, it is not an unexpected result that opinion leaders in this study were more likely than others to disagree in politics with some close friends. That opinion leaders influenced the vote intentions of their friends is a moot point, for no data are provided on this. In fact, the authors reported that those conversing with people of unlike views were themselves more likely to defect to a position discrepant from their predispositions and social group than were those who talked with like-minded people. (Maccoby, 1956, raised the possibility that statistical regression can account for some of these presumed defections.) Unfortunately, they have no information concerning who initiated these conversations.

Milne and Mackenzie (1958) reported that, in their discussions with others, opinion leaders claimed to have talked about campaign issues, particularly those salient for their preferred party. Also, discussions were as likely to be characterized mainly by expressions of agreement on political matters as by expressions of disagreement; but who instigated the discussions was not determined. Of particualr interest is the authors' observation that the proportion of opinion leaders who changed from one party to another was not markedly different from the proportion of changers in the sample as a whole; in fact, among opinion leaders, a relatively high number had shifted party preference during their "voting lives." Along with evidence that, although they remained partisan on principal party stands, opinion leaders deviated privately on selected issues, these data imply the possession by opinion leaders of a thoughtful, questioning attitude on political matters. Personal communication received mention as a source of influence by the small percentage of people who wavered or changed parties; noteworthy was the influence of husbands on wives in this group.

Though there are no direct data indicating why people ordinarily discuss political matters during an election campaign, there is some information about the justifications they offer for not talking about politics at that time. On the basis of the sample used in the 1948 election study, Baxter (cited in Berelson, Lazarsfeld, and McPhee, 1954) reported the following reasons: lack of sufficient knowledge, lack of opportunity, knowledge of a difference between own views and those of associates, other interests, lack of time, unwillingness to talk politics in business situations, and tension or unpleasantness associated with political discussions. To be sure, some of these may be no more than justifying rationalizations. But at least two characteristics seem implicated: (1) lack of interest and information, and (2) awareness of differences in views, with the possibility of a disagreeable interchange. Since those who admitted to discussions about the 1948 campaign were more likely to be in disagreement with their friends and to be opinion leaders, Baxter's evidence suggests that disagreement coupled with high interest leads to discussion; but when interest is low, disagreement may produce avoidance of discussions. This conjecture is consistent with the speculations of Lazarsfeld, Berelson, and Gaudet (1948) concerning the joint effects of cross pressures and interest.

Though the two-step hypothesis links media exposure to opinion leadership and then opinion leadership to informal communication, it is of interest to examine the relationship between media exposure and informal communication. Information of this sort is available from a number of studies.

Berelson, Lazarsfeld, and McPhee (1954) found that three times as many people who were high on an index of exposure to political communications "often" discussed politics than did those who were less exposed (35 percent versus 11 percent). Trenaman and McQuail (1961) reported that the two-thirds of their sample who admitted to discussing politics at work or at home were more exposed to television, newspapers, and local sources of information than were the nondiscussers. In a 1960 study (Converse, 1962), people were asked whether they had talked to anyone to convince them of reasons for voting for a particular party or candidate. Of those claiming exposure to four different media for information, 52 percent were opinion givers; of those claiming three media, 44 percent were; two media, 23 percent were; one medium, 15 percent; and no media, 0 percent.

The preceding evidence reflects the relationship between discussion and nonspecific exposure to political stimuli. Of greater value are data on the stimulation of discussion by a specific political event. Deutschmann (1962) found that 56 percent of the people in his panel who watched the first Kennedy-Nixon debate reported having conversations about it. Of those who talked about the debate, 47 percent did so with others of like views, 42 percent with others of mixed political opinions, and 11 percent solely with others of unlike views. Also, people who were generally high media users were much more likely to have talked about the debate than were those who used the media less. (A similar relation is reported by Deutschmann and Danielson, 1960, in regard to nonpolitical news events.) In fact, talking about the debate followed this order: those who either watched or heard the debate *and* also read about it > those who were exposed in only one way > those who were not exposed at all to a mass medium. Only 4 percent reported hearing about the debate through conversation alone; these are pure cases of the transmission function of informal communication. Deutschmann suggested that their small number implies that conversation acts as a supplement rather than as an alternative to the formal media. Katz and Feldman (1962) suggested that Deutschmann's data imply that, when the media are so pervasive or formal communications so attention-getting, there is little room for interpersonal transmission to operate. (As noted previously, this is not true in respect to the diffusion of unanticipated news events.)

Besides serving to transmit information, informal communication may also influence vote intentions. Lazarsfeld, Berelson, and Gaudet (1948) reported several instances of voting decisions resulting from personal influence. Berelson, Lazarsfeld, and McPhee (1954) suggested that the political homogeneity of primary groups may be due to discussions within the groups. However, Trenaman and McQuail (1961) found no relation between discussion and change in vote intentions. Deutschmann (1962) reported that 30 percent of the people who reported no conversation about the first Kennedy-Nixon debate changed their vote intention, while only 19 percent changed who reported having talked about it. But none of the six people who knew about the debate only through conversation changed their vote intention. In fact, more of those who were exposed to the debate only through the formal media changed (34 percent) than did those who were exposed through the media and talked about it (19 percent) or were not exposed at all (21 percent). (The previously mentioned data by Converse, 1962, bear a similarity to this finding.) This led Deutschmann to suggest that discussion may not be a particularly potent force for changing vote intentions, and that the media may function more as a change influence and discussion, since it tends to occur with like-minded people, as a reinforcer of existing intentions. Katz and Feldman (1962) agreed with the latter point (concerning discussion as a maintainer of the status quo), but they averred that it is primarily among those of low interest and little "initiative" that changes in voting intention are due to the media directly rather than to personal influence.

Despite their assertion of the two-step hypothesis, Lazarsfeld, Berelson, and Gaudet (1948) found that more than half of their respondents made no mention of personal contact, and approximately three out of four did not select a personal source as most important, when asked to select from a list of named sources the ones from which they obtained most of their information on the campaign or which were most influential in determining their vote intentions. When mentioning personal sources, women tended to name relatives and, particularly, husbands (*cf.* Katz and Lazarsfeld, 1955, on public affairs leadership), and men to mention business associates primarily and neighbors more than relatives; in general, manual workers mentioned personal contacts more than did other groups.

Milne and Mackenzie (1958) reported that only about 12 percent of their sample mentioned discussions as the chief source of information about the election, whereas over 80 percent named a mass medium. Newspapers were mentioned twice as often as television, which was named twice as often as radio.

The degree of attitudinal homogeneity of the primary group or the personal environment in known to be positively associated with stability of vote intentions. But how media exposure affects this relationship and its culmination in actual voting behavior is unknown. Some suggestive data are provided by Janowitz and Marvick (1956) based on nationwide interviews before and after the 1952 election. They designated as "media fans" those who claimed to have used a mass medium to follow the campaign closely *and* named it as their most important source of political informa- tion. Being a media fan had no effect on candidate preference when people were under conflicting pressures involving heterogeneity of viewpoints among their friends and others. But it did when their primary groups were homogeneous in voting preference. When the views of relevant others were uniformly pro-Eisen- hower, media fans gave 94 percent of their vote to him, while nonfans gave only 77 percent. When uniform pro-Stevenson views obtained, media fans gave him 82 percent of their vote, while nonfans cast only 67 percent for him.

Lazarsfeld, Berelson, and Gaudet (1948) suggested that one advantage of per- sonal influence is that some people will vote because of the pressure brought upon them by others. This implies that voting turnout is enhanced by social influence channeled through personal relations. There is little doubt that this occurs or that some people would not vote were it not for such pressures. This is implied in the joint voting turnout of families and friends and the strenuous efforts of party workers to personally urge people to vote. But how does personal contact compare with formal appeals in this regard?

This question was taken up in two experiments by Eldersveld (1956). People received four mailed appeals to vote in a forthcoming local election, or were con- tacted once by telephone or by a personal visit, or by mailed appeals and a visit, or were not contacted at all. The people making the personal contacts were strangers to the members of the sample. In both studies, voting turnout was markedly higher among those receiving some form of personal contact than among those sent printed appeals or not contacted at all. In the higher-stimulus election involving the mayor- alty, when a higher percentage of the electorate voted, the turnout among those receiving mailed appeals was only slightly above that of people who received no appeal at all; in the lower-stimulus election, it was considerably above that of the noncon- tacted group. People contacted by mail received either factual and somewhat intel- lectual appeals ("rational") or appeals emphasizing the citizen's duty to vote ("moral"); neither type of appeal was more effective than the other. Coupling a mailed appeal to personal contact was no more effective than personal contact alone; nor were there differences between the types of personal contact. Not only was personal contact effective with the politically informed, but also with those of little political knowledge who did not ordinarily vote in local elections. However, it was successful principally with those who believed in the efficacy of political participation.

Eldersveld also reported that people were more likely to recall having been per- sonally contacted than having received the mailed appeals. Unfortunately, there is no way of determining whether those receiving the mailed appeals did more than glance at any one, if even that. Of particular interest is the finding that those per- sonally contacted tended to be more exposed to or aware of campaign coverage in the media, particularly in the newspapers; this suggests an interplay between personal communications and media exposure through aroused interest.

TELEVISION

Though studies concerning the effects of television on political behavior have been cited, when and where relevant, the considerable importance of this medium in political campaigns justifies some commentary on its special characteristics and effects.

In discussions of television's impact on voting behavior, one theme has come up again and again: the personality and television style of the candidate is to become of increasing if not predominant importance, overshadowing issues and personal competence for the office. The televised "image" of the candidate is presumably to become the crucial determinant of his being nominated by a party and of his chances of winning an election. Furthermore, if his natural image is not all it should be, it will be modified by professionals who are expert in such matters and in the use of deliberate format and "props" to give the desired impression. Emphasis on the candidate as a television performer is based on the assumption that, to a great extent, people will naturally evaluate the political credentials of a candidate in terms of the personality he seems to possess. In this pseudo-face-to-face relationship (*cf.* Horton and Wohl, 1956), apparent character and style will dominate the viewer's evaluation of the person's suitability for office. Bradford (1956) suggested that television can reveal insincerity and bunkum, perhaps because of its greater intimacy and demandingness and because it brings the viewer perceptually close to the speaker. Burdick (1962) worried that television would lead to personality-cult politics, and Lang and Lang (1956), that television may aggravate the tendency toward pseudo-personalization of social issues (see Wiebe's comments, 1958, on people's reactions to the televised Army-McCarthy hearings of 1954). But all commentators agree that television has the remarkable ability of transforming a previously unknown or only sectionally known individual into a national personality. Senator Kefauver was projected to national prominence by the televised hearings of the crime committee; and, in 1952, television helped to rapidly establish Stevenson as a national figure. Thomson (1956) suggested that television can create political personalities more quickly than any other medium and seems better able to project personalities than demonstrate issues. Of relevance to the latter point is Carter's (1962) assumption that the first Kennedy-Nixon debate was liked less than the others because it contained less of a clash of personalities.

Lang and Lang (1956) proposed three conceptual ingredients as the basis for people's judgments of the personality of a televised candidate: "performance," or the style and manner of presentation and delivery; "political role," or skill in handling political questions or stating a political position; and "personal image," or imputed personal qualities and traits. They pointed out that the relation between a candidate's personal image and his political effectiveness is an empirical question, and that one does not necessarily imply or entail the other.

Assertions about the effects of television on a candidate's image are derived from presumptions by professional publicists and others, from qualitative analyses of televised performances of candidates, and, in general, from observation coupled with assumptions about effects. To be sure, Eisenhower's personal qualities were significant in his election, but people's image of him antedated his candidacy and his televised speechmaking (*cf.* Hyman and Sheatsley, 1954). What is the evidence from research on the effects of television on people's perceptions of political candidates?

In November, 1952, Pool (1959) compared the perceptions of college students who exposed themselves to the Presidential candidates principally through television ("watchers") with those who used radio primarily ("listeners"). From a list of adjectives, the students checked those which they believed applied to each candidate. Watchers and listeners were comparable in the general pattern of traits assigned to Eisenhower and to Stevenson. Pool conjectured that this uniformity of perceptions may mean that all media project the same image or that the characteristics projected over television and radio were assimilated to the images developed through exposure to other media. There is some suggestion in the data that television increased partisanship, for differences between supporters' and opponents' assignments of attributes to either candidate were greater among watchers than among listeners. However, Stevenson fared better on radio, for the listeners' image was more favorable than the watchers', regardless of which candidate they favored.

While not comparable to people's perceptions of the personal characteristics of individual candidates, television's effects on their perceptions of a political party are also of interest. In the 1959 general election, one of the tactics of the Labour Party was to develop the conception that, unlike the Conservatives, Labour's top candidates were of diverse types. Labour attempted to bring this out *implicitly* in their programs. However, Trenaman and McQuail (1961) reported that this perception was not among the qualities of the party broadcasts commented upon by their sample. (The previously mentioned research on the effectiveness of explicit conclusion-drawing seems relevant to this result.)

The Kennedy-Nixon debates of 1960 provided an unusual opportunity to determine television's effects on perceptions of the personal qualities of candidates. Nixon, as the Vice-President of the United States for eight years, was a widely known public figure; Kennedy, though receiving considerable publicity because of the primary contests, the televised proceedings at the convention, and the "religious issue," was not so well known or so clearly defined a personality. Tannenbaum, Greenberg, and Silverman (1962) found that, in general, the first debate had only a slight effect on people's image of Kennedy. However, there was a marked increase in their ascription to him of the adjective "experienced." Since this characteristic was considered a strength of Nixon, by virtue of his tenure as Vice-President, and a weakness of Kennedy, the change constituted a politically significant gain for Kennedy. In addition, though the changes in Kennedy's image were slight, they were all in the direction of the pattern people laid down for their "ideal President." In contrast, the changes in Nixon's image were erratic. The difference between people's conceptions of "Kennedy as President" and "Nixon as President" became sharper as the campaign progressed. Nixon's image was farther from that of the "ideal President" at the end than at the beginning of the campaign. Most of the changes in the perceptions of the Democrats resulted from the first debate; their characterizations of Kennedy increased in favorableness, while their characterizations of Nixon decreased in favorableness. A similar but less strong change was exhibited by the independents. Of particular interest is the finding that changes in people's conceptions of Kennedy were sharper for those who viewed the debates than for those who did not.

Carter (1962) obtained results which to a great extent parallel those of Tannenbaum, Greenberg, and Silverman. The image of Nixon held by Democrats and

Republicans changed relatively little over all debates. In contrast, both groups showed large positive changes in their images of Kennedy, particularly in respect to "experienced" and "industrious." Apparently, the debates helped to make Kennedy's image as clear-cut and definite as Nixon's, and most of this change was due to the first debate.

COMMENTARY

When the effects of the media on the outcomes of political campaigns in an open society are limited to conversions of vote intentions from one party to another, the media seem relatively ineffective. Few people appear to be converted merely through exposure to formal political communications. The available evidence suggests that the preponderance of total media effects is contributed by the reinforcement or substantiation of vote decisions brought about by other factors, such as habitual patterns of voting or social and personal influences. However, focusing on the voting effects of the media represents an unfruitful perspective, for the role of the media extends to contributions to attention, cognition, and diverse kinds of behavior. Also, the grossness of the research and the lack of frequent assessment of effects throughout the course of a campaign precludes a more thorough examination of the media's significance. In addition, the campaign period is of too short a duration and too filled with communications and countercommunications to permit much change. Since dispositions are strong, the brief and intense period of political activity preceding an election is unlikely to overcome their conservative influence. However, even within these limitations, the media can activate predispositions and strengthen "natural" vote preferences, as was evidenced in the 1948 election and is suggested by studies of the 1960 debates. For somewhat similar viewpoints, see Lang and Lang (1959) and Pool (1959).

A number of critics have argued that an appreciation of the effects of the media on voting preferences requires an examination of their contributions *between* campaigns, and not merely an examination of their influence during the campaign. As has been pointed out by Lang and Lang (1959), the media do not merely transmit messages, but structure "reality" by selecting, emphasizing, and interpreting events. This pervasive influence of the media may lead to small, cumulative changes between campaigns, at a time when political identifications and partisanship may not be salient; the net result may be to affect the dispositions themselves (Pool, 1959) or to set the perceptual frame in which the campaign is interpreted and responded to (Truman, 1951). The data of Milne and Mackenzie (1958) and of Trenaman and McQuail (1961) give force to this argument concerning the need to examine the effects of the media between campaigns. Both studies found that most of the change to the Conservatives in the 1955 and 1959 elections took place during the preceding inter-campaign periods; the campaigns themselves had little effect.

Emphasis on personal influence and assertions of the greater influence of informal over formal means of communication have also been criticized. For instance, Pool (1959) has argued that the data of the 1940 election (Lazarsfeld, Berelson, and Gaudet, 1948) do not provide adequate support for the assertion by Katz and Lazarsfeld (1955) that personal influence had a greater effect on voting behavior than did the media. In fact, in Pool's view, the research evidence leaves open the question of whether or not the media have indirect effects through the activities of opinion leaders. Lang and Lang (1959) suggested that an undue emphasis on opinion leaders may have resulted from excessive concern with the few people who change from one party to another and who are uninterested in the campaign and also underexposed to the media. Little attention has been given to those who vote against their dispositions or in opposition to apparent social and primary group influences; these may be the ones influenced by the media over time.

Luce (1959) has pointed out that much of the body of data on which evidence of personal influence is based is correlational. Hence, change in vote intention could have preceded and led to discussion with people holding the new vote preference, rather than discussion influencing change, as Berelson, Lazarsfeld, and McPhee (1954) asserted. Luce also suggested that, while discussion within a primary group may contribute to some extent to homogeneity of political preferences, the main basis for such uniformity rests in similar social identifications and similar environmental influences.

REFERENCES

Abelson, H. I., and W. D. Rugg (1958). Self-designated influentiality and activity. *Publ. Opin. Quart., 22*, 566–567.

Abelson, R. P., and M. J. Rosenberg (1958). Symbolic psycho-logic: a model of attitudinal cognition. *Behav. Sci., 3*, 1–8.

Albert, R. S. (1957). The role of mass media and the effect of aggressive film content upon children's aggressive responses and identification choices. *Genet. Psychol. Monogr., 55*, 221–285.

Anderson, B. (1962). Opinion influentials and political opinion formation in four Swedish communities. *Int. soc. Sci. J., 14*, 320–336.

Arnheim, R. (1944). The world of the daytime serial. In P. F. Lazarsfeld and F. N. Stanton (Eds.), *Radio research 1942–1943.* New York: Duell, Sloan, and Pearce. Pp. 34–85.

Attneave, F. (1959). *Applications of information theory to psychology.* New York: Holt.

Bailyn, Lotte (1959). Mass media and children: a study of exposure habits and cognitive effects. *Psychol. Monogr., 73*, No. 1 (whole No. 471).

Bandura, A. (1962). Social learning through imitation. In M. R. Jones (Ed.), *Nebraska symposium on motivation, 1962.* Lincoln: Univ. of Nebraska Press. Pp. 211–269.

_____ (1965). Influence of models' reinforcement contingencies on the acquisition of imitative responses. *J. Pers. soc. Psychol., 1*, 589–595.

Bandura, A., and Aletha C. Huston (1961). Identification as a process of incidental learning. *J. abnorm. soc. Psychol., 63*, 311–318.

Bandura, A., Dorothea Ross, and Sheila Ross (1961). Transmission of aggression through imitation of aggressive models. *J. abnorm. soc. Psychol., 63*, 575–582.

_____ (1963). Imitation of film-mediated aggressive models. *J. abnorm. soc. Psychol., 66*, 3–11.

Bandura, A., and R. H. Walters (1963). *Social learning and personality development.* New York: Holt, Rinehart, and Winston.

Banta, T. J. (1964). The Kennedy assassination: early thoughts and emotions. *Publ. Opin. Quart., 28*, 216–224.

Bartlett, F. C. (1932). *Remembering.* Cambridge, Eng.: Cambridge Univ. Press.

Bauer, R. A. (1961). Risk handling in drug adoption: the role of company preference. *Publ. Opin. Quart., 25*, 546–559.

—————— (1964). The obstinate audience: the influence process from the point of view of social communication. *Amer. Psychologist, 19*, 319–328.

Bauer, R. A., and Alice H. Bauer (1960). America, mass society and mass media. *J. soc. Issues, 16*, No. 3, 3–66.

Becker, S. L., and G. J. Wolfe (1960). Can adults predict children's interest in a television program? In W. Schramm (Ed.), *The impact of educational television.* Urbana: Univ. of Illinois Press. Pp. 195–213.

Belson, W. A. (1956). Learning and attitude changes resulting from viewing a television series, "Bon Voyage." *Brit. J. educ. Psychol., 26*, 31–38.

—————— (1957). The hurt mind. British Broadcasting Corporation, Audience Research Department. (Mimeo)

—————— (1958). The effect of television on cinema going. *A-V Communic. Rev., 6*, 131–139.

—————— (1959a). Effects of television on the interests and initiative of adult viewers in Greater London. *Brit. J. Psychol., 50*, 145–158.

—————— (1959b). Television and the family. British Broadcasting Corporation, Audience Research Department. (Mimeo)

—————— (1961). The effects of television on the reading and the buying of newspapers and magazines. *Publ. Opin. Quart., 25*, 366–381.

—————— (1963). A reply to Parker's note. *Publ. Opin. Quart., 27*, 321–329.

Ben-Zeev, S., and I. S. White (1962). Effects and implications. In S. Kraus (Ed.), *The great debates.* Bloomington: Indiana Univ. Press. Pp. 331–337.

Bennett, Edith B. (1955). Discussion, decision, commitment, and consensus in 'group decision.' *Hum. Relat., 8*, 251–273.

Berelson, B. (1942). The effects of print upon public opinion. In D. Waples (Ed.), *Print, radio and film in a democracy.* Chicago: Univ. of Chicago Press. Pp. 41–65.

—————— (1949a). Events as an influence on public opinion. *Journalism Quart., 26*, 145–148.

—————— (1949b). What 'missing the newspaper' means. In P. F. Lazarsfeld and F. N. Stanton (Eds.), *Communications research 1948–1949.* New York: Harper. Pp. 111–129.

—————— (1961). The great debate on cultural democracy. *Stud. Publ. Communic., 3*, 3–14.

Berelson, B., P. F. Lazarsfeld, and W. N. McPhee (1954). *Voting.* Chicago: Univ. of Chicago Press.

Berger, S. M. (1962). Conditioning through vicarious instigation. *Psychol. Rev., 69*, 450–466.

Berkowitz, L. (1962). *Aggression: a social psychological analysis.* New York: McGraw-Hill.

―――― (1964a). Aggressive cues in aggressive behavior and hostility catharsis. *Psychol. Rev., 71*, 104–122.

―――― (1964b). The effects of observing violence. *Sci. Amer., 210*, 35–41.

―――― (1965a). Some aspects of observed aggression. *J. Pers. soc. Psychol., 2*, 359–369.

―――― (1965b). Some experiments in automatism and intent in human aggression. Unpublished manuscript.

Berkowitz, L., R. Corwin, and M. Hieronymous (1963). Film violence and subsequent aggressive tendencies. *Publ. Opin. Quart., 27*, 217–229.

Berkowitz, L., and R. G. Geen (1966). Film violence and the cue properties of available targets. *J. Pers. soc. Psychol., 3*, 525–530.

Berkowitz, L., and Edna Rawlings (1963). Effects of film violence on inhibitions against subsequent aggression. *J. abnorm. soc. Psychol., 66*, 405–412.

Berlyne, D. E. (1960). *Conflict, arousal, and curiosity.* New York: McGraw-Hill.

Blumer, H. (1933). *Movies and conduct.* New York: Macmillan.

―――― (1959). Suggestions for the study of mass-media effects. In E. Burdick and A. J. Brodbeck (Eds.), *American voting behavior.* Glencoe, Ill.: Free Press. Pp. 197–208.

Blumer, H., and P. M. Hauser (1933). *Movies, delinquency, and crime.* New York: Macmillan.

Bogart, L. (1950). The spread of news on a local event: a case history. *Publ. Opin. Quart., 14*, 769–772.

―――― (1957a). Comic strips and their adult readers. In B. Rosenberg and D. M. White (Eds.), *Mass culture.* Glencoe, Ill.: Free Press. Pp. 189–199.

―――― (1957b). Measuring the effectiveness of an overseas information campaign: a case history. *Publ. Opin. Quart., 21*, 475–498.

―――― (1958). *The age of television.* New York: F. Ungar.

―――― (1959). Changing markets and media in Latin America. *Publ. Opin. Quart., 23*, 159–167.

―――― (1962). American television: a brief survey of research findings. *J. soc. Issues, 18*, No. 2, 36–42.

Bonjean, C. M., R. J. Hill, and H. W. Martin (1965). Reactions to the assassination in Dallas. In B. S. Greenberg and E. B. Parker (Eds.), *The Kennedy assassination and the American public.* Stanford: Stanford Univ. Press. Pp. 178–198.

Bradford, R. F. (1956). Politics and television: a fable. In W. Y. Elliott (Ed.), *Television's impact on American culture.* East Lansing: Michigan State Univ. Press. Pp. 185–193.

British Broadcasting Corporation (1964). The 1964 general election. (Mimeo)

Brodbeck, A. J. (1961). An exception to the law of 'adult discount': the need to take film content into account. *Psychol. Reports, 8*, 59–61.

Bruner, J. S., and R. Tagiuri (1954). The perception of people. In G. Lindzey (Ed.), *Handbook of social psychology.* Vol. 2. Cambridge, Mass.: Addison-Wesley. Pp. 634–654.

Burdick, E. (1962). The presidential campaign—1960. In E. Burdick *et al., The eighth art.* New York: Holt, Rinehart, and Winston. Pp. 241–259.

Buss, A. H. (1961). *The psychology of aggression.* New York: Wiley.

Campbell, A. (1962). Has television reshaped politics? *Columbia Journalism Rev., 1,* No. 2, 10–13.

Campbell, A., P. E. Converse, W. E. Miller, and D. E. Stokes (1960). *The American voter.* New York: Wiley.

Campbell, A., G. Gurin, and W. E. Miller (1954). *The voter decides.* Evanston, Ill.: Row, Peterson.

Campbell, A., and R. L. Kahn (1952). *The people elect a president.* Ann Arbor: Survey Research Center, University of Michigan.

Cantril, H. (1940). *The invasion from Mars.* Princeton: Princeton Univ. Press.

Cantril, H., and G. W. Allport (1935). *The psychology of radio.* New York: Harper.

Caplow, T., and J. J. Raymond (1954). Factors influencing the selection of pharmaceutical products. *J. Marketing, 19,* 18–23.

Carter, L. F. (1953). Leadership and small group behavior. In M. Sherif and M. O. Wilson (Eds.), *Group relations at the crossroads.* New York: Harper. Pp. 257–284.

Carter, R. E. (1958). Newspaper gatekeepers and the sources of news. *Publ. Opin. Quart., 22,* 133–144.

Carter, R. E., and O. Sepúlveda (1964). Some patterns of mass media use in Santiago de Chile. *Journalism Quart., 41,* 216–224.

Carter, R. F. (1957). The perceived appeals of television program content. Madison: Univ. of Wisconsin Television Laboratory, Research Bulletin No. 8.

———— (1962). Some effects of the debates. In S. Kraus (Ed.), *The great debates.* Bloomington: Indiana Univ. Press. Pp. 253–270.

Carter, R. F., and B. S. Greenberg (1965). Newspapers or television: which do you believe? *Journalism Quart., 42,* 29–34.

Cartwright, D. (1949). Some principles of mass persuasion: selected findings of research on the sale of U.S. war bonds. *Hum. Relat., 2,* 253–267.

Charters, W. W. (1933). *Motion pictures and youth.* New York: Macmillan.

Coffin, T. (1955). Television's impact on society. *Amer. Psychologist, 10,* 630–641.

Coleman, J. S., E. Katz, and H. Menzel (1957). The diffusion of an innovation among physicians. *Sociometry, 20,* 253–270.

Colley, R. H. (1961). *Defining advertising's goals.* New York: Association of National Advertisers.

Converse, P. E. (1962). Information flow and the stability of partisan attitudes. *Publ. Opin. Quart., 26,* 578–599.

Cooper, Eunice, and Helen Dinerman (1951). Analysis of the film "Don't Be a Sucker": a study in communication. *Publ. Opin. Quart., 15,* 243–264.

Cooper, Eunice, and Marie Jahoda (1947). The evasion of propaganda: how prejudiced people respond to anti-prejudice propaganda. *J. Psychol., 23,* 15–25.

Copp, J. H., M. L. Sill, and C. J. Brown (1958). The function of information sources in the farm practice adoption process. *Rural Sociol., 23*, 146–157.

Crile, Lucinda (1953). *Some findings from television studies.* U.S. Department of Agriculture, Extension Service Circular 490.

Cutlip, S. C. (1954). Content and flow of AP news—from trunk to TTS to reader. *Journalism Quart., 31*, 434–446.

Dale, E. (1933). *The content of motion pictures.* New York: Macmillan.

———— (1935). *Children's attendance of motion pictures.* New York: Macmillan.

Danielson, W. (1956). Eisenhower's February decision: a study of news impact. *Journalism Quart., 33*, 433–441.

Davison, W. P. (1956). Political significance of recognition via mass media—an illustration from the Berlin blockade. *Publ. Opin. Quart., 20*, 327–333.

———— (1959). On the effects of communication. *Publ. Opin. Quart., 23*, 343–360.

———— (1965). *International political communication.* New York: Praeger.

DeFleur, M. L. (1964). Occupational roles as portrayed on television. *Publ. Opin. Quart., 28*, 57–74.

DeFleur, M. L., and O. N. Larsen (1958). *The flow of information.* New York: Harper.

DeSoto, C. B. (1960). Learning a social structure. *J. abnorm. soc. Psychol., 60*, 417–421.

DeSoto, C. B., and J. L. Kuethe (1958). Perception of mathematical properties of interpersonal relationships. *Percept. mot. Skills, 8*, 279–286.

———— (1959). Subjective probabilities of interpersonal relationships. *J. abnorm. soc. Psychol., 59*, 290–294.

Deutschmann, P. J. (1962). Viewing, conversation, and voting intentions. In S. Kraus (Ed.), *The great debates.* Bloomington: Indiana Univ. Press. Pp. 232–252.

Deutschmann, P. J., and W. A. Danielson (1960). Diffusion of knowledge of the major news story. *Journalism Quart., 37*, 345–355.

Dexter, L. A. (1955). Candidates must make the issues and give them meaning. *Publ. Opin. Quart., 19*, 408–414.

Dodd, S. C. (1958). Formulas for spreading opinions. *Publ. Opin. Quart., 22*, 537–554.

Dollard, J., L. Doob, N. Miller, O. Mowrer, and R. Sears (1939). *Frustration and aggression.* New Haven: Yale Univ. Press.

Doob, L. W. (1948). *Public opinion and propaganda.* New York: Holt.

———— (1961). *Communication in Africa.* New Haven: Yale Univ. Press.

Dunn, S. W. (1952). Qualitative analysis of listening in radio class programming. *Journalism Quart., 29*, 175–180.

Dysinger, W. S., and C. A. Ruckmick (1933). *The emotional responses of children to the motion picture situation.* New York: Macmillan.

Eldersveld, S. J. (1956). Experimental propaganda techniques and voting behavior. *Amer. polit. Sci. Rev., 50*, 154–165.

Emery, F. E. (1959a). Psychological effects of the Western film: a study in television viewing: I. The theoretical study: working hypotheses on the psychology of television. *Hum. Relat., 12*, 195–214.

——— (1959b). Psychological effects of the Western film: a study in television viewing: II. The experimental study. *Hum. Relat.,* 215–232.

Emery, F. E., and O. A. Oeser (1958). *Information, decision and action.* New York: Cambridge Univ. Press.

Emmett, B. P. (1966). A brief history of broadcasting research in the United Kingdom, 1936–1955. In Y. Kumugai and S. Takashima (Eds.), *Studies of broadcasting.* Radio and TV Culture Research Institute, Japan Broadcasting Corporation. Pp. 77–100.

Epstein, S. (1962). Comments on Dr. Bandura's paper. In M. R. Jones (Ed.), *Nebraska symposium on motivation, 1962.* Lincoln: Univ. of Nebraska Press. Pp. 269–272.

Eron, L. D. (1963). Relationships of TV viewing habits and aggressive behavior in children. *J. abnorm. soc. Psychol., 67,* 193–196.

Evans, R. (1962). A new tool for politics. In E. Burdick *et al., The eighth art.* New York: Holt, Rinehart, and Winston. Pp. 173–181.

Fagen, R. R. (1964). Relation of communication growth to national political systems in the less developed countries. *Journalism Quart., 41,* 87–94.

Fearing, F. (1954). Social impact of the mass media of communication. In N. B. Henry (Ed.), *Mass media and education.* Chicago: Univ. of Chicago Press. Pp. 165–191.

Feshbach, S. (1955). The drive-reducing function of fantasy behavior. *J. abnorm. soc. Psychol., 50,* 3–11.

——— (1956). The catharsis hypothesis and some consequences of interaction with aggressive and neutral play objects. *J. abnorm. soc. Psychol., 24,* 449–462.

——— (1961). The stimulating versus cathartic effects of a vicarious aggressive activity. *J. abnorm. soc. Psychol., 63,* 381–385.

——— (1964). The function of aggression and the regulation of aggressive drive. *Psychol. Rev., 71,* 257–272.

Festinger, L., D. Cartwright, *et al.* (1948). A study of a rumor: its origin and spread. *Hum. Relat., 1,* 464–486.

Fine, B. J. (1957). Conclusion-drawing, communicator credibility, and anxiety as factors in opinion change. *J. abnorm. soc. Psychol., 54,* 369–374.

Fine, B. J., and N. Maccoby (1952). Television and family life. Boston University, School of Public Relations and Communications. (Mimeo)

Flowerman, S. H. (1947). Mass propaganda in the war against bigotry. *J. abnorm. soc. Psychol., 42,* 429–439.

Forsey, S. D. (1963). Plan 5. The influence of family structures upon the patterns and effects of family viewing. In L. Arons and M. A. May (Eds.), *Television and human behavior.* New York: Appleton-Century-Crofts. Pp. 64–80.

Freidson, E. (1953). The relation of the social situation of contact to the media in mass communication. *Publ. Opin. Quart., 17,* 230–238.

Fujinama, S. (1964). Research in Japan—1963. In A. Katagiri and K. Motono (Eds.), *Studies of broadcasting.* Radio and TV Culture Research Institute, Japan Broadcasting Corporation. Pp. 156–160.

Furu, T. (1962). *Television and children's life.* Radio and TV Culture Research Institute, Japan Broadcasting Corporation.

———— (1965). Research on 'television and the child' in Japan. In A. Katagiri and S. Takashima (Eds.), *Studies of broadcasting*. Radio and TV Culture Research Institute, Japan Broadcasting Corporation. Pp. 51–81.

Galbraith, J. K. (1958). *The affluent society*. Boston: Houghton Mifflin.

Gibb, C. A. (1954). Leadership. In G. Lindzey (Eds.), *Handbook of social psychology*. Vol. 2. Cambridge, Mass.: Addison-Wesley. Pp. 877–920.

Gieber, W. (1956). Across the desk: a study of 16 telegraph editors. *Journalism Quart.*, *33*, 423–432.

Glaser, W. A. (1965). Television and voting turnout. *Publ. Opin. Quart.*, *29*, 71–86.

Glynn, E. D. (1956). Television and the American character—a psychiatrist looks at television. In W. Y. Elliott (Ed.), *Television's impact in American culture*. East Lansing: Michigan State Univ. Press. Pp. 175–182.

Goldberg, H. D. (1951). The role of 'cutting' in the perception of the motion picture. *J. appl. Psychol.*, *35*, 70–71.

Gordon, J. E., and F. Cohn (1963). Effect of fantasy arousal of affiliative drive on doll play aggression. *J. abnorm. soc. Psychol.*, *66*, 301–307.

Gordon, J. E., and E. Smith (1965). Children's aggression, parental attitudes, and the effects of an affiliation-arousing story. *J. Pers. soc. Psychol.*, *1*, 654–658.

Gosnell, H. F. (1927). *Getting out the vote*. Chicago: Univ. of Chicago Press.

Goto, K. (1966). The state of broadcasting research. In Y. Kumagai and S. Takashima (Eds.), *Studies of broadcasting*. Radio and TV Culture Research Institute, Japan Broadcasting Corporation. Pp. 113–121.

Greenberg, B. S. (1963). Dimensions of informal communication. In W. A. Danielson (Ed.), *Paul J. Deutschmann memorial papers in mass communications research*. Cincinnati: Scripps-Howard Research. Pp. 35–43.

———— (1964a). Diffusion of news of the Kennedy assassination. *Publ. Opin. Quart.*, *28*, 225–232.

———— (1964b). The effects of communicator incompatibility on children's judgments of television programs. *J. Broadcasting, 8*, 157–171.

———— (1964c). Person-to-person communication in the diffusion of news events. *Journalism Quart., 41*, 489–494.

———— (1964d). Voting intentions, election expectations and exposure to campaign information. Unpublished manuscript, Institute for Communications Research Stanford University.

———— (1965a). Television for children: dimensions of communicator and audience perceptions. *A-V Communic. Rev., 13*, 385–396.

———— (1965b). Voting intentions, election expectations and exposure to campaign information. *J. Communic., 15*, 149–160.

Greenberg, B. S., and E. B. Parker (1965). Social research on the Kennedy assassination. In B. S. Greenberg and E. B. Parker (Eds.), *The Kennedy assassination and the American public*. Stanford: Stanford Univ. Press. Pp. 361–382.

Haefner, D. P. (1956). Some effects of guilt-arousing and fear-arousing persuasive communications on opinion change. Technical Report No. 1, Office of Naval Research, Contract No. Nonr-668(12), University of Rochester. (Mimeo)

Handel, L. A. (1950). *Hollywood looks at its audience.* Urbana: Univ. of Illinois Press.

Handlon, J. H. (1962). Hormonal activity and individual responses to stresses and easements in everyday living. In R. Roessler and N. S. Greenfield (Eds.), *Physiological correlates of psychological disorder.* Madison: Univ. of Wisconsin Press. Pp. 157–170.

Hartley, Ruth L. (1964). The impact of viewing aggression: studies and problems of extrapolation. Office of Social Research, CBS. (Multilith)

Heider, F. (1958). *The psychology of interpersonal relations.* New York: Wiley.

Heisler, Florence (1947). Comparison of comic book and non-comic book readers of the elementary school. *J. educ. Res., 40*, 458–464.

———— (1948). Comparison of the movie and non-movie goers of the elementary school. *J. educ. Res., 41*, 541–546.

Helson, H. (1964). *Adaption-level theory.* New York: Harper and Row.

Herzog, Herta (1944). What do we really know about daytime serial listeners? In P. F. Lazarsfeld and F. N. Stanton (Eds.), *Radio research 1942–1943.* New York: Duell, Sloan, and Pearce. Pp. 3–33.

Hicks, D. J. (1965). Imitation and retention of film-mediated aggressive peer and adult models. *J. Pers. soc. Psychol., 2*, 97–100.

Hill, R. J., and C. M. Bonjean (1964). News diffusion: a test of the regularity hypothesis. *Journalism Quart., 41*, 336–342.

Himmelweit, Hilde T. (1962). A theoretical framework for the consideration of the effects of television: a British report. *J. soc. Issues, 18*, 16–28.

———— (1963). Plan 4. An experimental study of taste development in children. In L. Arons and M. A. May (Eds.), *Television and human behavior.* New York: Appleton-Century-Crofts. Pp. 46–62.

Himmelweit, Hilde T., A. N. Oppenheim, and Pamela Vince (1958). *Television and the child.* New York: Oxford Univ. Press.

Hoban, C. F., Jr., and E. B. van Ormer (1950). Instructional film research, 1918–1950. Port Washington, N.Y.: U.S. Naval Training Device Center, Office of Naval Research. Technical Report No. SDC 269-7-19.

Holaday, P. W., and G. D. Stoddard (1933). *Getting ideas from the movies.* New York: Macmillan.

Horton, D., and R. Wohl (1956). Mass communication and para-social interaction. *Psychiatry, 19*, 215–229.

Hovland, C. I. (1948). Psychology of the communication process. In W. Schramm (Ed.), *Communications in modern society.* Urbana: Univ. of Illinois Press. Pp. 59–65.

———— (1954). Effects of the mass media of communication. In G. Lindzey (Ed.), *Handbook of social psychology.* Vol. 2. Cambridge, Mass.: Addison-Wesley. Pp. 1062–1103.

———— (1959). Reconciling conflicting results derived from experimental and survey studies of attitude change. *Amer. Psychologist, 14*, 8–17.

Hovland, C. I., I. L. Janis, and H. H. Kelley (1953). *Persuasion and communication.* New Haven: Yale Univ. Press.

Hovland, C. I., A. A. Lumsdaine, and F. D. Sheffield (1949). *Experiments on mass communication.* Princeton: Princeton Univ. Press.

Hovland, C. I., and W. Mandell (1952). An experimental comparison of conclusion-drawing by the communicator and by the audience. *J. abnorm. soc. Psychol., 47*, 581–589.

Hyman, H. H., and P. B. Sheatsley (1947). Some reasons why information campaigns fail. *Publ. Opin. Quart., 11*, 413–423.

——— (1954). The political appeal of President Eisenhower. *Publ. Opin. Quart., 17*, 443–460.

Jacobs, N., Ed. (1961). *Culture for the millions?* Princeton: Van Nostrand.

Janis, I. L. (1962). Psychological effects of warnings. In G. W. Baker and D. W. Chapman (Eds.), *Man and society in disaster.* New York: Basic Books. Pp. 55–92.

Janowitz, M., and D. Marvick (1956). *Competitive pressure and democratic consent.* University of Michigan, Institute of Public Administration. Michigan Governmental Studies, No. 32.

Jones, Dorothy B. (1942). Quantitative analysis of motion picture content. *Publ. Opin. Quart., 6*, 411–428.

Kagan, J. (1958). The concept of identification. *Psychol. Rev., 65*, 296–305.

Kagan, J., and W. Phillips (1964). Measurement of identification: a methodological note. *J. abnorm. soc. Psychol., 69*, 442–444.

Katz, E. (1957). The two-step flow of communication: an up-to-date report on an hypothesis. *Publ. Opin. Quart., 21*, 61–78.

——— (1961). The social itinerary of technical change: two studies on the diffusion of innovation. *Hum. Organizat., 20*, 70–82.

Katz, E., and J. J. Feldman (1962). The debates in the light of research: a survey of surveys. In S. Kraus (Ed.), *The great debates.* Bloomington: Indiana Univ. Press. Pp. 173–223.

Katz, E., and D. Foulkes (1962). On the use of the mass media as 'escape': clarification of a concept. *Publ. Opin. Quart., 26*, 377–388.

Katz, E., and P. F. Lazarsfeld (1955). *Personal influence.* Glencoe, Ill.: Free Press.

Katz, E., M. L. Levin, and H. Hamilton (1963). Traditions of research on the diffusion of innovation. *Amer. sociol. Rev., 238*, 237–252.

Kaufman, Helen J. (1944). The appeal of specific daytime serials. In P. F. Lazarsfeld and F. N. Stanton (Eds.), *Radio research 1942–1943.* New York: Duell, Sloan, and Pearce. Pp. 86–107.

Kaufmann, H. (1965). Definitions and methodology in the study of aggression. *Psychol. Bull., 64*, 351–364.

Kelley, S. (1956). *Professional public relations and political power.* Baltimore: Johns Hopkins Press.

——— (1962). Campaign debates: some facts and issues. *Publ. Opin. Quart., 26*, 351–366.

Kelman, H. C. (1958). Compliance, identification, and internalization: three processes of attitude change. *J. Confl. Resol., 2*, 51–60.

Kendall, Patricia L., and Katherine M. Wolf (1949). The analysis of deviant cases in communications research. In P. F. Lazarsfeld and F. N. Stanton (Eds.), *Communications research 1948–1949.* New York: Harper. Pp. 152–179.

Kimball, P. (1959). People without papers. *Publ. Opin. Quart., 23,* 389–398.

Klapper, J. (1960). *The effects of mass communication.* Glencoe: Free Press.

Knower, F. H. (1935). Experimental studies of changes in attitude: I. A study of the effect of oral argument on changes of attitude. *J. soc. Psychol., 6,* 315–347.

_____ (1936). Experimental studies of changes in attitude: II. A study of the effect of printed argument on changes in attitude. *J. abnorm. soc. Psychol., 30,* 522–532.

Krech, D., R. S. Crutchfield, and E. L. Ballachey (1962). *Individual in society.* New York: McGraw-Hill.

Kriesberg, M. (1949a). Cross-pressures and attitudes: a study of the influence of conflicting propaganda on opinions regarding American-Soviet relations. *Publ. Opin. Quart., 13,* 5–16.

_____ (1949b). Dark areas of ignorance. In L. Markel (Ed.), *Public opinion and foreign policy.* New York: Harper. Pp. 49–64.

Kumagai, Y., and S. Takashima (1966). Research in Japan 1964–1965. In Y. Kumagai and S. Takashima (Eds.), *Studies of broadcasting.* Radio and TV Culture Research Institute, Japan Broadcasting Corporation. Pp. 126–128.

Lang, Gladys E., and K. Lang (1955). The inferential structure of political communications: a study in unwitting bias. *Publ. Opin. Quart., 19,* 168–183.

Lang, K., and Gladys E. Lang (1956). The television personality in politics: some considerations. *Publ. Opin. Quart., 20,* 103–112.

_____ (1959). The mass media and voting. In E. Burdick and A. J. Brodbeck (Eds.), *American voting behavior.* Glencoe, Ill.: Free Press. Pp. 217–235.

_____ (1960). The unique perspective of television and its effect: a pilot study. In W. Schramm (Ed.), *Mass communications.* Urbana: Univ. of Illinois Press. Pp. 544–560.

_____ (1962). Reactions of viewers. In S. Kraus (Ed.), *The great debates.* Bloomington: Indiana Univ. Press. Pp. 313–330.

_____ (1965). The impact of expectations and election day perceptions on voting behavior. Paper read at American Association for Public Opinion Research meetings.

Larder, Diane L. (1962). Effect of aggressive story content on nonverbal play behavior. *Psychol. Reports, 11,* 14.

Larsen, O. N., and R. J. Hill (1954). Mass media and interpersonal communications in the diffusion of a news event. *Amer. sociol. Rev., 19,* 426–433.

Lasswell, H. D. (1949). The structure and function of communication in society. In W. Schramm (Ed.), *Mass communications.* Urbana: Univ. of Illinois Press. Pp. 102–115.

Lazarsfeld, P. F. (1940). *Radio and the printed page.* New York: Duell, Sloan, and Pearce.

_____ (1942). The effects of radio on public opinion. In D. Waples (Ed.), *Print, radio, and film in a democracy.* Chicago: Univ. of Chicago Press. Pp. 66–78.

———— (1948). Communication research and the social psychologist. In W. Dennis (Ed.), *Current trends in social psychology*. Pittsburgh: Univ. of Pittsburgh Press. Pp. 218–273.

———— (1955). Why is so little known about the effects of television on children and what can be done? *Publ. Opin. Quart., 19*, 243–251.

———— (1963a). Afterward: some reflections on past and future research on broadcasting. In G. A. Steiner, *The people look at television*. New York: Knopf. Pp. 409–422.

———— (1963b). Trends in broadcasting research. In A. Katagiri and K. Motono (Eds.), *Studies of broadcasting*. Radio and TV Culture Research Institute, Japan Broadcasting Corporation. Pp. 49–64.

Lazarsfeld, P. F., B. Berelson, and Hazel Gaudet (1948). *The people's choice*. New York: Columbia Univ. Press.

Lazarsfeld, P. F., and Helen Dinerman (1949). Research for action. In P. F. Lazarsfeld and F. N. Stanton (Eds.), *Communications research 1948–1949*. New York: Harper. Pp. 73–108.

Lazarsfeld, P. F., and H. Field (1946). *The people look at radio*. Chapel Hill: Univ. of North Carolina Press.

Lazarsfeld, P. F., and Patricia L. Kendall (1948). *Radio listening in America*. New York: Prentice-Hall.

Lazarsfeld, P. F., and R. K. Merton (1948). Mass communication, popular taste and organized social action. In L. Bryson (Ed.), *The communication of ideas*. New York: Harper. Pp. 95–118.

Lazarus, R. S., and Elizabeth Alfert (1964). Short-circuiting of threat by experimentally altering cognitive appraisal. *J. abnorm. soc. Psychol., 69*, 195–205.

Lazarus, R. S., E. M. Opton, M. S. Nomikes, and N. O. Rankin (1965). The principle of short-circuiting of threat: further evidence. *J. Pers., 33*, 622–635.

Lerner, D. (1958). *The passing of traditional society*. Glencoe, Ill.: Free Press.

Leuba, C., and C. Lucas (1945). The effects of attitudes on descriptions of pictures. *J. exp. Psychol., 35*, 517–524.

Levin, H. J. (1954). Competition among mass media and the public interest. *Publ. Opin. Quart., 18*, 62–79.

Lewin, K. (1953). Studies in group decision. In D. Cartwright and A. Zander (Eds.), *Group dynamics*. Evanston, Ill.: Row, Peterson. Pp. 287–301.

Lewin, K., and P. Grabbe (1945). Conduct, knowledge and acceptance of new values. *J. soc. Issues, 1*, 53–64.

Lionberger, H. F. (1960). *Adoption of new ideas and practices*. Ames: Iowa State Univ. Press.

Lippmann, W. (1922). *Public opinion*. New York: Macmillan.

Louis, R., and J. Rovan (1955). *Television and tele-clubs in rural communities: an experiment in France*. Paris: UNESCO.

Lovaas, O. I. (1961). Effect of exposure to symbolic aggression on aggressive behavior. *Child Develpmt., 32*, 37–44.

Lowenthal, L. (1944). Biographies in popular magazines. In P. F. Lazarsfeld and F. N. Stanton (Eds.), *Radio research 1942–1943*. New York: Duell, Sloan, and Pearce. Pp. 509–548.

Luce, R. D. (1959). Analyzing the social process underlying group voting patterns. In E. Burdick and A. J. Brodbeck (Eds.), *American voting behavior.* Glencoe, Ill.: Free Press. Pp. 330–352.

Lumsdaine, A. A. (1958). Gauging the effects of films on reading interests. In M. A. May and A. A. Lumsdaine (Eds.), *Learning from films.* New Haven: Yale Univ. Press. Pp. 185–194.

————, Ed. (1961). *Student response in programmed instruction.* Washington: National Academy of Sciences, National Research Council.

Lyle, J. (1962). Immediate vs. delayed reward use of newspapers by adolescents. *Journalism Quart., 39,* 83–85.

Lyness, P. I. (1952). The place of the mass media in the lives of boys and girls. *Journalism Quart., 29,* 43–54.

McCandless, B. R. (1944). A study of non-listeners. In P. F. Lazarsfeld and F. N. Stanton (Eds.), *Radio research 1942–1943*. New York: Duell, Sloan, and Pearce. Pp. 407–418.

Maccoby, Eleanor E. (1951). Television: its impact on school children. *Publ. Opin. Quart., 15,* 421–444.

———— (1954). Why do children watch television? *Publ. Opin. Quart., 18,* 239–244.

———— (1956). Pitfalls in the analysis of panel data: A research note on some technical aspects of voting. *Amer. J. Sociol., 59,* 359–362.

Maccoby, Eleanor E., H. Levin, and B. M. Selya (1955). The effect of emotional arousal on the retention of aggressive and nonaggressive movie content. *Amer. Psychologist, 10,* 359.

———— (1956). The effects of emotional arousal on the retention of film content: a failure to replicate. *J. abnorm. soc. Psychol., 53,* 373–374.

Maccoby, Eleanor E., and W. C. Wilson (1957). Identification and observational learning from films. *J. abnorm. soc. Psychol., 55,* 76–87.

Maccoby, Eleanor E., W. C. Wilson, and R. V. Burton (1958). Differential movie-viewing behavior of male and female viewers. *J. Pers., 26,* 259–267.

McGinnies, E., and I. Altman (1959). Discussion as a function of attitudes and content of a persuasive communication. *J. appl. Psychol., 43,* 53–59.

McGinnies, E., R. Lana, and C. Smith (1958). The effects of sound films on opinions about mental illness in community discussion groups. *J. appl. Psychol., 42,* 40–46.

MacLean, M. S. (1954). Mass communication of public affairs news. Unpublished doctor's dissertation, University of Wisconsin.

Mahony, Katherine St. J. (1953). Elementary school pupils' TV habits and choice. *Catholic educ. Rev., 51,* 234–245.

Mandler, G. (1962). From association to structure. *Psychol. Rev., 69,* 415–427.

Marcus, A. S., and R. A. Bauer (1964). Yes: there are generalized opinion leaders. *Publ. Opin. Quart., 28,* 628–632.

Marx, H. L., Jr., Ed. (1953). *Television and radio in American life.* New York: H. W. Wilson.

Mathur, J. C., and P. Neurath (1959). *An Indian experiment in radio farm forums.* Paris: UNESCO.

Mathur, J. C., and H. P. Saksena (1963). *Social education through television: an all India Radio-UNESCO pilot project.* Paris: UNESCO.

May, M. A., and N. L. Jenkinson (1958). The reading of a book based on a film. In M. A. May and A. A. Lumsdaine (Eds.), *Learning from films.* New Haven: Yale Univ. Press. Pp. 195–203.

Mehling, R., S. Kraus, and R. D. Yoakam (1962). Pre-debate campaign interest and media use. In S. Kraus (Ed.), *The great debates.* Bloomington: Indiana Univ. Press. Pp. 224–231.

Meine, F. J. (1941). Radio and the press among young people. In P. F. Lazarsfeld and F. N. Stanton (Eds.), *Radio research 1941.* New York: Duell, Sloan, and Pearce. Pp. 189–223.

Mendelsohn, H. A. (1964). A critical review of the literature and a proposed theory. In M. Blumenthal (Ed.), *The Denver symposium on mass communications research for safety.* Chicago: National Safety Council. Pp. 1–138.

―――― (1965). Exposure to election broadcasts and terminal voting decisions. Paper read at American Association for Public Opinion Research meetings.

Menzel, H., and E. Katz (1955). Social relations and innovation in the medical profession: the epidemiology of a new drug. *Publ. Opin. Quart., 19,* 337–352.

Merrill, I. R. (1961). Broadcast viewing and listening by children. *Publ. Opin. Quart., 25,* 263–276.

Merton, R. K. (1946). *Mass persuasion.* New York: Harper.

―――― (1949). Patterns of influence. In P. F. Lazarsfeld and F. N. Stanton (Eds.), *Communications research 1948–1949.* New York: Harper. Pp. 180–219.

Miller, D. C. (1945). A research note on mass communications. *Amer. sociol. Rev., 10,* 691–694.

Miller, N. E., *et al.* (1957). Graphic communication and the crisis in education. *A-V Communic. Rev., 5,* Special edition.

Miller, W. E. (1965). Analysis of the effect of election night predictions on voting behavior. University of Michigan, Survey Research Center. Unpublished report, Political Behavior Program.

Milne, R. S., and H. C. Mackenzie (1958). *Marginal seat, 1955.* London: Hansard Society for Parliamentary Government.

Mitnick, L. L., and E. McGinnies (1958). Influencing ethnocentrism in small discussion groups through a film communication. *J. abnorm. soc. Psychol., 56,* 82–90.

Mullen, J. J. (1963). Newspaper advertising in the Kennedy-Nixon campaign. *Journalism Quart., 40,* 3–11.

Murray, H. A. (1933). The effect of fear upon estimates of the maliciousness of other personalities. *J. soc. Psychol., 4,* 310–329.

Mussen, P. H., and Eldred Rutherford (1961). Effects of aggressive cartoons on children's aggressive play. *J. abnorm. soc. Psychol., 62*, 461–464.

Nafziger, R. O., W. C. Engstrom, and M. S. Maclean (1951). The mass media and an informed public. *Publ. Opin. Quart., 15*, 105–114.

Noelle-Neuman, Elisabeth (1959). Mass communication media and public opinion. *Journalism Quart., 36*, 401–409.

Nowlis, V. (1965). Research with the mood adjective check list. In S. S. Tomkins and C. E. Izard (Eds.), *Affect, cognition, and personality.* New York: Springer. Pp. 352–389.

Nowlis, V., and Helen H. Nowlis (1956). The description and analysis of mood. *Ann. N.Y. Acad. Sci., 65*, 345–355.

Okabe, K. (1963). Broadcasting research in post-war Japan. In A. Katagiri and K. Motono (Eds.), *Studies of broadcasting.* Radio and TV Culture Research Institute, Japan Broadcasting Corporation. Pp. 7–47.

———— (1964). Broadcast research today. In A. Katagiri and K. Motono (Eds.), *Studies of broadcasting.* Radio and TV Culture Research Institute, Japan Broadcasting Corporation. Pp. 7–21.

Ono, T. (1959). An analysis of Kimi No Na Wa (What is your name?). In H. Kato (Ed.), *Japanese popular culture.* Rutland, Vt.: C. E. Tuttle. Pp. 151–164.

Parker, E. B. (1963a). The effects of television on magazine and newspaper reading: a problem in methodology. *Publ. Opin. Quart., 27*, 315–320.

———— (1963b). The effects of television on public library circulation. *Publ. Opin. Quart., 27*, 578–589.

Passin, H. (1959). Preface. In H. Kato (Ed.), *Japanese popular culture.* Rutland, Vt.: C. E. Tuttle. Pp. 15–26.

Peterson, Ruth C., and L. L. Thurstone (1933). *Motion pictures and the social attitudes of children.* New York: Macmillan.

Pittman, D. J. (1958). Mass media and juvenile delinquency. In J. S. Roucek (Ed.), *Juvenile delinquency.* New York: Philosophical Library. Pp. 230–247.

Pool, I. de S. (1959). TV: a new dimension in politics. In E. Burdick and A. J. Brodbeck (Eds.), *American voting behavior.* Glencoe, Ill.: Free Press. Pp. 197–208.

———— (1963). The mass media and politics in the modernization process. In L. W. Pye (Ed.), *Communications and political development.* Princeton: Princeton Univ. Press. Pp. 234–253.

Pye, L. W. Ed. (1963). *Communications and political development.* Princeton: Princeton Univ. Press.

Renshaw, S., V. L. Miller, and Dorothy P. Marquis (1933). *Children's sleep.* New York: Macmillan.

Riley, Matilda W., and J. W. Riley (1951). A sociological approach to communications research. *Publ. Opin. Quart., 15*, 445–460.

Riley, J. W., F. V. Cantwell, and Katherine F. Ruttiger (1949). Some observations on the social effects of television. *Publ. Opin. Quart., 13*, 223–234.

Robinson, W. S. (1941). Radio comes to the farmer. In P. F. Lazarsfeld and F. N. Stanton (Eds.), *Radio research 1941*. New York: Duell, Sloan, and Pearce. Pp. 224–294.

Rogers, E. M. (1962). *Diffusion of innovations*. Glencoe, Ill.: Free Press.

———— (1965). Mass media exposure and modernization among Columbian peasants. *Publ. Opin. Quart., 29*, 614–625.

Rogers, E. M., and D. G. Cartano (1962). Methods of assessing opinion leadership. *Publ. Opin. Quart., 26*, 435–441.

Rogers, E. M., and W. Herzog (1966). Functional literacy among Colombian peasants. *Econ. Developmt. cult. Change, 14*, 190–203.

Rogers, E. M., and Leticia Smith (1965). Bibliography on the diffusion of innovations. East Lansing: Michigan State Univ. Department of Communication. (Mimeo)

Roper, E., and associates (1965). *The public's view of television and other media 1959–1964*. Television Information Office, New York.

Rosen, I. C. (1948). The effects of the motion picture "Gentleman's Agreement" on attitude toward Jews. *J. Psychol., 26*, 525–536.

Rosenberg, B., and D. M. White, Eds. (1957). *Mass culture*. Glencoe, Ill.: Free Press.

Rosten, L. C. (1937). *The Washington correspondents*. New York: Harcourt.

Ryan, B., and N. C. Gross (1943). The diffusion of hybrid seed corn in two Iowa communities. *Rural Sociol., 8*, 15–24.

Salant, R. S. (1962). The television debates: a revolution that deserves a future. *Publ. Opin. Quart., 26*, 335–350.

Samuelson, M., R. F. Carter, and L. Ruggels (1963). Education, available time and use of mass media. *Journalism Quart., 40*, 491–496.

Sarbin, T. R. (1954). Role theory. In G. Lindzey (Ed.), *Handbook of social psychology*. Cambridge, Mass.: Addison-Wesley. Pp. 223–258.

Sargent, S. S. (1939). Stereotypes and the newspapers. *Sociometry, 2*, 69–75.

Schachter, S., and J. E. Singer (1962). Cognitive, social, and psychological determinants of emotional state. *Psychol. Rev., 69*, 379–399.

Schachter, S., and L. Wheeler (1962). Epinephrine, chlorpromazine, and amusement. *J. abnorm. soc. Psychol., 65*, 121–128.

Schramm, W. (1954). Mass communications and their audiences in other countries. In W. Schramm (Ed.), *The process and effects of mass communication*. Urbana: Univ. of Illinois Press. Pp. 74–83.

———— (1957). *Responsibility in mass communications*. New York: Harper.

———— (1960). The audiences of educational television. In W. Schramm (Ed.), *The impact of educational television*. Urbana: Univ. of Illinois Press. Pp. 18–35.

———— (1962). Television in the life of the child—implications for the school. In C. R. Carpenter *et al., New teaching aids for the American classroom*. Washington, D.C.: Government Printing Office. Pp. 50–70.

———— (1964). *Mass media and national development*. Stanford: Stanford Univ. Press.

———— (1965). Communication in crisis. In B. S. Greenberg and E. B. Parker (Eds.), *The Kennedy assassination and the American public.* Stanford: Stanford Univ. Press. Pp. 1–25.

Schramm, W., and R. F. Carter (1959). The effectiveness of a political telethon. *Publ. Opin. Quart., 23,* 121–127.

Schramm, W., J. Lyle, and E. B. Parker (1961). *Television in the lives of our children.* Stanford: Stanford Univ. Press.

Schramm, W., J. Lyle, and I. de S. Pool (1963). *The people look at educational television.* Stanford: Stanford Univ. Press.

Schramm, W., and D. M. White (1949). Age, education, economic status: factors in newspaper reading. *Journalism Quart., 26,* 149–166.

Scollon, R. W. (1956). A study of some communicator variables related to attitude restructuring through motion picture films. Unpublished doctoral dissertation, Pennsylvania State University.

Scott, E. M. (1957). Personality and movie preference. *Psychol. Reports, 3,* 17–19.

Seldes, G. (1962). Some impressions of television. *J. soc. Issues, 18,* 29–35.

Sheatsley, P. B., and J. J. Feldman (1964). The assassination of President Kennedy: a preliminary report on public reactions and behavior. *Publ. Opin. Quart., 28,* 189–215.

———— (1965). A national survey on public reactions and behavior. In B. S. Greenberg and E. B. Parker (Eds.), *The Kennedy assassination and the American public.* Stanford: Stanford Univ. Press. Pp. 149–177.

Sheffield, F. D. (1961). Theoretical considerations in the learning of complex sequential tasks from demonstration and practice. In A. A. Lumsdaine (Ed.), *Student response in programmed instruction.* Washington, D.C.: National Academy of Sciences, National Research Council. Pp. 13–32.

Shuttleworth, F. K., and M. A. May (1933). *The social conduct and attitudes of movie fans.* New York: Macmillan.

Siebert, J. C., *et al.* (1954). *The influence of television on the election of 1952.* Oxford, Oxford Research Associates.

Siegel, Alberta E. (1956). Film-mediated fantasy aggression and strength of aggressive drive. *Child Develpmt., 27,* 365–378.

———— (1958). The influence of violence in the mass media upon children's role expectations. *Child Develpmt., 29,* 35–56.

Simon, H., and F. Stern (1955). The effect of television upon voting behavior in Iowa in the 1952 presidential election. *Amer. polit. Sci. Rev., 49,* 470–477.

Smith, C. H. (1944). The CBS forecast panels. In P. F. Lazarsfeld and F. N. Stanton (Eds.), *Radio research 1942–1943.* New York: Duell, Sloan, and Pearce. Pp. 419–438.

Smythe, D. W. (1954). Reality as presented by television. *Publ. Opin. Quart., 18,* 143–156.

Spain, Frances L., and Margaret C. Scoggin (1962). They still read books. In E. Burdick *et al., The eighth art.* New York: Holt, Rinehart, and Winston. Pp. 173–181.

Speier, H. (1939). Morale and war propaganda. In H. Speier and A. Kahler (Eds.), *War in our time.* New York: Norton. Pp. 299–326.

Speisman, J. C., R. S. Lazarus, A. Mordkoff, and L. Davison (1964). Experimental reduction of stress based on ego-defense theory. *J. abnorm. soc. Psychol., 68*, 367–380.

Star, Shirley A., and Helen M. Hughes (1950). Report on an educational campaign: The Cincinnati plan for the United Nations. *Amer. J. Sociol., 55*, 389–400.

Steiner, G. A. (1963). *The people look at television.* New York: Knopf.

Stempel, G. H. (1961). Selectivity in readership of political news. *Publ. Opin. Quart., 25*, 400–404.

Stewart, J. B. (1964). *Repetitive advertising in newspapers.* Boston: Harvard Business School, Division of Research.

Stouffer, S. A. (1955). *Communism, conformity, and civil liberties.* New York: Doubleday.

Stycos, J. M. (1952). Patterns of communication in a Greek rural village. *Publ. Opin. Quart., 16*, 59–70.

–––––– (1965). The potential role of Turkish village opinion leaders in a program of family planning. *Publ. Opin. Quart., 29*, 120–130.

Suchman, E. A. (1941). Invitation to music. In P. F. Lazarsfeld and F. N. Stanton (Eds.), *Radio Research 1941.* New York: Duell, Sloan, and Pearce. Pp. 140–188.

Swank, T. E. (1961). An analysis of the social diffusion of an audio-visual message through a church congregation. Unpublished doctoral dissertation, Indiana University.

Swanson, C. E. (1954). Procedures and effects of the printed media. In N. B. Henry (Ed.), *Mass media and education.* Chicago: Univ. of Chicago Press. Pp. 139–164.

Swanson, C. E., J. Jenkins, and R. L. Jones (1950). President Truman speaks: a study of ideas vs. media. *Journalism Quart., 27*, 251–267.

Tannenbaum, P. H., and Eleanor P. Gaer (1965). Mood change as a function of stress of protagonist and degree of identification in a film-viewing situation. *J. Pers. soc. Psychol., 2*, 612–616.

Tannenbaum, P. H., B. S. Greenberg, and F. R. Silverman (1962). Candidate images. In S. Kraus (Ed.), *The great debates.* Bloomington: Indiana Univ. Press. Pp. 271–288.

Taplin, W. (1960). *Advertising.* London: Hutchinson.

Thomson, C. A. H. (1956). *Television and presidential politics.* Washington: Brookings Institution.

Thorp, Margaret F. (1939). *America at the movies.* New Haven: Yale Univ. Press.

Thrasher, F. M. (1949). The comics and delinquency: cause or scapegoat? *J. educ. Sociol., 23*, 195–205.

Trenaman, J., and D. McQuail (1961). *Television and the political image.* London: Methuen.

Troldahl, V. C., and R. Van Dam (1965). A new scale for identifying public-affairs opinion leaders. *Journalism Quart., 42*, 655–657.

Truman, D. B. (1951). Some political variables for election surveys. *Int. J. Opin. Attitude Res., 5*, 241–250.

UNESCO (1956). *Cultural radio broadcasts.* Paris: UNESCO.

–––––– (1960). *Rural television in Japan.* Paris: UNESCO.

———— (1965). *Radio broadcasting serves rural development.* Paris: UNESCO.

U.S. Information Agency (1961). The impact of Hollywood films abroad. PMS-50. (Mimeo)

———— (1962). The impact of American commercial television in Western Europe. R-163-62(R). (Mimeo)

U.S. Senate, Subcommittee to Investigate Juvenile Delinquency (1964). Television and juvenile delinquency. Interim Senate Report, 88th Congress, Second Session.

Wall, W. D., and W. A. Simonson (1950). The emotional responses of adolescent groups to certain films. *Brit. J. educ. Sociol., 20,* 153–163.

———— (1951). The responses of adolescent groups to certain films. *Brit. J. educ. Sociol., 21,* 81–88.

Walters, R. H. (1966). Implications of laboratory studies of aggression for the control and regulation of violence. *The Annals, 364,* 60–72.

Walters, R. H., Marion Leat, and L. Mezei (1963). Inhibition and disinhibition of responses through empathetic learning. *Canad. J. Psychol., 17,* 235–243.

Walters, R. H., R. D. Parke, and Valerie A. Cane (1965). Timing of punishment and the observation of consequences to others as determinants of response inhibition. *J. exp. Child Psychol., 2,* 10–30.

Walters, R. H., and E. L. Thomas (1963). Enhancement of punitiveness by visual and audiovisual displays. *Canad. J. Psychol., 17,* 244–255.

Walters, R. H., E. L. Thomas, and C. W. Acker (1962). Enhancement of punitive behavior by audiovisual displays. *Science, 136,* 872–873.

Waples, D., B. Berelson, and F. R. Bradshaw (1940). *What reading does to people.* Chicago: Univ. of Chicago Press.

Warner, W. L., and W. E. Henry (1948). The radio day time serial: a symbolic analysis. *Genet. Psychol. Monogr., 37,* 3–71.

Warshow, R. (1954). Movie chronicle: the Westerner. *Partisan Rev., 21,* 190–203.

Wertham, F. (1954). *Seduction of the innocent.* New York: Rinehart.

———— (1962). The scientific study of mass media effects. *Amer. J. Psychiat., 119,* 306–311.

Westley, B. H., and W. J. Severin (1964a). A profile of the daily newspaper non-reader. *Journalism Quart., 41,* 45–51.

———— (1964b). Some correlates of media credibility. *Journalism Quart., 41,* 325–335.

White, D. M. (1950). The 'gatekeeper': a case study in the selection of news. *Journalism Quart., 27,* 383–390.

Wiebe, G. D. (1958). The Army-McCarthy hearings and the public conscience. *Publ. Opin. Quart., 22,* 490–502.

Wilke, W. H. (1934). An experimental comparison of the speech, the radio, and the printed page as propaganda devices. *Arch. Psychol., N.Y.,* No. 169.

Wilkening, E. A., Joan Tully, and H. Presser (1962). Communication and acceptance of recommended farm practices among dairy farmers of Northern Victoria. *Rural Sociol., 27,* 116–197.

Williams, R. M. (1947). The reduction of intergroup tensions. Social Science Research Council Bulletin No. 57.

Wirth, L. (1948). Consensus and mass communication. *Amer. sociol. Rev., 13,* 1–15.

——— (1956). *Community life and social policy* (ed. E. W. Marvick and A. M. Reiss). Chicago: Univ. of Chicago Press. Pp. 368–391.

Witty, P. A., P. Kinsella, and Anne Coomer (1963). A summary of yearly studies of televiewing—1949–1963. *Element. English, 40,* 590–597.

Wolfe, Katherine M., and Marjorie Fiske (1949). The children talk about comics. In P. F. Lazarsfeld and F. N. Stanton (Eds.), *Communications research 1948–1949.* New York: Harper. Pp. 3–50.

Wolfenstein, Martha, and N. Leites (1950). *Movies: a psychological study.* Glencoe, Ill.: Free Press.

Zajonc, R. B. (1954). Some effects of the 'space' serials. *Publ. Opin. Quart., 18,* 367–374.

39

Industrial Social Psychology

VICTOR H. VROOM, Carnegie-Mellon University

Psychologists have been studying and attempting to explain the behavior of persons in industrial organizations for over half a century. By the early 1930's industrial psychology had emerged as a legitimate and significant field of inquiry within psychology. Much of the early work by industrial psychologists was concerned with the technology of personnel selection and placement, and with the associated problems of test construction, job analysis, and criterion development. Industrial psychology had its origins in the psychology of individual differences, and shared with this field both a highly empirical, atheoretical orientation and the use of correlational methods.

During the past ten or twenty years there has been a tendency for psychologists with vastly different backgrounds, interests, and theoretical and methodological persuasions to become interested in the systematic study of behavior in industrial and other types of organizations. Experimental psychologists have applied their methods and concepts to problems of human factors in machine and system design; clinical psychologists have discovered applications of their diagnostic and therapeutic skills in industrial settings; and social psychologists have studied various forms of social influence within formal organizations. The net result has been not only a substantial increase in the range of behavioral phenomena studied by psychologists in industry, but also a healthy cross-fertilization of concepts and methods among the subdisciplines of psychology.

Our objective in this chapter is to provide a picture of the field which has come to be known as industrial social psychology (Haire, 1954; Vroom and Maier, 1961) or organizational psychology (Bass, 1965; Leavitt, 1962; Leavitt and Bass, 1964; Schein, 1965). We will not attempt at this point to draw a precise boundary around the subject matter signified by these terms, except to say that the phenomena of interest are manifestations of the processes of social influence within large-scale formal organizations.

Preparation of this chapter was supported in part by Ford Foundation Grant 140055 to Carnegie-Mellon University for research on organizational behavior. The author is also indebted to J. Stacy Adams, Marvin Dunnette, Harold Leavitt, Lyman Porter, Frank Scalia, and Karl Weick for their helpful comments and suggestions.

Selecting these phenomena for separate examination in a chapter such as this in no way implies that the processes affecting behavior in organizations are different than those which have been demonstrated in less complex behavior settings, including the laboratory. Ultimately, statements about the determinants of behavior in organizations should be derivable from general theories capable of explaining behavior in other situations. However, now, and for the foreseeable future, organizations provide social psychologists both with an opportunity to test basic propositions about the determinants of behavior in complex environments and with a chance to contribute in a direct way to knowledge about how to organize human activity to achieve particular objectives.

Since publication of the first edition of the *Handbook of Social Psychology* (Lindzey, 1954), behavioral-science research in organizations has been conducted at an extremely vigorous rate. There are now literally hundreds of books and articles reporting original research on the social determinants of behavior in organizational settings. As is frequently the case, this increase in our reservoir of empirical findings has far outstripped the development of theories capable of explaining them. The inherent complexity of the problems studied, the variety in research methods used, and the absence of standardization of concepts or measures combine to produce a situation which to the outsider appears chaotic and to the insider seems like a challenging, if perhaps insoluble, puzzle.

It is our task in this chapter to put the pieces of the puzzle together or, to put it more modestly, to fit as many pieces as possible into a coherent framework. To simplify this task we will distinguish three somewhat different classes of problems which have been subjected to research by social psychologists interested in the study of industrial and other types of organizations. These three problems are defined not in terms of the specific nature of the processes studied but in a more gross fashion corresponding to the size of the system about which one is asking questions and seeking answers. Thus, social psychologists have been concerned with (1) the behavior of individual organization members, (2) internal processes which take place in the small face-to-face work groups in organizations, and (3) the structure and functioning of large-scale formal organizations.

To be sure, these problems are interrelated. Individuals are components of groups and groups are components of organizations. However, the complexity of the problems increases markedly as one moves from smaller to larger systems, and there are commensurate changes in concepts used and processes studied. While ultimately it will be desirable to have mutually consistent and compatible theories of phenomena occurring at these different levels, we are far from having reached this interdisciplinary utopia. The safer course, and the one which we shall pursue, is to treat separately the results of research on individuals, on small work groups, and on formal organizations.

THE INDIVIDUAL IN THE ORGANIZATION

In one sense an organization is nothing more than a set of individuals who share the property of organizational membership. Of course, these individuals occupy interdependent roles and typically interact with one another in ways which are indicative of a highly coordinated complex system. However, there are some purposes for which it is analytically desirable to treat the individual as the system of interest and to relegate the remainder of the organization to the status of the environment in which the individual is behaving.

This approach is clearly psychological in nature. It seeks to explain, and ultimately to control, individual behavior in an organizational context. In organizations, as elsewhere, persons perceive, learn, think, solve problems, and make decisions. Though what they perceive or learn and the kinds of problems they solve or decisions they make may be different in organizational settings, there is no reason to believe that the underlying processes are any different.

The initial attempts by social psychologists to explain individual behavior in organizations were distinguishable in two major respects from earlier efforts by industrial psychologists. Social psychologists have been primarily interested in stimulus-response relationships, where the responses are observed behaviors on the part of organization members and the stimuli are measured or experimentally created attributes of their work environment, such as the supervision they receive, the tasks they are assigned, and the behavior of their coworkers. This approach stands in sharp contrast to the search by industrial psychologists for response-response relationships, specifically, correlations between test scores and job performance. In addition, social-psychological research has focused almost exclusively on the motivational bases of behavior in organizations, whereas more attention has been given to perceptual, cognitive, and motor skills in traditional industrial psychology.

Empirical research within the scope of this approach has utilized two broad classes of dependent variables: (1) the attitudes of individual members toward their roles in the organization, and (2) the effectiveness with which individual members perform their roles in the organization. We will examine, in turn, the empirical evidence which has been obtained with respect to each of these variables, and the concepts and propositions necessary to account for this evidence.

ATTITUDES TOWARD ORGANIZATIONAL ROLES

As noted by Allport (1954), the concept of attitude has occupied a central place in the history of social psychology. While there has been, and continues to be, considerable disagreement over the most useful conceptual definition of this concept, there is a great deal of uniformity among the kinds of measures used by different investigators. The attitudes of persons toward objects or events are commonly assumed to be revealed by their verbal responses to direct questions, asked in interviews or in questionnaires, concerning their feelings, desires, or preferences among these objects or events.

Our primary interest here is in the determinants and correlates of the attitudes of organization members toward their roles in organizations. Accordingly, in the investigations to be discussed, questions have been asked of workers concerning their feelings about the supervision they receive, the policies of the company for which they work, their promotional opportunities, their relations with their coworkers, and more inclusive referents such as their job and their membership in the organization. It should be noted that other terms have frequently been used to designate the same type of measure. Some writers (Morse, 1953; Smith, 1963) refer to such verbal reports as measures of job satisfaction, while others (Guion, 1958; Likert and Willits, 1940) prefer the concept of morale.

Attitudes and performance

Twenty years ago it was assumed that the attitudes or satisfaction of organization members and their role effectiveness were positively correlated with one another. An individual who liked his job, his supervisor, the company for whom he worked, and his coworkers was assumed to have a significantly higher probability of being effective on his job than one who had negative attitudes toward these role-related referents. An even stronger *causal* assumption was implicit in the writings of some of the early advocates of "better human relations" in American industry. The Hawthorne experiments and other early studies led many to the conclusion that satisfying the needs of workers would *result in* a higher level of productivity.

There is now sufficient evidence to indicate that both of these assumptions are gross oversimplifications of the actual state of affairs, if not totally in error. Measures of job attitudes, job satisfaction, and morale have been found not to bear any invariant positive relation to measures of effectiveness (Brayfield and Crockett, 1955; Kahn, 1960; Vroom, 1964). Positive relationships have been reported in some investigations, no relationship has been reported in others, and negative relationships in still others. Vroom (1964) has summarized the results of 20 investigations reporting product-moment correlation coefficients between measures of employee attitudes or job satisfaction and criteria of effectiveness. The median correlation between these two variables was found to be 0.14, with a range of 0.86 to −0.31. No systematic difference was observed between the results of investigations using groups and using individuals as units of analysis.

More recently, investigators have attempted to specify the conditions under which different relationships between attitudes and effectiveness would be found. Likert (1961) has suggested that the relationship between satisfaction and performance becomes more positive as the level of skill required by the job increases, and Triandis (1959) has proposed that the relationship will vary with the range of values of pressure for high production exerted on the population studied. At present, the available data do not provide an adequate test of either of these positions.

The causal assumption is further weakened by evidence from field experiments that social environments which produce high levels of productivity do not necessarily produce favorable attitudes or high levels of job satisfaction (Lewin, Lippitt, and White, 1939; Morse and Reimer, 1956). Similarly, in laboratory experiments it is clear that experimental conditions which produce a high level of task performance do not necessarily produce a high level of liking for the task, and vice versa (Freedman, 1963; Kaufmann, 1963; Leavitt, 1951). Finally, as the writer has previously pointed out (Vroom, 1964), a consideration of evidence concerning the effects of such properties of organizations as wage policies and promotional systems, as well as the effects of various properties of the face-to-face work group of which the individual is a member, leads to the inescapable conclusion that the conditions necessary to make membership in a system attractive and satisfying to a person are not identical with those which are necessary to motivate the person to perform effectively within his role. Measures of attitudes or of job satisfaction appear to be markedly affected by the amount of rewards that people derive from their roles, while measures of performance are more highly related to the basis for the attainment of rewards, specifically, the instrumentality of high performance for reward attainment.

While attitude measures have not been found to be consistently correlated with measures of performance, there is substantial evidence that they are negatively related to turnover. Several investigators (Fleishman, Harris, and Burtt, 1955; Giese and Ruter, 1949; Kerr, Koppelmeir, and Sullivan, 1951) have reported negative correlations between mean satisfaction scores for organizational units and turnover rates for these units. Weitz and Nuckols (1953) have also shown a negative relationship between job-satisfaction scores for individuals and the probability that these individuals would subsequently leave the organization.

To be sure, relinquishing one's membership in an organization is not a necessary consequence of dissatisfaction, nor is maintenance of membership a necessary result of satisfaction. The alternative of remaining in one's role is undoubtedly compared with other alternatives and the resultant choice is dependent on the consequences which are expected to follow from each. Thibaut and Kelley (1959) have used the concept of comparison level for alternatives (Cl_{alt}) to refer to the standard used by participants in a social relationship in deciding whether to remain in or leave that relationship. The value of Cl_{alt} is assumed to depend on the perceived quality of the best of the member's available alternatives, and he is predicted to leave the relationship when the level of outcomes which he derives from it (measured in terms of rewards and costs) drops below this value. To derive from this formulation testable predictions about the conditions under which individuals will leave organizations requires information which is seldom, if ever, available, namely, the alternatives available to that individual and the process which he uses in comparing and evaluating roles which are different on several outcome dimensions. Nonetheless, the general formulation is consistent with the observation that turnover rates vary not only with satisfaction levels and with measures of conditions internal to the organization, but also with labor market conditions (Behrend, 1953; Brissenden and Frankel, 1922; Woytinsky, 1942).

Measures of attitudes toward roles have also been found to bear a fairly consistent negative relationship with absence rates (Fleishman, Harris, and Burtt, 1955; Harding and Bottenberg, 1961; Metzner and Mann, 1953; Van Zelst and Kerr, 1953). This suggests the tentative conclusion that the attitudes of individuals toward their organizational roles are reasonably predictive of their decisions to occupy such roles. Such measures are not, however, predictive of the specific way in which the role will be performed or of the effectiveness of that performance.

These results would appear to make it mandatory to distinguish between the conditions which attract persons to their roles, binding them into the organization of which they are members, and the conditions which produce dependable and effective role performance on their part. Let us then proceed with a consideration of the evidence regarding the determinants of individuals' attitudes toward their roles in complex organizations.

Inducements and contributions

Barnard (1938) and Simon (1947) have provided a language for the identification and analysis of conditions under which an organization can induce persons to participate in its activities. Called the inducements-contributions theory, it views each member or participant in the organization as receiving inducements for his participation (which in the case of employees may include pay, recognition, prestige, etc.) and as making payments or contributions to the organization (including the "cost" to him of his effort and of lost opportunities stemming from his participation in the organization). The individual's decision to participate in the system is determined by the relative magnitude of inducements and contributions when both are measured in terms of the participant's values or motives.

While the language is different, the basic idea is seemingly indistinguishable from statements by social psychologists regarding the conditions affecting a person's attraction to a group (Bass, 1960; Cartwright and Zander, 1960; Thibaut and Kelley, 1959). The common ingredient is the notion that the attractiveness of a social system to a person and the probability that he will voluntarily withdraw from participation in it are related to the consequences of organizational membership, specifically, the rewards and punishments, or satisfactions and deprivations, incurred as a result of organizational membership.

While such a proposition may appear to be a tautology, it can be made testable by the addition of assumptions about motives which are common to all or at least a majority of persons. Thus, if an economic motive is assumed, namely, that more money is preferred to less money, then the finding that attitudes toward roles in organizations are positively correlated with the pay of the occupant (Barnett *et al.*, 1952; Miller, 1941; Thompson, 1939) can be explained. Similarly, other rather plausible assumptions about motives could account for the observed positive relationships between attitudinal measures and (1) amount of acceptance by coworkers (Van Zelst, 1951; Zaleznik, Christensen, and Roethlisberger, 1958), (2) amount of consideration shown by their superiors (Fleishman, Harris, and Burtt, 1955; Halpin and Winer, 1957; Likert, 1961; Seeman, 1957), (3) number of different operations performed in jobs (Walker and Guest, 1952; Wyatt, Fraser, and Stock, 1929), (4) amount of influence in decision making (Baumgartel, 1956; Jacobson, 1951; Vroom, 1960), and (5) level in the organization (Centers, 1948; Gurin, Veroff, and Feld, 1960; Hoppock, 1935; Kornhauser, 1965; Morse, 1953; Paterson and Stone, 1942; Porter, 1962; Super, 1939; Uhrbrock, 1934).

There is considerable evidence that these same work-role variables are negatively related to objective indicators of the decision not to participate in the organization, such as absences and turnover. Wickert (1951) and Ross and Zander (1957) found that people who reported that they had little influence on decision making had a higher probability of resigning from the organization than those who reported greater influence; Kerr, Koppelmeir, and Sullivan (1951) found the highest turnover among persons with the least opportunity for informal interaction; Baldamus (1951) found a positive correlation between the repetitiveness of jobs and the rate of turnover among their occupants; Fleishman, Harris, and Burtt (1955) found a negative relationship between supervisory consideration and absenteeism; and Fleishman and Harris (1962) found a negative relationship between consideration and turnover.

While these investigations are all correlational in nature and do not demonstrate that the designated properties of work roles "cause" the attitudes of their occupants, there is some evidence from field experiments that attitudes do change in the expected direction following changes in these work-role variables. Thus Walker (1950), Elliot (1953), and Guest (1957) reported increased job satisfaction following job enlargement; Morse and Reimer (1956) reported more favorable worker attitudes following an increase in their influence in decision making and less favorable attitudes following increased hierarchical control; and Meyer, Kay, and French (1965) reported more favorable attitudes toward management and toward the appraisal system on the part of employees as a consequence of the introduction of a work-planning and review

system which provided a greater opportunity for subordinates to participate in problem solving and in the setting of performance goals.

While each of the aforementioned variables (pay, acceptance, variety, influence,
status) may be safely regarded as dimensions on which larger amounts are preferred
to smaller amounts by most persons, it is not unreasonable to assume that individuals
may differ in their preferences among them. Individual differences in preferences
or motives have proven extremely useful in accounting for differences in people's
choices among work roles (Vroom, 1964), and similar reasoning would suggest that
they are influential in determining people's affective responses to the work role which
they have chosen. While measurements of individual differences in motives have not
yet played a major role in research on the determinants of attitudes toward organizations, the few studies which have been conducted have yielded quite promising results.

A recent field study by Turner and Lawrence (1965) illustrates the importance
of including both work-role variables and individual-difference measures in the
same investigation. These researchers set out to determine through correlational
methods the consequences of task attributes, such as amount of autonomy, responsibility, and variety, on the job satisfaction and absenteeism of rank-and-file workers.
A rating scale was developed to measure these task attributes and was used by the
researchers in rating 47 jobs in 11 companies. The existence of strong positive
intercorrelations among the ratings on the dimensions used made it necessary to
combine the separate scores into an index score which Turner and Lawrence called
the Requisite Task Attribute (RTA) index. Low-RTA jobs were simple and un-
demanding, while high-RTA jobs were more complex and required greater knowledge and skill. Contrary to expectations, no relationship was found between the RTA
scores of jobs and the job satisfaction of their occupants, and only a weak negative relationship was found between the RTA index and absenteeism. Subsequent analyses
indicated that these overall relationships masked two contrasting patterns of response
to task variables. The sample of 470 workers studied included two major subgroups:
those living and working in rural or small town settings, who were predominantly
Protestant; and those living and working in urban settings, who were predominantly
Roman Catholic. When the results for these two groups are analyzed separately, the
predicted results are obtained for the rural Protestant population and the reverse is
obtained for the urban Catholic population. The urban workers tended to express
more satisfaction with and exhibit less absenteeism on low-RTA jobs, while the rural
workers tended to be more satisfied with and be absent less frequently from high-
RTA jobs.

One of the explanations offered by Turner and Lawrence for the unanticipated
findings for urban workers utilizes the concept of anomie, originally introduced by
Durkheim. Conceivably, the urban workers could be characterized by a state of
normlessness brought about by industrialization. Sociologists have frequently pointed
to the state of normlessness which accompanies lower-class urban industrialized social
systems. Perhaps highly industrialized and unpleasant conditions of urban life foster
alienation from the traditional norms of society, most particularly a lack of concern
with upward mobility and self-actualization in work, attributes commonly associated
with the American middle class.

Further evidence for this explanation came from a study by Blood and Hulin
(1967). The subjects were male blue-collar workers in 21 different plants located

in different communities throughout the eastern United States. From census data, several indices were found which appeared likely to represent the degree of alienation prevalent in each community. These indices included degree of urbanization, population density, and evidence of slum conditions. The results indicate substantial variation in the responses of workers in different communities to apparently similar job situations—variation which is, at least in part, predictable from measures of the alienation in the community. In general, the pattern of results is consistent with that obtained by Turner and Lawrence. Workers in communities low in alienation appear to place a high value on demanding, involving jobs, while those in communities high in alienation tend to be more satisfied with jobs which are less personally involving and demand less responsibility.

The Turner-Lawrence and Blood-Hulin studies illustrate the difficulty of explaining a person's attitude toward his role solely in terms of objective properties of that role, and suggest that measures of individual or community differences *and* work-role variables can account for a larger proportion of variance in attitude than can either of these sets of variables considered alone. They do not, however, shed much light on the psychological processes underlying the contrasting patterns of response. One wants to know the nature of the psychological dispositions which are associated with the subcultural groupings in these investigations, and how these dispositions are acquired and can be measured.

Other investigators have had considerable success using self-report measures of relevant motives in predicting or explaining the effects of work-role variables on the attitudes of role occupants. In conjunction with a large-scale field experiment designed to determine the effects on attitudes and productivity of increased and decreased influence in decision making by rank-and-file workers, Tannenbaum and Allport (1956) used a self-report measure of motivation in an attempt to predict the attitudes of organizational members toward each of two experimentally induced programs of change. Persons were classified as suited or unsuited to each experimental program on the basis of their response to 26 questions about what they were "characteristically trying to do." This measure was found to be significantly related to the attitudes of individuals toward each experimental program as measured one year later. Individuals classified as suited to a program tended to express greater satisfaction with the program and a stronger desire for it to continue.

Additional evidence of an interaction between a situational variable and a self-report motivational measure was obtained by Vroom (1960). The size of the correlation between supervisors' judgments of the amount of influence they could exercise over their superiors and their attitudes toward their jobs was found to vary systematically with the strength of their need for independence as measured by a 16-item questionnaire. The correlations between these two variables were 0.55, 0.31, and 0.13, respectively, for supervisors high, moderate, and low in need for independence. A similar interaction was found between influence in decision making and the *F*-scale score of the supervisor. No relationship between influence and attitude toward the job was found for supervisors high in authoritarianism; a moderate positive relationship was found for supervisors intermediate in authoritarianism; and a marked positive relationship was found for supervisors low in authoritarianism.

The results of these studies indicate quite clearly that persons' attitudes toward their work roles and the probability that they will choose to continue to occupy them are dependent on both situational and personality variables. The situational variables correspond to the amounts of different kinds of outcomes (for example, pay, influence, variety) provided by the work roles, and the personality variables correspond to individual differences in the strength of their desire or aversion for these outcomes.

Social comparison processes

Thus far we have been viewing the attitudes of the organization member as determined solely by the nature of his individual transactions with the organization. The value he places on organizational membership, as expressed in his statements of the extent to which he is satisfied with his job and the organization, is determined solely by the rewards he derives and the costs he incurs from that membership. There is some evidence that indicates a limitation to this point of view.

Stouffer *et al.* (1949) found numerous instances in which the attitudes of soliders toward their roles were not predictable from the objective situation which they were facing. For example, there was greater dissatisfaction with promotional opportunities in the Army Air Corps than in the Military Police, despite the fact that the probability of promotion was much higher in the former branch of the service. Furthermore, high school graduates, who typically were assigned to better jobs and had significantly greater chances for advancement than those with less education, expressed greater dissatisfaction with their status and jobs.

Such findings were interpreted, in *ad hoc* fashion, as support for the fact that individuals develop conceptions of proper or equitable levels of reward at least partly from information about the rewards received by others. Dissatisfaction occurs when one's level of reward falls below the proper or equitable level. Translation of such ideas from the realm of a system for accounting for discrepancies between empirical findings and predictions from simpler theories has undoubtedly been aided by the recent development of more precise models of the process (Homans, 1961; Patchen, 1961; Adams, 1963). Problems remain, however, in the coordination of the abstract concepts contained in these models to measurable or manipulable events.

One of the issues that needs to be resolved before predictions can be made and tested concerns the process by which other persons are selected for comparison. It is intuitively obvious that a person does not compare the level of rewards which he receives with all other persons. Information about the reward levels of others is necessary to permit the comparison to occur. It is also likely that further selection takes place within the subset of others about whom information is available. But what are the variables which determine the selection process? This problem has been discussed by others (for example, Festinger, 1954; Merton and Kitt, 1952), and there has been some research relevant to the industrial scene. Patchen (1961) studied the wage comparisons made by hourly workers in an oil refinery, and Andrews and Henry (1963) studied those of lower- and middle-level managers. In both investigations it was found that persons compare their wages not only with the wages of others in the same organization but also with the wages of those who are not organization members. In the latter study, "outside" comparisons were most typical of highly educated managers.

The specific people used in wage comparisons can be assessed by direct questions or, indirectly, by determining the relative predictability of attitudes from various difference measures. Lawler and Porter (1963) found that the difference between the amount of pay received by a manager and that received by others at his level was a better predictor of the manager's satisfaction with his pay than was the absolute amount of pay that he received. First-line supervisors making more than $12,000 were more satisfied than were company presidents making less than $49,000. In their study of managers in five firms, Andrews and Henry (1963) found that overall satisfaction with pay was more highly related to the difference between their wages and the average amount received by others at their level in all five companies than to the difference between their wages and the average received by others at the same level in their own company.

Given that a person has compared the level of reward which he is receiving with that received by another, what determines the affective consequences of the comparison? The more recent theories put forth by Adams, Patchen, and Homans assume that the amount of satisfaction or dissatisfaction is not solely a function of differences in reward levels between the two persons, but is also influenced by differences in such variables as merit, seniority, ethnic background, etc., which are considered by the individual to be "proper" bases for reward allocation. A common theoretical solution has been to treat feelings of inequity or injustice as a response to perceived discrepancies between the ratios of rewards to such "inputs" or "investments" on the part of individuals. Thus, in a simple system consisting of only two persons each of whom has perfect information about the reward levels and other attributes of the other, the proper or equitable level of reward for each is predicted to be dependent on four sets of variables: (1) the level of reward received by the other, (2) the extent to which the other possesses attributes which are potential inputs or investments, (3) the extent to which the individual himself possesses the same attributes, and (4) the rules used by the individual for translating differences in attributes possessed (2 and 3 above) into a proper reward differential. The degree of inequity experienced by the person and his attitude toward the reward system are, in turn, predicted to be a function of each of these variables and of his own reward level.

Needless to say, difficulties in identifying and scaling the relevant variables make it presently impossible to subject the mathematical properties of this model to a definitive test. A crucial problem is found in the measurement of the fourth set of variables listed above. In order to test the theory, it is necessary to know the attributes which are believed by all persons to be proper bases for reward allocation or, alternatively (and perhaps more realistically), to have a method by which differences among persons can be assessed. An unsuccessful attempt by Zaleznik, Christensen, and Roethlisberger (1958) to predict the satisfaction of 47 workers from a reward-investment index obtained by subtracting from the wage level a number of worker attributes assumed to represent "investments" in their jobs (for example, age, seniority, education) seems more likely to be attributable to their scaling methods than to deficiencies in the theory which they sought to test.

Adams (1965b) has recently conducted some research on salaried employees in General Electric which constitutes an attempt to determine empirically the relative weight which people believe should be assigned to various attributes in salary decisions. Manager-subordinate pairs were asked to consider the last time the manager changed the salary of the subordinate and to rate the importance given to each of 45 factors and the importance which should have been given to each of these factors.

The results indicate some differences between managers and subordinates in "proper" bases for salary decisions, as well as some differences between persons in high- and low-level positions and among those working in different functional areas.

Homans (1961) and Adams (1963) postulated that perceived discrepancies in ratios of rewards to investments produce feelings of inequity, and consequently negative affect, *regardless of the direction of the discrepancy.* In other words, tension is produced by relative gratification as well as relative deprivation. Discrepancies produced by "overreward" are associated with feelings of guilt, while those produced by "underreward" are associated with feelings of anger or unfairness. Most of the empirical evidence concerns the latter situation. In fact, using differences between reports of levels of reward that one should and one is receiving from one's job as a criterion, Porter (1962) and Porter and Lawler (1968) found considerable evidence of underreward but none of overreward on the part of managers in American firms, a finding which may reflect defensiveness on the part of the respondents or the fact that the overreward situations are exceedingly short-lived. In a series of experiments to be reported later in this chapter, Adams (1963, 1965a) induced the belief on the part of subjects that they were being overcompensated, but these experiments are concerned with effects on performance, not on attitudes. Jaques (1961) reported that a state of disequilibrium is created by discrepancies between actual and equitable levels of pay which vary in intensity with the size of the discrepancy but are independent of its sign. While such a conclusion is consistent with the proposition under discussion, its significance must be tempered by the absence of any indication in the report of the measures used or of the number of subjects on whom observations were made.

The idea that statements of liking for or satisfaction with a role are influenced by relative rather than absolute reward levels can hardly be disputed when stated in its most general form. The problems remaining concern the specific nature of this comparison process. A complete explanation of the role of social comparisons in determining individuals' attitudes toward their roles must specify how specific others are selected for comparison, how information about self and others is combined to yield judgments of the equity or fairness of any reward differential, and by what mechanisms inequity or unfairness will be reduced or eliminated. The last of these questions is explored at some length in a recent paper by Adams (1965a), which discusses six alternative modes of inequity reduction and presents some assumptions which can provide a basis for initial predictions concerning the choices that will be made among them.

Expected level of reward

In the previous section we were concerned with the affective consequences of discrepancies between the level of reward that a person believes he should receive and that which he does receive. From the time of William James, psychological theorists have assumed that individuals compare the level of reward which they receive with that which they expected to receive. Positive discrepancies, in which the attained level of reward exceeds what was expected, have been predicted to produce satisfaction, whereas negative discrepancies, in which the attained level of reward is less than what was expected, have been predicted to produce dissatisfaction. Applying this proposition to the problem under consideration, we would not expect the attitudes of a single member toward his role in the organization to be a linear function of the level of reward which he receives. The relationship between these two variables should be represented by a monotonically increasing piecewise linear function, with the slope being steepest around the expected level.

The basic idea is similar in one respect to that discussed in the previous section. Affective responses to a given level of reward are assumed to be highly variable, and it is assumed that this variation can be accounted for by reference to a standard with which the attained or received level is compared and evaluated. The differences between these two formulations concern the nature of the standard of comparison, its predicted determinants, and the predicted consequences of discrepancies between the standard and attained level.

To test the proposition that a person's affective response to a given level of reward varies with the level that he expected, it is necessary to make some additional assumptions about the way in which expectations are formed and are altered by experience. Thus, if we assume that a person's expected level of reward in a given situation is determined solely by the reward levels which he has previously attained in that situation, we can expect that the affective consequences of a given reward level will vary predictably with prior reward levels. Substantial support for this prediction has been obtained from laboratory experiments on contrast effects (Crespi, 1942; Zeaman, 1949) and on extensions of Helson's concept of sensory adaptation levels to the problem of reinforcement (Bevan and Adamson, 1960; Black, Adamson, and Bevan, 1961; Collier and Marx, 1959; Helson, 1964). Also consistent with the prediction is evidence that experiences of success and failure are not dependent on the absolute amount of achievement, but on the relationship between achievement and level of aspiration, where the latter variable is, in large part, determined by previous achievement (Lewin *et al.*, 1944).

While the level-of-aspiration concept has played an important role in theories about behavior in organizations (Cyert and March, 1963; March and Simon, 1958), there has been little systematic empirical investigation of the way in which attitudes toward or satisfaction with outcomes of organizational membership are affected by previously obtained outcomes or other cues regarding the outcomes which will be obtained. A laboratory experiment conducted by Spector (1956) is suggestive of the kind of results that might be obtained if more explicit attention were given to this variable in research on behavior in organizations. He assigned subjects to four-person groups to work on a simulated military intelligence problem. They were instructed to operate as a team with each man decoding a different part of a series of messages given to the team. The level of reward expected by subjects was manipulated not by controlling rewards received on earlier trials, but by verbal communications from the experimenter. Some groups were told that three of the four men would be promoted after completion of the first message, while others were told that only one of every four men would be promoted. Subsequent to completion of the first message, all the members of half of the groups were promoted. This manipulation was independent of the manipulation of the probability of promotion, yielding four experimental conditions corresponding to the various combinations of high and low subjective probability of promotion and attainment or nonattainment of promotion. The dependent variable was a six-item morale measure which was similar to those used in industrial studies. Morale was found to be highest among subjects who received but did not expect a promotion, and lowest among subjects who expected but did not receive a promotion. There was no interaction between the two independent variables, and mean morale scores were a function of the amount and sign of the discrepancy between attainment and expectation.

Summary

To recapitulate, we have identified four classes of variables which, on the basis of existing evidence, appear to determine the attitude of a person toward his role in an organization and the probability that he will leave it, permanently or temporarily. These four variables are (1) the amounts of particular classes of outcomes, such as pay, status, acceptance, and influence, attained by the person as a consequence of his occupancy of that role, (2) the strength of the person's desire or aversion for outcomes in these classes, (3) the amounts of these outcomes believed by the person to be received by comparable others, and (4) the amounts of these outcomes which the person expected to receive or has received at earlier points in time.

The nature of the functional relationship between attitudes and these four variables can only be estimated from existing data. Given an outcome or outcome class which is desired by the person, the evidence reviewed suggests that the strength of his attraction toward his role and the probability of his remaining in it increase as the amount of the outcome received increases; decrease as the amount of the outcome received by comparable others exceeds the amount he receives; and increase as the difference between the amount of the outcome received and the amount which he expected and/or has been accustomed to receiving becomes more positive or less negative. On the other hand, if the person is indifferent to the outcome or outcome class, these relationships may be expected to disappear, and if the person has an aversion to the outcome, the signs of the relationships may be expected to reverse.

EFFECTIVENESS OF ROLE PERFORMANCE

Occupants of any work role, whether they are salesmen, managers, secretaries, or assemblers, vary in the effectiveness with which they accomplish their assigned duties. Some of this variation is attributable to what are often referred to as differences in ability or skill. These include differences in people's capacities to discriminate between stimuli requiring different responses, differences in knowledge of the "correct" responses to these different stimuli, and differences in capacities to execute the "correct" responses. Of greater interest to social psychologists have been the so-called motivational influences on performance, that is, aspects of the person and the situation which determine the amount of effort or energy which the person will direct toward the performance of his role.

Externally mediated rewards and punishments

One of the principal mechanisms used by organizations for motivating their members to perform their roles effectively is the linking of the rewards received or punishments incurred by an individual to the effectiveness of his performance. Those behavior patterns which contribute to the attainment of organizational goals are rewarded, while those which do not contribute to or interfere with the attainment of these goals are not rewarded or are punished. The clearest example of this approach can be found in the use of individual wage incentives, though it is by no means limited to this type of reward.

While individual wage incentives played a central role in the "blueprint" for organizations by Taylor and his followers in scientific management, they have not received much attention in the normative "theories" of management proposed by behavioral scientists (Likert, 1961; McGregor, 1960). Nevertheless, there is a fair amount of evidence of several different kinds to indicate that people do perform tasks or jobs more effectively when their wages are made conditional on their performance than when wages are independent of performance. Such findings have been obtained in laboratory experiments with college students (Atkinson, 1958; Atkinson and Reitman, 1956; Kaufmann, 1963) and in field experiments carried out on workers on production jobs (Wyatt, 1934). There is also evidence from a field study by Georgopoulos, Mahoney, and Jones (1957) that production workers who report on a questionnaire that there is a positive relationship between how well they perform and how much money they make tend to be better performers than those who report no connection between these events. Furthermore, most surveys of companies' experience with wage incentive plans indicate that substantial increases in productivity have followed their installation (Viteles, 1953).

The evidence concerning the effects of economic incentives on those performing more complex jobs, such as managers, engineers, and scientists, is much less clear. Considerable controversy remains about the possibility of eliciting a higher degree of effort from such persons by increasing the dependence of their wages on their performance. To be sure, the incentive properties of compensation systems which exist for managerial personnel are far different from those in use for production workers. Stock option plans, year-end bonuses, and annual salary increments which are contingent on "merit" provide much less dependence of income on performance than the traditional wage incentive systems used with production workers and salesmen. The rewards are temporally separated from the performance, they are in the form of increments to salary rather than total compensation, and they are typically based on subjective judgments by superiors of performance, rather than tied to objective criteria of output.

The principal evidence for the influence of compensation systems on managerial behavior and performance comes from a large-scale field study carried out by Porter and Lawler (1968). Using data collected by questionnaires from managers in both private industry and government, they found a consistent tendency for managers who believed that their job performance would have an important influence on their pay to be rated by their superiors as more effective than managers who believed that their job performance was relatively unimportant in determining their pay. This difference was found to be more marked for managers who rated pay as important to them than for those who rated it as less important, and the measure of the dependence of pay on job performance was found to be more strongly related to ratings of the amount of effort that they expended on their jobs than to ratings of the effectiveness of their performance.

Somewhat at variance with these findings, which point to the efficacy of economic incentives, are the results of a series of case studies conducted by Whyte and his associates (Whyte, 1955). Using participant observation methods, they observed numerous instances of restriction of output among production workers on incentive payment systems. They found that work groups tend to develop norms concerning an "appropriate" level of production, and individuals who exceed the norm of their group are pressured to reduce their production.

Group norms regarding appropriate levels of output represent, at best, a partial explanation of the origin of restriction of output among workers on wage incentive systems. One must also inquire into the motivational basis of the norms. Why, and under what conditions, do individuals attempt to influence their coworkers to hold down their level of output? On the basis of interviews with workers (Mathewson, 1931), it would appear that one of the major factors is a fear that high levels of performance will result in the tightening of rates by management. While labor contracts typically preclude such rate changes unless other changes in work methods are introduced, they do not prevent the possiblity of making a minor change in work methods in order to justify a reexamination of rates.

The use of wage incentives is, of course, restricted to roles where a quantitative measure of performance is available. It is also necessary that this measure be comprehensive, embracing all aspects of performance which are necessary for the organization to attain its goals. A study by Babchuk and Goode (1951) of the introduction of individual incentive payment in a department store indicates how functions which are not explicitly rewarded may be neglected in favor of those which "pay off" financially. When wages were tied to individual sales, the clerks devoted their energies to competing for customers and neglected such unrewarded, but nonetheless necessary, functions as stockwork and arranging merchandise for displays.

Wages represent but one kind of reward which can be made contingent on individual performance. Promotions can also be based on merit and accomplishment. There is some evidence that such promotional incentives are effective in motivating individuals to perform their roles effectively. In a study of over 600 workers in an appliance factory, Georgopoulos, Mahoney, and Jones (1957) found a higher proportion of "high producers" among workers who believed that low productivity would hurt their chances for promotion than among those who believed that productivity was irrelevant to promotion. While this finding is correlational and consequently not unequivocal evidence of the causal process in which we are interested, a causal interpretation is strengthened by the fact that the difference in productivity between those believing that productivity was instrumental to promotions and those believing that it was irrelevant to promotion was greatest for those describing a promotion as relatively important to them and who had control over their pace of work.

There would seem, however, to be some problems in creating a system in which promotional decisions are tied exclusively to effort and accomplishment on the present job. Individual differences regarding duties and responsibilities, the fact that receipt of a promotion by A is also dependent on the performance of worker B, and the difficulty in predicting promotional opportunities until they actually occur make it impossible to specify with any degree of certainty for a given person the behaviors which are necessary and sufficient for him to move "up" in the organization. Unlike wage incentives, which are clearly tied to one or more dimensions of performance, promotions are allocated on the basis of criteria which are highly subjective and are seldom explicitly stated in advance. The observations of Dalton (1959) suggest that, in awarding promotions within the managerial ranks, considerable weight is attached to "informal" factors which have nothing to do with actual performance. He found that managers tend to recommend and select for higher-level positions those who share their ethnic and religious background and political affiliation, participate in the same civic activities, and share the same recreational tastes.

Even if it were possible to award promotions solely on the basis of measurable and relevant aspects of role performance, it is not clear that it would always be wise to do so. There are undoubtedly instances in which performance at one level is not predictive of performance at a higher level. The qualifications for success in one position may be very different from those necessary in a lower position.

There are many other outcomes which have the properties of rewards and punishments and which are contingent on role performance within the organization. In the military, for example, medals and decorations are given those who exhibit heroism beyond the call of duty, and failure to conform to rules or obey orders makes one subject to disciplinary action. Similarly, in industrial organizations, managers and supervisors extend praise or give criticism, give or withhold approval, and engage in a wide range of behaviors which undoubtedly have affective consequences for their subordinates and probably bear some relation, albeit an imperfect one, to the behavior of the subordinate.

While there have been theoretical analyses of the problem of authority using concepts of contingent reward or reinforcement (for example, Adams and Romney, 1959), there has been far too little research on the effects on the behavior of subordinates of the actions that are rewarded or punished by their superiors. Most of the research on the consequences of different supervisory behaviors has conceptualized this behavior in general or "average" terms, for example, as punitive, supportive, considerate, etc., rather than in terms of the extent to which the supervisor discriminates between and responds differentially to different levels of effort or accomplishment on the part of his subordinates. There are, however, some findings which point to the power of supervisors to control the behavior of their subordinates, and which suggest that the consistency between the behavior patterns necessary to attain rewards or avoid punishments controlled by the supervisor and those required to perform the functions which make up the role may have an important bearing on the effectiveness of the resultant performance. Thus, several investigators (Fleishman, 1953; Mann and Hoffman, 1960) have observed that supervisors tend to pattern their behavior after that of their superior, and Kahn (1958) notes that workers in highly productive groups tend to describe their foreman as having more of an interest in production than did workers in less productive groups.

Galbraith and Cummings (1967) sought to test the proposition advanced by this author (Vroom, 1964), that a person's motivation to perform a job effectively is a multiplicative function of the valence of outcomes and of the perceived instrumentality of effective performance for the attainment of these outcomes. Studying 32 workers in a plant manufacturing heavy equipment, they measured, by individual questionnaires, the valence of a set of job-related outcomes such as pay, support and consideration from one's immediate supervisor, promotion, and acceptance by co-workers. Similar measures were obtained of workers' conceptions of the extent to which effective job performance was instrumental to the attainment of each of these outcomes. While the overall results provide considerable support for the multiplicative model, the interaction between valence and instrumentality was most marked in the case of support and consideration from the supervisor. Thus the actual output of these workers tended to be at the highest level when they valued the support of their superior *and* when they believed that this support was contingent on their performance. Lower output characterized those workers who reported less interest in the support of their superior and/or believed such support to be independent of their performance.

The most impressive evidence of the possibility of increasing productivity by punishing ineffective performance comes from a recent series of field experiments conducted by Miller (1965) in a plant manufacturing household refrigerators. While lacking some of the controls found in most laboratory investigations, this set of experiments constitutes an excellent example of the meaning and organizational usefulness of "action research" (Lewin, 1948). The subjects in the first experiment were operators responsible for classifying muffle boxes according to bore size. A problem had developed in this operation, stemming from the fact that many muffle boxes were being misclassified. A number of different approaches were tried sequentially in an attempt to reduce the frequency of these misclassifications. First, the foreman tried to solve the problem using communication and persuasion. He talked to each operator individually, showed him examples of misclassified parts, reviewed his work methods with him, and stressed the need for improvement. The results showed no significant or lasting improvement in performance. Consequently, a second approach was undertaken, in which each operator was provided with rapid feedback concerning his misclassifications. There was a marked initial improvement in performance but, by the end of the seven-week experimental period, the percentage of lots rejected because of misclassifications had increased to a point close to its previous level. The third method involved the combination of feedback with reprimands and warnings by the foreman for poor performance. When this was done, the number of lots rejected for misclassification dropped abruptly to zero and remained there for the remaining six weeks of observation.

Similar results were obtained in a second experiment on operators responsible for finishing cylinder bores. While attempts by the foreman to persuade operators through verbal communication to improve the quality of their performance did not have any effect, when individual operators were required to shut down their machine when one of their lots was rejected (thereby incurring a loss in their piecework income) and sort the parts contained in the rejected lot, the number of rejected lots dropped to zero and remained at that level for the remaining twelve weeks of the experimental period.

Comparable results were obtained in two other experiments in which only group performance could be measured and in which all operators were penalized for failures by any one. In one of these experiments, each time a lot was rejected a different operator was required to sort the lot on a day-rate basis. In the other experiment, whenever the percentage of defective parts exceeded a specified upper limit, the entire assembly line was shut down, experts converged on the area to analyze the cause of the difficulty, and immediate corrective actions were taken. Marked reductions in the number of rejected parts were effected in both situations.

It is apparent from these investigations that work quality can be improved by attaching penalties to errors in performance. Unfortunately, the report of these results contains no mention of the consequences of the experimental programs on quantity of production. It is quite likely that the improvement in quality was accompanied by a reduction in quantity, though Miller's discussion of the savings effected implies that the net effect was positive.

   The effectiveness of any system in which rewards and punishments are contingent on specified performance outcomes appears to be dependent on the degree of control which the individual has over these performance outcomes. The increment in performance to be expected from an increase in the extent to which an individual is rewarded for favorable results and/or punished for unfavorable results is directly related to the extent to which the individual can control the results of his performance.

   There are three distinguishable sources of lack of control over results, which appear, from existing evidence, to reduce the effectiveness of wage incentives or other organizationally produced reward-punishment contingencies. One source lies in the role interdependencies which are characteristic of formal organizations. Worker *A* receives information or materials, transforms or processes it in some way, and gives it to worker *B*, who processes it further and gives it to worker *C*, and so on. In such instances, it is difficult or impossible to trace errors or superior performance to a single individual. It is only the group or team effort which can be adequately evaluated, and each person has but partial control over the team outcome. While group incentives may be utilized in a situation involving interdependent roles, the larger the group, the smaller the increment in individual effort or performance. Studying workers on group-incentive payment systems in two British factories, Marriott (1949) has found that the mean level of individual performance decreases as group size increases.

   The amount of control that an individual has over the results on the basis of which he is being rewarded or punished also varies with the nature of the task or job that he is performing. In many tasks or jobs there is less than a one-to-one relationship between the behavior of the incumbent and the results he achieves. Other states, not under his control, also affect these results. The physician may perform a "perfect" operation but the patient may die; the salesman may make an effective sales pitch but fail to make the sale; and the manager may do an unusually effective job of administering his division but fail to make a profit because of adverse market conditions. Other "external" factors also influence the results, and the relationship between the individual's behavior and the rewards and punishments he receives becomes probabilistic rather than deterministic. While there has been little effort to study such phenomena directly in formal organizations, extrapolation from laboratory results would suggest that the presence of such external determinants of results would impede the acquisition of skill in performing the task and, given a previously acquired level of skill, would attenuate the performance increment resulting from the establishment of the reward-punishment system. Favorable results would be a matter of "luck," having a desirable territory, a favorable market, etc., rather than skill or conscientious application of effort.

   The third source of imperfect control over results lies in the set of variables that we have loosely referred to (Vroom, 1964) as representing the ability or skill of the individual to perform the job. The degree to which a particular set of results or performance outcomes are controllable depends, at least in part, on who is doing the controlling. An experienced pilot can control the behavior of a large commercial jet airliner during take-off and landing—an impossible feat for an individual who has never attempted to pilot an aircraft. There is considerable evidence (Fleishman, 1958; Wyatt, 1934) that the increment in performance resulting from the introduction of a system in which rewards and/or punishments are contingent on performance is greater for those of higher than for those of lesser ability. Such data, along with other investigations of a correlational nature (Galbraith and Cummings, 1967; Lawler, 1966; Vroom, 1960), are highly suggestive of a multiplicative relationship between ability and motivation in determining performance.

The evidence that we have been discussing has concerned the role of organizationally mediated rewards and punishments in the control of individual behavior in organizations. It has not been collected with a view toward testing any basic propositions about behavior, though the results, in the main, are consistent with learning theories in which reinforcement is accorded a major role, as well as performance or decision theories in which persons are assumed to make choices between alternatives in order to maximize the subjective expected utility of the outcomes. Its principal relevance is to an evaluation of approaches to the managerial process, such as McGregor's Theory X and Taylor's Scientific Management, in which organizationally mediated rewards and punishments allocated on the basis of merit and performance are assigned the task of effecting a reconciliation between individual and organizational goals.

In general, the evidence suggests that making effective performance on a task or job instrumental to the attainment of organizationally mediated rewards or the avoidance of punishments will improve productivity to the extent that (1) the relevant aspects of individual performance are measurable and the bases for the allocation of rewards and punishments are mutually understood and followed; (2) individuals have control over the performance outcomes on the basis of which the rewards and punishments are allocated; (3) the rewards are sufficiently attractive to overcome the effects of the added effort required to attain them; (4) there is no conflict, either actual or perceived, between those behaviors necessary to attain a short-term reward (for example, higher wages this week) and those required to avoid a longer-term punishment (for example, a tightening of standards).

Internally mediated rewards and punishments

While linking performance on a task or job to the attainment of rewards or the avoidance of punishments is one approach to motivating organizational members to direct their energies toward the objectives of the organization, it is by no means the only method. Likert (1961), McGregor (1960), and Maier (1963) are perhaps the principal proponents of approaches to the management of organizations which are based on somewhat different assumptions about human motivation. The starting point for these views is the idea that successful performance on a task or job can be a goal as well as a means to the attainment of a goal. Under some conditions, individuals derive satisfaction from effective performance of their roles in organizations and experience anxiety or tension when they are ineffective in their performance, independent of the immediate externally mediated consequences of this behavior. Many different terms have been used to label this hypothetical psychological state, some referring to a person's orientation toward his job or role, such as ego involvement (Vroom, 1964), intrinsic job satisfaction (Katz, 1964; Morse, 1953), and internalized motivation (Slater, 1959), while others, such as commitment to organizational objectives (McGregor, 1960), refer to his orientation toward the formal goals of the system. But, as Maier (1960) has pointed out, giving a phenomenon a name does not explain it. It is also necessary to determine the conditions under which it occurs. In this case it is necessary to specify when a person will persist in directing his effort toward the performance of his role in the absence of direct pressure from his social environment to do so.

Social psychologists doing research in industrial organizations have tended to approach this problem with an environmental bias. It has been implicitly assumed that the extent to which an individual is involved in his role or committed to the objectives of the organization of which he is a member is dependent on the content of that job and on the nature of the social relationships between its occupant and other organizational members. Two specific classes of variables have received particular attention. The first of these is the behavior of the leader in interactions with his subordinates, specifically, the extent to which he is considerate and supportive and encourages participation in goal setting and in problem solving and decision making. The second class of variables refers to the nature of the individual's duties and responsibilities. Since participation in decision making has implications for processes other than the motivation of subordinates, we will postpone a discussion of this issue until a later section. At this point we will focus on the motivational effects of task variables.

It is commonly assumed that jobs or tasks which are challenging and interesting and require skill create involvement on the part of those performing them. On the other hand, those which are simple, dull, uninteresting, or routine produce little or no involvement. Two problems are presented by such a formulation. First, the terms used to describe jobs assumed to produce a high degree of involvement refer to psychological responses to jobs rather than to objectively measurable properties of the job itself. A task or job which is challenging or interesting to one person may be dull and uninteresting to another. Thus, the proposition becomes circular. A challenging or interesting job becomes one which creates a high degree of involvement on the part of its occupants.

The second problem stems from the difficulty in inferring effects of task variables on such hypothetical motivational states as involvement. If we assume that the strength of a person's motivation to perform a task or job effectively can be observed only insofar as it is reflected in his actual level of performance on that task or job, then the research necessary to test propositions about the effects of task variables on motivation would require objective measures of performance which can be applied across tasks. However, traditional measures of performance are task-specific and permit comparisons of performance within but not across tasks. To be sure, it may be possible to determine the relative efficiency of different ways of dividing a set of functions among a set of persons, but the specific role of motivation is likely to be hard to isolate.

A somewhat different starting point for research on the determinants of involvement or intrinsic motivation has been taken by McClelland *et al.* (1953) and by Atkinson (1958). Individual differences are stressed and situational or environmental effects play a minor role. The basic assumption is that individuals vary in the strength of their achievement motivation (n Ach), which is assumed to be a relatively stable personality characteristic defined as a predisposition to derive satisfaction from "success in competition with some standard of excellence." A number of different methods have been used in the measurement of this personality variable, all of which involve the analysis of fantasy. The thematic apperception method (Murray, 1938) is the principal device for eliciting this fantasy. Subjects are requested to tell stories about pictures, and the content of their stories is scored according to the frequency with which different kinds of imagery appear.

Measures of achievement motivation have been found to be correlated with a number of other variables, including child-rearing practices (Winterbottom, 1958), demographic variables (McClelland, 1961; Meyer, Walker, and Litwin, 1961; Veroff *et al.*, 1960), occupational preferences (Burnstein, 1963; McClelland, 1955), and risk preferences (Atkinson *et al.*, 1960; Atkinson and Litwin, 1960; McClelland, 1958; Scodel, Ratoosh, and Minas, 1959). In addition, scores on this variable obtained from an analysis of popular literature in different countries and at different points in history have been found to be predictive of subsequent rates of economic growth (McClelland, 1961). Our interest here is in the relationship of achievement-motivation scores to the effectiveness with which individuals perform tasks or jobs. If, in fact, measures of this variable do reflect differences in the amount of satisfaction that individuals derive from success in task situations, then they should predict, at least to some degree, the effort expended by individuals in task performance and the effectiveness of that performance.

Much of the evidence on this question comes from laboratory experiments utilizing rather simple tasks under highly controlled conditions. A number of experiments (Atkinson and Raphelson, 1956; French, 1955; Lowell, 1952) have found that individuals with a high level of achievement motivation tend to perform more effectively in such situations than those with lower scores. The relationship is not, however, a perfect one, nor is it invariant with the nature of the task or the conditions under which it is given. The difference in performance between persons high and low in achievement motivation is most consistently found where subjects are given the task under achievement-orienting instructions (French, 1955), when other motives are not aroused (Atkinson and Reitman, 1956), and when the task is a relatively difficult one (Atkinson, 1958).

There has been little research on the relationship between achievement-motivation scores and the effectiveness with which individuals carry out their assigned roles in industrial organizations. McClelland (1962, 1963) has argued that achievement motivation contributes to success in a managerial career. However, the published data on this question are scanty and provide only limited support for the argument.

Conceivably, the strength of a person's motivation to perform a task or job effectively in a situation where no externally mediated rewards are promised for high performance and no externally mediated punishments threatened for low performance is neither a general personality characteristic independent of the task or task situation nor an invariant response to objectively defined task or situational properties. It is most likely that both personality and situational variables are necessary to account completely for this phenomenon and, furthermore, that there are significant interactions between them. The study by Turner and Lawrence (1965), previously described, identified marked differences between workers in urban and rural environments in the relationship between task attributes and perceptions of tasks by those performing them. Similar interactions between task and individual-difference variables appear likely to be at the root of differences in the amount of effort allocated to effective task performance. The kind of job which is perceived as challenging by one person and into which he directs a substantial portion of his available energies may be perceived as boring by another and elicit nothing but lethargy.

It is necessary, however, to go beyond such a broad programmatic statement to specify the properties of persons and of their roles which are relevant to this problem, and to indicate the manner of their interaction. This is a large order and existing evidence falls far short of the mark. Greatly needed is some kind of guiding theoretical framework in terms of which available results can be integrated and new research conducted.

There are a number of promising avenues of approach to this problem which are based on concepts and experimental findings in other areas of psychological research. Three such possibilities can be mentioned here:

1. *Effective performance on a job may acquire secondary reinforcing properties as a result of its association in space and time with previously established rewards.*

The idea that previously neutral events which are contiguously associated with primary rewards and punishments acquire affective properties similar in sign to those with which they have been associated has been fairly well established in experiments with both animals and humans. Its application to the problem under consideration—the satisfaction that some persons derive from effectively performing tasks assigned to them—has not been well explored. Conceivably, as Woodworth suggested almost half a century ago (Woodworth, 1918), complex behavior patterns such as those necessary to effectively perform a role in an organization acquire intrinsic motivational properties as a result of prior association with rewards. Thus, a child who is continually reinforced for application of a particular talent or skill such as music, baseball, or leading others may in his subsequent adult life seek out roles in which he has an opportunity to use this skill and apply it diligently despite the absence of immediate rewards and punishments for so doing.

2. *Effective performance on a job may be a natural consequence of attempts to seek and produce variation in one's sensory environment.*

As White (1959) and Seward (1963) have pointed out, the last ten or fifteen years have witnessed a remarkable change in the kinds of motivational phenomena studied by experimental psychologists and in the kinds of theories which have been proposed to explain these phenomena. While earlier work was based on the premise that the primary source of satisfaction lay in the reduction of tissue needs (Hull, 1943) or in the strength of drives produced by strong stimulation (Miller and Dollard, 1941), more recent research has pointed to the existence of strong and primary curiosity or exploratory motives (Harlow, 1953; Harlow, Harlow, and Meyer, 1950) and activity drives (Hill, 1956; Kagan and Berkun, 1954). The basic notion is that higher organisms, including man, derive satisfaction from exploring and manipulating their environment. Hebb (1949) and McClelland *et al.* (1953) have attempted to reconcile the observation that persons prefer variation and change in their sensory environment with other evidence that persons fear the strange and unusual. They have advanced the proposition that the amount of satisfaction or dissatisfaction generated by any stimulus is dependent on the size of the discrepancy between the stimulus and a hypothetical neural organization or adaptation level, which has been acquired as a result of past experience. If the stimulus is mildly different from the adaptation level, it is pleasant; if it is highly different from the adaptation level or very similar to the adaptation level, it is unpleasant. Evidence concerning this position may be found in Dember and Earl (1957), Hunt (1960), and Fiske and Maddi (1961).

The implications of this proposition for conditions which would produce a low level of performance are more obvious than for conditions which would produce a high level. If an individual were performing a highly repetitive operation, the sources of stimulation, from kinesthetic as well as other sense modalities, would be highly constant, and virtually no disparity between stimulation and adaptation levels could be assumed. The predicted result, varying behavior to produce somewhat different stimulation and thereby interfering with performance, has been observed on the part of subjects in an experimental situation by Karsten (1928).

3. *The knowledge that one has performed effectively on a job may be consistent with other cognitions, whereas the knowledge that one has performed ineffectively would be inconsistent.*

The assumption that inconsistency among cognitions is a source of tension and produces behavior or cognitive reorganization to remove the inconsistency has been common to a number of theories put forth by social psychologists (Brehm and Cohen, 1961; Festinger, 1957; Heider, 1958; Osgood and Tannenbaum, 1955). One type of inconsistency is that which can potentially exist between an individual's knowledge of his behavior or the outcomes which resulted from that behavior and his previously acquired beliefs, opinions, or attitudes. Conceivably, a person will be motivated to perform effectively on a task or job when effective performance would be more consistent with his other beliefs and opinions than would ineffective performance. Task performance may be a means of reducing existing inconsistency among cognitions or of obtaining information which is consistent with previously held cognitions.

Of these three working assumptions, the third has been most influential, not only in social-psychological research in general, but also in research on the specific problem of the motivational determinants of role performance. Adams (1963, 1965a) has taken this assumption as a point of departure for an imaginative series of experiments on the effects of wage inequities on individual productivity. His theoretical framework, which was briefly discussed early in this chapter, has been used to derive predictions concerning the motivational effects of one kind of cognitive inconsistency, namely, the belief on the part of a person that he is being overcompensated relative to others. "Overcompensated" subjects are assumed to experience tension and to attempt to reduce that tension by changing one or more of the components of the inconsistent relationship. If they are being paid on an hourly basis this can be achieved by increasing their performance on their job. Thus, when compensation is based on time worked, "overcompensated" persons are predicted to turn out a larger volume of work than "equitably compensated" persons.

To test this prediction, Adams and Rosenbaum (1962) hired university students to conduct standardized interviews with members of the general public. Each subject was led to believe that he was working on a public opinion survey and that his employment would continue for several months. During the hiring interview, half the subjects were led to believe that they were being overcompensated by being told that they lacked the training and experience necessary for the job, but because of time pressure would have to be hired and would receive the advertised $3.50 hourly rate.

The other half of the subjects were led to believe that they were being equitably compensated by being told during the hiring interview that they were fully qualified by virtue of their superior education and intelligence for the job and for the attractive hourly rate.

Despite rather small numbers of subjects (eleven in each condition), significant differences in performance were obtained. The "overcompensated" subjects collected significantly more interviews in the two-and-a-half-hour work period than the "equitably compensated" subjects. Since there is a possibility that the "overcompensated" subjects were working harder in order to protect their jobs, Arrowwood (reported in Adams, 1963) conducted a similar experiment in which subjects who were either "overcompensated" or "equitably compensated" performed the same work under "public" or "private" conditions. In the public condition the subjects submitted their interviews directly to the employer, whereas in the private condition they were permitted to mail them to another city and were under the impression that their employer would never see their work. The results show that the overcompensated subjects performed more effectively under both conditions. This finding does not rule out the possibility that the superior performance of the overcompensated subjects resulted from the "challenge" inherent in the instructions to them during the hiring interview. Conceivably, the mere fact that the college students were told that they lacked the necessary qualifications for the job motivated them to prove to themselves, if not to the experimenter, that this judgment was incorrect.

It follows from Adams' formulation that the superiority in performance of overcompensated persons should hold only on performance dimensions which are not the basis for compensation. If an "overcompensated" person in the above studies were being paid on a piece-rate basis, that is, in accordance with the number of interviews he conducted, an increase in performance would not decrease, and would probably increase, inequity. Supporting this view is experimental evidence that "overcompensated" subjects who are paid on the basis of the quantity of work they accomplish turn out a smaller quantity of work than subjects who are "equitably compensated" (Adams and Jacobsen, 1964; Adams and Rosenbaum, 1962). There is also evidence that, under such conditions, overcompensated subjects direct their attention toward and demonstrate superior performance on dimensions of performance, such as quality of work, which do not increase their level of compensation (Adams and Jacobsen, 1964).

Opposite predictions are derivable from the theory about the effects of undercompensation. Persons believing themselves to be undercompensated would be expected to turn out a lower quantity of work than those believing themselves to be equitably compensated when paid on an hourly basis, and a higher quantity of work when paid on a piece-rate basis. A recent experiment by Lawler and O'Gara (1967) was designed to test the latter prediction. Equity of compensation was established by amount paid per interview rather than by the experimental induction of perceived differences in qualifications to do the work, as in the experiments of Adams and his associates. As predicted, the undercompensated subjects collected significantly more interviews, but their interviews were of lower quality than those collected by the equitably compensated subjects.

Andrews (1967) also manipulated feelings of equity by actual pay rather than by instructions regarding qualifications. Subjects, all of whom worked on a piece rate, were either overcompensated (30 cents per piece), equitably compensated (20 cents per piece), or undercompensated (15 cents per piece). The results were consistent with those previously reported and with the equity formulation. Quantity of work was negatively related and quality of work was positively related to rate of compensation. Regardless of experimental treatment, those subjects who reported having received high hourly wage levels in the past turned out a higher quantity and a lower quality of work than those who reported lower past wage levels.

At present, the evidence reported concerning overcompensation and undercompensation pertains to its short-term effects on performance. It has been argued by Vroom (1964) that the effects of overcompensation on performance may be short-lived, since the feelings of inequity which are assumed to be produced by this condition can easily be reduced by cognitive changes which enhance the self-esteem of the subject. An experiment by Lawler *et al.* (1968) addressed itself to the question of the persistence of the performance effects. The experiment described above by Adams and Jacobsen on differences in work quantity and quality of overcompensated and equitably compensated subjects on piece rates was replicated, but instead of terminating the work after one session, subjects returned for two additional sessions after intervals of one or two days. The results obtained in the first experiment—lower quantity but higher quality of performance by overcompensated subjects—were also obtained in this experiment during the first work session. However, these differences dissipated very quickly thereafter. It is possible that the effects might have been prolonged by repeating the experimental instructions prior to each task session, but this experiment rather clearly demonstrates the transient nature of the effects of the manipulations used in other research.

Further evidence that effective task performance may be a means of reducing inconsistency among cognitions is found in a laboratory experiment by Weick (1964). The basic notion underlying this experiment is that people who choose to perform a task even though they are underrewarded for doing so will develop greater interest in the task and will work harder on it than those who are appropriately rewarded. This prediction is based on the assumption that underrewarded people will experience inconsistency stemming from the fact that they have chosen to work on a task with insufficient extrinsic justification, and will seek to reduce the inconsistency by enhancing the intrinsic value of the task and by directing greater effort toward its successful execution. In Weick's experiment, two groups of undergraduate subjects were assigned a concept-attainment task. One group received credit toward a course requirement for participation in the experiment and were treated in a professional manner by the experimenter. Those in the second group were told that they would be given no credit for participation (contrary to their expectations in volunteering) and were treated in a brusque, aloof manner by the experimenter. The results show that the second group completed more trials, took less time per problem, made fewer errors, set more realistic goals, persisted longer on an insoluble problem, and rated the task as more interesting than the first group.

While the Weick and Adams experiments both stemmed from the assumption that people strive to reduce inconsistency among cognitions, the nature of the inconsistency with which they deal is different. Adams assumes that the inconsistency lies in discrepant ratios between a person's cognition of his inputs to and outcomes from a task or job and his cognitions of the inputs and outcomes of others with whom he compares himself. Weick, on the other hand, regards the inconsistency as occurring between the person's behavior (he has chosen to perform the task or job) and his conception of his justification for doing so (he is being insufficiently rewarded). Despite the fact that both views stem from a single basic assumption about behavior, a situation could be created in which they would lead to diametrically opposite predictions. Do people who are being paid an hourly rate to perform a task or job but who perceive that they are being underrewarded (either through compensation or some other attribute of the situation) reduce their performance in order to increase the equity of the transaction or increase their performance in order to justify their decision to perform the task? Perhaps the answer depends on the extent to which they have information about the reward levels of others performing the same task or have acquired norms about equitable reward levels from past experience in similar task situations. In any event, further research is needed in order to establish more clearly the limits within which predictions from each of these ideas may be expected to hold.

If inconsistency (or dissonance) among cognitions is unpleasant, it follows that individuals will seek not only to reduce it (as has been implied by the experimental findings already cited) but also to avoid its occurrence. People may be motivated to do well on a task or job because failure to do so would create inconsistency with previously held beliefs. For example, there are situations in which effective performance of an assigned task would be consistent with a person's conception of his aptitudes or abilities, whereas ineffective performance would be inconsistent. If, in fact, people try to avoid information which threatens their self concept, then one ought to be able to predict their motivation to perform tasks or jobs effectively by knowing their beliefs about the attributes which they possess and by knowing their beliefs about the relevance of these attributes to effective performance of the tasks or jobs. Furthermore, to the extent that it is possible to manipulate these variables experimentally, one should be able to demonstrate significant effects on level of performance.

The view that people prefer consistent to inconsistent information about themselves was originally advanced by Lecky (1945) and has been elaborated by Vroom (1961, 1962, 1964). In support of this position are the results of an experiment by Kaufmann (1963). He attempted to induce on the part of subjects, through false feedback of test scores, the belief that they had a high degree of a fictitious attribute called "speed of closure." Subsequently they were all given a digit-symbol task to perform, half being told that speed of closure was highly relevant to performance on the second task, while the other half were told that speed of closure was irrelevant to the second task. It was predicted that subjects who believed that speed of closure was relevant to successful performance on the second task would be more highly motivated to do well, since ineffective performance on the second task would be inconsistent with their prior cognition. The results support the prediction. Subjects told that the digit-symbol task required speed of closure performed at a much higher level than those told that speed of closure was irrelevant to performance on the digit-symbol task. A recent experiment by Scalia (1966) replicated Kaufmann's results and provided further support for the proposition by showing that superiority in performance of subjects told that the digit-symbol task required speed of closure was not obtained for subjects induced to believe that they had a low degree of speed of closure. Aronson and Carlsmith (1962) have also obtained evidence of a "self-consistency motive" in an experiment which shows that subjects who had been led to believe, through false feedback, that they lacked social sensitivity tend to behave in such a way as to confirm rather than disconfirm this feedback, even though it was presumably unpleasant.

While the aforementioned experiments indicate that persons behave in task situations in such a way as to maintain their existing self-conceptions, there is also some evidence that they strive to implement favorable self-conceptions. A number of investigators (Lowin and Epstein, 1965; Ward and Sandvold, 1963) seeking to replicate the Aronson and Carlsmith findings described in the previous paragraph have found evidence of success-seeking behavior rather than consistency-seeking behavior. Thus, subjects tended to behave in such a way as to obtain information that they had a high degree of social sensitivity regardless of the previous experimental manipulation concerning the amount of this attribute possessed by the subject. Apparently, social sensitivity is a desired attribute and subjects strive to control the outcomes of the experimental situation so as to achieve those indicative of a high level of this attribute.

A similar conclusion is suggested by experiments concerning the effects of instructions regarding the nature of the task on the effectiveness of task performance. Several investigators (Alper, 1946; French, 1955; Kaustler, 1951; Atkinson, reported in McClelland *et al.*, 1953) have found evidence of higher performance when subjects were told that the task was a measure of some highly desirable ability or trait, for example, intelligence, than under neutral or relaxed instructions. Other investigators (Castaneda and Palermo, 1955; Russell, 1952) have failed to replicate this finding, but these exceptions appear attributable to conditions in which increases in performance would not be expected to result from increased motivation, for example, inadequate training. We can tentatively conclude that credible instructions to experimental subjects to the effect that a task they are about to perform requires an attribute which they believe themselves to possess *or* which they value and would like to possess increases the amount of effort which they will direct toward effective task performance. The conditions under which each of these two motives will be dominant in cases where they are in conflict, that is, where the task requires an attribute which is possessed but not valued or valued but not possessed, are somewhat less clear from existing research.

It is of course intuitively obvious that persons in actual work settings who have had extensive experience in the role they are performing would not be so easily "taken in" by false information concerning role requirements. Their judgments of the attributes necessary for success on their jobs would be controlled by different cues. It is conceivable, however, that similar processes could be at work. Perhaps individuals who describe their assignments or duties as challenging or intrinsically interesting and who persistently direct their available energies toward effective performance in the absence of externally mediated rewards and punishments are, in fact, in situations in which their jobs provide a source of important information about themselves, specifically, the degree to which they possess abilities and skills which are part of their actual or ideal self-conceptions.

The problem of achieving an understanding of the sources of satisfaction and dissatisfaction that are intrinsic to organizational roles is one of the most important and one of the most neglected areas of inquiry in industrial social psychology. Its importance is becoming increasingly evident as the psychologist extends his purview beyond the rank-and-file worker to include the scientist, the engineer, the entrepreneur, and the manager. Inconsistency theories have provided a promising but by no means the only avenue of attack on this problem. The outstanding difficulties with these formulations, which are not specific to their application in this context, are the lack of precision in rules for specifying when two cognitions are inconsistent, and incompleteness in specifying which of a number of alternative modes of inconsistency reduction will be exhibited in a given situation.

WORK GROUPS

In the previous section an organization was assumed to be composed of individual participants. It is also possible to view organizations as made up of small work groups, where each group corresponds roughly to what Mann and Dent (1954) have called an organizational family consisting of a supervisor and his immediate subordinates. The high level of interaction which often occurs among members of these groups and their resultant interdependence make it possible to make statements about the environment, structure, and behavior of groups and to seek generalizations or laws which are applicable to these miniature social systems.

Interest in groups as units of study and analysis in organizations was sparked by the writings of Elton Mayo and by the now famous series of investigations conducted by Mayo and his colleagues in the Hawthorne plant of the Western Electric Company. Of perhaps greater significance from the point of view of social psychologists, however, was the fact that Kurt Lewin in his later years turned his attention to problems of group dynamics. The research conducted by Lewin and his associates in group decision (Lewin, 1947) and democratic leadership (Lewin, Lippitt, and White, 1939) undoubtedly contributed in large measure to the conviction that group behavior in organizations could be studied in systematic fashion, and also helped to shape the particular group phenomena which have subsequently been selected for more intensive study.

GROUP NORMS AND GROUP COHESIVENESS

The observation that interaction among persons tends to decrease the variance in their behavior and, in the extreme, can produce highly standardized behavior patterns, has been made repeatedly by social psychologists (Newcomb, 1943; Sherif, 1947). In accounting for this phenomenon extensive use is made of the concept of group norm or group standard. Through interaction, group members acquire and transmit information concerning the actions which will be met with approval or disapproval. In groups in which members have been interacting with one another for an extended period of time, some behaviors tend to be rewarded or punished regardless of the actor or observer, and under such circumstances one can reasonably speak of a group norm with respect to that behavior.

Among industrial work groups most of the attention has been directed toward group norms concerning production. It is clear that codes with regard to appropriate levels of production are often developed in such groups. They are manifest in the outcomes of group activity, specifically, limited within-group variance in individual performance (Allport, 1934; Seashore, 1954), as well as in such aspects of group process as the fact that group members attend to the level of performance of others in their group and consistently reward those performing at appropriate levels while punishing those performing at "inappropriate" levels.

Many of the observations of group norms regarding production reported in the literature can be described as instances of organized restriction of output (Collins, Dalton, and Roy 1946; Mathewson, 1931; Roethlisberger and Dickson, 1939; Roy, 1952; Whyte, 1955). Workers are subjected to pressure from coworkers to hold down their production. Those who conform to these standards are accepted and are "popular" with their fellow workers, while those who violate them by producing at a high level are rejected and are "unpopular."

Although most descriptions of restriction of output have involved production workers on incentive payment, this phenomenon is not restricted to such situations. French and Zander (1949), for example, reported evidence of low performance norms among girls in a large business office. The correlation between popularity as measured by a sociometric questionnaire and productivity was found to be −0.67. Furthermore, as a consequence of a general reshuffling of personnel it was observed that high-performing girls lost friends while low performing girls gained. The correlation between level of performance and change in popularity following the reshuffling was found to be −0.85.

While low performance norms have received a great deal of attention in the literature, it would be incorrect to assume that all pressures from peers have the consequence of lowering productivity. Informal norms may act in opposition to formal administrative pressures, as suggested in the research described or in such popular labels as "gentleman's C" or "rate-buster." However, even a casual observation of groups of research scientists, professors, or managers would be likely to lead to the conclusion that the informal pressures which are prevalent in such situations are likely to induce a higher level of performance rather than restriction of output. Even on the shop floor, group norms may be congruent with formal administrative pressures. The Hawthorne experiments in the Relay Assembly room (Roethlisberger and Dickson, 1939) for example, showed that a small group of workers placed in an isolated experimental environment achieved a high level of productivity and showed a more or less continual increase during the experimental period. While the experimental design did not permit an unequivocal interpretation of this finding, the investigators attributed it, at least in part, to the development of a new set of norms regarding behavior on the job. These norms were consistent with, rather than antithetical to, the economic objectives of the formal organization of which the group was a part.

The precise role which group norms did play in the productivity increases in the Relay Assembly room experiments has not been and cannot be accurately estimated from the data obtained in this investigation. The contribution of these and subsequent investigations in the Hawthorne plant stems from the attention which they drew to a previously overlooked class of phenomena—the social pressures exerted on individuals by their coworkers to conform to production norms. In addition, the sharp contrast between the interaction patterns in the Relay Assembly and Bank Wiring rooms highlighted the fact that the direction of these pressures—toward high productivity or restriction of output—was, in fact, highly variable.

Two questions relevant to the role of group norms in performance have received some systematic attention from social psychologists. The first of these concerns the conditions associated with conformity to group norms regarding production. Under what circumstances do group members adhere to the informal standards regarding level of performance held by their peers? The second question concerns the determinants of the direction of group norms. Under what conditions are these informal social pressures consistent with or inconsistent with the objectives of the larger system?

Determinants of conformity to production norms

Schachter *et al.* (1951) conducted a laboratory experiment which sheds some light on the first of these questions. The experiment was designed to test a hypothesis originally proposed by Festinger, Schachter, and Back (1950), that the power of a group to influence its members is directly related to the cohesiveness of the group.

Each group, made up of three female undergraduates, was given the task of making cardboard checkerboards. Four experimental conditions were employed: (1) high group cohesiveness with high production norms, (2) low group cohesiveness with high production norms, (3) high group cohesiveness with low production norms, and (4) low group cohesiveness with low production norms. Cohesiveness was manipulated by instructions regarding the congeniality of other group members, while the direction of norms was manipulated by intercepting notes sent from one member to another and substituting prewritten sets of notes designed to influence members to increase or decrease their level of production. The results show that the experimentally created norms tended to have the expected effects, that is, increasing production in the case of the high production norms and decreasing production in the case of the low production norms. As predicted, the degree of conformity with the norm was greater in the high- than in the low-cohesiveness groups. Individuals who had been induced to be attracted to their coworkers were more influenced by pressures regarding performance which they believed to be emanating from these coworkers than were individuals who were induced to be indifferent to their coworkers. The effect of group cohesiveness on conformity was in the same direction for both high and low production norms, but reached statistical significance only for the low production norm.

Berkowitz (1954) replicated the Schachter *et al.* experiment using male subjects, a different task, and an extended production period to determine whether the social influences on production would persist after "communication" Between group members had ceased. While differences in production between groups with high and low norms were less striking than in the previous experiment, the results show significantly greater conformity in the highly cohesive groups than in the low-cohesiveness groups, regardless of the directions of the norm. Furthermore, it is clear from the Berkowitz results that the differential conformity of high- and low-cohesiveness groups persists after the induction of norms has ceased.

These two laboratory experiments provide quite strong support for the proposition that conformity to group norms regarding production will be directly related to the cohesiveness of the group. Further evidence in support of this proposition has been obtained in a field study by Seashore (1954). By means of questionnaires, he measured the cohesiveness of 228 work groups in a factory manufacturing heavy machinery. He also obtained, from company records, measures of the productivity of each group member for a three-month period. While there was little or no relationship between group cohesiveness and mean productivity of group members, there was a fairly marked negative relationship between group cohesiveness and within-group variance in productivity. Workers in highly cohesive groups were more likely to produce at or about the same level as their coworkers than were workers in groups that were low in cohesiveness. In the light of the experimental evidence reported above, it seems quite likely that these findings reflect the greater power of the highly cohesive groups to induce conformity to group norms regarding productivity.

Determinants of the direction of production norms

Most social scientists who have tried, after the fact, to account for differences in norms between groups have stressed the functional character of norms. Norms and the influence attempts which accompany them are internal mechanisms by which group members seek to attain their goals for the group. Thus, a norm of restricting output may be expected to serve some purpose, typically protecting its members against rate cuts or layoffs.

While seeking explanations for group norms in terms of their actual or expected consequences may be a source of useful hypotheses about the antecedents of group norms, it does not deal directly with the questions of how and under what conditions these norms are formed. Unfortunately, there has been little empirical work on the determinants of work-group norms regarding performance. In the field study partially described above, Seashore (1954) attempted to account not only for differential conformity to norms regarding productivity, but also for differences in the nature of the norms. He predicted high productivity norms to occur most frequently among work groups whose members were highly cohesive and who perceived the company as highly supportive. On the other hand, he predicted low productivity norms among work groups whose members were high in cohesiveness but who perceived the company as providing a low degree of support. Two different measures were taken to represent productivity norms: mean level of actual productivity of group members, and mean response of group members to a question dealing with the level of productivity which they believed to be reasonable. In addition, two different measures, both from questionnaires, were obtained concerning the degree to which the larger organization provided a secure and supportive environment for the group: one of these measures concerned the relationship of group members with the company; the other concerned their relationship with the union. The results are not striking, and in many cases not significant, but are generally in the direction predicted. The highest levels of actual and perceived reasonable productivity were found among groups which were high in cohesiveness and whose members perceived the company or union as supportive. The lowest levels of actual and perceived reasonable productivity tended to occur among highly cohesive groups perceiving the company and/or union as unsupportive. Unfortunately, the heterogeneity of the questions used in the two support measures makes it difficult to gain much insight into the actual mechanisms which might be involved in the emergence of high and low productivity norms.

In another field study concerned with the effects of supervisory methods on group performance norms, Patchen (1962) used a questionnaire to measure the performance norms of work groups in a company manufacturing plastic materials. Support for the validity of this measure is indicated by its positive correlation with work-group productivity and its negative correlation with incidence of absences, lateness, and leaving the job early. Measures of the behavior of the foreman in charge of each group were obtained from questionnaire descriptions by group members. Three of these measures—the extent to which the foreman encourages efficiency on the part of his subordinates, the extent to which the foreman "goes to bat" for his subordinates, and the power of the foreman—were found to have small but not significant positive correlations with the level of group performance norms. However, further analyses revealed substantial interactions among these three variables. Each variable was positively correlated with the measure of norms at high values of the other variables, and uncorrelated or negatively correlated at low values of the other variables. For example, the correlation between norms and the extent to which the foreman was described as "going to bat" for his men was $+0.86$ in groups where the foreman was seen as high on encouraging efficiency and -0.50 in groups in which he was seen as low on encouraging efficiency. The foremen of work groups with high performance norms tended to have high scores on all three indices, that is, to be described by their men as encouraging work efficiency, trying to obtain rewards for them, and having the power to obtain these rewards.

Likert (1961) has stressed the administrative importance of creating within organizations highly cohesive work groups with high performance norms. His book *New Patterns of Management* contains a set of proposals whereby managers could create effectively functioning work groups that have a high degree of group loyalty and high performance goals. Likert's conception of the managerial process calls for the manager in charge of a unit to (1) adopt a group rather than a man-to-man system of operation in which he meets with his subordinates as a group and uses the group as a problem-solving and decision-making instrument, (2) behave in a supportive manner in all interactions with subordinates so that subordinates will view their relationships as contributing to their sense of personal worth and importance, and (3) shorten "feedback" cycles through the use of measurements of the sociotechnical system, the particular measurements to be obtained being determined by the group and being used by the group for performance evaluation and goal setting.

The probable consequence of the implementation of these proposals is difficult to estimate for a number of reasons, not the least of which are the complexity of the problems with which they purport to deal, the inadequacy of existing data, and the lack of specificity or operationality in the proposals themselves. In the following section we will consider the evidence bearing on a more limited but still complex aspect of the Likert proposal, namely, the use of groups for problem-solving and decision-making purposes, or what is more frequently called participation in decision making.

PARTICIPATION IN DECISION MAKING

One of the most persistent and controversial issues in the study of management concerns the issue of participation in decision making by subordinates. Traditional models of the managerial process have been autocratic in nature. The manager makes decisions on matters within his area of freedom, issues orders or directives to his subordinates, and monitors their performance to ensure conformity with these directives. Scientific management, from its early developments in time and motion study to its contemporary manifestations in linear and heuristic programming, has contributed to this centralization of decision making in organizations by focusing on the development of methods by which managers can make more rational decisions, substituting objective measurements and empirically validated methods for casual judgments.

Most social psychologists and other behavioral scientists who have turned their attention toward the implications of psychological and social processes for the practice of management have called for greater participation by subordinates in the problem-solving, decision-making process. Pointing to evidence of restriction of output and lack of involvement under traditional managerial systems, they have argued for greater influence in decision making on the part of those who are held responsible for decision execution.

The empirical evidence provides some, but not overwhelming, support for beliefs in the efficacy of participative management. Field experiments on rank-and-file workers by Coch and French (1948), Bavelas (reported in French, 1950), and Strauss (reported in Whyte, 1955) indicate that impressive increases in productivity can be brought about by giving workers an opportunity to participate in decision making and goal setting. In addition, several correlational field studies (Katz, Maccoby, and Morse, 1950; Vroom, 1960) indicate positive relationships between the amount of influence which supervisors afford their subordinates in decisions which affect them and individual or group performance. On the other hand, in an experiment conducted in a Norwegian factory, French, Israel, and As (1960) found no significant differences in production between workers who did and workers who did not participate in decisions regarding introduction of changes in work methods; and in a recent laboratory experiment, Sales and Rosen (1965) found no significant differences between groups exposed to democratic and autocratic supervision. To complicate the picture further, Morse and Reimer (1956) compared the effects of two programs of change, each of which was introduced in two divisions of the clerical operations of a large insurance company. One of the programs involved increased participation in decision making by rank-and-file workers, while the other involved increased hierarchical control. The results show a significant increase in productivity under both programs, with the hierarchically controlled program producing the greater increase.

Reconciliation of these discrepant findings is not an easy task. It is made complex by different empirical interpretations of the term "participation" (Strauss, 1963) and by great differences in the situations in which it is applied. It appears highly likely that an increase in participation of subordinates in decision making may increase productivity under some circumstances but decrease productivity under other circumstances. Identification of the situational conditions which determine the efficacy of participative management requires the specification of the decision-making processes which it entails and of the various mechanisms by which it may influence the extent to which the formal objectives of the organization are attained.

To structure the problem, consider a manager of a unit in a formal organization. He is faced with a continuing series of problems to solve or decisions to make. Let us simplify our task by considering only the subset of problems which affect all the individuals reporting to him. From the standpoint of the interactions which they entail, one can identify a number of different processes by which the problem can be solved or the decision made which differ in the amount of influence (or participation) afforded subordinates. At the low end of the participation scale are so-called autocratic methods, in which the manager makes the decision by himself and issues an order or directive to his subordinates. At the high end of the participation scale is what Maier (1952, 1955, 1963) has called the group decision method, in which the manager shares the problem with his subordinates as a group and permits the group to make the decision.

As Tannenbaum and Schmidt (1958) have pointed out, there are many intermediate possibilities. The term "consultative management," for example, is often used to refer to a process in which subordinates individually or as a group take an active part in generating alternative courses of action and/or evaluating these courses of action, but the final choice is made by the manager. The consequences of this method are difficult to discuss because of the large number of different forms which it may take and because the weight attached to the ideas and opinions of subordinates is unspecified. Generally, it may be assumed to fall between autocratic and group decision methods in both the amount of influence or participation afforded subordinates and in the various consequences to be discussed. For the sake of convenience and clarity we will examine the issues involved in debates about participative management by focusing on the two extremes on the participation scale-autocratic and group decision making.

Having defined the methods to be compared, it is necessary to specify the criterion or criteria to be used in the comparison. Concepts like productivity or, to be even more general, effectiveness, are, of course, of ultimate concern, but both are determined by a multitude of other variables which may be affected in different ways by participation. From a pragmatic standpoint, however, it seems best to hold in abeyance the knotty problem of what is meant by effectiveness and how it can be determined, and to consider the evidence bearing on probabilities of different kinds of specific outcomes occurring as a consequence of different decision-making methods.

There are three classes of outcomes which are generally relevant to what is meant by effectiveness and which, on the basis of existing evidence, seem likely to be affected by participation in decision making. These are (1) the quality of decisions reached, (2) the execution of decisions reached, and (3) the amount of time required to make the decision.

Participation and decision quality

It is clear that the amount of influence afforded subordinates in the decision-making process can have important effects on the nature of the decisions reached. A manager who makes a decision autocratically may adopt a different course of action than if he had consulted his subordinates prior to making the decision, and both of these decisions may differ from that resulting from the use of group decision.

If, in fact, different courses of action are adopted as a result of these three processes, it is possible that these decisions differ in quality. The term "quality of decision" has been used by Maier (1963) to refer to the "objective or impersonal" attributes of the decision. For groups embedded within formal organizations with specified objectives, the relative quality of a set of alternative decisions made could be expressed in terms of their effects, if implemented with equal expenditure of human and physical energy, on the attainment of these objectives.

Autocratic and group decision methods differ in the number of persons who participate in the decision-making process and in the amount of interaction among persons which occurs prior to the decision. The autocratic method is essentially an individual decision-making process and involves no interaction among persons prior to the decision. On the other hand, in the group decision method, all members take part in the problem-solving or decision-making activity in a manner which entails a great deal of interaction among these members prior to the decision.

There are two related questions to be answered about the difference between decisions made by individuals and by groups. The first question concerns evidence that, in fact, group and individual decisions are distinguishable from one another in a systematic way.   How reliably is it possible to classify decisions as having been made by individuals or by groups solely from a knowledge of the nature of the decision?

Perhaps the most consistent evidence that group decisions tend to have somewhat different properties than individual decisions may be found in a series of experiments on risk taking by individuals and by groups.   Contrary to the popular stereotype of group decision making as cautious and conservative, the results of a fairly sizable number of experiments (Bem, Wallach, and Kogan, 1965; Stoner, 1961; Wallach and Kogan, 1965; Wallach, Kogan, and Bem, 1962, 1964) indicate that a group tends to select a riskier course of action than would have been selected by the average member of that group.   While at present there remains some controversy concerning the process or processes underlying this phenomenon (Brown, 1965; Kogan and Wallach, 1967), it is clear that groups do tend to select alternatives with higher payoffs but with lower probabilities of attainment than do individuals.   It should be noted, however, that there remains considerable overlap between the distribution of group and individual decisions.   Group decisions tend to be "riskier" than the mean of its members but not "riskier" than all of its members.

The fact that group decisions do, on the average, have at least one distinguishing feature from individual decisions makes it possible to raise the second question. What is the evidence that group decisions are more or less rational than individual decisions?   To what extent is there a difference between the quality of decisions made by individuals and by groups?   To answer this question, it is necessary to look at research in which comparisons are made between the solutions of groups and individuals to problems which have correct solutions, or to which reasonably objective judgments can be made concerning the relative quality of different solutions.   The risk-taking experiments do not have this property, since either the expected value of all alternatives was identical ((Wallach, Kogan, and Bem, 1964) or, as in the majority of experiments, it was indeterminate.

This literature has been reviewed extensively elsewhere (Lorge *et al.,* 1958) and will not be examined in depth here.   For our purposes it is sufficient to report a very frequent, though not unanimous, finding, that the mean quality of decisions reached by groups exceeds the mean quality of decisions reached by individuals.   Similar results have been obtained on such varied problems as a case in human relations (Lorge *et al.,* 1960), mathematical puzzles (Davis and Restle, 1963; Marquart, 1955; Shaw, 1932), finding a way to get a squad of soldiers across a mined road (Lorge *et al.,* 1955), and playing the game of "twenty questions" (Taylor and Faust, 1952).   The superiority of groups over individuals results in part from statistical consequences of the fact that, in groups, the activities of a large number of individuals are brought to bear on problem solution, and in part from social-psychological phenomena stemming from the fact that these individuals are interacting with one another during the problem-solving process.

While seemingly favoring the quality of decisions obtained by the group decision method over those obtained by the individual autocratic method, such a conclusion does not appear warranted.   The experimental evidence cited suggests superiority in the quality of decisions reached by the average group to those reached by the average group member.   However, in no sense can the manager of a group be considered to be an average group member.   He has been selected by different criteria, exposed to different training, and has access to different information than other group members.

While the mean quality of group decisions tends to be of higher quality than the mean of the individual solutions, there is some evidence that group decisions are inferior to those of the best group member (Tuckman and Lorge, 1962).

On theoretical grounds it seems highly likely that differences in quality of autocratic decisions and those reached by the group decision process are dependent on a number of other factors. Since quality is defined in terms of the organizational consequences of the decision if implemented, differences between the manager and his subordinates in amount of information relevant to judging these consequences and in the adequacy of their "programs" for processing that information would appear to be of crucial importance. In the extreme situation in which the manager has all the information bearing on the solution of the problem and has learned the rules for combining that information so as to achieve an optimal solution, consulting with subordinates or permitting one's subordinates to make the decision is not likely to improve decision quality and, at least in the latter case, may seriously impair the quality of the resulting decision. On the other hand, at the other extreme, in which the information relevant to the problem is widely distributed among group members and no single person, including the manager, possesses any more than a fraction of the needed information, participation by subordinates in the decision-making process is, almost by definition, necessary to attain a high-quality decision.

The possession of information by the decision-making system and the availability of "programs" for processing that information may be necessary conditions for the attainment of high-quality solutions, but they are not sufficient. One would expect the quality of decisions to depend not only on the knowledge or ability of the decision maker but also on his motivation to use his knowledge or ability to attain the most rational solution from an organizational point of view.

It would be unrealistic to assume that all organization members are solely committed to the attainment of organizational objectives. There are, for example, situations in which the organizational objectives and the desires of a particular group of its members are in conflict. The optimal solution to a problem from an organizational standpoint may be to eliminate their jobs, or reduce their pay or responsibility. It is difficult in such a situation to see how increasing the amount of influence which such persons have on the decision could increase the quality of the decision, and in fact, the opposite effect seems more likely. These considerations are relevant to the consequences for quality of decision of participation in decision making by subordinates when the manager and those who report to him are differentially disposed toward selecting among alternative courses of action on the basis of their organizational consequences, as opposed to personal gains and losses.

A case in point may be found in the field experiment conducted by Morse and Reimer (1956), cited earlier in this section. The experimenters attributed the increased productivity under the autocratic program to an administrative decision to cut staff by 25 percent. Since there was, at any one time, a fixed volume of work to be done, a reduction in staff was a highly effective means of increasing productivity and this decision was, from a productivity standpoint, of high quality. Understandably, there was greater reluctance to reduce staff in the divisions in which rank-and-file workers were accorded greater influence in decision making. To be sure, reduction in staff was effected but it was of much more modest proportions.

Maier (1963) has argued that the skill of the leader is an important variable in determining the quality of decisions obtained by the group decision method. He has presented a series of principles to guide leaders in stating problems for group discussion, conducting the discussion, and reaching the final decision. In a series of laboratory experiments, Maier and his associates (Maier, 1950, 1953; Maier and Hoffman, 1960) have shown that leaders trained in these principles achieve higher-quality group decisions than those who are untrained or who have had less training.

There is some evidence that interaction among individuals such as occurs in the group decision procedure may be functional at some stages of problem solving but dysfunctional at others. Taylor, Berry, and Block (1958) showed that interaction among group members inhibits the generation of alternative solutions to problems. Using college students as subjects, they compared the performance of 12 real groups, whose members interacted with one another, and 12 nominal or statisticized groups, whose members worked separately. Each group, made up of four persons, was instructed to use Osborne's brainstorming procedure, which calls for generation of as large a number of alternative solutions as possible within the fixed time limit and a moratorium on the evaluation of solutions generated. The results show that, for each of the three problems used, the nominal groups generated a larger number of different solutions, a larger number of high-quality solutions, and a larger number of unique solutions than did the real groups.

Dunnette, Campbell, and Jaastad (1963) replicated this experiment using industrial employees as subjects and employing an experimental design which called for each subject to work both as a member of a real and as a member of a nominal group. The results are highly consistent with those obtained by Taylor, Berry, and Block (1958), and add further support to the idea that interaction inhibits the "creative" phase of problem solving, that is, the process of generating alternative solutions to the problem.

On the other hand, interaction may be beneficial when the task involves evaluating rather than generating alternative solutions. In an early experiment, Thorndike (1938) gave subjects a set of problems and required each subject to choose between two answers, only one of which was correct. The subjects were then divided into groups and each group was asked to make a group choice. The results show clearly that the proportion of correct answers obtained by groups following discussions exceeded the proportion of cases in which the majority of group members had the right answer preceding discussion. Timmons (1942) and Hall, Mouton, and Blake (1963) obtained similar results in experiments in which subjects were asked to rank a set of alternatives on the basis of a criterion established by the experimenter. In both experiments, group rankings made following discussion were higher in quality than pooled rankings (that is, group average or group majority) of the same individuals prior to discussion. Apparently, individuals with more accurate evaluations of alternatives tend to have more influence on the group ranking than those with less accurate evaluations.

To test conclusively the possibility that interaction among group members facilitates one phase of problem solving and hinders another, it is highly desirable to hold the problem constant and to examine separately the effects of social interaction on each phase. An experiment by Vroom, Grant, and Cotton (1969) utilized this method. Four-man groups worked on complex administrative problems under four conditions: (1) members interacted during the generation of solutions but were prevented from interacting during the evaluation of solutions; (2) members were prevented from interacting during the generation of solutions but did interact during the evaluation of solutions; (3) members interacted during both the generation and the evaluation of solutions; (4) members were prevented from interacting during both the generation and the evaluation of solutions.

The results corroborate previous evidence that interaction during the generation phase of problem solving is dysfunctional. Groups in which members interacted with one another during generation produced a smaller number of different solutions, fewer high-quality solutions, and a smaller number of different kinds of solutions than groups in which members were restrained from interacting during generation. There was also some evidence that interaction during the evaluation process aids in discriminating high- and low-quality solutions; however, this effect was not as striking, and it varied with the manner in which individual evaluations were combined in non-interacting groups.

In summary, it appears that differences between the quality of autocratic and group decisions are dependent on a large number of variables, including (1) the extent to which the manager and those reporting to him have information relevant to judging the organizational consequences of different courses of action, (2) the extent to which their interests are consistent with organizational objectives, and (3) the skill of the manager in leading the group discussion. There is some evidence that interaction among individuals is dysfunctional during the creative phase of problem solving, in which alternative solutions are being generated, but may be functional during the evaluative phase, in which solutions are screened and chosen.

Participation and the execution of decisions

The effectiveness of a decision-making process is dependent not only on the quality of decisions which it generates but also on the speed and efficiency with which they are implemented. Many highly rational solutions to organizational problems have been ineffective because they were resisted and opposed by those who had to carry them out.

Most analyses of participation in decision making have dealt with its consequences for the motivation of participants to carry out the decision. Thus Coch and French (1948) treated participation as an influence on the field of forces acting on the individual; French, Israel, and As (1960) hypothesized that participation in a decision increases the "own forces" on the individual to carry out the decision; and Maier (1963) argued that group decision produces higher acceptance of the decision by group members.

The idea that participation in a decision by a person or group increases the probability that the person or group will execute the decision received empirical support from an early series of studies by Lewin and his associates which compared the effectiveness of lecture and group decision methods in changing behavior. Lectures in which people were presented with arguments to induce them to adopt new food habits (Lewin, 1947; Radke and Klisurich, 1947; Simmons, 1954) or change their practices in merit rating of subordinates (Levine and Butler, 1952) proved to be less effective in producing change than did group discussions concluded by a request from the leader for decisions regarding individual intentions of taking such action in the future. As a number of writers (Lorge *et al.*, 1958; Miller, 1951) have observed, the two experimental conditions, lecture and group decision, are different in a number of respects and the crucial variables responsible for the obtained differences are not obvious from these results.

In an experiment designed to deal with this problem, Bennett (1955) experimentally varied (1) the nature of the influence attempt (group discussion, lecture, none), (2) whether the subject was asked to make a decision regarding his willingness to engage in the behavior in question (no decision, decision), and (3) within the decision conditions, the extent to which the decision was public (anonymous, partially anonymous, public). The criterion behavior and the focus of the influence attempts was volunteering as subjects for psychological experiments. The only experimental variable related to probability of volunteering was whether the subject was asked to make a decision regarding his willingness to engage in this action. The proportion of persons performing the action was higher among those who were than among those who were not asked to make a decision. The nature of the influence attempt (group discussion versus lecture) was found to be irrelevant, as was the degree of public commitment. The only other variable which was predictive of the criterion behavior was the degree of actual and perceived group consensus regarding intention to act. Subjects who subsequently volunteered tended to come from groups where there had been a high degree of consensus that the criterion behavior was desirable, and tended to estimate the percentage of others in their group who would volunteer to be high.

It should be noted that, in each of the experiments described, the actions to which persons committed themselves concerned their future behavior as individuals rather than as group members. Unlike most decisions made in organized work groups, no interaction among group members was required during decision execution. Each person could execute his decision independent of the actions taken by other group members, and typically could not observe the extent to which others were engaged in similar behaviors. Nonetheless, these experiments do indicate that the probability that persons will execute decisions can be increased by a procedure in which they actively make decisions in a social situation in which there is substantial consensus among group members that the execution of the decisions is worthwhile.

Bavelas (reported in French, 1950) studied the effects on production of the setting of production goals by organized work groups. Groups of women sewing-machine operators, ranging in size from four to 12 workers, met with the experimenter in the management conference room. In these meetings, the experimenter asked the group if they would like to set a group goal for higher production. In most cases the group members agreed and then proceeded to make group decisions about the level of production which they hoped to reach and the length of time in which they would try to reach it. The experimenter then arranged for further meetings with the group in which he provided them with graphs showing changes in group productivity. Each experimental group was matched with a control group for type of job, social setting, and supervision. An analysis of the changes in productivity for experimental and control groups showed striking differences. In the control groups the level of production remained relatively constant during the four-month period of observation. On the other hand, in the experimental groups there was an average increase in production of 18 percent following the goal settings, and this was maintained over two months. As Viteles (1953) has pointed out, the effects of group goal setting and of knowledge of results are confounded in this experiment. It is impossible to determine the extent to which the production increase in the experimental groups was due to their participation in the goal setting or to the fact that they received continual feedback concerning their level of achievement.

The results of Lawrence and Smith (1955) are consistent with those of Bennett described above in showing the limitations of group discussion unless accompanied by decision making. The groups participated in weekly meetings for the purpose of setting production goals and, in addition, discussed a wide range of employee and company matters. Two other groups participated in group discussions without making decisions concerning production. The groups setting production goals showed a significantly greater increase in production than those not setting goals.

An experiment by Coch and French (1948) in the Harwood manufacturing company suggests the value of employee participation in the introduction of change. Four groups of workers about to undergo a change in work methods were used in the experiment. These groups were roughly equivalent with respect to their efficiency before the change and in the amount of change required. In one of the four groups, the control group, the change was introduced in the usual manner. The jobs were modified by the production department, new rates were set, and a meeting was held with workers at which they were told of the change. The other three groups, designated as experimental groups, were given an opportunity to participate in making decisions concerning some aspects of the change. In one of these experimental groups, workers were permitted to influence the change only through their elected representatives. They were told of the necessity for the change and selected two of their members to assist in working out the details. In the other two experimental groups, each operator could participate directly in making decisions concerning the change.

An analysis of the productivity of the four groups on the new job revealed marked differences. The productivity of the control group dropped substantially following introduction of the change and did not improve appreciably with time. This behavior pattern was typical of responses to changes in work methods in the past. The productivity of the first experimental group who participated through their elected representatives also dropped when they were placed on the new job, but after 14 days they had regained their previous production level. The most favorable results were achieved in the two experimental groups whose members had participated fully in making decisions regarding the change. These groups recovered their prechange level after four days and continued to improve until they reached a level of performance that was 14 percent above that which they had attained before the change. Evidence that the inferior performance of the control group was not attributable to the specific personnel involved was obtained when the control group became an experimental group for a later experiment. They then exhibited the same quick recovery and attained a new production high, as had previous groups participating in decisions regarding the change.

A recent and somewhat less controlled experiment by Fleishman (1965) raises questions about the generality of the Coch and French results, particularly the difference between the experimental groups directly participating in decisions regarding the change and the group who participated through their elected representatives. The subjects were also women sewing-machine operators, but were considerably older than in the previous experiment. The situation was also different in that changes in product were a much more frequent factor in the production process. A common element, however, was the sharp drop in productivity following a change in work methods. Twenty women, selected from among the 60 sewing-machine operators, all of whom were about to undergo the same change in the style of dress on which they were working, were told that a new procedure would be followed in the introduction of the change. The workers, rather than the management, would determine such things as the sequence of operations and the bundling procedures and would also be permitted to decide what portions of a total price set by management would be paid to those performing each operation. The remaining 40 operators, matched on the basis of a number of relevant variables, were not involved directly in participation in these decisions, though they worked side by side with those who were. The results show virtually no evidence of the characteristic drop-off in productivity for either those directly participating or those who did not. In fact, the entire lot of production was completed in three days rather than the eight days anticipated by management on the basis of experience with similar styles. Furthermore, both groups, when later returned to the style of dress they had been working on prior to the change, not only attained their previous level but also reached a new plateau. It is unfortunate that there was no control group who did not participate in the change and who worked separately from those who did. But nonetheless these results lend support to the author's conclusion that "direct participation of individual workers may not be as important an incentive as their perception of the group's participation in these work changes" (Fleishman, 1965, p. 266).

Bass and Leavitt (1963) conducted a series of laboratory experiments to determine differences in performance between teams which developed their own plan of organization and those which were given a plan devised by another team. Three tasks were used: the production of word-sentences, the common-target game, and a numbers game. The results show small but consistent differences in performance in favor of teams which were carrying out plans they had developed themselves.

The results which we have considered in this section suggest a fairly consistent effect of participation in decision making on the probability that decisions will be effectively implemented. Other things being equal, a person has a higher probability of carrying out decisions which he has made or helped to make than decisions that have been made for him by others. Less clear from these studies are the effects of participation in one decision on the motivation of group members to carry out other decisions. Whether having an influence on a decision affects only the execution of that decision or, as has been suggested by some writers, increases the strength of a generalized motivation to produce on the job cannot be determined from existing evidence.

Also subject to debate is the nature of the process by which participation affects decision execution. While social psychologists have tended to emphasize the motivational consequences of participation, it is possible that some of the experimental differences reported (for example, Bass and Leavitt, 1963) are due to greater understanding of decisions on the part of those who have shared in making them. Even within the realm of motivation there is some controversy about the extent to which demonstrated effects are attributable to "induced" or "own" forces (Lewin, 1938). Likert (1961) has argued that the use of groups as problem-solving, decision-making instruments creates work groups with high cohesiveness and with norms or standards which are consistent with, rather than opposed to, the organization's objectives. Thus, each group member is subject to forces induced by his peers to carry out the decision speedily and efficiently. It is also possible that these effects are independent of social influence and are due to a tendency for individuals to become "ego-involved" in decisions to which they have contributed. Something akin to the latter process is suggested by evidence that participation by a single person in decision making with a superior affects the subsequent performance of that person (Bachman, 1964; Meyer, Kay, and French, 1965; Vroom, 1960).

An interesting parallel exists between the effects of participation on the acceptance of decisions and the phenomenon of postdecision dissonance. Festinger (1957) has asserted that, when a person is confronted with two or more mutually exclusive alternatives which are similar in attractiveness but different in other properties, cognitive dissonance is created by the act of choice. This dissonance stems from an inconsistency between the person's knowledge of the alternative that he has chosen, and his knowledge of the relatively attractive properties of the unchosen alternative or alternatives. One method of reducing this postdecision dissonance is to reevaluate the alternatives, increasing the attractiveness of the chosen alternative and decreasing the attractiveness of the rejected alternatives. Supporting this prediction are the results of laboratory experiments by Brehm (1956), Brehm and Cohen (1959), and Brock (1963). If making a decision increases the attractiveness of the chosen alternative relative to those that are unchosen, it is possible that a similar, though possibly less intense, change will be produced by sharing or participating in the making of the decision. Thus a person who participates in decision making may experience postdecision dissonance and restructure alternatives in a manner analogous to a person making a decision. If, in fact, such a process underlies the effects of participation on decision acceptance and execution, the magnitude of these effects should be sensitive to differences in the initial attractiveness of alternatives and in the initial similarity among alternatives—variables which are predicted to determine the amount of postdecision dissonance and have been demonstrated to affect the amount of reevaluation of alternatives.

While the participation of individuals or of groups in decisions which affect them appears to be positively related to their acceptance of decisions and to the efficiency with which the decisions are executed, *other things being equal*, it is possible, if not likely, that in actual organizational situations other things will not be equal. Autocratic decision-making procedures tend to be accompanied by much stronger external controls over decision execution than democratic procedures. There are mechanisms by which the performance of those responsible for the execution of decisions can be monitored and appropriate application of rewards and punishments made.. Augmenting the autocratic decision-making method by the conditions necessary for the induction of forces on individuals to carry out decisions may be expected to attenuate differences in probability and efficiency of decision execution associated with different degrees of participation. If the manager has what French (1956) has called reward or coercive power over his subordinates and can monitor the decision-execution process, differences in execution should be smaller than if he lacks these bases of power and/or is unable to monitor decision execution. Thus, Lewin, Lippitt, and White (1939) found a slight advantage in productivity for autocratic over democratic leadership when the leader was in the room observing performance, but a strong superiority of democratic leadership when the leader was absent from the room.

Participation and decision time

The extent to which a manager involves his subordinates in decision-making processes can be expected to affect the time required to make the decision. Two dimensions of time are relevant to evaluation of the effectiveness of decision-making mechanisms: (1) the length of elapsed time for the presentation of a problem to the obtaining of a solution from the decision-making system, and (2) the number of man-hours taken by the decision-making system to transform a problem into a solution.

Laboratory experiments on elapsed time for problem solving by individuals or groups have provided mixed results. Taylor and Faust (1952) had individuals, groups of two, and groups of four play the game of twenty questions. Four problems a day were given for each of four consecutive days. Individuals were found to require more time per problem than groups of either two or four persons, with no significant difference between the two sizes of groups.

On the other hand, Davis and Restle (1963) found no difference between groups of four and individuals in working times on three Eureka-type problems. While groups obtained the correct solutions with higher frequency, the differences in elapsed time were not significant either for those groups and individuals solving or for those not solving the problem.

In neither of these experiments is there support for the common assumption among managers that group decision making is incompatible with a common requirement in organizations for fast decisions. There are, however, several features of the problems and methods employed in both experiments which deviate from problem-solving or decision-making situations found in organizations and which may have favored the performance of groups. First, there was a single correct solution to each of the problems used. Subjects could determine whether a given solution was the correct one by asking a question of the experimenter (in the twenty questions game) or by performing simple cognitive operations on that solution (in the Eureka problems). Consequently, little if any of the elapsed time of groups was spent in exchanging opinions concerning the relative value of alternative solutions, an activity which is very common in most group decision making in industry.

Second, the problem was presented simultaneously to all group members. None of the recorded elapsed time was spent in convening the group or in acquainting them with the problem. Typically in organizations, the problem first comes to the attention of the manager. In deciding whether to solve the problem or to present it to his subordinates as a group for solution, he must take cognizance not only of the time required for the group to solve the problem but also for him to convene the group and to communicate the problem to them. Finally, the situation in both laboratory experiments was such as to minimize conflict among group members. Each person was assigned the single goal of solving the problem and, as we have previously noted, had a basis for determining when that goal had been obtained. However, in a great many problem-solving or decision-making situations in organizations there is a disagreement among group members concerning the objectives to be attained or the means of attaining them. March and Simon (1958) put forth the highly tenable hypothesis that this interindividual conflict increases decision time, given pressure for joint decision making.

The difference in elapsed time between individuals and groups in problem solving would seem to be dependent on a number of additional factors, including the nature of the problem, the measure of elapsed time used, the criterion used in terminating problem-solving activity (for example, attaining correct solution, majority vote, consensus, etc.), and the amount of conflict both within and among individuals. There are undoubtedly conditions in which group decision making is "ruled out" because of time constraints. The quarterback on a football team who attempted to select each play by group decision would probably incur a succession of penalties for delay of the game. On the other hand, there are situations in which group interaction would reduce the amount of time required for information acquisition and would consequently reduce elapsed time.

While the results for elapsed time are conflicting, the evidence regarding man-hours taken by groups and individuals in the solution of problems is much more consistent. In the experiment described above, Taylor and Faust (1952) found that the mean number of man-minutes taken per problem was positively related to group size, being largest for groups of four and smallest for individuals. These results are similar to those obtained by Davis and Restle (1963). While both investigators found that the probability of a correct solution was somewhat higher for groups, it is apparent that this greater probability of success is not achieved without a substantially higher investment in man-hours.

It is not unreasonable to expect similar if not greater differences to be obtained in actual organizational situations. For a group of four to equal the man-hour investment of a single individual, it would have to solve the problem in one-quarter of the time. Similarly, a group of eight would have to solve the problem in one-eighth of the time, and so on. Considering only man-hours expended, group decision making is not an efficient means of solving organizational problems.

SUMMARY

We have considered the efficacy of participation in decision making from the standpoint of its effects on decision quality, decision execution, and decision time. The results suggest that allocating problem-solving and decision-making tasks to entire work groups, as compared with the leader or manager in charge of the groups, requires a greater investment of man-hours but produces higher acceptance of decisions and a higher probability that the decisions will be executed efficiently. Differences between these two methods in quality of decisions and in elapsed time are inconclusive and probably highly variable. With respect to both of these criteria, specific variables affecting differences in outcomes were discussed.

What implications does this analysis have for arguments concerning the overall effectiveness of participative management or group decision making in formal organizations? We have hesitated up to now to deal with such a global criterion as effectiveness, since the effects of participation can be more easily identified on such subcriteria as the quality of decisions which it produces, the acceptance of decisions or the probability that they will be executed efficiently, and the time required to make them. To be sure, the weight attached to each of these subcriteria in any overall assessment of decision effectiveness will vary from situation to situation. Quality will be weighted heavily in strategic decisions which are not reversible and in which the variance in contribution to organizational objectives of alternative courses of action is large; acceptance will be weighted heavily in decisions which must be executed by persons other than the manager in situations in which his monitoring of their behavior is difficult or impossible; elapsed time will be weighted heavily in decisions with binding time constraints; and time in man-hours will be weighted heavily in situations in which the opportunity costs of a given increment in man-hours is substantial.

It would be naive to think that group decision making is always more "effective" than autocratic decision making, or vice versa; the relative effectiveness of these two extreme methods depends both on the weights attached to quality, acceptance, and time variables and on differences in amounts of these outcomes resulting from these methods, neither of which is invariant from one situation to another. The critics and proponents of participative management would do well to direct their efforts toward identifying the properties of situations in which different decision-making approaches are effective rather than toward wholesale condemnation or deification of one approach.

THE ORGANIZATION AS A SYSTEM

In previous sections we have been concerned with what might be called the building blocks of organizations: individuals and small face-to-face work groups. Those social systems typically referred to as organizations are, in fact, much larger and more complex than either individuals or small groups. An organization is made up of multiple groups linked together in interdependent activity. It is set up for the purpose of attaining objectives and possesses a describable structure, for example, a relatively stable division of labor differentiating the behaviors of its members.

The systematic study of organizations is a meeting ground for representatives of many different disciplines, each bringing to it his own concepts, methods, and interests. Economists have been concerned with economic decision making by business firms and have sought to explain decisions regarding output, price of products or services, and product mix in terms of market factors. In the classical economic theory of the firm, an organization is treated as a single entrepreneur with the single goal of maximizing profits and with complete knowledge of the consequences of alternative courses of action. Sociologists have been much more catholic in their selection of problems. While their theories have emphasized the properties, antecedents, and consequences of bureaucracy, empirical research has covered a wide range of phenomena, including the relations between the organization and its environment, the socialization of organization members, conflict between subparts of organizations, and the development of "informal" organizations. In addition, administrative theorists have directed their attention toward problems confronting the executive in administering a complex organization and have asserted, unfortunately often without empirical justification, "principles" or "axioms" of organizational design.

Social psychologists have traditionally been concerned with smaller social systems than complex organizations. Their units of analysis have been principally the individual and the small group. Research on the latter, while potentially relevant to explanation of organizational behavior, has tended to neglect some of the basic properties of organized activity, such as a formally defined system of interdependent roles, mediated communication, and stable role assignments. In recent years, however, there have been signs of growing interest among social psychologists in theory and research on the behavior of complex formal organizations. A recent major work by Katz and Kahn (1966) entitled *The Social Psychology of Organizations* is representative of this interest, and illustrates the potential value of conceiving of organizations as open systems which import energy from their environments, transform this energy into some product form, and export it back into the environment, thereby re-energizing the system. It is too early to assess the influence of this point of view on empirical research on organizational behavior, but the unifying framework contained within the volume serves to identify problems previously overlooked by social psychologists, and provides an original framework for interpreting new findings.

In the remainder of this chapter we will not attempt any comprehensive or integrative review of research on organizations. The present diversity in interests and methods, both within and between disciplines, makes such an effort unfeasible in the space available for this task. We will rather restrict our examination to two different kinds of research activity involving organizations in which social psychologists have participated to a significant degree. The first of these is the adaptation of the laboratory experiment to the study of the structure and functioning of organizations. The second is the development and evaluation of methods of creating change in organization. The reader interested in other aspects of organizational behavior is referred to the aforementioned volume by Katz and Kahn (1966), to the *Handbook of Organizations* edited by March (1965), or to Chapter 8 in Volume 1 of this *Handbook.*

ORGANIZATIONS IN THE LABORATORY

The unique advantages of experimental methods in the development of scientific knowledge and the long tradition of laboratory experimentation in social psychology make it understandable that social psychologists should seek to understand the behavior of complex systems by bringing them into the laboratory for examination under controlled conditions. It is possible to create in the laboratory, at least in their simplest and most elementary forms, the basic properties of an organization. The organization members are the subjects in the experiment, the organization objectives are the task given the subjects to perform, and the organization structure is the pattern of activities and interactions imposed on participants or allowed to evolve over time. One or more of these three sets of variables—persons, task, and structure—can serve as independent variables in the experiment. Person variables may be manipulated by systematic selection of members for the organization or for key roles therein (Roby, Nicol, and Farrell, 1963) or by different amounts or kinds of preliminary training (Maier, 1953). The task may be varied by setting different objectives for the participants, by providing them with different resources for the attainment of these objectives, or by altering the environmental conditions under which the objectives are to be attained. Finally, structure may be varied by such methods as placing different restrictions on communication among subjects (Leavitt, 1951) or splitting the total task into different sets of subtasks and assigning them to subjects (Lanzetta and Roby, 1956b; Thomas, 1957). The ultimate objective is to determine, at least for the kinds of systems which can be constructed in the laboratory, the main effects of and interactions among person, task, and structural variables. While there have been a few cases in which investigators have attempted to create large organizations in the laboratory and to study their operations over a period of months (for example, Chapman *et al.,* 1959), the most significant findings to date have resulted from experimentation with much smaller administrative units set up over a much shorter period of time. In the balance of this section, we will examine two aspects of organizational behavior which have received considerable attention by experimenters. The reader interested in a broader treatment of the problems and potential of laboratory experimentation with organizations is referred to Weick (1965, 1967).

The effects of structure on performance

Structural variables have received considerable attention in experiments conducted to date. The problem to which these experiments are addressed is to determine the effects on organizational performance of different structural arrangements among members.

Stemming from theoretical formulations by Bavelas (1948, 1950), a large number of experiments have been conducted on the relative efficiency of different communication structures for solving simple problems. A communication structure is defined as a set of positions with specified communication channels. Such structures can be created by seating subjects around a table partitioned into as many sections as there are participants. Slots between participants permit the passage of notes. The slots which are open on any given trial define the communication structure for that trial. A typical task used in these experiments is the identification of a common symbol from lists given to each subject before the start of the trial. The problem is considered solved only when each member has identified the correct solution to the problem. The usual procedure is to conduct a series of trials under the same network, with new sets of symbols on each trial.

Glanzer and Glaser (1961) and Shaw (1964) have provided comprehensive reviews of the extensive literature dealing with the effects of different networks of communication. Direct comparison of the results of these experiments is made difficult by differences in number of participants, in the particular networks and dependent variables employed, and in tasks or other details of experimental procedure. The reader interested in a comprehensive review of research on this problem is referred to these more detailed treatments. We will restrict ourselves here to an examination of some of the key experiments and to results bearing on the relative efficiency of different networks.

Using five-man networks and common-symbol problems, a number of investigators (Cohen, Bennis, and Wolkon, 1961; Guetzkow and Simon, 1955; Leavitt, 1951; Mohanna and Argyle, 1960; Morrissette, Switzer, and Crannell, 1965) have found that centralized structures (for example, the Wheel), in which participants are differentiated in the centrality of their positions, are more efficient, as measured by speed of attaining solution or number of messages, than are decentralized structures (for example, the Circle), in which there is no differentiation. The centralized structures more rapidly organize to solve the problems. Participants in peripheral positions send information to the center of the network, where a decision is made and sent out to the periphery. Furthermore, this pattern of organization tends to be highly stable once developed. In less centralized structures the organization problem is more difficult and observed interaction patterns are less stable, as well as less efficient.

The results of other experiments suggest that the magnitude and direction of differences in efficiency between centralized and decentralized structures varies with the kind of task used. Shaw (1954b) found a tendency for four-man Circles to be somewhat faster in solving arithmetic problems than four-man Wheels—just the opposite of what had been found in the experiments described above. A similar result was obtained in an experiment conducted in Holland (Mulder, 1960), though Wheels tended to become relatively more efficient than Circles with continued practice. In an attempt to reconcile his data with those of the other investigators Shaw (1954a), conducted another experiment with three-man networks in which he varied problem complexity. His hypothesis, that decentralized structures will require less time than centralized structures to solve complex problems but more time to solve simple problems, was generally supported by the data. Similar evidence of greater efficiency of decentralized networks on complex problems has been obtained by Macy, Christie, and Luce (1953).

The implication, albeit a tentative one, is that no single network is most efficient for all tasks. Decentralized structures have an advantage for tasks which are difficult, complex, or unusual, while centralized structures are more effective for those which are simple and highly routinized. Further research on network performance, using a wider range of tasks, is needed to determine the specific task attributes which interact with centrality. Complexity has not been well defined and fails to capture the vast and subtle differences which can exist between group tasks. An experiment by Faucheux and Moscovici (1960), while different in method from those described above, sheds light on the types of tasks in which centralized and decentralized organizational forms evolve, and the results may have some bearing on the relative effectiveness of these decision-making processes. Twelve four-man groups were given two tasks to perform in counterbalanced order. One task was of a "deductive" nature, the solution requiring only the strict application of a set of rules furnished by the experimenter. The other task was "inferential" in nature, requiring the generation of all possible combinations of a set of elements. Centrality was not experimentally manipulated as in the network experiments, but observed from the actual communications addressed by members to one another. The results indicate that groups tend to develop a centralized organization when carrying out the "deductive" task, and tend to develop a decentralized organization on the "inferential" task. Furthermore, an internal analysis showed that groups failing to centralize in the deductive task performed less efficiently than those who centralized. Similarly, groups who centralized in the inferential task performed less efficiently than those who did not.

An experiment by Roby, Nicol, and Farrell (1963) lends further support to the idea that differences in performance between centralized and decentralized structures vary with the nature of the task. Different structures were created, not by restricting communication among members as in the experiments cited above, but by the assignment of individual roles. The subjects were divided into four-man teams and were given simple problems, the solution of which required obtaining environmental state information from display lights and setting response switches to meet specifications contained in the problem. Each team operated with two types of structures, centralized and distributed. In the centralized structure, problem-solving responsibility rested in only one team member. His task was to obtain the information from the display lights, determine from the problem the appropriate settings for the response switches, and direct the other team members in making these settings. (Two members of each team performed this leadership role at different points in time—one judged best, the other worst, by the experimenter on the basis of performance on practice problems.) Under the distributed structure, responsibility for solving the problem was divided equally among team members, with each man being given one part of the problem to solve.

All teams worked, under each structure, on two different types of problems: E-type and R-type. The former were those problems whose solutions required reaction only to environmental state information (settings of display lights), while the solution of R-type problems required team members to coordinate their responses (for example, appropriate setting of a given switch depended on settings of other switches). The results show distributed structures to be substantially faster than centralized structures in solving E-type problems. However, centralized structures with high-aptitutde leaders were far more efficient in solving R-type problems. For both types of problems, the centralized structure with the low-aptitude leader proved to be least effective.

One of the fundamental problems in the design of an organization is specifying the most efficient locus for each decision or class of decisions. Many practices used in complex organizations are aimed at bringing together decision-making responsibility and information relevant to the decision. Thus, under some conditions, roles (for example, sets of decisions to be made by a single member) are assumed to be fixed and attempts are made to select and place in each role an individual posssessing the relevant information or knowledge. Alternatively, the persons are treated as given, and decisions are assigned to persons in such a way as to maximize the possession of information relevant to each decision by the person making it, subject to "overload" constraints. Finally, both persons and roles can be regarded as fixed and information flows adjusted to get information to the "right place" quickly and with minimum distortion.

Lanzetta and Roby (1956a) have examined, under controlled laboratory conditions, the consequences of structures in which members have direct or indirect access to information required for decision making. Their basic task, which was much more complex and more realistic than those employed in the experiments described above, was modeled after that confronting a bomber crew. It required scanning readings on aircraft instruments projected onto displays and executing appropriate responses on control devices. Each subject was seated in a separate booth and could communicate with other team members by means of telephone. Two types of structures were created: (1) a low-autonomy structure in which each subject had two controls for which none of the four necessary input readings was directly available from displays in the subject's booth and all had to be acquired from other crew members, and (2) a high-autonomy condition in which three of the four input readings were directly available and only one had to be acquired from others. The results, not surprisingly, show substantially more errors under the low-autonomy structure, a finding which was obtained under four different task conditions. Similar evidence of inefficiencies caused by a structure in which members are dependent on others for relevant information has been obtained in other experiments by the same investigators (Lanzetta and Roby, 1957; Roby and Lanzetta, 1957).

Feedback and organizational performance

The role of feedback or knowledge of results in promoting individual learning and performance has been widely recognized. The modification of individual behavior through changes in response-outcome contingencies is the cornerstone of reinforcement theories of learning and of many viable methods of training.

The consequences of feedback for organizational performance have been less intensively examined. Like individuals, organizations acquire information concerning the consequences of their actions on the external environment. The crew of a submarine can, for example, observe whether their torpedoes hit their targets. Similarly, members of an industrial organization can observe changes in sales following modification in prices or advertising. The unique quality of organizational feedback stems from the fact that the environmental changes which occur are not dependent on the actions of one organization member but rather on the coordinated actions of a number of such members. Depending on the particular feedback contingencies involved, it is possible for an individual to observe a positive environmental change (that is, be reinforced) for incorrect responses on his part or observe a negative environmental change (that is, not be reinforced) for correct responses. The interesting psychological questions raised by such an analysis concern the consequences of different feedback arrangements on organizational performance.

Within the last ten years a number of investigators have sought to study these questions experimentally under controlled laboratory conditions. In these experiments organizational structure, the variable of interest in the preceding section was held constant. The independent variable was the feedback system (that is, the basis for appraising members of correct performance), and the dependent variable was the performance of the organization or work team.

Rosenberg and Hall (1958) carried out one of the first experiments of this kind, using Air Force trainees as subjects. Two subjects were run simultaneously on a task which required each to turn a micrometer knob a constant number of units. Subjects were randomly assigned to one of three feedback conditions: (1) direct feedback, in which each subject was informed at the end of each trial of the magnitude and direction of the error in his own response, (2) confounded feedback, in which each subject was informed of the average of his own and his partner's errors, and (3) other's feedback, in which each subject was informed of the magnitude and direction in error of his partner. The results show that other's feedback produced significantly lower average team accuracy over the 50 trials than either direct or confounded feedback. There was no significant difference in team accuracy between the latter two feedback conditions. A similar experiment by Hall (1957 also yielded no difference in team performance under direct and confounded feedback.

Glaser, Klaus, Egerman (1962) conducted an experiment on three-man teams, using a variant of the confounded-feedback condition. The objective of the investigation was to determine whether phenomena which have been reliably observed in investigations of individual learning, that is, response acquisition, extinction, and spontaneous recovery, would also be exhibited in the performance of organized teams. Since the same apparatus has been employed in a series of investigations to be discussed, we will describe it in some detail. The basic unit of investigation was a simulated three-man military work team. Two of the team members were assigned to the roles of monitor. Their task was to observe stimulus display panels and independently depress a switch for either two seconds or four seconds, depending on the nature of this display. The third team member, called the operator, could not observe the displays directly but could observe the length of presses from his two monitors in the light signals on his own panel. He was instructed to depress his own control switch for four seconds if and only if the information received from his two monitors was identical and accurate.

The critical element in both monitors' and operator's tasks was the length of the switch press. Strict tolerances were established for correct length and individual responses were treated as incorrect if they exceeded these tolerances. Each team member was given individual training in depressing switches for two- and four-second intervals until he reached a criterion level of a 63 percent accurate response prior to performing in the team setting.

The independent variable in the first investigation was team feedback. A bell would ring and a large wall counter visible to all team members would advance one point each time *all three team members performed correctly* on a trial. No individual feedback was provided and the nature of the task deprived each team member of cues concerning the correctness of his own response. The dependent variable was change in team proficiency. Removal and reinstatement of team feedback over time made it possible to treat each team as a single experiment, though six teams were run one and

one-half hours a day over an average of 37 days. The results indicate that team performance can be manipulated using methods found to be effective for individuals.
When teams were provided with team feedback, the rate of correct team response
progressively increased; when such feedback was withdrawn, the rate of correct
response progressively diminished. An unexpected finding was a decline in rate of
correct team performance when initially placed in the team condition over what was
predicted from a mathematical combination of the performance levels of component
members during individual training.

A subsequent experiment (Egerman, Klaus, and Glaser, 1962) dealt with the
consequences of team feedback on the performance of "redundant" teams. A
"redundant" team is operationally defined, for the purposes of the experiment, as one
in which the performance of each monitor is redundant whenever the other monitor
has performed correctly. Thus, a correct team response is one in which the operator
and at least one monitor have performed correctly. While feedback also is "confounded" in this experiment, as in the previous one, the theoretical consequences of
the confounding are quite different. In the previous experiment, each team member
was on an aperiodic reinforcement schedule for correct responses. A correct response
by an individual team member was a necessary but not sufficient condition for positive
team feedback. In the present experiment, correct performance by individual monitors is neither necessary nor sufficient for positive team feedback. A monitor can be
reinforced for an incorrect response if both the operator and the other monitor have
made correct responses. To the extent that this in fact occurs, a decrement in monitor
performance with continued practice would be expected which should be reflected
subsequently in a decrement in team proficiency. The results are consistent with this
prediction. While the addition of a redundant member to a two-man team initially
increased its performance, continued performance of the three-man team was accompanied by a marked decrement in team performance.

These results indicate that organized teams learn to perform efficiently under
confounded feedback provided that this feedback consists of appropriate indication
of correct individual performance. However, when team feedback inappropriately
reinforces incorrect individual responses, as in the redundant team arrangement,
team performance is likely to decrease.

A follow-up experiment (Egerman, Glaser, and Klaus, 1963) corroborated these
findings using two-person teams. Three feedback conditions were employed: (1) a
"series" condition in which both of the team members were required to perform
their task correctly to complete the task, (2) a "parallel" condition in which correct
performance by either member was sufficient to complete the task, and (3) an "individual" condition in which one specified member of the team was required to perform
correctly in order to complete the task.

As in the previous experiment, teams working under the parallel feedback
arrangement, whose members received continuous reinforcement of correct responses
and aperiodic reinforcement of incorrect responses, showed a significant decrement
in performance from initial to final periods. Similarly, teams working under the
series feedback arrangement, whose members received aperiodic reinforcement of
correct responses, showed an increment in performance from initial to final periods,
though the difference was not statistically significant. The results for teams working
under the individual feedback arrangement revealed a slight increment in performance of the specified team member who received continuous reinforcement for
correct responses and a marked decrement (40 percent) in the performance of the

nonspecified members who received aperiodic reinforcement of both correct and incorrect responses.

The series and parallel feedback conditions employed in the preceding arrangements are analogous to types of confounded feedback studied by Zajonc (1962). Using a group reaction-time task, he compared the performance of seven-man groups on easy and difficult tasks. On the difficult task, which is comparable to the series condition discussed above, each team member had to depress a reaction key in response to the onset of a stimulus light within a specified time interval in order to achieve a successful trial; on the easy task, which is similar to the parallel condition, correct performance by only one of the seven members was necessary for the trial to be successful. There was a slight improvement in performance under both conditions, with the difficult task producing the greater increase. The decrement in performance observed under the parallel condition in the previous experiments is not evident in these data, a finding which may be attributable to the fact that the nature of the task provided more cues to individual subjects concerning the correctness of their individual performance or to the relatively short number of trials used. Zajonc's experiment also calls into question the generality of the previously reported findings (Hall, 1957; Rosenberg and Hall, 1958) of no difference in team performance under direct and confounded feedback. Very substantial differences were observed in this investigation, favoring direct feedback. These conflicting results probably reflect the different kinds of tasks employed. In the confounded feedback condition used in the Hall and Rosenberg-Hall experiments, the optimal response by an individual was dependent on the response being made by his partner. Hence, mutual compensation of errors was possible. In the Zajonc experiment, a correct response by an individual was defined independently of the responses of other team members and mutual compensation of errors was not possible.

The experiments cited in this section constitute a promising attempt to explain the performance of highly structured and organized work teams in terms of concepts of feedback and reinforcement which have demonstrated their utility in explaining individual behavior. At present, the systems that have been analyzed in these terms have been small, and the tasks assigned to and structural arrangements created among team members for experimental purposes have been exceedingly simple and unrepresentative of those found in actual organizations. There are, for example, few real tasks which deprive their operator of any cues of the correctness of his individual performance and which make him completely dependent on feedback contingent on team performance. Thus, a baseball player can judge how well he has played independent of whether his team has won the game, and a worker on an automobile assembly line receives visual cues regarding the effectiveness of his performance and rarely sees the final vehicle. It appears highly likely that such individual feedback would attenuate, if not erase, the effects of the various team feedback arrangements observed in the experiments that have been reported in this section. The usefulness of concepts derived from the study of individual learning in explanation of organizational behavior will depend on the extent to which they can be elaborated to handle larger social systems and multiple feedback sources.

Summary

The relatively short history of laboratory experiments on organizations and the complexity of the processes that they are intended to illuminate make it difficult to point to significant advances in knowledge which they have produced. At least for the present, scientific questions about the relative efficiency of different structures or feedback systems are largely unanswered, and the related technology of organizational design remains an art rather than a science. However, the potential of laboratory methods should not be confused with their present achievement. To do so would be to throw out a healthy infant because he has not yet learned to walk. While the structural complexity of a General Motors and the subtleties and uncertainties of its economic, political, and social environment are undoubtedly impossible to simulate in the laboratory, such simulations are by no means necessary for, and may be irrelevant to, advances in general knowledge.

The basic assumption underlying laboratory experimentation on any system—physical, biological, or social—is that complex phenomena may be explained by reducing them to their basic and most elementary forms and by studying these forms under highly controlled conditions. The experiments cited in this section illustrate that systems having some of the properties of organizations can be created in the laboratory and that the behavior of these systems varies in a predictable and reliable manner with experimental conditions. The principal objections to laboratory experimentation stem not from their internal validity but from what Campbell (1957) has called external validity, that is, the extent to which valid inferences can be drawn about processes in highly complex "real life" organizations from observations made in "artificial" laboratory settings. The assumption implicit in these objections is that some of the differences between the social systems created in the laboratory and actual organizations interact with the independent variables being examined.

Criticisms of this nature are not easily answered. Parallel experiments in both field and laboratory settings constitute the most direct approach to determining the generalizability of laboratory findings. There are some examples of this parallel experimentation to be found in the literature (for example, Latané and Arrowood, 1963; Schachter *et al.*, 1961), but many of the independent variables utilized in laboratory experiments, including the structural and feedback variables discussed in this section, are rarely subject to experimenter control in field settings. Perhaps the most promising approach is to increase the authenticity of laboratory simulations of organizations and to determine whether similar relations are obtained between independent and dependent variables. Even if findings fail to replicate, the evidence of interactions obtained in this manner would provide a stronger foundation for inferences regarding applicability to other situations.

CREATING CHANGE IN ORGANIZATIONS

Social psychologists and other behavioral scientists have, with increasing frequency, been faced with situations which call for the application of their accumulated knowledge in improving the effectiveness of ongoing organizations. As Leavitt (1964) has pointed out, there are three somewhat different "entry points" for changing organizations and effecting improvements in their performance. One can begin with the *technology* of the system and seek to "strengthen" the organization by introducing new tools (for example, drill presses, computers) to perform functions previously carried out by people. Alternatively, one might start with the *structure* of the organization with a view toward increasing its effectiveness through legislatively induced modifications in the division of labor and in systems of authority and communications. Finally, the "targets" of the change could be the *people* in the organization.

The objective might be to improve organizational performance by increasing the interpersonal skills of managers and creating more effective interpersonal and inter-group relations. It should be noted that these three approaches are distinguishable only as starting points for change, and not as final outcomes. Major changes in any one of these subsystems are likely to result in changes in each of the others.

During the last 20 to 30 years, behavioral scientists have played a number of different roles in planned attempts at organizational change. In some cases, they have acted as consultants to organizations and participated in a relationship similar to that of a physician or psychoanalyst with his patients or clients (Jaques, 1951; Sofer, 1961). In other cases, they have acted in the role of researcher, collecting data about the organization and feeding it back in such a way as to implement change (Mann, 1957). In still other cases, the behavioral scientist has played the role of trainer and has sought to increase the human-relations skills (Maier, 1952), inter-personal competence (Argyris, 1962), or social sensitivity (Tannenbaum, Weschler, and Massarik, 1961) of members of one or more organizations. While the persons exposed to the training are most frequently managers and supervisors, the methods of training vary considerably from one program to another. Since the training approach is most common and has been most frequently evaluated, we will devote most of the balance of this section to a consideration of the various methods that have been used and to a consideration of the evidence regarding their effects.

Early attempts to improve the interpersonal skills of managers consisted largely of lectures supplemented by case discussions. Evaluation studies of such programs have not provided much evidence of their effectiveness. Canter (1951) conducted a 20-hour human-relations training course for 18 supervisors, using lecture-discus-sion methods. Before and after the training, these supervisors and a control group of supervisors who did not receive the training completed a battery of pencil-and-paper tests of psychological and supervisory knowledge. On most of the tests, the trained group improved to a significantly greater extent than the control group. However, a companion study by Tyler (1950) designed to measure any effects of the training on the morale of subordinates found no significant differences between trained and untrained groups.

Fleishman (1953) also found significant changes in supervisory attitudes as a result of training. Before and after an intensive two-week training course using lecture-discussion methods, supervisors completed a leadership opinion question-naire designed to measure how each supervisor thought he should lead his own work group. These questionnaires yielded scores on two dimensions: Considera-tion and Initiating Structure. Following training, scores on the Consideration dimen-sion increased while scores on Initiating Structure decreased. These results are consistent with the objectives and nature of the training. However, some additional analyses, intended to shed some light on the long-term effects of the training on the supervisors' behavior on the job, provided a different picture of the training effectiveness. Questionnaires given to subordinates of trained and untrained super-visors provided no evidence that the trained group were seen as higher in Considera-tion and lower in Initiating Structure. In fact, there was a statistically significant tendency for those supervisors who had been trained most recently to be described as less considerate than untrained supervisors.

Clearly, human-relations training programs using lecture-discussion methods can have an effect on the supervisors' statements of how they should behave, but it is not at all clear that such training does produce any change in their behavior on the job. Other studies that failed to find evidence of significant changes in subordinates' descriptions of their supervisor's behavior relative to control groups have been carried out by Hariton (1951) and by Harris and Fleishman (1955).

In the forms of training that we have considered, the trainer plays a very active and directive role. Most of the interaction which takes place within the training sessions occurs between the trainer and trainees. More recently, new training methods have been developed in which the trainer's role is nondirective and interaction among trainees plays a very central part. The fundamental unit of this method is the T-(training) group. Originally developed in the late 1940's by staff members of the National Training Laboratories for summer workshops in community relations, T-group training has, within the last decade, been widely used for developing interpersonal skills on the part of managers and supervisors. The procedure has been described in detail elsewhere (Bradford, Gibb, and Benne, 1964; Marrow, 1964; Schein and Bennis, 1965) and will only be touched upon here. Briefly, a T-group is an unstructured group in which group members acquire information about the consequences of their behavior on others through feedback from other group members. The trainer is not a lecturer or even a discussion leader. He permits the group members to develop their own structure and encourages them to develop a feedback system through which their reactions to the behavior of other group members can be communicated within the group.

T-group training is far from being standardized. In addition to the variability which inevitably results from the combination of differences in group composition and the unstructured environment, there are important differences in trainer style. There have also been a number of "offshoots" of the T-group method which retain the element of face-to-face feedback but modify other aspects of the process. Tannenbaum, Weschler, and Massarik (1961) use the term "sensitivity training" to refer to their approach, which places greater emphasis on interpretations of individual psychodynamics; and Blake and Mouton (1962) have "experimented" with instrumented T-groups in which the trainer is removed from direct participation in the group.

Considering the paucity of data available on the effects of most educational and therapeutic methods and the strong emotional commitment on the part of many T-group leaders, there has been a surprising number of studies which try to assess the effects of this training method. Many of these investigations have yielded positive results but have utilized criteria which provide little indication of the organizational consequences of the training. Changes over the course of training have been reported in interaction patterns among participants (Back, 1948), participants' descriptions of their emotional states (Bass, 1962), participants' descriptions of other group members (Bennis *et al.,* 1957; Harrison, in Argyris, 1962), and participants' descriptions of themselves (Burke and Bennis, 1961).

Of greater interest than changes in behavior in the T-group or short-term changes in responses to questionnaires is the effect of training on the person's behavior in other situations, particularly in the organization from which he came. Does the T-group experience have any effect on the manager's behavior in situations involving his subordinates, peers, or superiors? Recent research suggests that this method of training may "transfer" to the job situation. Miles (1960) evaluated a two-week program conducted at Bethel, Maine for 34 elementary school principals. A control group was obtained by asking each participant in the program to nominate a comparable person from the same organization who had not received the training. In addition, another control group was obtained by selecting a random sample of 148 principals selected from a directory. Each subject, both experimental and control, was asked to name six to eight associates who could describe his job behavior. Using an open-ended perceived-change measure given to the associates, changes in job behavior were detected on the part of 73 percent of the trained subjects as compared with 17 percent and 29 percent of the matched and random controls respectively.

Bunker (1965) also used an open-ended perceived-change measure, but his study was conducted on a much larger and more heterogeneous population. Judgments of change were obtained from the associates of 346 T-group participants and an equal number of nominated controls. Reported changes were substantially more frequent on the part of associates of the trained subjects than of associates of the untrained subjects. A content analysis of these changes suggested that those who had participated in T-groups were seen as improving in listening, in their degree of cooperation and tact, and in their willingness to encourage participation by others to a greater extent than the controls.

It is, of course, likely that the observers in both the Bunker and Miles studies knew whether the subject had participated in T-group training. Possibly this knowledge, rather than changes in behavior, produced the different amounts of reported change. While it would seem to be impossible to conceal the fact of training from associates close enough to the subject to detect changes in his interpersonal behavior, one can compare the amounts and kinds of change reported by associates of persons receiving different kinds of leadership training. Boyd and Elliss (1962) found a significant difference in the frequency with which observers (peers, subordinates, and superiors) reported changes in the behavior of managers who had participated in T-group training as opposed to those who had participated in a more traditional program entitled "Men and Administration." Six months after the conclusion of the training, 65 percent of observers of T-group trainees reported behavior change, compared with 51 percent of observers of those participating in the conventional program and 34 percent of observers of controls who received no training.

An important new development in training consists of programs for organizational families, persons who normally work with one another in the same organization. Such programs have the apparent advantage of reducing the problem of transfer of training to the actual work environment. Mann (1957) was one of the first proponents of training actual organizational units rather than collections of individuals from different organizations or different parts of the same organization. He has also conducted what is, to date, the only evaluation of this kind of training which uses adequate criteria and reasonable controls. Mann's approach, which he calls organizational feedback, evolved as a solution to the problem of how to use attitude survey data in effecting organizational change. The evaluation of the method was conducted in the accounting departments of a large public utility. Attitude survey data provided the focus of a series of meetings which began with the manager in charge of these departments and his department heads and progressed downward to the rank-and-file level. Each meeting included a manager and his immediate subordinates and was conducted by the manager. The meetings focused on the meaning of the attitude data and on their implications for ways in which working relationships could be improved.

Four departments participated in the feedback program and two others served as controls. A second attitude survey conducted at the conclusion of the program revealed that significant changes in attitudes had occurred in the four experimental departments but not in the controls. The changes included more positive attitudes toward supervision, higher assessments of the group's ability to get the job done, and more favorable attitudes toward job content and responsibility.

The most critical question, and also the one most difficult to answer conclusively, concerns the effects of change procedures on organizational effectiveness. The skeptic might concur with evidence that managers become more sensitive to the feelings of others and more participative, and conclude that their effectiveness in their organizations is reduced or impaired by these changes. To overcome these objections one must show that the training of organization members increases the effectiveness of the organization.

The available evidence that is relevant to this question is promising but inconclusive. In the field experiment conducted by Morse and Reimer (1956), described earlier in this chapter, an average increase in productivity of 10 percent occurred in two divisions of a large insurance company following an intensive and apparently successful effort by both company and research personnel to increase the influence of the rank and file in decision making. The implications of this result are, however, obscured by the fact that another change program conducted in two similar divisions of the same organization and intended to decrease rank-and-file influence was followed by an average productivity increase of 14 percent. The results for employee attitudes and satisfaction are more consistent with the hypotheses underlying the experiment. The attitudes of rank-and-file employees generally became more favorable in the divisions in which their influence in decision making was increased, and less favorable in the divisions in which their influence was decreased.

Seashore and Bowers (1963) evaluated a change program designed to apply Likert's "theory" of management to selected departments in a company manufacturing packaging materials. Three departments served as experimental units and were subject to a multifaceted change program which included organizational feedback meetings (Mann, 1957), individual counseling, a formal training course for supervisors in principles of human behavior, and T-group training for key managers. Two other departments did not participate in these programs and were treated as controls. A comparison of before- and after-questionnaire results for both experimental and control departments provides evidence that the change programs did have an effect on working relationships in the experimental departments. It is also clear that employee attitudes became more positive in the experimental departments relative to the controls. The results for productivity measures, for example, machine efficiency and waste, are much more equivocal and do not provide convincing evidence of the effectiveness of the change program.

Barnes and Greiner conducted an evaluation of Blake and Mouton's managerial grid approach to organization development (Blake *et al.*, 1964). The method, which is described in detail elsewhere (Blake and Mouton, 1964), bears some similarity to T-group training in its emphasis on feedback, but is more structured, more intensive, and focuses on managerial styles rather than on behavior which may not be relevant to management. A total of 800 managers and technical men in a plant of a large company participated in the training. Questionnaire data obtained at the end of the program indicated that those persons who took part "felt" that interpersonal relationships were different after the change. They reported improvements in such dimensions as the way they worked together with their boss, the quality of decisions made by their group, and the degree of profit and loss consciousness of their group.

Inspection of the calendars of a sample of the managers showed an average of 31 percent more time spent in meetings, and an analysis of the demographic characteristics of the 50 most highly rated managers before and after the program was strongly suggestive of a change in promotional criteria favoring younger managers in line positions. Of most interest, however, is the fact that profits more than doubled during the year in which most of the training was done. As the authors pointed out, there are a number of factors which may have been responsible for this increase, some of which (for example, increased market prices, lower materials costs, taxes, and depreciation) were not under management control and could in no way be attributed to the learning program. Corporate records show that approximately 44 percent of the increase in profits was achieved through management actions, in particular, a large-scale manpower reduction involving 600 employees. It is unclear to what extent these decisions were the result of the training program. The plant management had been under pressure from its parent organization to reduce personnel for some time before the program began and, while management tended to give credit to the training for the quality of the particular decision reached, one can only speculate about what would have happened without the training.

Marrow, Bowers, and Seashore (1967) have provided a highly readable account of an attempt to change an organization through an intensive integrated program of organizational, psychological, and technological change. In 1962 the Harwood Manufacturing Company, of which Marrow is Chairman of the Board, acquired a competitor—the Weldon Manufacturing Company—of approximately equal size. Shortly after the takeover it became apparent that the managerial styles of the two organizations differed widely. While Harwood encouraged participation in decision making, Weldon operated under a traditional authority-obedience system. Furthermore, a comparative study of the two companies on such criteria as man-hour productivity, turnover, and waste showed that Harwood was superior in every respect.

Following the acquisition, several different consulting and service organizations were engaged for extended periods in an attempt to introduce necessary changes in the newly acquired organization. The various change activities covered a wide range and included reorganization of the work flow in the plant, reorganization of the shipping department, the introduction of "vestibule" training for new operators, and sensitivity training for managers and staff. A team of behavioral scientists from the Institute for Social Research of the University of Michigan was engaged to evaluate the effects of the change program and of its parts on the attitudes and behavior of employees and on the performance of the organization.

All indicators of organizational performance show marked improvements between 1962, the year in which Weldon was acquired, and 1964, after the change program was terminated. Return on invested capital changed from a loss of 15 percent during 1962 to a return of 17 percent during 1964, turnover and absence rates were cut in half during the same period, and production efficiency changed from 19 percent below standard in 1962 to 14 percent above standard in 1964.

Further indications of change were revealed in attitude measurements obtained from random samples of nonsupervisory employees at Weldon in 1962, 1963, and 1964. While most changes were moderate and in fact were matched by equivalent changes in Harwood during the same period, they were in a direction congruent with the goals of the change program: they included more favorable attitudes toward the company, toward fellow employees, and toward the compensation system. Marrow, Seashore, and Bowers suggested that positive changes in attitudes and satisfaction of employees may be harder to achieve than gains in cost performance and work output.

The unequivocal evidence of the beneficial effects of the overall change program on organizational performance raises questions about the specific processes underlying the changes. What components or combination of components of the rather diverse collection of things done in the Weldon organization produced the marked improvements? The fact that the various change programs were part of a "total package" and were not introduced in a manner which would permit an evaluation of their separate and joint effects makes it difficult to reach a definitive answer to such questions. However, the different change programs were introduced at different points in time and, if one assumes that their effects would be exhibited in the short run, some conclusions could be drawn about the relative effects of components of the "package" by examining daily and weekly changes in relation to the occurrence of specific change programs. The results of this analysis reveal increases in productivity following several program components (arranged in decreasing order of magnitude): (1) individual counseling and training of operators whose performance was low in relation to standard, (2) the termination of employees with chronically low production records and histories of frequent absence, (3) training of supervisors and staff in interpersonal relations, and (4) the introduction of group problem-solving meetings between supervisors and operators, in which they attempted to define their joint work problems and to develop solutions for them.

What conclusions can be drawn about the effectiveness of the kinds of methods of creating change in organizations which have been developed by social psychologists and other behavioral scientists? To the "tough-minded" investigator, the answer may be "None." He could point, in any given investigation, to problems with the measures used or to the absence or inadequacy of control populations. On the other hand, his more "tender-minded" colleague, accustomed to the uncertainties created by unavoidable departures from orthodox experimental design in field experimentation, might be expected to give a more positive answer. He could point to the absence of evidence of behavioral change resulting from formal lecture-discussion training programs and to the more promising results obtained from less structured programs in which participants played a more active role and received feedback concerning the effects of their behavior on others. He might also note the evidence that change programs in which the training unit is an organizational family produce not only behavioral changes but also increased satisfaction and more favorable attitudes. Finally, he might argue, though perhaps more tentatively, that the impressive productivity increases obtained concurrently in at least two companies with massive training justify their very serious consideration as a means of increasing organizational effectiveness. An immediate choice between these two positions is up to the reader. The final choice rests with social science.

REFERENCES

Adams, J. S. (1963). Toward an understanding of inequity. *J. abnorm. soc. Psychol.,* 67, 422–436.

———— (1965a). Inequity in social exchange. In L. Berkowitz (Ed.), *Advances in experimental social psychology.* Vol. 2. New York: Academic Press. Pp. 267–300.

_____ (1965b). A study of the exempt salary program. General Electric Company, Behavioral Research Service.

Adams, J. S., and Patricia R. Jacobsen (1964). Effects of wage inequities on work quality. *J. abnorm. soc. Psychol., 69,* 19–25.

Adams, J. S., and A. K. Romney (1959). A functional analysis of authority. *Psychol. Rev., 66,* 234–251.

Adams, J. S., and W. B. Rosenbaum (1962). The relationship of worker productivity to cognitive dissonance about wage inequities. *J. appl. Psychol., 46,* 161–164.

Allport, F. H. (1934). The J-curve hypothesis of conforming behavior. *J. soc. Psychol., 5,* 141–183.

Allport, G. (1954). The historical background of modern social psychology. In G. Lindzey (Ed.), *Handbook of social psychology.* Cambridge, Mass.: Addison-Wesley. Pp. 3–56.

Alper, T. G. (1946). Task-orientation vs. ego-orientation in learning and retention. *Amer. J. Psychol., 59,* 236–248.

Andrews, I. R. (1967). Wage inequity and performance. *J. appl. Psychol., 51,* 39–45.

Andrews, I. R., and M. M. Henry (1963). Management attitudes toward pay. *Indust. Relat., 3,* 29–39.

Argyris, C. (1962). *Interpersonal competence and organizational effectiveness.* Homewood, Ill.: Irwin, Dorsey.

Aronson, E., and J. M. Carlsmith (1962). Performance expectancy as a determinant of actual performance. *J. abnorm. soc. Psychol., 65,* 178–182.

Atkinson, J. W. (1958). Towards experimental analysis of human motivation in terms of motives, expectancies, and incentives. In J. W. Atkinson (Ed.), *Motives in fantasy, action, and society.* Princeton: Van Nostrand. Pp. 288–305.

Atkinson, J. W., J. R. Bastian, R. W. Earl, and G. H. Litwin (1960). The achievement motive, goal setting, and probability preferences. *J. abnorm. soc. Psychol., 60,* 27–36.

Atkinson, J. W., and G. H. Litwin (1960). Achievement motive and test anxiety conceived as motive to approach success and motive to avoid failure. *J. abnorm. soc. Psychol., 60,* 52–63.

Atkinson, J. W., and A. C. Raphelson (1956). Individual differences in motivation and behavior in particular situations. *J. Pers., 24,* 349–363.

Atkinson, J. W., and W. R. Reitman (1956). Performance as a function of motive strength and expectancy of goal attainment. *J. abnorm. soc. Psychol., 53,* 361–366.

Babchuk, N., and W. J. Goode (1951). Work incentives in a self-determined group. *Amer. sociol. Rev., 16,* 679–687.

Bachman, J. G. (1964). Motivation in a task situation as a function of ability and control over the task. *J. abnorm. soc. Psychol., 69,* 272–281.

Back, K. (1948). Interpersonal relations in a discussion group. *J. soc. Issues, 4,* 61–65.

Baldamus, W. (1951). Type of work and motivation. *Brit. J. Sociol., 2,* 44–58.

Barnard, C. I. (1938). *The functions of the executive.* Cambridge: Harvard Univ. Press.

Barnett, G. J., I. Handelsman, L. H. Stewart, and D. E. Super (1952). The occupational level scale as a measure of drive. *Psychol. Monogr., 66,* No. 10 (whole No. 342).

Bass, B. M. (1960). *Leadership, psychology, and organizational behavior.* New York: Harper.

——— (1962). Mood changes during a management training laboratory. *J. appl. Psychol., 46*, 361–364.

——— (1965). *Organizational psychology.* Boston: Allyn and Bacon.

Bass, B. M., and H. J. Leavitt (1963). Some experiments in planning and operating. *Managemt. Sci., 9*, 574–585.

Baumgartel, H. (1956). Leadership, motivations, and attitudes in research laboratories. *J. soc. Issues, 12*, 24–31.

Bavelas, A. (1948). A mathematical model for group structures. *Appl. Anthropol., 7*, 16–30.

——— (1950). Communication patterns in task-oriented groups. *J. Acoust. Soc. Amer., 22*, 725–730.

Behrend, H. (1953). Absence and labour turnover in a changing economic climate. *Occupat. Psychol., 27*, 69–79.

Bem, D. J., M. A. Wallach, and N. Kogan (1965). Group decision making under risk of aversive consequences. *J. Pers. soc. Psychol., 1*, 453–460.

Bennett, Edith Becker (1955). Discussion, decision, commitment, and consensus in 'group decision.' *Hum. Relat., 8*, 251–273.

Bennis, W., R. Burke, H. Cutter, H. Harrington, and J. Hoffman (1957). A note on some problems of measurement and prediction in a training group. *Group Psychother., 10*, 328–341.

Berkowitz, L. (1954). Group standards, cohesiveness and productivity. *Hum. Relat., 7*, 509–519.

Bevan, W., and R. Adamson (1960). Reinforcers and reinforcement: their relation to maze performance. *J. exp. Psychol., 59*, 226–232.

Black, R., R. Adamson, and W. Bevan (1961). Runway behavior as a function of apparent intensity of shock. *J. comp. physiol. Psychol., 54*, 270–274.

Blake, R. R., and Jane S. Mouton (1962). The instrumented training laboratory. In I. Weschler and E. Schein (Eds.), *Issues in human relations training.* National Training Laboratories, Selected Reading Series, No. 5. Pp. 61–76.

——— (1964). *The managerial grid.* Houston: Gulf.

Blake, R. R., Jane S. Mouton, L. B. Barnes, and L. E. Greiner (1964). Breakthrough in organization development. *Harvard Bus. Rev., 42*, 133–155.

Blood, M. R., and C. L. Hulin (1967). Alienation, environmental characteristics and worker responses. *J. appl. Psychol., 51*, 284–290.

Boyd, J. B., and J. D. Elliss (1962). Findings of research into senior management seminars. Hydro-Electric Power Commission of Ontario. Internal Document.

Bradford, L. P., J. R. Gibb, and K. D. Benne (1964). *T-group theory and laboratory method: innovation in re-education.* New York: Wiley.

Brayfield, A. H., and W. H. Crockett (1955). Employee attitudes and employee performance. *Psychol. Bull., 52*, 396–424.

Brehm, J. (1956). Post-decision changes in the desirability of alternatives. *J. abnorm. soc. Psychol.*, *52*, 384–389.

Brehm, J. W., and A. R. Cohen (1959). Re-evaluation of choice alternatives as a function of their number and qualitative similarity. *J. abnorm. soc. Psychol.*, *58*, 373–378.

————— (1962). *Explorations in cognitive dissonance.* New York: Wiley.

Brissenden, P. F., and E. Frankel (1922). *Labor turnover in industry.* New York: Macmillan.

Brock, T. C. (1963). Effects of prior dishonesty on post decision dissonance. *J. abnorm. soc. Psychol.; 66*, 325–331.

Brown, R. (1965). *Social psychology,* New York: Free Press.

Bunker, D. R. (1965). Individual applications of laboratory training. *J. appl. behav. Sci., 1*, 131–148.

Burke, R. L., and W. G. Bennis (1961). Changes in perception of self and others during human relations training. *Hum. Relat., 14*, 165–182.

Burnstein, E. (1963). Fear of failure, achievement motivation, and aspiring to prestigeful occupations. *J. abnorm. soc. Psychol., 67*, 189–193.

Campbell, D. T. (1957). Factors relevant to the validity of experiments in social settings. *Psychol. Bull., 54*, 297–312.

Canter, R. R., Jr. (1951). A human relations training program. *J. appl. Psychol., 35*, 38–45.

Cartwright, D., and A. Zander (1960). *Group dynamics* (2nd ed.). Evanston, Ill.: Row, Peterson.

Castaneda, A., and D. S. Palermo (1955). Psychomotor performance as a function of amount of training and stress. *J. exp. Psychol., 50*, 175–179.

Centers, R. (1948). Motivational aspects of occupational stratification. *J. soc. Psychol., 28*, 187–217.

Chapman, R. L., J. L. Kennedy, A. Newell, and W. C. Biel (1959). The systems research laboratory's air defense experiments. *Managemt. Sci., 5*, 250–269.

Coch, L., and J. R. P. French, Jr. (1948). Overcoming resistance to change. *Hum. Relat., 1*, 512–532.

Cohen, A. M., W. G. Bennis, and G. H. Wolkon (1961). The effects of continued practice on the behaviors of problem-solving groups. *Sociometry, 24*, 416–431.

Collier, G., and M. H. Marx (1959). Changes in performance as a function of shifts in magnitude of reinforcement. *J. exp. Psychol., 57*, 305–309.

Collins, O., M. Dalton, and D. Roy (1946). Restriction of output and social cleavage in industry. *Appl. Anthropol., 5* (3), 1–14.

Crespi, L. P. (1942). Quantitative variation of incentive and performance in the white rat. *Amer. J. Psychol., 55*, 467–517.

Cyert, R., and J. G. March (1963). *A behavioral theory of the firm.* Englewood Cliffs, N.J.: Prentice-Hall.

Dalton, M. (1959). *Men who manage: fusions of feeling and theory in administration.* New York: Wiley.

Davis, J. H., and F. Restle (1963). The analysis and prediction of group problem solving. *J. abnorm. soc. Psychol., 66*, 103–116.

Dember, W. N., and R. W. Earl (1957). Analysis of exploratory, manipulatory, and curiosity behaviors. *Psychol. Rev., 64*, 91–96.

Dunnette, M. D., J. P. Campbell, and Kay Jaastad (1963). The effect of group participation on brainstorming effectiveness for two industrial samples. *J. appl. Psychol., 47*, 30–37.

Egerman, K., R. Glaser, and D. J. Klaus (1963). Increasing team proficiency through training: 4. A learning-theoretic analysis of the effects of team arrangement on team performance. Pittsburgh: American Institute for Research.

Egerman, K., D. J. Klaus, and R. Glaser (1962). Increasing team proficiency through training: 3. Decremental effects of reinforcement in teams with redundant members. Pittsburgh: American Institute for Research.

Elliott, J. D. (1953). Increasing office productivity through job enlargement. In *The human side of the office manager's job.* New York: American Management Association, Office Management Series, No. 134. Pp. 3–15.

Faucheux C., and S. Moscovici (1960). Etudes sur la créativité des groupes: II. Tâche, structure des communications et réussite. *Bull. CERP, 9*, 11–22.

Festinger, L. (1954). Motivations leading to social behavior. In M. R. Jones (Ed.), *Nebraska symposium on motivation, 1954.* Lincoln: Univ. of Nebraska Press. Pp. 191–218.

——— (1957). *A theory of cognitive dissonance.* Evanston, Ill.: Row, Peterson.

Festinger, L., S. Schachter, and K. Back (1950). *Social pressures in informal groups.* New York: Harper.

Fiske, D. W., and S. R. Maddi (1961). *Functions of varied experience.* Homewood, Ill.: Dorsey.

Fleishman, E. A. (1953). Leadership climate, human relations training, and supervisory behavior. *Personnel Psychol., 6*, 205–222.

——— (1958). A relationship between incentive motivation and ability level in psychomotor performance *J. exp. Psychol., 56*, 78–81.

——— (1965). Attitude versus skill factors in work group productivity *Personnel Psychol., 18*, 253–266.

Fleishman, E. A., and E. F. Harris (1962). Patterns of leadership behavior related to employee grievances and turnover. *Personnel Psychol., 15*, 43–56.

Fleishman, E. A., E. F. Harris, and H. E. Burtt (1955). *Leadership and supervision in industry.* Columbus: Ohio State University, Bureau of Educational Research.

Freedman, J. L. (1963). Attitudinal effects of inadequate justification. *J. Pers., 31*, 371–385.

French, E. G. (1955). Some characteristics of achievement motivation. *J. exp. Psychol., 50*, 232–236.

French, J. R. P., Jr. (1950). Field experiments: changing group productivity. In J. G. Miller (Ed.), *Experiments in social process: a symposium on social psychology.* New York: McGraw-Hill. Pp. 79–96.

_____ (1956). A formal theory of social power. *Psychol. Rev., 63,* 181–194.

French, J. R. P., Jr., J. Israel, and D. As (1960). An experiment on participation in a Norwegian factory. *Hum. Relat., 13,* 3–19.

French, J. R. P., Jr., and A. Zander (1949). The group dynamics approach. In A. Kornhauser (Ed.), *Psychology of labor management relations.* Champaign, Ill.: Industrial Relations Research Association. Pp. 71–80.

Galbraith, J., and L. L. Cummings (1967). An empirical investigation of the motivational determinants of task performance: interactive effects between instrumentality-valence and motivation-ability. *Organizat. Behav. hum. Perform., 2,* 237–257.

Georgopoulos, B. S., G. M. Mahoney, and N. W. Jones (1957). A path-goal approach to productivity. *J. appl. Psychol., 41,* 345–353.

Giese, W. J., and H. W. Ruter (1949). An objective analysis of morale. *J. appl. Psychol., 33,* 421–427.

Glanzer, M., and R. Glaser (1961). Techniques for the study of group structure and behavior: II. Empirical studies of the effects of structure in small groups. *Psychol. Bull., 58,* 1–27.

Glaser, R., D. J. Klaus, and K. Egerman (1962). Increasing team proficiency through training: 2. The acquisition and extinction of a team response. Pittsburgh: American Institute for Research.

Guest, R. H. (1957). Job enlargement: a revolution in job design. *Personnel Admin., 20* (2), 9–16.

Guetzkow, H., and H. A. Simon (1955). The impact of certain communication nets upon organization and performance in task-oriented groups. *Managemt. Sci., 1,* 233–250.

Guion, R. M. (1958). Industrial morale (a symposium): 1. The problem of terminology. *Personnel Psychol., 11,* 59–64.

Gurin, G., J. Veroff, and Sheila Feld (1960). *Americans view their mental health.* New York: Basic Books.

Haire, M. (1954). Industrial social psychology. In G. Lindzey (Ed.), *Handbook of social psychology.* Cambridge, Mass.: Addison-Wesley. Pp. 1104–1123.

Hall, E. J., Jane S. Mouton, and R. R. Blake (1963). Group problem solving effectiveness under conditions of pooling vs. interaction. *J. soc. Psychol., 59,* 147–157.

Hall, R. L. (1957). Group performance under feedback that confounds responses of group members. *Sociometry, 20,* 297–305.

Halpin, A. W., and B. J. Winer (1957). A factorial study of the leader behavior descriptions. In R. M. Stogdill and A. E. Coons (Eds.), *Leader behavior: its description and measurement.* Columbus: Ohio State University, Bureau of Business Research, Research Monogr. No. 88. Pp. 39–51.

Harding, F. D., and R. A. Bottenberg (1961). Effect of personal characteristics on relationships between attitudes and job performance. *J. appl. Psychol., 45,* 428–430.

Hariton, T. (1951). Conditions influencing the effects of training foremen in human relations principles. Unpublished doctoral dissertation, University of Michigan.

Harlow, H. F. (1953). Mice, monkeys, men and motives. *Psychol. Rev., 60,* 23–32.

Harlow, H. F., Margaret Kuenne Harlow, and D. R. Meyer (1950). Learning motivated by a manipulation drive. *J. exp. Psychol., 40*, 228–234.

Harris, E. F., and E. A. Fleishman (1955). Human relations training and the stability of leadership patterns. *J. appl. Psychol., 39*, 20–25.

Hebb, D. O. (1949). *The organization of behavior.* New York: Wiley.

Heider, F. (1958). *The psychology of interpersonal relations.* New York: Wiley.

Helson, H. (1964). *Adaption-level theory.* New York: Harper and Row.

Hill, W. F. (1956). Activity as an autonomous drive. *J. comp. physiol. Psychol., 49*, 15–19.

Homans, G. C. (1961). *Social behavior: its elementary forms.* New York: Harcourt, Brace, and World.

Hoppock, R. (1935). *Job satisfaction.* New York: Harper.

Hull, C. L. (1943). *Principles of behavior.* New York: Appleton-Century.

Hunt, J. M. (1960). Experience and the development of motivation: some interpretations. *Child Develpmt., 31*, 489–504.

Jacobson, E. (1951). Foreman-steward participation practices and worker attitudes in a unionized factory. Unpublished doctoral dissertation, University of Michigan.

Jaques, E. (1951). *The changing culture of a factory.* London: Tavistock.

——— (1961). *Equitable payment.* New York: Wiley.

Kagan, J., and M. Berkun (1954). The reward value of running activity. *J. comp. physiol. Psychol., 47*, 108.

Kahn, R. L. (1958). Human relations on the shop floor. In E. M. Hugh-Jones (Ed.), *Human relations and modern management.* Amsterdam: North-Holland. Pp. 43–74.

——— (1960). Productivity and job satisfaction. *Personnel Psychol., 13*, 275–287.

Karsten, Anitra (1928). Psychische Sättigung. *Psychol. Forsch., 10*, 142–254.

Katz, D. (1964). The motivational basis of organizational behavior. *Behav. Sci., 9*, 131–146.

Katz, D., and R. L. Kahn (1966). *The social psychology of organizations.* New York: Wiley.

Katz, D., N. Maccoby, and Nancy C. Morse (1950). *Productivity, supervision, and morale in an office situation.* Ann Arbor: Univ. of Michigan, Institute for Social Research.

Kaufmann, H. (1963). Task performance and responses to failure as functions of imbalance in the self-concept. *Psychol. Monogr., 77*, No. 6 (whole No. 569).

Kaustler, D. H. (1951). A study of the relationship between ego-involvement and learning. *J. Psychol., 32*, 225–230.

Kerr, W. A., G. Koppelmeir, and J. J. Sullivan (1951). Absenteeism, turnover, and the morale in a metals fabrication factory. *Occupat. Psychol., 25*, 50–55.

Kogan, N., and M. A. Wallach (1967). Risk taking as a function of the situation, the person and the group. In *New directions in psychology.* Vol. 3. New York: Holt, Rinehart, and Winston. Pp. 111–278.

Kornhauser, A. W. (1965). *Mental health of the industrial worker: a Detroit study.* New York: Wiley.

Lanzetta, J. T., and T. B. Roby (1956a). Effects of work-group structure and certain task variables on group performance. *J. abnorm. soc. Psychol., 53*, 307–314.

―――― (1956b). Group performance as a function of work-distribution patterns and task loads. *Sociometry, 19*, 95–104.

―――― (1957). Group learning and communication as a function of task structure 'demands.' *J. abnorm. soc. Psychol., 55*, 121–131.

Latané, B., and A. J. Arrowood (1963). Emotional arousal and task performance. *J. appl. Psychol., 47*, 324–327.

Lawler, E. E. (1966). Ability as a moderator of the relationship between job attitudes and job performance, *Personnel Psychol., 19*, 153–164.

Lawler, E. E., C. A. Koplin, T. F. Young, and J. A. Fadem (1968). Inequity reduction over time in an induced overpayment situation. *Organizat. Behav. hum. Perform., 3*, 253–268.

Lawler, E. E., and P. W. O'Gara (1967). The effects of inequity produced by under-payment on work output, work quality and attitudes toward the work. *J. appl. Psychol., 51*, 403–410.

Lawler, E. E., and L. W. Porter (1963). Perceptions regarding management com-pensation. *Indust. Relat., 3*, 41–49.

Lawrence, Lois C., and Patricia C. Smith (1955). Group decision and employee par-ticipation. *J. appl. Psychol., 39*, 334–337.

Leavitt, H. J. (1951). Some effects of certain communication patterns on group performance. *J. abnorm. soc. Psychol., 46*, 38–50.

―――― (1962). Toward organizational psychology. In Gilmer B. von Haller (Ed.), *Walter Van Dyke Bingham.* Pittsburgh: Carnegie Institute of Technology. Pp. 23–30.

―――― (1964). Applied organizational change in industry: structural, technical and human approaches. In W. W. Cooper, H. J. Leavitt, and M. W. Shelly, II (Eds.), *New perspectives in organization research.* New York: Wiley. Pp. 55–71.

Leavitt, H. J., and B. M. Bass (1964). Organizational psychology. *Annu. Rev. Psychol., 15*, 371–398.

Lecky, P. (1945). *Self-consistency: a theory of personality.* New York: Island.

Levine, J., and J. Butler (1952). Lecture vs. group decision in changing behavior. *J. appl. Psychol., 36*, 29–33.

Lewin, K. (1938). The conceptual representation and the measurement of psycho-logical forces. *Contrib. psychol. Theory, 1*, No. 4.

―――― (1947). Group decision and social change. In T. M. Newcomb and E. L. Hartley (Eds.), *Readings in social psychology.* New York: Henry Holt. Pp. 330–344.

―――― (1948). *Resolving social conflicts.* New York: Harper.

Lewin, K., Tamara Dembo, L. Festinger, and Pauline S. Sears (1944). Level of aspiration. In J. M. Hunt (Ed.), *Personality and the behavior disorders.* Vol. 1. New York: Ronald. Pp. 333–378.

Lewin, K., R. Lippitt, and R. K. White (1939). Patterns of aggressive behavior in experimentally created social climates. *J. soc. Psychol., 10*, 271–299.

Likert, R. (1961). *New patterns of management.* New York: McGraw-Hill.

Likert, R., and J. M. Willits (1940). *Morale and agency management.* Vol. 1: Morale —the mainspring of management. Hartford: Life Insurance Sales Research Bureau.

Lindzey, G., Ed. (1954). *Handbook of social psychology.* Cambridge, Mass.: Addison-Wesley.

Lorge, I., L. Aikman, Gilda Moss, J. Spiegel, and J. Tuckman (1955). Solutions by teams and by individuals to a field problem at different levels of reality. *J. educ. Psychol., 46,* 17–24.

Lorge, I., D. Fox, J. Davitz, and M. Brenner (1958). A survey of studies contrasting the quality of group performance and individual performance: 1930–1957. *Psychol. Bull., 55,* 337–372.

Lorge, I., Paula Weltz, D. Fox, and K. Herrold (1960). Evaluation of decisions written by ad hoc groups and simulated commanders. In A. H. Rubenstein and C. J. Haberstroh, *Some theories of organization.* Homewood, Ill.: Irwin. Pp. 448–451.

Lowell, E. L. (1952). The effect of need for achievement on learning and speed of performance. *J. Psychol., 33,* 31–40.

Lowin, A., and G. F. Epstein (1965). Does expectancy determine performance? *J. exp. soc. Psychol., 1,* 248–255.

McClelland, D. C. (1955). Some social consequences of achievement motivation. In M. R. Jones (Ed.), *Nebraska symposium on motivation, 1955.* Lincoln: Univ. of Nebraska Press. Pp. 41–64.

———— (1958). Risk taking in children with high and low need for achievement. In J. W. Atkinson (Ed.), *Motives in fantasy, action, and society.* Princeton: Van Nostrand. Pp. 306–321.

———— (1961). *The achieving society.* Princeton: Van Nostrand.

———— (1962). Business drive and national achievement. *Harvard Bus. Rev., 40,* 99–112.

———— (1963). Why men and nations seek success. *Nation's Bus., 51,* 32–33.

McClelland, D. C., J. W. Atkinson, R. A. Clark, and E. L. Lowell (1953). *The achievement motive.* New York: Appleton-Century-Crofts.

McGregor, D. (1960). *The human side of enterprise.* New York: McGraw-Hill.

Macy, J., L. S. Christie, and R. D. Luce (1953). Coding noise in a task-oriented group. *J. abnorm. soc. Psychol., 48,* 401–409.

Maier, N. R. F. (1950). The quality of group decisions as influenced by the discussion leader. *Hum. Relat., 3,* 155–174.

———— (1952). *Principles of human relations.* New York: Wiley.

———— (1953). An experimental test of the effect of training on discussion leadership. *Hum. Relat., 6,* 161–173.

———— (1955). *Psychology in industry* (2nd ed.). Boston: Houghton Mifflin.

———— (1960). Maier's Law. *Amer. Psychologist, 15,* 208–212.

———— (1963). *Problem-solving discussions and conferences: leadership methods and skills.* New York: McGraw-Hill.

Maier, N. R. F., and L. R. Hoffman (1960). Using trained 'developmental' discussion leaders to improve further the quality of group decisions. *J. appl. Psychol.*, *44*, 247–251.

Mann, F. C. (1957). Studying and creating change: a means to understanding social organization. In C. M. Arensberg *et al.* (Eds.), *Research in industrial human relations.* New York: Harper. Pp. 146–167.

Mann, F. C., and J. K. Dent (1954). The supervisor: member of two organizational families. *Harvard Bus. Rev., 32*, 103–112.

Mann, F. C., and L. R. Hoffman (1960). *Automation and the worker.* New York: Holt.

March, J. G., Ed. (1965). *Handbook of organizations.* Chicago: Rand McNally.

March, J. G., and H. A. Simon (1958). *Organizations.* New York: Wiley.

Marquart, Dorothy I. (1955). Group problem solving. *J. soc. Psychol., 41*, 103–113.

Marriott, R. (1949). Size of working group and output. *Occupat. Psychol., 23*, 47–57.

Marrow, A. J. (1964). *Behind the executive mask.* New York: American Management Association.

Marrow, A. J., D. G. Bowers, and S. E. Seashore (1967). *Management by participation,* New York: Harper and Row.

Mathewson, S. B. (1931). *Restriction of output among unorganized workers.* New York: Viking Press.

Merton, R. K., and Alice S. Kitt (1952). Contributions to the theory of reference behavior. In G. E. Swanson, T. M. Newcomb, and E. L. Hartley (Eds.), *Readings in social psychology* (rev. ed.). New York: Holt. Pp. 430–444.

Metzner, Helen, and F. Mann (1953). Employee attitudes and absences. *Personnel Psychol., 6*, 467–485.

Meyer, H. H., E. Kay, and J. R. P. French, Jr. (1965). Split roles in performance appraisal. *Harvard Bus. Rev., 43*, 123–129.

Meyer, H. H., W. B. Walker, and G. H. Litwin (1961). Motive patterns and risk preferences associated with entrepreneurship. *J. abnorm. soc. Psychol., 63*, 570–574.

Miles, M. B. (1960). Human relations training: processes and outcomes. *J. counsel. Psychol., 7*, 301–306.

Miller, D. C. (1941). Economic factors in the morale of college-trained adults. *Amer. J. Sociol., 47*, 139–156.

Miller, L. (1965). The use of knowledge of results in improving the performance of hourly operators. General Electric Company, Behavioral Research Service.

Miller, N. E. (1951). Learnable drives and rewards. In S. S. Stevens (Ed.), *Handbook of experimental psychology.* New York: Wiley. Pp. 435–472.

Miller, N. E., and J. Dollard (1941). *Social learning and imitation.* New Haven: Yale Univ. Press.

Mohanna, A. I., and M. Argyle (1960). A cross-cultural study of structured groups with unpopular central members. *J. abnorm. soc. Psychol., 60*, 139–140.

Morrissette, J. O., S. A. Switzer, and C. W. Crannell (1965). Group performance as a function of size, structure and task difficulty. *J. Pers. soc. Psychol., 2*, 451–455.

Morse, Nancy C. (1953). *Satisfactions in the white-collar job.* Ann Arbor: Univ. of Michigan, Institute for Social Research, Survey Research Center.

Morse, Nancy C., and E. Reimer (1956). The experimental change of a major organizational variable. *J. abnorm. soc. Psychol., 52,* 120–129.

Mulder, M. (1960). Communication structure, decision structure and group performance. *Sociometry, 23,* 1–14.

Murray, H. A. (1938). *Explorations in personality.* New York: Oxford Univ. Press.

Newcomb, T. M. (1943). *Personality and social change.* New York: Holt, Rinehart, and Winston.

Osgood, C. E., and P. H. Tannenbaum (1955). The principle of congruity in the prediction of attitude change. *Psychol. Rev., 62,* 42–55.

Patchen, M. (1961). *The choice of wage comparisons.* Englewood Cliffs, N.J.: Prentice-Hall.

——— (1962). Supervisory methods and group performance norms. *Admin. Sci. Quart.,* 276–290.

Paterson, D. G., and C. H. Stone, (1942). Dissatisfactions with life work among adult workers. *Occupations, 21,* 219–221.

Porter, L. W. (1962). Job attitudes in management: I. Perceived deficiencies in need fulfillment as a function of job level. *J. appl. Psychol., 46,* 375–384.

Porter, L. W., and E. E. Lawler (1968). *Attitudes of effective managers.* Homewood, Ill.: Irwin, Dorsey.

Radke, Marian, and Dana Klisurich (1947). Experiments in changing food habits. *J. Amer. Dietet. Assoc., 23,* 403–409.

Roby, T. B., and J. T. Lanzetta (1957). Conflicting principles in man-machine system design. *J. appl. Psychol., 41,* 170–178.

Roby, T. B., Elizabeth H. Nicol, and Francis M. Farrell (1963). Group problem solving under two types of executive structures. *J. abnorm. soc. Psychol., 67,* 550–556.

Roethlisberger, F. J., and W. J. Dickson (1939). *Management and the worker.* Cambridge: Harvard Univ. Press.

Rosenberg, S., and R. L. Hall (1958). The effects of different social feedback conditions upon performance in dyadic teams. *J. abnorm. soc. Psychol., 57,* 271–277.

Ross, I. C., and A. Zander (1957). Need satisfactions and employee turnover. *Personnel Psychol., 10,* 327–338.

Roy, D. (1952). Quota restriction and gold bricking in a machine shop. *Amer. J. Sociol., 57,* 427–442.

Russell, W. A. (1952). Retention of verbal material as a function of motivating instructions and experimentally-induced failure. *J. exp. Psychol., 43,* 207–216.

Sales, S. M., and N. A. Rosen (1965). A laboratory investigation of the effectiveness of two industrial supervisory patterns. Unpublished manuscript, Cornell University.

Scalia, F. (1966). Self-consistency and task performance. Unpublished Master's thesis, Carnegie Institute of Technology.

Schachter, S., N. Ellertson, D. McBride, and D. Gregory (1951). An experimental study of cohesiveness and productivity. *Hum. Relat., 4*, 229–238.

Schachter, S., B. Willerman, L. Festinger, and R. Hyman (1961). Emotional disruption and industrial productivity. *J. appl. Psychol., 45*, 201–213.

Schein, E. H. (1965). *Organizational psychology.* Englewood Cliffs, N.J.: Prentice-Hall.

Schein, E. H., and W. G. Bennis, Eds. (1965). *Personal and organizational change through group methods: the laboratory approach.* New York: Wiley.

Scodel, A., P. Ratoosh, and J. S. Minas (1959). Some personality correlates of decision-making under conditions of risk, *Behav. Sci., 4*, 19–28.

Seashore, S. (1954). *Group cohesiveness in the industrial work group.* Ann Arbor: Univ. of Michigan, Institute for Social Research, Survey Research Center.

Seashore, S. E., and D. G. Bowers (1963). *Changing the structure and functioning of an organization.* Ann Arbor: Univ. of Michigan, Institute for Social Research, Survey Research Center.

Seeman, M. (1957). A comparison of general and specific leader behavior descriptions. In R. M. Stogdill and A. E. Coons (Eds.), *Leader behavior: its description and measurement.* Columbus: Ohio State Univ., Bureau of Business Research, Research Monogr. No. 88. Pp. 86–102.

Seward, J. P. (1963). The structure of functional autonomy. *Amer. Psychologist, 18*, 703–710.

Shaw, Marjorie E. A. (1932). A comparison of individuals and small groups in the rational solution of complex problems. *Amer. J. Psychol., 44*, 491–504.

Shaw, M. E. (1954a). Some effects of problem complexity upon problem solution efficiency in different communication nets. *J. exp. Psychol., 48*, 211–217.

—————— (1954b). Some effects of unequal distribution of information upon group performance in various communication nets. *J. abnorm. soc. Psychol., 49*, 547–553.

—————— (1964). Communication networks. In L. Berkowitz (Ed.), *Advances in experimental psychology.* Vol. 1. New York: Academic Press. Pp. 111–149.

Sherif, M. (1947). Group influences upon the formation of norms and attitudes. In T. M. Newcomb and E. L. Hartley (Eds.), *Readings in social psychology.* New York: Holt. Pp. 77–90.

Simmons, W. (1954). The group approach to weight reduction: I. A review of the project. *J. Amer. Dietet. Assoc., 30*, 437–441.

Simon, H. A. (1947). *Administrative behavior.* New York: MacMillan.

Slater, Carol W. (1959). Some factors associated with internalization of motivation towards occupational role performance. Unpublished doctoral dissertation, University of Michigan.

Smith, Patricia C. (1963). Cornell studies of job satisfaction: strategy for the development of a general theory of job satisfaction. Unpublished manuscript.

Sofer, C. (1961). *The organization from within.* London: Tavistock.

Spector, A. J. (1956). Fulfillment and morale. *J. abnorm. soc. Psychol., 52*, 51–56.

Stoner, J. A. F. (1961). A comparison of individual and group decisions involving risk. Unpublished Master's thesis, Massachusetts Institute of Technology.

Stouffer, S. A., E. A. Suchmann, L. C. DeVinney, Shirley A. Star, and R. M. Williams (1949). *The American soldier: adjustment during army life.* Vol. 1. Princeton: Princeton Univ. Press.

Strauss, G. (1963). Some notes on power equalization. In H. J. Leavitt (Ed.), *The social science of organizations.* Englewood Cliffs, N.J.: Prentice-Hall. Pp. 39–84.

Super, D. E. (1939). Occupational level and job satisfaction. *J. appl. Psychol., 23,* 547–564.

Tannenbaum, A. S., and F. H. Allport (1956). Personality structure and group structure: an interpretive study of their relationship through an event-structure hypothesis. *J. abnorm. soc. Psychol., 53,* 272–280.

Tannenbaum, R., and W. H. Schmidt (1958). How to choose a leadership pattern. *Harvard Bus. Rev., 36,* 95–101.

Tannenbaum, R., I. R. Weschler, and F. Massarik (1961). *Leadership and organization.* New York: McGraw-Hill.

Taylor, D. W., P. C. Berry, and C. H. Block (1958). Does group participation when using brainstorming facilitate or inhibit creative thinking? *Admin. Sci. Quart., 3,* 23–47.

Taylor, D. W., and W. L. Faust (1952). Twenty questions: efficiency in problem solving as a function of size of group. *J. exp. Psychol., 44,* 360–388.

Thibaut, J. W., and H. H. Kelley (1959). *The social psychology of groups.* New York: Wiley.

Thomas, E. J. (1957). Effects of facilitative role interdependence on group functioning. *Hum. Relat., 10,* 347–366.

Thompson, W. A. (1939). Eleven years after graduation. *Occupations, 17,* 709–714.

Thorndike, R. L. (1938). The effects of discussion upon the correctness of group decision where the factor of majority influence is allowed. *J. soc. Psychol., 9,* 343–362.

Timmons, W. M. (1942). Can the product superiority of discussions be attributed to averaging or majority influences? *J. soc. Psychol., 15,* 23–32.

Triandis, H. C. (1959). A critique and experimental design for the study of the relationship between productivity and job satisfaction. *Psychol. Bull., 56,* 309–312.

Tuckman, J., and I. Lorge (1962). Individual ability as a determinant of group superiority. *Hum. Rel., 15,* 45–51.

Turner, A. N., and P. R. Lawrence (1965). *Industrial jobs and the worker: an investigation of response to task attributes.* Boston: Harvard Univ. Graduate School of Business Administration, Division of Research.

Tyler, B. B. (1950). A study of factors contributing to employee morale. Unpublished Master's thesis, Ohio State University.

Uhrbrock, R. S. (1934). Attitudes of 4,430 employees. *J. soc. Psychol., 5,* 365–377.

Van Zelst, R. H. (1951). Worker popularity and job satisfaction. *Personnel Psychol., 4,* 405–412.

Van Zelst, R. H., and W. A. Kerr (1953). Workers' attitudes toward merit rating. *Personnel Psychol., 6,* 159–172.

Veroff, J., J. W. Atkinson, Sheila C. Feld, and G. Gurin (1960). The use of thematic apperception to assess motivation in a nationwide interview study. *Psychol. Monogr., 74,* No. 12 (whole No. 499).

Viteles, M. S. (1953). *Motivation and morale in industry.* New York: Norton.

Vroom, V. H. (1960). *Some personality determinants of the effects of participation.* Englewood Cliffs, N.J.: Prentice-Hall.

———— (1961). The self-concept: a balance-theoretical treatment. Unpublished manuscript, University of Pennsylvania.

———— (1962). Ego-involvement, job satisfaction, and job performance. *Personnel Psychol., 15,* 159–177.

———— (1964). *Work and motivation.* New York: Wiley.

Vroom, V. H., L. D. Grant, and T. S. Cotton (1969). The consequences of social interaction in group problem solving. *Organizat. Behav. hum. Perform., 4,* 77–95.

Vroom, V. H., and N. R. F. Maier (1961). Industrial social psychology. *Annu. Rev. Psychol., 12,* 413–446.

Walker, C. R. (1950). The problem of the repetitive job. *Harvard Bus. Rev., 28*(3), 54–58.

Walker, C. R., and R. H. Guest (1952). *The man on the assembly line.* Cambridge: Harvard Univ. Press.

Wallach, M. A., and N. Kogan (1965). The roles of information, discussion, and consensus in group risk taking. *J. exp. soc. Psychol., 1,* 1–19.

Wallach, M. A., N. Kogan, and D. J. Bem (1962). Group influence on individual risk taking. *J. abnorm. soc. Psychol., 65,* 75–86.

———— (1964). Diffusion of responsibility and level of risk taking in groups. *J. abnorm. soc. Psychol., 68,* 263–274.

Ward, W. D., and K. D. Sandvold (1963). Performance expectancy as a determinant of actual performance: a partial replication. *J. abnorm. soc. Psychol., 67,* 293–295.

Weick, K. E. (1964). Reduction of cognitive dissonance through task enhancement and effort expenditure. *J. abnorm. soc. Psychol., 68,* 533–539.

———— (1965). Laboratory experimentation with organizations. In J. G. March (Ed.), *Handbook of organizations.* Chicago: Rand McNally. Pp. 194–260.

———— (1967). Organizations in the laboratory. In V. H. Vroom (Ed.), *Methods of organizational research.* Pittsburgh: Univ. of Pittsburgh Press. Pp. 1–56.

Weitz, J., and R. C. Nuckols (1953). The validity of direct and indirect questions in measuring job satisfaction. *Personnel Psychol., 6,* 487–494.

White, R. W. (1959). Motivation reconsidered: the concept of competence. *Psychol. Rev., 66,* 297–333.

Whyte, W. F. (1955). *Money and motivation: an analysis of incentives in industry.* New York: Harper.

Wickert, F. R. (1951). Turnover and employees' feelings of ego-involvement in the day-to-day operations of a company. *Personnel Psychol., 4*, 185–197.

Winterbottom, Marian R. (1958). The relation of need for achievement to learning experiences in independence and mastery. In J. W. Atkinson (Ed.), *Motives in fantasy, action, and society.* Princeton: Van Nostrand. Pp. 453–478.

Woodworth, R. S. (1918). *Dynamic psychology.* New York: Columbia Univ. Press.

Woytinsky, W. S. (1942). *Three aspects of labor dynamics.* Washington, D.C.: Social Science Research Council.

Wyatt, S., assisted by L. Frost and F. G. L. Stock (1934). *Incentives in repetitive work: a practical experiment in a factory.* London: His Majesty's Stationery Office. Industrial Health Research Board, Report No. 69.

Wyatt, S., J. A. Fraser, and F. G. L. Stock (1929). *The effects of monotony in work.* London: His Majesty's Stationery Office. Industrial Fatigue Research Board, Report No. 56.

Zajonc, R. B. (1962). The effects of feedback and probability of group success on individual and group performance. *Hum. Relat., 15*, 149–161.

Zaleznik, A., C. R. Christensen, and F. J. Roethlisberger (1958). *The motivation, productivity, and satisfaction of workers: a prediction study.* Boston: Harvard Univ. Graduate School of Business Administration.

Zeaman, D. (1949). Response latency as a function of the amount of reinforcement. *J. exp. Psychol., 39*, 466–483.

40

Psychology and Economics

HERBERT A. SIMON, Carnegie-Mellon University

ANDREW C. STEDRY, University of Texas

In discussing the mutual relations of psychology and economics, we shall make use of psychological categories as organizing concepts. After considering the extent to which the two fields have areas of common interest, we shall devote three sections to the motivation of the consumer, of the producer or entrepreneur, and of the employee, respectively. There follows a discussion of *oligopoly* (competition among the few) viewed as a conflict phenomenon. The final section reviews the cognitive aspects of economic behavior, including some important recently proposed modifications in the characterization of rational economic action. The relations between psychology and economics run both ways. We are not concerned merely with possible applications of psychological methods to economics, but equally with the use of economic theory and data about economic behavior in psychology.

Economic behavior, family behavior, political behavior, and organizational behavior are all forms of human behavior. Each can be explained partly in relatively general terms that cut across these categories, and partly in terms that apply only to a particular area of behavior. The fruitfulness of the interaction between economics and other social sciences hinges on whether the same mechanisms operate in all these areas of behavior, and on how far human behavior in one area is relevant for testing theories in the others. The question is a pragmatic one that has to be asked and re-asked as the sciences of man develop, and as our understanding of their interrelationship deepens.

THE SUBSPECIES OF ECONOMIC MAN

Psychology enters economics through the characteristics that are postulated for the several subspecies of economic man. These subspecies include (1) the buyer or seller of commodities in a market, (2) the entrepreneur or producer, (3) the consumer, and (4) the worker. In certain areas of economic theory the categories overlap, but they are convenient for classifying and examining economic man.

269

We must look first at the distinction between producer and consumer. When we understand this, we can study the motivations of each kind of economic man, and then the cognitive aspects of his behavior.

The separation of producer and consumer

It is not strictly accurate to state that in economic theory there are producers or workers and consumers. Rather, each person is assumed to be both, but the roles are kept quite distinct. The line between them is defined by the clock: during the working day, economic man is a worker or producer; during the remainder of the 24 hours he is a consumer.

Interactions between the producer or worker and the consumer

In a strict version of the theory, there are only two possibilities for interaction between John Doe, producer or worker, and John Doe, consumer. First, the length of his workday—be he entrepreneur or worker—and, hence, the time boundary between his roles, may depend on an economic decision that weighs the utility of the income obtainable by working longer against the disutility of substituting work for leisure. This decision is an essential part of any economic theory that seeks to explain the length of the workweek. Second, when he makes decisions as a consumer, John Doe's income is one determinant of his spending and saving behavior. Theories of consumer choice typically take income as a given, determined by the production segment of the economy.

The masters of classical economic theory were well aware that separating producer from consumer, and vice versa, oversimplifies the facts of the real world but still permits a tolerable approximation to human behavior throughout most of the economic sphere. Alfred Marshall (1920), for example, was careful to discuss the possible "psychic income" that the entrepreneur receives from his activity, and was also aware that the daily work activity of the laborer might alter his tastes, and hence his utility function. Ricardo assumed that, in the long run, wages must sink to a subsistence level; hence, the wage rate might really be regarded as a "marginal cost of producing labor." In the Ricardian theory, the consumer was thus almost swallowed by the producer.

A few important economic theorists have rejected all or most of this classical analysis, Thorstein Veblen and John R. Commons being prominent examples. The vast majority of contemporary economic theorists may be regarded, however, as disciples of the classical tradition; and, like most disciples, they sometimes ignore or underemphasize the qualifications that the masters were careful to acknowledge. In extreme cases, the result has been to change economics from an empirical science to a vast tautology in which entrepreneurs maximize profit by definition—for profit is defined as "that which entrepreneurs maximize"—and consumers maximize utility by definition—for the same reason.

The other subspecies

We have mentioned four subspecies of economic man. One of these is the consumer, who tends not to be further differentiated in the theory. On the production side of the economy, however, the distinction between the entrepreneur and the worker is significant. About the buyer and seller, little needs to be said except that they observe the classical maxim, "Buy cheap and sell dear." For the rest, they do not require separate discussion. We have omitted the investor as a separate subspecies. As a person who saves, his behavior is part of that of the consumer. As a person who lends to others, he is buyer and seller of the services of capital. As a person who holds the residual equity in a business in anticipation of profit, he is an entrepreneur.

Speaking strictly, this multiple role is incompatible with most of classical theory. In Ricardian theory, for example, where wages are driven to the subsistence level, it is inconceivable that a worker could save or invest in his own or another's company. In contemporary society, workers (in the sociological sense) may own a substantial portion of one enterprise, while in another enterprise managers (workers, as defined by economic theory) actually perform the entrepreneurial activities without any substantial ownership interest. This state of affairs is effectively ruled out by the classical theory, which contains no means of dealing with it.

What distinguishes the worker from the entrepreneur in the theory is that the former sells to the latter the right to apply his time and effort during working hours to the goal of the enterprise. In agreeing to accept authority in the workplace, the laborer's productive services become "disembodied" from him, so to speak, and are turned over to the entrepreneur. In terms of this distinction, the hired executive, however exalted his position in the administrative hierarchy, is a worker and not an entrepreneur. We shall see that economists have become increasingly uneasy with this classification of roles, both with its factual inaccuracy and with its economic consequences.

THE GOALS OF ECONOMIC SCIENCE

Economics can be defined as the discipline that purports to describe, predict, and explain behavior in the marketplace. The *a priori* assumption that each human being behaves like "economic man" underlies both the descriptive and predictive aspects of economic analysis, and raises questions of how far economics, in its present state, conforms to the norms of a science. G. P. E. Clarkson (1963), for example, has suggested that the theory of consumer demand falls short of these norms because its assumptions of rational behavior have repeatedly been shown to be empirically invalid. This crucial interrelation between economic assumptions and observable behavior will be dealt with in detail later in this chapter.

The definition itself does not really describe the major focus of economic literature. Work in economics may be classified as dealing with (1) descriptions of the economy or its major segments as a whole (*macroeconomics*), or of the behavior of the individual economic man and the individual firm (*microeconomics*); or (2) prescriptions for the economy and economic behavior within it, either for purposes of public policy (*normative macroeconomics*) or as advice to the consumer or businessman (*normative microeconomics*).

In large part, normative macroeconomics has been the central concern of economists while, at the same time, descriptive microeconomics has provided the theoretical basis for prescription. Virtually all of pre-Keynesian economics, and much contemporary work, is based on extrapolating the hypothesized behavior of the individual consumer or entrepreneur to the economy as a whole. Descriptive macroeconomics should, of course, be the essential basis for policy prescription, but specific research endeavors in this area have been largely determined by direct relevance to normative policy issues (for example, business-cycle theory). Normative microeconomics, while it has only recently been cultivated on any intensive scale, is now a flourishing area of economic research, overlapping statistical decision theory and other relatively new areas such as "management science," "logistics," and "operations research."

Economists have usually been interested in descriptive microeconomics, understanding the behavior of individual economic agents only to the extent necessary to provide a foundation for macroeconomic analysis. Hence, economic research at the micro level stems largely from a recognition that at least some aspects of the economy can be understood only if a certain sector of individual behavior can be explained. We shall see this mechanism operating with particular clarity when we come to the topic of expectations.

Two economic principles operate to keep to a minimum the macroeconomist's concern with individual behavior (Bowen, 1955, pp. 6–8). The first is the assumption of objective rationality, which permits strong predictions to be made about human behavior without the painful necessity of observing people. The second is the assumption of competition, for where competition exists, the individuals who behave in conformity with the principle of rationality survive at the expense of the others. Hence, the classical economic theory of markets with rational agents and perfect competition is a deductive theory that requires almost no contact with empirical data—once the underlying assumptions are accepted or verified—to establish its propositions.

The preoccupation of economists with the economy as a whole has led them to be satisfied with these two principles whenever the deduced theory provides a satisfactory mechanism for predicting macroeconomic phenomena. That this ability to predict does not say anything about the validity of the theory and its underlying principles has been pointed out by Clarkson (1963, especially pp. 83–85). He further pointed out (pp. 99–101) that economists have frequently denied the necessity for verification of the underlying principles on grounds that they are "obvious." Others have suggested that certain phenomena, for example, commodity prices, are determined by rational agents at the "margin," so that only a small fraction of the consumers or producers need be rational to produce agreement with theory (Machlup, 1946, 1947). Furthermore, the theory suggests that, since only the rational will survive, the study of the irrational is the study of transient phenomena. It is also frequently argued that, if there are people who do not behave rationally, they should be taught to do so (Coombs and Beardslee, 1954).

Thus, because economists have little concern with actual individual behavior, they have not much sought interaction with psychologists. Some justification for ignoring individual behavior is also provided by the vast number of variables involved and the difficulty of identifying observed macro data with underlying micro phenomena (Theil, 1964), particularly without recourse to sophisticated statistical techniques. (See Goldberger, 1964, for an extensive discussion of the inadequacy of the most commonly used techniques in econometrics and a survey, with extensive bibliography, of more sophisticated techniques.) As we proceed, we shall also consider how far this independence of economics from the behavioral sciences may be explained by the present state of knowledge in the latter fields.

Our task, then, is to explore what has been a no-man's-land between economics and behavioral science: the area of descriptive microeconomics. Of course, we are not the first explorers and we shall be guided by what has already been learned of the territory, particularly by the economists who are usually called "institutionalists." The assumptions of economic theory that have been most challenged are its motivational assumptions, particularly the consistency of preferences of humans and their exclusive preoccupation with monetary rewards. In fact, there have been perhaps an excessive preoccupation with motivation and insufficient attention to the cognitive aspects of economic behavior. Hence, we shall pay particular attention to the psychological study of the limits of humans, regarded as learning and information-processing organisms, in their capacities for rational choice.

MOTIVATION: THE CONSUMER

We shall discuss separately the motivation of the consumer and the motivation of the producer, taking up the consumer first. A first section describes the apparatus—based on the concept of utility function—used by the economist to discuss consumer behavior. The second section explores psychology to determine what concepts in that field, if any, correspond to the economist's "utility." A third section considers the economist's interest in consumer behavior and the possible relevance of psychological research in answering his questions.

THE UTILITY FUNCTION

The fundamental postulate in microeconomics about the consumer is that he possesses a *utility function*. This is roughly equivalent to saying that, for any pair of alternatives of action presented to him, he can tell which he prefers. In some variants of the theory, alternatives are assumed to be presented in the form of "bundles of commodities"; in others, as alternative courses of action with consequences attached.

For example, Modigliani and Brumberg (1954) have developed a theory of consumption and saving that assumes that each consumer estimates the present value of his expected future stream of income; he then chooses among all possible time patterns of saving and spending consistently with his assumption. The consumer, in this theory, is assumed to be able to ascertain his preferences among these alternative streams of spending and saving.

Cardinal and ordinal utility

There has been much discussion as to whether a *cardinal* utility function should be postulated, or only an *ordinal* function. Suppose that we assign the utility x_1 to one of the consumer's alternatives, and the utility x_2 to another, where x_1 is greater than x_2 and the first alternative is the one he prefers. We say that the utility function is *ordinal* if the numbers x_1 and x_2 could equally well be replaced by any numbers y_1 and y_2 such that y_1 is greater than y_2. The set of functions y that have this property in relation to the function x are called the *monotonic increasing transformations* of x. By "equally well," we mean that the new function y leads to exactly the same predictions of the consumer's behavior as the function x.

Suppose, on the contrary, that only *linear transformations* of x preserve all the properties of the consumer's behavior:

$$y_i = ax_i + b,$$

where a is a positive constant and b is an arbitrary constant. In this case, the quantity of utility attached to alternatives is uniquely defined, except for the unit of measurement a and the zero point of the scale, fixed by b. It is defined to just the same extent that temperature is defined by the Fahrenheit and centigrade scales. When utility is defined up to a linear transformation, we say that the utility function is *cardinal*.

Let us suppose that four alternatives are open to a consumer. If he has only an ordinal utility function, then a statement such as "The first alternative has greater utility than the third" is meaningful; but a statement such as "The advantage of the first alternative over the second is greater than the advantage of the third over the fourth" is not meaningful. For, by monotonic transformations of the utility scale, we can make the difference in utility between one pair of alternatives greater or less, as we please, than the difference between another pair of alternatives.

It follows that, if utility is ordinal, statements about increasing or decreasing marginal utility are meaningless; that is, we cannot say that a man gets more or less utility from his sixth dollar than from his one million and sixth. (The *marginal* utility of a commodity or money is the amount the utility will be increased by an increase of one unit in the amount of the commodity or money; that is, it is the first partial derivative of utility with respect to the other variable.) Conversely, it can be shown that, if such statements are meaningful, then—implicitly or explicitly—a cardinal utility function has been defined.

Until about two decades ago, there was a tendency to prefer the ordinal function on grounds of parsimony and because Slutsky, Hicks, and other economists had demonstrated that no significant proposition in the accepted theory of consumer choice depended on the cardinal measurement of utility. This trend was reversed in 1944 with the publication of von Neumann and Morgenstern's *The Theory of Games and Economic Behavior* (1944). Up to that time, the theory of consumer choice had been concerned primarily with choice where no uncertainty about future events was involved. Von Neumann and Morgenstern treated the more general case where uncertainty was admitted. They showed that, if a decision maker could make consistent choices among uncertain prospects (for example, lottery tickets at various odds for various bundles of commodities), then cardinal utilities could be assigned to the commodity bundles after observing a sufficient variety of such choices (see also Luce, 1959; Marschak, 1959; Restle, 1961).

The von Neumann–Morgenstern proposal provided cardinal utility with the same operational status that had previously been held by ordinal utility: utilities could be measured simply by observing acts of choice. Further study has shown that, where uncertain prospects are involved, there is an important interaction between subjective probabilities and cardinal utilities; to measure either one operationally calls for an experimental design that, in effect, permits the measurement of both. In the next paragraphs we shall consider this point more fully. (A rather comprehensive discussion of the literature and issues on the topics considered in this and the following section will be found in Luce and Suppes, 1965. See also Arrow's chapter, 1963, and his review, 1958.)

Utility and subjective probability

To understand the issues involved in utility measurement and their implications for psychology, let us consider them in a psychological framework. We confront a subject with a number of alternatives (for example, we offer him any one of several phonograph records or, as suggested above, a choice among lottery tickets, each having different odds and different payoffs) and we observe the choices he makes. We wish to construct scales to measure the probabilities he has assigned to the occurrence of the various possible outcomes and the utilities he attaches to them.

Now if there were *objective* probabilities attached to each of the possible outcomes, and if the subject accepted these probabilities as the basis for his choices, then we would be faced with a straightforward task of constructing a utility scale. However, we must consider the possibility that there are no objective probabilities attached to events or that, if there are, they are not identical with the subjective probabilities that the subject himself attaches to the same events. A subject may prefer a particular risky alternative because one of the possible outcomes has a low subjective probability but a very high utility, or because this same outcome is judged to have a high probability of occurrence but only a moderately high utility.

It is not at all obvious that this interacting expectational-preference system can be analyzed into its components, but a rigorous formal examination of the question shows that in fact it can be. If we propose an appropriate set of alternatives to the subject, we can measure operationally both his probability estimates and his utility. This was first shown some decades ago by the English philosopher Frank Ramsey (1931), but his proposal was not clearly understood and was largely neglected until the rediscovery of cardinal utility by von Neumann and Morgenstern (1944).

There is one important "if" to be attached to this statement, an "if" involved in all psychophysical measurement. The scales can be measured operationally *provided that* the subject can make consistent choices. For example, no utility scale would be compatible with a preference for *A* over *B*, for *B* over *C*, and for *C* over *A*. By adopting a statistical viewpoint (that is, percentage of trials in which *A* is preferred to *B*), we can weaken somewhat the requirements of consistency, but basically the possibility of constructing such a scale hinges on the consistency of the subject, and his consistency hinges on the transitivity and the stability of his choices (Luce, 1958; Luce and Edwards, 1958).

Thus the issue has been shifted. The question is no longer one of cardinal versus ordinal utility. If a utility scale can be defined, the additional assumption that it can be defined for choices among uncertain prospects guarantees its cardinality. The question now is whether a utility scale "exists" at all: Is the behavior of consumers over the range of situations relevant for economics sufficiently consistent, and are consumer choices sufficiently transitive, to make the concept of utility empirically meaningful?

Phrasing the issue in these terms has given it interest for both economists and psychologists, and a number of philosophers and mathematicians as well, with the result that considerable empirical work has gone forward (Davidson, Suppes, and Siegel, 1957; Marschak, 1959; Mosteller and Nogee, 1951). More recently, empirical work has emphasized the existence of "subjective probability" and the notion of "subjective utility," which, if combined properly under the proper experimental conditions, provide evidence of rational behavior (Coombs and Beardslee, 1954; Edwards, 1953). (It is, in fact, almost impossible to define irrational behavior given sufficiently broad definitions of subjective utility and probabilities.) The earliest investigation predates the present surge of interest; it was an attempt in 1931 by the psychologist L. L. Thurstone to establish the ordinal utility function of a single subject.

The evidence available at the present moment is too scanty to permit very definite conclusions. The following observations are at least consistent with the experimental results:

1. *Under a number of experimental conditions, significant differences can be observed between the probability estimates used by the subjects (subjective probabilities) and the objective probabilities known to the experimenter.*

2. *A fairly high degree of consistency is observed in choices when the payoff is in money; consistency is much lower with multidimensional payoffs (for example, choice among phonograph records or among marriageable young ladies).*

PSYCHOLOGICAL ANALOGS OF UTILITY

The term "utility" has, until recently, had little currency in psychology, though similar constructs are to be found in theoretical and empirical work in the field. The notion that reward and punishment influence behavior is found in the earliest psychological work, that is, in learning theory (for a summary, see Mosteller and Nogee, 1951). Indeed, the notion that the type of reward, its frequency of bestowal, and the way in which it is administered are determinants, not only of *behavior,* but also of the cognitive process of *learning,* remained virtually unchallenged among psychologists in the classical tradition prior to the contrary empirical evidence of Tolman (1949).

The relatively simplistic interpretation of reward-punishment determinism in learning theory is, in many ways, closer to the behavioral determinism hypothesized by classical economists than to the recent attempts to incorporate nonmonetary variables into a more generalized utility function. In experiments conducted with animals, it is typically assumed that the food reward or the electric shock punishment causes, say, the rat to learn the maze; there is no assumption that he receives additional satisfaction from the learning process (but see Berlyne, 1954). In experiments on human learning, monetary reward has been used extensively with an implicit assumption that the amount of money received is the appropriate reward measure; in terms of utility theory, this is equivalent to stating that utility is a linear function of money. The notion of "psychic income" is ignored in the psychological theory as in classical economic theory. In both fields possible intangible utilities have been largely neglected.

Another similarity between the classical treatments in both fields, which has tended to disappear with the attempts to marry them, is the absence of explicit treatment of the cognitive processes underlying rational behavior. It is not assumed that the rat knows his utility function and, knowing all the alternatives, consciously maximizes his utility. Classical economics, while incorporating an assumption of rationality, tends to avoid explicit consideration of mental processes, but rather depends on the marketplace to produce rationality. These theories resemble the "principle of least effort" in physics, which serves as a convenient proposition from which to deduce testable hypotheses without the implication that the molecules, individually or collectively, consciously minimize effort. The maximization principle has been used to deduce empirically testable hypotheses about socioeconomic phenomena (Zipf, 1949) without literally requiring individual behavior to be explained on this level.

Lewin (1951), in his theory of "valences," treated individual choice with competing rewards and punishments as analogous to the situation in physics where a number of nonparallel forces converge on the same body. If the analogy were carried out strictly, the net valences of the Lewinian theory would have the formal properties of additive linear utilities. In both psychology and economics, however, new variables are introduced. Intangible rewards, which cannot be expressed in terms of money or commodities, enter into both the Lewinian theory and contemporary treatments of utility theory (see, for example, the multidimensional utility functions employed by Chipman, 1960).

A further difficulty arises for the force analogy because Lewin and those who have used his theoretical formulations as the basis for empirical work have not followed the physical analogy to its appropriate conclusion. For example, if *both* a large reward and a smaller punishment are attached to a particular course of action, Lewinians and most other psychologists would predict that behavior will be different from what it would be if only a small reward—representing the difference between the original reward and punishment—were attached to the action (Lewin, 1936). The "resultant of forces" analogy disappears; notions of individual conflict, quite removed from either the physical or (classical) economic behavioral formulations (Maier, 1949), are introduced, so that the "utility" of a situation depends both on the resultant of forces and on the absolute values of the utilities and disutilities of the rewards and punishments.

In the area opened up by Lewin (1936) and his followers, however, utility constructs have had much application in psychology. The idea of an aspiration level, or goal, whose attainment was desired originated in psychology (Frank, 1935). In a subsequent attempt to explain the existence of this target, Lewin *et al.* (1944) suggested that the aspiration level is that particular goal which is arrived at by maximizing the sum of the satisfaction achieved from attainment of the goal (success) and the dissatisfaction from nonattainment (failure). The close analogy between the valence theory and economic utility theory has been thoroughly explored by Starbuck (1963) in this context. The use of utility theory to explain the existence of aspiration levels or goals has been pursued by psychologists to the extent of actually viewing the aspiration level as a point of inflection on a utility curve (Becker and Siegel, 1958).

In borrowing from economic theory, psychologists have, by and large, both in the empirical studies cited above relating to probabilistic utility measurements and in the process of explaining the existence of goals, assumed the additivity of utilities. While the works cited represent an attempt to apply economic theory to psychological concepts, the qualifications placed by economic theorists on their theories have not been accepted in their entirety by the psychologists who have sought to borrow therefrom.

The laboratory rat usually faces a rather simple set of alternatives; he goes for the cheese or receives an electric shock. A construct like the utility function is only needed to explain choice in the face of complex alternatives when the subject is trying to select the "best" alternative. If the alternatives cannot all be scaled along a single dimension (for example, in terms of money), or if the subject is supposed to be trying to maximize the satisfaction obtainable from setting a particular level of aspiration, the computational powers attributed to the individual become formidable indeed. In most laboratory experiments where the subject is faced with a choice among alternatives, the situation is one of reward versus no reward, and even where alternative rewards are present, the consistency of the subject's preference is not tested over a wide range of circumstances or a long stretch of time. These experiments can hardly be expected to predict human behavior in real-life situations where the alternatives are multitudinous and the rewards have a multiplicity of dimensions.

We can contrast the classical theories and experiments with the contemporary treatments of behavioral experimentation in which utility is used as a behavioral determinant. In describing current empirical work involving decision making under uncertainty, Coombs and Beardslee stated (1954, p. 255): "The three variables, prize, stake, and probability of winning, are each regarded as psychological variables, not necessarily linearly or even monotonically related to their 'real' properties, e.g., 'dollar' values or 'objective' probabilities." They later go on (p. 262) to state that "The basic hypothesis is that in deciding between uncertain outcomes or events the individual chooses that offer or alternative which maximizes his expected utility . . . . This hypothesis is precisely analogous to the assumption frequently made in economics, save that the quantity maximized here is one involving [the utility of the prize, the utility of the stake, and psychological probability], all of which are psychological magnitudes."

There is good reason for departing, in empirical work, from the assumption that individuals maximize expected utility where both utilities and probabilities are defined in objective terms. In addition to studies already cited, indicating that the utility of money is nonlinear, experiments show that subjects refuse to maximize expected (objective) utility even where the stakes are clear and the objective probabilities stated (see Feldman, 1959, including references; Edwards, 1953; and others). Thus, it has been necessary to generalize the meaning of expected utility to develop an empirically valid theory incorporating the basic assumption of utility maximization.

Unfortunately, it is almost impossible to test the resulting psychological theory. If the monotonicity assumption is dropped, for example, then an individual may prefer less money to more. The empirical content of the hypothesis of rationality is diluted to some very weak requirements that the subject, when confronted with a whole sequence of choices, behave consistently, so that his subjective utilities and his subjective probabilities can be induced from his actual behavior. If a certain amount of inconsistency is actually observed, this may be interpreted as refuting the hypothesis of rationality, or alternatively, as providing evidence that during the sequence of trials the subject's preferences or his assessments of probabilities underwent change. Utilities and probabilities can be estimated only if they remain invariant, an assumption that is implausible in situations of any complexity.

Requirements of calculation

The topic of cognition will be discussed at some length in a later section of this chapter. It is necessary to comment at this point, however, on the implications of the assumption of rationality for the cognitive capacities of the decision maker. Trying to maximize expected utility, whether in the psychological or economic sense, would place an enormous burden on the limited computing power of a human being. In a complex situation, it would require that the individual be aware of *all* the possible alternatives, and assess the value of each possible outcome associated with each of them as well as the probabilities of the various outcomes. Consider, for example, the decision of an incipient college graduate who has job possibilities with, say, 400 firms, and might eventually obtain any one of a hundred positions in each. It is unreasonable to think that he can assess all the alternatives and probabilities involved and then proceed to maximize his expected utility by picking the "best" job.

The assumption of cognitive rationality at this level was not explicitly stated in the classical theories. It is associated with relatively recent developments in psychology and economics, but is inadequate either for explaining behavior or for deriving testable hypotheses, except possibly in experiments involving the simplest individual choice decisions. It is possible to design experiments in which the alternatives are arbitrarily limited and the computational requirements minimal. It is not, however, possible to assume that the complex problems an individual faces in everyday affairs fit this neat pattern.

Rather, it is reasonable to assume that an individual adopts a behavior pattern which requires neither complex computation nor knowledge of all the alternatives. A construct like the utility function is needed to explain choice of the "best" alternative. If the individual is merely looking for a "good" alternative, a theory of his choice can be constructed that dispenses entirely with a utility scale (Simon, 1955). In this "satisficing" theory of behavior, the individual examines the alternatives available to him, and if a subset of these is perceived as satisfactory, he selects one of them (presumably the best of the subset, though this is not necessary for the theory) and proceeds to act. If none of the alternatives is perceived as satisfactory, he institutes "search" behavior which ceases when a satisfactory alternative is found. The definition of "satisfactory" determines the aspiration level. Both aspiration-level theory and experiments predict this kind of behavior. If search does not produce better alternatives, the aspiration level will decline, so that some alternative, possibly a previously rejected one, will now be "satisfactory" and will be selected. There may also be other mechanisms to terminate the search process; for example, a decision may be reached after some specified time period.

This theory of behavior can be tested in complex situations. Since much of the evidence which exists in support of the theory has been collected in the context of management decision making, we shall defer presenting it to later sections where we discuss entrepreneurial motivation. The point we wish to stress here is that the theory requires neither omniscience on the part of the individual nor superhuman computational capabilities, but defines a process by which decisions can actually be made.

Quasi-rational models of behavior

In recent years, attempts have been made to reconcile the complete cognitive rationality implied by utility theory with the bounded rationality implied by satisficing theory. One approach to such a reconciliation focuses on the individual's search behavior, on how he allocates his effort among the many needs and goals that concern him. The problem can then be formulated of allocating effort *optimally* in order to achieve all goals *satisfactorily*. The theory assumes that satisfactory levels of goal attainment are defined, and introduces a reward function, dependent on the goal attainments, that is to be maximized. In order to have a convenient label for the behavior described by this combined approach, we shall call it "quasi-rational."

In quasi-rational behavior, the optimization procedure provides a unique solution to the effort-allocation problem (Charnes and Stedry, 1964a), and thus predicts the amount of search effort that will be allocated to each goal. The search itself will be a satisficing process of finding, within the search time allotted, an alternative that attains the goal satisfactorily (Charnes and Stedry, 1966b). It has been demonstrated that, for many situations, heuristic solution methods will find the optimal effort-allocation plan using calculations within the scope of human computational ability, and compatible with a theory of bounded rationality (Charnes and Stedry, 1964b). Some data are now available from a field experiment (Stedry and Kay, 1966) showing actual behavior that conforms closely to the quasi-rational model.

THE ECONOMIST'S INTEREST IN UTILITY

Having explored the various notions of utility currently prevalent in both psychology and economics, we now return to the basic interest of the macroeconomist in utility theory. At the present time, neither "subjective utility" nor "subjective probability" can be used operationally for macroeconomic predictions or prescriptions. Nor has the work on quasi-rational behavior developed to the point where aggregation is possible or even attempted. Essentially, the macroeconomist is left with what he has had for half a century—a tight, readily workable concept of consumer behavior whose properties lend themselves readily to deductive predictions in the large.

The macroeconomist is ordinarily rather uninterested in detailed information about the shapes of consumers' utility functions. Perhaps this is both justified and understandable in view of the fact that there seems to be little agreement among either psychologists or economists on what the shape of this function should be. Rather, the macroeconomist uses, by and large, the theory of consumer behavior that has existed for a couple of centuries: that the consumer is rational in a rather restricted sense, that he optimizes his spending in such a way as to maximize his utility, given his income, and that, in general, he behaves as a "rational man." For purposes of economic prediction it is only necessary that the theory, deduced from somewhat crude notions of rationality, provide acceptable empirical hypotheses for testing. If these can be validated, the niceties of understanding the underlying phenomena may be irrelevant. Error is committed only when the empirical fits are cited as evidence for the validity of the underlying assumptions. The aspects of consumer behavior, treated in the large, which the macroeconomist is actually concerned with are discussed in the following paragraphs.

CONSUMER RATIONALITY

An important application of economic theory to policy is to determine under what circumstances economic mechanisms allocate resources efficiently. This question is the main focus of the branch of economic theory known as welfare economics. The important postulate, used in virtually all the literature of welfare economics, is that consumers are rational—that consumers maximize utility, that they attempt to allocate their incomes so as to purchase, from all possible collections of commodities, the basket that will give them the greatest satisfaction. This assumption provides a deductive basis for macroeconomic theory whose convenience and consistency cannot be questioned.

Whether individual consumers are literally rational in this sense is not important. The overall question of interest to the macroeconomist is whether the assumptions of consumer rationality, however tentative in view of the empirical evidence to the contrary, provide an adequate mechanism for predicting behavior in the large.

Elasticity of demand

In economics, the consumer enters the market through his demand schedule, the schedule of quantities of a commodity he will buy at various prices. The summation of these quantities for all consumers gives the market demand schedule. For many applications, it must be assumed that the market demand schedule has a negative slope, that the quantity demanded decreases as price increases. For other purposes, it may be necessary to know the elasticity of demand, that is, how sensitively the quantity demanded depends on price. The tendency, even in these matters, is to deal in generalities; only occasionally is the economist concerned with the numerical measurement of the elasticities of demand for specific commodities.

Many attempts have been made to derive certain characteristics of the demand schedule by deductive reasoning from the theory of consumer choice. However, where it is necessary to measure the elasticity of demand numerically, the usual procedure is to infer the elasticity from direct measurements of quantities purchased in the market at various prices. Hence, the empirical study of demand has rested much more on the direct accumulation and analysis of data than on inferences from underlying psychological principles (Schultz, 1938).

Saving and spending

In the modern, post-Keynesian theory of the business cycle, the consumer's decision as to what proportion of his income he will spend and what proportion he will save is of very great importance. The number of cents he will spend out of each dollar of income at the "marginal" decision is the "marginal propensity to consume" of Keynes. In certain versions of Keynesian theory, an additional crucial assumption is made: that spending increases less than proportionately as income increases. Considerable effort has been devoted, over the past two decades, to testing this assumption (Katona, 1951, Chapters 7 and 8).

On the one hand, there have been attempts to measure spending and saving behavior by obtaining empirical data from consumers or analyzing secondary data from the economy. On the other hand, there have been attempts to deduce the spending and saving behavior of the consumer from the theory of rational consumer choice. The first course involves no particular framework of theory and, while it may yield data of interest to psychologists, it has borrowed little or nothing from psychology.

The second course, the deduction of the theory of saving from the theory of consumer choice, has also evolved almost independently of work in psychology. It illustrates the characteristic approach of the economist to individual behavior and the reason why he can formulate his assumptions with so little dependence on empirical observation (even though he may use aggregative data to test the consequences derived from his assumptions).

Modigliani and Brumberg (1954) assumed that the only motive for saving is retirement income and that the consumer adjusts his saving to give him a level annual expenditure over his lifetime. During periods of high income, he saves; during periods of low or no income, he dissaves. These are plausible assumptions, at least as approximations, and it is their introspective plausibility that the economist takes as his justification for adopting them. From these assumptions, together with assumptions as to how income expectations are formed and data on length of life and length of adult earning period, numerical estimates can be made of the fraction of total income that will be saved; that is to say, the saving-consumption function can be deduced from these assumptions. Up to the present time, the model has held up fairly well in explaining the actually observed data on consumer expenditure and savings.

Similar approaches have been used by economists to explain the fact (or supposed fact) that some individuals both gamble in lotteries and buy insurance (Luce and Suppes, 1965, p. 393). The explanation, like that outlined above, consists in showing that circumstances exist (that is, can be postulated) under which the behavior in question *would be* rational behavior for a consumer bent on maximizing his utility. It is quite uncharacteristic of the economic theorist to test his explanation further by studying the consumer's attitudes or subjecting him to experimental situations. On the other hand, the psychological assumptions that underlie theories of this kind are not difficult to identify, and there are many possibilities here for direct testing by psychologists of the economic models.

Expectations

The third aspect of the consumer's behavior in which the macroeconomist has substantial interest is the formation of expectations. (Expectations really belong to the cognitive rather than the motivational sphere, but it is convenient to discuss them here to round out our picture of contemporary research. For a panorama of recent approaches to the theory of expectations, see Bowman, 1958.) In a world of uncertainty, a theory cannot make a consumer's expenditure depend on future income, but only on *expectations* of future income. Hence, the predictions of the theory will depend on assumptions about the formation of expectations.

Studies have been made of how both consumers and businessmen form expectations. We will have more to say in the next section about businessmen's expectations, but a comment is relevant here before we turn, again, to consumers' income. Modigliani and Sauerlender (1955) have shown that expectations involving the statements of businessmen, their intentions, and other factors presumed to be relevant to actual decisions were poorer predictors of the actual behavior than were "naive" models which simply assumed that "next year" and "this year" would be the same or that "next year" could be approximated by adding this year's figures with the difference between this year's and last year's data. This does not, of course, preclude the possibility of basing forecasts on business expectations; it merely serves as an indication that such expectations must be tempered by some form of correction to compensate for the errors usually found in such forecasts.

Returning to the area of consumer motivation, a similar skepticism may be presumed. Though, over the past decade, considerable data have been accumulated on consumers' plans and expectations from the Survey of Consumer Finances conducted for the Board of Governors of the Federal Reserve System by the Survey Research Center of the University of Michigan (Bowman, 1958; Katona, 1951, Chapter 5), these statements are subject to the same qualifications as those observed in Modigliani and Sauerlender (1955). It is not clear that actual consumer behavior could not be predicted as well by simple extrapolation. However, these and similar data obtained by others begin to inform us to what extent consumers plan their expenditures in advance and for what kinds of purchases; what expectations they hold about their own income; and how well the expenditure plans predict actual behavior. It can hardly be said that these data have been linked with psychological generalizations from other areas of behavior; at present, they simply stand as brute facts.

Marketing

Thus far we have left out of account the study of consumer behavior that has been carried out for its practical utility to the business firm, namely, market research. The literature on selling and advertising has generally had a closer tie to psychology than has the economic literature on consumer demand. There have been attempts to apply principles of motivation and learning to the design of effective selling procedures.

The validity of general psychological principles applied to marketing behavior has had limited empirical test. There have been, for example, a number of controlled experiments comparing the relative effectiveness of different advertising copy or methods. An interesting development of the past few years has been the application of projective techniques to the study of consumer motivation. An early study of this sort, carried out by Mason Haire, showed that housewives had a quite different perception of a woman (otherwise unidentified) who bought instant coffee than of a woman who bought ground coffee.

Many of the data of market research do not see the light of day, since they are gathered and analyzed for proprietary purposes. Hence, in spite of the great amount of discussion in the marketing field concerning "motivation research" and other applications of psychology to marketing, the number of good empirical studies in the literature is not large.

An important study, which may be a prototype of research to come on innovation and consumer adoption of new commodities, was carried out by the Bureau of Applied Social Research at Columbia University to determine the influence processes involved in the adoption of a new antibiotic by physicians (Coleman, Katz, and Menzel, 1957). While this study will hardly fit within the traditional static framework of utility theory, it points the way to possible approaches to the dynamics of consumer choice.

SUMMARY: CONSUMER MOTIVATION

Macroeconomics does not require, for most purposes, a detailed theory of consumer choice. The utility function has been a central theoretical construct in this area, but only a limited number of features of the function are required for the macro theories derived from it. Much of the work on consumer demand is independent of the concept of utility entirely, and deals with commodities and money in a form which renders the concept irrelevant. What is apparent, in either case, is that the macro theories have been derived from those micro theories which readily lend themselves to an inductive process, that is, those theories whose variables and functions are sharply defined and sufficiently unambiguous that they may be treated as axioms in an orderly proof.

The predisposition of economists to deduce behavior from assumptions of rationality and other "plausible" assumptions about behavior is thus readily explicable. The interaction between economics and psychology has been limited (in large part, it would seem) by the fact that, when one introduces complexities into the behavioral pattern without adequate specificity, testable macroeconomic propositions can no longer be derived. The lack of predictability implied in the loose definitions of utility, for example, associated with subjective utilities and probabilities that bear no resemblance to their objective counterparts, makes prediction on an aggregative level virtually impossible.

The greatest potentialities for work of mutual value to the two disciplines would thus appear to lie in (1) endeavoring to find a workable behavioral approach to utility theory which would be amenable to aggregation; (2) exploring behavior in conflict situations to develop predictability as good as that which can be obtained from the axioms underlying the economic theory of games; (3) extending the study of the actual spending-saving behavior of consumers and the formation of consumer expectations; (4) extending the study of consumer market behavior in the large (in numbers of individuals), but in relation to individual products and specific marketing techniques; and (5) extending the theories of quasi-rational and satisficing behavior as possible substitutes for the axioms of rationality.

MOTIVATION: THE ENTREPRENEUR

In economic theory, the entrepreneur is the man who holds the residual equity in the business firm. After all the other factors of production, including labor and an imputed rent or interest rate on his invested capital, have been paid, his share is the remainder, be it large or small. Most important for the theory, he is the man who controls the decision variables of the basic productive unit, the firm.

Just as the central assumption about consumption is that the consumer strives to maximize his utility, so the central assumption about production is that the entrepreneur strives to maximize his residual share, his profit (Papandreou, 1952, pp. 205–210). But the assumption of profit maximization is even more essential to the validity of classical economic theory than the assumption of utility maximization; hence, the attack upon and the defense of classical theory have tended to focus on the former postulate.

The hypothesis that the entrepreneur seeks to maximize his profit is a simple corollary to the general postulate of economic rationality. Attacks on the hypothesis have been frequent, and they range over many issues (Katona, 1951, Chapter 9; Papandreou, 1952):

1.   The theory leaves ambiguous whether short-run or long-run profit is to be maximized. If long-run profit is the criterion, then it is extremely difficult, because of the uncertainty in long-run consequences of action, to determine what course of action maximizes profit or to test whether a particular firm is in fact using the criterion. This is a serious difficulty for both descriptive and normative microeconomics.

2.   The entrepreneur may obtain all kinds of "psychic income" from the firm, quite apart from monetary rewards. If he is to maximize his utility, then he will sometimes balance a loss of profits against an increase in psychic income. For example,

the high return from ownership of slum property is sometimes attributed to the negative psychic income attached to such ownership. But if we admit psychic income into the picture, the criterion of profit maximization loses all its definiteness and becomes identical with (and as ambiguous as) utility maximization.

3.   The entrepreneur may not care to maximize, but may simply want to earn a return that he regards as "satisfactory." By sophistry and an adept use of the concept of psychic income, the notion of seeking a satisfactory return can be translated into utility maximization, but not in any operational way. As we shall see, the notion of seeking "satisfactory" levels of profits or sales is more meaningfully related to the psychological concept of aspiration levels than is any notion of maximization.

4.   Under modern conditions, the equity owners and the active managers of an enterprise are usually separate and distinct groups of persons—the managers are really "labor" and not "entrepreneurs." Under these circumstances, there is no reason to postulate an identity of interests between entrepreneurs and managers or to assume that the latter are motivated to maximize profits.

5.   In the actual payment systems in operation in firms, the rewards to the managers who are the actual decision makers are usually determined by procedures which are at variance with, if not detrimental to, profit maximization.

All these objections concern motivation; they assume, more or less, that the entrepreneur or the manager *could* aim at profit maximization if he wanted to. We shall see in the section on cognition that there are also serious cognitive questions as to the capacity of economic man to maximize profit, but we shall focus on questions of motivation for the moment.

Few data from psychology outside economics bear directly on the issues at hand. There have been some investigations, however, that are worth mentioning. These fall in two categories: (1) attempts to determine the relative importance of economic and noneconomic motivation and (2) studies of the dynamics of aspiration levels.

In addition to these psychological studies, there have been a number of inquiries directed specifically at these economic issues and carried out primarily by economists. Among these are studies of the formation of expectations by managers and business firms and studies of the making of particular classes of business decisions (pricing decisions, investment decisions, etc.). We shall consider each of these four classes of investigations, the two "psychological" and the two "economic," in turn. In a final part of this section, we shall discuss the identity and conflict of interest between owners and managers.

ECONOMIC AND NONECONOMIC MOTIVATION

The past 20 years have seen a strong reaffirmation of the importance of noneconomic as against economic motivation, for employees as well as managers and entrepreneurs. This is one of the central points—certainly one of the most widely quoted—of Barnard's *The Functions of the Executive* (1938). It was earlier emphasized by Veblen and other institutionalists.

It is hard to determine the relative role of noneconomic and economic motivations because we do not have a really satisfactory metric for comparing them. We are confronted again with the task of constructing a utility function in which monetary gain is one dimension in the commodity space and status, prestige, power, and all the other things that men are supposed to work for are the other dimensions. Since no one has made the measurements needed to establish the shape of this function, the usual statements about the relative importance of the various motivations are nonoperational. They have about the same semantic status as the assertion, "It is later than you think."

The situation is not so hopeless if we reject the economists' assumptions, which are implicit above, that there must be some marginal rate of substitution between profit and other goals and that "measuring the importance of the profit motive" is synonymous with measuring this *a priori* marginal rate of substitution. From an institutionalist point of view, it would be equally satisfactory if we could simply describe the situations where profit would be sacrificed for other goals. Unfortunately, even this descriptive task has not been carried out in any comprehensive fashion. About the best we can say is that enough illustrations of response to other motivations have been collected to rule out the hypothesis that profit maximization (even long-run profit maximization) is an all-encompassing goal of business management. A measure of the "importance" of the deviations remains to be constructed.

SATISFICING VERSUS MAXIMIZING

The notion of "satiation" plays no role in classical economic theory. However, in the treatment of motivation in psychology, this concept enters rather prominently. First, there is the widely accepted idea that motivation to act stems from *drives,* and that action terminates when the drive is satisfied. Second, there is the idea that the conditions for satisfaction of a drive are not necessarily fixed, but may be specified by an aspiration level that adjusts itself on the basis of experience (Diggory, 1935; Festinger, 1942; Gardner, 1940; Lewin *et al.,* 1944; Siegel, 1957; Simon, 1955; Stedry, 1960, 1964).

The prevalent psychological treatments of motivation, then, hypothesize that drive satisfaction is an all-or-none phenomenon, but that the boundary between the satisfied and unsatisfied states (the level of aspiration) is variable. If we apply this point of view to the business firm, we would expect its goals to be stated, not in terms of maximizing profit, but in terms of reaching a certain level or rate of profit, holding a certain share of the market, a certain level of sales, or the like (Cyert and March, 1962; Katona, 1951, Chapter 9). There is considerable empirical evidence—most of it, unfortunately, of an anecdotal kind—that supports this interpretation of the goals of the business firm (Early, 1956).

Here is one of the most interesting areas of relationship between economics and psychology. First, it does not seem unfeasible to test whether business behavior is governed by maximizing or by satisficing criteria. Second, the economic data required to choose between these hypotheses would extend previous theorizing about aspiration levels to a new area of human behavior.

It has sometimes been argued that the distinction between satisficing and maximizing behavior is not important for economic theory. In the first place, the psychological evidence shows that aspirations tend to adjust to the attainable. Hence, in the long run, the argument goes, the level of aspiration and the attainable maximum will be very close together.

A second argument is that, even if some firms behaved in the manner of the aspiration-level hypothesis, they would gradually lose out to the maximizing firms, which would make larger profits and grow more rapidly than the others (Alchian, 1950).

Both of these arguments assume that (1) firms know how to go about maximizing if they want to and (2) the economic environment of firms changes slowly enough that the long-run position of equilibrium will be approached. Both hypotheses are dubious, but their discussion will have to be postponed to a later section where cognitive matters will be considered in detail. If we retain a reasonable skepticism, at least until the evidence is in, toward arguments that lean heavily on long-run equilibrium, then the test of the aspiration-level hypothesis is of substantial interest to economic theory as well as to psychology.

BUSINESS EXPECTATIONS

Business expectations, like consumer expectations, are variables of crucial importance to macroeconomics and, unlike most other psychological concepts, cannot be exorcised from the economic model by assumptions of rationality. A considerable part of business-cycle theory hinges on postulates, most of them constructed in the comfort of armchairs, about the way in which business expectations are formed and how they change under changing environmental circumstances. (For an exploration of relations between business forecasting and partial reinforcement situations, see Feldman, 1959; Cyert, March, and Starbuck, 1961.)

Business expectations are currently a very active object of economic research, and several periodic surveys are now being conducted of business forecasts of business conditions (Katona, 1951, Chapters 9 through 13). Unfortunately, for reasons that are not yet fully understood, forecasts of the future behavior of businessmen that rely on the statements of businessmen as to their future plans are frequently inaccurate. In an unpublished study conducted by one of the authors, expected investment gleaned from interviews of executives published monthly by the *Survey of Current Business* was compared with actual investment for the corresponding periods published in the same journal. In the 48-month period studied (1957–1960), which included both "good" and "bad" years, the businessmen's investment plans exceeded the actual investment in 46 out of 48 of the months examined.

We need not, however, rely on such casual evidence. As mentioned previously, Modigliani and Sauerlender (1955) have shown that the "railroad shippers' forecasts" of expected carloadings could be improved simply by assuming that last year's actual shippings would be equal to this year's. The *Fortune* forecasts of business activity were better than these particular naive forecasts. But assuming that next year's activity would equal last year's activity plus the differential between last year's activity and that of the previous year gave better predictions than the *Fortune* forecasts. When such naive economic models are capable of besting the informed judgment of businessmen, the inability of businessmen to forecast expected profit— a necessary concomitant of the assumption that they should be able to maximize it —buttresses the argument that it would be impossible for entrepreneurs to maximize expected profit even if they so desired.

While not dismissing businessmen's own forecasts as relevant data, the evidence cited above tends to question the validity of the forecasts, without some qualification, at least to the point of allowing for optimistic bias. This evidence becomes extremely significant when one considers the high likelihood that businessmen's expectations become *a priori* self-fulfilling prophecies; other businessmen look at them. If, for example, a downturn is expected by the businessmen polled, other businessmen are likely to take this as an indication that they, too, should cut down on capital expenditures, expansion plans, etc.

The actual decision making of businessmen seems, therefore, to deserve considerable study. While clearly not independent of forecasts, much business decision making appears to be based on considerations quite removed from forecasts. Therefore, we shall turn our attention to actual studies of business decision making in the context of the ongoing operations of business firms.

STUDIES OF BUSINESS DECISIONS

We commented earlier on the significance of Keynesian economic theory for the empirical study of consumer behavior. The controversy over the validity of the Keynesian formulation has had a similar impact on the study of business behavior. One of the heretical doctrines of Keynes was that the amount of investment was nearly independent of the rate of interest. Another aspect of Keynesian theory dealt with liquidity preference, that is, the desire to hold cash rather than securities as interest rates diminish. Liquidity preference was the central issue, among economic theorists, in the monetary theory controversy of the late 1940's. A major problem in that controversy was to decide which interest rate was most appropriate for estimating the liquidity-preference function. A comprehensive treatment of such studies up to 1950 will be found in Hayes (1950). More recently, Tobin (1947) and Stedry (1959) have dealt with this problem, using short-term interest rates with differing formulations of other factors affecting liquidity preference.

The extent of liquidity preference depends heavily on the desire of firms to hold cash. Recent theory and research on policies with respect to cash holding has focused on the possibility of a "liquidity trap," that is, limitations on minimum and maximum cash holdings that might set both lower and upper bounds on interest rates. This hypothesis is supported on the behavioral level in studies conducted by Chambers and Charnes (1961) and Clarkson (1962) of actual institutions that provide mechanisms for the liquidity of firms.

Stemming from a pioneering study by Hall and Hitch (1939), there have also been a number of attempts to determine whether or not businessmen actually use marginalist principles in pricing their products. (Under classical assumptions, profits will be maximized if the quantity produced is set so that the cost of producing one more unit would just equal the increase in revenue from selling the additional product.) Different investigators have returned from the field with quite differing conclusions. Hall and Hitch (1939) found average costs to be more significant in determining prices than marginal costs, while Early (1956) found, by questionnaire, that businessmen claim to make extensive use of marginalist procedures. The use of average costs can easily be traced to standard works in accounting (Bennett, 1930; Cadmus and Child, 1953; Kohler, 1957).

In the broader area of management decision making in general, Cyert, Dill, and March (1958) reported observations of management decision-making behavior that are quite remote from either marginal or average costing. Cyert and March (1956) reported pricing decisions that are clearly made by programmed decision rules whose relation to marginalist principles of economic behavior are, at best, remote.

Many other studies might be cited which indicate that firms do not, in fact, behave as the classical economic theory of entrepreneurship would predict. Of particular interest is the work of Cooper (1951), who pointed out the discrepancy between the assumptions of classical theory and the actual measurement tools available to business firms for measuring the activities of the firm's participants. The classical theory assumes that the entrepreneur has all his factors of production under complete control; they are cooperative and automatically assure the entrepreneur of cooperation in his desire for profit maximization. Considering the often antagonistic aims of labor and management (which will be dealt with more fully below), the assumption of cooperation breaks down and a more appropriate notion of factor rivalry (dealt with by Cooper, 1951) becomes relevant. We shall treat this problem in considerable detail in the following sections of this chapter.

CONFLICT OF INTEREST

The actual or potential conflict of interest between owner and hired manager has been considered at length in the economics literature (Papandreou, 1952) and has, in fact, supplied the impetus for much of the development in accounting practice (Bennett, 1930; Cadmus and Child, 1953; Kohler, 1957) designed to "protect" the absentee owner from mismanagement of funds by his employees, at both managerial and lower levels in the hierarchy.

Three questions are involved:

1. *Is the reward that the top management of modern industrial firms actually receives closely related to the effects of their actions on the firm's profits?*

2. *Insofar as the correlation between management rewards and company profits is imperfect, what do members of top management in fact maximize or, alternatively, what are their goals for the firm and themselves?*

3. *If, in fact, a conflict of interest exists between the theoretical entrepreneur (or an actual group of stockholders who represent his legal equivalent in the contemporary corporation) and top management, what can or should be done about it?*

Gordon (1945) was able to show pretty conclusively that the correlation between management rewards and company profits is relatively low. On the second point, the evidence is less clear; it takes us back to some of our earlier questions about measuring the relative strengths of different motivations where there is a conflict of interest. A formal comparison between the classical theory of the firm and organizational theories that come out of behavioral science, such as those of Barnard (1938) and Simon (1947), shows that they differ precisely at this point. Both the economic theories and the organizational theories of the firm assume that the firm will adopt a *viable* course of action, a course that will enable it to satisfy its various groups of participants (customers, investors, employees, suppliers) so that they will continue to participate. In general, any such course of action yields a *surplus*, that is, income over and above that needed for distribution to the participants. Cyert, Dill, and March (1958) have provided empirical evidence that a viable course of action is aimed at producing an *adequate* surplus for the satisfaction of participants, a motive which has been formalized in Williamson (1964). The organizational theories leave indeterminate whether (1) the managers will try to maximize this surplus or (2) all of it will be captured by the entrepreneur. The classical theory of the firm takes a definite stand on both points, asserting that the firm will be conducted in such a way as to maximize the surplus and that the surplus will go to the entrepreneur (Simon, 1952).

However inconclusive and anecdotal the evidence, most observers are persuaded that the organizational theory provides a more realistic picture of the behavior of large corporations than does the classical theory. The former is also consistent with a satisficing theory of the firm's decision making, while the latter is not.

Related to both the second and third points is the question whether or not the entrepreneur actually wishes the firm to maximize profits. Under the assumptions of the classical theory, he is a single individual who expects maximal profit because he is taking risk. The neoclassical theory, in general, accepts the notion that the entrepreneur is in fact a collection of investors whose interests are to select a portfolio which maximizes their return subject to some form of discounting for risk. The departure from the classical theory is noteworthy in that the *investor* replaces the entrepreneur as both owner and supplier of capital for the firm; furthermore, the investor (or, perhaps more aptly, portfolio selector) shares in a variety of ways in the profit and risk, and provides, via the purchase of bonds, loans to the same or other entrepreneurs.

Attempts have been made to define the portfolio selector as a maximizer of return subject to a constraint on risk. Markowitz (1959), for example, defined risk in terms of variance of returns. Empirical studies show that the portfolios actually selected by sophisticated investors do not fit this pattern. Chambers and Charnes (1961) showed that the loan portfolios of a bank are much more conservative than any maximization of return assumption could explain; Farrar (1962) found that the portfolios of mutual funds frequently departed from the maximum return that could be obtained at a given risk level.

This finding may result, in part, from errors in measurement, since, as has been pointed out by Solomon (1966), the relationship between the "true" rate of return assumed by economists and the accounting rates of return used by them in empirical studies rarely coincide. Though aggregated data have provided reasonable confirmation of empirical hypotheses derived from both theories, the controversy between the theories of Modigliani and Miller (1958) and Gordon (1962) has shown how difficult it is to define who this new variety of entrepreneur actually is or what precisely he desires from his portfolio. A study by Clarkson (1962), cited above, indicates that the behavior of a sophisticated investor—once again a trust officer selecting portfolios for his clients—can be simulated by a set of decision rules only remotely related to a theory of return maximization. Rather, the observed behavior fits the notion that the investor was seeking an adequate rate of return with some reasonable probability.

Viewing the investor as an individual seeking an adequate return on his investment, that is, a satisficer, raises real questions as to the extent of the conflict of interest between investor and management. Stability of management, company prestige, regular payment of dividends, and avoidance of stockholder discontent may well be joint goals of management and investor. To attain these goals may call for the design of appropriate subgoals for subunits within the organization (Charnes and Stedry, 1966a).

It is difficult to determine, in the modern widely held corporation, whose entrepreneurial profit is being maximized. In neoclassical economic theory, maximization of "expected long-run profit" is postulated and frequently defined as "maximization of discounted expected cash flows." It is difficult to translate these terms into criteria for actual management decision making in some basic areas, for example, in funds for capital expenditures (Weingartner, 1963). Going further, the particular discount rate to be used may differ considerably from stockholder to stockholder so that, even if a true discount rate could be determined for the firm, it would not be relevant to the "partial holder of entrepreneurship" in most cases.

Consider, for example, the elderly stockholder with no estate motive, compared with one with an estate motive. The former would probably desire high present profits and high dividend payout, and would thus prefer that the firm return to the stockholder all amounts which could not justify investment at a very high rate of return. The latter, however, would prefer that the firm reinvest its profits, implying decision making based on a lower discount rate for the firm.

In view of the difficulty of defining the motives of the contemporary entre-preneur, however inconclusive and anecdotal other evidence may be, most observers are persuaded that organization theory provides a more realistic basis for explaining the behavior of large corporations than does classical economic theory. The former is also consistent with a satisficing theory of the firm's decision making, while the latter is not.

ROLE STRUCTURES

Perhaps one of the most interesting psychological or sociological aspects of this topic is its connection with role theory. The conclusions of classical economics about the behavior of the firm can be valid in a world in which there is considerable divorce of management from ownership only if the role of the owner can be defined, and the members of management are willing to play the role of profit-maximizing entrepreneurs in the face of the difficulties of definition that have been enumerated. A thorough treatment of role structures in an economic context will be found in Smelser (1963).

On the other hand, if the classical conclusions are wrong, then it becomes an empirical question to determine what premises the members of management do, in fact, employ in their decision making. Do they identify with the interests of some particular group of participants (for example, investors), or do they perceive them-selves as arbiters seeking to make a "fair" and acceptable division of the firm's surplus among its various participants? Again, the answers will have to come out of continu-ing empirical study of the firm's behavior.

SUMMARY: ENTREPRENEURIAL MOTIVATION

Over the past 20 years the motivational assertions embedded in the classical theory of the firm have been widely challenged. The challenge has stemmed partly from theory, and partly from a substantial body of data that is far from consistent with the classical theory. First, there has been emphasis on the noneconomic, as contrasted with the economic, motivations of the entrepreneur. Second, there has been argument that firms and individual persons do not maximize, but satisfice. Third, data on actual decision-making processes in firms have failed to confirm the universality or even the prevalence of marginalist principles of choice. Fourth, data on management and ownership have shown that, in large segments of modern business, those who hold active managerial control have no great personal economic inducement to maximize profits.

There has been some resistance among economists to accepting the cogency of the evidence for these assertions—and even more resistance to admitting their relevance to normative macroeconomics if they are true. Edward S. Mason (1952), for example, in commenting on Papandreou's essay, "Some Basic Problems in the Theory of the Firm" (Papandreou, 1952, pp. 221–222), stated his defense as follows: "The writer of this critique must confess a lack of confidence in the marked superiority, *for purposes of economic analysis,* of this newer concept of the firm over the older conception of the entrepreneur." The italics are Professor Mason's, and the italicized phrase can be translated—we think without violence—as "for purposes of normative macroeconomics."

The matters discussed in these paragraphs are relevant for business-cycle theory largely for understanding how businessmen form their expectations and how these expectations affect their investment and pricing decisions. This is perhaps the weakest point in the empirical verification of business-cycle theories, and a point at which much ongoing empirical work is directed.

The theory of the firm is relevant also for welfare economics, for determining under what circumstances the behavior of the firm will lead to efficient allocation of resources. The departure of the firm's behavior from the classical model vitiates all the conclusions about resource allocation that are derivable from that model when perfect competition is assumed. Hence, the indifference of Professor Mason (and numerous other economists) is justified only if the firm's behavior turns out to be about the same in the newer theories as in the old ones. There is no reason so far for supposing that this will be so.

There are other questions of long-run economic policy which have been only slightly investigated in economics and for which an accurate understanding of motivation in the business firm may well have even more important implications than any mentioned thus far. The separation of ownership from control may well affect the risk-taking behavior of the firm. Most commentators on this point—solid evidence is almost completely lacking—assume that "business bureaucrats" will be more conservative in their attitudes toward risk and innovation than entrepreneur-owners. There is no very solid basis in psychological theory for making a definite prediction on this point, and the question can be answered only through empirical work.

MOTIVATION: LABOR

More can be said about the relations of economics and psychology in the area of labor relations than in the two areas previously discussed. By the same token, what has to be said is already well known to the specialists in labor relations, who have been less respectful of disciplinary boundaries than most of their colleagues in psychology and economics. We shall try here to steer a middle course. We shall not attempt a full exposition of the role of economics, psychology, and sociology in labor economics and industrial relations, but point instead to a few key issues.

The motivation of the employee can be and has been approached from the classical standpoint as a pure question of "labor economics." At the other extreme, the same topic can be and has been approached as a pure question of the psychology of motivation. The field of labor economics and industrial relations is today an area of active communication—though not always complete agreement—for economists, psychologists, and sociologists (Coleman, 1955).

The central issues are very similar to those considered in the two previous sections. We are interested in the job-taking and job-leaving behaviors of the employee, in his behavior while employed on the job, and in his activity in and through unions. Numerous predictions can be made about all these segments of behavior if we make the classical assumptions about economic rationality. The classical theory, for example, predicts movement from one job to another in terms of wage-rate differentials, and predicts the absence in equilibrium of differentials in wages for comparable jobs. The classical theory also permits predictions as to how employees will respond to wage incentive schemes, and most of the theorizing about piece rates in the early scientific management movement was thoroughly consistent with classical economic theory.

The empirical evidence, on the other hand, only partly supports these classical predictions. Geographical movements of the labor force, for example, are responsive to many forces other than wage differentials, though the influence of the latter, as one of several factors, is clearly demonstrable. In the matter of wage incentive schemes, employee responses have been shown to be far more complicated and dependent on far more complex relations than can be accounted for by a simple economic calculus.

A recent study by Nealey (1964) has attempted to establish a relation between money and various employee benefits, both tangible and intangible, via a questionnaire approach which attempts to establish tradeoffs between incremental hourly pay and improvements in other areas. This study has been plagued with the problems we have noted above in attempts to combine psychological and economic constructs in providing a unidimensional utility scale—for example, intransitivity of choices. Again, it would appear, though the evidence is scanty, that an employee desires a satisfactory level of pay, satisfactory working conditions, and so on, and that tradeoffs between the economic variables and the noneconomic concomitants of employment are difficult to measure even "at the margin."

Unfortunately, we have as a substitute for the classical model only a mass of empirical specifics that do not permit sharp predictions beyond the particular phenomena to which the data themselves relate. An attempt to combine these specifics into a cogent whole has been provided by Vroom (1964), but he, too, recognizes the absence of a cohesive body of theory to provide a framework within which the empirical results may be analyzed for prediction and understanding. Thus, the situation remains much the same as that described in March and Simon (1958); the motivation of labor is in a state of theoretical development similar to that of the areas of consumer and entrepreneurial motivation.

LABOR UNIONS

In discussing the employment relation, we cannot neglect labor unions. The effect of unions on the relation will be discussed in a different context in the next section, where we consider the topic of competition among the few. Again, we shall see that the existence of unions provides new reasons for lowering the walls between economics and the other behavioral sciences and for bringing social and political considerations to bear on an economic relationship.

In particular, we note the work of Fouraker and Siegel (1963), which generalizes to collective bargaining their earlier work (1960) in two-person or two-group bargaining situations conducted in the laboratory. This work combines the psychological notions of aspiration level and utility along the lines described earlier (Edwards, 1954; Siegel, 1957). The economic conditions of the 1930's, combined with the political structure whose evolution can also largely be traced to the Depression, have provided a legal framework within which collective bargaining can be treated as a major, if not *the* major, vehicle for negotiation between the firm and the worker. This set of events has been a major factor in altering the treatment of the laborer-firm relationship in both psychology and economics: the former can extrapolate two-group bargaining laboratory situations to collective bargaining; the latter can treat laborer-firm negotiations as a problem in oligopolistic rather than perfectly competitive market behavior.

THE VARIETIES OF LABOR

In the classical theory there is the entrepreneur, who manages, and labor, who does the work. We have discussed one aspect of this relation in connection with entrepreneurial motivation. A second aspect is relevant here. The "group leader," who performs a certain managerial role for three to 50 people, is in many plants, a member of the labor union. In some plants foremen and even their supervisors belong to the labor union. In others, engineers, time-study men, and their supervisors belong to a labor union, perhaps the same one as the "blue collar" workers. The precise line of demarcation between identification with management and identification with labor is frequently difficult to draw. Thus, if one considers identification a psychological variable, the line drawn in classical theory between labor and entrepreneur is difficult to interpret indeed. In the following discussion, therefore, we will use evidence drawn from studies of labor and their immediate supervisors with the assumption that supervisors identify with labor as often as with management.

THE AUTHORITY RELATION

One peculiar feature of the employment relation, which distinguishes it from most other economic arrangements and transactions, is this: the employee sells his "services" to the employer and then becomes a "factor of production" (Simon, 1951). Here the classical assumption of the separation of production behavior from consumption behavior is clearly open to question.

The economic model of the employee, once the employment bargain has been struck, is that of a passive and neutral agent of production who will accept the authority of the employer. A considerable body of psychological evidence shows that the behavior of employees typically departs from the model of passivity and neutrality in a number of ways (Homans, 1950; March and Simon, 1958, Chapters 3 and 4). Among the hypotheses that have been pretty well validated are these:

1. *The Hawthorne effect.* When special attention is given to a group of workers by management (say, by enlisting them in an experimental situation), production is likely to rise independently of changes in actual working conditions.

2. *The interaction hypothesis.* High morale and productivity in organizations are promoted if the employees have opportunities for interaction with each other. Con-

versely, when the work is organized in such a way as to discourage cooperation, teamwork, or social intercourse, low morale is likely to result.

3. *The participation hypothesis.* Significant changes in human behavior can be brought about rapidly only if the persons who are expected to change participate in deciding what the change shall be and how it shall be made.

4. *The cross-pressures hypothesis.* When the same individual has occasion for frequent and close contact with two or more groups that hold conflicting values and attitudes, he will find himself in internal personal conflict. The conflict is often evidenced by symptoms of frustration: withdrawal, aggressive behavior, and the like.

The Hawthorne studies are probably best summarized in Roethlisberger and Dickson (1939). A group of studies summarized by Likert (1961) provide insight into the relation between morale and productivity. Participation has been advocated by Leavitt (1958) and McGregor (1960), while the specific areas in which participation improves performance have been studied by Vroom (1960) and others (French, Israel, and As, 1960; French, Kay, and Meyer, 1966; Kay, Meyer, and French, 1965). The notion that authority and control are entirely antithetical to the workings of an organization has been advanced by Argyris (1964) and others (Bennis *et al.*, 1964). Finally, conflicting pressures have been shown to cause frustration (Maier, 1949), and have been investigated in terms of allocating effort (Charnes and Stedry, 1964b, 1966) and in a field study of actual behavior under the pressures of attaining difficult goals in one or more areas (Stedry and Kay, 1966). The cited studies represent only a subset of those available, though each contains a comprehensive bibliography pertaining to these topics.

In view of the prominence of phenomena like these in research data, and in the everyday practice of management as well, there is less tendency to apply the economic calculus to supervisory problems than to most other areas of economic behavior. On the other hand, however significant these phenomena may be for the practice of management, they do not appear to have important implications for macroeconomics. Or, to state the conclusion in a more precise way, if this revision of our picture of the employment relation has implications for public policy, these implications cannot be explored via the classical economic model for discussing welfare questions.

CONFLICT OF INTEREST: OLIGOPOLY

Economic theory avoids any assumption of common goals and parallel interests among the participants in the economic system. Through the authority relation, employees can agree to accept the goals of their employers as guides to behavior; apart from this, each consumer is assumed to maximize his personal utility, each producer his profit. (This does not rule out the possibility of nonselfish goals, for one person's pleasure may enter into another person's utility function; but since the utility functions are givens of economic analysis, their content is irrelevant to the theory.)

The conflict of interests creates no particular problems of theory so long as each participant in the system treats the other participants as parts of his given environment, and does not try to predict their behavior and anticipate it. But when this restriction is removed—when it is assumed that a seller takes into account the reactions of buyers to his actions—the precision of prediction of the classical theory vanishes. The only case where the classical theory can then be applied with complete safety is to situations of perfect competition, where the number of competitors is so large that each competitor may safely assume that the market price is a given which is not affected by his own actions. Note that we are not concerned here with the usual antimonopoly argument that competition is desirable from a welfare standpoint; what we are saying is that competition is an essential condition for unambiguous prediction of behavior from the classical assumptions of economic rationality.

The very assumptions of omniscient rationality that provide the basis for deductive prediction in economics when competition is present lead to ambiguity when they are applied to competition among the few. Awareness of this problem goes back a century to Augustin Cournot, but recognition of its fundamental character and sweeping consequences stems from von Neumann and Morgenstern's *The Theory of Games and Economic Behavior* (1944). The central difficulty in competition among the few is familiar to every bridge or poker player: rational play requires one to outguess one's opponents, but not to be outguessed by them—clearly not a consistent requirement, if it is applied to all the players.

Von Neumann and Morgenstern proposed a solution in the case of a game with two players and a zero-sum payoff, that is, a payoff in which one player would lose what the other won. In this case "omniscient" rationality generally calls for each player to randomize his play in a specified way in order to prevent the opponent from discovering his intentions. If the players accept this definition of rationality and behave this way, then their behavior is predictable at least in an average sense.

But when we attempt to extend the theory to situations that are not zero-sum or that involve more than two players, the ambiguities appear in new forms (specifically in the form of bargaining among actual or potential coalitions of players), and the pure theory no longer makes specific predictions of behavior. In fact, new conceptions of optimality have had to be developed to substitute for the classical notion of Pareto optimality (Nash, 1950). Attempts to extend the mathematical theory of games have been numerous (Kuhn and Tucker, 1954), but the incorporation of actual behavior in these models is rare. The development of "team theory," originated by Marschak (1955), represents one response in economics to the existence of coalitions.

A further objection to the theory of games, at least as a descriptive theory, is that it requires of economic man powers of reasoning far beyond that required by the classical theory. To eliminate the ambiguities that "outguessing" introduces into prediction, we must seek more realistic assumptions that stem from limitations on human capacity for rational calculation (Luce and Raiffa, 1957, Chapter 10; Simon, 1955). The relationship between game theory and the actual behavior of subjects in experiments has been analyzed by Shubik (1962).

Analyses of economic behavior in situations of oligopoly draw, at least implicitly, upon theories of power and bargaining—initially developed to explain political phenomena—as well as upon economic theory. This is true of both competition among producers (for example, the automobile, steel, or aluminum industries) and between unions and employers (particularly industry-wide collective bargaining). An excellent example of the latter kind of analysis is provided by Fellner (1947), who conceived of the degree of relative power of union and employer as critical for determining the point at which agreement is reached. Unfortunately, it is unclear how "degree of power" is determined. The amount of power held by members of coalitions, firms in an industry, etc., has been implicitly assumed but rarely measured. Power as a variable has remained within the province of investigation of sociologists and social psychologists. The lack of combination of measures in these fields with predictions of behavior based on them makes it impossible to deduce specific predictions of behavior from available theory. The consequence is dependence on description and actual observations of behavior for making predictions. (Examples of the weakness of predictions derived deductively from a few "plausible" assumptions about human behavior may be found in Chamberlain, 1955; Schelling, 1956; Siegel and Fouraker, 1960.)

Four important areas of social science and social policy—two in economics and two more closely related to political science—have as their central concern the phenomena of power and the processes of bargaining, the theory of political parties, labor-management relations, international politics, and oligopoly theory. Any progress in the basic theory applicable to one of these is certain to be almost equally important to the others.

COGNITION: THE CHALLENGE TO RATIONALITY

Up to this point we have emphasized primarily the relations between economics and motivational theory in psychology. It is true that cognitive considerations have not been absent (for example, the formation of expectations by the economic actor), but they have played a secondary role in the discussion. In the present section, cognitive matters will have the central place, while motivation and affect will be considered only as they interact with cognition. This shift in emphasis will allow us to view the relation of economics to psychology from a standpoint suggested by important recent trends in research on both sides of the interdisciplinary boundary.

Classical economics minimized its dependence on motivational theory in psychology by taking utility maximization (for the consumer) and profit maximization (for the entrepreneur) as the sole motives of economic man. Similarly, economics got along almost without psychological hypotheses about economic man's intellective qualities, by assuming him to be "objectively" rational, that is, rational in dealing with a given external environment as viewed by an omniscient being gifted with unlimited powers of computation (Simon, 1947, Chapter 4). Given these basic assumptions, motivational and cognitive, nothing more need be known about economic man to predict his behavior; it suffices to have information about his environment, for example, the prices in the markets in which he trades, his production function, and so on.

Economists can claim, with considerable justification, that the classical model has had great predictive power in the areas of behavior with which they have been concerned. But economics has been moving steadily into newer areas where the power of the model has never been demonstrated and where its adequacy must be considered anew. Labor economics has been such an area, oligopoly or imperfect competition theory another, decision making under uncertainty a third, and the theory of economic development a fourth. We have already noted some difficulties the theory has encountered in these new territories:

1. When the assumptions of perfect competition were removed, even the definition of rationality became ambiguous. New definitions had to be constructed (by no

means as "obvious" intuitively as was simple maximization) to extend the theory of rational behavior to bargaining and outguessing situations. Moreover, these new game theory formulations do not give an unequivocal prediction of how a rational man would behave.

2.   When the assumptions of perfect foresight were removed, the definition of rationality had to be extended in another direction to handle uncertainty about the environment. (There has been a strong tendency, under the influence of game theory, to wrap these two problems into one by treating "nature" as a malevolent opponent. While this solution appeals to some mathematicians and statisticians on esthetic grounds, its logical or empirical basis is hard to find.)

But extending the classical theory to these new areas requires more than broadening the definition of rationality. It requires, in addition, a distinction between the objective environment in which the economic actor "really" lives and the subjective environment that he perceives and to which he responds. When this distinction is made, we can no longer predict his behavior, even if he behaves rationally, from the characteristics of the objective environment; we also need to know something about his perceptual and cognitive processes (Simon, 1955, 1956).

The classical model is a theory of a man choosing among fixed and known alternatives, to each of which are attached known consequences. When perception and cognition intervene between the decision maker and his objective environment, this model is no longer adequate. Then we need a description of the choice process that recognizes that alternatives are not given but must be sought, and a description that takes into account the arduous task of determining what consequences will follow on each of the alternatives (Clarkson and Meltzer, 1960).

The decision maker's information about his environment is much less than an approximation of the real environment. The term "approximation" implies that the subjective world of the decision maker resembles quite closely the external environment but lacks, perhaps, some fineness of detail. The psychological evidence contradicts this view—the perceived world is fantastically different from the "real" world. The differences involve both omissions and distortions and arise in both perception and inference.

Psychological research has paid most attention to the sins of commission, to the distortions of the external environment in perception and inference. For several years, experimental work (for example, Asch, 1952; Sherif, 1936) has emphasized *affect* as a cause of distortion. For our purposes, however—understanding the relations of psychology to economics—the sins of *omission* in perception are more important than the sins of commission. The decision maker's model of the world encompasses only a minute fraction of all the relevant characteristics of the real environment, and his inferences extract only a minute fraction of all the information that is present, even in his model. Under these circumstances, his choices cannot be predicted from a knowledge of the external environment without a knowledge also of the selective mechanisms that are part of his perceptual and problem-solving processes (March and Simon, 1958).

Perception is sometimes referred to as a "filter." This term is as misleading as "approximation," and for the same reason: it implies that what comes through into the central nervous system is really quite a bit like what is "out there." In fact, the filtering is not merely a passive selection of some part of a presented whole, but an active process involving attention to a very small part of the whole and exclusion, from the outset, of almost all that is not within the scope of attention. We need not argue the issue of "conscious" and "subconscious" perception; we need simply observe that every human organism lives in an environment that generates millions of bits of new information each second and that the bottleneck of the perceptual apparatus certainly does not admit more than 1000 bits per second, and probably much less.

Equally significant omissions characterize the processing that takes place when information reaches the brain. As every mathematician knows, it is one thing to have a set of differential equations and another to have their solutions. Yet the solutions are logically implied by the equations—they are "all there," if we only knew how to get at them! By the same token, hosts of inferences *might* be drawn from the information stored in the brain, but they are not. The consequences implied by information in the memory become known only through active information processing, and hence through active selection of particular problem-solving paths from the myriad that might have been followed. Attempts to find a relationship between classical learning theory and the concept of cognition are not necessarily new (Tolman, 1948), but the complexity of this relationship becomes quite apparent when viewed as a determinant of human behavior (Miller, Galanter, and Pribram, 1960).

If we have a rat in a very small maze, with cheese at one branch point, and if we give the rat plenty of time to explore, we can predict where he will finally go without any very deep knowledge of rat psychology. We simply assume that he likes cheese (a given utility function) and that he chooses the path that leads to cheese (objective rationality). If we now transfer the rat to a maze having a number of pieces of cheese in it, but a maze that is several orders of magnitude larger than the largest maze he could possibly explore in a rat's lifetime, then prediction is more difficult. We must now know how a rat solves problems in order to determine where he will go. We must understand what determines the paths he will try and what clues will make him continue along a path or go back.

Classical economics was highly successful in handling small-maze problems without depending on psychology. Labor relations, imperfect competition, uncertainty, and long-run dynamics encase the decision maker in a much larger maze than those considered in classical short-run static theory. In these new areas the economist and the psychologist have numerous common interests in cognitive theory that they have not shared previously.

THE GOVERNMENT OF ATTENTION: ROLES

Short-run predictions of behavior, where there is a large discrepancy between subjective and objective rationality, require information both about the environment and about the frame of reference of the decision maker. In the longer run, the frame of reference may itself become the dependent variable for prediction, but a variable not easily eliminated from the analysis. For even if the environment is one of the long-run determinants of the frame of reference, there is no reason to suppose that there is any simple one-to-one relation between them. Though the individual and the social system to which he belongs must meet long-run tests of survival and efficiency, there are certainly multiple solutions to the survival problem (as evidenced, in another realm, by the large number of distinct biological species).

Though the distinction between the perceived environment and the objective environment is important in many parts of sociology, social psychology, and individual psychology, there has been little consensus as to what terms should be used to denote the perceived environments. Those in common use include "frame of reference," "set," "definition of the situation," and "role." None of these terms is exactly synonymous with the others—at least in the usage of a single writer—but all are used in a variety of meanings, and each has a large area of overlap with the others.

For the purposes of this essay, we need not solve this terminological problem; we can use the four terms above more or less interchangeably. But we must clarify the concepts to which the terms refer. Indeed, this clarification opens important possibilities for contributions of economics to psychology and vice versa. (Bruner *et al.*, 1956, provide a somewhat different example of important conceptual borrowing of psychology from economics and game theory.) In the following paragraphs we shall propose a revision in the concept of "role" or "frame of reference" that appears to us essential to the fruitful application of that concept. (For a more detailed discussion of the proposal set forth here, see Simon, 1947.) In the next section, the redefined concept will be used to interpret some of the significant relevant current research.

A current definition of *role* (Newcomb, 1950, p. 278) that is representative of definitions in use in social psychology and sociology reads: "Each position carries with it definite prescriptions for behaving toward other persons in related positions . . . . Such ways of behaving toward others . . . are called *roles*." For brevity, we may say that roles are usually defined as *positionally prescribed sets of behaviors*.

There is, up to the present time, a great poverty of propositions about the characteristics of roles (as distinguished from propositions about how roles are acquired). This poverty can be traced in large part to the unsatisfactory nature of the definition of role. The definition provides a name or label for a phenomenon, but not a useful tool for its analysis. The difficulty resides in the term "behaviors," which designates the unit for the description of roles. A "behavior" or "action" is not a satisfactory unit for describing the cognitive orientations of persons to their environments. A summary of recent work relating roles and behavior, as well as a study which indicates the strong effect on behavior which can be produced by a simple change in role, will be found in Gold and Stedry (1964).

The inadequacy of role description becomes apparent when we try to apply the role concept to *rational* and *adaptive* behavior. If roles were prescribed sets of behaviors, then there would be no place for rational calculation in role behavior. A person could decide whether he would conform to a role (and this is the topic most prominently discussed in the literature on roles), but having decided that he would conform, the role prescription would itself determine his behavior in that role.

A concept of role that does not admit processes of rational choice is obviously useless for describing the behavior of economic or administrative man. We need something like the role concept, for we need to distinguish between the objective and subjective environments of choice. At the same time, we must avoid substituting, in the theory, socially prescribed sets of behaviors for choice. We need a definition of role that accomplishes the former without implying the latter.

The difficulties with the role concept disappear if we introduce the *decision premise* as the unit of role description in place of the *behavior*. *A role, in terms of this definition, is a social prescription of some, but not all, of the premises that enter into an individual's choices of behaviors* (Dearborn and Simon, 1958; Simon, 1947, pp. 221–228). Any particular concrete behavior is the result of a large number of premises, only some of which are prescribed by the role. In addition to role premises, there are premises about the state of the environment based directly on perception, premises representing beliefs and knowledge, and idiosyncratic premises that characterize the personality. (For a specific example of concrete behavior in an actual industrial situation, see Rubin, Stedry, and Willits, 1965.)

A fanciful (but only slightly fanciful) example will help to make clear both the distinction between the new definition and the usual one, and the reason for making it. Suppose we were to construct a robot incorporating a modern digital computer and to program (that is, instruct) the robot to take the role of a business executive in a specified company. What would the program look like? Since no one has yet done this (Clarkson and Meltzer, 1960; Cyert, Simon, and Trow, 1956), we cannot say with certainty. However, several points are fairly clear. The program would *not* consist of a list of prescribed and proscribed behaviors, since what an executive does is highly contingent on information about a wide variety of circumstances. Instead, the program would consist of a large number of *criteria* to be applied to possible and proposed courses of action, of programs for *generating* possible courses of action, of computational procedures for *assessing* the state of the environment and its implications for action, and the like. Hence, the program—that is, the role prescription—would interact with information to produce concrete behavior adapted to the situation. The elements of such a program take the form of what we have called "decision premises," and what the computer specialist would call "instructions and data" (Newell and Simon, 1956).

ROLES AND THE PROCESS OF RATIONAL DECISION

The definition of role in terms of decision premises is useful not only for clarifying concepts, but also for constructing actual detailed descriptions of concrete roles preparatory to analyzing the structure of these roles and their specific content. We can study the form of the role prescription and the cognitive and other central processes through which it is translated into action; at this point we can expect some genuine congruence to develop between the "economic" or "administrative" man and the "problem-solving" man who has been studied in psychology.

This is not a mere prospectus to be realized at some undefined future date. A substantial number of current research efforts in different fields are converging toward this point, as the following examples show.

Economics

Normative microeconomics seeks to advise the businessman in his decisions—whether to buy a piece of equipment, how much inventory to hold, what price to pay for a product, etc. Hence, theories in this field take the form of decision-making procedures for handling particular problems. To mention just one example, linear programming theory has been used to construct a computational model for determining the most profitable blending policies in an oil refinery (Charnes, Cooper, and Mellon, 1952). A summary of over 60 actual applications, along with the underlying mathematical and economic theory, is contained in Charnes and Cooper (1961).

These decision models are not merely abstract "theories" of the firm, but actual decision-making devices. We can think of any such device as a simulation of the corresponding human decision maker, in which the equations and other assumptions that enter into the formal decision-making procedure correspond to the decision premises, including the role prescription, of the decision maker (Clarkson, 1962; Clarkson and Simon, 1960).

In particular, the problems of subjective rationality must be faced in constructing normative decision models: (1) the latter can require for their application only data that are obtainable; (2) they can call only for practical computations; (3) insofar as they utilize forecasts, they must specify a method of forecasting. These models, then, share many of the properties of less formal decision-making roles described in terms of the premises used in deciding, the data, and the rules of computation.

The evolution of normative microeconomics—perhaps better termed management science or operations research—has, in fact, been remarkable over the relatively short period from its inception during World War II. The earliest operations research approaches, as depicted, say, in Arrow, Harris, and Marschak (1951), were based almost entirely on classical economics, which assumed profit maximization on the part of the firm with absolutely no constraints whatever on the possible decision-making behavior of firms. Later applications (Dorfman, Samuelson, and Solow, 1958) admitted technological constraints. In what was a pioneering work, Charnes, Cooper, and Miller (1959) considered a cash balance constraint, an arbitrary decision of management, as appropriate for inclusion in a management science model. Since then, the work on chance-constrained programming (Charnes and Cooper, 1959, 1963) has admitted policy constraints on a rather broad basis; and the recent work of Ijiri (1966) on programming to goals (rather than profit maximization) and the treatment by Charnes and Stedry of multiple goals (Charnes and Stedry, 1964a, 1964b, 1966b) have added a new dimension in the use of maximization techniques within what are, in effect, satisficing models. This evolution has been traced in detail in Charnes and Stedry (1966a).

Higher mental processes

Students of human problem solving have tried to describe in some detail the stages of the process and the steps taken by the problem solver. Though the studies that have been reported to date fall far short of complete descriptions of the process—in many respects less complete than the normative economic models mentioned above—they point clearly in the direction of describing the problem solver in terms of his "program," that is, the premises that determine the course of the process (Bruner, Goodnow, and Austin, 1956; de Groot, 1965).

Electronic computers

Until very recently, the electronic digital computer was a device that, if instructed in in painful detail by its operator, could be induced to perform rather complicated and tedious arithmetical operations. Recent research has enabled the computer to interpret and execute instructions given to it in languages that begin to have some of the power and flexibility of natural languages, and to carry out tasks that, if performed by humans, would certainly be called "thinking" and "learning."

A few items will illustrate the stage that such research has reached. Several computers have been programmed to design industrial equipment (for example, small motors and transformers), and the persons who have devised these programs believe that their main processes simulate the decision procedures previously followed by the design engineers, and hence, describe the role of design engineer in these situations. Situations exist where the computer is being used to simulate production schedulers, people who manage to solve problems which have eluded solution by algorithmic methods within reasonable bounds of computer time constraints. Heuristic approaches to problems whose combinatorial possibilities are unmanageable in terms of developing optimal solutions have used heuristic techniques which provide satisfactory (and probably near-optimal) solutions, as suggested, for example, in Tonge (1961).

Second, a computer program, the General Problem Solver (Newell, Shaw, and Simon, 1958; Newell and Simon, 1960), is able to reason in rather general terms, solving problems of discovering proofs for mathematical theorems, proving trigonometric and algebraic identities, and a variety of other problems by applying means-end analysis. The program has been shown to simulate the main processes used by college students in solving some novel problems of moderate difficulty. Another computer program (Clarkson, 1962; Clarkson and Meltzer, 1960) simulates the decision processes used by a bank officer in investing the assets of a trust fund. A third (Feldman, 1959) shows that the same basic cognitive processes can be used to explain, on the one hand, certain economic predictions of businessmen and, on the other, the behavior of subjects in partial-reinforcement experiments.

These computer programs contribute to economic theory by providing very concrete explanations of significant economic decision-making processes. At the same time, they are laying the foundations for an operational and rigorous information-processing theory of human thinking and problem solving. They bring promise of a far closer relation between economic and psychological theories of decision making than we have had in the past (Sprowls, 1962). So long as economics emphasized macroscopic events and ignored detailed process within the business firm, and so long as psychology avoided the complexities of higher mental process in favor of rigorous experiments on simple learning and choice situations, the two fields had little common ground. With the appearance of computer programming as a tool powerful enough to allow the study of thinking and learning processes in situations as complex as those of everyday life, it will no longer be acceptable to explain the same phenomena with two different, and often contradictory, bodies of theory.

THE STRUCTURE OF ORGANIZATIONAL AND ECONOMIC ROLES

We see that the *role* of a person who is behaving rationally or adaptively can be identified in large part with the decision premises he applies to the substance of his problem and the decision premises that govern his problem-solving processes. We see also that rapid progress is being made toward a more accurate and complete description of certain economic, executive, and technical roles (or parts of them). Apart from normative applications (for example, substituting computers for humans in decision-making tasks), we are not primarily interested, as psychologists or economists, in the detailed description of the roles, but in broader questions: characterizing the structure of roles in general terms, understanding how roles come to be structured in the particular ways they do, and tracing out the implications for macroeconomics and other large-scale social phenomena of this version of role theory.

Characterizing role structure

Here we are concerned with generalizations about cognitive processes, particularly generalizations that are relatively independent of the substantive content of the role. A classical example is Dewey's description of stages in the problem-solving process and its use in Bales's categories for coding group discussions (Bales, 1950; Lazarsfeld, 1954). Another example, of particular interest to economics, is the hypothesis that economic man is a *satisficing* or *quasi-rational* animal whose problem solving is based on search activity to meet aspiration levels, rather than a *maximizing* animal whose problem solving involves finding the best alternatives in terms of specified criteria (Simon, 1955). A third hypothesis is that *operative goals,* associated with observable criteria of success and relatively definite means of attainment, play a much larger part in governing choice than *nonoperative goals,* which lack concrete measures of success or programs for attainment (March and Simon, 1958, Chapter 6).

Understanding how roles emerge

Within almost any single business firm, certain characteristic roles will be represented: selling, production, accounting, and so on (Cyert, March, and Starbuck, 1961; Dearborn and Simon, 1958). This consistency may be explained partly in functional terms: a model that views the firm as producing a product, selling it, and accounting for its assets and liabilities simplifies the real world and provides the members of the organization with a workable frame of reference. Imitation within the culture provides an alternative explanation. It is exceedingly difficult to test hypotheses as to the origins and causal conditions for roles as universal in the society as these, but the underlying mechanisms could probably be explored effectively by studying less common roles—safety director, quality control inspector, and the like—that are found in some firms, but not in all.

With our present definition of "role," we can also speak meaningfully of the role of an entire business firm, of decision premises that underlie its basic policies (Bowen, 1955, Chapter 3; Cyert, Simon, and Trow, 1956). In a particular industry, we find that some firms specialize in adapting the product to individual customers' specifications; others specialize in product innovation. The common interest of economics and psychology includes not only the study of individual roles, but also the explanation of organizational roles of these sorts.

Tracing the implications for macroeconomics

If basic professional goals remain as they are, the interest of the psychologist and the economist in role theory will stem from somewhat different ultimate aims. The former will use various economic and organizational phenomena as data for studying the structure and determinants of roles; the latter will be primarily interested in the implications of role theory for the model of economic man and, indirectly, for macroeconomics.

Let us consider, by way of example, the economic theory of the size of firms. The classical theory is a static equilibrium theory. Firms of optimum size, in terms of average cost per unit of output, drive other firms to this size or out of business. Hence, the "typical" size of firm in an industry will be that at which average cost per unit is a minimum. Attempts to determine empirically what this size is in specific cases have not been very successful; the theory is further embarrassed by the fact that in almost all industries there is an extremely wide dispersion of firms by size.

The empirical data are more easily reconciled with a model that assumes that the firm searches for growth opportunities than with one that assumes equilibrium at an optimum (Bowen, 1955, pp. 72–73). Thus, research at the micro level on the actual mechanisms of decision making and problem solving has important implications at the macro level for the size distributions of firms (Ijiri and Simon, 1964). The implications extend both to the explanation of the phenomena and the consequences for economic welfare of various kinds of governmental interventions to alter the size distributions of firms (Simon and Bonini, 1958).

The topics of innovation and technological change provide somewhat more obvious links than the one just discussed between the firm and individual decision maker, on the one hand, and the economy and society, on the other. The factors determining the rate of a nation's economic and technological development are still very much matters of speculation. In particular, classical economics, built upon basically static models of the economy, does not readily handle the processes of invention, growth, and diffusion of knowledge as determinants of productivity or of the rate of capital investment. Some progress has been made in exploring the processes by which innovations are diffused through a culture (Coleman, Katz, and Menzel, 1957; Griliches, 1957). Recent work by Mansfield and Brandenburg (1966) has succeeded in tracing some of the determinants of diffusing innovation within the culture of industrial firms. Other work (Brandenburg and Stedry, 1966) has attempted to relate the accumulation of knowledge to its development and application *within* a research and development organization. It is probably fair to say, however, that little is known about the determinants of the rate and direction of research or other inventive activity, or how this is translated into technical know-how; still less is known about how this last is stored and reproduced by society. A better understanding of these processes would have obvious implications for the decisions that individual firms have to make in budgeting and directing research and development activities, for the decisions of governments relating to economic development, and for the encouragement of technological progress. Hence, improved theories of human thinking and problem solving may have a major impact on economic and business policy.

CONCLUDING COMMENTS

This discussion of the mutual interests of economics and the behavioral sciences in cognitive processes, and particularly those of the rational decision maker, has necessarily been more speculative than earlier sections of this article. Here we are examining an area of investigation that is just emerging, just becoming an important element in the social scientist's model of the world. In describing this area, we have tried to point to a number of the diverse research activities that testify to its growing significance and its possible implications for the social sciences.

The relative lack of communication between economists and behavioral scientists on the topic of motivation can be attributed in considerable part to the economist's belief that his purposes are served by a very rudimentary theory of motivational processes, a theory he can construct without much outside help. Cognitive theory has been of great concern both to economics (rationality) and to behavioral scientists (learning, problem solving). What has limited communication here has been the great difference between the models of rational behavior that have prevailed in the several disciplines. There are strong indications today that a more realistic description of human rationality is emerging, one that may serve as a common ground for a wide variety of social scientists (Bruner, Goodnow, and Austin, 1956; de Groot, 1946; Newell and Simon, 1960).

METHODOLOGICAL BORROWINGS

A person who has occasion to wander into various territories in the social sciences is struck not only by the diversity of tribal customs relating to substantive matters—concepts and theories—but by the diversity of methodologies as well. If a social scientist is discovered computing a regression coefficient, he is almost certainly an economist; a factor analysis identifies him as a psychologist, probably working with test data; a t or chi-square test, as a social or experimental psychologist, probably working with experimental data, etc. Mathematical statistics has provided a common meeting ground for the statistically sophisticated of all disciplines, but the statistical techniques they have brought back to their own tribes have tended to be somewhat specialized. Scaling techniques and latent-structure analysis are hardly known outside social psychology, the country of origin; the work that has been done on the statistical identification problem is an even more closely held secret of the econometricians. The highly technical nature of some of these developments and the language in which they must be described have hindered their diffusion. As examples of impressive theoretical development, though couched in language virtually incomprehensible to the psychologist, one might cite the work of Theil (1961, 1964), Van de Panne (1965), and others.

The same may be said about empirical methodology. For a traditional economic theorist, an empirical study means going to the reports of the U. S. Census or the Bureau of Foreign and Domestic Commerce. A social psychologist generates new data by experimenting with small groups of college sophomores in a laboratory. The anthropologist-sociologist buys a ticket to New Guinea or Newburyport. The ecologist-sociologist and the demographer-sociologist behave more like the economist, looking largely to official tabulations of aggregative data for their information. The public opinion specialist constructs a stratified random sample and asks questions of a number of respondents. These are some of the principle varieties of social scientists, viewed as data seekers.

Recent years have seen an increasing amount of borrowing of empirical methodologies among disciplines, though the average experience of social scientists trained in one discipline, but using the data-gathering techniques of the others, is very slight. A few economists are now using questionnaires and the interview as a means of learning about economic behavior. An even smaller group is exploring the possibilities of actually observing behavior within the business firm. A few studies, easily counted on the fingers, have attempted to elucidate economic phenomena by laboratory experimentation.

All these activities seem to be growing—amidst a certain healthy skepticism of traditionally trained economists—and growing not merely in quantity but in sophistication of technique. For example, the belief that the way to learn how a businessman makes decisions is to ask him (comparable to earlier beliefs in most public opinion polling studies) is gradually waning; one or two of the most carefully designed and controlled studies of utility functions show a high degree of sophistication with respect to introspective evidence.

The borrowing in the other direction, from economics to the behavioral sciences, lies more in the direction of statistics and mathematical formalization than empirical techniques.   Mathematical theorizing is undoubtedly most highly developed in economics, where it has been intimately involved in the advance of theory over the last 50 years.   Recently, the trend toward mathematical formalization of theories has spread to psychology and, to a lesser extent, sociology (Lazarsfeld, 1954) and anthropology (Udy, 1964).   Recent discussions of the use of mathematics in sociology are contained in White (1963, 1964). The number of social scientists capable of handling mathematics as consumers and as producers is increasing rapidly, and we may expect it to continue to do so under the impetus it has been given by the Social Science Research Council and the Ford Foundation.

As we survey the various aspects of methodology, then, we observe a slow but significant diffusion of empirical techniques from the behavioral sciences to economics and a return traffic in statistics and mathematics.   These streams of diffusion of knowledge are bringing about important advances in the technical level of both empirical and theoretical work in the social sciences.

CONCLUSION

We shall not try to summarize further what is already a compressed survey of an alarmingly wide range of topics. The word "interdisciplinary" is in fashion again in the social sciences, but our review of the literature has not revealed any great excess of interdisciplinary fervor on the whole. On the contrary, the disciplinary boundaries remain rather effective barriers to the sharing of knowledge in areas that are certainly of common concern to economics and the behavioral sciences, and areas in which all these disciplines have much to contribute. It is doubtful whether the existing disciplines constitute a satisfactory frame of reference for the sciences of man. If the subjective rationality of the social scientist is to be adequate to the task of interpreting the objective facts of the real world of social phenomena, a more effective set of role definitions than those in current use needs to be found.

REFERENCES

Alchian, A. A. (1950). Uncertainty, evolution, and economic theory. *J. polit. Econ.,* *58,* 211–221.

Argyris, C. (1962). *Interpersonal competence and organizational effectiveness.* Homewood, Ill.: Dorsey.

———— (1964). *Integrating the individual and the organization.* New York: Wiley.

Arrow, K. J. (1958). Utilities, attitudes, choices: a review note. *Econometrica, 26,* 1–23.

———— (1963). Utility and expectation in economic behavior. In S. Koch (Ed.), *Psychology: a study of a science.* Vol. 6. New York: McGraw-Hill. Pp. 724–752.

Arrow, K. J., T. Harris, and J. Marschak (1951). Optimal inventory policy. *Econometrica, 19,* 250–272.

Asch, S. E. (1952). *Social psychology.* Englewood Cliffs, N.J.: Prentice-Hall.

Bales, R. F. (1950). *Interaction process analysis.* Cambridge, Mass.: Addison-Wesley.

Barnard, C. I. (1938). *The functions of the executive.* Cambridge: Harvard Univ. Press.

Becker, S., and S. Siegel (1958). Utility of grades: level of aspiration in a decision theory context. *J. exp. Psychol., 55,* 81–85.

Bennett, G. E. (1930). *Fraud: its control through accounts.* New York: Century.

Bennis, W. G., E. H. Schein, D. E. Berlew, and F. I. Steele, Eds. (1964). *Interpersonal dynamics: essays and readings on human interaction.* Homewood, Ill.: Dorsey.

Berlyne, D. E. (1954). A theory of human curiosity. *Brit. J. Psychol., 45,* 180–191.

Borko, H., Ed. (1962). *Computer applications in the behavioral sciences.* Englewood Cliffs, N.J.: Prentice-Hall.

Bowen, H. R. (1955). *The business enterprise as a subject for research.* New York: Social Science Research Council.

Bowman, M. J. (1958). *Expectations, uncertainty, and business behavior.* New York: Social Science Research Council.

Brandenburg, R. G., and A. C. Stedry (1966). Toward a multi-stage information conversion model of the research and development process. *Naval Res. Logistics Quart., 10,* 129–146.

Bruner, J. A., J. T. Goodnow, and G. A. Austin (1956). *A study of thinking.* New York: Wiley.

Cadmus, B., and A. J. E. Child (1953). *Internal control against fraud and waste.* Englewood Cliffs, N.J.: Prentice-Hall.

Chamberlin, N. W. (1955). *A general theory of economic process.* New York: Harper.

Chambers, D., and A. Charnes (1961). Inter-temporal analysis and optimization of bank portfolios. *Managemt. Sci., 7,* 393–410.

Charnes, A., and W. W. Cooper (1959). Chance-constrained programming. *Managemt. Sci., 6,* 73–80.

———— (1961). *Management models and industrial applications of linear programming* (2 vols.). New York: Wiley.

———— (1963). Deterministic equivalents for optimizing and satisficing under chance constraints. *Operations Res., 11,* 18–39.

Charnes, A., W. W. Cooper, and B. Mellon (1952). Blending aviation gasolines. *Econometrica, 20,* 135–159.

Charnes, A., W. W. Cooper, and M. H. Miller (1959). Application of linear programming to financial budgeting and the costing of funds. *J. Bus., 32,* 20–46.

Charnes, A., and A. C. Stedry (1964a). Exploratory models in the theory of budgetary control. In W. W. Cooper, H. J. Leavitt, and M. W. Shelly (Eds.), *New perspectives in organization research.* New York: Wiley. Pp. 212–249.

_____ (1964b). Investigations in the theory of multiple budgeted goals. In C. P. Bonini, R. K. Jaedicke, and H. M. Wagner (Eds.), *Management controls: new directions in basic research.* New York: McGraw-Hill. Pp. 186–204.

_____ (1966a). The attainment of organization goals through appropriate selection of sub-unit goals. In J. R. Lawrence (Ed.), *Operational research and the social sciences.* London: Tavistock. Pp. 147–164.

_____ (1966b). Search-theoretical models of organization control by budgeting multiple goals. *Managemt. Sci., 12*, 457–482.

Chipman, J. S. (1960). The foundations of utility. *Econometrica, 28*, 193–224.

Clarkson, G. P. E. (1962). *Portfolio selection: a simulation of trust investment.* Englewood Cliffs, N.J.: Prentice-Hall.

_____ (1963). *The theory of consumer demand: a critical appraisal.* Englewood Cliffs, N.J.: Prentice-Hall.

Clarkson, G. P. E., and A. H. Meltzer (1960). Portfolio selection: a heuristic approach. *J. Finance, 15*, 465–480.

Clarkson, G. P. E., and H. A. Simon (1960). Simulation of individual and group behavior. *Amer. econ. Rev., 50*, 920–932.

Coleman, J. R. (1956). The role of the local industrial union in contemporary collective bargaining. *Proc. VIIIth annual meeting of Industrial Relations Research Association, 1955.* Madison, Wisc.: Industrial Relations Research Association. Pp. 274–286.

Coleman, J., E. Katz, and H. Menzel (1957). The diffusion of an innovation among physicians. *Sociometry, 20*, 253–270.

Coombs, C., and D. Beardslee (1954). On decision-making under uncertainty. In R. M. Thrall, C. H. Coombs, and R. L. Davis (Eds.), *Decision processes.* New York: Wiley. Pp. 255–285

Cooper, W. W. (1951). A proposal for extending the theory of the firm. *Quart. J. Econ., 65*, 87–109.

Cooper, W. W., H. J. Leavitt, and M. W. Shelly, Eds. (1964). *New perspectives in organization research.* New York: Wiley.

Cyert, R. M., W. R. Dill, and J. G. March (1958). The role of expectations in business decision making. *Admin. Sci. Quart., 3*, 307–340.

Cyert, R. M., and J. G. March (1956). Organizational factors in the theory of oligopoly. *Quart. J. Econ., 70*, 44–64.

_____ (1962). *A behavioral theory of the firm.* Englewood Cliffs, N.J.: Prentice-Hall.

Cyert, R. M., J. G. March, and W. Starbuck (1961). Two experiments on bias and conflict in organizational estimation. *Managemt. Sci., 7*, 254–264.

Cyert, R. M., H. A. Simon, and D. B. Trow (1956). Observation of a business decision. *J. Bus., 29*, 237–248.

Davidson, D., P. Suppes, and S. Siegel (1957). *Decision making: an experimental approach.* Stanford: Stanford Univ. Press.

Dearborn, D. C., and H. A. Simon (1958). Selective perception: a note on the departmental identification of executives. *Sociometry, 21*, 140–144.

de Groot, A. D. (1965). *Thought and choice in chess.* The Hague: Mouton.

Diggory, J. C. (1935). Responses to experimentally induced failure. *Amer. J. Psychol., 47,* 48–61.

Dorfman, R., P. A. Samuelson, and R. M. Solow (1958). *Linear programming and economic analysis.* New York: McGraw-Hill.

Early, J. S. (1956). Marginal policies of 'excellently managed' companies. *Amer. econ. Rev., 46,* 44–70.

Edwards, W. (1953). Probability-preference in gambling. *Amer. J. Psychol., 66,* 349–364.

—————— (1954). The theory of decision making. *Psychol. Bull., 51,* 380–417.

—————— (1961). Behavioral decision theory. *Annu. Rev. Psychol., 12,* 473–498.

Farrar, D. E. (1962). *The investment decision under uncertainty: portfolio selection.* Englewood Cliffs, N.J.: Prentice-Hall.

Feldman, J. (1959). An analysis of predictive behavior in a two-choice situation. Unpublished doctoral dissertation, Carnegie Institute of Technology.

Fellner, W. J. (1947). Prices and wages under bilateral monopoly. *Quart. J. Econ., 61,* 503–532.

Festinger, L. (1942). A theoretical interpretation of shifts in the level of aspiration. *Psychol. Rev., 49,* 235–250.

Fouraker, L. E., and S. Siegel (1963). *Bargaining behavior.* New York: McGraw-Hill.

Frank, J. D. (1935). Individual differences in certain aspects of the level of aspiration. *Amer. J. Psychol., 47,* 119–128.

French, J. R. P., Jr., J. Israel, and D. As (1960). An experiment on participation in a Norwegian factory. *Hum. Relat., 13,* 3–19.

French, J. R. P., Jr., E. Kay, and H. H. Meyer (1966). The effects of threat and participation in a performance appraisal situation. *Hum. Relat., 19,* 3–20.

Gardner, J. W. (1940). The use of the term 'level of aspiration.' *Psychol. Rev., 47,* 59–68.

Gold, M. M., and A. C. Stedry (1964). The effect of role-playing in a problem-solving situation. *Indust. Managemt. Rev., 6,* 81–101.

Goldberger, A. S. (1964). *Econometric theory.* New York: Wiley.

Gordon, M. J. (1962). *The investment, financing and valuation of the corporation.* Homewood, Ill.: Irwin.

Gordon, R. A. (1945). *Business leadership in the large corporation.* Washington, D.C.: Brookings Institution.

Griliches, Z. (1957). Hybrid corn: an exploration in the economics of technological change. *Econometrica, 25,* 501–522.

Hall, R. L., and C. J. Hitch (1939). Price theory and business behavior. *Oxford Econ. Papers, 2,* 12–14.

Hayes, S. P., Jr. (1950). Some psychological problems of economics. *Psychol. Bull., 47,* 289–330.

Hilgard, E. R. (1956). *Theories of learning* (2nd ed.). New York: Appleton-Century-Crofts.

Homans, G. C. (1950). *The human group.* New York: Harper.

Ijiri, Y. (1966). *Management goals and accounting for control.* Amsterdam: North-Holland.

Ijiri, Y., and H. A. Simon (1964). Business firm growth and size. *Amer. econ. Rev.,* *54,* 77–89.

Katona, G. (1951). *Psychological analysis of economic behavior.* New York: McGraw-Hill.

Kay, E., H. H. Meyer, and J. R. P. French, Jr. (1965). Effects of threat in a performance appraisal interview. *J. appl. Psychol.,* *49,* 311–317.

Kohler, E. L. (1957). *A dictionary for accountants* (2nd ed.). Englewood Cliffs, N.J.: Prentice-Hall.

Kuhn, H. W., and A. W. Tucker (1954). *Contributions to the theory of games.* Vol. 3. Princeton: Princeton Univ. Press.

Lazarsfeld, P. F., Ed. (1954). *Mathematical thinking in the social sciences.* Glencoe, Ill.: Free Press.

Leavitt, H. J. (1958). *Managerial psychology.* Chicago: Univ. of Chicago Press.

Lewin, K. (1936). *Principles of topological psychology.* New York: McGraw-Hill.

———— (1951). *Field theory in social science.* New York: Harper.

Lewin, K., T. Dembo, L. Festinger, and P. S. Sears (1944). Level of aspiration. In J. M. Hunt (Ed.), *Personality and the behavior disorders.* Vol. 1. New York: Ronald. Pp. 333–378.

Likert, R. (1961). *New patterns of management.* New York: McGraw-Hill.

Luce, R. D. (1958). A probabilistic theory of utility. *Econometrica,* *26,* 193–224.

———— (1959). *Individual choice behavior.* New York: Wiley.

Luce, R. D., and W. Edwards (1958). The derivation of subjective scales from just noticeable differences. *Psychol. Rev.,* *65,* 222–237.

Luce, R. D., and H. Raiffa (1957). *Games and decisions.* New York: Wiley.

Luce, R. D., and P. Suppes (1965). Preference, utility, and subjective probability. In R. D. Luce, R. R. Bush, and E. Galanter (Eds.), *Handbook of mathematical psychology.* Vol. 3. New York: Wiley. Pp. 249–410.

McGregor, D. (1960). *The human side of enterprise.* New York: McGraw-Hill.

Machlup, F. (1946). Marginal analysis and empirical research. *Amer. econ. Rev.,* *36,* 519–554.

———— (1947). Rejoinder to an antimarginalist. *Amer. econ. Rev.,* *37,* 148–154.

Maier, N. R. F. (1949). *Frustration.* Ann Arbor: Univ. of Michigan Press.

Mansfield, E., and R. G. Brandenburg (1966). The allocation characteristics and outcomes of the firm's R & D portfolio: a case study. In *Proc. Conf. on Microeconomics of Technological Change and Economic Growth.* New York: Ford Foundation.

March, J. G., and H. A. Simon (1958). *Organizations.* New York: Wiley.

Markowitz, H. M. (1959). *Portfolio selection.* New York: Wiley.

Marschak, J. (1955). Elements for a theory of teams. *Managemt. Sci., 1*, 127–137.

―――― (1959). Binary-choice constraints and random utility indicators. In K. J. Arrow, S. Karlin, and P. Suppes (Eds.), *Mathematical methods in the social sciences.* Stanford: Stanford Univ. Press. Pp. 312–329.

Marshall, A. (1920). *Principles of economics* (8th ed.). New York: St. Martin's.

Mason, E. S. (1952). Comment on A. G. Papandreou, "Some basic problems in the theory of the firm." In B. F. Haley (Ed.), *A survey of contemporary economics.* Vol. 2. Homewood, Ill.: Irwin. Pp. 221–222.

Menzel, H., J. Coleman, and E. Katz (1955). On the flow of scientific information in the medical profession. Columbia University, Bureau of Applied Social Research. (Mimeo)

Miller, G. A., E. Galanter, and K. H. Pribram (1960). *Plans and the structure of behavior.* New York: Holt.

Modigliani, F., and E. Brumberg (1954). Utility analysis and the consumption function. In K. K. Kurihara (Ed.), *Post-Keynesian economics.* New York: Knopf.

Modigliani, F., and M. H. Miller (1958). The cost of capital, corporation finance and the theory of investment. *Amer. econ. Rev., 48*, 261–297.

Modigliani, F., and O. H. Sauerlender (1955). Economic expectations and plans of firms in relation to short-term forecasting. In L. R. Klein (Ed.), *Short-term economic forecasting.* Princeton: Princeton Univ. Press. Pp. 261–351.

Mosteller, F., and P. Nogee (1951). An experimental measurement of utility. *J. polit. Econ., 59*, 371–404.

Nash, J. (1950). Equilibrium points in *n*-person games. *Proc. Nat. Acad. Sci., 36*, 48–49.

Nealey, S. M. (1964). Pay and benefit preference. Berkeley: Univ. California, Institute of Industrial Relations, Reprint No. 200.

Neumann, J. von, and O. Morgenstern (1944). *The theory of games and economic behavior.* Princeton: Princeton Univ. Press.

Newcomb, T. M. (1950). *Social psychology.* New York: Dryden.

Newell, A., J. C. Shaw, and H. A. Simon (1957). Empirical explorations of the logic theory machine. In *Proc. Western Joint Computer Conf.* New York: Institute of Radio Engineers. Pp. 218–230.

―――― (1958). Elements of a theory of human problem solving. *Psychol. Rev., 65*, 151–166.

Newell, A., and H. A. Simon (1956). The logic theory machine. *IRE Trans. Information Theory, IT-2*, 61–79.

―――― (1960). The simulation of human thought. In *Current trends in psychological theory.* Pittsburgh: Univ. Pittsburgh Press. Pp. 152–179.

Papandreou, A. G. (1952). Some basic problems in the theory of the firm. In B. F. Haley (Ed.), *A survey of contemporary economics.* Vol. 2. Homewood, Ill.: Irwin. Pp 183–219.

Ramsey, F. P. (1931). *The foundations of mathematics and other logical essays.* New York: Harcourt, Brace.

Restle, F. (1961). *Psychology of judgment and choice.* New York: Wiley.

Roethlisberger, F. J., and W. J. Dickson (1939). *Management and the worker.* Cambridge: Harvard Univ. Press.

Rubin, I. M., A. C. Stedry, and R. D. Willits (1965). Effort allocation of R & D supervisors. *IEEE Trans. Engineering Managemt., EM-12,* 70–78.

Schelling, T. C. (1956). An essay on bargaining. *Amer. econ. Rev., 46,* 281–306.

Schultz, H. (1938). *The theory and measurement of demand.* Chicago: Univ. of Chicago Press.

Sherif, M. (1936). *The psychology of social norms.* New York: Harper.

Shubik, M. (1962). Some experimental non-zero sum games with lack of information about the rules. *Managemt. Sci., 8,* 325–343.

Siegel, S. (1957). Level of aspiration and decision making. *Psychol. Rev., 64,* 253–263.

Siegel, S., and L. Fouraker (1960). *Bargaining and group decision-making.* New York: McGraw-Hill.

Simon, H. A. (1947). *Administrative behavior.* New York: Macmillan.

—————— (1951). A formal theory of the employment relation. *Econometrica, 19,* 293–305. (Reprinted in H. A. Simon, *Models of man.* New York: Wiley. Chapter 11.)

—————— (1952). A comparison of organization theories. *Rev. econ. Studies, 20,* 40–48. (Reprinted in H. A. Simon, *Models of man.* New York: Wiley. Chapter 10.)

—————— (1955). A behavioral model of rational choice. *Quart. J. Econ., 69,* 99–118. (Reprinted in H. A. Simon, *Models of man.* New York: Wiley. Chapter 14.)

—————— (1956). Rational choice and the structure of the environment. *Psychol. Rev., 63,* 129–138. (Reprinted in H. A. Simon, *Models of man.* New York: Wiley, 1957. Chapter 15.)

—————— (1957). *Models of man.* New York: Wiley.

Simon, H. A., and C. P. Bonini (1958). The size distribution of business firms. *Amer. econ. Rev., 48,* 607–617.

Smelser, N. J. (1963). *The sociology of economic life.* Englewood Cliffs, N.J.: Prentice-Hall.

Smith, A. (1911). *The wealth of nations.* London: G. Bell and Sons, Ltd.

Solomon, E. (1966). Accounting measurements and the evaluation of profitability: true yield versus book yield. In Y. Ijiri, R. K. Jaedicke, and O. Nielson (Eds.), *Research in accounting measurement.* Menasha, Wisc.: American Accounting Association. Pp. 232–243.

Sprowls, R. C. (1962). Business simulation. In H. Borko (Ed.), *Computer applications in the behavioral sciences.* Englewood Cliffs, N.J.: Prentice-Hall. Pp. 78, 510, B63C.

Starbuck, W. H. (1963). Level of aspiration. *Behav. Sci., 8,* 128–136.

Stedry, A. C. (1959). A note on interest rates and the demand for money. *Rev. Econ. Statist., 41,* 303–307.

———— (1960). *Budget control and cost behavior.* Englewood Cliffs, N.J.: Prentice-Hall.

———— (1964).   Budgeting and employee behavior: a reply. *J. Bus., 35,* 195–202.

Stedry, A. C., and E. Kay (1966). The effect of goal difficulty on performance: a field experiment. *Behav. Sci., 11,* 459–470.

Theil, H. (1961). *Economic forecasts and policy* (2nd rev. ed.). Amsterdam: North-Holland.

———— (1964). *Optimal decision rules for government and industry.* Amsterdam: North-Holland.

Thurstone, L. L. (1931). The indifference function. *J. soc. Psychol., 2,* 139–167.

Tobin, J. (1947). Liquidity preference and monetary policy. *Rev. Econ. Statist., 29,* 124–131.

Tolman, E. C. (1948). Cognitive maps in rats and men. *Psychol. Rev., 55,* 189–208.

———— (1949). There is more than one kind of learning. *Psychol. Rev., 56,* 144–155.

Tonge, F. M. (1961). *A heuristic program for assembly line balancing.* Englewood Cliffs, N.J.: Prentice-Hall.

Udy, S. H., Jr. (1964). Administrative rationality, social setting and organizational development. In W. W. Cooper, H. J. Leavitt, and M. W. Shelly (Eds.), *New perspectives in organization research.* New York: Wiley. Pp. 173–192.

Van de Panne, C. (1965). Optimal strategy decisions for dynamic linear decision rules in feedback form. *Econometrica, 33,* 307–320.

Vroom, V. H. (1960). *Some personality determinants of the effects of participation.* Englewood Cliffs, N.J.: Prentice-Hall.

———— (1964). *Work and motivation.* New York: Wiley.

Weingartner, H. M. (1963). *Mathematical programming and the analysis of capital budgeting problems.* Englewood Cliffs, N.J.: Prentice-Hall.

Weisskopf, W. A. (1955). *The psychology of economics.* Chicago: Univ. Chicago Press.

White, H. (1963). Uses of mathematics in sociology. In J. C. Charlesworth (Ed.), *Mathematics and the social sciences.* Philadelphia: American Academy of Political and Social Science. Pp. 77–94.

———— (1964). The cumulation of roles into homogenous structures. In W. W. Cooper, H. J. Leavitt, and M. W. Shelly (Eds.), *New perspectives in organization research.* New York: Wiley. Pp. 195–211.

Williamson, O. E. (1964). *The economics of discretionary behavior.* Englewood Cliffs, N.J.: Prentice-Hall.

Zipf, G. K. (1949). *The principle of least effort.* Cambridge, Mass.: Addison-Wesley.

41

Political Behavior

DAVID O. SEARS, *University of California, Los Angeles*

The primary purpose of this chapter is to present a social-psychological account of the formation and change of political opinion. It emphasizes the political socialization of children and postadolescents, public political sophistication, political information processing, voting behavior, and electoral change. A secondary concern is the socialization of democratic ideals, such as tolerance for minorities and respect for their rights.

The chapter is intended to address only a portion of the broad field described as "political behavior." The simplest typology of this field is Lane's (1963), based on a distinction among six political processes: electoral and public opinion, legislative, administrative, judicial and legal, international, and integrative. Only the first is dealt with here. This is not too unrepresentative of the field as a whole, since "electoral and public opinion processes" have received considerably more systematic empirical attention than all the others combined. Research on the others is growing, however, and the potential utility of social-psychological approaches should become increasingly obvious as it does.

The emphasis throughout will be upon the presentation of political data, analyzed in terms of some rather simple psychological ideas. The explorer of interdisciplinary terrain usually has the option of emphasizing descriptive data from the more "applied" discipline or the explanatory concepts of the more "basic" one. Today, the empirical information available on political behavior is extensive, while social psychology is in general rather modest about its theories. Exotic interpretations of commonplace political phenomena should not, therefore, be expected. However, the

The author wishes to express thanks to Ronald P. Abeles for assistance with the library research, to Raymond Wolfinger, Fred I. Greenstein, and Robert Riley for their comments, and to Judith Azen and Karen Stanley Ebeling for secretarial assistance. Preparation of the manuscript was supported by National Science Foundation grant GS-232 to the author. It was completed while the author held a visiting appointment in the Department of Social Relations at Harvard University, whose support is gratefully acknowledged.

context furnished by contemporary experimental social psychology should deepen the understanding of these phenomena.

The literature on which this chapter concentrates faces three main problems of generality. The first is the problem of distinguishing real from chance effects. Significance tests are not typically used in evaluating nonexperimental data on political behavior. The precaution used below, in general, is to restrict the discussion to large differences obtained in large and representative samples. However, these criteria can be applied only intuitively.

The second is the problem of generalizing across political systems. Enthusiasm for empirical social science (or "behavioralism," in the lingo of political science) has been primarily, though not exclusively, an American phenomenon. Thus most data have been collected in the United States. With rare exceptions, data from other nations are not cited below. Limiting one's aspirations to the understanding of American political behavior scarcely reduces the size of the task, but greater generality may occasionally be implied below. It is not usually intended.

The third problem lies in generalizing across elections. Most of the available evidence has been gathered on Presidential elections since 1940. These are of considerable current interest, but indeterminate historical generality; and they differ in some crucial respects from other elections (for example, for County Assessor). This is not a particularly serious handicap, since, as will be seen, it is very likely that the principles are about the same across elections, though the values of the parameters change somewhat (presence or absence of party label, variations in turnout rate, volume of mass media coverage, etc.). Nevertheless, we are partly at the mercy of history. To the extent that recent history has only incompletely sampled political stimuli, we run the risk of embarrassing inaccuracies should conditions change in the future. The political events of 1968 have been unnerving for this as well as other reasons; at the moment they seem not to force a fundamental revision in what follows, but only time can tell.

One final limitation should be mentioned. Almost all the studies cited are survey studies rather than experimental studies. Experimental research on political behavior is quite feasible, and has been attempted on occasion. It is to be hoped that those occasions will become more frequent. In the meantime, the primary mode of analysis must be correlational, with causal explanations based on the use of partial correlations or other controls. Again, caution is in order: the discussion below may occasionally be misleading if it is taken literally in this respect.

THE INDIVIDUAL VOTE DECISION

Perhaps the most common question about the political behavior of American citizens asks what determines their votes. Partly this is because voting is the main form of political participation for most citizens, and partly it is because the most dramatic political changes in America usually derive from elections.

Since the refinement of sample survey techniques in the 1940's and 1950's, a considerable volume of research has been done on the behavior of the individual American voter. The first modern study was a panel survey conducted in Erie County, Ohio, on the 1940 Presidential contest between Roosevelt and Willkie. Each of 600 respondents was interviewed seven times between May and November 1940, in an effort to account for changes in preference as they occurred rather than retrospectively (as is necessary if only a single preelection interview is used). The results were reported by Lazarsfeld, Berelson, and Gaudet in *The People's Choice* (1948).

The main finding was that very little change occurred during the campaign. Sixty-nine percent indicated the same vote intention (Democrat, Republican, or undecided) in October that they had given in May, and only 5 percent indicated a change in partisan preference. The other 26 percent either became undecided, or started with no preference and later acquired one (Lazarsfeld, Berelson, and Gaudet, 1948, p. 102).

The mass media seemed to have little to do with these changes. In the first place, the absolute level of exposure to campaign propaganda was low; about half the people were not exposed to the main flood of campaign oratory and written material disseminated in the last frantic days of the campaign (p. 121). Second, campaign propaganda mainly reached those who were highly interested in the campaign; since these tended also to be the most committed partisans, the propaganda rarely reached the vulnerable. Instead of having a converting effect, then, campaign propaganda seemed primarily to activate latent predispositions or reinforce existing candidate preferences. The main mediating variable used in this connection was selective exposure, that is, the notion that people expose themselves primarily to propaganda favoring their own initial positions (pp. 82, 90).

The voter's social characteristics were invoked to account for his vote. The Index of Political Predisposition (IPP) simply added the respondent's standing on three demographic variables: religion, social class, and urban or rural residence. The maximum pro-Democratic predisposition was held by Catholic, working-class, urban residents; the maximum pro-Republican, by Protestant, middle-class, rural residents. Individual votes were closely associated with the Index, according to the aggregate data presented. The proportions voting Democratic at its six successive levels were, respectively, 83, 70, 56, 39, 27, and 26 percent (p. 26).

People with politically contradictory predispositions (for example, middle-class Catholics) tended to vacillate in their preferences, deciding relatively late in the campaign. They were described as being under "cross pressures," and seemed to have less interest in the campaign, be less attentive to the mass media, and be more dependent on personal influence than those who maintained constant partisan preferences throughout the campaign. From such findings came the impression that "changers" cast thoughtless, near-random votes, rather than being sensitive spectators to the hue and cry who cast their votes carefully and deliberately.

From this early research, and later work in its tradition, Rossi (1966) culled six main generalizations about voting behavior. The first four are particularly important because they counter common lay observations: (1) campaign issues are not important contributors to electoral choice: "by and large voters assimilate their stands on issues to their long standing loyalties to parties and their candidates" (p. 72); (2) relatively few voters change candidate preferences during political campaigns, and those that do tend to be the less attentive and knowledgeable; (3) the mass media do not change many votes during campaigns; and (4) personality variables have not been demonstrated to relate strongly to partisan choice. The primary determinants of the vote are viewed as being social, and of long standing: (5) partisan choice correlates clearly and consistently with membership in certain social groups and aggregrates (for example, Catholics are more Democratic than Protestants); and (6) primary groups (such as the family or work group), rather than personality structure or political ideology, provide the major sources for longstanding political loyalties. Voters reflect the political complexions of their immediate surroundings.

Later in this chapter, the first two of these assertions, deprecating the role of campaign issues and minimizing the number and quality of changers, will be considered in more detail. The next two, minimizing the roles of the mass media and of personality variables, have not been challenged in an important way since the Erie County study was published (see Greenstein, 1967; Klapper, 1960), and consequently will not be addressed in this chapter. It is the last two of these, attributing partisan choice to longstanding loyalties to primary and to secondary groups, that we now turn to. The most obvious shortcoming they present is that they offer too rigid a view of the determinants of voting behavior; they do not offer a clear way of accounting for the radical (and seemingly systematic) swings that occur regularly in electoral outcome.

A simple way to operationalize this question is to ask how much weight to give each of several potential ingredients in the vote decision. Obviously, every campaign provides a number of standard inputs: candidates, campaign issues, recommendations made by primary and secondary groups, predispositions within the voter, and so on. A common, if perhaps chimerical, assumption is that some are regularly much more influential over individual votes than others. The following represents an assessment of efforts to establish such causal priorities. There are two basic questions: (1) Is one of these inputs regularly more closely related to the vote? (2) What is the causal sequence among them? For example, are attitudes toward campaign issues just rationalizations for party-line voting, or for a commitment to a charismatic leader? We will limit the discussion to partisan choice as a dependent variable, ignoring variations in turnout [a lengthy subject in itself, though its importance in Presidential races may have been exaggerated (*cf.* Andrews, 1966; Fuchs, 1966; Kelley, Ayres, and Bowen, 1967)]. Also, we will consider Presidential rather than lesser races, only because existing research has concentrated on them. The main efforts are considered in historical sequence.

The IPP

Using the three demographic predictors has the disadvantage that their partisan implications are quite variable both over geography and over time, and are not always impressively large. When applied to national samples in 1944 and 1948, the association between the IPP and the vote was not striking (Janowitz and Miller, 1952; Lazarsfeld, Berelson, and Gaudet, 1948, p. xvi). Social class was apparently only modestly related to partisan preference before the Depression, and again is declining in importance (Campbell *et al.*, 1960; Key, 1955). In the South the relationship is not so clear (Converse, 1963a). In fact, in the United States as a whole, the correlation is rather weak, especially as compared to several European nations (Thompson, 1967). Religion sharply differentiated the parties in 1960, but not so clearly in 1952 and 1956 (Converse, 1966c), and perhaps even less so prior to the 1920's (Key, 1959). Whatever the limitations of the IPP, however, *The People's Choice* must be regarded as a landmark venture. Its findings anticipate much of the more detailed work to be reviewed below, and the book itself is a model of clear scientific exposition (even if the data presentation is sometimes obscure).

"Voting": the Elmira study

The same research group did a panel study of the 1948 Presidential contest in El-mira, New York (Berelson, Lazarsfeld, and McPhee, 1954). Their analysis was in many ways more thorough than their previous study, but will not be considered in this context, since no single model of the individual voting decision was derived and tested.

"The Voter Decides"

Researchers at the Survey Research Center of the University of Michigan have pur-sued another general approach. They view the decision sequence as one in which all inputs (whether new information or preexisting attitudes and predispositions) are translated into partisan attitudes favoring one side or the other. These partisan attitudes in turn determine the individual's vote decision. As will be seen, these authors conceptually treated all inputs in much the same way initially. In later studies, party identification was distinguished from those partisan attitudes that dealt pri-marily with the stuff of the campaign (principally the candidates, campaign issues, and group appeals).

In the first study, three dimensions were used: party identification, issue orien-tation, and candidate orientation. Data were from a nationwide sample in 1952 (Campbell, Gurin, and Miller, 1954).

Party identification. Party identification is "the sense of personal attachment which the individual feels toward the [party] of his choice" (Campbell, Gurin, and Miller, 1954, pp. 88–89). A single item was used to measure it, and this item is worth quoting because it is central to numerous later analyses: "Generally speaking, do you usually think of yourself as a Republican, a Democrat, an Independent, or what?" If the respondent answered "Republican" or "Democrat," he was asked: "Would you call yourself a strong Republican (Democrat) or a not very strong Republican (Demo-crat)?" If, on the other hand, he had answered "Independent," he was further asked: "Do you think of yourself as closer to the Republican or Democratic party?" A seven-point scale emerges: strong and weak Democrats; Independents leaning toward the Democrats, neither party, or Republicans; and weak and strong Republi-cans.

This measure correlated closely with the 1952 Presidential votes, as shown in Table 1. Its validity is further suggested by the "strong" party identifiers' claims that they would more readily support disagreeable candidates of their own party, and more often vote straight party tickets, compared to "weak" party identifiers or independents. Also, it is closely related to the respondent's recall of his past party regularity, and to the party for which he first voted (Campbell, Gurin, and Miller, 1954, pp. 97–107).

Issue orientation. The relevance of political issues to the vote decision was described in terms of two dimensions. "Issue partisanship" was based on the extent to which the respondent took a consistently Republican or Democratic party line on four se-lected campaign issues, and on whether or not he correctly perceived the policy differences between the two parties on two given issues. Hence, a person who took the same policy positions as the Democratic party and was aware of the true party differences in policy stands would be classified as a strongly Democratic issue partisan;

TABLE 1

PARTY IDENTIFICATION AND CANDIDATE PREFERENCE IN 1952

	Democrat		Independent			Republican	
	Strong	Weak	Demo-crat leaning	Inde-pendent	Repub-lican leaning	Weak	Strong
Eisenhower	15%	38%	35%	74%	89%	90%	99%
Stevenson	83	59	61	20	9	10	1
Other responses	2	3	4	6	2	—	—
	100%	100%	100%	100%	100%	100%	100%

Source: Campbell, Gurin, and Miller, 1954, p. 109. The figures represent percent voting, or if not voting, preferring a given candidate. Data are from the 1952 Survey Research Center election study.

on the other hand, if he either took positions favoring neither side consistently, or was insensitive or mistaken about party differences, he would be a weak issue partisan. The vote turned out to be substantially correlated with issue partisanship.

The second dimension, "extent of issue orientation," was based on a combination of sensitivity to party differences and how many issues the respondent took a position on. Hence, the highly issue-oriented person was both sensitive and opinionated; low issue orientation implied insensitivity and few issue stands (Campbell, Gurin, and Miller, 1954, p. 130).

Candidate orientation. The voter's attitudes toward the candidates were also described in terms of two variables: "candidate partisanship," the extent to which his expressed comments about the two candidates favored one or the other, and the "extent of candidate orientation," based simply on the number of all positive and negative personal references made to the candidates (Campbell, Gurin, and Miller, 1954, p. 137). Candidate partisanship, too, was related strongly to the vote.

Thus each of these three dimensions of attitude was associated with the vote. In combination, they were simply treated as additive motivational constructs. And indeed, the greater their consistency, the more likely the indicated vote. When inconsistent, no response or an ambiguous response was expected, and conflict between the three was in fact related to vacillation about candidate choice, later decisions, and split-ticket voting (pp. 157–164).

Our primary concern here, however, is with the relative contribution of each dimension to the vote. The authors offer some data, but they are not very helpful. All three partisan orientations were positively correlated with each other (p. 145), but the magnitude of correlation was not assessed. Another test was to see which partisan attitudes were most prominent among those who switched to a Republican vote in 1952. Their Republican sentiments show up more clearly on candidate partisanship than on either of the other dimensions (pp. 168–170), suggesting that 1948–1952 candidate differences might have been particularly important in electoral change (a suggestion supported by Hyman and Sheatsley, 1953, on the basis of other convincing data). Thus, the data from this study yield neither a quantitative comparison of the power of these several dimensions nor a causal sequence.

TABLE 2

CORRELATION OF PARTISAN ATTITUDES WITH 1952 PRESIDENTIAL CHOICE

	Simple correlation	*Partial correlation (other four held constant)*
Party identification	+ 0.59	+ 0.42
Domestic-issue partisanship	0.48	0.23
Foreign-issue partisanship	0.38	0.20
Orientation to Eisenhower	0.35	0.16
Orientation to Stevenson	0.23	0.12

Source: Campbell and Stokes, 1959, p. 356. $N = 1522$, and includes all respondents expressing a preference for a major-party candidate. Multiple correlation of five attitudes with choice is 0.68. Data are from the 1952 Survey Research Center election study.

Unique variance

A later refinement attempted to determine more directly how much variance each partisan attitude contributed to the vote (Campbell and Stokes, 1959). Party identification was clearly the most influential, correlating 0.59 with candidate preference, whereas the multiple correlation based on all partisan attitudes (expanded to five for this analysis) was only 0.68. Partial correlations were used to index the amount of unique variance each dimension contributed to candidate preference. This procedure simply exaggerated the dominant status of party identification, as shown in Table 2. Note that data are from 1952, a year when defection from party commitments was at a relatively high level; thus perhaps they even underestimate the power of party identification. It was not just the "least admirable" voters who used party identification to guide their votes: it was the most important variable for those who "cared very much" as well as for those who "didn't care at all" about the election (p. 364), and for those who decided during the campaign as well as for those who "knew all along." Its supremacy was slightly less marked at higher educational levels, but still held (p. 360).

Party identification thus appears to account for the lion's share of variance in individual vote decisions. The major exception seems to be those who decide at the last moment; their votes are not highly correlated with party identification (or *any* partisan attitudes). Party identification seems also to account for much of the correlation between the vote and the other partisan attitudes. It is the only partisan attitude controlling much independent or unique variance; the correlations between the others and candidate preference tend to wash out with party identification held constant. This again suggests a process whereby campaigns activate and reinforce longstanding partisan predispositions, and align attitudes toward the partisan stuff of the campaign with them.

It might be noted in passing that the other partisan attitudes were measured in a different way in this study, and that all subsequent studies used this revised procedure. At the beginning of each interview, eight open-ended questions had been asked about the two political parties and about the two Presidential candidates: for example, "I'd like to ask you what you think are the good and bad points about the two parties.

Is there anything in particular that you (like, don't like) about the (Democratic, Republican) Party? What is that?" (Campbell, Gurin, and Miller, 1954, p. 215). Partisan attitudes toward a given candidate or issue area were measured by subtracting the number of pro-Democratic references to it from the number of pro-Republican references.

"The American Voter"

In a third effort by the Survey Research Center (Campbell *et al.*, 1960, Chapters 3 and 4; Stokes, Campbell, and Miller, 1958), all partisan attitudes were derived from these open-ended questions. The six partisan attitudes used again yielded a high multiple correlation with Presidential preference ($r = 0.71$ in 1956). Also, the best-predicting combination of these dimensions correctly classified 86 per cent of the respondents' votes (Campbell *et al.*, 1960, p. 74). This analysis does not try to measure in detail the variance uniquely attributable to any given partisan attitude.

Campbell *et al.* repeated the finding that conflicting partisan attitudes are associated with later decisions, split-ticket voting, and indifference to the election outcome (1960, pp. 82–86). And, as in the Campbell and Stokes (1959) analysis, partisan attitudes explained the individual's vote powerfully if he "knew all along" whom to vote for (multiple $r = 0.80$ and 0.79 for 1952 and 1956, respectively), but weakly if he "decided within two weeks of the election" ($r = 0.29$ and 0.21) (Campbell *et al.*, 1960, p. 79).

The conceptual status of party identification is changed in this analysis. It is now seen not as one of the partisan attitudes, but as an antecedent factor that partially organizes them. Party identification correlates highly with the partisan attitudes, accounting for about half the variance in them (Goldberg, 1966, p. 97). Campbell *et al.* (1960) conclude: "the voting act can be explained in an immediate sense by the strength and direction and consistency of attitudes toward the political objects this act touches. We find now that an important part of the variation in the partisanship and internal coherence of these attitudes may in turn be accounted for by stable partisan identifications" (p. 136). Over the long term, or at occasional critical junctures of history, partisan attitudes may influence party identification. More typically, however, the direction of influence is otherwise: party loyalty determines much of the content of the transitory partisan attitudes concerned with any given election.

A causal inference model

Goldberg (1966) has applied the causal inference technique (see Blalock, 1964) to these questions. The technique permits the posing of various alternative causal models, then testing them with partial correlations. Goldberg used five variables from the 1956 Survey Research Center election study to predict Presidential vote: father's sociological characteristics and party identification, and the respondent's sociological characteristics, party identification, and partisan attitudes (as defined in Campbell *et al.*, 1960).

Three distinctive alternative models were tested. The first was essentially that of *The American Voter* (Campbell *et al.*, 1960, pp. 24–37). The vote was seen as a direct product of partisan attitudes, which in turn were a joint product of father's and own social characteristics, and own party identification. That is, the "attitude field is taken to be the result of two causal streams, one consisting in the sociological conditioning of childhood and adult life [Berelson, Lazarsfeld, and McPhee, 1954], and the other consisting in affective conditioning to the party label [Lane and Sears, 1964]" (Goldberg, 1966, p. 915). The model seems to fall short at several points, but most notably in not asserting a direct causal link between the respondent's party identification and his vote; evidently all such effects of party identification on the vote are *not* mediated by his partisan attitudes.

A second model sees party identification as the final mediator, whose immediate precursors are current partisan attitudes, own social characteristics, and father's party identification. Essentially, this model asserts that people vote on the basis of their party preferences, which are reorganized for each election to take account of new developments. This model is plausible but something of a straw man, since, as will be seen later, party identification is quite stable and is not usually adjusted to fit current vote intentions. In any case, the model falls short, mainly through the large unexplained variance caused by partisan attitudes reflected directly in the vote (not mediated through party identification), and the influence of party identification on partisan attitudes.

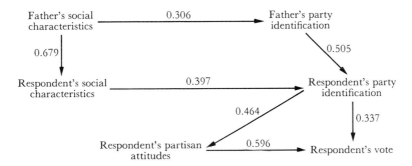

Fig. 1. Voting model. The numbers are the beta weights for the causal relationships specified. Only those significant beyond the 0.01 level are shown. Data are from the 1956 Survey Research Center election study. (From Goldberg, 1966.)

The final, and most satisfactory, model sees the vote as jointly a product of party identification and partisan attitudes, with the latter also in part a result of the former. This model is diagrammed in Fig. 1. Perhaps most important, according to this model, is that "father's sociological characteristics, father's party identification, and respondent's sociological characteristics have almost no impact upon voting behavior save as they act through respondent's party identification" (Goldberg, 1966, p. 919). Hence, it emphasizes the role of political socialization in producing durable party loyalties rather than "a conscious evaluative relating of political means to ends" (p. 919) or the simple translation of sociological characteristics into the vote, as in *The People's Choice*.

This optimal model, using these six variables, accounts for 50 percent of the variance in voting. This represents enormous power by the normal standards of behavioral science, but it does leave plenty of room for improvement. Goldberg noted two shortcomings in particular. It does not provide for any impact of partisan attitudes on party identification, and thus is unable to take account of "critical" or "realigning" elections in which large population groups switch or acquire new party allegiances (Key, 1955). However, these are relatively uncommon events (Campbell, 1966a).

More serious, it does not take account of political events in the environment. Like all analyses discussed in this section, it views the vote only as a reflection of predispositions (party identification, social characteristics, residues of socialization, etc.) and the respondent's evaluative response to stimuli (partisan attitudes). The process by which events in the external world are translated into partisan attitudes falls outside its purview. This second shortcoming is, of course, more severe, since party identification is known to be quite stable, while partisan attitudes fluctuate considerably from year to year.

PROCESSING OF POLITICAL INFORMATION

The optimal model discussed above turns attention back upon the antecedents of partisan attitudes and of party identification. As is implied in the model, party identification is perhaps best accounted for in historical terms, and this will be dealt with later when we discuss political socialization. Partisan attitudes, though, appear to represent some resultant of party identification and the individual's perception of political events. In this section we consider first how sophisticated, complex, and veridical these perceptions typically are, and second, the process by which external events are generally translated into partisan attitudes and a vote.

THE PUBLIC'S POLITICAL SOPHISTICATION

Popularized versions of democratic theory often presuppose what Hennessey (1965) has called the "omnicompetent" citizen. In particular, they have assumed three things about the voter: (1) that he is attentive to and informed about the persons and issues in public life, (2) that he accurately perceives the alternative positions taken by each political party or major faction in important policy disputes, and (3) that he holds some one of the apparently common versions of political ideology (for example, he stands somewhere on the liberal-conservative continuum), so that he can assess political alternatives by referring to his own ideological predispositions. In this section some evidence on these assumptions will be reviewed.

Salience

The first and most important point is that politics, or public affairs in general, represents a world to which most citizens are quite indifferent. They rarely think or talk about political issues, and as a consequence their political opinions tend not to be deeply considered. Cantril (1965, p. 36), trying to describe "human concerns," asked Americans what their fondest hopes and worst fears were. Political matters were mentioned by two percent and five percent in these two contexts, respectively, and the international situation by ten percent and 24 percent. Much more salient than either, of course, were their own families' economic and health situations. Better economic status was most hoped for by 65 percent, better health by 48 percent. Worse health was feared by 56 percent, and economic difficulties by 46 percent. Thus, personal lives are far more salient in the average person's thinking than political matters; this implies not only that political matters are generally of low salience, but also that they can become of great salience when they have direct personal relevance.

Information level

How aware are American citizens of the persons, issues, and events that presumably form the bases for periodic electoral choices? In 1962 and 1963 Erskine summarized results from numerous representative samples in her useful regular feature on "The Polls" in the *Public Opinion Quarterly*. The data in the following discussion are all drawn from those summaries, though the source for each one is not cited individually. Tables 3, 4, and 5 give some representative items. The exact levels of familiarity depend to some extent on the details of the interview situation, but these items should permit some intuitive grasp of the amount of information possessed by the general public. For other useful interpretations, see Hyman and Sheatsley (1954) and Bell, Hill, and Wright (1961).

The chronic know-nothings. Hyman and Sheatsley (1954) have described a "hard core of know-nothings," familiar with virtually nothing political, as follows: "In almost every instance where the polls have tested public information, at least 20 percent of the population have revealed complete ignorance" (p. 36). While there is much truth in this observation, Tables 3, 4, and 5 reveal occasional exceptions. Incumbent Presidents or major-party Presidential candidates are known to virtually everyone, as are war heroes such as MacArthur and Eisenhower. Occasional headline events such as the downing of the U-2 plane or the 1961 Berlin crisis reach almost everyone. Similarly, 99.8 percent of a National Opinion Research Corporation (NORC) national sample had heard of President Kennedy's assassination within five hours of its occurrence (Sheatsley and Feldman, 1965). However, these are exceptions; only rarely is a public this well aware of public persons or events. In 1955, only 90 percent could identify Christopher Columbus and 67 percent Napoleon (Erskine, 1963a). And the "know-nothings" had not heard of medicare or the Peace Corps by 1962.

The informed layman. The same tables give a fairly accurate picture of what the average, moderately well-informed layman knows, as indicated by those political stimuli familiar to 50 to 75 percent of the public. He is likely to be familiar with the most salient person in any given category. He knows of Walter Reuther, but not David MacDonald; before the 1956 Democratic convention, Adlai Stevenson but not one of his major rivals, Averill Harriman; Estes Kefauver, but not Adlai Stevenson before the 1952 conventions. He will be able to identify an occasional foreign leader, but usually not Congressional leaders. Many, but far from all, will surpass the rather rudimentary hurdle of knowing which party controls Congress: between 43 and 61 percent (depending on whether or not one corrects for guessing), according to a 1958 study (Stokes and Miller, 1962). The informed layman will recognize the most salient cabinet officers (for example, Dean Acheson in 1950) and usually knows the Vice-President's name (69 percent in 1952). The average citizen does not possess more esoteric bits of knowledge, such as (in 1948) who Norman Thomas was.

Political issues and events obey the same rule. The periodic Congressional sideshows do reach most people in some form or another. Senator McCarthy's charges about the State Department, the Kefauver crime investigation, or the House Committee on Un-American Activities were all known to 60 percent or more in their heydays. Highly controversial policy issues, however, may not have the currency often assumed for them, as Table 4 shows. Only 72 percent were familiar with the Taft-Hartley law in 1948 and 66 percent with the term "right-to-work" in 1957, though these were among the "hottest" and most controversial domestic issues of their day.

TABLE 3

PERCENTAGE OF RESPONDENTS IDENTIFYING NAMES OF PUBLIC PERSONS

	Poll date *(month/year)*	*Percent*
Presidency		
Harry S. Truman	11/47	98%
Adlai Stevenson	6/56	88
Dwight Eisenhower	6/52	83
Estes Kefauver	6/52	67
Adlai Stevenson	6/52	34
Nonpolitical		
Douglas MacArthur	11/47	97%
Dwight Eisenhower	11/47	95
John L. Lewis	4/57	93
Walter Reuther	4/57	70
Domestic politics		
Gov. Orval Faubus	10/57	57%
Sen. Lyndon Johnson	6/56	32
Sen. Harry S. Byrd	11/47	32
Foreign affairs		
Dean Acheson	12/50	66%
Sen. Arthur Vandenberg	11/47	65
V. M. Molotov	9/47	62
Marshal Tito	10/51	43
Andrei Gromyko	9/47	34
Warren Austin	9/47	11

Source: Erskine, 1962. Data are mainly from Gallup polls.

The data presented by Erskine suggest that the average citizen, not unusually involved in politics, attends to only the most salient headline issues of the day. Beyond that level, his knowledge is exhausted. Perhaps a good rule of thumb is that, in most domains, only the single most vivid person or issue reaches the average American's awareness.

The attentive public. Except in unusual circumstances, cabinet members, ambassadors, powerful Senators and Congressmen, and leaders of foreign nations are likely to be known only to a fraction of the public. For example, the U.S. Ambassador to the United Nations, Warren Austin, could be identified by only 11 percent of the public in 1947. As majority leader of the Senate, and thus a leading opposition leader to the Eisenhower Administration in 1956, Lyndon Johnson was known by only 32 percent of the public. Earlier, House Speaker Joseph Martin was known only to 33 percent, the very powerful Senator Harry S. Byrd to 32 percent, and so on. In 1955, only 22 percent of the general public had ever heard of Sigmund Freud.

TABLE 4
PERCENTAGE OF RESPONDENTS FAMILIAR WITH SELECTED ISSUES AND EVENTS

	Date of poll (month/year)	Percent
Highly visible		
U-2 plane downed	6/60	96%
U.N. or United Nations	5/48	89
Berlin crisis	9/61	89
Army-McCarthy hearings	5/54	87
Marshall Plan	11/48	82
Kennedy's medicare plan	8/62	81
McCarthy's charges about Reds in the State Department	7/50	78
Medium visibility		
Kefauver crime probe	4/51	72%
Taft-Hartley law	6/48	72
Peace Corps	11/62	71
Right-to-work laws	8/57	66
House Committee on Un-American Activities	1/49	64
Voice of America broadcasts	6/51	46
Low visibility		
Hoover Commission reports	5/49	28%
The term "bipartisan foreign policy"	6/50	26
Americans for Democratic Action	2/48	23
Truman's Point Four program	5/50	23
Common Market	12/61	22
Bricker amendment	10/53	19

Source: Erskine, 1962, 1963b, 1963c. The figures represent the percentage of people who said that they had heard or read about the item. Data are mainly from Gallup polls.

Even extremely important issues often do not penetrate beyond those few who are most concerned with them. The "bipartisan foreign policy" concept was familiar to only 26 percent in 1950; and the Bricker Amendment, a truly revolutionary effort to change procedures for making foreign policy, was known to only 19 percent. Therefore, there is no reason to assume widespread public awareness of an issue even when legislative circles are hotly and deeply split on it. In fact, a good rule of thumb is that one almost invariably overestimates public awareness, and probably by large margins in most cases.

Candidates' visibility. Awareness of candidates for elective office is of particular importance. The 1948 data, shown in Table 5, are probably representative. At the Presidential level, usually about 10 percent of the population are unable to recall the name of a major party candidate, and far more do not know the name of the Vice-Presidential candidate. Presidential candidates' visibility prior to the national conventions is highly variable, as shown by some examples in Table 3. The "dark horse" Stevenson

TABLE 5

PERCENTAGE OF RESPONDENTS CORRECTLY
RECALLING CANDIDATES' NAMES, AUGUST, 1948

	Presidential	*Vice-Presidential*
Republican Party (Dewey, Warren)	88%	58%
Democratic Party (Truman, Barkley)	91	49
Progressive Party (Wallace, Taylor)	67	30
Socialist Party (Thomas, Smith)	21	0

Source: Erskine, 1962. Data are from Gallup poll.

was known to 34 percent in 1952, but four years later, after he had been defeated once, to 88 percent.

Of course, a wise Presidential vote does not necessarily depend on knowledge of the Vice-Presidential candidates, or even of the rivals for a nomination. But ignorance is a serious problem in races for lesser offices. Relatively few people know who their United States Senators and Congressmen are. Typical percentages cited by Erskine (1963a) are 35 percent accurately naming both Senators, 38 percent their Congressman, and 57 percent one of their two Senators.

Most surprising is how few people are exposed to any information at all about each Congressional candidate during an election campaign. Table 6 gives data from the 1958 campaign, and shows that only 24 percent meet the traditional criterion for a democratic election—that is, hearing or reading something about each candidate—and 46 percent are exposed to *no* information about *either* candidate. There are dramatic if rare exceptions: Miller and Stokes (1966, p. 369) cite the 1958 Little Rock Congressional race, which had gotten mixed up in the local school integration controversy. There, virtually every voter seems to have heard something about each candidate.

While familiarity with Congressional candidates seems rare, familiarity with the candidates for the many obscure state and local offices for which voters are asked to cast ballots must be even rarer. Theoretically, local offices are closer to home and the issues and candidates should be much more familiar. This seems unlikely in the extreme. Wise voting in these races must be based on something other than detailed familiarity with the alternatives. In this connection, the advantage accruing to the Congressional incumbent is an interesting sidelight of Table 6. Obviously, the system would be vastly more unstable if for some reason incumbents never succeeded themselves, provided that information about the candidates remained as rare as it is.

Finally, we might remind ourselves that the American public is as affluent, as unpreoccupied with subsistence needs, as literate and well-educated, and as politically involved as any in modern times. In fact, Almond and Verba's (1963, p. 96) data suggest that Americans are unusually well-informed voters by the standards of other Western nations. Yet their level of political attentiveness is so low that no excuse or rationalization can rescue it. One possible implication is that, unsatisfactory as it is, this level represents some kind of upper limit of public attentiveness in relatively peaceful mass democracies. Certainly one should not assume in the voter too complex a perception of the current flow of political persons and events.

TABLE 6

PERCENTAGE OF RESPONDENTS WHO HAD READ OR HEARD
SOMETHING ABOUT THE CONGRESSIONAL CANDIDATES IN THEIR DISTRICT, 1958

| | | *About incumbent* | | |
		Yes	No	Total
About nonincumbent	Yes	24%	5%	29%
	No	25	46	71
	Total	49%	51%	100%

Source: Miller and Stokes, 1966, p. 367. Includes contested districts only. Data are from the
1958 Survey Research Center election study.

Attitude structures and ideology

The manifestly low information level of the general public might conceivably be compensated for by efficient information processing, based on overall guiding ideological principles or even some integrated clusters of attitudes. How widespread are abstract political ideologies or coherent and integrated attitude structures in the general public?

Recognition of standard descriptive terms. First, how widespread is public comprehension of the conventional terms "liberal" and "conservative"? In one nationwide sample, direct questions were asked about them. Converse (1964) characterized the responses as follows: 17 percent had "an understanding of its breadth," another 35 percent had the terms "rather well under control but [with] a fairly limited set of connotations for them," and the remaining 48 percent of the sample could not be said to have satisfactory understanding of the terms as they are used in American politics. They either could not define the terms, or incorrectly linked party and label, or both (Converse, 1964, p. 223).

Ideology. A very similar tabulation follows from coding free responses concerning differences between the parties (based on the questions cited earlier) for their "level of conceptualization" (Campbell *et al.*, 1960, pp. 216–265). In this now well-known effort, four major categories were defined: $11\frac{1}{2}$ percent of the public was defined as "ideological" or "near-ideological," and another 42 percent described party differences in terms of "group benefits": group interest, direct benefit to specific groups, etc. The least ideological category ($17\frac{1}{2}$ percent) responded in terms wholly irrelevant to policy issues; for example, they just mentioned candidates or could think of no difference between the parties. The remainder (24 percent) were placed in an intermediate category; they often referred to a policy controversy, but without reference to the possible implications of ideological concepts or group interests. This classification, then, identifies only a small fraction of the electorate as conceiving of party differences in ideological or abstract terms.

Much more sophistication is found in political "elites." Converse (1964, p. 226) simulated a typical political rally on the basis of the two dimensions just described. Over 80 percent of the "rally public" are at a level essentially comparable to the most sophisticated half of the general public. Educational differences are equally striking: the percent giving ideological responses is 32 percent for those with some college,

10 percent for those with high school only, and five percent for those with grade school only (Campbell *et al.,* 1960, p. 250). Thus it is not surprising that many political analysts and academics chronically overestimate the electorate's political savvy; they mainly encounter the sophisticates.

Attitude structures. Even if policy attitudes are not usually bound together by underlying abstractions, they may covary together in politically meaningful clusters. In one effort to test this possibility on Survey Research Center data, several domestic policy items were successfully Guttman-scaled, as were several items on internationalism (Campbell *et al.,* 1960, pp. 195–209). However, a surprising number of seemingly related items did not scale. Contradictions between specific items that seem logically connected were also quite common. Those most enthusiastic about foreign aid or increasing domestic welfare programs were not always among those most unwilling to have taxes cut (Key, 1961, pp. 159, 167). Whether or not the government should guarantee employment was unrelated to attitudes toward the influence of big business in government (Key, 1961, p. 169). Hero's (1966, pp. 449–455) analysis of the numerous Gallup polls on the United Nations during 1954 to 1966 reveals some consistency among views on the United Nations itself, but much inconsistency between views on the United Nations and opinions about other related aspects of foreign policy. Hero noted that such relationships are usually statistically significant but weak. And despite the obvious correlation between domestic liberalism and internationalism during the 1950's in Congress and among political activists, the two clusters seem to have been essentially unrelated in the general public, according to the 1952 and 1956 Survey Research Center data (Key, 1961, pp. 157–158).

Axelrod (1967), using cluster analysis on the same data, also found weak domestic-liberalism and foreign-internationalism clusters, but even clearer was a "populism" dimension (following Hofstadter, 1955). The complete populist favors welfare issues but opposes taxes, foreign involvement, and civil liberties. It is a provocative thought that the main "popular" dimension of political coherence is one quite different from that stressed by political analysts. But none of the three clusters was of very great strength.

Perhaps a less demanding test is simply to see whether policy attitudes are systematically correlated at all. Converse (1964, pp. 228–229) reported correlations among seven standard Survey Research Center policy items. The average correlation was 0.23 for domestic issues and for foreign issues, and 0.16 for the whole set. Thus, major policy attitudes seem only modestly interrelated in the general public. Even among the French the interrelations are no higher (Converse and Dupeux, 1962). Bogart (1967, p. 342) concluded aptly that people hold a variety of opinions on any given topic. They may be contradictory and arouse a sense of conflict or discomfort, or they may simply reflect "the opposing view points to which we are subject through mass media and conversation." None of this holds necessarily for more central beliefs, especially (apparently) those referring to social groups. Sheatsley (1966, p. 231) demonstrated very clearly the close relationship between generalized attitudes toward racial integration and specific attitudes toward racial issues. Scores on a prointegration scale (a scale of general attitudes toward the desirability of racial integration) are closely related to such other attitudes as whether or not Negro groups are asking too much, whether the Negro movement has been violent or peaceful, and whether demonstrations have helped or hurt the Negro cause.

In party elites the level of interdependency is much higher, as might be expected. The average correlation in 1958 was 0.53 for congressional candidates on domestic issues, and 0.37 on foreign issues. Converse (1964) suggested that, among such political sophisticates, ideological or abstract principles may assume greater importance as a basis for opinion formation, and group-related attitudes may decline somewhat in centrality. He cited the lower correlation between two civil rights issues (the Fair Employment Practices Commission and school desegregation) among Congressional candidates ($r = 0.31$) than in the general public ($r = 0.57$).

However, in most political situations, greater information sophistication is associated with greater alignment of votes with group memberships. Several examples may make the point. The correlation between vote preference and either subjective social status or occupational status (Campbell *et al.*, 1960, p. 352; Converse, 1964, p. 232) increases at more abstract "levels of conceptualization." Attitudes toward a California fair housing law and a referendum measure to repeal it were inconsistent eight months before the 1964 election for 46 percent of those without a high school diploma, and for only 28 percent of those with more than two years of college (Wolfinger and Greenstein, 1968). McClosky (1964) noted, on the basis of data comparing convention delegates and voters at large, that "the capacity to recognize sympathetic or hostile reference groups is not highly developed among the public at large" (p. 373). A reasonable modification thus suggested by Converse (1964) is that greater sophistication or information increases reliance on group cues, but only up to a point. At extremely high levels of sophistication, more complex and abstract cues take over.

Instability of policy attitudes. If abstract organizing principles are difficult to find, and policy attitudes cohere only in a vague manner, possibly the attitudes themselves are not very meaningful. Again, a simple test has been performed to determine whether or not most policy attitudes are stable in the absence of systematic external pressure to change (as defined by constant marginal divisions of opinion over successive measurements). Attitudes toward specific government policy matters are not particularly stable. Converse (1964, p. 240) reported that test-retest correlations over a two-year period on six policies such as federal aid to education and foreign economic aid ranged from 0.40 to about 0.28. Miller (1967) presented additional data on more general foreign policy stances. The correlation between 1956 and 1960 attitudes about American international involvements was only 0.17; about "the chances of our country getting into war," 0.29; and whether or not "our chances of staying out of war have been getting better," only 0.16 (Miller, 1967, pp. 222–223). These data come from a Survey Research Center panel study conducted from 1956 to 1960. Converse (1963a) used the extravagant but perhaps justified term "nonattitudes" to describe such interview responses. In fact, he argued that the data fit a statistical model in which the vast majority of respondents is responding randomly to these policy questions, and only a minority has "real and stable" attitudes on the matter (p. 15).

Too little research has been done on the cognitive characteristics of popular political thinking (though the force of affective dispositions has been so impressive, and probably controls so large a proportion of the variance, that the emphasis on them is quite understandable—see Osgood, 1962). Lane conducted very lengthy depth interviews with 15 working-class men and published his analyses as *Political*

Ideology (1962). He emphasized in particular two characteristics of American working-class thinking. The working-class time perspective, he found, tended to emphasize "the day after tomorrow." He found little interest in long-range Utopias, or in "bread-circuses," rather "a worried trust in their own future situations and concentration on the problems of the moment" (Lane, 1962, p. 288). This, of course, avoids the most shortsighted selfishness, but it does not facilitate long-range planning, or at least does not precipitate much popular support for it.

Another aspect of American working-class thinking noted by Lane is the lack of "contextualizing" of problems. He found that current political issues were rarely related to historical events, to other policies, or to more fundamental values or ideological dimensions (Lane, 1962, Chapter 22). This held even when democratic values, such as freedom of speech, were at issue. It may be, as Turiel, Kohlberg, and Rest (in press) have suggested, that passive comprehension exists without active spontaneous expression, but there seems to be general agreement about the absence of the latter.

In broad terms, there can be little dispute about the generalization that few citizens organize their political ideas in an abstract ideological framework recognizable to sophisticated political thinkers. Nevertheless, it should be noted that three aspects of the Survey Research Center analysis cited above may underestimate the depth of popular thinking. High correlations between policy items in the general public would depend on a *shared* ideological conception; idiosyncratic ideas, however abstract, would depress the correlations. Axelrod's "populist" ideology is somewhat orthogonal to the conventional liberalism sought by Key (1961), Campbell *et al.* (1960), and Converse (1964), but each shows up as "mush" in the other's analysis. Converse elsewhere (1966c) has begun to look for such idiosyncratic organizations.

Second, the major analysis here (Campbell *et al.*, 1960, pp. 216–265) rests on responses to several open-ended items posed near the beginning of the interview. Spontaneous expression of complex ideas is generally much less common than passive comprehension (Turiel, Kohlberg, and Rest, in press), but either may form a basis for opinion formation. The respondent may not be able to articulate his ideas, but they may nonetheless provide a context for organizing incoming information. And ideas flow more freely with some "warm-up," as Lane (1962) found when he used several interviews per respondent.

Finally, the policy questions used in these Survey Research Center studies were more sophisticated and specialized than those normally used in political polls. This is one advantage, because the issues have not gone out of date quickly. But it may be that policy attitudes on the more visible (if more transitory) issues of the day are more meaningful and more coherently related to basic political perspectives than are attitudes toward these longer-standing questions of fundamental public policy (compare, for example, the question whether or not the federal government should intervene in school segregation, with the question whether or not Negroes are "moving too fast").

However, these cautions should not be interpreted as suggesting any basic doubts about the authors' general conclusions from these studies. The only question is whether or not other estimates, using other data bases, would reveal somewhat more complex thinking.

Stability of party identification. By far the most stable attitude yet reported from this panel study is party identification. The rank-order correlation between 1958 and

1960 was 0.70. Even so, a substantial amount of turnover among the three categories, Democrat, Independent, and Republican, seems to be occurring all the time. In the four-year period between 1956 to 1960, 22.6 percent of the white electorate changed from one to another category (recomputed from data presented by Converse, 1963b).

Most of this change consists of people moving in and out of the Independent category, rather than from party to party. Of those who classified themselves as Independents in 1956, 60 percent changed at least once when retested in 1958 and 1960. Of those with a partisan preference in 1956, 18 percent changed once by 1960. In short, 74.4 percent of the American public retained over three interviews in 1956, 1958, and 1960 the same position in a three-way party classification (recomputed from data presented by Jennings and Niemi, 1966, p. 98).

The next most stable attitudes measured refer to Negroes. The two items regarding establishment of a federal Fair Employment Practices Commission and the federal government's role in school desegregation yielded test-retest correlations over 0.40. Again, the implication is that group-related attitudes are the most meaningful and stable attitudes held to any wide degree in the general public; party identification is perhaps the clearest of these in the political arena.

Perceptions of political parties' positions

The emphasis thus returns to party identification as a key to political opinion formation. This raises the general question of what cognitions are associated with each party's image among the general public. The American political parties and their candidates often differ in policy proposals and/or general ideological stances. To how much of this is the electorate sensitive? What do voters think they are endorsing when they express a party preference or "vote party" for some obscure office?

Generalized party images. Spontaneous descriptions of the parties do yield a certain amount of consensus on a distinctive image for each party. In one large sample, Southerners, white and Negro alike, responded to open-ended questions by associating the Democratic party with liberalism, social welfare policies, spending, good economic conditions, and being good (or too good) to Negroes and workers. Almost no one applied the *opposite* of any of these descriptions to it. The Republican image was, for the most part, just the inverse of this, with the single exception that many also thought the Republicans good or too good to Negroes (Matthews and Prothro, 1966a). Non-Southern data were not presented in detail, but "a comparison of Southern and non-Southern images of the parties reveals that they are highly similar" (p. 157).

This might suggest that the policy, ideological, and group-interest alternatives offered by the two parties are mirrored in the electorate's perceptions. Indeed, little gross distortion occurs. Republicans are rarely viewed as social welfare enthusiasts, for example. However, any given image content appears relatively infrequently. In the Southern white sample, only 29 percent mentioned something about the Democrats in the area of liberalness, social welfare, and spending, and only 24 percent mentioned something about the Republicans' conservatism. The Democrats' alleged goodness to the working man was cited by 29 percent in this sample (Matthews and Prothro, 1966a, pp. 151, 154) and 33 percent nationwide in 1952 (Campbell, Gurin, and Miller, 1954, p. 209). And the precise content of the image depends to some extent on the content of any given campaign. For example, from 1960 to 1964 the Democratic party became markedly more associated with civil rights, and the Republicans less with peace (Campbell, 1966b, p. 267). Most elements of party images do not change much, however.

Similarly, when asked directly, only about 50 percent knew how the terms "liberal" and "conservative" are conventionally used in today's politics, and could correctly assign them to the Democratic and Republican parties, respectively (Converse, 1964, p. 222; about 10 percent were "wrong" by conventional standards). Even the 1964 campaign, supposedly conducted around these ideological terms, seems not to have increased public understanding of them (Converse, Clausen, and Miller, 1965, p. 335). Thus, the parties' images seem only rarely to be erroneously perceived, but few voters emphasize the longstanding ideological or group commitments made by each party.

Party policy positions. A clear test of voters' perceptions on specific policy issues occurred with two highly salient campaign issues in 1948: the Taft-Hartley Act and price control. However, in Elmira only 16 percent accurately perceived both candidates' very distinctive positions on the two issues. More than a third of the sample could give, at best, the correct answer on one issue for one candidate (Berelson *et al.*, 1954, p. 227). However, these data were collected in August before formal campaigning had really begun, and accurate recognition would presumably have been higher later in the campaign.

A more detailed list of policy issues dividing the two parties was presented to respondents in the 1956 Survey Research Center election study. On each issue, about 30 percent expressed an opinion, felt they knew what the government was doing about the matter, *and* perceived party differences on the issue (Campbell *et al.*, 1960, p. 182). One might quibble about taking this absolute level too seriously, but it is probably not far off.

It might be more reasonable to expect voters to pick up the different general stances adopted by the parties toward broad classes of government problems. Campbell, Gurin, and Miller (1954, p. 129) asked respondents in 1952 about the two parties' general stances on governmental social welfare activity and internationalism. The correct difference ("Democrats will do more") was perceived in both areas, or in one area with no difference perceived in the other, by 36 percent of their nationwide sample. A figure around 30 percent seems to recur in these studies.

The racial issue in 1960 and 1964 offers another ready test. In 1960 the two candidates did not differ sharply, but in 1964 the difference was clear. This change apparently was perceived accurately by the public. A measure of perceived association between party and position showed highly significant differences in 1964 but none in 1960 (Converse, Clausen, and Miller, 1965, p. 329).

Parties' group appeals. How clear are the parties' traditional differential appeals to major population groupings? Reliable data indicate that (1) there is little disagreement about which party best serves the interests of, and gets the most votes from, various economic groups, but that (2) substantial numbers of voters are not able to distinguish the two parties in each respect. Key (1961, p. 434) presented 1959 Gallup data indicating clear consensus among "business and professional" people that the Republicans serve their interests best (58 percent to 15 percent for the Democrats); and Campbell, Gurin, and Miller (1954, p. 211) found that 55 percent of their 1952 sample thought "big businessmen" would vote Republican, with only

12 percent predicting a Democratic vote. Similarly, "unskilled workers" saw the Democrats as serving their interests best by a 54 percent to 15 percent margin, and in the Survey Research Center sample "working-class people" were predicted as more likely to vote Democratic by a 51 percent to 7 percent margin. However, on each of these four questions the insensitive proportion was around 30 percent, and the "wrong" link was perceived by 10 percent or so.

The ethnic bases of the two parties are apparently less clear. Campbell, Gurin, and Miller (1954) found only 44, 25, and 19 percent able to make a directional prediction for the voting of Negroes, Catholics, and Jews, respectively.

Hence, relatively few people seem to get the two parties' images, group appeals, general policy stands, or ideological orientations backwards. The proportion who perceive them correctly varies considerably, with about half the electorate having accurate perceptions of differential economic group appeals and ideological labels. About half also seem to know which party controls Congress. On other dimensions the proportion with a clear perception is considerably smaller. These figures would seem to set some upper limits on the particular kind of voting behavior that involves judging a party's acceptability by its perceived relationship to policies or groups about which the voter has some affect. However, the ties between various ethnic, religious, racial, economic, or regional groups and a particular party do not necessarily rest on the group member's perceiving an advantage of that party for that group's members, as will be seen below.

Preferences among factions or multiple parties

In the light of this apparent insensitivity to ideological matters, it is paradoxical that aggregate voting switches often seem to follow ideological lines. The postmortems of political editors after elections usually describe an electorate expressing its "will" in ideological terms, or at least such meaning is often painfully extracted from a complex pattern of results. A related effect would obtain if most respondents indicated preferences among factions or candidates (or parties, in a multiparty nation) that corresponded to their relative ideological or policy positions. Both effects would be hard to understand if one did not impute to the voters a sophisticated set of perceptions.

Aggregate electoral change. In the literature, there are many instances of interelection changes which seem deliberate and rational as described by aggregate, nonsurvey data. One particularly clear example is based on a series of elections for various offices in Atlanta (Jennings and Zeigler, 1966a, 1966b). A relatively liberal Democrat, Charles Weltner, successfully challenged the conservative incumbent Congressman in a first and then a runoff primary in 1962. In the primaries, he seems to have drawn upon the coalition that had sustained moderate mayors in Atlanta, combining well-educated, high-income whites with the Negro vote. In Atlanta's Fulton County, the correlation over precincts of the vote with the percentage of Negro voters was +0.92; with median educational level, +0.55 (both partial correlations holding the other variable and median income constant); and with the 1961 vote for Ivan Allen, the moderate Atlanta mayor, +0.76. Weltner evidently had the same kind of support in the two primaries, since their voting outcomes correlated +0.73.

Against a Republican in the general election, his support changed abruptly; precinct outcomes in the runoff primary and the general election correlated only

+0.19. Race and education were no longer highly correlated with his vote ($r = +0.15$ and -0.36), nor was the 1961 vote for mayor ($r = -0.04$). Rather, he drew more upon traditional Democratic party allegiances, which implied a loss of some Negroes and, of course, of most of the white middle class. The 1960 Kennedy vote, one index of Democratic voting, correlated -0.42 with Weltner's primary vote but $+0.40$ with his general election vote. Thus aggregate data seem, at least, to describe coalitions that shift in a meaningful and deliberate (or at least consensual) way from election to election. The question is whether or not the aggregate shifts represent individual shifts that are meaningful in terms of being tied to relevant attitudes.

Factional preferences. An analogous case for which individual data exist is defection in the general election by disappointed backers of another candidate for the nomination. From the individual data in this case, it looks as if voters are behaving with considerable sophistication; defection rates bear a surprisingly strong relationship to the ideological gap between preferred and nominated candidate.

In 1964, the nomination of Barry Goldwater by the Republicans ultimately led to sizable defections to the Democrats. Backers of Rockefeller and Romney, the most liberal rivals of Goldwater, defected at a rate four times the usual Republican defection rate. Those who had preferred Scranton and Lodge defected at three times the normal rate; and the supporters of the least liberal alternative, Nixon, defected at only double the normal rate (Campbell, 1966b, p. 265; Converse, Clausen, and Miller, 1965, p. 326).

The same thing had occurred in 1948. Taft and Dewey supporters both defected to Truman at a rate of eight percent, while supporters of the more liberal Vandenberg and Stassen defected at rates of 23 and 33 percent, respectively (Berelson *et al.,* 1954, p. 205).

Were the differential defection rates created by the disaffected voter's sense of ideological distance between himself and the nominee? In both 1948 and 1964, supporters of various Republican candidates for the nomination held distinctive ideologies or policy positions. In 1948, Vandenberg drew heavily from "international liberals" and very lightly from "international conservatives" (defined in terms of specific policy questions), and equally from "domestic liberals" and "domestic conservatives." Taft's support was almost entirely from "domestic conservatives" and was not related to international attitudes (Berelson, Lazarsfeld, and McPhee, 1954, p. 204). In 1964, "ideological differences plainly existed between grass-roots supporters of the various factions, and these differences were indeed correlated with defections from a Goldwater vote" (Converse, Clausen, and Miller, 1965, p. 327). In addition, preconvention choices for the nomination were correlated with the "appropriate" ideological positions on the Birch Society: Rockefeller's supporters were most antagonistic, and Goldwater's supporters were most favorable (Lipset, 1963b, p. 359).

However, it is true that no compelling data have been presented to indicate a systematic link between an individual's ideology or policy attitudes and his defection as a member of a disenchanted party faction. It would require that voters perceive the candidates' positions as arrayed over some ideological continuum, and that their own preferences among the candidates be systematically related to the distances along that continuum. Relevant though discouraging data come from a study in which Finnish voters were asked which party they would vote for if they were unable to vote for the party of their choice. The aggregated data resembled the pattern one would expect if each voter perceived the several parties as arrayed along a left-to-right dimension. However, the individual orders were chaotic: "The 317 Finnish respondents who gave full preference orders managed to generate 202 distinct patterns, each ranking eight parties" (Converse, 1966b, p. 188).

It is probably a mistake to impute too much ideological sophistication to those defectors. For example, the seemingly deliberate anti-Goldwater defectors were actually less politically informed than the nondefectors (Benham, 1965, p. 194). Hence, it is not at all clear that these defections have a policy or ideological root. What they *do* represent is less clear. Perhaps the use of aggregate data overemphasizes the systematic nature of the shift; a few deliberate voters thinking in similar terms, and a great many random voters, might produce a highly "rational" aggregate pattern. Or the defectors may have been weaker party identifiers from the start. However, a more complete empirical analysis is needed to clear up this paradox.

Four conclusions are suggested by this discussion: (1) Only the most salient political stimuli are recognized by the general public. The day-to-day stuff of politics, its transitory persons, events, and issues, reaches the mass public only occasionally and then superficially. (2) Only a small minority can be said to apply manifestly political ideological principles to the elements of ongoing political life. (3) Most voters have only superficial and unstable preferences at the concrete policy level. In the public as a whole, policy attitudes on different issues are usually not systematically related. (4) The most stable and meaningful political attitudes are those referring to groups, especially the political parties. The content of these commitments does not focus on policy issues in most cases, and the policy implications of the commitments are likewise recognized only by a minority.

PARTISANSHIP IN POLITICAL INFORMATION PROCESSING

The "average voter" thus seems to have some clear attitudes toward groups, but not much information or many clearly relevant organizing principles. This would suggest that the most important cues in processing political information involve group-related predispositions rather than stimulus attributes or abstract principles. Thus, it appears that simple political partisanship accounts for much political opinion formation.

In this section, the most relevant social-psychological model of information processing is briefly outlined (for a more comprehensive treatment, see Chapter 21), then applied to selected political situations. Finally, an attempt is made to determine whether or not this is the typical manner of processing political information.

Consistency theories

The most obvious formal bases for analyzing partisan information processing are the several cognitive consistency theories: dissonance theory (Festinger, 1957), congruity theory (Osgood and Tannenbaum, 1955), and balance theory (Abelson and Rosenberg, 1958; Heider, 1946; Newcomb, 1953). In commonsense terms, each theory simply asserts that people prefer to agree with those whom they like and respect, and to disagree with those they dislike and do not respect.

In more specific terms, three basic ideas are proposed. First, simultaneously holding cognitions which are psychologically inconsistent produces pressure to change. For our purposes, the important cognitions refer to (1) opinions on political issues, (2) evaluations of sources of information, and (3) the positions of such sources on such political issues. When, in any given instance, these three are inconsistent (for example, when a revered leader takes a position disagreeable to his followers), pressure to change is created. The second idea is that change occurs most commonly in the least intense or weakest of these sets of cognitions (Osgood and Tannenbaum, 1955). Finally, changes in any of these cognitions are functionally equivalent and thus interchangeable. To the extent that opinion change occurs, for example, the source need not be reevaluated nor his position distorted. Some controversy surrounds the detailed implications of each of these three ideas (McGuire, 1966), but there is a good deal of consensus about the specific empirical consequences of the general consistency principle.

Strong opinions and trusted sources. Opinions are hard to change when they are intense, strong, matters of personal certainty, or when the individual is ego-involved in them or committed to them (Kelley and Lamb, 1957; Miller, 1965). High ego involvement reduces opinion change most noticeably when the opinions of the source and of the subject are initially highly discrepant (Freedman, 1965). The other side of the coin should also be stressed; opinions about which an individual is uninvolved or uncertain are highly unstable and responsive to seemingly weak or transitory influences.

The same holds for source evaluations. Sources regarded as expert, trustworthy, or likable are more influential (Hovland and Weiss, 1951; Osgood and Tannenbaum, 1955). This added influence is especially noticeable when the individual's position is initially highly discrepant from the source's (Aronson, Turner, and Carlsmith, 1963). Again, the other side of the coin might be noted; when a source is previously unknown or neutrally evaluated, his evaluation is highly susceptible to change.

Modes of resolution. Perhaps the three most important outcomes of inconsistency are opinion change, source reevaluation, and distortion of the source's position. Opinion change is most likely when prior opinions are relatively weak (for example, on unfamiliar issues), when the source has a good reputation, and when his position is fairly clear. However, little opinion change normally occurs in initially strong opinions. In such cases, other responses to pressure to change are to be expected.

One important alternative is reevaluation of the source, which is especially likely if he is initially neutral, unknown, or anonymous. In political life, of course, source reevaluation is an especially important mode of resolution, since the desired outcome is often election of a candidate rather than change of public opinion toward some policy position. When taking an unpopular position, the source becomes more negatively evaluated; when taking a popular position, more positively evaluated (Tannenbaum, 1966; Tannenbaum and Gengel, 1966). The more radically such weak sources disagree with the subject on important issues, the more they are derogated (Hovland, Harvey, and Sherif, 1957). But the source's reputation is less dependent on the position he takes when the subject has a clear initial evaluation of him (Aronson, Turner, and Carlsmith, 1963).

Systematic distortion of the source's position has been demonstrated most often when the subject has had a strong initial opinion or firm evaluation of the source. Two kinds of distortion may occur: assimilation, in which disagreement with the source is underestimated; and contrast, in which it is exaggerated (Hovland, Harvey, and Sherif, 1957). Consistency should be maximized, of course, by assimilating positions of low discrepancy from that held by the subject, especially when the source is favorably evaluated. Such effects have been demonstrated in a number of settings, though the magnitude of distortion has not always been very dramatic (Hovland, Harvey, and Sherif, 1957; Kelman and Eagly, 1965; Manis, 1960, 1961; Sherif, Sherif, and Nebergall, 1965). Consistency should also derive from contrasting highly discrepant positions, particularly from negatively evaluated sources. Here the data are much less clear. Another possible form of contrast has been described by Turiel, Kohlberg, and Rest (in press), who found children transmuting disliked moral advice into more simplistic form. They clearly reproduced the position advocated, but the rationale was unimpressive and simpleminded.

Aside from the lack of evidence on contrast, though, data from experimental studies support the conclusion that opinion change, source reevaluation, and distortion of sources' positions are all used as mechanisms for restoration of consistency. Typically, the changes increase agreement with favorably evaluated people, and disagreement with the unfavorably evaluated.

Reference-group influence. The impact of reference groups can easily be interpreted as a special case of the consistency principle. Harold Kelley, in several papers, and Converse and Campbell (1960) have offered rather explicit models for reference-group influence. Their variables correspond closely to those emphasized here, but refer to a group rather than an individual as the source of information. "Strength of identification with the group" (Converse and Campbell, 1960) or "valuation of the group" (Dittes and Kelley, 1956; Kelley and Volkhart, 1952) are analogous to the evaluation of the source. "Transmission of group standards" (Converse and Campbell, 1960) or clarity of group norms (Kelley and Woodruff, 1956) correspond to perceptions of the source's position.

These authors do introduce two other variables, relevant for groups, but perhaps less so for individual communicators. One is the "salience" of the group (Kelley, 1955); for example, candidates with Catholic names make Catholicism salient to the voter. The other is the "legitimacy of group political activity," that is, whether or not the voter feels it is legitimate for the group to take political stands, as in controversies surrounding political intervention by the Catholic Church (Converse and Campbell, 1960). The evidence regarding these two variables is quite weak, however. In fact, when Catholic voting for a Catholic candidate was at perhaps an all-time high, in 1960, lay Catholics' beliefs in the legitimacy of Catholic political activity nosedived (Converse, 1966c, p. 112). Such beliefs may well be particularly susceptible to the need for rationalizing other commitments (for example, the desire to reduce anti-Kennedy feelings based on religious prejudice during the 1960 campaign).

Formation of political opinions

The main implication of consistency theories for political partisanship is that strong predispositions control opinion formation. Two questions are thus raised: what predispositions are especially important, and how strong is their effect on opinion formation relative to other variables (for example, objective stimulus differences)?

Political predispositions. Three kinds of partisan predispositions seem likely to be of special importance: *party identification,* group-related attitudes (especially *racial attitudes,* currently), and attitudes toward specific *political persons.* Their unusual strength seems apparent by several criteria. All are acquired early in life: party identification and basic racial attitudes are apparently acquired during grade school (see pp. 370–374 below), and the tendency to personalize is particularly prominent in children's political thinking (see pp. 416–419 below). They are unusually stable over time in comparison to other attitudes, as has been indicated above regarding party identification and other group-related attitudes, and as may be inferred from the stability of candidate preferences once adopted (see pp. 354–355 below). And there is some evidence that each is related more strongly to other attitudes than are others; this too has already been suggested above but will be discussed in more detail in this section.

Two others have not generally been so clearly matters of partisan conflict, but they may be just as powerful in opinion formation. Young children learn a form of *political chauvinism* which evidently persists through life in only slightly modified form. It may be a special case of the stability of group-related attitudes, with the nation as referent. Finally, *generalized democratic principles* seem to be learned fairly early and persist in some unanimity. Most people believe in the general principles of democratic voting, freedom of religion, and so forth. Both of these will be considered in more detail below.

These predispositions should affect two kinds of political evaluations in particular. One is *issue stands*. Most voters care little about most issues, with the most noteworthy exceptions being those that affect them directly (Campbell *et al.*, 1960, Chapter 14) and group-related issues (Converse, 1964). They have especially little ego-involvement in issues of foreign policy (Lipset, 1966). The other obvious target is evaluations of *new candidates*. First impressions of political persons should be especially vulnerable to the operation of the predispositions cited above, and may therefore represent a major source of electoral change (Stokes, 1966b).

The effects of predispositions on evaluations of political candidates, issues, perceptions, and the vote are discussed below. The point is to estimate the force of these predispositions, in terms of the magnitude of the relationships, and to suggest that many evaluations thus affected have little independent status. That is, they are simply creatures of a momentary association with a strong predisposition.

Evaluations of candidates. Nothing is clearer than that political candidates are evaluated in large part according to their party. A graphic example comes from a 1960 Detroit sample survey (*n* = 1350) by Sigel (1964, p. 494). She found voters only infrequently able to cite liabilities of their favored candidate or assets of his opponent, when asked standard open-ended questions. The preferred candidate was assigned no liabilities by 82 percent of the Democrats and 88 percent of the Republicans, and the nonpreferred candidate, no assets by 72 percent and 74 percent, respectively. Though this is more extreme partisanship, it is in the same direction as that obtained nationwide by the Survey Research Center in 1952 (Campbell, Gurin, and Miller, 1954, pp. 53–54). The clearest nationwide data are presented by Stokes (1966b).

Evaluations of candidates' appearances in the mass media are apparently usually made on the same simple partisan basis. Table 7 shows dramatically the effects of predispositions on judgments of who won the first Kennedy-Nixon televised debate in 1960. Obviously most people saw the debate as confirming their prior opinions. (Though these responses were based on a single interview with each respondent and depend on his recall of his predebate preference, only slightly less partisanship emerged from respondents interviewed by Kraft before the first debate and again

TABLE 7

"WHO WON" FIRST 1960 TELEVISED DEBATE,
DEPENDING ON PRIOR CANDIDATE PREFERENCE

Predebate preference	Kennedy	No choice	Nixon	Total
Favored Kennedy	71%	26%	3%	100%
Undecided	26	62	12	100
Favored Nixon	17	38	45	100

Source: Katz and Feldman, 1962, p. 199. Data are from a Gallup survey.

after the second; *cf.* Katz and Feldman, 1962, p. 199. Thus the data in Table 7 are probably quite accurate.) Schramm and Carter (1959) asked viewers of a 28-hour-long telethon by a 1958 Republican gubernatorial candidate what had impressed them. Of the Democrats interviewed, 58 percent said "nothing" or made some other negative comment, while of the Republicans only 27 percent did. The media themselves are evaluated on the same basis. Media coverage of the Kennedy assassination tended to be rejected as "slanted" more often by Republicans than by Democrats (Anderson and Moran, 1965, pp. 145–146), and working-class men quite reasonably think the predominantly Republican press a less trustworthy source than other media (Kornhauser, Sheppard, and Mayer, 1956, pp. 88–91).

The entry of previously nonpolitical persons into political candidacy clearly illustrates how quickly partisan predispositions take effect. Generals Eisenhower and de Gaulle were evaluated on a sharply partisan basis soon after their entries into politics in 1952 and 1958. That is, respondents' party identifications and their parties' stances toward the generals were good predictors of respondents' evaluations of these new candidates (Converse and Dupeux, 1966, p. 330; Hyman and Sheatsley, 1953).

None of these examples explicitly tests the relative power of response predispositions and stimulus attributes in producing candidate evaluations. McGrath and McGrath (1962) did so, obtaining ratings of Kennedy and Nixon in 1960 on 50 attributes from a sample of highly partisan college students. They found 29 agreed on by the two sets of partisans (stimulus-determined), while for the other 21, the ratings were more favorable to the preferred candidate than to his opponent (response-determined). In this form the outcome depends on how the attributes are selected, but the question is appropriate.

Issue positions. As indicated earlier, many people simply are not familiar with the main political issues or events of the day. Hence, it is unrealistic to expect them to have stable opinions about such matters. When they are asked to express an opinion, they use whatever cues are available. Often party preference is the handiest cue. Key (1961, p. 450) has offered an especially obvious case. Gallup offered the question, in 1935, "Are you in favor of the present administration's agricultural policy as embraced in the AAA?" Key, probably correctly, assumed that most respondents were not familiar with the details of the AAA program, and therefore, responded primarily on the basis of their attitudes toward the administration. The proportion of Democrats supporting it was 70 percent; of Republicans, 8 percent. Numerous other such examples are shown in Table 14 (see p. 363 below).

However, the parties' followers do genuinely differ on some issues, primarily those concerned with domestic issues. For example, Berelson, Lazarsfeld, and McPhee (1954, pp. 209–211) found that Elmira Democrats and Republicans differed on several domestic issues regarding labor unions, price controls, housing projects, and antitrust legislation. Matthews and Prothro (1966a, pp. 143–145) found that Southern Democrats and Republicans of both races differed on socioeconomic liberalism, but not on segregationism. Perhaps the clearest data are those obtained by Campbell *et al.* (1960, p. 198), who found that party identification correlated with domestic liberalism, but not foreign policy internationalism, in the 1950's. Pool, Abelson, and Popkin (1964, p. 140), sampling a wider variety of issues from the 1950's, also reported that foreign policy attitudes were not related to party. Even attitudes toward Senator Joseph McCarthy were not strongly related to foreign policy attitudes (Lipset, 1963b, pp. 338–340).

Thus it would appear that the predispositions cited earlier do contribute to cleavage on policy preferences, but given the relatively low information and sophistication level typical in the electorate, their effects are not especially powerful on any given issue, nor extensive across issues (McClosky, Hoffman, and O'Hara, 1960). The clearest effects seem to appear when cues evoking the predisposition are momentarily salient, for example, when the party or candidate is cited in the question on policy preference (as in Key's example), or in some highly publicized campaigns, as in the 1964 California referendum to repeal fair housing (Wolfinger and Greenstein, 1968).

Partisan attitudes of the various kinds measured in election campaigns show the effects of party identification more clearly, as already suggested. The point is made most clearly in Goldberg's (1966) computation that party identification and a composite measure summing six dimensions of partisan attitude (candidate, issue, group, and party attitudes) were correlated +0.71 in the 1956 Survey Research Center election survey. Since party identification is highly stable, it accounts for a very large proportion of variance in the way people evaluate the transient features of politics and embody them in partisan attitudes.

Perceptual distortions: voting norms and candidates' positions. Perceptions of group voting norms often seem to be distorted in the service of consistency. People seem to expect others like themselves, or groups they like, to vote the same way they do. Berelson, Lazarsfeld, and McPhee (1954, p. 78) asked Elmira respondents how they thought various groups would vote in 1948: rich people, college people, farmers, factory workers, and poor people. Assimilation generally occurred: Republicans thought each group would vote predominantly Republican, while in all but one case, Democrats estimated them as more Democratic by an average of more than 20 percent per group. In the sole contrast effect, 91 percent of the Democrats expected rich people to vote Republican.

When de Gaulle reentered political life in France in 1958, it was not at all clear initially where he would locate himself on the partisan continuum. Thus, all but his most extreme opponents tended to assume he would resemble them. For example, 91 percent of all those who thought he was a Socialist were themselves Socialists (Converse and Dupeux, 1966, pp. 335–336). Only the Communists contrasted him;

30 percent assigned him to "the right," while no more than eight percent in any other party did so.

The same principle accounts for the fact that partisans almost invariably over-estimate their own candidate's chances of being elected (Lazarsfeld, Berelson, and Gaudet, 1948, p. 106). Most people assume that most other people will support the same man they do. In October 1964, for example, 93 percent of the Johnson supporters expected Johnson to win, but only 46 percent of the Goldwater supporters did (Benham, 1965, p. 193), despite the fact that many highly publicized polls at that time were predicting a Johnson sweep. More generally, Burnstein (1967) has shown that people expect interpersonal imbalances to be redressed by changing the attitude discrepant from their own. Upon learning that two hypothetical friends disagree about a candidate, a subject does not expect the friendship to dissolve, nor does he expect the person favoring his own candidate to change; instead, he expects the person favoring his opponent to change.

Candidates' policy positions also seem often to be distorted. The Elmira study offers a typical example of the data used to indicate distortion. Republicans and Democrats alike tended more often to see their candidate as supporting their issue position, and the opposite candidate as opposing it, than the reverse. However, this result could as easily be explained by assuming that voters adopt their own candidate's policy position if they know it.

Froman and Skipper (1962) assumed that distortion will be greater when reality is less confining, and when the individual has strong predispositions. Indeed, they found more distortion on three "style" issues (war, depression, and corruption in government), where leaders of both parties claim the same virtuous alternative, than on three "position" issues (farm price supports, public ownership of natural re-sources, and federal aid to education), on which party leaders, in fact, differ sub-stantially (McClosky, Hoffman, and O'Hara, 1960). Also, strong party identifiers were more accurate than weak identifiers on position issues, presumably because they were better informed, but distorted more on style issues, presumably because of their greater partisanship. The differences were small in magnitude, however, and no significance tests were given.

An even more poignant case is Matthews and Prothro's (1966a) report, from a survey done in 1961, that Southern Negroes strongly prefer integration and South-ern whites strongly prefer "strict segregation" (pp. 332–333), yet few whites feel that a majority of Negroes favor integration, and almost half the Negroes think there is no majority support among whites for segregation (p. 352).

Still, distortion is by no means universal. Sheatsley (1966, p. 231) showed that white Americans are generally more likely to deal with this cognitive "problem" by rejecting Negro demands than by denying they exist or otherwise distorting them. And the liberal racial position of the Boston Catholic hierarchy is clearly evident and undistorted to even the most prejudiced Boston lay Catholics (Ross, Crawford, and Pettigrew, 1966). Johnson and Goldwater supporters alike agreed that Johnson had the better chance, and Democrats and Republicans alike agreed that college people were more likely than poor people to vote for the Republicans. Also, regarding some groups there is a surprising amount of consensus. Catholics were expected to be Democratic by 78 percent of the Elmira Democrats and 77 percent of the Republi-cans. Perceptions of class voting norms follow the same pattern: some distortion by exaggerating the likelihood of one's own class supporting one's candidate, alongside considerable consensus on the basic Republican and Democratic loyalties of middle-and working-class persons, respectively (Eulau, 1962, p. 99).

The difficulty of distorting a clear position is illustrated in a study using two extreme partisan communications and a "fence-straddling" communication, each delivered by an anonymous source, in the 1960 campaign. The extreme positions were not systematically distorted, while the "fence-straddling" communication tended to be assimilated (Sherif, Sherif, and Nebergall, 1965, pp. 153, 161). Similarly, Elmira Democrats and Republicans alike, regardless of their own position, correctly saw Truman favoring price control more often than Dewey, and Dewey favoring Taft-Hartley more often than Truman. It is easy to overestimate the amount of distortion that occurs in the service of consistency restoration. Often what seems to be distortion is likely to be just ignorance. Perhaps, when distortion takes place, it is likely to operate more on the rationale for the position than on the position itself (Turiel, Kohlberg, and Rest, in press). In any case, evaluative changes seem more common than perceptual distortions.

Voting. Obviously, many people vote in line with their enduring party preferences. The number who do is surprisingly high, though. Of the Survey Research Center election sample in 1952, 82.6 percent voted for their party's candidate, and 83.6 percent did so in 1956 (Campbell *et al.*, 1960, p. 139; these figures ignore Independents). In both years many Democrats had defected to Eisenhower; hence, these are reasonable minimal estimates of a population baseline. (See Table 1.) Defections were of the same order of magnitude, but in the opposite direction, in 1964 (Campbell, 1966b, p. 276). For lesser offices the proportion of defectors may be even lower. In the 1958 Survey Research Center survey, 88.4 percent voted for their party's congressional candidate (Stokes and Miller, 1962), and this higher figure is characteristic of off-year partisan elections (Campbell, 1960).

The regularity of party voting is considerably greater for strong party identifiers (Campbell, 1966a, pp. 50, 56; Campbell *et al.*, 1960, p. 125). Consistency of party-line voting up and down the ballot at any given election is also highly correlated with party identification. Table 8 illustrates the point; it also shows that the boost in straight-ticket voting produced when the ballot form allowed one act (for example, pulling a party lever) to register a vote for the entire ticket, instead of requiring separate choices for each office, was greater for those whose internal motivation was less, that is, the weak party identifiers and independents. (An interesting sidelight is Walker's demonstration, 1966, that votes cast for lesser offices decline substantially when there is no simple provision for straight-ticket voting.) The greater impact of the form of ballot on less involved voters is illustrated by the fact that Northern nonwhites actually voted at a slightly higher rate than whites in the 1964 Presidential contest, but at the Congressional level, the nonwhite vote was about 11 percent below the white level.

Other group-related predispositions play an important part in determining the vote. Currently the racial issue is a highly salient one. Ross, Crawford, and Pettigrew (1966) found basic racial attitudes clearly related to voting for Mrs. Louise Day Hicks, a Boston School Committeewoman who had strongly opposed busing and other mechanisms of school desegregation. It is important that anti-Negro sentiment was not expressed in blatant terms, but emerged in terms of resistance to schooling white children in heavily Negro schools. Becker and Heaton (1967) found, in a

TABLE 8

STRAIGHT-TICKET VOTING BELOW THE PRESIDENTIAL LEVEL, 1956

| | Ballot style for party-line vote | |
	Single choice	Multiple choice
Strong identifiers	77%	77%
Weak identifiers	70	55
Independents	48	30
N	319	485

Source: Campbell and Miller, 1957, p. 307. Data are for Northern respondents only, from the 1956 Survey Research Center election study. In "single choice" ballot styles, only a single act is required to cast a vote for a given party's entire ticket.

careful study of the election of Massachusetts' Negro Senator Brooke in 1966, that racial attitudes made a sharp difference in level of support. In mid-October, 39 percent of the "most prejudiced" supported Brooke, while 68 percent of the "least prejudiced" did. As with Mrs. Hicks, though, it is easy to exaggerate the absolute level of bigotry, as well as its political effects (Senator Brooke was elected, and Mrs. Hicks failed in her 1967 effort to be elected mayor of Boston). Campbell (1966b) reported 1964 data that clearly indicate a close relationship between racial attitudes and Presidential voting, though the absolute amount of defection of Northern Democrats to Goldwater over the race issue was small. In the South it was considerably greater, as might be expected.

The point here is that racial predispositions have strong effects, but not invariably crucial or even stronger than more mundane matters (for example, bad candidate images, as in the case of Brooke's and Johnson's opponents). Nevertheless, the virtual absence of any white support given recent Negro candidates (Mayors Hatcher and Stokes, of Gary, Indiana and Cleveland, respectively) suggests that this issue is potentially an extremely explosive and divisive one in Northern and Western, as well as Southern, elections.

Case study: religion and the vote in 1960. The "religious issue" in the 1960 Presidential campaign offers a clear instance of the effect of predispositions on the vote. Protestants voted heavily for Nixon, changing little from their massive support of Eisenhower in 1956. Catholics gave much more support to Kennedy (about 80 percent) than they had to Stevenson (about 50 percent). In the previous three Presidential elections, the difference between Catholics and non-Southern white Protestants had been about 20 to 25 percent, but it soared to about 50 percent in 1960 (Converse, 1966c, p. 97). Let us consider here the "religious vote" interpretation of this change, that the Nixon-Protestant and Kennedy-Catholic votes were unusually large relative to any "normal" baseline expectations. This discussion is largely drawn from two papers based on Survey Research Center data (Converse, 1966c; Converse *et al.*, 1961).

Consider first the Protestants. Their vote for Nixon (63 percent) closely resembled their 1956 vote for Eisenhower (64 percent). Presumably the maximum "anti-Catholic" vote of any political consequence would be among Democratic Protestants defecting to Nixon. According to the view of reference-group influence presented above, (1) defection to the Republicans would be a positive function of involvement in Protestantism, hence, greatest among strong Protestants; and (2) defection on religious grounds would be a negative function of Democratic party identification, hence, greatest among weak Democrats.

The clearest data are on the first point. Converse *et al.* (1961) reported that about six percent of Protestant Democrats who "never" attended church defected to Nixon, a level approximately equal to the "normal" defection rate for each party, when everything else is equal. Hence, Converse *et al.* reasoned, this is defection unrelated to religion. As regularity of Protestant church attendance increased, so did defection to Nixon; among "regular" attenders, over 35 percent of Northern and over 40 percent of Southern Protestant Democrats voted for Nixon. Since regular attendance is more common in the South, the electoral impact of this relationship was greater there. Scoble and Epstein (1964) repeated this finding among Wisconsin voters, using more diverse indices of Protestant religious involvement: frequency of attendance, membership in a church, and parochial school education. And Converse (1966a, p. 33) demonstrated the presumed intervening mechanism, that deviations from votes expected on the basis of party identification were closely related to anti-Catholic feeling. Data on the second point, that religious-based defections should be more common among weak Democrats than strong Democrats, are given only in aggregate form by Converse (1966c, pp. 102, 103) and Stokes (1966b, p. 24), and in that form they are ambiguous.

The level of anti-Catholic feeling was surprisingly high in this election. Nearly half the white Protestants interviewed in the 1960 Survey Research Center survey introduced "the Catholic question" spontaneously; and of these, over three-fourths were unequivocally hostile. Kennedy's election apparently dampened these fires, however. Erskine (1965, p. 495), in her summary of religious attitudes, reported that the proportion saying that they would not vote for a Catholic for President because of his religion slipped from 24 percent to 13 percent in the period from 1959 to 1961.

The other side of the coin is that Catholics could be expected to vote unusually heavily for Kennedy because of the increased salience of Catholicism. One must assume that the rank and file was aware of his Catholicism; this was not true of the general public in 1959 (47 percent in April), but generally was by 1960 (84 percent in July), according to Erskine (1961, p. 129).

Kennedy got about 80 percent of the Catholic vote, which is 17 percent more than a Democratic Presidential candidate would normally be expected to get (Converse *et al.*, 1961). Presumably, the added Catholic votes should have come primarily from those highly identified with Catholicism. Several measures of religious involvement have been used: frequency of church attendance (though this is more useful for Protestants than for Catholics), subjective identification with Catholicism, and parochial school education.

With 1958 data, the baseline "expected" Democratic vote is not significantly related to involvement in Catholicism, calculated on the basis of either frequency of church attendance or a subjective measure of "identification with the Catholic community" (Converse, 1966c, p. 109). Here the "expected" baseline is computed by assuming that defection rates are entirely a function of party identification; hence, the "normal vote" for any grouping of voters is a simple function of the distribution of party identification in the group (Converse, 1966a). On the other hand, deviations in the 1960 Presidential vote from this "normal vote" base are markedly

TABLE 9

KENNEDY PERCENT OF TWO–PARTY VOTE, 1960:
DEVIATION FROM DIVISION EXPECTED FROM PARTY IDENTIFICATION

	Outside the South	*South*	*Nation as a whole*
Gains from Catholics	+5.2%	+ 0.7%	+4.3%
Losses from Protestant Democrats and Independents	−3.6	−17.2	−6.5
Balance	+1.6%	−16.5%	−2.2%

Source: Converse *et al.*, 1961, p. 278. Each column sum is a proportion of that region's voters. Data are from the 1960 Survey Research Center election study.

associated with these measures of religious involvement, especially the latter. "High" Catholic identifiers were 23 percent more pro-Kennedy than expected, while "low" identifiers were only three percent more (Converse, 1966a, p. 108). Scoble and Epstein (1964) also replicated this finding, using parochial school education as a measure of relgious involvement. Thus, there is substantial evidence here that the strong Catholic vote for Kennedy was not just a return to the usually pro-Democratic stance of Catholic voters suppressed by Eisenhower's popularity. It was a genuinely pro-Catholic vote.

The precise cumulative magnitude of the impact of religion on the 1960 election is of no theoretical, but some practical, interest. Converse *et al.* (1961, p. 278) estimated that the religious issue overall raised Nixon's vote by 2.2 percent, as shown in Table 9. These figures do not include Kennedy's lost potential converts among Protestant Republicans. The outcome of the election makes good sense in these terms. Nixon made substantial inroads into the normally Democratic South, while Kennedy did unusually well in the industrial Northeast.

Clearly, then, the 1960 election provides a clear instance of electoral "pull" when group membership is salient. It parallels the recruitment of Catholics to the cause of such Catholic public figures as Father Coughlin and Senator Joseph McCarthy. Even with occupation or party identification controlled, Catholics were far more favorable to Coughlin and to McCarthy than were Protestants. Nor was this just a result of militant anti-Communism in the Catholic Church. No overrepresentation of Catholics was found in non-Catholic anti-Communist movements such as the John Birch Society or the Christian Anti-Communism Crusade (Lipset, 1963b; Wolfinger *et al.*, 1964).

Conclusion. The data covered in this section do not suggest that party identification or other predispositions are inviolable, but they do indicate a dominant role for them in voting and other occasions of opinion formation. Even in presidential voting, with all the attendant publicity, a vast majority "vote party," and in lesser elections it is even greater (though the role of party label in municipal and state elections has not received as much attention). This has a variety of consequences. One is that electoral outcomes are much more stable than they would be otherwise (Campbell, 1960). Another is that less relevant determinants of the vote decision are overwhelmed.

It is easy to take a derogatory stance toward those who vote a "party line" or otherwise simply implement their predispositions in their votes. But, in fact, party labels enable people to organize their perceptions and preferences, and emerge with a meaningful gesture, about a subject matter they have little interest in and usually less information about. In nonpartisan elections, in referenda, or in one-party areas, voting tends to be more capricious, and the quality of government is not superior to any obvious degree (Greenstein, 1963; Key, 1949; Wolfinger and Greenstein, 1968).

Information flow and opinion change

Clearly, consistency pressures often make evaluations of new information little more than creatures of predispositions. And the effect is often surprisingly strong. The further question is whether or not this is the characteristic way in which people interpret political information. That is, what difference does exposure to political information *typically* make in the individual's opinions (by "information" we mean any incoming political stimuli)?

A model: the debate. Perhaps the simplest simulation of an extended period of exposure to controversy is the debate. Like an election campaign, it presents both sides in a clearly partisan atmosphere. The following is one hypothesis about the effects of debates which may serve as a useful model for understanding the impact of political information. This model might best be illustrated by considering the effects of a major political debate, the first 1960 televised campaign debate. Three clear effects emerged. First, the sharply partisan response to it has already been noted in Table 7; initial partisan commitments tended to be reinforced by exposure to the debate (see also the several other polls reviewed by Katz and Feldman, 1962, pp. 206–207). Information that can be interpreted so easily as favoring either side might be thought to make it more difficult for people to choose a candidate. On the contrary, a second clear effect is that the debates helped previously uncertain people to choose. Roper's poll found that 41 percent, after seeing the four debates, were "more sure their choice was right," and only five percent were "less sure" (Katz and Feldman, 1962, p. 212). These and other debates have reduced the number of "undecided" people (Ben-Zeev and White, 1962; Millson, 1932). A third effect, also clear from Table 7, is that Kennedy fared better than Nixon by every criterion: in attracting the undecided, in restraining his own partisans from defection, and in attracting defections from the other side.

Two processes may account for these effects, one holding for those with strong partisan predispositions or commitments, and one for those with no strong initial preference. For strong partisans, a debate obviously reinforces and polarizes initial prejudices (an effect that may actually begin in anticipation of the debate, according to data presented by Sears, Freedman, and O'Connor, 1964).

The uncommitted or weak partisans, on the other hand, may move freely to the more persuasive side. Again, some data suggest they may suspend judgment and moderate their opinions in anticipating a debate, thus leaving themselves free to join the "winner" (Sears, Freedman, and O'Connor, 1964). Therefore, the postdebate division of opinion among the previously uncommitted may often be quite disproportionate. The first 1960 debate (see Table 7) and others (Millson, 1932) are cases in point. Presumably, the degree of disproportionality would depend on how much more persuasive one side was than the other.

In short, debates seem to reinforce the committed and push the initially undecided to choose sides, often disproportionately to the more compelling side.

Polarization around predispositions in natural situations. Available evidence on exposure to information in most natural situations suggests, however, that it has only one dominant effect: it polarizes opinion along predispositional lines. A clear explicit statement of the point has been made by Gamson and Modigliani (1966) in their "cognitive consistency model": "Increasing knowledge will change people in *different* directions leading to a greater polarization of opinion among the more knowledgeable" (pp. 190–191). "Conceptual sophistication" is the major intervening variable: "poorly informed individuals, even with different ideological orientations, will have difficulty relating their orientation to specific policies . . . however, among the sophisticated, those with different predispositions will rally around different specific policies" (p. 192).

All the relevant evidence need not be reviewed here. A few examples may illustrate the point. First, informational level has been indexed by differences in factual information on the issue in question, and in educational level (or socioeconomic status, which is closely related). Gamson and Modigliani (1966, p. 195) divided Detroit respondents in 1963–1964 on the basis of factual information and basic predispositional beliefs about Communism (whether the U.S.S.R. is basically trying to dominate the world, expand its influence in a limited way, or just defend itself). Policy beliefs (on China's admission to the United Nations, trade with the U.S.S.R., military strength) were essentially uncorrelated with predispositions among those with low information (contingency coefficients were 0.14, 0.19, and 0.14), but were highly correlated for those with high information (0.46, 0.51, and 0.31).

Relevant predispositions also made more difference in evaluations of various "radical right" groups and personalities among high-socioeconomic-status or better-educated respondents than among low. Catholics and Protestants were more sharply split on Father Coughlin, high and low authoritarians on McCarthy, and Democrats and Republicans on the Birch Society, among such high information groups than among the less educated and less well-off (Lipset, 1963b). Pool, Abelson, and Popkin (1964, p. 139) also found that followers of the two parties are split more on "party-dominated" issues among high-information than low-information groups; for example, more among men and upper-status voters than among women and lower-status voters. McClosky (1964) found that the well-educated followers of the two parties are split more on domestic policy than are the less educated. And Campbell *et al.* (1960, p. 352) found that people with higher "levels of conceptualization" vote most in line with their subjective social status.

Second, propaganda or election campaigns should add to people's fund of information. Yet they tend also to polarize the public along predispositional lines. Klapper (1960), in his extensive review of the literature on mass communications, concluded that they usually reinforce predispositions. This was a central conclusion of the original Erie County voting study, of course. And Stricker (1964) has presented some evidence of increasing partisan polarization over the course of a campaign.

Campaigns and higher chronic information levels also increase the internal consistency of political opinions. Wolfinger and Greenstein (1968) found Californians' attitudes toward a referendum measure and attitudes toward a fair housing law it was designed to repeal became considerably more consistent as the campaign wore on. Consistency was initially greater among the better educated, and the campaign increased the consistency of the other voters' attitudes. Sullivan (1966) found that the 1960 campaign increased the consistency of various partisan attitudes. Racial prejudice became more closely related to votes regarding a Negro candidate for Senator in

1966 in Massachusetts (Becker and Heaton, 1967) as the campaign wore on. And in a nationwide survey on Vietnam, Verba *et al.* (1967) found that logically incompatible "escalation" and "deescalation" scores were more negatively correlated for people with high factual information ($r = -0.47$) than for people with less ($r = -0.25$). However, information level had little effect on consistency in matters where the logical consequences were more obscure; for example, correlations between willingness to pay the costs of military buildups and desire to escalate the war.

Miller's conclusion seems appropriate, therefore: "The alert, informed, fully socialized, political man will become aware of many more new pieces of information and will behave much more predictably, usually by incorporating them into his prior system of values and beliefs" (1967, p. 228). The rather surprising conclusion, then, is that it is the *best*-informed people who form opinions most closely aligned to their predispositions (as opposed, for example, to what an "objective observer" might feel to be the merits of the case). It might be noted, though, that some writers have emphasized consistency with basic values, and internal consistency, as criteria for "rational" opinions (Scott, 1958).

Why should information primarily increase polarization in these studies, whereas this is only part of the story with debates? The studies of debates cited above differ from the normal course of events in the political world primarily in that exposure to the debates was fairly complete. In 1960, for example, about 80 percent of the adult population saw or heard at least one campaign debate. Even so, the poorly educated individual of low occupational status often did not watch, and "independent voters" were "far less likely to hear the debates" (Katz and Feldman, 1962, pp. 190–192). This is typical of natural situations, that strong partisans are more likely than the uncommitted to be exposed to information, and given *de facto* selectivity, information generally reinforces or polarizes partisan opinion. The uncommitted do not have as good an opportunity to respond to information, since they are less often exposed to it.

The slightly informed change most. These data would suggest a simple positive relationship between information exposure and attitude stability. However, Converse (1962) has proposed that in natural situations the two are related in a U-shaped function. His reasoning is based on the empirical correlation between political involvement, strength of predispositions, and information intake. Attitude stability at any given level of involvement depends on the relative balance between predispositional strength and intake. At low involvement, intake tends to be low and even relatively weak predispositions go unchallenged. With slightly greater involvement, the individual is normally exposed to some information, and his predispositions are relatively weak; hence, his opinions tend to be unstable. At high levels of involvement, information intake is high, but so is resistance to change, and thus attitude stability is again high.

As supporting data, Converse first presented the now standard finding that stability of vote intentions is positively related to information level. This is shown in Table 10. The more critical data show the U-shaped curve regarding stability of the individual's vote intention through a campaign. Those who were exposed to the campaign in *none* of the mass media were perfectly stable; the vote intentions they expressed during the campaign predicted perfectly their final votes. The most instability occurred among those exposed to the campaign in one medium; they presumably had both superficial information intake (primarily television) and weak partisan predispositions. Beyond this point, stability increased with greater number of media used, to a

TABLE 10

CHANGE IN PRESIDENTIAL VOTING AND POLITICAL INFORMATION LEVEL, 1956-1960

Information level	Voted twice for same party	Voted twice, shifted	Failed to vote once	Twice a nonvoter
High	49%	33%	19%	11%
Medium	32	32	35	17
Low	19	35	46	72
Total	100%	100%	100%	100%
N	712	207	220	201

Source: Converse, 1962, p. 581. "Information level" is a scale based on such knowledge as which regions Kennedy and Nixon came from and which party controlled the 1960 Congress. The table is restricted to noninstitutionalized persons who were over the age of 21 at both elections. Data are from the 1956-1960 Survey Research Center panel survey.

high correlation between vote intention and actual vote of about 0.94 for those using all four major media (radio, television, newspapers, and magazines).

This, then, confirms and elaborates the basic point of this section. There are those who have strong partisan feelings and are highly involved; they are typically exposed to a great deal of information, but, in the main, it reinforces or even polarizes their prior beliefs, because they force it into a consistent, partisan view of things. Those with little or no interest who are exposed to no new information are also highly stable; their predispositions go unchallenged (or they use some simple cue such as incumbency; see Jones, 1966, and Miller and Stokes, 1966, for data). The ones who change are those with weak involvement, weak partisanship, and some exposure to relevant information. Thus, substantial defection from predispositions is likely only when information reaches many low-involvement voters, for example, in what Campbell (1960) has called a "high-stimulus" election campaign.

A special case: foreign policy opinions. There is some evidence that additional information on foreign policy issues, rather than polarizing opinion, increases support for official government policy. In one global attack on this problem, Rosi (1965) used several indices of information level, such as education, awareness of events, and interest in events, in relation to opinions on nuclear weapons tests and fallout in the period 1954–1963. There were no "drastic cleavages" between the attentive and inattentive, but "more of the attentive public appeared to respond positively and rapidly to the firm setting of policy by the administration." Also, "when policy was in flux, compared to the attentive the less informed members of the public at times took stronger—or even opposing—positions" (p. 293). For example, in 1961–1962 the informed increasingly favored test resumption, but switched more sharply to the test ban treaty in 1963 when the Administration endorsed it.

Higher information levels, as indexed by amount of factual information, have been associated with greater support of official policy in several studies. This held on the six items regarding Korea, aid to Yugoslavia, the United Nations, and Communist China, cited from 1951 and 1957 Gallup polls by Back and Gergen (1963a). Similarly, in 1963–1964, high-information people in Gamson and Modigliani's sample (1966) tended more to support official policy on three issues concerning Communist China, the U.S.S.R., and U.S. military strength. The fact that in these polls the alternatives to official policy were sometimes more bellicose, and sometimes less so, suggests that the critical dimension was support of official policy rather than "toughness."

When educational level or socioeconomic status is taken as the index of information level, the results are similar. In 1956, college-educated respondents were vastly more likely to reject isolationism than were the less educated (Key, 1961, p. 337). They also supported official policy more in 1953 and 1954 on United Nations atomic energy control and nuclear arms treaties with Russia, according to Gallup polls (Gamson and Modigliani, 1966). In May 1966, college-educated persons were more likely than the public as a whole to support the nation's involvement in Vietnam (Armor *et al.*, 1967, p. 172). And Lipset (1966, p. 44) quoted several polls as indicating that, up to that time, college students had supported the Vietnam war more than the general public, a finding that might seem paradoxical except for the general relationship between education and support for official policy. One apparent exception to the rule comes from a 1963 survey in nine Northeastern communities on fallout shelters. Respondents of low socioeconomic status were considerably more favorable to fallout shelters than were those of high socioeconomic status, thus supporting government policy more. Respondents of low socioeconomic status also tended more to "over-support governmental policy," endorsing harsh penalties for failing to take cover in civil defense drills, watching antishelter people for possible Communist leanings, and supporting any fallout shelter program the government proposed (Levine and Modell, 1965, p. 277). However, this may mainly reflect the harsher treatment less educated people typically recommend for deviants and nonconformists (Lipset, 1960; Stouffer, 1955), rather than greater support for the details of official policy.

All these comparisons deal only with members of the general public. Those who are still more informed—elite groups and decision makers themselves—are not simply still more supportive of official policy. In some respects, they do react more quickly and consensually to support changes of official policy. For example, Rogers, Stuhler, and Koenig (1967) found that a panel of knowledgeables (chosen for their prime interest in foreign affairs) supported the policies of the new Kennedy administration more than did the general public. They agreed more with Kennedy's position that America's prestige had slipped, they wished to avoid resuming nuclear tests despite the lack of a test ban treaty, and they were more militant over Communist penetration in Berlin and Latin America. It is also noteworthy that here the gap between elite thinking and college-educated lay thinking was larger than that between attentive and inattentive members of the general public. For example, 79 percent of the panel felt the United States should risk war over Berlin, as against 55 percent of the college public and 51 percent of the total public (Rogers, Stuhler, and Koenig, 1967, p. 246).

But the "elite" or "superattentive" public is also more likely to criticize the government's foreign policy. In a fairly large ($N = 152$) and representative 1966 sample of professors from the Boston area, 66 percent thought it was a mistake for the United States to become involved in Vietnam in the first place, as opposed to 36 percent of the general public. Similarly, about 72 percent of the professors felt that troops should not have been sent to the Dominican Republic in 1965. Yet they were strikingly agreed (80 percent) in approving the government's blockade of Cuba during the 1962 missile crisis (Armor *et al.*, 1967, p. 163). A 1967 survey of University of Michigan faculty found less consensus, but only 22 percent explicitly supported the then-current Administration policy. Rogers, Stuhler, and Koenig (1967) also found that the general public, as compared with the panel of experts, was inclined to support long-held United States policies and not to criticize American actions. For example, after the Bay of Pigs invasion, 73 percent of the elite panel disapproved of "the way the United States government has dealt with Fidel Castro and his government in Cuba," while only 28 percent of the poll did so. The same principle may account for the observation that intellectuals were considerably more upset by shifts in Communist party ideology, and more likely to drop out of the party, than were workers (Lipset, 1960).

These data thus suggest a fairly sharp distinction between persons with special expertise and involvement in foreign policy, and the general public, even including the attentive, well-informed, and highly educated. The general public seems primarily disposed to support official government foreign policy. Low levels of criticism are usually found. In times of crisis, as Rogers, Stuhler, and Koenig indicated, "The mass public would seem to close ranks around the President ... perhaps echoing Nathan Hale's 'My country, right or wrong'" (1967, pp. 248–249). Sometimes war policy does become a partisan issue, but the circumstances for this are not clear (see Belknap and Campbell, 1952). Two apparent instances of this rallying-round are the increases in public approval of the President following two minor national disasters: the U-2 shooting and the Bay of Pigs invasion (see Katz and Piret, 1964). Levine and Modell (1965) perhaps overstated the point only slightly in describing the "oversupportive" individual thus: "[he] believes that the public should accept without question suggestions from authority. When asked for his opinion ... he seemed actually less to be voicing a stand on this particular issue than to be giving a vote of confidence in the government" (1965, p. 277).

Thus, as information increases within the general public, foreign policy opinions too seem to become more consistent with predispositions. But in this case, the main relevant predisposition is not divisive: it is generalized support for the government as an embodiment of the nation. The effect is to make the better-educated, more informed members of the public seem more reactive, and indeed more acquiescent. On some issues information may be so widespread that the entire public swings with gross changes in official policy. Lipset (1966) suggested that this had been the case in the early stages of the Vietnam war. He said, "Johnson makes opinion, he does not follow it" (1966, p. 44). Subsequent events raise questions about the limitations of this observation. However, normally the better educated will seem more docile, and the poorly educated more refractory.

One usually expects the better educated to examine issues more critically. With foreign policy, though, criticism appears to be limited largely to those with extreme levels of involvement in foreign affairs—the cadre of experts. Thus, as Rosi (1965) says, "To the extent that the permissiveness of public opinion in this case is generalizable to foreign policy-making in the nuclear age, the responsibility rests heavily upon elites—political, communications, interest group, individual—to offer relevant criticism of Administration policies and to generate new alternatives" (1965, p. 296). And potentially dangerous constraints exist on the freedom to criticize or dissent: Lipset noted the finding of a nationwide survey in March 1966, that only 34.5 percent agreed "with the right of an American citizen to demonstrate against the war in Vietnam," while 62 percent disagreed.

ISSUES, CANDIDATES, AND ELECTORAL CHANGE

The assertion that voters mainly evaluate incoming information in terms of long-standing partisan predispositions does not explain the radical changes in election outcome that occur from one year to the next. A considerable amount of year-to-year stability in people's voting preferences could particularly be expected from the high correlation between party identification and the vote, and the relative stability of party identification. Yet people who "stand pat" obviously do not contribute to electoral change. For this we must look to people who change preferences or who do not vote consistently.

Number of floating voters

First, how many people do not typically "stand pat" and vote for the same party's candidate from year to year in Presidential elections?

Between-election switchers. A four-year panel study is the only way of pinning down the actual number of people who change from one election to the next. Converse *et al.* (1961, p. 272) reported, from the Survey Research Center panel study, that 23 percent shifted from 1956 to 1960 (this figure includes only those who voted both times), 17 percent to the Democrats and six percent to the Republicans. Key reported more extensive Gallup poll data, based on voters' retrospective claims about their previous votes, for all elections from 1940 through 1960 except 1956. He divided all those voting in a given election into two groups: those who did not vote in the previous election, and those who did vote for the same party or shifted to it. The smallest number of shifters was 10 percent (1944) and the largest was 19 percent (1960), with an average of 13 or 14 percent (Key, 1966, p. 20). These figures are based on postelection reports of votes rather than preelection vote intentions, but both give approximately the same picture. Incidentally, Key's data for the 1960 election, comparable to the 23 percent reported above from Converse *et al.* (1961), show that 22 percent shifted. This provides some confidence that Key's figures for the other elections, on which panel data do not exist, are accurate enough to be of use.

Within-campaign switchers. Three panel studies of campaigns provide the main source of data on within-campaign changers. Lazarsfeld, Berelson, and Gaudet (1948, pp. 65–66) reported that eight percent changed parties from May to November, 1940, and Berelson, Lazarsfeld, and McPhee (1954, p. 23), in their study of Elmira, found that eight percent changed from June to August, 1948, and three percent from August to October. Benham (1965) has perhaps the most reliable data, based on nationwide panels. He found that seven percent changed from August to November, 1960, and 10 percent in the comparable period of 1964. These figures, then, give quite a consistent picture. Of course, some of these changers may also be included in the between-election estimates of change. Others may simply be "returning home" during the campaign after flirting with the opposition during the period between elections.

Larger fractions are reported for persons changing from a neutral, no-preference, no-opinion, or "don't know" stance to a preference. They are 28 percent, 10 percent, and 11 percent for the community studies, and 13 percent and 11 percent in Benham's larger and thus more reliable panels.

New voters. The third reason why one outcome differs from another is that some people vote in one election and not in another. Over the 1940–1960 span of elections, Key (1966, p. 20) reported, an average of 16 percent of the total vote was cast by those not voting in the previous election, ranging from 13 percent in 1944 to 20 percent in 1952. The proportion of the electorate that consists of "new voters" at any given election (that is, voters who had not voted in the previous election) is very large. Key's figures (1966, p. 20) suggest that new voters and switchers each constitute about one-sixth of the electorate (though the variability is extreme), and standpatters about two-thirds. Hence, one should look as carefully at "new voters" as at switchers to determine the basis for an electoral shift. A large fraction of them are young, of course. In 1952, 41 percent of the new voters were under 30, while only 13 percent of those who had also voted in 1948 were under 30 (Key, 1966, p. 105).

Locus of electoral change

These fluctuations could help one side as much as the other, and thus generally balance each other, or they could be highly systematic. Do the changers and new voters usually go disproportionately to one side or the other?

The switchers. As indicated above, the Converse *et al.* (1961, p. 272) panel data indicate about a three-to-one margin for the Democrats in 1960. This could be due to the abnormally strong Republican vote in 1956, which was bound to regress somewhat. However, Key's data (1966, p. 24) indicate, if anything, that this ratio was unusually low. Since 1940, the previously victorious party has lost disproportionately each time, with margins running from 2.2-to-1 (1944) to 8.1-to-1 (1940). The others were 2.6-to-1 (1948), 6.5-to-1 (1952), and 3.9-to-1 (1960), thus averaging 4.6-to-1.

   One must conclude that the rate of exodus is usually far greater from one partisan camp than from the other. Similarly, the percentage of each side's vote which is made up of defectors from the other side is invariably highly unequal (Key, 1966, p. 27).

The sometime voters. Do the new voters also usually flock disproportionately to one side rather than the other? According to Converse *et al.* (1961), they were about equally divided in 1960, as were those who voted in 1956 but did not vote in 1960, whether by reason of death or lack of interest (pp. 271–272). Key's (1966, p. 24) data indicate that new voters generally swing to the winner, but usually not by a great margin. The proportion of each party's vote that is made up of new voters tends to be rather similar at any given election, though its level in the two parties varies considerably from election to election (p. 27). Note that in "realigning elections" (see p. 362 below) the division of new voters may be dramatically disproportionate. The 1932 and 1936 elections are perhaps the most recent examples, and the authors of *The American Voter* report (on the basis of retrospective data) that over 80 percent of the "new votes" then were for Roosevelt, the Democrat (Campbell *et al.,* 1960, p. 155). These radically unequal divisions are rare, and extremely important for that reason.

   If the "new voters" usually split rather evenly between the two parties, and the "shifters" tend to divide very disproportionately, then large-scale electoral shifts (whether or not sufficient to roust out the incumbent party) have come about recently mainly from disproportionate switching rather than from disproportionate division of the new voters. Hence, we give greater attention to the former here in attempting to account for short-term electoral change. New voters may have a greater long-term impact, though, as is suggested later in this chapter.

Characteristics of changers and Independents

What kind of people are the changers (or the Independents, who switch around a great deal)? The classic assertion was made by Lazarsfeld, Berelson, and Gaudet (1948, p. 69): "These people [the two-party changers], who in a sense were the only ones of the entire electorate to make a complete change during the campaign were: the least interested in the election; the least concerned about its outcome; the least attentive to political material in the formal media of communication; the last to settle upon a vote decision; and the most likely to be persuaded, finally, by a personal contact, not an 'issue of the election.'" In other analyses, the authors attributed lack of interest and other indices of low involvement and indecisiveness to "cross pressures." Subsequently, attention has focused on these two sets of variables separately.

Cross pressures and conflict. Conflicts of various kinds seem to be correlated with instability of vote preference and with late vote decisions. Conflicting partisan attitudes often have this effect. Berelson, Lazarsfeld, and McPhee (1954, p. 20) and Lazarsfeld, Berelson, and Gaudet (1948, p. 58) gave such data on conflicts involving subjective socioeconomic status, images of the candidates, previous Presidential vote, and attitudes on campaign issues. Campbell *et al.* (1960, p. 82) found conflicting partisan attitudes in 1956 associated with late voting decisions; similarly, partisan attitudes correlated with the vote far better among the early deciders (the more consistent) than among the late deciders (who had more highly conflicting partisan attitudes).

Conflicts between the normal political consequences of objective social characteristics also are found more frequently in changers and late deciders. Lazarsfeld, Berelson, and Gaudet (1948, p. 55) found conflicts between religion, objective socioeconomic status, and occupation to be associated with change (instability) within a campaign. Berelson, Lazarsfeld, and McPhee (1954, p. 128) and Campbell *et al.* (1960, p. 88) have repeated such findings. This relationship would be expected from the centrality of group-related attitudes in political opinion formation.

Persons whose immediate social environments are politically mixed or inconsistent with their own preferences also are more likely to change. Berelson, Lazarsfeld, and McPhee (1954, pp. 119–122) found that vote intentions are more likely to change when they conflict with the views dominant among family or friends than when they fit. Thus, campaigns tend to increase the homogeneity of primary groups.

It might be noted parenthetically that each of these conflicts seems also to be associated with relatively little interest in the campaign (Lazarsfeld, Berelson, and Gaudet, 1948, p. 62). This, of course, is the often repeated "cross pressures" idea, based on the notion that psychological conflicts often lead to leaving the psychological field. However, in many cases, the direction of causality may actually be the reverse; for example, an uninterested person may not bother to tidy up his attitudes.

Interest and information. Perhaps the most striking generalization one can make is that interest is especially low among changers and late deciders (Berelson, Lazarsfeld, and McPhee, 1954, p. 20; Lazarsfeld, Berelson, and Gaudet, 1948, pp. 53–54). Similarly, Lazarsfeld, Berelson, and Gaudet (1948, p. xviii) reported data from a NORC study of the 1944 election to the effect that changers are more likely than constants to say that it makes little difference which candidate wins, and also more likely to say that they could see no real difference between the candidates.

Data from more recent elections support these early findings. Key (1966, p. 100) found (on the basis of personal recall of vote) that voters switching parties from

1948 to 1952 were as interested in the election as those who stuck with the same party. These data will be considered further in a moment. Those who switched from 1956 to 1960, however, were considerably less interested than the stand-patters (p. 143). In both elections Key found switchers less concerned about the outcome and feeling less strongly about their choice (pp. 103, 144). However, the elections are different in that switchers in 1952 did not differ from standpatters in "thought given to the election" (p. 102) or in the number of "no opinion" responses given to policy questions (p. 96). In 1960 the switchers were more likely to give "no opinion" responses (p. 143). Even the Republican defectors from Goldwater in 1964, who supposedly thereby demonstrated ideological sophistication, turn out to have been less informed than nondefecting Republicans (Benham, 1965, p. 194). Perhaps the most compelling data come from Converse's report of the 1956–1960 Survey Research Center panel study. They are shown in Table 10. The shifters are clearly lower than the standpatters in information level (and thus presumably in information exposure as well).

These data suggest that 1952 was an important exception to the general rule. However, a closer look reveals this is not so. Presumably, the "switcher" category is normally composed largely of low-involvement persons, but also of some high-involvement persons. The former group would necessarily be depleted following a low-turnout election, since many would not have voted before, and as they reenter the electorate would be regarded as "new voters." This would fit the pattern of the 1948–1952 transition, of course. The turnout was very low in 1948, and very high in 1952, and the vote division markedly switched to the Republicans. However, the switch was to an unusual degree composed of Republican new voters rather than defecting 1948 Democrats. Key's (1966, p. 20) data indicate that the number of new voters was far greater in 1952 than in any other election in the span treated (1940–1960). The number of shifters (16 percent) was greater, to be sure, than in the years of Democratic reelection (13, 10, and 11 percent in 1940–1948), but not by much, and lower than for the 1956–1960 changeover (19 percent). So 1952 turns out to be an exception only because the turnout was relatively low in 1948.

Hence, changers both within and between campaigns are unusually uninvolved. This manifests itself in two primary ways: (1) low interest in the campaign, lack of concern about outcome, and less perceived difference between candidates; (2) low exposure to media, low information level, and more "no opinion" responses to policy questions. Note also the extreme unpredictability of the uninvolved and/or late-deciding voter. Their votes bear little relation to their partisan attitudes (Campbell and Stokes, 1959), and are probably based mostly on late social influences.

Independents. The evidence with regard to self-proclaimed "Independents" is similar and equally convincing. They are generally less interested in election campaigns and less concerned about their outcomes (Berelson, Lazarsfeld, and McPhee, 1954, p. 27; Campbell *et al.*, 1960, pp. 143–145). Table 11 gives some representative data. Some evidence from 1952 indicates that, when compared separately with Democrats and Republicans, Independents may be intermediate on some of these dimensions, such as campaign participation, interest in campaign, media consumption, and caring about outcome (Agger, 1959). However, this is probably due to their also being intermediate in education and socioeconomic status, because of the different class appeals of the two parties; and both variables are themselves good predictors of interest and participation.

TABLE 11

RELATION OF STRENGTH OF PARTY IDENTIFICATION TO CONCERN OVER OUTCOME, 1956

	Strong party identifiers	*Weak party identifiers*	*Independents*
Care very much or care pretty much	82%	62%	51%
Don't care very much or don't care at all	18	38	49
Total	100%	100%	100%
N	609	621	395

Source: Campbell *et al.*, 1960, p. 144. Data are from the 1956 Survey Research Center election study.

Sporadic voters. Analyses of chronic nonvoters or sporadic voters indicate they are even less involved and less attentive than switchers or Independents. As shown in Table 10, Converse reported that both sporadic voters and nonvoters are less informed than repeat voters. Table 12 shows the strength of difference in involvement between repeat voters and new voters over several elections.

The general proposition, then, is that the probability of change in partisan choice, or even in turnout, is negatively related to interest in and information about politics. Thus, in this sense, the electorally most decisive groups are those least equipped to make informed decisions.

Exceptions. Two important exceptions have been noted by Converse, who has suggested that at extreme levels of either high or low interest and information, this simple function may reverse. Some data (1962) already mentioned suggest little instability of party preference or vote intention among persons with no mass media exposure (who are also known to be very low in interest and involvement). Presumably, these are persons with little information intake, and hence with little instigation to defect from a standing party loyalty. At higher levels of information intake, these data indicate the relationship suggested above: the greater the exposure, the less the change. And at extremely high joint levels of conceptualization and abstraction, Converse's (1964) data indicate a decline in strength of party identification. This suggests that the most involved persons may do slightly more switching than the more loyal persons who are slightly less ideologically inclined.

In American Presidential races, neither of these exceptional groups seems likely to be numerically significant, if one considers simply their own votes. The level of information outflow is high and almost ubiquitous, and the highly ideological group is a very small fraction of the total American electorate.

However, in practical terms, these exceptions are not at all trivial. In many other partisan races, information is much more difficult to come by. Converse has wryly noted (1962, p. 586) that a content analysis of newspaper references to local Congressional candidates failed in 1958 because such references were "printed only sporadically and then usually buried in a remote section of the paper." State and local

TABLE 12

PERCENTAGE OF STANDPATTERS, SWITCHERS, AND
NEW VOTERS WHO ARE POLITICALLY UNINVOLVED

	Standpatters (D–D, R–R)	Switchers (D–R, R–D)	New voters (O–D, O–R)
Interest in politics, 1952	16%	19%	42%
Thought given to the election, 1956	20	22	44
Interest in politics, 1960	19	21	43

Source: Key, 1966, pp. 99, 102, 141. The figures represent the percentage of voters who said "only a little" or "none," as opposed to "a great deal" or "a fair amount" of interest or "quite a lot" or "some" thought. Voters are classified by their reported votes in two consecutive Presidential elections (for example, 1948 and 1952). Data are from preelection Gallup polls. N varies between 395 and 4409.

partisan races below, say, the gubernatorial and mayoralty level receive a similar lack of media attention. Hence many non-Presidential contests may meet this minimal-information, party-label criterion. Consequently, as Stokes and Miller (1962) have shown, party-line voting is a more important determinant of electoral outcome in off-year Congressional races than in Presidential elections.

The less intense party identification of the extremely involved may not affect large numbers of voters directly, but most of them may be highly influential in one or another political "elite." They may be leaders of reference groups with great power (for example, ethnic groups or labor unions), or wealthy men with financial power in politics. Scoble (1963) noted that the most involved members of the National Committee for an Effective Congress are not the most committed to the Democratic party. Grupp (1966) reported a similar finding regarding members of the John Birch Society; and Braungart (1966), regarding members of two extremist student activist organizations. The efforts of such activists generally have political effects out of proportion to the small fraction of the electorate they represent; but again it should be emphasized that it is an extremely small fraction.

The analysis thus far has emphasized built-in stability in partisan elections due to the existence of stable and effective party loyalties. These, and other group-related predispositions of somewhat less political relevance (or power), seem to be of long standing in the individual's life, and control much of his political opinion formation. They seem also to be rather contentless commitments; "party images" are neither particularly differentiated nor do they generally appear to be very ideological. Electoral change occurs primarily when defection occurs from these standing loyalties. The "short-term forces" that create defection may be visible in the voter's partisan attitudes concerning any given electoral choice, but at this point in the analysis their antecedents are not clear. It seems evident that the defectors are usually switchers rather than sporadic voters, and that they are usually less informed and less interested than those upholding their commitments, but it is not yet clear what kinds of information are critical to them. Here let us consider some of the alternative possibilities, and see if there is any evidence about their relative power.

TABLE 13

PERCENTAGE OF RESPONDENTS WHOSE PRESIDENTIAL PREFERENCE
WAS CONSISTENT WITH THEIR ISSUE POSITIONS

	Percent voting in accord with own issue position		
	Democratic position	Republican position	*N*
Which party will do the best job maintaining prosperity (October 1960)	92.5%	93.5%	2183
Which Presidential candidate could handle Korea best (October 1952)	92.6	76.8	2239
Sympathies generally with unions or companies (October 1952)	66.7	76.6	3874
U.S. entry into Korean War, a mistake or not (October 1952)	57.4	66.6	4399

Source: Key, 1966, pp. 73, 78, 127. Data are based on Gallup polls conducted prior to the elections indicated. A few respondents are omitted for reasons irrelevant to the point made by the table, for example, because they could not recall for whom they had voted in the prior election. The figures represent a percentage of all those holding a given issue position.

Issues and the vote

One traditional theory about the operation of a democracy is that candidates or parties offer policy alternatives, from which the public then indicates, by appropriate voting, which policies they approve. Electoral change depends on the issues selected. Obviously, this does happen sometimes: Agger (1959) and Converse (1964) were able to identify some highly issue-oriented independent voters, and Senator Goldwater's success in the South in 1964 seems to have derived partly from his popular racial stand (Converse, Clausen, and Miller, 1965). Similarly, Louise Day Hicks' successes in Boston are attributed in part to the fear of neighborhood desegregation on the part of white Bostonians (Ross, Crawford, and Pettigrew, 1966). Yet people do not generally refer to policy positions in explaining what they like or dislike about a candidate (Campbell, 1966c). Hence, we must ask how often policy alternatives play a critical role.

Change in issue stands. It is most tempting to assume an association when voters' issue positions change between elections toward positions favored by the party that improves its vote over the same period. Miller (1967) cited two examples from the 1956–1960 period. Voters' partisan attitudes on foreign policy favored the Democrats increasingly from 1952 to 1960, paralleling the increasing Democratic vote (p. 226). Voters also became increasingly pessimistic about America's chances of staying out of war, and increasingly thought that the Democrats would be more effective in keeping the nation out of war (pp. 217–220). While these changes might warm the hearts of Democrats, by themselves they provide no evidence of issue-based changes in votes.

Issue stands and Presidential preference. A more direct approach is to correlate voters' issue stands with their Presidential preferences, as in the Campbell, Gurin, and Miller (1954) "issue partisanship" analysis cited above. The 1964 California senatorial race was one example. The defeat of the Democratic candidate, Pierre Salinger, was blamed by some on his stand against a referendum opposing fair housing. The vote clearly was correlated with attitudes on the referendum. Defection from Salinger among Democrats amounted to 36 percent of those favoring the referendum and 13 percent opposed. He received Republican defectors in almost the reverse ratio: 10 percent of its supporters and 34 percent of its opponents (Anderson and Lee, 1965, p. 466). The critical voters in the race were the proreferendum Democrats, many of whom defected. Table 13 provides a more extensive set of examples making the same general point: issue position and candidate preferences are often very highly correlated. However, even those correlations do not prove a causal connection. For example, 1964 California Presidential voting was correlated even more closely than Senatorial voting with the fair housing referendum, and neither Presidential candidate had taken a position on the referendum. Moreover, the Democratic Presidential candidate won a smashing victory, while the Senator and fair housing were decisively defeated.

Issue stands and voting change. Key (1966) has gone further, attempting to establish that issue positions are correlated with *changes* in the voter's Presidential preferences. Using data from preelection Gallup polls, he presented the policy positions held by those who defected from their previous Presidential vote, and those held by voters who did not vote in the previous election.

Substantial correlations do appear between a wide variety of policy positions and vote changes during the period 1936–1960. According to Key's analysis, in 1940 the important issues concerned the domestic programs of the New Deal and the "third term." Similarly, the "campaign of 1948 shaped antagonisms along New Deal and anti-New Deal lines" (p. 49). Defections to Eisenhower in 1952 were attributed to voters' derogation of the Truman Administration, to concern about the Korean situation, and to feelings of assurance that Eisenhower would continue much of the New Deal–Fair Deal domestic program. In 1952 the "electorate looked at the public scene, did not like what it saw, and . . . threw the ins out" (p. 63). The 1956 election was regarded as a vote of confidence for Eisenhower, based particularly on peace and prosperity. And 1960, Key says, was marked by "fluffy and foggy political stimuli" (p. 113); consequently, the important grounds for decision were party, religious, and other group loyalties, rather than policy issues.

The question is whether in these cases the issue stands antedated, and controlled, candidate preferences. The obvious alternative is that the voter adopted appropriate policy positions after the fact, to rationalize a candidate preference arrived at for other reasons. Key's data, if anything, probably maximize the probability of rationalization, for two reasons. First, they depend on the voter's recall of his vote or nonvote four years earlier, and any systematic distortions in recall are likely to maximize the intelligibility of the vote by relating it to other attitudes. Second, the data were all gathered in single interviews in October of the election year. Since most vote intentions are final by October (Benham, 1965; Campbell *et al.*, 1960; Lazersfeld, Berelson, and Gaudet, 1948), even those whose vote is determined by issues are likely to use other issues as added rationalizations.

What might be most convincing is a comparison of issues that controlled many vote changes with issues that controlled very few, rather than simply listing a series of issues, all of which correlate with vote change. A crude step in this direction may be taken with Key's data by comparing issues in terms of how much "correct" switching or recruiting was done relative to how much "incorrect" movement occurred—defining "correctness" in terms of correspondence between issue stand and candidate preference.

The relative consistency of positions on each of Key's issues with the votes cast by new voters is shown in Table 14 (the degree of consistency is approximately the same with "switchers," but data for new voters are simpler to present). The issues seem to divide into three categories. Issue stands relate very closely to the vote when they essentially just rephrase the candidate or party preference question, especially in the form, "Which candidate (party) could handle (X) best?" Less closely correlated are a number of domestic issues that do not invoke the candidates or parties explicitly. And least related to changing votes are the few foreign issues also phrased without mentioning party or candidate. The only apparent exception to this ordering is the "third term" issue in 1940, which correlated closely with change without explicitly mentioning Roosevelt, but which obviously applied to him personally.

This ordering closely resembles the pattern one would expect if voters were responding, in October of an election year, to issue questions largely as vehicles for justifying their own candidate choice. Voting changes correlate closely with those policy positions that are transparently votes of confidence in the candidate, and indifferently on foreign policy questions where the link is obscure.

The most direct way of ruling out rationalization as an explanation for these correlations would be to show that the appropriate policy opinion preceded the voting change. Miller (1967) took a first step in this direction by relating policy opinion changes to vote changes over a four-year period. Unhappily, the two kinds of change are barely correlated, though when both do change, the direction of change is usually the same. Miller concluded that the issue positions often represent "a *post hoc* rationale for a vote decision reached on other grounds" (p. 226).

Classification of elections

Once the central role of party identification has been accepted, substantial variations in the outcome of Presidential elections seem likely to reflect one of two kinds of underlying patterns. One is basic change in the distribution of party loyalties, whether toward a given party or in the form of compensating shifts toward each party. Campbell (1966a) has described this as a "realigning" election. The second is a sudden swing of the vote without marked disturbance in party loyalties; Campbell terms this a "deviating" election. The third logical possibility, of course, is an election in which the vote mirrors party preference, described by Campbell as a "maintaining" election. The analysis of electoral change, then, sets two tasks. One is to describe the circumstances for marked realignment of party loyalty; and the second, to determine the conditions for substantial numbers of defections from party preference.

Secular realignment. Several interesting essays have described historical realignments of the parties, and need not be summarized here (Campbell, 1966a; Key, 1955, 1959; Sellers, 1965). The evidence does suggest, however, that large-scale changes of party loyalty are rare. For example, the status polarization that evidently occurred

TABLE 14

PERCENTAGE OF "NEW" VOTERS WHOSE POLICY POSITIONS AND PRESIDENTIAL
CHOICES WERE CONSISTENT LESS THE PERCENTAGE WHOSE POLICY POSITIONS AND
PRESIDENTIAL CHOICES WERE INCONSISTENT

Issues explicitly invoking candidates: "Which candidate would be . . . ?"	
Better for providing postwar jobs (1944)	92%
Better wartime President (1940)	89
Better for winning war (1944)	84
Better for handling Korea (1952)	74
Issues explicitly invoking parties: "Which party would be . . . ?"	
Better for people like yourself (1960)	78%
Better for the country's most important problem (1960)	76
Better for maintaining prosperity (1960)	72
Party identification (1960)	69
Better for keeping the U.S. out of World War III (1960)	62
Domestic policy issues phrased without explicit reference to parties or candidates:	
Third term (1940)	78%
FDR's farm program (1940)	67
Approval of Truman as President (1952)	50
Federal regulation of business (1940)	41
Approval of Eisenhower as President (1960)	38
Favor unions or companies more (1952)	33
Social Security (1936)	24
Foreign policy issues phrased without explicit reference to parties or candidates:	
Mistake to enter Korea (1952)	18%
Mistake to enter World War I (1940)	15
Stay out of war or help England (1940)	5

Source: Key, 1966, pp. 43–139. The figures represent the percentage voting in line with their policy position on the issue cited less the percentage voting inconsistently with their policy position. Only those who failed to vote in the previous Presidential election are included. However, almost exactly the same ordering of "power" of issues occurs for respondents who switched from one election to the next, voting both times. The magnitude of effect is also comparable.

as a consequence of the Depression of the 1930's seems mainly to have involved persons voting for the first time. The "first vote ever," at least as recalled in the Survey Research Center surveys of the 1950's, switched from strongly Republican in the 1920's to strongly Democratic in the 1930's. Campbell *et al.* concluded: "the Great Depression swung a heavy proportion of the young electors toward the Democratic party and gave that party a hold on that generation, which it has never fully relinquished" (1960, pp. 153–155). For example, from 1948 through 1956, this "generation" voted more in line with their social class than did older or younger people (1960, pp. 356–360). The older Republicans who defected to Roosevelt in 1932 and 1936 mostly did *not* change their party preferences, and later resumed voting for the Republican party. (The more general issue of the stability of party preference throughout a lifetime is considered in detail below.)

Key (1955) contrasted the period of the 1920's and 1930's, which realigned the basic party division more along class and religious lines, with the election of 1896, which simply moved people of every kind into the Republican camp. Key's analysis is an excellent example of the clever use of aggregate data, all that is available from presurvey days. However, the evidence regarding individual change can only be inferential. Survey data indicate that changes in party preference have been minor in the period 1952–1964, despite large electoral swings (Converse, 1966a, p. 13). Thus "deviating elections" seem to be much more common than "realigning elections."

"Deviating elections" and candidate appeal. The probability of a "deviating election" (that is, one in which the minority party wins without substantially affecting the basic distribution of party identification) has been estimated to be 0.28, given the normal variability in Presidential election outcomes during the period 1892–1960 and the current four percent advantage in party identification held by the Democrats (Stokes, 1966a). The question is what makes the critical difference.

In 1952 and 1964, large numbers of voters defected from the losing party to vote for the winner. In each case party identification was not importantly affected (Converse, 1966a). Stokes' (1966b) analyses of the data from these elections suggest that the most variable partisan attitude, by far, was candidate attitude. The net advantage accruing to each side from the other partisan attitudes was relatively stable ("domestic policy" helping the Democrats, "foreign policy" helping the Republicans, and so on). But the net impact of candidates favored the Republicans tremendously in 1952 and 1956, and the Democrats equally strikingly in 1964.

Similarly, Stokes and Miller (1962) found that votes in off-year Congressional elections are dominated by two variables: party loyalty, and knowledge or impression of the candidate. Policy references to the candidate are extremely rare. And Sellers (1965), considering all American Presidential elections, concluded that Presidents elected in deviating elections, "Washington, Jackson, Harrison, Taylor, Grant, and Eisenhower—were 'popular hero' candidates who were widely revered for their military achievements and personal characteristics before entering politics" (p. 22). The cases of two such candidates on whom survey data exist, de Gaulle and Eisenhower, confirm the point quite clearly. Voters' "images" of these generals were dominated by personal references; policy references were comparatively rare (Converse and Dupeux, 1966, p. 300); and each was evaluated partially on partisan grounds after entry into politics, but the overall level of evaluation was strongly favorable in each case.

The general point, then, is that short-term electoral change most commonly derives from what Stokes calls a "turnover of objects" rather than from attitude change. It comes more often from the entry of new candidates, new issues, and new events into the political scene than from changed evaluations of old ones. And among these, apparently new candidates are especially important. This conclusion is a little startling; why should candidates be so central, and policies more peripheral?

Image politics

Two kinds of explanation will be offered here for the centrality of personalities. One is that persons represent unusually simple stimuli, easily cognized and retained. This is important because most political stimuli are too complex to be handled comfortably by the majority of voters. The other is that voters have a penchant for relating the abstract and remote to their own personal experience, which means they have a tendency to personalize politics. First, we deal with the problem of complexity.

Opinion without information. An interesting phenomenon in survey research is that many respondents give political opinions without being able to specify any reasons for them, or indeed give evidence of having any relevant information. This shows up clearly on policy issues. In one Minnesota poll, 87 percent had definite opinions on whether or not Communist China should be admitted to the United Nations, but 64 percent could give no reasons why she should be admitted, and 30 percent could give no reasons why she should not (Rogers, Stuhler, and Koenig, 1967, p. 247). In the 1956 Survey Research Center election survey, respondents were asked what the government *should* be doing about 16 general issues (segregation of schools, aid to neutral nations, etc.), and then what the government *was* doing. On the average, about 20 percent had an opinion, but without any idea, even a mistaken one, of what the government was doing (Campbell *et al.,* 1960, p. 174).

Very often people cannot even give a rationale for their votes. Campbell, Gurin, and Miller (1954, pp. 43, 53–54) found that an average of 18 percent could not make favorable comments about their candidate and/or party in 1952, and 29 percent could not make unfavorable comments about the opposition. It is more understandable that some respondents are not able to cite counterattitudinal arguments, but surprising that most cannot: 67 percent were unable to cite anything unfavorable about their side, and 59 percent unable to mention anything good about the opposition. As a general rule, according to Hyman and Sheatsley (1954, p. 37), one-third of the electorate cannot say why they like or dislike their own party. The point is perhaps put most engagingly by Almond and Verba (1963, p. 98) in describing their American, English, German, and Mexican respondents: "the willingness to express opinions is widespread, affecting even the uninformed . . . even the cognitively incompetent feel free to express opinions."

Why do opinions exist without informational basis? First, the opinion may be based on simple affective conditioning without any transmission of information, such as occurs when young children adopt their parents' opinions, a wife doubles her husband's vote, or people adopt the standards of their reference groups (Lane and Sears, 1964, p. 70). Incidentally, this resembles McGuire's (1964) analysis of "cultural truisms." The other possibility is that the opinion was originally formed in response to both information and affect, but only the affect has been retained. It has been demonstrated in both impression-formation (Anderson and Hubert, 1963) and attitude-change (Hovland and Weiss, 1951) experiments that affective change is sometimes retained even when the informational basis for it is lost (see also Chapter 21). And retention, presumably, is partly a function of stimulus simplicity. (It may also be that the interview situation sometimes "pulls" a response where only a "non-attitude" exists; see Converse, 1963a; Bogart, 1967.)

Affects toward persons and groups. Of all political opinions, simple affects toward groups and candidates seem to be retained most stably. They are more stable than other opinions, and more widespread than information or rationales. Perhaps they are retained because they are so simple and easy to remember. Groups and candidates alike can be denoted briefly and in concrete terms. Even the cognitive contents attached to the affects tend to be simple. The most common contents of "candidate images" seem to stress general leadership qualities and personal qualities (*cf.* Converse and Dupeux, 1966, p. 300) or vague impressions of special competences such as the general impression in 1960 that Nixon could "handle" Russia better (Pool, Abelson, and Popkin, 1964, p. 84). "Party images" tend also to be rather simple, largely describing "broad postures of government" and perceptions of how much the party "does for" any given group (Matthews and Prothro, 1966a). Thus, stable attitudes toward groups and candidates come rather easily. The main difference between the two, of course, is that groups themselves are rather stable, while candidates come and go.

Personalizing. One gets the impression that voters prefer to think about politics in terms of individual persons rather than abstractions or collectivities. Lane (1959b) hypothesized that people discuss politics more in terms of important people than in terms of issues, and that they "follow political news when it deals with figures with whom they can identify and whom they 'understand'" (pp. 87, 296). He also presented some evidence (p. 279), as did Lazarsfeld, Berelson, and Gaudet (1948), that an unusual amount of space in the media is given over to personal, "human interest" stories about political persons. (Elsewhere he suggested that *blame* is typically assigned to conditions, not persons; see Lane, 1962. This may be part of a general reluctance to criticize; see pp. 424–443 below. Participants in the Watts riot did personalize blame for it more than did nonparticipants; perhaps blaming is generally understood to demand action. See Sears and McConahay, 1967b.)

For another thing, the President seems to be an extremely important focus of political attention for Americans. When asked who was "in the best position to see what the country needs," 61 percent indicated the President, and only 17 percent chose Congress. On the other hand, only 10 percent thought the President had "most to say in the way our government is run," while 52 percent indicated Congress had (Survey Research Center surveys in 1958 and 1959, cited by Sigel, 1966, p. 128). In images of Presidential candidates, personal character references are much more prominent than anything else (Converse and Dupeux, 1966; Hyman and Sheatsley, 1953, 1954). And Americans responded to President Kennedy's death more in personal than in political terms; for example, 91 percent of a national sample said that they had felt deeply sorry for his wife and children, while only 44 percent worried as much about how his death would affect our relations with other countries (Sheatsley and Feldman, 1965, p. 156). This personalizing, as will be indicated in more detail below, is a chronologically immature way of dealing with political stimuli. Yet it offers another possible explanation for the centrality of candidate differences in promoting electoral change.

Content of candidate images. Still, the principal contents of candidate images seem to have to do with personal qualities rather than policy positions. In 1960 and 1964, the most common favorable images concerned Kennedy's education, Nixon's experience and presumed ability to handle world problems, Goldwater's integrity, and Johnson's record and experience. The unfavorable images were a little more concrete, especially Kennedy's religion and Goldwater's positions on social security and war, but also common were critiques of Goldwater's impulsivity, poor speeches, and unclear positions (Campbell, 1966b, pp. 261–262). Images in 1952 and 1956 had emphasized much the same kind of content, except that there was more emphasis on what Converse and Dupeux (1966) describe as the "generalized worship" deriving from military achievements that characterized the images of both de Gaulle and Eisenhower. At least one effort has been made to factor-analyze candidate images, the result being two primary factors (across six candidates): (1) a general evaluative dimension and (2) personal assertiveness. Moderately clear idiosyncratic factors also emerged for each candidate (Anderson and Bass, 1967).

Valence issues. The issue contents found in party or candidate images often tend to refer to "valence issues." This is a useful term that Stokes (1963) has proposed to describe "the linking of the parties with some condition that is positively or negatively valued by the electorate." Depression and recovery in the New Deal years, or Korea, corruption, and Communism in 1952, or prestige abroad in 1960 were issues of this kind: almost everyone favors prestige and recovery and opposes depressions, corruption, Communism, and so on. Thus, the important variable is not which party has the more popular policy position, but whether or not the "issue" content becomes established as a part of the candidate or party image. Can Hoover and the Republican party successfully be associated with depression and economic deprivation, or not?

Position issues. Those issues that present reasonable and popular policy alternatives are termed "position issues" by Stokes. Simple positions on such issues are sometimes prominent aspects of candidates' images. For example, in 1964, nuclear war was thought more likely under Goldwater; many thought Goldwater opposed to social security, especially those aged 60 and over; and his position on civil rights was salient in his image in the South (Benham, 1965, pp. 191–192; Converse, Clausen, and Miller, 1965). In all three cases, his "image" represented a highly simplified version of his positions.

Perhaps, as a general rule, such issue stands are translated into broad "postures" in the voters' versions of the candidate's image. They think of him as likely to do more or less, go farther or less far along a given line, or be good or bad for a given group, be "softer" or "tougher" with some other group. But the affect transferred to the candidate's image may depend on congruence between the direction of his posture and the voter's rather than on consideration of concrete policy. The voter may in fact have been exposed to a more detailed version of the candidate's position and even shifted his affective impression of the candidate appropriately. However, all but the simplest implications are quickly lost from the content of the image, even if the affective change is stable. In any case, it is clear that the details are rarely retained; on 16 policy issues, Campbell *et al.* (1960, p. 182) found that an average of only about 30 percent of the electorate had an opinion *and* had some idea (even if mistaken) about what current government policy was *and* saw the parties as differing on the issue (even if the direction of difference was incorrectly perceived).

Thus, electoral success depends, in part, on the affects that are implanted in the images of upcoming candidates. The contents associated with the affects tend to be highly simplified and to refer to (1) personal interest material, (2) valence issues, or (3) rudimentary policy preferences. All of these tend to be resistant to change once established, probably because contradictions would be complicated and the voter is not exposed to enough information to make them effective. By this view, the critical issue in image formation is which of these contents are "sold" most effectively, that is, which become most salient to the voter.

This emphasis on "images" does not contradict the earlier emphasis on partisan predispositions. Rather, these latter are probably the single most important sources of affective commitments to candidates. The present analysis is oriented toward explaining defections from party preference. And defections seem most easily produced by introducing new objects, since impressions of the familiar are resistant to change, and impressions of the new are manipulable. New candidates are especially likely to produce defections, since persons are so easily and happily cognized relative to other political stimuli.

Conclusions: origins and effects of images. Most often, the image of a particular candidate is built up around particular personal qualities. The image is based partly on "issues," but these tend to be valence issues or vaguely stated positions. The primary purpose of raising issues at all may be simply to provide something for the candidate to talk about while he exemplifies his integrity, experience, decisiveness, etc. Even then, too many issues may confuse things: Anderson and Lee (1967) quoted one successful image maker as claiming three issues is the optimum number for a successful campaign. In any case, the contents of the images seem to be transitory and unimportant; their primary role is to contribute to the affects associated with the candidate.

An important exception concerns those position issues which have direct personal relevance. The race issue, for example, may involve events with tangible and personal consequences, such as neighborhood desegregation, school deterioration, or lack of personal safety in the streets. In this form, issues may have a genuine and important effect, even though the real issue may be rationalized in quite different (and more noble) terms (Ross, Crawford, and Pettigrew, 1966; Wolfinger and Greenstein, 1968).

But even this degree of direction is uncommon; more often the outcome of an election is most reasonably interpreted as a vaguer statement. In 1952, for example, "The voters were not asking for any specific program of legislation; they just wanted a new bunch of fellows to run things better" (Campbell, 1964, p. 755).

Conclusion

The model presented initially for the influence of issues in campaigns is not Utopian, considering the gross characteristics of American society. The levels of education and literacy are astonishingly high, and mass media penetrate to every corner of the society to an unprecedented degree. Since the basic characteristics of the political system have remained essentially unchanged for several generations, voters have not had to learn a whole new set of cues every few years. Yet it seems as if popular intellectual participation in the electoral process is at a rather low level.

Political party identification is clearly the most stable determinant of the vote, as well as the most important determinant in any given partisan election. However, it is a longstanding commitment rather than the result of a "fit" between party positions and the voter's policy preferences. In fact it does not relate strongly to policy stands in the general public. Hence, party preference does not seem notably responsive to policy considerations.

The public is not familiar with very many public persons or issues, and exposure to media information on public affairs is surprisingly occasional. Those who change sides between elections or in response to an election campaign seem to be the least attentive, least informed, and least interested.

Most voters reach a stable Presidential preference before the campaign even begins. Available data on policy opinions suggest that, with rare exceptions, they are much more volatile than candidate or party preferences.

Two explanations for correlations between policy opinions and vote intentions, when they exist (a sometime thing), would therefore seem most plausible. First, insofar as the policy attitudes are stable, they probably derive more often from candidate or party loyalties than vice versa. Second, many policy preferences as expressed in opinion surveys are probably not very stable or meaningful. What appears to be a policy question may, to the respondent, be little more than a slightly indirect way of asking for candidate or party preference. Key discounted the possibility that many voters try to "make things look tidy" by trying to make themselves look consistent, "for a voter must have a fair amount of information to simulate a consistent pattern of preferences" (p. 150). However, in most cases it does not take a great deal of information to deduce that one's favorite party should be best for maximizing prosperity.

The most powerful variables in electoral choice appear to be party identification and candidate image. Stokes (1966a) has estimated that the probability of a minority-party Presidential victory is 0.28, given the variance of outcomes since 1892, and given the current four percent Democratic advantage in party identification. The short-term force that seems to have accounted for the most variance in the outcomes of recent Presidential elections is candidate image (Stokes, 1966b).

The antecedents of party identification will be discussed in more detail in the next section. Candidate images seem to be particularly important because they are so simple: voters like to personalize their politics, and often the informational basis for a feeling about a candidate is forgotten. In any case, the content that may be most influential in candidate images may be the "valence issue," which is merely a matter of trying to stick one's own candidate with things that everyone agrees are good, and the opposition with things everyone agrees are bad. The critical variable, then, seems to be what sticks and what does not—critical, of course, within the constraints imposed by the basic distribution of party preferences. The absence of these constraints is what makes "image politics" so important in primary or nonpartisan elections, or in areas where one party does not exist or the two parties are evenly divided.

Policy (or "position") issues may have some influence over candidate images (especially when they have some personal relevance to the voter), and, as asserted by Key, "The only really effective weapon of popular control in a democratic regime is the capacity of the electorate to throw a party from power. . . . This probably permits the electorate to be utilized to its best advantage in the process of popular government" (1966, p. 76). It is not clear that the electorate has an accurate or sophisticated view of party performance when it "throws the rascals out" (see Stokes and Miller, 1962). But the rascals have not been appallingly rascally, nor the nation in truly desperate straits, in recent times. Perhaps in such situations more attention, if not more perspicacity, would mark the electorate. The experience of the 1930's suggests that realignment of long-standing predispositions would not be unlikely.

THE LIFE HISTORY OF PARTISAN PREDISPOSITIONS

In voting behavior, party identification and other group-related attitudes are the most central determinants of partisan decision. The same is true for opinion formation on many other issues. If such predispositions control so much variance in public opinion, what in turn controls them? Goldberg's (1966) voting model viewed an adult's party identification as a joint function of his father's party identification and his own social characteristics, thus emphasizing youthful political socialization and adult social location. But Goldberg's model was based on a restricted set of variables. The main goal of this section is to determine what contributes most, and particularly to determine whether or not youthful socialization is the primary source of partisan commitments.

DEVELOPMENT OF PARTISANSHIP IN CHILDHOOD

Perhaps the commonest assumption is that most Americans adopt, in childhood, a lifelong commitment to their parents' party. Hyman (1959) and Hess and Torney (1965), for example, cited West's observation that "a man is born into his political party just as he is born into probable future membership in the church of his parents." The reliable evidence on the childhood phase of this generalization is briefly summarized in the following discussion. As will be seen, the evidence is quite incomplete, and probably does not sustain the rather exaggerated claims that have sometimes been made for it.

Early perceptions of parties

Awareness that two parties exist and that they are supposed to differ in some way comes rather early. In one sample, 28 percent of the third-graders said they "do not know what Democrat and Republican mean," but by the fifth grade, only nine percent did not understand the terms. Under both Eisenhower and Kennedy, less than 20 percent of the third-graders could not identify the President's party. And they soon came to believe that the parties differ in some way (Hess and Torney, 1967, pp. 82, 90, 278).

However, schoolchildren are vague about just how they differ. Perhaps the primary policy differences between the parties, or at least the features of their "party images" most distinctive to adults, fall on the dimension of "helping the rich" as opposed to "helping the unemployed." A substantial minority of adults distinguish the parties in this way (Campbell, Gurin, and Miller, 1954, p. 125), but there is little evidence that children do before the eighth grade (Hess and Torney, 1967, p. 81). Rather, the primary contents of early party images seem to refer to candidates and incumbents, especially the President (Greenstein, 1965a, p. 67).

Party identification

When do children first develop party identification? The data suggest fairly rapid increases in the proportion claiming a party preference up to about the fifth grade (age 11), and then a more gradual increase during the rest of life. In Hess and Torney's (1967, p. 90) sample, 36 percent of the second-graders had a party preference, increasing to a fairly stable level of around 55 percent in grades five to eight. Greenstein (1965a, p. 73) found that about 60 percent in grades four to eight had a party preference, but he offered them no "Independent" or "don't know what a party is" alternative. Jennings and Niemi (1968) found that 64 percent in grade twelve had a party preference. Data from several surveys in the 1950's suggest that this is just slightly below the level for young adults; the number of party identifiers increased consistently from 69 percent of the youngest age group, those aged 21 to 24, to 84 percent in the oldest, those aged 75 and over (Campbell *et al.*, 1960, p. 162). In short, self-proclaimed party preference seems to rise sharply to about 50 or 60 percent of the population by grade five (about age 11), and then the increase continues, much more gradually, throughout life. Evidence that these data reflect age differences, rather than historical changes, will be considered later.

The proportion of persons claiming independence of party label appears to be related to age in an inverted U-function. It increases with age in grade school, from nine percent in grade two to 32 percent in grade eight (Hess and Torney, 1967, p. 90), reaches 36 percent in grade twelve (Jennings and Niemi, 1968), but diminishes among adults from 31 percent to 16 percent over the age range cited above from the Campbell *et al.* (1960) data.

The process by which these early preferences are acquired is suggested by analogy from the acquisition of attitudes toward nationality groups. Lambert and Klineberg (1967) found that six-year-olds differentiate their own group from all others on a simple "we-them" basis; Americans, for example, are "like me," whereas Japanese, Russians, or African Negroes are "not like me," to white American children. Feelings of similarity or dissimilarity are based most clearly on gross physical differences, and apparently have little affective significance. By age 10, children feel positively about most groups. By age 14, however, feelings of dissimilarity are phrased in terms of political and personality attributes, as is the case for adult stereotypes. And they are consistent with affects; similar nationalities are liked, and dissimilar ones tend to be disliked. Perhaps such preferences are normally acquired, first, by a perception of "me-ness" regarding the membership group, then later the appropriate affects and conventional rationales.

The power of early commitments

These early party preferences are relatively contentless, since the child has virtually no information about partisan politics. Thus they conceivably could be transitory, affectless preferences that are easily changed and without power to shape other opinions. The childhood acquisition of party identification would be meaningful only if early preferences share some of the stability and intensity of adult commitments.

One general test is whether or not children's reactions to an election outcome follow a partisan pattern. By grades five and six, their affective reactions to Kennedy's election ("Did you feel happy or sad when Kennedy was elected?") were polarized along party lines almost as much as were their teachers' (Hess and Torney, 1967, p. 210). Few children reported they "didn't care" about it (less than 20 percent at each grade level studied). These reactions also meet the important test of attitude stability (Converse, 1964), at least over a period of up to two weeks. The children's reactions were measured on a simple five-point scale, and the test-retest correlations were +0.83 for grade four, +0.85 for grade six, and +0.81 for grade eight (Hess and

Torney, 1965, p. 423). Over 70 percent of the children gave exactly the same response on both occasions. These data suggest that partisan reactions to the election
outcome were not ephemeral, even at grade four. Unfortunately, there is no comparable evidence on the stability of party preference.

Strong party preferences should have the power to determine other issue positions when paired with them, especially when the "issue" is explicitly an evaluation
of party competence (see Table 14 for some examples with adults). In response to
such questions as which party "does most for the United States" or "does most to
help keep us out of war," children from the third grade through the eighth grade
showed highly significant tendencies to ascribe greater virtue to their own party
(Hess and Torney, 1965, p. 369).

These are useful preliminary indicators. They are not wholly convincing, but
they certainly suggest that early party preferences have some durability and strength.
Additional research is required before one can have great confidence that stable partisan predispositions are implanted in childhood. It could be, for example, that they
are potentially highly unstable at this age, but relatively unused and unchallenged,
and that firm commitments are usually not made until late adolescence. However,
insofar as they are durable, they again represent the pattern of opinion formation in
the absence of information. Children have only the vaguest idea of how the parties
might differ, but apparently do not hesitate to express a preference.

Parents as agents of socialization

Parents are usually cited as the most important influence on the development of
party preference (Campbell, Gurin, and Miller, 1954; Hyman, 1959; Lane and
Sears, 1964). Indeed, retrospective parent-child agreement tends to be high, and
most grade-school children report the same party preference as their fathers. However, no solid data currently exist on agreement between parents and preadolescent
children.

Existing indirect evidence suggests that the parents' role is relatively large,
though far from all-encompassing. Children in two studies were asked where they
would go for voting advice (Greenstein, 1965a; Hess and Torney, 1967). The data
are shown in Table 15. In both studies it is apparent that most young children
think their parents are reliable sources of information, and would be inclined to look
to them for advice. This is presumably the age when they are acquiring party preferences. By grade eight, many children have learned to say that they would make up
their own minds, or decide for themselves. Like most adults, they here begin to resist
admitting they take help or advice from others.

Parental influence might also be inferred from agreement between siblings.
Hess and Torney (1965, p. 440) measured sibling agreement on affective reactions
to Kennedy's victory, but not, unfortunately, on party preference. Siblings were
moderately closely agreed ($r = +0.50$, $N = 117$), while unrelated pairs of children,
matched for sex, grade, and social status, were not ($r = +0.04$).

Neither these data nor those reporting the child's perception of his agreement
with his parents (Hess and Torney, 1965, p. 175) give a precise estimate of how
often preadolescent children simply copy their parents' party preferences. They do

TABLE 15

CHILDREN'S PREFERRED SOURCES OF VOTING ADVICE

	Grade level		
	4	6	8
If you had to vote, who would be best to ask for voting advice?			
One or both parents	83%	71%	61%
Teacher	6	10	14
Would decide myself (written in)	1	6	4
N	111	115	180
If you had to vote, where would be the best place to look for help in making up your mind?			
One or both parents	58%	39%	27%
Other people	6	4	4
Mass media	5	10	16
Make up own mind	31	47	53
N	1231	1643	1589

Sources: Greenstein, 1965a, p. 104; Hess and Torney, 1967, p. 86.

suggest, however, that it is far from a universal pattern (though, as will be seen, party preference is shared with parents much more than are most other attitudes).

Other agents: teachers, peers, and mass media

Neither teachers nor peers are mentioned very often as potential sources of voting advice (though lower-status children are much more likely to mention teachers than are higher-status children; *cf.* Greenstein, 1965a, p. 104; Hess, 1963, p. 554). Beyond that, the critical datum really is how much contact children have with the political opinions of anyone outside the home, and this is not very clear. At each age level, about the same proportion reported having "talked about a candidate" with friends as with parents (Hess and Torney, 1967, p. 71). These data do not reflect frequency or intensity of discussion. Moreover, they conflict with earlier data suggesting that political discussion with parents is more frequent until the later years of high school, when the rates became more equal (Hyman, 1959, p. 101). More data on this point are badly needed. The resemblance of the parents' and offspring's social environment is quite great (Goldberg, 1966), and this alone could produce much parent-offspring political agreement, even in the absence of any transmission between the two (Hyman, 1959).

Whatever the relative exposure to parents' views and those of other sources, clearly, exposure to the latter increases dramatically as the child gets older. Hess and Torney (1967, pp. 71, 86) reported particularly sharp increases between grades three and five in political discussion with parents or friends, and, a little later, in reading about candidates in newspapers or magazines. In another study, children at age six reported that they got most of their information about nationality groups from parents and television, but those aged 10 and 14 rarely mentioned their parents, primarily citing television and school (Lambert and Klineberg, 1967, p. 35). How much influence this additional exposure to nonfamilial ideas has is unknown.

The role of election campaigns

One influence that has not been explored very vigorously is the role of elections. It might well be that each child's early partisan commitments become crystallized only during Presidential campaigns, when politics is discussed more in school, mock elections are held, campaign buttons worn, discussion with peers increases, etc. One implication of this "critical period" notion would be that the parents' candidate preferences in that election might be more crucial for the child's ultimate party identification than the parents' party identifications. The vividness of the former is illustrated by Niemi's (in press) report that high school students have a rather accurate perception of their parent's candidate preference (in 1964, in a large nationwide sample, tau-beta = 0.82), but not so accurate a perception of his party identification (tau-beta = 0.59). Ninety-two percent could accurately name the candidate for whom the parent voted, but only 71 percent could name the parent's party identification. Further, the inaccuracies were primarily in the direction of attributing a vote for the winner, which might further exaggerate the lasting effect of a momentary electoral swing. Children of the 1950's might be unusually Republican, of the early 1960's unusually Democratic, etc. A competing hypothesis (Campbell *et al.*, 1960) suggests that the "first vote" is unusually influential in determining long-term commitments. In this view, an election campaign has its most enduring effects upon young adults.

INTERGENERATIONAL CONTINUITY

An implication of the finding that young children have political opinions is that such early opinions persist, more or less unchanged, well into adulthood. By themselves, of course, such data do not justify this conclusion. Yet the question is extremely important: how much influence do preadult political opinions, and the parents that are presumably responsible for many of them, have on adult opinions?

Parent-offspring agreement

A first step is to determine just how close the agreement between parents and offspring is in childhood, and in adulthood as well. If it should turn out that children do agree very closely with their parents on party preference, the political system would appear to be very stable indeed, if not inflexible for some purposes. Thus, the exact extent of parent-to-offspring attitude transmission would seem to be of more than idle interest.

There are three important sources of data. Hyman (1959) has reviewed a large number of studies using a variety of techniques, but mostly with small, unrepresentative samples. There are data from large samples of schoolchildren (Hess and Torney, 1967) and adults (Campbell, Gurin, and Miller, 1954) who reported on both their own and their parents' party preferences. This procedure probably overestimates parent-child agreement somewhat, because recall of parents' opinions is

TABLE 16

RELATIONSHIP BETWEEN PARENT AND OFFSPRING PARTY PREFERENCES

| | Adult respondents (N = 1281) | | | |
Parents (as recalled by respondent)	Democratic	Independent	Republican	Total
Both Democrats	36.9%	8.2%	6.2%	51.3%
Split, one uncertain, both shifted	7.1	6.1	5.6	18.8
Both Republicans	4.8	6.0	19.0	29.8
Total	48.8	20.3	30.8	99.9

| | High school seniors (N = 1852) | | | |
Parent (as independently reported)	Democratic	Independent	Republican	Total
Democratic	32.6%	13.2%	3.6%	49.4%
Independent	7.0	12.8	4.1	23.9
Republican	3.4	9.7	13.6	26.7
Total	43.0	35.7	21.3	100.0

Sources: Campbell, Gurin, and Miller, 1954, p. 99 (data from the 1952 Survey Research Center election survey); Jennings and Niemi, 1968, p. 173 (data from the 1965 Survey Research Center survey).   About 14% of the adult sample was excluded because the respondent's preference was unknown or of a minor party, or the parents' preferences were unknown. About 2% of the high school sample is excluded because parent and/or offspring is apolitical or undecided.

likely to be distorted. And in the best available study, the Survey Research Center (Jennings and Niemi, 1968; Niemi, 1967; Niemi, in press) interviewed a national probability sample of 1669 high school seniors. A total of 1992 parents were also interviewed (in some cases, one, and in other cases, both parents). This study combines the advantage of a representative sample with that of independently gathered information from parents and offspring.

Party preference. The level of agreement reported in these latter two studies is shown in Table 16. Obviously, it is rather substantial ($r = +0.59$ for the high school data, for example). Perhaps more interesting, considering the hypothesis that children blindly adopt party preferences from their parents, is the proportion who agree exactly. In the adult sample, 61 percent reflect the parental pattern: the appropriate partisan preference when the parents agreed on one, and Independence when the parental partisanship was equivocal. High school seniors and their parents, interviewed separately, yield a similar figure: 59 percent of the offspring agree with their parents. The number of persons who take the *opposite* party preference from their parents is rather low in both cases: 11 percent for the adults and seven percent for the high school seniors.

Comparable data from other studies are given in Table 17. Two were questionnaire studies in classrooms, Hess and Torney (1965) sampling metropolitan grade schools, and Goldsen *et al.* (1960), undergraduate students at eleven major universities. Maccoby, Matthews, and Morton (1954) interviewed young adults in Cambridge, Massachusetts in 1952. National mail surveys were done on college graduates by

TABLE 17

PERCENT AGREEMENT BETWEEN PARENTS AND OFFSPRING ON PARTY PREFERENCE

Source	Respondents	Parent	Of those with complete data				Of complete sample		
			Agreeing (DD,II,RR)	Opposite (DR,RD)	Other (DI,RI,IR,ID)	Total	N	Incomplete data*	Agreeing (DD,II,RR)
Hess and Torney (1965, p. 175)	grades 2–4	father	81%	4%	16%	101%	424	38%	50%
Hess and Torney (1965, p. 175)	grades 5–7	father	78	3	19	100	649	16	66
Jennings and Niemi (1968, p. 173)	grade 12	one†	59	7	34	100	1852	2	58
Goldsen et al. (1960, p. 256)	college students	father	61	5	32	98	2975	15	52
Maccoby, Matthews, and Morton (1954, p. 27)	ages 21–24	one	74	12	13	99	339	18	61
Campbell, Gurin, and Miller (1954, p. 99)	adults	both	61	11	27	99	1490	14‡	52
Havemann and West (1952, p. 117)	college graduates	father	58	10	32	100	9064	—	—
McClintock, Spaulding, and Turner (1965, p. 213)	psychologists	both	51	25	24	100	339	5	49
Turner, McClintock, and Spaulding (1963, p. 278)	sociologists	both	45	31	25	101	298	12	39
Turner, Spaulding, and McClintock (1963, p. 654)	political scientists	both	41	26	33	100	213	4	39

* Unless otherwise specified, exclusions are due to the respondents' being unable to characterize their parents' political preferences, or having none themselves.

† Independent interviews of parent and offspring. Other data are based on offspring's report only.

‡ See Table 16 for explanation.

Havemann and West (1952), and on academic psychologists, sociologists, and political scientists by McClintock, Spaulding, and Turner (1965; Turner, McClintock, and Spaulding, 1963; Turner, Spaulding, and McClintock, 1963). In all of these studies, the respondent's recall was the sole measure of parental party preference.

The results are strikingly consistent. Considering only those respondents whose data are complete, a little under 80 percent of the grade school children report agreement with their fathers (Hess and Torney, 1965). In the national samples of late adolescents or adults, about 60 percent report agreement (Campbell, Gurin, and Miller, 1954; Goldsen *et al.,* 1960; Havemann and West, 1952; Jennings and Niemi, 1968). Greater agreement was found in the survey of Cambridge, perhaps because, in a preponderantly Democratic community, offspring are likely to become Democrats whether influenced by parents or not (Maccoby, Matthews, and Morton, 1954). The three samples of social scientists average around 45 percent agreement with parents.

Perhaps the more meaningful question, though, is what proportion of the entire sample in each study share (or think they share) a party preference with parents. This probably gives a maximum population estimate of parent-offspring transmission of party preference. This figure is given in the last column of Table 17. It appears that about 55 percent of the adult population think they share their parents' preferences, given the three standard alternatives: Democrat, Republican, and Independent.

Defection from a definite parental party preference to the opposite party is normally rare. Few in the grade school, high school, and college samples defect; none of these studies found more than seven percent. In the large adult samples, the figure tends to be a little higher, around 10 percent. However, among the social scientists it is very high, averaging over 25 percent.

Party preference, therefore, does not show the dramatic degree of continuity between generations usually assumed for it in discussions of political change. Already, at age 17 and 18, 42 percent of the population does not share the position taken by one parent selected at random. However, only rarely does the defection lead the offspring to the opposite political party.

Group-related opinions. Are other kinds of political and social attitudes transmitted from parents to offspring? One probable limitation on intergenerational transmission is the instability of most such attitudes among adults (Converse, 1963a, 1964). If a parent is himself highly inconsistent, he is unlikely to transmit a consistent position to his child. Since the most stable adult opinions seem to be those which refer to some group as an object, perhaps the greatest amount of imitation will be found in attitudes toward groups.

In fact, however, the correlations between children and parents on other group-related issues are unimpressive. Jennings and Niemi (1968) reported parent-offspring correlations varying over eight stimulus groups from +0.36 for "Catholics" to +0.12 for "big business." Even correlations for the most distinctive minority groups, "Negroes" ($r = +0.26$) and "Jews" ($r = +0.22$), seem rather modest. For party identification the correlation had been much higher, $r = +0.59$. Correlations on two group-related policy issues, on the federal government's role in school integration and on prayers in the public schools, are of the same order of magnitude (tau-beta = +0.34 and +0.29, respectively; Jennings and Niemi, 1968). These two questions revolve around racial and religious issues, of course. These relatively low correlations are surprising, since ethnic and racial attitudes appear to follow the same developmental pattern as party identification; that is, they are learned and become stable rather early (Harding *et al.*, 1954, pp. 1034–1037; Proshansky, 1966). More direct evidence on the role of parents in transmitting such attitudes would be very desirable.

Religious beliefs are often held up as the model of parent-child belief transmission. Jennings and Niemi (1968) found that 74 percent of their parent-student pairs shared the same denominational preference; this represents a higher degree of agreement than holds for party preference. However, as one moves from the central question, denominational preference, to more abstract and esoteric matters of dogma, the level of agreement falls off. The contingency coefficient for denominational agreement was +0.88, but for an item regarding the literal and divine nature of the Bible, it was only +0.34. As with politics, then, transmission from parents seems most successful with simple, group-related cues (a vote, party membership, or denomination), and less clear on the subtler, more abstract matters.

Other political opinions. Two other issues were used in which principles of civil liberties were invoked, and here parent-child agreement is almost random. The issues concerned whether or not a legally elected Communist should be allowed to take office, and whether or not speakers against churches and religion should be allowed. The tau-betas were +0.13 and +0.05, respectively. These low correlations are predictable, in a sense, because most Americans appear not to have coherent and integrated beliefs about such democratic fundamentals, as will be seen below. Yet it is unsettling that so little intergenerational continuity exists on such fundamental derivations from basic democratic ideology.

A similar pattern of relatively low correlation characterizes Hess and Torney's analysis of siblings' attitudes (1965, pp. 192, 439–442). They found 13 percent of 113 intersibling correlations to be statistically significant ($p < 0.05$), while three percent of a like number of attitudes held by randomly matched pairs were significantly correlated. There is no obvious explanation for most of the significant correlations, except for the one on reactions to Kennedy's election cited earlier, or several rating the siblings' father.

Political cynicism is of particular interest because it is one of the dimensions on which children seem to show marked attitudes in grade school. Hess and Torney (1965, pp. 439–442) did not find a systematic pattern of correlations between siblings on various items measuring trust in leaders and the political system. Similarly, Jennings and Niemi (1968) found a low parent-child correlation, tau-beta = +0.12. It would seem from this that parents do not play so central a role in the development of attachment to the system as has been thought. Another possibility is that children's attitudes on such matters are not very stable, even in high school.

These data seem to contradict Hyman's conclusion that the studies he reviewed "establish very clearly a family correspondence in views that are relevant to matters of political orientation. Over a great many such correlations from the different studies, the median value approximates 0.5. The signs, almost without exception, are *never negative*" (1959, p. 72). The discrepancy between this conclusion and the findings cited above is hard to reconcile. There are several possibilities: many of the studies Hyman cited were conducted on college students and their relatively sophisticated parents; the samples tended to be small and unrepresentative; and published studies usually overemphasize positive results. The Jennings and Niemi results seem more likely to be representative of the general population than the smaller studies summarized by Hyman. The best current guess would seem to be that the level of agreement on party preference shown in Table 17, and the low correlations on political issues and group attitudes obtained by Jennings and Niemi, are representative of data that will be obtained in future large-scale studies.

Accuracy of perceived parental positions

Presumably, one upper limit on the ability of parents to determine their children's opinions is the clarity of their own expressed opinions. How accurately are parents' opinions perceived by their children?

Again, the best data come from the Survey Research Center survey in 1965 of high school seniors and their parents. These students ought to be in an optimal position to report their parents' opinions; younger children are less politically aware, and older persons often have left the parental home to set up their own household, do military service, attend college, etc. (Niemi, in press). Still, the accuracy of perception is not terribly impressive. Table 18 gives the simplest three-way breakdown of parental party preferences, and shows that 70.9 percent of the students are able to classify their parents accurately. This table (recomputed from Niemi, in press, pp. 20, 39) does not include the students (a little under 10 percent) who were unable to report the appropriate parent's party preference. Presumably, this means that at maximum less than two-thirds of American parents convey their party preferences to their children clearly enough that the child, as he leaves adolescence and enters the electorate, has a clear and accurate perception of them. The fact that *agreement* between parents and children is as high as it is at this stage (58 percent, using the same three-way breakdown of party preferences; see Table 16) testifies to the fact that other influences (for example, shared social class, ethnic group, region, place of domicile) support the parent's position more often than not. But it is a mistake to overemphasize the direct role of the family.

This, then, raises the question of how much retrospective agreement (column one of Table 17) is accounted for by biases in the respondent's recall of his parents' preference. The most obvious possibility is that the adult respondent simply projects his own preference upon his dim memory of his parents' politics. How serious a bias

TABLE 18

STUDENT'S PERCEPTION OF PARENT'S PARTY IDENTIFICATION

Parent's actual party identification	*Democrat*	*Independent*	*Republican*	*Total*
Democrat	39.9%	6.5%	3.5%	49.9%
Independent	8.4	9.7	4.6	22.7
Republican	3.1	3.1	21.3	27.4
Total	51.4%	19.2%	29.4%	100.0%

Source: Niemi, in press. Data are from independent interviews with parents and high school seniors. They exclude students unable to report on the parent's preference. $N = 1664$.

TABLE 19

STUDENT–PARENT SIMILARITY IN POLITICAL ATTRIBUTES,
CONTRASTING STUDENTS' PERCEPTIONS WITH PARENTS' OWN REPORTS

	1964 Presidential vote preference	*Party identification*	*Political interest*
Subjective agreement (as perceived by students)	+0.68	+0.58	+0.18
Objective agreement (independent interviews)	+0.59	+0.47	+0.10

Source: Niemi, 1967, p. 119. Entries are tau-beta correlations.

is this likely to be? Niemi (1967; in press) has carefully analyzed students' perceptions of parental politics from these same Survey Research Center interviews. Table 19 gives some representative data. Over a large number of such comparisons, he found that students typically overestimated the amount of agreement between their political attributes and their parents' (69 percent of the errors in vote reports favored the student's own preference; Niemi, 1967, p. 23), and the magnitude of the bias tended to inflate the tau-beta correlations by 0.05 to 0.15 most of the time (see Table 19). It may be conjectured that this inflation is at a minimum for high school seniors, as indicated above, because such perceptions are probably maximally accurate at this age. This would suggest that those parent-offspring correlations based on offspring recall, shown in Table 17, are inflated somewhat more than this. Just how serious the bias is for a representative sample of adults is not perfectly clear, but it must lower somewhat the 52 percent agreement given for the Campbell, Gurin, and Miller (1954) study in column seven of Table 17.

Determinants of continuity

Much evidence indicates that a group's influence over the opinions of its members depends in large part on three variables: (1) the extent to which the individual values or identifies with the group, (2) the clarity of the group norms as communicated to the member, and (3) the strength of position taken by the group (see pp. 337–339 above). If family influence is analyzed as a special case of group influence, political defection should occur with unclear family norms, and with clear norms only when the child does not value or identify with the family.

Clarity of parental positions. The clarity of parental positions varies widely depending to some extent on family politicization (Niemi, in press). Moreover, there is some evidence that defection is more common with unclear positions. McClosky and Dahlgren (1959, pp. 764–766) used three indices of clarity: a global measure of intrafamilial political communication, stability of parental party preference, and physical distance between the adult respondent's and his parents' place of residence. In each case, the less clear the norms, the greater the defection and the greater the instability of the respondent's final partisan preference.

Converse and Dupeux (1962) were puzzled by the finding, in comparable surveys of French and American voters, that the French showed much less tendency to identify with a party. In the United States, 75 percent expressed a party preference, while in France only 45 percent did so. The confusions of the French multiparty system seemed inadequate as an explanation, because party identification is about as common in the equally multipartied Norwegian system as in the United States (Campbell and Valen, 1961). However, only 29 percent of the French respondents could characterize their father's typical voting behavior (perhaps because many French parties are short-lived), whereas 91 percent of the Americans could. And in each country there was a strong relationship between knowing the father's party and having a personal party preference. Hence, the French father's lack of communication of political norms to his children may be partly responsible for their low level of commitment to parties.

In general, it would appear that only a few political and social attitudes are expressed in sufficiently vivid form in the average American family to be adopted by the children. Hyman (1959, pp. 70–75) and Jennings and Niemi (1968) alike indicated that parents and offspring often share party preference but agreement seems random on most other political issues. The dimension that makes the difference seems intuitively clear, but has resisted clear definition. It has been described variously as "centrality" (Converse, 1963a), "group-relatedness" (Converse, 1964), and "concreteness" (Jennings and Niemi, 1968). It would seem to be the same dimension discussed above in connection with variations in the internal consistency and stability of adult opinions.

The parent-child relationship. Do disordered family relations and hostility toward the parents in fact eventuate in political rebellion? Survey studies have not strikingly demonstrated that they do. Maccoby, Matthews, and Morton (1954) sampling young persons aged 21 to 24, and Middleton and Putney (1963a) sampling college students, found extremes of parental discipline, either too harsh or too permissive, to be slightly associated with defection. A much clearer finding, in the latter study, was that closeness to parents was clearly associated with conformity to family political norms, particularly when the parents were interested in politics. Adolescent rebellion (at least as indexed by the number of overt acts of defiance in high school) proved a poor predictor of political rebellion, even among families highly interested in politics.

The most comprehensive study, again, is the Jennings and Niemi (1968) survey of high school seniors. Their measures of the two critical variables, the quality of the parent-child relationship and the level of political interest and involvement in the home, were exceptionally thorough. However, none of their indices of these variables was strongly related to defection rates. They concluded that the quality of the parent-child relationship, as perceived by either the parent or the child, and the degree of parent and student political involvement, do not bear any simple relationship to the congruency of parent and child political opinions. Also, they did not find any evidence of the interaction of parent-child closeness and degree of family politicization suggested by the Middleton and Putney data. (In a more recent analysis of these data, though, Jennings, 1968, reports that children defect from the father to the mother when she is the closer parent and more politicized, especially when the child is a girl.) It should also be noted that parents and offspring often do not agree about the quality of their relationship: the tau-beta correlation between parents' and high school seniors' reports on student-mother closeness was +0.29; on student-father closeness, +0.28; and on how well the student gets along with his parents, +0.12 (see Niemi, 1967, p. 34).

These results are inconclusive. Lane's (1959a) analysis of depth interviews with 15 working-class men is suggestive, however. He identified four who probably had experienced "seriously damaged" relations with their fathers. However, they did not simply move to the opposite party. Rather, these men were characterized by low political information and involvement, inhibition of critical attitudes toward political leaders, pessimistic views of the future of the social order, and authoritarian orientations.

Lane's analysis of these effects is interesting. He assumed that there generally is relatively little rebellion directed against the father in America, because the society is relatively permissive and because fathers are not such domineering figures in the home. The rebellion that does occur is unlikely to take a political form because politics is of low salience to all concerned; delinquency and "dropping out" are much more relevant and effective modes of rebellion. Moreover, the adolescent boy with damaged relations with his father often expends much attention and energy on personal problems, and thus does not devote very much to an area so remote from personal preoccupations as politics. Hence, he is unlikely to develop any complicated intellectualizations explaining a rebellious partisan choice. The faulty relationship with the father presumably promotes skepticism about the trustworthiness of authority, disposing the son to political pessimism. But it also promotes fear of authority, thus inhibiting the expression of displaced aggression toward political authority. In this analysis, "adolescent rebellion" is usually apolitical. More recently, the Vietnam war, affecting many adolescents personally, seems to have politicized many rebellions.

THE LATER LIFE HISTORY OF PARTY IDENTIFICATION

There are no longitudinal data in existence that would enable one to estimate how stable, over a lifetime, is the typical individual's party preference. For example, Benjamin Bloom's (1964) estimable book on the stability of human characteristics offers virtually nothing on the stability of attitudes, and McGuire's discussion of attitude change in this *Handbook* (Chapter 21) does not consider a time span greater than a few months. Using retrospective data, however, Campbell *et al.* (1960, p. 150) found that 80 percent of the electorate claimed they had never changed party preference. Key (1961, p. 300) presented Survey Research Center data indicating that defection in party identification from parental politics does not increase with age; it is no more likely among those over 55 years of age than among those under 35. Other data to be considered here will also suggest that the party preference with which a voter enters the electorate, no matter what its source, tends to be highly stable. A variety of influences have often been assumed to operate on adults and to change their preferences substantially, but on closer examination it is not at all clear that such changes do in fact occur with any great frequency.

Aging

One common hypothesis is that people become more conservative as they age. Since there is a demonstrable and consistent relationship between age and Republicanism (see below), it has sometimes been assumed that people drift toward the Republican party as they age. Crittenden (1962), however, has followed the party preference of four-year "generations" (or "age cohorts") as they age, by using Gallup poll data on voting and party preference from 1946 through 1958. He reports that four-year "generations" (for example, those aged 21 to 24 in 1946) generally become more Republican over eight-year periods, relative to the overall trends over these elections toward more Democratic party preferences and more Republican Presidential voting.

However, the main point here is to explain the overall time trends in party preference. If one computes the changes over four-year periods (1946 to 1950, 1950 to 1954, and 1954 to 1958) for each four-year "generation" (controlling for educational level), it turns out that 30 of the changes are pro-Republican, three favor neither party, and 33 are pro-Democratic (data from Crittenden, 1962, p. 651). Hence over this 12-year span, any given "generation" remained constant, on balance, in its party preference.

This suggests that a given age group enters the electorate with a given distribution of party identifications, which remains more or less constant with age. A more detailed look at the relationship of date of birth to adult party identification also suggests this view. It reveals a curve with two obvious components: a long-term, rather slow, linear increase in the percentage of Democratic voters, and a distinct curvilinear component in which the percentage of Democratic voters reaches a peak among those born, roughly, between 1912 and 1922. This is essentially the "Depression generation," aged seven through 17 when the Depression struck, and 19 through 29 when it ended with the start of World War II. They cast their "first votes" overwhelmingly for Roosevelt in 1932 and 1936. Over 80 percent of those going to the polls for the first time in each year now recall voting for Roosevelt (Campbell *et al.*, 1960, pp. 154–155). Scoble (1963) found that defection to the Democrats among people who became liberal activists was maximal among people in their late twenties or early thirties at the outset of the Depression. These data suggest, then, that the voter's early commitment may be highly stable.

Social mobility

Vertical social mobility, whether intergenerational or within the individual's lifetime, is usually thought to have a considerable effect on partisan predispositions. The hypothesis most often cited with respect to social mobility is based on the personal difficulties caused by status change: that the upwardly mobile are even more conservative than the stable members of the class to which they move, because they overidentify with middle-class norms to achieve security and recognition, and that the downwardly mobile are more conservative than their class of destination, because they wish to retain middle-class values (Lipset and Zetterberg, 1959). An alternative hypothesis is that people retain the partisan predispositions they acquired in childhood and adolescence, unless as young people they move into environments politically discrepant with these predispositions. Then they adjust their views to a position intermediate between their childhood and adult environments. A third hypothesis is that people do not adjust their party preferences to suit changes in adult social location, but remain true to initial commitments.

The best data are from Barber's (1965) secondary analysis of 1952, 1956, and 1960 Survey Research Center surveys. With respect to party preference, the intergenerationally mobile are clearly intermediate between the classes of origin and destination. Stable professional-business respondents (or their wives) are 46 percent Democratic, while those upwardly mobile into this group are 56 percent Democratic. Those downwardly mobile to blue-collar occupations, and stable blue-collar respondents, are 60 percent and 70 percent Democratic, respectively (Barber, 1965, p. 114). Comparable data for other nations have been given by Lipset and Zetterberg (1959), Lopreato (1967), and Thompson (1967). Presidential voting follows the same pattern, though less consistently; as Barber says, "voting habits are probably retained with less tenacity than the party identification" (p. 134).

Other studies in America have yielded the same intermediate result. McClosky and Dahlgren (1959, p. 769) and Berelson, Lazarsfeld, and McPhee (1954, p. 91) indicated that mobile voters wind up, on the average, somewhere between the political preferences of the classes of origin and destination, but are somewhat less stable partisans. Maccoby, Matthews, and Morton (1954, pp. 33–36) found some indication that young people mobile in either direction hold Republican party preferences and working-class ideological positions. However, the number of cases in these three studies is insufficient to allow much confidence in more detailed statements.

The mobile groups are also intermediate on a number of class-related specific economic policy issues. On government guarantees of full employment, medicare, and the desirability of public power and housing, the blue-collar respondents are more liberal than the business-professional class, and the downwardly mobile more than the upwardly mobile, though both are intermediate between the stable respondents (Barber, 1965, pp. 175–195). On foreign policy issues (isolationism and foreign aid) the upper-status respondents are more liberal, but all differences are rather small (pp. 199–210). Race prejudice and attitudes toward civil liberties will be discussed in more detail below, but in brief, upper-status groups are more liberal, and mobile groups are, once again, intermediate.

The simplest explanation for these findings might be that the mobile respondent is socialized into class-appropriate beliefs as a youth, and then adjusts them partially but not completely when he moves into new social surroundings as an adult, to adjust to friends with new preferences, etc. However, very little such adjustment may, in fact, take place. For this process to occur, the parents would be expected to support the political norms of the class of origin, while the respondent's current friends should support the norms of his new class. But, in fact, both parents and current friends are politically intermediate between the two classes, just like the respondent. Furthermore, with age, the respondent should move closer to his new class, but no important age differences of this sort appear (Barber, 1965, pp. 135–146). This would suggest that the mobile respondents were not completely mobile after all, and that their political ideas reflect the political socialization of intermediate social origins.

Indeed, there are several suggestions in these data that the mobile are, in fact, intermediate in social location as well as in political preferences, and are actually not completely mobile. The upwardly mobile are more often Catholic, and have less income or education, than the stable business-professional respondents. Similarly, the downwardly mobile are more often Protestant, and have more income and education than stable blue-collar workers (Barber, 1965, p. 110). And both mobile groups significantly more often "misclassify" themselves subjectively than do the stable respondents (p. 162).

Other evidence indicates that the politically intermediate status of the mobile results from preselection; the most politically conservative workers tend to be upwardly mobile, and the most leftist middle-class members downwardly mobile (Thompson, 1967). Hence, adult circumstances may not be particularly important. The 1956 Survey Research Center data on mobility within the individual's lifetime also reveal no correlation with changes in party identification. The Republicans gain about equally among the upwardly and the downwardly mobile (Campbell *et al.*, 1960, p. 459), but just about in the proportion one would expect from the greater number of Democrats to begin with.

Again, conclusions must be tentative in the absence of more complete longitudinal data. But if these retrospective data may be trusted, they suggest again the continuity of partisan predispositions from preadult commitments, and rather little change resulting from adult changes in social status. It would appear that the mobile were socially and politically intermediate between the classes as children, on the average, and that they also wind up in that position as adults.

Migration

Migration by mature voters into a region with distinctive political norms ordinarily does not change their partisan identification (Converse, 1963b). This conclusion is supported by a detailed analysis in *The American Voter*. Neither migrants to the West from other Northern states, or from the South, as of the 1950's, had adapted very much to the mildly Democratic complexion of the area. The Northern emigrants continued to vote Republican and the ex-Southerners remained strongly Democratic. Similarly, upper-status whites migrating to the South and low-status white Southerners migrating to the Midwest or the Northeast remained Republican and Democratic, respectively.

The only important group of migrants that appears to have changed are Negroes moving from the South to North, who politically are much closer to Northern than Southern Negroes (Campbell *et al.*, 1960, pp. 447–453). It seems likely that their flexibility derives from weak youthful political socialization among Southern Negroes, who for many years were excluded from participation in electoral politics.

Suburbanization of previously Democratic urban residents is another such change. Greer (1961) found that suburbanized St. Louis Catholics did not differ from urban Catholics in party loyalty to the Democratic party, though they tended to defect to the Republicans in their voting more often than did urban Catholics. Defections in party preference occurred only among those groups thoroughly resocialized in other respects—third generation or more in America, highly educated, etc. Another study comparing urban and suburban residents (Greenstein and Wolfinger, 1958) had, unfortunately, too few cases to make a detailed comparison controlling for ethnic background, but did yield one crucial piece of data. Suburban Democrats associated with Republicans much more than suburban Republicans did with Democrats. This would be expected on the basis of availability alone. However, if party preference were to change, one would assume it would occur only if primary group relationships provided little or no support for the initial party commitment. Indeed, Greer suggested that persistence of Democratic party preference among suburbanized Catholics is in part contingent on differential associations which reinforce prior political habits.

If party preference is not generally altered by aging, adult social mobility, or migration, racial attitudes may be. Sheatsley (1966, p. 226) reported scores on a pro-integration scale from an NORC survey in 1963, which proved migrants to the North or South to be intermediate between lifelong residents of the two regions. However, contrary to the pattern seen above for party preference, current residence seems to have a greater effect than residence of origin. Perhaps the clarity and uniformity of regional norms are greater for the race issue than they are for party preference.

Marriage

The same may be true for marriage. The degree of reported political agreement between spouses is remarkable. McClosky and Dahlgren (1959, p. 769) reported 84 percent, and Maccoby, Matthews, and Morton (1954, p. 31) 77 percent agreement in party preference (despite the relatively short married lives of these young respondents). In Presidential voting, 90 percent agreement was reported by Campbell, Gurin, and Miller (1954, p. 201) in 1952, and even more than that in 1940 by Lazarsfeld, Berelson, and Gaudet (1948, p. 141). Among Bennington alumnae, 91 percent voted with their husbands in 1960 and 90 percent in 1964, proving that exalted levels of education are no insurance against marital concord (Newcomb *et al.,* 1967). In these cases, self-selection no doubt accounts for part of the agreement, but as for the rest of it, someone must have changed. However, no one has followed the process in detail, and all that is really known is that husbands and wives both agree, perhaps conspiratorially, that women are more likely to change. One might hypothesize that young people with conflicting party preferences adjust them when they marry, but that older people do not. There is no systematic evidence on this point, however.

In short, whereas initially adult party identification seemed to be a joint function of preadult socialization and adult social location, these data suggest that the latter is not usually so powerful a variable. Possibly most adult social locations do not present sufficiently homogeneous political climates to pressure the individual out of earlier beliefs (Key, 1961); the individual can almost always find a political ally.

GENERATIONS AND HISTORICAL CHANGE

The image of public opinion developed earlier emphasized its stability. Parents transmitted predispositions to children, and the flow of information, rather than changing opinion, tended to polarize opinion around predispositions. The finding that many adult opinions are rather volatile and unpredictable simply meant that the picture had to be enlarged to encompass a substantial component of randomness. This still leaves little provision for systematic long-term changes in public opinion on important issues—and it is clear that substantial long-term changes do take place. The race issue is a good example, particularly since individual attitudes on it tend to be relatively stable, at least over short periods of time (see pp. 332–340 above).

Liberal replies to the question, "Do you think white students and Negro students should go to the same schools or to separate schools?" increased from 30 percent in 1942 to 49 percent in 1956, and to 63 percent in 1963. An even more spectacular change has occurred subsequently among Southern whites: in 1963, 30 percent favored integrated schools, while in June 1965, 55 percent did (Sheatsley, 1966, pp. 219, 235). These changes are representative of numerous others that could be cited.

The relative imperviousness of such attitudes to changes of circumstance in adulthood suggests a more serious look at the much mistreated "generational" hypothesis. This rests on the joint operation of two essential variables, as Hyman (1959, p. 129) has suggested in his excellent presentation. The maximum susceptibility to influence should occur when the flow of incoming information is at adult levels, but before age rigidifies the individual. (As may be recalled, short-term influence is viewed by Converse, 1962, as a joint function of two very similar variables—information flow and mass of stored information from the past.) Most writers would place the outer bounds of this period as puberty and age 30.

If this hypothesis is correct with respect to party identification, evidence should exist that (1) political information begins to reach adult levels only around the age of puberty, (2) susceptibility to influence should diminish after age 30 or so, and consequently, (3) opinions adopted by the individual during this "critical period" should be unusually persistent. On the first point, the evidence is convincing but not definitive (see Greenstein, 1965a; Hess and Torney, 1967; Sigel, 1968). The other points are considered below.

Youthful receptivity

On the basis of the evidence summarized above, late adolescents and young adults would seem to enter the electorate with relatively few family-based political predispositions. At that age, the number who do not clearly share even a party preference with their parents is almost as great as the number who do, and on more esoteric matters the continuity is even slighter. This would suggest a relative openness of mind, though latent predispositions might exist which later would come to full strength. On the other hand, mere lack of parent-child continuity does not exclude the possibility of strong predispositions formed on other grounds. In this section let us consider the possibility that people acquire durable predispositions only about the time they reach voting age. This would facilitate a "generational" effect, with the current *Zeitgeist* markedly influencing young people.

Evidence was reviewed earlier on the relation between party identification and age. It clearly indicated that the proportion of party identifiers increases rather sharply around age 10, then rises slowly but consistently with age. The proportion of Independents also rises until approximately age 21, but then it diminishes steadily with age. Thus college students, in particular, are likely to be self-proclaimed Independents. Indeed, Jennings and Niemi (1968) found that 36 percent of high school seniors were Independents; Goldsen *et al.* (1960) found that 42 percent of a large sample of college students were Independents; and among adults, 29 percent of the college-educated and 17 percent of the grade-school-only respondents were found to be Independents (Campbell and Cooper, 1956, p. 49).

The lesser partisanship of young voters is also suggested by several other findings. Key (1966, p. 83) found young voters a little more likely to switch from one party to another between Presidential elections. Considering the six elections from 1940 to 1960, he found an average of 19 percent switching among those aged 21 to 39, 18 percent of those aged 40 to 59, and 14 percent of those 60 and over. These data are based on large Gallup polls and are probably quite reliable. Negative affect about a loss by one's Presidential candidate seems to increase with age, as indicated by Hess and Torney's (1965) data on schoolchildren, and Berelson, Lazarsfeld, and McPhee's (1954, p. 92) findings on disgruntled Dewey supporters in Elmira. Young voters in Elmira were also more likely to cast votes inconsistent with their attitudes on the major campaign issues (Taft-Hartley and price control) (Berelson, Lazarsfeld, and McPhee, 1954).

In these data there is some slight suggestion of a discontinuity such that aging does not increase partisanship so much after a person is in his thirties. Crittenden (1963) noted that straight-ticket voting increased among persons over 40, but the 40 to 59 and 60-plus groups were very similar. Campbell and Cooper (1956) found no age differences in defection from party identification when they split the sample at age 45. The proportion of Independents decreased most sharply from age 21 to 30, though the proportion of strong identifiers seems to increase consistently across the entire age range of voters (Campbell *et al.*, 1960, p. 162).

The authors of *The American Voter* suggested that strong party identification is a function simply of duration of identification with a party, rather than of the rigidities of advanced chronological age. Using voters' recall of past changes in party prefer- ence, they showed that younger voters are actually somewhat more strongly identified with their party than are older voters, once length of membership is controlled. Thus, older people who switch become no more partisan than younger people who stick with their initial choice (Campbell *et al.*, 1960, p. 163). The lesser partisanship among younger voters in general may be due to the relatively short history of their affiliation with a party.

Young people are also less interested and involved in political life than are their elders. The difference shows up most notably in voting rates. Over the entire age span, turnout is related to age in an inverted-U function: voting rates are quite low for those in their early twenties, but starting with the late twenties, they rise gradually to about age 60, where they drop off somewhat (Campbell *et al.*, 1960, p. 494; Milbrath, 1965, p. 134). Measures of interest, involvement, and attention to the campaign in the mass media seem to show the same pattern. They are low for people in their early twenties, but soon thereafter attain the level typical for older people (Berelson, Lazars- feld, and McPhee, 1954, pp. 25, 92; Campbell *et al.*, 1960, p. 496). Again, note here the discontinuity in the age function around age 30.

Thus, it appears that adolescents and young adults have not yet acquired the rela- tively durable partisan attachments more characteristic of mature persons, nor are they as involved in politics. This means that they are unusually susceptible to change at this age. However, rather sharp increases in partisanship and involvement seem currently to occur in the first few years after people reach voting age. It might be noted that these conclusions are reached on the basis of naturalistic observations, and with the voting age set typically at 21. It is surprising to note that there has been very little systematic experimental work attempting to determine the relationship between chronological age and receptivity to information—for example, on persuasibility, suggestibility, or influenceability in general (see Chapter 21).

Climate of opinion

For systematic political change to occur, receptivity presumably is not enough; there must also be a systematically biased informational environment. Any political environ- ment in which opinion is preponderantly on one side may be described as a distinctive "climate of opinion," or, more grandiosely, as a *Zeitgeist*. The distinctive political tra- ditions of different regions or geographical localities have been especially prominent in this connection. Key, in his classic *Southern Politics in State and Nation* (1949), demon- strated remarkable continuity over many years in partisan divisions within geograph- ical units, for example, within counties or large areas of Southern states. Later, he demonstrated impressive continuities in the relative partisan divisions of Indiana counties, going back as far as the Civil War. This is described as "a standing decision by the community" (Key and Munger, 1959, p. 286). Wolfinger and Greenstein (1969) have made a similar analysis of political differences between Northern and Southern California.

Climates of opinion seem to operate by attenuating parental influence for whichever political group is locally deviant or in the minority (Hyman, 1959, p. 113). This is accomplished, presumably, by biasing the individual's political environment at the primary group level. Hyman cited the contrast between predominantly Republican Elmira and predominantly Democratic Cambridge. In each case, members of the majority party were considerably more likely than members of the minority to have friends and coworkers who shared their party preferences. And indeed, Elmira Democrats with politically homogeneous friends defected no more than did Republicans. But among those with politically mixed friends, Republicans were more faithful to their party. This advantage to the majority is termed the "breakage effect" by Berelson, Lazarsfeld, and McPhee (1954, p. 89). Presumably, it operates at maximum efficiency on young voters, though the data on this point are scant.

Distinctive climates of opinion within high schools or colleges ought to be particularly influential, since they would meet both informational and open-mindedness criteria. Unfortunately, the data here are not at all clear. One example, though, is evidence presented by Langton (1967) of "resocialization" of working-class high school students to middle-class political norms by their middle-class peers. The optimal conditions for "resocialization" were social class heterogeneity both of friendship groups and of the school as a whole. This occurred with both Jamaican students' attitudes toward support of the political system and Detroit students' attitudes toward the Presidency and toward Lee Harvey Oswald. Langton suggested that peer resocialization may be especially significant as the child grows older, with lower-status children, and on beliefs that are not firmly anchored at home (that is, probably less on party identification and race, for example, than on other attitudes).

However, it should be emphasized that the effects of climates of opinion in this period of life are very poorly understood at present. The results often seem confused and contradictory (Hyman, 1959; Jacob, 1957). In particular, research in this area has been unable to define the effective political environment; for example, different college majors are often compared, but rarely different college peer groups. A promising area of future work would treat the interactions of curricular, structural, and peer influences.

Party realignment

Earlier the view (held by Campbell *et al.*, 1960) was expressed that party realignments occur particularly when the initial loyalties of voters entering the electorate are affected. New voters and old voters alike swung to Roosevelt in 1932 and 1936, but only the new voters (even those who were not young in age) stayed on as Democratic party identifiers. Wolfinger (1965) has suggested that the same process accounts for enduring ethnic ties to one party or the other. In a "critical election" the voters are polarized along ethnic lines, and if this polarization persists over a few years (Campbell, 1966c, speaks of a "critical era" rather than a "critical election"), it may affect permanent party loyalties as well as more transitory candidate preferences.

Wolfinger cited the New Haven case of Italian-American defection to the Republican party because of an Italian mayoralty candidacy on the Republican ticket in several elections in the 1940's and 1950's. Initially, the Italian Republican vote depended on this candidate's presence on the ticket, but ultimately it became autonomous. Today "most Italians not only vote for Republican candidates but consider themselves Republicans. Their party identification was changed and fixed by Celantano's several campaigns" (p. 903). Since the analysis is based largely on aggregate data, there is no way to check on the interpretation that would be consistent with our more general argument: that older Italians voted for Celantano while maintaining Democratic party allegiance, while younger ones entered the electorate as Republicans. These latter commitments would be "functionally autonomous" of the original reason for the ethnic party tie, and would normally tend to be highly persistent. Indeed, Wolfinger argued that ethnic voting differences are *not* rapidly disappearing, particularly in the ethnically homogeneous neighborhoods, where they receive primary group support.

As indicated earlier, "first votes" do not seem to divide disproportionately in normal times. The important question for realignment, then, is what causes disproportionate divisions—such as those in the 1930's, and that of Negroes in 1964 —and what promotes the persistence of these deviations. It may be, though, that every national election creates some bias in later "first votes." Levin (1961), in a 1957 survey of high school students, found that defections from parental attitudes were (1) generally toward the position dominant in the high school and (2) predominantly pro-Republican. He suggested that the incumbent national administration sets a "national climate of opinion," which in this case worked to the advantage of the Republicans. This might also explain the disproportionately pro-Democratic defections reported from the 1965 Jennings and Niemi (1968) survey. Also, inaccuracies in the students' perceptions of the parents' beliefs favored the victorious Democrats (Niemi, in press).

Persistence and regression of youthful changes

Assuming that something does "resocialize" the individual during adolescence or early adulthood, what determines whether the changes will persist or whether the individual will revert to his previous way of thinking?

Perhaps the prototype of a generational effect in political socialization is Newcomb's account of students attending Bennington College during the 1930's. As freshmen, Bennington girls were as conservative as those at comparable colleges, but during college they became markedly less conservative than students at other colleges. Liberalism was associated with being respected by other students, involvement in the college, and duration of attendance; thus, it appeared that the college had somehow been responsible for the change (Newcomb, 1943). Newcomb's hypothesis was that the persistence of change would depend on the political complexion of the adult environment. Therefore, he collected longitudinal data by reinterviewing in 1960 a sample of Bennington graduates of 1938, 1939, and 1940 (Newcomb, 1963; Newcomb *et al.*, 1967).

The overall liberalism of the group did remain about constant over the 20-year period. In 1940, 51 percent had supported Roosevelt, and in 1960, 60 percent supported Kennedy. A majority indicated they had supported a Republican in *at most* one Presidential election since leaving college, and only 27 percent said that they had supported Republicans in at least five. Also, 77 percent considered themselves "liberal" or "somewhat liberal," and only 17 percent "conservative" or "somewhat conservative" (Newcomb *et al.*, 1967, pp. 25–26).

The stability of individual attitudes is also impressive. Their collegiate conservatism, as measured in their senior year, correlated +0.47 with their conservatism over 20 years later in 1960, and +0.48 with the number of Republican candidates supported in the interim. Newcomb is clearly justified in saying that over a span of more than 20 years this "degree of individual stability is startling" (1963, p. 7).

Change might have been especially common among those who had become liberals during college, as a form of regression to earlier attitudes. However, those who changed away from conservatism in college were later about as pro-Democratic as those who entered and left college as liberals, supporting Kennedy at rates of 81 percent and 86 percent, respectively. In fact, senior-year conservatism predicts adult attitudes better than do freshman-year attitudes. Thus, the impact of college was critical for the final, relatively stable level achieved by adult attitudes.

Why had these attitudes persisted? One possibility might be that, in general, the voters' demographic characteristics guaranteed their being in a politically supportive environment. However, by this criterion, the Bennington alumnae should have lived in highly conservative circumstances. Socioeconomically, they were in the top one percent of the American population, nearly all from Protestant backgrounds, and aged 40 to 45, typically. On the basis of national Survey Research Center data, less than 30 percent of "women like our Bennington graduates of 1938, 1939, and 1940" voted for Kennedy in 1960. In 1964, 53 percent of the college-educated, nationally, voted for Johnson, while 89 percent of these Bennington graduates did (Newcomb *et al.*, 1967, pp. 45–50).

But their immediate social environments were themselves a little deviant, and thus politically supportive. Both husbands and friends were unusually liberal for their social circumstances, though somewhat more conservative than the Bennington alumnae. And the alumnae opinions were closely associated in 1960 with husbands' and friends' opinions. Over 90 percent of the husbands and wives voted the same way in 1960 and 1964, and there was even a correlation of +0.32 between the wives' senior-year conservatism and the husbands' 1960 conservatism (Newcomb, 1963).

The key to the puzzle is that the husbands were comparable to their wives in demographic terms, but atypical of that stratum. Fifty percent had attended Ivy League colleges, but only 33 percent were in the strongholds of conservatism: management or business positions. Unusual numbers were in the professions, communications, entertainment, and the arts (Newcomb *et al.*, 1967, p. 19). Those in such "atypical" occupations were considerably more liberal than those in business. Hence, Newcomb (1963) concluded that the persistence of youthful change depended on selection of a social environment that would be politically supportive. Presumably, husbands and friends are selected for some other reasons as well, but this dimension is crucial politically.

Newcomb (1963) invoked the notion of "autistic hostility" to explain why newly liberalized Bennington alumnae were no longer influenced by their conservative parents' views. He assumed that parents and offspring simply stopped talking about such divisive matters as political and social issues. Niemi's (in press) data suggest that the same thing may happen between husbands and wives. High school students have quite imprecise ideas of their parents' party identifications when the parents themselves disagree completely. Perhaps the parents themselves do not discuss politics very much. Such offspring would, of course, be good candidates for later re-socialization.

One other example of the persistence of such radical change, closer to home, might be of interest. Social scientists do not generally come from economically or ethnically disadvantaged backgrounds, yet they too turn out to be highly liberal. The majority of academic psychologists, political scientists, and sociologists had fathers who were Republicans, in the highest status occupations, and themselves came from "native," Anglo-Saxon stock. As adults, the social scientists are well-off by the standards of the average American. Yet they are strongly Democratic: only 10 percent of the academic sociologists, 16 percent of the political scientists, and 21 percent of the psychologists claimed Republican identification, though nationally around 35 percent of those with any college education at all are Republican (Campbell and Cooper, 1956, p. 4; McClintock, Spaulding, and Turner, 1965; Turner, McClintock, and Spaulding, 1963; Turner, Spaulding, and McClintock, 1963). Thus, American social scientists, too, constitute a paradox in terms of conventional formulas for political socialization. Their background is conservative, but their adult politics liberal. There are perhaps historical reasons for this (see Lipset, 1960, pp. 310–343, for an interesting speculative account), but the mechanisms by which this continues to be implemented in successive generations of social scientists are unknown. Self-selection is a good possibility, but then, so too is resocialization during the college, graduate school, and young-academic years.

The "generation gap" today

This notion of generational effects has been subjected to an unfortunate amount of abuse as a result of its undisciplined and exaggerated use in recent years. However, it is useful to inquire just how much variance is being contributed to contemporary public opinion by generational differences. The "generation gap" is supposed to occur along a dimension that is vaguely left to right, with the libertarian and egalitarian positions supposedly upheld more by youth. A first question, then, is whether or not substantial age differences of this kind really exist.

Youthful liberalism. There is indeed considerable evidence that young people are more liberal, tolerant, and favorable to change than are older people. A few examples will illustrate. Republican voting, one possible (if dubious) index of conservatism, does increase with age, though not always very dramatically (Campbell and Cooper, 1956, p. 22; Campbell, Gurin, and Miller, 1954, p. 70; Crittenden, 1962, p. 65). Republican party identification increases substantially with age relative to the proportion of people selecting a Democratic preference (Campbell *et al.*, 1960, p. 162; Crittenden, 1962, p. 650). For example, in Survey Research Center surveys over a period of years, the Democrats had an advantage of 48 to 21 percent among those aged 21 to 24, but only 46 to 31 percent among those aged 45 to 49, and both parties drew 42 percent of those 75 years and over (Campbell *et al.*, 1960, p. 162).

Substantial age differences are especially prominent in issues of civil liberties. Stouffer (1955, pp. 89–93) found spectacularly greater willingness among young people to tolerate nonconformists. For example, of those aged 21 to 29, 47 percent were classified as "more tolerant," while only 18 percent of those aged 60 and over were; and 10 percent of the younger group were "less tolerant," while 21 percent of the older group were. Most significant, substantial age differences remain even with education controlled (young people have, on the average, considerably more schooling than their elders). In 1965, high school seniors were considerably more liberal than their parents on three civil liberties issues: allowing legally elected Communists to take office, banning prayers from public schools, and allowing atheists to speak (Jennings and Niemi, 1968). Other data (Jennings, 1966) indicate that these parents were liberal relative to the electorate as a whole, underscoring the liberalism of their children. Jennings and Niemi (1968) found less political cynicism among high school students than among their parents. Also, Dennis (1966) found support for the party system greater among young people, again suggesting greater tolerance for conflict.

Racial prejudice is substantially lower among the young. Sheatsley (1966, p. 226) found large age differences in both the North and the South (though without education controls). In the North, youth was considerably more prointegrationist. In the South, the same held, except for those under 25, who were more segregationist than those aged 25 to 44. Sheatsley suggested that this derived from the younger Southerners' being members of a generation that was exposed to the stormy post-1954 years of "massive resistance" to racial change in the South, during the sensitive period of their own lives. Other data, though, suggest less prejudice among the young (Erskine, 1962; Jennings and Niemi, 1968; Morris and Jeffries, 1967; see also the dissent by Noel and Pinkney, 1964).

Finally, reliable age differences seem also to appear in recommended child-rearing practices; older people favor discipline-oriented practices more than younger people do (Gergen and Back, 1965; Stouffer, 1955, p. 97). Thus, on party preference, civil liberties, and racial questions, younger people seem considerably more liberal than their elders, though on other matters the pattern is more mixed (Hyman, 1959).

Perception of rebellion to the left. In reality, only about seven percent at age 18 seem to have selected the party opposite to their parents. Adult respondents perceive only slightly more rebellion; about 11 percent feel they have selected a party opposite to that shared by their parents, as shown in Table 16. One might then assume that most people would perceive themselves as essentially agreeing with their parents. And one would not expect offspring to see themselves as systematically shifting to the left or the right, at least not very much.

Yet the results of a major survey in 1961 reveal that a very large proportion of American college students see themselves as to the left of their parents. Middleton and Putney (1963a, 1963b, 1964) gave anonymous questionnaires to 1440 students in a cross-sectional sample of American colleges and universities. Each student classified himself and his parents as socialists, highly liberal, moderately liberal, moderately conservative, highly conservative, or having no political views. Many more students classified themselves as socialist or liberal (60 percent) than classified their parents that way (30 percent), and the students were more inclined to describe their parents (49 percent) than themselves (32 percent) as conservatives.

But the most interesting finding is that 33 percent of the students saw themselves as to the left of their parents, and only eight percent to the right. A later survey of 316 Negro students at Howard University revealed a similar pattern: 23 percent to

TABLE 20

STUDENTS' PERCEPTIONS OF THEIR POSITIONS
RELATIVE TO THEIR PARENTS' POSITIONS

Students' position	*Relative to parents they are:*				
	Rebelling to left	Rebelling to right	Conforming	Other	Total
Socialist, highly liberal, liberal (N = 869)	50%	4%	36%	11%	101%
Moderately conservative, highly conservative (N = 468)	9	17	64	10	100

Source: Middleton and Putney, 1963b, p. 382. The "Other" category includes all respondents without political views and those who could not report their parents' views.

the left, and seven percent to the right, of their parents (Levitt, 1967). The asymmetry of this intergenerational change is indicated by the fact that the conservative students were predominantly conforming to conservative parents, whereas liberal students either conformed to liberal parents or were rebelling against conservative parents. This is shown in Table 20. What this means, essentially, is that most liberal parents keep their offspring on the left, while children of conservative parents divide between the left and the right.

It also means that students who remain conservative are primarily in agreement with their families, whereas many liberal students must disagree with their families. Members of rightist student political organizations also describe their relationships with their parents as being closer and more open than do members of leftist organizations. Also, more rightist students describe their parents as supporting and approving their political activity, while the leftists report parental opposition more often (Braungart, 1966). The evidence on objective liberalization relative to parents is much harder to come by. However, Jennings and Niemi (1968) did find modest marginal differences between parents and children on civil liberties and racial issues.

The incumbent administration, as indicated before, might be one of the more visible embodiments of the political *Zeitgeist*. However, some other data from the Middleton and Putney survey of college students suggest that their rebellion, at least, is not simply a movement toward what they see as the current national consensus. Among those who defected from their parents, 50 percent saw themselves as moving *away* from what they perceived as the "conventional political views in the United States," and 35 percent felt they were moving toward them (1963b, p. 383). Thus, the national consensus, at least in the sense of a statistical average of the electorate's views, is not necessarily an attractive nonfamilial source of influence for young people. This might seem to be an unnecessarily ponderous way of dealing with what must seem to be some fairly obvious effects: namely, the love affair between young Americans and John F. Kennedy, or disputes over draft laws and the legitimacy of the war in Vietnam, or apparent widespread use of hallucinogenic drugs, etc. However, available data do not reveal how widespread these feelings are, nor how radical a departure they represent from the previous generation, at least not beyond the cock-tail-party-anecdote level of data presentation. These are interesting questions to research, even if they often seem discredited by wild claims.

If, however, one does accept the notion that young people are generally (or at least currently) to the left of their elders, then one must ask how this comes about. It seems extremely unlikely that secondary schools are responsible for very much of it, and the effects of college education on values or political and social attitudes are at present very poorly understood (Jacob, 1957). College students do attribute consid-erable influence to traditional sources. Middleton and Putney (1964) reported that college students often cite their parents (42 percent) and friends (19 percent) as sources of their political views. But the other most frequently cited sources could be expected to reflect somewhat more up-to-date or unconventional thinking: pro-fessors (30 percent) and mass media and books (21 percent).

One would expect exposure to parents to reinforce traditionalism, if anything, relative to exposure to nonfamilial sources. Indeed, liberal students cite college professors, mass media, and books more often (57 percent) than do conservative students (40 percent), while conservative students are more likely to cite their parents (51 percent) than are liberal students (38 percent). Other data also suggest that the liberal bias of the current *Zeitgeist* may be just an accident of history. Students who cite books or mass media are likely to be more extreme at either end of the political continuum than are students who cite their parents as prime sources of political influence (Middleton and Putney, 1964).

These data suggest that *discontinuities* in the political experience of young people are of critical importance in modernizing public opinion. Marc Bloch's explanation for the traditionalism of French peasant villages focuses on the fact that grand-parents do most of the caretaking, while parents work. Children then reflect the traditional ideas of the grandparents, while the parents are the "sponsors of change" (Hyman, 1959). Rettig (1966) has found some evidence that moral attitudes in the *kibbutz* in Israel change more, from generation to generation, than they do in the *moshava*, because in the latter children have more contact with their parents. And Dawson (1966) cites the conflicts of young Africans, torn between the traditional ideas of their villages and the modern, urbanized ways of the large cities.

In theory, the American college education should fulfill the requirements for severing some of the ties between the young adult and traditional ideas. In some data, the amount of defection from parental party is related simply to the amount of edu-cation, but it is not clear that this is a universal finding.

Personalizing and female traditionalism

Women are less inclined than men to rebel. Even as young girls, they are more con-cerned with "keeping things as good as they are" (Hess and Torney, 1967, p. 189), a difference that increases with age, and hence, may be a part of the developing sex role. Middleton and Putney (1963b, p. 381) found 37 percent of their male college students ($N = 824$) rebelling to the left of their parents, and 27 percent of their females ($N = 616$) did so.

Women appear to be much more influenced by those in their immediate social environment, especially in the family. For one thing, women more freely express the desire for such discussions. Greenstein (1965a, p. 199) found young girls more likely than boys to say they would seek the voting advice of a parent. Lambert and Klineberg (1967, p. 154) found girls got more information about foreign peoples from parents, and that boys got more information from television and movies. Among married adults who said they were willing to discuss the campaign with someone else, Berelson, Lazarsfeld, and McPhee (1954, p. 103) found that 53 percent of the women named a family member, while only five percent of the men did. Also, women (69 percent) more readily admit having discussed politics with a family member than do men (41 percent), and having been influenced by their spouse (27 percent of the women, six percent of the men), according to Campbell, Gurin, and Miller (1954, p. 205).

This greater receptivity to familial influence may explain the sex difference in perceived political rebellion. College girls were much more likely than boys to report that their own political views were influenced by specific persons, especially parents (Middleton and Putney, 1964). Fifty-three percent of the coeds, and only 34 percent of the males, reported being influenced by parents. Boys were slightly more likely to cite professors, mass media, or books, presumably the carriers of the *Zeitgeist*; and they were much more likely to "claim independent evolution of views" (22 percent to nine percent), which probably means that they were basing their opinions on something nonfamilial and likely not very traditional. Indeed, this response was given most by the students on the left: twice as often by socialist as by conservative students, and almost as frequently by those self-classified as "highly liberal" (Middleton and Putney, 1964, pp. 488–491).

This may be part of a general tendency for women to personalize politics more than men. They were more candidate-oriented and less issue-oriented in 1952 (Campbell, Gurin, and Miller, 1954, p. 155); they think of government more in personal terms as children (Hess and Torney, 1967); and they tended more to attribute personal rather than political motives to Lee Harvey Oswald (Feshbach and Feshbach, 1965, p. 296).

Finally, there is some evidence that women are less tolerant of conflict and deviation than are men. Perhaps they are more traditionally oriented and do not understand why everyone should not agree with them. Dennis (1966, p. 610), for example, found that men and women support the party system in the abstract to about the same degree, but women are considerably more antagonistic to the idea that partisan conflict is a good and healthy standard diet. Stouffer (1955, pp. 131–155) found that women are considerably less tolerant on civil liberties questions, regardless of whether age, occupation, education, or church attendance is controlled.

Men simply seem to like politics and conflict more. They are more militant on foreign policy questions (Hero, 1966, p. 463; Rosenberg, 1965, pp. 305–307; Verba *et al.,* 1967). Men are more active than women (Campbell *et al.,* 1960; Lane, 1959b; Milbrath, 1965). Even in childhood, boys adopt political attitudes, interests, and activities earlier and more intensely than girls. And they are more likely to select a figure from public life as an exemplar (Greenstein, 1965a, p. 117; Hess and Torney, 1965). Children in father-dominated families have more interest in and information about politics, earlier political opinions, and are more likely to discuss politics (Hess and Torney, 1967, p. 101).

Thus, women tend to be oriented toward persons they know, particularly in the family, and less interested in more impersonal stimuli such as mass media or books.

Their orientation toward the family prevents them from being fully exposed to the *Zeitgeist,* and they seem to reject innovation, deviation, and conflict.

CONCLUSIONS

These data suggest some general hypotheses about distinctive stages in the political life cycle.

Childhood and adolescence

Relatively early in life, the child adopts a party preference. Currently, there is no reason to think that this early adoption of a party preference lends it any special strength. It seems more likely that, at this age, partisan preferences are rather unthinking and not very intense. Their apparent stability (though some data on the point would be helpful) may result primarily from ecological accident, or "de facto selective exposure" (Sears and Freedman, 1967), rather than from constant exposure to parental politics. The child's faint partisanship is rarely challenged, because politics is not discussed very much, and because he tends to be surrounded by people of his own social location and political preference.

Throughout the period of childhood and adolescence, his preference is correlated with his parents' preferences, but there is a surprising amount of disagreement with them (42 percent at age 17 or 18, according to Jennings and Niemi). Apparently, the child is often unaware of the disagreements, and it is not clear what he makes of them when he is aware of them. In any case, the disagreements tend to be moderate rather than extreme; only in very rare instances are parents and offspring at the opposite ends of the continuum. Agreement is so slight on many other political issues that the parents' contribution truly seems minimal.

If party preference in this period is not very intense and is potentially unstable, disagreements with parents should not really be classified as meaningful "rebellions." By this argument, then, the early adoption of party preference in this country has little long-term significance, since it remains pallid and potentially volatile through adolescence. However, the need for additional direct data on this point cannot be overemphasized.

Early adulthood

The individual, then, normally reaches late adolescence or early adulthood without strong party commitments. Much depends on the exact nature of his informational environment during this crucial period. This tends to minimize change, since his social environment normally resembles his parents' rather closely. For example, Goldberg (1966) composed an index of political predisposition based on social characteristics, much like the old IPP of Lazarsfeld, Berelson, and Gaudet (1948) but broader and more up-to-date. On this index, the political implications of adult respondents' social characteristics correlated extremely strongly with their fathers' ($r = +0.81$) in the 1956 national Survey Research Center survey. This would suggest that considerable intergenerational political continuity is guaranteed by shared social locations alone. Probably the direct role of parents in promoting this continuity has been exaggerated. It seems likely to derive more commonly from the acquisition of a mild preadult predisposition, reinforced later on by a supportive adult environment.

Still, the opportunities for discontinuities to occur are manifold in this stage of life. More esoteric and varied educational experiences, departure from the family home as residence, marriage, entry into an occupation, and possibly vertical social mobility upward or downward, offer the potential for exposure to a much wider set of ideas. In most cases, though, this potential is not realized.

However, two conditions seem particularly likely to produce discontinuities: (1) a climate of opinion in which childhood ideas are in a distinct minority (the condition of the conservative Bennington freshman, or the political liberal joining a police force); and (2) a charismatic Presidential candidacy or some other "critical election." Neither of these has been adequately explored, but both seem likely to have lasting effects, especially if reinforced later by supportive peer groups. Everything else being equal, any such influences are likely to have a more marked and lasting effect, the earlier they occur. Perhaps for most relatively simple affective dispositions (for example, party, race, and most other group-related attitudes), the "critical period," if there is one, comes during late adolescence. For more esoteric matters (for example, whether one owes one's loyalty to cognitive or S-R psychology), the critical point may not come until a little later. In either case, though, influence is much more likely to be successful at this stage than later on (especially after age 30).

On other political issues, however, the young adult does not usually have even a mild family-based predisposition. This means he should be unusually receptive to new information at this age, though not too interested in political issues. Often this will lead him to the position appropriate for his parents, since their social environments tend to be similar. But his receptivity to information means that he is more influenced by the *Zeitgeist* than are his more hardened parents. Thus, each generation as a whole is influenced to some degree by current thinking at an age when the parents' potential for influence has suddenly dropped, and usually before strong partisan predispositions have developed.

Beginning at this age also, offspring interpret the discrepancy between their positions and their parents' in a more meaningful way. Thus, one finds differences in the defection rates resulting from variables that should theoretically produce them, such as closeness of the parent-offspring relationship, or sex roles. But the magnitude of defection is not very great. Very rarely do extremist ideologues come from families at the other end of the continuum, as will be seen in the next section. It is equally a mistake to overestimate the magnitude of each generation's movement away from traditional ideas to more current ones. The "generation gap" on political matters is usually not very great in absolute terms.

Maturity

As the individual ages, his partisan dispositions become less vulnerable. He typically settles into an environment in which marriage, job, residence, friends, and social status all tend to become increasingly stable and politically homogeneous. To some degree, perhaps, he has selected a comfortable adult political environment, and to some degree he has simply adjusted to it. With the passage of time, partisan dispositions become increasingly strong. The general principle may be that resistance to change of a given set of partisan beliefs depends on their having been maintained for a certain length of time. But in fact, most people adopt fairly firm beliefs during their twenties, and they do not change much after their early thirties (Converse, 1966a, puts the point of reaching stability at age 30 or 35). New information has little impact, minority political status does not produce defection in basic loyalties (Miller, 1956), and radical changes in the political complexion of the environment tend not to affect partisan predispositions.

Therefore, a plausible though unverified hypothesis is that each generation marches through life with a more or less constant set of beliefs. New events, persons, and issues are interpreted with a set of predispositions acquired in adolescence and early adulthood. Basic historical changes thus depend on affecting the political stimulation and political environments of young people. Presumably, this is why radical attempts to alter societies have focused especially on the youth, as in the cases of the Hitler Youth and the Soviet boarding schools (*cf.* Bronfenbrenner, 1962).

SOCIAL ORIGINS OF UNDEMOCRATIC BELIEFS AND THE RADICAL RIGHT

One of the main concerns of this chapter is the socialization of democratic, tolerant beliefs. As will be seen, the level of public tolerance is not overwhelmingly high regarding specific cases, though in the abstract everyone seems to agree that tolerance is the proper attitude. There is some suggestion that society currently socializes young people so as to give them slightly more liberal beliefs than their predecessors had. But where do the most markedly *illiberal* people come from? What was their socialization experience and what aspects of American society are responsible for their beliefs? An inquiry of this sort will not only aid in understanding current antidemocratic opinion, but also perhaps will aid in estimating how broad the potential support for such leadership is.

A number of areas of illiberalism have been studied. The research to be reviewed here focuses on four areas: (1) *support for right-wing movements*—the followers of Father Coughlin (Lipset, 1963a), the John Birch Society (Grupp, 1966; Lipset, 1963a), the followers of Senator Joseph McCarthy (Campbell and Cooper, 1956; Lipset, 1963a; Polsby, 1963; Trow, 1958), voters for California's Proposition 24 in 1962, an anti-Communist measure (Ferguson and Hoffmann, 1964), the Christian Anti-Communism Crusade (Koeppen, 1967; Wolfinger *et al.*, 1964), the followers of Senator Barry Goldwater (Benham, 1965; Converse, Clausen, and Miller, 1965; Crespi, 1965; Wolfinger and Greenstein, 1969), and members of the Young Americans for Freedom (Braungart, 1966; Westby and Braungart, 1966); (2) *racial antagonisms*, as displayed by voters for Proposition 14 in California, a 1964 referendum measure designed to overthrow fair housing legislation (Wolfinger and Greenstein, 1968), and by voters for Governor George Wallace (Rogin, 1966), and racial prejudice (Barber, 1965; Bettelheim and Janowitz, 1964; Hodge and Treiman, 1966; Stember, 1961; Treiman, 1966); (3) *anti-democratic attitudes* in general (Barber, 1965; Kelly and Chamblis, 1966; Lipset, 1960; Lipsitz, 1965; Rush, 1967; Stouffer, 1955; Selvin and Hagstrom, 1960); and (4) the use of "*status politics*" ideas to explain Abolitionists (Donald, 1956), early twentieth-century Progressives (Hofstadter, 1955; Mowry, 1963), the effects of social mobility on class attitudes (Wilensky and Edwards, 1959), and voting (Johnson, 1962, 1964, 1966; Lenski, 1954, 1967; Lipset and Zetterberg, 1959; Lopreato, 1967; Thompson, 1967).

The emphasis in this section will be on a review of existing data rather than on the many interesting theoretical speculations that have appeared in the literature.

These, unfortunately, have often proved difficult to test, or unfounded when tested adequately (see Koeppen, 1967; Polsby, 1963; Wolfinger *et al.*, 1964). No particular effort is made initially to distinguish between the various versions of illiberal opinions; these distinctions emerge as the differences in origin become clear. As Lenski (1963), Lipset (1960), and others have noted, they are by no means all manifestations of the same thing.

It should be noted that there is a large literature on the characteristics of political activists and of political elites quite independent of their ideological predilections. This literature also considers the question of who votes at all and who does not. This material has been reviewed in several excellent summaries elsewhere (Lane, 1959b; Lipset, 1960; Lipset *et al.*, 1954; Matthews, 1954; Milbrath, 1965). Because these summaries are so thorough, this literature is not covered in this chapter, though generally it is classified as of the same genre as the material dealt with here. A second relevant area which is largely ignored below considers personality dispositions as productive of illiberal ideas. The reason for omission here is an absence of reliable data (see Greenstein, 1967, for a recent discussion of this area of research).

Status and education

One hypothesis, expounded in most detail by Lipset (1960), is that illiberal opinions are most prevalent among lower-status and poorly educated persons. Lipset presented suggestive evidence on a wide variety of noneconomic issues, such as support of one-party systems, nationalism, anti-Semitism, opposition to free speech, and religious fundamentalism. (Of course, status is generally *negatively* related to liberalism on economic issues, but they fall outside the purview of this section.) In a statistically more explicit description of this pattern of opinions, Axelrod (1967) found a moderately coherent "populism" by doing a cluster analysis on Survey Research Center policy items. Axelrod's results closely resemble the pattern found by Lipset, finding liberalism on economic issues but not on noneconomic issues. The "populist" favors medicare, job opportunity, and federal aid to education, but opposes taxes, civil liberties, and an internationalist foreign policy. These positions cluster most among nonvoters (who tend to be of low status) and least among college graduates.

Lipset's explanation is that low-status, poorly educated people have unsophisticated political and social perspectives, and that they are unusually hostile. Lack of sophistication comes primarily from lack of exposure to a diversity of ideas, people, or other stimuli. Low educational levels, little reading, relatively isolated occupations and lives, and little participation in voluntary organizations all mean that the low-status person is exposed to a narrow set of views, primarily reinforcing his own. Lack of sophistication is manifested in a view of politics that is oversimplified and based on short time perspectives, thus rendering incomprehensible the rather complicated rationales normally given by liberals for tolerance or gradualist political strategies. There is scant empirical evidence bearing directly on this interpretation, though Back and Gergen (1963b, pp. 440–442) found several indices of time perspective correlated with education and occupational status and Schuman and Harding (1963) found "sympathetic identification with the underdog" to be related to education. In addition, lack of education and low income both decrease "emotional sensitivity" and "psychological responsiveness to the environment" (Bradburn and Caplovitz, 1965).

TABLE 21

PARTY IDENTIFICATION AND VOTE INTENTION ON PROPOSITION
14 WITH EDUCATION CONTROLLED: WHITE GENTILES ONLY

| | Percent intending to vote "no" | |
Educational level	Republicans	Democrats
More than 2 years of college	33%	64%
1 to 2 years of college	27	32
High school graduates	8	30
Less than high school	10	29

Source: Wolfinger and Greenstein, 1968, p. 760. "Don't know" responses excluded from the bases. A "no" vote would support fair housing legislation. Data are from the statewide California poll.

The hostility presumably derives both from authoritarian child-rearing practices (though perhaps indifference is also a factor, as suggested by Bronfenbrenner, 1962) and from economic insecurity. Both income and education do relate positively to expressions of feelings of happiness (Bradburn and Caplovitz, 1965, p. 23).

The proposition that status is positively associated with noneconomic liberalism is persuasively supported by available evidence. By any of the normal indicators of status (income, occupation, or education), anti-Negro racial prejudice is substantially greater in the working class than in the middle class (Bettelheim and Janowitz, 1964; Hodge and Treiman, 1966; Sheatsley, 1966; Treiman, 1966; Wolfinger and Greenstein, 1968). See Table 21 for an example. Lower-class children are more hostile toward foreign peoples, according to one study (Lambert and Klineberg, 1967, p. 156).

Support for civil liberties is vastly greater at upper status levels than at lower levels (Dynes, 1967; Key, 1961; Prothro and Grigg, 1960). For example, in a large nationwide sample, 66 percent of the college graduates were scaled as "more tolerant," and only 16 percent of those who never went past grade school were so scaled (Stouffer, 1955, p. 90). Kelly and Chamblis (1966), in a Seattle survey, found socioeconomic status positively related to attitudes on civil liberties, civil rights, and internationalism. After John Kennedy's assassination, more lower-status people favored capital punishment for Jack Ruby, and they preferred more repressive postassassination actions (Lipsitz and Colfax, 1965, p. 373). Even children showed this pattern; working-class Detroit children were more likely to be "glad" that Ruby killed Oswald, and to want to see Kennedy's murderer "shot or beat up" (Langton, 1967, p. 758). In a survey in Manhattan, respondents of higher socioeconomic status were found to be more tolerant of behavioral deviance (that is, psychological disorder) as indexed by social-distance items (Dohrenwend and Chin-Song, 1967). Kohn (1963) also reported middle-class parents to be less concerned with conformity and the display of "respectable" behavior (though greater restrictiveness may not always have marked working-class parents; see Bronfenbrenner, 1965).

Most, but not all, of the evidence on ultraconservative beliefs follows the same pattern. Low-status persons were much more favorable to Father Coughlin and to

TABLE 22

SUPPORT FOR JOSEPH McCARTHY BY EDUCATION AND PARTY PREFERENCE

| | *Party identification* | | |
Education	Democrat	Independent	Republican
Graduate school	− 59%	− 44%	− 28%
College	− 44	− 24	− 19
Vocational	− 41	− 20	− 19
High school	− 27	− 8	− 5
Grammar school	− 18	− 8	+ 6

Source: Lipset, 1963b, p. 331. Entries are percentage differences between approval and disapproval of McCarthy. For example, among Democrats with graduate school education, 8% were pro-McCarthy and 67% anti-McCarthy, yielding − 59% net support. Data are from the 1954 INRA survey.

Senator McCarthy (Lipset, 1963b, pp. 320, 331–333; Polsby, 1963, p. 819). An example is given in Table 22. Similarly, Braungart (1966) and Westby and Braungart (1966) found that college students who belonged to the ultraconservative Young Americans for Freedom were much more likely to come from medium-status, low-income homes, with less educated fathers, than were members of leftist organizations. This is shown in Table 23. In a suburban sample, Ferguson and Hoffmann (1964) reported a modest income difference in support of an anti-Communist referendum measure. Hero (1966, p. 460) reported extremely strong education differences in anti-Communist attitudes; for example, college-educated respondents were much more likely to advocate admitting Communist China to the United Nations, or to acquiesce to a majority vote to do so.

Three studies suggest that education may be more important in this relationship than other indicators of status. In one, neither income nor occupation was related to "right-wing extremism," though education was (Rush, 1967). In another, differences in political authoritarianism between middle- and working-class respondents disappeared when education was controlled (Lipsitz, 1965). And in Stember's (1961) copious secondary analysis of educational differences in poll data on racism and anti-Semitism, the same picture emerges, except that the highly educated seem less heroic. Stember concluded that social status has no uniform effect of its own on attitudes toward the rights of Negroes, once education is controlled (1961, p. 81). The highly educated are indeed less prejudiced, but primarily on racial stereotypes, legal or formal discrimination, and issues of government policy [though Barber's results with Survey Research Center items on federal racial policy reveal substantial high-status opposition to federal intervention, apparently not based on racial prejudice (1965, pp. 260–284)]. The liberalism of the highly educated, however, is less clear with regard to intimate social relations. As Stember says (1961, p. 17), "It appears that the educated . . . are more open to relations with Negroes only where intimacy is limited."

In three cases, higher-status, better-educated people have been found less liberal. Those attending "schools" of the Christian Anti-Communism Crusade were overwhelmingly of high status, whether judged by education, income, or occupation (Koeppen, 1967; Wolfinger *et al.*, 1964). Supporters of the John Birch Society in California also tended to be relatively high in education and economic level, though there was no nationwide status difference (Lipset, 1963b, pp. 352, 356). Perhaps most confusing was the preconvention support for Senator Goldwater in 1964. There is some indication that high-status persons in the South and West favored him most, while in the East they seem to have opposed him most (Crespi, 1965, p. 532). Segregationist Governor George Wallace drew more votes in the 1964 Presidential primary in middle-class suburbs of Wisconsin than he did in working-class areas, but Rogin's (1966) analysis strongly suggests that this was mainly due to the fact that high-status Republicans voted in the Democratic primary to embarrass the very unpopular Democratic governor who ran against Wallace.

The upper strata of each socioeconomic level also seem somewhat more liberal by several criteria. They were more antagonistic to Father Coughlin (Lipset, 1963b, p. 321) and to the anti-Communist Francis Amendment (Ferguson and Hoffmann, 1964), and they tend generally to be less prejudiced against Negroes (Bettelheim and Janowitz, 1964). Newcomb *et al.* (1967, p. 49) reported a Survey Research Center finding that graduates of high-status colleges were much more "unhappy" over Goldwater's selection in 1964 as Republican nominee than those from low-status colleges. One dissenting report is that support for McCarthy increased with status within educational or occupational categories, but no data are given (Lipset, 1963b, p. 333).

Liberalism on noneconomic issues is, therefore, associated rather strongly with high status; at least, this has been true in recent years. Educational level is the variable most closely associated with the effect. The major exception seems to be contemporary Western extreme conservatism. Of course, the association of liberalism with high status does not hold for economic issues, where the middle class is more favorable to business and private enterprise, and the working class more socialistic and egalitarian (though even they are not overwhelmingly so, according to Lane, 1962). For data on economic liberalism, see Key (1961, pp. 121–152) and Barber (1965).

Status discrepancy. Status discrepancies or inconsistencies have been thought by numerous writers to motivate both ethnic prejudice and radical political attitudes, especially ultraconservatism. The hypothesis takes several forms (see Bettelheim and Janowitz, 1964; Hofstadter, 1963; Lenski, 1954). Status inconsistency has been defined in terms both of simple inconsistency between one's standing on various status dimensions (for example, the college-educated blue-collar worker) and of transitional status (that is, downwardly or upwardly mobile persons). Mobility will be considered separately here.

Barber (1965), Hodge and Treiman (1966), and Treiman (1966) offer a simple way of testing the hypothesis. Higher-status people are less racially prejudiced, as indicated above. A simple "additive model" would assume that inconsistencies between status dimensions, or transitions between them, would produce a level of prejudice somewhere between the levels expected from either alone. For example, a person downwardly mobile from middle to working class should be intermediate in anti-Negro prejudice. The alternative, suggested by the "status discrepancy" hypothesis, is that inconsistent or transitional statuses produce special tensions which are unusually productive of prejudice and radicalism. Hence, the input status dimensions should interact (an "interaction model").

The best data on anti-Negro prejudice, from 1230 NORC interviews in a 1963 nationwide sample, fit the additive much more closely than the status-discrepancy ("interaction") model. The status dimensions are income, education, occupation, and spouse's education. Interestingly enough, a 1944 NORC survey found the most status-discrepant (education and income) respondents *most* racially liberal. The highest acceptance of Negroes as next-door neighbors was among those from the upper class with only grade-school education and from the lower class with college education (Stember, 1961, p. 133).

Ultraconservatism and status discrepancy do not seem consistently related. Kelly and Chamblis (1965), in a Seattle mail sample, found socioeconomic status a better predictor than status inconsistency for attitudes on social welfare, civil liberties, and civil rights. Dynes (1967), in a Southern sample, found no interaction between status and education with respect to freedom of speech, though each had the usual main effect. Lipset (1963b, pp. 334, 363), an original proponent of the status-discrepancy hypothesis, found no solid data in its favor among supporters of Joseph McCarthy and the John Birch Society. Wolfinger *et al.* (1964) and Koeppen (1967) found no support for it in data on the Christian Anti-Communism Crusade. Occupation and educational attainment were as consistent with each other among the Crusaders as in comparable national samples.

On the other hand, Rush (1967) did find inconsistencies among education, income, and occupation to be related to right-wing attitudes. Unfortunately, his mail sample had a high nonresponse rate, and his analysis is dependent on very small numbers of cases in some cells. In a somewhat related finding, Trow (1958) found antagonism toward big business and big organized labor related to support for McCarthy. Lipset (1963b, p. 341) was unable to replicate this finding with a larger sample, but Wolfinger *et al.* (1964) and Koeppen (1967) found some evidence for it among their Crusaders. However, it is not clear whether the feeling is centered on "antibureaucratic" sentiments or "old-fashioned individualism," as Wolfinger *et al.* and Trow would have it, or simply on generalized hostility, negativism, and biliousness.

Lenski (1954, 1967) offers the more general hypothesis that voting in favor of social change (usually for the left) predominates among those with inconsistent status on ethnicity, income, occupation, and education. His data support the hypothesis, but the support is apparently due mainly to continued left voting by otherwise high-status members of ethnic minority groups; low-status members of the majority ethnic group do not differ much from those with consistent status. The difference between these and the preceding studies arises from the fact that only Lenski has used ethnicity as a status variable. Marx (1967, p. 57), in a large survey of urban Negroes in 1964, found racial militancy to be a positive function of both education and occupational prestige, but no interaction was present, and hence, there was no status-discrepancy effect.

This general hypothesis, that status discrepancies are major determinants of attitudes favorable to political change (whether in a reactionary or progressive direction), has been explored provocatively by some historians. Donald's (1956) analysis of the Abolitionists, and Mowry's (1963) and Hofstadter's (1955) of the

Progressives, are most noteworthy. The statistical support has been rudimentary in each case, consisting largely of demonstrations that particular occupational, educational, and religious groups were dominant in the leadership of these movements, with no comparable data presented for their opponents or for uninvolved persons. However, any use of quantitative techniques and sociological theory in analyzing historical phenomena must be applauded, especially when it parallels so closely analyses made of contemporary political opinions on which the hypotheses can be thoroughly tested on large, representative samples.

It seems fair to conclude that status discrepancies, anxieties, and inconsistencies have not been shown to contribute in any important, general way to the development of racial prejudice or ultraconservative political attitudes. The main effects of status and education are strong and consistent, however.

Social mobility. The most frequent hypothesis has been that persons either mobile upwardly or downwardly are unusually conservative. Variants include Bettelheim and Janowitz (1964), who expected downward mobility, but not upward mobility, to produce unusual amounts of racial prejudice; and Lipset and Zetterberg (1959), who assumed that the upwardly mobile would be more conservative than either the class of origin or the class of destination, but that the downwardly mobile would only be more conservative than the latter.

The "additive" alternative, as suggested earlier, assumes that the individual is socialized into the norms of his class of origin, then is influenced somewhat by his class of destination; thus, he is left finally somewhere in between. Most data support this latter notion. The clearest are based on a 1963 nationwide NORC sample (Hodge and Treiman, 1966), in which mobility was tested by comparing the respondent's occupation with his father's. Mobile persons were intermediate in racial prejudice. Bettelheim and Janowitz (1964, pp. 32–33) reviewed seven studies, six of which they cited as supporting their original (1950) hypothesis that downwardly mobile people are more prejudiced than stable persons, even those in the class of destination. Since each study was done with a sample of limited size and in a small geographical region, they do not seem so representative as the NORC survey. However, the data do contradict the NORC findings. On upward mobility there is no contradiction; Bettelheim and Janowitz (1964, pp. 35–36) found no obvious deviations from additivity in the same seven studies.

More confusing data were presented by Barber (1965), from Survey Research Center surveys. The items used to measure racial feeling concerned government racial policy, and elsewhere (Key, 1961, p. 165) have been shown to fit as part of an economic welfare scale. Indeed, Barber showed that the class differences were those to be expected of economic rather than noneconomic issues; that is, higher-status respondents were more conservative. In any case, the non-Southern data seem to support Bettelheim and Janowitz' (1950) notion that the downwardly mobile are the most prejudiced, and the upwardly mobile intermediate. However, a separate analysis of an item concerning the civil liberties of government employees reveals the usual intermediate outcome, with higher-status persons more liberal.

One clear confirmation of Lenski's (1954) idea about status inconsistencies leading to pressure for change, as applied to mobility, is found in Marx's 1964 survey of urban Negroes (Marx, 1967, p. 60). Both upwardly and downwardly mobile respondents were considerably more racially militant than status-stable respondents.

With respect to radical right organizations, though, there is little indication that mobility is an important factor. Wolfinger *et al.* (1964) and Koeppen (1967) found that Christian Anti-Communism Crusaders were unusually status-stable, and within their samples, the mobiles were *less* conservative than the status-stable respondents.

Thus, the only evidence that status-discrepancy tensions are significant, politically, for mobile persons is that found among Negroes, and some rather ambiguous evidence with regard to downwardly mobile persons' attitudes toward Negroes (which, however, is contradicted by the thorough NORC nationwide survey). Here again, it appears that the "additive" socialization model described in the previous section fits the data most closely.

Alienation and migrancy. One popular hypothesis, partly growing out of mass society theory (see Kornhauser, 1959, pp. 60–73), is that socially isolated groups or individuals are especially susceptible to extremist appeals. One implication is that right-wingers should be low in political participation. However, it is obvious that in this country there is no great dearth of ultraconservative activists. The Crusaders had extremely high rates of voting, sense of efficacy, activism in Republican party affairs, and political letter writing, even relative to the national college-educated population (Koeppen, 1967; Wolfinger *et al.*, 1964). Grupp (1966, p. 9) described members of the Birch Society as "singularly active politically." The most active political letter writers and among the most consistent voters in this country are the extreme conservatives (though letter writers are not unusually extreme on matters of foreign policy concerning the Vietnam war) (see Converse, Clausen, and Miller, 1965; Verba *et al.*, 1967).

The further question is really whether or not the nonparticipants in America can potentially be enlisted behind the extremists. Only suggestive evidence is available, but McCarthy supporters were only slightly lower in interest and previous voting record than his opponents, and the slight difference could be accounted for by status differences alone (Polsby, 1963, p. 817).

Geographical mobility has been thought to create rootlessness, alienation, and loneliness, and thus to motivate angry efforts to restore a past golden era. Yet all the evidence suggests that it has no such extreme effect. Newcomers to California did not, in 1964, prefer Goldwater to the other Republican candidates more than did the old inhabitants, did not prefer Goldwater to Johnson more, and were actually somewhat more liberal on Proposition 14. Even high intrastate mobility did not increase support for Goldwater or increase opposition to the fair housing law (Wolfinger and Greenstein, 1969). The national evidence on migration is similar. Migrants retain about the same party allegiances they had originally, and seem to vote about as regularly (Campbell *et al.,* 1960). Southern-born whites moving to the North are considerably more liberal than Southerners, and Northerners who move South are only slightly less liberal than stable Northern residents (Sheatsley, 1966). Negroes active in the 1965 Watts rioting tended proportionately to come more often from Los Angeles than from other areas of the country (Sears and McConahay, 1967b). Detroit rioters in 1967 tended to be native Detroiters, not recent migrants (National Advisory Commission on Civil Disorders, 1968). Finally, Wolfinger and Greenstein (1969) noted that the rapidly growing Northern California city of San Jose is unequivocally more liberal politically than Los Angeles or San Diego, though not differentiable on standard demographic measures. Thus, rapid population growth and geographical mobility do not necessarily, or perhaps even usually, have a conservatizing or radicalizing effect.

Republicanism

Besides education and status, Republican party identification consistently relates to ultraconservatism. The relationship is extremely strong in most cases. In the Christian Anti-Communism Crusade, Republicans outnumbered Democrats 66 percent to eight percent (Wolfinger *et al.*, 1964, p. 268), and only six percent of the Birch Society membership claimed to be Democrats (Grupp, 1966, p. 2). In April 1954, a Gallup survey indicated that a majority of the nation's Republicans were favorable to McCarthy, whereas only 25 percent of the Democrats were (Polsby, 1963, p. 819). This gross difference appeared repeatedly in surveys done on Mc-Carthy (Campbell and Cooper, 1956, p. 92; Lipset, 1963b, p. 329). Table 22 gives one example. Among Father Coughlin's supporters in 1938, 49 percent expected to vote for a Republican Congressman, whereas only 37 percent of his opponents did (Lipset, 1963b, p. 323). In 1962, the anti-Communist Francis Amendment was supported by 55 percent of those who voted for the Republican gubernatorial candidate, Richard Nixon, and by only 22 percent of those voting for the Democrat, "Pat" Brown (Ferguson and Hoffmann, 1964).

The race question, at least in 1964 (and perhaps it was a landmark year in this respect), showed the same correlation with Republicanism. Table 21 shows the extremely strong relationship between party preference and vote on the anti-fair-housing measure, Proposition 14. It was opposed by 51 percent of those planning to vote for President Johnson, and by 12 percent of the Goldwater supporters (Wolfinger and Greenstein, 1968, p. 760). However, in the past, race has not been so evidently correlated with party preference (Converse, Clausen, and Miller, 1965).

Traditional Americans

Numerous other demographic measures have been used, of course. The impression they convey is that a nativist, traditionalist segment of American society is most attracted to these illiberal ideas. This is manifested in several ways.

Salience of religion. Religious affiliation relates to such attitudes in two general ways. First, Father Coughlin and Senator McCarthy, both obviously Catholic, received far stronger support from Catholics than from Protestants, even with social class or party affiliation controlled (Lipset, 1963b, pp. 319, 320, 335). Similarly, the Christian Anti-Communism Crusade, explicitly religious and Protestant, received scarcely any support from non-Protestants. On the other hand, Barry Goldwater and the John Birch Society have been shown not to attract Protestants and Catholics differentially (Crespi, 1966; Lipset, 1963b, p. 357). These, then, seem simply to be instances of differential group salience, rather than any general link between Protestantism or Catholicism and the right wing.

Protestant fundamentalism. It has often been speculated, however, that authoritarian political attitudes are particularly common in fundamentalist Protestant sects and among Catholics, because their religious dogmas are highly authoritarian. There is little evidence that Catholics are unusually authoritarian politically, aside from the cases just mentioned. The fundamentalists are another story, however.

In several surveys the major Protestant denominations have ordered themselves consistently, in terms of liberalism on civil liberties, foreign relations, racial issues (Allinsmith and Allinsmith, 1948; Glock and Stark, 1966), and antagonism to Father Coughlin and Senator McCarthy (Lipset, 1963b, pp. 319, 335). Episcopalians and

Congregationalists were the most liberal, followed by the Presbyterians, Methodists, and Lutherans, with the Baptists being the most illiberal. However, the same ordering seems to have held for antagonism to Franklin D. Roosevelt, for members' socio-economic status, and in fact for the status of the various denominations (Allinsmith and Allinsmith, 1948; Lipset, 1963b, p. 335), thus leading to the suspicion that denominational differences simply reflect the greater pro-Democratic allegiance, and greater authoritarianism on most other issues, that are characteristic of lower-status persons.

Johnson (1962, 1964) has controlled for social status in surveys done in Eugene, Oregon and Tallahassee, Florida. He found distinctive norms operating in "liberal" and "fundamentalist" Protestant congregations, as evidenced by the fact that high frequency of attendance (an index of religious involvement) was related to increased Democratic voting for religious liberals and increased Republican voting for fundamentalists. This held for blue-collar and white-collar workers alike, in both Oregon and Florida. Among Baptists and Methodists, "liberal" and "neo-orthodox" ministers voted considerably more Democratic than did "conservative" ministers, even when the class composition of their congregations was controlled (Johnson, 1966, p. 205). They were also more liberal on such issues as segregation, capital punishment, and federal aid to education (Johnson, 1967). A rather interesting incidental finding is that almost all the "conservative" pastors were Republican, while only the younger "liberal" and "neo-orthodox" Methodist pastors were predominantly Democratic (Johnson, 1966, p. 207). Therefore, all the older pastors, as well as the younger conservative ones, were aligned against the young liberals.

Jews and Negroes. Jews are almost invariably the strongest opponents of illiberal views (Crespi, 1966, p. 528; Lipset, 1963b, pp. 319–377 *passim;* Wolfinger and Greenstein, 1968). They are vastly overrepresented in leftist movements (Braungart, 1966; Glazer, 1961; Grupp, 1966; Scoble, 1963; Watts and Whittaker, 1966) and underrepresented in the right (Braungart, 1966; Grupp, 1966; Koeppen, 1967; Wolfinger *et al.,* 1964). As an aggregate, Jews are unusually high in status, yet unusually liberal on economic and noneconomic issues alike. However, note Litt's (1961) suggestive conclusion from a survey study: "Jews who feel socially and psychologically subordinate because of their ethnic affiliation are least likely to be tolerant of political nonconformists and altruistic toward other deprived groups" (p. 280). Perhaps Jews' liberalism is not merely due to solidarity among underdogs.

Fewer data are available on Negroes, yet they were unusually anti-McCarthy (Lipset, 1963b, p. 337), anti-Proposition 14 (Wolfinger and Greenstein, 1968), and anti-Goldwater (Crespi, 1966, p. 527). Samples of Negroes large enough to be conclusive are rarely asked questions extending much beyond racial matters, but a test of the "working-class authoritarianism" hypothesis among Negroes might yield some surprises. Another surprise is that Mexican-American and Oriental voters were opposed to Proposition 14 (Wolfinger and Greenstein, 1968). Apparently they were not as resentful of Negroes as was generally thought.

Aging. As indicated earlier, young people tend to be considerably more liberal than older people, at least currently (and at least on civil liberties and race prejudice; this hypothesis is not so clear regarding Goldwater and the Birch Society; see Crespi, 1965, and Lipset, 1963b). This may be due to a generational effect, or it may be due to the inherent effects of aging itself. Back and Gergen (1963a, 1963b; Gergen and Back, 1965, 1966) have explored the possible consequences of shorter time perspectives on the part of older people, in terms that would lead them politically to support ultraconservative thinking. They found some evidence in secondary analyses of poll data that older people prefer dramatic, immediate, short-range solutions to public problems; that they prefer extreme or total solutions; that they are more pessimistic; and that they are less involved in public affairs (at least after a certain age).

There are other differences between age groups that might contribute to illiberal thinking. Bradburn and Caplovitz (1965) found younger people happier, on the whole, and more emotionally reactive (pp. 9, 23). Schuman and Harding (1963) devised a test of "sympathetic identification with the underdog" to see how people empathize with minorities. They found a fairly substantial correlation with age, with younger people being more empathic. These findings, however, only scratch the surface of orientations that are linked to age and are of great potential significance in public opinion. Also it should be noted that there are dramatic age differences in exposure to higher education, which itself should affect some of these dispositions.

Provincialism. In most of these studies, farmers and residents of small towns or rural areas were among the strongest adherents to ultraconservatism, and residents of urban areas most hostile to it. Farmers were among Coughlin's and McCarthy's staunchest supporters (Lipset, 1963b, pp. 322, 332), and were most enthusiastic about Goldwater and the Birch Society (Crespi, 1966, p. 529; Lipset, 1963b, pp. 355–356). Stouffer (1955, pp. 112–113) found rural and small town dwellers considerably less liberal than city dwellers on civil liberties issues. Wolfinger *et al.* (1964) and Koeppen (1967) did not find an unusual proportion of farm or small town backgrounds among their Crusaders, though.

Region, on the other hand, has no simple effects. McCarthy did best in the East and Midwest, and worst in the West; Goldwater did worst in the first two, and best in the South and West (Crespi, 1965; Polsby, 1963, p. 813). In both cases the safest guess would be that regional differences are largely produced by other variables, especially racial attitudes. On the racial issue, there is, of course, an enormous difference between the South and the rest of the country, contrary to many Southern protestations (Sheatsley, 1966).

However, some interesting and seemingly inexplicable regional differences have been noted. Southern California is more conservative than Northern California in many political and social matters. If the obvious background factors are examined, they do not explain the differences at all well. Elite groups differ most of all, suggesting the existence of different "political cultures" which pervade the informational environment in ways which, however, cannot now be measured very rigorously (Wolfinger and Greenstein, 1969).

Attitudinal recruitment and consensus

One important question is whether or not people are recruited to such movements on the basis of longstanding political or social attitudes. A related question is how great the degree of consensus is within the rank and file on ultraconservative ideology. The data unequivocally indicate that ultraconservatives are considerably more alarmed about, and adopt a tougher policy stance toward, domestic Communism than do comparable nonadherents. The Christian Anti-Communism Crusaders, not surprisingly, believe to an extraordinary degree that the danger from domestic Communists is serious: 66 percent believe it "a very great danger," as opposed to 18 percent of college-educated Americans nationwide. And 91 percent agreed that "Communists have a lot of influence in [American] colleges and universities" (Wolfinger *et al.*, 1964, pp. 269–270). Birch Society supporters thought the internal Communist threat much more serious than did opponents of the Birch Society (Lipset, 1963b, p. 360). Perception of the Communist threat was also quite strongly related to votes on the anti-Communist Francis Amendment (Ferguson and Hoffmann, 1964). A tougher international line toward Communists was taken, as well, by the Crusaders and supporters of Father Coughlin and Senator McCarthy (Lipset, 1963b, pp. 322, 339; Wolfinger *et al.*, 1964, p. 271). Yet it is not at all clear that supporters of ultraconservative leaders uniformly hold ultraconservative opinions on other issues. Polsby (1963, pp. 823–824), for example, cross-tabulated responses to six different items on McCarthy used in a 1954 Gallup survey. McCarthy supporters showed rather little consistency, in absolute terms, and considerably less than his opponents. Lipset (1963b, p. 338) correlated McCarthy support with a series of policy items and concluded, "Perhaps more significant than the fact that support of McCarthy correlated with conservative and isolationist political attitudes is that these relationships are on the whole so weak."

Father Coughlin's charismatic appeal also camouflaged a chaos of dissension among his followers on his main themes. Few of them opposed Franklin D. Roosevelt, supported his position in the Spanish Civil War, or voted for his third-party candidate (and of those who did, relatively few were overtly anti-Semitic). Here too, then, it would be misleading to translate his enthusiastic personal following into an equivalent level of approval for his political positions.

Radical right organizations similarly give the impression of representing cohorts of semihysterical partisans of the nineteenth century. Yet the Crusaders are far from agreed on a conservative domestic stance. Sizable minorities supported medicare, unions, and federal aid to education, and a majority opposed the South's position on integration (Wolfinger *et al.*, 1964, p. 272). When Grupp (1966) asked a large sample of members of the Birch Society, "What changes in federal policy would you like to see?" 65 percent failed to mention a single one of the Society's six major programs.

In short, followers of right-wing leaders and organizations seem united in their belief that Communism is a threat, and that a hard line must be taken against it. Aside from that, there seems to be little consensus on more detailed ultraconservative ideology, at least among the rank and file. This, of course, is what we have come to expect of any rank and file.

One other interesting question on which there are, unfortunately, too few data concerns whether or not illiberal positions draw substantial support on the basis of racial or ethnic prejudice, even when their manifest appeal is of some other kind. Proposition 14 seems to have been supported most by those most prejudiced against Negroes (though by many relatively less prejudiced, as well) (Wolfinger and Greenstein, 1968), and Father Coughlin by the anti-Semitic (Lipset, 1963b, p. 326). However, anti-Semitism and McCarthy support were related in contradictory ways across several studies, and apparently McCarthy support was not related to anti-Negro prejudice (Lipset, 1963b, pp. 342–347). Hence, it is not obvious from available data that ultraconservatism is just masking any unusually intense or widespread prejudice against minorities (though this is not to say ultraconservatives are particularly liberal in such matters).

The high-status ultraconservative

The data pose a paradox. On the one hand, ultraconservatism includes some attitudes most prevalent in the working class, especially chauvinism and intolerance. On the other hand, there is much about it that is characteristic of the middle class: opposition to economic liberalism, Republican party identification, white Anglo-Saxon Protestantism. And in the South and West, at least, it seems to be quite popular among relatively well-off people.

A provocative possibility is offered from surveys of college student activist organizations by Braungart (1966) and Westby and Braungart (1966). Their data suggest that ultraconservative activists may often be people socialized in Republican, Protestant, small-town, lower-middle-class or working-class environments, with the political and social opinions characteristic of that segment of society. However, they may carry these illiberal attitudes with them as they move up into more visible and higher-status positions. Thus, they wind up showing no dramatic "status discrepancy" effects, in terms of the "interaction model" described above. But they are highly illiberal relative to those who have maintained a stable high-status position. In other words, high-status ultraconservatism is the residue of socialization into provincial, low-status, Protestant, Republican, less educated beliefs, combined with mobility into a visible high-status location.

Westby and Braungart sampled college students attending the national conventions of right-wing (Young Americans for Freedom) and left-wing (Students for a Democratic Society and SENSE) organizations. The contrast in social backgrounds is clear, as indicated by the data given in Tables 23 and 24. Right-wing activists are more likely to be highly religious Protestants, and much less likely to be Jewish or nonreligious. They come predominantly from "middle, lower-middle, and respectable working class" homes (Braungart, 1966, p. 12), while leftists more often come from high-status homes. Rightists also tend to attend lower-status colleges; this is reminiscent of the finding cited above that Goldwater found more favor among the alumni of such colleges (Newcomb *et al.*, 1967). Also, rightists tend much more often to come from Republican, and leftists from Democratic, families.

The contrast is highlighted by two other surveys of leftist or liberal organizations, one on the Berkeley Free Speech Movement (Watts and Whittaker, 1966), the other on the National Committee for an Effective Congress (Scoble, 1963). Contrasted with a cross section of Berkeley students, members of the Free Speech Movement were more Jewish or nonreligious (75 percent compared to 41 percent) and more often had fathers with advanced academic degrees (36 percent compared to 23 percent) and college-graduate mothers (44 percent compared to 28 percent). Similarly, members of the National Committee for an Effective Congress were unusually Jewish, "other," or "none" in religion (46 percent as opposed to about seven percent nationally), and "exceptionally high by conventional measures of social status" (Scoble, 1963, p. 236); for example, 70 percent were college graduates and 84 percent professional-managerial (Scoble, 1963, pp. 232–233). Another study of student activists on the left reveals that their parents are considerably more liberal than is customary for persons of their high status (Flacks, 1967).

TABLE 23

SOCIAL BACKGROUND OF RIGHT–WING AND LEFT–WING STUDENT ACTIVISTS

	Young Americans for Freedom (right-wing)	*Students for a Democratic Society (left-wing)*
Own religion		
Protestant	61%	32%
Jewish or "none"	8	52
Currently attend church or synagogue	82	26
Social class		
High (class I or II)	31%	62%
Middle (class III)	38	23
Low (classes IV or V)	31	15
Father's education		
College graduate	33%	52%
Some college	22	21
No college	45	27
Father's occupation		
Executive, proprietor, professional	29%	58%
Administrative, clerical	49	28
Skilled, unskilled labor	19	7

Source: Braungart, 1966, pp. 17–27. Total sample is 180 from Students for a Democratic Society and 155 from Young Americans for Freedom. Entries are percentages of each group.

Perhaps much right-wing extremism can be accounted for, then, as a simple, additive function of socialization experiences peculiar to a "traditional American" location of origin (fundamentalist Protestant, Republican, small town, middle or lower-middle class), and an adult location in relatively affluent, suburban, college-educated circumstances. This change would not seem impressive if measured by the standard indicators of vertical social mobility; it is scarcely a rags-to-riches story. It might even be too subtle to be measured in terms of intergenerational mobility at all.

But the difference between these locations of origin, and those of the more affluent people, with higher-status occupations, educated at high-status colleges, and dwelling in the urban upper-middle class, may be critical in terms of early political socialization. Westby and Braungart (1966, p. 692) say: "As members of a fully 'arrived' stratum, upper-middle-class individuals can afford the luxury of 'deviance' from a straight-line conformist politics, especially if their position is relatively well-established, and their mobility not too recent" (note that this parallels the experimental finding that maximum conformity occurs at intermediate status levels; Dittes and Kelley, 1956). This feeling of the "luxury of deviance" may set the tone for political socializa-

TABLE 24

PARENTAL AND STUDENT POLITICAL AFFILIATIONS

	Leftist students (Students for a Democratic Society) (N = 180)		Rightist students (Young Americans for Freedom) (N = 155)	
	Parents	Students	Parents	Students
Democrat, Radical, Socialist, Communist	53%	55%	12%	—
Independent, split	31	37	25	12%
Republican, Conservative	13	—	61	88
Total ("other" excluded)	97%	92%	98%	100%

Source: Braungart, 1966, p. 20.

tion in high-status families, and thus orient the child toward the more esoteric forms of liberalism such as are represented in the Free Speech Movement, opposition to the censorship of pornography, and anti-Vietnam peace marches.

Finally, it may be that liberalism is a clearer high-status political norm in some localities than others (though regional differences in elite attitudes have only begun to be explored). The feeling of "noblesse oblige," however modest its aspirations, that seems characteristic of high-status groups in New England and the San Francisco Bay area (*cf.* Newcomb *et al.*, 1967; Wolfinger and Greenstein, 1969) may not be so prevalent in many parts of the South and West; this perhaps accounts for the high-status ultraconservatism in these latter areas.

Conclusions

The clearest evidence about the social origins of illiberal ideas is that they result from socialization in lower-status, less educated, fundamentalist Protestant, Republican, small-town or farm circumstances. There is little evidence that any special contribution is made by strains attendant upon vertical social mobility or migration from one area to another. However, those who are mobile from the above-described origins into a social location in which liberalism is a clear norm will obviously stand out like a sore thumb, and perhaps mislead their peers into believing that the mobility itself (rather than the origins) was responsible for their illiberal notions. Similarly, racial prejudice among Northerners can often be explained rather simply in terms of the Southern working-class origins of many who today are Northerners in the upper-working or lower-middle class. And, in general, older people are less liberal, though as yet it is not clear how much of this is due to their age, and how much to changing times.

The common error of psychologists oriented toward individual differences lies in invoking complex personality explanations for intolerance, ethnocentrism, and so on, when much simpler explanations based on distinctive political socialization experiences may serve as well. Such experiences surely have their personality concomitants as well, but there is no use explaining racial prejudice on the basis of adult personality when it turns out that the individual in question has been prejudiced ever since he was a small boy in Alabama.

Finally, it should be noted that the explanation offered above for the high-status ultraconservative does not by any means explain all data of this kind. For example, the Crusaders (Koeppen, 1967; Wolfinger *et al.*, 1964) had high-status parents, and thus remain something of a mystery in these terms.

CONFLICT, CONSENSUS, AND COMMITMENT TO THE SYSTEM

The question of internal partisanship is a major preoccupation in the domestic politics of the United States, but the experience of newly created nations (and, indeed, the instability of much older ones) has made it clear just how important a stable basic framework of rules and conventions can be. The institution or maintenance of a democratic system is not contingent in any immediate sense upon public opinion. In the long run, though, it may well be that democracy thrives only where people actively support it. The question to be raised in this section is: What precisely is the nature of this support in the United States? Upon what symbols does it focus; and how far into the details of our constitutional and governmental structure does the support reach? What is the course of development of support for the system? (This is a critical issue for new nations, because here intervention is possible.) And how do people feel about conflicts within the system, and about dissent over its nature?

ATTACHMENT TO THE POLITICAL SYSTEM

The early socialization of attachment

In one way or another, the child's attachment to the political system is enhanced by almost any experience that furthers the internalization of conforming, normative patterns of thinking and action. Here, however, we are merely concerned with identifying those attitudes that are explicitly political and that are acquired in childhood.

Simple chauvinism. Apparently the earliest concepts of nation, or of the political system more generally, are of a simple "we-they" quality. Lambert and Klineberg (1967, p. 184) found that six-year-olds in a variety of countries tended to think of all other nationality groups as dissimilar from themselves. By age ten, dissimilarity was perceived less often, and was attributed primarily to those foreign peoples with distinctively different physical characteristics or to political opponents, for example, Chinese, African Negroes, Indians, and Russians (pp. 145–150). Hess and Torney (1967, p. 26) reported similar findings.

As the child moves through the grade school years, he acquires and maintains a strong positive feeling toward his nation, with relatively vague conceptual content. Hess and Torney (1967, p. 26) found that nearly 95 percent of their large sample of white school children, at every level from grade two through grade eight, agreed with the statements that the "American flag is the best flag in the world" and that "America is the best country in the world." [Note that in many cases attitude acquisition must simply be a function of exposure, since familiarity is a good predictor of preference, acceptability, or liking (Greenwald and Sakumura, 1968; Lambert and Klineberg, 1967; Zajonc, 1968).] These opinions are characterized initially by superlative positive affect and by attachment of the concept "America" to conventional symbols (for example, the flag or the Statue of Liberty). That the primary focus of the attachment is to something clearly "American" but otherwise vague is suggested by the fact that from 30 to 50 percent at each grade level thought it all right "for the government to lie to another country if the lie protects the American people." Affects toward nationality groups are initially highly favorable, but by age 10 this is less true, and they begin to become correlated with feelings of similarity or dissimilarity toward them (Lambert and Klineberg, 1967, p. 188).

Only later are the conventional rationalizations for patriotic feelings acquired. Second-graders gave a wide variety of responses to the question, "What makes you proud to be an American?" but eighth-graders gave the standard answers ("freedom" and the "right to vote") as often as their teachers did. Similarly, the U.S.A. and U.S.S.R. were seen only as "good" and "bad," respectively, in the second grade, but by eighth grade they were differentiated in terms of "freedom" and "democracy" (Lambert and Klineberg, 1967, p. 30). Another primitive aspect of this patriotism is intolerance of dissent. Only 15 percent of the fourth-graders felt "you can say things against the government," while 54 percent of the eighth-graders did (p. 66). Perhaps younger children cannot distinguish intrasystemic conflict from antisystemic polemic; the term "government" may not be differentiated from authority in general (*cf.* Kohlberg, 1963).

Apparently, grade schools try to contribute to this patriotism; all but one of the sample of 119 teachers displayed the United States flag prominently in the classroom, over 85 percent at each grade level required their pupils to pledge allegiance to the flag daily, and patriotic songs were sung daily in most classrooms in the younger grades (Hess and Torney, 1967, p. 108). There is, however, no direct evidence indicating what the primary sources of this naive patriotism are. Hess and Torney concluded that this "strong positive attachment to the country" is stable, shows little change through elementary school years, and is "exceedingly resistant to change or argument." They considered it the most basic and essential aspect of political socialization.

Government: the benevolent monolith. Children have a strikingly favorable view of the government. Ninety percent of the third-graders agreed that "what goes on in the government is all for the best," and in eighth grade 76 percent agreed (Hess and Torney, 1967, p. 63) Similarly, 72 percent of the fourth-graders said that the government makes mistakes "almost never" or "rarely," as opposed to "sometimes," "often," "usually," or "almost always." And 77 percent agreed that the "government usually knows what is best for people." With age, some naiveté disappears (among eighth-graders these percentages were 59 and 84 percent, respectively), but the affect remains highly favorable (Easton and Dennis, 1965, pp. 52–54).

Children do not think conflict within the country is desirable. They do not think that in a democracy you can say things against the government. After the 1960 campaign, 70 percent of the third-graders said that Kennedy and Nixon "never said anything bad about each other." Older children are less restrictive about conflict: they agreed that one can disagree with the government, and 60 percent of the eighth-graders said Kennedy and Nixon "said bad things about each other because they did

not agree about everything" (Hess and Torney, 1967, p. 78). Young children, failing
to perceive conflict, do not understand discontent and the need for change. Giving
"to change things that are not good" as a motive for running for office is rare for third-
graders (15 percent), but not so rare for eighth graders (37 percent) (p. 76). The public's vague, generalized approval of government, to be discussed later, and its distaste
for domestic conflict, are both anticipated here in childish attitudes.

It seems that parents and teachers alike try to protect children from the sordid
realities of political life. One illustration is a study of parents' explanations to their
children of the assassination of President Kennedy (Orren and Peterson, 1967). A
nationwide sample of parents, a majority of whom personally believed that more than
one man was involved in the slaying, apparently failed altogether to mention a conspiracy to their children (under age 12). Children themselves, probably as a consequence, failed to give conspiratorial explanations for it, though their reactions resembled adults' in most other respects (Sigel, 1965). Similarly, Hess and Torney
(1967, p. 65), who asked elementary school teachers how they presented material,
found that emphasis on the positive was very great in the early grades, with critical
emphasis dominating only later on. Material was presented to "emphasize the positive" by 54 percent in grade two, and by only 14 percent in grades seven and eight.
Material was presented "critically, to point out both the good and bad," by 18 percent
in grade two, and by 68 percent in grades seven and eight.

The benevolent leader

A second set of attitudes focuses on the most salient national leader. As indicated
earlier, attitudes toward political candidates seem to play a central role in electoral
decision. It is, therefore, not merely of academic interest that children seem first to
conceptualize government in terms of its leaders, and to personalize many governmental functions. Again, affect precedes information. Children express strong positive affect toward leaders, and only later acquire supporting rationalizations.

Salience. Familiarity with high leaders is one of the few political contents that is practically at adult levels by the second grade; Hess (1963, p. 555) found that 95 percent
of those aged seven through nine recognized and correctly identified the President's
name, and the level of recognition of national leaders was similarly high for smaller
samples in Chile, Japan, and Australia. Similarly, Greenstein (1965a, p. 32) found
that 96 percent of his fourth-graders could name the President, and 90 percent
could name their unusually popular and visible mayor (Richard Lee of New Haven).

Personalizing government. Young children tend to see government in terms of people,
not in terms of institutions, roles, laws, or buildings (Hess and Easton, 1960). As they
get older, personalizing declines and other symbols take over. For example, Easton
and Dennis (1965, p. 45) found that second-graders, asked to pick the "two best pictures of government" from a variety of symbols, tended to pick the pictures of George
Washington and then-President Kennedy (86 percent). Eighth-graders rarely picked
these leaders (25 percent). But appropriate informational inputs may decrease personalizing; of a large Detroit sample, 32 percent "remembered most" something political about President Kennedy shortly after his assassination, and 55 percent cited
some personal quality. Here there was a rather sharp break about grade eight (about
age 14), with personalizing much more characteristic before than after (Sigel, 1968).

As might, therefore, be expected, young children overestimate the President's
importance in government. The President is cited as "running the country" by 86 per-

cent of the second-graders, but by only 58 percent of the eighth-graders (Hess and Torney, 1967, p. 35). Easton and Dennis (1965, p. 48) found 76 percent of the second-graders, but only five percent of the eighth-graders, thinking that the President makes the laws.

As the child grows older, he increasingly thinks of government in terms of institutions rather than individuals. Ninety-six percent of the eighth-graders chose "voting" and "Congress" as "the two best pictures of government"; these had been chosen only rarely by second-graders (10 percent). Congress was thought to make the laws by 35 percent of the eighth-graders and only 5 percent of the second-graders. Evidently the age trend continues, because Sigel (1966) found adults citing Congress much more often than the President as making the laws, and Easton and Dennis (1965, p. 48) found that grade school teachers particularly emphasize Congress in their own thinking.

Overidealizing the President. Initially, children express extremely favorable affect toward the President. In one second-grade sample, over half indicated that the President was "about the best person in the world." The President, along with "Father" and "Policeman," was rated as close to "my favorite of all" in the second grade (Hess and Torney, 1967, p. 43). This overidealization appears also to occur in Chile, Puerto Rico, Japan, and Australia, according to some early data (Hess, 1963, p. 549). However, it seems very definitely *not* to occur in Appalachia. There, young children have a negative image of political authority, and their cynicism persists throughout school (Jaros, Hirsch, and Fleron, 1968). This is not simply due to poverty: very often lower-status castes or classes reveal more trust than higher-status ones. American Negroes, adults and children alike, were more grief-stricken by the death of President Kennedy than were whites (Sheatsley and Feldman, 1965; Sigel, 1965). Working-class students were more likely to idealize the role of the President and to feel that all American Presidents have "done their job well" than were middle- or upper-class students (Langton, 1967, p. 758). In Jamaica, schoolchildren of lower status were more supportive of the political system than middle- or upper-status children (Langton, 1967, p. 753). Jaros (1967, p. 381) reported that Detroit Negro children do not regard the President as less benevolent than do white children—"Clearly, Negro children do not regard the President as a symbol of a resented, white-dominated regime"—and in the same study there were no class differences in attitudes toward the President. This contrasted with Greenstein's finding (1965a) that lower-class New Haven children idealized the President more than middle-class children did. Working-class children were more likely to agree that "the President is my favorite" when the President was John F. Kennedy (Hess and Torney, 1967, p. 135); it is not so clear how they would feel about a Republican. In other respects, class differences in trust of the system are less marked in this latter study (Hess and Torney, 1967, p. 137). Most of these class or caste differences may simply reflect special appeals: the Jamaican regime was most popular among the lower classes, as was Kennedy, who also had a special appeal to Negroes. [Similarly, the disrespect for the President (a Democrat) in Appalachia may be due to its predominantly Republican complexion.]

One specific aspect of these positive feelings is that the President is seen as benevolent, protective, and interested in taking care of the child. The President "cares a lot what you think if you write to him," according to 75 percent of the second-graders; the President was similarly rated high on "would always help me if I needed it" (Hess and Torney, 1967, p. 40). In a Detroit sample (grades four through eight), an even more prominent aspect of the Presidential image than his benevolence was his power and strength (for example, "the President can tell *everyone* what to do"; Jaros, 1967). However, the image of President Kennedy shortly after his assassination included virtually no spontaneous references to his concern for children, his role as a family man, etc. (Sigel, 1968). If children especially admired him for these child-oriented aspects of his public behavior, their verbal admiration nevertheless did not reflect it.

This idealized image is not characteristic of all authorities. The President is rated higher than several other authority figures (policeman, government, Supreme Court, and Senator) in the early grades, and maintains this superiority as the child grows older. Two changes worth noting do occur, however. One is that the generalized expressions of positive affect become less common, though evaluations of job compe-tence (for example, knowing a lot, rarely making mistakes) remain consistently high (Hess, 1963). Overestimation of the President's strength and power evidently de-clines more rapidly than does overestimation of his benevolence (Jaros, 1967). The other is that trust turns increasingly from persons to institutions. In fact, by fifth grade, the Supreme Court and "government" are regarded as more knowledgeable and less likely to err than the President (Hess and Torney, 1967, pp. 92, 97). The reason for this change is not clear, but it may be noted that it coincides temporally with the development of partisan dispositions.

As in the case of early nationalism, the highly favorable affect develops initially without supporting cognitive content of any consequence. Greenstein says of his fourth-graders: "using the most generous coding standards, less than a fourth of them could describe the President's duties." Substantial amounts of information about the Presidency become evident only from sixth grade on (1965a, pp. 33, 58–59). For example, after the Kennedy assassination, 41 percent of Sigel's fourth-graders, and 62 percent in the sixth grade, knew Kennedy's stand on James Meredith's ad-mission to the University of Mississippi (Sigel, 1968).

Favorable evaluations of other politicians. Other offices, and politicians in general, also receive favorable evaluations from children. They initially view candidates as moti-vated by the public welfare, not by selfish gain. Most fourth-graders rate "people who try to get elected" as "more honest than most people," "less selfish than most," and say that they "almost always" or "always" keep their promises. By the eighth grade, though, adult cynicism about politicians becomes more manifest, and only minorities endorse these favorable positions (Hess and Torney, 1967, p. 76). More generally, as Greenstein noted (1965a, p. 67), children are reluctant to evaluate leaders unfavorably.

Conclusions. The personalizing of politics by young children is striking. Yet it is not at all clear why children focus attention and feeling on political leaders rather than on other political objects. One possibility is simply that leaders are highly visible and adults generally speak well of them. Adults' familiarity with political matters does not go far beyond the most visible national leaders, and Greenstein (1965a, pp. 58–59) noted that children could describe the President's and mayor's roles considerably better than those of Congressmen or aldermen. Also, adults' attitudes toward such leaders are more likely to be positive than negative (and especially so in what they tell children; see Orren and Peterson, 1967; Hess and Torney, 1967). So perhaps small children just repeat what they hear most often. This is strongly suggested by the Appalachia children's negativism and cynicism. A related possibility is that children being tested in schools tend to try to reiterate what their teachers have said, which is perhaps not very much on politics until the later grades.

Another possibility is that persons are easier perceptual objects to handle than are aggregates or abstractions. If this is true, it seems likely also to be true for adults (but perhaps not to the same degree). Thus it would not be surprising if adults, thinking more about the simpler objects, communicated more frequently about them to their children. There is some evidence that low-IQ children personalize government more at all ages' (Greenstein, 1965a, pp. 228–230). Finally, the child may generalize his feelings about a given personal relationship (for example, with his father) to political stimuli (for example, to the President). The data here are notoriously difficult to gather and, to date, they do not really provide even a foothold (see Greenstein, 1965b). In their study of Appalachia children, Jaros, Hirsch, and Fleron (1968) found no relationship between father image and Presidential image; and father absence produced, if anything, more positive Presidential images. This might be interpreted as fulfilling some compensatory function, but it is doubtful that politics are salient enough to serve such an important psychological need. Rather, the absence of the father probably breaks the transmission chain in an area of socialization dominated by men. (It is not clear that political cynicism usually is salient enough to follow a simple transmission line from a father to his son; see Jennings and Niemi, 1968. However, cynicism may be somewhat more salient, and fueled by partisanship, in Appalachia than elsewhere.)

Children's personalizing of politics may later sensitize them, as adults evaluating the flow of political events, to interperson differences. This might explain the lability of candidate orientation relative to other partisan attitudes (Stokes, 1966b). Personalizing is indeed more characteristic of politically "immature" adults. Girls are less informed and interested in politics than boys even as early as the third grade, and thereafter personalize government more than do boys. They are especially likely, in comparison with boys, to view individuals as more benevolent than institutions (Hess and Torney, 1967, pp. 173ff). As adults, women are more candidate-oriented than men (Campbell, Gurin, and Miller, 1954).

The attachment to leaders is highly positive and appears to be rather durable. The intense emotional attachment to the Chief of State is seen in the remarkable intensity of mourning following John F. Kennedy's death (Sheatsley and Feldman, 1965). The implication often drawn from these findings is that this early idealizing is the basis for a lifelong attitude of support for the political system. Yet it does not necessarily follow that the young child's ideals are a galaxy of political and patriotic heroes. For example, Greenstein (1965a, p. 138) reported that George Washington was the "exemplar" of 29 percent of a large sample of children in 1902, but of only three percent of a similar sample in 1958. Perhaps it is easy to overestimate the symbolic importance of a "father of the country." Hence, children's acquisitions of attitudes supporting the political system may not depend on their being able to identify the national unit with a hero or ideal person. However, such interdependencies are poorly understood at present.

Approval of government and governors

How persistent is this early approval of government and public officials? Do people continue to have generally favorable attitudes toward them? The common impression is that people are often cynical and distrusting of government—for example,

TABLE 25

PERCEIVED IMPACT OF NATIONAL GOVERNMENT ON RESPONDENT'S DAILY LIFE

		Nation			
	U.S.A.	United Kingdom	Germany	Italy	Mexico
Improves conditions	76%	77%	61%	66%	58%
Sometimes improves, sometimes does not	19	15	30	20	18
Better off without it	3	3	3	5	19
Other	2	4	5	8	5
Total	100%	99%	99%	99%	100%
N	821	707	676	534	301

Source: Almond and Verba, 1963, pp. 80, 82. Those indicating the national government had no effect on their daily lives are excluded; this represents 11%, 23%, 17%, 19%, and 66% of these five samples, respectively.

"various surveys on public attitudes toward political leadership show, at best, an ambivalent attitude" (Bell, Hill, and Wright, 1961, p. 134). What actually is the case? *Global approval of government.* The overall level of confidence in the government seems high. McClosky (1964, p. 370) found 90 percent agreeing that "I usually have confidence that the government will do what is right." This seems to be characteristic of at least the four other Western nations tested by Almond and Verba. As shown in Table 25, most respondents see their national government as having a positive effect. Almond and Verba's data with regard to local bureaucrats and police are considerably more mixed. Local bureaucrats and police were favorably evaluated in the United States and England, but negatively evaluated in Mexico (1963, p. 108). Lane's depth interviews (1962, p. 84) reveal more than just approval; they reveal a positive zeal for justifying the American political and social system. Clearly, American commitment to this system is very powerful, however unfocused it may be.

This commitment appears to be related to Americans' belief in responsibility for their own status. This was central to Lane's respondents' definitions of "freedom." They were hostile to radical egalitarianism, indifferent to the fact of differential life chances from birth, and imbued with the notion that whatever they were was a product of their own doing. This general belief in personal responsibility for one's own lot is characteristic of most Americans, not just the upwardly mobile (for Survey Research Center data, see Barber, 1965, p. 313ff). Perhaps it derives from the "land of opportunity" stereotype, and from the legacy of immigrant generations, for whom the choice of the American system was a deliberate, meaningful, and costly decision. It is perhaps understandable, from the perspective of dissonance theory, that people would approve of and provide justifications for a system they feel voluntarily committed to (Brehm and Cohen, 1962).

TABLE 26

EVALUATIONS OF LEGISLATIVE BODIES BY LOS ANGELES COUNTY RESIDENTS

	Positive *(yes, represents* *well or a little)*	*Negative* *(no, does not* *represent)*	*Difference*
Negroes (N = 586)			
U.S. Congress	82%	10%	+72%
California State Legislature	70	13	+57
L.A. County Board of Supervisors	70	16	+54
L.A. City Council	73	15	+58
Whites (N = 578)			
U.S. Congress	86%	6%	+80%
California State Legislature	79	6	+73
L.A. County Board of Supervisors	66	6	+60
L.A. City Council	62	9	+53

Sources: Morris and Jeffries, 1967; Sears, 1967. Based on the following question: "Here are several parts of government. Do you feel they generally represent you and speak for you?"

Lane, though, attributes this strong commitment, not to conditioning or dissonance, but to a general sense of satisfaction, to good mental health, and to a sense of leading a rewarding life (Lane, 1962, 1965a). Whether or not these are the explanations, the commitment is impressive; witness Negroes' willingness to fight for the United States (Brink and Harris, 1966) or their confidence that the American system will take care of their problems (Beardwood, 1968; Cantril, 1965; Brink and Harris, 1966).

It is not clear that this commitment is just "patriotism" as it is conventionally defined. Lane (1965b, pp. 752–756) argued that Americans have vague and ill-defined referents for the term "patriotism" that primarily concern wartime duty to serve in the military or otherwise serve the country. He found little discussion of "Americanism" or railing against subversion and communism, and argued that the "cool definition" of "patriot" follows from the freedom of the country and the fact that no repressive measures are necessary to ensure overt expression of fealty.

Approval of officials and institutions. Specific political roles or agencies almost invariably receive majority approval. When respondents in a 1944 NORC poll were asked, "Are you satisfied with the way most people who hold political office in this state are doing their jobs?" 51 percent said that they were satisfied, and 32 percent not satisfied (Mitchell, 1959). A mixed sample of Los Angeles whites and Negroes was asked, shortly after the 1965 Watts riot, "Do you think elected officials can generally be trusted?" In a total sample of 1164, 66 percent said "Yes" and 31 percent "No" (unpublished data).

More specific roles and institutions are also evaluated favorably. The same Los Angeles sample was asked to evaluate various legislative bodies. As shown in Table 26, both whites and Negroes gave predominantly favorable ratings to Congress, the legislature, the City Council, and the County Board of Supervisors. Even so serious an event as a rebellion had not drastically upset support of government in the black community—but note that it was viewed as, and was in fact, a rebellion by a minority, though favorably regarded by the majority in some respects (Sears and McConahay, 1967a; Sears and Tomlinson, 1968). Key (1961, p. 31) reported extremely small percentages of "outspokenly critical evaluations" of schools, police, and other governmental agencies. In the Watts survey, Sears (1967) found favorable evaluations of almost all categories of officials and agencies asked about, especially service agencies and legislators. Jennings, Cummings, and Kilpatrick (1966) found ratings of federal appointees, Congressmen, and top-level civil servants all highly positive in a variety of samples, including the general public.

Finally, political roles rank very high in occupational prestige. In a 1946 NORC poll, government officials were ranked higher than any other occupational group (Mitchell, 1959, p. 689). This has been a consistent finding in subsequent years (Hodge, Siegel, and Rossi, 1964). Inkeles and Rossi's (1956) data suggest that, if anything, the agreement across six nations on the high status of political roles is greater than for most other kinds of roles.

Cynicism about politicians. On the other hand, it is true that many observers have thought American adults cynical about politics, and about politicians in particular (Mitchell, 1959). McClosky (1964, p. 370) has presented some representative data, indicating that over half his sample of the general public agreed with such statements as "Most politicians are looking out for themselves above all else," "Most politicians don't seem to me to really mean what they say," and "There is practically no connection between what a politician says and what he will do once he gets elected." Delegates to the national party conventions, most of them politicians themselves, not surprisingly took a far more charitable view, though 25 percent of them agreed that politicians don't mean what they say. The same derogation of party politicians emerges from a Wisconsin sample: 36 percent agreed, and 33 percent disagreed, that "party leaders make no real effort to keep their promises once they get into office" (Dennis, 1966, p. 605). So there seems to be a widespread tendency to regard "politicians" as untrustworthy, thus distinguishing them from officeholders with more dignified titles.

Yet Lane (1962) noted that his working-class interviewees did not tend to blame individual politicians if something went wrong; they blamed conditions beyond anyone's control, or at worst, such individual characteristics as lack of education. Lane sees a sort of bemused acceptance of the probable occasional malfeasance of politicians, without very much moralizing. (It is interesting to note that Kingdon, 1967, found victorious political candidates "congratulating" the electorate, perceiving the public as being well-informed, interested in politics, and so on, while losers "rationalized" in part by blaming the public for ignorance, indifference, etc. Also, according to the winners, candidate attributes were the decisive factor; according to the losers, party label was the main factor in the outcome. Perhaps losing politicians are not as gracious as the public is.)

Loci of most mistrust. Many attempts have been made to establish what political objects are most likely to be mistrusted, and who the most cynical persons are. Space precludes mentioning more than those few that are of most interest. Local governments, especially obviously corrupt ones, are not generally trusted very much, and Negroes tend on the whole to be less trusting than whites.

The public is sometimes described as feeling the federal government has too much power, and preferring that local governments take on more of the government's activities. In fact, however, most people do not feel the federal government is getting too strong (Converse, Clausen, and Miller, 1965), and it is the more trusted level of government by an extraordinary margin. In a nationwide sample of 2062 high school seniors, 79 percent had "more faith and confidence" in the national government (Jennings, 1967); and in Watts, 58 percent thought the federal government did "the best job for you and your problems" (Sears, 1967). In these two studies, only 17 percent and 10 percent, respectively, cited *either* state or local governments.

Where do individual differences in cynicism and mistrust come from? One possibility might be parents, but a thorough, large-sample study by Jennings and Niemi (1968) appears to rule out any strong systematic correlation between parents' political cynicism and that of their adolescent children. Litt (1963b), taking another tack, has conducted an especially provocative study of Boston politics which leads to the ingenuous suggestion that cynicism comes from living in a corrupt world. Length of residence in Boston, as an index of exposure to corrupt politics, was positively related to political cynicism, but length of residence in the politically "clean" suburb of Brookline was not.

It is thus not surprising to find American Negroes considerably more cynical about government than whites. Marvick (1965, p. 119) has compared matched subsamples of Negroes and whites on the Almond and Verba data cited earlier. Among whites, 85 percent and 90 percent expected "equal treatment" from police and bureaucrats; among Negroes, only 60 percent and 49 percent expected it. Exactly 50 percent of the sample of Watts Negroes said they "trusted" elected officials, while 79 percent of the white sample did (Morris and Jeffries, 1967; Sears, 1967). More of the Negro respondents indicated trust in Negro elected officials (62 percent) than in officials in general—a mild surprise, considering the contention often made that rank-and-file Negroes do not trust Negro leadership.

Still, Negroes have not typically been nearly so pessimistic about white society as might be thought. In a 1967 survey published in the Christmas issue of the *Boston Globe*, Louis Harris reported that 50 percent of the Negroes believed that "hate can be removed from people's minds," while only 31 percent of the whites did. After the Watts riot, 51 percent of the Watts sample of Negroes thought the riot had made whites more sympathetic to Negro problems, and 12 percent felt it had diminished sympathy (Sears and Tomlinson, 1968). A survey of urban Negroes in 1967 reported that 53 percent thought Negroes could get what they wanted under the American system, and 43 percent thought they could not—but the poor were much more optimistic than those better-off (Beardwood, 1968, p. 148). Brink and Harris (1966, p. 135) reported that Negroes scored as less "alienated" (in terms of feeling powerless or hopeless) than low-income whites, and only slightly more "alienated" than the public as a whole. In the same survey, 69 percent expected white attitudes toward Negro rights to be better in five years, and two percent thought they would be worse (p. 258). It is not yet clear why Negro children seem so approving of government, as indicated earlier, or Negro adults so optimistic. It may be that lower-status people, being on the whole intellectually unsophisticated, may respond with superficial approval to remote matters they rarely give much thought to. But these sharp differences between lower-status whites and Negroes, and those given earlier between children in Appalachia and the more representative sample of white children recruited by Hess and Easton, suggest that something more important is going on. Distinctive patterns of political socialization seem to be present, with Negroes currently (or at least until recently) being socialized into the conventional optimistic, opportunity-oriented, system-supporting set of American ideas about government.

Rallying around the government. Despite some areas of mistrust and cynicism, the American public as a whole seems sufficiently attached to the government to rally to its support at critical junctures. The example of foreign policy crises has already been cited (see p. 351 above). Another instance is the tendency to draw around the winner after an election. This is a general norm of American life, as suggested by the fact that most children learn it is desirable at an early age (Hess and Torney, 1965, p. 153). It is not yet clear, despite several studies, that people boost their evaluations of the winning candidate in order to support him. Voters clearly distort their past votes so as to claim having voted for a winner—Key's data are persuasive on this point (1966, p. 14)—and partisan polarization diminishes after an election (Paul, 1956; Raven and Gallo, 1965; Sears and Freedman, 1961; Stricker, 1964); but it is not clear that anything of a more energetically supportive nature happens (and unhappily, relevant survey data do not have adequate preelection baseline measures; *cf.* Katz and Piret, 1964). In fact, one study even suggests that the office of the Presidency is boosted in voters' esteem when their candidate is elected to it, rather than that the candidate gets an added boost of support by becoming President (Hetherington and Carlson, 1964). Data from another study (Anderson and Bass, 1967) indicate that postelection changes represent primarily an increase for the winner and a loss for the loser in perceived political power and influence, and a slightly more favorable evaluation of the winner. There was little evidence of evaluative depolarization regarding the three 1964 electoral contests investigated by Anderson and Bass. However, elections are rather pallid stimuli for evoking latent supportive attitudes.

Positivity in political evaluation

These data reopen the question of political evaluation. On the basis of partisanship, one could expect political persons and groups to be evaluated according to relevant predispositions. However, partisanship only insists that the preferred side be evaluated more favorably than the nonpreferred. Conceivably, both sides could be approved, both disapproved, or the former approved and the latter disapproved. These three alternatives would lead to quite different consequences, according to the cognitive consistency theories (and the substantial empirical support behind them). For example, if both are generally approved, one would expect better compliance with governmental policy. It would also imply that even the nonpreferred party and its leadership would normally command respect and possess some credibility in the eyes of its opponents. This might facilitate governmental succession; it would certainly enhance the persuasive power of the "outs" (and thus perhaps their ability to block programs they oppose); and it should increase the variability of electoral outcomes, by making it not very disagreeable to cross from one party to the other. So is there any evidence of systematic biases one way or the other in political evaluations?

Political persons. The regular Gallup polls ask citizens whether they approve or disapprove of the job the President is doing. These ratings are almost invariably positive (Bell, Hill, and Wright, 1961, p. 136; Dahl, 1967, p. 107); that is, more people

TABLE 27

PERCENTAGE OF RESPONDENTS MAKING ANY FAVORABLE OR
UNFAVORABLE REFERENCES TO EACH PRESIDENTIAL CANDIDATE IN 1952

	Favorable	*Unfavorable*	*Difference*
References to Eisenhower			
Eisenhower voters ($N = 687$)	89%	33%	+56%
Stevenson voters ($N = 494$)	53	67	−14
Total sample ($N = 1614$)	68	45	+23
References to Stevenson			
Eisenhower voters ($N = 687$)	38%	57%	−19%
Stevenson voters ($N = 494$)	70	19	+51
Total sample ($N = 1614$)	47	35	+12

Source: Campbell, Gurin, and Miller, 1954, pp. 53–54. References elicited in response to four open-ended questions, for example, "Is there anything in particular about (Stevenson) (Eisenhower) that might make you want to vote (for) (against) him?" Data are from the 1952 Survey Research Center election study.

say they "approve" than "disapprove" (the major exceptions have been Truman and Johnson, bogged down in Asian wars toward the ends of their terms). Even Presidential candidates are normally rated positively. In 1952 more respondents in the Survey Research Center sample made favorable references to each candidate than made unfavorable references. For Eisenhower the excess was 23 percent and for Stevenson, 12 percent (Campbell, Gurin, and Miller, 1954, pp. 53–54). (See Table 27.)

This has been a characteristic pattern in the period during which such ratings have been gathered. In fact, experienced poll watchers (Becker and Heaton, 1967, p. 349) report surprise when as many as 37 percent report unfavorable evaluations of a candidate (former Governor Peabody of Massachusetts).

From 1952 through 1964 all major-party Presidential candidates were rated positively, on balance, except Stevenson in 1956 (who was rated about neutral) and Goldwater in 1964 (sharply negative) (Stokes, 1966b). There are other counterexamples, of course. In June 1967, a Gallup poll showed segregationist ex-governor George Wallace of Alabama rated favorably by only 24 percent and unfavorably by 58 percent nationwide. But apparent negative evaluations are often not what they seem. A survey was done of Boston voters during the 1959 mayoralty election, at a time when Boston voters were popularly said to be quite alienated and cynical. Yet when voters were asked for their impressions of the candidates, the number who failed to make unfavorable comments exceeded those who failed to make favorable comments (Levin, 1960, pp. 39–42).

A rough idea of the extent of this bias toward favorable ratings is given by data collected from 350 college students in October 1963 and June 1964. They were given a list of 16 American politicians, eight from each party. They tended to rate most leaders of their own party as acceptable, but only about half of those from the opposite party as objectionable (Sears, 1965a). Similar results were obtained in 1960 and 1961 during a follow-up study of Bennington graduates (Newcomb *et al.*, 1967, p. 24).

This may indicate a general skewness in American political evaluations, whereby leaders of one's own party are rated favorably but the opposition is not rated sharply negatively. Lane (1965a, p. 885) separated "approval" ratings of Eisenhower, Kennedy, and Johnson by the respondent's party preference. He found extremely high approval by the leader's own party, of course, but a consistent majority from the opposite party also "approved" Presidential performance. Among Republicans in 1962, 56 percent approved, and only 19 percent disapproved, "of the way Adlai Stevenson is handling his job as ambassador to the U.N." (Hero, 1966, p. 449), despite their rough treatment of him as a Presidential candidate a few years earlier. Converse and Dupeux (1966, p. 325) ascribed this phenomenon to the entry of nonpolitical heroes into political life, but it seems to be far more general than that.

Even in aggrieved circumstances, Americans seem generally to evaluate their politicians favorably. In the survey of Watts residents shortly after the 1965 riot, 586 Negro respondents were asked to evaluate 13 elected officials ranging from the President to a local school board member. Only two were evaluated negatively: the Mayor of Los Angeles, who had been notoriously unsympathetic to Negro demands, and a Republican United States Senator (the sample was 84 percent Democratic and two percent Republican). Even so, neither was as sharply negatively evaluated as the others were positively evaluated. For example, positive ratings exceeded negative ones by 92 percent for President Johnson and 43 percent for a Negro member of the Los Angeles School Board. Negative ratings exceeded positive ones by 41 percent for Mayor Yorty and only 12 percent for Senator George Murphy (Sears, 1967).

Particularly revealing in this study are data from another sample from which particular hostility might be expected. Interviews were conducted with 124 Negro respondents who had been arrested during the rioting. While not all had been criminally active in the riot, a substantial number had been, and there is other evidence that they were unusually hostile (Sears and McConahay, 1967a; Sears and Tomlinson, 1968). Yet they too generally rated leading white Democrats and local Negro elected officials positively (Sears, 1967). Again only two of 13 politicians were rated unfavorably, on balance.

Thus two conclusions stand out. Most people are favorable to their own candidate and many are unfavorable to his opponent. However, they tend to be more positive about their candidate than they are negative about the opposition. Thus, both candidates are rated positively overall if we consider the average of supporters' views and opponents' views. Second, the proportion of negative references is not only smaller than the proportion of positive references, but it is low in absolute terms. In 1952, 50 percent made no negative comments at all about Eisenhower and 61 percent made none about Stevenson (Campbell, Gurin, and Miller, 1954, p. 61).

The political parties. The same predominance of positive evaluations (or bias toward "positivity," to use Zajonc and Burnstein's term, 1965) holds, but much less impressively, for the political parties. In 1952, each set of partisans made more favorable than unfavorable references to its own party, and the reverse was true for the opposition; the balance was slightly on the positive side (Campbell, Gurin, and Miller, 1954, p. 43). Both remained positive until 1964, when the Republicans became

TABLE 28

EVALUATIONS OF POLITICAL PARTIES BY LOS ANGELES NEGROES

	Positive	Negative	Difference	N
Democratic party				
Strong Democrats	97%	3%	+94%	302
Weak or Independent Democrats	98	2	+96	127
Independents, Republicans	81	19	+62	16
Republican party				
Strong Democrats	32%	68%	−36%	282
Weak or Independent Democrats	39	61	−22	111
Independents, Republicans	63	37	+26	19

Source: Unpublished data from Los Angeles Riot Study. Data collected in late 1965 and early 1966. Positive responses to the question, "How good a job is X doing?" were "does well" or "does fairly well." Negative responses were "does nothing" or "does harm."

negative as a result of Barry Goldwater and his bellicose image (Campbell, 1966b). The highly partisan Watts sample evaluated the Democratic party positively, on balance, and the Republican Party negatively. Yet negative feeling about the latter was not nearly so marked as was positive feeling about the Democratic Party, as shown in Table 28.

Data on other politically relevant reference groups are not easy to come by. Freeman and Showel (1951) collected data on how willing people would be to take voting advice from various voluntary associations, but only in rank-order form. Gallup has now and then reported evaluations of such associations. One in 1965 yielded positive ratings for the ADA, DAR, AMA, and FBI; CORE was neutral, the NAACP slightly negative, and only the Ku Klux Klan and the Birch Society were highly negative. Ratings of the major civil rights groups have been gathered from samples of Negroes. Marx (1967, pp. 26–27) reported that only the Black Muslims consistently received negative evaluations from Negroes in New York, Chicago, Atlanta, Birmingham, and a "metropolitan sample" representative of metropolitan Negroes generally. In Watts, Negroes gave overwhelmingly positive evaluations of all civil rights groups (NAACP, 95 percent positive; Urban League, 83 percent; SNCC, 60 percent; CORE, 80 percent; and Martin Luther King's SCLC, 83 percent). Again, the Muslims were not viewed so favorably, only 30 percent rating them positively (Sears, 1967). Campbell and Schuman (1968) obtained very similar results in their 1968 survey of Negroes in 15 cities for the Kerner Commission.

Partisanship and positivity around the globe. Almond and Verba (1963) have presented some data on this combined pattern of partisanship and positivity in ratings of the nonpreferred party in four other nations. Each respondent was told, "We're interested in what sorts of people support and vote for the different parties," and was given a list of statements and asked to choose those most appropriate for describing the supporters of the competing parties in his own country. The overwhelming tendency was to attribute favorable qualities to supporters of the respondent's party

TABLE 29

EXCESS OF POSITIVE OVER NEGATIVE STATEMENTS
IN DESCRIPTIONS OF NONPREFERRED PARTY

	Evaluating party of left	*Evaluating party of right*	*Both*
U.S.A.	+ 53%	+ 40%	+ 45%
United Kingdom	− 22	− 6	− 14
Germany	+ 17	− 4	+ 8
Italy	− 72	− 41	− 68
Mexico	− 31	− 5	− 9

Source: Almond and Verba, 1963, p. 131. Respondents selected descriptive statements from a prepared list. Some respondents selected more than one. The entries are based on at least 700 statements from each nation.

and less favorable ones to the opposition. However, the ratings of the opposition parties are most interesting to us here, and are shown in Table 29. Obviously, the outcome is quite variable across nations and even within nations. Americans think unusually well of the supporters of the opposite party. In Italy, where apparently the most hostility toward the opposition exists, religious and party differences are highly correlated, and this contributes to the severity of cleavage.

Another index of antagonism toward the opposition is the extent to which the respondent would feel pleased or displeased with the marriage of his child across party lines. Here the responses are considerably more uniform across countries. Except in Mexico, people feel more pleased about an intraparty marriage than displeased about an interparty marriage. Americans, again, seem to be the least displeased with the opposition.

These differences might suggest some emotional blandness regarding partisan conflict in this country. This does not seem to be the case. Rather, the American respondents claimed more emotional reactivity of every sort in partisan conflicts than did respondents of any of the other nations, and far more than the average (Almond and Verba, 1963, p. 146). Thus, United States citizens seem to be relatively emotionally involved in their partisanship, but are unusually accepting of the opposition.

Influence of parties and politicians. As indicated above, the importance of a pattern of "positivity" would lie in its consequences for how readily groups and leaders could influence both their followers and the general public. So, what kind of influence do they generally have over political opinions?

One could think of three alternative hypotheses about the direction of influence parties and leaders might have when they take a position. First, if simple partisanship was the rule, one's own party would generally have positive influence, and the opposite party negative influence. Or, if people are in fact generally cynical about the parties and about politicians, perhaps both parties and their leaders would have negative influence. But the implication of the general bias toward positive evaluations of political persons and groups is that one's own party would have much more positive influence than the opposition would have negative influence. The opposition might have some slight positive or negative influence, but the main effect would be the clear positive influence of the preferred party. Presumably, the same hypotheses would hold for political leaders.

To test this hypothesis, 228 college students were tested in a simple experimental situation over a period extending from April 1963 through December 1964 (Sears, 1965a, 1965b). The main goal was to determine the kind of influence the parties and politicians generally have in political opinion formation. Each subject was given a series of trials, on each of which he was presented with a hypothetical situation in which one or both political parties took positions on an unspecified bill before Congress. The subject then indicated his own opinion on the "bill," knowing nothing beyond how one or both parties stood on it. Other subjects were presented with positions taken by one or two well-known political leaders.

The "positivity" hypothesis was broadly sustained throughout the data. The positions taken by each party, when the other party's positions were unknown, positively influenced a majority of the subjects. Fifty-six percent were positively influenced by their own party when its positions were given, and by the opposite party when its positions were given. The simple partisan response (that is, being positively influenced by their own party, but negatively influenced by the opposition) was given by 24 percent of the subjects. The hypothesis of general cynicism must also be rejected; only one percent were negatively influenced by their own party.

The bias toward positivity also emerged when subjects were presented with the positions of political leaders. As indicated earlier, a majority of the political leaders had been rated as "acceptable" (including about half the leaders from the opposition party) rather than "objectionable" in a premeasure. In the experimental situation, the "acceptable" leaders by and large had positive influence, while "objectionable" leaders had negative influence. Thus a substantial number of leaders from the opposite party, and almost all the leaders from the preferred party, had positive influence. Of course, the most extreme opposition leaders (for example, Robert Welch and Barry Goldwater, for Democratic subjects) had clear negative influence.

The bias toward positivity came through even more clearly when the subjects were given the positions of both parties or of two political leaders on any given issue. Eighty-seven percent were positively influenced by both parties' positions under such circumstances, and only five percent were positively influenced by their own party and negatively influenced by the opposition. The same kind of finding held with political leaders.

A closer look at these situations in which two sources' positions were given reveals two quite different processes. When the opposition agreed with the position taken by the preferred party or leader, the position was not given the "kiss of death"; rather, its plausibility was enhanced. This supports Dahl's observation (1961, p. 316) that the public assumes that agreement between political authorities indicates everything is all right. One can imagine being suspicious of such agreements, thinking that the leadership is in collusion against the public or that the representative of one's own party has "sold out." However, Americans evidently do not think that way, if these students are representative in this respect; they assume that agreement is good.

On the other hand, when the "acceptable" opposition leaders, or the nonpreferred party, disagree with the preferred party or leader's position, it weakens support for that position. The subject tends to compromise between the two positions, though naturally he lines up closer to the preferred party or leader. This exaggerated power of the moderate opposition (which is much less clear for the extreme opposition) suggests again that Americans do not feel entirely comfortable with intrasystemic disagreements or with the partisan party system in general. They do not take disagreement between the parties necessarily as indicating that their party is right and the opposition is wrong. Rather, they settle somewhere between the most visible partisan rivals.

Communication content. If people have more positive than negative political attitudes, probably the communications environment is also skewed in this direction. Lane (1959b, p. 291) concluded from a number of content analyses that positive, supportive themes are more typical of media content during election campaigns than is negative, critical material. Similarly, in 1960 each candidate gave more positive than negative material in the first three debates and in two major speeches (their acceptance speech and a major speech on farm policy). In the last debate, however, both candidates emitted more criticism than positive arguments; in this respect, it resembled propaganda in the 1940 campaign, which became increasingly negative toward the end (Lazarsfeld, Berelson, and Gaudet, 1948, p. 111). Also, criticism was more characteristic of the debates than the speeches, and was made more frequently by the challenger, Kennedy, than by Nixon, the member of the incumbent administration (Ellsworth, 1965).

Finally, there is some evidence that people generally prefer positive messages to negative messages. This preference appears to decline with greater information levels; that is, the more informed people tend to prefer negative messages (Freedman and Sears, 1965; Sears, 1966). This, too, parallels the report that campaign propaganda became more negative as the campaign wore on, presumably as the voters became better informed.

Explanations for positivity. This bias toward positive evaluations has not received much direct attention, and therefore no conclusive explanation is available for it at this stage; the following merely represent some good possibilities.

Two possible explanations are specifically political. First, partisan dispositions may focus on the favored object rather than the nonfavored one; that is, partisanship is based on favoring the preferred, rather than opposing the nonpreferred. This would seem to follow from the pattern of attitude acquisition by exposure to only one side, as suggested earlier in connection with chauvinism. Thus, reactions to the nonpreferred are naturally more variable. McGrath and McGrath (1962) did find greater variance in ratings of the nonpreferred Presidential candidate than in ratings of the preferred one. Sigel (1964) reported that the image of the preferred candidate was highly correlated with the image of the "ideal candidate," whereas the image of the nonpreferred candidate was not significantly correlated with the "ideal" one way or the other. A second possible explanation is that political officials and parties have some credibility by virtue of being authorities, even if they are known to be biased. Thus, even the opposition is likely to be correct on occasion just because it is well-informed.

There is probably some truth in both of these explanations, but the positivity bias has also been noted in a variety of nonpolitical experimental situations. Anderson and Jacobson (1965) found subjects rejecting a negative description more readily than a positive description when, in an impression-formation situation, it contradicted the other information at their disposal. Zajonc and Burnstein (1966) found it easier for subjects to learn triadic relationships between positively related hypothetical stimulus persons than between negatively related persons. In attitude-change experiments, Kelman and Eagly (1965) and Manis (1961) both failed to find contrast effects for negative or low-prestige communicators, as would be expected from consistency theories.

Three other explanations are more general, and might apply to political and non-political evaluations alike. One is that positive evaluations simply provide more information in opinion-formation situations. Hovland (1952) has applied this hypothesis to concept-formation situations. A second is that Americans, at least, feel some trepidation about intrasystemic conflict. This begins with early socialization experiences, which stress positive rather than negative affects. To illustrate, Lane (1965b, p. 748) offered several popular phrases (for example, "boost, don't knock," "accentuate the positive") and concluded that the "good citizen" role does not include criticism. Hess and Torney (1967, p. 89) showed that only beginning about fourth or fifth grade do substantial numbers of children begin to express negative affect about the victory of the opposition candidate in an election. This affect increases with age and, in fact, older people may be rather negativistic. The positivity effect in the non-political experiments cited depended on the subjects' rejecting negative affects, and especially on their rejecting consistency when it involved interpersonal conflict. Lane (1962, Chapter 21) is talking about much the same thing when he refers to "the lost sense of evil." His working-class interviewees did not convey a sense of moralized politics. They were reluctant to blame people or to choose scapegoats, and would rather see things as beyond political leaders' control. A third is that favorable attitudes are a simple function of exposure. Hence people feel most positively toward those ideas with which they are most familiar (Greenwald and Sakumura, 1967; Zajonc, 1968). Because of *de facto* selective exposure (Sears and Freedman, 1967), people tend regularly to be exposed more to one side than to its opposite, and thus develop mainly positive attitudes supporting that side.

Attachment to the President: the assassination of John F. Kennedy

The President seems to play an especially central role in Americans' attitudes toward their political system. He initially symbolizes the concept of government for young children (Greenstein, 1960, 1965b; Hess and Easton, 1960). Lipset suggested, with particular reference to George Washington, that a charismatic leader is necessary in new nations to act "as a symbol which represents and prolongs the feeling of unity developed prior to the achievement of independence" (1963a, p. 23). The material reviewed earlier suggested that affects are especially likely to become invested in political persons.

Perhaps this was most vividly demonstrated in the assassination of President Kennedy. The subsequent public grief and emotionality was extreme relative to the deaths of any comparable non-Presidential persons. Fortunately, good data on these reactions exist from a nationwide NORC survey which was conducted almost entirely within eight days of his death (Sheatsley and Feldman, 1965). A considerable number of other studies were published, mostly in collections edited by Greenberg and Parker (1965) and by Wolfenstein and Kliman (1965).

Attention. Considering the public's normally low level of interest in public affairs, the attention paid to the assassination was phenomenal. The *median* time spent watching television or listening to the radio was at least eight hours on each of the four days following the President's death. This, of course, does not include time spent reading newspapers or talking with friends. A significant minority was completely immersed in the events; about a quarter of the people devoted 13 or more hours per day to radio and television. Even the "know-nothings" were attentive to this event; as already indicated, 99.8 percent reported having heard of the event within five hours of its occurrence.

Profound emotional upset. Most American citizens reported that they were profoundly emotionally upset by the assassination. Most (54 percent) said they did not continue with their normal activities, and only 19 percent said they were able to carry on "pretty much as usual." Thirty percent said they were "*more* upset than most people," as opposed to eight percent who said that they were less upset than most. A majority "could not recall any other time in their lives when they had the same sort of feelings," and of those who could, most referred to the death of a parent, close friend, or other relatives (Sheatsley and Feldman, 1965, p. 154). Most (54 percent) said they "felt like talking with other people about it," while 40 percent "felt more like being by myself." Previous Kennedy supporters felt more like being alone; 51 percent of the Negroes, but only 28 percent of the Southern whites who voted for Nixon in 1960, wanted to be alone (p. 154).

Table 30 summarizes some of the physical and emotional symptoms reported during the four days. It also shows how common the same symptoms were later on, thus giving some kind of baseline. Sheatsley and Feldman (1965, p. 167) concluded, quite justifiably, that "the President's assassination seems clearly to have engaged the 'gut feelings' of virtually every American." This level of involvement is, of course, extraordinary in American public affairs.

Political norms were obeyed. The assassination afforded an opportunity for emotional behavior to overrule "good" civic attitudes. This did not happen. First, and perhaps most important, the response was more personal and emotional than it was political or governmental. Few people said that they were deeply concerned about the country's future or international relations; there was more concern about the Kennedy children than about "how the United States would carry on without its leader" (Sheatsley and Feldman, 1965, p. 156). Even explanations for his assassination, or attributions of the assassin's motives, tended not to be political or ideological, despite Lee Harvey Oswald's glaring political commitment (pp. 163–164).

Due process ruled the day in response to Oswald and Ruby. Only four percent thought Ruby should be punished lightly or set free, less than 20 percent gloated over Oswald's death or regretted that he had not suffered more, and many elaborated on the need for fair trials in both cases (pp. 165, 172).

Idealization of Kennedy. Half the population called Kennedy "one of the two or three best Presidents the country ever had"; only two percent termed him "somewhat below average" or "one of the worst Presidents the country ever had." The public had approved of his performance as President much more modestly prior to his death, according to the regular Gallup poll soundings (Sheatsley and Feldman, 1965, p. 166).

Partisanship. Even those who had opposed Kennedy in 1960 reacted emotionally, but less so. They averaged six to seven hours per day with radio and television. Sixty-two percent of the Southern whites who had opposed Kennedy in 1960 "felt the loss of someone very close and dear," and Table 30 shows that on other dimensions they reacted strongly, but not so strongly as the public as a whole. Dallas residents

TABLE 30

PHYSICAL AND EMOTIONAL SYMPTOMS DURING FOUR DAYS FOLLOWING KENNEDY
ASSASSINATION, COMPARED WITH SYMPTOMS AT TIME OF INTERVIEW

	During four days			At time of interview
Symptom	Nationwide sample	Dallas sample	White Southern Kennedy opponents	Nationwide sample
Felt very nervous and tense	68%	82%	56%	24%
Cried	53	56	34	20
Trouble getting to sleep	48	53	39	18
Kept forgetting things	34	35	22	12
Headaches	25	26	12	9
Upset stomach	22	26	14	5
Lost temper more than usual	19	21	10	4
N	1384	212	138	1384

Sources: Bonjean, Hill, and Martin, 1965, p. 186; Sheatsley and Feldman, 1965, p. 158. Based
on data from surveys in Dallas and nationwide conducted shortly after November 22, 1963.

did not react differently from the nation as a whole, as is also shown in Table 30.
For example, 77 percent "felt angry that any one should do such a terrible deed"
(Sheatsley and Feldman, 1965, p. 188), as opposed to 73 percent of the national
sample (Bonjean, Hill, and Martin, 1965, p. 186; Sheatsley and Feldman, 1965,
p. 156). By almost any standard, Democrats and Kennedy supporters reacted much
more intensely than did Republicans (Greenberg and Parker, 1965, pp. 373–376),
but Verba (1965, p. 357) is probably right in saying that "it would be hard to find
evidence that the crisis was in any important sense a partisan matter." Though adequate data have not yet been presented, it might be hypothesized that such strong
reactions to the King and Robert Kennedy assassinations were less common.

Data on the changes in political partisanship following the assassination reveal
more decreased partisanship by Republicans than by Democrats. Sears (1965a)
compared college students tested immediately before the assassination with comparable students tested two to three weeks afterward. Republicans became less
partisan and were more concerned with observing the moratorium on partisanship.
Democrats, on the other hand, remained as partisan as before, and were even less
willing to use the Republican party as a reference group. The main effect on Democrats was that they became more sensitive to the expression of opposition by either
party and by previously objectionable opposition leaders. Perhaps this anticipated
President Johnson's "politics by consensus." According to national poll data, public
approval of bills advocated by both Presidents increased rather sharply; an example
is the public accommodations bill, which had been rather stable for some time prior
to the assassination.

The assassination, as Verba (1965) has noted, seemed to arouse a diffuse emotional commitment to something. It is not clear whether it was specific to Kennedy

or not, but previous assassinations or Presidential deaths seem to have aroused similar feelings (Sheatsley and Feldman, 1965). This need not necessarily relate to the institution of the Presidency, but in some important sense the President does in fact symbolize the nation. Greenstein (1965b) speaks of the President in similar terms, especially as symbolizing national unity, stability, and predictability. The extent to which our commitment to the nation is focused on or symbolized by the President still remains unclear; it is possible to disapprove of the President (and occasionally even vote him out of office), but his death is the occasion for mass intense national mourning.

Finally, the grief focused both upon the President and upon the man. Again, the men in political life seem to be the most vivid content in public opinion (and note Stokes and Miller's observation, 1962, that the women are even more vivid, simply because they are more unusual).

CONSENSUS AND DEMOCRATIC PRINCIPLES

It is possible that attachment to the political system is based on a general consensus among American citizens about basic democratic principles. Is there such a consensus? The clearest data come from three surveys done in the 1950's: a nationwide survey of 4933 citizens (Stouffer, 1955), a survey of 244 registered voters in the two academic communities of Ann Arbor, Michigan and Tallahassee, Florida (Prothro and Grigg, 1960), and a nationwide mail-return survey of 1484 respondents (McClosky, 1964). The latter two samples overrepresented the highly educated (and thus should simply overestimate support for democratic principles) but are not otherwise seriously biased.

The general public

At a very broad, general level, the American public is overwhelmingly agreed on general democratic principles regarding majority rule, minority rights, freedom of speech, and the superiority of democracy as a form of government. Prothro and Grigg (1960) reported that over 95 percent of their samples agreed with each of the following statements: "Democracy is the best form of government," "Public officials should be chosen by majority vote," and "The minority should be free to criticize majority decisions." McClosky (1964) found 89 percent agreeing that "I believe in free speech for all no matter what their views might be."

The public is not so agreed upon specific procedural rules. Prothro and Grigg found that 79 percent would restrict voting to taxpayers, and 51 percent to the well-informed. Other data of this kind are shown in Table 31. A surprisingly large number endorsed such obviously totalitarian (but admittedly ambiguous) principles as permitting the abolition of minorities. The authors noted hopefully that a Negro ran (unsuccessfully) for mayor of Tallahassee, without a peep of protest, shortly after 42 percent had agreed in their survey that "a Negro should not be allowed to run for mayor of this city." However, in more recent cases, Negro legislators have been forbidden to serve under rather ambiguous circumstances, a fact which suggests that such attitudes are implemented on occasion.

Specific applications of freedom of speech have a special importance, since they must contradict the well-documented human tendency for people *not* to tolerate

TABLE 31

PERCENTAGE OF RESPONDENTS SUPPORTING RULES OF THE GAME

	General public	*Convention delegates*
"In dealing with dangerous enemies like the Communists, we can't afford to depend on the courts, the laws, and their slow and unreliable methods" (disagree)	74%	93%
"The majority has the right to abolish minorities if it wants to" (disagree)	72	93
"People ought to be allowed to vote even if they can't do so intelligently" (agree)	48	66
"Any person who hides behind the laws when he is questioned about his activities doesn't deserve much consideration" (disagree)	24	44
N	1484	3020

Source: McClosky, 1964, pp. 365, 367.

opinions discrepant from their own (*cf.* Festinger, 1950; Hovland, Harvey, and Sherif, 1957). The Bill of Rights extends legal protection to minorities for this reason. The need for such protection is clear from public hostility to free speech in concrete, meaningful situations. The best data are from Stouffer's study (1955); some items are shown in Table 32. Large majorities do not think that Communists or atheists should be allowed to speak publicly, keep their books in the public library, or teach in college. The removal of a book by a known Communist from the public library is favored by 66 percent (Stouffer, 1955, p. 40). Presumably this extravagance would exclude Marx, Lenin, and Sartre, among others. The American sense of "fair play," in 71 percent of the sample, gives a forum to a man whose loyalty has been questioned, but who swears that he has never been a Communist. When it is clear that a man has deviant opinions, however, most people wish to restrict sharply his freedom of speech. This anticipates a theme that will emerge more clearly later. An ostensible virtue of the American political system is its ability to regulate and even protect political conflict. Even so, Americans do not like political conflict.

Political elites

This apparent anomaly has turned attention to the attitudes and behavior of political "elites." Clearly, freedom of speech is protected quite well (if not perfectly) in the United States, but not because of great popular fervor for it. The late V. O. Key, Jr., put the point well: "The longer one frets with the puzzle of how democratic regimes manage to function, the more plausible it appears that a substantial part of the explanation is to be found in the motives that actuate the leadership echelon, the values that it holds, in the rules of the political game to which it adheres" (1961, p. 537).

The best data on the attitudes of elites are from the Stouffer and McClosky studies. In the first, interviews were held with 1500 community leaders holding 14

TABLE 32

PERCENTAGE OF RESPONDENTS SUPPORTING
SPECIFIC APPLICATIONS OF CIVIL LIBERTIES

	General public	Community leaders
Freedom of speech		
"If a man wanted to make a speech in your community favoring government ownership of all the railroads and big industries, should he be allowed to speak, or not?" (yes)	58%	84%
"Consider a man whose loyalty has been questioned before a Congressional Committee, but who swears under oath he has never been a Communist. Should he be allowed to make a speech in your community, or not?" (yes)	70	87
"Suppose an admitted Communist wants to make a speech in your community. Should he be allowed to speak, or not?" (yes)	27	51
Civil liberties for atheists		
"If a person wanted to make a speech in your community against churches and religion, should he be allowed to speak, or not?" (yes)	37%	64%
"If some people in your community suggested that a book he wrote against churches and religion should be taken out of your public library, would you favor removing the book or not?" (no)	35	64
"Should such a person be allowed to teach in a college or university, or not?" (yes)	12	25

Source: Stouffer, 1955, pp. 29, 33, 36, 41. Data are from 1954 Gallup and National Opinion Research Corporation surveys. Total N = 4933.

specific local roles, such as the local political party chairmen, mayor, commander of the American Legion, newspaper publisher, and president of the school boards. McClosky received mailed questionnaires from 3020 delegates (and their alternates) to the two political parties' 1956 national conventions.

Community leaders and convention delegates are vastly more protective of the "rules of the game" and of civil liberties than is the public as a whole, as shown in Tables 31 and 32. Most impressive, though, is Stouffer's (1955, p. 52) finding that *every* one of his 14 categories of leaders was more tolerant than is the general public, measured on a "willingness to tolerate nonconformists" scale. The least tolerant leaders were officers of the Daughters of the American Revolution, but even so, 48 percent were classified as "relatively more tolerant," as opposed to 31 percent of the

TABLE 33

PERCENTAGE OF RESPONDENTS ENDORSING INHUMANE POSITIONS

	General public	Convention delegates
"We might as well make up our minds that in order to make the world better a lot of innocent people will have to suffer"	42%	27%
"To bring about great changes for the benefit of mankind often requires cruelty and even ruthlessness"	31	19
"The true American way of life is disappearing so fast that we may have to use force to save it"	35	13
"Almost any unfairness or brutality may have to be justified when some great purpose is being carried out"	33	13

Source: McClosky, 1964, p. 365. See Table 31 for *N*'s.

general public. Hence, the cleavage between the public and almost any group of its leaders on matters of civil liberties is enormous.

Support for civil liberties and rules of the game is also highly correlated with both age and education independently. For example, 66 percent of the college graduates were "more tolerant," while 16 percent were of those who only went to grade school. Similarly, 47 percent of those aged 21 to 29 were "more tolerant," while only 18 percent of those aged 60 and over were (Stouffer, 1955, pp. 89–90). However, large numbers even of the college-educated are rather undemocratic. Of the college-educated, 38 percent opposed letting the uninformed vote (Prothro and Grigg, 1960) and 23 percent favored forbidding a speech against religion (Stouffer, 1955). Prothro and Grigg reached the discouraging conclusion that on only three of ten items is there a consensus among those with some college education on support of specific application of procedural rights.

Finally, it is encouraging to note that political influentials are less cruel and inhumane than the general public, as well as more committed to formal democratic principles. Some data given by McClosky (1964) are shown in Table 33. This dimension, incidentally, has not received very much research attention, though it would seem to be of substantial intrinsic interest.

What these data add up to, as Dahl (1961, p. 312) has noted, is that Americans are agreed on general principles, but not on specific applications. In fact, on many matters a majority holds views contrary to the rules of the game actually followed in the political system. There is much higher agreement on democratic norms in the "political stratum" than among voters in general. Yet even there the agreement is not overwhelmingly high.

It should be noted that the operation of the political system depends to a very great extent on the attitudes and behavior of "elites," that is, those who actively participate in political life beyond mere voting. The study of elites is a rapidly growing and fascinating area, and perhaps no less fascinating are those questions that try to explain political decisions as a complex function of elite dispositions, role requirements, and public opinion. Both of these areas are well beyond the scope of this chapter. It should be made very clear, however, that public opinion's lukewarm zeal for dissent, minorities, or deviant behavior does not imply that the national policy is one of intolerance. The United States has a mixed record in most of these matters, but a considerably better one than the rest of the human race.

AMBIVALENCE ABOUT POLITICAL CONFLICT

Despite their approval for government, Americans tend to be somewhat cynical about politicians. This unfavorable attitude may be part of a more general distaste for political conflict. For example, pressure groups and "lobbyists" have long had a notoriously bad reputation. Prothro and Grigg (1960) noted that only 45 percent of their sample agreed that "a professional organization like the AMA has a right to try to increase the influence of doctors by getting them to vote as a bloc in elections." Sigel (1966, p. 129) asked whether various groups had "a right" to try to make the President change his mind on a matter of public policy after he has made it up. Majorities felt Congress, the cabinet, or the public had the right, but only 21 percent thought "business leaders and union leaders" did.

Even the hallowed American party system is not thoroughly reputable. Dennis (1966) has analyzed attitudes toward the party system in terms of general or diffuse support for the principle, and support for the norm of partisanship ("people can and ought to take opposing sides on political matters, and there should be regular means for doing so"; p. 601). His data are based on various items presented to a probability sample ($N = 702$) of Wisconsin residents in 1964.

As with other elements of democratic ideology, a majority supported the general principle of the party system. About two-thirds agreed that "people who work for parties during political campaigns do our nation a great service," that "democracy works best where competition between parties is strong," and disagreed that "it would be better if, in all elections, we put no party labels on the ballot" (Dennis, 1966, pp. 602–603). However, support again does not extend beyond these vague statements of general principle. Some representative items are given in Table 34. They indicate that a substantial majority feels the parties confuse people, hurt the country, and that things would be better if the parties did not take opposite stands quite so often. As Dennis says, "party competitiveness is desired only at an abstract level" (p. 608).

Correlations between these attitudes and demographic variables tend to be on the low side. Most noteworthy, perhaps, is that general support (as indexed by such items as those given at the top of Table 34) is higher among the young and better educated. This recalls Stouffer's (1955) finding that tolerance on matters of civil liberties is also substantially greater among the young and the well-educated. These groups may be better able to tolerate deviation or conflict in general, though, if so, it is not clear why.

It appears, then, that America's "ambivalence toward politics" is quite circumscribed. It crops up in some cynicism about the motives of politicians and in negative attitudes toward deviation or conflict. The bulk of Americans cannot be said to support the civil liberties of those who disagree with them, nor are they happy with the idea that politics should always be an arena of conflict. These negative attitudes toward partisanship do not necessarily transfer to the actual use of partisan persons or

TABLE 34

PERCENTAGE OF RESPONDENTS HOLDING FAVORABLE
AND UNFAVORABLE ATTITUDES TOWARD THE PARTY SYSTEM

	Favorable	*Unfavorable*
General support		
"The conflicts and controversies between the parties hurt our country more than they help it"	35%	47%
"The parties do more to confuse the issues than to provide a clear choice on them"	21	54
"The best rule in voting is to pick the man regardless of his party label"	10	82
Norm of partisanship		
"Democracy works best where competition between parties is strong"	68%	12%
"Things would be better if the parties took opposite stands on issues more than they do"	31	43
"Our system of government would work a lot more efficiently if we could get rid of conflicts between the parties altogether"	34	53

Source: Dennis, 1966, pp. 605–606. Data are from a 1964 probability sample of Wisconsin, $N = 702$. The rows include all those expressing an opinion.

groups as bases for opinion formation, as indicated earlier. But there remains constant pressure to move political life to a more monolithic, consensual, majoritarian basis. The question, then, is whether or not the American political culture transmits a systematic set of norms of this kind to children.

The rational-independent norm

As they get older, children increasingly adopt a "rational-independent" norm, according to which the ideal citizen is independent of fixed party loyalties, is primarily candidate-oriented, and "makes up his own mind" in voting rather than being swayed by his parents or others around him. For example, older children seem less attracted to party membership. They increasingly say it is "not too important" or "not important at all" for grown-ups to belong to one of the parties, and the proportion of children who are "Independents" constantly increases throughout the grade school years, whereas the proportion of party adherents stabilizes around grade five. They apparently learn candidate orientation instead. Given the alternatives, "Join a party and always vote for its candidate" or "Not join a party; vote for the men he thinks are best," to describe a "good citizen," 51 percent of the fourth-graders chose candidate orientation, as did 74 percent of the eighth-graders and 87 percent of the teachers (Hess and Torney, 1967, p. 84).

The child also learns that he should "make up his own mind" rather than be socially influenced, as shown in Table 15. Most children thus initially believe that it is all right to take on the parents' preference, but by grade eight they feel it is a bad idea. The main increases are in the proportion saying "make up own mind" and "mass media." The rational independent presumably informs himself about the candidates by attending to the mass media, and then he picks the best man.

Lane's observation, based on his interviews with adults, is similar. He noted that they have a "fear of being influenced," that they are reluctant to attribute their opinions to other people or to groups, that they seem reluctant even to admit seeking advice, and wish to view themselves as independent and responsible for their own opinions. The consequence is that their political opinions seem "parthenogenic" (Lane, 1962, pp. 134, 338, 376).

Those children who adopt the rational-independent norm seem to have a number of coherently related ideas. Relative to those who take a partisan preference, Independents see less difference between the parties, think party membership less important for adults, and believe more in voting for the candidate rather than the party. Also, more of them see "voting" as the symbol of the government, subscribing to what Hess and Torney term the "personal clout illusion" (1967, p. 209).

Teaching of conflict

In each of the respects cited above from the Hess and Torney data, the children's teachers personally support the rational-independent norm more than do even the older children. They do not think party membership is especially important, they are more likely to be political Independents (55 percent claimed to be Independents in the Hess and Torney sample, p. 90; in the nation as a whole, according to Converse, 1966a, p. 13, who used a somewhat different question, less than 30 percent typically claim to be Independents), and they believe more in voting for the candidate than for the party. This does not constitute direct evidence that schools tend to socialize children toward the rational-independent norm, but it seems like a good possibility. There is growing evidence that many of these attitudes hostile to political partisanship and the expression of conflict stem from a simplistic view of the political process taught in elementary and secondary schools.

That the camouflaging of conflict has been normative in American schools in the past is suggested by Jennings and Zeigler's (1968) study of high school teachers. They found that classroom expression of conflict (in terms of speaking favorably or unfavorably about such controversial matters as atheism, civil rights, or the criticism of local officials) is *least* endorsed by those who have been teaching longest, those who were education majors in college, and those teaching in small towns, the South, or the Midwest. The most expressive are the novitiate teachers in the metropolitan school districts—scarcely the carriers of the educational culture.

Litt (1963a) has provided a compelling demonstration of the low salience of political conflict in "civics" classes, and, even more interesting, of how this is especially characteristic of low-status schools. In three New England towns varying in class composition (from predominantly upper-middle class to working class), he interviewed "potential civic and educational influentials" regarding the content of proper civic education courses and did a content analysis of the texts then in use. The primary emphasis mentioned by leaders in all communities and in all texts used was upon "fundamentals of the democratic creed"—the abstract principles of democratic ideology cited by Prothro and Grigg (1960). Themes concerning the conflictful, rather than consensual, aspects of politics were emphasized only slightly by upper-status community leaders and in their texts, and virtually not at all in the others. These referred to "politics as the resolution of group conflict" within agreed-upon rules of the game, and to politics as the use of power and influence by politicians and political officials (as opposed to mechanical allocation of services to citizens). Finally, the upper-status community's leaders and texts emphasized "citizen political participation," whereas the lower-status community's leaders and texts did not.

These data highlight the emphasis placed in American political socialization on a commitment to the American system that in the preadolescent years has rather slim content and stresses consensus, rather than conflict, as the ideal and even normal state of the system. In terms of this limited goal, American children seem to be successfully socialized. However, children do not accept the desirability of intrasystemic conflict, and they appear ambivalent about established mechanisms for channeling and regulating conflict, such as "politicians" and the party system. The schools, for some reason, are overly cautious about this aspect of democratic life. It is worth noting that the schools seem *most* cautious, and most dedicated to minimizing exposure to partisanship and conflict, in those years that seem (see pp. 370–374 above) to be crucial for the development of partisan commitments, roughly grades four through eight.

Some, perhaps, are concerned that too early an exposure to intrasystemic partisan conflict will impair the child's attachment to the system as a whole. This remains to be tested thoroughly. But children who early commit themselves to a party are just as supportive of authority and the nation on a variety of dimensions as are Independents. They are also just as interested in politics, just as concerned and likely to have opinions about specific issues, and so on (Hess and Torney, 1967, pp. 200–203). Participation in school politics on mock elections or other semipolitical activity similarly seems anything but harmful.

Accentuating the positive

As well as minimizing conflict, American political socialization seems to "accentuate the positive." The image children initially have of political authority is highly benevolent as well as powerful, even in aggrieved and depressed subgroups of the population, such as urban Negroes (but evidently not in other such groups, for example, poor whites in Appalachia). Their images of other nationality groups are uniformly more positive than negative (Lambert and Klineberg, 1967, p. 34). There is some evidence that both derive from highly selective teaching; for example, the fact that parents evidently did not transmit their own fears of a conspiracy behind the Kennedy assassination, or that children can assemble facts to describe attractive nationality groups but not those they feel unfavorably toward (pp. 122–125), or that grade school teachers consciously try to emphasize the positive (Hess and Torney, 1967). One highly benign consequence of this pattern of training is that American children apparently like other peoples even when they regard them as highly dissimilar (for example, the Chinese or African Negroes; Lambert and Klineberg, 1967, pp. 144–150). However, the primacy of the positive and consensual may leave the child naive about conflict and cleavage when he becomes more aware of it.

The fearful partisans and positivity

In his interviews with some upper-working-class men, Lane (1962) saw a decline of partisan predispositions as bases for political choice. "One reason for the low political tension . . . in the United States [is that] politics has not been moralized; the parties have not been invested with strong moral feeling; the issues are not seen as moral issues; the political leaders have not been made moral heroes and villains" (p. 344). Almond and Verba (1963) did not find Americans living in a black-and-white political world, as clearly indicated in our discussion of positivity. Americans have relatively strong political feelings but, as Lane says, they are not exclusionist moral feelings—they can like their side, but that does not exclude liking the opponent as well (or having one's daughter marry one). It is not that consistency pressures are inoperative, it is just that they start off from a benign point of general positive evaluations.

Lane suggested a reason for the rational-independent norm in the theme he observed: "the *fear of partisanship,* and its obverse, the search for independence. Where there is conflict, the culture seems to instruct these men, there is probably something to be said for both sides, and the proper course is to *search for middle ground*" (1962, p. 134). This follows, psychologically, when there is something to be said on each side, that is, when each side is evaluated positively.

The uses and abuses of partisanship

In at least one version of the ideals visualized by Americans, all group identifications will disappear in a melting pot, to be replaced by independent thinking and rationalism. Lane's interviewees, mostly of recent Irish, Italian, and Polish descent, tended to view their ethnic ties as illegitimate and transitory (1962, p. 392), and as melting away. Many scholars have been impressed by the persistence of these ties (*cf.* Glazer and Moynihan, 1963; Parenti, 1967; Wolfinger, 1965), but it does seem that the norms of American society are against them.

The political consequences of diffused group identity are to complicate the individual's political thinking, not to unshackle it. In Lane's words, "these men are not speaking of being torn between various attractive or hateful alternatives; they are speaking of uncertainty and doubt. Partisanship might serve as a great clarifier, but these men are not partisan. They are supposed to listen to all sides, to understand some of it, to decide on the merits; but they haven't the time to listen, they haven't the equipment and background to understand, they aren't guided by their experience to a decision" (1962, pp. 34–35).

Given the politically sparse informational environment most Americans live in, what are the political consequences of removing from consideration such a simple cue as party, as in nonpartisan elections? Greenstein (1963, pp. 57–60) has outlined several: "celebrities" become more successful (for example, ex-shortstops, movie actors, or the relatives of famous men); meaningful protest voting is considerably harder to accomplish, because it is more difficult for the voter to comprehend whom to vote for in order to protest; other kinds of factions or interest groups become more powerful, and are perhaps less well known to the voter; incumbency may become even more powerful a variable than it already is (*cf.* Stokes and Miller, 1962); and public opinion may become extremely unstable and volatile, as in Presidential primaries (Abelson, 1968). There is some evidence that the politically irrelevant ethnic label may replace party as the primary cue for the voter when elections are non-partisan (Greenstein, 1963; p. 59; Pomper, 1966). There is indeed much that is unthinking about a simple party-line response to a Presidential campaign, but this may seem sophisticated indeed in comparison to a high school dropout wandering about at the tail end of a ballot among nonpartisan candidates for Superior Court Judge, Office Number Six.

Yet there is some advantage in a system which does not place too great a reliance on party or other group memberships. Lane (1962, p. 32) cited the individual voter's tolerance of ambiguity; he does not instantly see events through the partisan's glasses. Berelson, Lazarsfeld, and McPhee (1954) and Key (1966) saw a considerable advantage in electoral flexibility; changing conditions can be reflected in changing popular expression of opinion when voters are not inflexibly wedded to a particular party (or even a particular ideology). But there seems little doubt that the norms by which American children have typically been socialized do not serve well the goal of training citizens to satisfy their needs through individual or collective action in the political system.

REFERENCES

Abelson, R. P. (1968). Computers, polls, and public opinion—some puzzles and paradoxes. *Transaction, 5*, No. 9, 20–27.

Abelson, R. P., and M. J. Rosenberg (1958). Symbolic psycho-logic: a model of attitudinal cognition. *Behav. Sci., 3*, 1–13.

Agger, R. E. (1959). Independents and party identifiers: characteristics and behavior in 1952. In E. Burdick and A. J. Brodbeck (Eds.), *American voting behavior.* Glencoe, Ill.: Free Press. Pp. 308–329.

Allinsmith, W., and B. Allinsmith (1948). Religious affiliation and politico-economic attitude. *Publ. Opin. Quart., 12*, 377–389.

Almond, G. A., and S. Verba (1963). *The civic culture.* Princeton: Princeton Univ. Press.

Anderson, L. F., and E. Moran (1965). Audience perceptions of radio and television objectivity. In B. S. Greenberg and E. B. Parker (Eds.), *The Kennedy assassination and the American public.* Stanford: Stanford Univ. Press. Pp. 142–146.

Anderson, L. R., and A. R. Bass (1967). Some effects of victory or defeat upon perceptions of political candidates. *J. soc. Psychol., 73*, 227–240.

Anderson, N. H., and S. Hubert (1963). Effects of concomitant verbal recall on order effects in personality impression formation. *J. verb. Learn. verb. Behav., 2*, 379–391.

Anderson, N. H., and A. Jacobson (1965). Effect of stimulus inconsistency and discounting instructions in personality impression formation. *J. Pers. soc. Psychol., 2*, 531–539.

Anderson, T. J., and E. C. Lee (1965). The 1964 election in California. *West. polit. Quart., 18*, 451–474.

———— (1967). The 1966 election in California. *West. polit. Quart., 20*, 535–554.

Andrews, W. G. (1966). American voting participation. *West. polit. Quart., 19*, 639–652.

Armor, D. J., J. B. Giacquinta, R. G. McIntosh, and E. H. Russell (1967). Professors' attitudes toward the Vietnam war. *Publ. Opin. Quart., 31,* 159–175.

Aronson, E., J. A. Turner, and J. M. Carlsmith (1963). Communicator credibility and communication discrepancy as determinants of opinion change. *J. abnorm. soc. Psychol., 67,* 31–36.

Axelrod, R. (1967). The structure of public opinion on policy issues. *Publ. Opin. Quart., 31,* 51–60.

Back, K. W., and K. J. Gergen (1963a). Apocalyptic and serial time orientations and the structure of opinions. *Publ. Opin. Quart., 27,* 427–442.

———— (1963b). Individual orientations, public opinion, and the study of international relations. *Soc. Problems, 11,* 77–87.

Barber, J. A., Jr. (1965). Social mobility and political behavior. Unpublished Ph.D. dissertation, Stanford University.

Beardwood, R. (1968). The new Negro mood. *Fortune, 78,* 146ff.

Becker, J. F., and E. E. Heaton, Jr. (1967). The election of Senator Edward W. Brooke. *Publ. Opin. Quart., 31,* 346–358.

Belknap, G., and A. Campbell (1952). Political party identification and attitudes toward foreign policy. *Publ. Opin. Quart., 15,* 601–623.

Bell, W., R. J. Hill, and C. R. Wright (1961). *Public leadership.* San Francisco: Chandler.

Benham, T. W. (1965). Polling for a presidential candidate: some observations on the 1964 campaign. *Publ. Opin. Quart., 29,* 185–199.

Ben-Zeev, S., and I. S. White (1962). Effects and implications. In S. Kraus (Ed.), *The great debates.* Bloomington: Indiana Univ. Press. Pp. 331–337.

Berelson, B. R., P. F. Lazarsfeld, and W. N. McPhee (1954). *Voting: a study of opinion formation in a presidential election.* Chicago: Univ. of Chicago Press.

Bettelheim, B., and M. Janowitz (1950). *Dynamics of prejudice.* New York: Harper.

———— (1964). *Social change and prejudice.* New York: Free Press.

Blalock, H. M., Jr. (1964). *Causal inferences in nonexperimental research.* Chapel Hill: Univ. of North Carolina Press.

Bloom, B. S. (1964). *Stability and change in human characteristics.* New York: Wiley.

Bogart, L. (1968). No opinion, don't know, and maybe no answer. *Publ. Opin. Quart., 31,* 331–345.

Bonjean, C. M., R. J. Hill, and H. W. Martin (1965). Reactions to the assassination in Dallas. In B. S. Greenberg and E. B. Parker (Eds.), *The Kennedy assassination and the American public.* Stanford: Stanford Univ. Press. Pp. 178–198.

Bradburn, N. M., and D. Caplovitz (1965). *Reports on happiness.* Chicago: Aldine.

Braungart, R. G. (1966). SDS and YAF: backgrounds of student political activists. Paper presented at meeting of the American Sociological Association, Miami.

Brehm, J. W., and A. R. Cohen (1962). *Explorations in cognitive dissonance.* New York: Wiley.

Brink, W., and L. Harris (1964). *The Negro revolution in America.* New York: Simon and Schuster.

———— (1966). *Black and white.* New York: Simon and Schuster.

Bronfenbrenner, U. (1962). Soviet methods of character education: some implications for research. *Amer. Psychologist, 17,* 550–564.

———— (1965). Socialization and social class through time and space. In H. Proshansky and B. Seidenberg (Eds.), *Basic studies in social psychology.* New York: Holt, Rinehart, and Winston. Pp. 349–365.

Burnstein, E. (1967). Sources of cognitive bias in the representation of simple social structures: balance, minimal change, positivity, reciprocity, and the respondent's own attitude. *J. Pers. soc. Psychol., 7,* 36–38.

Campbell, A. (1960). Surge and decline: a study of electoral change. *Publ. Opin. Quart., 24,* 397–418.

———— (1964). Voters and elections: past and present. *J. Politics, 26,* 745–757.

———— (1966a). A classification of presidential elections. In A. Campbell, P. E. Converse, W. E. Miller, and D. E. Stokes, *Elections and the political order.* New York: Wiley. Pp. 63–77.

———— (1966b). Interpreting the presidential victory. In M. C. Cummings, Jr. (Ed.), *The national election of 1964.* Washington, D.C.: Brookings Institution. Pp. 256–281.

Campbell, A., P. E. Converse, W. E. Miller, and D. E. Stokes (1960). *The American voter.* New York: Wiley.

Campbell, A., and H. C. Cooper (1956). *Group differences in attitudes and votes.* Ann Arbor: Univ. of Michigan, Institute for Social Research.

Campbell, A., G. Gurin, and W. E. Miller (1954). *The voter decides.* Evanston, Ill.: Row, Peterson.

Campbell, A., and W. E. Miller (1957). The motivational basis of straight and split ticket voting. *Amer. polit. Sci. Rev., 51,* 293–312.

Campbell, A., and H. Schuman (1968). Racial attitudes in fifteen American cities. In *Supplemental studies for the National Advisory Commission on Civil Disorders.* Washington, D.C.: Government Printing Office.

Campbell, A., and D. E. Stokes (1959). Partisan attitudes and the presidential vote. In E. Burdick and A. J. Brodbeck (Eds.), *American voting behavior.* Glencoe, Ill.: Free Press. Pp. 353–371.

Campbell, A., and H. Valen (1961). Party identification in Norway and the United States. *Publ. Opin. Quart., 25,* 505–525.

Cantril, H. (1965). *The pattern of human concerns.* New Brunswick, N.J.: Rutgers Univ. Press.

Converse, P. E. (1962). Information flow and the stability of partisan attitudes. *Publ. Opin. Quart., 26,* 578–599.

———— (1963a). Attitudes and non-attitudes: continuation of a dialogue. Paper presented at meeting of the International Congress of Psychology, Washington, D.C.

———— (1963b). A major political realignment in the South? In A. P. Sindler (Ed.), *Change in the contemporary South.* Durham, N.C.: Duke Univ. Press. Pp. 195–222.

———— (1964). The nature of belief systems in mass publics. In D. E. Apter (Ed.), *Ideology and discontent.* New York: Free Press. Pp. 206–261.

———— (1966a). The concept of a normal vote. In A. Campbell, P. E. Converse, W. E. Miller, and D. E. Stokes, *Elections and the political order.* New York: Wiley. Pp. 7–39.

———— (1966b). The problem of party distances in models of voting change. In M. K. Jennings and L. H. Zeigler (Eds.), *The electoral process.* Englewood Cliffs, N.J.: Prentice-Hall. Pp. 139–174.

———— (1966c). Religion and politics: the 1960 election. In A. Campbell, P. E. Converse, W. E. Miller, and D. E. Stokes, *Elections and the political order.* New York: Wiley. Pp. 96–124.

Converse, P. E., and A. Campbell (1960). Political standards in secondary groups. In D. Cartwright and A. Zander (Eds.), *Group dynamics* (2nd ed.). Evanston, Ill.: Row, Peterson. Pp. 300–318.

Converse, P. E., A. Campbell, W. E. Miller, and D. E. Stokes (1961). Stability and change in 1960: a reinstating election. *Amer. polit. Sci. Rev., 55,* 269–280.

Converse, P. E., A. R. Clausen, and W. E. Miller (1965). Electoral myth and reality: the 1964 election. *Amer. polit. Sci. Rev., 49,* 321–336.

Converse, P. E., and G. Dupeux (1962). Politicization of the electorate in France and the United States. *Publ. Opin. Quart., 26,* 1–23.

———— (1966). De Gaulle and Eisenhower: the public image of the victorious general. In A. Campbell, P. E. Converse, W. E. Miller, and D. E. Stokes, *Elections and the political order.* New York: Wiley. Pp. 292–345.

Crespi, I. (1965). The structural basis for right-wing conservatism: the Goldwater case. *Publ. Opin. Quart., 29,* 523–543.

Crittenden, J. (1962). Aging and party affiliation. *Publ. Opin. Quart., 26,* 648–657.

———— (1963). Aging and political participation. *West. polit. Quart., 16,* 323–331.

Dahl, R. A. (1961). *Who governs? Democracy and power in an American city.* New Haven: Yale Univ. Press.

———— (1967). *Pluralist democracy in the United States: conflict and consent.* Chicago: Rand McNally.

Dawson, R. E. (1966). Political socialization. In J. A. Robinson (Ed.), *Political Science Annual.* Vol. 1. Indianapolis: Bobbs-Merrill.

Dennis, J. (1966). Support for the party system by the mass public. *Amer. polit. Sci. Rev., 60,* 600–615.

———— (1967). Recent research on political socialization: a bibliography. Unpublished manuscript, Lincoln Filene Center, Tufts University.

Dittes, J., and H. H. Kelley (1956). Effects of different conditions of acceptance upon conformity to group norms. *J. abnorm. soc. Psychol., 53,* 629–636.

Dohrenwend, B. P., and E. Chin-Shong (1967). Social status and attitude toward psychological disorder: the problem of tolerance of deviance. *Amer. sociol. Rev., 32,* 417–432.

Donald, D. (1956). *Lincoln reconsidered* (2nd ed.). New York: Vintage.

Dynes, W. (1967). Education and tolerance: an analysis of intervening factors. *Soc. Forces, 46,* 22–34.

Easton, D., and J. Dennis (1965). The child's image of government. *Ann. Amer. Acad. Polit. Soc. Sci., 361,* 40–57.

Ellsworth, J. W. (1965). Rationality and campaigning: a content analysis of the 1960 presidential campaign debates. *West. polit. Quart., 18,* 794–802.

Erskine, Hazel G. (1961). A revival: reports from the polls. *Publ. Opin. Quart., 25,* 128–139.

———— (1962). The polls: the informed public. *Publ. Opin. Quart., 26,* 669–677.

———— (1963a). The polls: textbook knowledge. *Publ. Opin. Quart., 27,* 133–141.

———— (1963b). The polls: exposure to domestic information. *Publ. Opin. Quart., 27,* 491–500.

———— (1963c). The polls: exposure to international information. *Publ. Opin. Quart., 27,* 658–662.

———— (1965). The polls: religious prejudice, part I. *Publ. Opin. Quart., 29,* 486–496.

Eulau, H. (1962). *Class and party in the Eisenhower years.* Glencoe, Ill.: Free Press.

Ferguson, Jenniellen, and P. J. Hoffmann (1964). Voting behavior: the vote on the Francis amendment in the 1962 California election. *West. polit. Quart., 17,* 770–776.

Feshbach, S., and Norma Feshbach (1965). Personality and political values: a study of reactions to two accused assassins. In B. S. Greenberg and E. B. Parker (Eds.), *The Kennedy assassination and the American public.* Stanford: Stanford Univ. Press. Pp. 289–304.

Festinger, L. (1950). Informal social communication. *Psychol. Rev., 57,* 271–282.

———— (1957). *A theory of cognitive dissonance.* Stanford: Stanford Univ. Press.

Flacks, R. (1967). The liberated generation: an exploration of the roots of student protest. *J. soc. Issues, 23,* 52–75.

Freedman, J. L., and D. O. Sears (1965). Selective exposure. In L. Berkowitz (Ed.), *Advances in experimental social psychology.* Vol. 2. New York: Academic Press. Pp. 58–97.

Freeman, H. E., and M. Showel (1951). Differential political influence of voluntary associations. *Publ. Opin. Quart., 15,* 703–714.

Froman, L. A., Jr., and J. K. Skipper, Jr. (1962). Factors related to misperceiving party stands on issues. *Publ. Opin. Quart., 26,* 265–272.

Fuchs, D. A. (1966). Election-day radio-television and Western voting. *Publ. Opin. Quart., 30,* 226–236.

Gamson, W. A., and A. Modigliani (1966). Knowledge and foreign policy opinions: some models for consideration. *Publ. Opin. Quart., 30,* 187–199.

Gergen, K. J., and K. W. Back (1965). Aging, time perspective, and preferred solutions to international conflicts. *J. Confl. Resol., 9,* 177–186.

———— (1966). Communication in the interview and the disengaged respondent. *Publ. Opin. Quart., 30,* 385–398.

Glazer, N. (1961). *The social basis of American Communism.* New York: Harcourt, Brace.

Glazer, N., and D. P. Moynihan (1963). *Beyond the melting pot.* Cambridge: M.I.T. Press.

Glock, C. Y., and R. Stark (1966). *Christian beliefs and anti-Semitism.* New York: Harper and Row.

Goldberg, A. S. (1966). Discerning a causal pattern among data on voting behavior. *Amer. polit. Sci. Rev., 60,* 913–922.

Goldsen, R. K., M. Rosenberg, R. M. Williams, and E. A. Suchman (1960). *What college students think.* Princeton: Van Nostrand.

Greenberg, B. S., and E. B. Parker (1965). Summary: social research on the assassination. In B. S. Greenberg and E. B. Parker (Eds.), *The Kennedy assassination and the American public.* Stanford: Stanford Univ. Press. Pp. 361–382.

Greenstein, F. I. (1960). The benevolent leader: children's images of political authority. *Amer. polit. Sci. Rev., 54,* 934–943.

―――― (1963). *The American party system and the American people.* Englewood Cliffs, N.J.: Prentice-Hall.

―――― (1965a). *Children and politics.* New Haven: Yale Univ. Press.

―――― (1965b). Popular images of the President. *Amer. J. Psychiat., 122,* 523–529.

―――― (1967). The impact of personality on politics: an attempt to clear away underbrush. *Amer. polit. Sci. Rev., 61,* 629–641.

Greenstein, F. I., and R. W. Wolfinger (1958). The suburbs and shifting party loyalties. *Publ. Opin. Quart., 22,* 473–482.

Greenwald, A. G., and J. S. Sakumura (1967). Attitude and selective learning: where are the phenomena of yesteryear? *J. Pers. soc. Psychol., 7,* 387–397.

Greer, S. (1961). Catholic voters and the Democratic party. *Publ. Opin. Quart., 25,* 611–625.

Grupp, F. W., Jr. (1966). Political activists: the John Birch Society and the ADA. Paper presented at meeting of the American Political Science Association, New York.

Harding, J., B. Kutner, H. Proshansky, and I. Chein (1954). Prejudice and ethnic relations. In G. Lindzey (Ed.), *Handbook of social psychology.* Cambridge, Mass.: Addison-Wesley. Pp. 1021–1061.

Havemann, E., and P. West (1952). *They went to college.* New York: Harcourt.

Heider, F. (1946). Attitudes and cognitive organization. *J. Psychol., 21,* 107–112.

Hennessey, B. (1965). *Public opinion.* Belmont, Calif.: Wadsworth.

Hero, A. O., Jr. (1966). The American public and the U.N. 1954–1966. *J. Confl. Resol., 10,* 436–475.

Hess, R. D. (1963). The socialization of attitudes toward political authority: some cross-national comparisons. *Int. soc. Sci. J., 25,* 542–559.

Hess, R. D., and D. Easton (1960). The child's changing image of the President. *Publ. Opin. Quart., 24,* 632–644.

Hess, R. D., and Judith V. Torney (1965). *The development of basic attitudes and values toward government and citizenship during the elementary school years, part I.* Chicago: Univ. of Chicago.

―――― (1967). *The development of political attitudes in children.* Chicago: Aldine.

Hetherington, E. Mavis, and Mary Carlson (1964). Effects of candidate support and election results upon attitudes to the presidency. *J. soc. Psychol.*, *64*, 333–338.

Hodge, R. W., P. M. Siegel, and P. H. Rossi (1964). Occupation prestige in the United States, 1925–1963. *Amer. J. Sociol.*, *70*, 286–302.

Hodge, R. W., and D. J. Trieman (1966). Occupational mobility and attitudes toward Negroes. *Amer. sociol. Rev.*, *31*, 93–102.

Hofstadter, R. (1955). *The age of reform.* New York: Knopf.

_____ (1963). The pseudo-conservative revolt. In D. Bell (Ed.), *The radical right.* Garden City, N.Y.: Doubleday. Pp. 63–80.

Hovland, C. I. (1952). A "communication analysis" of concept learning. *Psychol. Rev.*, *59*, 461–472.

Hovland, C. I., O. J. Harvey, and M. Sherif (1957). Assimilation and contrast effects in reactions to communication and attitude change. *J. abnorm. soc. Psychol.*, *55*, 244–252.

Hovland, C. I., and W. Weiss (1951). The influence of source credibility on communication effectiveness. *Publ. Opin. Quart.*, *15*, 635–650.

Hyman, H. H. (1959). *Political socialization.* Glencoe, Ill.: Free Press.

Hyman, H. H., and P. B. Sheatsley (1953). The political appeal of President Eisenhower. *Publ. Opin. Quart.*, *17*, 443–460.

_____ (1954). The current status of American public opinion. In D. Katz, D. Cartwright, S. Eldersveld, and A. M. Lee (Eds.), *Public opinion and propaganda.* New York: Holt, Rinehart, and Winston. Pp. 33–48.

Inkeles, A., and P. H. Rossi (1956). National comparisons of occupational prestige. *Amer. J. Sociol.*, *61*, 329–339.

Jacob, P. E. (1957). *Changing values in college: an exploratory study of the impact of college teaching.* New York: Harper.

Janowitz, M., and W. E. Miller (1952). The index of political predisposition in the 1948 election. *J. Politics*, *14*, 710–727.

Jaros, D. (1967). Children's orientations toward the president: some additional theoretical considerations and data. *J. Politics*, *29*, 368–387.

Jaros, D., H. Hirsch, and F. J. Fleron, Jr. (1968). The malevolent leader: political socialization in an American subculture. *Amer. polit. Sci. Rev.*, *62*, 564–575.

Jennings, M. K. (1966). Observations on the study of political values among preadults. Unpublished manuscript, University of Michigan.

_____ (1967). Pre-adult orientations to multiple systems of government. *Midwest J. polit. Sci.*, *11*, 291–317.

_____ (1968). Political values and the family circle. Paper presented at meeting of the American Psychological Association, San Francisco.

Jennings, M. K., M. C. Cummings, Jr., and F. P. Kilpatrick (1966). Trusted leaders: perceptions of appointed federal officials. *Publ. Opin. Quart.*, *30*, 368–384.

Jennings, M. K., and R. G. Niemi (1966). Party identification at multiple levels of government. *Amer. J. Sociol.*, *72*, 86–101.

_____ (1968). The transmission of political values from parent to child. *Amer. polit. Sci. Rev.*, *62*, 169–184.

Jennings, M. K., and L. H. Zeigler (1966a). Class, party, and race in four types of elections: the case of Atlanta. *J. Politics, 28*, 391–407.

_____ (1966b). Electoral strategies and voting patterns in a Southern congressional district. In M. K. Jennings and L. H. Zeigler (Eds.), *The electoral process*. Englewood Cliffs, N.J.: Prentice-Hall. Pp. 122–138.

_____ (1968). Political expressivism among high school teachers: the intersection of community and occupational values. Unpublished manuscript.

Johnson, B. (1962). Ascetic Protestantism and political preference. *Publ. Opin. Quart., 26*, 35–46.

_____ (1964). Ascetic Protestantism and political preference in the deep South. *Amer. J. Sociol., 69*, 359–366.

_____ (1966). Theology and party preference among Protestant clergymen. *Amer. sociol. Rev., 31*, 200–208.

_____ (1967). Theology and the position of pastors on public issues. *Amer. sociol. Rev., 32*, 433–442.

Jones, Charles O. (1966). The role of the campaign in Congressional politics. In M. K. Jennings and L. H. Zeigler (Eds.), *The electoral process*. Englewood Cliffs, N.J.: Prentice-Hall. Pp. 21–41.

Katz, E., and J. J. Feldman (1962). The debates in the light of research: a survey of surveys. In S. Kraus (Ed.), *The great debates*. Bloomington: Indiana Univ. Press. Pp. 173–223.

Katz, F. E., and F. V. Piret (1964). Circuitous participation in politics. *Amer. J. Sociol., 69*, 367–373.

Kelley, H. H. (1955). Salience of membership and resistance to change of group-anchored attitudes. *Hum. Relat., 8*, 275–289.

Kelley, H. H., and T. W. Lamb (1957). Certainty of judgment and resistance to social influence. *J. abnorm. soc. Psychol., 55*, 137–139.

Kelley, H. H., and E. H. Volkhart (1952). The resistance to change of group-anchored attitudes. *Amer. sociol. Rev., 17*, 453–465.

Kelley, H. H., and Christine L. Woodruff (1956). Members' reactions to apparent group approval of a counternorm communication. *J. abnorm. soc. Psychol., 52*, 67–74.

Kelley, S., Jr., R. E. Ayres, and W. G. Bowen (1967). Registration and voting. *Amer. polit. Sci. Rev., 61*, 359–379.

Kelly, K. D., and W. J. Chamblis (1966). Status consistency and political attitudes. *Amer. sociol. Rev., 31*, 375–382.

Kelman, H. C., and A. H. Eagly (1965). Attitude toward the communicator, perception of communication content, and attitude change. *J. Pers. soc. Psychol., 1*, 63–78.

Key, V. O., Jr. (1949). *Southern politics in state and nation*. New York: Vintage.

_____ (1955). A theory of critical elections. *J. Politics, 17*, 3–18.

_____ (1959). Secular realignment and the party system. *J. Politics, 21*, 198–210.

——— (1961). *Public opinion and American democracy.* New York: Knopf.

——— (1966). *The responsible electorate.* Cambridge: Harvard Univ. Press.

Key, V. O., Jr., and F. Munger (1959). Social determinism and electoral decision: the case of Indiana. In E. Burdick and A. J. Brodbeck (Eds.), *American voting behavior.* Glencoe, Ill.: Free Press. Pp. 281–299.

Kingdon, J. W. (1967). Politicians' beliefs about voters. *Amer. polit. Sci. Rev., 61,* 137–145.

Klapper, J. T. (1960). *The effects of mass communications.* Glencoe, Ill.: Free Press.

Koeppen, S. R. (1967). Dissensus and discontent: the clientele of the Christian Anti-Communist Crusade. Unpublished Ph.D. dissertation, Stanford University.

Kohlberg, L. (1963). Moral development and identification. In H. W. Stevenson (Ed.), *Child psychology.* The 62nd Yearbook of the National Society for the Study of Education, Part I. Chicago: Univ. of Chicago Press. Pp. 277–332.

Kohn, M. L. (1963). Social class and parent-child relationships: an interpretation. *Amer. J. Sociol., 68,* 471–480.

Kornhauser, A., H. L. Sheppard, and A. J. Mayer (1956). *When labor votes.* New York: University Books.

Kornhauser, W. (1959). *The politics of mass society.* Glencoe, Ill.: Free Press.

Lambert, W. E., and O. Klineberg (1967). *Children's views of foreign peoples.* New York: Appleton-Century-Crofts.

Lane, R. E. (1959a). Fathers and sons: foundations of political belief. *Amer. sociol. Rev., 24,* 502–511.

——— (1959b). *Political life: why people get involved in politics.* Glencoe, Ill.: Free Press.

——— (1962). *Political ideology: why the American common man believes what he does.* New York: Free Press.

——— (1963). Political science and psychology. In S. Koch (Ed.), *Psychology: a study of a science.* Vol. 6: Investigations of man as socius. New York: McGraw-Hill. Pp. 583–638.

——— (1965a). The politics of consensus in an age of affluence. *Amer. polit. Sci. Rev., 59,* 874–895.

——— (1965b). The tense citizen and the casual patriot: role confusion in American politics. *J. Politics, 27,* 735–760.

Lane, R. E., and D. O. Sears (1964). *Public opinion.* Englewood Cliffs, N.J.: Prentice-Hall.

Langton, K. P. (1967). Peer group and school and the political socialization process. *Amer. polit. Sci. Rev., 61,* 751–758.

Lazarsfeld, P. F., B. Berelson, and Hazel Gaudet (1948). *The people's choice* (2nd ed.). New York: Columbia Univ. Press.

Lenski, G. E. (1954). Status crystallization: a non-vertical dimension of social status. *Amer. sociol. Rev., 19,* 405–413.

——— (1963). *The religious factor.* Garden City, N.Y.: Doubleday.

———— (1967).   Status inconsistency and the vote: a four nation test.   *Amer. sociol. Rev., 32,* 298–301.

Levin, M. B. (1960).   *The alienated voter: politics in Boston.*   New York: Holt, Rinehart, and Winston.

———— (1961).   Social climates and political socialization.   *Publ. Opin. Quart., 25,* 596–606.

Levine, G. N., and J. Modell (1965).   American public opinion and the fallout-shelter issue.   *Publ. Opin. Quart., 29,* 270–279.

Levitt, M. (1967).   Negro student rebellion against parental political beliefs.   *Soc. Forces, 45,* 438–440.

Lipset, S. M. (1960).   *Political man.*   Garden City, N.Y.: Doubleday.

———— (1963a).   *The first new nation.*   New York: Basic Books.

———— (1963b).   Three decades of the radical right: Coughlinites, McCarthyites, and Birchers, 1962.   In D. Bell (Ed.), *The radical right.*   Garden City, N.Y.: Doubleday.   Pp. 313–378.

———— (1966).   Doves, hawks, and polls.   *Encounter, 27,* 38–45.

Lipset, S. M., P. F. Lazarsfeld, A. H. Barton, and J. Linz (1954).   The psychology of voting: an analysis of political behavior.   In G. Lindzey (Ed.), *Handbook of social psychology.*   Vol. 2.   Reading, Mass: Addison-Wesley.   Pp. 1124–1175.

Lipset, S. M., and H. L. Zetterberg (1959).   Social mobility in industrial societies.   In S. M. Lipset and R. Bendix (Eds.), *Social mobility in industrial society.*   Berkeley and Los Angeles: Univ. of California Press.   Pp. 11–75.

Lipsitz, L. (1965).   Working class authoritarianism: a re-evaluation.   *Amer. sociol. Rev., 30,* 103–109.

Lipsitz, L., and J. D. Colfax (1965).   The fate of due process in a time of crisis.   In B. S. Greenberg and E. B. Parker (Eds.), *The Kennedy assassination and the American public.*   Stanford: Stanford Univ. Press.   Pp. 327–335.

Litt, E. (1961).   Ethnic status and political perspectives.   *Midwest J. polit. Sci., 5,* 276–283.

———— (1963a).   Civic education, community norms, and political indoctrination.   *Amer. sociol. Rev., 28,* 69–75.

———— (1963b).   Political cynicism and political futility.   *J. Politics, 25,* 312–323.

Lopreato, J. (1967).   Upward social mobility and political orientation.   *Amer. sociol. Rev., 32,* 586–592.

McClintock, C. G., C. B. Spaulding, and H. A. Turner (1965).   Political orientations of academically affiliated psychologists.   *Amer. Psychologist, 20,* 211–221.

McClosky, H. (1964).   Consensus and ideology in American politics.   *Amer. polit. Sci. Rev., 58,* 361–382.

McClosky, H., and H. E. Dahlgren (1959).   Primary group influence on party loyalty.   *Amer. polit. Sci. Rev., 53,* 757–776.

McClosky, H., P. J. Hoffman, and Rosemary O'Hara (1960).   Issue conflict and consensus among party leaders and followers.   *Amer. polit. Sci. Rev., 54,* 406–427.

Maccoby, Eleanor, R. E. Matthews, and A. S. Morton (1954).   Youth and political change. *Publ. Opin. Quart., 18,* 23–29.

McGrath, J. E., and M. F. McGrath (1962). Effects of partisanship on perceptions of political figures. *Publ. Opin. Quart., 26,* 236–248.

McGuire, W. J. (1964). Inducing resistance to persuasion: some contemporary approaches. In L. Berkowitz (Ed.), *Advances in experimental social psychology.* Vol. 1. New York: Academic Press. Pp. 192–229.

_____ (1966). The current status of cognitive consistency theories. In S. Feldman (Ed.), *Cognitive consistency: motivational antecedents and behavioral consequences.* New York: Academic Press. Pp. 1–46.

McGuire, W. J., and D. Papageorgis (1961). The relative efficacy of various types of prior belief defense in producing immunity against persuasion. *J. abnorm. soc. Psychol., 62,* 327–337.

Manis, M. (1960). The interpretation of opinion statements as a function of recipient attitude. *J. abnorm. soc. Psychol., 60,* 340–344.

_____ (1961). Interpretation of opinion statements as a function of recipient attitude and source prestige. *J. abnorm. soc. Psychol., 63,* 82–86.

Marvick, D. (1965). The political socialization of the American Negro. *Ann. Amer. Acad. Polit. Soc. Sci., 361,* 112–127.

Marx, G. T. (1967). *Protest and prejudice: a study of belief in the black community.* New York: Harper and Row.

Matthews, D. R. (1954). *The social background of political decision-makers.* New York: Random House.

Matthews, D. R., and J. W. Prothro (1966a). The concept of party image and its importance for the Southern electorate. In M. K. Jennings and L. H. Zeigler (Eds.), *The electoral process.* Englewood Cliffs, N.J.: Prentice-Hall. Pp. 139–174.

_____ (1966b). *Negroes and the new Southern politics.* New York: Harcourt, Brace, and World.

Middleton, R., and S. Putney (1963a). Political expression of adolescent rebellion. *Amer. J. Sociol., 68,* 527–535.

_____ (1963b). Student rebellion against parental political beliefs. *Soc. Forces, 41,* 377–383.

_____ (1964). Influences on the political beliefs of American college students: a study of self-appraisals. *Il Politico, 29,* 484–492.

Milbrath, L. W. (1965). *Political participation.* Chicago: Rand McNally.

Miller, N. (1965). Involvement and dogmatism as inhibitors of attitude change. *J. exp. soc. Psychol., 1,* 121–132.

Miller, W. E. (1956). One-party politics and the voter. *Amer. polit. Sci. Rev., 50,* 707–725.

_____ (1964). Majority rule and the representative system of government. In E. Allardt and Y. Littunen (Eds.), *Cleavages, ideologies, and party systems.* Helsinki: The Academic Bookstore. Pp. 343–376.

_____ (1967). Voting and foreign policy. In J. N. Rosenau (Ed.), *Domestic sources of foreign policy.* New York: Free Press. Pp. 213–230.

Miller, W. E., and D. E. Stokes (1966). Constituency influence in Congress. In A. Campbell, P. E. Converse, W. E. Miller, and D. E. Stokes, *Elections and the political order.* New York: Wiley. Pp. 351–372.

Millson, W. A. D. (1932). Problems in measuring audience reaction. *Quart. J. Speech, 18,* 621–637.

Mitchell, W. C. (1959). The ambivalent social status of the American politician. *West. polit. Quart., 12,* 683–698.

Morris, R. T., and V. Jeffries (1967). The white reaction study. Los Angeles Riot Study, Institute of Government and Public Affairs, University of California, Los Angeles.

Mowry, G. E. (1963). *The California progressives.* Chicago: Quadrangle Books.

Murphy, R. J., and R. T. Morris (1961). Occupational situs, subjective class identification, and political affiliation. *Amer. sociol. Rev., 26,* 383–392.

National Advisory Commission on Civil Disorders (1968). *Report of the National Advisory Commission on Civil Disorders.* New York: Bantam.

Newcomb, T. M. (1943). *Personality and social change.* New York: Dryden.

_____ (1953). An approach to the study of communicative acts. *Psychol. Rev., 60,* 393–404.

_____ (1963). Persistence and regression of changed attitudes: long-range studies. *J. soc. Issues, 19,* 3–14.

Newcomb, T. M., Kathryn E. Koenig, R. Flacks, and D. P. Warwick (1967). *Persistence and change: Bennington College and its students after 25 years.* New York: Wiley.

Niemi, R. G. (1967). A methodological study of political socialization in the family. Unpublished Ph.D. dissertation, University of Michigan.

_____ (in press). Collecting information about the family: a problem in survey methodology. In J. Dennis and F. W. Frey (Eds.), *Political socialization: a reader of theory and research.* New York: Wiley.

Noel, D. L., and A. Pinkney (1964). Correlates of prejudice: some racial differences and similarities. *Amer. J. Sociol., 69,* 609–622.

Orren, K., and P. Peterson (1967). Presidential assassination: a case study in the dynamics of political socialization. *J. Politics, 29,* 388–404.

Osgood, C. E. (1962). Studies on the generality of affective meaning systems. *Amer. Psychologist, 17,* 10–28.

Osgood, C. E., and P. Tannenbaum (1955). The principle of congruity and the prediction of attitude change. *Psychol. Rev., 62,* 42–55.

Parenti, M. (1967). Ethnic politics and the persistence of ethnic identification. *Amer. polit. Sci. Rev., 61,* 717–726.

Paul, I. H. (1956). Impressions of personality, authoritarianism, and the fait accompli effect. *J. abnorm. soc. Psychol., 53,* 338–344.

Polsby, N. W. (1963). Toward an explanation of McCarthyism. In N. W. Polsby, R. A. Dentler, and P. A. Smith (Eds.), *Politics and social life.* Boston: Houghton Mifflin. Pp. 809–824.

Pomper, G. (1966). Ethnic and group voting in nonpartisan municipal elections. *Publ. Opin. Quart., 30,* 79–98.

Pool, I., R. P. Abelson, and S. L. Popkin (1964). *Candidates, issues, and strategies.* Cambridge: M.I.T. Press.

Proshansky, H. M. (1966). The development of intergroup attitudes. In Lois W. Hoffman and M. L. Hoffman (Eds.), *Review of child development research.* Vol. 2. New York: Russell Sage Foundation.

Prothro, J. W., and C. W. Grigg (1960). Fundamental principles of democracy: bases of agreement and disagreement. *J. Politics, 22,* 276–294.

Raven, B. H., and P. S. Gallo (1965). The effects of nominating conventions, elections, and reference group identifications upon the perception of political figures. *Hum. Relat., 18,* 217–229.

Rettig, S. (1966). Relation of social systems to intergenerational changes in moral attitudes. *J. Pers. soc. Psychol., 4,* 409–414.

Rogers, W. C., Barbara Stuhler, and D. Koenig (1967). A comparison of informed and general public opinion on U.S. foreign policy. *Publ. Opin. Quart., 31,* 242–252.

Rogin, M. (1966). Wallace and the middle class: the white backlash in Wisconsin. *Publ. Opin. Quart., 30,* 98–108.

Rosenberg, M. J. (1965). Images in relation to the policy process: American public opinion on cold-war issues. In H. C. Kelman (Ed.), *International behavior: a social-psychological analysis.* New York: Holt, Rinehart, and Winston. Pp. 277–334.

Rosi, E. J. (1965). Mass and attentive opinion on nuclear weapons tests and fallout, 1954–1963. *Publ. Opin. Quart., 29,* 280–297.

Ross, J. M., T. Crawford, and T. Pettigrew (1966). Negro neighbors—banned in Boston. *Transaction, 3,* No. 6, 13–18.

Rossi, P. H. (1966). Trends in voting behavior research: 1933–1963. In E. C. Dreyer and W. A. Rosenbaum (Eds.), *Political opinion and electoral behavior.* Belmont, Calif.: Wadsworth. Pp. 67–78.

Rush, G. B. (1967). Status consistency and right-wing extremism. *Amer. sociol. Rev., 32,* 86–92.

Schramm, W., and R. F. Carter (1959). Effectiveness of a political telethon. *Publ. Opin. Quart., 23,* 121–126.

Scoble, H. M. (1963). Political money: a study of contributors to the National Committee for an Effective Congress. *Midwest J. polit. Sci., 7,* 229–253.

Scoble, H. M., and L. D. Epstein (1964). Religion and Wisconsin voting in 1960. *J. Politics, 26,* 381–396.

Scott, W. A. (1958). Rationality and non-rationality of international attitudes. *J. Confl. Resol., 2,* 8–16.

Schuman, H., and J. Harding (1963). Sympathetic identification with the underdog. *Publ. Opin. Quart., 27,* 230–241.

Sears, D. O. (1965a). Effects of the assassination of President Kennedy on political partisanship. In B. S. Greenberg and E. B. Parker (Eds.), *The Kennedy assassination and the American public*. Stanford: Stanford Univ. Press. Pp. 305–326.

―――― (1965b). The influence of opposition parties and leaders. *Amer. Psychologist, 20,* 540. (Abstract)

―――― (1966). Opinion formation and information preferences in an adversary situation. *J. exp. soc. Psychol., 2,* 130–142.

―――― (1967). Political attitudes of Los Angeles Negroes. Los Angeles Riot Study, Institute of Government and Public Affairs, University of California, Los Angeles.

Sears, D. O., and J. L. Freedman (1961). Organizational and judgmental modes of cognitive conflict resolution. *Amer. Psychologist, 16,* 409. (Abstract)

―――― (1967). Selective exposure to information: a critical review. *Publ. Opin. Quart., 31,* 194–213.

Sears, D. O., J. L. Freedman, and E. F. O'Connor, Jr. (1964). The effects of anticipated debate and commitment on the polarization of audience opinion. *Publ. Opin. Quart., 28,* 615–627.

Sears, D. O., and J. B. McConahay (1967a). Riot participation. Los Angeles Riot Study, Institute of Government and Public Affairs, University of California, Los Angeles.

―――― (1967b). The politics of discontent: blocked mechanisms of grievance redress and the psychology of the new urban black man. Los Angeles Riot Study, Institute of Government and Public Affairs, University of California, Los Angeles.

Sears, D. O., and T. M. Tomlinson (1968). Riot ideology in Los Angeles: a study of Negro attitudes. *Soc. Sci. Quart., 49,* 485–503.

Sellers, C. (1965). The equilibrium cycle in two-party politics. *Publ. Opin. Quart., 29,* 16–38.

Selvin, H. C., and W. O. Hagstrom (1960). Determinants of support for civil liberties. *Brit. J. Sociol., 11,* 51–73.

Sheatsley, P. B. (1966). White attitudes toward the Negro. *Daedalus, 95,* 217–238.

Sheatsley, P. B., and J. J. Feldman (1965). A national survey of public reactions and behavior. In B. S. Greenberg and E. B. Parker (Eds.), *The Kennedy assassination and the American public*. Stanford: Stanford Univ. Press. Pp. 149–177.

Sherif, C. W., M. Sherif, and R. E. Nebergall (1965). *Attitude and attitude change: the social judgment-involvement approach*. Philadelphia: W. B. Saunders.

Sigel, Roberta S. (1964). Effect of partisanship on the perception of political candidates. *Publ. Opin. Quart., 28,* 483–496.

―――― (1965). An exploration into some aspects of political socialization: school children's reactions to the death of a president. In Martha Wolfenstein and G. Kliman (Eds.), *Children and the death of a president*. Garden City, N.Y.: Doubleday. Pp. 30–61.

―――― (1966). Image of the American presidency: part II of an exploration into popular views of presidential power. *Midwest J. polit. Sci., 10,* 123–137.

―――― (1968). Image of a president: some insights into the political views of school children. *Amer. polit. Sci. Rev., 62,* 216–226.

Stember, C. H. (1961). *Education and attitude change.* New York: Institute of Human Relations.

Stokes, D. E. (1963). Spatial models of party competition. *Amer. polit. Sci. Rev., 57,* 368–377.

———— (1966a). Party loyalty and the likelihood of deviating elections. In A. Campbell, P. E. Converse, W. E. Miller, and D. E. Stokes, *Elections and the political order.* New York: Wiley. Pp. 125–135.

———— (1966b). Some dynamic elements of contests for the presidency. *Amer. polit. Sci. Rev., 60,* 19–28.

Stokes, D. E., A. Campbell, and W. E. Miller (1958). Components of electoral decision. *Amer. polit. Sci. Rev., 52,* 367–387.

Stokes, D. E., and W. E. Miller (1962). Party government and the saliency of Congress. *Publ. Opin. Quart., 26,* 531–546.

Stouffer, S. A. (1955). *Communism, conformity, and civil liberties.* New York: Doubleday.

Stricker, G. (1964). The operation of cognitive dissonance on pre- and post-election attitudes. *J. soc. Psychol., 63,* 111–119.

Sullivan, D. G. (1966). Psychological balance and reactions to the presidential nominations in 1960. In M. K. Jennings and L. H. Zeigler (Eds.), *The electoral process.* Englewood Cliffs, N.J.: Prentice-Hall. Pp. 238–264.

Tannenbaum, P. H. (1966). Mediated generalization of attitude change via the principle of congruity. *J. Pers. soc. Psychol., 3,* 493–499.

Tannenbaum, P. H., and R. W. Gengel (1966). Generalization of attitude change through congruity principle relationships. *J. Pers. soc. Psychol., 3,* 299–304.

Thompson, K. H. (1967). Class change and party choice: a cross-national study of the relationship between intergenerational social mobility and political party choice. Unpublished Ph. D. dissertation, University of Wisconsin.

Treiman, D. J. (1966). Status discrepancy and prejudice. *Amer. J. Sociol., 71,* 651–664.

Trow, M. (1958). Small businessmen, political tolerance, and support for McCarthy. *Amer. J. Sociol., 64,* 270–281.

Turiel, E., L. Kohlberg, and J. Rest (in press). Level of moral development as a determinant of preference and comprehension of moral judgments made by others. *J. Pers. soc. Psychol.*

Turner, H. A., C. G. McClintock, and C. B. Spaulding (1963). The political party affiliation of American political scientists. *West. polit. Quart., 16,* 650–665.

Turner, H. A., C. B. Spaulding, and C. G. McClintock (1963). Political orientations of academically affiliated sociologists. *Sociol. soc. Res., 47,* 273–289.

Verba, S. (1965). The Kennedy assassination and the nature of political commitment. In B. S. Greenberg and E. B. Parker (Eds.), *The Kennedy assassination and the American public.* Stanford: Stanford Univ. Press. Pp. 348–360.

Verba, S., R. A. Brody, E. B. Parker, N. H. Nie, N. W. Polsby, P. Ekman, and G. S. Black (1967). Public opinion and the war in Vietnam. *Amer. polit. Sci. Rev., 61,* 317–333.

Walker, J. L. (1966). Ballot forms and voter fatigue: an analysis of the office block and party column ballots. *Midwest J. polit. Sci., 10*, 448–463.

Watts, W. A., and D. Whittaker (1966). Free speech advocates at Berkeley. *J. appl. behav. Sci., 2*, 41–62.

Westby, D. L., and R. G. Braungart (1966). Class and politics in the family backgrounds of student political activists. *Amer. sociol. Rev., 31*, 690–692.

Wilensky, H. L., and H. Edwards (1959). The skidder: ideological adjustments of downward mobile workers. *Amer. sociol. Rev., 24*, 215–231.

Wolfenstein, M., and G. Kliman, Eds. (1965). *Children and the death of a president.* Garden City, N.Y.: Doubleday.

Wolfinger, R. E. (1965). The development and persistence of ethnic voting. *Amer. polit. Sci. Rev., 59*, 896–908.

Wolfinger, R. E., and F. I. Greenstein (1968). The repeal of fair housing in California: an analysis of referendum voting. *Amer. polit. Sci. Rev., 62*, 753–769.

——— (1969). Comparing political regions: the case of California. *Amer. polit. Sci. Rev., 63*, 74–85.

Wolfinger, R. E., Barbara Kaye Wolfinger, K. Prewitt, and Sheila Rosenhack (1964). America's radical right: politics and ideology. In D. Apter (Ed.), *Ideology and discontent.* New York: Free Press. Pp. 262–293.

Zajonc, R. B. (1968). The attitudinal effects of mere exposure. *J. Pers. soc. Psychol. Monogr. Suppl.,* part 2, 1–27.

Zajonc, R. B., and E. Burnstein (1965). The learning of balanced and unbalanced social structures. *J. Pers., 33*, 153–163.

42

A Social Psychology of Education

J. W. GETZELS, University of Chicago

It is a peculiar fact that until recently education seems to have been omitted from the systematic theoretical and empirical concerns of social psychologists. This is not to say that there have not been social-psychological studies of matters relevant to education. Indeed, what is there of interest to social psychology that is irrelevant to education? Our surprise, from the perspective of 1965, is that there has been so little attempt to deal with the relationship between social psychology and education in an orderly way. For example, though there was a chapter on "Industrial Social Psychology" in the preceding *Handbook* (Lindzey, 1954), there was none on "Educational Social Psychology"; and though there was a chapter on "The Psychology of Voting: An Analysis of Political Behavior," there was no parallel chapter on, say, "The Psychology of Schooling: An Analysis of Educational Behavior." What is even more surprising is that the Index to the *Handbook,* containing some 2000 items, includes altogether only three references to education ("and mass media," "and prejudice," "and sociometry") and only one to teaching ("nondirective *vs.* traditional")—all incidental to the issue of education as a central institution in the social and psychological life of a people and in the development of its children. There are no references to school, classroom, teacher, or students.

It might perhaps be expected that the chapter entitled "Socialization," which begins with the statement, "Socialization refers to a problem which is old and pervasive in human life—the problem of how to rear children so that they will become adequate adult members of the society to which they belong" (Child, 1954, p. 655), might deal with education as we know it. But again, the words school, teacher, student are mentioned only in passing. There is nothing to indicate that the ordinary human being in our society spends the greater portion of his waking hours from the age of six (which is rapidly being extended downward to four or five) to the age of 16 (which is rapidly being extended upward to 18 or more) as a "student" in a place provided by "society" called a "school" where he is expected to be "educated" under the guidance of "teachers" directed by "administrators" answerable to "board members" responsible to the "public."

In 1959, the Society for the Psychological Study of Social Issues took note of this gap between social psychology and education, and commissioned "a research-oriented book of readings to include existing empirical studies from preschool to the college level," on the grounds that social-psychological phenomena pervade educational problems (Charters and Gage, 1963, p. xvi). It is, of course, self-evident that social-psychological phenomena from cognition and learning to leadership and group interaction, and that social-psychological concepts from role and personality to motivation and level of aspiration, do in fact bear on all manner of educational affairs. But it is by no means self-evident just how to define the area that may distinctively be called the *social psychology of education*.

As Charters and Gage (1963), who undertook the Society's commission, rightly pointed out, there is a difference between social psychology for educators and a social psychology of education. Social psychology for educators would include anything in social psychology having explicit or implicit significance for education. Labor-management strife in a community, family fertility rates, leadership, and group performance all have a bearing on what goes on in school. A social psychology of education requires some delimitation, some set of concepts and variables that are simultaneously and distinctively social-psychological and educational.

One way of delimiting this area is to take an inventory of social-psychological topics of relevance to educators and of educational settings to which these topics might apply. Charters and Gage (1963, p. xvii) compiled such an inventory. Their list of social-psychological topics includes the following:

1. *Social aspects of perception, including interpersonal perception.*
2. *Social aspects of cognitive processes, including problem solving, intelligence, memory.*
3. *Social aspects of motivation (excluding attitudes).*
4. *Personality development, self, and self concept.*
5. *Language and stereotypes.*
6. *Mass communication and public opinion.*
7. *Modes of face-to-face communication.*
8. *Modes of interpersonal influence.*
9. *Attitude formation and change.*
10. *Multiple-group membership, reference group.*
11. *Role, role conflict, role set.*
12. *Ideology, value systems, national character.*
13. *Socialization—child and adult, professionalization.*
14. *Social stratification.*
15. *Division of labor, occupations, social psychology of work.*
16. *Small group structure.*
17. *Small group process.*
18. *Leadership.*
19. *Group conflict, segregation, discrimination, prejudice.*

Their inventory of educational settings is as follows:

1. *Teacher-pupil relationship (including parent-child).*
2. *Classroom group.*
3. *Peer group, gangs.*

4. *Student society of the school.*
5. *Social organization of adults in the school.*
6. *Community in relation to education and the school.*
7. *Profession of education.*
8. *Society and the institution of education.*

This inventory is surely indicative of the many ways in which matters of concern to social psychology are also related to matters of concern to education. But the lists do not in themselves provide an articulated framework—a systematic scheme—within which to see the relationships among the topics, among the settings, and between the topics and the settings. From one point of view this is an advantage, for it permits the greatest diversity of concepts and the widest coverage of empirical findings to be brought to bear upon educational problems. From another point of view, however, this advantage becomes a severe disadvantage, for the lack of any theoretical restriction may have the consequence of making the social psychology of education only a grab bag of social-psychological notions and data perhaps relevant to education but unrelated in any systematic way to each other. In the face of this, almost any attempt at a systematic scheme, however modest its merit, may be more helpful than none at all. But there is a risk here too: matters of relevance may be omitted because they do not fit into the categories given by the scheme. And so we are faced with the usual choice in a field where there is little prior conceptualization: to deal primarily with already existing topics which seem to us in some way relevant or interesting, or to attempt to formulate an explicit scheme which will provide some conceptual unity to the field, guide our selection of topics, and hopefully have the residual value of serving as a stimulus for more fruitful alternate schemes.

Our own inclination is in the latter direction, even with all the risks it entails. Accordingly, we shall first present a framework within which to view the social psychology of education; on the basis of this framework, we shall derive a number of systematic issues for further examination; we shall then review selected portions of the existing literature relevant to these issues and call attention to areas where work still needs to be done, at least from the particular point of view of the scheme we set forth.

A FRAMEWORK FOR A SOCIAL PSYCHOLOGY OF EDUCATION

One tentative framework was initially formulated by Getzels and his associates (Getzels, 1952, 1958, 1963; Getzels and Guba, 1957; Getzels and Thelen, 1960) and has been applied to a number of aspects of education (for example, see Campbell, Corbally, and Ramseyer, 1962; Guba and Bidwell, 1957; Shaplin, 1964). The most general context of interpersonal or social behavior, whether in education or elsewhere, is taken to be a given *social system* (Parsons and Shils, 1951). The term "social system" is conceptual rather than descriptive and must not be confused with society or state, or thought of as applicable only to large aggregates of human interaction. Specifically with respect to education, for one purpose a given community may be considered a social system, with education a particular institution within this system; for another purpose the school itself (or a single classroom within the school) may be conceived as a social system. Most broadly considered, the social psychology of education deals with behavior in the educational setting conceived as a social system.

THE SCHOOL AS A SOCIAL SYSTEM: INSTITUTION AND INDIVIDUAL

We may think of a social system as involving two classes of phenomena which are at once conceptually independent and phenomenally interactive. There are, on the one hand, institutions with certain roles and expectations that will fulfill the goals of the system. On the other hand, there are individuals with certain personalities and dispositions inhabiting the system, whose interactions comprise what is called social behavior. Behavior in the school can be understood as a function of these major variables: (1) institution, role, and expectation, which together refer to the normative dimension of activity in a social system; and (2) individual, personality, and disposition, which together refer to the personal dimension of activity in a social system. From this point of view, one may study the specific role of pupil, for example, without reference to *particular* children (this may be thought of as the institutional, or sociological, level of analysis); or one may study the personality of particular children without reference to the *specific* role of pupil (this may be thought of as the individual, or psychological, level of analysis). When we study the two in concert—interactively— we are dealing with what may be thought of uniquely as the *social-psychological* level of analysis, though *the distinctions among the three levels in practice are by no means so hard and fast as they appear schematically here.* The relevant elements of the framework may be represented pictorially as in Fig. 1.

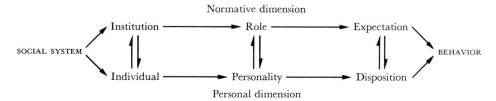

Fig. 1. Elements of the framework, showing the normative and personal dimensions of behavior in a social system. (From Getzels, 1958.)

In order to comprehend behavior in a social system we need to understand the relations of the indicated conceptual elements. The term institution has received a variety of definitions. Here it is sufficient to point out only that all social systems, and surely educational systems, have certain imperative functions that come in time to be carried out in certain routinized patterns. These functions and patterns are said to be "institutionalized," and the agencies for carrying out these functions and patterns are termed institutions. The most important analytic units of an institution are the roles. The term role has also received a variety of definitions, but within the present formulation roles are conceived, to use Linton's (1936, p. 14) terminology, as the "dynamic aspects" of the positions, offices, and statuses in an institution delineating the normative behavior for the role incumbent. The role itself is defined by the expectations attaching to it, that is, the rights, privileges, and obligations to which the incumbent of the role must adhere. Roles are complementary and form "role sets" (Merton, 1957), each role deriving its definition and meaning from other roles in the set. Thus the role of teacher and the role of pupil cannot be understood or implemented except in relation to each other. In performing the role behavior expected of him, the teacher "teaches" the pupil; in performing the role behavior

expected of him, the pupil "learns" from the teacher. At this level of analysis, it is sufficient to conceive of the role incumbents as devoid of personalistic or other individual-
izing characteristics, as if all incumbents of a given role were alike and implementing
the given role in the same way.

But roles are implemented by particular flesh-and-blood individuals, and no two
individuals are alike even when they are presumably performing the same role. Each
individual stamps the role with the characteristic style of his own personality. Not all
teachers "teach," not all pupils "learn"—at least not in the same way. Social behavior
is a function not only of normative expectations but also of personal dispositions, and
the two may not coincide. It is therefore not enough to know only the nature of the
roles and expectations within a social system—though, to be sure, behavior in the system cannot be understood apart from these—but we must know also the nature of the
individuals inhabiting the roles, and how they perceive and react to the expectations.

Just as the institutional dimension was analyzed into the component elements of
role and expectation, so the individual dimension may be analyzed into the component
elements of personality and disposition. The term personality, like the term role, has
received a variety of definitions. Here it is sufficient to conceive of it as the dynamic
aspects of the individual—his pattern of needs, motives, and dispositions—that govern
his reactions to the environment and its expectations. The central analytic units of
personality in the present formulation are the cognitive and affective dispositions
which we may define, with Parsons and Shils, as "individual tendencies to orient and
act with respect to objects in certain manners and to expect certain consequences of
these actions" (1951, p. 114). At this level of analysis, we may conceive of the individual as devoid of specific roles or other generalizing characteristics, as if he were on
a desert island freed of any outside institutional constraints.

From the point of view of the present framework, in order to understand the behavior of particular role incumbents in specific institutions, we must know both the
role expectations and the individual dispositions. A clarifying analytic distinction may
be made between the emphases of educational sociology, educational psychology, and
a social psychology of education. Where educational sociology is primarily concerned
with the normative role patterns in school (institutional differences) and educational
psychology with the distinctive personal patterns (individual differences), a social
psychology of education is concerned with the interaction of role and personality in
the school or classroom as a social system in the context, as we shall see, of the cultural
or community values.

THE SCHOOL IN THE COMMUNITY CONTEXT:
ROLE, PERSONALITY, AND VALUE

The school as a social system is part of a particular community, and the nature of the
educational roles and the character of the teacher-pupil interactions are integrally
related to other aspects of the community. To cite one obvious instance, the school is
inextricably related to the political system. On the one hand, it is expected that the
school will prepare children for the wise execution of political power; on the other,
the school itself depends for its existence on the political system. Similarly, it is expected that the school will prepare children for participation in the economic system,
but the school in turn depends on the economic system for its support. It is expected
that the school will instruct the children, but whether the children will be ready for

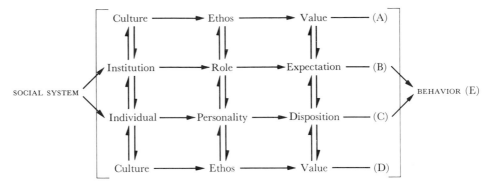

Fig. 2. Elements of the framework, showing normative, personal, and cultural dimensions of behavior in a social system. (From Getzels, 1963.)

instruction may depend more on the motives they acquire from the family than on anything the school itself does. In short, the school and the classroom seem almost unique in the symbiosis of their relationships, at least theoretically, to the other aspects of the social order.

At the most general level, these interrelated systems may be seen as embedded in a culture with a certain *ethos* defined by the constituent patterns of *values*. The quality of institutional roles and individual personalities in the school system, as in all other systems, is related to the ethos of the particular culture, and the specific role expectations and personal dispositions to its values. On the one hand, the expectations of the school derive, at least in part, from the values of the culture in which the school is situated; and on the other, the dispositions of the child are also, at least in part, internalizations of the values (or subvalues) of the culture (or subculture) in which the child is reared. One may understand a great deal about the requirements of the curriculum and the motivations of the pupils if one knows the character of the culture. The school, for example, cannot devote itself to a classical curriculum when this kind of education is no longer supported by the culture. The pupil will ordinarily not learn for the sake of learning when learning itself is not a value in the culture or subculture in which he is brought up.

Thus it must be borne in mind that, although the social psychology of education may focus on the internal system of the school or classroom, the system is inevitably related to external systems and most generally to what we have called the culture, with its attendant ethos and the component values. By way of summary, we may present the structural dimensions and central concepts of the framework schematically as in Fig. 2.

BEHAVIOR IN THE SCHOOL: EFFECTIVENESS, EFFICIENCY, AND EFFECTANCE

The indicated elements of the school as a social system are not only related to each other structurally, but are also related dynamically to the quality of performance in the system. Three basic criterion concepts of performance may be applied: effectiveness, efficiency, and effectance (Barnard, 1938; White, 1959). Each of these expresses a relationship between the primary elements of the model (A, B, C, D) and the nature of the observed behavior (E).

Effectiveness is an expression of the correlation between the values (A), the expectations (B), and the actual behavior (E). When the correlation is high, the behavior is effective; that is, the behavior is in keeping with the values and expectations, and thus contributes to the goals of the system and reflects the aspirations of the culture. When the correlation is low, the behavior is ineffective; that is, it is not in keeping with the values and expectations, and thus fails to contribute to the goals of the system and to reflect the aspirations of the culture.

Efficiency is an expression of the correlation between the subvalues (D), the dispositions (C), and the actual behavior (E). When the correlation is high, the behavior is efficient; that is, the behavior is congruent with the individual's values and dispositions, and thus fulfills his cognitive and affective needs. When the correlation is low, the behavior is inefficient; that is, it is incongruent with the individual's values and dispositions, and thus fails to fulfill his cognitive and affective needs.

To the extent that there is discrepancy between (1) the values serving as the context for the school, with the consequent role expectations, and (2) the values available to the child for internalization, with the consequent personality dispositions, behavior may conform to the one or to the other, or to some compromise between the two. When behavior conforms to the dispositions, it appears "natural," "authentic," "pleasurable," and is forthcoming with a minimum of strain or expenditure of psychic energy; in this sense, it is efficient. But it may not fulfill the role expectations or contribute to the goals of the system—the behavior may not be effective. The child who is permitted to do just as he wishes may not necessarily learn what the school was set up for him to learn. When behavior conforms to the expectations, and there is a discrepancy between the dispositions and the expectations, the behavior seems "unnatural," "unauthentic," "painful," and is forthcoming with a maximum of strain and expenditure of psychic energy; the behavior is inefficient. But it may fulfill the role expectations and contribute to the goals of the system; in this sense, the behavior is effective. The artist or musician forced to teach against his will in order to make a living may do so exceedingly well but at great cost in personal frustration and disappointment. It is clear that it is possible for performance in the school to be effective without necessarily being efficient, and to be efficient without necessarily being effective. A critical issue in the social psychology of education is the factors making for effectiveness and efficiency, and the relation between the two in the school system.

We may borrow the term *effectance* (White, 1959) to refer to the general relation between efficiency and effectiveness. Behavior is effectant when it is simultaneously efficient and effective; behavior is not effectant to the degree that there are discrepancies between its effectiveness and its efficiency. The aim of the school is to maximize behavior that is educationally effectant, that is, behavior that is individually efficient and institutionally effective. The social psychologist of education hopes not only to understand educational activity as it is, but also to contribute to its greater effectance.

A SOCIAL PSYCHOLOGY OF EDUCATION: SYSTEMATIC ISSUES

Despite its obviously primitive nature, the preceding formulation permits us to see a number of educational issues dealt with previously in discrete terms as conceptually related, and to derive a number of previously unformulated issues which still need to be dealt with. It will be noted that these issues encompass within the single set of concepts and relations the greater number of social-psychological topics and educational settings included in the initial inventory of topics and settings.

CULTURE AND SCHOOL: SOCIALIZATION AND EDUCATION

The first issue is the effect of the community on the expectations of its schools and the dispositions of its children, that is, the interaction of B and A, and of C and D, in our model. This includes, on the one hand, the impact of the values of the culture on the curriculum, and on the other, the impact of socialization practices in the family on the ability and willingness of the pupils to learn. It includes also the relation between the child's position in the social structure and the child's position in the school structure.

From the point of view of the relations between community values, educational expectations, and the child's dispositions, the situation of two children in the school setting may be very different indeed. Here, for example, is the situation approximated by the majority middle-class child:

1. $A \cong D$; *that is, the culture within which the child is socialized and the culture which is the context for the school tend to be congruent.*

2. $D \cong C$; *that is, the dispositions that are internalized and the values of the culture tend to be congruent.*

3. $A \cong B$; *that is, the expectations of the school and the values of the culture tend to be congruent.*

4. $B \cong C$; *that is, the expectations of the school and the dispositions of the child tend to be congruent.*

Presumably, in a well-functioning system the cultural values are internalized by the children through the process of socialization and enter the psychic economy of the individual as cognitive and affective dispositions for value-relevant behavior. The role expectations are defined in relation to the same values that had entered into the socialization process, so that what is required of the child for role performance in the school is congruent with his dispositions for behavior. This situation leads to functional behavior—functional in relation to what the cultural values require, the institutional expectations include, and the individual's dispositions make attractive in the form of preferred behavior. The behavior is likely to be both effective and efficient—that is, effectant, as previously defined.

Consider now, in the same terms, the situation of the minority lower-class or so-called culturally deprived child who is said to be socialized in a subculture whose values and cognitive experiences are different from those of the dominant culture:

1. $A \not\equiv D$; *that is, the culture in which the child is socialized and the culture which is the context for the school tend to be incongruent.*

2. $D \cong C$; *that is, the dispositions that are internalized tend to be congruent with the values of the subculture (D here is the minority lower-class subculture).*

3. $A \cong B$; *that is, the expectations of the school and the values of the prevailing middle-class culture tend to be congruent.*

4. $B \not\equiv C$; *that is, the expectations of the school and the dispositions of the child tend to be incongruent.*

The situation here leads to dysfunctional behavior—dysfunctional for the culture, the institution, and the individual, at least from the point of view of the values and experiences represented in the school. We are not asserting that these differences exist, or if they exist that the postulated effects are inevitably the case. These are empirical questions to which we shall turn when we consider the empirical work in this area. What the framework does is point, in systematic terms, to a possible interaction between the socialization patterns in the family, the educational expectations of the school, and behavior in the school in relation to the culture as a whole. In this sense, for example, we may see the recent movement toward compensatory preschool experiences for the lower-class child (as exemplified in Head Start) as an attempt to bring the values and experiences within which the child is socialized (D) into greater congruence with the values and experiences within which he will be educated (A). We can see too that change in the educational situation of the lower-class child might also be achieved by bringing the institutions and role expectations of the school (B) into greater congruence with the child's dispositions (C)—a possibility which seems largely neglected.

ROLE RELATIONS IN THE SCHOOL: THE PROBLEM OF INSTRUCTION

In the preceding section we dealt with the relation between the external system and the internal system of the school, that is, the relations between A and B and between D and C. We consider now the internal system of the school itself, and especially the normative aspect of the system (B) and its possible impact on the pupils (C).

Numerous role relationships or "role sets" provide the context for behavior in the school. Among the sets are board of education and superintendent, superintendent and principal, principal and teacher, teacher and parents, and so on, and of course all sorts of combinations of these. But the central relationship (or role set) in the school is the one involving teacher and student, and student and student, that is, the classroom itself.

In a famous passage on "teaching as institutionalized leadership," Waller (1965, p. 196) described the classroom as follows:

> Teacher and pupil confront each other with attitudes from which the underlying hostility can never be altogether removed. Pupils are the material in which teachers are supposed to produce results. Pupils are human beings striving to realize themselves in their own spontaneous manner, striving to produce their own results in their own way. Each of these hostile parties stands in the way of the other; in so far as the aims of either are realized, it is at the sacrifice of the aims of the other.
>
> Authority is on the side of the teacher. The teacher nearly always wins. In fact, he must win, or he cannot remain a teacher.

There is no doubt that the teacher is a highly powerful figure in the classroom. But whether he is quite as decisive a factor, or whether there need inevitably be the kind of pitched battle that Waller envisioned, was brought into question by Lewin's classic investigations of styles of leadership showing that such a clash between the leader and the led and presumably the teacher and the taught was by no means inevitable. There are such intervening issues as the particular organization of roles within the school, the nature of the "student culture" and "classroom climate," and the different effects of "authoritarian" or teacher-centered and of "democratic" or learner-centered instruction.

We shall deal with the specific findings of the relevant studies when we turn to the empirical work in this domain. Here we wish to put the issues of the role structure of the school and classroom instruction within the concepts and relations of the present framework (Getzels and Guba, 1957). From this point of view, three ideal-type school and classroom orientations may be identified. It will be noted that the various extant descriptions of school structure, classroom climate, and instruction as "formal-informal," "dominative-integrative," and "teacher centered–student centered" may all be subsumed under these orientations:

1.   One orientation emphasizes the normative dimension of behavior and accordingly places stress on the roles and expectations within the institution rather than on the personality and dispositions of the individuals in the system. If one writes the equation $B = f(R \times P)$, where B is observed behavior, R is a given role, and P is the personality of the particular role incumbent, in this orientation R is maximized, P minimized. It is assumed that, given the institutional purpose, appropriate procedures can be discovered through which the role is taken, despite possible personal dispositions of the learner to the contrary. The relationships in the role set are *universalistic* and the criterion of performance is *effectiveness*.

2.   A second orientation emphasizes the personal dimension of behavior and accordingly places stress on the personality and cognitive and affective dispositions of the individual rather than on the roles and expectations of the institution. In the equation $B = f(R \times P)$, R is minimized, P maximized. The assumption is that the greatest ultimate accomplishment will ensue not through enforced adherence to normatively defined roles but through letting each person seek out what is most relevant to him. The relationships in the role set are *particularistic* and the criterion of performance is *efficiency*.

3.   Essentially, neither of the preceding orientations deals with the classroom as a group or social system; the one emphasizes uniform adherence to a relationship between teacher and pupil in role terms, and the other in personality terms. The condition that roles and personalities exist in the classroom within a group context is more or less irrelevant. The third orientation attempts simultaneously to take into consideration both role and personality by focusing on the classroom as a social system. Since the goals of the system must be carried out, roles and expectations must be made explicit; since the roles and expectations will be carried out by people, the personalities and dispositions of the people must be taken into account. But this cannot be just a compromise, an average or halfway point, between the two. In the equation $B = f(R \times P)$, R and P are maximized or minimized as the situation requires. The relationships in the role set are *transactional* and the criterion of performance is not only effectiveness *or* efficiency but what we have referred to as *effectance*.

PERSONALITY RELATIONS IN THE SCHOOL: THE PROBLEM OF LEARNING

We have been dealing with the interaction between the school as a social system and other systems to which it is related, and with the role structure and relationships in the school itself, that is, with the interactions between A and B and between C and D, and with B. We turn now to some issues pertaining to the characteristics of the individuals in the system and their effect on the nature of behavior in the school, that is, to dimension C in the framework.

By the time the child is ready to take his place in the educational system and assume the role of pupil, he is ready to react to it in a particular way (Getzels, 1956). All children of a particular grade level may be exposed to the same expectations, but they do not therefore perceive the expectations in the same way. Instead, each child comes with a characteristic set of cognitive and affective dispositions which determine in a large measure his particular relationship to the role of learner—what he will see and hear, what he will remember and forget, what he will think and say, and what he will do gladly with others and what he will do only under duress.

The critical differences between the reactions of one child and those of another to the expectations imposed by the school are not only a function of differences in their intelligence—differences with which we shall deal below—but also of differences in their affective dispositions: differences in their pattern of preferences, attitudes, drives, needs, values, and perhaps chiefly of their interests. The child who remembers the batting averages, to the third decimal place, of a dozen members of his favorite baseball team may also be the one who cannot remember the single date of the discovery of America. It is shortsighted to think of him as having baseball memory and history forgetfulness, or baseball intelligence and history stupidity. What he has is baseball *interest* and history *indifference*.

To understand the effect of dispositions on role performance in school, it is necessary to know not only something of the generic concept of disposition but also the several types of dispositions. In view of its central importance, we shall take the concept of interest as a starting point and examine its relation to other dispositions which have been identified. In this way we may at once make clear its specific meaning as well as indicate the range and nature of dispositions affecting behavior in the school setting.

We may begin by distinguishing between an interest and a preference (Getzels, 1956). We have a preference for broccoli over asparagus, but we may have no interest in either. We would not expend the slightest effort to learn more about the one than about the other. The child faced with a choice of subjects already available in school may admit to a preference for one subject over another, but he may have no interest in either. The difference between a preference and an interest is that a preference is relatively passive, while an interest is inevitably dynamic. A preference is a disposition to *receive* one object as against another; it does not induce one to *seek out* the particular object for study or acquisition. In contrast, the basic nature of an interest is that it does induce one to seek out particular objects and activities.

Again, despite considerable usage to the contrary, there is a significant distinction between an interest and merely a positive attitude. We may, for example, have a positive attitude toward the Eskimos but have no particular interest in them. In contrast, we may have a decidedly negative attitude toward the Soviets but be keenly interested in them. This is, of course, not to say that attitudes do not influence the child's behavior in school or the kind of learning he will or will not do. His attitudes toward the Eskimos will influence what he will and will not learn about them, as his attitudes toward the Soviets will influence what he will or will not learn about them. There is, however, an important conceptual difference between an attitude as a disposition and an interest as a disposition. An attitude implies a disposition to react in a particular direction with respect to a given object. We do not ordinarily speak of being driven by an attitude; we are necessarily driven by our interests.

We may also distinguish between a drive, a need, and an interest. A drive has its source in a specific physiological disequilibrium. An interest has its source in experience and challenges us to exert ourselves even though there is no necessity in any biological sense. Technically speaking, we may say that a drive is a function largely of our instinctual processes, an interest a function largely of our ego processes. There is a distinction also between a need and an interest, though the distinction here is more subtle. A need is a disposition or force within the organism which consistently impels him toward one type of activity as against another. Thus we may speak of an individual as having a high or a low need for achievement or for affiliation. Insofar as the force is not necessarily biological but may have its source in experience, it is distinct from a drive; insofar as it disposes the individual toward a general type of activity rather than toward a specific object or goal, it is distinct from an interest. The need for achievement may find expression in the school situation, for example, in the arts, sciences, athletics, or extracurricular activities. The need is the same; the interests are different. Against this background, we may define interest as a characteristic disposition, organized through experience, which impels an individual to seek out particular objects, activities, skills, understandings, or goals for attention and acquisition. Finally, a distinction may be made between an interest and a value. A value is a conception of the desirable (that is, of what ought to be desired) which influences the selection of behavior (Kluckhohn, 1951, p. 395). Thus it is possible for an interest and a value to be quite incompatible: an interest disposes us toward what we *want* to do, a value toward what we *ought* to do. In short, the dispositions which are brought by the various individuals into the role structure of the school tend to determine the definition of the roles, and affect not only *how much* or *how well* the learner will learn and the teacher will teach but also the *particular kind* of learning and teaching that will be done.

ROLE, PERSONALITY, AND VALUE
RELATIONS IN THE SCHOOL: TYPES OF CONFLICT

On the basis of the foregoing formulations, it is possible to derive a number of systematic types of conflict to which the school is liable: (1) conflict between the cultural values and the institutional expectations, that is, between dimensions A and B of the framework; (2) conflict between the personality dispositions and the role definitions, that is, between B and C of the framework; (3) conflict between roles and within roles, that is, within dimension B, which may take the form of disagreements within a single group defining a given role, among several groups defining a given role, or contradictions between two or more roles a given individual is occupying at the same time; (4) conflict arising from the incompatibility of dispositions within the role incumbent, that is, within a single individual in C; (5) conflict arising from personality differences, incongruent interpersonal perceptions, and idiosyncratic definitions of complementary expectations, that is, among individuals in C. A central issue in the social psychology of education is the nature and effect of these conflicts in the school setting, a subject to which we shall return in detail when we consider the relevant empirical literature.

SOCIAL PSYCHOLOGY AND EDUCATION: EMPIRICAL STUDIES

We have outlined a tentative framework within which to see the relationship between social psychology and education. This framework suggested a number of issues for analysis. We turn now to a consideration of empirical work relevant to these issues. A word must be said first, however, about the choice we faced in attempting to bring to bear a vast number of relevant pieces of prior research within a single framework. We could either undertake an exhaustive citation of the literature and within the limitations of space comment briefly on as many studies as possible, or we could focus on a selected number of studies and already existing reviews of the relevant work in particular areas, and discuss those in some detail. The advantage of the first alternative is comprehensive, even if brief, coverage of primary sources; the consequent disadvantage is that within the limits of space it would result, as is so often the case, in not much more than an annotated bibliography. The advantage of the second alternative is that it permits consideration of major studies and comprehensive areas of work in some detail; the consequent disadvantage is that there will necessarily be omissions in coverage of primary sources and considerable reliance on already existing reviews. We have sought a compromise between the alternatives, discussing some studies in depth but attempting to mention as many additional studies as possible or at least to cite the sources for such studies. However, where a compromise was inexpedient, we tended to favor the second over the first alternative.

SOCIAL STRUCTURE, SOCIAL CLASS, SOCIALIZATION, AND EDUCATION: EARLY WORK

A primary issue in the social psychology of education is the nature of the interaction between the school and other systems in the community. Empirically the issue has taken the form of two questions: First, and more generally, what is the relation between the social stratification of a community and its educational system, and second, and more specifically, what is the relation between the socialization practices in the family and the child's behavior in the school setting?

Social class

An annotated bibliography of early work on stratification and education is available for ready reference, and we need not review the content here (Dixon, 1953). Instead it will be more useful to focus attention on three classic studies which not only represent the salient issues but had, and continue to have, a preeminent impact on thinking in this domain (Brookover and Gottlieb, 1963). These are *Middletown* (Lynd and Lynd, 1929), *Who Shall Be Educated?* (Warner, Havighurst, and Loeb, 1944), and *Elmtown's Youth* (Hollingshead, 1949).

The monumental study by the Lynds in 1924–1925 of Middletown, a Midwestern industrial city of about 38,000 inhabitants, dealt with a number of issues involving social stratification and education which have prevailed to this day: the nature of social concern with education, the effect of social structure on the curriculum, the effect of social class status on school achievement, the relation between social class status and participation in school activities, the nature of social class differences in intellectual functioning.

The Lynds (1929, p. 182) pointed out that Middletown was very concerned that all its young "have an education"—a concern reflected in the fact that no less than 45 percent of all money expended by the city was devoted to its schools. Though little empirical evidence of social class variation in educational attitudes was presented, the difference was described as follows: "If education is oftentimes taken for granted by the business class, it is no exaggeration to say that it evokes the fervor of a religion, a means of salvation, among a large section of the working class" (p. 187). But if there is this fervor for education among the working class, why then do their children leave school? At least two reasons are related to the socioeconomic class factor. One reason is direct: the lower-class children leave school because their financial help is needed at home. Another reason is indirect yet perhaps more potent: the school is dominated by middle-class values of dress, behavior, and associations which tend to suppress the educational aspirations of the lower-class children (pp. 186, 216–17). Not only did the Lynds find socioeconomic differences in intellectual achievement after the children got to school, they found striking differences in intellectual ability even before children came to school. For example, when tested in the first grade, 25.8 percent of business-class children and 6.5 percent of working-class children had an IQ of 110 or above, and 45.5 percent of working-class children and 13.4 percent of business-class children had an IQ of 89 or below (p. 37). The Lynds did not deal directly with the significant question: What is the source of these variations? But they did refer to the possibility that the differences in intelligence may be due to social conditions rather than to native endowment, and insisted that this must be taken into account in dealing with children of different social class status (p. 36).

Who Shall Be Educated? (Warner, Havighurst, and Loeb, 1944) extended the preceding work, especially in arguing that the educational system was essentially an instrument of social mobility and stratification: "the schools are elevators in a hardening social structure"; they do not serve all children equally (p. 49). Ninety-eight percent of the teachers in the Midwestern community under study, 97 percent of those in the Eastern community, and 92.5 percent of those in the Southern community came from the middle class (p. 101). The investigators argued that these teachers selected certain children for promotion in the social hierarchy in line with their middle-class values; the rest were trained to adjust to the status in which they were born. In the Eastern community, for instance, all upper-upper children were in private college preparatory schools, all lower-upper pupils in the public high school, and 80 percent of the upper-middle-class children were in college preparatory courses, but 45 percent of the lower-middle and only 28 percent of the upper-lower and 26 percent of the lower-lower children were in these college preparatory courses. The others were in the commercial or general courses preparing for vocations—courses which suffered from lack of community support and were held less prestigeful by teachers and administrators. The authors concluded: "There seems to be no doubt that the powerful middle class, by their influence on the schools, tend to contribute to the subordination of the lower classes by refusing equipment to schools which are predominantly lower class" (p. 76).

This series of early studies of education in the community context, which set the pattern for many more limited pieces of research during the 1940's and 1950's (see Dixon, 1953), probably had its culmination in Hollingshead's *Elmtown's Youth* (1949). The locus of the study was a Midwestern community of some 10,000 inhabitants. The investigator found a powerful socioeconomic prestige structure dividing the inhabitants sharply into five classes in which their children were socialized and grew up as adolescents. There were significant relationships between these socioeconomic class levels and the adolescents' intelligence-test performance, school attendance and achievement, membership in cliques and dating patterns, church, occupational, and recreational behavior. The findings corroborated preceding studies, and subsequent work by Davie (1953) in New Haven supported the Elmtown conclusions: for example, only 1.6 percent of adolescents aged 16 in the highest social class but fully 42.6 percent in the lowest class were not in school. More specifically, Hollingshead raised the question: Is school failure in the lower classes linked to lack of intellectual capacity? There was a significant association between social class and IQ and between social class and rate of school failure. But even if it is assumed that those with an IQ below 90 are unable to do high school work, only 11 percent of the adolescents for whom scores were available in the lowest class had an IQ below 90, yet 89 percent of those who completed a semester or more of high school failed at least one course. In short, Hollingshead (1949, p. 175) concluded, "Behind the stark figures of grades received in courses and scores made on intelligence tests lies the Elmtown social system."

Three aspects of the social structure were held responsible for the educational plight of the lower-class adolescent. First, the control of education was in the hands of a board composed only of members of the middle and upper classes: "the relationship between the well-being of the community as a whole and the education of approximately four-fifths of the children was not comprehended by the classes the Board members represented" (p. 126). Second, the teachers themselves came from the middle classes, abetting the incongruence between the behavior the children were expected to exhibit in school and the life they actually experienced at home (p. 128). Third, the lower-class parents believed that they were powerless to challenge the position of the "inner ring"; to speak up was to risk reprisal not only upon themselves economically but upon their children in school. A minority in next to the lowest class who did speak up were likely to be called "radicals" and "trouble makers" by both those in the higher and those in their own class. As for parents in the lowest class, they "were so far removed from the main current of community opinion and so much preoccupied with their own affairs that they took little interest in things of a civic nature" (pp. 145–146).

Socialization

In addition to documenting distinct relations between the several social classes and the educational system of the community, and variations in the educational behavior of the children themselves, each of the preceding studies suggested the existence of social class differences in preparing children for school. Children of the upper and middle classes were trained in the family to respond positively to the school situation, whether it be the taking of a general intelligence test or a specific arithmetic examination, or responding in a classroom recitation. The lower-class children were not; they were not trained to do their best, nor were they ingrained with the idea that, if they were to succeed in life, they must do well in school (Warner, Havighurst, and Loeb, 1944; Hollingshead, 1949, pp. 175f). In terms of our model, the children of the one subculture acquired through the process of socialization the cognitive and affective dispositions congruent with the expectations of the school; the children of the other subculture did not.

These observations, for the most part, were quite specific to school behavior, and without reference to any general theory relating child-rearing practices to personality formation. But contemporary cultural anthropologists and social psychologists were making comparative studies of the relationship between socialization and personality, and arguing that there was a profound effect of particular early infant experiences on later behavior. Accordingly, in 1943 Davis and Havighurst (1946) undertook a systematic investigation of "social class and color differences in child-rearing" in the Chicago area. Though there had been earlier studies of American child-rearing practices, for almost a decade the results of this work were taken, in Bronfenbrenner's (1958, p. 400) words, "as the definitive statement of class differences in socialization."

On the basis of interviews with 48 white and 50 Negro middle-class, and of 52 white and 50 Negro lower-class mothers, the investigators found significant class differences in infant training and socialization practices. More lower-class than middle-class babies were breast-fed only; more lower-class babies were fed at will; lower-class children were weaned later; bowel and bladder training were begun earlier in the middle-class families; middle-class children were expected to help at home and assume responsibility earlier. In addition, middle-class children were expected by their parents to achieve a higher occupational status and more of the middle-class children were expected to go to college. The central conclusions were: first, although there were some Negro-white variations, the critical differences were by social class; second, and more important, lower-class socialization was more "permissive" and less achievement-oriented, middle-class socialization was less "permissive" and more achievement-oriented. As we shall see, the second conclusion was later to be sharply challenged and in significant aspects reversed, but as Sewell (1961, p. 344) says, "The findings of the Chicago group and the inferences made from their findings were widely accepted and held sway without competition for some time." They had a profound effect on research and thinking regarding not only social class differences in personality structure but also, at least by implication, on mental functioning and school performance.

Social class, socialization, and mental functioning

Though not directly concerned with cognitive processes *per se*, the work on social stratification and socialization suggested that socioeconomic factors were related to differences in mental functioning, at least as reflected in performance on intelligence tests. Thus, the Lynds presented data showing differential IQ's by economic level, and in passing asked whether these differences might not be due to environmental conditions (see p. 472 above). Hollingshead (1949, p. 176) adduced similar data, and concluded: "We believe that such factors as these [distinctive home environments] have as much influence on the differences observed in the test scores as 'native intelligence,' but this is essentially an impression . . . ."

This is not the place to review the massive literature on the nature-nurture controversy with respect to intellectual development, but in an educationally influential monograph entitled *Social Class Influences upon Learning*, initially given as the Inglis Lecture at Harvard University, Allison Davis (1948) took the unequivocal position: First, "just as the culture of a particular social-class group influences the emotional system of the human individual, so does the culture likewise guide his mental activities" (p. 38); and second, the prevailing types of mental tests "penalize most heavily the pupils of the lower socio-economic group, because these groups have the least training and motivation to solve academic problems" (p. 39). An analysis of ten standard paper-and-pencil group intelligence tests showed that a large proportion of the items "discriminated between" children from the highest and lowest socioeconomic levels, but on some tests almost all the items, while on others only about half the items, showed such discrimination. On the highly verbal Henmon-Nelson test, 93 percent of the items showed significant socioeconomic differences; on the nonverbal Otis Alpha, 46 percent of the items showed such differences. The conclusion was that, in view of the wide variations, depending on what test was used, at least part of the differences must be due to the nature of the material in the tests themselves. A further analysis of the content of specific items suggested the reason for the variations. An item requiring the children to be familiar with the word *sonata,* a word which is clearly more prevalent in the high than in the low socioeconomic home, brought 78 percent correct responses for high socioeconomic children and only 28 percent from low socioeconomic children; but an item involving the concept of *cutting tool,* an implement common to all socioeconomic groups, showed no differences in correct response by socioeconomic status.

Davis (1948, pp. 63–65) then postulated three types of mental "phenomena" entering into a response to a cognitive problem and therefore responsible for the intelligence-test status of one pupil as compared with another: (1) hereditary phenomena, determining certain complex organic functional relationships, but not segregated by socioeconomic level; (2) cultural phenomena, including experiential and motivational factors acquired at home and school, which are segregated by socioeconomic level; (3) the phenomena of "speed," which are a complex function of hereditary factors, the physical condition of the testee, his cultural habits of work, his familiarity with the forms and content of the problem, and his previous training with the specific types of problems. If intelligence is not to be mistaken for differential cultural experiences, an attempt must be made to equalize the cultural elements of the test problems and the test situation. A full account of the empirical and theoretical work underlying and extending the preceding concepts is given by Eells *et al.* (1951), and of the construction of a "culture-fair" test of mental functioning by Davis and Eells (1953). We shall have occasion to return to some of the issues raised by this general line of thinking and investigation in the latter part of the following section.

SOCIAL STRUCTURE, SOCIAL CLASS, SOCIALIZATION, AND EDUCATION: CRITICISM OF EARLY WORK AND MORE RECENT STUDIES

The work on social stratification and education became at once controversial and evoked a body of criticism which seems, at least in retrospect, almost inexplicable in its personal rancor and partisanship. For example, at the 1952 Invitational Conference of the Educational Testing Service, Haggard (1953) presented for discussion a paper on "Techniques for the Development of Unbiased Tests." The discussant reacted with such acrimony that Haggard (1953, p. 127) felt compelled to remark that he hoped in the future the discussant would behave "in keeping with his stature in the field." Or again, in a symposium on Social Class Structure and American Education, Loeb (1953) described some unattractive features of middle-class culture; the discussant (Gross, 1953, p. 308) replied that the description was "an excellent caricature of certain phases of the 'home life culture' of a good many assistant and associate professors . . . ," presumably Loeb being one—as if this comment took care of the basic point. To be sure, there were the inevitable problems of the representativeness of the sampling, of the reliability of the observations, of the cogency of the inferences in the work in question, but one cannot help wondering why the criticism included so much personal reference and nervous humor. From the hindsight of 1965, one cannot help wondering also what current educational conditions in the inner city might be, had the warnings implicit in the early studies of social class bias in the schools been heeded.

Social class

At least five points of criticism were raised with respect to the social-class analysis of education. The issues may be put in the form of the following questions: (1) How may social class be defined most fruitfully for such analysis? (2) How adequate are the criteria for distinguishing among social classes in the prevailing studies? (3) How representative are the findings from the community studies? (4) How valid are the inferences drawn from the empirical data? (5) Finally, and this is more an extension than an issue in criticism, what emendations of the original work must be made in the light of more recent research?

The first and perhaps basic issue is: How is one to define social class most fruitfully? Kurt Mayer (1953) charged that studies like *Who Shall Be Educated?* based on the Warner classification were misleading, since they confused three different types of stratification: the social or *prestige* status of any given individual, his *economic* class position, and his position in the *power* structure. Prestige, wealth, and power may be closely related in the long run, but there are no automatic one-to-one correlations among them at any given moment of time in every instance. May not some of the inconsistencies in the available studies—say, the finding of high motivation for education on the part of "lower-class" parents in one study and of low motivation in another study—be due to the confusion in stratification by economic, prestige, and power indices?

The second issue is related to the first. The criteria for distinguishing one class from another are said to be, for the most part, vague and unsystematic. Mayer (1953, p. 156), for example, charged that any careful reader of the studies deriving from the Warner classification cannot escape the conclusion that the classificatory scheme is arbitrarily imposed upon the community: "it is definitely not a substantive arrangement recognized by the members of the community themselves."

How representative are the findings from the community studies? Warner was quite emphatic that the findings are representative. He stated (Warner and Bailey, 1949, p. xv): "To study Jonesville is to study America . . . . The social structure governing American capitalism lies within the actions of its people, for the lives of ten thousand citizens of Jonesville express the basic values of 140,000,000 Americans." Mayer (1953) contended that the assumption that there is no difference between the large society and the local community has its roots in the functional school of anthropology. He argued that, although such an assumption may perhaps be adequate in the investigation of a preliterate tribe, it is unwarranted in a complex industrial society like the United States. As he put it, "community reputational analysis is feasible only in small communities where most inhabitants know each other personally, or at least by sight. Certainly any rating procedure where local informants rate the status reputation of their fellow citizens becomes manifestly unworkable in large cities where even neighbors do not know one another" (p. 157).

In a widely cited paper, Charters (1953) argued further that the inferential structure which supported the proposition that the middle class controls education was seriously flawed. He accepted the raw data that board members, administrators, and teachers are recruited predominantly from the middle classes, but he asserted that it does not therefore follow, as the proposition requires, that the attitudes they hold in their private status determine their behavior as public officers in the school system. Inferring the proposition from these data entails four assumptions, none of which is tenable. The first assumption is that agents filling the office of board member, administrator, or teacher also occupy positions in the social stratification of the community. School board members are necessarily an integral part of the community, but in the case of the professional personnel this is by no means so clear. They are *in* the community but not *of* the community, and serious question must be raised against the first assumption of the argument. The second assumption is that a person classified in a particular social group has internalized the values of that group. Charters contended that persons do not always adhere to the values or norms appropriate to their group membership. It may very well be that some board members fall into this category, their behavior being influenced more by their "reference groups" than by their "membership groups." The third assumption is that values relevant to the operation of the school differ from one class stratum to another. There is no question that there are differences, but one additional notable finding must be considered: persons in the lower strata are generally less critical of the schools than are those in the higher class positions. If this is so, it may be argued, contrary to the proposition, that the American schools are *not* reflecting the values of the dominant class to the satisfaction of that class. The fourth assumption is that the values which agents of the school internalize by virtue of their class status are the prime determinants of their official acts in the school. If class position were the only factor in their behavior, there would be little variation among the agents who are largely of the same group. But patently, important differences do exist among school personnel from one time to another and from one place to another—differences for which a social-class analysis cannot account. And so this assumption, too, is highly questionable. Charters (1953, p. 279) concluded: "In reviewing the assumptions implicit in the argument of dominant class control of the school, we have found reason to question their unqualified applicability. Dominant class control has not been demonstrated to the satisfaction of the author."

Finally, there is the question of what emendations must be made in the original findings as a result of more recent research. A very complex methodological issue is involved here, for it is difficult to say whether the new observations are the result of shortcomings in the earlier studies or the result of changes in the schools and communities themselves—changes that ensued not only from the transformation of American society but indeed had their source, to some extent, in the influence exerted by the very work under question because of these changes. To cite but one instance, insofar as the early studies called attention to the segregation of children in school by the status position of their parents, and this influenced change toward greater "integration," then the later studies would necessarily be at variance with the earlier ones in this respect.

In general, the more significant of the studies are not content to show a relationship between the single factor of social class and some school variable. They endeavor to explore the influences accounting both for the relationship and the exceptions to the relationship. Typical of these studies was the one by Kahl (1953). He found the characteristic positive correlation between class status and the likelihood of college attendance, which prevails even when IQ is held constant. Whereas the preceding work might have stopped here, Kahl noted that prediction was good at the extremes, but it was not good in the middle. Though a boy in the top quintile of intelligence whose father was in the "major white collar" group had an 89 percent chance of aiming at a college career, and a boy of the same intelligence whose father was in the "other labor and service" group had only a 29 percent chance of aiming at a college career, a boy still with the same intelligence, whose father was in the "common man" group, had almost a fifty-fifty chance of aiming at a college career. This observation raised the important problem: What influenced the differential aspirations within the one group? Why did half aim at college and the other half not? Accordingly, Kahl selected 24 of these boys for intensive study. He found that there was, in fact, a general way of life identifying the "common man" class, but there were also significant differences within the class. Parents who were discontented with their status tended to train their sons from the earliest years to take school seriously and to use education as a means of climbing into the middle class. Only the sons who internalized such values were sufficiently motivated to aspire to college. The point, of course, is not that parents influence their children, which, as Kahl pointed out, is "obvious," but that parents within the same social class may influence their children differently. Thus we have both the operation of the social-class factor and, within a single class, quite disparate dispositional influences.

The earlier studies had consistently shown marked segregation of children in the informal "life" of the school by the status position of their parents. Brookover and Gottlieb (1963) pointed to more recent work, showing that there are internal norms in the school culture which cut across the external social class categories. For example. Coleman (1959) examined the "climate of values" among students in nine public high schools. He found that adolescents do not always reflect the values and attitudes of their parents, and social class alone will not predict their social relationships in school. Again, the earlier studies had tended to emphasize that the schools were "social elevators in a hardening social structure" acting selectively against the lower-class child to reinforce the prevailing social class structure. But more recent theoretical analyses suggest that the schools serve an allocating function in American society (Parsons, 1959). A study of graduate students in a sample of universities supports this contention by showing that approximately two-thirds of the students in natural science, social science, and the humanities came from lower-middle and lower-class backgrounds; not only is the total college population composed from all strata, but increasingly larger proportions are from the lower strata (Brookover and Gottlieb, 1963, p. 10). And finally, with respect to social class and school achievement, Rosen (1956) found the "achievement syndrome" to be associated with class position but also to act independently of it, and Strodtbeck (1958) showed that there are striking achievement differences between boys of Italian and of Jewish extraction, indicating that social class factors may be attenuated by ethnic and religious values cutting across the class lines. Moreover, Brookover and Gott ieb (1963) reported a recent study of high- and low-achieving students showing the typical relationship with socioeconomic background, but also a sizable proportion of those from the lower-class families excelling in school. They concluded: "Certainly factors other than those identified as social class are operating in determining school grades" (p. 11).

It is impossible to adjudicate in categorical terms between the proponents and detractors of social-class analysis of education. Our impression is that, if the one claimed too much, the other is willing to grant too little: the criticisms of both the conceptual and empirical works are not themselves immune from criticism. We may briefly comment on each of the preceding points at issue. Undoubtedly, there are differences between the social order and the economic order, and a reputational study is more directly related to the one than to the other. Yet, as Weber (Gerth and Mills, 1946, p. 181) pointed out, "the social order is of course conditioned by the economic order to a high degree, and in turn reacts to it." If the two orders are sep- arable conceptually, they are nonetheless sufficiently interrelated empirically that the data may not be so egregiously in error as some claim. Again, it is charged that the criteria of class are vague and unsystematic, and that the status classificatory scheme is imposed arbitrarily and not recognized by the members of the community them- selves. Yet relevant studies (for example, Hollingshead, 1949, p. 74) state explicitly and in detail that the members of the community did assert the existence of classes and gave them names, identified particular persons and themselves as members of specific classes, and associated characteristic behavior with the classes they named. Similarly, the charge that the local community studies are inevitably unrepresentative of any- thing except the particular community where the study was done may also be open to question. Not that absolute representativeness can be claimed, yet the data adduced from such different communities as Elmtown, Middletown, and New Haven do show considerable overlap.

There is no question that many of the conclusions reached by the social-class analyst were inferential. A critic cannot be denied his right to assert that a particular inference, say a positive relationship between the social class status of a school official and the manner in which he performs his educational duties, has "not been dem- onstrated to his satisfaction." On the other hand, several of the studies do provide material demonstrating that the manner in which the school official performs his duties apparently is influenced by the values he has internalized. The critic (Charters, 1953, pp. 272–273) then comments regarding this material, "Although this type of demonstration reads well and perhaps convincingly, it allows the investigator to select his evidence to prove his point"—a grave charge but one which can be neither proved nor disproved in the particular case. We are then put in the awkward position of either accepting the evidence as cited by the social-class analyst and appearing gul- lible by disregarding the critic's imputation, or disregarding the evidence as cited by the social-class analyst and appearing astute by acquiescing to the critic's contrary judgment. Perhaps all one may say with any certitude here is "More research is needed."

Finally, there is the criticism that the studies overemphasize the relation between social stratification and education, a criticism that is buttressed by evidence showing that other factors also account for differential participation in school activities, mobility, and achievement, and that there is an increasing proportion of lower-class youth in higher education. There is surely no doubt that factors other than social class account for differential school behavior, but it is doubtful that any social-class analyst ever implied otherwise. There is no question that changes in the relation between social stratification and education have taken place over the years—changes which, as we have already observed, may have been influenced by the very studies which were later brought into question by the transformation they helped to bring about. More lower-class youth are in fact in college today than a decade or two ago. Yet, as the following comparative data on college entrants make clear, the changes have not been of such an order that the social-class factor can be altogether discarded. The percentage of males of a given social class who entered college in 1948 and 1960 respectively were as follows: upper and upper-middle, 80 and 85 percent; lower-middle, 50 and 55 percent; upper-lower, 15 and 25 percent; lower-lower, 6 and 10 percent (Havighurst, 1961, p. 123). One may look at the *increase* from 6 percent to 10 percent in college entrance for the lower-lower-class youth during the period and conclude that social class is not so great a factor in educational differences as it used to be; but one may also look at the remaining *discrepancy* between the 85 percent in college entrance by the upper classes and the 10 percent by the lower-lower class even in 1960, and permit oneself to wonder whether the social-class factor is indeed as disposable in the analysis of educational behavior as several of the critics have suggested.

This is not to gainsay the validity of the criticism that many social-class studies of education are univariate in nature, or the need for emending preceding conclusions in the light of changing conditions and more refined analyses. A great deal more must be known regarding the selective process of education and the relation between education and social mobility, especially in the light of the rapidly changing technological requirements (Floud and Halsey, 1961, p. 4). Three types of studies seem particularly useful: at the most macroscopic level, cross-national studies; at an intermediate level, cross-community studies; at a more microscopic level, personalistic studies. Thus, for example, at the macroscopic level, Anderson (1961) compared a number of occupational groups in some two dozen populations in different nations varying in economic development. He found that, although farm and labor groups in the United States enjoyed unusually favorable opportunities, even here there were definite inequalities, and he concluded: "The striking fact that emerges from these data is that as the economy becomes tertiary (and even as university attendance expands) there is at most a sluggish tendency for the more disadvantaged sections of the population to contribute an increasing relative proportion of students. . . . The present results certainly demonstrate that inequality of opportunity for higher education is a widespread, and stubborn, characteristic of societies" (p. 263). At the intermediate level, Rogoff (1961) studied the relation of three factors to educational selection: scholastic ability, family status, and the processes arising from community and school structures. She found, as others had before her, that both scholastic ability and family status were significant factors in the students' plans to continue with their education. But what was more important, she demonstrated the crucial role played by the particular community—small town, suburb, or city— within the national milieu in the children's scholastic aptitude and educational aspirations. No matter what the family status, children in the large suburbs had the highest scholastic aptitude and more of them planned to go to college. And finally, at the microscopic personalistic level, a topic to which we shall return, Strodtbeck (1958), for example, showed the relation of need achievement to academic performance. In short, although for some purposes each level of analysis may be applied independently (and because of methodological difficulties often must be), it is ultimately necessary, as our basic model suggests, to consider educational phenomena in cultural, institutional, and personalistic terms interactively.

Socialization

Social scientists may disagree about the rigidity of the American class structure, but few would deny that there are variations in the way children in the different classes are brought up. The method of handling by the parents, the style of life, the material comfort, and the intentional and unintentional instruction the child receives vary depending on the social class of the family. All conceptions of child development, from simple conditioning to psychoanalysis, suggest that these differences may eventuate in distinctive personality characteristics. Numerous investigations have accumulated in this area, often with contradictory emphases and conclusions (Sewell, 1961, p. 186, has reported a selected bibliography of some 195 items by 1961).

The empirical work anchoring discussion of American social class differences in child rearing is the study by Davis and Havighurst (1946), to which reference has already been made. The results were reported in 1946, and, as has been indicated, for almost a decade they remained the definitive statement of specific status differences in socialization (Bronfenbrenner, 1958; Sewell, 1961). But in 1954 Maccoby and Gibbs (1954) published the first part of a large study of child-rearing practices in the Boston area (Sears, Maccoby, and Levin, 1957) which almost completely contradicted the Davis-Havighurst findings. There were no differences in infant feeding practices, and in opposition to the earlier observations, there was greater severity in toilet training, less indulgence in sex play, more restriction of aggression, greater imposition of demands, more physical punishment, deprivation of privileges, and ridicule by the lower-class parents than by the middle-class parents. It was the middle rather than the lower class that was more "permissive." Havighurst and Davis (1955) attempted a reanalysis of their data for a subsample more comparable in age to the subjects of the Boston study, but concluded that "the disagreements between the findings of the two studies are substantial and important" (p. 441). They speculated that these differences could be attributed either to genuine changes in child-rearing practices over time or to variations in sampling and item equivalence. Sears, Maccoby, and Levin (1957, p. 446) argued, however, that the basic interpretation of the earlier data had been in error: rejection, a pushing of the child out of the way, had been mistaken for permissiveness.

A number of ensuing investigations (for example, Kohn, 1959; Littman, Moore, and Pierce-Jones, 1957; Miller and Swanson, 1958; White, 1957) attempted to resolve the questions raised by the Chicago and Boston interpretations, with results from the separate studies generally confirming the Boston conclusions (Havighurst and Neugarten, 1962, p. 109). There the matter stood until, in a compelling analysis of 18 separate published and unpublished studies in relation to each other, the first in 1932 and the last in 1957, Bronfenbrenner (1958) demonstrated that class differences in feeding, weaning, and toilet training show "a clear and consistent trend" over time: "From about 1930 till the end of World War II, working-class mothers were uniformly more permissive than those of the middle class. They were more likely to breast feed, to follow a self-demand schedule, to wean the child later both from breast and bottle, and to begin and complete both bowel and bladder training at a later age. After World War II, however, there has been a definite reversal in direction; now it is the middle-class mother who is the more permissive in each of the above areas" (p. 424). These shifts in infant care, especially on the part of middle-class mothers, showed a striking correspondence to the changes in practices advocated by expert opinion. Two other conclusions were also noteworthy: first, although more tolerant of their children's expressed impulses and desires, the middle-class parents throughout the period continued to have higher expectations for them. Their children were expected to learn to take care of themselves earlier, to accept responsibility about the home, "and—above all—to progress further in school" (Bronfenbrenner, 1958, p. 424). Second, there were indications that the gap between the social classes may be progressively narrowing.

The relationship between such specific child-rearing practices as feeding habits, weaning, or toilet training and global personality characteristics remains controversial, some studies showing no or only slight relationships (Orlansky, 1949), and Sewell (1961) has argued that a change in research orientation is called for. Future work must increasingly concern itself with intraclass as well as interclass differences, and with variables like interests and aspirations as well as the global aspects of personality structure like "adjustment," which figured prominently in preceding work. Considerable evidence is already available regarding differences in the school-related belief systems of students, and work along these lines should be pursued. For example, as compared with middle-class adolescents, lower-class adolescents appear to have lower achievement needs (Rosen, 1956, 1959); they are more likely to have lower occupational and educational aspirations, even when such factors as IQ, parental pressure, urban-rural background, and peer influences are taken into account (Sewell, Haller, and Straus, 1957; Sewell, 1961); they are less likely to place a high value on college education (Hyman, 1953); they are less willing to defer gratifications (Schneider and Lysgaard, 1953). It would be fruitful to study in depth how these apparently class-linked dispositions develop differentially through the period of socialization and how responsive they are to intervention by the school and other forces (Sewell, 1961).

Mental ability

Davis (1948) had argued that mental functioning was culturally determined and hence there were at least two reasons why the mental ability of lower-class children could not be assessed by the conventional criteria. First, the available measures dealt with problems favoring the cultural experiences and language forms of the middle class, and second, the measures called for the kind of work habits and motivation which are not valued or taught in the lower-class culture. Accordingly, Davis and his colleagues undertook a twofold empirical attack on the problem: one was to construct a "culture-fair" measure, and the other, to examine the effects of motivation, practice, and other conditions on the test performance of lower-class children. It is outside the scope of this chapter to enter into the psychometric issues involved in the construction of a culture-fair test of intellectual functioning or to review the results obtained with the use of such instruments (see, for example, Charters, 1963; Dreger and Miller, 1960; Lorge, 1953). The actual test that was constructed (Davis and Eells, 1953), as has been the case with similar tests, produced disappointing though not consistently negative results, and Charters (1963, p. 20) was able to conclude, in his assessment of work with this instrument, that it "could not be counted on to equalize the IQ's between classes." But there was the other major issue in the argument: Could the motivation, prior training, and test forms be manipulated to affect the intelligence scores of lower-class children? Haggard (1954) studied the changes in test scores as a function of four conditions: when the test items were in the language and experience of the lower-class children, when the items were read aloud, when practice was given, and when the children were motivated by the promise of material reward for good performance. Though the social class differences were not fully accounted for by such matters as motivation, practice, test form, and rapport, the study showed that the test scores of children, whether of low or high status, could be influenced by these factors. The investigator concluded that test performance depends on the experiences children bring with them and on psychological factors in the testing situation itself. The revision of intelligence tests to remove middle-class bias might not be sufficient to produce an adequate instrument for measuring the mental ability of lower-class children; but changing the motivations of the children, increasing their familiarity with tests and test forms, and improving their rapport in the testing situation might. Similar effects of training on test scores were reported by Boger (1952) and Brazziel and Terrell (1962); and of the effect of monetary rewards as against praise, by Klugman (1944). The effect of "compensatory preschool education" will be dealt with in greater detail below (pp. 488–494).

But the question of specific training and education aside, there is an ever-increasing number of studies pointing to the significance of social and cultural factors in intellectual development. To cite only a sampling of relevant work, Nisbet (1953) confirmed the hypothesis that the environment of large families—the limited amount of contact between parent and child, and the consequent retardation of the child's verbal development—tends to depress intelligence-test scores; Bernstein (1961) analyzed the role of differential social-class language patterns in the thought processes of children, and concluded that the lower-class child is handicapped in conceptual thinking; Deutsch and Brown (1964) found significantly lower intelligence-test scores for children in father-absent homes as compared with intact families; Clarke and Clarke (1953) reported that an environment that is antagonistic toward the child retards mental development, but after removal from such conditions the retardation tends to fade and IQ increments occur; Vera John (1963) studied the differential sorting patterns of lower and middle-class children and concluded that the acquisition of more abstract and integrative language seems to be handicapped by the living conditions of the lower-class children; McCandless (1952) discussed the effect of environment on the development and maintenance of intellectual functioning, and suggested that the frustrating experiences of the lower-class child interfered with his problem-solving ability; Riessman (1962, p. 73) drew on personal experience and empirical studies to delineate the following portrait of the deprived child's "style": (1) "physical and visual rather than aural," (2) "content-centered rather than form-centered," (3) "externally oriented rather than introspective," (4) "problem-centered rather than abstract-centered," (5) "inductive rather than deductive," (6) "spatial rather than temporal," (7) "slow, careful, patient, persevering (in areas of importance), rather than quick, clever, facile, flexible."

In general, as Charters (1963, pp. 12–13) pointed out, psychologists had been explaining the relationship between social class and intelligence either by postulating hereditary factors, the persons with a higher level of innate intelligence reaching the upper social levels, or by postulating that the environment itself could be ranked in "mental stimulation value" by social class, and the development of differential intelligence levels by children attributed to the greater amount of stimulation in one environment over another. There is, however, a third possibility proposed by Davis and his colleagues, which, as Lorge (1953, p. 76) said, "motivated anew serious re-examination of intelligence and of intelligence tests." Environmental influences may differ not only in *amount* of stimulation but in *kind* of stimulation, with the consequence that different kinds of environment foster different kinds, or "styles," of thinking. The relationship between mental functioning and social class may lie in the *cultural* differences among the social classes. The crux of work in this domain may consist not in continuing to demonstrate differences in IQ but in exploring other aspects of intellect.

SEGREGATION AND EDUCATION

Whatever the judgment may be regarding the existence of subcultural dominant and subordinate groups as defined by socioeconomic status and the relation of these factors to education, there can be little doubt about the manifest existence of sub-cultural dominant and subordinate groups as defined by color and caste status, and the relation of *these* factors to education. In the South, caste discrimination was enforced by law and educational segregation was legislated. Segregation was *de jure*, and despite the "separate but equal" doctrine, educational discrimination against the Negro child is easily demonstrable in financial terms. As recently as 1940, the annual expenditure in the South per white pupil was $50.14 and per Negro pupil $21.54 (in Mississippi, the respective figures were $41.71 and $7.24), the capital out-lay per white pupil was $4.37 and per Negro pupil $0.99 (in Alabama, the respective figures were $6.68 and $0.62), the number of volumes in school libraries per white pupil was 3.3 and per Negro pupil 0.8 (Ashmore, 1954, pp. 153f). The provisions for higher education were even more discriminatory. As late as 1952, when the South was trying to overcome the evidence being presented in pending court cases that their schools were not only separate but also unequal, substantial fiscal distinc-tions, to say nothing of other forms of discrimination, remained (Ashmore, 1954, pp. 153f). In the North, the caste distinctions were informal and less rigid but no less real (Warner, Havighurst, and Loeb, 1944, p. 120). If educational discrimination was not *de jure*, it was *de facto*, as the numerous shabby all-Negro schools in New York's Harlem, Chicago's South Side, and the Watts area of Los Angeles to this day readily attest. The effects of educational segregation could be seen not only in the inferior status of the Negro in every aspect of school achievement but, as Chief Justice Warren wrote in the 1954 public school desegregation ruling, in every aspect of his being: "To separate [Negro children] from others of similar age and qualifica-tions solely because of their race, generates a feeling of inferiority as to their status in the community that may affect their hearts and minds in a way unlikely ever to be undone."

Even where *educational* segregation is not enforced, the Negro faces *personal* discrimination. He is often automatically considered mentally inferior and incapable of learning—as one who need not be dealt with as a differentiated human being. It is this, as a number of Negro writers point out, that is most shattering to the concep-tion of one's self. "I am an invisible man," writes Ralph Ellison (1952, p. 7). "No, I am not a spook like those who haunted Edgar Allen Poe; nor am I one of your Hollywood-movie ectoplasms. I am a man of substance, of flesh and bone, fiber and liquids—and I might even be said to possess a mind. I am invisible, understand, simply because people refuse to see me. . . . When they approach me they see only my surroundings, themselves, figments of their imagination—indeed, everything and anything except me." James Baldwin puts this even more directly: "the Negro in America does not really exist except in the darkness of our minds . . . . He is a social and not a personal or a human problem; to think of him is to think of statistics, slums, rapes, injustices . . ." (see Lott and Lott, 1963, p. 1). Sensitive white writers also see this; thus, William Faulkner (1959, p. 308) observed: "No white man understood Negroes and never would so long as the white man compelled the black man to be first a Negro and only then a man. . . ."

Segregation, personality development, and school achievement

Pettigrew (1964a) contended that, despite the importance of the problem and the numerous studies, many of the most crucial questions about the personality of the Negro American have not received even tentative answers. There are three reasons for this failure: First, the greater bulk of research is directed toward various practical problems devoid of theoretical perspective. Second, there are at least two formidable methodological difficulties; the race of the interviewer is a complicating factor, and it is virtually impossible to control for such factors as education, Southern subculture, and socioeconomic class. Third, there is a great need for a social-psychological theory that will take into account not only the history and cultural position of Negro Americans as these are reflected in individual personality, but will also specify the mediating mechanisms among the factors. An inadvertent but telling example of how real these difficulties are is provided by two papers published side by side in the journal containing Pettigrew's article: on the basis of one set of empirical data, one paper (Noel, 1964) concluded that the ethnic identification of Negroes *increases* with their social status; on the basis of another set of empirical data, the other paper (Parker and Kleiner, 1964) concluded that the ethnic identification of Negroes *decreases* with their social status.

Despite the conceptual and methodological difficulties, which must always be borne in mind, there is at least one recurring conclusion regarding the psychological development and characteristics of the Negro child in relation to his education: what is true for the lower-class child can be applied in extreme form to the Negro child. As the Ausubels (1963) pointed out in their perceptive paper on Negro ego development, caste status places the average Negro in an inferior subculture even within the lowest socioeconomic class: well over 50 percent of Negro families live at the very lowest level of the lower-class standard. Physical surroundings are more likely to be inferior, intellectual stimulation less available, homes more likely to be broken, fathers more often absent, family life less stable (Ausubel and Ausubel, 1963; Dai, 1953; Hill, 1957). The child's opportunity of "learning to learn" in preparation for school under these conditions is at a minimum. But segregation by caste has more far-reaching implications for development than just lower-class membership. The Negro child perceives himself as socially rejected by the prestigeful elements of society and develops a sense of his own worthlessness (Bernard, 1958; Clark and Clark, 1965; Lott and Lott, 1963; Riessman, 1962; Wertham, 1952). The white lower-class child may hope to escape and surmount his class membership, even if the hope is often illusory, but for the Negro the stigma of caste membership is "inescapable and insurmountable" (Ausubel and Ausubel, 1963, p. 119). The Negro cannot

realistically compete in the labor and professional market with whites of equal intelligence and education.   Unfavorable socialization experiences, unequal school
opportunities, and manifest occupational discrimination all conspire to depress the
educational motivation and academic achievement of Negro children, especially
Negro boys. They attend school less regularly, they drop out in greater numbers, and
on the average they learn much less than white children (see Ausubel and Ausubel,
1963; Bloom, Davis, and Hess, 1965; Bullock, 1950; Dreger and Miller, 1960;
Kennedy, Van de Riet, and White, 1961; Osborne, 1960; Pettigrew, 1964b).

There is no doubt that Negro pupils are also handicapped in school by significantly lower IQ's than comparable white pupils have (Dreger and Miller, 1960;
Kennedy, Van De Riet, and White, 1961; Klineberg, 1963; Shuey, 1958). Though
a contrary view is expressed by some investigators (Shuey, 1958), most hold that environmental conditions contributing to the lower academic achievement also
contribute to the lower IQ (Ausubel and Ausubel, 1963; Dreger and Miller, 1960;
Klineberg, 1963; Pettigrew, 1964b). In a recent study, Deutsch and Brown (1964)
demonstrated once more that there are significant differences in IQ between Negro
and white children. But, in addition, their findings show: (1) Negro children at each
socioeconomic level score lower than white children; (2) Negro-white differences
increase at each higher socioeconomic level; (3) for the lower-class Negro there is a
decrement in IQ from the first to the fifth grade; (4) there is a consistent trend for
the IQ's of children without fathers in the home to be lower than for those with
fathers in the home; (5) there is a significant effect of preschool experience on IQ—
children who attended a nursery or kindergarten score higher than those who did
not, the difference being greater at the fifth grade than at the first grade level. These
data seem to support the "cumulative deficit hypothesis" previously advanced (Deutsch,
1963): deprivational influences have a greater impact at later than at earlier developmental stages. As Deutsch and Brown (1964, p. 31) put it, differences that are not
significant in the first grade "are simply not significant *yet*."

Desegregation and the American dilemma

If segregation has serious manifest effects on the Negro, it has no lesser latent effects
on the white (Myrdal, 1944). The social psychology of education must deal as much
with one as with the other. Rose (1956, p. 312) pointed out: "what is important in
the Negro problem is what is in the minds of white people, and . . . changes for good
or evil in the Negro problem depend primarily on changes in people's beliefs and
values." Studies (Cook, 1957) of the response of presumably similar border communities to the Supreme Court desegregation decision showed an enormous range
of reaction depending on "what was in the minds" of the people. In Cairo, Illinois,
for instance, desegregation was initiated only by threat of legal action, the local
school authorities, the entire white population, and even much of the Negro population apparently being opposed to desegregation; in Carlsbad, New Mexico, desegregation was begun two years before the Supreme Court decision, no groups in the
community being opposed; in Hoxie, Arkansas, the school authorities favored
integration but general public opinion was strongly opposed (Williams and Ryan,
1954).

Campbell and Pettigrew (1959) investigated one aspect of this "American dilemma" in some depth by examining the role of ministers in the desegregation of

Little Rock. Of the 29 clergymen interviewed, only five were segregationist, yet most ministers were far less active than their value systems would lead one to anticipate. The study revealed almost a classic case of role-personality conflict: the self-reference or dispositional system of the ministers typically favored integration; the professional-reference system as represented by ministerial associations was without sanctions; the membership-reference system represented by the ministers' congregations was strongly opposed to desegregation. Personal dispositions alone, then, would lead the liberal ministers to defend integration and condemn as un-Christian those who supported segregation. But the ministers were obligated to consider the expecta-tions of their church membership, and the church members could apply sanctions. In view of the multiplicity of pressures, the investigators concluded that it was not surprising that most ministers were less vocal than their own values would predicate. Rather, what was surprising to them was that a small number of the ministers con-tinued to express the moral imperative in the face of threatened social reprisal.

Desegregation and education

Though the threat of reprisal for acting upon moral imperative remains, and there is a "hard core" of opposition to school desegregation which would use force against attempts to mix Negro and white children in the same schools (Tumin, 1958), opinion on school desegregation and the estimate of the Negro child seem to have undergone significant alteration in recent years. Hyman and Sheatsley (1964) reported that, on the question whether Negro and white children should attend the same school, the shift toward positive responses from 1942 to 1963 in the North was from 40 to 75 percent, and in the South from 2 to 30 percent. On the question whether they themselves would object to sending their children to a school where a few of the children were Negro, the shift in "would not object" responses in the two years between 1963 and 1965 was from 87 to 91 percent in the North, and from 38 to 62 percent in the South (Pettigrew, 1965). And perhaps most noteworthy, the notion re-garding the innate inferiority of the Negro has also undergone radical transforma-tion. In 1942, 50 percent of white Northerners and 21 percent of white Southerners believed the Negro to be as intelligent as the white; in 1963, the respective figures were 80 percent and 59 percent (Hyman and Sheatsley, 1964).

Nonetheless, there is a paradox between these verbal reports and what appears to be happening. As Pettigrew (1965) suggested, the problem of racially separate schools is growing more, not less, complex, and seems increasingly to be evolving from *de jure* to *de facto* segregation. This is especially true of the great urban centers. There are cities like Washington, major divisions of cities like Manhattan in New York, and sections of cities like Woodlawn in Chicago which are very largely Negro in resi-dential composition. How is school integration to be achieved in these ghettos? And there is the flight of white (and sometimes Negro) middle-class families from the urban centers to suburban communities, leaving the city schools to the lower-class and Negro populations. The situation is further complicated by the fact that, in addi-tion to the white segregationists, there are Negro separatists who also advocate educa-tional segregation on principle, albeit a different principle. The battle against *de jure* segregation may be won at the cost of *de facto* segregation, and the war against educa-tional discrimination on the grounds of color may yet be lost for the near future. It is not inconceivable that the present separate school systems may evolve into two other types of separate school systems: urban and suburban. The problems of segregation seem to be transformed into the problems of urbanization.

Though the ultimate evidence is by no means yet available, this much seems clear: despite the very real psychological difficulties faced by Negro children in desegregated schools (Katz, 1964), and perhaps by some white children as well, the dire effects on education that some predicted have not eventuated. On the contrary, Pettigrew (1964b, pp. 127f) has shown that the evidence is in the reverse direction. Educational administrators in communities ranging from Logan County, Kentucky, and Muskogee, Oklahoma, to Baltimore and Washington reported that their academic standards had not been lowered by desegregation—in fact, the standards had improved for *both* groups. Factual assessment of achievement scores in Washington after desegregation also showed improvement for both Negro and white students. Louisville similarly showed substantial gains in Negro performance and slight gains in white performance after only one year of desegregation (Stallings, 1959). As Pettigrew (1964b, p. 128) pointed out, desegregation as such does not accomplish this feat. There are numerous factors at work: the new and healthier self-image the Negro is said to gain in the process, encouragement of the Negro parents and teachers, a more vital interest on the part of the community as a whole in education. But even so, these improvements do not lift the average Negro-performance to white norms. Desegregation prepares the way, but it is not *by itself* a panacea for the problems faced by Negro and white lower-class—or so-called "culturally deprived" or educationally disadvantaged—children.

SOCIALIZATION AND COMPENSATORY PRESCHOOL EDUCATION

Many proposals for doing something educationally distinctive for lower-class children have been made through the years, including smaller classes, specially trained teachers, particular emphasis on reading, learning materials based on the experiences of the children, special facilities and help with homework, and almost any other devices that might conceivably be productive in bringing their level of academic achievement up to that of middle-class children. However, these measures seemed to many only to pose the dilemma rather than to provide a viable solution. The measures were *remedial* rather than *preventive;* they were directed at doing something *after* the child was in school rather than *before.*

Latterly there has been a vigorous movement—some would say an almost too vigorous movement—for preschool education to compensate for the lack of preschool preparation of these children (see, for example, Bloom, Davis, and Hess, 1965; Deutsch, 1964; Hunt, 1964). Supporting the movement are two lines of argument drawn from social-psychological theory and investigation. First is the evidence for the preeminent impact of early experience; it is during the early period that the child not only acquires a characteristic set of values, language, and fund of information, but literally *learns to learn.* It is during this period that he acquires the basic cognitive and affective dispositions for meeting the expectations he will face upon coming to school. Second is the claim that the values, language, information, and style of learning acquired by the middle-class child are *continuous* with what will be required of him in school; the values, language, information, and style of learning acquired by the lower-class child are *discontinuous* with what will be required of him in school.

In a paper at the 1965 White House Conference on Education, Getzels (1965) examined the assumptions and current status of preschool education in the context of five basic issues: (1) What is the effect of early experiences on the development of school-related abilities?   (2) How early must the opportunity for school-related experiences be available? (3) What are the differences between "deprived" and "non-deprived" children in the continuity and discontinuity of preschool experiences and school expectations? (4) What is the nature of compensatory school education, and what are the empirical results?   (5) What are some of the long-range ideological issues? These questions may be dealt with in turn here.

Early experiences and school-related abilities

Numerous studies attest to the view that the development of both specific and general cognitive dispositions—the dispositions required for success in school—is determined in many critical ways by the availability of relevant experiences in the preschool environment. Work along this line has steadily increased in frequency and rigor. To mention only a sampling of studies in several school-related abilities, Irwin (1948) found a systematic relationship between mastery of speech sounds in infants one to 30 months of age and the occupational status of the family; Milner (1951) found a significant relationship between the reading readiness of first-grade children and the "verbal environment" at home; Montague (1964) found a similar relationship between the arithmetic concepts of kindergarten children and the socioeconomic status of their families; Brown and Deutsch (1965) have gone a step further in specificity and shown that not only are there differences in cognitive performance between social class and race groups, but also, within the groups, a "particular level of cognitive performance reflects certain specific environmental characteristics"; Hess (1964) reported the same relationship for the acquisition of language and the nature of the mother-child interaction. Hunt (1964, p. 223) suggested that "it looks now as though early experience may be even more important for the perceptual, cognitive, and intellective functions than it is for the emotional and temperamental functions."

Timing of school-related experiences

How *early* should the opportunity for relevant experiences be available? For example, is the present school age—the magic number six—time enough? Little is known about this for any specific ability, or, of course, in view of different rates of maturation, for any given individual. Nonetheless, an increasing number of studies are showing that it is the lack of *early* experience that may be most damaging not only in learning such specific habits as linguistic accents but, as Hunt (1964, p. 220) has said, in "'programming' [the] intrinsic portions of the cerebrum so that they can later function effectively in learning and problem-solving."

The most direct studies of the "timing" of experience come from experiments with animals—experiments that cannot be done with humans. For example, Riesen (1947, 1958) deprived animals of light at various stages in their growth, and found that early and sustained stimulus deprivation resulted in perceptual deficit. Thompson and Heron (1954) compared the adult problem-solving ability of Scotty pups reared as pets in human homes from the time of weaning until eight months of age with that of their litter-mates reared in isolation in laboratory cages for the same period. The adult tests were made when the animals were 18 months old, after both groups had been together in the dog pasture for a period of 10 months. The early experience seemed decisive: the pet-reared animals performed better than the cage-reared animals. There is relevant if less direct evidence for humans as well. Bloom (1964, pp. 72f) estimated the long-term overall effect of living in a "culturally deprived" as against a "culturally abundant" environment to be 20 IQ points, and hypothesized that this effect was spaced developmentally as follows: from birth to four years, 10 IQ units; from four to eight years, 6 IQ units; from eight to 17 years, 4 IQ units. The rank-order correlation between the hypothesized effects and empirical data from a number of studies was 0.95, the absolute amount of the observed effects being substantially greater even than the estimates.

But the evidence that is perhaps most suggestive for humans comes from a number of "natural experiments." Hebb (1949) cited the studies by Senden of congenitally blind individuals who were given sight as adults but had to *learn to see.* Dennis (1960) compared the onset of walking among Hopi children who were cradled and not cradled, and the onset of walking among children brought up in Teheran orphanages where stimulus variation was minimal. He concluded that the reason why there was no difference in the age of onset of walking between the cradled and the noncradled Hopi children but there was retardation in the orphanage children was that both groups of Hopi children experienced a rich variety of stimulation from their mothers, which the orphanage children did not get. Hunt (1961, pp. 258f) argued that Piaget's conception of the organism-environment interaction through assimilation and accommodation is neither hereditarian nor is it environmentalistic; it is both. He (1964, p. 226) drew attention to Piaget's emphasis on looking and listening in the first phases of development and offered the aphorism: "the more a child has seen and heard, the more he wants to see and hear" (see Piaget, 1952, pp. 276).

The question here is not whether there are constitutional determinants of perception or cognition (see Fantz, 1961, 1963; Gibson, 1963). The point rather is that, given the same potentialities at birth, the availability and timing of experience appear to facilitate or inhibit the expression of the potentiality. Much of what may appear as somehow arising "innately"—perception, language, temperament, what has been called the child's characteristic "learning set" or what may be called his "codes for future learning"—is affected by the mediation of multiple and early experiences. There are significant differences in this respect in different environments: the necessary experiences tend to be available for some children and not for others. Indeed, the term "culturally deprived," which for want of a better one seems to have been widely applied to children in this disadvantaged situation, should be taken to mean not the lack of a culture in general but the lack of availability of school-related experiences at the appropriate time. Perhaps it might be better to refer to the situation not as culturally deprived but as educationally deprived or disadvantaged.

Value and language experiences
of educationally deprived and nondeprived children

The third question was: What are the differences between so-called "culturally" or educationally deprived and nondeprived children in the continuity or discontinuity of preschool experiences and school expectations, or more specifically, what is the nature of the differences in the "codes for future learning" acquired by the two groups? Attention has already been called to such specific differences as are measured by vocabulary, arithmetic, reading readiness, and intelligence tests. There are two *more general* differences that must be considered. Through early contacts with the environment, the child learns two pervasive "codes" that become the substratum for behavior: one is a *language code*, the other a *value code*. The language code gives him the categories for structuring and communicating his experiences. The value code tells him what in his experiences is important, worth attending to. It is precisely with respect to the character of these crucial codes that the disadvantaged child may differ most sharply from the advantaged child and from school requirements.

Explicitly or implicitly, the school requires an *achievement* ethic, with consequent high valuation of the *future, deferred gratification,* and *symbolic commitment to success.* Not only are these the values of the school, but they are the values of the environment in which most middle-class children are brought up. In contrast to this, the lower-class child is likely to experience only a *survival* or *subsistence* ethic (not an achievement ethic) with consequent high valuation on the *present* (not the future), on *immediate gratification* (not deferred gratification), and *concrete commitment* (not symbolic commitment). Empirical evidence shows that the children do in fact reflect these experiences. Thus, lower-class children tend to have lower "need achievement" than middle-class children (Rosen, 1956, 1959), and their educational and occupational aspirations also tend to be lower (Sewell, Haller, and Straus, 1957); they tend to learn more quickly when given material than nonmaterial incentives, while the reverse is true for middle-class children (Terrel, Durkin, and Wiesley, 1959); their time orientation is shorter (LeShan, 1952), and they are less willing to defer gratification than are middle-class children (Schneider and Lysgaard, 1953). In short, the lower-class in contrast to the middle-class child may face a severe discontinuity between the values he has internalized and the values that are functional in the school setting, a discontinuity which may affect not only his behavior toward the school but the school's behavior toward him.

What has been said of values is applicable as well to language. One line of work that is relevant here is that of Bernstein (1961, 1962), which is consonant with other observations in this area. He argued that different social strata generate different speech systems or linguistic codes, regulating the selection an individual makes from what is available in the language as a whole. These linguistic codes, which develop early and are stabilized through time, come to play an important role in the intellectual, social, and affective life of the child. There are two language codes: one "elaborated," the other "restricted." In the restricted code, the vocabulary and syntactic structure are drawn from a *narrow* range of possibilities, the organizing elements of the speech are *simple,* and there is *considerable dependence on extraverbal channels of communication* such as gestures. In the elaborated code, the vocabulary and syntactic structure are drawn from a *wide* range of possibilities, the organizing elements of the speech are *complex,* and there is *little reliance on extraverbal channels of communication:* the message must be given and sought in the verbal material itself. A middle-class child is likely to experience and acquire an elaborated language code; a lower-class child, a restricted language code. The school is of course predominantly concerned with elaborated language codes. In language as in values, then, for one child school is *continuous* with his early experience, and for the other child school is *discontinuous* with his early experience. From this point of view, compensatory preschool education may be seen as an effort to bring the experience of the lower-class child into greater continuity with the expectations of the school—expectations that presuppose middle-class value and language codes for its children—not only to increase learning but to avoid the frustrating consequences of incongruence between what he has experienced and what the school expects.

Compensatory preschool educational programs

The current rapid rate of growth and diversity of preschool projects precludes saying anything about the nature of the programs or the research without risk of oversimplifying and being out of date almost at once. Despite the wide variability in specific activities, the programs may be classified (at least for analytic purposes) into three broad categories. In one, the predominant assumption seems to be that the observed deficiencies of the educationally disadvantaged child are more superficial than fundamental—the differences are in quantity rather than in kind—and the preschool experiences that are needed are *supplementary*; from this viewpoint, if a nursery or preschool activity is good for the middle-class child, it is good also (if perhaps at some simpler level) for the lower-class child. In a second, the assumption is that the significant deficiencies reside in the lack of familiarity with school-related objects and activities—say, pencils, books, the use of crayons, following directions—and the preschool experiences the child needs are predominantly *academic-preparatory*. In the third, the assumption is that, because of powerful environmental effects, the disadvantaged child becomes fundamentally different in self concept, language, value, and perceptual process; from this point of view, neither the supplementary nor the academic-preparatory activities in themselves are sufficient: what is required is *specialized activity* that will *compensate for*, in the sense of *counteract*, the deleterious environmental effects.

In view of the theoretical and procedural differences, it might be expected that research in this domain would be abundant. Regrettably, there are as yet no systematic comparisons of the relative effectiveness of the several types of programs nor of different points of intervention within a given type of program. However, two relevant observations from the research that is available so far can be made. One is that early educational enrichment tends to be effective in raising intelligence-test scores, vocabulary level, expressive ability, arithmetical reasoning, and reading readiness. Independent current reports by Bereiter *et al.* (1965), Gray and Klaus (1963), Weinart, Kamii, and Radin (1964), and Larson and Olson (1965) all point to one or more of these effects, as do the studies by Kirk (1958) with mentally retarded children and the earlier investigations at the Iowa Child Welfare Station, which were ridiculed at the time but are now being reexamined (see Hunt, 1964, p. 209). All this is encouraging, even though the studies used different procedures and it is impossible to say what it is specifically in the preschools that accounts for the positive effects. The second observation is less encouraging. Though Deutsch (1962) has reported differences in the fifth grade favoring children who attended preschool over those who did not, the evidence is apparently from an uncontrolled study, and two more recent experimental studies (Weinart, Kamii, and Radin, 1964; Larson and Olson, 1965) which have followed their children through kindergarten and first grade report that the initial differences tended *not* to be maintained in the regular school situation. Larson and Olson (1965) bluntly stated that their data indicated "one shot" compensatory programs would seem to be a "waste" unless the entire curriculum of urban schools is revised. It must be emphasized that this is but one exploratory study done with only a handful of subjects at the kindergarten rather than an earlier period. Nonetheless, this and the preceding observations raise questions that must be faced: What are criteria for selecting preschool activities from the available alternatives? On what basis will the effectiveness of what is being done be evaluated? May not long-term mischief be done to the idea of compensatory preschool education if the possible lack of educational effects is interpreted erroneously for want of careful research? To pose these questions is not to derogate what is being done, but it does suggest that a more solid base in conceptualization, long-term planning, and empirical study is needed. In any case, whatever the effects of the prevailing preschool programs, these efforts must not become substitutes for making the radical alterations needed in all aspects of the inner city schools.

School expectations as the criterion for pupil dispositions

Getzels (1965) raised a last ideological issue, which ought perhaps to have been the first issue. The preceding questions have all dealt with problems of means, assuming the ends—the ends being, to put it most sharply, to transform the dispositions of the preschool lower-class child in accordance with the role expectations of the prevailing school. But this raises two troublesome issues, the first concerned with the nature of the transformation that is to be imposed on the child, and the other with the character of the school that will presumably serve as the standard for the transformation.

The concept of cultural deprivation (or whatever other term is used) presumes that there is a normative or dominant middle-class culture, and that some children are deprived of experience with *this* culture (not *all* culture). From this viewpoint, the middle-class child is also culturally disadvantaged—disadvantaged in relation to the values and experiences of *another* culture, say intimacy and cooperativeness as against aloofness and competitiveness. It is a *relational* not a quantitative concept, and cultural deprivation in the present context refers only to deprivation of school-related middle-class values and experiences. It does not mean that the culturally deprived child has fewer values, nor that he may not have other values and experiences that are assets.

This raises the first issue. Assume with Frank Riessman (1962, p. 48), among others, that the lower-class child *does* have certain assets in the way of values and experiences that are both functional and also of intrinsic worth—say "equalitarianism, informality, and warm humor" or "lessened sibling rivalry." What will be the effect of imposing contrary attitudes such as achievement anxiety on these assets or on the child's functioning in his environment? Can a program of compensatory education, even at its best, be salutary in any ultimate way without altering the racism and the disadvantaged environment giving rise to the disadvantaged child? Will the child's conception of life and of himself disappear if Appalachia, Harlem, and Watts are permitted to remain?

The second issue is not unrelated to the first. Compensatory early education is predicated on the criterion of success in school as the measure of fruitful socialization; the children are to be raised according to the modes of behavior and thought rewarded in the classroom. But the demands of the present school are themselves contradictory: on the one hand, the school rewards conformity and docility, and on the other, it implies later success through ingenuity and daring. And more, the school is said to be defective educationally; it can hardly serve as a model. Thus, Bettelheim (1961, p. 393) suggested that "learning inhibitions can come from a child's desire for honesty and truth in the light of his own life experience and of clear-cut desires and values." Do Sally, Dick, and Jane represent honesty and truth for the Negro child or, for that matter, any child? Henry (1957) showed how relentlessly honest feeling and originality are stamped out in the elementary school by the prevailing rivalry, which is at once stimulated and feared by the teacher herself. Friedenberg (1959, p. 69) questioned whether the social and intellectual way of life reflected in the school should be taken as a "Given of the Natural Order." In the face of this, one may well ask: Can the standards of today's schools be taken safely as the model for the transformation of the disadvantaged child, and more broadly, is this what we want for our children, or should not some thought be given, even in the present context, to the transformation of the school itself? We may put the issue in the terms of our framework. Assuming, as seems justified, that certain cultural values provide inappropriate criteria for satisfactory socialization and personality formation, are the expectations of the school system as it is presently constituted likely to provide more satisfactory criteria for socialization and personality formation, considered as more than just learning to read and write? The vulnerability of the schools in this respect has become increasingly apparent. Particularly, the urban scene in 1965 is undergoing vast changes in mood and militancy, and we may anticipate transformations in the educational system at all levels.

THE SCHOOL AS A SOCIAL SYSTEM

In the preceding sections we dealt with the relation of the school as a system to the community in which it is embedded, and to other systems with which it is in contact. In the present section we shall deal with empirical studies of the school itself, and in the following section with the classroom as the teaching-learning unit within the school. We shall consider first the elementary and secondary school, and then the college and university.

Elementary and secondary school: the informal student society

Wayne Gordon (1957) analyzed the social system of a suburban high school in a Midwestern metropolitan community. He accepted Hollingshead's (1949) argument that behavior in the school was fundamentally related to family status in the community, but he felt that this said nothing about the manner in which conformity and adjustment in the school actually occur. Accordingly, he focused his study on the structure of the institution itself, a major hypothesis being that the social behavior of students is functionally related to the *general social position they occupy in the status system of the school.* He suggested that there are two sets of expectations: first, those deriving from the formal structure of the school as an organized social system, and second, the expectations deriving from the informal associations and organized extracurricular activities of the student culture. The two sets of expectations are integrated in such way as to determine the social prestige of individual students. The dominant motivation to action is to meet the expectations of the *informal* structure.

 Gordon found that grade-point rank contributed least, extracurricular activity most, to general social status. For boys, the primary determinant of status was athletics, combined with such other characteristics as grade level, dress, dating, and friendship. For girls, the determinants of status were more diffuse, including a complex of personality, school service, dress, and morality exemplified by selection in the senior year as Yearbook Queen. Though the friendship patterns for both boys and girls moved steadily toward a more integrated system of prestige strata from freshman to junior year, for boys the solidarity of team accomplishment in athletics maintained the friendship pattern through the senior year, but for girls competition for Yearbook Queen tended to disrupt former friendship patterns.

The dominance of informal considerations in student status did not eliminate conformity to teacher expectations in the classroom—the teacher could enforce compliance through the power of the grade—but the student subculture redefined the meaning of achievement and grades in three substantial ways. First, the students acquired a lore about "what it takes to pass" and "how to get a grade" with which they manipulated teachers into giving them better grades than their objective achievement warranted (p. 37). Second, students varying in social status—say, "big wheels" and "nonwheels"—had distinctive personal associations with the teachers affecting both classroom interaction and the distribution of rewards (p. 47). Third, the requirements of the two sets of expectations, those presented by the formal system and those defined by the informal system, resulted in classroom conflict (pp. 34f).

The complexities presented by the informal "alien subculture" in the formal system added up to a situation of continuous stress in the teacher's role, forcing the teacher to seek adjustment to the various pressures in order to protect his personality. Some teachers dealt with their problems privately; others, in the "intimate congeniality" of selected colleagues. Some teachers sought support from the principal and relied on official authority; others attempted to attain student control through personalized relationships. But the reality of the informal student subculture remained and had to be taken into account if the nature of the formal educational process and the education obtained by the students of Wabash High School were to be understood. As Bidwell (1965, p. 982) pointed out, these results confirm Waller's (1932) ideas regarding the pervasive conflict between official procedures and the affective components of pupil-teacher interaction.

Gordon focused on the student culture of a *single* high school. Coleman (1961), citing his indebtedness to both Hollingshead and Gordon, undertook to compare student cultures in ten diverse high schools ranging in size from 150 students to almost 2000, and in locality from a farm community of 1000 inhabitants to a major city of several million. Data including interests, attitudes, and peer ratings were collected by questionnaire and sociogram from the entire student body in each school, and supplementary data by questionnaire from samples of parents and teachers in each school. Some parts of the analysis dealt with all schools together; other parts with each school separately. Thus both the commonality and variation of student cultures were examined.

The observations in the schools taken together were in essential agreement with Gordon's. Once more there was the characteristic organization of the student system into groups of greater or lesser prestige, and once more the boys' groups were more closely integrated than the girls' groups. The *content* of the student culture was again found to center on nonacademic values: in all cases athletics was extremely important for the boys, and social success with boys was extremely important for girls (p. 314). Scholastic success received differing rewards, and sometimes punishments, in the different schools, but in no instance did it "count" as much as other activities (p. 265).

Coleman demonstrated a striking effect of peer-group rewards for academic excellence—that is, the frequency with which "good grades" were mentioned as a criterion for being in the leading crowd—and the utilization of academic ability by the students. In the school where social rewards for good grades were highest, the boys whose average grades were A or A− had IQ's 1.53 standard deviations above the school mean; in the school where social rewards for good grades were lowest, the boys with an average of A or A− had IQ's only about a third (0.59) of this distance above their school mean (p. 262). There was no reason to suppose that good grades were valued less by the teachers in one school than by those in the other. The implication seems clear: the student culture has a direct impact on how much a student will "put out"—when the student culture devalues good grades, there is a strong deterrent to academic achievement.

Coleman placed much of the blame for the alienation of student culture from academic values simultaneously on the peculiar status of athletics and the attempt by schools to do away with competition as a motivating device for academic effort. He argued that organized athletics provides virtually the only avenue available to the *student body as a unit* for positive competitive action, and this action carries its own discipline with it. What is left in the classroom is only the unpleasantness of negative competitive action by *students as individuals against each other*, that is, grade grubbing. Coleman suggested that the structure of rewards in the school must be shifted from interpersonal competition, with its conflict-producing effects, to intergroup competition, in which group rewards reinforce achievement. More important even is the general principle: "motivations may be sharply altered by altering the structure of rewards, and more particularly . . . among adolescents, it is crucial to use informal group rewards to reinforce the aims of education rather than to impede them" (p. 322).

The studies by Gordon and by Coleman are the only systematic investigations of any scope into the student society. There is a large body of more narrowly focused work, for the most part using sociometric techniques, which consistently indicates the presence of sex, age-grade, prestige, and leadership subgroups in the school system. There seem to be no inquiries into the teacher colleague society to match those of the student society (see Bidwell, 1965, pp. 984–985, 992).

Elementary and secondary school: the formal adult structure

To understand the structure and operation of the school, it is necessary to analyze the hierarchical and collegial relations among the superintendent and principal, and principal and teacher, as well as the impact of these relations on the student. Peculiarly, as Bidwell (1965) pointed out, there seems to be no published work in this area. There are, however, a number of discrete studies of superintendent–school board and of principal-teacher relations that do provide some insight into the formal operation of the school system. Gross, Mason, and McEachern (1958) reported interview and questionnaire data bearing on consensus within and between 105 school superintendents and nearly all of the 517 members of their boards of education on two main variables: the division of responsibility between board and superintendent in the policy-making and in the executive functions. The degree of consensus was related to a variety of personal and organizational factors. Among the findings were the following: (1) there was greater overall consensus among superintendents than among board members; (2) the greater the homogeneity of the board along such dimensions as religion, political orientation, level of education, and motivation for service, the greater their agreement on educational matters; (3) the better educated the board member and the more motivated he was for civic service, the greater his approval of the professional ideology of school administration; (4) with respect to agreement or disagreement between board and superintendent, boards similar in motives and education were especially likely to endorse professional points of view and to agree on such matters with the superintendent; (5) such characteristics as common religion or political orientation, which tended to produce high agreement among boards, did not directly affect agreement with the superintendent, thus casting school board–superintendent relations in organizational-role rather than in personal-status terms.

Work by Carlson (1961, 1962) shows the systematic relationship between the criteria used by school boards to hire superintendents and (1) the career patterns of the superintendents and (2) the nature of their performance. On the basis of observations, interviews, and sample surveys, Carlson distinguished two career-line characteristics of school superintendents: place-bound and career-bound. The place-bound superintendent was recruited from within the school system in which he was serving at a lower echelon; the career-bound superintendent was recruited from another school system. In the first case, the board usually wanted a man to consolidate changes already introduced in the system; in the second case, the board usually wanted a man to introduce changes that needed to be made. The attitudes and characteristics of the two types of superintendents differed systematically, the one being unwilling to assume risks either for himself or his office, the other willing to do so. The career-bound people were given a broad mandate as to goal and wide latitude in method of attaining the goal; the place-bound people were not given such freedom, and were required to be more responsive to the wishes of the board and to the already existing staff. Accordingly, career-bound superintendents tended early in their tenure to make new rules and add new members to their personal staff, while the place-bound superintendents seemed content with maintaining the established rules and making few personnel changes.

Halpin (1956) compared the expectations held for the administrative behavior of the superintendent by his board of education and his subordinate staff, and their perceptions of his actual performance. The subjects of the study were 50 Ohio public school superintendents, the 237 members of their school boards, and 350 members of their staffs. The instrument used was the Leader Behavior Description Questionnaire (LBDQ), which provides two measures similar in meaning to the role and personality dimensions of our model: Initiating Structure (IS), referring to the extent that a leader organizes the role activity of subordinates, and Consideration (C), referring to the extent that a leader maintains personal relationships and grants autonomy to his subordinates. The respondents answered the questions in two ways: according to the perceptions of the superintendent's actual behavior and the expectations of how he should behave. Though board members tended to stress Initiating Structure in their expectations, the staff members tended to stress Consideration, thus, it would seem, providing the superintendent with a dilemma—whether to adhere to superordinate or subordinate expectations. Moreover, although staffs and board members tended to agree among themselves with respect to the superintendents' actual performance, they did not agree with each other. Staff members perceived the superintendent as low in Consideration; the board members perceived him as high, thus reversing their expectations and further confounding the role and personality dilemmas within the school system—a subject to which we shall return in a later section.

College and university

The preceding studies dealt with elementary and secondary school systems. We now turn to studies of college and university systems. With the change in level of education comes a transformation in the character of the typical issues under investigation. The elementary and secondary studies were concerned with the formal and informal structures of the school, and with the administrative interaction. Only infrequently did they touch on the relation of these observations to differential educational output. The hard-boiled practitioner may be tempted to remark, "All right, this school has high consensus and that one low, but what difference does it make in any performance variable?" Indeed, both from a theoretical and from a practical point of view, either high or low consensus may be more conducive to productivity. Much of the theoretical and practical inconclusiveness of educational research probably has its source in the lack of an acceptable criterion of productivity to which observations can be anchored. What *is* the criterion to be applied in evaluating the productivity of one elementary or secondary school against another—personal adjustment, academic achievement, vocational preparation, social awareness, creative aspiration, admission to an Ivy League college?

The studies of colleges and universities begin with differences in productivity and output, and raise the question of how to account for the observed differences. The point of departure for most recent studies is the work of Knapp and Goodrich (1952), who showed that a relatively small number of higher institutions were especially productive of scholars and scientists, and by Knapp and Greenbaum (1953), who devised an index of institutional productivity of "younger American scholars" and demonstrated enormous variability among colleges and universities in such productivity. The index was based on the number of students per thousand graduates from 1946 to 1951 who later received Ph.D. degrees, university, government, or foundation fellowships. When this index was applied to some 377 undergraduate schools, the obtained distribution was striking in its large positive skew: only a very small number of schools were productive by *this* criterion. When the 50 institutions with the highest indices for male graduates and the 13 institutions with the highest indices for female graduates were designated as "institutions of high productivity," some interesting characteristics of these schools were observed. For example, for the male group, only four of the schools were publicly controlled, 31 of the 50 were liberal arts colleges, 18 had some religious affiliation, the very top five schools were coeducational, and in the first 12 institutions the fraternity system was either nonexistent or extremely weak. However, Knapp and Greenbaum (1953) suggested that ultimately the differential productivity of schools, and especially of the small liberal arts colleges, lay in the "climate of values" which "elevated the scholar and the intellectual to the position of 'culture hero'" (p. 97).

The more recent studies focus on the differential climate of "value" or "expectation" or "environmental press" among institutions and the relation of these to differential outcomes in student achievement. Typically, Pace (1963) reported the results of a long-term investigation of differences in the "atmospheres" of 32 colleges as measured by the College Characteristics Index (CCI), a 300-item instrument based on

Murray's concept of "environmental press" and paralleling the previously available Activities Index (AI) measuring "personality needs." Among the major results were that, beyond a few common characteristics (for example, student leaders do not have many special privileges), colleges are vastly different from one another. The range of correlations of the 30 subsections of the CCI for the 32 institutions was from 0.93 to −0.87, differences between college environments tending to fall into several distinctive clusters—humanistic, scientific, practical, welfare, and rebellious. These in turn form patterns of interrelations such that (for example), though the humanistic and scientific clusters are positively related in an intellectual pattern, the humanistic cluster is unrelated and the scientific cluster is negatively related to the social-welfare cluster. In short, one may think about college environments as "whole cultures" having distinctive "atmospheres." More than this, there are "predictable and demonstrable consequences" which follow from the differences: the correlation between the intellectual-humanistic cluster and the percentage of men who go on to graduate school was 0.80, and of women 0.84 (p. 77).

But a crucial question may be raised: Are the different rates of productivity due to the nature of the institution *per se* (the "institutional productivity" hypothesis), or to the nature of the students in the institutions (the "student quality and motivation" hypothesis)? In the terms of our general model, the one hypothesis argues for the primacy of the institutional role expectations in student achievement, the other for the primacy of personalistic need dispositions. The work of Knapp and of Pace was predicated on the first hypothesis. An ingenious study by Holland (1957) tends to support the second hypothesis. Using data from the National Merit Scholarship students for the years 1955 and 1956, Holland sought answers to three fundamental questions regarding institutional productivity. First, are different rates of college productivity a function of differential attendance rates by scholastically superior students? Holland calculated the "expected" rate and the "observed" rate of attendance by his talented students at "high" and "low" productive colleges, and found that they attended "high" productive institutions in frequencies 3 to 15 times the "expected" frequencies (p. 434). Second, are differential rates of institutional productivity a function of differential socioeconomic status in the student populations? Knapp and Goodrich had suggested that scientists may originate more often in "lower" than in "higher" socioeconomic groups and, conceivably, institutions with high productivity may attract larger proportions of such students, but Holland found no evidence for this (p. 434). Third, are differential rates of productivity a function of parental vocational motivations and their implied attitudes and values concerning scholarly achievement? Holland found that the students in "high" productive colleges tended to have fathers in physical-activity, scientific, and social-welfare occupations, and students in "low" productive institutions tended to have fathers in persuasive, sales, and supervisory occupations. It is not unreasonable to believe that the differential backgrounds of the parents have significant implications for their children's interest in scientific and scholarly attainment (p. 435). All in all, he concluded, the evidence argues strongly against the "institutional productivity" hypothesis; variations in college productivity are probably due to the divergent proportions of high-aptitude students in these colleges and to differences in their educational motivations.

Heist *et al.* (1961) further explored the hypothesis that colleges are differentially selective, not only with respect to scholastic aptitude, which may be self-evident, but also with respect to underlying attitudes, values, and intellectual dispositions. Their sample of 268 subjects was drawn from Merit Scholarship students who had been part of Holland's population. Relevant personality tests and questionnaires were administered prior to college entrance and before the first year in college was completed. When the students were divided into two subsamples matched for scholastic aptitude, one attending "high" and the other "low" productive colleges, highly significant differences in the hypothesized directions were found. The investigators concluded that students of high ability in "high" and "low" productive colleges tend to differ significantly in dispositions related to serious intellectual pursuits, thus supporting the explanation that differential college productivity resides in *who the students are* rather than in *what the institutions do.*

But this by no means settled the issue. On the basis of a series of equally ingenious studies also utilizing Merit Scholarship data, Thistlethwaite (1959a, 1959b, 1960) reached an opposing conclusion, that even if the quality of students is equated, there still remains an appreciable institutional effect. He devised an index of institutional productivity independent of student quality based on the discrepancy between a school's expected rate of Ph.D. output as predicted by its enrollment of talented students and its actual rate of output (1959a, p. 72). Two such indices were developed: one for the natural sciences (NS) and the other for the arts, humanities, and social sciences (AHSS). When he applied these indices to different types of institutions, Thistlethwaite found wide variations in productivity independent of the quality of the student body. For example, a comparison of 81 Catholic institutions with 157 Protestant institutions showed the latter to be significantly more productive both in NS and AHSS (1959a, p. 73). When the median scores on each of the 30 scales of the College Characteristics Index as filled out by 916 Merit students in 36 colleges were correlated with the NS and AHSS measures, 12 of the 30 scales were significant at the 0.01 level with at least one of the productivity measures (1959b, p. 185). One type of college environment was associated with achievement in the natural sciences, while a different kind of environment was associated with achievement in the arts, humanities, and social sciences. Productivity in the humanities was positively related to humanism, reflectiveness, sentience, harm avoidance, and understanding, and negatively related to pragmatism, deference, and abasement. Productivity in the natural sciences was positively related to scientism, aggression, and impulsion, and negatively related to order, deference, and sentience (1959b, p. 186). This again suggests that there are differences in institutional productivity not accounted for by differences in student quality.

Since CCI is a composite of items describing both student and faculty, it was impossible to tell whether faculty influences or student-culture influences, or both, are related to productivity. Thistlethwaite (1959b) therefore constructed two separate scales: one descriptive of student culture, the other of faculty culture. The findings with each scale were once more consistent with the hypothesis that scientific achievement and scholarly achievement thrive in different types of environments. The investigator concluded that the college environment is an important determinant of educational productivity, at least as measured by the students' motivation to seek advanced intellectual training. Moreover, there are differences in the college environments which stimulate productivity in the natural sciences or in the arts, humanities, and social sciences.

In many ways these studies provide the strongest available evidence that differential environments have differential effects on the behavior of students (Pace, 1963). However, although the studies controlled for scholastic aptitude, they did not control for motivational factors, nor did they deal directly with the effect of college environment on educational motivation. In a subsequent study, Thistlethwaite (1960) investigated the effect of differential college environments on student motives by examining the relationship between the college experiences of 1500 Merit students in 327 colleges and changes in their major field of study and level of training sought. The results provide interesting data regarding the distribution of talented students in the various subject-matter fields, changes in field of study during college, characteristics of teachers having greatest influence on students, and so on. But in the present context, the salient findings were that all predictions regarding the effect of faculty press on student motivation to seek graduate training in certain fields were confirmed: college environments characterized by faculty affiliation, emphasis on achievement, enthusiasm, and independence were associated with increased student level of academic aspiration in the arts, humanities, and social sciences; college environments characterized by lack of faculty emphasis on compliance were associated with increased student level of academic aspiration in the natural sciences. There was no evidence that student press influenced the level of aspiration, at least so far as Merit students are concerned. It seems quite clear, as Pace (1963, p. 78) pointed out, that different environments do have a demonstrable consequence on student behavior over and above the student culture which is part of the total college culture.

We have suggested that behavior in a social system is a function of *both* the institutional role expectations and the individual personality dispositions. One set of the preceding studies focused on the institutional dimension and found that *it* contributed to the behavior of college students, and the other set on the personalistic dimension and found that *it* contributed to the behavior of college students. The crucial question, then, is not which set of data is correct to the exclusion of the other, but rather what is the interaction between the two factors (to say nothing of other variables). What, for example, is the effect on productivity when student dispositions and institutional expectations are congruent or discrepant? As part of his notable series of studies of college environments as milieus for learning, Stern (1962, pp. 713f) examined the relative congruence or discrepancy between student needs (or dispositions) and environmental press (or expectations) of some 32 colleges of various types. Among the findings were the following: students in the same institution tend to have similar need scores; the perceptions of press are not projections of needs; different types of institutions vary in the uniqueness of student needs and environmental press; institutions vary in the relative congruence or discrepancy between needs and press. With respect to the last two findings, business administration students are least like any other students; liberal arts colleges are most distinctive in press; the discrepancy between student needs and institutional press is greatest in the liberal arts colleges, least in schools of engineering.

No consideration of research into the American college, however brief, can be concluded without mention of the volume *The American College* (Sanford, 1962), which contains some 30 informative papers on various aspects of higher education, including changes in the character of the American college student. A number of the papers supplement the more quantitative work on higher education with perceptive reports in depth of individual institutions: Riesman and Jencks (1962) on the University of Massachusetts, Boston College, and San Francisco State College; Brown (1962) and Freedman (1962) on Vassar; Jencks and Riesman (1962) on Harvard; Hughes, Becker, and Greer (1962) on medical education. More recently, Knapp

(1964) combined the "statistical" and "case history" methods of inquiry in a study of the baccalaureate origins of individuals taking the doctorate in the humanities and the origins of the doctorate itself. Included in the results were factorial typologies of 95 institutions by "style of scholarly production" and other statistical analyses showing major distinctions between two classes of institutions: privately supported institutions of high cost usually in the East, and publicly supported state universities typically in the Midwest and West, the one a prolific source of humanistic scholars, the other identified more with the production of scholars in the sciences and technologies. But over and above the presentation of the statistical findings, a third of the monograph was devoted to comparative case studies of three Eastern universities (Yale, Harvard, Catholic University), two Western universities (Berkeley and Stanford), and three Midwestern state universities (Wisconsin, Indiana, Ohio State). Knapp calls his work a study in the "ecology" of humanistic education, and as such it may well serve as a model for the study of other areas of higher education.

THE CLASSROOM AS A SOCIAL SYSTEM

Two general observations may be made about research on the classroom, on teaching, and on teacher-pupil interaction: first is its vastness—there are literally thousands of studies—and second is the noncumulative nature of most of the work. The first characteristic attests to the importance of the issues, the second to the paucity of integrative concepts. It is noteworthy that, although there are many systematic theories of learning, there are few such theories of teaching (Bruner, 1964). For analytic purposes, empirical inquiry into the classroom may be divided into the following overlapping categories: (1) observations and ratings of classroom behavior, (2) sociometric structure, (3) classroom climate, (4) group process and interaction, (5) the classroom as a pattern of role and personality relationships.

Observations and ratings of classroom behavior

Extensive reviews of the literature on the observation and rating of classroom behavior are contained in the *Handbook of Research on Teaching* (Gage, 1963). The simplest method of comparing classrooms is to make a global rating of teacher skill, but such ratings have proved uniformly unsuccessful in yielding measures that correlate significantly with any other observation of teacher effectiveness or classroom behavior (Medley and Mitzel, 1963, p. 257). Attempts were therefore made to replace the global ratings with objective indices of what teachers and pupils "actually do." But this, too, did not prove very fruitful. For example, it was found that, of numerous observations of teacher and pupil verbal and nonverbal behavior, only items like student "looks around," "ignores instructor," "sleeps or dozes" had any relationship to measures of student achievement (see Medley and Mitzel, 1963, pp. 261f). On the basis of earlier work by Cornell, Lindvall, and Saupe (1952) and Withall (1949), Medley and Mitzel (1963, pp. 278f) constructed an omnibus instrument called OScAR (Observation Schedule and Record) to help the observer see and hear as much of what was going on as possible and to record as much of it as he could "without assumptions as to its relative importance or relevance to any known dimension." Though a number of the observations seemed to account for some of the differences in teacher-pupil rapport and in principals' ratings, none succeeded in getting at any aspect of classroom behavior related to pupil achievement of cognitive objectives. Medley and Mitzel (1963, p. 288) suggested that recent work of a more systematic nature involving the "logic" of class-room discourse (Smith, 1959) and of verbal behavior in mathematics (Wright and Proctor, 1961) may prove more useful in developing a much-needed theory of instruction.

Though the early omnibus ratings and observations of global classroom behavior did not provide very fruitful results, such methods have been applied with significant effect in research on specific problems in teacher-pupil interaction. For example, in a study founded in "equilibrium" theory and using rating scales, Gage, Runkel, and Chatterjee (1963) examined the effect of feedback on teacher performance. They found that giving teachers feedback by informing them how they were rated by their pupils not only produced change in teacher behavior but improved teacher accuracy in the perception of their pupils' opinions. Hoehn (1954) used a classroom observation schedule to test the often repeated judgment that teachers accord better treatment to pupils of high than of low socioeconomic status. The investigator tabulated five hours of observations in each of 19 third-grade classrooms and found both quantitative and qualitative differences in teacher-pupil contacts, but these were due more to variations in achievement than in socioeconomic status. Meyer and Thompson (1956) were interested in studying the differential responses of teachers to girls and to boys. On the basis of prior socialization theory, they hypothesized that the "masculine" behavior of boys will result in male pupils receiving a larger number of dominative, or punitive, contacts than girls from their teachers, who are primarily women from the middle socioeconomic stratum of society. To test this hypothesis, three sixth-grade teachers and their pupils were directly observed for a total of 30 hours per classroom. In all three schools, the boys did in fact receive significantly more disapproval than the girls. Making insightful use of direct observations of a number of elementary school classrooms, Henry (1957) showed how the teacher's needs for acceptance by her children and her fear of inability to control free discussion often compel her to push children into uncritical docility, while they seek her approval. It was the formulation of important problems and the application of relevant concepts that gave meaning and fruitfulness to the observations in these studies.

Sociometric structure

The observation method provides an "outsider's view" of the relations in a group; the sociometric method provides an "insider's view" of the relations in the group. The school class involves relations in a group, and it was only natural that sociometry be applied to studying the structure and dynamics of the classroom. Extensive reviews of the literature are given by Lindzey and Borgatta (1954) and by Gronlund (1959), and more recently, specialized reviews have been given by Remmers (1963), Withall and Lewis (1963), and Bidwell (1965). Some studies do little more than describe the sociograms of classrooms in different localities, with results consistently indicating the presence of sociometric cliques and subgroups within the formal organization of the class, more clear-cut clique structure at the secondary than at the elementary level, and higher sociometric status for the more intelligent, socially adept, and peer-conforming children (Bidwell, 1965, pp. 984–985). Gronlund (1959, pp. 93–113) found typical sociometric patterns among classes and across schools: a larger percentage of the pupils appear in the lower (few positive choices) than in the higher (many positive choices) sociometric status categories, boys and girls both show preferences for their own sex, there is an increase in mutual choices in the higher grades. But there are also indications of idiosyncratic influence by the school on certain classroom patterns. For example, the percentage of cross-sex choices in seating, work, and play in sixth-grade classrooms varied from 21, 15, and 7 percent in one school to 6, 4, and 2 percent in another. Moreover, within the classroom, although the teacher's perception of high and low status children is not the same as the children's own, the sociometric status of a child is related to his contacts with the teacher and to the teacher's contacts with the child. Bonney (1947) investigated whether teachers could identify students who were high and low in sociometric status by comparing the estimates of 13 teachers and the actual choices of 291 of their students. He found that teachers tended to overrate students who were active in class and conformed highly to teacher standards of behavior, but who were looked on as outsiders by other students. They tended to underrate students who had good interpersonal relationships in their own cliques and those who were well liked by peers, but who were likely to disregard teacher regulations. Lippitt and Gold (1959) showed that teachers more often pay attention to the social (rather than the performance) behavior of low status pupils than of high status pupils. Apparently this aspect of their behavior is as salient for teachers as it is for classmates. How the teacher reacts to such children depends on whether they are boys or girls. Low status boys receive more criticism than their high status classmates, but low status girls receive more support.

In view of the differential perceptions and responses of teachers to pupils according to sociometric status, it would seem that there should be systematic relation between achievement and status. Buswell (1953) administered a battery of intelligence and achievement measures and a sociometric test of best-liked peers to examine the relation between pupils' intellectual performance in class and their status with peers. She found that the highly accepted pupils were significantly higher than the rejected pupils in mean achievement. Schmuck (1962) also studied the issue of sociometric status and achievement, especially the utilization of academic abilities. The elementary school classrooms in his sample varied in the pattern of sociometric structure, some being "diffuse" (wide distribution of negative and positive choices) and others "central" (narrow distribution of choices). Pupils were able to perceive their status more accurately in the sociometrically "central" than in the "diffuse" classrooms. The investigator found that low utilization of academic ability was an interaction effect of low sociometric status and accurate perception of the status, but high utilization was not related in the same way to these factors. It is possible that the relations between sociometric rank and intellectual performance are artifactual, both variables appearing as effects of other student attributes such as intelligence or emotional stability (Bidwell, 1965, p. 989). Nonetheless, the observations are provocative in suggesting that classroom structures have important consequences for student achievement and in generating significant hypotheses for further inquiry.

Classroom climate

A number of influences converged to stimulate the study of "classroom climate." One almost forgotten influence seems to have been the work of Dorothy S. Thomas, who as early as 1929 initiated the study of social interaction and formation of groups among nursery school children (see Medley and Mitzel, 1963, p. 263). A second was the introduction of sociometric techniques with the publication in 1934 of Moreno's

Who Shall Survive? A third was the work in mental hygiene, child development, and education by such people as Prescott (1938) and subsequent studies showing the effect of knowledge of children's attitudes and emotional problems on the teacher's effectiveness (Ojemann and Wilkinson, 1939). A fourth, less direct but unquestionable, influence was the work by Roethlisberger and Dickson (1939) demonstrating the effect of group climate on industrial productivity. A fifth was the introduction of Rogerian nondirective counseling which, as Stern (1963, p. 426) says, "appeared to offer a point of departure for classroom instruction supported by psychological theory, educational practice, and ethical belief." The sixth and by far the most potent influence was the work in group dynamics, and especially the study by Lewin, Lippitt, and White (1939) on the different behaviors of children in differing social climates, a study which had an enormous impact on educational practice and inquiry.

Lewin, Lippitt, and White (1939) examined the effect of three leadership roles and the consequent group climates by observing the behavior of four "clubs" of five 10- or 11-year-old boys each under three leadership conditions: "democratic," "autocratic" ("authoritarian"), and "laissez-faire." Groups were matched to control for individual differences, and leaders were rotated to control for treatment variation. Records were kept of relevant behavior, including the interaction within the group, between the leader and individual boys, the expression of aggression, and productivity in club projects. One observation stood out above all others. The social climates resulting from the different leader styles produced significant differences, which can be briefly summarized as follows: (1) aggressive behavior was either very high or very low under authoritarian conditions, extremely high under laissez-faire conditions, and intermediate under democratic conditions; (2) productive behavior was higher than or as high in authoritarian climates when the leader was present as in democratic climates but much lower when the leader was absent, moderately high and independent of the leader's presence or absence in the democratic climates, and lowest in the laissez-faire climates.

A major limitation of the study—a limitation that was to persist in a long line of work deriving from this study—was that the authoritarian leader seemed not only to have been "directive" but also "unfriendly." Though the authoritarian pattern was not intended to be personally disagreeable, as performed experimentally it manifested a personal harshness that need not necessarily accompany autocratic rule (Wallen and Travers, 1963, p. 476). Despite this, the theoretical and applied issues raised by the study led to a fruitful body of work reexamining the nature of interaction in the classroom. A notable series of studies was undertaken by Thelen and his associates (see Thelen, 1950, 1951; Thelen and Withall, 1949). Withall (1949) developed a Climate Index involving the transcription and analysis of the verbal behavior of teachers into seven categories, further divisible into two classes: learner-supportive or -centered and teacher-supportive or -centered statements. If more teacher statements were of the first kind, the classroom climate was said to be "learner-centered"; if of the second, the climate was said to be "teacher-centered." Significant relationships were found between the Climate Index and other measures of group process, pupil reactions, expert ratings, and styles of problem-solving activity (Withall, 1949; Thelen and Withall, 1949; Flanders, 1949). The work of H. H. Anderson and his associates on "dominative" and "integrative" teaching styles, the one producing aggressive behavior in the classroom, the other cooperative and self-directed behavior, had come before this. Recently instruments for categorizing pupil-teacher interaction and studies of classroom climate have been reported on such functions as "positive and negative affectivity" by Hughes (1959) and on "direct and indirect teacher influence" by Flanders (1960). Whether the dimensions of classroom inter-action dealt with in these studies are called "authoritarian-democratic," "teacher-centered–student-centered," "dominative-integrative," or "direct–indirect influence," there is little question that they refer to similar phenomena, and the phenomena are of importance in educational theory and practice (Medley and Mitzel, 1963, p. 274), though not so simple or decisive as some would maintain (Anderson, 1959).

Group process and interaction

In addition to the observation of classroom climates in the "natural" context of the school, there is also the observation of experimentally manipulated learning groups and laboratory classes. These studies have been founded primarily in classic small-group concepts and methods, but include influences from T-group theory (Miles, 1964), person perception (Tagiuri and Petrullo, 1958), and individual versus group learning and problem solving (Hare, 1962, pp. 339–373). The relevant literature is immense, the *Handbook of Small Group Research* (Hare, 1962) listing some 1300 studies. A recent text (Bany and Johnson, 1964) devoted exclusively to "group dynamics and education" reviews many of the small-group studies especially relevant to education. Here we can attempt only a brief description of illustrative work and some generalized conclusions for several of the conceptual categories given by Hare (1962, pp. 374–391) as they reflect on classroom learning.

Group size. To select the appropriate size group for a given problem, Thelen (1949) suggested the "principle of least group size." That is, the group should be just large enough to include all the relevant skills necessary to solve the problem; larger groups provide less opportunity for individual participation and greater opportunity for con-flict, and therefore are less efficient. Hare (1962, p. 388) cited two studies, one with a physical, the other with an intellectual task, to make the point of "diminishing re-turns." In the first study, one person could pull 63 kilograms using 100 percent of capacity, but eight persons were able to pull only 248 kilograms, 49 percent of average individual capacity. In the other study, a similar effect was obtained as eight groups of different sizes discussed an intellectual problem and recorded their contributions on a blackboard. The average number of individual contributions decreased as the size of the group increased. McKeachie (1963, pp. 1131–1132, 1142–1143) reviewed the literature on size of lecture and discussion classes, and concluded that group size is a much more relevant variable in classes taught by discussion than in those taught by lecture.

Group cohesiveness. A number of studies (see Cartwright and Zander, 1960) have ex-amined the nature of group cohesiveness and its effect on productivity. In general, highly cohesive groups are found to have many beneficial aspects such as responsible activity, interpersonal influence, and individual security, but the relation to actual productivity is less certain. The consequence specifically of cooperation and compe-tition has also been examined. Morton Deutsch (1960), for example, investigated the effects of cooperation and competition in experimental classroom situations. In one condition, the students were told that they would be graded individually in relation to each other's performance. In the other condition, the students were told they would be given a single grade depending on the performance of the group as a whole. The cooperative group was superior in coordinated effort, diversity of contribution per member, achievement pressure, and attentiveness to their classmates. There was no significant difference, however, in the amount of learning, "though the tendency was in favor of the cooperative group" (p. 447).

Group communication. Interaction in a group depends on the communication patterns available to the members. For example, Leavitt (1951) constructed five-member groups and placed them in circular, linear, cross-over, and Y-type communication linkages, and found systematic variations in the number of errors made and in morale among the groups. Bavelas (1960) summarized the findings from this and similar studies by suggesting that the available communication patterns make for distinctive locations of recognized leadership, probability of error in performance, and general satisfaction of the group members. In this sense, the character of the physical arrangement of a classroom—whether it is the conventional rows of seats facing the teacher's desk or the circular arrangement of a seminar table—necessarily influences the nature of the interaction (Getzels, 1960).

Group composition. One of the salient pedagogic problems is the composition of classroom groups. Classrooms are normally composed by age-grade and curriculum characteristics. But what about grouping within age and grade by similar ability or by sex or interest or personality? Or is there some optimum "mix" that is superior to either similarity or randomness? This is, of course, the ancient dilemma of homogeneous versus heterogeneous grouping, and the research findings here are inconclusive. Though general opinion favors homogeneous grouping, at least by ability, there is contrary evidence as well (McKeachie, 1963, pp. 1143–1144; Russell and Fea, 1963, pp. 909–914). Torrance and Arsan (1963) studied the effect of grouping children homogeneously or heterogeneously by intelligence and creative ability on their performance in creative scientific tasks. The findings with respect to productivity were ambiguous, seeming to depend for significant results on type and level of ability, but for all types and levels of ability there was greater disruptive social stress in the heterogeneous groups. It may well be that optimal group composition lies not in the issue of homogeneity versus heterogeneity but in the "compatibility" between the person's dispositions and the expectations of the role he is to play in the group. In an experiment with "compatible" and "noncompatible" groups formed by selecting individuals by intelligence and personality according to their prospective roles in the group interaction, Schutz (1958, pp. 128–135) confirmed his hypothesis that the compatible group would be more productive. Thelen (1963), in a classroom experiment of compatible grouping for "teachability," found that the differences between "teachable" and regular classes did not lie in one or two outstanding traits such as IQ or past achievement; rather the differences were many but small and were distributed over a wide range of measurable traits.

Group leadership. That type of leadership—authoritarian-democratic, direct-indirect, dominative-integrative—has an effect on group interaction and performance was demonstrated by the work of Lewin, Lippitt, and White (1939) and the multitude of studies that followed. The implications of these studies for the classroom were held to be straightforward: "democratic" methods were better than "autocratic" methods, discussion methods better than recitation methods, the seminar better than the lecture. Educational textbooks (see, for example, Burton, 1952, p. 297; Mursell, 1954,

p. 146) generalized from the available findings and reported unequivocally that learners accomplished more both in subject-matter and personal-social learning in the "permissive" setting, and they accordingly advocated "democratic" over "authoritarian" classroom organizations, often almost without any qualification as to the nature of the task or of the character of the students or teacher.

Others argued that this was educational sentimentalism and name-calling on the basis of political value implications of the terms themselves. Direct methods of instruction need not be "authoritarian" in the nasty sense of the word, and in fact teacher-centered procedures *can* be more satisfactory than other methods. In an effort to shed light on the controversy, Anderson (1959) examined 49 experimental studies in which authoritarian leadership was compared with democratic leadership, focusing on 32 investigations especially relevant to the classroom situation. Though Hare had concluded from a similar extensive review that democratic leadership was associated with low productivity and high morale whereas authoritarian leadership was associated with high productivity and low morale, Anderson (1959, p. 204) concluded that "it is still impossible to demonstrate that either of the two styles is more closely associated with high productivity or high morale." More particularly with respect to the 32 investigations dealing with learning as an outcome, 11 studies showed greater learning for the student-centered groups, 13 studies showed no difference, and eight showed greater learning with the teacher-centered methods (Anderson, 1959, p. 209). In general, morale is higher in the learner-centered groups, but not when there is anxiety about grades awarded on the basis of final examinations. Anderson remarked that "the results of twenty years of investigation remain embarrassingly non-cumulative" (p. 209), and concluded that the "authoritarian-democratic construct, as far as education is concerned at least, has far outlived its usefulness either as a guide to research or as an interpretation of leadership behavior" (p. 212).

Stern (1963) reviewed 36 educational studies about half of which overlapped with those dealt with by Anderson. He concluded (pp. 427–428) that cognitive gain was largely unaffected by whether the teaching was directive or nondirective but, regardless of whether the investigation was concerned with attitudes toward a cultural outgroup, other participants in the class, or toward oneself, the results generally indicated that nondirective instruction facilitated a shift in a favorable direction. McKeachie (1963) also reviewed the literature, especially with respect to lecture versus discussion methods at the college and university level. He suggested that work in this area has dealt with *the* lecture method and *the* discussion method but not with significant variations within each method which might make a difference. For example, such lecture variables as credibility of the speaker, order of presentation, presentation of one side of an issue or both sides, and the emotionality of the argument (see Hovland, 1963) all might have an effect on the observed results in lecture-versus-discussion research. More generally, McKeachie (1963, p. 1127) raised the issue of whether the question regarding the merit of one method as against the other as presently put—that is, "Which is better?"—might not more usefully be stated as "For what goals?" One method might be better if the expectations are for "simple" learning, the other if they are for "complex" learning.

To this one may add the further question, "And for whom?" Students with varying dispositions will react differently to similar expectations. The point is nicely made by Wispe's (1951) study of eight matched sections of an introductory college social-science course, four of which were taught "directively" and four "permissively." Though there were no differences between the methods when taken as a whole, there were two findings that are crucial to the present question: first, when the two methods were analyzed for their effects on the "better students" and the "poorer students," the directive sections were more beneficial to the latter; and second, students who were personally dependent, insecure, and intropunitive preferred directive instruction, while students who were personally independent, secure, and extrapunitive preferred permissive instruction. The significant observation lay not in the situational factors alone, nor in the personalistic factors alone, but in the interaction between the two.

The classroom as a pattern of role and personality relationships

One need not accept Anderson's (1959) low estimate (see p. 508) of the democratic-authoritarian construct as related to research on the classroom to suggest that we shall probably have to depart from this as well as other dichotomous formulations if further progress in this field is to be made. To characterize a classroom in such global terms is to obscure the complexities of the teaching-learning situation. A number of alternatives have been proposed. One alternative is to study the classroom in terms of ecological concepts, linguistic analyses, or teacher behavior categories that are more differentiated than "directive-permissive" leadership (for example, Barker, 1963; Bellack, 1965; Jackson, 1964; Kounin, Gump, and Ryan, 1961; Smith and Meux, n.d.). Another is to apply the kind of need-press variables used by Stern, Stein, and Bloom (1956) which have been found especially fruitful in the study of school environments. But Lavin (1965, p. 161) suggested that this too may be too gross for the analysis of the specific face-to-face role and interpersonal systems of the classroom. A third possibility is to conceive of the classroom as a miniature society or social system with differentiated role and personality relationships linked to differentiated educational goals (Getzels and Thelen, 1960). This formulation speaks directly to three of the salient issues of classroom structure left largely unanswered in preceding work: (1) McKeachie's question, "For what goals?" (2) Wispe's question, "For whom?" and (3) the more general problem of the nature of instructional styles going beyond the democratic-authoritarian construct.

Goals of instruction: "what" is involved. In the conception of the classroom as a social system presented here, behavior is seen as a function of teacher and student attempts to cope with an environment composed of patterns of roles and patterns of personalities to achieve institutional effectiveness and individual efficiency (see pp. 461–465 above). The proportion of role and personality factors determining behavior will vary with the specific goal, the specific role, and the specific personality. The interaction we have in mind may be illustrated by the representation shown in Fig. 3 of the relation between role and personality factors involved in the course of, say, a class in English.

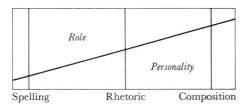

Fig. 3. The relation between role and personality factors in a class in English. (After Getzels and Thelen, 1960.)

In these terms, activity in the classroom may be defined along a continuum from objectives requiring maximum adherence to expectations, as in learning to spell, where the opportunity for personal idiosyncrasy as to acceptable outcome is minimal, through tasks like acquiring a characteristic rhetorical style, where individual idiosyncrasy in outcome is acceptable but only within an expected grammatical structure, to creative expression, where the greatest freedom of personal idiosyncrasy may be encouraged and for which there is no single "right" expectation as there is in spelling. The conception of the classroom as a social system in specific role and personality terms may provide for an orderly analysis of the relation between educational goal, instructional style, and classroom structure.

Individual differences: "who" is involved. This conception also provides for systematic entry into Wispe's question of the interaction between situational factors and individual variables, for it is clear that, insofar as behavior in the classroom is a function of role *and* personality, some teachers and students simply because of *who* they are will perform better in, say, a spelling-type or directive situation which is defined primarily in role terms, and other teachers and students will perform better in a more permissive situation which allows greater opportunity for individual expressiveness. As we shall see in the following section, there are individuals of apparently similar general ability who not only function better in one classroom atmosphere than another but who characteristically do better in one subject than another, depending on the types of role-personality proportions involved in the subject matter.

Styles of instruction. Classroom instruction is concerned with producing change in behavior, that is, learning. The teacher is the designated leader in this. The present formulation suggests that three ideal-type orientations are available to him: what we have called institutional (universalistic), personal (particularistic), and transactional (see pp. 467–468 above). The first emphasizes the role dimension and is universalistic with respect to individual differences; the second emphasizes the personal dimension and is particularistic with respect to individual differences; the third moves from the one to the other, depending on the behavior change to be achieved. In these terms, one may view directive and permissive leadership styles, which have served as the constructs for so much of classroom research, as special cases of only the first two possibilities, and omit the third possibility. This conceptual omission has had two results: (1) in practice, widespread belief that directive instruction (for example, the lecture) is inherently bad and permissive instruction (for example, the discussion) inherently good, no matter *what* or *who* is involved; and (2) in research, endless comparisons of directive and permissive teaching methods, with only infrequent analysis of what and who is involved, as if these were irrelevant issues. Whether the conception of the classroom as a social system in role and personality terms or some other conception will prove more fruitful is difficult to say, but what seems certain, as Anderson (1959, p. 212) suggested, is that the conception of the classroom as either authoritarian or democratic seems to have reached a point of diminishing returns and that we are now forced to explore new avenues of inquiry.

PERSONALITY AND THE EDUCATIONAL PROCESS

We have dealt with a number of salient aspects of the value dimension in education, with the relation between the value dimension and the role dimension, and with the role dimension, though we could not discuss these without some reference to the personality of the role incumbent as well. We turn now to a consideration of the personality dimension itself, especially as related to the central role incumbents in the educational process, the teacher and the pupil. The twofold issue is: What is the relationship of the personal characteristics of the teacher to performance in teaching, and what is the relationship of the personal characteristics of the pupil to performance in learning?

Teacher characteristics and teaching

As in other areas of educational research, there is no dearth of studies of teacher personality and characteristics. The annotated bibliography by Domas and Tiedeman (1950) mentions some 1000 items, and a more recent review of the literature by Getzels and Jackson (1963) refers to the addition of at least 800 items since then. We shall discuss the pertinent results under two headings: (1) cognitive dispositions, and (2) noncognitive or affective dispositions. The former deals with intellectual variables such as intelligence, divergent thinking, and verbal understanding, the latter with personalistic variables such as attitudes, preferences, interests, and needs, though of course the two are not unrelated.

Cognitive dispositions. As a group, teachers and teacher-trainees score higher on standardized measures of intelligence than does the population at large, but they score lower than other professional groups (Wolfle, 1954). However, reliance on mean scores in these comparisons may be misleading, since the overlap among the various groups is great. For example, the average AGCT scores of graduate students in medicine is exceeded by about 35 percent of the graduate students in education (Getzels and Jackson, 1963, p. 570). Relatively little is known about the cognitive abilities of different subgroups of teachers, though Ryans (1960) indicates some superiority in "verbal understanding" on the part of female teachers over male teachers, graduates of liberal arts colleges over graduates of state and teachers colleges, teachers in large cities over those in smaller communities, teachers in the upper grades over those in the lower grades. The differences are small, even when statistically significant, and do not seem to be of either great predictive or great theoretical importance.

A more important question is the relationship between intellectual ability and performance in teaching. Morsh and Wilder (1954) reviewed 55 studies appearing between 1927 and 1952 in which an attempt was made to relate intelligence-test scores to measures of teaching effectiveness. The results were confusing, 16 studies showing positive correlations exceeding 0.30, but these were balanced by at least 15 studies reporting negative correlations. What is more, Shea (1955) found that for 110 graduates of a four-year teachers college program the correlation between practice-teaching grades and the nonverbal-reasoning section of the National Teacher Examination and with the L and Q scores of the American Council of Education Psychological Examination were 0.00, −0.08, and −0.17. The correlations between on-the-job ratings of effectiveness with the same measures were 0.06, 0.34, and 0.29 respectively. It would seem that continuing to correlate global intelligence-test scores with teaching achievement will not contribute much to our understanding of teaching. It may be more profitable to explore other cognitive variables, and Knoell (1953), for one, attempted to do just this by examining the relation between a number of the Guilford-type "ideational fluency" tests and several measures of teaching performance, with promising results. It is not that the empirical data are so compelling in themselves, but the observations lend themselves more readily to a conceptualization of teaching than do observations with many other measures of mental ability. It is easier to understand why the "ability to call up many new ideas in a situation" should be related to teacher success than to understand why, say, the "ability to memorize digits" should be so related. In any event, the relevance of the conventional measures of intelligence within the range of those who usually enter teaching has been explored over and over without producing very fruitful results, and other approaches must be sought for an understanding of how the cognitive dispositions of teachers relate to their teaching performance (Getzels and Jackson, 1963, p. 573).

Noncognitive or affective dispositions. It is probably safe to say that, if there is any measure of personality anywhere, it has been given to a teacher somewhere and correlated with some criterion of teaching performance. The assumption seems to be that there is an ideal "teachership personality," something like the presumed ideal "leadership personality," equally effective with all students in all subjects under all conditions. Underlying much of the work in this domain is the search for this personality.

Perhaps the most popular of the measures is the Minnesota Teacher Attitude Inventory, an instrument designed to assess how well a teacher will get along with pupils in interpersonal relations, and indirectly how well satisfied he will be with teaching as a vocation (Cook, Leeds, and Callis, 1951). It is an empirically constructed scale, the items involving "cold" and "warm" reactions to children. There are at least 50 studies relating scores on the MTAI to "good" and "poor" teachers, successful and unsuccessful student-teachers, various teacher characteristics, and other personality measures (see Getzels and Jackson, 1963, pp. 508–522). The results are inconsistent. For example, in two studies with teachers (Leeds, 1950; Leeds, 1952), the correlations between the MTAI and supervisor ratings are 0.43 and 0.46, but in two other studies (Callis, 1953; Chappell and Callis, 1954) the correlations are 0.19 and 0.18. Again, one study with student teachers concluded that the MTAI has a "fair degree of both validity and reliability" (Stein and Hardy, 1957, p. 326), but three other studies reached quite contrary conclusions, finding no relation between MTAI scores and performance (Fuller, 1951; Oelke, 1956; Sandgren and Schmidt, 1956). Similar inconsistent and unexplained results are reported in studies relating the MTAI to teacher characteristics and other instruments. For example, in an investigation of the relation between the MTAI and the MMPI, Cook and Medley (1955) found that teachers high on the MTAI tend to have high K scores, and they tend to score higher than do teachers low on the MTAI in the "subtle" items of the hysteria, psychopathic-deviate, and paranoia scales; teachers low on the MTAI tend to score higher on the depression scale and the "obvious" items in general. No explanation for these relationships is given, and one is left with the question of why a high MMPI score on the hysteria or psychopathic-deviate scales should be related to "desirable" rather than to "undesirable" teacher-pupil relations, that is, to high rather than to low MTAI scores.

What has been said about the indiscriminate application of the MTAI holds also for other instruments. For example, the Kuder Preference Record does not claim to be highly diagnostic for teachers *qua* teachers, but is sensitive to differences among various subgroups of teachers by subject-matter field. Nonetheless, researchers persist in lumping teachers together, no matter what their subject-matter field or who their students, administering the instrument, and comparing the profiles of those who are "good" and those who are "poor." Thus, Hedlund (1953) found that female "good" teachers scored lower in musical preferences than did other teachers. No reason is advanced for this, and we are left to wonder why good teachers are less interested in music than other teachers, or for that matter why this is true of female teachers but not of male teachers. Not only are there unexplained, but there are often contradictory findings. Gowan (1957) reported that 20 outstanding female elementary teachers showed lower mechanical and higher persuasive preferences than did normative groups, but Stewart and Roberts (1955) reported that student teachers who remained in the teacher-training program, as compared with those who did not, were significantly higher in mechanical and lower in persuasive preferences. Similarly with respect to the MMPI, Gough and Pemberton (1952) reported that a paranoia score in the middle range is a "sign" predictive of success in practice teaching. But Hedlund (1953) reported that a low paranoia score differentiated student teachers who became good teachers from those who became poor teachers or who failed to complete the program satisfactorily. Schmid (1950) reported that low practice-teaching ratings were associated with high MMPI introversion scores, and suggested that "teaching requires an extravertive individual" (p. 315). But a study by Singer (1954) found that there was a positive correlation between introversion and ratings of teacher effectiveness. Contradictory conclusions are also often reported when different instruments are used, even though the variable measured bears the same name and definition. For example, Sheldon, Coale, and Copple (1959) gave the TAT and the Edwards to two groups of students, one having the highest and another the lowest scores on "warm teacher scales" like the MTAI that had previously been used to discriminate between "good" and "poor" teachers. The high group had lower need for dominance and higher need for aggression on the TAT, but this was reversed on the Edwards. Shapiro, Biber, and Minuchin (1957) administered a projective Cartoon Situation Test to teachers in training and compared the responses with ratings they had received in practice teaching. They found that subjects who identified with the children in the Cartoon Situations seemed to overidentify with children in their classrooms, and were rated least prepared to teach. But Ohlsen and Schultz (1955), using a modification of the TAT, found that identification with the children in the pictures was a "good" sign; it was positively related to supervisory ratings of student-teachers.

We have not attempted a full inventory of the contradictory findings in this search for "good teacher" traits, but it is probably not unfair to say that the inconsistent nature of the results is the single consistent conclusion that can be drawn from the work in this domain. The point of our instances is not to reiterate the well-known methodological caution that the same label on different types of tests may refer to different responses (Getzels and Walsh, 1958), or to call attention to the obvious confounding effects of applying different criteria of teacher effectiveness as if they were interchangeable, or to warn of the evident danger of generalizing from samples of nursery school teachers to samples of secondary school teachers. Nor in so emphasizing the anomalous aspects of research on teacher personality have we intended to imply that all work is of this order, or that there are not leads toward theory formation in the existing studies (see, for example, Tyler, 1954, and Michaelis, 1954). The point rather is that the appearance of these contradictions over and over again in an area of inquiry calls attention to the need for some guiding set of concepts within which such inconsistencies may be noted systematically and further work designed accordingly. Merely continuing to pile up empirical studies without relation to each other is to mistake the accumulation of data for the development of understanding.

It is not impossible that a start toward such conceptualization might be analogous to the one suggested for the teaching situation to which we have already referred (see pp. 509–510 above). To the ubiquitous question, "Who is teaching?" must be added at least two other questions: "Who is teaching what?" and "Who is teaching whom?"—and perhaps a third question as well: "Who is teaching what to whom by which method?" Indeed, Strong (1943) raised exactly the question, "Who is teaching what?" He pointed out that the notion of a global "teaching personality" is shortsighted both theoretically and empirically, despite the commonly held belief in the existence of such an ideal type. There are significant and appropriate differences among teachers by subject-matter fields. For example, male high school teachers of mathematics and physical science belong in Strong Interest Group IV, but male high school teachers of social science belong in Group V. The correlation between the interest patterns of, say, female high school teachers of English and female elementary school teachers is 0.05. The personality of teachers *qua* teachers may be less important than the personality of teachers differentiated by what they are teaching (Strong, 1943, pp. 161–162).

Similarly with respect to the second question, "Who is teaching whom?" Della Piana and Gage (1955) argued that it is not the teacher attitudes alone that must be looked at, but the *relation* between the teacher attitudes and the pupil attitudes. Teacher attitudes appropriate for one pupil may not be appropriate for another. In our terms, what is at issue in a complementary role relationship is not merely the dispositions of each role incumbent separately, but the *fit* between the two sets of dispositions interactively. The investigators examined the relations between some 100 teachers divided by MTAI score and 2700 of their pupils divided by whether they preferred cognitively oriented or affectively oriented teachers. The findings supported the interaction hypothesis: the correlation between the MTAI scores and the effectiveness ratings of the teachers by their pupils was a function of the cognitive and affective orientations of the pupils. Along the same lines, Washburne and Heil (1960) posed the hypothesis that the influence of teachers on pupils is conditioned not only by the personality of the teacher, but by the interaction of different types of teacher personality with different types of pupil personality. They classified 55 elementary school teachers as "turbulent," "self-controlling," and "fearful," their pupils as "conformers," "opposers," "waverers," and "strivers," and observed the nature of the achievement forthcoming from the various teacher-pupil combinations. Though the investigators did not cite specific data, they (1960, p. 425) reported: "The results verified the major hypothesis of the study—that different kinds of teachers get varying amounts of achievement from different kinds of children." The issue for us is not whether the particular typology used by Della Piana and Gage or by Washburne and Heil is the optimal one. Rather it is that efforts such as these shift the important problem from the continued search for predictors of the "teaching personality," which has not proved too fruitful, to the analysis of the interaction between the personality of teachers and pupils, which may be more promising. The focus of inquiry becomes not merely *who* is teaching, but *who* is teaching *what* to *whom where* and by *which method.*

Learner characteristics and learning

Virtually all the methodological and conceptual issues met with in the study of teachers hold in the study of students. The exception seems to be that, generally speaking, there is firmer confidence in the criterion of performance. There are teacher grades and standardized achievement tests. But even here the issue is not so simple as the multitude of correlational studies between "something" and grades or tests would imply. Are the grades in one school interchangeable with the grades in another? Indeed even within one school, are the grades from one teacher the same as those from another? And if standardized achievement tests are used, which presumably would overcome the unreliability and other errors associated with teacher grades, is a combination or average of scores in one set of subjects interchangeable with those in another set of subjects? Further, there are some investigators (Lavin, 1965, p. 15) who would raise the prior and even more complex question: "Why, and for what, are grades important?" On the basis of an empirical study of some 7262 college freshmen attending 24 colleges and universities, Holland and Richards (1965, p. 165), for example, took the extreme position that the results "strongly suggest that academic and non-academic accomplishment are relatively independent dimensions of talent." Nor are these issues new. There is no prior analysis that does not raise similar problems (see, for example, Bloom and Peters, 1961; Harris, 1940; Lavin, 1965; St. John, 1930; Stein, 1963; Stuit *et al.*, 1949; Travers, 1949). It is at once fascinating and disheartening to read the work in this area seriatim, and see the same issues appear, fade away, and reappear, but for the most part remain unresolved.

Cognitive dispositions. Consider the conclusions of a review of studies of the relationship between intelligence and achievement before 1930 (St. John, 1930) and the conclusions of a recent review of studies published between 1953 and 1961 (Lavin, 1965). In the former, the mean of some 320 correlations at the elementary and secondary levels is given as 0.56 when the criterion of achievement is standardized achievement tests; when the criterion is teacher marks, the mean of some 600 correlations at the elementary, secondary, and higher education levels is 0.40 (St. John, 1930, pp. 38–41). But the means obscure important variations in the relationships by types of students, subject matter, level of schooling, and numerous other factors. For example, with standardized tests as the criterion, the range of 106 correlations from six studies of reading was 0.51 to 0.72, and of 57 correlations from five studies of arithmetic it was 0.13 to 0.91. With respect to educational level, the criterion this time being teacher marks, the range of 77 correlations at the elementary level was 0.09 to 0.91 with a mean of 0.54, the range of 263 correlations at the secondary level was −0.23 to 0.90 with a mean of 0.36, and the range of 257 correlations at the higher level was 0.00 to 0.83 with a mean of 0.40. With respect to subject matter, the mean correlation in natural sciences at the secondary and higher levels was 0.46, in English it was 0.38, in mathematics it was 0.32, and in fine arts it was 0.27. There were differences in the degree of relationship by the sex of the students, the coefficients being higher for girls than for boys (St. John, 1930, p. 140). There also seemed to be variations by personality, as suggested by the following array of correlations between intelligence and university grades: for "average" students, 0.49; "indolent" students, 0.34; "diligent" students, −0.05; girls with "most dates," 0.13; girls with "no dates," 0.43; students with "psychoneurotic symptoms," 0.32; students scoring as the "healthiest mentally," 0.61 (St. John, 1930, p. 45). Though the data are far from conclusive statistically, they are surely suggestive. The reviewer also cited work raising the possibility that the relation between intelligence and achievement is not linear over the entire range. In short, the association between intelligence and performance in school was found to depend, at least in part, on the criteria of intelligence and achievement applied, the level of schooling, the subject matter, the personal qualities of the students, perhaps even the level of intelligence itself, and numerous unidentified factors (St. John, 1930, p. 60).

A generation and many, many studies later, a review of the relevant research (Lavin, 1965, pp. 47–63) does not modify the foregoing observations in any substantial way, nor are any of the issues left open then much closer to resolution. The correlation between global measures of intelligence and achievement is again given as about 0.50 with a range from 0.30 to 0.70, the best single predictor of future achievement in school remaining prior achievement in school. Though attempts have been made to construct differential batteries for particular ability and subject-matter areas, the results are controversial, some holding that this is a useful approach while others adduce data to show that multifactor tests of abilities like those by Guilford (1959) add little to the prediction of performance. Current work again points to differential relationships at different levels of education; different relationships by sex of student, the relationship being higher for females than for males; the possibility that the relationship is nonlinear, intelligence possibly being a "threshold variable" such that after a certain level of ability is reached it may no longer play a highly significant role in school performance (Lavin, 1965, pp. 58–59). The greater confidence with which we can now state a specific cause-and-effect or antecedent-consequent relationship, or even a consistent degree of relationship, as compared with a generation ago, hardly seems commensurate with the increase in the number of studies. Perhaps we have gone as far as we can with our present cross-sectional methods, and what is needed in this domain are some other approaches—perhaps longitudinal semi-clinical work with a *total range of children,* as in Terman's (1954) work with gifted children. In any case, as Lavin (1965, p. 59) concluded, measures of intellectual ability and dispositions account for about 35 to 45 percent of the variation in academic performance. This is a generous estimate, but still leaves more than half of the variation to be explained.

Noncognitive or affective dispositions. It is even more hazardous to generalize from the volume of studies dealing with personality and achievement than it is from the studies dealing with intelligence and achievement. There are too many instruments, procedures, varieties of subject matter, types of students, institutions, and levels of education for which findings are available—findings which are often inconsistent with one another. The inconsistencies sometimes make perfectly good sense, but to show this, individual studies must be examined in some detail, and this is not feasible within the present limitations of space. To take one example for many, 13 studies report that socioeconomic class is *directly* related to academic performance, but six studies report that socioeconomic class is *inversely* related to academic performance (Lavin, 1965, pp. 125–127). This contradiction can be resolved by reference to the particular studies themselves—whether the samples were from public or private secondary schools and whether the colleges were Eastern Ivy League or not. It is then evident that the relationship is positive through most of the socioeconomic range but inverse at the upper socioeconomic levels. This difference is meaningful on theoretical grounds when the socioeconomic class categories are taken to symbolize a variety of values, attitudes, and motivations related to academic performance. Eastern upper classes hold values that are not in keeping with the predominant American success orientation (McArthur, 1960). Whereas for other students "success" is a primary motivation, for the upper-class private school student "being" is a primary motivation. The one type of student strives for A's if it is in his power to get them; the other is satisfied with "gentlemen's C's" even if he could get A's. When a study does not include the upper-class private school segments, positive relations are found; when it does include the upper-class segments and does not go below the middle class, inverse relations are found. The inconsistency between the separate studies is more apparent than real and "can be resolved on both a statistical and a theoretical level" (Lavin, 1965, p. 127). We cannot go into similar extensive analyses for other inconsistencies in this domain, nor can we even summarize the major studies. There are two recent reviews that have done this, one for all levels of education (Lavin, 1965) and the other specifically at the college level (Stein, 1963), upon which we shall draw to indicate the direction of work relevant to the personality dimension of our framework.

Lavin (1965) suggested that five types of variables have been applied to the study of personality and achievement: (1) variables referring to motivational states, such as need achievement or interest; (2) personality "styles," such as degree of independence or introversion; (3) self concepts, such as self-acceptance or self-confidence; (4) study habits, including both the actual mechanisms of study and attitudes toward schoolwork; (5) manifestations of psychopathology as measured by such instruments as the MMPI. Most studies assess the relationship between a single variable and academic performance, though there are some investigations which use anywhere from two to ten variables in multivariate designs. Among the more notable multivariate studies is that of Stern, Stein, and Bloom (1956), who formulated two contrasting patterns of personality: stereopathic and nonstereopathic. Individuals of the former type were expected to have difficulty with academic tasks involving ambiguity, abstraction, spontaneity, and departures from convention. Specifically the hypothesis was that individuals of this kind would have greater difficulty in the humanities and social sciences, would make a poorer adjustment to liberal education, and would tend to seek vocations such as medicine, law, and engineering. When stereopaths and nonstereopaths were matched in ability and observed in the college situation, the hypothesis was by and large confirmed.

A synthesis of the numerous single-variable and multivariable studies permits a limited number of generalizations to be drawn (Lavin, 1965, pp. 105–111). Higher levels of performance tend to be associated with (1) social maturity in the school role, as reflected in better study habits and positive attitudes toward academic performance; (2) emotional stability; (3) cognitive styles involving greater flexibility in problem solving; (4) achievement via conformity; (5) achievement via independence, including more autonomy, more introversion, and less impulsivity. Findings from the single-variable studies alone show that better achievement is related to positive self-image, less defensiveness, and greater interest in particular content areas. But it must be emphasized that the relationships on which this summary is based are at best quite weak and often inconsistent. Lavin (1965, p. 111) suggested that this "disappointing state of affairs" may be due to the circumstance that virtually all studies "conceive of the individual as if he were operating in a social vacuum," and that the same personality factors might be more useful if the social setting in which educational performance takes place were conceptualized and used as a significant variable with which personality interacts.

Stein (1963) attempted to integrate the literature from a different point of view. He suggested that four major approaches characterize efforts to relate personality and college achievement: (1) the pilot-experience approach, (2) the social and demographic approach, (3) the psychological approach, and (4) the transactional approach. The pilot-experience approach assumes continuity of performance among educational levels such that, when appropriate correction factors for institutional differences are taken into account, correlations as high as 0.70 to 0.80 between high school and college achievement are obtained. Presumably, if the objective of educational research is only prediction, these correlations could be increased by increasing the similarity of high school and college experiences. When personality factors are included in these investigations, however, it turns out that a major factor common to both high school and college achievement may be the disposition for *conformity*. Holland (1960) found that the personality characteristics of college achievers are unrelated to the personality characteristics of "more creative" people, and he argued against the indiscriminate use of high school grades for college selection, since this only reinforces the status quo and delays development of more adequate criteria of personal worth and of educational objectives.

The social and demographic approach includes studies in which socioeconomic status, urban-rural residence, religious affiliation, birth order, and other such descriptive factors are related to achievement. We have already cited illustrative studies of this kind, and numerous others are mentioned by both Lavin and Stein. This approach has a signal advantage—it is easy to gather data. But there are certain disadvantages. The work tends to be of the single-variable kind and, as in the case of the social class studies to which we referred, may provide misleading conclusions unless related to factors which will add "psychological meaning" to the purely descriptive variables.

The psychological approach attempts to relate personality characteristics *directly* to achievement criteria. For example, Roe's (1957) studies of creativity led her to the belief that *interests* are more important than *aptitudes* in vocational aspirations. The sources of interest are the child's early experiences in the family; these foster two basic orientations, one "toward persons" and the other "not toward persons." Roe found that it was more difficult to obtain free play of creativity from individuals with "personal" than from those with "nonpersonal" interests. Since interests and aptitudes generally correlate only 0.30, more effective work would be possible if more information on interests were available (see Stein, 1963, p. 17). Other studies utilizing the psychological approach relate differential achievement to such variables as adjustment, anxiety, need achievement, masculinity-femininity, and various typologies of personality (Lavin, 1965, pp. 64–121; Stein, 1963, pp. 16–49). This approach too has certain advantages, notably in overcoming some of the disadvantages of the other approaches by adding "dynamic" factors to the more "descriptive" variables. But there are again disadvantages. Most of the studies concentrate on the relationship between single personality characteristics and some criterion of achievement. This approach fails to deal with the problem that behavior is not determined only by the personality of the individual, as if it operated in a social vacuum, but is more likely to be a function of the pattern of the individual's personality characteristics engaged with the pattern of particular situational characteristics.

Thus both Stein and Lavin, from their different points of vantage, concluded that what is needed is an approach that will deal with the "person" and the "place" or, in our specific terms, with the "personality dispositions" and "role expectations" in interaction. But their solutions vary somewhat. Stein suggested that the transactional approach, as reflected in his own work and in that of Stern, Stein, and Bloom (1956) and Stern and Pace (1958), has the greatest potential. Typically this approach involves two kinds of measures: one examines the structure of personality needs, and the other the structure of environmental press, both as derived from Murray's need-press schema. It is then possible to think of these two structures as "criteria" for one another, and to assess the relative congruence or incongruence between them. But Lavin (1965, p. 161) argued that the need-press conception "oversimplifies the social environment" in that "institutional characteristics are described on the most general basis rather than in specific role systems." He suggested that it is necessary to look at "counterpositions" in the educational setting, including student to student, student to teacher, student to administrative officials. These counterpositions may define different and possibly conflicting expectations for the student role as well as for others within the school system, with important consequences for educational outcome.

Though Lavin's suggestion is more akin to our own formulation in social-system terms rather than in need-press terms, there is no reason to make a categorical judgment between the two approaches here. Indeed, it is desirable that alternative formulations not be prejudged without empirical application; it may very well be that for one purpose the one approach may be superior, and for another purpose the other. In any event, no matter which theoretical position is taken, two conclusions seem clear from the foregoing analyses: First and most generally, there is convergence of opinion that we must add to the measurement model, where the primary aim of empirical work is *classification* and *prediction,* a conceptual model, where the primary aim of empirical work will be *understanding* and *explanation.* Second and more specifically, a central issue seems to be the problem of continuity and discontinuity or congruence and incongruence among roles and personalities in the educational setting—that is, most simply, the problem of the nature and sources of *conflict* in the school. It is to this issue that we turn in the following section.

SOURCES OF CONFLICTS IN THE SCHOOL SYSTEM

To focus on the problem of conflict is not to suggest that the conflicts and discontinuities in the school are necessarily greater than in other systems. Rather the concept of conflict may provide heuristic leverage into the operation of the system quite as the concept of deviance provides leverage into the functioning of personality, or the concept of dissonance into the process of cognition (Festinger, 1957). It suggests a point of entry not only into the kinds of issues noted in the preceding section but, more generally, into the dynamic relations among the value, role, and personality elements of social behavior. Accordingly, we return here more directly to our initial formulation (see pp. 461–470 above; also Getzels, 1963) and point to five types of conflict derived from the framework, and for each type refer to studies illustrating the relevant research issues in empirical terms.

Incongruity between cultural values and institutional expectations

One type of conflict, or at least discontinuity, is between the values of the community or of subgroups within the community and the expectations of the school to which it sends its children (that is, between dimensions A and B of the framework). An obvious instance of this is the discontinuity between the orientations giving rise to the so-called culturally deprived or educationally-disadvantaged child and the requirements of the school which he is likely to attend (see pp. 488–494 above). But the incongruities between the cultural values and the school expectations are sometimes more pervasive, if less visible, than this. Spindler (1955), for example, analyzed the prevailing conception of the "ideal American boy." He found that such qualities as "sociability," "popularity," and "well-roundedness" were mentioned far more frequently than "high intelligence," "high academic aptitude," or "creativity." But it is exactly these devalued characteristics—intellectuality and individuality—which education is supposed to foster. In this sense, the presumed criteria of social worth and of educational worth are incongruent, and to the extent that they are, there is a source of conflict in the school.

Incongruity between personality dispositions and role expectations

Conflicts of this type (between dimensions B and C of the framework) occur as a function of discrepancies between patterns of expectations attaching to a role and patterns of dispositions characteristic of the incumbents of the role. Consider, for example, the case of the authoritarian teacher in a permissive school, or, in the work already cited, of the stereopathic student in the liberal arts curriculum, the child with low need achievement in a highly competitive school, the independent student in a lecture as against a discussion group. In such cases there is a mutual interference between the institutional demands and the personal inclinations, and the individual must choose to fulfill the one or the other. If he fulfills role requirements, he becomes frustrated and dissatisfied; he is inefficient. If he chooses to fulfill the personality dispositions, he is liable to unsatisfactory role performance; he is ineffective. On the basis specifically of this model, Lipham (1960), for example, defined the role of school administrators in terms of a number of crucial expectations. He hypothesized that administrators whose dispositions are congruent with the expectations will suffer less strain and therefore be more productive than administrators whose dispositions are not congruent with the role expectations. The results of a study with principals in a large Midwestern city as subjects confirmed the hypothesis.

Incongruity between roles and within roles

There is a range and variety of conflicts (within dimension B itself) which occur when a role incumbent is required to conform simultaneously to a number of expectations which are mutually exclusive, contradictory, or inconsistent; in this situation performance of one set of requirements makes performance of another set of requirements impossible, or at least difficult. These role conflicts may arise in a number of ways of which the following three are illustrative:

Disagreement within a single reference or alter group in defining a given role. There are numerous examples of this type of conflict in the school. The principal may be expected by some teachers to visit them regularly as the "supervisor of instruction," and by other teachers to treat them as "professional personnel," which by definition means that they are not in need of "supervision"; the pupil may be expected by some teachers to emphasize the mechanisms of writing, the substance being useful only for the practice of correct form, and by other teachers to emphasize content, the form being merely a vehicle for the communication. At a more fundamental level, the entire purpose of the school (and consequently of the roles within it) may be defined differently by various individuals even within the same school. Consider, in this connection, the apparently simple problem of age differences. Prince (1957) asked the question: Are there differences in the basic beliefs among educators of different age groups? When he dichotomized beliefs and value orientations into "emergent" and "traditional," he found that the younger the teacher or the principal, the more likely were his beliefs to be "emergent"; the older he was, the more likely they were to be "traditional." Such differences would surely have an effect on the nature of the expectations they would hold for the school.

Disagreement among several reference or alter groups defining a given role. To illustrate with an example which is currently much in the news, the university faculty member may be expected by his academic dean to emphasize publications, by his department head to emphasize committee duties, and by his students to emphasize teaching. Though these sets of expectations for the same role are not necessarily opposed to each other, time taken to implement one set may be seen as taking time from another, and to this extent they are in conflict. Or consider the administrator role as viewed by superintendents and by school board members. Gross, Mason, and McEachern (1958) found significant differences with respect to a variety of expectations. For example, with respect to the expectation that the administrator "keep a watchful eye on the personal life of his subordinates," 66 percent of board members as contrasted with 26 percent of superintendents gave positive responses; with respect to the expectation that the administrator "defend teachers from attack when they try to present the pros and cons of various controversial social and political issues," 70 percent of superintendents and 29 percent of the board members gave "absolutely must" responses.

Contradictions between two or more roles the individual is occupying at the same time. It is here that we have the problems arising from the circumstance that role incumbents in the school are inevitably also occupying roles in other systems, which may have expectations opposed to those of the school. For example, the adolescent cannot ordinarily be an outstanding student and maintain respectable membership in the "gang" (Coleman, 1961); the teacher often cannot be an active member of a minority political party—and sometimes not even of the two majority parties—and remain a teacher in good standing (Getzels and Guba, 1955b); a school board member often finds it difficult to fulfill the universalistic expectations of his role on the board and the particularistic expectations of his role as friend, or business associate, or communicant of a particular church (Gross, 1959).

Conflicts deriving from personality disorder

The preceding types of conflict derive primarily from dislocations in the institutional dimension of behavior. There are also conflicts deriving from the personal dimension of behavior (that is, within a single individual in dimension C). One such type occurs as a function of conflicting dispositions within the individual. The effect of such personal instability is to keep the individual at odds with the institution because he cannot maintain a durable relationship to a given role, because he misperceives the expectations of the role, or because he feels excessive strain in a situation where others under the same circumstances do not. An obvious instance of this is the extremely disturbed child as pupil (see, for example, Bettelheim, 1955). Though the literature for less manifestly disturbed individuals is less consistent, there is evidence showing positive relations between personality adjustment and school performance (Stein, 1963, pp. 22–28). Similarly, though the literature is again inconsistent and the effects may be related to particular situational factors, there is evidence showing that, at least in a military school, teachers who are "conflict prone" as against those who are "conflict immune" tend to be less masculine, less free from nervousness, more introverted, more depressive, and more cycloid in temperament as these are measured by the Guilford-Martin Inventories; more inclined to authoritarian aggression and ethnocentrism as measured by the California E and F scales; and tend toward extrapunitiveness and ego defensiveness rather than impunitiveness, intropunitiveness, and need persistence as measured by the Rosenzweig Picture-Frustration Study (Getzels and Guba, 1955a).

Conflict arising from personality differences, incongruent interpersonal perceptions, and idiosyncratic definitions of expectations

There is a second, more subtle but more pervasive, type of conflict deriving from the personality dimension. Disagreement in a role set, that is, among complementary role incumbents—or, in terms of the framework, among "personalities" in dimension C—as to their mutual rights and obligations is not the result solely of personality disorder in any pathological sense. There may be selective perception of expectations just as there is selective perception of other objects and events in the environment. Complementary role relationships—or, more broadly, relationships in a role set—function at two levels of interaction. The first level derives from the roles involved in the interaction—pupil and teacher, teacher and teacher, teacher and principal. This is the formal or normative level. The second, but no less important, level derives from the particular people as individuals in the roles involved in the interaction—this particular pupil and this particular pupil, this teacher and this teacher, this teacher and this principal. This is the personalistic or informal level. The publicly prescribed relationships are thus enacted in two separate private situations, the one embedded in the other. These private situations are related through those aspects of the existential objects and events that overlap in the perceptions of the members of the role set. Depending on the nature of the selective perceptions involved, there may be greater or lesser overlap. When the overlap is high, there is congruence in the complementary role definitions and interpersonal perceptions, with concomitant understanding; when the overlap is low, there is incongruence in the complementary role definitions and interpersonal perceptions, with concomitant conflict.

Involved here is, of course, the entire problem of interpersonal perception (Tagiuri and Petrullo, 1958). To cite only one study in the educational setting directly related to the present formulation, Ferneau (1954) investigated the interaction of school consultants and administrators. He asked consultants and administrators who were known to have had a consultantship relation to describe their definition of the consultant role, and then to evaluate the outcome of the consultantship. He found that, when the administrators and the consultants agreed on the expectations, they tended to rate the actual consultantship favorably; when they disagreed on the expectations, they tended to rate it unfavorably. And apparently the evaluation of success or failure was unrelated to the particular expectations, provided that the participants' perceptions of the expectations overlapped.

Two comments may be added to this brief account of varieties of conflict or disagreement in the school as a social system. First, we have not intended to imply that conflict is inevitably an evil. On the contrary, certain types of conflict give rise to productive transformations in the system. Second, we have not intended to imply that the present model and the classification of conflict derived from it is the only possible formulation, or that it is even in some ultimate sense the "right" one. It does, however, seem moderately useful at this time in clarifying various phenomena within a single set of concepts and relations, and in providing an explicit point of departure for more fruitful theoretical and empirical work in this domain.

SUMMARY AND CONCLUSION

Of all the social institutions, the one that seems to have been most seriously neglected as an object of *systematic* theoretical and empirical concern by social psychology has been education. Though there were sizable chapters on the social psychology of industry and of politics in the preceding *Handbook of Social Psychology,* there was none at all on education—in fact, the school, the teacher, and the pupil were hardly mentioned as subjects for programmatic social-psychological inquiry. Accordingly, we opened this chapter by presenting a framework which, however primitive, might point to some of the significant theoretical and empirical problems of education within a related set of categories and concepts. The framework conceived of the school as a social system in role and personality terms in a value context. We then derived a number of social-psychological issues, and reviewed illustrative empirical studies relevant to the issues. Thus we dealt with such problems as social class, socialization, and education; segregation and compensatory preschool education; the school and the classroom as social systems; the role and personality of teachers and students; and the sources of conflict and discontinuity in society and the school. Throughout, our intention has not been to suggest that the particular point of view we were utilizing is in some ultimate sense the "right" one or even a "good" one. Rather our hope has been that it would serve as a locus of departure—an invitation, as it were, for more useful formulations—so that, if the present chapter has done no more (from the perspective of 1965) than call attention to the void of ten years ago, ten years hence when presumably a new *Handbook* will be compiled, our attempt will be superseded by a chapter on the social psychology of education which will be seen not merely as filling a preceding void, but will make a conceptual and empirical contribution worthy of the central function of education in the development of the individual and of society.

REFERENCES

Anderson, C. A. (1961). Access to higher education and economic development. In A. H. Halsey, Jean Floud, and C. A. Anderson (Eds.), *Education, economy, and society: a reader in the sociology of education.* New York: Free Press. Pp. 252–265.

Anderson, R. C. (1959). Learning in discussions: a résumé of the authoritarian-democratic studies. *Harvard educ. Rev., 29,* 201–215.

Ashmore, H. S. (1954). *The Negro and the schools.* Chapel Hill: Univ. of North Carolina Press.

Ausubel, D. P., and Pearl Ausubel (1963). Ego development among segregated Negro children. In A. H. Passow (Ed.), *Education in depressed areas.* New York: Teachers College Bureau of Publications, Columbia University. Pp. 109–141.

Bany, Mary A., and Lois V. Johnson (1964). *Classroom group behavior.* New York: Macmillan.

Barker, R. G., Ed. (1963). *The stream of behavior.* New York: Appleton-Century-Crofts.

Barnard, C. I. (1938). *The functions of the executive.* Cambridge: Harvard Univ. Press.

Bavelas, A. (1960). Communication patterns in task-oriented groups. In D. Cartwright and A. Zander (Eds.), *Group dynamics: research and theory* (2nd ed.). Evanston, Ill.: Row, Peterson. Pp. 669–682.

Bellack, A. A. (1965). *The language of the classroom.* New York: Institute of Psychological Research, Teachers College, Columbia University. U.S. Office of Education, Cooperative Research Project No. 2023.

Bereiter, C., J. Osborn, S. Engelman, and P. Reidford (1965). An academically-oriented pre-school for culturally deprived children. Paper presented at Annual American Educational Research Association Meetings.

Bernard, Viola W. (1958). School desegregation: some psychiatric implications. *Psychiatry, 21,* 149–158.

Bernstein, B. (1961). Social class and linguistic development: a theory of social learning. In A. H. Halsey, Jean Floud, and C. A. Anderson (Eds.), *Education, economy, and society: a reader in the sociology of education.* New York: Free Press. Pp. 288–314.

―――― (1962). Linguistic codes, hesitation phenomena, and intelligence. *Lang. and Speech, 5,* 31–46.

Bettelheim, B. (1955). *Truants from life: the rehabilitation of emotionally disturbed children.* Glencoe, Ill.: Free Press.

―――― (1961). The decision to fail. *School Rev., 69,* 377–412.

Bidwell, C. E. (1965). The school as a formal organization. In J. G. March (Ed.), *Handbook of organizations.* Chicago: Rand McNally. Pp. 972–1022.

Bloom, B. S. (1964). *Stability and change in human characteristics.* New York: Wiley.

Bloom, B. S., A. Davis, and R. Hess (1965). *Compensatory education for cultural deprivation.* New York: Holt, Rinehart, and Winston.

Bloom, B. S., and F. R. Peters (1961). *The use of academic prediction scales for counseling and selecting college entrants.* New York: Free Press.

Boger, J. H. (1952). An experimental study of the effects of perceptual training on group IQ scores of elementary pupils in rural ungraded schools. *J. educ. Res., 46,* 43–53.

Bonney, M. E. (1947). Sociometric study of agreement between teacher judgments and student choices: in regard to the number of friends possessed by high school students. *Sociometry, 10,* 133–146.

Brazziel, W. F., and Mary Terrell (1962). An experiment in the development of readiness in a culturally disadvantaged group of first-grade children. *J. Negro Educ., 31,* 4–7.

Bronfenbrenner, U. (1958). Socialization and social class through time and space. In Eleanor E. Maccoby, T. M. Newcomb, and E. L. Hartley (Eds.), *Readings in social psychology.* New York: Holt, Rinehart, and Winston. Pp. 400–425.

Brookover, W. B., and D. Gottlieb (1963). Social class and education. In W. W. Charters, Jr., and N. L. Gage (Eds.), *Readings in the social psychology of education*. Boston: Allyn and Bacon. Pp. 3–11.

Brown, B. R., and M. Deutsch (1965). Some effects of social class and race on chilren's language and intellectual abilities: a new look at an old problem. Paper read at Biennial Meeting of the Society for Research in Child Development.

Brown, D. (1962). Personality, college environments, and academic productivity. In N. Sanford (Ed.), *The American college*. New York: Wiley. Pp. 536–562.

Bruner, J. (1964). The new educational technology. In A. De Grazia and D. A. Sohn (Eds.), *Revolution in teaching: new theory, technology, and curricula*. New York: Bantam Books. Pp. 1–7.

Bullock, H. A. (1950). A comparison of the academic achievement of white and Negro high school graduates. *J. educ. Res., 44,* 179–192.

Burton, W. H. (1952). *The guidance of learning activities* (2nd ed.). New York: Appleton-Century-Crofts.

Buswell, Margaret M. (1953). The relationship between the social structure of the classroom and the academic success of the pupils. *J. exp. Educ., 22,* 37–52.

Callis, R. (1953). The efficiency of the Minnesota Teacher Attitude Inventory for predicting interpersonal relations in the classroom. *J. appl. Psychol., 37,* 82–85.

Campbell, E. Q., and T. F. Pettigrew (1959). Racial and moral crisis: the role of Little Rock ministers. *Amer. J. Sociol., 64,* 509–516.

Campbell, R. F., J. E. Corbally, and J. A. Ramseyer (1962). *Introduction to educational administration* (2nd ed.). Boston: Allyn and Bacon.

Carlson, R. O. (1961). Succession and performance among school superintendents. *Admin. Sci. Quart., 6,* 210–227.

———— (1962). *Executive succession and organizational change.* Chicago: Midwest Administration Center, University of Chicago.

Cartwright, D., and A. Zander (1960). Group cohesiveness: introduction. In D. Cartwright and A. Zander (Eds.), *Group dynamics: research and theory* (2nd ed.). Evanston, Ill.: Row, Peterson. Pp. 69–94.

Chappell, T. L., and R. Callis (1954). The efficiency of the Minnesota Teacher Attitude Inventory for predicting interpersonal relations in a naval school. Columbia: University of Missouri, Report No. 5, ONR 649(00).

Charters, W. W., Jr. (1953). Social class analysis and the control of public education. *Harvard educ. Rev., 23,* 268–283.

———— (1963). Social class and intelligence tests. In W. W. Charters, Jr., and N. L. Gage (Eds.), *Reading in the social psychology of education*. Boston: Allyn and Bacon. Pp. 12–21.

Charters, W. W., Jr., and N. L. Gage, Eds. (1963). *Readings in the social psychology of education*. Boston: Allyn and Bacon.

Child, I. L. (1954). Socialization. In G. Lindzey (Ed.), *Handbook of social psychology*. Vol. 2. Cambridge, Mass.: Addison-Wesley. Pp. 655–692.

Clark, K. B., and Mamie P. Clark (1965).   Racial identification and preference in Negro children.   In H. Proshansky and B. Seidenberg (Eds.), *Basic studies in social psychology.* New York: Holt, Rinehart, and Winston. Pp. 308–317.

Clarke, A. D. B., and A. M. Clarke (1953). How constant is the I.Q.? *Lancet, 2,* 877– 880.

Coleman, J. S. (1959).   Academic achievement and the structure of competition. *Harvard educ. Rev., 29,* 330–351.

———— (1961). *The adolescent society.* New York: Free Press.

Cook, S. W. (1957).   Desegregation: a psychological analysis. *Amer. Psychologist, 12,* 1–13.

Cook, W. W., C. H. Leeds, and R. Callis (1951). *The Minnesota Teacher Attitude Inventory.* New York: Psychological Corp.

Cook, W. W., and D. M. Medley (1955). The relationship between Minnesota Teacher Attitude Inventory scores and scores on certain scales of the Minnesota Multiphasic Personality Inventory. *J. appl. Psychol., 39,* 123–129.

Cornell, F. G., C. M. Lindvall, and J. L. Saupe (1952). *An exploratory measurement of individualities of schools and classrooms.* Urbana: Bureau of Educational Research, College of Education, University of Illinois.

Dai, B. (1953). Some problems of personality development among Negro children. In C. Kluckhohn and H. A. Murray (Eds.), *Personality in nature, society, and culture* (2nd ed.). New York: Knopf. Pp. 545–566.

Davie, J. S. (1953).   Social factors and school attendance. *Harvard educ. Rev., 23,* 175–185.

Davis, A. (1948). *Social class influences upon learning.* Cambridge, Mass.: Harvard Univ. Press.

Davis, A., and K. Eells (1953). *Davis-Eels tests of general intelligence or problem-solving ability.* Yonkers, N.Y.: World Book Co.

Davis, A., and R. J. Havighurst (1946).   Social class and color differences in child rearing. *Amer. sociol. Rev., 11,* 698–710.

Della Piana, G. M., and N. L. Gage (1955). Pupils' values and the validity of the Minnesota Teacher Attitude Inventory. *J. educ. Psychol., 46,* 167–178.

Dennis, W. (1960). Causes of retardation among institutional children: Iran. *J. gen. Psychol., 96,* 47–59.

Deutsch, Martin (1962). The influence of early social environment on school adaptation. Paper presented at Symposium on School Dropouts, Washington, D.C.

———— (1963). The disadvantaged child and the learning process. In A. H. Passow (Ed.), *Education in depressed areas.* New York: Teachers College Bureau of Publications, Columbia University. Pp. 163–179.

———— (1964). Facilitating development in the pre-school child: social and psychological perspectives. *Merrill-Palmer Quart., 10,* 249–263.

Deutsch, Martin, and B. Brown (1964). Social influences in Negro-white intelligence differences. *J. soc. Issues, 20,* 24–35.

Deutsch, Morton (1960).   The effects of cooperation and competition upon group process.   In D. Cartwright and A. Zander (Eds.), *Group dynamics: research and theory* (2nd ed.).   Evanston, Ill.: Row, Peterson.   Pp. 414–448.

Dixon, N. R. (1953).   Social class and education: an annotated bibliography.   *Harvard educ. Rev., 23,* 330–338.

Domas, S. J., and D. V. Tiedeman (1950).   Teacher competence: an annotated bibliography.   *J. exp. Educ., 19,* 101–218.

Dreger, R. M., and K. S. Miller (1960).   Comparative psychological studies of Negroes and whites in the United States.   *Psychol. Bull., 57,* 361–402.

Eells, K., A. Davis, R. J. Havighurst, V. E. Herrick, and R. W. Tyler (1951).   *Intelligence and cultural differences: a study of cultural learning and problem-solving.*   Chicago: Univ. of Chicago Press.

Ellison, R. (1952).   *Invisible man.*   New York: New American Library (Signet).

Fantz, R. L. (1961).   The origin of form perception.   *Sci. Amer., 204,* 66–72.

————— (1963).   Pattern vision in newborn infants.   *Science, 140,* 296–297.

Faulkner, W. (1959).   *The mansion.*   New York: Random House.

Ferneau, E. (1954).   Role-expectations in consultations.   Unpublished doctoral dissertation, University of Chicago.

Festinger, L. (1957).   *A theory of cognitive dissonance.*   Evanston, Ill.: Row, Peterson.

Flanders, N. A. (1949).   Personal-social anxiety as a factor in experimental learning situations.   Unpublished doctoral dissertation, University of Chicago.

————— (1960).   *Teacher influence, pupil attitudes, and achievement.*   Minneapolis: University of Minnesota.   U.S. Office of Education, Cooperative Research Project No. 397.

Floud, Jean, and A. H. Halsey (1961).   Introduction.   In A. H. Halsey, Jean Floud, and C. A. Anderson (Eds.), *Education, economy, and society: a reader in the sociology of education.*   New York: Free Press.   Pp. 1–12.

Freedman, M. B. (1962).   Studies of college alumni.   In N. Sanford (Ed.), *The American college.*   New York: Wiley.   Pp. 847–886.

Friedenberg, E. Z. (1959).   *The vanishing adolescent.*   Boston: Beacon Press.

Fuller, Elizabeth M. (1951).   The use of teacher-pupil attitudes, self-rating, and measures of general ability in the preservice selection of nursery school-kindergarten-primary teachers.   *J. educ. Res., 44,* 675–686.

Gage, N. L., Ed. (1963).   *Handbook of research on teaching.*   Chicago: Rand McNally.

Gage, N. L., P. J. Runkel, and B. B. Chatterjee (1963).   Changing teacher behavior through feedback from pupils: an application of equilibrium theory.   In W. W. Charters, Jr., and N. L. Gage (Eds.), *Readings in the social psychology of education.*   Boston: Allyn and Bacon.   Pp. 173–181.

Gerth, H. H., and C. W. Mills, Eds. (1946).   *From Max Weber: essays in sociology.*   New York: Oxford Univ. Press.

Getzels, J. W. (1952).   A psycho-sociological framework for the study of educational administration.   *Harvard educ. Rev., 22,* 235–246.

_____ (1956). The nature of reading interests: psychological aspects. In H. M. Robinson (Ed.), *Developing permanent interest in reading.* Proceedings of Annual Conference on Reading held at the University of Chicago. Supplementary Educational Monograph No. 84. Pp. 5–9.

_____ (1958). Administration as a social process. In A. W. Halpin (Ed.), *Administrative theory in education.* Chicago: Midwest Administration Center, University of Chicago. Pp. 150–165.

_____ (1960). Theory and practice in educational administration: an old question revisited. In R. F. Campbell and J. M. Lipham (Eds.), *Administrative theory as a guide to action.* Chicago: Midwest Administration Center, University of Chicago. Pp. 37–58.

_____ (1963). Conflict and role behavior in the educational setting. In W. W. Charters, Jr., and N. L. Gage (Eds.), *Readings in the social psychology of education.* Boston: Allyn and Bacon. Pp. 309–318.

_____ (1965). Pre-school education. In *White House conference on education.* Washington, D.C.: Government Printing Office. Pp. 116–125.

Getzels, J. W., and E. G. Guba (1955a). Role conflict and personality. *J. Pers., 24,* 74–85.

_____ (1955b). The structure of roles and role conflict in the teaching situation. *J. educ. Sociol., 29,* 30–40.

_____ (1957). Social behavior and the administrative process. *School Rev., 65,* 423–441.

Getzels, J. W., and P. W. Jackson (1963). The teacher's personality and characteristics. In N. L. Gage (Ed.), *Handbook of research on teaching.* Chicago: Rand McNally. Pp. 506–582.

Getzels, J. W., and H. A. Thelen (1960). The classroom as a unique social system. In N. B. Henry (Ed.), *The dynamics of instructional groups.* The 59th Yearbook of the National Society for the Study of Education, Part II. Chicago: Univ. of Chicago Press. Pp. 53–82.

Getzels, J. W., and J. J. Walsh (1958). The method of paired direct and projective questionnaires in the study of attitude structure and socialization. *Psychol. Monogr., 72,* No. 1 (whole No. 454).

Gibson, Eleanor J. (1963). Development of perception; discrimination of depth compared with discrimination of graphic symbols. *Monogr. Soc. Res. Child Develpmt., 28,* No. 2, 5–24.

Gordon, W. (1957). The social system of the high school. Glencoe, Ill.: Free Press.

Gough, H. G., and W. H. Pemberton (1952). Personality characteristics related to success in practice teaching. *J. appl. Psychol., 36,* 307–309.

Gowan, J. C. (1957). A summary of the intensive study of twenty highly selected elementary women teachers. *J. exp. Educ., 26,* 115–124.

Gray, Susan W., and R. A. Klaus (1963). Early training project: interim report. George Peabody College. (Mimeo)

Gronlund, N. E. (1959). *Sociometry in the classroom.* New York: Harper.

Gross, N. (1953). A critique of "Social Class Structure and American Education." *Harvard educ. Rev., 23*, 298–329.

——— (1959). Some contributions of sociology to the field of education. *Harvard educ. Rev., 29*, 275–287.

Gross, N., W. S. Mason, and A. W. McEachern (1958). *Explorations in role analysis: studies in the school superintendency role.* New York: Wiley.

Guba, E. G., and C. E. Bidwell (1957). *Administrative relationships.* Chicago: Midwest Administration Center, University of Chicago.

Guilford, J. P. (1959). Three faces of intellect. *Amer. Psychologist, 14*, 469–479.

Haggard, E. A. (1953). Techniques for the development of unbiased tests. In *Proceedings of the 1952 invitational conference on testing problems.* Princeton, N.J.: Educational Testing Service. Pp. 125–127.

——— (1954). Social-status and intelligence: an experimental study of certain cultural determinants of measured intelligence. *Genet. Psychol. Monogr., 49*, 141–186.

Halpin, A. W. (1956). *The leadership behavior of school superintendents.* Columbus: Ohio State Univ. Press.

Hare, A. P. (1962). *Handbook of small group research.* New York: Free Press.

Harris, D. (1940). Factors affecting college grades: a review of the literature, 1930–37. *Psychol. Bull., 37*, 125–166.

Havighurst, R. J. (1961). Social class influences on American education. In N. B. Henry (Ed.), *Social forces influencing American education.* The 60th Yearbook of the National Society for the Study of Education, Part II. Chicago: Univ. of Chicago Press. Pp. 120–143.

Havighurst, R. J., and A. Davis (1955). A comparison of the Chicago and Harvard studies of social class differences in child rearing. *Amer. social. Rev., 20*, 438–442.

Havighurst, R. J., and Bernice L. Neugarten (1962). *Society and education* (2nd ed.). Boston: Allyn and Bacon.

Hebb, D. O. (1949). *The organization of behavior.* New York: Wiley.

Hedlund, P. A. (1953). *Cooperative study to predict effectiveness in secondary school teaching: third progress report.* Albany: Univ. of the State of New York and State Education Department.

Heist, P., T. R. McConnell, F. Master, and Phoebe Williams (1961). Personality and scholarship. *Science, 133*, 362–367.

Henry, J. (1957). Attitude organization in elementary school classrooms. *Amer. J. Orthopsychiat., 27*, 117–133.

Hess, R. D. (1964). Educability and rehabilitation: the future of the welfare class. *J. Marriage and Family, 26*, 422–429.

Hill, M. C. (1957). Research on the Negro family. *Marriage and Family Living, 19*, 25–31.

Hoehn, A. J. (1954). A study of social status differentiation in the classroom behavior of nineteen third grade teachers. *J. soc. Psychol., 39*, 269–292.

Holland, J. L. (1957).   Undergraduate origin of American scientists.   *Science, 126,* 433–437.

—————— (1960).   The prediction of college grades from personality and aptitude variables.   *J. educ. Psychol., 51,* 245–254.

Holland, J. L., and J. M. Richards, Jr. (1965).   Academic and nonacademic accomplishment: correlated or uncorrelated?   *J. educ. Psychol., 56,* 165–174.

Hollingshead, A. (1949).   *Elmtown's youth.*   New York: Wiley.

Hovland, C. I. (1963).   Yale studies of communication and persuasion.   In W. W. Charters, Jr., and N. L. Gage (Eds.), *Readings in the social psychology of education.* Boston: Allyn and Bacon.   Pp. 239–253.

Hughes, E., H. Becker, and B. Greer (1962).   Student culture and academic effort. In N. Sanford (Ed.), *The American college.*   New York: Wiley.   Pp. 515–530.

Hughes, M. (1959).   *Assessment of the quality of teaching in elementary schools.*   Salt Lake City: Univ. of Utah Press.

Hunt, J. M. (1961).   *Intelligence and experience.*   New York: Ronald.

—————— (1964).   The psychological basis for using pre-school enrichment as an antidote for cultural deprivation.   *Merrill-Palmer Quart., 10,* 209–248.

Hyman, H. H. (1953).   The value system of different classes: a social psychological contribution to the analysis of social classes.   In R. Bendix and S. M. Lipset (Eds.), *Class, status, and power: a reader in social stratification.*   Glencoe, Ill.: Free Press.   Pp. 426–442.

Hyman, H. H., and P. B. Sheatsley (1964).   Attitudes toward desegregation.   *Sci. Amer., 211,* 16–23.

Irwin, O. C. (1948).   Infant speech: the effect of family occupational status and of age on use of sound types.   *J. Speech and Hearing Disorders, 13,* 224–226.

Jackson, P. W. (1964).   The conceptualization of teaching.   *Psychol. in the Schools, 1,* 232–243.

Jencks, C., and D. Riesman (1962).   Patterns of residential education: a case study of Harvard.   In N. Sanford (Ed.), *The American college.*   New York: Wiley.   Pp. 731–773.

John, Vera P. (1963).   The intellectual development of slum children: some preliminary findings.   *Amer. J. Orthopsychiat., 33,* 813–822.

Kahl, J. A. (1953).   Educational and occupational aspirations of common man boys. *Harvard educ. Rev., 23,* 186–203.

Katz, I. (1964).   Review of evidence relating to effects of desegregation on the intellectual performance of Negroes.   *Amer. Psychologist, 19,* 381–399.

Kennedy, W. A., V. Van De Riet, and J. C. White (1961).   *The standardization of the 1960 revision of the Stanford-Binet intelligence scale on Negro elementary-school children in the southeastern United States.*   Florida State University, Human Development Clinic.

Kirk, S. A. (1958).   *Early education of the mentally retarded.*   Urbana: Univ. of Illinois Press.

Klineberg, O. (1963).   Negro-white differences in intelligence test performance: a new look at an old problem.   *Amer. Psychologist, 18,* 198–203.

Kluckhohn, C. (1951). Values and value-orientation in the theory of action: an exploration in definition and classification. In T. Parsons and E. A. Shils (Eds.), *Toward a general theory of action.* Cambridge: Harvard Univ. Press. Pp. 388–433.

Klugman, S. F. (1944). The effect of money incentives vs. praise upon the reliability and obtained scores of the Revised Stanford-Binet test. *J. gen. Psychol., 30,* 255–269.

Kohn, M. L. (1959). Social class and parental values. *Amer. J. Sociol., 64,* 337–351.

Knapp, R. H. (1964). *The origins of American humanistic scholars.* Englewood Cliffs, N.J.: Prentice-Hall.

Knapp, R. H., and H. B. Goodrich (1952). *Collegiate origins of American scientists.* Chicago: Univ. of Chicago Press.

Knapp, R. H., and J. J. Greenbaum (1953). *The younger American scholar, his collegiate origins.* Chicago: Univ. of Chicago Press.

Knoell, Dorothy M. (1953). Prediction of teaching success from word fluency data. *J. educ. Res., 46,* 674–683.

Kounin, J. S., P. V. Gump, and J. J. Ryan, III (1961). Exploration in classroom management. *J. Teacher Educ., 12,* 235–246.

Larson, R. G., and J. L. Olson (1965). Final report: a pilot project for culturally deprived kindergarten children (tentative draft). Racine, Wisc.: Unified School District No. 1. (Mimeo)

Lavin, D. E. (1965). *The prediction of academic performance: a theoretical analysis and review of research.* New York: Russell Sage Foundation.

Leavitt, H. J. (1951). Some effects of certain communication patterns on group performance. *J. abnorm. soc. Psychol., 46,* 38–50.

Leeds, C. H. (1950). A scale for measuring teacher-pupil attitudes and teacher-pupil rapport. *Psychol. Monogr., 64,* No. 6 (whole No. 312).

———— (1952). A second validity study of the Minnesota Teacher Attitude Inventory. *Element. School J., 52,* 398–405.

LeShan, L. L. (1952). Time orientation and social class. *J. abnorm. soc. Psychol., 47,* 589–592.

Lewin, K., R. Lippitt, and R. White (1939). Patterns of aggressive behavior in experimentally created social climates. *J. soc. Psychol., 10,* 271–299.

Lindzey, G., Ed. (1954). *Handbook of social psychology.* Cambridge, Mass.: Addison-Wesley.

Lindzey, G., and E. F. Borgatta (1954). Sociometric measurement. In G. Lindzey (Ed.), *Handbook of social psychology.* Vol. 1. Cambridge, Mass.: Addison-Wesley. Pp. 405–448.

Linton, R. (1936). *The study of man.* New York: D. Appleton-Century.

Lipham, J. M. (1960). Personal variables related to administrative effectiveness. Unpublished doctoral dissertation, University of Chicago.

Lippitt, R., and M. Gold (1959). Classroom social structure as a mental health problem. *J. soc. Issues, 15,* 40–49.

Littman, R. A., R. A. Moore, and J. Pierce-Jones (1957). Social class differences in child rearing: a third community for comparison with Chicago and Newton, Massachusetts. *Amer. sociol. Rev., 22,* 694–704.

Loeb, M. B. (1953). Implications of status differentiations for personal and social development. *Harvard educ. Rev., 23,* 168–174.

Lorge, I. (1953). Difference or bias in tests of intelligence. In *Proceedings of the 1952 invitational conference on testing problems.* Princeton, N.J.: Educational Testing Service. Pp. 76–82.

Lott, A. J., and Bernice E. Lott (1963). *Negro and white youth: a psychological study in a border-state community.* New York: Holt, Rinehart, and Winston.

Lynd, R. S., and Helen M. Lynd (1929). *Middletown: a study in contemporary American culture.* New York: Harcourt, Brace.

McArthur, C. C. (1960). Sub-culture and personality during the college years. *J. educ. Sociol., 33,* 260–268.

Maccoby, E. E., and P. K. Gibbs (1954). Methods of child-rearing in two social classes. In W. E. Martin and Celia B. Stendler (Eds.), *Readings in child development.* New York: Harcourt, Brace. Pp. 380–396.

McCandless, B. (1952). Environment and intelligence. *Amer. J. ment. Defic., 56,* 674–691.

McKeachie, W. J. (1963). Research on teaching at the college and university level. In N. L. Gage (Ed.), *Handbook of research on teaching.* Chicago: Rand McNally. Pp. 1118–1172.

Mayer, K. (1953). The theory of social classes. *Harvard educ. Rev., 23,* 149–167.

Medley, D. M., and H. E. Mitzel (1963). Measuring classroom behavior by systematic observation. In N. L. Gage (Ed.), *Handbook of research on teaching.* Chicago: Rand McNally. Pp. 247–328.

Merton, R. K. (1957). *Social theory and social structure* (rev. ed.). Glencoe, Ill.: Free Press.

Meyer, W. J., and G. G. Thompson (1956). Sex differences in the distribution of teacher approval and disapproval among sixth-grade children. *J. educ. Psychol., 47,* 385–396.

Michaelis, J. U. (1954). The prediction of success in student teaching from personality and attitude inventories. *Univ. Calif. Publ. Educ., 11,* 415–481.

Miles, M. B. (1964). The T-group and the classroom. In L. P. Bradford, J. R. Gibb, and K. D. Benne (Eds.), *T-group theory and laboratory method.* New York: Wiley. Pp. 452–476.

Miller, D. R., and G. E. Swanson (1958). *The changing American parent.* New York: Wiley.

———— (1960). *Inner conflict and defense.* New York: Holt.

Milner, Esther (1951). A study of the relationship between reading readiness in grade one school children and patterns of parent-child interactions. *Child Develpmt., 22,* 95–122.

Montague, D. O. (1964). Arithmetic concepts of kindergarten children in contrasting socioeconomic areas. *Element. School J., 64,* 393–397.

Moreno, J. L. (1934). *Who shall survive?* Washington, D.C.: Nervous and Mental Disease Publishing Co.

Morsh, J. E., and Eleanor W. Wilder (1954). Identifying the effective instructor: a review of the quantitative studies, 1900–1952. USAF Personnel Training Research Center, Research Bulletin No. AFPTRC-TR-54-44.

Mursell, J. (1954). *Successful teaching: its psychological principles* (2nd ed.). New York: McGraw-Hill.

Myrdal, G. (1944). *An American dilemma* (2 vols.). New York: Harper.

Nisbet, J. (1953). Family environment and intelligence. *Eugenics Rev., 45,* 31–40.

Noel, D. L. (1964). Group identification among Negroes: an empirical analysis. *J. soc. Issues, 20,* 71–84.

Oelke, M. C. (1956). A study of student teachers' attitudes toward children. *J. educ. Psychol., 47,* 193–198.

Ohlsen, M. M., and R. E. Schultz (1955). Projective test response patterns for best and poorest student-teachers. *Educ. psychol. Measmt., 15,* 18–27.

Ojemann, R. H., and F. R. Wilkinson (1939). The effect on pupil growth of increase in teacher's understanding of pupil behavior. *J. exp. Educ., 8,* 143–147.

Orlansky, H. (1949). Infant care and personality. *Psychol. Bull., 46,* 1–48.

Osborne, R. T. (1960). Racial differences in mental growth and social achievement: a longitudinal study. *Psychol. Reports, 7,* 233–239.

Pace, C. R. (1963). Differences in campus atmospheres. In W. W. Charters, Jr., and N. L. Gage (Eds.), *Readings in the social psychology of education.* Boston: Allyn and Bacon. Pp. 73–79.

Parker, S., and R. Kleiner (1964). Status position, mobility, and ethnic identification of the Negro. *J. soc. Issues, 20,* 85–102.

Parsons, T. (1959). The school class as a social system. *Harvard educ. Rev., 29,* 297–318.

Parsons, T., and E. A. Shils, Eds. (1951). *Toward a general theory of action.* Cambridge: Harvard Univ. Press.

Pettigrew, T. F. (1964a). Negro American personality: why isn't more known? *J. soc. Issues, 20,* 4–23.

———— (1964b). *A profile of the Negro American.* Princeton: Van Nostrand.

———— (1965). School desegregation. In *White House conference on education.* Washington, D.C.: Government Printing Office. Pp. 108–116.

Piaget, J. (1952). *The origins of intelligence in children* (transl. M. Cook). New York: International Univ. Press.

Prescott, D. A. (1938). *Emotion and the educative process.* Washington, D.C.: American Council on Education.

Prince, R. (1957). A study of the relationships between individual values and administrative effectiveness in the school situation. Unpublished doctoral dissertation, University of Chicago.

Remmers, H. H. (1963). Rating methods in research on teaching. In N. L. Gage (Ed.), *Handbook of research on teaching.* Chicago: Rand McNally. Pp. 329–378.

Riesen, A. H. (1947). The development of visual perception in man and chimpanzee. *Science, 106,* 107–108.

―――― (1958). Plasticity of behavior: psychological aspects. In H. F. Harlow and C. N. Woolsey (Eds.), *Biological and biochemical bases of behavior.* Madison: Univ. of Wisconsin Press. Pp. 425–450.

Riesman, D., and C. Jencks (1962). The viability of the American college. In N. Sanford (Ed.), *The American college.* New York: Wiley. Pp. 74–192.

Riessman, F. (1962). *The culturally deprived child.* New York: Harper.

Roe, Anne (1957). Early differentiation of interests. In C. W. Taylor (Ed.), *The second (1957) University of Utah research conference on the identification of creative scientific talent.* Salt Lake City: Univ. of Utah Press. Pp. 98–108.

Roethlisberger, F. J., and W. J. Dickson (1939). *Management and the worker.* Cambridge: Harvard Univ. Press.

Rogoff, Natalie (1961). Local social structure and educational selection. In A. H. Halsey, Jean Floud, and C. A. Anderson (Eds.), *Education, economy, and society: a reader in the sociology of education.* New York: Free Press. Pp. 241–251.

Rose, A. (1956). *The Negro in America.* Boston: Beacon Press.

Rosen, B. C. (1956). The achievement syndrome. *Amer. sociol. Rev., 21,* 203–211.

―――― (1959). Race, ethnicity, and the achievement syndrome. *Amer. sociol. Rev., 24,* 47–60.

Russell, D. H., and H. R. Fea (1963). Research on teaching reading. In N. L. Gage (Ed.), *Handbook of research on teaching.* Chicago: Rand McNally. Pp. 865–928.

Ryans, D. G. (1960). *Characteristics of teachers.* Washington, D.C.: American Council on Education.

St. John, C. W. (1930). *Educational achievement in relation to intelligence as shown by teachers' marks, promotions, and scores in standard tests in certain elementary grades.* Cambridge: Harvard Univ. Press.

Sandgren, D. L., and L. G. Schmidt (1956). Does practice teaching change attitudes toward teaching? *J. educ. Res., 49,* 673–680.

Sanford, N., Ed. (1962). *The American college.* New York: Wiley.

Schmid, J., Jr. (1950). Factor analysis of prospective teachers' differences. *J. exp. Educ., 18,* 287–319.

Schmuck, R. (1962). Sociometric status and utilization of academic abilities. *Merrill-Palmer Quart., 8,* 165–172.

Schneider, L., and S. Lysgaard (1953). The deferred gratification pattern: a preliminary study. *Amer. sociol. Rev., 18,* 142–149.

Schutz, W. C. (1958). *FIRO: a three-dimensional theory of interpersonal behavior.* New York: Holt.

Sears, R. R., Eleanor E. Maccoby, and H. Levin (1957). *Patterns of child rearing.* Evanston, Ill.: Row, Peterson.

Sewell, W. H. (1961). Social class and childhood personality. *Sociometry, 24,* 340–356.

Sewell, W. H., A. O. Haller, and M. A. Straus (1957). Social status and educational and occupational aspirations. *Amer. sociol. Rev., 22,* 67–73.

Shapiro, Edna, Barbara Biber, and Patricia Minuchin (1957). The Cartoon Situation Test: a semi-structured technique for assessing aspects of personality pertinent to the teaching process. *J. proj. Tech., 21,* 172–184.

Shaplin, J. T. (1964). Toward a theoretical rationale for team teaching. In J. T. Shaplin and H. F. Olds, Jr. (Eds.), *Team teaching.* New York: Harper and Row. Pp. 57–98.

Shea, J. A. (1955). The predictive value of various combinations of standardized tests and sub-tests for prognosis of teaching efficiency. *Cath. Univ. Amer. Educ. Res. Monogr., 19,* No. 6.

Sheldon, M. S., J. M. Coale, and R. Copple (1959). Current validity of the warm teacher scales. *J. educ. Psychol., 50,* 37–40.

Shuey, A. M. (1958). *The testing of Negro intelligence.* Lynchburg, Va.: Bell.

Singer, A., Jr. (1954). Social competence and success in teaching. *J. exp. Educ., 23,* 99–131.

Smith, B. O. (1959). A study of the logic of teaching: a report on the first phase of a five-year research project. Washington, D.C.: U.S. Office of Education. Department of Health, Education, and Welfare, Project No. 258.

Smith, B. O., and M. O. Meux (n.d.). *A study of the logic of teaching.* Urbana: Bureau of Educational Research, College of Education, University of Illinois. U.S. Office of Education, Project No. 258 (7257).

Spindler, G. D. (1955). Education in a transforming American culture. *Harvard educ. Rev., 25,* 145–156.

Stallings, F. H. (1959). A study of the immediate effects of integration on scholastic achievement in the Louisville schools. *J. Negro Educ., 28,* 439–444.

Stein, H. L., and J. A. Hardy (1957). A validation study of MTAI in Manitoba. *J. educ. Res., 50,* 321–338.

Stein, M. I. (1963). *Personality measures in admissions.* New York: College Entrance Examinations Board.

Stern, G. G. (1962). Environments for learning. In N. Sanford (Ed.), *The American college.* New York: Wiley. Pp. 690–730.

——— (1963). Measuring noncognitive variables in research on teaching. In N. L. Gage (Ed.), *Handbook of research on teaching.* Chicago: Rand McNally. Pp. 398–447.

Stern, G. G., and C. R. Pace (1958). *College characteristics index.* Syracuse: Psychological Research Center, Syracuse University.

Stern, G. G., M. I. Stein, and B. S. Bloom (1956). *Methods in personality assessment.* Glencoe, Ill.: Free Press.

Stewart, L. H., and J. P. Roberts (1955). The relationship of Kuder profiles to remaining in a teachers' college and to occupational choice. *Educ. psychol. Measmt., 15,* 416–421.

Strodtbeck, F. L. (1958).   Family interaction, values and achievement.   In D. C. McClelland, A. L. Baldwin, U. Bronfenbrenner, and F. L. Strodtbeck (Eds.), *Talent and society.* New York: Van Nostrand. Pp. 135–194.

Strong, E. K., Jr. (1943).   *Vocational interests of men and women.*   Stanford: Stanford Univ. Press.

Stuit, D. B., G. S. Dickson, T. F. Jordan, and L. Schloerb (1949).   *Predicting success in professional schools.*   Washington, D.C.: American Council on Education.

Tagiuri, R., and L. Petrullo, Eds. (1958).   *Person perception and interpersonal behavior.* Stanford: Stanford Univ. Press.

Terman, L. M. (1954).   Discovery and encouragement of exceptional talent. *Amer. Psychologist, 9,* 221–230.

Terrel, G., Jr., Kathryn Durkin, and M. Wiesley (1959).   Social class and the nature of the incentive in discrimination learning. *J. abnorm. soc. Psychol., 59,* 270–272.

Thelen, H. A. (1949).   Group dynamics in instruction: principle of least group size. *School Rev., 57,* 139–148.

―――― (1950).   Educational dynamics: theory and research. *J. soc. Issues, 6,* 5–95.

――――, Ed. (1951).   Experimental research toward a theory of instruction. *J. educ. Res., 45,* 89–136.

―――― (1963).   Grouping for teachability. *Theory into Practice, 2,* 81–89.

Thelen, H. A., and J. Withall (1949).   Three frames of reference: the description of climate. *Human Relat., 2,* 159–176.

Thistlethwaite, D. L. (1959a).   College environments and the development of talent. *Science, 130,* 71–76.

―――― (1959b).   College press and student achievement. *J. educ. Psychol., 50,* 183–191.

―――― (1960).   College press and changes in study plans of talented students. *J. educ. Psychol., 51,* 222–234.

Thompson, W. R., and W. Heron (1954).   The effects of restricting early experience on the problem-solving capacity of dogs. *Canad. J. Psychol., 8,* 17–31.

Torrance, E. P., and K. Arsan (1963).   Experimental studies of homogeneous and heterogeneous groups for creative scientific tasks. In W. W. Charters, Jr., and N. L. Gage (Eds.), *Readings in the social psychology of education.*   Boston: Allyn and Bacon. Pp. 133–140.

Travers, R. M. W. (1949).   Significant research on the prediction of academic success. In Wilma T. Donahue, C. H. Coombs, and R. W. Travers (Eds.), *The measurement of student adjustment and achievement.*   Ann Arbor: Univ. of Michigan Press. Pp. 147–190.

Tumin, M. M. (1958).   Readiness and resistance to desegregation: a social portrait of the hard core. *Soc. Forces, 36,* 256–263.

Tyler, F. T. (1954).   The prediction of student-teaching success from personality inventories. *Univ. Calif. Publ. Educ., 11,* 233–314.

Wallen, N. E., and R. M. W. Travers (1963).   Analysis and investigation of teaching methods. In N. L. Gage (Ed.), *Handbook of research on teaching.*   Chicago: Rand McNally. Pp. 448–505.

Waller, W. W. (1965). *The sociology of teaching.* (Originally published 1932.) New York: Wiley.

Warner, W. L., and W. C. Bailey (1949). *Democracy in Jonesville.* New York: Harper.

Warner, W. L., R. J. Havighurst, and M. B. Loeb (1944). *Who shall be educated?* New York: Harper.

Washburne, C., and L. M. Heil (1960). What characteristics of teachers affect children's growth? *School Rev., 68,* 420–428.

Weinert, D. P., C. K. Kamii, and N. L. Radin (1964). Perry pre-school project progress report. Ypsilanti, Mich.: Ypsilanti Public Schools. (Mimeo)

Wertham, F. (1952). Psychological effects of school segregation. *Amer. J. Psychother., 6,* 94–103.

White, Martha S. (1957). Social class, child-rearing practices, and child behavior. *Amer. sociol. Rev., 22,* 704–712.

White, R. W. (1959). Motivation reconsidered: the concept of competence. *Psychol. Rev., 66,* 297–333.

Williams, R. M., Jr., and Margaret W. Ryan, Eds. (1954). *Schools in transition: community experiences in desegregation.* Chapel Hill: Univ. of North Carolina Press.

Wispe, L. G. (1951). Evaluating section teaching methods in the introductory course. *J. educ. Res., 45,* 161–186.

Withall, J. (1949). Development of a technique for the measurement of socio-emotional climate in classrooms. *J. exp. Educ., 17,* 347–361.

Withall, J., and W. W. Lewis (1963). Social interaction in the classroom. In N. L. Gage (Ed.), *Handbook of research on teaching.* Chicago: Rand McNally. Pp. 683–714.

Wolfle, D. L. (1954). *America's resources of specialized talent.* New York: Harper.

Wright, Elizabeth M., and Virginia H. Proctor (1961). *Systematic observation of verbal interaction as a method of comparing mathematics lessons.* St. Louis, Mo.: Washington University. U.S. Office of Education, Cooperative Research Project No. 816.

43

Social-Psychological Aspects
of International Relations

AMITAI ETZIONI, *Columbia University*

The study of the conditions under which a just and stable peace can be achieved constitutes the main core of contemporary analyses of international relations; hence, the following discussion focuses on the issues and problems in applying social psychology to the prevention of war. It is evident, however, that the discussion and reported findings have implications for other aspects of international relations. For example, questions that we raise about the ability of actors to control their behavior apply as readily to international trade or to competition in outer space as they do to war and peace.

The discussion consists of four main parts: (1) a review of the debate over the rationality of international actors (what is their nature?); (2) a note on the level of generalization of social-psychological statements and their applicability to various units of analysis; (3) a discussion of the units of analysis (who are the international actors?); and (4) an extended sample of a substantive approach to our subject.

Our procedure is to present the main arguments that have been put forth in these subject areas and then to indicate our own position. In general, our perspective is relatively more sociological than psychological, more theoretical than empirical, more inclined toward the engaged scholar than toward the pure scientist, more in favor of multilateral disarmament than either arms control or unilateral pacifism (Etzioni, 1962; 1968, pp. 553–613).

In the social psychology of international relations, more than in most fields of study, social-science findings are unevenly distributed among various subfields and basic theoretical assumptions are not agreed upon. Hence, a mere survey of findings would give a very lopsided view of the field and would tend to conceal the divergent assumptions behind the various findings. In any case, there are already several

---

This article was written during my fellowship at the Center for Advanced Study in the Behavioral Sciences. I greatly benefited from the various services of the Center and the comments of my fellows, especially Robert Abelson, Richard Watson, John Holland, and Julian Stanley. I am especially grateful to comments by Milton J. Rosenberg. I am indebted for research assistance to Fred DuBow and Horst Hutter. This work is a by-product of Project DA-DSS-W-49-083-66-01 of the Advanced Projects Research Agency of the Department of Defense.

reviews of those subfields in which many of the data lie. We therefore choose (1) to focus on issues that are actively discussed, (2) to report in some detail one or two *recent* key studies rather than attempt an exhaustive survey, and (3) to refer the reader to review works for detailed coverage. Even within these limits, we cannot do justice to this important and rich field. This essay at best will serve to open some doors; it aims to close none.

Among the publications that devote most of their space to social-science research relevant to the prevention of war are the *Journal of Conflict Resolution* (Ann Arbor) and the *Journal of Peace Research* (Oslo). See also *Background,* a publication of the International Studies Association. Abstracts of peace research are available from the Canadian Peace Research Institute. A semiannual digest, *Current Thought on Peace and War,* is published in Durham, North Carolina. For an important bibliography of earlier work, see Bernard *et al.* (1957) and Snyder and Robinson (n.d.). The most important recent work is that of Kelman (1965), published for the Society for the Psychological Study of Social Issues. A fair number of the articles published in the *Bulletin of Atomic Scientists* are of interest. The U.S. Department of State and the Arms Control and Disarmament Agency publish various bibliographical guides. See also a special issue of the *International Social Science Journal* (1965) on peace, edited by Peter Lengyel, and of *Social Problems* (1963), edited by Peter I. Rose and Jerome Laulicht. For reviews of contributions of social scientists to the study of war, without a specific focus on its prevention, see Janowitz (1959) and Bowers (1967).

DEGREE OF SELF-CONTROL: THE NATURE OF THE ACTORS

A key general question lying behind the myriad of more specific ones that concern students of international relations is the degree to which man controls his fate as compared to the degree to which he is controlled by it. Though the same question has been asked in many other studies of human relations, especially of the relations between man and his work, it is more pivotal in the understanding of international relations than in any other study area, for here man might be not only alienated or subjugated but eliminated as well. Work technologies which man has created, but over which he has lost control, reduce him to the level of an instrument, but at least he possesses the status of a utensil which commands some attention. However, the strategic literature about nuclear warfare refers to millions of men to be annihilated and millions of new ones presumably to be grown to order to replace them; in this context individuals are not granted even the status of objects that have an instrumental value.

The basic question of man's control of his fate appears specifically in the discussion of his capacity to avoid wars he does not desire and to limit wars he did initiate to the levels he desires. This issue has been stressed because all sides to the debate concerning man's nature agree that an increasing number of international actors command, or are about to command, weapons whose use would have consequences irrational by anyone's standards. These weapons are able to wipe out completely the actors involved; hence, their use cannot advance the goals to which the actors themselves adhere. Psychological assumptions about the nature of man and his relations to others, as well as data which psychological research provides, play a significant role in this debate.

We shall use the term *rationalistic* to refer to the set of assumptions that lies at the core of the position that man can engage in various threatening and warring acts without losing control of his conduct or the ensuing interaction; and *nonrationalistic* to refer to those who maintain that these activities, once initiated, have a propelling power and dynamic of their own which leads to the loss of self-control. While it should be noted that the differences between these two positions are considerable, they are not mutually exclusive. The rationalists recognize instances of loss of control, but consider them so improbable that they can be disregarded, or expect that some limited precautions will suffice to counter these tendencies, or they argue that all and any alternative systems available would be more dangerous than the existing one. Many nonrationalists, at least by implication, recognize that rational decisions are made, but suggest that their effectiveness declines once a hostile mood and vicious cycle of hostile acts have "taken off"—an effect analogous to the decline in the braking power of a car with the increase of its speed.

Specifically, the controversy over the degree of actors' self-control in situations of international conflict appears in three main subject areas: intranational control systems, international interaction, and generalized strategic assumptions.

INTRANATIONAL COMMUNICATION AND ITS DISTORTIONS

Social scientists have pointed out that the national military control systems, at least in the West, are based on the assumption that messages issued by command posts will be understood and followed by the receivers (M. Deutsch, 1961; Etzioni, 1964, pp. 167–171; Horowitz, 1961; Michael, 1962). Initial national efforts in the United States, for instance, focused almost exclusively on engineering attempts to ensure that messages broadcast would reach the intended receivers and be relayed with enough power for them to be clearly audible, without "noise" on the line or enemy jamming, and also to ensure coding and decoding of the messages to prevent unauthorized listening by a foe. Social scientists have played a major role in bringing to bear well-known findings about distortions of communication messages due to personality and cultural factors. Similarly, the danger of unauthorized use of nuclear weapons, following unauthorized messages or without any messages being received at all, has been stressed on the basis of general theories of deviance. The danger of projecting interpretations on the basis of ambiguous signals has also been pointed out (for example, interpreting unaccounted radar blips as an incoming missile attack).

Until recently, little actual research on national control systems was conducted. Social scientists mainly applied knowledge from other areas (for example, the social psychology of rumors) to that of national control systems. The effect of their publications was to encourage some limited revisions of the control systems in order to safeguard against these dangers. For instance, locks were put on the doors of missile silos which only the command post could open. Efforts to make unauthorized use of weapons less likely and to screen out people with psychological disorders from positions of access to nuclear arms were intensified. Melman (1961, p. 15) reported that, during one year alone, the U.S. Air Force discharged 4213 men on disability grounds; one-fourth of this total were released because of psychotic disorders, psychoneurotic difficulties, or anxiety reactions. Etzioni presented some data on the influence of social scientists on policy making in this area (see Etzioni, 1967, pp. 806–830).

INTERNATIONAL INTERACTION: ESCALATION

Of more general interest is the debate over one particular form of loss of control, that of escalation. This is the case (1) because the arguments on both sides are directly applicable to other forms of loss of control in international conflict situations, (2) because it is believed that this particular form of loss of control is more likely to lead to all-out war than distorted national communication or unauthorized use of weapons, and (3) because escalation of conflicts is of interest both to those who seek to prevent the transformation of nonarmed conflicts into armed ones (disarmers) and to those who seek to limit the scope of war if it does occur (arms controllers). Obviously, disarmers also would prefer a "limited" to an all-out war, and arms controllers—under most conditions—would prefer no war to a limited one. The difference is in what the two schools consider feasible and where they focus their efforts. There is also a difference in judgment as to whether war might still serve the national interest; the disarmers are more inclined to deny the utility of war than are the arms controllers. Donald Brennan, a leading researcher of the arms-control school, after identifying his arms-control position, added: "The great majority of us accept the idea that national military force may sometimes be used with justice in defense of important national goals or human values" (1965, pp. 25–26). (See also Ikle, 1962.)

The argument over escalation is brought into focus by Herman Kahn's book, *On Escalation* (1965), and by a major review of the book by Charles E. Osgood (1965) in which he summarizes the main nonrationalist arguments. Kahn's position is that, if one side's interests are threatened, it might escalate the level of conflict as a way of protecting or advancing its position without being dragged all the way up the escalator into all-out war. Kahn provided a ladder of 44 rungs, with several major thresholds. At rung 22 a limited nuclear war is declared. At the top looms "spasm or insensate war." Escalation of one or more rungs is expected to yield the desired results because moving up some steps communicates the strength of the escalating actor's resolve to the other(s). It indicates that he might be willing to escalate further, up to a level of conflict the opposite side is unwilling to face—unwilling, either because, at that level, the opposition estimates that, even if it prevailed, its losses would outweigh the gains such a confrontation would yield, or because such escalation might lead to all-out war, which all sides fear. Finally, if the conflict is actually further escalated, the escalating actor is expected to be "prepared" so that, at some level, he will win because the opposite side will be disadvantaged. China in 1965, for instance, might have been *relatively* willing to engage in a conventional war with the United States over Vietnam, but quite reluctant to face a tactical nuclear war (Brody, 1966). Thus, escalation is expected to work in the United States' favor, for she either can threaten a tactical nuclear war if China begins moving with conventional troops (thereby avoiding even the conventional stage), or, if the threat is called, can actually use nuclear weapons, which are expected to be superior to China's force.

In part, the very conception of escalation is a psychological concept and rests on psychological premises. Some of these Kahn himself pointed out. For instance, the less credible to the other side is a particular threat to escalate (assuming that the first side is not bluffing), the more likely it is that actual additional escalation will occur ("additional" referring to rounds beyond those initially used to communicate resolve). Second, the thresholds that mark some rungs of the ladder as particularly critical for escalation (that is, those where raising the level of conflict by one rung is particularly likely to generate several additional raises) are psychological. The main threshold is the taboo against use of nuclear weapons. A step up here fundamentally changes the definition of the situation. On the one hand, actors are particularly likely to pause before taking a postthreshold step, since the escalation that will follow will be particularly high, and hence the threat to escalate is particularly frightening. On the other hand, transgressions, especially repeated ones, will tend to erase the pause (or escalation-slowing) effects of the thresholds by changing the attitude toward them.

While Kahn's own concepts are not bereft of psychological considerations and insights, the basic psychological assumptions on which the use of escalation as a rational strategy rests are invalid. As Osgood (1965, p. 13) has pointed out:

> Military escalation produces the very conditions, both internally and externally, which make it harder and harder to stop and de-escalate. Internally, if early escalations fail and produce counter-escalation, anger and frustration impel one upward; and if escalation succeeds, one is learning to use this means at the expense of others, until we find ourselves trying to police the world. Externally, the early stages of escalation are more likely to produce hardening rather than softening of the opponent's resolve, thus forcing us to higher steps on the ladder than we had originally intended to reach. This is precisely what appears to be happening in Vietnam. The analogy with sexual arousal may be disturbing, but it is valid; as every practiced seducer knows, each threshold whose passage can be induced makes it easier to induce passage of the next.

Thus, three mechanisms are suggested that might turn an escalation process from a tool into a trap. If your side is being *frustrated,* the public might demand more escalation than the strategy (and, in this sense, rationality) calls for; if your side is being successful, that is, *rewarded,* the pressure might be for more frequent use of the pressure-and-threat strategy than cool calculations advise. Finally, it is suggested, escalation alters the conduct of the opponent, whose resolve, at least initially, is hardened rather than weakened. This point is also supported by studies of the effect of bombing on the morale of citizens in Japan and Germany during World War II (U.S. Strategic Bombing Survey, 1947a, 1947b). Wright (1965) listed among the factors that promote escalation relative equality in forces immediately available and the belief that superior forces will eventually be available.

One might add that the problems of communication between nations are even more severe than in national control systems (Bauer, 1961; Wedge and Muromcew, 1965). An act that might appear to one side as a minor escalation might appear to another as a major one. For instance, the U.S.S.R. might well have considered positioning of its missiles in Cuba, the way the United States did on U.S.S.R. borders in Turkey, at worst a minor escalation of the Cold War; the United States considered it a major one (*cf.* Holsti, Brody, and North, 1964). Actually, once tension is high, even what one side considers or presents as a deescalation might be misperceived as a trap or even an escalation. United States discontinuation of bombing of North Vietnam in 1965 was perceived by the West as a deescalatory step, but as major new troop commitments were made at the same time in the South, and as major operations were carried out against North Vietnamese troops there, it is not clear at all that the deescalation was credible to the other side.

While escalations have rarely been studied as such, *arms races* and the role of psychological factors in their upward spiraling are more often a subject of research.

It is often argued that arms races, once initiated (for whatever reason), generate forces of their own leading to higher levels of armaments which sooner or later are likely to trigger war. In its simplest and most basic formulation, the concept suggests that the hostile act of actor A (who raises his level of armaments) is a sufficient cause for actor B to raise the level of his armaments, a raise which in turn suffices for actor A to increase his arms further.

A pioneering study of arms races, building on the simplest formulation, was conducted by Lewis F. Richardson (1939, 1960), who used mathematical models (especially differential equations) to study the interaction between two or more competing units, much as modern economists do. Indeed, arms races have been compared to price wars (Boulding, 1962, p. 25; Cassady, 1963; Etzioni, 1964, pp. 24–27; Shubik, 1959). Both, when they break through various points of potential equilibrium and continue to escalate, lead to conflicts which are ruinous often not only to the victim but also to the aggressor.

Richardson started with a two-actor model; his projections attain a good fit with data on the 1909–1914 arms race leading to World War I. Developing his model to include more countries, Richardson showed that the increase in the number of actors, beginning even with three, makes the international system less stable; that is, arms races become more prone to lead to war (1960, p. 155). His "enlarged" model gives a fair fit for the 1932–1939 arms race leading to World War II, though Harsanyi has pointed out that the same fit might be achieved on the basis of different assumptions, so long as the costs of armaments in both periods rose in strength exponentially (1962, p. 695).

Richardson's work is very rudimentary despite, and perhaps because of, the relative subtlety of his mathematical model. The data he fed into his models were poor and uneven. They had to be taken, in his own words, on a basis of give or take 20 percent (1960, p. 4); thus, when plotted on a scattergram, they could "fit" similarly well (or similarly poorly) a variety of curves that differ considerably from his (the paucity of Richardson's data is widely recognized—see K. W. Deutsch, 1963, pp. 39, 44–45; Boulding, 1962, p. 35). Moreover, Richardson made several highly untenable assumptions in order to be able to use the available quantitative data at all. The assumption most widely challenged is that the amount of trade between two nations is an indicator of the friendliness of their relations, and that expenditure on arms is an indicator of hostility. Some expenditures seem to have a stabilizing effect; for example, hardening of missile sites allows a nation to sit out a first strike and is believed to reduce significantly the danger of a nation's preemptive strike on the basis of a misconception that it is about to be attacked. Other expenditures (for example, arming an indigenous opposition in the opponent's land) can be highly destabilizing (Schelling, 1963, p. 474). Richardson's most central assumption was that arms races are a function of hostility or friendliness of the people of the nations involved. He explicitly assumed that these sentiments are nonconscious, not policies or postures. His model seeks to describe mathematically how the change of mood of one nation changes that of the other. The reaction of the second nation is assumed to be automatic and immediate (*cf.* Pool, 1952, p. 61).

Boulding (1962) refined the Richardson model by adding a "preference function" of the actors (see also Rapoport, 1957). While these preferences are presented by Boulding as character profiles, they can also be viewed as alternative strategies an actor might follow. Boulding, for instance, characterized actors as saints, evil, or "publicans." Saints react in a friendly manner to all actions, including hostile ones;

evil actors react in a hostile fashion to all actions, including friendly ones; publicans give what they get (and thus approximate what Richardson assumed all actors to be like). The level of the arms race and the probability that it will lead to a breakdown, to a war, depend on the nature of the actors. The probability is obviously highest when two evil actors clash, inconceivable when two saints meet. More interesting are the encounters between saints and evils or between saints and publicans, which lead to less upward spiraling than do encounters in which the more hostile of each pair is met by an actor responding in kind. The arms-race cycle runs out "earlier" (that is, with less escalation and probability of a breakdown), the more "underescalating" the reaction is, and earliest (Boulding pointed out) if escalation by actor A is met by deescalation on the part of actor B (see also Triska and Finley, 1965).

Some students of the arms race assume that the actors react automatically and on the basis of a formed character; others see the actors as commanding strategies which they can alter more or less at will. I advocate a third approach which is a "mix" of these two: under some conditions the first view seems to be more valid; under others, the second view. Specifically, when relations are relatively "neutral" (no intense friendships or hostilities), actors will act relatively rationally and be relatively free to change strategies. When "involvements" are intense, for example, in military alliances, even initially rational alliances often lead to "entanglements" in which commitment to allies leads to conduct that is "nonrational." At the other end of the friendship-hostility spectrum, the more hostile the relationship, the less control the actors have; that is, the less the Kahn-Schelling model applies and the more the actors live in a Richardson-Boulding-Osgood world. The capacity to brake a car within a given distance (to avoid collision) under varying degrees of speed seems to provide a good analog (maybe even a mathematical equation): the higher the speed, the smaller the braking capacity (for a given distance). The car analog highlights my proposition that the major decisions are made in the *early* part of an escalation process; thus he who steps on the first rungs had better take into account the increased loss of control that additional steps tend to entail. (Thresholds might be seen as "step functions" that break up the unilinear progression and give increased opportunities for slowing down before major increases in loss of control; in this sense they are like steep upgrades in the road before sharp declines.)

The arms-race model raises the question of the wisdom of unilateral deescalation and disarmament. Richardson suggested that for any country to increase its armaments, even in response to the increase of another, is irrational, for there is an "automatic" reciprocation from the other side. His model depicts, he says, "what people would do if they did not stop to think" (1960, p. 12). Not to reciprocate is the obvious policy implication.

Huntington (1958), using historical case studies rather than mathematical models, argued that not all arms races lead to wars and that, in effect, some raises in armament levels by one actor have the effect of preventing war by communicating to the other side the first actor's resolve and his willingness to stabilize the level of armament on a specific, though high, level (see also Kissinger, 1961, p. 217). Discussing the British-French arms race in the late nineteenth century, Huntington concluded that, after several Richardson-like rounds, the British finally succeeded in communicating to the French the British capacity and resolved to maintain a certain ratio of arms above whatever the level the French might amass, and thus the race petered out, leading to equilibrium rather than war.

One's view of the danger of arms races is greatly affected by one's estimate of the probability of breakdown versus attaining balance short of war. Those in favor of deterrence strategies argue that the probability of war is low (Kahn, 1960, pp. 208–209); those opposed to them argue that it is high. For instance, on December 27, 1960, C. P. Snow stated that "within, at the most, ten years, some of these bombs are going off. I am saying this as responsibly as I can. *That* is the certainty . . ." (*New York Times*, December 28, 1960). Aside from disagreement about the level of the probability itself, the capacity to determine this probability has also been questioned.

In my judgment, the major difference between prenuclear and nuclear arms races lies not so much in the probability of a breakdown, which might well be low (perhaps even lower in nuclear than in prenuclear times), but in the "utility" of the outcome. In prenuclear days the question about which proportion of arms races leads to war might have been meaningful, since war was one way, however costly, to restore the equilibrium. Nations were rarely wiped out and war objectives were often limited. Relatively shortly after a war, the actors could return to normal domestic and international life, including arms racing. Nuclear wars, it is widely acknowledged, might entail the complete devastation of the actors. Hence, it would seem that probabilities of breakdown that were "acceptable" within the limits of prenuclear systems might be quite unacceptable in the nuclear world.

THE ACTORS AS STRATEGISTS

The question of actors' rationality (or self-control) is most directly confronted in the debate concerning their capacity to implement strategies, whatever they are, as against being caught in forces beyond their control. Thomas C. Schelling's (1960) work is a typical example of the rationalistic approach, drawing on game theory. Schelling dealt with strategies which rational actors might adopt in any conflict situation (from maneuvering in traffic jams to husband-wife warfare), but application to international conflicts was his main concern. He stressed that zero-sum games, the preoccupation of traditional game theorists, provide poor models for a theory of conflict because they apply only to limited situations. Most situations more closely approximate variable-sum games, involving both conflicting and common interests between actors. Schelling actually considered both mixed interest and cooperative games, but the mixed interest ones are more applicable to international situations.

The central psychological factors with which he dealt are threat and interactor communication. In Richardson's world, actors work directly on each others' feelings; in Boulding's world, the impact and response are screened by the actors' respective characters. (In this sense, Richardson is much closer to a stimulus-response model, and Boulding to the study of interaction among systems which have structures or "character.") Schelling's actors have "minds"; they do not merely react to other actors' moves, but study them, work out strategies, manipulate, send false signals, etc. The actors realize that a credible threat has an effect similar to actual exercise of power but entails only some of the costs and risks of its application. While this is generally true, it is especially so in the relationship among nuclear powers, where the sides have a strong common interest to avoid nuclear war; hence, much more can be achieved by credible threats than in situations in which the actors are more inclined to test out a threat by calling it, even if it entails risking a showdown. The more credible one can make one's threats, the more productive they are in terms of the ego's goals.   In addition to credibility, Schelling considered the intensity of the threat, that is, how closely one actually approaches the point of showdown as a means of communicating resolve.   Again, intensity and output of threat were claimed to be associated.

With these basic assumptions in mind, Schelling viewed two or more actors who face each other in a conflict situation as engaged in psychological warfare with the purpose of gaining as much as they can by threat behavior (1960, 1965).   In this context, Schelling has argued repeatedly and adamantly that it is advantageous to follow a strategy that will make one appear reckless, obtuse, and willing to commit suicide; in short, it is rational to act irrationally.   The basic reason is that such conduct forces the other side, if it seeks to avoid a showdown, to take the brunt of the concessions that need to be made.   Striking workers who seek to block a train are most credible if they chain themselves to the track and throw away the key to the locks in full sight of the driver; the countermove for the driver would be to put the train in low gear and leave it, in full sight of the workers (Schelling, 1960, p. 139).   A motorist who wishes to gain the right of way at an intersection should approach it with so much speed that it is evident he could not slow down even if he wanted to (1960, pp. 12, 37).   Other drivers will give way if they act rationally and not from "mere spite."   Similarly, it is deemed advantageous to give nuclear arms to reckless allies over whom one does not have full control (1960, p. 142).

Schelling presented almost no data in support of the various conclusions he drew from analogies taken from the behavior of kidnappers, blackmailers, and inmates of mental hospitals.   He disregarded the fact that game theory deals with games that have an end, while international relations are more like a chain of unending games where the success of a threat in one round might greatly increase the probability of a blow-up in the next one.   Schelling seemed to imply that acts of spite (and, more generally, not succumbing to threats when that might be rational) are marginal situations, but international conduct seems to suggest that such acts are rather common.   K. W. Deutsch (1963, pp. 68–69) has pointed out that repeated frustration of an actor increases the likelihood that he will act irrationally.   It is easy to see that, if two actors were to follow a Schelling strategy, let us say at street intersections, neither would survive.

If Schelling is both a leader and representative of the rationalistic school, Rapoport occupies a similar position on the other side of the argument.   While he nominated Kahn as the "archvillain" of his critique (1965, p. 36), Schelling, Kissinger, and others are also named (1964).   At the root of many specific points which Rapoport raised are two propositions: (1) the strategists are not mere analysts of international relations, but have an important effect on the interaction itself; (2) the disaster of nuclear war would be so great that all other value differences between the sides pale in comparison, and this should be—but is not—the key premise from which strategists start their work.

Strategists affect political and military decision makers as well as the public at large, which comes to perceive international problems in terms and from viewpoints which the strategists provide.   Thus, for instance, by making the unthinkable thinkable, a major threshold against nuclear war is eroded.   And, by thinking in terms of threats and counterthreats, the world is viewed as if it were a zero-sum situation, though in fact common interests (especially avoidance of nuclear war) should be overriding: "[Thermonuclear war] could not occur if the strategists of both sides did not put forward convincing arguments about the necessity of possessing 'nuclear capabilities' and the will to use them" (1964, p. 191). Rapoport also emphasized the idea of self-fulfilling prophecies and the conception of paranoia. The actors, under tension (generated by strategists' inspired amassing of arms and their aggressive interpretations), come to view each other as under the spell of an "all-consuming passion of the enemy to destroy us," and the theory of deterrence rests squarely, according to Rapoport, on the assumption that "only the realization of his vulnerability prevents him from doing so" (1964, p. 106).

Decision-making theories, Rapoport (1964, pp. 5–6) pointed out, are of three kinds: descriptive, formal, and normative. The first two are used in scientific research but, as such, provide no criteria for action. Any decision-making theory that seeks to guide action cannot do so exclusively on scientific-rational grounds, but must also introduce normative principles. Strategists are manifestly in the business of guiding action, not just research, and therefore inevitably evoke normative principles. Here Rapoport's first and second assumptions meet: strategists under the guise of rational theories introduce their value preferences by attributing to the actors psychological traits that suit their theories. In effect, the rationalists advocate an approach that maximizes conflict and makes nuclear war more likely, just as the world situation warrants an approach that would emphasize common interests—above all, peace—as the key normative principle. (For counterarguments see Brennan, 1965; and for a counter to the counterarguments, Rapoport, 1965. For an exchange between representatives of both sides, including Schelling, Wohlsetter, Rapoport, and others, see Archibald, 1966, pp. 137–220.)

THE GRADUALIST APPROACH

Strategists include some who share at least several of Rapoport's value premises and who, in direct opposition to Schelling, attempt to devise strategies that, rather than use the irrational rationally to test the limits within which conflicting interests can be advanced, seek to use the nonrational factors rationally to reduce the level of threats and tensions and to expand the realm of common interests. Etzioni (1962, 1964, 1967), Finkelstein (1962), Fisher (1962), Millis (1965), Osgood (1960, 1962), Singer (1962), and Sohn (1962) fall in this category.

Gradualist strategists assume that one of the factors preventing reduction of international tensions, settlement of conflicts, and reduction of armament is the Cold War frame of reference. Developed by both sides, it has lost its connection with international reality, if indeed such a connection ever existed. The sides, it is argued, reinforce each other's misinterpretations. Finally, it is suggested, the upward spiraling of tensions, generated and felt by the mutual reinforcing of hostile images, the psychological "arms race," can be reversed, leading to a gradual reduction of arms and a build-up of international institutions.

According to the gradualist theory, when a high level of hostility generates psychological blocks that prevent the sides from facing international reality, various defense mechanisms are activated. For one, a high level of tension tends to produce a *rigid* adherence to a policy chosen under earlier conditions. Both sides increase armaments and hold to a hostile posture ("Cold War"), even though armaments have been procured beyond military needs and hostile feelings are no longer justified in view of changes in the opponent's character and intention (Almond, 1960, p. xvi). These changes are *denied*—another mode of defensive behavior—to make continuation of the earlier policy psychologically possible.

Furthermore, fears of nuclear war, *repressed* because they are too threatening to be faced, express themselves in stereotyping and paranoia, indications of which can be found in the conduct of nations entrapped in a state of high international tension. *Stereotyping* is represented by the division of the world into black and white, good and bad nations. Information is manipulated by selecting among and distorting the content of communications, so that positive information about one's adversary is ignored and negative information about one's own side is disregarded. Bronfenbrenner found that, when American schoolchildren were asked why the Russians planted trees alongside a road, they responded that the trees blocked vision and "made work for the prisoners," whereas American trees were planted "for shade" (1961, p. 96). Ralph K. White (1961) provided impressive evidence for the "mirror image" in American-Soviet relations. His statements are documented by quotations from leaders and experts on both sides. Forty-five percent of the themes and subthemes on the American side have almost identically worded counterparts on the Soviet side, and another 32 percent have counterparts that are similar if not identical. The six major mirror-image resemblances are: (1) attributing aggressive intent to the other; (2) attributing peaceful intent to the self; (3) judging both self and other in terms of essentially the same criteria (truthfulness, unselfishness, material well-being, strength, unity, courage, etc.); (4) having a "black top" image of the other (it is the enemy *leaders* who are evil, not the people); (5) saying that we must not listen to the other because he always tells lies; (6) refusing to believe that the other side is motivated by fear of our side.

At the same time, White pointed out that there are real differences in viewpoint between the Russians and ourselves. As Osgood has summarized (1962, pp. 139–140):

> For one thing, we have quite different conceptions of "democracy": they give lip service to government of and for the people, but seldom mention the essential individual freedoms that give meaning to this conception. For another, we have different attitudes toward deception: they accept rational and skillful deception in the interest of Communism as moral, whereas for us deception is always immoral (and we become outraged when our own transgressions are pointed out to us). We have a higher regard for facts than they do: for us, facts are more sacred than theories, political as well as scientific, while for them the reverse seems to hold true. And finally, according to White, the Russians cling to a warm feeling of friendliness toward the American people which we do not seem to reciprocate— a point well worth keeping in mind.

All in all, blocked or distorted communication prevents "reality testing" and correction of false images.

Stereotyping is often accompanied by *paranoia*. Whatever one side offers is interpreted as an effort to advance its own goals and as a trap for the other. If the Soviets favor complete and general disarmament, this in itself leads Americans to regard disarmament as a Communist ruse (Spanier and Nogee, 1962, pp. 32–55). The possibility of a genuine give-and-take is ignored. The same repressed fear, the gradualist analyst continues, causes even reasonable concessions to the other side, made as part of a give-and-take, to be seen as submission or (to use the political term) appeasement. The labeling of bargaining behavior as disloyal or treacherous impedes negotiations that require open-mindedness, flexibility, and willingness to make concessions which do not sacrifice basic positions and values.

What kind of therapy is possible? How can the vicious circle of hostile moves and countermoves be broken? The answer is similar to that implied by psychoanalytic techniques: increased and improved communication. Communication can be increased by visits of Americans to Russia and Russians to America, by exchange of newspapers, by publication of American columns in Soviet newspapers and vice versa, by summit conferences, and the like (Mills, 1958, pp. 103ff). Communication will become less distorted and tensions will be reduced if one of the sides begins to indicate a friendly state of mind. While such indications will be initially mistrusted, if continued they will be reciprocated, reducing hostility; this in turn will reduce counterhostility, thus reversing the Cold War spiral. Once the level of tension is reduced and more communication is received from the other side, there will be an increased ability to perceive international reality as it is, which will further lessen tensions. Joint undertakings are also helpful; psychological experiments with children, it is said, have shown that the introduction of shared tasks assists in reducing hostility. Here reference is often made to a study by Sherif and Sherif (1953; see also Sherif, 1958, 1966, and Blake, 1959). International cooperative research, joint exploration of the stars, oceans, and poles, and joint foreign aid under United Nations auspices, rather than competitive aid, are therefore favored.

There are significant differences in the extent to which this theory claims to explain international behavior. Strongly put, it suggests that "war starts in the minds of men" and "the situation is what we define it to be." In this interpretation, the causes of war are psychological and can be fully explained in psychological terms. Arms are merely an expression of these attitudes of mind (Fromm, 1961, p. 8). If attitudes are modified, arms either will not be produced or will have no threatening impact. The people of New Jersey do not fear nuclear arms held by New Yorkers.

More moderate versions of the theory consider psychological factors as one aspect of a situation that contains economic, political, and military dimensions as well. Just as triggers without hostilities do not make a war, so hostilities without arms cannot trigger battles. Moreover, even if armaments were initially ordered to serve a psychological motive, once available they generate motives of their own which impel hostile attitudes or even wars. Thus one can hold the gradualist theory with varying degrees of strength (Waskow, 1963, pp. 74–82). Osgood, in most of his writings on this subject, has advanced the stronger version (1962), while this author subscribes to the more moderate one (Etzioni, 1962, Chapter 4; 1964, pp. 21–26, 62–68, 209–212).

A second line of variation centers on where the blame for triggering the spiral is placed. Some writers tend to view the sides as being equally at fault, with no "real" reason for a Cold War other than misunderstanding. Stalin, for example, wished only to establish weak friendly governments on his Western borders, a desire which the West misperceived as expansionist. Others tend to put more blame on the West or on the East. All these interpretations can be coupled with gradualist analysis on the grounds that, regardless of the initiator or the validity of the initial cause, the same process of psychological escalation is at work. The therapy, therefore, remains the same. To insist that the side that triggered the process be the one to take the initiative to reverse it is viewed as immature behavior.

Next, there are important differences in the steps suggested to break the cycle. It is generally agreed that measures which require multilateral negotiations are not appropriate for the initiation of tension reduction. The high level of hostility and mutual suspicions invariably disrupts the negotiations, and the mutual recriminations that follow increase rather than reduce the level of international tensions. Unilateral steps, therefore, are needed. The important differences between the two versions of the theory concern the nature of these steps. Jerome Frank (1960), for instance, stressed that the initiatives must be clear, simple, and dramatic to overcome the psychological barriers, for any minor concession will be seen as a trap to encourage the opponent to lower his guard. In Frank's judgment, unilateral renunciation of nuclear weapons might well be the only step large enough to break the vicious cycle (1960, pp. 263–265). More moderate interpretations call for significant reductions of arms as initiatives; still more moderate interpretations seek to restrict the unilateral steps to purely symbolic gestures not involving a weakening of the initiator's military strength, even though some arms reduction, such as the cutting of arms surpluses, might well fulfill this function (see Etzioni, 1962, especially Chapter 7).

The pattern of events between June 10 and November 22, 1963 provides an opportunity for a partial test of the gradualist theory, one we refer to as the Kennedy experiment. The details are analyzed elsewhere. (We draw here on Etzioni, 1967. For historical background, see Sorensen, 1965, especially Chapter XXV, and Schlesinger, 1965, pp. 888–923.) Briefly, the experiment began with a hint from the White House that the President was about to make a major foreign policy address, which attracted the public to television and radio sets. Then, on June 10, at the American University in Washington, President Kennedy made what has since become known as the "Strategy for Peace" speech.

The speech, which came only eight months after the Cuban blockade, called attention to the dangers of nuclear war and took a reconciliatory tone toward the Soviet Union. President Kennedy said "constructive changes" had taken place which "might bring within reach solutions which now seem beyond us." He was carefully optimistic about the prospect of peace: "Our problems are man-made . . . and can be solved by man." But the President's concern was not limited to changes in the other camp; the speech was directed as much to the American people as it was to the Russian government. United States policies, declared the President, must be so constructed "that it becomes in the Communist interest to agree to a genuine peace"; and he explicitly called on the American people to "reexamine," that is, modify, their attitudes toward the U.S.S.R. and the Cold War. He also informed his listeners that the United States had halted all nuclear tests in the atmosphere and would not resume them unless another country did so.

The U.S.S.R. reciprocated immediately. Kennedy's speech was published in full in the government newspaper *Izvestia*, an opportunity for communication with the Russian government rarely accorded a Western leader. The next day the Soviets reversed their earlier objection to a Western-favored proposal that the United Nations send observers to wartorn Yemen. The United States then removed, for the first time since 1956, its objection to the restoration of full status to the Hungarian delegation to the United Nations. Premier Khrushchev announced that he had ordered production of strategic bombers halted.

A brief study of the headlines these speeches, announcements, moves, and steps generated around the world, and a limited review of the millions of words of interpretation they inspired, shows that they indeed had a "relaxing" effect (*New York Times*, June 16, 1963; July 6, 1963, p. 1E; July 14, 1963, pp. 1E and 5E; *Washington Post*, September 16, 1963). Newspapers told their readers about a "thaw" in the Cold War, a "pause," the beginning of an East-West *détente*, a renewal of "the Camp David atmosphere." While many commentators warned their readers not to expect too much, most hastened to affirm their support of the "liquidation of the Cold War." In short, an atmosphere congenial to negotiation and, even more important, to public acceptance of the results of negotiation was created.

From mid-1963 on, the psychological atmosphere was reinforced by such steps as the actual ratification of the limited nuclear test-ban treaty by the original signatories, discussions of joint Russian-American exploration of space, the sale of American wheat surpluses to the Soviets, consideration of a new American consulate in Leningrad and a Russian one in Chicago, and, not least, continual press reports on meetings between the sides and new plans they were rumored to be considering.

The experiment was slowed down with the approach of an election year (*New York Times,* December 23, 1964, p. 1), halted with the assassination of President Kennedy, and undermined by the escalation of the war in Vietnam between 1964 and 1966. (For a study of a longer application of the gradualist strategy, see Etzioni, 1966, pp. 57–58. For a comparison of this strategy with the unilateral-disarmament approach, see Senghaas, 1961.)

What conclusions can be drawn from this brief and incomplete test of the theory? Certain of the central hypotheses were supported: (1) unilateral gestures were reciprocated; (2) unilaterally reciprocated gestures reduced tensions; (3) unilaterally reciprocated gestures were followed by multilateral-simultaneous measures, which further reduced tensions; (4) initiatives were "suspected," but, when continued, they "got across"; (5) the gestures and responses created a psychological momentum that led to pressures for more measures, a reversal of the Cold War or hostility spiral; (6) when measures were stopped, tension reduction ceased (we shall see the significance of this point below); (7) the relatively more consequential acts were initiated multilaterally or were transformed from an initially informal, unilaterally reciprocated basis to a formal, multilateral one.

Not all the assumptions and derivations of the theory were so clearly supported. Most important, it is impossible to tell, without rerunning history for "control" purposes, whether multilateral negotiations could have been undertaken successfully without the "atmosphere" first having been improved by unilateral steps. The fact, however, that both the test treaty and the space ban were first introduced on a unilateral-reciprocal basis and that even in such conditions these measures were hard to defend before Congress suggests that, if not preceded by tension reduction, they either might have failed or the risks of failure would have been sufficiently high for the Administration to refrain from introducing them. (Attempts to advance a test ban in earlier periods failed; see Spanier and Nogee, 1962, pp. 118–159.)

Also, the Kennedy experiment was only a partial application of the theory: the gestures were not the clear signals a full test of the theory would require. To gain the Senate's consent for a test-ban treaty, for instance, its value for *American* security was stressed. During the entire period, American observers provided alternative interpretations of the gestures: for example, rather than consisting of efforts to communicate a desire for peaceful coexistence, the *détente* was seen as a method of exacerbating the Sino-Soviet rift. Above all, it is argued that, since the process was halted, one cannot tell whether psychological measures open the door to "real" give-and-take or are relatively meaningless in the absence of basic and lasting settlements of differences and conflicts. The fact remains, however, that gestures which were almost purely psychological in nature opened the door to an American-Soviet *détente*. Whether more of the same could have brought about more fundamental changes cannot be learned from this case.

Even though the adoption of the measures advocated by the theory yielded the expected psychological results, there still remains the possibility of spuriousness. Hence, we ask: What other factors could account for the *détente?* Two alternative sources of tension reduction most often cited are "catharsis" and "substitution." According to the "catharsis" interpretation, the stage was set for a *détente,* so far as the United States was concerned, after the Cuban blockade discharged a large amount of frustration that Americans had accumulated over the Cold War years. Traditionally, Americans have expected that wars will be short, end with an American victory, and be followed by the restoration of peace. In contrast, the Cold War requires a continual state of mobilization and prolonged tensions without the prospect of victory. The resulting frustration was deepened by the widely held belief that the Communists were being more successful than the West in Asia, Latin America, and Africa. Under the pressure of these frustrations, it is often suggested, efforts to reach accommodation with Russia came to be viewed as "weakness," and a "tough" *verbal* posture was popular. The establishment of a Communist government in Cuba, Soviet successes in space, the fiasco of the 1961 Bay of Pigs invasion, and the positioning of Soviet missiles in Cuba in 1962 all further deepened American frustration. While the 1962 blockade initially raised many fears, once it proved not to lead to war and to yield a Soviet retreat, it became the first American victory in a long time. While the success of the blockade was widely perceived as supporting the "tough" line, the psychological effect (it is argued) was in the opposite direction, namely, one of cathartic release.

The other interpretation associates the initiation of the *détente* with the increased visibility of the disintegration of the blocs. In 1962 Communist China attacked the Soviet Union publicly, criticizing Soviet involvement in Cuba as "adventurism" and its retreat as "defeatism." About the same time, the American-French dispute forced itself on the attention of the public. As the rifts gained recognition, the hostile rejection of Mao and of de Gaulle partially replaced (or "drained") the hostility focused earlier on the Soviet Union (Kautsky, 1965, p. 14). The Soviets now seemed "reasonable" and "responsible" compared to Communist China, for Russia appeared willing to share with us the concern over nuclear proliferation and dangers of war provoked by over-eager allies (*New York Times,* October, 1963, p. 1E; July 7, 1963, p. 1E; August 14, 1963, p. 1E; August 25, 1963, p. 4).

But the consciousness of deep differences of interest within the blocs, even when they agitated against specific agreements between the United States and the U.S.S.R., had the psychological effect of reducing interbloc tensions. The recognition of the splits in the alliances undermined the prevailing simplistic image of the forces of light fighting the forces of darkness. As a result, it is suggested, the ideological fervor of the international atmosphere declined, tension was reduced, and *détente* enhanced.

For the initiation of negotiations which involve give-and-take, such a weakening of ideological fervor is important, because otherwise politicians find it hard to face their voters with the outcomes of the negotiations. At the same time, bifurcation of the bloc images shifted the focus of the xenophobia. Within the Communist camp, China became the villain; in the West, the focus of American self-righteousness became de Gaulle. These two replaced the previous preoccupation with Russia.

All these psychological processes may have been feeding into each other. Catharsis, bifurcation of images, and unilateral initiatives may all have contributed to the *détente* as well as to each other. For instance, catharsis may have eased the inception of a policy of unilateral initiatives, and in turn the resultant reduction of interbloc tensions may have accelerated bifurcation of the bloc images, thus facilitating the further reduction of tensions through additional unilateral initiatives.

We still remain with the difficult question of the relative weight of the three processes in bringing about the *détente*. While it is impossible to answer this question with precision, it seems that, while catharsis and bifurcation may have helped, they were not prerequisites of the resultant situation; unilateral initiatives alone could have produced the effect. The best evidence for this is found in the examination of two other occasions in which a thaw was achieved: the 1959 Camp David spirit and the 1955 Geneva spirit (Rovere, 1956). These cannot be analyzed here, but they seem to support the proposition that unilateral initiatives can bring about a *détente* and major agreements (for example, disengagement in Austria) without the support of the other two psychological processes.

It also should be noted that the 1963–1964 thaw did not immediately follow the termination of the Cuban crisis, in the sense that no *détente* existed between November 1962 and June 1963 (though this still would not rule out the role of catharsis as a preparatory condition). Similarly, while the bifurcation of the bloc images was deepened in 1962, it existed before and was as much caused by the *détente* as it affected the *détente*. Above all, the effect can be traced most directly to the unilateral initiatives; it started with them, grew as they grew, and slowed down only as they decreased.

THE ACTORS: CHARACTER AND SITUATION

The various works discussed so far share one assumption: that man's conduct is largely affected by the nature of the situation and, above all, by the conduct of interaction with other actors. The very interest in strategy presumes that the basic course of action— and not just details—is not predetermined, that actors are free within broad limits to reset their course. A considerable number of social scientists, however, do not take this assumption for granted; they debate and engage in research on the question of the relative weight of innate drives versus situational factors, either directly in the field of war and peace or by applying findings from studies in other areas to international relations. It is of interest to note that the "strategistic" literature and the innate-versus-situational studies rarely refer to each other. We treat this latter approach only briefly because there are several fine and up-to-date survey works (for example, Lawson, 1965; McNeil, 1965b; Yates, 1962).

The sources of the insights and findings applied vary considerably and include the conduct of social animals, preliterate tribes, and children, as well as experiments in social laboratories. Historically, the development of the basic position seems to us to have taken a typical dialectical form. Initially it was argued that, if one frustrated a living thing by preventing a satisfaction of one of its needs, it would engage in aggressive behavior, and that the occurrence of such behavior would be an indication that the person or animal had been frustrated (for example, see Dollard *et al.*, 1939). The more frustration, it was said, the more aggression one could expect. The antithesis was that while basic needs (in this instance, expression of or outlet for aggression) might be universal and, in that sense, "natural," the outlets are learned, that is, culturally and socially determined. Hence, one can learn to find constructive outlets for aggressive predispositions, for the pressures generated by frustration. Moreover, it was pointed out that there are many kinds of frustration and, even more important, of aggression, including self-oriented aggression (from suicide to alcoholism), and that there is release of tension without aggression, that is, catharsis. Thus, not all frustration leads to violence and conflict. And, one might add, aggression might be a mode of conformity and hence might neither be generated by frustration nor necessarily serve as an outlet. In fact, for a person not aggressively inclined, to have to participate in an aggressive act might be a *source* of frustration. We need to know more about what kind of frustration leads to what kind of aggression. While frustration might well be universal and unavoidable, the kinds that are more likely to lead to violence might not be universal, or perhaps we could learn to avoid them. We could, for example, try to avoid prolonged mass unemployment or uncontrolled inflation, and not demand total surrender of an enemy when a fight does occur (a humiliation which tends to spawn a sense of revenge and to plant the seeds of the next fight— harsh peace terms for Germany after World War I are believed to be one source of World War II). So long as we do not seek a world without tensions and tolerate institutionalized conflict (for example, in sports), aggression can be channeled away from *lethal* conflict.

If the first school might be labeled pessimistic and the second optimistic, then the third position, which comes close to a synthesis, is more cautiously optimistic or less intractably pessimistic. An anecdote from a kindergarten presents this position in capsule form: a boy who was hitting other boys was given a rubber doll and a stick and was encouraged to hit the doll. After a few minutes, he came back and said: "I want a doll that will cry Ouch!" In terms of the third line of argument, then, limiting aggression to nonviolent outlets may well be much more difficult than the optimists imply, though not impossible (Ross, 1955). To stress the difficulty involved, social scientists have pointed out that war has existed throughout all human ages and at least in most societies (Bramson and Goethals, 1964; Clarkson and Cochran, 1941; Vagts, 1937; *cf.* Wright, 1942). The same outlet of aggression—war—has been found in societies and cultures that vary immensely. These facts must give some pause to those who believe in easy sublimation or institutional containment of violence. Above all, we need specific knowledge of when and how violence can be marshaled rather than more assurance that, in principle, there is nothing in human nature to prevent its control.

It should be noted that, while the three approaches arrange themselves logically in a dialectic sequence, and while their popularity probably follows the same order historically, all three schools coexist today. Thus Berkowitz (1962) might be said to represent a latter-day, sophisticated pessimistic position, Buss (1961) a latter-day, sophisticated optimistic one, with both moving toward the middle group in later publications (Berkowitz, 1965; Buss, 1966). In part, a researcher's position about the capacity to contain violence can be predicted from his general metatheoretical or theoretical positions. The average social psychologist, for instance, seems to be more optimistic than those who take a clinical approach, though there are many exceptions. We do not seek to review here the extensive literature on frustration-aggression, but some of the most recent findings deserve brief attention, both for the purpose of illustrating the preceding remarks and for the purpose of calling attention to some recent and representative studies not covered by earlier review publications.

One line of studies draws on the social behavior of *animals*. A key argument here centers on what seems to be considered a dated issue in other fields of social psychology: Is aggression an instinct, and do animals and humans alike tend involuntarily to share it? Lorenz (1964, 1966) represents those who view aggression both as an instinct and as given. He states: "There cannot be any doubt, in the opinion of any biologi-cally-minded scientist, that intraspecific aggression is, in Man, just as much of a spon-taneous instinctive drive as in most other higher vertebrates" (1964, p. 49). It can be remarked that, even if this is the case, the conclusion is much less pessimistic in regard to prevention of war than it might at first seem. Lorenz himself (1964, 1966), Hall (1964), and others have shown that the aggression of social animals tends toward forms which usually involve little harm to the participants. Destructive fighting is reported to be extremely rare among lions, wolves, fish, reptiles, birds, and primates.

J. P. Scott is a major representative of the more optimistic school. As a matter of principle, he states, in direct opposition to Lorenz (Scott, 1965, p. 820):

> The concept of a "drive" is at best a symbol of an unknown group of internal stim-uli and physiological mechanisms affecting behavior. All that we know indicates that the physiological mechanisms associated with fighting are very different from those underlying sexual behavior and eating. There is no known physiological mechanism by which spontaneous internal stimulation for fighting arises. Rather, the physiological mechanisms for fighting are triggered by immediate external stimuli. There is much evidence that fighting can be suppressed by training while the physiological mechanisms are operating, and, on the other hand, that fighting can be induced by training in the absence of these physiological mechanisms.

In his own study of the social behavior of dogs (Scott, 1965), which was conducted over a period of 13 years and included a training school for dogs, Scott concluded that aggression can be both learned and unlearned. Stress is put not only on training tech-niques in the narrow sense of the term, but on the learning effects of the ecology—an approach somewhat like that of the therapeutic community in mental hospitals (Scott, 1965). Hall (1964) concluded that baboons who live in well-organized societies under natural conditions will show very little inclination to fight among themselves. When an invader or predator approaches, an alarm is given and the adult males at-tack the outsider. But baboon societies either avoid each other or, if they meet, for instance, next to a common source of water, they are tolerant of one another. On the other hand, if a disorganized group of strange baboons in captivity is forced into one environment, intense and destructive fighting does take place.

The analog to human societies is ever-present in these studies. Webster (1965, p. 10) commented that Scott's study of young dogs "may provide a new method for deeper understanding of our own evolutionary past and present, especially in regard to juvenile behavior." He warned, however, against the "too-prevalent anthropomor-phism of canine behavior." J. Fisher (1964) demonstrated that societies of similar fish are less likely to fight each other than they are to fight less similar fish, a situation which reminded Fisher of race relations. King (1954) was similarly affected by a paral-lel finding for like and unlike groups of dogs, as was Scott (1965), who quoted King's study. Lorenz went further than most in anthropomorphizing the animals he ob-served. In reading these studies, I was often amazed by the similarities in the conduct of social animals and humans, until I asked what was the significance of the parallels, what was the analytic status of the analog? Since this question applies also to the other analogies to be discussed here, we shall confront it later.

Studies of *preliterate tribes* traditionally were limited to one or a few tribes at a time. Can a society exist without war, or is war a universally necessary outlet for aggression?

This is a question that was answered by pointing to a society which knows no war, for instance, the Hopi (Eggan, 1943). A Hopi is educated to use "sweet words" and a "low voice" when speaking to his enemies. When this does not suffice, "with a tongue as powerful as a poison arrow, he carries on a constant guerilla warfare with his fellows" (Eggan, 1943, p. 373). In short, conflict is limited to nonviolent forms. The Comanche are reported to have been peaceful as plateau tribes but to have learned warfare, including all-out war, when they moved to the plains (Kardiner *et al.*, 1945, p. 49). This suggests that war is "learned" and not "inevitable." For a recent review essay of such studies see Mead and Metraux (1965); for an earlier work, Turney-High (1949); and for a recent case study, Vayda (1961).

The increased concern in anthropology with quantitative data has led over the past few years to a greater use of large numbers of preliterate societies for one study, sometimes at the cost of valid information on each of the tribes involved (Leach, 1960). An example of these recent studies is Raoul Naroll's, which is part of a research project supported by the United States Navy, referred to as Project Michaelson. Naroll's (1966) study covers 48 preliterate tribes all over the world. The tribes were selected so as to minimize diffusion effects and to ensure that each tribe would constitute an independent case for the study of the relations between "traits" (preparation for war) and aggressive behavior (frequency of wars). A test to measure similarities in traits of tribes ecologically close to one another was designed to screen out those tribes that appear to have borrowed significantly from each other.

The following traits were defined as warlike and indicative of a military orientation (similar to Boulding's definition of evil character): use of fire-and-movement tactics (firing at the foe from a distance before moving in for hand-to-hand combat), surprise attack tactics, fortification and military readiness, and "multiple expectations." The latter trait refers to a Guttman scale set of attitudes identified in an earlier study by Quincy Wright (1942): (1) All warring tribes expect to fight to defend their territory and to revenge injuries. (2) Some also expect to fight in order to plunder. (3) Some fight for these two preceding reasons and also for prestige. (4) Some add political control, that is, incorporation of the defeated tribe into the victorious one. Frequency of war was determined according to phrases used in ethnographic writings about the tribes. War, for example, was reported as "perpetual" or "periodic" versus "rare" or "sporadic."

As for overall correlations between warlike traits and frequency of wars, Naroll reported: "If the deterrence hypothesis were correct, then societies with strong military orientations would have less frequent war. This study gives no support at all to the deterrence theory. Very few of the measures of military orientation seem to have any impact, one way or the other, on the frequency of the war" (1966, p. 18). Nor does the study support the arms-race or the unilateral-disarmament propositions, since neither the presence nor absence of preparations for war affects the frequency of wars.

Possibly the most important conclusion is that the frequency of war seems to be determined by factors other than the tribes' militant or pacific nature. It should also be noted that the data, as reported by Naroll so far, do not cover the relations *between* tribes. Thus we have no comparisons of the frequency of war among tribes who face tribes that score higher or lower than they do on the war-trait index.

"Situational" explanations of generation of aggression and alternative outlets have focused on applications of group dynamics and structural-functional frames of reference, the first using as a main variable the relations among intraunit cohesion and interunit tensions, the second centering on alternative structural answers to the same basic functional need for an outlet for aggression. More specifically, the following positions, derived from Tanter (1966), have been taken: Rosecrance (1963, p. 304) argued that international instability is associated with intranational instability (see also Wright, 1942). Sorokin (1937) contended that there is little association between foreign and domestic conflict. Huntington (1962) suggested that there is a negative association, and McKenna (1962) that there is a positive one. Haas and Whiting (1956, pp. 61–62) added a directionality to the proposition: as they saw it, foreign policies promoting interunit conflict are used by groups that seek to promote their intraunit stability. Coser (1956, pp. 82–93) took a similar position, while Simmel (1955a, p. 97) reversed the direction, arguing that conflicts whose source is external preserve internal cohesion (see also Galtung, 1965). K. W. Deutsch *et al.* (1957, pp. 44–46) found from studying historical cases that, when communities were formed to counter enemies, they tended to disintegrate once the external threat passed, while those that formed because of more "constructive" reasons tended to be more stable. Etzioni's (1965) study of four contemporary unions supports this conclusion (see also van Doorn, 1966; Guetzkow, 1957).

Rummel (1963, 1966) and Tanter (1966) applied sophisticated statistical tools, including factor analysis and multiple regression, to data on inter- and intranational conflict of 83 nations in the period 1946–1960. Rummel (1963) found very little correlation between foreign and domestic "conflict behavior"; Tanter (1966) found a "small" relationship between the two; Rummel (1966) further supported the conclusion that there was very little correlation (see also Chadwick, 1966; Feierabend and Feierabend, 1966).

These studies are statistical in nature, and the basic procedure is to dimensionalize the two main variables, domestic and foreign conflicts, and attempt to relate the dimensions to each other. This approach allows for little analytic explanation in terms of the underlying dynamics of regularities (if any) which are found. Two values of these studies are (1) to warn against quick assumptions often made in qualitative studies about associations between internal and external conflict, which data like the above do not support, and (2) to focus attention on the fact that data about conditions and intervening variables must be added to the analysis before the relationship between internal conflict and external aggression can be more fully explored.

Finally, there is a large and rapidly growing literature whose findings are based on the study of interpersonal behavior in *social-science laboratories.* Frustration and aggression, trust and suspicion, cooperation and conflict are produced, usually among students whose conduct is observed under experimental conditions. A large and growing body of theoretical considerations and experimental data has been accumulated on "mixed"-interest situations, where the parties to a relationship have both common and conflicting interests, a situation which is by far the most common. Variations on two-person nonzero-sum games, widely referred to as the "prisoner's dilemma," are the most frequently used experimental situations. Our main concern here is not with the detailed development of the findings themselves, but with their applicability to international relations. Hence, we draw on the basic findings, disregarding many additions and refinements. (For review works, see Rapoport and Chammah, 1965; M. Deutsch, 1965a. Regular reports on further developments are presented in current issues of the *Journal of Conflict Resolution.*)

For those unfamiliar with the "dilemma," Luce and Raiffa (1957, p. 95) described it as follows:

> Two suspects are taken into custody and separated. The district attorney is certain they are guilty of a specific crime, but he does not have adequate evidence to convict them at a trial. He points out to each prisoner that each has two alternatives: to confess to the crime the police are sure they have done or not to confess. If they both do not confess then the district attorney states that he will book them on some very minor trumped-up charge ... ; if they both confess, they will be prosecuted, but he will recommend less than the most severe sentence; but if one confesses and the other does not, then the confessor will receive lenient treatment for turning state's evidence, whereas the latter will get the "book" slapped at him.

Morton Deutsch, who conducted many such experiments himself and whose associates and students followed with related ones, described the basic experimental situation as follows (1958, p. 269):

> In our experimental work to test our hypotheses, we have been utilizing a two-person non-zero-sum game, in which the gains or losses incurred by each person are a function of the choices made by one's partner as well as the choices made by one's self.

The game is illustrated schematically as follows:

	A	B
X	(+9, +9)	(−10, +10)
Y	(+10, −10)	(−9, −9)

In this scheme, Deutsch continues,

> Person I has to choose between rows X and Y; Person II has to choose between columns A and B. The amount of (imaginary) money each person wins or loses is determined by the box they get into as a result of their respective choices. For example, if Person I chooses row X and Person II chooses column A, they get into the AX box, and they each win $9.
>
> If you examine the possibilities of choice for Person I, you will notice that he can win most and lose least by choosing Y. Similarly, Person II can win most and lose least by choosing B. However, if I chooses B and II chooses Y, they both lose $9. Both can win only if they end up in the AX box. If I is reasonably sure that II is going to choose X, he can win more by choosing B. Analogously, if II is confident that I is going to choose A, he can win more by choosing Y rather than B!

In a large number of experiments, various factors affecting the basic game are altered, including the players' orientations to each other (on a hostile-friendly or trust-suspicion dimension), the amount of communication allowed, its accuracy, the nature of the players (individuals versus groups), the amount of rewards and punishments, and the number of rounds played. The main findings of studies by Deutsch and his associates (Deutsch, 1960, 1962; Deutsch and Krauss, 1962; Ravich, Deutsch, and

Brown, 1965; Krauss and Deutsch, in press; Hornstein and Deutsch, 1967), to draw on a summary by Deutsch himself (1965a), are as follows: Conflicts can be resolved in either a cooperative or a competitive mode. Both modes are found mixed but one tends to prevail. A major reason is that each mode tends to be self-perpetuating once it establishes itself, despite differences in original conditions. This is the case, Deutsch says, because of mirror-image-like factors. Hence, one major way to elicit cooperation is to act cooperatively.

Factors affecting the outcomes in the Deutsch studies include: (1) the larger the "size" (or stake) and rigidity of the issues involved, the less likely is cooperation; (2) the weaker the links between the actors and the less salient they are, the less likely is cooperation; (3) the greater is intra-actor conflict, the less likely is interactor cooperation; (4) the attitudes, strength, and resources of interest and relevant third parties affect the level of cooperation in a variety of ways, basically as one would expect on common-sense grounds.

We would like to register here a minor semantic objection. As we see it, these are two modes of conflict termination, not resolution. While cooperative interaction might well result in resolution, competitive interaction ends the conflict and produces an outcome (mainly because the experimental situation ends), but not a resolution. Under competition, should the parties continue to interact, as they almost inevitably do in nonexperimental situations, they would continue to be in conflict.

To refer to the noncooperative mode of interaction as competitive seems inadvisable because competition is widely understood as conflict under agreed-upon rules or shared norms. That is, competition itself involves a mix of cooperative and conflicting interests and may be thought of as an intermediary state between cooperation and uncontained conflict. Finally, from a normative viewpoint, asking for a world with no conflict might be neither desirable (some conflicts are useful) nor pragmatic. On the other hand, working toward a world without uncontained conflict might be both. (On the transition from uncontained to contained conflict or competition, but not necessarily to cooperation, see the following discussion on encapsulation.)

The second major body of relevant data comes from the work of Rapoport, his associates and students. Rapoport reported, on the basis of about 200 experimental sessions and nearly 100,000 responses, that (1) the player's typical first response is practically random; (2) the short run (ten games) decreases cooperation; (3) after about 50 games cooperation rises steadily; (4) the modal frequencies, however, are at the extremes—most pairs lock in a tacit collusion to cooperate, others to fight; (5) responses of the two players are "typically" interdependent; (6) cooperation increases with increased rewards and with punishment for defection (1963, pp. 574–577). These are only some of the numerous findings (see also Marlowe, 1963; Pilisuk *et al.*, 1965). Many more could be listed and many more surely will be made, since the basic experimental procedure lends itself to many variations.

FROM ANALOG TO INTERNATIONAL REALITY

The implications for international relations of all these studies, from animals to children, from primitive tribes to sophomores in social-science laboratories, need to be explored. There is little doubt that all these researchers see significant implications of their findings for international relations in general, and for the nuclear age in particular. Lorenz closed his book about animal aggression (1966) with some advice for avoiding nuclear holocaust (for example, increase international sports). Naroll (1966) applied his findings on primitive warfare to an evaluation of deterrence and unilateral disarmament. Deutsch explicitly stated: "I started this paper with the assumption that one could not only speak in the same terms about conflict at different levels—intraphysic, interpersonal, intergroup, and international—but that it is useful to do so. . . . There are some general principles which can be used to characterize conflict and the processes of conflict resolution which are applicable in a wide variety of contexts" (1965a, p. 41). Deutsch concluded his research reports with discussions of their implications for international politics (1962, 1965b), including a suggestion for termination of the war in Vietnam (1965b, pp. 44–46).

The following quotation includes two statements which typically succeed one another, one dealing with persons and the other with international blocs: "Our research indicates that mutual trust is most likely to occur when people are positively oriented to each other's welfare—i.e., when each has a stake in the other's doing well rather than poorly. Unfortunately, the East and West, at present, appear to have a greater stake in each other's defects and difficulties than in each other's welfare" (Deutsch, 1961, p. 110). The most important critique of the Deutsch studies, that by Kelley (1966), focuses on various experimental procedures (for example, was the imaginary money used of motivational significance?) and inferences made in terms of the general theory of conflict, but the application of the findings to international actors is not questioned (see also Deutsch's rejoinder; Deutsch, 1966).

Generalization from one to another set of units can rest on the following main grounds: (1) strictly pragmatic considerations, (2) heuristic needs, (3) logical validity, and (4) theoretical validity. Before we explore these, it should be noted that many of the researchers who make the transition from their particular analog (the units they actually study) to international actors are not explicit as to which of these claims they make. Many of those who do face the issue do not claim to meet the more stringent requirements of logical or theoretical validity, but proffer only a pragmatic or heuristic value for their extrapolations. *However, after various disclaimers, the researchers often use procedures, arguments, and a general tone of presentation strongly implying that their findings, on the analog level, have validity for international relations.* While the problems of extrapolation appear in any inductive generalization and in transference of generalizations from one body of data to another—even replication of findings for the same kinds of actors under laboratory conditions has proven difficult—the situation in this area of study is much more complex than in most because of the considerable difference between the observed actors and international ones, nations armed with nuclear weapons (*cf.* Rapoport, 1963, p. 574). It might be argued that in laboratories we do not study actors (or are free not to generalize about actors) and that, hence, the difference between the laboratory and the international setting does not matter. We study variables and the relations among them, and these are universal. We shall see below that, even if this claim were valid, the problem of differences in indicators would still have to be faced, and these differences vary in proportion to the difference in *actors* (or units), not variables. More fundamental, we suggest, is that, at least in the subject area here explored, among the variables which interact with each other are significant contextual (or emergent) variables by virtue of which the analog and international units differ considerably (Etzioni, 1967; 1968, Chapters 19 and 20). We turn now to explore these points in some detail.

The *pragmatic* defense of extrapolation is that the regularities discovered on the analog level "work" on the international level, that is, fit data about international conduct, and that this is sufficient to justify the procedure. In opposition, it might be said that what "works" is a relative concept. Often the fit between the model, induced from whatever units, and data about international actors is rather poor. Or, in order to produce a better fit, extremely tenuous assumptions and "pseudo-constants" are introduced (K. W. Deutsch, 1963, p. 39). Second, since we seek to explain processes or to advise, we need to understand the underlying factors and mechanisms.

These criticisms apply, for instance, to Richardson's finding (1960, p. 153) that more people die in large "deadly quarrels" than in small ones. (This conclusion is not tautological because, if the small fights had been much more numerous than the large ones, the relationship would be reversed.) Richardson's finding might even be of some pragmatic value: for example, we should perhaps first concentrate on eliminating large wars and those conflicts that lead up to them. All disciplines that treat applied problems, from medicine to engineering, make considerable use of such information. (For more such information on international actors, see Russett *et al.*, 1964.) It is hence not a question of being against or in favor of pragmatic research, but a question of how much effort should go into it as against other kinds. Clearly, it is necessary to realize that such research alone will not do; information is valuable, but it is not a substitute for understanding.

The position that a study on the analog level is a *heuristic device* for international study is represented by Rapoport. He stated that "no extrapolation of the results obtained from it [the experiment] to any real situation can be seriously depended on. The most one can expect from simulation is hints on what sort of psychological processes may be pertinent" (1963, p. 574). Such a modest stand may at first seem unassailable. If researchers find such heuristic study helpful in their formulation of new propositions, for which they claim no validity so far as international actors are concerned, what possible exception could anyone take?

One might argue that some heuristic devices are much more expensive than others, not just in research budgets but in research years, and that, hence, the rule of economy should direct more efforts to the less expensive devices. Getting hundreds of thousands of responses from students is a rather arduous way to formulate a proposition. But a counterargument seems to be well-taken: we are dealing here with the psychology of discovery; what one researcher finds stimulating the next one might not, and therefore each should use what best fits his creative skills, from historical novels to man or machine simulation of wars. Moreover, it might be said that each heuristic device has some typical blind spots, and that the use of a variety of devices (by the same or different researchers) enhances the likelihood that international relations will be explored from a large number of possible views, and that the blind spot of our joint knowledge will be reduced (Campbell and Fiske, 1959; Webb *et al.*, 1966, pp. 1–5). (Hence, by the way, the considerable amount of disdain among those who use one kind of analog against those who use others, especially between the "humanist," qualitative types and the "scientific," quantitative ones, is quite ill-founded.) The previous discussion of the supplemental character of Richardson's and Huntington's respective work—one using statistical, the other historical, data—is a case in point.

Eventually, research will be needed to determine, through testing on the international level, the relative power of various heuristic devices to generate valid propositions. While one could hardly expect to find any one analog from which one could derive propositions which need not be verified on the international level, such research—aside from its interest for the psychology of creativity—might serve to rechannel research efforts toward the more productive devices. These research efforts are not allocated in a laissez-faire fashion, as is sometimes implied, with each researcher picking up whatever device he finds most useful. Various mechanisms, from boards allocating research funds to committees which approve dissertation proposals, affect the direction of these efforts. The tendency now seems to be to focus research where there are new tools, such as computers and gaming (Alger, 1965; for a review, see Brody, 1965). Whether these provide for the most productive analogs is not known. In general, validation of extrapolations is treated in this field with the same lack of enthusiasm as evaluation studies are in psychoanalysis, except that here the claim that such an assessment would spoil the therapeutic relationship cannot be advanced. Research on the relative productivity of various analogs would, of course, not lead to the abandonment of work with the less productive devices, but might direct more effort toward the more useful ones.

Even more fundamental questions are raised by the implied claim for validity of statements about international conduct based only on *validation* on the analog level. This claim appears in two major forms. In some instances, the researcher states that his findings (for example, about two groups of fish) are "useful" for or "applicable" to the understanding of international relations. These are ambiguous terms, allowing the researcher first to use "useful" to mean a source of insight, discovery, etc., but then to discuss international conduct as if "useful" meant "valid," without presenting any evidence of validation on the international level. Such studies are reported as if they were validating, but no justification is so much as indicated for the implied stand that they are valid for international actors.

In the second form, an explicit claim is made, on either logical or theoretical grounds, for an ability to derive valid statements from the study of one unit about others. On *logical* grounds, it is stated that the "structure" all actors confront is the same; hence, two sophomores and the United States and China face the same choices (for example, they may either cooperate or compete, either suspect or trust each other). (We assume that the terms are defined so that they are mutually exclusive and exhaust the particular dimensions.) Moreover, the relations between such variables can be logically spelled out (for example, there are four possible combinations of the two variables just listed, if we treat them as dichotomous).

The value of logical derivations, especially when there is a large number of variables and when mathematical techniques and computers are used to spell out the various possible relations among the variables—which is impossible to do otherwise— might well be considerable (for example, see Galtung, 1964; Smoker, 1964). The statements thus derived, however, have no empirical validity in themselves and cannot be used either to explain the behavior of or to advise international actors unless these statements are coupled with empirical ones.

By far the most interesting suggestion is that the units actually studied and the international ones are isometric in substantive *theoretical* terms—interesting in that, if this were the case, international theory indeed could be greatly advanced by studies of other units, and we hardly need to add that it is much easier to analyze interaction between students than between superpowers. There are two primary ways in which this argument can be stated. One is that the study of interpersonal interaction provides an isometric model for international interaction because, after all, nations are made of people and therefore can be expected to act like people. This is manifestly wrong, however, because groups of people obviously interact differently than individuals. Nations are much more than combinations of individuals: for instance, they have an internal structure (for example, a military-industrial establishment) and collective possessions (for example, nuclear weapons) which persons do not; and differences in these, we suggest, significantly affect international relations, but not necessarily in the same way as they would affect interpersonal ones.

A position we find much more defensible is that psychological variables which appear on the interpersonal level account for *part* of the variance in international conduct, and these variables can be studied effectively on the interpersonal level. (Similarly, cultural variables might be studied in primitive tribes. I do not see what applicability validating animal studies might have for international relations, but they cannot be ruled out in principle.)

It should be noted, however, that if one takes this "partial-isometric" stand, *no statement induced from the analog level can be directly extrapolated to international actors.* First one must ask what other factors, which either do not appear or are difficult to study on the analog level, affect the international processes? This is necessary not only because these other factors (for example, differences in available weapons technology) may account for part of the variance, but also because the relations among psychological variables might well be affected by, or "interact" with, these nonpsychological variables. It is not enough to say, for instance, that just because two sophomores trust each other more when they cooperate more, if China and the United States were to show greater mutual trust, disarmament would be more likely. We must also ask what effect disarmament would have, let us say, on the economy of the countries involved, and to what degree their awareness of the economic consequences "blocks" disarmament and prevents them from coming to "trust" each other.

The fact that study of international relations is an applied study leads to the same conclusion: that direct transition from psychological research to understanding of international conduct is not possible. The conclusions of applied research are inevitably synthetic and interdisciplinary, while the disciplines of psychology, sociology, and economics are analytic; that is, they deal with subsets of variables. It is not enough to acknowledge the existence of other factors and to suggest holding them constant while we advise and explain international actors on the basis of a subset. We can study the relations among psychological variables without having to look at nonpsychological ones if our purpose is to enrich psychology; this is the analytic procedure. But if we seek to contribute to the study of international relations, we must relate our variables to those of other analytic disciplines before international propositions can be validated. The analogs, in which subsets of variables are studied, are helpful only for studying components of synthetic propositions. Herein lies the virtue of combining the findings of a variety of studies conducted with a variety of analogs in a variety of disciplines. From an abstract viewpoint, there is no reason why, if all the relevant variables were studied with the help of one analog, or combined on the basis of a validated interdisciplinary theory, verified statements about international actors could not be derived. In practice, however, this is an ideal which cannot even be approximated. Hence, ultimately, the need for validation of all propositions, however derived and partially supported, on the international level itself seems inescapable.

The second claim is that a generalized theory, though it is not necessarily psychological in nature, applies to all units and might be studied in any unit for the sake of the others. System and cybernetic theories, for instance, have been said to apply to persons, groups, and nations (Mack and Snyder, 1957, p. 108). More or less the same points made above apply to this claim. We suggest that there are systematic differences among the various units. Hence, a general theory might explain part of the variance in the action of any and all units; but if induced from studies of one kind of unit, it will still tend to include both too much (because of unique properties of that kind of unit) and too little (because of lack of information about those properties particular to the applied field). Second, we suggest that a significant part of the variance of international conduct is to be explained by "emergent," macroscopic variables, while other important segments of the variance can be accounted for by theories developed on the basis of intrasocietal, interpersonal, and intrapersonal research. The fact that one can study, on an analog level, variables rather than populations—psychological factors, for instance, rather than persons—does not ensure safe extrapolation from the laboratory to international "populations." It allows us to extrapolate to psychological variables as they affect (jointly with nonpsychological ones) international conduct. Hence, *psychological study is, on the one hand, a necessary, integral part of the study of international relations, and is, on the other hand, always segmental.*

When variables are transposed from one unit to another, the question of indicators must be considered. A common danger is for indicators that are inclusive on the personality or microunit level to be only segmentally so on the macroscopic level. Once we learn to guard against this danger, it seems, the related danger for studies that use research on the analog level—personifying international actors—greatly diminishes. An example might illustrate this point.

A central concept for interpersonal studies is "trust." As Deutsch pointed out (1958, pp. 266–269), it holds both an element of predictability and an expectation of conduct of another actor (or of other actors). When players trust each other, one finding reads, they are more likely to come out of a conflict on the cooperative side. What does this finding suggest for the conduct of international actors? To answer this question, the variables first have to be "translated" into international terms. Three possible indicators could be used to estimate the trust international actors have in each other: (1) the trust that the citizens of one country have in those of the other; (2) the trust that the elites of the two countries have in each other; (3) the existence of some organizational or institutional arrangements such as mutual "partisan" inspection (Finkelstein, 1962) or simultaneous destruction of weapons at a neutral spot (for example, Stone, 1966), which will have the same effect for international actors *as if* they trusted each other, but might entail no change of citizen or elite sentiments. (Actually, such an arrangement may be necessary precisely because sentiments such as trust are weak.) Moreover, one might suggest that an index of international trust must include all three kinds, weighing more heavily for the third indicator, less for the second, and least for the first, because of their relative significance for the particular conduct. To change the attitude of the citizens or the elites may often not be feasible, but working out a procedure of enforcement could be comparatively easy.

The danger in personification can be seen in the fact that the first indicator, citizens' mutual trust, is most often used in psychological discussions of international relations, the second less often, and the third almost never. Actually, the third indicator comes to mind mainly when one systematically guards against personification. More generally, every analog has, so to speak, a dis-heuristic effect. In general, guarding against the specific blind spots of one's analog may permit its use without unwarranted extrapolations.

Once it is made clear that all international conduct is a mixture of personal, microscopic-social, and macroscopic-social variables, it is quite easy to see that the experimental situation allows us to study more than psychological variables. Other variables can be "simulated" in the laboratory. Thus, experiments which deal with more than two actors are more "international" than those which deal with only two. Those which deal with groups of actors playing against other groups of actors (where the group formation is a variable) are more "international" than those which deal with individuals. Similarly, it has been shown that cross-cultural differences and bureau-cratization or institutionalization can be simulated in the laboratory and their effect on interaction studied (Benson, 1962; Bloomfield, 1960; Gladstone, 1953; Guetzkow and Bowers, 1957; Verba, 1964; Zelditch and Hopkins, 1961; for a review of simula-tion in international relations, see Snyder, 1963). (No attempt is made in this chapter to review the simulation material or to explore the problems of its methodology. For a treatment of these issues, see Chapter 12 of this *Handbook*.)

The relationship between these studies and psychology should be delineated. Methodologically, there is no necessary relationship between the study of organiza-tional aspects of, let us say, interactions between a decision maker and his staff, or a chief-of-state and Congress (Guetzkow, 1963), and psychology; it could be subsumed under sociology or political science. There is, however, a pragmatic link. Each of the social-science disciplines seems to have developed an expertise in one research tech-nique. Thus the study of documents, which are used by all disciplines, for example, to study the psychology of presidents and secretaries of states (Kuenzli, 1956; Link, 1966), is considered the specialty of historians. Survey methods are often considered the domain of sociologists even though they are used, for instance, in economic and political science research. Similarly, experimental techniques seem to be the specialty of psychologists, and we therefore can expect that more of the experimental work which deals with variables of international theory will be conducted by psychologists than by members of other disciplines.

Finally, it might be asked: Since we are interested in explaining international con-duct, why use analogs in the first place? Why not study international actors "outright"? In response, several arguments in favor of having both "direct" and "analog" studies can be made. First of all, since the study of international relations is synthetic, it draws on a variety of analytic studies, psychology included. Or, to put it differently, some of the international variables are psychological. While these variables might also be studied on the international level, it is more economical to study them on the analog level. Indeed, this is often the only level on which they can be relatively freely ex-plored. The same would hold for the contribution of other analytic disciplines to the study of international relations. Second, most international studies which do not use analogs have so far been highly descriptive. To the degree that theories have evolved at all from international data, they have not proven to be more powerful than those which have used interpersonal or other "outside" analogs. Moreover, "outright" international theories have some blind spots of their own.

First of all, international theories, like analogs, disregard some factors (especially psychological variables) in favor of playing up others. Hence, it is fruitful to draw both on "outside" analogs and on theories induced from international data.

Second, much of international theory tends to be conservative in that it sees as its prime model those situations which existed in the past, particularly balance-of-power situations. While there are numerous definitions of the balance-of-power concept, all seem to assume that the regulation of the system's condition is based on the attributes and relations of the member units, with next to no regulatory power of the system itself; this means that the system bonds tend to break down and can be maintained only with a probability of war. While this model reflects quite accurately the weight of historical evidence (though it usually underplays historical change in actors, especially where two or more have merged into one community), its projection into the future tends to neglect the possibility of transformation of the system. Various contemporary factors increase the probability of breakdowns in the international system as compared to the nineteenth century, the century of peace; and because of changes in technology of weapons and means of delivery, these breakdowns may become much more devastating than those of previous periods. However, those who use international models, especially since World War II, tend to view all system models which assume more system regulation of conflict than is provided by the balance of power as unrealizable. The conditions tending to produce more centrally regulated systems (which make breakdowns less likely) can be studied much better where they have actually evolved, that is, in intrasocietal and regional systems rather than on the world level. (We shall illustrate this point below.) Thus, a major corrective provided by "outside" analogs is the realization that fundamentally different systems of human relations from those prevailing in international relations are, in principle, feasible.

THE UNITS OF ANALYSIS AND LEVEL OF GENERALIZATION

The theories and studies explored so far focus on the nature of the actor—is he in control of forces he can trigger but cannot marshal? Is he inherently aggressive and, if so, can his aggression find outlets other than acts of violence? The same works already mentioned, as well as numerous others, can also be reviewed with respect to another major issue of the social-psychological studies of international relations, namely, their assumptions as to who the actor actually is, to what unit the analysis refers. For those studies which recognize various kinds of units, it might be asked to which units and to what part of the universe of such units the findings claim applicability, that is, are generalized.

The most elementary outline of this controversy entails again a three-step, dialectic process. The core difference involves disparate views as to what is the place of psychology in the study of international relations. What might be referred to as the *maximalist* position is that the study of psychology is the study of man, and hence there is in principle no limitation to the contribution psychology can make to the study of international relations. The more typical representatives of the maximalist approach are not greatly concerned with methodological questions, at least not in this context. They tend to make statements about international conduct as if the nations were persons writ large, usually without making an explicit claim for the interlevel generalizability of their findings or insights: "U.S. pride was hurt by impressment of American sailors" (an example provided by Perry, 1956).

The *minimalist* approach, generally emphasizing that nations are very different from persons, doubts the relevance of studying personal or interpersonal conduct for understanding national behavior. The minimalists grant that citizens act like individuals, but view their effect on foreign policy and international conduct as small. More methodological awareness characterizes this group, though minimalism too is often expressed by implication rather than stated outright. Many of the *realpolitik* writings suggest that symbolic and psychological factors are at best ephemeral and marginal; economic and military forces are what really count. The tradition of inventories of sources of power, as bases for foreign policy in general and war in particular, typically pays little attention to psychological factors, such as identification of the population with the particular warring unit and its goals (Jones, 1954). The maximalists tend to assume that psychological factors and mechanisms account for much if not all of the variance of the conduct under study, while the minimalists tend to assume that non-psychological factors account for most of it.

A third position, approaching a synthesis, is not simply an intermediary one. It argues that psychological factors are "real" and do account for a significant part of the variance, but not for most or even the majority of it. More important, it makes specific suggestions as to how the two sets of variables, psychological and nonpsychological, relate in terms of both the units of analysis and the nature of the generalizations made (Almond, 1954; Etzioni, 1967; Kluckhohn, 1955, pp. 112–113; Parsons, 1962).

As with the study of situational and innate attributes, here, too, all three positions exist simultaneously, though the tide seems to be turning in favor of the third position. Rather than cover the vast literature reviewed often before, we shall illustrate the maximalist and minimalist approaches from recent publications and devote more attention to the development of the synthetic approach.

We choose the following study (Group for the Advancement of Psychiatry, 1965) to represent the maximalist position because it is by a group of eminent scholars, because it was published after the debate about the nature of the units of analysis was well under way, and because the presentation is a moderate one; many maximalist publications are much more extreme. The main statement concluding the study refers to the functional alternatives to war (p. 307):

> War is a social institution; it is not inevitably rooted in the nature of man. Although war has traditionally served as an outlet for many basic human psychological needs, both aggressive and socially cohesive ones, the increasing mechanization and automation of modern warfare has rendered it less and less relevant to these needs. There are other social institutions and other means of conducting conflict between groups of people, or between nations, that can serve these psychological needs more adaptively in our modern world.
>
> Many of the traditional stereotypes concerning the courage and manliness involved in the pursuit of war are psychologically questionable. As psychiatrists we know that the resort to violence is apt to stem not only from anger or feelings of strength but also from feelings of fear and inner weakness. It requires great strength and moral courage to carry on some forms of conflict without resorting to violence. . . .

Specific propositions and mechanisms studied are the following (pp. 307–308):

> 1. Psychological defense mechanisms, such as denial, emotional isolation, and habituation that enable large numbers of people to live in the shadow of imminent nuclear annihilation without searching for appropriate adaptive measures that might remove or reduce the awesome danger.

2. The primitivizing effects of extreme fear or panic that can lead to impulsive or irrational behavior to ward off an immediate threat, without regard to the long-term consequences of such behavior.

3. The increasing dehumanization, both of man and society, that depersonalizes the horrors of war and mass suffering and treats them as statistics. . . .

4. Ethnocentric perceptual distortions, exaggerated nationalism, group identifications and pressures, and a basic human need to fit perceptions into one's pre-existent frame of reference. Inherent in these distortions, *which exist on both sides,* is the danger that they lead to stereotyped conceptions, both of one's self and of the adversary, hamper communication, and lead to mutual distrust and a biased perception of what is fair and reasonable.

5. The fact that distorted perceptions and mutual distrust tend to provoke reciprocal behavior from the adversary, so that the mutual expectation that "the other side doesn't really want peace and can't be trusted" tends to become self-fulfilling.

6. The fact that the above-mentioned psychological factors, in addition to political and military ones, exert a significant pressure upon political leaders, who are caught in a conflict between the things they have to say and do to maintain their power and prestige at home, and the taking of the kinds of initiative that might lead to a lessening of tension with the adversary.

The authors make clear in their concluding lines where they stand in regard to the relative weight of psychological factors (pp. 388–389):

> We recognize, of course, that many other disciplines—political science, law, economics, the physical and biological sciences, and military science itself—are involved in the ultimate resolution of the complex problems we face. We realize also that the contribution of the behavioral sciences must be viewed in the total context of all these other considerations. But, as the preamble to the Constitution of UNESCO says, "Wars begin in the minds of men." Since this is so, the minds of men must also be capable of ending war.

Note that, with few exceptions, particularly conclusion 6 (regarding the freedom of political leaders to act in a nonviolent direction or to respond to citizens' demands for such conduct), the question of the unit of analysis is largely disregarded. Needs and mechanisms that can be attributed to persons are directly associated with acts that are attributed to societal units; for example, "denial" is associated with a nation's predisposition toward war. This is the typical character of maximalist analysis (Alexander, 1941; Dunn, 1950; Frank, 1960; Fromm, 1960; Strachey, 1957). Moreover, statements may be made in such a way that it is impossible to determine whether they refer to individuals, nations, or both, and if both, whether they are expected to hold in equal strength for all these units. Most commonly, the studies simply refer to "man" as an undifferentiated concept. A typical sample is the following statement: "This time the choice between violent-irrational, or anticipatory-rational behavior is a choice which will affect the human race and its cultural, if not physical, survival" (Fromm, 1961, p. 8). Whose choice—yours and mine, the government's, mankind's?

It might be said that such statements imply a set of intermediary steps and mechanisms that leads from personality needs and mechanisms to national acts (Perry, 1956). The group of psychiatrists quoted above have suggested a mechanism: intra-personality processes affect public opinion, which in turn sets a context for decision makers. That most maximalists, however, are less than fully aware of the units-of-analysis issue can be learned from their tendency to make substantive statements and assumptions which studies of the *relations* among the units find unwarranted. They tend, by and large, to assume a very close association among the different units; for example, change in personal sentiments is expected to lead to considerable change in public opinion on foreign policy matters, which in turn is expected to have considerable effect on the decision makers. The assumption of tight association makes it possible to disregard the difference between the units of analysis once it is formally recognized, because if changes in one unit almost automatically produce changes of about the same magnitude in the others, the units may indeed be treated as though they were one and the same actor.

The main findings of empirical studies of the relations between units, however, are that (1) the relationship is far from close and (2) the direction of the effect seems to be different from that assumed by most maximalist interpretations. Thus, for instance, the relationship between changes in public opinion and national decision making in regard to foreign policy, most students of the subject agree, is tenuous (Almond, 1960; Rosenau, 1961). And public opinion is said to be determined to a greater extent by communication elites, political leaders, and interest groups than the decisions of these actors are determined by public opinion (Cornwell, 1965; Rosenau, 1961, Chapter 5; Sussmann, 1959). For instance, national elites are viewed as able both to decide to engage in war and to mobilize public opinion in its support, including the drumming up of national paranoia, promotion of misconceptions, etc. All this is often not taken into account by writers in the maximalist tradition.

The minimalists charge the maximalists with disregarding the differences between the units of analysis and/or assuming them to link tightly, and with assuming a causality to exist in a direction which conflicts with the one shown by the data (Farber, 1955, pp. 323–337; Waltz, 1959; Wolfers, 1962, pp. 8–12). In addition, the minimalists argue that factors which are nonpsychological in nature are much more important in determining foreign policy.

The third, synthetic approach takes into account the differentiation among the units of analysis and the need to study the relations among them; it sees psychological factors as affecting the properties of all the units involved and their relations, though some more than others. The specific list of units used varies considerably according to which specific sociopolitical theory is applied and the degree of detail aimed at. A typical list includes personalities, cohesive collectivities, and organized political groups (the nation-state) (Mack and Snyder, 1957, p. 107). Singer (1959) uses subsystems, systems, and suprasystems (see also Singer, 1965). It should be noted, however, that, whatever list one uses, the relationship among the units is hierarchical (subunit to unit) and not across boundaries (interunit), in the sense that "higher" units (for example, nations) set a context for "lower" ones, and "lower" ones act within the "higher" ones.

For example, one might take as the lowest unit a *role* (or a role segment); at the next level, social microunits such as the family, work teams, and peer groups; and at the next level, social macrounits such as subsocieties, societies, and suprasocietal units. Now if one seeks to study the relationship between two role segments, the microscopic and macroscopic contexts must in principle be taken into account, for the relationship would tend to be systematically different if it occurred in different cultures or in different historical and societal environments. (Of course, it is not necessary in any one empirical study to cover the full range. One way to "take into account" is to hold the contextual variables constant.) At the same time, it is fruitful to view even the most macroscopic unit as consisting of various combinations of roles and micro-units and to view their state as, in principle, having an effect on the conduct of the macroscopic unit. The level of *societal* cohesion, for instance, is directly affected by—but far from identical with—the cohesion of the small groups (Etzioni, 1968, pp. 99–103). Pragmatically, we usually handle this complex relationship by holding constant at least one of the two main dimensions, either studying the "same" role (or microunit) in different macroscopic contexts, for example, in the cross-cultural or historical analysis of armies (Janowitz, 1964), or studying different roles (or micro-units) in the same macroscopic context (Smith, 1958), or studying the same units over time. But when we come to theory building or to applied problems, we have to draw the pieces together, to synthesize, or else limit our analysis and advice explicitly to a given context, for example, to modern pluralistic societies.

CITIZENS AND ELITES IN MODERN PLURALISTIC SOCIETIES

Citizens

With regard to modern pluralistic societies, several general statements can be made concerning the relationship between units which would not hold for totalitarian or premodern (nonmass) societies, where the population's effect on the decision makers is even smaller and more indirect. Here, *role studies* tend to focus on the citizen (Perry, 1956). There are literally hundreds of studies of attitudes which citizens maintain toward other nations and their own, toward alternative modes of conduct of foreign policy, and toward the United Nations and world government (these are occasionally related to other attitudes, for example, a conservatism-liberalism scale), and to various psychological mechanisms, personality traits, or status characteristics. Levinson (1957), in a typical study, found a correlation between an ethnocentrism (or pseudo-nationalism, anti-internationalism) scale and authoritarian personality charac-teristics (see especially p. 42). Such an association has also been reported by Farris (1960); see also Smith, Bruner, and White (1956, p. 22) and Doob (1964).

For the reader not familiar with this literature, the following two quotations will provide a sample of the findings. The first is a reproduction of the summary (with minor omissions) of what is a recent, highly sophisticated methodological study of foreign-policy attitudes in association with personality-trait categories, a study which covers both "mere" citizens and elite members. Isolationists and non-isolationists were compared on a large battery of personality and attitude scales, as well as on other measures. The samples employed in the surveys from which the data were taken in-cluded a national sample of 3020 political leaders, a cross-section sample of 1484 adults in the general population of the United States, and a cross-section sample of 1082 adults in the general population of Minnesota (McClosky, 1967, pp. 106–107):

> ... [Isolationism] is obviously a political attitude, influenced by political cir-cumstances, reference groups, demographic factors, and other such determi-nants, it is also shaped to a considerable extent by a complex set of personality variables, primarily of an aversive nature. Such personality states as misan-thropy, psychological inflexibility, manifest anxiety, and low self-esteem have a powerful influence on the attitudes one adopts towards other nations and foreign

policy in general. Such personality factors, together with social opportunity and intellectual endowment, affect cognitive capacity and function, and these, in turn, further influence one's disposition to favor withdrawal from, or entrance into, international involvements.

Isolationism was also found to be part of a network of attitudes that are related to common underlying personality dispositions. Among these are classical and welfare conservatism, radical doctrines of the extreme right and extreme left, and attitudes critical of democratic beliefs and practices. Despite its strong chauvinistic overtones, isolationism is frequently associated with feelings of disappointment in one's own society and disaffection from the political institutions of one's country. The isolationist orientation parallels closely other forms of belief that rely heavily upon dichotomous thought processes, that lack breadth of perspective, and that seek to exclude whatever is different, distant, or unfamiliar. It also parallels other attitudes that are marginal or deviant in relation to the society. Like other deviant orientations, it signifies for some of its proponents a failure of socialization and an inadequate internalization of the norms. It is more common among those who are, by any criterion and for any reason, parochial, and less common among those who are open to experience and cosmopolitan in their perspective.

Although isolationism manifestly appears as a peaceful withdrawal from international entanglements and has been frequently interpreted as a simple desire to keep one's country from becoming militarily embroiled, it is characteristically xenophobic and belligerent in its posture toward foreign affairs. It represents, for the most part, a rejection of other men rather than a concern for them, a disavowal of responsibility and a strong urge to disengage oneself from obligations toward others. One can scarcely begin to understand the phenomenon, therefore, if one confines his analysis to the familiar political categories.

A subgroup of so-called pacific isolationists was located and analyzed. While this group possesses characteristics closer to those of non-isolationists, and displays less of the bullying militancy that marks the jingoist isolationist, its members nevertheless possess many of the same personality and attitude characteristics found among the jingoist isolationists, though in lesser degree.

The preceding discussion does not imply that the correlation between personality traits and attitudes has been established beyond reasonable doubt. Several social scientists raised doubts that they exist, on theoretical grounds, and some studies found no such correlation (Gamson, 1964).

The more sophisticated studies, especially McClosky's, make no claim whatsoever that differences in attitude or personality have an effect on international conduct.

The second kind of study reports attitudes toward foreign policies as related to other attitudes or socioeconomic-status data, but gives no data on personality traits. An example of this type is one by Withey (1962b), who conducted several other such studies (Withey, 1962a; Scott and Withey, 1958). While there are several studies of "specialized" groups, especially of students, many of them deal with a national probability sample. In the following case, the number of respondents is 1474 adults. Withey commented that such a sample is expected to give a national picture accurate within 1.5 percent of standard error. Here are some of the findings, first regarding the way U.S.–U.S.S.R. relations are seen (Withey, 1962b, p. 10).

Five ways of looking at U.S.–U.S.S.R. relations were posed. These five are by no means exhaustive of perspectives but they do range over the scale of viewpoints and they provide a check on the more spontaneously expressed opinions already reported and encountered early in the interview. The five in the order of their acceptance are as follows:

"The Cold War with Russia is a fight between two very different ways of life with different values and ideas." 89 percent agree.

"Our problems with Russia are just like having trouble with a 'bad guy' or a delinquent who won't behave." 63 percent agree.

"We have a Cold War with Russia because the United States and Russia are each trying to do what they want and their interests interfere with each other." 55 percent agree.

"Our troubles with Russia are just a question of which country is going to survive as a powerful nation." 49 percent agree.

"We have a Cold War with Russia because the United States and Russia don't really try to work together and understand one another." 29 percent agree.

Quotations regarding nuclear exchange between the two superpowers and related issues yielded the following answers (pp. 12–13):

If the U.S. were to get into some direct armed conflict with Russia, even if the involvement was highly localized, relatively few—only 15 percent—thought it likely that nuclear bombs could be kept out of it. In other words, people thought that if the U.S. and U.S.S.R. ever became involved in direct rather than proxy armed conflict, the chances of escalation to nuclear war would be high. This is undoubtedly the reason why the Berlin crisis was seen as particularly alarming.

Questions were not asked on the strategy of attack if a nuclear war were precipitated, i.e., military versus population targets, etc., but respondents were asked whether they thought that the area where they lived would be better off, about the same, or worse off than major target areas elsewhere in the United States. One adult in five expects to be in an area hit worse than other areas of the country. Forty percent expect their condition to be about the same as most of the United States or about average, with some places worse and some better off. Only one in four thinks it will be better off than most of the country.

On the other hand, few people indeed expect to be virtually immune from attack hazards. About 44 percent of the adult population of the U.S. expect annihilation. Another 15 percent give themselves about as much chance as the residents of Hiroshima. Eleven percent more see heavy damage, fire and fallout dangers but the possibility of survival.

Only about 21 percent can be categorized as foreseeing conditions of slight hazard. About one in ten expects no danger at all though most predict confusion, fear and "hard times." Thus, there is no doubt that the majority of the U.S. public thinks that a nuclear exchange would be catastrophic for the nation.

Information about fallout or international affairs seems to make very little difference in one's estimates about the seriousness of attack when possible "local" conditions are described. Looking at just the 20–25 percent of the population most informed about international affairs, 58 percent expect an attack locally which would be as bad as or worse than World War II atomic attacks; 59 percent of the general public fall into the same category.

Most surveys of this kind provide a one-time, two-variable, descriptive account. Actually, the single largest body of psychological and social-psychological research on international relations is of this kind. (For good surveys of these numerous works, see Kelman, 1965; Paul and Laulicht, 1963; Rosenberg, 1967.)

A small fraction of the existing surveys are more "complex." Some are cross-cultural; Evan (1958), for instance, reported attitudes toward disarmament in six countries. Some sample the same population at different points in time. They show a trend of increased interest among American voters in foreign affairs even in nonwar years. Few employ advanced statistical analysis. Most are straightforward one-country, one-point-in-time, two-variable, "cross-tab" reports.

These surveys have several values. From their inception, surveys have served as a means of communication; originally, they enabled the middle class to find out what the poor felt in a more systematic fashion than by simply asking their maids. Studies of privates told army commanders what soldiers think, and studies of workers proved informative for management as well as for union leaders. Now, in the same vein, the United States uses survey techniques to discover what the citizens of allied (Free, 1959) and nonallied (Nehnevajsa, 1960) nations think about the U.S.S.R., the United States, and the United Nations (Cory, 1957; Lentz, 1950), and about alternative foreign policies (for example, more versus less moderate). The main effect of such surveys is to provide a more accurate picture of "public" opinion than did earlier means, such as reports by diplomats based on local newspaper clippings and informal interviewing. It seems reasonable to conclude that surveys make the elite more responsible to the public, not by increasing public influence *per se*, but by sampling a "public" that is closer to the real public, with its wants and desires, than were earlier conceptions.

Indirectly, the surveys are also of interest in connection with a central question which appears in many ways both in the professional-technical literature and in more popular writings on the subject: is the public "better" or "worse" than the governments? Critiques of society and its foreign policy, especially from left and anarchist traditions, have often implicitly or explicitly assumed that elites are dragging nations into war, but that if the public voice could be heard, peace would be established. Conservatives have often taken a more pessimistic view of man and have argued that it is necessary to guard against "mass" instincts, that the governments are the voice of authority which prevents hotheaded action. (For a review of both positions, see Claude, 1964, pp. 276ff.) Surveys have not, to our knowledge, been conclusively analyzed from this viewpoint. So far as we can tell, their main virtue is to show that both views are somewhat naive.

The views of the public do not exist independently of the actions of the elites. If the public is agitated and fearful, its choice of deescalation or escalation is itself greatly affected by the elites, in terms of both immediate specific responses and longer-range views. Second, the public seems not to hold one monolithic view, "for peace" or "for war." Not only are there numerous subpublics, some more militant and some more moderate than the government, but one and the same person might hold views which, if taken in isolation, would classify him simultaneously as a "dove" and a "hawk." A large majority of Americans, for instance, tend to favor a stronger United Nations *and* United States engagement in nuclear war for the sake of West Berlin. Further studies of the public's "mind," taking into account differences in macro-sociological variables, may bring us closer to the answer to the question, not of whether man is good or evil "by nature," but under what conditions the public at large has a moderating versus a militarizing effect on various kinds of governments.

Survey findings are also employed to argue for changes in policy, and have been used in campaigning by various sides for alterations in policies. For instance, various polls on public views on the war in Vietnam, including one conducted by a group of political scientists at Stanford, were used to advocate more as well as less escalation. Thus these studies are of pragmatic political interest.

The surveys also have a descriptive value for social-science-oriented efforts. For example, for those who study differences among generations, sexes, classes, etc., the reports on differences in attitudes among these groups on foreign affairs comprise relevant descriptive data which complement information about their attitudes toward other matters, from religion to narcotics. Finally, for students of societal action and international interaction, these surveys are, of course, important building blocks.

Relatively little generalized international analysis, however, has been built so far with these "blocks." One main reason is that most of the studies do not take into account the units-of-analysis problem. Information about what citizens feel and say is not, as a rule, systematically related to a model of how such atomistic role states affect international relations. A first step in this direction (which the survey studies themselves rarely take) is to break away from the one-man, one-attitude weighting approach (*cf.* Roper, 1953). When we wish to move from a static description of aggregates of attitudes to a societal action analysis—be it the community's willingness to celebrate the birthday of the United Nations, or voters' reactions to changes in U.S.–China relations—we need to take into account (1) that not all citizens' attitudes have the same weight in shaping societal action, (2) that citizens' attitudes change in the very process which societal action entails, and (3) that those which have less weight to begin with are most likely to change in the direction of those which have more weight to begin with.

Probably the most important way in which citizens in modern pluralistic societies affect international relations is by voting. But, as is all too well known, the citizens' vote is not the simple result of an aggregation of atomistic preferences, but of various societal processes and interaction among them. If we look at an election as a *societal* action, as a way in which society chooses among its elites and among alternative courses of action, we must start with the notion that not all the members of the societal body share equally in making these decisions (Milbrath, 1965, p. 21):

> About one-third of the American adult population can be characterized as politically apathetic or passive; in most cases, they are unaware, literally, of the political part of the world around them. Another 60 percent play largely spectator roles in the political process; they watch, they cheer, they vote, but they do not do battle. In the purest sense of the word, probably only 1 or 2 percent could be called gladiators.

In general, citizens with more education, a better standard of living, higher social status, more leadership skills and experience, and key positions in organizations, have more effect on the societal course than those who fall lower in these dimensions. As for psychological mechanisms and personality traits, the data show that these are not randomly distributed among the various sociological and political activation categories. For instance, it is not sufficient to know that x percent of the American public scores high on an "isolationist" scale. We need also to ascertain whether these individuals are those who rarely vote, whether few of them are opinion leaders, etc., or whether they vote more frequently than others, include active and higher-ranking groupings, etc. Only after we relate the psychological data to such a sociological structure can we learn much of their societal and international importance.

(The preceding discussion stresses the role of ideological contexts. It is widely held among students of political behavior that party affiliation and the personality of the candidate are more important in determining the vote than the "issues": see Campbell *et al.*, 1960; *cf.* Key, 1966. While this is not the place to explore this question, we suggest that ideological contexts affect party affiliation and perhaps also preferences for varying personalities of candidates. "Issues" do not exhaust the role of contexts in shaping the vote; clearly, other factors are also at work.)

In passing, it should be noted that elite data, in order to be compared with data on the followers, need to be coupled with samples of the same sociopolitical units. Stouffer (1955) stated that the leadership of certain American voluntary associations is more liberal than the followers, and hence one would expect the action of these associations to be more liberal than would be indicated by a simple averaging of public opinion in which leaders and followers are lumped together. But the study loses part of its value because leaders and followers were sampled in such a way that no direct leader-follower comparison is possible.

A second relevant dimension for one who studies public attitudes in relation to societal action (let us say, the 1963 test ban treaty or construction of public fallout shelters) is to what degree the attitudes have already been "processed." In general, we would expect that, the "older" an issue is, and the more it has been exposed to mass media and to interpersonal and leadership processes, the closer an aggregate analysis of a random sample of the population would come to predicting the course of societal action. Conversely, the less an issue has been socially "processed" (or if a new critical event creates a turning point for an "old" issue), the less informative such an analysis would be for purposes of predicting the direction of societal action, because these attitudes themselves would still be subject to influence. A simple illustration would be a public opinion poll conducted a short time before an election versus one conducted a long time before an election. Moreover, since a societal action which has transpired will still alter some attitudes, postaction attitudes also have to be considered before the effect of a discrepancy between attitudes and a societal act can be fully understood. One cannot derive from preaction resistance the notion that the public will necessarily protest, vote against, or otherwise object to, let us say, United States acceptance of the seating of Communist China in the United Nations. Obviously, some attitudes shift *post hoc* to favor a societal act (for example, the 1963 test ban treaty), while others do not (for example, United States intervention in Korea). Which do and which do not, and under what conditions, is still largely an open question. But without such dynamic study of public opinion, it is difficult to assess its potential importance for international conduct and relations.

So far, we have discussed ways to study citizens' attitudes. The obvious next question is to ask how influential they are in determining the actions of decision makers, especially, in our context, those actions dealing with foreign policy. The data so far seem largely to support those who take a "downward flow" position, suggesting that various elites and interest groups shape the public view *and* make the societal decisions (both with regard to the policy to pursue and how to "sell" it to the public), and to go against the notion that the public at large participates effectively in national decision making in general and foreign policy matters in particular (Padover, 1958; Rokkan, 1960; Stokes and Miller, 1962). The public debate, it is said, is limited to those few alternatives over which the elites disagree, and these do not include most important foreign policy questions. Thus, both Republicans and Democrats espouse several variations of the containment-plus-deterrence doctrine, and the American public interprets the world and the proper ways to approach it within the limits set by this doctrine.

If this view is valid, then citizens' preferences, personalities, and even votes, the main subjects covered so far by the social psychology of international relations, would be of little importance. And if this is the case in modern pluralistic societies, it could be argued that the same holds even more strongly for earlier or other contemporary societies. On the other hand, it may be argued that, while public opinion does not participate effectively in many specific foreign policy decisions, it does serve as *a context that sets significant limits* on the maneuverability of the national decision makers; and that changes in the public "mind" which are not generated by the elites themselves do affect their "degrees of freedom." And even if past action of an elite helped to mold the public mind, once formed, it is much less given to manipulation, even by that elite. Is there any way to reconcile this notion, which seems to me intuitively correct, with many of the data pointing in the opposite, elitist direction?

This is not an either-or question, but one of the relative degree to which the variance in public opinion can be accounted for by elite versus "mass" factors. The basic decision on this question will determine where social-psychological study of international relations should be concentrated. Obviously, if changes in the attitudes of the average citizen are largely elite-produced, this would suggest a relative focus of research on elite activities and "psychology." But if the citizens' intra- and interpersonal processes are more autonomous, continued focusing of attention on them would be justified, though elite roles and conduct, of course, would still need to be studied.

The following speculative considerations seem to deserve empirical testing. Let us assume that the citizens' minds (at least those of the educated and active citizens who lead the others) work in terms of a contextual theory; that is, they maintain a small set of broad and vague contextual conceptions such as "appeasement" and "the American way of life." These conceptions are supported by various *bits* of knowledge (such as what happened historically at Munich, though no accuracy is assumed) and a generalized emotional disposition (for example, negative) in a specific degree of intensity (which changes over time). Now it seems that the relationship between the bits and their respective contexts is loose, much looser than the interpretations of many public opinion polls seem to imply. (A good insight into what these contexts are like can be gained from a study by Lane, 1962.) Bits can be dropped with relative ease and new ones substituted; partially conflicting bits can be held simultaneously, but the context stays.

Under what conditions *contexts* change is relatively unknown. Contextual transformation may be the result of accumulation in a specific subject area of a large number of bits which do not fit and a context strained to a breaking point, at which either this subfield is disorganized or another context introduced. Or transformation may follow along the lines of "dissonance theory" (Festinger, 1957). Perhaps contexts fade and new ones are imprinted on top of them, in a gradual rather than an abrupt manner.   In any case, for us the main point is that the importance of a bit or single attitude cannot be assessed unless we know the general state of its context.   Remove a bit when the context is well reinforced, and nothing much happens; remove it when it is eroding, and this act may tip the balance in favor of, let us say, the introduction of a new one.

Now let us relate this contextual conception to the fact that political leaders are elected on a one-shot basis; this implies for the citizen that he must choose on the basis of a generalized context and *not* bits.   He obviously cannot vote against a candidate on Vietnam, for him on Medicare, against him on civil rights, for him on educational policy, etc.   Hence, if there is little correlation between some specific attitudes which citizens hold and the action of elites, this is not necessarily an indication that citizens' attitudes have no effect.   Before the relationship between the numerous attitudes and generalized action, such as voting, can be studied dynamically, the bits (or specific attitudes) would have to be weighted in terms of the contexts in which they appear. To put it differently, the act of voting is like subconscious indexing in which different attitudes have different weights, and the weights are in part determined by the state of some generalized views (contexts) and the conceived relationship between the specific attitudes and the generalized views.   Party loyalty may well be the single most important such context.

If such contexts are important, what implications does this have for constraints on the actions of national decision makers in modern pluralistic societies?   We would expect the elites to have considerable freedom of action but only within the limits of established contexts, and only so long as their specific actions do not disorganize these contexts or create a countercontext.   Thus, Kennedy was relatively calm about the 1961 Cuban fiasco (and public opinion in his support even rose after the crisis), but he also realized in 1962 that another fiasco, this time in the missile crisis, might associate him with an appeasement or "soft" context (Sorensen, 1965, pp. 669–70, 696).   (In the 1960 election, six ultraliberal Congressmen were elected.   Most of them were not reelected.   One of the survivors explained to the author that each year he voted on one major issue out of line with his less liberal voters: one year against increase of the defense budget, and one year for abolishing the House Committee on Un-American Activities.   He felt that, if he were to do both in the same year, he would be ousted because he would "trigger" the contextual reaction of his voters.   His analysis might not be scientifically valid, but I suggest it is worth some consideration, and it certainly affected his decision making and vote in Congress.)

Case studies of national decision makers in modern pluralistic societies suggest that at least some leaders very much wish to keep their decisions, not just in domestic but also in foreign policy, well within the limits of existing contexts, aware (or believing) that there are high political risks and costs involved in attempting to change them. When a new event occurs for which there is no ready context, such as Soviet expansionism in 1946–1947 or Soviet orbiting of a satellite in 1957, the national decision makers seem relatively free to interpret it.   But once a bit is placed in a context or a context is established, the public feeds it back to the leaders (and here the various psychological mechanisms on the citizen level come into play), who, under most circumstances, are boxed in or are compelled to invest much effort to alter it.   Kennedy's 1963 experiment to loosen the public conception of what was in line with U.S. national interest, to move from a Cold War approach to a "strategy for peace," is of particular interest from this viewpoint because it suggests both the limitations and the success of such an effort. Most of the specific steps taken (the new bits) were fed into the prevailing context. Thus, the test ban treaty and increased trade with the U.S.S.R. (the wheat deal) were introduced as serving the nationalistic interests of the United States. At the same time, an effort was made to establish a new context, of peaceful coexistence. Whether Kennedy could have advanced more in accumulating bits that could be introduced into both contexts, and then have shifted gradually from one to another, we shall never know. Surely we do not wish to imply that such a transition is impossible; see, for instance, de Gaulle's termination of the war in Algeria, changes in French-German relations since 1945, and Roosevelt's mobilization of support for his introduction of the United States into World War II. Studies of such contextual shifts might cast new light on the relationship between attitudes, voters, and national decision making, and on the degree to which one level (citizens at large) affects the other (national leadership). Holsti and North (1965) argued that, with the development of the use of computers, simulation techniques, and the employment of historical data, such studies would become more feasible. (See also Verba, 1964, and Brody, 1966.)

It should be stressed at this point, however, that two minimalist arguments seem to be valid. First of all, many decisions that appear as bit decisions when they are made have context-setting effects, and the voters who treat them as bit decisions are in effect thus foregoing their ability to participate in molding policies, or limiting it to a *post hoc* reaction. For instance, the decision to build anti-missile missiles may be seen as merely a decision to buy one more weapons system, but it actually reopened the strategic U.S.-U.S.S.R. arms race. Second, voting is a very atypical national activity in that millions of citizens have a specific and comparatively individualistic and effective role in it. Many other decisions, such as specific appropriations made by Congressional committees and myriad administrative decisions, are "cleared" or negotiated mainly with various interest groups and out of the public eye (Schilling, 1961). The public probably has less influence on these than on general contextual policy decisions. Still, from time to time the public is mobilized—for instance, in the war on poverty, in favor of car safety, and against fallout shelters—without anyone being able to point to any specific interest group or mass medium interested in such mobilization (and with strong coalitions working against it); and is led by unattached intellectuals, professionals, and religious leaders, who form a kind of lobby for societally critical perspectives (Moynihan, 1966). The simple notion that this can or cannot be done on foreign policy matters is not justified, for, just as there are instances where such mobilization failed, there are instances where it was effective—for example, in curbing the shelter race and in supporting the test ban treaty, and in Truman's and Johnson's decisions not to stand for reelection.

On the other hand, it should be pointed out, in support of those who attribute a greater role to citizens than do the minimalists, that, while interaction among nations probably is mediated more through institutional and governmental channels than most interactions between other groups (not to mention most interpersonal relations), there is a certain amount of direct interaction among the citizens of various nations. This includes tourism (which even for the U.S.S.R. included about a million citizens a year by 1965, half of whom visited "capitalist" countries), student and other exchange programs, symbolic interaction through the mass media, etc. Here the psychological mechanisms of the citizens come into play more directly because "international" conduct in these instances is interpersonal. There are several studies of such contacts, including student exchange programs and the effect of travel on attitudes (French and Zajonc, 1957; Hero, 1959; Lerner, 1956; Taba, 1955; Terhune, 1964).

It should be noted, however, that (1) these contacts themselves are greatly affected in scope and shape by the macroscopic factors, especially by the action of governments (for example, restriction on travel); (2) the influence of these interpersonal contacts on those who do come into cross-national contact is small in terms of change in their preconceptions and attitudes (Ram and Murphy, 1952, pp. 13–16; Saenger, 1953); and (3) the impact of the small group which acquires more "internationalist" attitudes on the societal and political interaction among nations, under most conditions, is small. The idea that cultural, social, and economic contacts between the citizens of two countries will bring the countries closer together is widely held, but there is little to support it. Even when contacts are unusually numerous or effective, which itself is often possible only when the governments of two nations are friendly and the institutions of the respective societies are tolerant of each other, nations whose citizens thus interact have shown themselves capable of engaging in the most hostile act of all—outright war (for example, France and Germany in 1914). In earlier ages, travel, trade, and cultural contacts among citizens continued while their countries were at war.

Even more massive, in terms of the number of citizens affected, are "direct" symbolic cross-national interactions—from being exposed to a cross-national television program, to listening to the news about developments in other countries. Again, many of the studies of such images of other nations and their dynamics have not taken sufficient account of the macroscopic variables, such as governmental management and interpretation of the news (Cohen, 1961; Pool, 1952), societal and cultural interpretations imposed on it, etc. (Galtung and Ruge, 1965). There actually is very little direct cross-national symbolic interaction. Most citizens, even of the relatively attentive and active public, interact through filters which their societies erect. This is to suggest not that their personal and interpersonal interpretations do not matter, but that, if we are to link up studies of these personal processes with international conduct and relations, the articulation of these processes with the macroscopic dynamics of the national filters has to be considered.

In short, while citizens' predispositions are to be taken into account as a "raw material" which is subjected to societal and political processing, and as a source of limits and constraints on the action of other units, it seems that the basis for explanation of variations in international conduct does not rest here. Psychological factors, however, do appear in the other units of analysis as well, and hence the relatively limited role the average person plays in shaping international conduct is not a measure of the limits of psychology in explaining these relations.

Elites

The second set of units in which psychological variables and explanations play a role lies at the other end of the scale: the units of decision makers or elites. (For "role" studies of senators, see Matthews, 1960, and Huitt, 1961.) There is surprisingly little systematic information on whether (and, if so, to what degree) the psychological mechanisms of elites are different from or similar to those of other citizens.

McClosky (1967) supported Stouffer (1955) in his contention that American leaders are more liberal and less isolationist than the population at large; these attitudes correlated negatively with need for aggression, paranoia, rigidity, and other variables.

One reason why elite members can be expected to have different personalities than the population at large is that they are selected in ways which make some personality types more likely to be recruited and others to be screened out. But there is little evidence to support this proposition, and even less on what effect these differences in elite personalities have on those interactions between nations that are mediated through the decision makers. There are some psychoanalytically oriented case studies of leaders, for instance, of President Wilson (Link, 1966), but it is difficult to generalize from them. (Leites' study, 1953, deals with nondemocratic elites.)

More "situational" interpretations also apply to studies of the elites and their international function. A president, on his own, might act very much like a next-door neighbor when he hears a piece of upsetting news (Szulc, 1966, p. 45). But between a national leader and societal action there are usually filter mechanisms, unavailable to common citizens, such as staff and advisors, Congressional committees, and pressures of military services. These filters might "cool out" a leader or magnify his agitation, but can hardly be without effect. The mechanisms and patterns of interaction among decision makers and between decision makers and their staff have been studied historically, from the viewpoint of play between the elites and interest groups or of rivalry among the military services (for example, Posvar, 1964; Smith, 1966, Chapter VI), but very rarely from a social-psychological viewpoint (for one of the few, see Alger, 1961, 1965). In part, this is because access to the necessary data is difficult. But this obstacle might be somewhat overcome if more social psychologists were interested in exploring the proposition that institutionalized interpersonal behavior is different from noninstitutionalized interpersonal behavior.

Societal units

Some of the available data concern units, links, and processes which are "in between" the citizen and the national elites, and which together constitute the societal units or international actors. Much of this body of data is not psychological in itself, though it deals with variables which both affect and are affected by psychological variables. Psychological studies of societal units focus on the societal images of the elite members, their "public opinion" models, and their interaction with the citizens' images and fantasies (a perspective examined by Edelman, 1964, and by Klapp, 1964). Nonpsychological studies deal with the selection of elites from among the population in terms of sociological background (for example: Are members recruited exclusively from a ruling class or from all classes?), power analysis (Does one or more societal grouping monopolize the control of the state? Is there a military-industrial power elite?), and circulation of elites (Is it regularly or rarely changed, orderly or only following violence, etc.?), and associate these variables with predisposition to war with other nations (for example, see Janowitz, 1957).

Further exploration of these nonpsychological studies, of which the preceding list is just a small random sample, would lead us far beyond the limits of this essay. The same holds for studies of national culture, control of mass media, theories of relations between interest groups, internal organization of political parties, and the effect of all these on international conduct (for a recent review, see McClelland,

1966). Each of these units, however, is affected by psychological factors, which can be seen as "working" on the roles of the members either of these units (which are like those of the citizens) or of their respective elites, or on the relations among them. Thus, the whole preceding discussion can be applied over and over again. For instance, questions about the psychological consequences of the ways elites are selected can be asked about labor union leaders, not just about senators and presidents, and these in turn can be related to the labor unions' foreign policy positions and their impact on the national scene.

In addition, global factors, especially cultural and environmental factors, are studied, and the interaction between these and psychological factors is explored with a view to determining their effect on international relations (on global factors and their measurement, see Lazarsfeld and Menzel, 1961). Much has been made, for instance, of the effect of the ecology of islands on communication and interaction and how this influences the development of nationalist identities; nationalist identities, in turn, help determine what social units (tribes, regions) it is considered legitimate to use violence against. (For a social-psychological analysis of the significance of these factors, see Etzioni, 1965, pp. 27–30.) Another group of studies, in which one major variable is environmental, deals with the impact of disasters on communities, from which conclusions are drawn regarding society's capacity to survive various degrees of nuclear war. (For review works, see Barton, 1963; Grosser, Wechsler, and Greenblatt, 1964. For a critical study of overly optimistic conclusions, see Dentler and Cutright, 1963.)

Cultural patterns have been studied, mainly by anthropologists. For a while, notions about "national character" were largely disregarded, and differences in the behavior of members of the same societal unit—even highly monolithic, small and well-integrated tribes—were stressed. It seems now that criticism of the national-character idea may have been somewhat overreactive and that members of nations do have modal responses. This is not to deny differences, subgroups, and atypical behavior, but differences in modal West German, British, and Mexican reactions to the same set of international stimuli, for instance, might in part be explained by differences of cultural patterns, socialization, etc. (Almond and Verba, 1963). (For a comparison of American and Japanese views of peace issues, see Lentz, 1965.) Most social-psychological studies conducted since the popularity of the national-character approach declined, with the exception of some good work on the Soviet Union and China (Bauer, Inkeles, and Kluckhohn, 1956; Inkeles, 1958; Skinner, 1965), fall mainly into one of the categories reviewed earlier: they either are role studies of nonelites, studies of elites or of social-psychological interactions between them, or studies of economic, social, or political development that are cross-national and not international.

All in all, the multi-unit approach can be summarized in an analog. So long as we deal with the interaction among groups, where the main contact among members is indirect, representational, and institutionalized—characteristic of most international interactions—the members' psychological states and predispositions can be treated as, in principle, unprocessed *raw material*. (The degree to which they have been processed is a secondary variable.) Interaction processes among citizens, among the more and less active ones, among them and organized societal groupings and the mass media—under various environmental and cultural conditions—are to be treated as *half-processed*. (The product is, of course, affected both by the qualities of the "raw material" and by the processing techniques and tools.) Finally, the national elites and society-wide institutions *complete the processing* and "turn out" most of the significant international acts, especially those concerning war and peace. There are situations in which interaction among members of two nations is "raw" or "half-processed," as when American and Russian tourists meet, or scientists of several nations confer, relatively free from macroscopic societal controls (but not from much of their respective national cultures). By and large, however, the more important international interactions take place through the "final" processing filters and are affected by their nature. This is especially so in the case of war and peace.

ENCAPSULATION: CONTAINING INTERSOCIETAL CONFLICT

In the preceding discussion much attention was paid to the role of citizens, less to elites, and least to societal, ecological, and cultural factors, because this has been the distribution of research efforts in the social psychology of international relations. We hold, though, that much of the variance in international conduct has to be explained by a more macroscopic, that is, societal, analysis, interwoven with psychological considerations. In the closing section of this essay we provide a lengthy example of such an approach, drawing on our own previous work (1964; see also Burton, 1965).

This discussion serves a second purpose as well. We indicated earlier that one of the major shortcomings of prevailing international theory, as we see it, is that it tends to assume that the actors are basically given; their moods and strategies may change, but not the units themselves (*cf.* Wolfers, 1962, pp. 3–24). The following discussion seeks to illustrate an approach which takes into account the partial and changing bonds among the actors. The approach is one of a theory of conflict which entails the transformation of the adversaries and of the system they create. Developments of international relations since 1945 provide historical illustrations for the analytic propositions of the conflict theory.

As we see it, armaments technically could be reduced to those needed for internal security in one year. The United States disarmed within a year following World War II, in 1945–1946. Attitudes toward other nations can be changed fairly rapidly, as the United States' alliance with its previous enemies Germany and Japan suggests, though basic contexts seem more difficult to alter. The thorniest bush hindering disarmament appears to grow on the institutional level, for unless a supranational source of security can be provided as national ones are surrendered, disarmament will be followed by rearmament, civil war, or both. The establishment of a worldwide security force, in turn, requires development of the elements of a world community to provide legitimization and support to the law-enforcing machinery, and to assist in advancing the necessary changes in the world society—especially assistance in the development of "have-not" countries, which is essential if world authority is to be stabilized. To meet these prerequisites for stable and just peace, that is, to evolve a world community, seems to be a most stringent task. The question is whether or not we can point to any model that might indicate under what conditions such evolution might occur. We are far from confident that such a transformation of international relations will indeed take place, but there seems to be some value in pointing out the processes which promote or hinder it.

SELF-ENCAPSULATION AND ITS SOURCES

Encapsulation is the process by which conflicts are modified so that they become limited by rules (the "capsule"). The rules exclude some modes of conflict practiced earlier and legitimize others. Conflicts that are "encapsulated" are not solved in the sense that the parties become pacified; that is, not all conflict is eliminated. But the use of arms, or some uses of some arms, are effectively ruled out. To illustrate, many observers expect the normative views of Communism and the West to remain unreconciled, and therefore suggest that the basis for disarmament is lacking. They see two possibilities: two or more powers that basically are either hostile or friendly. Encapsulated conflicts point to a third kind of relationship. Here, differences of belief or interests and a mutually aggressive orientation may well continue, but the sides effectively rule out some means and some modes of conflict. In this sense encapsulation is less demanding than pacification, since it does not require that the conflict be resolved or extinguished, but only that the range of its expression be curbed; hostile parties are more readily "encapsulated" than pacified.

At the same time, encapsulation tends to provide a more lasting solution than does pacification (*cf.* Timasheff, 1965, p. 233). When pacified, the parties remain independent units and, after a period of time, their differences may again lead to conflict. Once encapsulated, the parties lose some of their independence in that the capsule which has evolved limits future conflicts, though the possibility of breaking a capsule, of undermining the formed rules and bonds, remains.

Capsules differ considerably in their scope and hence in their strength. Some minimal rules govern many unrestrained conflicts, such as consent on the proper use of the white flag and the Geneva convention regarding prisoners of war. In the present context these minimal capsules are of little interest, since by themselves they do not provide a basis on which a world society capable of significantly curbing international conflict can grow. The following discussion is concerned with capsules strong enough to rule out war.

The containment of conflict must be self-propelling. Once a third superior authority is assumed, once a world government or powerful United Nations police force is organized, an authority is introduced that can impose rules on the contending parties and thus keep their conflicts limited to those expressions allowed by the particular capsule. But such universal authority is not available and thus the analysis must turn to *conflicts that curb themselves.* In other words, through the very process of conflict the participants work out a self-imposed limitation on the means and modes of strife.

How could a conflict curb itself? Park advanced one theoretical answer. (Park's exact position is difficult to determine because he developed his theory in a large number of articles written at different dates. For a collection of these articles see Park, 1950.) He pointed out that conflict generates interaction between the parties to the conflict. Conflict "forces" the parties to know and to communicate with each other, and this in turn leads to the evolution of shared perspectives and bonds, until the conflict turns into competition limited by a set of rules (see also Williams, 1964). Homans (1950, pp. 110–117) supported this line of analysis by suggesting that communication breeds affinity.

The theorem that increased communication between parties is the mechanism through which conflicts are encapsulated, and that this mechanism emerges from the conflict itself, seems valid only under special conditions. If the parties to a conflict exhibit similar values and sentiments, for example, communication can make them aware of this latent consensus, and can draw on it to build up procedures for conflict settlement and for legitimation of resolutions passed. Under these circumstances, communication may also serve to work out limited differences of interest or viewpoint within the framework of shared values and sentiments.

But when the conflicting parties' basic values, sentiments, and interests are not compatible, increased communication only highlights this incompatibility, dispels hopes of a settlement or an accommodation, makes the parties more conscious of the deep cleavages that separate them, and increases hostilities. To reformulate this point: the greater the differences between parties to a conflict, the smaller the encapsulation attainable through increased communication (Blake, 1959, p. 90; Fedder, 1964). Or, to put it more sharply, the greater the need for communication, the less effective is it likely to be. The inability of communication to serve as the propelling force for self-encapsulation when conflict is pervasive limits its relevance to international conflicts, which are often all-encompassing, with few values shared by all parties. Compared to most intrasocietal conflicts, international conflict tends to be boundless.

For encapsulation of international conflicts, the distribution of power among the parties seems to be more important than communication. Encapsulation is advanced when it serves to protect the more powerful participants against demands of the rising participants for a greater share of the power. In this sense encapsulation is analogous to the introduction of welfare legislation by the Tories in Britain or by Bismarck in Germany when the political power of the labor movement was on the rise.

PLURALISM AND ENCAPSULATION

The number of actors participating in a system has often been related to the system's stability. The balance-of-power system seems to require at least five participants (Kaplan, 1957, pp. 684–693). Systems with three participants tend to lead to the coalition of two against the third (Simmel, 1955b, p. 45; Thibaut and Kelley, 1961, pp. 200–204; see also Gamson, 1964; Riker, 1962). Bipolar systems, that is, systems with two participants, have been shown to be particularly difficult to pacify. Single-actor systems are by definition pacified. The participation of a large number of actors, on the basis of application of a full-competition model to the international scene, has been considered especially conducive to peace (Russett, 1963). (Richardson, we saw, argued the opposite: the more actors, the less stable the system.) Observe, however, that these propositions assume that the actors are interchangeable in that they have the same or similar power. The most outstanding characteristic of the international system is that the participants differ drastically in their power; the relative power of any two nations is, moreover, significantly different according to the sector of international relations under discussion and the particular matter at hand. A more realistic model must therefore take into account the relative power of the participants relevant to the issues at hand, rather than focus on the number of participants. To reformulate our encapsulation proposition in this context: encapsulation seems to be enhanced by the transition from a bipolar state of power to one in which the distribution is more pluralistic, a transition to be referred to as depolarization.

International relations approximated a state of bipolarity between 1946 and 1956. It was in this period, the height of the Cold War, that the two fairly monolithic camps, one directed from Moscow and the other from Washington, both armed with nuclear armaments which no other bloc commanded, faced each other across the globe. While there were quite a few countries that were not aligned with either camp, their military and political weight was small. The sides focused their attention on keeping their respective blocs integrated and on enjoining third countries from swelling the ranks of the opposite camp. Each bloc checked the other, hoping for an opportunity to expand its own area of influence while waiting for collapse of the other. There was little inducement for encapsulation in this bipolar system.

The shift toward pluralism generated a constellation of power more conducive to encapsulation. Between 1956 and 1964, in each of the two major camps a secondary power rebelled. There were immense differences between de Gaulle's France and Mao's China in their relations to their respective nuclear overlords, as well as in cultural, economic, and military qualities. Both, however, were formerly weak powers and had followed a foreign policy formulated in foreign capitals; both, under re-awakening nationalism, increased their power and correspondingly followed a foreign policy of their own. The net effect of the rebellion of the secondary powers was to draw together the two overlords. Seeking to maintain their superior status and fearing the consequences of conflicts generated by their rebelling vassals, the over-lords set out to formulate some universal rules they wanted all parties to observe. The treaty of partial cessation of nuclear tests that the United States and the U.S.S.R. tried to impose on France and Communist China constitutes a case in point, as do efforts to stem the availability of nuclear weapons to additional powers. The Geneva disarmament negotiations, in which Communist China and France did not participate, were typical of this period.

One characteristic which these measures share is the service of the more "narrow" needs of the superpowers and the simultaneous advance of the "general welfare" of the world. They can therefore be presented in terms of universal values and implemented in world institutions. Thus, the prime motivation of the 1963 nuclear test ban treaty might have reflected the desire of the United States and the U.S.S.R. to remain the only superpowers, but it also indirectly reduced the dangers of nuclear war and was presented to world public opinion as if the prime motive were the advancement of peace and disarmament. This is a familiar pattern, one in which interest groups in a body politic, whether a nation-state or a village community, work out solutions. They seek to find community values in terms of which they can couch their causes. However, this is not without significance for encapsulation. Indirectly, these values affect the selection of the course of action followed by an interest group and provide a common basis on which similar interests of divergent powers can be harmonized and their ties in the shared community deepened.

The period of encapsulation terminated in 1964 with escalation of the war in Vietnam. Whether the war's effects on encapsulation were only temporary is not possible to tell at this time.

International floating vote

The significance of the existence of a sizable floating vote (not committed to any one party) for the *maintenance* of a democratic political system has often been pointed out. It is less often recognized that the *emergence* of a significant floating vote accelerates encapsulation. In the same period in which the internal solidarity of the East and the West declined, the bipolar system was further weakened by the increase in the number of nonaligned countries. The group of nonaligned countries grew to be the largest, and the status of nonalignment was built up as both the East and the West increasingly recognized its legitimacy.

The growth in number and weight of the floating votes made several contributions to encapsulation. Around them evolved a major shared norm between East and West (and the third countries). This norm limits the conflict between East and West by declaring one major sector of the international system outside the conflict, as far as armed means are concerned. While the norm was violated in Vietnam, Laos, and in a few other places, it was widely observed and violations became less frequent. At the same time reliance on nonviolent means such as trade, aid, and propaganda commanded an increasing proportion of United States and U.S.S.R. efforts in third countries, moving roughly from above a quarter of their total investment in foreign efforts in the mid-1950's to close to three-quarters in the mid-1960's.

The norm supporting nonalignment is of special interest to the study of encapsulation, since it does not bar conflicts but only rules out intervention by force. Peaceful appeals, especially those aimed at internal changes in the country, such as progress toward freedom and social justice or socialism, are "allowed." This quality of the norm had a double effect. First, it forbade (and quite successfully) forcing countries into a bloc, which would have weakened the general movement toward regulation of the conflict and, if continued, would have reduced and potentially exhausted the floating vote. Second, the norm left room for the expression of both sides' ambitions without violating the rules curbing the conflict.

The "open frontier" proposition applies here. The proposition states that, when the parties to a conflict have an open "space" in which they can make gains more readily than by encroaching on each others' domain, and in which the rewards of expansion are at least as high, conflict between the parties is reduced. This is true so long as the parties to the conflict do not have the same commitment to expansion and refrain from the use of force toward each other in the competition over the previously undivided space. The courting of nonaligned countries without territorial conquest or annexation provided an "endless," that is, inexhaustible, "frontier." This is not to imply that the parties will be engaged in an endless contest over the favors of these countries. The decline in the amount of foreign aid that both the United States and the U.S.S.R. were willing to give in the early 1960's as compared to the late 1950's suggests that they were growing tired of the contest. (The U.S.S.R. has increased aid somewhat following the intensification of its contest with Communist China over the same territories.) The "frontier" seems to deplete the energies devoted to conflict. There was no evidence that, as the sides grew tired of this mode of conflict, they became reinterested in other, especially more violent, modes.

Buffer states are particularly important for prevention of limited wars that might escalate into an all-out war. Contrary to a widely held belief, the presence of buffer states, such as Austria, Afghanistan, Finland, and Burma, did not create a dangerous vacuum in the period under study, but kept the superpowers apart. This was so partly because the buffer states, in effect, were protected by an implicit agreement of both superpowers to come to their defense if they were attacked by the other. (It was activated in support of India in 1962.) This "remote deterrence" was at least as effective as the positioning of troops in curbing a field of influence; it has less retarding effects on social change in the particular country and, the record shows, is less prone to escalation.

In addition to defining major segments of the international system out of the zone of armed conflict between the two camps, the several nonaligned territories were so located that they provided a pacifying buffer zone between East and West. A comparison of the relations between the two blocs as they eyed each other across nonaligned Austria, Cambodia, or Burma, with situations in which they faced each other without such a buffer, as in Germany, Korea, and Vietnam, illustrates the point.

Above all, the increase in the floating vote, like the decrease in bloc solidarity, largely increased the range of political activities and sharply reduced the pressures to turn to military alternatives. The more rigidly the sources of power (for example, votes) and the rewards to be had (for example, economic assets) are divided between two parties, and the more integrated these parties are, the less can the weaker of the two expect to gain in power and to improve its share in the allocation of assets by nonviolent means. The more the avenues of political efforts such as campaigning (to appeal to the floating vote) and bargaining (to split away a segment of the opposing party) are or seem to be futile, the greater the pressure toward armed showdown. The less open are constitutional or otherwise legitimate avenues of expression, the higher the pressure toward change by force.

These general rules apply with special strength on the international level. Here the use of armed means is considered less illegitimate than in a national society ("war is the continuation of diplomacy by other means"). The normative bonds among the actors are much weaker and the hostility more totalistic; there are few constitutional avenues for expression and no force controlled by the system to curb drives toward violent "solutions." The decrease in bloc solidarity and the increase in the number and appeal of nonaligned countries were therefore of special importance in reducing the pressure toward armed advances and increasing the premium on other political efforts.

The floating vote is to be viewed as a reward that shifts to the favored side; the values according to which the floating vote shifts become the values the competing sides seek to promote, or at least seek to appear to be promoting. In the period under study, the nonaligned countries, on balance, rewarded moderation insofar as they, as floating voters often are, were politically "between" the sides to the conflict. The nonaligned countries stand to lose from a U.S.–U.S.S.R. war, and to gain from peaceful competition between the United States and the U.S.S.R. over the favor of third countries. Hence, it is not surprising that, between 1956 and 1964, the third countries frequently used their growing influence to encourage encapsulation. Non-aligned countries tended to favor reduction of armaments and of Cold War tensions, increase in the capacities, power, and status of the United States, and cessation of hostilities and exclusion of armed interventions in international conduct (Wilcox, 1962, pp. 127–130).

Other factors

Given a proper psychological state (see the discussion of the Kennedy experiment above, pp. 551–552), encapsulation can proceed as a sociopolitical process of community-building and as a process of formalization of implicit rules and strengthening of sanctioning institutions. Each of these subjects deserves a major analysis in its own right but here can only be briefly outlined. Formalization cannot advance greatly without community-building; thus, this process is charted first.

Sociopolitical processes supporting encapsulation are those which reduce the differences of interest and viewpoint of the conflicting parties and build shared ties among them. The evolution of intermediary bodies for consensus formation is of

special value for encapsulation. The formulation of an agreed-on policy always requires a process; even when basic values are shared, differences of interests and
viewpoints among various subgroups must be worked out. A government whose
policy is not backed by such a process of consensus formation will find the implementation of its policy expensive and difficult, if feasible at all. For the formation of a
new community, of new authorities and rules (which a peace system requires), consensus formation is indispensable, since the number of policies to be agreed upon is
much larger than in an existing community, and the normative basis on which to
build is much narrower. Herein lies the special significance of consensus formation
for encapsulation.

For a consensus-formation structure in a society, corporation, or village to be
effective, it must take place simultaneously on several levels of the societal unit.
Rather than attempt to reach consensus among all parties in one general assembly,
the "population" (which might consist of individuals, plants, departments, or nations)
is divided into subgroups that are more homogeneous than the population at large.
These groups work out a consensus among their respective members and are then
represented, on the next level of consensus formation, as if they were basically a single
unit. Such interlevel processing might be repeated several times. In the American
political system, for instance, the primaries, national conventions, and, to a degree,
postelection negotiations over participation in the cabinet provide such a multi-
layer consensus-formation structure.

Regional organizations, communities, and blocs might serve as "intermediary
bodies" for the international community. We are studying here a developing and not
an existing consensus-formation structure; thus, the intermediary bodies are considerably more advanced than the "top" layer. Several factors affect the contribution
of these bodies to the community-building and encapsulation: (1) Transient blocs have
much less such value than lasting federations. (2) Regional organizations with narrow
scopes of function have much less value than those broad in scope. (3) Only regional
organizations with an initial functional scope large enough to serve as a basis for take-
off will continue to grow into communities broader in scope (though not necessarily
into full-fledged peace systems). (For the best discussion of functionalism of international organizations, see Haas, 1964, Chapters I through IV.) (4) Regional bodies
formed against other regional bodies, whether the goals are offensive or defensive,
tend to retard rather than to advance encapsulation, since they repeat on a large scale
the features of nationalism, including the interunit conflict. (5) Finally, only regional
bodies that allow "upward transfer" to continue are ultimately productive for encapsulation. *Upward transfer* is a process in which units that join a larger system
transfer some of their power, rights, and sentiments to the center of the system of
which they are a part. Studies of social structures as different as the American
federal government and the Southern Baptist Association (Harrison, 1959) have
shown that, once a center of effective authority is established, it tends (under circumstances and for reasons that cannot be discussed here) to grow in power, rights, and
command of loyalties. The center has to be effective, for if the initial authority is weak
it will not trigger the upward-transfer process.

At this stage of our knowledge and history, the last phase of this upward-transfer
process is particularly difficult to chart because, while some crude contours of regional
communities have started to appear, failures still outnumber successes by a large
margin, and there are only the most tenuous signs of what the top layer might be like.
The nature of the last phase is particularly obscure at the transitional stage, for in

the development of intermediary bodies, the flame of regional and bloc chauvinism often melts away some nationalistic sovereignty in favor of regional organizations or regional states. But without such chauvinism, or without the Cold War, initiatives to form the Atlantic Community, the East European Community, and many other regional bodies would not have been undertaken. Similarly, a major driving force behind attempts to form common markets in Central America, in various parts of Africa, in the Far East, and elsewhere is the desire to counter actual or anticipated consequences of the European Economic Community. Progress, in short, might not be unilinear but dialectical. Rather than states forming regional bodies that serve as a smooth transition to a global body, the regional bodies might first move apart, exhibiting hostility and generating interregional tension. This may seem opposed to the need for global integration, but this very conflict can prepare the ground for the ultimate "synthesis" of regional blocs.

The existence and strengthening of *cross-cutting international organizations*, organizations with members from two or more regions, would enhance the development of a global society under certain conditions and have a dampening effect on interregional conflict. The conflict-reduction effect of cross-cutting multiple memberships is often stressed, but it should be noted that, in this context, this effect is not automatically ensured. Actually, conflict may be exacerbated rather than reduced if the cross-cutting organizations are not universal but serve to tie two or more regions, for example, North America and Western Europe, into a bloc. Such cross-regional organizations could, for instance, serve to sustain bipolarity and retard the emergence of pluralism, to strengthen the parties to a global conflict rather than set limits to interregional conflict.

Second, these cross-cutting organizations are effective only if their functions are sociologically important in the sense that they affect the allocation of assets and attract ideological commitments. A universal postal service or a board for allocations of radio frequencies has little, if any, conflict-dampening effect. On the other hand, a General Agreement on Tariffs and Trade, extended to all nations of all regions, might have some such effect.

But even a universal organization serving many important functions would be more a source of tension and conflict than a basis for their limitation if it were dominated by one region or group of regions, to the partial or complete loss of responsiveness to the others. Actually, an organization that does not allow politically effective regions to participate and to gain representation more or less proportional to their power would provoke more conflict, the more powerful it is and the more loyalty it commands.

Another major aspect of encapsulation is the *evolution of the rules and of agencies for their enforcement*. Here there is much room for the application and development of the sociology of law. There are some obvious applications, such as theorems concerning change through legislation, suggesting that one need not wait until all the units involved are ripe for progress before change can be initiated, but also warning against excessive reliance on legislation when there is only a narrow foundation of political consensus. A premature world law might be treated like prohibition, providing large profits to arms smugglers and leading to the law's repeal rather than lasting disarmament.

Less often discussed among sociologists and rarely studied empirically is the comparative effectiveness of various sanctions for the evolution and enforcement of various laws. These questions are of special relevance for the verification of disarmament treaties and alternative responses to violation (Woods Hole Summer Study, 1962). The concern in these instances is, first of all, with protecting the existing international law from erosion, and with accelerating its growth and therefore providing mechanisms for its formulation. Here a key problem is the conversion of implicit and "understood" rules into explicit and enforced law.

When rules are formalized, effective verification and response machinery must still be created. The formal 1954 agreements to neutralize Laos and limit arms supplies for Vietnam were supervised by an understaffed, underfinanced, ill-equipped, politically deadlocked commission. Since 1959, each side has accused the other of violating these agreements; the completely inadequate enforcement machinery provided a clear picture neither of who was first to violate the agreements nor of what a proper response should be, short of disregarding the agreement.

A transition course from the presocietal stage of the international system to one that answers the full list of functional requirements of a global society has been outlined here. It is not suggested that the international system necessarily will follow this course or, if it starts on this path, will follow it all the way to its end. There are, however, some signs that it will turn this way, and charting the course is helpful to those who seek a better understanding of international relations and to those interested in understanding how to better them.

The transition involves not the elimination of conflict but its encapsulation. The evolution of the capsule which could keep conflict unarmed might be initiated when the configuration of power is favorable—for this, the rise of pluralism and a sizable floating vote seem important—and when the psychological atmosphere is ripe. Once initiated via encapsulation, the full evolution of an international societal system requires the formulation and enforcement of rules and the construction of social foundations which such formulation and enforcement would necessitate. This, in turn, might take place when regional bodies provide intermediary levels for a global consensus-formation structure. The top layer of this structure might emerge out of a process of upward transfer of power, rights, and loyalties to a central organ of the emerging world community.

REFERENCES

Alexander, F. (1941). Psychiatric aspects of war and peace. *Amer. J. Sociol., 46,* 504–520.

Alger, C. F. (1961). Non-resolution consequences of the United Nations and their effect on international conflict. *J. Confl. Resol., 5,* 128–145.

———— (1965). Decision-making theory and human conflict. In E. B. McNeil (Ed.), *The nature of human conflict.* Englewood Cliffs, N.J.: Prentice-Hall. Pp. 274–292.

Almond, G. A. (1954). *The appeals of communism.* Princeton: Princeton Univ. Press.

———— (1960). *The American people and foreign policy.* New York: Praeger.

Almond, G. A., and S. Verba (1963). *The civic culture: political attitudes and democracy in five nations.* Princeton: Princeton Univ. Press.

Archibald, K., Ed. (1966). *Strategic interaction and conflict.* Berkeley: Univ. of California Press.

Barton, A. H. (1963). *Social organization under stress: a sociological review of disaster studies.* Washington, D.C.: National Research Council.

Bauer, R. A. (1961). Problems of perception and the relations between the United States and the Soviet Union. *J. Confl. Resol., 5,* 223–229.

Bauer, R. A., A. Inkeles, and C. Kluckhohn (1956). *How the Soviet system works: cultural, psychological and social themes.* Cambridge: Harvard Univ. Press.

Benson, O. (1962). Simulation of international relations and diplomacy. In H. Borko (Ed.), *Computer applications in the behavioral sciences.* Englewood Cliffs, N.J.: Prentice-Hall. Pp. 574–595.

Berkowitz, L. (1962). *Aggression: a social psychological analysis.* New York: McGraw-Hill.

––––––– (1965). The concept of aggressive drive: some additional considerations. In L. Berkowitz (Ed.), *Advances in experimental social psychology.* Vol. 2. New York: Academic Press. Pp. 301–329.

Bernard, J., F. H. Pear, R. Aron, and C. Angell (1957). *The nature of conflict: studies on the sociological aspects of international tensions.* Paris: UNESCO.

Blake, R. R. (1959). Psychology and the crisis of statesmanship. *Amer. Psychologist, 14,* 87–94.

Bloomfield, L. P. (1960). Political gaming. *U.S. Naval Inst. Proc., 86,* 57–64.

Boulding, K. E. (1962). *Conflict and defense: a general theory.* New York: Harper.

Bowers, R. V. (1967). The military establishment. In P. F. Lazarsfeld, W. H. Sewell, and H. L. Wilensky (Eds.), *The uses of sociology.* New York: Basic Books. Pp. 239–274.

Bramson, L., and G. W. Goethals, Eds. (1964). *War: studies from psychology, sociology, anthropology.* New York: Basic Books.

Brennan, D. G. (1965). Strategy and conscience. *Bull. atom. Scientists, 21,* 25–30.

Brody, R. A. (1963). Varieties of simulations in international relations research. In H. Guetzkow *et al., Simulation in international relations: developments for research and teaching.* Englewood Cliffs, N.J.: Prentice-Hall. Pp. 190–223.

––––––– (1965). International relations as a behavioral science. In G. Sperrazzo (Ed.), *Psychology and international relations.* Washington, D.C.: Georgetown Univ. Press. Pp. 53–61.

––––––– (1966). Cognition and behavior: a model of international relations. In O. J. Harvey (Ed.), *Experience, structure, and adaptability.* New York: Springer. Pp. 321–348.

Bronfenbrenner, U. (1961). The mirror image in Soviet-American relations: a social psychologist's report. *J. soc. Issues, 17,* 45–56.

Burton, J. W. (1965). *International relations: a general theory.* Cambridge, Eng.: Cambridge Univ. Press.

Buss, A. H. (1961). *The psychology of aggression.* New York: Wiley.

––––––– (1966). Instrumentality of aggression, feedback, and frustration as determinants of physical aggression. *J. Pers. soc. Psychol., 3,* 153–162.

Campbell, A., P. E. Converse, W. E. Miller, and D. E. Stokes (1960). *The American voter.* New York: Wiley.

Campbell, D. T. (1966). Pattern matching as an essential in distal knowing. In K. R. Hammon (Ed.), *The psychology of Egon Brunswik.* New York: Holt, Rinehart, and Winston. Pp. 81–106.

Campbell, D. T., and D. W. Fiske (1959). Convergent and discriminant validation by the multitrait-multimethod matrix. *Psychol. Bull., 56,* 81–105.

Cassady, R., Jr. (1963). Price warfare in business competition: a study of abnormal competitive behavior. Michigan State University, Bureau of Business and Economic Research. Occasional Paper No. 11.

Chadwick, R. W. (1966). The development of a partial theory of international behavior: a test, revision and extension of the international simulation theory. Unpublished Ph.D. dissertation, Northwestern University.

Clarkson, J. D., and T. C. Cochran, Eds. (1941). *War as a social institution: the historian's perspective.* New York: Columbia Univ. Press.

Claude, I., Jr. (1964). *Swords into plowshares: the problems and progress of international organization.* New York: Random House.

Cohen, B. C. (1961). Foreign policy makers and the press. In J. N. Rosenau (Ed.), *International politics and foreign policy.* Glencoe, Ill.: Free Press. Pp. 220–228.

Cooper, J. B. (1955). Psychological literature on the prevention of war. *Bull. Res. Exch. Prevention of War, 3,* 2–15.

Cornwell, E. E., Jr. (1965). *Presidential leadership of public opinion.* Bloomington: Indiana Univ. Press.

Cory, R. H., Jr. (1957). The role of public opinion in United States policies towards the United Nations. *Int. Organizat., 11,* 220–227.

Coser, L. A. (1956). *The functions of social conflict.* Glencoe, Ill.: Free Press.

Dentler, R. A., and P. Cutright (1963). *Hostage America.* Boston: Beacon Press.

Deutsch, K. W. (1963). *The nerves of government: models of political communication and control.* Glencoe, Ill.: Free Press.

Deutsch, K. W., et al. (1957). *Political community and the North Atlantic area: international organization in the light of historical experience.* Princeton: Princeton Univ. Press.

Deutsch, M. (1958). Trust and suspicion. *J. Confl. Resol., 11,* 265–279.

——— (1960). The effect of motivational orientation upon trust and suspicion. *Hum. Relat., 13,* 123–139.

——— (1961). Psychological alternatives to war. *J. soc. Issues, 18,* 97–119.

——— (1962). Cooperation and trust: some theoretical notes. In M. R. Jones (Ed.), *Nebraska symposium on motivation, 1962.* Lincoln: Univ. of Nebraska Press. Pp. 275–320.

——— (1965a). Conflict and its resolution. Paper presented to annual meeting of American Sociological Association.

——— (1965b). A psychological approach to international conflict. In G. Sperrazzo (Ed.), *Psychology and international relations.* Washington, D.C.: Georgetown Univ. Press. Pp. 1–20.

——— (1966). Rejoinder to Kelley's comments. In K. Archibald (Ed.), *Strategic interaction and conflict.* Berkeley: Univ. of California Press. Pp. 44–48.

Deutsch, M., and R. M. Krauss (1962). Studies of interpersonal bargaining. *J. Confl. Resol., 6,* 52–76.

Dollard, J., L. W. Doob, N. E. Miller, O. H. Mowrer, and R. R. Sears (1939). *Frustration and aggression.* New Haven: Yale Univ. Press.

Doob, L. (1964). *Patriotism and nationalism: their psychological foundations.* New Haven: Yale Univ. Press.

Dunn, F. S. (1950). *War and the minds of men.* New York: Harper and Row.

Edelman, M. (1964). *The symbolic use of politics.* Urbana: Univ. of Illinois Press.

Eggan, D. (1943). The general problem of Hopi adjustment. *Amer. Anthropologist, 45,* 357–373.

Etzioni, A. (1961a). *A comparative analysis of complex organizations: on power, involvement and their correlates.* Glencoe, Ill.: Free Press.

————, Ed. (1961b). *Complex organizations: a sociological reader.* New York: Holt, Rinehart, and Winston.

———— (1962). *The hard war to peace: a new strategy.* New York: Collier.

———— (1964). *Winning without war.* Garden City, N.Y.: Doubleday.

———— (1965). *Political unification: a comparative study of leaders and forces.* New York: Holt, Rinehart, and Winston.

———— (1966). War and disarmament. In R. K. Merton and R. A. Nisbet (Eds.), *Contemporary social problems* (rev. ed.). New York: Harcourt, Brace, and World. Pp. 723–773.

———— (1967). Nonconventional uses of sociology as illustrated by peace research. In P. F. Lazarsfeld, W. H. Sewell, and H. L. Wilensky (Eds.), *The uses of sociology.* New York: Basic Books. Pp. 806–838.

———— (1968). *The active society: a theory of societal and political processes.* New York: Free Press.

Evan, W. M. (1958). An international public opinion poll of disarmament and 'inspection by the people': a study of attitudes toward supranationalism. In S. Melman (Ed.), *Inspection for disarmament.* New York: Columbia Univ. Press. Pp. 231–250.

Farber, M. L. (1955). The anal character and political aggression. *J. abnorm. soc. Psychol., 51,* 486–489.

Farris, C. D. (1960). Selected attitudes on foreign affairs as correlates of authoritarian and political anomie. *J. Politics, 22,* 50–67.

Fedder, E. H. (1964). Communication and American-Soviet negotiating behavior. *Background, 8,* 105–120.

Feierabend, I. K., and Rosalind L. Feierabend (1966). Aggressive behaviors within politics, 1948–1962: a cross-national study. *J. Confl. Resol., 10,* 249–271.

Festinger, L. (1957). *A theory of cognitive dissonance.* New York: Row, Peterson.

Finkelstein, L. W. (1962). The uses of reciprocal inspection. In S. Melman (Ed.), *Disarmament: its politics and economics.* Boston: American Academy of Arts and Sciences. Pp. 82–98.

Fisher, J. (1964). Interspecific aggression. In J. D. Carthy and F. J. Ebling (Eds.), *The natural history of aggression.* New York: Academic Press. Pp. 7–14.

Fisher, R. (1962). Internal enforcement of international rules. In S. Melman (Ed.), *Disarmament: its politics and economics.* Boston: American Academy of Arts and Sciences. Pp. 99–120.

Frank, J. D. (1960). Breaking the thought barrier: psychological challenges of the nuclear age. *Psychiatry, 23,* 245–266.

Free, L. A. (1959). *Six allies and a neutral.* Glencoe, Ill.: Free Press.

French, J. R. P., Jr., and R. B. Zajonc (1957). An experimental study of cross-cultural norm conflict. *J. abnorm. soc. Psychol., 54,* 218–224.

Fromm, E. (1960). The case for unilateral disarmament. *Daedalus, 89,* 1015–1028.

———— (1961). *May man prevail?* Garden City, N.Y.: Doubleday.

Galtung, J. (1964). A structural theory of aggression. *J. Peace Res., 2,* 95–119.

———— (1965). Institutionalized conflict resolution. *J. Peace Res., 4,* 348–397.

Galtung, J. M., and M. H. Ruge (1965). The structure of foreign news: the presentation of the Congo, Cuban and Cyprus crises in four Norwegian newspapers. *J. Peace Res., 1,* 64–91.

Gamson, Z. A. (1964). Experimental studies of coalition formation. In L. Berkowitz (Ed.), *Advances in experimental social psychology.* Vol. 1. New York: Academic Press. Pp. 81–110.

Gladstone, A. (1953). Can the prevention of war be studied experimentally? *Bull. Res. Exch. Prevention of War, 1,* 1–3.

Grosser, G. H., H. Wechsler, and M. Greenblatt, Eds. (1964). *The threat of impending disaster.* Cambridge: M.I.T. Press.

Group for the Advancement of Psychiatry (1965). Psychiatric aspects of the prevention of nuclear war. *Int. J. Psychiat., 1,* 341–390.

Guetzkow, H. (1957). Isolation and collaboration: a partial theory of inter-nation relations. *J. Confl. Resol., 1,* 38–68.

———— (1963). A use of simulation in the study of inter-nation relations. In H. Guetzkow *et al., Simulation in international relations: developments for research and teaching.* Englewood Cliffs, N.J.: Prentice-Hall. Pp. 24–42.

Guetzkow, H., and A. Bowers (1957). The development of organizations in a laboratory. *Management Sci., 3,* 380–402.

Haas, E. B. (1964). *Beyond the nation state.* Stanford: Stanford Univ. Press.

Haas, E. B., and A. S. Whiting (1956). *Dynamics of international relations.* New York: McGraw-Hill.

Hall, K. R. L. (1964). Aggression in monkey and ape societies. In J. D. Carthy and F. J. Ebling (Eds.), *The natural history of aggression.* New York: Academic Press. Pp. 51–64.

Harrison, P. M. (1959). *Authority and power in the free church tradition: a social case study of the American Baptist Convention.* Princeton: Princeton Univ. Press.

Harsanyi, J. C. (1962). Mathematical models for the genesis of war. *World Politics, 14,* 687–699.

Hero, A. O. (1959). *Studies in citizen participation in international relations.* Vol. 6. Boston: World Peace Foundation.

Holsti, O. R., R. A. Brody, and R. C. North (1964). Measuring affect and action in international reaction models: empirical materials from the 1962 Cuban crisis. *J. Peace Res., 1,* 170–190.

Holsti, O. R., and R. C. North (1965). The history of human conflict. In E. B. McNeil (Ed.), *The nature of human conflict.* Englewood Cliffs, N.J.: Prentice-Hall. Pp. 155–171.

Homans, G. C. (1950). *The human group.* New York: Harcourt, Brace, and World.

Hornstein, H. A., and M. Deutsch (1967). Tendencies to compete and to attack as a function of inspection, incentive, and available alternatives. *J. Pers. soc. Psychol., 5,* 311–318.

Horowitz, I. L. (1961). Arms, policies, and games. *Amer. Scholar, 31,* 94–107.

Huitt, R. K. (1961). The outsider in the senate: an alternative role. *Amer. polit. Sci. Rev., 55,* 566–590.

Huntington, S. P. (1958). Arms races: prerequisites and results. In C. J. Friedrich and S. E. Harris (Eds.), *Public policy: a yearbook of the Graduate School of Public Administration.* Cambridge: Harvard Univ. Press. Pp. 41–86.

———— (1962). Patterns of violence in world politics. In S. P. Huntington (Ed.), *Changing patterns of military politics.* New York: Free Press. Pp. 17–50.

Ikle, F. C. (1962). Arms control and disarmament. *World Politics, 14,* 713–722.

Inkeles, A. (1958). *Public opinion in Soviet Russia: a study in mass persuasion* (enlarged ed.). Cambridge: Harvard Univ. Press.

Janowitz, M. (1957). Military elites and the study of war. *J. Confl. Resol., 1,* 9–18.

———— (1959). *Sociology and the military establishment.* New York: Russell Sage Foundation.

———— (1964). *The military in the political development of new nations: an essay in comparative analysis.* Chicago: Univ. of Chicago Press.

Jones, S. B. (1954). The power inventory and national strategy. *World Politics, 6,* 421–452.

Kahn, H. (1960). *On thermonuclear war.* Princeton: Princeton Univ. Press.

———— (1965). *On escalation: metaphors and scenarios.* New York: Praeger.

Kaplan, M. A. (1957). Balance of power, bipolarity and other models of international systems. *Amer. polit. Sci. Rev., 51,* 684–695.

Kardiner, A., *et al.* (1945). *The psychological frontiers of society.* New York: Columbia Univ. Press.

Kautsky, J. H. (1965). Myth, self-fulfilling prophecy, and symbolic reassurance in the East-West conflict. *J. Confl. Resol., 9,* 1–17.

Kelley, H. (1966). Comments on M. Deutsch's bargaining, threat and communication. In K. Archibald (Ed.), *Strategic interaction and conflict.* Berkeley: Univ. of California Press. Pp. 41–43.

Kelman, H. C., Ed. (1965). *International behavior: a social-psychological analysis.* New York: Holt, Rinehart, and Winston.

Key, V. O. (1966). *The responsible electorate.* Cambridge: Harvard Univ. Press.

King, J. A. (1954). Closed social groups among domestic dogs. *Proc. Amer. Philos. Soc., 98*, 327–336.

Kissinger, H. A. (1961). *The necessity for choice.* New York: Harper.

Klapp, O. E. (1964). *Symbolic leaders: public dramas and public men.* Chicago: Aldine.

Kluckhohn, C. (1955). Politics, history, and psychology. *World Politics, 8,* 112–123.

Krauss, R. M., and M. Deutsch (in press). Communication in interpersonal bargaining. *J. Pers. soc. Psychol.*

Kuenzli, A. E. (1956). The mobilization of sentiments: Roosevelt and Churchill. *Bull. Res. Exch. Prevention of War, 4,* 17–20.

Lane, R. E. (1962). *Political ideology: why the American common man behaves as he does.* Glencoe, Ill.: Free Press.

Lawson, R. (1965). *Frustration: the development of a scientific concept.* New York: Macmillan.

Lazarsfeld, P. F., and H. Menzel (1961). On the relation between individual and collective properties. In A. Etzioni (Ed.), *Complex organizations: a sociological reader.* New York: Holt, Rinehart, and Winston. Pp. 422–440.

Leach, E. R. (1960). Review of S. H. Udy, Jr.'s "Organization of Work: A Comparative Analysis of Production among Non-Industrial Peoples." *Amer. sociol. Rev., 25,* 136–138.

Leites, N. (1953). *A study of Bolshevism.* Glencoe, Ill.: Free Press.

Lentz, T. F. (1950). The attitudes of world citizenship. *J. soc. Psychol., 32,* 207–214.

––––––– (1965). Japan vs. USA: a comparative public opinion study. *J. Peace Res., 3,* 288–294.

Lerner, D. (1956). French business leaders look at EDC: a preliminary report. *Publ. Opin. Quart., 20,* 212–221.

Levinson, D. J. (1957). Authoritarian personality and foreign policy. *J. Confl. Resol., 1,* 37–47.

Link, A. S. (1966). *Wilson: campaigns for progressivism and peace, 1916–1917.* Princeton: Princeton Univ. Press.

Lorenz, K. (1964). Ritualized fighting. In J. D. Carthy and F. J. Ebling (Eds.), *The natural history of aggression.* New York: Academic Press. Pp. 39–50.

––––––– (1966). *On aggression.* New York: Harcourt, Brace, and World.

Luce, R. D., and H. Raiffa (1957). *Games and decisions: introduction and critical survey.* New York: Wiley.

McClelland, C. A. (1966). *Theory and the international system.* New York: Macmillan.

McClosky, H. (1967). Personality and attitude correlates of foreign policy orientation. In J. Rosenau (Ed.), *Domestic sources of foreign policy.* New York: Free Press. Pp. 51–109.

Mack, R. W., and R. C. Snyder (1957). Introduction. *J. Confl. Resol., 1,* Special issue, 105–110.

McKenna, J. C. (1962). *Diplomatic protest in foreign policy.* Chicago: Loyola Univ. Press.

McNeil, E. B. (1965a). The nature of aggression. In E. B. McNeil (Ed.), *The nature of human conflict.* Englewood Cliffs, N.J.: Prentice-Hall. Pp. 14–41.

———, Ed. (1965b). *The nature of human conflict.* Englewood Cliffs, N.J.: Prentice-Hall.

Marlowe, D. H. (1963). Commitment, contract, group boundaries and conflict. In J. H. Masserman (Ed.), *Violence and war with clinical studies.* New York: Grune and Stratton. Pp. 43–55.

Matthews, D. R. (1960). *U.S. senators and their world.* Chapel Hill: Univ. of North Carolina Press.

Mead, M., and R. Metraux (1965). The anthropology of human conflict. In E. B. McNeil (Ed.), *The nature of human conflict.* Englewood-Cliffs, N.J.: Prentice-Hall. Pp. 116–138.

Melman, S. (1961). *The peace race.* New York: Ballantine.

Michael, D. N. (1962). Psychopathology of nuclear war. *Bull. atom. Scientists, 18,* 28–29.

Milbrath, L. W. (1965). *Political participation.* Chicago: Rand McNally.

Millis, W. (1965). *An end to arms.* New York: Atheneum.

Mills, C. W. (1958). *The causes of World War III.* New York: Simon and Schuster.

Moynihan, D. P. (1966). The war against the automobile. *Publ. Interest, 1,* 10–26.

Naroll, R. (1966). Does military deterrence deter? *Trans-Action, 3,* 14–20.

Nehnevajsa, J. (1960). *Further analysis of the U-2 incident: effects of an event.* New York: Columbia Univ. Press.

Osgood, C. E. (1960). A case for graduated unilateral disengagement. *Bull. atom. Scientists, 16,* 127–131.

——— (1962). *An alternative to war or surrender.* Urbana: Univ. of Illinois Press.

——— (1965). Escalation as a strategy. *War/Peace Report, 5,* 12–14.

Padover, S. K. (1958). *U.S. foreign policy and public opinion.* New York: Foreign Policy Association.

Park, R. E. (1950). *Race and culture.* Glencoe, Ill.: Free Press.

Parsons, T. (1962). Polarization of the world and international order. In Q. Wright, W. M. Evan, and M. Deutsch (Eds.), *Preventing World War III: some proposals.* New York: Simon and Schuster. Pp. 310–331.

Paul, J., and J. Laulicht (1963). *In your opinion: leaders' and voters' attitudes on defense and disarmament.* Clarkson, Ont.: Canadian Peace Research Institute.

Perry, S. E. (1956). International relations and game theory. *Bull. Res. Exch. Prevention of War, 4,* 1–8.

Pilisuk, M., P. Potter, A. Rapoport, and J. A. Winter (1965). War hawks and peace doves: alternate resolutions of experimental conflicts. *J. Confl. Resol., 9,* 491–508.

Pool, I. de S. (1952). *The 'prestige papers': a survey of their editorials.* Stanford Univ. Press.

Posvar, W. W. (1964). The impact of strategy expertise on the national security policy of the United States. *Publ. Policy, 13,* 36–68.

Ram, P., and G. C. Murphy (1952). Recent investigations of Hindu-Muslim relations in India. *Hum. Organizat., 11,* 13–16.

Rapoport, A. (1957). Lewis F. Richardson's mathematical theory of war. *J. Confl. Resol., 1,* 249–299.

––––––– (1963). Formal games as probing tools for investigating behavior motivated by trust and suspicion. *J. Confl. Resol., 7,* 520–579.

––––––– (1964). *Strategy and conscience.* New York: Harper and Row.

––––––– (1965). The sources of anguish. *Bull. atom. Scientists, 21,* 31–36.

Rapoport, A., and A. M. Chammah (1965). *Prisoner's dilemma: a study in conflict and cooperation.* Ann Arbor: Univ. of Michigan Press.

Ravich, R., M. Deutsch, and B. Brown (1965). An experimental study of decision-making and marital discord. Paper delivered at meeting of Association for Research in Psychiatry.

Richardson, L. F. (1939). Generalized foreign politics. *Brit. J. Psychol., Monogr. Suppl., 23,* 1–87.

––––––– (1960). *Arms and insecurity: a mathematical study of the causes and origins of war.* Pittsburgh: Boxwood Press.

Riker, W. H. (1962). *The theory of political coalitions.* New Haven: Yale Univ. Press.

Rokkan, S., Ed. (1960). Citizen participation in political life. *Int. soc. Sci. J., 12,* Special issue, 7–99.

Roper, E. (1953). American attitudes on world organization. *Publ. Opin. Quart., 17,* 405–442.

Rosecrance, R. N. (1963). *Action and reaction in world politics.* Boston: Little, Brown.

Rosenau, J. N. (1961). *Public opinion and foreign policy.* New York: Random House.

Rosenberg, M. J. (1967). Attitude change and foreign policy in the cold war era. In J. N. Rosenau (Ed.), *Domestic sources of foreign policy.* New York: Free Press. Pp. 111–159.

Ross, H. L. (1955). Some evidence against the sublimation of aggression. *Bull. Res. Exch. Prevention of War, 3,* 74–76.

Rovere, R. H. (1956). *The Eisenhower years: affairs of state.* New York: Farrar, Straus, and Cudahy.

Rummel, R. J. (1963). The dimensions of conflict behavior within and between nations. *Gen. Systems Yearbk., 8,* 1–50.

––––––– (1966). Dimensions of conflict behavior within nations, 1946–1959. *J. Confl. Resol., 10,* 67–73.

Russett, B. M. (1963). *Toward a model of competitive international politics.* New Haven: Yale University Political Science Research Library, Yale Paper in Political Science No. 8.

Russett, B. M., H. Alker, K. W. Deutsch, and H. Lasswell (1964). *World handbook of political and social indicators.* New Haven: Yale Univ. Press.

Saenger, G. (1953). *The social psychology of prejudice: achieving intercultural understanding and cooperation in a democracy.* New York: Harper.

Schelling, T. C. (1960). *The strategy of conflict.* Cambridge: Harvard Univ. Press.

—— (1963). War without pain, and other models. *World Politics, 15,* 465–487.

—— (1965). Signals and feedback in the arms dialogue. *Bull. atom. Scientists, 21,* 5–10.

Schilling, W. R. (1961). The H-bomb decision: how to decide without actually choosing. *Polit. Sci. Quart., 76,* 24–46.

Schlesinger, A. M., Jr. (1965). *A thousand days: John F. Kennedy in the White House.* Boston: Houghton Mifflin.

Scott, J. P. (1965). On the evolution of fighting behavior. *Science, 148,* 820–821.

Scott, W. A., and S. B. Withey (1958). *The United States and the United Nations: the public view.* New York: Manhattan Publishing Co.

Senghaas, D. (1961). Unilateralismus and Gradualismus: zur Strategie des Friedens. *Neue Politische Literatur, 1,* 1–15.

Sherif, C., and M. Sherif (1953). *Groups in harmony and tension: an integration of studies on intergroup relations.* New York: Harper.

Sherif, M. (1958). Superordinate goals in the reduction of intergroup conflict. *Amer. J. Sociol., 63,* 349–356.

—— (1966). *In common predicament: social psychology of intergroup conflict and cooperation.* Boston: Houghton Mifflin.

Shubik, M. (1959). *Strategy and market structure: competition, oligopoly, and the theory of games.* New York: Wiley.

Simmel, G. (1955a). *Conflict.* Glencoe, Ill.: Free Press.

—— (1955b). *The web of intergroup affiliations.* Glencoe, Ill.: Free Press.

Singer, J. D. (1959). International conflict: three levels of analysis. *World Politics, 12,* 453–461.

—— (1962). *Deterrence, arms control, and disarmament: toward a synthesis in national security policy.* Columbus: Ohio State Univ. Press.

—— (1965). *Human behavior and international politics.* Chicago: Rand McNally.

Skinner, G. W. (1965). Compliance and leadership in rural Communist China: a cyclical theory. Paper presented at annual meeting of American Political Science Association.

Smith, B. L. R. (1966). *The Rand Corporation: a case study of a nonprofit advising organization.* Cambridge: Harvard Univ. Press.

Smith, M. B. (1958). Opinions, personality and political behavior. *Amer. polit. Sci. Rev., 52,* 1–17.

Smith, M. B., J. S. Bruner, and R. W. White (1956). *Opinions and personality.* New York: Wiley.

Smoker, P. (1964). Fear in the arms race: a mathematical study. *J. Peace Res., 1,* 55–63.

Snyder, R. C. (1963). Some perspectives on the use of experimental techniques in the study of international relations. In H. Guetzkow *et al., Simulation in international relations: developments for research and teaching.* Englewood Cliffs, N.J.: Prentice-Hall. Pp. 1–23.

Snyder, R. C., and J. A. Robinson (n.d.). *National and international decision-making.* New York: Institute for International Order.

Sohn, L. D. (1962). Progressive zonal inspection: basic issues. In S. Melman (Ed.), *Disarmament: its politics and economics.* Boston: American Academy of Arts and Sciences. Pp. 121–133.

Sorensen, T. C. (1965). *Kennedy.* New York: Harper and Row.

Sorokin, P. (1937). *Social and cultural dynamics.* Vol. 3. New York: Bedminster.

Spanier, J. W., and J. L. Nogee (1962). *The politics of disarmament: a study in Soviet-American gamesmanship.* New York: Praeger.

Stokes, D. E., and W. E. Miller (1962). Party government and the saliency of Congress. *Publ. Opin. Quart., 26,* 531–546.

Stone, J. J. (1966). *Containing the arms race: some specific proposals.* Cambridge: M.I.T. Press.

Stouffer, S. (1955). *Communism, conformity and civil liberties: a cross-section of the nation speaks its mind.* Garden City, N.Y.: Doubleday.

Strachey, A. (1957). *The unconscious motives of war.* London: Hillary.

Sussmann, L. (1959). Mass political letter writing in America: the growth of an institution. *Publ. Opin. Quart., 23,* 203–212.

Szulc, T. (1966). *Dominican diary.* New York: Delacorte.

Taba, Hilda (1955). *Cultural attitudes and international understanding: an evaluation of a study tour.* New York: Institute of International Education.

Tanter, R. (1966). Dimensions of conflict behavior within and between nations 1958–60. *J. Confl. Resol., 10,* 41–64.

Terhune, K. W. (1964). Nationalism among foreign and American students: an exploratory study. *J. Confl. Resol., 8,* 256–270.

Thibaut, J. W., and H. H. Kelley (1961). *The social psychology of groups.* New York: Wiley.

Timasheff, N. S. (1965). *War and revolution.* New York: Sheed and Ward.

Triska, J. F., and D. D. Finley (1965). Soviet-American relations: a multiple symmetry model. *J. Confl. Resol., 9,* 37–53.

Turney-High, H. H. (1949). *Primitive war: its practice and concepts.* Columbus: Univ. of South Carolina Press.

U.S. Strategic Bombing Survey (1947a). *The effects of strategic bombing on German morale.* Washington, D.C.: Government Printing Office.

———— (1947b). *The effects of strategic bombing on Japanese morale.* Washington, D.C.: Government Printing Office.

Vagts, A. (1937). *A history of militarism: romance and realities of a profession.* New York: Norton.

van Doorn, J. A. A. (1966). Conflict in formal organization. In A. de Rueck and J. Knight (Eds.), *Conflict in society.* London: J. and A. Churchill. Pp. 111–132.

Vayda, A. P. (1961). Expansion and warfare among Swidden agriculturists. *Amer. Anthropologist, 63,* 346–358.

Verba, S. (1964). Simulation, reality, and theory in international relations. *World Politics, 16,* 490–519.

Waltz, K. (1959). *Man, the state, and war: a theoretical analysis.* New York: Columbia Univ. Press.

Waskow, A. I. (1963). *The worried man's guide to world peace: a Peace Research Institute handbook.* Garden City, N.Y.: Anchor.

Webb, E. J., D. T. Campbell, R. D. Schwartz, and L. Sechrest (1966). *Unobtrusive measures: nonreactive research in social sciences.* Chicago: Rand McNally.

Webster, D. B. (1965). Review of J. P. Scott and J. L. Fuller's "Genetics and the Social History of the Dog." *Natural History, 74,* 10.

Wedge, B., and C. Muromcew (1965). Psychological factors in Soviet disarmament negotiation. *J. Confl. Resol., 9,* 18–36.

White, R. K. (1961). Misconceptions in Soviet and American images. Paper presented at meeting of American Psychological Association.

Wilcox, F. O. (1962). The nonaligned states and the United Nations. In L. W. Martin (Ed.), *Neutralization and nonalignment: the new states in world affairs.* New York: Praeger. Pp. 121–151.

Williams, J. A., Jr. (1964). Reduction of tension through intergroup contact: a social psychological interpretation. *Pacific sociol. Rev., 7,* 81–88.

Withey, S. B. (1962a). Public opinion on war and shelters. *N.Y. Univ. Thought, 2,* 6–18.

_____ (1962b). *The U.S. and the U.S.S.R.* Ann Arbor: University of Michigan, Survey Research Center.

Wolfers, A. (1962). *Discord and collaboration: essays on international politics.* Baltimore: Johns Hopkins Press.

Woods Hole Summer Study (1962). *Verification and response in disarmament agreements.* Washington, D.C.: Institute for Defense Analysis.

Wright, Q. (1942). *A study of war* (2 vols.). Chicago: Univ. of Chicago Press.

_____ (1965). The escalation of international conflicts. *J. Confl. Resol., 9,* 434–449.

Yates, A. J. (1962). *Frustration and conflict.* New York: Wiley.

Zelditch, M., Jr., and T. K. Hopkins (1961). Laboratory experiments with organizations. In A. Etzioni (Ed.), *Complex organizations: a sociological reader.* New York: Holt, Rinehart, and Winston. Pp. 464–477.

44

Psychology of Religion

JAMES E. DITTES, Yale University

Religion has always provided an important focus for applied psychology. Question-naire, scaling, and case study procedures, oedipal theories and factor analysis not only found immediate application to religion as soon as devised; their development was, in fact, prompted in no small part by the search for ways to study religion (see, respectively, Starbuck, 1899; Thurstone and Chave, 1929; James, 1902; Freud, 1913; Thurstone, 1934). More of psychology's pioneers gave earnest attention to religion than might be supposed (for example, Galton, G. S. Hall, Wundt), and the profession's leaders continue to do so. At least one-fourth of the presidents of the American Psychological Association have given attention to religion at some point in their careers, and this rate persists about equally in every decade. The first of dozens of books to carry the title *Psychology of Religion* appeared in 1899 (Starbuck), almost certainly before any other "Psychology of . . ." and, indeed, before there was much "psychology" to be applied. One of the earliest journals in psychology was the *American Journal of Religious Psychology and Education* (1904–1911).

Psychologists' attraction to religion should not be hard to understand. Religion offers rich, sometimes dramatic, instances of key psychological processes such as the development and change of attitude and belief, the arousal and reduction of anxiety and guilt, personality change, the development of integrative and self-referent processes in personality, and, above all, many instances of the interrelation between cognitive and motivational variables. Furthermore, these are frequently in important interaction with group processes (Gregory, 1952). Phenomenological reports of religious life (and theological formalization and elaboration of such reports) offer both data and theories expressed in terms of a "dynamic," "functional" language highly congenial to the terms of contemporary motivational and personality theories.

Appreciation is due Mrs. Fawn Hewitt, Mrs. Elizabeth Powers, Mrs. Jane Smith, and James Vaughan for assistance in surveying the literature and improving the manuscript. Gordon Allport also made several helpful comments on a late revision of the manuscript.

To specify just one example: many religious phenomena are understandable as postcommitment elaboration and protection of belief, a process which has been made popular for study in our decade by "dissonance theory." Most religious commitments in our culture are reached by processes of socialization and influence under conditions maximizing the importance, commitment, and perceived freedom of choice; but the commitments are held under circumstances providing high likelihood of encountering contradictory data and beliefs, and hence, high dissonance. Many processes of ritual, group formation, and cognitive elaboration may be interpreted as prime instances of "dissonance reduction." The phenomenon of dissonance-reducing proselytizing has, in fact, been inspected by dissonance theorists in an intensive study of one case, comprising a book-length report (Festinger, Riecken, and Schachter, 1956).

Yet the same complexity and intensity of important processes which attract psychological investigation of religion also frustrate it. The field has been marked largely by brief flurries of interest as one investigator after another is attracted to it, then bewildered by the difficulties of study. There has not been sustained development of theory, empirical findings, or research techniques. Publications today are not substantially advanced over the earliest writings. All surveys of the field agree, whether in apology or in indictment, on the primitive state of the study of the psychology of religion, and the material to be presented in this chapter provides little basis for disputing this judgment.

Explanations for this primitive condition vary. The sheer quantity of publications (for example, as indexed in any volume of *Psychological Abstracts* or *Dissertation Abstracts*) and other evidence of the cordiality of editors and program chairmen to the study of religion dispute both the contention (Douglas, 1963) of a kind of resistance or taboo within psychology to the study of religion and also the argument (Clark, 1958) that there is a short supply of empirical data. Rather, the chief problem appears to be in the realm of theory and in the theoretical relevance of data. The critical psychological questions and the categories of data by which they can be answered simply have not yet been specified.

Systematic conceptual development has been impeded by a number of general problems which deserve brief mention here. There is, most obviously, the practical difficulty of unraveling the complex phenomena to discover the important variables and relations among them. The psychological richness of religious processes, which makes them attractive for study, also makes them persistently baffling to comprehend. Beyond this, however, systematic progress has been stymied by disagreement or uncertainty over several general questions of strategy or approach. Four of these will be mentioned, the last three closely related to the first.

HOW UNIQUE IS RELIGION?

In religion, are there unique psychological variables, and relationships among variables, different from those in other phenomena? Should the units of analysis and the theories be those derived from more general, basic psychological theory and then applied to religion; or should they be categories and theories suggested by the particular material of religion itself? Four types of answers may be identified. They are listed here in the order of increasing degree of contention for the uniqueness of religion and lessening degree of respect for parsimony. The correct choice among these is empirically available, in principle, and eventually there will be grounds for a decision. But at present it is made by each investigator on varying grounds of hunch and preference.

1. *Instancing.* In events regarded by participants as religious, the same variables and relationships are found as in other events. For example, the same effects of the salience of group membership are found when the group is the Catholic Church as when the group is the student body of a particular college. This position might be called the most "reductionistic" or the most "parsimonious," depending on the values being emphasized.

2. *Uniquely prominent relationships.* Certain relationships among certain variables, which may exist outside religion, are particularly discernible within religious events. For example, the evocation of affiliative behavior by ambiguous or stress situations may be especially prominent in religious phenomena. The relationships discerned in religion may hold in other situations, though in attenuated or masked or otherwise less observable fashion, so that their study in religion may help to illuminate other behavior. This is analogous to the study of abnormal psychology, in which particular relationships, such as defensive reactions to anxiety, may be discernible and their study illuminating for normal behavior as well.

3. *Unique relationships.* The basic variables in religious behavior are essentially those found in any behavior, but they interact with some variables within religion (for example, absolute sanctions, or freedom ensuing from absolute acceptance) to provide relationships unlike those found elsewhere.

4. *Basically unique variables.* The basic variables operating within religion (for example, a "religious" sentiment) are different and separate from those discerned outside religion.

Descriptive versus theoretical starting points

Phenomena-based descriptive strategies. The third and fourth positions above emphasize the uniqueness of religion and are likely to be associated with a strategy of study which is essentially descriptive. The argument, valid if one accepts one of the assumptions specified in paragraphs 3 and 4 above, is that the study of religion is still so primitive that descriptive, taxonomic tasks need to be completed before more sophisticated theorizing is possible. This is a position likely to be taken by those most sympathetic with religion, and with the claims of the perception of events by religious participants, and hence, those most impressed with the "richness" and "irreducibility" of religious phenomena. William James's analysis of religion (1902) is essentially an example of this position, though his own methodological arguments about the field of psychology of religion are consistent with paragraphs 1 and 2 above.

Theory-based strategies. The first two positions are much more likely to lead to theoretical work, rather than descriptive, because the categories and theories are available as already developed in the study of behavior other than religion. By the same token, such a strategy is sometimes seen as overly reductionistic and blind to important variables and relationships existing within the rich area of religion.

Freud's views provide a good example of this approach. The two most fully stated general theories of religion are both associated with Freud, though neither is by any means exclusively his. One theory, associated with Freud's second book on religion (1927) and with the writings of such others as Marx, Tawney, and Weber, is essentially a theory of compensation, on the grand unchallengeable scale provided by religious dimensions, for frustrations and stresses of various kinds. The compensation primarily emphasized is that of a protective parent figure, but other satisfactions, such as the resolution of cognitive ambiguities, or self-enhancement, are also provided in deferred or fantasied satisfactions. The other theory, associated with Freud's other two books on religion (1913, 1939), emphasizes the hostile rather than the dependent relations with parents, and proposes that religion represents an elaborate projection of oedipal motivation. Various elements of belief and of practice are analyzed, respectively, as allowing for the expression of hostility, for its control, for punishment, and for forgiveness. Both theories assume a projection of attitudes toward parents.

Relation to practical concerns

Much of the sustained and comprehensive work in the psychology of religion has developed out of the applied demands of religious institutions. These have included such concerns as the religious education of children; pastoral counseling provided by clergy; the effective expression of liberal social values; the selection, recruiting, and career guidance of clergymen; and the definition of the role of religious institutions in contemporary culture. Concern for these demands has sometimes taken the form of an argument for position 3 or 4 in the paragraphs above.

Nonpsychological questions

The argument for the uniqueness of religion may be associated, in extreme forms, with the contention that religion is not accessible to psychological study at all. Such an argument is likely to betray a confusion between psychological and philosophical (or theological) questions and to make the supposition that psychological analysis is to be used as a basis for answering philosophical questions. Such a confusion is common enough to require at least brief attention here.

Logically, the distinction between the two disciplines seems clear. Though psychology and philosophy may be concerned with the same phenomenon, such as a particular belief or a particular ritual, they are asking different questions about it. Psychology is concerned with such questions as the psychological history and function of the belief or ritual; philosophy is concerned with such questions as the truth or goodness of the belief or ritual. Judgments of the latter kind are based on their own criteria, and there is no clear logic by which the answers to the psychological questions can either imply or presuppose answers to the philosophical questions. Knowledge of the patterns of social influence and personal motivation in the history of the particular belief is not relevant to the criteria by which that belief must be judged true or false. The "genetic fallacy" has been soundly discounted by every major writer in the psychology of religion, including Freud (1927) and James (1902). That the confusion persists, both among those who propose and those who oppose psychological study of religion, may itself be a psychological question worth exploration (Dittes, 1968).

DEFINITION: CHOICE OF UNITS AND VARIABLES

A majority of the studies surveyed for this chapter have implicitly assumed that "religion" is a single, quantifiable variable. The degree of religion has been assessed by one or another readily convenient index, such as frequency of church attendance, scales measuring attitude to the church, or assent to traditionally orthodox statements. This has been done without explicit attention to the questions whether religion may be so regarded as a single, quantifiable variable; if so, how defined; and whether the measures employed are suitable indices of the concept, however defined. As Glock (1962) has stated it, "In our zeal to study the correlates of religion and to understand its effects, we have somehow ignored the phenomenon itself." Many difficulties in research—in formulating hypotheses, in developing indices and designs, in interpreting diffuse, sometimes contradictory results—arise out of the obscuring, in such a procedure, of potentially important distinctions. More substantive problems cannot be addressed in this chapter until a major portion of it has been devoted to questions of definition.

IS RELIGION A DISCRETE, UNITARY VARIABLE?

In particular, the question needs to be raised whether "religion" can be fruitfully regarded as a single *variable* or as a general *area of research* within which various hypotheses and variables can be identified. The problem is perhaps parallel with that of such terms as "small groups," "mass media," or "mental health," which are sometimes taken as single variables, but which are more often and more fruitfully regarded as areas of research. In general, it will be seen in the following sections (1) that theoretical considerations argue strongly for a complex multitude of variables within the domain of religion and make the use of "religion" as a single variable appear as conceptual or operational laziness and naiveté; but (2) that there is some empirical warrant for treating religion as a single variable, especially when it is appropriate to regard it as an object of general cultural perception.

Conceptual considerations

The problem of definition is enhanced by the great variety of phenomena to which one culture or another applies the word "religion." Every culture and subculture finds reasonably clear—and, for its own practical purposes, valid—bases for designating particular phenomena with this label. Attempts at definition which start from this array of phenomena labeled "religion" seem fated to founder upon one of two shoals. One strategy is to search for the essential or universal elements within a multicultural array of phenomena. Such a tactic invariably reduces everything to a thin and low common denominator which is doubly flawed: on the one hand, it excludes elements (for example, personal relation to a single deity, or particular standards of social relations) that are regarded as absolutely essential by one tradition or another; on the other hand, it includes instances (Communism being the most popularly cited example) which no culture commonly regards as religious. The alternative strategy—and peril—is to regard the characteristics of one tradition as definitive for all instances of religion. Such a cultural bias is at work even when supranatural reference is made part of the definition, or, as is currently popular, in the imposition of contemporary Western existentialist notions—"meaning to life," values, ultimate concerns, etc.—as controlling definitions (see, for example, a compilation of such definitions in Chapter 1 of Glock and Stark, 1965).

It is likely that the purposes of the social scientist differ from the practical needs of a culture in such a way as to require different categories and criteria of definitions. Perhaps the field of abnormal psychology provides a useful guide. Abnormal psychology has had, first of all, to reckon with diversity of phenomena and with the futility of trying to regard "abnormality" itself as a single or definable variable. Second, abnormal psychology has gradually shaken loose from phenomena-based categories defined in terms most relevant to participants and casual observers and useful for practical purposes of patient management, and has begun to devise more genotypical, scientifically useful categories.

The diversity of phenomena within religion has been catalogued dramatically by Paul Johnson (1959, pp. 47–48):

> In the name of religion what deed has not been done? For the sake of religion men have earnestly affirmed and contradicted almost every idea and form of conduct. In the long history of religion appear chastity and sacred prostitution, feasting and fasting, intoxication and prohibition, dancing and sobriety, human sacrifice and the saving of life in orphanages and hospitals, superstition and education, poverty and wealthy endowments, prayer wheels and silent worship, gods and demons, one God and many gods, attempts to escape and to reform the world. How can such diametrical oppositions all be religious?

Johnson's catalog of contradictions could easily be extended. Even within the relatively homogeneous Judeo-Christian tradition, one finds firm insistence on the importance of obedience to regulation and on freedom from regulation, on inculcation of guilt feelings and on freedom from guilt feelings, on autonomy and on "absolute dependence," on the conservation of social values and on the overthrow of social values, on individual mystical aloofness and on the interdependence and responsibilities of group membership, on fear and on trust, on intellect and on emotion, on salvation by passively received "justification" and on salvation by energetically pursued "good works." The catalog is almost endless.

The difficulty, if not the presumption, of finding among these phenomena a single, discrete variable seems formidable. The possibility of finding herein a variety of problems of substantial interest to any psychologist also seems great.

Perhaps the most elaborately developed argument for multidimensionality has been made by Glock (1959, 1962), who has proposed five independent dimensions. Glock derived his categories and definitions from the norms and traditions of one or more of the world's religions themselves. His analysis illustrates well the range of problems and likely variables, and is rich and clear enough to warrant outlining in some detail; this is attempted in Table 1. Some additional refinements will be suggested in this chapter, especially in the section on belief (pp. 642–645).

Though Glock argues for the discreteness of these dimensions, he also seems to propose, in a general way, some relation among them. The relation most clearly suggested is with the dimension of religious knowledge. In effect, he proposes a curvilinear relation between religious knowledge and the other dimensions of religiosity, with greatest religiosity on other dimensions likely to be found among those

TABLE 1

ARRAY OF POSSIBLE RELIGIOUS VARIABLES (AFTER GLOCK, 1962)

Religious beliefs (the ideological dimension)
Content and scope of beliefs
  Type of belief and unbelief
    Traditional
      Warranting beliefs: concerned with existence and character of divine

      Purposive beliefs: explaining divine purpose and defining man's role with regard to that purpose

      Implementing beliefs: proper conduct toward God and fellow man for the realization of the divine purpose
    Nontraditional
      Any beliefs adopted to meet needs to discover purpose and meaning of life

      Any deep commitment to a set of values
Degree or strength of personal belief
Saliency of belief

Religious practice (the ritualistic dimension)—public and private "practices expected of religious adherents . . . such activities as worship, prayer, participation in special sacraments, fasting . . ."

Frequency and patterns of practice
  Practices common to different traditions

  Practices unique to one tradition
Variation in nature of a practice: for example, qualitative differences in the practice of praying

Meaning of ritual acts for the individual: for example, prayers of praise or prayers of petition

---

Religious feeling (the experiential dimension)
Overt and extreme forms: for example, conversion experience, glossolalia, other ecstasy

More subtle and less public feelings
  Concern: for example, a wish to believe, a seeking after a purpose in life, or a sense of deprivation

  Awareness of the divine

  Trust or faith, that life is somehow in the hands of a divine power in which trust can be reposed
    Measured by direct report

    Measured indirectly by such "fruits of faith" as freedom from worry, a feeling of well-being
  Fear
    Measured by direct report

    Measured indirectly by representation on other dimensions, for example, in beliefs about the nature of God

---

TABLE 1 (Continued)

Religious knowledge (the intellectual dimension)

Knowledge of origin, dogma, practices of own tradition

Attitudes toward knowledge
  The importance of knowledge

  Openness to literature critical of tradition
Degree of intellectual sophistication: for example, biblical literalism in interpretation of Scripture

---

Religious effects (the consequential dimension)—implications of religion for "conduct" in "secular" affairs

Rewards
  Experience of immediate rewards: for example, peace of mind, freedom from worry

  Saliency of future rewards: salvation, eternal life, higher reincarnation
Responsibilities
  Obedience to concrete and specific prescriptions

  Application of general principles

---

with moderate knowledge about their own faith. This is consistent with the findings of at least one empirical study (Martin and Nichols, 1962). With a sample of undergraduates, Martin and Nichols measured religious information with 120 true-false items, half of them on the Bible; they measured religious belief with items covering a wide variety of doctrines, such as efficacy of prayer, afterlife, nearness of God, divinity of Jesus, and the importance of church. Among the third of the subjects highest on religious information, there was a significant negative correlation between belief and information. Among the third lowest on religious information, there was a significant positive correlation between belief and Bible information.

   Godin (1962, 1964) has also offered a noteworthy argument for multidimensionality, especially in a compelling essay (1964) on the variety of psychological "meanings" which might be inferred from the most commonly used index, that of church affiliation.

Factor analysis

The question of the unidimensionality of religion invites, and has received, factor-analytic study. Such studies can be divided into two types which may be characterized, somewhat crudely but not inaccurately, as those which view religion from the "outside" and those which view religion from the "inside."

   The former, which tend to be earlier, are characterized by the following conditions: (1) The instruments contain relatively few religious items, among other items assessing social attitudes which produce contrasting factors and which tend to make the religious items seem relatively clustered. (2) The items have most typically measured attitudes toward the church, including reports of church attendance, or consent to elementary conventional theistic or christocentric statements. These tend to be terms typically used by the culture in general and by nonreligious persons (and psychologists?) to characterize religion. The creedal statements, in fact, are commonly stated in crude and simplistic terms which a theologically sophisticated and committed person might have trouble interpreting unambiguously or assenting to. (3) Samples have been representative of the culture in general, heterogeneous with respect to religious commitments or affiliations, if any. (4) Furthermore, and of special relevance to the typical finding of these studies, the samples have generally been late adolescents, for whom issues of autonomy versus institutional loyalty and conventional orthodoxy would seem to be especially keen.

Viewing religion from the "outside," such studies have typically produced a single, general proreligious factor which seems best interpreted as representing favorableness of *attitudes toward religious institutions,* forms, personnel, and official doctrine. This may be taken as a fair indication of how the culture at large defines religion. (Something like this must be the criterion by which *Time* magazine assigns some news to its "Religion" department. It has been, until recently, the criterion by which laws—those dealing, for example, with conscientious objection to military service, with taxation, and with constitutional religious freedom—have regarded religion.) The dominant defining items are institutional affiliation and "belief in God."

By contrast, those studies which have viewed religion from the "inside"—with more sophisticated samples and items and by analyzing religion items alone—have, understandably, tended to produce multiple factors. These researchers (especially Armatas, 1962; Ashbrook, 1966; Broen, 1957; King, 1967; Shand, 1953) have gone to considerable effort to collect systematically a heterogeneous pool of sophisticated items from religiously committed persons. They have also deliberately limited their sample to religious persons by using clergymen (Shand); laymen nominated by clergymen (Ashbrook, Broen); persons identified as actively involved and committed in church activities (Allen and Hites); persons scoring high on the Thurstone scale and also rating themselves as religious and rating religion as important to them (Allen and Spilka); or, simply, the relevant and (from this point of view) welcome self-selection (48 percent) of church members who comply with a pastor-signed request to complete the questionnaire (King). Probably the work which has most systematically made an effort to use sophisticated items and sophisticated samples has been that directed by Bernard Spilka at the University of Denver.

This restriction of subjects to those actively involved and committed in church activities has probably had two effects. Statistically, absence of variability in church activity precludes this from emerging as a factor. More important, however, is the apparent likelihood that active and committed persons are likely to make more subtle distinctions, especially if the investigator provides items which permit such finer distinctions.

Two important studies (Cline and Richards, 1965; Keene, 1967b) have been "inside" with respect to using a broad range of sophisticated items, but have used a more heterogeneous, cross-section sample. They have consequently each found a massive general religious factor (defined, especially in the case of the former, by church attendance), with a series of much smaller but interpretable factors trailing off. When Keene (1967a) analyzed only those data deriving from members of a sect (the Baha'is) attracting highly committed, mostly first-generation members, he found five nearly equally weighted factors quite different from those found in the general sample (Keene, 1967b). They resemble in some respects the categories suggested by Glock (see Table 1).

Cline and Richards' (1965) study is especially important for two reasons: (1) they used a random sample of a city population, not just college students, though the city happened to be Salt Lake City, comprised largely of Mormons; (2) they used three very different types of data: the conventional questionnaire, judges' ratings of responses to projective materials, and judges' ratings of a great many variables emerging from interview transcripts. A massive general religious factor emerged, loaded most heavily by church attendance, with variables represented from all three types of data.

They found that all religious belief and activity items loaded on this first general religious factor more exclusively for females than for males. For males, the first factor was somewhat more exclusively an "activity" factor, with belief items producing another factor.

Keene (1967b) used a large sample (681) divided about equally among Jews, Protestants, Catholics, nonaffiliateds, and Baha'is. He does not say what, if any, criteria were used with respect to degree of commitment to the respective traditions. His massive first factor was loaded with highly diverse items: committed-like items ("motivating your daily activities with religious feelings and ideas," "feeling committed to your religion"), institutionally loyal behavior (contributing funds, attending services), extrinsic-like items ("finding relief from physical pains or ailments through the support of religious faith, conviction, or experience"), mystical, and moralistic. (See the section following this one for discussion of the distinction between committed, or intrinsic, and consensual, or extrinsic, dimensions.)

His second factor suggests a conservative- (or fundamentalistic- or orthodox-) versus-liberal belief factor. On this and the first factor, factor scores showed Baha'is, Catholics, Protestants, Jews, and nonaffiliateds scoring in that order, as would be expected for both general religiosity and orthodoxy of belief. This factor is defined by flat affirmation of conventional orthodox beliefs (immortality, soul, existence of God). The third factor is something of an artifact, loaded with only two items almost identically worded, "questioning the validity of . . . religion." The fourth factor suggests loyalty to institutional forms of religion, attributing primary importance to doctrine, creed, ceremony, ritual, and remaining in the same religion as parents. Catholics, Jews, Baha'is, Protestants, and nonaffiliateds scored on this factor in that order.

Among studies "inside" with respect to both items and samples, King (1967) has provided the most thorough mapping yet of religious space. He developed a pool of 121 items from a search of previous studies, submitted these to a large sample of Southern Methodists, and performed both factor analysis and cluster analysis. He found eleven meaningful factors. The first three (creedal assent and personal commitment, participation in congregational activities, and personal religious experience) correspond remarkably closely to the first three of Glock's proposed dimensions (Table 1). Most others also correspond to distinct categories which have been identified in previous theoretical-empirical work: for example, personal ties in the congregation (Lenski's "communal involvement"), openness to religious growth, dogmatism, extrinsicness, financial behavior and attitudes, and a final factor that King proposes as indicating the salience or importance of religion. (King also includes a large bibliography on the question of definition and measurement.)

Ashbrook worked not just "inside" religion, but "inside" the factor of institutional affiliation. His items all concerned church membership and church activities. But his results demonstrated that, given suitably differentiating items, active church members do distinguish many different and meaningful factors in their activity. Important evidence that the many factors are meaningful is the pattern of correlation Ashbrook found between these factors and independent indices of the organizational effectiveness of the church.

Gray (1964) also developed more refined distinctions among attitudes toward the church and devised a 54-item scale measuring a conception of the church (combining traditional christocentric statements of its constituency with activistic, nonmoralistic views of its role in culture) derived from certain theological formulations, and apparently distinguishable statistically (though he did not factor-analyze) from similar pro-church attitudes only subtly different conceptually.

Monaghan (1967) factor-analyzed a Q-sort of 56 items reporting attitudes toward the church and one's participation in it, finding three clear factors he called "authority-seeker," "comfort-seeker," and "social participator." Both his items and sample were "inside." He derived his items from interviews with church members, and used as his sample the members of a single fundamentalist church.

Other "inside" studies suggest other specific, interpretable factors. Broen found two factors. One of these, called "nearness of God," represented the immanence, accessibility, and mercy of God, contrasted with His remoteness or judgment. The second factor correlated +.32 with the first and was described as "fundamentalism-humanitarianism." It contrasted a view of man as essentially sinful along with a view of a punishing God versus a view of man as potentially good and able, "thus having little need for much outside intervention in the form of some Deity."

Shand found four clear factors, two of which he labeled fundamentalistic and two of which emphasize broad interpersonal values such as brotherliness and truth. Of the two fundamentalistic factors, the first was labeled "righteous-formalistic fundamentalist," defining religion in terms of conversion, scriptures, and institutionally based forms, such as creeds and rituals. Shand labeled the second factor "practical fundamentalist," defining it in terms of well-defined behavioral, moralistic, and trait characteristics. The other two factors both defined religion in terms of broadly personal and ethical characteristics of brotherliness, truth, and honesty, and in terms of a belief in God. These two factors differed in presence or absence of a belief in Christ.

Both Broen and Shand found, as did Keene, that factor scores were correlated with denominational membership, in ways predictable from an understanding of the official doctrines and general reputations of different denominations. Broen's nearness-of-God factor was correlated with the liberalism factor. Something of the same personalism and immanence is implied in Shand's liberal factors. Perhaps they do not emerge more clearly for Shand because his sample included only clergymen (who might show little variance on an institutionalism-versus-personal difference) and no females (who loaded heavily on Broen's first personalistic factor). Allen and Hites (1961) found a dozen factors, representing different topics and different arenas of religious activity (for example, relation with God, church activity, family religious life).

Factors which have emerged prominently in several of these studies (Broen, 1957; Keene, 1967a, 1967b; Shand, 1953) seem to represent a distinction within

American religious groups between what are most often called liberalism and conservatism. Perhaps this can be attributed to the same characteristics of sample and
of items—one step removed—as have been invoked above to explain the emergence
of a single, institution-oriented religion factor among the earlier studies. Just as
using a broad cultural sample produces a principal factor representing the broad
cultural categories, so does using a diverse Protestant sample produce principal factors which have primarily characterized American Protestant history and ideology.
If a study were to use a more homogeneous sample within one of the Protestant
traditions and use items more sophisticatedly representative of it, still more subtle
factors would be likely to emerge. This is suggested by the studies which have used
more homogeneous samples (Allen and Hites, 1961; Keene, 1967a; King, 1967) and
perhaps by the small factors found by Cline and Richards, working with a predominantly Mormon sample.

However, the conservative-liberal distinction is a real difference, significant both
psychologically and theologically. It has more than an arbitrary or accidental relation
to denominational membership. It presumably represents the consequence of successful instruction and socialization by the denominational institution and, to a lesser
extent, some degree of selection by individuals of institutions which are congenial
with their religious orientation. The difference might be characterized in gross
psychological terms as a difference between "superego" and "ego" types of religion.
(The personality differences implied by such a characterization require discussion
elsewhere.) The "conservative" religion tends to represent a restriction of spontaneous personal expression and a reliance on authority and on prescribed procedures
and rules in personal conduct. Involved are literalism of scripture, pietism, moralism, legalism, and ritualism. The conservative's emphasis on conversion (see Shand's
first two factors) implies a greater concern with guilt. Shand's first two factors distinguish between the focus of this authority and prescription on institutional forms
and the focus on moralistic behavior. The more liberal or "ego" emphasis is on the
support of persons and of broad personal and interpersonal values. The distinction
has clear parallels, or perhaps better, roots, in various types of theological thinking.
On the one hand is emphasis on the transcendance, aloofness, majesty, and judgment
of God; on objective, institutionally controlled means of sustaining the relations between God and man; and on the need to remedy man's sinfulness, by careful obedience and self-surveillance and by sacramental or other means of grace. On the other
hand, there is an emphasis on the immanence of God and on his liberating grace.

Correlation among common measures

The question of the homogeneity of religion as a discrete variable may also be addressed by studies reporting correlation among specific commonly used indices.
We shall cite those which have used large and representative samples and/or have
used the most common indices and/or have been most influential and most cited.

Lenski (1961) based his study on extended interviews with 656 persons selected
as a probability sample representative of the Detroit area. He generated four measures from his own conceptual distinctions by distinguishing between commitment
to a socioreligious group and commitment to a "type of religious orientation," and
then making a distinction within each of these categories. Commitment to a religious
group might be called "communal"; this was measured by the proportion of relatives

and friends belonging to the same religious group—Catholic, Protestant, or Jewish. Or it might be "associational"; this was measured by frequency of attendance at worship and other church activities.   Lenski selected two "religious orientations." One of these was "doctrinal orthodoxy," measured by a six-item questionnaire asking about beliefs in God, life after death, divinity of Christ, etc.   The other was "devotionalism," measured by two items reporting frequency of prayer.

Lenski found virtually zero correlation between his "communal" and "associational" measures, within separate faith groups as well as in the total sample. He found doctrinal orthodoxy and devotionalism correlated only slightly (equivalent to a Pearson r of .23).   In a personal communication, Lenski has kindly provided correlations between church attendance and his measures of orthodoxy and devotionalism.   These are equivalent to Pearson r's of about .30 and .40, respectively, for his total sample.

Lenski's findings have been often cited (Allen and Spilka, 1967; Allport, 1966; Cline and Richards, 1965; Douglas, 1963; Glock, 1962) as evidence for the multidimensionality of religiosity, even within the relatively simple and cohesive realm of institutionally oriented activity.   But a few reservations should be entered here. For one thing, as noted above but not reported in Lenski's book, church attendance is significantly correlated with both orthodoxy and devotionalism.   For another thing, Lenski worked only with dichotomization of his variables and tended to dichotomize at strict cutting points.   This procedure obscures much possible variability that would be relevant to the question of correlation among indices.   Lenski's study is notable, however, for having a cross-faith sample, breaking beyond the single-faith restriction of most samples.

Fukuyama (1960, 1961) attempted to provide operational measures for the first four of Glock's categories (see Table 1), using a sample of 4000 members of 12 Congregational churches in seven cities.   Belief was assessed by agreement with three dogmatic statements on life after death, Jesus Christ, and the Bible.   Practice was assessed by frequency of attendance, regularity of giving, and participation and leadership in church organizations.   "Feeling" was assessed by items reporting devotional practice, faith in the power of prayer, and belief in the necessity of conversion.   Knowledge was measured by three questions concerning the Bible.   Fukuyama renamed these categories as creedal, cultic, devotional, and cognitive orientations.   Though his measures do not follow Glock's categories closely, they do represent an array in one study with a large sample of several frequently used measures. Fukuyama trichotomized his distributions.   He found a substantial contingency coefficient of .47 between his belief and "feeling" indices—not too surprising in view of the fact that two of his "feeling" measures were essentially statements of belief (in prayer and in the importance of conversion).   Otherwise, he found only low positive contingency coefficients among his various indices, ranging between .12 and .17, significantly different from zero for his large sample.

In an analysis that seems illuminating for the question of multidimensionality, Fukuyama trichotomized his distribution according to whether subjects tended to be high on none, one, or more than one of his four indices.   He apparently found that this provided a single meaningful scale, showing a linear correlation with most of his other variables.   The more dimensions on which a person scored high, the more likely that person was to be female, older, divorced or widowed, a college graduate, of higher socioeconomic status, and a nonurban resident. Since the intercorrelations among the indices were almost all low, and since this pattern of correlation with social variables is unlike the correlations of any single index, we may infer that there is a kind of interchangeability represented here, that persons scoring high on any two or more of these indices (and they apparently differ as to which two) have something in common, which might be construed as a general religiousness factor.

Salisbury (1962) also undertook to check the relation among the categories suggested by Glock, using a sample of about 2000 Protestant students from Northern and Southern schools. Belief was assessed by separating the extremes who assented to (15 percent) or dissented from (19 percent) all four orthodox statements derived from Allport, Gillespie, and Young (1948). This measure was significantly related with reported church attendance and with a report of an emotional religious awakening or crisis experience; Salisbury reported no measure corresponding to knowledge.

Faulkner and DeJong (1966) devised a four- or five-item Guttman scale for each of Glock's categories, with a sample of introductory sociology students, and found the scales substantially intercorrelated (*r*'s ranging between .36 and .58). Because their subjects and items were probably the least sophisticated religiously of these several attempts to measure Glock's dimensions, it is predictable from the previous discussion of "outside" and "inside" studies that they would find the highest intercorrelations.

Allen (1965) attempted to code interviews for three of Glock's categories, renamed "creedal, communal, experiential." He abandoned the effort when he failed to establish interjudge reliability and when other findings in his data proved highly significant. But he reported his coding categories in an appendix.

Though he did not proceed to factor analysis, Welford (1957) reported that church attendance was the one variable most highly correlated with other measures of religion, most of them the kind here being reviewed. [This apparently is the study mentioned by Argyle (1958, p. 13) to justify, in his survey, the interchangeable use of various indices.] This was also true in Allen's data (1965, Table 3). It is perhaps of interest that Barron (1963), in developing the ego-strength scale for the MMPI, scored church attendance positively, but five other religious items negatively, including frequent prayer and suggestions of biblical literalism. He did not report intercorrelations between these items, but the scale as a whole has impressive validity correlations.

Practical, and sometimes polemic, concerns have generated some research intended to demonstrate that institutional affiliation is or is not related to institutionally sanctioned beliefs or behavior. The classically quoted studies were done by Hartshorne and his associates (for example, Hartshorne and May, 1928). They found a pattern of slight or negligible correlation between attendance at church or church school and behavior in a wide variety of tasks intended to measure character and ethical behavior. Ross (1950), in a survey of young men, expressed dismay at values, attitudes, and practices held by religious adherents inconsistent with professed beliefs. Goldsen *et al.* (1960, p. 228) found no relation between religiousness and confession of cheating on an examination.

In a commonly cited study, Fichter (1951), looking impressionistically at group effects rather than individual results, concluded that there is a general correspondence between religious practice of parishioners and their adherence to doctrinal and ethical positions. He proposed the possibility of a single quantitative scale (1953) that would range from the "nuclear" through the "modal" and "marginal" to the "dormant" Catholic, with positions defined both by practice and by belief.

Construction of scales

The ease with which scales can be constructed of seemingly heterogeneous items itself provides some evidence for unidimensionality. In constructing a Thurstone scale on "favorable attitude toward organized religion," Holtzman and Young (1966) found judges (sophomore introductory psychology students) able reliably to place items referring to theistic belief, devotional practice, conventional views of immortality, and general proreligious attitudes, as well as items referring to the church as an institution. In use, the scale proved to be very highly correlated with church attendance (Young, Dustin, and Holtzman, 1966).

Goldsen *et al.* (1960) found it possible to derive a Guttman scale, implying a single factor, from four items given to a large sample of students at eleven universities. The four items, in decreasing order of assent, were:

> Do you, personally, feel you need to believe in some sort of religious faith or philosophy?
>
> I believe in a divine God, creator of the universe, who knows my innermost thoughts and feelings, and to whom one day I shall be accountable.
>
> [My] church or . . . religion . . . has its own personality, something over and above the individual members in it.
>
> Religious beliefs or activities [comprise one of] three things or activities in your life . . . you expect to give you the most satisfaction.

The only item these authors report as falling outside the pattern is, oddly enough, reported frequency of attendance at religious services. However, though specific information is not given about the degree of correlation between this and the other items across all subjects, data presented for percentages at each of the schools suggest a significant correlation, across schools, between attendance and the other items. Calculation, for example, with the given data, yields a Spearman rho of .77 between attendance and the first item. These authors report (1960, pp. 162, 226) close correlation between this religiousness scale and the scale of "religious belief" assessing attitudes toward prayer, God, church, clergy, faith, and salvation of the soul.

College students are, of course, a particularly unrepresentative sample with which to assess the relation of church attendance and other variables. This is indicated especially in a unique study by Bender (1958). He replicated questionnaire and other measures, including the Allport-Vernon-Lindzey, on a sample of men when they were college seniors and again 15 years after graduation. Church attendance was correlated highly significantly (.79) with the Allport-Vernon-Lindzey measure of religious interest at the 15-year follow-up, but not during college.

The two most commonly used scales—the Allport-Vernon-Lindzey and the Thurstone-Chave scales—seem to be highly representative of an institution-oriented religious factor. Thurstone and Chave (1929; Chave, 1939) present straightforward items assessing attitude toward church, attitude toward God, and attitude toward

Sunday observance. The Study of Values (Allport, Vernon, and Lindzey, 1960) segregates religion as one among six areas of social value. Though the manual's definition of the religious scale, following Spranger, is definitely noninstitutional and emphasizes personal, mystical attitudes, the actual items predominantly assess attitude toward the objective forms of religion. The majority of items assess the subject's preference for engaging in activity which is labeled religious. A minority of items assess preferences for more general concerns and activities, such as finding "meaning in life" or "introducing highest ethical principles." Perhaps these two types of items would separate into two subscales corresponding to Allport's own extrinsic-intrinsic distinction (see below).

Hunt (1968) has shown that the religion scale of the Study of Values is closely correlated with institutional loyalty, church attendance, orthodoxy on theology, and conventional acceptance of religion of parents, and not with items which might be regarded as tapping something more like the intrinsic, transcultural, noninstitutional, mystical kind of religion implied by the manual's quotation of Spranger. But he argues that the distinctions discovered by his factor analysis do not correspond with Allport's definitions of extrinsic-intrinsic. Brown (1964) found that the religious scale correlated .57 with a scale for "intrinsicness." But the extrinsic end of his scale is confounded with antireligious statements, attitudes which accounted for over one-third of his sample.

Professionalism and denominational differences

It is sometimes supposed (for example, by Argyle, 1958, p. 86) that professional religious activity may be taken as a kind of intense degree on a quantitative scale of religiosity. Certainly a general kind of allegiance to the institution—as is also measured by church attendance—may be one of the factors involved in such a vocational decision. But probably the vocational decision involves so many factors that it requires separate consideration (Menges and Dittes, 1965).

A special problem in studying the consequences or the effects of religion is to discern differential effects of different religious traditions. Relevant research arguing for important differences between denominations or between faith groups includes Argyle (1958), Broen (1957), Elkind (1964a, 1964b), Elkind and Elkind (1962), Goldsen et al. (1960), Lenski (1961), McLelland (1955), Poit (1962), Rokeach (1960), and Shand (1953). However, in most of these there is a serious question as to whether the differences are those which would be predicted from an understanding of the ideology, as distinguished from the social context, of the faith groups.

Consistency of relation with other variables

Another type of evidence on the unidimensionality of religion has to do with the consistency of the relationship found between one or another indicator of religion and other variables. Obviously, it is more efficient simply to keep this in mind as a question to be noted in studies to be reviewed subsequently than it is to consider them all here. But diverse relations within a single study may be of special interest. We will cite here three studies based on survey data with large samples.

Demerath (1965) surveyed previous research showing inconsistent findings as to the relation between religiosity and social class. He suggested that part of the diversity was due to varying indices of religiosity. His own study, based on survey data of about 9000 members of five Protestant denominations, showed similar inconsistent findings. Three of his measures of religiosity showed negative correlation with a standard index of social class based on income, education, and occupation. Two showed a positive correlation. And one—church attendance!—showed no relation, despite the substantial positive correlation Demerath has reported, in a personal communication, between attendance and other indices.

Lenski's (1961) four measures showed highly different patterns of correlation with his other variables of behavior and attitude. For example, economic attitudes and activities which Lenski regards as "the spirit of capitalism" were correlated positively with church attendance among Protestants but not among Roman Catholics, positively with level of devotional practice among both Protestants and Catholics, negatively with communal involvement among white Protestants and Catholics, with the suggestion of a negative relationship with doctrinal orthodoxy among both white Protestants and Catholics. The index of religiosity showing the most consistent strong relation with other variables was the familiar frequency of church attendance, in direct contrast to the data Demerath analyzed.

Fukuyama (1960, 1961) found that practice and knowledge were related positively to socioeconomic status and negatively with age, and that his other two indices showed significant relations in the opposite direction. Men were significantly higher than women on knowledge; women were higher on the other three dimensions.

Summary

Theoretical concerns and general sophisticated reflection (either theological or psychological) seem to offer compelling arguments for multidimensionality. This is clearly the bias of most researchers, including the present writer. Religion seems far too complex an arena of human behavior—as diverse and heterogeneous as human behavior itself—not to include many different and unrelated types of variables. Yet the net impact of much empirical work seems to suggest that, over fairly heterogeneous samples and using a variety of types of items, persons in a general population do tend to identify a common factor of religion or religiousness or religiosity.

Probably both interpretations are right. The common factor as discerned in factor-analytic studies should perhaps be construed simply as "religion as seen by the general population." It is based primarily on the affiliation with a highly visible institution and with a general understanding of the norms of that institution. The social scientist is still free and perhaps ought to be encouraged to discern more analytic, genotypical, discrete variables which may elude the general population. The distinctions developed by Glock and the factors discovered by King seem most worthy of further attention.

RELIGION AS EXPLICIT AND DIFFERENTIATED VERSUS SUBJECTIVE AND DIFFUSED

One particular dilemma of definition and measurement—the greatest dilemma for the social psychology of religion—is a distinction which has been persistently noted at least since the time when the Old Testament prophets distinguished between solemn assemblies and righteousness (Amos 5:21–24), between sacrifices and steadfast love, between burnt offerings and knowledge of God (Hosea 6:6).

On the one hand, there is "religion" in relatively explicit form, tending to be public, social, overt, manifest, institutionalized, formalized, and differentiated. This is "religion" as it is readily and conveniently identified within the culture, tending to be segregated into a particular behavior, formal belief, or institutional connection which is identified by the culture as exclusively religious and as distinguished from "nonreligious" activity. Such religion provides a social psychologist with reasonably reliable, objective, and familiar indices. Perhaps all the measurements discussed in the preceding section fall into this category.

On the other hand, there is "religion" in more subjective form, more a matter of personal attitudes, orientation, set, frame of reference, response expectancy, values and loyalties and commitments, fundamental motivations or standards—the "spiritual" dimension of all life. "Religion is one's system of devotions, reverences, allegiances, and practices—whether avowed or implicit, conscious or unconscious" (Appel, 1959, p. 1777). This is "religion" as it is more commonly regarded by religious spokesmen. It is also the "religion" implied by most comprehensive psychological theorists (for example, Freud). This "religion" may be identified within or without more explicit and institutionalized "religion" of the kind discussed above. "Few men can avoid the problem of struggling with questions of 'salvation' (how can man be saved from his most difficult problems?), or the nature of reality, of evil (why do men suffer?), and the like" (Yinger, 1957, p. 15). For reasons which will be made clearer later, this chapter will adopt the terms suggested by Allen and Spilka (1967; Allen, 1965) to designate this distinction: *consensual* religion versus *committed* religion. Terms suggested by others have included "primary" versus "secondary" (Clark, 1958), and "moral commitment" versus "calculative involvement" (adapted by Ashbrook, 1966, from Etzioni, 1961). Terms given common currency by Allport—"extrinsic" and "intrinsic"—will be discussed later.

Like the broad concept "religion" itself, many of the frequently studied phenomena and many of the most used categories themselves may be subject to the same distinction between the "consensual" and the "committed." For example, "conversion" may represent primarily a change of institutional allegiance or may take place, even if highly "emotional," within certain generally prescribed forms which an institution or culture makes normative; or conversion may refer to a much more subjective and private change of orientation and values. Similarly, "belief" may refer to assent to publicly formalized doctrines, or it may refer to much less articulate, personally held attitudes and expectations. The term "belief in God" may refer to formally held doctrines, or it may refer to a more generalized, diffused expectation or set as to whether the fundamental environment is basically hostile or benign. The term "faith" may refer to no more than the major religious groups—one might speak of an "interfaith sample" of Christians and Jews—or it may refer to the content of formal doctrines. On the other hand, "faith" may imply an attitude of trust without particular cognitive content or institutional implications, and pervading many roles and situations, not just those places or postures conventionally regarded as religious. Most of the categories in Glock's array (Table 1) might apply either to consensual or to committed forms.

The distinction here is sometimes considered a difference between religion and ethics or morals. For example, Hartshorne and May's (1928) classic study demonstrated only a slight relation between institutional religious activity (especially attendance at religious education) and varied indices of values and moral behavior. The most recent finding along these lines is reported by Black and London (1966), who found that, for a large student sample of Protestants, Catholics, and Jews, church attendance, prayer, respect for clergy, and creedal orthodoxy occupied a distinct "religious" factor (along with obedience to parents and laws, and patriotism) independent of judgments on a large array of moral decisions (except for disapproval of sexual activity, which was loaded moderately on the religion factor.)

But it should be noted that, within the area of ethics itself, a comparable distinction is found in what may be described as debate over whether the basis for ethical behavior lies in formal prescriptive explicit principles or in a kind of properly "tuned" existential responsiveness (see Gustafson, 1965, for a survey).

Most well-known typologies appear to be at least partially congruent with this distinction, including Fromm's (1950) distinction between authoritarian and humanitarian religion, and even James's (1902) distinction between the extroverted "healthy-minded" and more introspective "sick-souled," though James's preoccupation with individual religious experience made him relatively unconcerned with any form of institutional religion. Even the much overused church-sect distinction (see, for example, Demerath, 1965) has, among the many dimensions it embraces, something of the distinction here referred to.

Perhaps the most notable theological attempt to discern the relationship between the inner spiritual life and the more visible and public was made by Jonathan Edwards (1959; written 1746). Mistrustful of his contemporaries' reliance on dramatic conversion experiences (for which, ironically, his own preaching was so frequently responsible) as evidence of God's grace and the criterion for a true religious life, Edwards struggled to evolve twelve calmer and more objective "signs" or criteria.

The argument is sometimes inaccurately advanced—as a resistance to psychological investigation of religion at all—that scientific investigation must be restricted to the more formal and explicit, and that the spiritual dimensions are inaccessible to objective investigation. It is, of course, true that what has here been called the subjective is more difficult to assess reliably, but in principle is as accessible as any psychological phenomenon. Religion, even as spiritual life, remains a human phenomenon. There may be metaphysical or other philosophical and theological questions relevant to religious behavior or religious belief, but, as discussed earlier, the impossibility of psychology's answering these questions does not preclude the effort to address psychological questions.

Are the two types correlated?

Most persons who have made such a distinction have intended to imply by it the hypothesis that the two types are not closely correlated; sometimes there is the prophetic insistence that they are negatively correlated. However, the social scientist—perhaps like institutional church leaders—however much he may in principle concede the distinction and lack of correlation, may often act as though the distinction did not exist or as though the two types were closely correlated. The explicit, consensual religion is far more accessible and manageable. Because of the difficulty of developing well-defined concepts and reliable indices of the more subjective dimensions of religion, the social psychologist is strongly tempted to use an instance of the explicit or consensual as an index for the subjective or committed.

However, the validity of such an assumption is made dubious by frequent analysis, much of it by religious leaders themselves, which makes it appear that the relation between these two aspects of religion—the more explicit and formal, and the more subjective and pervasive—may range widely from a positive to a negative correlation.   The sequence appears to be common in which (1) particular personal orientations or attitudes or behavioral sets tend to develop and exist independently of any institution; (2) the patterns become formalized and institutionalized; (3) the institutions and structures tend to persist autonomously of the founding ideology and to promote attitudes and behaviors varying from, or even contradictory to, the founding theology.

It is the last development, when it allegedly occurs, producing an inverse correlation between the two types, that particularly prompts public attention to their distinction.   This was the occasion for the Old Testament prophets, quoted above, and—to span many eras of other prophets and reformers—for the distinction Kierkegaard proposed between "official Christianity" and "the radical Christian."

Within religious thinking in this generation, there happens to be particularly vigorous analysis asserting the negative correlation.   This may make the distinction seem particularly important in this period of the history of religion and make it particularly implausible for the social psychologist studying contemporary phenomena to use the readily measurable explicit and consensual as an index for the more subjective and committed.   Three examples may be cited.   (1) Among Roman Catholics, the radical institutional reforms occasioned by the second Ecumenical Council apparently represent long-smoldering criticism of the negative correlation.   (2) Among the three most noted Protestant European theologians, Bultmann, Brunner, and Barth (to which might be added Bonhoeffer), even the most conservative, Karl Barth (1956, pp. 280–361), has written of "the revelation of God as the abolition of religion." The others have been much more vigorous in their pleas for rescuing Christianity from the forms of religion.   (3) The most notable American Protestant theologian, Paul Tillich (1963), has been especially noted for his refusal to identify the Christian faith with the existing Christian church.   For example, he identified a "latent" church which may, on occasion, be expressing the purposes of God more readily through various "secular" movements than through the structural church.   Much of this discussion is reviewed by Daniel Jenkins in *Beyond Religion: The Truth and Error in "Religionless Christianity"* (1962), and has been reflected and encouraged by the writings of two American sociologists, Peter Berger (1961, 1967) and Gibson Winter (1961). The attack on conventions and forms of religion have come to popular attention in such phrases as *Honest to God* (Robinson, 1963), *Radical Theology and the Death of God* (Altizer and Hamilton, 1966), and *The Secular City* (Cox, 1965).   Shiner (1967) discusses systematically the dilemmas in definition produced by contemporary "secular" theology which embraces as "Christian" attitudes and behavior which social scientists may still be scoring as nonreligious or anti-religious and which celebrates as religious advance the decline of institutionally based behaviors and attitudes which have been central in empirical definitions of religion.   The problem may be especially acute when subjects are students who are particularly exposed to such contemporary secular theology and who may define their own religiousness in its terms.

Empirical studies, to be discussed shortly, have also addressed the question of correlation between the two types.   Scalers have tended to start with the supposition that they were dealing with two ends of a single dimension, and have been led by their data toward regarding the two categories as independent.

Distinction provoked by correlation with prejudice

Among social scientists, in recent years, the distinction between the explicit and the subjective has been most commonly recognized in connection with the interpretation of one persistent empirical finding. This is the correlation, discussed in more detail later in this chapter, between ethnocentrism and "religion." This empirical finding, which came to prominence in reports of *The Authoritarian Personality* (Adorno *et al.*, 1950), has produced some difficulty of interpretation for two reasons: (1) ethno-centrism is a negative social value and religion is commonly accepted as a positive value, and their positive correlation creates some "dissonance"; (2) furthermore, ethnocentrism contradicts the professed ideology of established religions.

In the report of *The Authoritarian Personality*, Sanford (pp. 215–221) discovered that, on an open-ended questionnaire item, "How important in your opinion are religion and the church?" some subjects distinguished, in their answers, between the church and "real" religion. Furthermore, he found that anti-Semitism scores were correlated with the amount of importance attached to the church, but not with the amount of importance attached to religion.

In analyzing interview data in the same publication, Adorno (pp. 728–743) formulated these observations: there is frequently a negative correlation between "conventional religious rigidity" and "personally experienced belief"; the prevailing pattern is for "the dissolution of positive religion" and "the transformation of religion into an agency of social conformity" (p. 730); and prejudice tends to be associated with those adhering to the social forms of religion, but not with those who "take religion seriously in a more internalized sense." Pointing to the "subordination of religion to extrinsic aims," Adorno suggested that prejudiced persons "seem to make use of religious ideas in order to gain some immediate practical advantage or to aid in the manipulation of other people" (p. 733).

The researchers of *The Authoritarian Personality* (specifically, Frenkel-Brunswik and Sanford) first reported this distinction between the "deeper" religion of the less prejudiced and the "utilitarian" religion of the anti-Semites in 1946 in a volume (Simmel, 1946) to which Allport wrote an interested preface.

Reflecting on these and other studies (for example, Allport and Kramer, 1946), Allport (1950) claimed that "the religious sentiment in these cases [of prejudiced persons] is blindly institutional, exclusionist, and related to self-centered values. Among people with reflective and highly differentiated sentiments, race prejudice is rarely found" (p. 59). Allport later elaborated this difference and introduced the terms "interiorized" and "institutionalized" (1954, p. 453), and still later reemployed the terms suggested by Adorno, "extrinsic" and "intrinsic" religion (Allport, 1959, 1963, 1966; Allport and Ross, 1967), with increasingly specific definitions and with some hints (reminiscent of William James's famous distinction between the sick-souled and healthy-minded) that intrinsicness and extrinsicness may be regarded as more general personality types. Hunt (1968) concluded that extrinsicness-intrinsicness is a personality variable.

At about the same time as the other writers, Bettelheim and Janowitz (1949), dealing with the same problem, made a similar distinction. They distinguished internal and external control of personality as the distinction applied both to social attitudes and to religion. They pointed out that a person whose religion was oriented primarily to the institution was likely to feel subject to external threats and demands in all areas. Correspondingly, they found that persons who had "internalized" religious teachings displayed an inner control and stability which also resulted in more tolerance.

Further refinement and distinction?

Considerable consensus, then, exists as to the distinction between the religious orientation which is focused on the more explicit, the more formalized, the more institutionalized, and the more differentiated, and the religious orientation which consists of a more internalized set of dominant attitudes which may affect behavior and attitudes in diffuse roles and activities, not just those connected with designated "religious" forms. But the next question is whether or not the distinction is to be regarded as identifying meaningful research categories or general clusters of categories within which important distinctions must yet be made. So long as effort has been directed primarily toward asserting the major distinction, relatively little attention has been given to distinctions or other refinements within each category. It is now possible, however, especially in empirical work to be described shortly, to begin to see such finer distinctions emerging.

For example, theoretical writings and scaling attempts appear to suggest at least three separate dimensions within the more explicit and differentiated dimension: (1) adherence to conventional belief or other norms of an institution or tradition; (2) favorable evaluation of the institution; and (3) the element of "self-serving" motivation behind such adherence, introduced by Adorno and by Allport partly as value judgment and partly as hypothesis.

Labels for the distinction

For the more general categories, this chapter will use the pair of terms originally introduced by Allen and Spilka (1967; Allen, 1965): consensual religion and committed religion. The connotations of these terms fit the various implicit and explicit definitions which have been made. More important, Allen and Spilka have provided clear and reliably scorable definitions and have demonstrated most unequivocally the utility of their variables in clarifying the relation of religion and prejudice.

The terms most commonly used to refer to this distinction have been the pair that Allport settled on: "intrinsic" and "extrinsic." But Allport has made it increasingly clear (Allport and Ross, 1967), in his conceptual definition of "extrinsic" and in the items he proposed to measure it with, that he wishes to restrict this term to the element of utilitarianism, which is what is most connoted by the term itself, as in Adorno's phrase "the subordination of religion to extrinsic aims." (As Allport would now have it, the extrinsically religious person "uses" his religion and the intrinsically religious person "lives" it.) Such refinement and differentiation is welcome progress, and it may be well to restrict the term "extrinsic" to this more limited factor of utilitarianism. Moreover, Allport clearly conceptualized his distinction as contrasting ends of the same dimension, whereas the more general distinction is perhaps best left open as regards the nature of the relations between the two categories.

Scaling efforts

Scaling efforts have begun to establish this distinction between the "consensual" and the "committed." Most of them have been generated by the effort to tease out the relation of religious variables with prejudice; hence, this section and that below on social attitudes necessarily overlap.

Jeeves (1957) developed two scales which measured attitudes toward the religious institution and toward "individualism." (Typical items for the two scales: "For the vast majority of people, in order to live a truly religious life, the church or some such other organized religious body is an essential," and "A man ought to be guided by what his own experience tells him is right rather than by what any institution, such as the church, tells him to do.") Jeeves's report implies that the negative correlation between institutional and individual preference was far from perfect; at least he calls attention to a substantial group who assent to both types of items. This is also the finding of Allport and Ross (1967), who labeled this group the "indiscriminately proreligious." It implies a general religious factor corresponding to that in factor analyses discussed above, as does the fact that Feagin (1964), in a study discussed below, found his intrinsic and extrinsic scales both correlated highly with his total set of items. (The relation with prejudice in Jeeves's data is apparently a negative correlation with the individualism scale rather than a positive correlation with institutionalism—the reverse of the situation reported by Sanford and Adorno.) Using a selection of Jeeves's items, Brown (1964) found a correlation between institutionalism and individualism of only −.16. Using Brown's items, Allen (1965) found that the two scales correlated −.17 (this is significant for his sample).

Wilson (1960) developed a 15-item extrinsic-religious-values scale. Some of the items reflect evaluation of the institution, presumably corresponding to Jeeves's institutionalism scale. (Typical item: "Some people say that they can be genuinely religious without being a member of any church.") Other items reflect Allport's allegation of a utilitarian, "self-seeking" orientation, extrinsicness as here more strictly defined (for example, "Prayer is, above all else, a means of obtaining needed benefits, protection, and safety in a dangerous world"). Wilson's report implies a close correlation of the two types of items in that he reports them as a single homogeneous reliable scale, rather than as two scales. However, not much can be made of this correlation except the observation that all the items apparently reflect the same positive attitude toward the church. It is difficult to tell how much the scale may be regarded as assessing any peculiarly extrinsic or consensual religious orientation, as distinguished from a more general proreligious attitude. Wilson apparently intended originally to regard intrinsicness as represented by low scores on his scale, and therefore provided no intrinsic, proreligious items from which extrinsicness could be distinguished.

Workers at Harvard developed a new scale, adding "intrinsically" worded items to the type used by Wilson. These added items ask for reports of devotional practice and church attendance, as well as reflecting Allport's more narrow definition of intrinsicness (for example, "I try hard to carry my religion over into all my other dealings in life"). This scale was apparently intended originally to represent a single dimension, with "intrinsically" worded items simply scored in the opposite direction from the others. But the analysis suggests otherwise.

Feagin (1964) factor-analyzed 21 of these items as administered to 286 Southern Baptists. He found that the two sets of items formed two distinct factors. One factor was defined primarily by the purely intrinsic items plus reported frequency of church attendance and private devotion. Perhaps this should be regarded more as a general devoutness characteristic cutting across (as does Southern Baptist ideology) the institutional and the personal distinctions. As Feagin pointed out, there is supposedly a large element of social desirability in this factor. The other factor is a more clear-cut statement of the "utilitarian" function served by religion, extrinsicness as now more narrowly defined, represented by such an item as "The purpose of prayer is to secure a happy and peaceful life." The six items loading most heavily on this factor clearly express this utilitarian motive. These were the only six which Feagin kept as an extrinsic scale, which he then showed correlated with a measure of racial prejudice. (In Allport's sample, discussed below, these same items showed the highest item-to-total correlation.) Feagin also kept as an intrinsic scale only the six items loading most highly on the first factor.

Allport and Ross (1967), however, retained all of the pool of items developed at Harvard (except, unaccountably, for one which had loaded heavily on Feagin's extrinsic scale). They divided these, apparently on the basis of face validity, into two scales, apparently not otherwise tested as to their psychometric properties, and in some instances contradicting the relative loading on Feagin's two factors. The two scales had median item-to-total correlations of .39 and .44, respectively, and were correlated with each other .21.

Allen and Spilka (1967; Allen, 1965) conceptualized the difference between committed and consensual orientations as a difference of expression or style (Allen, 1965, p. 14):

> The "committed" orientation, on the one hand, reflects an emphasis on the abstract, relational qualities of religious belief which tend to be nonambiguous, well differentiated or multiplex, and diversity-tolerant. It would also involve a personal, devotional commitment to religious values which suffuse daily activities. The "consensual" orientation, on the other hand, reflects an emphasis on the concrete, literal qualities of religious belief which tend to be vague and global, nondifferentiated and bifurcated, relatively restrictive and diversity-intolerant. It would also involve a detached or neutralized, magical or possibly vestigial commitment to religious values.

They developed coding categories for applying this distinction to five characteristics of a person's religious thought: content, clarity, complexity, flexibility, and importance. These categories were applied by judges to tape-recorded interviews. Subjects had been selected as religious persons by a set of questionnaire items, and were interviewed for up to an hour according to a schedule of open-ended questions which gave them an opportunity to discuss various aspects of religion. High inter-judge reliability was achieved (Allen, 1965, p. 102). The complete coding categories are given in Allen and Spilka (1967). Allen's "committed" subjects attended church significantly more often than his "consensual" (as did Feagin's and Allport and Ross's "intrinsic" subjects), and they scored higher on self-ratings of religiosity and attitudes toward the church. (But it should be remembered that this is within a relatively narrow range among subjects already selected for their high scores on these scales.)

Brown (1964) found that he could sort replies to incomplete sentences (for example, "In my everyday life, religious beliefs . . .") more or less along what he termed an "extrinsic-intrinsic" dimension. But he found that he had to adopt two "extrinsic" categories, one reflecting the utilitarian or self-serving function of the beliefs, the other reflecting their "conventional acceptance," apparently a combination of the acceptance of institutional authority and a general kind of conventionalism. He found that replies so scaled were correlated slightly with Jeeves's institutionalism and individualism.

Apparently quite independently of these other empirical studies, Whitam (1962) devised separate scales for "externalization" (for example, "A person should stick to the church even though he doesn't believe in most of the things it stands for"), for conventional morality, and for "utilitarianism" (for example, "Religion helps a person to get ahead in the world"). Only the latter two were significantly correlated with his measure of prejudice, and that not highly: .24 and .23, respectively. Unfortunately, Whitam has not calculated correlations between his scales.

Both of these last scaling efforts suggest the distinction (p. 623) among three types of "consensual" religion: conventionality, favorable attitude toward institution, and utilitarian motivation (Allport's extrinsicness).

Vernon (1962) compared what he called direct and indirect measures of religiosity, which may be related to the distinction under discussion here. The "direct" questions asked for ratings of attitudes towards religion. The "indirect" index consisted of a tally of occasions on which the subject offered some form of religious identification (for example, "I am a Christian," "I am an immortal soul") when asked to give 20 answers to the question, "Who am I?" Vernon found no correlation between the public attitudes and the more private, spontaneous identifications.

In the very limited context of examining a minister's vocational decision, one element of the explicit-objective dimension has been developed by Kling (1959; Dittes, 1964). He found it possible to scale the degree to which a theological student describes his "call" in the conventional evangelistic categories of a direct, immediate communication by God (committed?), as compared with the description of the "call" as a decision-making process not unlike any other decision (consensual?).

Factor analyses

Three factor analyses, in addition to Feagin's, are relevant to the distinction here under discussion.

With a heterogeneous sample and with questionnaire, projective, and interview data, Cline and Richards (1965) produced two results which are relevant here. One is the appearance on the same factor of all three elements which have sometimes been distinguished, as above, within the consensual variable. The factor is heavily loaded with institutionally related activity, with general attitude toward the church and religion, and with judges' ratings (based on interview transcript) as to "degree to which he uses or exploits religion to his advantage (for business, social, status, or similar reasons)"—Allport's refined extrinsic variable.

Their data also decidedly support the distinction between consensual and committed. After the strong first factor, just described, a clear second factor emerged, based primarily on judges' ratings of the kind of person and values which could be inferred from the interview transcript. This factor, which Cline and Richards called the "compassionate Samaritan," represents religiously endorsed values of helpful and warm interpersonal relations. It is highly loaded by such variables as the judges' ratings on "genuine love, compassion, sympathy for others," "degree to which he lives up to teachings of his religion," "degree to which he lives a good, moral life," "good Samaritan, do-er who really helps others," humility, and the degree to which the rater felt he personally liked the subject. The factor has substantial negative loadings on ratings of being self-centered or a religious phony, the "degree to which he uses or exploits religion" (especially among men), and questionnaire data on conventionality of belief in God (among women). By their effective combination of questionnaire and interview data, including an almost unique effort at scaling committed religion, Cline and Richards have provided the best empirical confirmation to date of the independence of consensual and committed factors.

King (1967) found that extrinsic items of the kind developed by Feagin and others at Harvard (see above) produced a clear and distinct factor when administered among a large pool of items to a homogeneous sample.

The distinction is not confirmed, however, in a study by Keene (1967b). Though he did not choose items to be relevant to this distinction, many of them appear to be so. Some could be regarded as measuring committed religion ("motivating your daily activities with religious feelings and ideas"), and others as measuring the institutional-loyalty element of consensual religion ("attending religious services and meetings") or the self-seeking utilitarian motive ("finding relief from physical pain or illness through the support of religious faith, conviction, or experience"). He found all these types of items, and others, mixed on a single large first factor.

Conclusion

The extended discussion above has been with reference to the single greatest dilemma in the definition and measurement of religion. Theoretical considerations have been presented which make it seem quite plausible to argue that easily accessible objective indices of religion are distinguishable from and probably not correlated with more subjective personal orientations which are usually regarded by theologians and psychologists alike as of more substantial interest. Attempts at empirical confirmation have suggested some support for the distinction, but have foundered on the problem that none of these dimensions—any more than "religion" itself—has proved a unitary, identifiable variable, but only a general area in which variables may be discovered.

Apparently the measures most commonly used, frequency of church attendance and attitude toward the church, are related with this distinction curvilinearly, consistent with the curvilinear relation between church attendance and prejudice, to be discussed below. Among heterogeneous samples, distinguishing largely at low levels of attendance and attitude, institutionally oriented behavior and attitudes appear related with what has here been called consensual religion. However, among homogeneous samples of persons scoring high on these variables, the most extremely high scores appear to be associated with "committed" religion.

RELIGION AND SOCIAL ATTITUDES

Two types of problems have dominated research in the social psychology of religion in the last few decades. One of these is the relation between personality characteristics and religion. The other is the relation between conservative social attitudes and religion. Both came into clear focus with the publication of *The Authoritarian Personality* (Adorno *et al.*, 1950) and the two are still related, or confounded, in the same way that they were in that publication: "authoritarianism" may be taken either as an attitude or as a personality variable.

Much of the research has involved the slow and gradual refinement of distinctions, including some of the distinctions in the definition of religion previously discussed. Much of the incentive for these distinctions has apparently come from the dissonance produced by the persistent finding of a correlation between religion and ethnocentrism (or other undesirable social attitudes). One resolution of this dissonance has been to refine the definition of religion, as previously discussed, so that some form of religion is left untainted by ethnocentric correlation. Indeed, it does appear that the studies showing a relation with conservative ideology, with a few notable exceptions, have been concerned with "consensual" religion, measured usually by institutional affiliation or by agreement with statements of conservative religious ideology.

Another resolution has been to refine the understanding of conservative social ideology, as, for example, in the distinction between the content of an attitude and the manner in which it is held. Thus, for example, the authors of *The Authoritarian Personality* decided that prejudice was more correlated with "the way" religion was adhered to than with the nature of the religion itself. Developing this, Rokeach (1960) distinguished between a conservative social ideology and a dogmatism with which it (or a liberal ideology) may be held, and he found that religion tends to be correlated with the dogmatism. A third resolution, overlapping the second, has been the effort to discover personality characteristics which may mediate the correlation between religion and prejudice. (This resolution was also proposed in *The Authoritarian Personality*.) To find a personality characteristic that tends to be productive of or attracted to a religious position, and also to a conservative social position, is to remove some of the imputed responsibility of religion for producing the conservative ideology. But first we will discuss the research with attitudes.

CORRELATION OF CONSERVATIVE AND PRORELIGIOUS ATTITUDES

When Thurstone introduced the scaling method which bears his name (Thurstone and Chave, 1929), he illustrated the technique with a scale measuring attitude toward the church. He also guided the development of scales measuring attitude toward God and attitude toward Sunday observance (Chave, 1939).

When Thurstone introduced factor analysis in his American Psychological Association presidential address (Thurstone, 1934), his major illustration of a factor space and his only application to attitudes used the data of an unpublished study by Thelma Gwynn Thurstone, producing a prominent first factor defined at one end by these three religious attitude scales and at the other end by favorable attitudes toward evolution, birth control, and divorce. He pointed out: "In naming the common factor which is most prominent in these attitude scales, there may be some question as to whether it should be called conservatism or religion."

Following Thurstone's lead, the application of scaling methods and factor analysis to attitude measurement during the next two decades typically included a religious attitude measurement and produced consistent confirmation of Mrs. Thurstone's discovery of the close relation between proreligious and conservative social attitudes. As prominent social concern has focused in the postwar years on ethnocentrism, either as anti-Semitism or as racial prejudice, so the studies in more recent years have tended to be restricted to the relation between ethnocentrism and religion.

Among the studies using religious attitude scales and demonstrating correlation between proreligion and conservative social attitudes are those by Allport and Ross

(1967), Ferguson (1939, 1944), Gardner (1960), Goldsen *et al.* (1960), Hadden (1963), Jeeves (1957), Kelly, Ferson, and Holtzman (1958), Kirkpatrick (1949), Kitay (1947), Putney and Middleton (1961), Sanai (1952), Siegman (1962), Struening and Spilka (1952), and Young, Benson, and Holtzman (1960). Their measurements of social attitude range over such issues as capital punishment, sex, divorce, conscientious objectors, race, admission of Communist China to the United Nations, and medicare.

There have been some notable exceptions. Prothro and Jensen (1950), in a sample of students in six Southern colleges, found a slight positive correlation between attitude toward church and attitude toward Negro and Jew. They reported that their sample varied in attitude toward the church within a relatively narrow range at the favorable end of the scale, thus introducing the possibility of a curvilinear relation between religiosity and conservative social attitudes, with the most extremely religious showing greater liberalism. Also with a Southern sample, all Catholics, and apparently all within the high range of religiosity, Liu (1961) found a positive correlation between religious orthodoxy and liberal racial views. Siegman (1962) failed to replicate, in an Israeli sample, the correlation he found in the United States. With a sample of subjects selected for their religiosity, Allen (1965, p. 62) found prejudice related significantly negatively with attitude toward the church and with self-ratings of religiosity.

Most measures of doctrinal orthodoxy show a face similarity to religious attitude scales. Studies using this measure have reported similar results (Droba, 1932; Feagin, 1964; Gregory, 1957; Keedy, 1958; Lenski, 1961; O'Neil and Levinson, 1954; O'Reilly, 1954; Putney and Middletown, 1961; Ranck, 1957; Salisbury, 1962; Whitam, 1962; Wilson, 1960). These have shown correlations with ethnocentrism. Though Glock and Stark (1966) purported to show a correlation between anti-Semitism and orthodoxy, their actual finding was a correlation between anti-Semitism and a "religious bigotry index" which was actually scored and weighted in such a way that three-fourths of its weight came from three anti-Jewish items and less than 10 percent from items assessing doctrinal orthodoxy.

One important exception is reported. Using a national sample of Lutheran young people, Strommen (1963, 1967) reported a sizable negative correlation (−.42) between a 17-item scale of doctrinal orthodoxy and an eight-item measure of conservative social attitudes. As with other such exceptions to the general findings, Strommen's sample appears to have been relatively homogeneous in the high range of orthodoxy, again suggesting the hint of a curvilinear relationship with the total range of orthodoxy.

The Allport-Vernon religious scale has shown a less clear relation with social attitude. This may have to do with the ambiguity, discussed earlier, of the significance of the scale. Gardner (1960) and Jones (1958) found only a slight correlation, Evans (1952) a slightly negative correlation with anti-Semitism. Prothro and Jensen found that among Protestants, but not among Catholics or Jews, the Allport-Vernon religious measure was correlated negatively with a Q-sort measure of attitude toward change.

Kirkpatrick's (1949) data, derived from large samples in Minneapolis, suggest that the relation between religious attitude and conservatism disappears when the effects of sex, education, and denominational affiliation are controlled. Feagin (1964) reported the relationship reduced but still significant when education was partialed out, as did Keedy (1958) and Stouffer (1955). Allport and Ross (1967) found the relation between general religious endorsement and prejudice largely mediated by education, but argued that this represents rather than obscures psychologically important variables.

A plausible interpretation, consistent with Thurstone's original dilemma as to what to label the factor, is to suppose that what is represented here has nothing uniquely to do with religion or religious institutions, but represents a general conservative attitude toward social structure, including religious institutions and their official doctrines. Whether this is related to social, economic, and educational influences or to more individual psychological characteristics is, of course, a much larger problem.

CORRELATION OF CONSERVATIVE ATTITUDE AND INSTITUTIONAL AFFILIATION

When frequency of church attendance is used as a measure, the relation with conservative social attitudes, especially in more recent studies of ethnocentrism, apparently depends on what range of the attendance scale is used. The relationship appears to be curvilinear, so that at low frequencies attendance is positively correlated with ethnocentrism, but at high frequencies a reversal is suggested. Very regular attenders appear to be more liberal than less frequent attenders, and sometimes even more liberal than nonattenders.

Several studies have measured variation in attendance primarily at low frequencies and have shown a positive correlation with conservative attitudes, usually racial prejudice or anti-Semitism (Sanford, Chapter 6 in Adorno *et al.*, 1950; Blum and Mann, 1960; Garrison, 1961; Gough, 1951; Hadden, 1963; Jones, 1958; Levinson and Sanford, 1944; Merton, 1940; Rokeach, 1960; Rosenblith, 1949; Ross, 1950; Sanford and Levinson, 1948; Stouffer, 1955; Turbeville and Hyde, 1946). This list includes those which use what amounts to the low extreme of the attendance scale, namely, a comparison of persons with no church affiliation and those with some affiliation. It also includes those studies which report attendance as a single linear variable with a heterogeneous sample across the full range of attendance; in such samples, very frequent or regular attenders (weekly or more) are in a minority, so that we may assume that an otherwise unspecified measure of attendance frequency is distinguishing largely among degrees of less frequent attendance. Allport and Kramer (1946) and Rosenblith (1949) also found recall of church influence during childhood correlated with prejudice, a finding Rosenblith (1957) failed to replicate.

Studies which have compared frequencies of attendance only at the high end of the scale have found negative correlations with ethnocentrism (Allen, 1965; Lenski, 1961; Parry, 1949; Rosenblum, 1958; Shinert and Ford, 1958).

A number of investigators have shown the curvilinear relation within a single study (Friedrichs, 1959; Glock and Stark, 1966, Table 52; Kelly, Ferson, and Holtzman, 1958; Pinkney, 1961; Sanford, Chapter 6 and p. 212 in Adorno *et al.*, 1950; Struening, 1957, 1963; Tumin *et al.*, 1958; Williams, 1964; Young, Benson, and Holtzman, 1960).

Most of these studies were done with subjects predominantly of one religious group, and no differences in the relation of church attendance and conservatism seem to show up as attributable to one group. However, Chein (in an unpublished study cited by Harding *et al.*, 1954, p. 1039) reported one study with a sample of New York City housewives (number not specified) in which the correlation between church attendance and anti-Negro attitude varied by faith group: there was a sizable negative correlation among Catholics, a slightly negative one among Jews, and there was no relation among Protestants. But this seems an exception, perhaps attributable to the particular interaction of the sample and the social attitudes being measured. Lenski (1961) found correlation between attendance and conservative political views among both Protestants and Catholics, though the relation between conservative economic views and attendance held only among Protestants. Goldsen *et al.* (1960) showed a relation within each of the faith groups between conservative position over a range of issues and a religious index significantly weighted by church attendance.

TWO TYPES OF RELIGION

A curvilinear relationship with conservative attitudes is hinted at by the data on religious attitudes and doctrinal orthodoxy, and decidedly demonstrated by the data on church attendance: the most intensely religious reverse the trend for religiosity to be associated with conservative attitudes. This raises the possibility of a distinction between two types of religiosity, one type, associated with moderately favorable attitudes and moderate attendance, correlated with conservative attitudes, and the other type, associated with more intense religiosity, correlated with more liberal attitudes. This possibility has been eagerly picked up by several researchers and has generated most of the attempts to formulate the distinction discussed in the last section under the labels "consensual" and "committed." We will see here how fruitful this distinction has been in demonstrating a differential relation with conservative attitudes, especially ethnocentrism.

Several earlier studies of prejudice made an impressionistic distinction of the two types with remarkable consensus. The authors of *The Authoritarian Personality* decided that prejudice was more correlated with "the way" religion was adhered to than with the nature of the religion itself. Specifically, they decided that ethnocentrism seemed low among the "subjects whose religion would appear to be 'genuine' in the sense that it was arrived at more or less independently of external pressure and takes the form of internalized values." Those who showed evidence of "conventionalism" and "submission" in the way they developed their religion were those who were found to be most ethnocentric. Bettelheim and Janowitz (1949, 1950) similarly found a correlation between "stable religious beliefs, either positive or negative, and tolerance" (p. 156). They interpreted stability as representing firm internalization of religious convictions. Allport (1954, p. 452) reported a small study in which a panel of parishioners selected because "their faith really meant something" were less prejudiced than those "who seemed influenced more by political and social aspects of religious activity." In a related study, Allport reported that regular attendants at a Bible class were less prejudiced than irregular attendants.

Other studies have dropped similar hints, incidental to other findings. Friedrichs (1959) found that members of church study groups were more tolerant than members of governing boards or Sunday school teachers. Lenski (1961) reported that "devotionalism" (meaning essentially reported frequency of prayer) correlated positively with a measure of racial tolerance while, at least among Catholics, adherence to doctrinal orthodoxy was related with prejudice. Other suggestions appear in studies by Jeeves and Whitam cited above.

Beginning the development of the intrinsic-extrinsic scales at Harvard (discussed above), Wilson (1960) found a correlation between his extrinsic-religious-values scale and a measure of prejudice. But, as pointed out above, the scale can probably be taken more as a measure of general proreligious attitudes than as an instrument for clearly distinguishing between types. Allport and Ross (1967) found several measures of prejudice correlated slightly more highly with their extrinsic scale than with an intrinsic scale. Feagin (1964) found a much more decisive difference, very likely related to the fact that his intrinsic and extrinsic scales were derived more systematically from a factor analysis. He found that an anti-Negro scale correlated .35 with his extrinsic scale, and −.01 with the intrinsic scale. (Further analysis showed this difference to be greatest among his oldest subjects.)

Allen (1965; Allen and Spilka, 1967) demonstrated an extremely strong relation between his committed-consensual distinction and measures of prejudice and of world-mindedness. In a factor-analytic study with a heterogeneous sample, Keene (1967b) found ethnocentrism particularly associated with religious factors emphasizing doctrine, creed, and ritual, especially among Jews and Catholics. Rejection of ethnocentrism was particularly associated with what Keene called "personal" religion, defined as a preference for "inner, personal experience" over doctrine, creed, ceremonies, and rituals as "the primary force in religion," coupled with the fact of not being a member of the same religion as parents. (The last item is reminiscent of one of the indicators Adorno *et al.* used to distinguish two types of religion.)

INTERPRETATION

Two sets of findings, then, invite interpretation which corresponds approximately to Allport's aphorism that religion "makes prejudice and it unmakes prejudice" (1954, p. 420) but does not, however, necessarily accept the direction of influence implied by Allport's language.

Little interpretive effort has been applied to the reduced conservatism associated with "committed" religion and most frequent attendance. It is not clear from the research just how "reduced" the conservatism is, whether the committed are less prejudiced than the nonreligious or only less prejudiced than the consensually religious. In general, it may be suggested that committed religion provides (or presupposes) enhanced personal security, self-esteem, and compensation, or otherwise tends to reduce the psychological motivation prompting prejudice. It might also be held that religious teachings of brotherhood are more attractive to or more influential on those who are more committed.

The more clearly established relation of prejudice with consensual religion and moderate attendance invites two types of explanation. One explanation attempts to show how such religion causes prejudice and other conservative attitudes. The other is an exploration of how they are common consequences of other factors. In fact, both types of theory have tended to propose similar mediating variables.

How (consensual) religion causes prejudice

Three related types of theory seem to be available:

1. Submission to a religious institution and ideology may foster a lulling of judgmental processes, an abdication of the independence and skill of ego processes which would otherwise presumably be more able to cut through social stereotypes and generalized fears which promote prejudice. To put it another way, habits of conformity,

acquiescence, conservatism, and closed-mindedness may generalize from religion to social judgments, which lie in the same general sphere of values and commitments, even when they do not generalize so far as to interfere, for example, with a business-man's vigorous independence of judgment in his occupational roles.

2.   Religious ideology tends to promote a concept of social exclusiveness or "particularism" (Glock and Stark, 1966), especially with notions of unique revelation or special election as a member of a divinely chosen group (Allport, 1959). Such doctrines might lead fairly directly to social exclusion and disregard for "others." Or it might be mediated and enhanced by an actual exclusive group membership which in turn needs to be justified and defended by even further well-defined boundaries and social distance. Olson (1963) has detailed the degree to which some hints of anti-Semitism persist in children's educational literature of Christian denominations.

3.   A third explanation belongs in the family of dissonance theories. Religious groups have two characteristics which tend to enhance dissonance: (a) they are generally entered with what a person perceives to be freedom of choice and volition; and (b) ideology and practice are subject to considerable challenge, implicit or explicit, in our culture. Dissonance reduction may include a justification or protection of the affiliation with a rationale of exclusiveness or even superiority. If it takes the form of social consensus, this may have to be bolstered (even at the risk of losing a larger consensus) by making membership highly visible and distinctive from non-membership. Such a process could well generalize to include attitudes measured as prejudice.

Common sources of prejudice and (consensual) religion

Most writers have worked with the conceptually more sophisticated assumption that the correlation between prejudice and consensual religion is to be accounted for by seeing them as common consequences or representations of some third factor. The data suggest that education and class differences can account for much of the correlation between prejudice and religion. Whether the presence of such mediating variables precludes or requires additional explanation in terms of personality variables is a matter for debate (Allport, 1966).

Insofar as conservative social attitudes seem to be correlated with those elements of religion which are closely associated with fairly casual institutional loyalty, the possibility exists that it is simply favorable attitude toward existing social institutions which is primarily captured both by measures of religion and by measures of conservative social attitude. In the context of the earlier discussion of problems of definition, we need to remember that these measures of religion, even the more refined distinctions, are derived from broad, popularly held cultural categories, not from the categories by which religiously sophisticated persons would define and analyze religion. From the latter point of view, most if not all of these indices of religion do not measure degree of religion any more than degree of mental health would be assessed by items reflecting attitudes toward such popular stereotypes as "peace of mind" and "personal adjustment." Favorable attitudes toward such cultural stereotypes, whether of "adjustment," of "religion," or of racial distinctions, may be all that is involved in such findings.

Perhaps most researchers have ventured interpretation in the direction suggested by *The Authoritarian Personality,* namely, in personality characteristics of social conformism (which may or may not be implied in the interpretation just above) and in intolerance of ambiguity. With hardly a perceptible transition from discussion of attitudes to discussion of personality factors, this has been the pattern of analysis used by Adorno *et al.* (1950), Allport (1954), Argyle (1958), Bettelheim and Janowitz (1949), and Goldsen *et al.* (1960). The discussion here, then, also anticipates that of the next section. The theories offered seem to be one form or another of an assertion of a "weak ego," a "constricted ego," or a severe superego, or some combination of these. The composite theoretical picture of the personality for whom conventional, institution-based religion and conservative ideology and prejudice are functional is something like the following: (1) a person threatened or overwhelmed by one or another external circumstance or internal impulse; (2) a person therefore responsive to and reliant upon controls, structures, self-supports, and identity clues, especially as these may be provided externally, clearly, and unambiguously; (3) thus, a person possessing a wide range of characteristics serving this latter function, including those described as suggestibility, rigidity, intolerance of ambiguity, need for definiteness, closure seeking, manipulativeness, reliance on social or institutional or other authorities, moralism, and other conventional indices of a severe superego. Any one of these latter characteristics can be readily discerned within religion or within prejudice.

Some of the evidence for such a conceptualization will be presented in the next section. We will mention those few implications which have been drawn with special reference to prejudice.

Such an interpretation should predict that particular elements of doctrine or of practice are emphasized by prejudiced more than by tolerant persons. Freud suggested some relations between particular elements of religious ideology (both Christian and Jewish) and anti-Semitism, and these have been elaborated somewhat by Berliner (1946) and Lowenstein (1951). Spilka and Reynolds (1965) discovered, with a sample of 200 Catholic girls deliberately chosen because they were all strongly religious, that the more prejudiced tended to perceive God as abstract, impersonal, and kingly, and the unprejudiced perceived God more as real, fatherly, human, and a benevolent ruler. This study is based on previous work (Armatas, 1962; Spilka, Armatas, and Nussbaum, 1964) in developing a reliable Q-sort of God concepts as derived from statements by persons relatively sophisticated and relatively committed religiously.

Several researchers have extended their analysis of a correlation between religion and prejudice in an effort to isolate the crucial factor of intolerance of ambiguity. However, firm demonstration of this point still awaits more systematic design. Gregory (1957) decided, after an item analysis of the items on his religion scale, that it was the most literalistic statements of belief which were most correlated with the F scale. Strommen (1967) discovered that the use of "?" as a response to a long belief questionnaire was correlated with more liberal attitudes on the social attitudes scale. The coding categories which define Allen's consensual religion (Allen, 1965; Allen and Spilka, 1967) rely heavily on the use of narrow and unambiguous conceptualization. Kottman (1966) found the Thurstone scales correlated with several indices of over-precision or preoccupation with verbal statement.

COMPARISON OF FAITH GROUPS

Differences in social attitudes among faith groups (Catholic, Protestant, Jewish) are readily measurable and may have some practical interest, though it is difficult to tell what illumination of religion is provided by discovering such differences. Clear, consistent results do not emerge from such studies.

Where differences are found, they tend to reveal Catholics, Protestants, and Jews ranking in that order on conservatism on racial issues (Allport and Kramer, 1946; Rokeach, 1960; Rosenblith, 1949, 1957; Sappenfield, 1944; Triandis and Triandis, 1960; Turbeville and Hyde, 1946) and issues of freedom of speech (Lenski, 1961; Pyron, 1961); and Protestants, Catholics, and Jews ranking in that order on other issues, including anti-Semitism (Glock and Stark, 1966; Goldsen *et al.*, 1960; Lenski, 1961).

The care and comprehensiveness of studies reporting no overall difference among groups is impressive (Adorno *et al.*, 1950; Pinkney, 1961; Stouffer, 1955; Williams, 1964). Furthermore, Blum and Mann (1960), Parry (1949), Sappenfield (1943), Spoerl (1951), and Triandis and Triandis (1960) have all presented data and analysis indicating that ethnocentric attitudes of a faith group are specific to the object group toward which attitude is measured.

This and many other obvious considerations suggest that any tendencies of association between one of the faith groups and ideology or prejudice is likely to be attributable to ethnic and class variables. Lenski (1961), for example, has made the important point that white and Negro Protestants are likely to have different social views. Allinsmith and Allinsmith (1948) found that denominational differences disappeared completely when social class was controlled.

Triandis and Triandis distinguished among different Jewish groups, finding, for example, that conservative Jews have significantly higher F scores and reformed Jews significantly lower F scores than Protestants.

Fetter (1964) undertook to compare social attitudes of Christians and Moslems living under similar village conditions in Lebanon, where commitment to the respective religious communities is intense. Interviewing a large random sample of 406 men in eleven villages, he found no significant differences within a range of economic and social attitudes relevant to village life. This contradicts an expectation that Moslem doctrinal fatalism would produce a difference (even though the Maronite form of Christianity in Lebanon, in remote relation with Roman Catholicism, is far from meeting the conditions for a strictly "Protestant ethic"). On attitudes toward education, cooperative farming, technical advice, etc., Moslems were likely to be as favorable as Christians. All were generally conservative, reflecting social, not religious, influences.

Lenski (1961) has energetically insisted that differences between faith groups may *not* be reduced to class differences and, in fact, may well be greater than differences due to class effects. His argument is offered as support for the Weberian theory of the influence of Protestantism on economic life. But to demonstrate this point is essentially to prove a kind of null hypothesis—that the commonly supposed effect of social class does not hold—and requires reliable assessment of social class. Lenski's procedure is explained only briefly in a footnote (Lenski, 1961, p. 73). It apparently was based exclusively on occupation, by which the sample was dichotomized into middle class and working class. If a casual and relatively unreliable index of social class is used, this does not provide decisive evidence against the influence of social class.

Greeley (1963), working with a broad range of attitudes and personal characteristics, has undertaken another kind of analysis to isolate the relative influence of religion as such. He reasoned that differences between Catholics, Protestants, and Jews, if they were attributable to some religious influence, should be greater among those who could be regarded as more religious within their tradition. To measure religiosity, he had only a single-item self-rating, so his execution may not be definitive.   He found that some traits which had distinguished Protestants (for example, plans to teach school, helpfulness, self-ratings of drive) *were* correlated with religiosity.   But in all three faith groups the majority of characteristics, including assessments of conservative and liberal attitudes, showed no relations with the religiosity measure.

The evidence is not overwhelming as to the fruitfulness or the reliability of studying gross differences between faith groups.

RELIGION AND PERSONALITY CHARACTERISTICS

It is a confession of the poverty and primitive state of this field to propose a section so grossly focused as the heading above indicates.   Particular personality and motivational variables are implied by any theory or problem in the understanding of religion. Research with such variables, and any review of research, such as this chapter, should be specific to particular theories or particular problems.   The procedure here, in lumping indiscriminately all research with personality variables, simply reflects the status of the field.   Furthermore, almost without exception, in empirical studies religion has been regarded as a single variable, and the design has, in effect, asked the question, "Who is, and who is not, religious?"   Empirical research has not really addressed the possibility, raised consistently by theoretical observers (for example, James, Freud), of particular doctrines or practices or types of religion being associated differentially with personality characteristics.   The above heading reflects this primitive state in another respect also, in that it implies, accurately, that research is restricted exclusively to correlational studies.

This section will be organized around the general supposition that religion is associated with deficiencies of personality, with a "weak ego" or "constricted ego." (This is also a rubric under which intense religious experience may be understood; see below.)   This theory is highly general, both in the sense that it subsumes a variety of more specific statements and also in the sense that it is widely held.   Religious proponents and detractors alike can agree that religion functions to meet the needs of those who feel frustrated, threatened, inadequate, or deprived.   The analyses of Freud and Marx ought not to be an insult to those whose highest religious celebrations commemorate a captivity or a crucifixion and whose scripture finds focus in such passages as the prophecy of the suffering servant in Isaiah or the Beatitudes of the Gospels, or whose doctrine and practice enhance recognition of man's fallen state and fundamental helplessness.   In other words, the most common theological and psychological themes coincide, at least in these general terms.

The psychological research reflects an overwhelming consensus that religion (at least as measured in the research, usually institutional affiliation or adherence to conservative traditional doctrines) is associated with awareness of personal inadequacies, either generally or in response to particular crisis or threat situations; with objective evidence of inadequacy, such as low intelligence; with a strong responsiveness to the suggestions of other persons or other external influences; and with an array of what may be called desperate and generally unadaptive defensive maneuvers. Here, perhaps, are the sick souls and divided selves, two types of religious predispositions described by William James (1902), and with which he felt particularly sympathetic.

A pair of early dissertations by Howells (1928) and Sinclair (1928) provides a striking keynote. Measuring religion, respectively, by report of mystical experience and by institutional allegiance, they found that the more religious subjects scored lower on measures of mental alertness and of intelligence, were more responsive to suggestion, were less able to endure electric shock and more disposed to acquire skills to avoid it, and were less adept at certain motor skills. The methodological rigor of these studies, however, is far enough from ideal that they are chiefly of historical and illustrative interest.

PERSONAL INADEQUACY

Self-esteem

In a large sample of 2842 graduate students in arts and sciences in 25 universities, Stark (1963) found that church attendance and affiliation were correlated negatively with the following indices: whether the student felt himself to be an "intellectual"; the degree to which the student wanted his future job to have opportunities for creativity and originality, freedom from pressure to conform, and freedom from extensive supervision; the degree to which the student aspired to be "respected . . . among specialists in your field at different institutions" rather than simply within the local institution. Among graduate students, all of these may be regarded as indices of self-esteem and confidence.

In a sociometric study, Bonney (1949) found that students with church affiliation received significantly fewer friendship choices than those without church affiliation. Cowen (1954) found that the Brownfain self-rating inventory was correlated negatively with the religious measure of the Allport-Vernon, and Strunk (1958) found the Brownfain correlated negatively with a seven-part index including church attendance and attitudes toward religion. Prothro and Jensen (1950) found that, among Protestants in their sample, the religion scale on the Allport-Vernon was correlated with an index of low self-reliance. Symington (1935) found that, in some of his samples, the more conservative subjects reported more problems on the Pressy Checklist.

Bender (1958), however, found that, when used with subjects who had been out of college for 15 years, the Allport-Vernon religious measure was correlated significantly with two ratings of ego strength based on interview material. These relationships did not appear when the men were seniors in college. Another slight hint of modified effects over time appears in a study by McKenna (1961), who found a correlation, only among women who had attended a Catholic college, between a measure of religious maturity and scales of the Guilford-Zimmerman selected as measuring self-objectification and self-extension.

Results employing conventional personality inventories appear too slight and too contradictory to report in detail. The trend, if any, is for measures of religion to be correlated with indices of pathology and deficiency.

Intelligence

Binnewies (1934), Brown and Lowe (1951), Kildahl (1957), Stark (1963), and Symington (1935) all report a negative correlation between conservative religious ideology and intelligence. Some of these studies, and many others, also demonstrate negative correlation with amount of education. A number of studies, ranging from Leuba

(1934) to Clark (1955), suggest that eminence, as measured by appearance in *Who's Who*, is associated with religious skepticism and nonaffiliation.

Kosa and Schommer (1961) provide one study in which intelligence was correlated positively with religious participation. But the participation was in college religious organizations, not in worship, and intelligence was also correlated, though less strongly, with participation in other activities, such as the student newspaper or liberal arts academic clubs.

Young, Dustin, and Holtzman (1966) report a negative but apparently curvilinear correlation between college grades and favorable attitudes toward organized religion; A students reversed the trend and showed more favorable attitudes than B+ students. The authors suggest that both high achievement and approval of organized religion may represent strong internalization of cultural (or, at least, parental) norms.

DEPENDENCE AND SUGGESTIBILITY

Two studies have concluded from a battery of clinical measures that more orthodoxly religious persons are more submissive and dependent in interpersonal relations (Dreger, 1952; Ranck, 1961). Goldsen *et al.* (1960, pp. 177–179) cite data characteristically reporting greater social conformity in attitudes among the more religious. With a three-faith sample of 300 students, Black and London (1966) found that all their indices of religion (church attendance, prayer, respect for clergy, and belief in God) occupied the same factor as obedience to parents and to unjust laws, patriotism, and disapproval of illicit sexual behavior. Most religious systems recommend humility and submissiveness. It is a good question whether such sanctions most likely produce, attract, or rationalize such personal characteristics.

A number of sociologists and social psychologists have felt constrained to demonstrate that increased American religious activity in recent decades may be interpreted as a crystallization of suburban religious participation, as part of general middle-class conformity (Berger, 1961; Lazerwitz, 1962; Nash and Berger, 1962; Rosenberg, 1957; Winter, 1961). Such analysis is less startling than might be supposed for Jewish and Christian theologians who work from a basic premise of the working of God in history through constituted social groups and through incarnation; that is, potentially through the very worldly processes which the social psychologist specifies.

Many types of self-rating and questionnaire data have produced results which might raise suspicion of social-desirability or acquiescent response set. Typical examples, more or less at random, would be the finding by Burchinal (1957) of a correlation between reported marital satisfaction and church attendance (reminiscent of billboard slogans, "Families that pray together stay together") and the finding by Carney (1961) of higher scores on attractive personality characteristics on various inventories and scales. Theological students characteristically score high on the *K* scale of the MMPI (Kania, 1965).

More direct evidence of acquiescence was provided by Fisher (1964), who found a strong correlation between the Bass social-acquiescence scale and three indices of religion: frequency of church attendance, self-rating of religiosity, and the Allport-Vernon religious scale.

Sanford's finding (1946) of greater general optimism associated with church affiliation and attendance might be interpreted as a kind of repressive denial, reminiscent of one strain of American religiosity (Meyer, 1965), dubbed variously "peace of mind" or "positive thinking" and labeled ironically by William James (1902) as "healthy-mindedness."

A number of intriguing miscellaneous findings can be reported here, if one grants the assumption that the behavior involved represents dependence in some form. Alcoholism is sometimes taken to be associated with dependent personality characteristics; Walters (1957) reported that alcoholic patients were more likely than control patients to have religious backgrounds. If ESP ever finds a home within psychological theory, it may well be within the general area of interpersonal dependency; Nash (1958) reports a correlation between ESP ability and religious scores on the Allport-Vernon. Two studies have demonstrated a correlation between church attendance and responsiveness to a placebo (Duke, 1964; Lasagna *et al.,* 1954).

The dramatic phenomena of religion—most noticeably the processes of mass evangelism and conversion and instances of healing—have, of course, frequently been analyzed as instances of hysteria-like or hypnotic-like suggestibility. Chronologically, such analyses have ranged at least from Coe (1916) to Sargant (1957). But such analyses have characteristically not gone beyond the stage of establishing descriptive similarities.

How is one to interpret suggestibility if it is involved in these phenomena? (1) It may represent a kind of general personal weakness or frustration looking for support anywhere, and finding it, on occasion, in such phenomena. This is reminiscent of the first general theory cited in the opening section, and of a kind of "weak ego" basis for religion. (2) It might represent a kind of inhibition of personal initiative and a submissiveness to authority, reminiscent of the kind of "superego" religion and of the second general theory cited in the opening section. (3) It might simply represent the fact that institutional religion is part of the cultural *status quo* and therefore is participated in by those who are, for one reason or another, adherents to the conventional.

MORE DESPERATE DEFENSES AND CONSTRICTED PERSONALITY

From various kinds of data, a generally consistent correlation has been reported between orthodox religious commitment and a relatively defensive, constricted personality (Adorno *et al.,* 1950, pp. 183, 193; Gregory, 1957; Jones, 1958; Prothro and Jensen, 1950; Putney and Middletown, 1961; Ranck, 1961; Rokeach, 1960; Spilka, 1958; Stanley, 1964; Swickard, 1963; Weima, 1965). The label of authoritarianism has become the most popular general term to describe these characteristics, which seem to be marked primarily by an intolerance of ambiguity and a reliance on structure, either internal or external. Freud (1907) first described the similarity of religious practices to obsessive symptoms.

Efforts to extend such characterization into issues of extrapunitiveness and intrapunitiveness (for example, Bateman and Jensen, 1958; Brown, 1966; King and Funkenstein, 1957) or into incidence of mental illness (Oates, 1955) have not produced decisive results.

Some exceptions to the general finding appear. Dreger (1958) was unable to confirm with questionnaire and inventory data his previous findings with projective tests. More significant are two recent studies which have used a range of established and apparently reliable measuring instruments, many of them identical with those of studies just cited, which have failed to confirm the relation between constricted personality characteristics and adherence to conventional beliefs. Martin and Nichols (1962) found a correlation between the F scale and conventional religious beliefs only among subjects low on "religious information." In a recent study, Brown (1966) has found that measures of authoritarianism, rigidity, and intolerance of ambiguity define a second factor distinct from the first general religious factor. However, this finding seems to contradict the results of an earlier study (Brown, 1962), in which the same measure of authoritarianism was loaded exclusively and highly on the first factor defined by orthodox Christian beliefs.

INTERPRETATION

Only the most general of interpretations can be made of such gross findings. It was suggested at the outset of this section that psychological theories implicit within theological views could readily predict the attraction of religion to persons betraying the evidence of "weak egos"—if that is a fair summary of the findings reported here. But many such theological positions would go on to claim that religion effectively functions to meet these deficiencies and that, therefore, involvement in an authentic religious relationship ought not to be correlated with, at least, the most maladaptive of the defensive reactions against such weakness. If religion effectively meets dependency needs, reduces anxiety, assures the self, and solves problems, then religious persons ought not to persist in dependence and feelings of inadequacy, or in constricted, defensive attempts to cope with such inadequacy. The general, normative pattern for the religious life is that of a passive dependence on God which results in an active, responsible, courageous stance toward life.

(Some theological positions would take exception to this implied psychological prediction. Within Christian theology, there are three radically different positions which would decline to predict measurable pragmatic effectiveness of religious faith along these lines: A radical orthodoxy, represented by Karl Barth, would deny that actions of God necessarily have anything to do with observable, natural phenomena such as personality characteristics. Existentialist thinking, represented by Kierkegaard, would deny any consistent lawful regularities in the psychic-spiritual life, so that any such predictions are not warranted. One thrust of Protestant thought, exemplified in Luther—*simul justus, simul peccator*—emphasizes the unlikelihood of certainty or completion in the religious pilgrimage.)

In other words, the implied prediction is of a curvilinear relation between such personality characteristics and depth or authenticity of involvement in religion. Persons not attracted to or rejecting religion should be low in these characteristics ("Those who are well have no need of a physician, but those who are sick: I came not to call the righteous, but sinners"; Mark 2:17). Those who are attracted to religion should show these characteristics. Among those who give evidence of a "successful" or authentic or deep religious involvement, these characteristics should either be reduced or else be unproductive of anxiety and defensive reactions. It seems likely, at the very least, that the same distinction between consensual and committed religion which has proved fruitful in demonstrating a differential relation with prejudice (see above) should also be relevant here. A few studies begin to show hints along these lines.

French (1947) undertook to distinguish subjects who showed highly differentiated and organized, and presumably generally more mature, religious sentiments. She found, judging from a battery of tests, interviews, autobiographies, etc., that these were more likely to "consciously recognize and accept both strengths and weaknesses as parts of their selves."

Allport and Ross (1967) found a $-.32$ correlation between degree of education and their measure of extrinsic religious orientation, and apparently no correlation with their intrinsic subscale. Keene (1967b) found the factor representing orthodox or institutionalized forms, creeds, and rituals, consistently related to neurotic and inhibitive personality factors, as well as to ethnocentric attitudes. His other religious factors showed no such relationship. Indeed, his general religious factor showed some tendency toward a negative relationship with these maladaptive personality factors.

Brown (1966) found that only one of his many religious measures was loaded on the factor representing authoritarianism, rigidity, and intolerance of ambiguity. This was a scale assessing positive evaluation of the institutional church.

Salzman (1953) and Allison (1966) distinguished two types of religious conversion, a distinction which could probably be applied more generally to religious involvement. One exploits the possibilities in religion for enhancing rigidity and authoritarianism and reliance on largely external supports. The other represents greater maturation and freedom. Barron (1963) has described the kind of authentic religion he terms "believing for oneself" and has found this to be correlated with various measures of independence, ego strength, and absence of authoritarianism. He contrasts these subjects with those who solved the crisis in belief by atheism or by a more simplistic return to religion, and who thereby retained their "slavery to the antinomies" and perpetuated the conflict "through acceptance of polarities as real," rather than achieving a higher-level integration. Barron tends to regard the religious adjustment as the dependent, rather than the independent, variable.

Since committed religion is generally defined in terms of a general personal orientation, and without regard to institutions and doctrines, it is very likely that many psychological studies deal with variables relevant to committed religion, even though this is unintended by the author. An experiment by Deutsch (1960) might be mentioned almost as a random example. He found that the F scale was related with apparently pervasive (religious?) attitudes toward one's environment. In a game experiment, subjects tended to be characteristically either "trusting and trustworthy or suspicious and untrustworthy in this essentially ambiguous situation with unknown others." (Many psychologists would be hard pressed to find a better definition of what they mean by a genuine, committed religious orientation.) Deutsch found lower F scores associated with the trusting orientation.

It seems odd that the experience of guilt has not been more directly studied in such research. Guilt is generally supposed in most theological analyses to constitute a primary motive for religious response. It comprised a prominent part of the analysis of earlier theorizing in the psychology of religion, especially, of course, as this centered on the conversion experience. Guilt is a natural counterpart to the low self-regard which has been discussed.

For the record, it should probably be reported in a section on "personality" that church attendance has been found correlated with such variables as sex (Protestant and Catholic women and Jewish men attend more), race (Negroes attend more than whites), indices of social class, and age (curvilinearly). The literature is surveyed by Argyle (1958) and by Lazerwitz (1961).

DEVELOPMENT AND FUNCTION OF BELIEF

It is perhaps paradoxical that the more specific the type of religious behavior which we consider, the more the question occurs as to what, if anything, unique attaches to the adjective "religious." Is there anything unique about the psychology of religious belief that does not belong to the more general study of belief and attitude? In principle, the answer to that question is almost certainly "No." The patterns of development, function, and structure of belief are hardly likely to be different because they bear a content that may be regarded as religious. But in practice, a consideration of religious beliefs may tend to raise or emphasize certain types of problems and interpretations not otherwise prominently considered. Of the four positions charted in the opening section on the uniqueness of religion, position number two (p. 604) is being suggested here.

As a device for designating some of the kinds of problems particularly relevant in the study of religious beliefs, Table 2 presents a chart generated by distinguishing three types of independent variables and three types of dependent variables. The classification of independent variables is adapted from one proposed by Smith, Bruner, and White (1956). It separates the sources of belief into (1) the objective reality of "the way things are," relatively uncathected, yet imposing certain structures and limits; (2) the social reality of parents, persons, and groups large and small which provide both important crucial satisfactions and also norms of belief and attitude, and which often make the former conditional upon adherence to the latter; and (3) the internal realm of motivations and impulses, insofar as these can be considered in isolation.

The distinction coincides with research by Putney and Middletown (1961), who developed scales for religious ideology comprising three dimensions: "acceptance . . . of the tenets; . . . orientation toward other persons with respect to . . . belief; the significance of beliefs to self-conception." (They also used a fourth variable, corresponding to the first column, the "degree of recognition of ambivalence.") It turned out that they found their attempts to measure these different dimensions highly intercorrelated with a large sample of 1200 students in several eastern states.

The dependent variables providing the three columns of the chart reflect two common distinctions. The first, between the intensity or style of a belief and the content of the belief, provides columns one and two. Whether or not any belief is held or closure imposed on a particular situation, and with how much intensity and certainty, is a variable likely to be quite independent of the content or the substance of that belief. At one end of the dimension (at which the question is whether or not any belief or closure exists), the variable may be called something like tolerance or intolerance of ambiguity, open- or closed-mindedness, need for definiteness, need for structure, or need for closure. At the other end of the dimension, representing the greater intensity, the variable may be called something like dogmatism or rigidity.

This distinction between the first two columns has sometimes been regarded as one between content-free and content-based characteristics of belief. It is the distinction which Rokeach (1960) has emphasized in his own consideration of the authoritarian personality in raising the possibility of an authoritarianism of the left, as well as of the right. It is perhaps the same distinction Eysenck (1944) has found between the tough-minded and tender-minded factor and the radical-conservative factor.

TABLE 2

IDENTIFYING DIFFERENT DESIGNATIONS OF THE FUNCTIONS OF BELIEF

	Dependent variables		
Independent variables	*Intensity of belief* (for example, open-mindedness, tolerance of ambiguity, dogmatism)	*Content of belief* (for example, benignness of God)	*Protection of belief* (for example, evidence of the benignness of God)
Reinforcement from objective reality	1. Disappointments are reduced by learning to read a train timetable (acquisition of elementary ego process of "reality mapping").	4. Highly varied experiences of personal support and satisfactions are generalized into a broader expectation and optimism.	7. Instances of benign experience are selectively recalled.
Social reinforcement	2. Parents praise child's skills of naming objects, solving problems; are less warm to "I don't know."	5. Parents reward expressions of "God is good," frown on alternatives.	8. Membership in like-minded group is sought, or others are proselytized to the view.
Intrapsychic reinforcement	3. The pain of indecision over internally conflicting motives, or the anxiety of overwhelming raw emotion is reduced by labeling, decision, control.	6. Oedipal anxieties are stilled by feeling assurance of a loving father.	9. Behavior and attitudes of gratitude and thanksgiving (for example, benevolence, prayer) are fostered as a "confirming response" to God's goodness.

It is the distinction which Dittes (1959a) has emphasized in suggesting that the effects of threat or anxiety on suggestibility, rigidity, and the like may be mediated through this closure variable.

The distinction between the first two columns and the third represents the difference between acquiring a belief and protecting it. This distinction, which itself may be more readily recognized in the study of religious beliefs than of other beliefs, acknowledges that a belief or attitude may arise out of one source but find expression, elaboration, and protection against challenges by using another source. Perhaps most characteristically, a person moves diagonally up the table—from the lower left to the upper right corner—finding the impetus for holding any belief from "intrapsychic" motives, acquiring the particular belief or attitude from social reinforcement, and expressing and defending the belief in terms of objective, rational considerations. But this is by no means the exclusive pattern (note the important role of social consensus—line 2—in protecting beliefs).

Perhaps a complete logic would require another column before the last, indicating the role of motivation for protecting the belief or attitude, corresponding to the role of intensity as a motivation for acquiring a belief or attitude. This column might be headed "vulnerability to challenge" or "vulnerability to dissonance." It would recognize that there are individual differences (related to the same array of independent variables) in the degree to which a person regards contradiction or challenge as motivating. The column is left out of the chart here because, at our present stage of knowledge, it appears that the variables involved here are the same as for the first column.

It might also be recognized that the three independent variables ranged along the side of Table 2 provide three different sources for dissonance and challenge to belief, and that the source for the challenge may be independent either of the source of belief or of the source of protection.

In the cells of the tables are entered what are presumably typical reinforcing and learning situations. For reference, the cells are numbered.

Perhaps most discussion of religious beliefs has concentrated on cells 5 and 7. Social norms and influencing processes are an obvious source of religious beliefs, and objective reality provides a major source of protective rationalization. Yet in these cells, religious beliefs may be the least unique in their functioning. (This, of course, has been part of the purpose of some analyses: to demonstrate that religious beliefs are subject to the same socializing and rationalizing processes as any other beliefs.)

Any discussion of cell 4 would seem to belong in the area of philosophy, and perhaps theology.

The study of religious beliefs, perhaps more than anything else a social psychologist might do, raises the left-hand set of variables to particularly prominent attention. For one thing, religion concerns an area of maximum ambiguity and minimum reinforcement of closure from objective reality. There is room for great variability in degree of closure to be attributed to social and intrapsychic sources (cells 2 and 3). Furthermore, theological doctrines themselves vary widely as to the degree of closure which is considered normative for a religious person. Some Protestant theology especially (for example, Luther, 1520) holds openness as a norm and offers a suspicion of closure. This can be construed (Dittes, 1959b) as providing a psychological theory for closure, relevant to the lower two left cells.

As such theological observation suggests, religion would seem to be a particularly significant area in which to assess the threat-reducing or esteem-enhancing functions of cognitive closure. Prejudice, of course, is another likely area, and it is certainly no accident that, as previously discussed, a correlation between these has been found. Empirical studies on this problem seem confined to those already discussed under the heading of "religion and personality characteristics," in which the most frequent measure of religion was conservative ideology—but a measure undifferentiated (except by Brown, 1962) between the variables represented by the columns of Table 2.

Cells 8 and 9 may also point to processes particularly, even though not uniquely, apparent in religion. One can observe fairly readily in religious groups the process of responding to challenge, for example, challenge of belief, with affiliative behavior (seeking social consensus, or seeking compensatory interpersonal satisfactions?) and with ritualistic or other behavior consistent with the belief (and presumably serving to confirm the belief). Festinger, Riecken, and Schachter (1956) provide one systematic account intended to demonstrate this process.

Cells 6 and 9 raise problems which have received particular attention in the context of Freud's projection theory. Empirical work has been essentially preliminary and has been more concerned with simply establishing a similarity between attitudes (for example, between attitudes toward father and toward God) without investigating the more specific conditions, especially ambivalence, which Freud regards as determinative of such projection to God. Nelson and Jones (1957), Peterman (1966), Strunk (1959), and Siegman (1961) have all used Q-sort or semantic-differential techniques to open up variability in attitudes toward God and toward parents, and to discover the degree of correspondence between the two. Results have not been startlingly supportive for a relationship which is so much taken for granted in speculative literature. Nelson and Jones found God concepts more closely related to mother than to father. Peterman found belief related equally with admiration of mother and of father. Siegman found God and father significantly correlated on the activity factor of a semantic differential with a United States sample, but not with an Israeli sample. He found a "fear of God" measure greater among females in Israel than among males, contrary to Freud's prediction.

Perhaps the problem here, as throughout, is that the measures are taken more or less out of the air rather than out of the stuff of the phenomenon being measured. Perhaps the general adjectives of the semantic differential as developed by Osgood are not particularly relevant to the specific attitudes toward father which may be projected toward God. An otherwise curious finding, consistent with this possibility, is reported by Siegman. Among the third of the subjects scoring lowest on a self-report religiosity scale, the correlations between God and father were statistically significant on all three factors on the semantic differential; they were virtually zero among the third of the subjects scoring highest. The more religiously sophisticated the subjects, the less relevant they may have found the items. To meet this kind of difficulty, Spilka, Armatas, and Nussbaum (1964) have undertaken a factor analysis of God concepts based on adjectives produced by religious persons and using religious persons in the factor analysis. Gorsuch (1968) used both the adjectives used by Spilka *et al.* and a group of the standard semantic-differential adjectives, and concluded that the latter were relatively fruitless for measuring a conceptualization of God.

INTENSE EXPERIENCE

In writing anything purporting to be comprehensive on the psychology of religion in the mid-1960's, it is as impossible as it was for William James in 1902 to overlook religious phenomena involving intense emotional experience. It was the phenomena of mysticism and conversion, especially as they were experienced by individuals in isolation, which mostly interested James. Various forms of "spirit possession," such as glossolalia (speaking in tongues), faith healing, trance states—all in a social context—are today apparently increasing in incidence, or at least in prominence, and in demand for psychological attention. Perhaps the psychologist is most likely to have his attention drawn to the mystical-like phenomena reported as a consequence of psychedelic drugs, such as LSD, mescaline, and psilocybin. The use of these drugs, interestingly enough, has almost always involved at least a dyadic group and itself has generated cultish group phenomena of no small proportion, so that the subject can hardly be ignored in a chapter on the social psychology of religion. Yet one is also hard pressed to find anything reliable to say on the subject.

The dramatic phenomena have always attracted special attention from psychologists, from William James on, and as such may represent a distraction from more fundamental processes in the psychology of religion. Conversion, for example, may be much more important to study as an exposed and accessible instance of such basic or genotypical processes as guilt reduction, or attitude change, or personality integration. But it is included here simply as one more instance—on a phenomenological level—of intense, overt, emotional behavior in a social and religious context.

PSYCHEDELICS AND RELIGION

The major dilemma in this area is still the search for relevant variables, definitions, and categories. (See Furgeson, 1965, for a survey with regard to conversion.) The situation with psychedelic drugs provides a good illustration. Here the dominant question in the literature has been one of definition: Is the psychedelic experience mystical and religious? Havens (1964), Leary (1964), and Smith (1964) have written careful surveys and concluded that the experience is religious. But by what criteria? And how are the criteria measured in the experience? Little conclusiveness seems to have emerged from such a discussion.

A fundamental problem is that the question as posed requires a research design which seems to amount to proving a kind of null hypothesis: the drug-induced experience is not different from "natural" mysticism (or religion). Such a task is the more precarious, the less reliably measured the variables are. In this case, in which the drug experience is so novel as to transcend conventional language categories and the mystical experience is by definition ineffable, the degree of precariousness would seem to approach infinity. The problem is particularly great when the evidence consists of the reports of subjects themselves that the experience has been religious. What they mean by "religious" is not systematically explored. One may suspect that this is simply the only word most subjects have available to apply to any kind of intensely emotional self-transcending experience.

The most systematic empirical effort to establish the religiousness (in this case, mysticalness) of the psychedelic experience was by Pahnke (1963; Pahnke and Richards, 1966). He devised reliable scoring procedures for nine categories (for example, transcendance of time and space, deeply felt positive mood) which appeared from the literature (primarily relying on Stace, 1960) to identify reported mystical experience. He found, using suitable control techniques of double-blind administration, that the reports of subjects receiving psilocybin during a Good Friday worship service were scored significantly higher on each of these categories than the protocols of control subjects. But this still seems a relatively feeble demonstration of a null hypothesis, that these subjects' experiences were like those of a mystic. An appropriate control would be to include scoring categories of intense, novel, but non-mystical experiences. It would be necessary to demonstrate that psilocybin produced effects identifiable as specifically mystical and not generally startling or novel. The experience may be simply a general phenomenon for which subjects can make use of mystical terms on a questionnaire—if those are the only terms that are supplied to them!—and which subjects can describe in spontaneous protocols which judges match with mystical terms—if those are the only terms that are supplied to *them!*

THEORY OF EGO CONSTRICTION

From the literature, some consensus seems to emerge about a general framework of interpretation—it is far too general even to be called a theory. These experiences are seen to involve a kind of constriction of the ego, a curtailment of the usual patterns of perception, judgment, and behavior control. These phenomena have been likened variously to hypnosis (Gill and Brenman, 1959), hysteria, thought control (Frank, 1961; Sargant, 1957), psychoses (Arieti, 1961), and regression in the service of the ego and sensory deprivation (Allison, 1966).

Consequent upon the curtailment of ego patterns, or loss of self, can be expected (1) greater expression of impulses otherwise controlled and (2) greater responsiveness to social influences. Both expectations seem amply confirmed by general observational data. Erotic or other impulse expression which is normally prohibited has been noted in such experiences, whether in extreme forms of the kind which intrigued Freud (1913) in his survey, or in the milder form, such as noted by Alland (1962), in which "possessed" persons engaged in something like the social dancing which was normally prohibited (see also Mischel and Mischel, 1958). It is equally clear that persons in these experiences are particularly responsive to the norms and the suggestions of the immediate social group as to the behavior appropriate once "possessed," whether hallucination, or trance, or stereotyped motor activity, such as dancing and glossolalia.

The *environmental conditions* that induce and encourage such a state can be catalogued, especially as these have evolved fairly standard patterns in one group or another. Conditions strikingly similar to hypnosis have been noted by Lang and Lang (1960) and by Alland (1962). These include: (1) gradual constriction of perception and attention to a very limited focus of sight and sound, sometimes self-produced, as in the repetition of stereotyped phrases; (2) the abandonment of individual decision making and judgment; (3) the gradual encouragement, as in singing and swaying, of the response of following the suggestions of the leader and the patterns of the crowd; (4) the isolation of cult members from broader social involvements; and (5) a general kind of weakening of self brought on by such privations as fasting, and heat and concentration of carbon dioxide. Such conditions have been given explicit statement in the induction procedures which mystics, such as in the yoga tradition, have established, and in such an elaborate philosophical system as that of Plotinus. Plotinus' neo-Platonic philosophical system, which has in fact been associated, by Plotinus and others, with mystical practice, is a kind of explicit representation of the systematic regressive constriction of attention, and withdrawal from peripheral involvement. The system construes all of reality as but emanations, or shadows, from a central monadic creative source, and recommends the discipline of withdrawal from the emanations and communion with the source. The system has obviously lent itself to Christian adaptation.

Such a general understanding of the processes of this intense religious experience implies predictions about the relative likelihood of different individuals participating, and thus introduces the question of *individual differences*. The prediction is

.that the experience will be more common among persons with predispositional characteristics that could be described as weak egos. This presumably might show up in dependence on others, in intrapsychic conflict, or in various manifestations of low self-esteem, including guilt, or deficiencies of "identity." (To tighten the theory a bit, the low self-esteem and guilt presumably can be traced to past severe internalization of norms and demands, which in turn can presumably be traced to the dependence.) Such a prediction accords fairly closely with various reported descriptions of the preconversion states and personalities of persons who have been involved in such an intense experience (Christensen, 1965; Coe, 1917; DeSanctis, 1927; James, 1902; Starbuck, 1899) and with the studies of personalities of classic mystics, necessarily based on documents (for example, see Spangler, 1961). Kildahl (1965) found converts less intelligent and scoring higher on the MMPI hysteria scale.

The *outcome* or function of such experience is less easily predictable and less clearly discernible in observations. Perhaps two types of resolutions can be very broadly distinguished corresponding roughly to the distinction that has been made earlier between structure-bound and freeing (that is, superego and ego) forms of religious maturation. One resolution might be construed as a perpetuation of the dependence pattern. A conversion experience, for example, may offer different but still specific group standards and practices, commonly guilt-reducing, which can be construed as meeting the dependency needs and bolstering the ego—in one of Erikson's terms, "over-commitment." Or a resolution may tend to show a greater liberation from past dependencies and an enhancement of independence and ego skills. Presumably, the dynamics of the latter process could be traced to a more fundamental regressive kind of dependency satisfaction—"basic trust" in Erikson's terms—analogous to that provided by an ideal parent or to the "acceptance" of a therapist, which leaves a person relatively self-confident and relatively liberated from further reliance on specific dependency objects. More recent observations have especially emphasized the constructive, integrative, or "problem-solving" functions of conversion (Allison, 1966; Christensen, 1965; Salzman, 1966; Stewart, 1966).

REFERENCES

Ackerman, N. W., and Marie Jahoda (1950). *Anti-Semitism and emotional disorder.* New York: Harper.

Adorno, T. W., Else Frenkel-Brunswik, D. J. Levinson, and R. N. Sanford (1950). *The authoritarian personality* (2 vols.). New York: Harper.

Alland, A., Jr. (1962). Possession in a revivalistic Negro church. *J. scient. Stud. Religion, 1,* 204–213.

Allen, E. E., and R. W. Hites (1961). Factors in religious attitudes of older adolescents. *J. soc. Psychol., 55,* 265–273.

Allen, Mary K. (1955). Personality and cultural factors related to religious authoritarianism. Unpublished Ph.D. dissertation, Stanford University.

Allen, R. O. (1965). Religion and prejudice: an attempt to clarify the patterns of relationship. Unpublished Ph.D. dissertation, University of Denver.

Allen, R. O., and B. Spilka (1967). Committed and consensual religion: a specification of religion-prejudice relationships. *J. scient. Stud. Religion, 6,* 191–206.

Allinsmith, W., and Beverly Allinsmith (1948). Religious affiliation and politico-economic attitude: a study of eight major U.S. religious groups. *Publ. Opin. Quart., 12,* 377–389.

Allison, J. (1966). Recent empirical studies of religious conversion experiences. *Pastoral Psychol., 17,* 21–33.

Allport, G. W. (1950). *The individual and his religion.* New York: Macmillan.

———— (1954). *The nature of prejudice.* Cambridge, Mass.: Addison-Wesley.

———— (1959). Religion and prejudice. *Crane Rev., 2,* 1–10. (Reprinted in G. W. Allport, *Personality and social encounter.* Boston: Beacon Press, 1960. Chapter 16.)

———— (1963). Behavioral science, religion, and mental health. *J. Religion and Health, 2,* 187–197.

———— (1966). The religious context of prejudice. *J. scient. Stud. Religion, 5,* 447–457.

Allport, G. W., and J. Gillespie (1955). *Youth's outlook on the future.* Garden City, N.Y.: Doubleday.

Allport, G. W., J. Gillespie, and J. Young (1948). Religion of the post-war college student. *J. Psychol., 25,* 3–33.

Allport, G. W., and B. M. Kramer (1946). Some roots of prejudice. *J. Psychol., 22,* 9–39.

Allport, G. W., and J. M. Ross (1967). Personal religious orientation and prejudice. *J. Pers. soc. Psychol., 5,* 432–443.

Allport, G. W., P. E. Vernon, and G. Lindzey (1960). *The study of values.* Boston: Houghton Mifflin.

Altizer, T. J., and W. Hamilton (1966). *Radical theology and the death of God.* Indianapolis: Bobbs-Merrill.

Appel, K. E. (1959). Religion. In S. Arieti (Ed.), *Handbook of psychiatry.* Vol. 2. New York: Basic Books. Pp. 1777–1782.

Argyle, M. (1958). *Religious behaviour.* New York: Free Press.

Arieti, S. (1961). The loss of reality. *Psychoanal. Rev., 48,* No. 3, 3–24.

Armatas, T. J. (1962). A factor analytic study of patterns of religious belief in relation to prejudice. Unpublished Ph.D. dissertation, University of Denver.

Ashbrook, J. B. (1966). The relationship of church members to church organization. *J. scient. Stud. Religion, 5,* 397–419.

Barron, F. (1963). *Creativity and psychological health.* Princeton: Van Nostrand.

Barth, K. (1956). *Church dogmatics.* Vol. 1, Part 2. New York: Scribner's.

Bateman, M. M., and J. S. Jenson (1958). The effect of religious background on modes of handling anger. *J. soc. Psychol., 47,* 133–141.

Bender, I. E. (1958). Changes in religious interest: a retest after fifteen years. *J. abnorm. soc. Psychol., 57,* 41–46.

Berger, P. (1961). *The noise of solemn assemblies.* New York: Doubleday.

———— (1967). A sociological view of the secularization of theology. *J. scient. Stud. Religion, 6,* 3–16.

Berliner, B. (1946). On some religious motives of anti-Semitism. In E. Simmel (Ed.), *Anti-Semitism.* New York: International Univ. Press. Pp. 79–84.

Bettelheim, B., and M. Janowitz (1949). Ethnic tolerance: a function of social and personal control. *Amer. J. Sociol., 55,* 137–145.

———— (1950). *Dynamics of prejudice.* New York: Harper. (Reprinted in B. Bettelheim and M. Janowitz, *Social change and prejudice.* New York: Free Press, 1964. Part II.)

Binnewies, W. G. (1934). Measuring the effect of a social force. *J. educ. Sociol., 8,* 83–93.

Black, M. S., and P. London (1966). The dimension of guilt, religion, and personal ethics. *J. soc. Psychol., 69,* 39–54.

Blum, B. S., and J. H. Mann (1960). The effect of religious membership on religious prejudice. *J. soc. Psychol., 52,* 97–101.

Bonhoeffer, D. (1953). *Letters and papers from prison.* London: SCM Press.

Bonney, M. E. (1949). A study of friendship choices in college in relation to church affiliation, in-church preferences, family size, and length of enrollment in college. *J. soc. Psychol., 29,* 153–166.

Broen, W. E., Jr. (1957). A factor-analytic study of religious attitudes. *J. abnorm. soc. Psychol., 54,* 176–179.

Brown, D. G., and W. L. Lowe (1951). Religious beliefs and personality characteristics of college students. *J. soc. Psychol., 33,* 103–129.

Brown, L. B. (1962). A study of religious belief. *Brit. J. Psychol., 53,* 259–272.

———— (1964). Classifications of religious orientation. *J. scient. Stud. Religion, 4,* 91–99.

———— (1966). The structure of religious belief. *J. scient. Stud. Religion, 5,* 259–272.

Burchinal, L. G. (1957). Marital satisfaction and religious behavior. *Amer. sociol. Rev., 22,* 306–310.

Carney, R. E. (1961). Some correlates of religiosity. *J. scient. Stud. Religion, 1,* 143–144.

Chave, E. J. (1939). *Measure religion.* Chicago: Univ. of Chicago Bookstore.

Christensen, C. W. (1965). Religious conversion in adolescence. *Pastoral Psychol., 16,* 17–28.

Clark, W. H. (1955). A study of some of the factors leading to achievement and creativity with special reference to religious skepticism and belief. *J. soc. Psychol., 41,* 57–69.

———— (1958). *The psychology of religion.* New York: Macmillan.

Cline, V. B., and J. M. Richards, Jr. (1965). A factor-analytic study of religious belief and behavior. *J. Pers. soc. Psychol., 1,* 569–578.

Coe, G. A. (1916). *The psychology of religion.* Chicago: Univ. of Chicago Press.

Cowen, E. L. (1954). The negative concept as a personality measure. *J. consult. Psychol., 18,* 138–142.

Cox, H. (1965). *The secular city.* New York: Macmillan.

Demerath, N. J. (1965). *Social class and American Protestantism.* Chicago: Rand McNally.

DeSanctis, S. (1927). *Religious conversion* (transl. H. Augur). New York: Harcourt, Brace.

Deutsch, M. (1960). Trust, trustworthiness, and the *F* scale. *J. abnorm. soc. Psychol., 61,* 138–140.

Dittes, J. E. (1959a). Effect of changes in self-esteem upon impulsiveness and deliberation in making judgments. *J. abnorm. soc. Psychol., 58,* 348–356.

_____ (1959b). Justification by faith and the experimental psychologist. *Religion in Life, 28,* 567–576.

_____ (1964). *Vocational guidance of theological candidates.* Dayton, O.: Ministry Studies Board.

_____ (1968). The psychology of religion. In D. L. Sills (Ed.), *International encyclopedia of the social sciences.* Vol. 13. New York: Crowell-Collier and Macmillan. Pp. 414–421.

Douglas, W. (1963). Religion. In N. Farberow (Ed.), *Taboo topics.* New York: Atherton. Pp. 80–95.

Dreger, R. M. (1952). Some personality correlates of religious attitudes as determined by projective techniques. *Psychol. Monogr., 66,* No. 3 (whole No. 335).

_____ (1958). Expressed attitudes and needs of religious persons compared with those determined by projective techniques. *J. gen. Psychol., 58,* 217–224.

Droba, D. D. (1932). Churches and war attitudes. *Sociol. soc. Res., 16,* 547–552.

Duke, J. D. (1964). Placebo reactivity and tests of suggestibility. *J. Pers., 32,* 227–236.

Edwards, J. (1959). *A treatise concerning religious affections.* (Written 1746.) New Haven: Yale Univ. Press.

Elkind, D. (1964a). Age changes in the meaning of religious identity. *Rev. religious Res., 6,* 36–40.

_____ (1964b). Piaget's semi-clinical interview and the study of spontaneous religion. *J. scient. Stud. Religion, 4,* 40–47.

Elkind, D., and S. Elkind (1962). Varieties of religious experience in young adolescents. *J. scient. Stud. Religion, 2,* 102–112.

Etzioni, A. (1961). *A comparative analysis of complex organizations.* Glencoe, Ill.: Free Press.

Evans, R. I. (1952). Personal values as factors in anti-Semitism. *J. abnorm. soc. Psychol., 47,* 749–756.

Eysenck, H. J. (1944). General social attitudes. *J. soc. Psychol., 19,* 207–227.

Faulkner, J. E., and G. F. De Jong (1966). Religiosity in 5-D: an empirical analysis. *Soc. Forces, 45,* 246–254.

Feagin, J. R. (1964). Prejudice and religious types: a focused study of southern fundamentalists. *J. scient. Stud. Religion, 4,* 3–13.

Ferguson, L. W. (1939). Primary social attitudes. *J. soc. Psychol., 8,* 217–223.

_____ (1944). A revision of the primary attitude scales. *J. Psychol., 17,* 229–241.

Festinger, L., H. W. Riecken, and S. Schachter (1956). *When prophecy fails.* Minneapolis: Univ. of Minnesota Press.

Fetter, G. C. (1964). A comparative study of attitudes of Christian and of Moslem Lebanese villagers. *J. scient. Stud. Religion, 4,* 48–59.

Fichter, J. H. (1951). *Southern parish.* Vol. 1: Dynamics of a city church. Chicago: Univ. of Chicago Press.

———— (1953). The marginal Catholic: an institutional approach. *Soc. Forces, 32,* 167–173.

Fisher, S. (1964). Acquiescence and religiosity. *Psychol. Reports, 15,* 784.

Frank, J. D. (1961). *Persuasion and healing.* Baltimore: Johns Hopkins Press.

French, Vera V. (1947). The structure of sentiments. *J. Pers., 15,* 247–282; *16,* 78–108, 209–244.

Frenkel-Brunswik, Else, and R. N. Sanford (1946). The anti-Semitic personality: a research report. In E. Simmel (Ed.), *Anti-Semitism.* New York: International Univ. Press. Pp. 96–124.

Freud, S. (1907). Obsessive acts and religious practices. In *Collected papers.* Vol. 2. London: Hogarth Press, 1953. Pp. 25–35.

———— (1939). *Moses and monotheism.* New York: Vintage Books, 1955.

———— (1927). *The future of an illusion.* Garden City, N.Y.: Doubleday, 1957.

———— (1913). *Totem and taboo.* New York: Norton, 1962.

Friedrichs, R. W. (1959). Christians and residential exclusion: an empirical study of a northern dilemma. *J. soc. Issues, 15,* No. 4, 14–23.

Fromm, E. (1950). *Psychoanalysis and religion.* New Haven: Yale Univ. Press.

Fukuyama, Y. (1960). The major dimensions of church membership. Unpublished Ph.D. dissertation, University of Chicago.

———— (1961). The major dimensions of church membership. *Rev. religious Res., 2,* 154–161.

Furgeson, E. H. (1965). The definition of religious conversion. *Pastoral Psychol., 16,* 8–16.

Gardner, L. A. (1960). Certain religious attitudes and beliefs of students in a Lutheran college, with reference to their value structures and personal values. Unpublished Th.D. dissertation, Boston University School of Theology. *Diss. Abs., 21,* 687–688.

Garrison, K. C. (1961). Worldminded attitudes of college students in a southern university. *J. soc. Psychol., 54,* 147–153.

Gill, M. M., and M. Brenman (1959). *Hypnosis and related states.* New York: International Univ. Press.

Glock, C. Y. (1959). The religious revival in America? In Jane Zahn (Ed.), *Religion and the face of America.* Berkeley: University Extension, University of California. (Reprinted in C. Y. Glock and R. Stark, *Religion and society in tension.* Chicago: Rand McNally, 1965. Chapter 4.)

———— (1962). On the study of religious commitment. *Religious Educ., Res. Suppl.,* S-98–S-110. (Reprinted in C. Y. Glock and R. Stark, *Religion and society in tension.* Chicago: Rand McNally, 1965. Chapter 2.)

Glock, C. Y., and R. Stark (1965). *Religion and society in tension.* Chicago: Rand McNally.

————— (1966). *Christian beliefs and anti-Semitism.* New York: Harper and Row.

Godin, A. (1962). Importance and difficulty of scientific research in religious education: the problem of the criterion. *Religious Educ., 57,* 163–171, 238. (Reprinted in *Religious Educ., Res. Suppl.,* 1962, S-166–S-174.

————— (1964). Belonging to a church: what does it mean psychologically? *J. scient. Stud. Religion, 3,* 204–215.

Goldsen, Rose K., M. Rosenberg, R. M. Williams, Jr., and E. A. Suchman (1960). *What college students think.* Princeton: Van Nostrand.

Gorsuch, R. L. (1968). The conceptualization of God as seen in adjective ratings. *J. scient. Stud. Religion, 7,* 56–64.

Gough, J. G. (1951). Studies of social intolerance: IV. Related social attitudes. *J. soc. Psychol., 33,* 263–269.

Gray, D. B. (1964). Factors related to a conception of the church held by Presbyterian laymen. Unpublished Ph.D. dissertation, University of Pittsburgh.

Greeley, A. M. (1963). A note on the origins of religious differences. *J. scient. Stud. Religion, 3,* 21–31.

Gregory, W. E. (1952). The psychology of religion: some suggested areas of research to psychology. *J. abnorm. soc. Psychol., 47,* 256–258. (Reprinted in O. Strunk, Jr., Ed., *Readings in the psychology of religion.* Nashville: Abingdon, 1959. Pp. 261–265.)

————— (1957). The orthodoxy of the authoritarian personality. *J. soc. Psychol., 45,* 217–232.

Gustafson, J. M. (1965). Context versus principles: a misplaced debate in Christian ethics. *Harvard theol. Rev., 58,* 171–202.

Hadden, J. K. (1963). An analysis of some factors associated with religion and political affiliation in a college population. *J. scient. Stud. Religion, 2,* 209–216.

Harding, J., B. Kutner, H. Proshansky, and I. Chein (1954). Prejudice and ethnic relations. In G. Lindzey (Ed.), *Handbook of social psychology.* Cambridge, Mass.: Addison-Wesley. Pp. 1021–1061.

Harrison, P. M. (1959). *Authority and power in the free church tradition.* Princeton: Princeton Univ. Press.

Hartshorne, H., and M. A. May (1928). *Studies in deceit.* New York: Macmillan.

Havens, J. (1961). The participant's vs. the observer's frame of reference in the psychological study of religion. *J. scient. Stud. Religion, 1,* 79–87.

————— (1964). A working paper: memo on the religious implications of the consciousness-changing drugs. *J. scient. Stud. Religion, 3,* 216–226.

Holtzman, W. H., and R. K. Young (1966). Scales for measuring attitudes toward the Negro and toward organized religion. *Psychol. Reports, 18,* 31–34.

Howells, T. H. (1928). Comparative study of those who accept as against those who reject religious authority. *Univ. Iowa Stud. Char., 2,* No. 2.

Hunt, R. A. (1968). The interpretation of the religious scale of the Allport-Vernon-Lindzey study of values. *J. scient. Stud. Religion, 7,* 65–77.

Jahoda, Marie (1958). *Current concepts of positive mental health.* New York: Basic Books.

James, W. (1902). *Varieties of religious experience.* New York: Longmans, Green.

Jeeves, M. A. (1957). Contribution on prejudice and religion. In *Proceedings of the XVth International Congress of Psychology, Brussels.* Pp. 508–510.

Jenkins, D. (1962). *Beyond religion: the truth and error in 'religionless Christianity.'* Philadelphia: Westminster.

Johnson, P. E. (1959). *Psychology of religion* (rev. ed.). New York: Abingdon.

Jones, E. M. (1957). The study of religious concepts. *Psychol. Reports, 3,* 293–297.

Jones, M. B. (1958). Religious values and authoritarian tendency. *J. soc. Psychol., 48,* 83–89.

Kania, W. (1965). An investigation of the *K* scale of the MMPI as a measure of defensiveness in Protestant theological seminary students. Unpublished Ph.D. dissertation, Michigan State University.

Keedy, T. C. (1958). Anomie and religious orthodoxy. *Sociol. soc. Res., 43,* 34–37.

Keene, J. (1967a). Baha'i world faith: redefinition of religion. *J. scient. Stud. Religion, 6,* 221–235.

—————— (1967b). Religious behavior and neuroticism, spontaneity, and worldmindedness. *Sociometry, 30,* 137–157.

Kelly, J. G., J. E. Ferson, and W. H. Holtzman (1958). The measurement of attitudes toward the Negro in the south. *J. soc. Psychol., 48,* 305–317.

Kildahl, J. P. (1957). Personality correlates of sudden religious converts contrasted with persons of gradual religious development. Unpublished Ph.D. dissertation, New York University.

—————— (1965). The personalities of sudden religious converts. *Pastoral Psychol., 16,* 37–44.

King, M. (1967). Measuring the religious variable. *J. scient. Stud. Religion, 6,* 173–185.

King, S. H., and D. H. Funkenstein (1957). Religious practice and cardiovascular reactions during stress. *J. abnorm. soc. Psychol., 55,* 135–137.

Kirkpatrick, C. (1949). Religion and humanitarianism: a study of institutional implications. *Psychol. Monogr., 63,* No. 9 (whole No. 304).

Kitay, P. M. (1947). Radicalism and conservatism toward conventional religion: a psychological study based on a group of Jewish college students. *Teach. Coll. Contrib. Educ.,* No. 919.

Kling, F. R. (1959). *The motivations of ministerial candidates.* Princeton, N.J.: Educational Testing Service. Research Bulletin 59–2.

Kottman, E. J. (1966). A semantic study of religious attitude. *J. Religion and Health, 5,* 119–129.

Kosa, J., and C. O. Schommer (1961). Religious participation, religious knowledge, and scholastic aptitude: an empirical study. *J. scient. Stud. Religion, 1,* 88–97.

Lang, K., and Gladys E. Lang (1960). Decisions for Christ: Billy Graham in New York City. In M. Stein, A. J. Vidich, and D. M. White (Eds.), *Identity and anxiety.* Glencoe, Ill.: Free Press. Pp. 415–427.

Lasagna, L., F. Mosteller, J. M. von Felsinger, and H. K. Beecher (1954). A study of the placebo response. *Amer. J. Med., 16,* 770.

Lazerwitz, B. (1961). Some factors associated with variations in church attendance. *Soc. Forces, 39*, 301–309.

–––––– (1962). Membership in voluntary associations and frequency of church attendance. *J. scient. Stud. Religion, 2*, 74–84.

Leary, T. (1964). The religious experience: its production and interpretation. *Psychedelic Rev., 1*, 324–346.

Lenski, G. (1961). *The religious factor.* Garden City, N.Y.: Doubleday.

Leuba, J. H. (1934). Religious beliefs of American scientists. *Harper's, 169*, 291–300.

Levinson, D. J. (1954). The inter-group relations workshop: its psychological aims and effects. *J. Psychol., 38*, 103–126.

Levinson, D. J., and R. N. Sanford (1944). A scale for the measurement of anti-Semitism. *J. Psychol., 17*, 339–370.

Liu, E. T. (1961). The community reference system, religiosity, and race attitudes. *Soc. Forces, 39*, 324–328.

Lowenstein, R. (1951). *Christians and Jews: a psychoanalytic study.* New York: International Univ. Press.

Lurie, W. (1937). A study of Spranger's value type by the method of factor analysis. *J. soc. Psychol., 8*, 17–38.

Luther, M. (1520). *Treatise on religious liberty.* Philadelphia: Muhlenberg, 1957.

McClelland, D. C. (1955). *Studies in motivation.* New York: Appleton-Century-Crofts.

McKenna, H. V. (1961). Religious attitudes and personality traits. *J. soc. Psychol., 54*, 378–388.

Martin, C., and R. C. Nichols (1962). Personality and religious belief. *J. soc. Psychol., 56*, 3–8.

Menges, R. J., and J. E. Dittes (1965). *Psychological studies of clergymen.* New York: Thomas Nelson.

Merton, R. (1940). Facts and factitiousness in ethnic opinionaries. *Amer. sociol. Rev., 5*, 13–28.

Meyer, D. (1965). *The positive thinkers.* New York: Doubleday.

Mischel, W., and F. Mischel (1958). Psychological aspects of spirit possession. *Amer. Anthropologist, 60*, 249–260.

Monaghan, R. (1967). The three faces of the true believer: motivations for attending a fundamentalist church. *J. scient. Stud. Religion, 6*, 236–245.

Nash, C. B. (1958). Correlation between ESP and religious value. *J. Parapsychol., 22*, 204–209.

Nash, D., and P. Berger (1962). The child, the family, and the 'religious revival' in suburbia. *J. scient. Stud. Religion, 2*, 85–93.

Nelson, M. O., and E. M. Jones (1957). An application of the Q-technique to the study of religious concepts. *Psychol. Reports, 3*, 293–297.

Oates, W. E. (1955). *Religious factors in mental illness.* New York: Association Press.

Olson, B. (1963). *Faith and prejudice.* New Haven: Yale Univ. Press.

O'Neil, W. M., and D. J. Levinson (1954). A factorial exploration of authoritarianism and some of its ideological correlates. *J. Pers., 22*, 449–463.

O'Reilly, C., and E. J. O'Reilly (1954). Religious beliefs of Catholic college students and their attitude toward minorities. *J. abnorm. soc. Psychol., 49,* 378–380.

Pahnke, W. N. (1963). Drugs and mysticism: an analysis of the relationship between psychedelic drugs and the mystical consciousness. Unpublished Ph.D. dissertation, Harvard University.

Pahnke, W. N., and W. A. Richards (1966). Implications of LSD and experimental mysticism. *J. Religion and Health, 5,* 175–208.

Parry, H. J. (1949). Protestants, Catholics and prejudice. *Int. J. Opin. Attitude Res., 3,* 205–213.

Peterman, D. J. (1966). Familial and personological determinants of orientations toward God. Unpublished Ph.D. dissertation, University of California, Berkeley.

Pinkney, A. (1961). The anatomy of prejudice: majority group attitudes toward minorities in selected American cities. Unpublished Ph.D. dissertation, Cornell University.

Poit, C. H. (1962). A study concerning religious belief and denominational affiliation. *Religious Educ., 57,* 214–216.

Prothro, E. T., and J. A. Jensen (1950). Inter-relations of religious and ethnic attitudes in selected southern populations. *J. soc. Psychol., 32,* 45–49.

Putney, S., and R. Middletown (1961). Dimensions and correlates of religious ideologies. *Soc. Forces, 39,* 285–290.

Pyron, B. (1961). Belief Q-sort, Allport-Vernon study of values and religion. *Psychol. Reports, 8,* 399–400.

Ranck, J. G. (1957). Some personality correlates of theological conservatism and liberalism. *Drew Gateway, 27,* 59–70.

––––––– (1961). Religious conservatism-liberalism and mental health. *Pastoral Psychol., 12,* 34–40.

Roberts, D. (1950). *Psychotherapy and a Christian view of man.* New York: Scribner's.

Robinson, J. A. T. (1963). *Honest to God.* Philadelphia: Westminster.

Rokeach, M. (1960). *The open and closed mind.* New York: Basic Books.

Rosenberg, M. J. (1957). The social sources of the current religious revival. *Pastoral Psychol., 8,* 31–40.

Rosenblith, Judy (1949). A replication of "Some roots of prejudice." *J. abnorm. soc. Psychol., 44,* 470–489.

––––––– (1957). How much invariance is there in the relations of 'prejudice scores' to experiential and attitudinal variables? *Psychol. Reports, 3,* 217–241 (Monogr. Suppl. No. 5).

Rosenblum, A. L. (1958). Ethnic prejudice as related to social class and religiosity. *Sociol. soc. Res., 43,* 272–275.

Ross, M. (1950). *The religious beliefs of youth.* New York: Association Press.

Salisbury, W. S. (1962). Religiosity, regional sub-culture, and social behavior. *J. scient. Stud. Religion, 2,* 94–101.

Salzman, L. (1953). The psychology of religious and ideological conversion. *Psychiatry, 16,* 177–187.

———— (1966). Types of religious conversion. *Pastoral Psychol., 17*, 5–20, 66.

Sanai, M. (1952). An empirical study of political, religious, and social attitudes. *Brit. J. Psychol., Statist. Sect., 5*, 81–92.

Sanford, R. N. (1946). Optimism and religion. *Amer. Psychologist, 1*, 451–452.

Sanford, R. N., and D. J. Levinson (1948). Ethnocentrism in relation to some religious attitudes and practices. *Amer. Psychologist, 3*, 350–351. (Abstract)

Sappenfield, B. R. (1943). Group differences in social attitudes. *Psychol. Record, 5*, 289–305.

Sargant, W. (1957). *Battle for the mind.* London: Heinemann.

Shand, J. D. (1953). A factor-analytic study of Chicago Protestant ministers' conceptions of what it means to be 'religious.' Unpublished Ph.D. dissertation, University of Chicago.

Shiner, L. (1967). The concept of secularization in empirical research. *J. scient. Stud. Religion, 6*, 207–220.

Shinert, G., and E. E. Ford (1958). The relation of ethnocentric attitudes to intensity of religious practice. *J. educ. Sociol., 32*, 157–162.

Siegman, A. W. (1961). An empirical investigation of the psychoanalytic theory of religious behavior. *J. scient. Stud. Religion, 1*, 74–78.

———— (1962). A cross-cultural investigation of the relationship between religiosity, ethnic prejudice and authoritarianism. *Psychol. Reports, 11*, 419–424.

Simmel, E., Ed. (1946). *Anti-Semitism.* New York: International Univ. Press.

Sinclair, R. D. (1928). A comparative study of those who report the experience of the divine presence and those who do not. *Univ. Iowa Stud. Char., 2*, No. 3.

Smith, H. (1964). Do drugs have religious import? *J. Philos., 61*, 517–530.

Smith, M. B., J. S. Bruner, and R. W. White (1956). *Opinions and personality.* New York: Wiley.

Spangler, J. (1961). Becoming a mystic: an analysis of developmental factors according to the Murray 'need-press' theory. Unpublished Ph.D. dissertation, Boston University.

Spilka, B. (1958). Some personality correlates of interiorized and institutionalized religious belief. *Psychol. Newsletter, 9*, 103–107.

Spilka, B., P. Armatas, and June Nussbaum (1964). The concept of God: a factor-analytic approach. *Rev. religious Res., 6*, 28–36.

Spilka, B., and J. Reynolds (1965). Religion and prejudice: a factor analytic study. *Rev. religious Res., 6*, 163–168.

Spoerl, D. T. (1951). Some aspects of prejudice as affected by religion and education. *J. soc. Psychol., 33*, 59–76.

Stace, W. T. (1960). *Mysticism and philosophy.* Philadelphia: Lippincott.

Stanley, G. (1964). Personality and attitude correlates of religious conversion. *J. scient. Stud. Religion, 4*, 60–63.

Starbuck, E. D. (1899). *The psychology of religion.* London: Walter Scott.

Stark, R. (1963). On the compatibility of religion and science: a survey of American graduate students. *J. scient. Stud. Religion, 3,* 3–20. (Reprinted in C. Y. Glock and R. Stark, *Religion and society in tension.* Chicago: Rand McNally, 1965. Chapter 14.)

Stewart, C. W. (1966). The religious experience of two adolescent girls. *Pastoral Psychol., 17,* 49–55.

Stouffer, S. (1955). *Communism, conformity and civil liberties.* New York: Doubleday.

Strommen, M. P. (1963). *Profiles of church youth.* St. Louis: Concordia.

——— (1967). Religious education and the problem of prejudice: a book discussion. *Religious Educ., 62,* 52–59.

Struening, E. L. (1957). The dimensions, distributions and correlates of authoritarianism in a midwestern university faculty population. Unpublished Ph.D. dissertation, Purdue University.

——— (1963). Anti-democratic attitudes in midwestern university. In H. H. Remmers (Ed.), *Anti-democratic attitudes in American schools.* Evanston, Ill.: Northwestern Univ. Press. Chapter 9.

Struening, E. L. and B. Spilka (1952). A study of certain social and religious attitudes of university faculty members. *Psychol. Newsletter,* No. 43, 1–18.

Strunk, O., Jr. (1958). Relation between self-reports and adolescent religiosity. *Psychol. Reports, 4,* 683–686.

——— (1959). Perceived relationships between parental and deity concepts. *Psychol. Newsletter, 10,* 222–226.

Swickard, D. L. (1963). A factor-analytic study of the patterns of religious belief, degree of prejudice, and perceived parent-child rearing practices. Unpublished Ph.D. dissertation, University of Denver.

Symington, T. A. (1935). Religious liberals and conservatives. *Teach. Coll. Contrib. Educ.,* No. 640.

Thouless, R. H. (1954). *Authority and freedom.* London: Hodder and Stoughton.

Thurstone, L. L. (1934). The vectors of mind. *Psychol. Rev., 41,* 1–32.

Thurstone, L. L., and E. J. Chave (1929). *Measurement of attitude.* Chicago: Univ. of Chicago Press.

Tillich, P. J. (1963). *Systematic theology.* Vol. 3. Chicago: Univ. of Chicago Press.

Triandis, H. C., and L. M. Triandis (1960). Race, social class, religion, and nationality as determinants of social distance. *J. abnorm. soc. Psychol., 61,* 110–118.

Tumin, M., *et al.* (1958). Education, prejudice, and discrimination: a study in readiness for de-segregation. *Amer. sociol. Rev., 23,* 41–49.

Turbeville, G., and R. E. Hyde (1946). A selected sample of attitudes of Louisiana State University students toward the Negro: a study in public opinion. *Soc. Forces, 24,* 447–450.

Vernon, G. M. (1962). Measuring religion: two methods compared. *Rev. religious Res., 3,* 159–166.

Walters, O. S. (1957). The religious background of fifty alcoholics. *Quart. J. Study of Alcohol, 18,* 405–416.

Weima, J. (1965). Authoritarianism, religious conservatism, and sociocentric attitudes in Roman Catholic groups. *Hum. Relat., 18,* 231–239.

Welford, A. T. (1957). On the measurement of religious attitude and behavior. In *Proceedings of the XVth International Congress of Psychology, Brussels.* Pp. 506–508.

Whitam, F. L. (1962). Subdimensions of religiosity and race prejudice. *Rev. religious Res., 3,* 166–174.

Williams, R. M., Jr. (1964). *Strangers next door.* Englewood Cliffs, N.J.: Prentice-Hall.

Wilson, W. C. (1960). Extrinsic religious values and prejudice. *J. abnorm. soc. Psychol., 60,* 286–287.

Winter, G. (1961). *Suburban captivity of the churches.* New York: Doubleday.

Woodruff, A. D. (1945). Personal values and religious background. *J. soc. Psychol., 22,* 141–147.

Wrightsman, L. S., Jr. (1963). The measurement of philosophies of human nature. Paper read to Midwestern Psychological Association Convention, Chicago. In S. Cook (Ed.), *Research plans.* New York: Religious Education Association, 1962. Pp. 118–122.

Yinger, J. M. (1957). *Religion, society and the individual.* New York: Macmillan.

———— (1963). Sociology looks at religion. New York: Macmillan.

Young, R. K., W. M. Benson, and W. H. Holtzman (1960). Change in attitudes toward the Negro in a southern university. *J. abnorm. soc. Psychol., 60,* 131–133.

Young, R. K., D. S. Dustin, and W. H. Holtzman (1966). Change in attitude toward religion in a southern university. *Psychol. Reports, 18,* 39–46.

Zimmermann, F. K. (1934). Religion: a conservative social force. *J. abnorm. soc. Psychol., 28,* 473–474.

45

Social Psychology of Mental Health

HOWARD E. FREEMAN, Brandeis University and Russell Sage Foundation

JEANNE M. GIOVANNONI, University of California, Los Angeles

Mental health covers an elusive and diffuse field and the term itself encompasses a multiplicity of meanings. It makes more sense, consequently, to regard it as a valuable rubric to head a chapter or describe an arena of work than as a concept to give orientation to research (Smith, 1961). Naturally, in the light of their heavy investment in the phenomenon of mental health, social psychologists have sought repeatedly to clarify the concept and the definition of the field (Jahoda, 1958; Scott, 1958a; Smith, 1961); but, beset as they are by powerful ideological imperatives, by the many public and private bodies that deal with mental health, by the partisan theories of most practitioners, and above all, by the limited current knowledge based on research, they have betrayed futility and confusion in their work. Mental health is an ascientific concept, and it is unlikely that present or future thinking and study in any of the behavioral and medical sciences are going to regularize its status. Thus, in this chapter, we shall look at the field of mental health as a social-psychological endeavor, and describe the relevant work of social psychologists in it.

It is not possible to develop an orderly analysis, however, without examining the basic issues and problems that plague the subject. At the outset, it is fair to observe that social psychologists agree neither on the meaning of "mental health" nor on the boundaries of the field; the discontinuities in social-psychological research in mental health are as severe as those in the rest of the field. At the heart of the problem lies the multiplicity of meanings given to the term "mental health." It is with the ambiguity of definition that we must first deal.

THE CONCEPT OF MENTAL HEALTH

For our purposes, the various definitions of mental health can be grouped into three categories: mental health can be considered as a medical, a psychological, or a social phenomenon. The confusion in definition is compounded by the overlapping and merging—unfortunately, there is no integration—of the three positions. The three views are presented with the caution that we are of necessity oversimplifying.

MENTAL HEALTH AS A MEDICAL PHENOMENON

Historically the medical practitioner's orientation has dominated the field and it continues to do so. In his orientation to mental health, he carries over his thinking about biophysiological phenomena and particularly the conception of systems, that is, groups of body organs and parts that together perform one or more vital functions. In medicine, judgment of an individual's health status is made on the basis of an assessment of the adequacy of functioning of these systems: the individual patient's responses are considered against supposedly usual or typical reactions, and sufficient and patterned deviation from these norms leads to a description of him as "ill." "Mental health," too, in its most rudimentary medical meaning, denotes that an individual's psychic system functions at a level deemed "satisfactory."

No system functions perfectly, of course. In making judgments about the health of an individual it is necessary to take into account his total functioning, for the malfunctioning of part of a system may be compensated for by other body mechanisms. A system functions satisfactorily so long as it is in "homeostatic balance," and illness is either the lack of or tenuousness of such a balance. Health and illness are seen to exist along a continuum: health is equated with an optimum, stable balance, and illness is seen as degrees of departure from the satisfactory homeostatic functioning of the system. Thus, for the psychiatrist, optimum mental health and severe mental illness are poles of a continuum. Though the psychiatrist does not expect to find many individuals at either extreme, he categorizes the individual by gauging where he falls along the illness-wellness continuum. In this narrow medical sense, the mentally healthy individual is one whose psychic system is functioning in ways that, as Szasz (1961) points out, one generation of psychiatrists has taught another are normal.

In the field of mental health the medical practitioner—legally, and for all practical purposes—has retained primary right to the role of diagnostician, including the making of judgments as to severity of illness. The importance of this role cannot be overestimated: his almost complete monopoly to pronounce individuals as "healthy" or as "ill" accounts for his continuing influence in research, and has allowed him, as will be discussed, to strongly influence both the psychological and the sociological orientations to the field.

The questionable applicability of the medical model to mental health underlies some of the thorniest issues in the field. While many of the same difficulties in diagnosis beset other branches of medicine, they are particularly pronounced in the field of psychiatry. Diagnosis, not only in psychiatry but in all of medicine, concerns itself with the appropriate definitions of "systems," and with the patterning of indicators or symptoms of illness. There is considerable controversy over the relative virtues of "tests" and clinical judgment in making diagnostic pronouncements. Tests presumably supply objective information. However, in the case of the circulatory system, for example, the diagnostician finds interpretation of levels of cholesterol beyond reasonable limits very difficult because of the lack of definitive knowledge of the role of abnormal quantities of it in circulatory illness (Dawber, Moore, and Mann, 1957). In the diagnosis of all illness, though there is a tendency to develop and rely on tests and other reproducible indicators of particular pathologies, many practitioners insist on the value of "intuition" and "clinical experience" in diagnosis. Consequently, the development of operational definitions for all disorders is exceedingly difficult.

The reliance on intuition and clinical experience is pronounced in the evalua-tion of mental health. Though intellectually the psychiatrist subscribes to rigor in diagnostic criteria, he operates at a disadvantage in comparison with other medical specialists. His "system" is much more an abstraction and, oriented as he is by psy-chodynamics, he struggles with a conceptual framework that straddles internal and external states, that is, intrapsychic and behavioral phenomena. In addition to the problems of observation of psychic phenomena, there remains the difficult task of interpreting the relative severity of the malfunctioning.

Further, the notion of a continuum of mental health and illness offers only the grossest categorization and, as is the case with the other body systems, more elaborate taxonomic classifications are provided (Jellinek, 1939). One example of this is the international classification of mental disorders into the organic and congenital and the so-called functional, with specific labels under each—all in an attempt to approxi-mate the complexity and respectability of other branches of medical practice (Lewis, 1953). However, at least when diagnosing patients suspected of so-called functional types of mental illness, the psychiatrist has at his command almost no reliable tests of intrapsychic functioning and only most inadequate norms by which to judge ob-servable behavior.

Discouraged by the failure of his colleagues in medicine and psychology to pro-duce reliable and, to his mind, valid tests, the psychiatrist typically ends by diagnosing on nonspecific and undefined grounds—less so in the case of organic disorders than of functional disorders. There is considerable evidence regarding the shortcomings of psychiatric diagnosis: numerous studies point out the unreliability of psychiatric diagnoses (Ash, 1949; Doering, 1934; Elkin, 1947; Mehlman, 1952); there have been many attempts, with little success, to develop mass screening devices that correlate with psychiatric judgment or outcome (Srole, 1962; Stouffer, 1949); and the excessive overlap among categories renders the taxonomic classification virtually useless ex-cept for the "ideal" case. Moreover, medical definitions of health and illness are uniform neither between one English-speaking country and another (Yap, 1951) nor even between one practitioner and another (Ash, 1949; Pasamanick, Dinitz, and Lefton, 1959).

We are not sure, of course, how most psychiatrists really diagnose for they, as do most physicians, usually practice their craft in private (Freidson, 1963). No doubt there is much variation in what information an individual practitioner takes into account and what weight he gives to the details in it. In particular, it is difficult to assess the extent to which extrinsic circumstances are considered, such as that a given diagnosis will assure the patient's admission into a public hospital, or be the least likely to stigmatize him. Thus, that the highest rate of schizophrenia is found in the lower social class may indeed be a function of the reluctance to so label "nice" people —those most like the diagnostician (Hollingshead, 1958)!

Damning the psychiatrist is easy, of course, but it should be pointed out that investigators oriented toward social science have made no major gains in solving these problems, though there have been attempts to develop a standard system for particu-lar diagnoses. Most of this work has been done on schizophrenia. For example, Wing (1961a) has developed a simple classification of chronic schizophrenia. Based on ratings of mental symptoms made during a standard interview, it has been shown to have satisfactory interrater and test-retest reliability, and the correspondence of the scale's scores with social behavior provides some evidence of its validity. Also notable is the work of Phillips and Rabinovitch (1958), who analyzed the tendency of specific behavioral symptoms to appear together or be mutually exclusive. On the basis of considerable work, they hypothesized that symptoms tend to occur in three major groups assumed to indicate "avoidance of others," "self-indulgence and turning against others," and "self-deprivation and turning against the self." Both of these studies use symptomatic behaviors as units of classification, independent of existing nosologies.

There is little reason to believe, however, that most medical practitioners are going to abandon their health-illness notion of mental disorders or their taxonomic classification (Barton, 1958; Lewis, 1953). In addition to tradition and naiveté, a lack of adequate alternatives perpetuates the current diagnostic procedures for all their shortcomings. In any case, these problems impinge on much research in mental health of a social-psychological character for, no matter how unreliable or meaningless the medical orientation happens to be, it nevertheless determines a set of "social facts." It contributes much to the categorization of individuals as mentally ill from the sociological standpoint, a point best illustrated by the use of the "fact" of hospitalization as a social characteristic: a person cannot be so categorized without the opinion of a medical practitioner. One must recognize, certainly, to the extent that medical diagnoses are a variable in a study or a criterion of a sample (Freeman and Simmons, 1963; Pasamanick, 1961), that social-psychological research is vulnerable to idiosyncratic findings, as are community studies when so oriented (Eaton and Weil, 1953; Leighton, 1959; Srole *et al.*, 1962). Moreover, the medical orientation is the springboard of those who view mental health as a psychological phenomenon; its influence is apparent, formerly and now, in abnormal and personality psychology (Roe, 1949; Smith, 1961), and here, too, the vagueness of it cannot be overcome.

MENTAL HEALTH AS A PSYCHOLOGICAL PHENOMENON

While indeed there is much overlap between the medical and psychological approaches to mental health, there are discernible differences. Historically, psychology has not been so bound to the health-illness notion as has medicine. Rather the focus of psychology has been on the formulation of general laws, and thus while the physician's primary focus has been on the deviant or the ill, much of the psychologist's interest in "mental illness" has been generated by the utility of data on mental patients for formulating principles about psychological functioning in general. The psychologist also is not faced with the necessity of fitting his conceptions of mental health into a prescribed model, as is the physician with his allegiance to the body systems approach. In psychology, for example, perceptual processes may be investigated without regard to other psychological processes such as concept formation.

If there is an analogous point in the psychological view to the systemic approach of medicine, it is that of personality integration. According to many, personality integration is the central point of the psychological orientation (Smith, 1959), and, of course, the psychodynamic frame of reference is heavily dominated by the work of psychiatrists. But in psychology there is obviously a variety of theoretical positions regarding "personality," and these views are reflected in the various ways in which the concept of mental health has been elaborated. Some psychologists look at personality as a set of discrete dimensions (Cattell, 1957). Others have tried to develop tests supposedly reflecting specific attributes of personality which they try to fit together to obtain an appraisal of the psyche as a unitary phenomenon (Shoben, 1957). Still others hold a "holistic" view, that personality is more than the sum of its parts (Maslow, 1954). Finally, there are those who view personality as the collation of learned behaviors. Perhaps what distinguishes the psychological from the medical approach more than anything else is the fact that there is no *one* psychological approach, as there is a clearly discernible medical one.

But in their research, and certainly in clinical practice, psychologists find it necessary to order persons along a continuum. It is at this point in the field of mental health that the medical and psychological orientations become inextricably involved. Whereas a sick-well continuum dominates the medical orientation, an "abnormal-normal" continuum characterizes the psychological approach. "Abnormal" is not always defined by deviation from statistical norms; rather the term frequently characterizes those who supposedly would be classified by the medical scheme as "ill." Thus the great body of research devoted to identifying differences in functioning between "normals" and "abnormals" is beset with all the problems noted regarding the medical processes of diagnosis—particularly since, in most of them, the definition of "abnormal" rests solely on the fact that the individual has already been labeled mentally ill by a medical practitioner. To be sure, a good deal of the effort by the psychologist to operationalize medical definitions of mental illness through the development of psychological tests is aimed at freeing him from dependence on the impressionistic judgments of psychiatrists. The reliability of most tests is low, however, and their validity usually questioned when judged by diagnostic criteria. Thus, while psychological theory concerning mental health may be distinguished from the medical stance by its diversity of meanings, its more relativistic approach to mental phenomena, and its comparative freedom from the biophysiological systems model, there is a considerable overlap, in both clinical practice and in research, with medical thinking.

As noted, because of the influence of medicine there has been a preoccupation with "illness"; health, in general, has been defined as the absence of illness. There is an increasing effort among psychologists, however, to come to grips with a "positive" definition of mental health. While considerable attention has been given to theoretical formulations of such a concept, little empirical work has been done (Schwartz and Schwartz, 1968; Smith, 1959). Most of the efforts to measure mental health have ended up as attempts to operationalize medical criteria of mental illness (Gurin, Veroff, and Feld, 1960; Srole *et al.*, 1962). Nevertheless, the work of Jahoda (1958), among others, provides sets of psychological statements that embrace the current thinking regarding positive definitions of mental health. According to her, measures defining health are many, including an individual's attitude toward himself, realization of potential, unification of function, independence of social influences, conception of the world, resilience, and mastery of life. One may anticipate much more research effort oriented toward a "positive" definition of health.

MENTAL HEALTH AS A SOCIAL PHENOMENON

A third approach to mental health is that which regards mental health as a social phenomenon. Unlike the medical and psychological emphasis on intrapsychic functioning, whether conceived of as systemic or as discrete dimensions, the social approach focuses primarily on overt behavior. This is not to say, of course, that both the medical and psychological orientations are not also concerned with behavior. The placing of an individual on the health-illness continuum by psychiatrists and the medical classification of patients according to a typology of disease are based primarily on the interpretation of symptoms and inferences about day-to-day interpersonal functioning. The psychologist likewise relies on the interpretation of behavior as indicating the relative strength of various personality dimensions and their organization. But behavior has a place in its own right in the concept of mental health.

One order of assessment of mental health according to social criteria is provided by measures of performance in social roles. These consist of estimates of the extent to which individuals follow and respond to the community's normative prescriptions and expectations of appropriate behavior in roles related to occupation and work, social participation, use of leisure, and family relations. Since social prescriptions and expectations most directly enter into definitions of the abnormal or deviant, mental health is thus viewed in its most relative terms and with the least concern for psychodynamic processes.

Related to but conceptually different from these instrumental roles is behavior of a more affective nature, behavior which is often referred to as the symptomatic expression of psychiatric illness. The most common manifestations are hallucinations, delusions, and withdrawal. While many students, of course, seek to interpret such behavior as characteristic of certain role sets or cultural variations, it is also clearly of direct concern to the psychiatrist and psychologist, leading, as it does, to the identification of an individual as a mentally disordered person or as one with an abnormal personality. It is clear that the two types, instrumental and affective behavior, are interdependent, yet they may occupy different places in the conceptualization of mental health. There is still to be demonstrated a one-to-one relationship between symptomatic state and instrumental performance. For example, in community follow-up studies, investigators have failed to find a strong association between employment status and symptomatic state or between employment and subsequent readmission to hospital (Brown, 1959; Freeman and Simmons, 1958; Giovannoni and Ullmann, 1963; Marks, 1963). Even more curious is the finding of Zigler and Phillips (1961) with regard to the association between psychiatric diagnosis and symptomatology. In an examination of the relationship between manifestation of symptoms and inclusion in a particular diagnostic category, the most striking finding was that, although relationships do exist between symptoms and diagnosis, they are generally so slight that membership in a particular diagnostic group conveys only minimal information about symptomatology.

A second order of behavior which is perhaps the most frequently used as a differential of mental health, not only in socially oriented research but by laymen as well, consists of acts that label an individual as unhealthy, including, of course, being admitted to a mental hospital or to ambulatory treatment (Cumming and Cumming, 1957). Relevant, too, are the duration and frequency of hospitalization and the acceptance or rejection of treatment. Clear identification as a mental patient, as one exposed to a treatment network, is a social characteristic widely used to distinguish the sick from the well.

Though hospitalization can properly be regarded as a social phenomenon, it is obvious that it is largely a consequence of the actions of persons who hold certain views of mental health. Certainly, with respect to hospital admission, to duration of treatment, and to referral for it, the decisive role of the psychiatrist with his medical orientation results in the labeling of the given individual as ill in a social as well as a medical sense (Davis, Freeman, and Simmons, 1957; Mishler and Waxler, 1963).

At first glance, measures of mental health in terms of treatment appear to be "hard" variables and a solution to the problem of measurement. As already pointed out, however, these measures are in varying degrees a function of the medical orientation: the illness-wellness formulation of the psychiatrist in making his diagnosis contaminates and impinges upon what he prescribes, that is, treatment. Moreover, a broad series of conditions affect the validity of these measures: the availability of treatment and resources (Albee, 1959); the degree to which the hospital adheres to the philosophy of the "therapeutic community" (Rapoport, 1960); the legal status of the patient (that is, committed or voluntary); the size of the hospital (Gurel, 1964) and whether it is public or private; aftercare and the hospital's interest in employability and eventual integration into the community; the hospital's affiliations with programs in which research or student groups would benefit from the release or retaining of patients; and the relative pressure and manipulation by physicians, families, and patients themselves to gain admission, readmission, or release (Freeman and Simmons, 1963). A given patient may be voluntarily committed to a state institution for 15 days' observation, receive a preliminary work-up and some situational counseling, be released as not mentally ill and never classified or even recorded as such; or he may be legally committed to a psychotherapeutically oriented private teaching hospital and remain there as long as his student therapist needs the case, a complete family and social history being obtained. He may then be returned to the community on a one-year "trial visit," or transferred to a day hospital, a night hospital, a weekend hospital, or a weekday hospital, depending on their availability. During these periods he may or may not be regarded officially as a "patient." These illustrations may be an exaggeration of what typically occurs; but in any case, many observers are clearly convinced of the weakness of these so-called "hard" measures (Mishler and Scotch, 1963; Rawnsley and Loudon, 1962; Sinnett and Hanford, 1962). Measures of hospital and other treatment experience, though often used as key measures of health, as criteria of validity in estimating the levels of health in a community (Leighton, 1959) and in estimating changes over time in rates of illness (Goldhamer and Marshall, 1953), are as questionable as any of the other indices we have already commented on.

The interrelationships of the medical, psychological, and social orientations to mental health are, of course, quite evident. Indeed, in psychiatry, there is the rapidly growing field of social psychiatry. Persons identified with this position usually take a broad perspective and make every effort to include concepts of social role as well as personality in their thinking about mental health (Leighton, 1960). It is obvious that an essential element of a social psychology of mental health is the concern with the interaction of individual and social variables, and thus there are many features common to social psychiatry and social psychology, though neither has handled well the problem of defining a workable concept of mental health.

A PRAGMATIC VIEW

Currently, in the social psychology of mental health, the different orientations are all reflected in various investigations. These studies are often undertaken with the most naive assumptions regarding measurement and sometimes without even awareness of the importance of problems of definition. In the development of comprehensive theories and—even more deplorable—in attempts at theoretical integration, there tends to be a lack of consciousness of the diversity of definition and the unclarity of the concept, as well as of the all-pervasive methodological problems of reliability and validity.

It is obvious that no single definition of mental health is going to be satisfactory to all individuals, given their various affiliations and orientations. Consensus about a single set of criteria to measure it is equally improbable. In practice, this means that each and every investigator, either for purposes of convenience and methodological rigor or because of the stimulus and support of the study, will select some combination for himself out of the array of possible criteria, choosing either from among the three sets or from within one. This, naturally, has led to chaos.

As it stands now, however, since practice and programs of treatment operate in the climate of medicine, medicine dominates much of the social psychology of mental health. At the same time, the very heart of psychology and the interest of many social psychologists centers about a concern with personality and consequently this orientation, too, cannot be ignored; moreover, the variables within the social frame of reference are important, not only as commonly accepted phenomena within social psychology, but also because of their significance to health and welfare policy makers and the general public. Thus, the lack of congruence among these three points of view would not justify us in dismissing any conceptualization at this time as outside the purview of the social psychology of mental health.

In selecting studies for review in a chapter such as this, it is of course necessary to limit the field of the social psychology of mental health, despite the vagueness that characterizes the boundaries of the field and definition of the term. In this chapter, for a study to be considered as being in the field of the social psychology of mental health it must, of course, have some measure of a social-psychological nature. Thus, population descriptions of mental illness along a medical health-illness continuum are beyond its scope, as are studies concerned only with individual characteristics of personality, unless they include social-psychological elements over and above individual measures. Also, studies that make reference solely to social characteristics such as hospital rates need not be included unless there are, again, some social-psychological elements.

Where the dependent variable constitutes some measure of mental health, to be considered as a social-psychological variable the definition of health must have some social-psychological content: a characteristic of interaction, for example, or a measure of role performance, or a measure of the social personality or attitudes of the given individual. And, regardless of orientation, it is necessary to include as appropriate investigations those that make use of independent variables of a social-psychological nature.

With few exceptions, most social psychologists would agree that measures reflecting social interaction, the performance of role, or values and attitudes fall within their domain. Moreover, many "personality" measures are, in the eyes of persons within the field, not individual qualities, but rather a function of the interaction between the individuals and the social structure, and consequently should be included under the rubric of the social psychology of mental health (Borgatta and Cottrell, 1957).

Often, explanatory or intervening variables of a social-psychological nature occupy such an important place in the reasoning behind studies that properly they must be included. But many times the intermediary social-psychological variables are not included in the actual empirical work. For example, Hollingshead and Redlich (1958) sought to relate a structural variable—social class—to the prevalence of mental illness, but underlying their view is the concept of "press." This social-psychological concept served as the explanatory variable between the independent and dependent variables. In a sense, however, the sequence is incomplete in their work, as in many others', because they offer no empirical measure of the intermediate variable. Yet, given the current status of the field, such studies must properly be examined. Similarly, in a large number of studies, the sequence is incomplete in that they involve relational analysis between a social-psychological variable and an intermediate one, assumed to be associated with some phenomenon viewed as mental health. For example, a study of the relationship of combat anxiety to stress could well be included in our analysis, though it is only an assumption that the connection between these two measures carries on to differences in mental health status (Ginzberg *et al.*, 1959). Here the inclusion of studies is a matter of discretion and, admittedly, in the pages that follow we have been selective.

While we have tried to limit our selection of studies for review to those which have some explicit, or at least implicit, social-psychological variable, it must be remembered that these same studies will almost always reflect some aspect from the medical, psychological, or social orientation. It is apparent that in reviewing individual investigations, one must carefully note the measures of mental health employed, assess their methodological and conceptual character, and not forget that:

1.   The illness-wellness concept of the psychiatrist, drawn from physical medicine, may be entirely irrelevant and handicapping; nevertheless, it has a dominant place, for it influences all other measures of health. Both the assessment of persons along such a continuum and the taxonomic classification employed in categorizing types of mental patients are of doubtful reliability, and thus are dubious measures in research.

2.   Psychological measures, that is, personality measures, impose a number of limitations: to the extent that they are derived from or dependent on the medical orientation, they suffer from the same limitation noted above. Moreover, scales bearing the same or similar labels may, in fact, turn out to be measuring different variables. Further, assessments based on structured measures may yield different findings than those based on impressionistic evaluations, interpretations of behavior, or nondirective devices. Finally, personality measures may be unrelated to the performance of a social role and to measures of illness based on treatment experience.

3.   Measures of hospital experience may reflect the external environment of the individual to a much greater extent than they measure mental health and, further, may be unrelated either to psychological conceptualizations of mental health or to measures of performance. Social measures include assessments of the performance of an instrumental role or of affective behavior, that is, symptomatic expressions of illness. These measures may be neither highly correlated with one another nor with various measures of hospital experience, personality assessment, or medical judgments of health and illness.

Regardless of the view of mental health, with the exception of general community studies of health status such as the "Midtown" research (Srole *et al.*, 1962), most concern has been with the "mentally ill," no matter how defined, and not with the healthy or general population of the community. If it were not this way, of course, there would be no distinction between the field of mental health and all the behavioral sciences—a position, by the way, that has actually been taken by some students of mental health (Miller and Mishler, 1959) and one which is sometimes reflected in the policies and awarding of grants of such groups as the National Institute of Mental Health. But the emphasis has been, as will be evident in this review, on the mentally ill, not the healthy, or rather what, by one definition or another, is viewed as the ill group. Indeed, our grouping of most studies under such terms as "etiology" and "treatment"—terms applicable to the investigation of an illness—is a reflection of the fact that the great preponderance of effort in the field of mental health has in actuality been devoted to mental illness.

MENTAL HEALTH AS A SOCIAL ATTRIBUTE

Despite the controversy over the experts' various and conflicting definitions of mental health and illness, there has been considerable effort among social psychologists toward ascertaining the general population's definition of mental health, and their attitudes and opinions about those they deem to be mentally ill. Since most of the population manifests some symptoms of maladjustment, there is extensive controversy over the process by which certain individuals are identified as ill. In particular, there has been a recent emphasis on examining the community reaction to the person labeled mentally ill, to the social undesirability of symptoms, and to stigmatization. A number of studies have been undertaken of conceptions of illness among persons who ordinarily are not in contact with so-called mental patients, among patients and their relatives, and among professionals and semiprofessionals whose work brings them into intimate contact with the mentally ill.

In 1950, Star (1955) assessed attitudes by presenting a national sample with a series of vignettes and asking what was wrong with the person described, what should be done about such a person, and whether the condition was curable. Star's conclusion was that the public is frightened of mental illness, considers it to be one of the worst things that could happen to anyone, and surrounds the area with mystique. At least two other studies using case descriptions report somewhat more favorable findings (Lemkau and Crocetti, 1962; Woodward, 1951): both find that the members of the community have reasonable knowledge of illness and are quite optimistic about recovery. Lemkau and Crocetti interpret their finding of less ignorance and hopelessness as a consequence of the increased knowledge and understanding of the past decade. Their study was confined to a Baltimore sample and local differences might account for the difference in findings. Gurin and associates (Gurin, Veroff, and Feld, 1960) used different techniques of data collection, and thus it is not possible to compare their work directly with Star's study of ten years before.

It is quite clear, however, that views and attitudes on mental illness, belief in its organic or functional basis, and optimism about recovery are correlated with the general enlightenment of community members. The more educated and intellectually sophisticated apparently have been the most receptive audience of the vast efforts of the mental hygiene movement and, at least as evidenced by verbal responses, seem likely to hold views consistent with those of the psychodynamically oriented practitioner (Freeman and Kassebaum, 1960; Gurin, Veroff, and Feld, 1960).

Several studies have assessed attitudes between and within selected groups. Dohrenwend, Bernard, and Kolb (1962), using Star's case descriptions, interviewed community leaders in New York and classified their responses according to type of leader, the extremes being the educational and the economic. The educational leaders were most "sympathetic," followed next by the political. "Sympathetic" was interpreted in this study as identifying more behavior as mental illness, regarding it as serious, and calling for professional help. With respect to the negative views of the economic group, a similar finding is reported in two other investigations (Olshansky, 1958; Whatley, 1963): employers are distrustful of mental patients and decline to hire them to perform duties of a personal nature.

In one of the most comprehensive studies of attitudes and levels of information, Nunnally (1961) found that, despite the unfavorable stance of a large part of the population, relatively high levels of information are quite common among people in general. In brief, then, there seems to be much information on the so-called facts of mental illness among the general public but unfavorable attitudes toward the patients, though this varies with social and personal characteristics.

At least three studies approached attitudes on a more analytical level. Cumming and Cumming (1956), using case descriptions of behavior, report that quantitatively rather than qualitatively disturbed behavior is less likely to be recognized by the lay population as illness. A second study (Phillips, 1964) included behavioral characteristics and sex identification in descriptions of mental illness. The findings suggest that individual deviation from socially prescribed norms, rather than the seriousness of the symptoms from the point of view of mental hygiene, is correlated with the favorableness of the evaluation; moreover, given the same behavior, men are more likely to be unfavorably judged than are women.

In a novel experimental study, Gergen and Jones (1963) asked 64 subjects to predict the behavior of particular persons identified as "normal" or as "mentally ill" and then to rank them on a behavior-rating scale. The findings were that, even in experimental situations, similar behavior is variously evaluated, depending on whether the person is characterized as ill or normal.

Differences in attitude are also revealed in studies conducted among professionals and semiprofessionals working in the mental health field. When Cohen and Struening (1962) administered a scale of opinions about mental illness, a factor analysis of responses made by samples of employees at two mental hospitals revealed five dimensions of attitude: authoritarianism (which accounted for the largest amount of common variance), benevolence, mental hygiene ideology, social restrictiveness, and interpersonal ideology. Occupation and education were substantially related to the first three in both hospitals, with education yielding curvilinear relationships on benevolence and mental hygiene ideology. The individual items in each factor suggest that attitudes and opinions among mental hospital personnel range from the belief that a lack of moral strength causes mental illness to the view that children of mental patients, if raised by normal families, would not become ill. In a similar way, Gilbert and Levinson (1957) investigated the interrelationships of ideology, personality, and institutional policy in two differently oriented hospitals, using scales measuring custodialism, family ideology, and authoritarianism. They found that a custodial orientation toward treatment was part of a broader configuration of authoritarianism, though responses varied according to occupation. Other differences within the groups were apparently related to more general personality domains. Middleton

(1953) administered a test of prejudice to state mental hospital employees and found that ward attendants were more prejudiced against patients than personnel without close contact with patients, and that education was negatively associated with prejudice.

There have been several investigations of attitude change following exposure to a mental hospital. A pretest and posttest of student nurses undergoing psychiatric training, and of nursing students in general hospital training, revealed favorable shifts in attitudes toward the mentally ill over a 12-week period among nurses in the psychiatric program but not among those in a general hospital (Hicks and Spaner, 1962). In a related study comparing medical students exposed to a mental hospital internship with those not so exposed, Gelfand and Ullmann (1961) reported that a more "mental-hygiene-oriented" view was created in the first group.

Though there is a body of literature suggesting that contact with patients, information on problems of mental illness, and community educational programs change the opinions of persons exposed to them, this generalization is tempered by studies that give evidence of the overriding importance of basic socialization experiences. For example, Cumming and Cumming (1957) report that a mental health educational program presenting to the community realistic descriptions of the behavior of the mentally ill produced opinions contrary to the goals of the program, though consistent with the community's norms. Attitudes toward mental illness apparently are anchored in the individual's basic emotional and social disposition and consequently, from a practical standpoint, experiments in changing attitudes must differentiate among audiences, and the scope, techniques, and messages must be specialized (Scott and Freeman, 1963).

An intensive investigation of psychiatric ideologies in various institutions combined both field observation and structured questionnaire responses (Strauss *et al.*, 1964). While individual experiences with the mentally ill were associated with the ideology of persons within treatment settings, both professional role commitments and the institutional structure accounted for more of the variance than did personal interaction.

Finally, attitudes and definitions of mental illness have been assessed in the persons presumed to be closest to the phenomenon, namely, mental patients and their relatives (Clausen and Yarrow, 1955; Cumming and Cumming, 1957; Freeman and Simmons, 1961; C. G. Schwartz, 1957; Yarrow *et al.*, 1955). These studies point out that clinical signs of illness are frequently interpreted as minor and explained away as "tension" even among members of the family who have frequent contact with mental patients.

Manis, Houts, and Blake (1963) investigated and compared the evaluation of mental illness among mental patients and the mental health staff responsible for them, with a control group of medical and surgical patients. They concluded that psychiatric and nonpsychiatric patients generally held similar opinions regarding mental illness, though severely disturbed mental patients viewed mental illness in more moralistic terms than did normal persons. An interesting finding of their study is that shifts in attitudes among patients in the direction of those held by the staff were correlated with the staff's ratings of gains in treatment and with length of hospitalization. Giovannoni and Ullmann (1963) administered the same scales that Nunnally had used in his community study of normal subjects to a sample of psychiatric patients and learned that patients are as well informed as normal respondents and equally as negative in their attitudes toward mental illness. Gallagher, Levinson, and Erlich (1957) found that a custodial orientation toward mental illness among patients was related to their social class and their degree of authoritarianism. As a generalization, it appears that patients and the normal are not very different in their view of mental illness and that the major correlations hold true, regardless of the group studied.

Two critical issues need further study. Do the response of members of the community to mental patients and the public's conceptions of the mentally ill individual relate to differential expressions of mental illness on the part of various cultural and social groups or to differential perceptions of comparable behavior in different social and cultural groups? Some argue that the unfavorable attitudes to symptomatic behavior are found equally throughout the general population; others insist that different cultural groups assess a given symptom in markedly different ways. Is mental illness itself manifested consistently across cultures or is it culture-bound? These questions become decisive, of course, if one assumes that attitudes are direct reflectors of behavior in the presence of a psychiatrically ill person. There is some evidence that in the real situation bizarre behavior is responded to consistently by all groups, though these data are limited (Freeman and Simmons, 1963).

There has been considerable concern with the issue of stigma (Freeman and Simmons, 1961; Goffman, 1963; Greenblatt, York, and Brown, 1955; Lemert, 1962; Schwartz and Schwartz, 1964), and much debate as to its importance as a barrier to recovery and its salience in the relations of patients with their families and primary group associates. It is apparent that mental illness is not an objective status, but there is little evidence to show whether this is a bar to the adequate reciprocal performance of roles between an individual patient and his close associates.

It should be noted that the value orientation of the research worker undoubtedly exerts an influence. Social psychologists generally have sought to expose authoritarianism and bureaucratic arrangements, and most of them are personally committed to a therapeutic community and a psychodynamic point of view. Given this situation, it is often hard to judge the extent to which interpretations of their studies are a function of personal ideology or a consequence of empirical findings.

These potential biases notwithstanding, it is apparent that, while the studies reviewed differed in the populations sampled and in the techniques of collecting data, one common finding is that mental illness is a social characteristic about which people in general have strong preconceptions. These attitudes derive less from what the mental patient does than from his having been labeled "mentally ill." It is his status, in large part, rather than his performance that differentiates him from others and results in special relations with members of the community.

ETIOLOGY

The major effort by investigators in mental health has been directed toward studying the causes of mental illness. Some have set themselves the relatively modest task of simply gathering descriptive data in order to elucidate the nature of the phenomena, while others have addressed themselves to the more ambitious goal of demonstrating causal links between some set of variables and mental illness.

Etiology has been investigated from a variety of theoretical vantages, with a broad range of methods, and focused on a wide gamut of substantive interests. Even studies that may be unequivocally called social-psychological range from the almost purely sociological to the almost exclusively psychological—from those which yield only inferential data on the individual to those whose findings are chiefly on individual characteristics, social attributes being treated only suggestively. Here the studies are ordered from the sociological to the psychological.

ECOLOGICAL RESEARCH

One of the earliest sociological explorations of mental disorder was through ecological investigation (Eliot, 1955), that is, studies which related mental disorder to the spatial distribution of local populations. An early interest was urban-rural differences; later it was intra-urban distributions.

Interest in rural-urban differences was stimulated by the theory that rural life is less conducive to mental disorder than is city life, because of the existence of a simpler and more stable social structure, greater clarity in definition of role, and a spirit of *Gemeinschaft*—all giving rise to lasting, intimate, and supportive personal relationships (Leacock, 1957).

In such studies the findings vary from one to the next, depending in part on the definition of mental disorder. While several studies show a positive correlation between incidence of hospital admissions and urbanization (Dayton, 1940; Malzberg, 1940; Pollack and Nolan, 1929), it is difficult to judge how closely this is related to the distribution of institutions and arrangements for treatment. At least two reviewers concur in the conviction that rural rates are lower for schizophrenia, but they question whether this is true of the affective disorders (Lemkau and Crocetti, 1958; Rose and Stub, 1955). Among studies challenging the doctrine of rural-urban differences is one by Love and Davenport (1920), who used the Army's rejection rates in World War I for the country as a whole as the measure of illness. They report no differences in rural-urban rates, with the exception of rates for the four largest cities, which were the highest. Using suicide as a criterion of mental disturbance, a reversal in the rate is reported (Schroeder and Beegle, 1955) in Michigan, where the suicide rate among rural males was almost double that among urban males.

Research workers have turned now to testing the general ecological hypothesis through the study of select populations, such as migrants, or through inter- and intra-community studies, with precise definitions of structural characteristics such as social class. Increasing urbanization and the disappearance of the supposedly idyllic rural community has rendered the question of "keeping 'em down on the farm" largely academic, and the demographic shift has reduced interest in urban-rural differences.

In a number of intra-urban investigations, areas of high and low incidence of mental illness were first located and then relevant social characteristics of residents specified. A now classic study of this type was undertaken in the 1930's by Faris and Dunham (1939). They calculated the rate by census tract in Chicago of first admissions diagnosed as schizophrenic during the years 1922 through 1934, and then classified the tracts according to housing, rental value, ethnicity, radio ownership, education, and so on. Their major findings, corroborated and extended in later reports (Dunham, 1947, 1953), show the highest incidence of mental illness in the center of the city, the rates declining as one approaches the periphery. Rates for schizophrenia alone show a similar distribution, but manic-depressive psychosis is more widely dispersed and the cases tend to cluster in the higher socioeconomic areas. Further, rates among foreign-born, the native whites, and those of mixed parentage were highest in the predominantly Negro section; conversely, rates were lower among Negroes in predominantly Negro areas than elsewhere.

The interpretation of these findings stimulated great controversy and led to a large number of further studies replicating and amplifying Faris and Dunham's work. Among the variables studied were social isolation, social change, social mobility, and socioeconomic status. One question was whether schizophrenics tend to be concentrated in the central part of the city and, if so, did life there cause schizophrenia? The alternative hypothesis was that certain characteristics of schizophrenics lead them to reside in the central part of the city; this came to be known as the "drift hypothesis" (Dunham, 1953; Faris and Dunham, 1939; LaPouse, Monk, and Terris, 1956). Studies of this issue present conflicting results. Gerard and Houston (1953), for instance, investigated spatial mobility in relation to life in familial or nonfamilial settings. They collected the histories of residence of 146 male schizophrenics admitted to Worcester State Hospital from 1931 to 1950 and compared them by city of birth and by place of residence, one and five years prior to admission. They related the concentration of schizophrenics in certain parts of the city to the high number of unattached males living there. These unattached men had rates of inter- and intra-city mobility significantly higher than those admitted to hospital from family households. Hare (1956) contributed to understanding of the problem in his study in Bristol of the influence of family settings on the distribution of 441 cases of schizophrenics hospitalized over a five-year period. The rate of hospitalization of persons living in nonfamily settings was higher than the rate of those with families, and the highest rates were observed in the central districts, where the largest proportion of single-person households were found.

These studies do not challenge the notion that living in certain parts of the cities is correlated with the likelihood of being hospitalized with the diagnosis of schizophrenia. Certainly the data on intra-urban differences are more consistent than those concerning urban-rural distinctions. However, despite the consistency of their findings, these investigators have failed to offer any adequate interpretation of etiological significance. Consequently, the contribution of the spatial data to the understanding of the etiology of schizophrenia is meager, as Dunham (1947) himself has stated. Many critics of the ecological method claim that this defect is inevitable (Clausen and Kohn, 1954; Mishler and Scotch, 1963; Robinson, 1950). They cite as its inherent weaknesses the fallacy of imputing the characteristics of communities to all their inhabitants; the impossibility of determining which of a number of interrelated demographic characteristics are etiologically important; and the differential disposition of the mentally ill in various communities.

In a somewhat different approach, Scott (1958b) pointed out that it is necessary, at this level of analysis, to regard the communities rather than the individuals as the elements to be studied, and that statistical tests should be based on the degrees of freedom representing the number of communities studied, rather than the number of residents. He illustrates his point with a study (Jaco, 1954) in which the number of subjects was used to determine the degrees of freedom. Mishler and Scotch (1963) reject the idea of the comparability of ecological studies with individual analyses.

SOCIAL ISOLATION

It is often suggested that a number of social determinants may reduce the amount of one's social interaction and impair the quality of interpersonal relationships, resulting in social isolation which then leads to mental illness. This line of thinking has been advanced particularly in connection with schizophrenia, partly because schizophrenics are so often socially withdrawn, isolated, and divorced from reality (Bleuler, 1950). Social isolation has been studied as a cause of mental illness, directly and indirectly—by way of personal case histories and the investigation of presumably causative social circumstances. It is considered to be a mediating link in the early work by Faris and Dunham (1939). Of particular note are two characteristics of residents in areas of high incidence: transiency and ethnic heterogeneity. Emigration also has been considered productive of social isolation: Malzberg and Lee (1956), using first admission rates to New York hospitals, found them highest for schizophrenia in the foreign-born, regardless of sex or race, and higher among recent migrants than among other residents; Robertson (1903) demonstrated a higher rate among migrants to California than among older residents; Lemert (1948) found a negative correlation between hospitalization among the foreign-born and the number of foreign-born of their own nationality living around them; and Gruenberg (1954) substantiates Faris and Dunham's findings concerning high rates among whites living in Negro areas and Negroes in white areas.

Kohn and Clausen (1955) studied social isolation more directly among 45 schizophrenics and 13 manic-depressives hospitalized between 1940 and 1952 in Hagerstown, Maryland and a nonhospital comparison group matched in age, sex, and occupation. Approximately one-third of the mental patients showed evidence of having been socially isolated from between the ages of 13 and 14, but the normals did not. They were unable to find any sign that the patients had been situationally isolated from their peers by lack of available playmates, excessive residential mobility, severe illness, or parental restriction. Further, they found no correlation between social isolation and relationships with parents or siblings among the isolated patients and the controls.

In a study in Texas (Jaco, 1954), several indices of social isolation were discovered to characterize residents in areas with high rates for schizophrenia. Unlike the Kohn and Clausen study, these findings had reference to adult rather than adolescent isolation. The work on social isolation is reminiscent of much of the work (to be discussed later) on the process-reactive continuum in schizophrenia, particularly the notion of the "shut-in adolescent" (Becker, 1959; Chapman, Day, and Burstein, 1961; Kantor and Winder, 1959). While social isolation may be characteristic of schizophrenics, or at least of some, it is difficult indeed to determine whether it is socially induced, a manifestation of the illness itself, or an etiological antecedent. A study in Puerto Rico among lower-class families again reveals differences between schizophrenics and their families, in contrast with normal individuals, but this careful study fails to document many prescribed differences (Rogler and Hollingshead, 1965). Thus, although there is evidence of an association between isolation and schizophrenia, whether it is of etiological significance or merely a descriptive characteristic is not easy to assess. It is commonly accepted as an etiological determinant, however, because of the ease with which it fits into psychosocial theories of the illness.

SOCIAL CHANGE

Major societal changes are assumed to result in varying degrees of personal aberration—one of Durkheim's (1951) postulates to explain high rates of suicide. The principal social-psychological concept bringing social change to bear upon individual disorder is role: changes in the social system are presupposed to burden the individual with new roles and role demands, and mental disorder is assumed to be the outcome in those who fail to adapt themselves. Every individual, of course, faces the demands of new and changing roles throughout his life, simply on the basis of his shifts in status at various stages of maturation (Cottrell, 1942). At any given period, however, a stable society is assumed to offer relatively clear role definitions together with orderly social institutions.

The individual can, of course, suffer rather abrupt changes in role definitions and expectations, quite apart from general social change, simply by moving from one culture to another or from one social stratum to another within the same culture. The investigation of the relationship of social change to mental disorder has focused on longitudinal studies of societies presumed to have undergone structural changes and on the study of groups who have moved from one culture to another.

While an enormous amount of social commentary has been devoted to the description of how social change in the United States, particularly in the last 150 years of industrialization and urbanization, has resulted in an increase in mental disorder, surprisingly few empirical studies have been undertaken to test the premise. One of the most definitive works is that of Goldhamer and Marshall (1953). They studied first admissions to Massachusetts state hospitals and the antecedent institutions—almshouses, county institutions, and so on—for the period 1840–1940. They found that rates of those aged under 50 were no higher in the latter half-century than in the former, though an increase was found in older age groups. Thus, at least in Massachusetts, during a century in which there was presumed to have been marked social change, no marked concomitant increase appears in the rate of confinement for psychoses. Dunham (1947) reported similarly that any increase in hospitalization between 1910 and 1950 can be accounted for by an increase in the number of persons hospitalized without psychoses. Reports by Kramer and associates (Kramer, Pollack, and Redick, 1961; Pugh and MacMahon, 1962) further corroborate the lack of correlation.

In one longitudinal study, at Virginia State Hospital (Wilson and Lantz, 1957), morbidity rates per thousand from 1918 to 1955 were calculated for Negroes and whites. The results suggest not only a consistently higher rate among Negroes than whites but also a considerably greater increase in the Negro rate. The increase among Negroes is related by the authors to social change: they state that it is due to segregation and to the torments of uncertainty suffered by Negroes in "crossing from one culture to another." It would seem logical that the "crossing" would accompany not segregation but desegregation. That the latter was a fact in Virginia during the years studied is questionable and the social-change interpretation of the findings remains unsubstantiated. The already noted studies of urban-rural rates have often been seen as indicating that the stresses of urbanization are conducive to a higher incidence of mental disorder. These explorations, however, are cross-sectional and cannot be generalized to an ongoing process of social change, such as urbanization. Furthermore, it is not the urban centers that are becoming urbanized but the rural areas, and consequently it would take an increase in rural rates to support the theory that urbanization contributes to mental illness.

The study of social change has been pursued in other (non-Western) cultures considered more stable, and in those in the throes of social change, for example, those moving from primitive to complex, nonliterate to literate. Various anthropological techniques are employed in the inquiries and they vary in case-finding techniques. Any sensible comparison of their findings to establish comparative rates of incidence or prevalence is out of the question, but it certainly can be observed that mental aberration is not unique to civilized man (Benedict and Jacks, 1954; Eaton and Weil, 1955; Lemkau and Crocetti, 1958), though its expression may vary (Lu, 1962). Eaton and Weil account for the low rates of mental disorder among the Hutterites by what they call "controlled acculturation," that is, a built-in tolerance of change through the entire society's values and institutions.

Social isolation is presumed to be an effect of social change and, at the same time, the process whereby it is related to mental illness. Generally, comparison of hospitalization rates of the foreign-born with those of the native-born indicates higher rates among the former (Faris and Dunham, 1939; Hammer and Leacock, 1961; Jaco, 1960; Malzberg, 1955; Malzberg and Lee, 1956; Rose and Stub, 1955). When rates are adjusted for age, sex, marital status, and education, the differences decrease but do not disappear (Lee, 1963; Locke, Kramer, and Pasamanick, 1960; Malzberg, 1956a, 1956b, 1959).

First admissions to mental hospitals among the Norwegian-born of Minnesota, native-born of Minnesota, and Norwegian-born of Norway have been intensively studied. Making the diagnoses himself from the records, Odegaard (1936) reported a higher incidence of senile and arteriosclerotic psychoses and of schizophrenia among the immigrants, but lower rates for manic-depressive psychoses among them than among the native-born Norwegians. However, his interpretation of these data does not suggest social change as the etiological agent. He argues that schizophrenia is constitutionally determined and posits that the "leptosomic schizoid type" is inclined to withdraw or to retreat into "dreams of greatness" which might lead him to seek his fortune in the New World. Essentially, what we seem to have here is a drift hypothesis, but on an international scale. He found no evidence of immigration-based trauma in the case material he reviewed nor any clustering of admissions immediately following immigration. The increase of psychotic older persons he attributes simply to the hardships of immigrant life.

A refugee population in Norway was studied by Eitinger (1959), who distinguished the refugee from the ordinary "voluntary" immigrant. Finding a higher incidence of mental disease among refugees than among a matched settled average population, he rejects the notion of a higher incidence among refugees when in their native land and offers data to substantiate his stand. He postulates an interaction between a predisposed personality and the mental and physical stresses of the uprooting.

The effect of demands on individuals forcibly dislodged by urban renewal in this country have been investigated by Fried (1963, 1964), who reports unmistakable and widespread grief among those forced to give up their slum homes, but little evidence of increased psychoses. Studies of housing in the United States (Wilner *et al.*, 1958) and in Britain (Hare and Shaw, 1965) again indicate that this type of upheaval is not correlated with severe mental disorder.

The concept of crisis brought about by rapid social and other change, and its consequences for the individual, have been elaborated by Lindemann and others (Caplan, 1961; Lindemann, 1944, 1960; Rapoport, 1963). Lindemann pointed to crisis in an individual's environment as a principal determinant of emotional disturbance, but evidence of the link between crisis and severe illness is scanty. Indeed, Lewis (1942) found no special effects of airraids on the mental health of the people in England.

It seems that there is little basis, despite the superficial reasonableness of the idea, for holding that either broad social change or sudden change is correlated with the severe disorder. Perhaps the lack of association between social change and mental illness is accounted for by the collective phenomenon of relative deprivation (Merton and Kitt, 1957); upheavals and crises, if they affect large aggregates with whom the individual identifies himself, may have a diminished impact on the social order and on his own personal circumstances.

SOCIAL CLASS

In spite of the differences in method, an association has repeatedly been found between social class and the prevalence of mental illness. It is a good bet that one's chances of being hospitalized with a diagnosis of schizophrenia are greatest if he is of the lower class. But while the findings are regarded by many as consistent and convincing, the etiological interpretation of the relationship remains unclear.

The ecological investigators have used different definitions of "mental illness" and various indices of social class. In Faris and Dunham's work (1939) some of the indices to categorize census tracts reflected social class and, certainly, spatial distribution itself cannot be considered independent of individual socioeconomic circumstances. Similarly, LaPouse's (LaPouse, Monk, and Terris, 1956) finding of a higher rate of hospitalized schizophrenia in areas of lower median rental may also be explained by social class.

In their Hagerstown, Maryland, ecological study, Clausen and Kohn (1959) used occupation as an index of socioeconomic status, and reported that the probability of being hospitalized with a diagnosis of schizophrenia did not vary significantly with the socioeconomic status of the neighborhood, nor with occupation. These findings are atypical. On the basis of a study done in England, Stein (1957) argued against the use of occupation as a single index of social class. He studied first admissions to mental hospitals from a group of East (low status) and West (high status) boroughs in London. Among men aged 15 to 59 years, the rates in East and West indicated a social-class gradient in incidence as well as in prevalence, the differences being particularly marked in the first-admission rates for schizophrenia. Yet the boroughs with higher status in the West end had higher rates of first admissions of patients aged 15 to 59 than boroughs in the lower-class East end, especially for schizophrenia and particularly among older women. Noting that household structure, marital status, number of persons living alone, and other social and demographic variables also varied greatly between the East and the West, he proposed that comparison by the single index of social class is not meaningful and that, in any case, occupation alone is a questionable index of social class in areas differing in status or tradition.

One ecological study raises questions not so much about social class as about the definition of mental illness. Instead of using hospitalization as the definition, Kaplan, Reed, and Richardson (1956) in two communities—one of high and one of low status—estimated the rates of hospitalized and nonhospitalized cases of psychosis. Their method of finding "nonhospitalized psychoses" was essentially reputational, that is, asking those who should know, who in the neighborhood was psychotic. They report that the incidence of hospitalized cases was significantly higher in the area of lower status, but that the incidence of nonhospitalized cases was higher in the higher-class community. The significance of their findings is somewhat mitigated by the fact that the lower-class sample had a two-thirds rate of attrition.

As to individual cases of psychoses: several studies of first admissions with a diagnosis of schizophrenia have demonstrated a relationship with socioeconomic status. All these used occupation of the patient as the indicator of social class (Clark, 1948; Frumkin, 1955; Jaco, 1960; Locke, 1960; Nolan, 1917; Odegaard, 1956), and all but Odegaard found a higher incidence of schizophrenia in all the lower-ranking occupations.

Attention has been focused on the association of social class and various diagnostic categories, chiefly schizophrenia, manic-depressive psychosis, and the psychoneuroses. While questions may be raised regarding reliability and validity of medical diagnoses, nonetheless, it is consistently shown that schizophrenia is a lower-class disease and that manic-depressive psychosis and the psychoneuroses are afflictions of those of higher socioeconomic standing. At the very least, one's socioeconomic status is related to the kind of label given him if hospitalized (Dayton, 1940; Hyde, Kingsley, and Chisholm, 1944; Lemkau, Tietze, and Cooper, 1943; Malzberg, 1940; Rose and Stub, 1955; Tietze, Lemkau, and Cooper, 1941).

Hollingshead and Redlich (1958) provide the most definitive data on the distribution of mental disorders by social class. Unlike some of the studies just reported, most of their figures are based not on incidence but on prevalence (the number of cases under treatment at a given point in time). Nonetheless, their findings were consistent with those just discussed. They found the rate of treated schizophrenia in New Haven to be roughly eight times as high in the lowest of five social strata as in the two highest. Larger portions of the upper classes were under treatment for neuroses, and they exhibited a greater frequency of manic-depressive psychoses. Again, the findings of Hollingshead and Redlich are based on cases under treatment and thus do not necessarily reflect "true" incidence. Their work also indicates that neither the kind of treatment nor the length of hospitalization are independent of social class. A ten-year follow-up study (Myers, Bean, and Pepper, 1964) of the hospitalized portion of the New Haven census supported the hypothesis of a significant relationship between social class and length of hospitalization. The higher the social class of the patients, the higher the proportion no longer hospitalized. Hardt and Feinhandler (1959), using education and occupation as measures of social class, found a similar correlation between social class and length of hospital stay.

Of course, as was touched upon in describing the Kaplan study, rates of both incidence and prevalence, based on treated populations, may not reflect the "true situation" regarding the association between social class and mental illness. The Midtown Manhattan survey (Srole *et al.*, 1962) attempted to establish prevalence of psychopathology among both treated and untreated cases, and part of the analysis dealt with social class. To assess psychopathology, responses obtained in a two-hour interview, including structured scales, were rated independently by two psychiatrists; traditional diagnostic categories were abandoned and in their place the respondents were categorized according to generalized anxiety symptoms, specific symptom constellations, gross typology, and severity of disturbance. The association between social class and all of these is reported as follows: (1) anxiety was found to be highly prevalent in the entire population and independent of social class; (2) symptom constellations were most prevalent in the lower class and least prevalent in the upper; (3) among the gross typologies the prevalence varied inversely with status, with the exception of the simple neurotic type, which was found to be significantly associated with the upper class; and (4) when a general mental health rating was made, more severe disturbance was found in the lower class, and significantly more of the symptom-free were found in the middle and upper classes. Additional data from this study have also been presented relating social-class status to certain physical conditions presumed to be psychosomatic (Rennie and Srole, 1956). Significant relationships were found between a particular illness and a particular status, but the overall prevalence of psychosomatic conditions was not associated with class.

In all the investigations noted here, the determination of an etiological link is *ex post facto* and based on little more than sophisticated speculation. Thus the associations they present between social variables and mental disorder may range from the purely biological, a kind of social Darwinism, to simple rejection of the social variables as artifacts of matters, like differential access to treatment and differential evaluation of a given symptom by intimates and gatekeepers. While an investigator's conviction of the potency of a social variable may account for his arguing that it is etiological, one must admit it is difficult to dismiss social class.

The most social-psychologically oriented interpretation of these findings posits that differential stresses of various life styles precipitate mental disorder; this is one of the more coherent explanations of the link between a structural variable and mental disorder. It is not possible to reject this point of view in the face of the relatively consistent results of various macro- and microscopic studies. Furthermore, in many studies which can be so interpreted and which yield stable findings, hospitalization rates and other measures of mental health were used. These are compatible with both the medical and psychological orientation, and they provide an opportunity to integrate the sociological view with the other two.

In a study of automobile workers (Kornhauser, 1965) in which structured measures of mental health were found to correlate well with psychiatric judgments of the workers' responses, the current position is well summed up; there apparently is a relationship between mental health and what a person wants, what he would like to be as a person, and what he actually sees himself as being and becoming. While individuals of all life styles and economic levels endure lifelong difficulties, compromises, and readjustments, these burdens fall disproportionately on the individual of the lower socioeconomic class. Thus, by reason of economic deprivation and limited experience with a broad range of life styles, he is more apt to be dissatisfied. All the same, Miller and Mishler's (1959) serious warning against the uncritical acceptance of a link between class and schizophrenia should be heeded.

Of all the variables reflecting structural situational factors, including spatial distribution, social change, and social isolation, certainly the findings on social class are the most consistent. Perhaps the second major group of consistent findings would be those of studies relating to intra-urban spatial distribution. But as already noted, it is difficult to separate place of residence from the socioeconomic status of the inhabitants; and the finding of higher rates of mental disorder in the central part of the city may simply be a reflection of social-class position.

The consistency of the findings on social class makes it difficult to reject the idea that factors in the social structure may be etiological determinants; and the discrepancies in findings on some of the other variables cannot be taken as evidence of their irrelevance, but rather of the extreme difficulty in operationalizing and measuring variables such as social change and social isolation. Even with social class, however, the problems of interpretation remain unsolved. Perhaps some of the work reviewed below, on the processes by which social factors are mediated through family interaction, is an approach to elucidating the link between structural variables and individuals' aberrations. At any rate, there yet remains to be developed a satisfactory theoretical formulation of the etiological significance of sociological variables in mental illness.

THE FAMILY

The family as the basic unit of socialization has long been considered of the utmost importance in the etiology of schizophrenia and other mental disorders. Viewpoints range from the sociological, from which the family is seen largely as the surrogate of noxious cultural and class strains and values, to the almost purely psychological, which focuses primarily on conscious and unconscious personal reactions to the parents.

Myers and Roberts (1959) undertook one of the more intensive studies of patterns of family interaction in relation to class and illness. Using case histories and interviews, they studied 50 middle-class and lower-class ambulatory schizophrenics and their families. They found the former to be dominated by perfectionistic mothers, who insisted on socially acceptable behavior, inhibition of aggressive and sexual impulses, overconformity, and extreme control. Though the father's role was passive and ambiguous, parents of both sexes spent a good deal of time with their children and frequently cherished unrealistic aspirations for them. This general pattern of values was further reinforced by social institutions, such as the church and school, into which at least one parent was well integrated.

The lower-class patients, on the other hand, came from large families in which neither parent had time to spend with the children; fathers were physically dominant, physical violence was frequent, and little affection or interest was shown by either fathers or mothers. Though at home there was far less censure of sexual and aggressive impulses, there were frequent clashes at school and similar institutions dominated by middle-class regard for control and conformity. These families were generally fearful and isolated from all institutions in the larger community.

Certain of these intrafamilial and community conditions were found more often among the schizophrenics than among the neurotics at each class level. In general, schizophrenia-related conditions were most common in the lower class; middle-class schizophrenics tend to be subjected to situations more characteristic of lower-class patients than of their neurotic peers: specifically, general disorganization at home, lack of parental affection, guidance, and control, and the shifting to children of the responsibilities of child rearing. Schizophrenics, even of the middle class, and all lower-class patients, suffered under similar stresses—neglect, rejection, isolation, and fear of parents.

The authors do not conclude that these life conditions caused schizophrenia, since schizophrenics come from all social levels and not all lower-class persons become schizophrenics. Rather, they allow for the possibility of some kind of constitutional or psychological predisposition in the schizophrenic that is likely to be brought out by the life conditions characteristic of the lower class.

Several investigators, using a variety of techniques, have assessed the differential effect of structural variables, such as social class and urban-rural setting, on personal relationships in the family (Beck, 1960; Clausen and Kohn, 1956; Lane and Singer, 1959; Query, 1961; Zuckerman, Oltean, and Monashkin, 1958). These studies frequently have compared families of schizophrenics and normals of different social backgrounds. While the great range of variables studied, such as dependence on the mother, her attitudes toward child rearing, domination by the father, and so on, makes comparison of the substantive findings impossible, the studies demonstrate that family differences are not solely related to the presence of a schizophrenic child in the family. Differences in family patterns were found to be related to both the presence of pathology and the family's social standing. At least the point is clear that family patterns, attitudes, and interaction are not independent of social status—a finding which challenges the judgment that pathological family life is solely the result of idiosyncrasies in the parents' personalities. This should be borne in mind in the following review of research which either used single-class samples or did not control class variables.

A considerable amount of effort has been devoted to studying aspects of interaction in families of schizophrenics, as distinct from normals, or within groups of schizophrenics. Lu (1962) observed 15 male and nine female chronic schizophrenic patients from a state hospital in Illinois who were part of a sample of 50 patients, their nonschizophrenic siblings, and at least one parent. All were from the lower class, under 35 years of age, and most were Catholics. She concluded that the interplay of three conditions contributes to the development of schizophrenic symptoms: (1) contradictory parental expectations regarding dependence and independence, coupled with the schizophrenic child's persistent efforts to comply with them all; (2) certain experiences at birth or during infancy that inclined the parents and the preschizophrenic child to interact in contradictory ways; and (3) certain sociocultural situations which heightened to the critical point the dilemma between dependence and independence to which the schizophrenic symptoms might be considered a response— such situations as exist where the mother has married "beneath" her or the parents are of different religions. She postulated a "quadruple-bind" hypothesis involving interaction between the parents' contradictory expectations of independence and dependence, and the child's efforts to comply.

In an earlier study, Gerard and Siegel (1950), after interviewing the parents of 71 schizophrenics and 30 normals, reported differences in family interaction between the two groups. In the families of schizophrenics there was relatively more discord, overt or covert, a heightened relationship with the mother, who dominated the family, a diminished relationship with the father, and marked overprotection and prohibition of social experimentation.

Caputo (1961) studied 20 couples with adult male chronic schizophrenic sons and 20 with normal sons. He tested them individually with a parent attitude inventory and later, in an interview, had them discuss their disagreements on the inventory. He scored the ensuing interaction between them by a modification of Bales's technique and found in the parents of schizophrenics more bilateral hostility, less consensus, and a greater tendency to see the son as like themselves. Attitudes of both parents of the patients were found to deviate from the attitudes of the parents of normal offspring.

Horner (1961) matched ten hospitalized schizophrenics with ten normals as to age, education, and occupation and used the Pascal-Jenkins Behavioral Scales to gather systematic histories, including scales on each grandparent, parent, and sibling. He reported that parents of schizophrenics were significantly less compatible than those of normals, that they denied their children affection, had little close personal contact with them, and taught them withdrawal and other maladaptive social responses. Winder and Kantor (1958) studied 48 women, 25 of whom were the mothers of schizophrenics and 23 were the mothers of normals, and found more pathology among the mothers of schizophrenics as inferred from the Rorschach.

Fisher, Walker, and Sheer (1959), studying the parents of 20 neurotic and 20 normal sons, reported that the parents of the normals were individually less maladjusted than those of the neurotic and the schizophrenic. There were no differences in this attribute between parents of neurotics and parents of schizophrenics. Parents of normals and of neurotics were distinguished from parents of schizophrenics by their closer and more harmonious marital relationships. McKeown (1950), who also studied parents of schizophrenics, neurotics, and normals, used case histories of the pathological groups and gathered data on the normals by interview. There were 42 subjects in each group, and it is one of the few studies of this type where social-class variables were controlled in the selection of the sample. Parental behavior was categorized as demanding and antagonistic, superficial, encouraging and protective, or indulgent. Among the patients, the parents of the schizophrenics were most often demanding and antagonistic, while among the parents of normals encouraging behavior predominated.

Patterns of role dominance and conflict in the parents of 12 hospitalized tuberculosis patients, 12 schizophrenics with favorable prognoses, and 12 schizophrenics with poor prognoses were established by Farina (1960) using problem situations involving hypothetical instances of a son's behavior; these situations were solved by the parents separately and then together. Dominance by the mother was most marked in the group with poor prognoses, controls were in an intermediate position, and patients with good prognoses were characterized by father dominance. Conflict was least marked in the normals, more so in the schizophrenics with good prognoses, and highest in those given poor prognoses. Myers (Myers and Goldfarb, 1962) studied the parents and siblings of 45 children between six and 11 in age, diagnosed as schizophrenic, whose state had been categorized as "organic" or "nonorganic"; he introduced as controls a group of 30 public school children. After the two had been differentiated by a neurologist and psychiatric ratings had been made of parents and siblings by a psychiatrist, interviews and ratings of adequacy in familial interaction were obtained. The incidence of parental schizophrenia was found greater among the mothers than the fathers, and twice as many mothers of "nonorganics" were rated schizophrenic as were mothers of "organics." The adjustment rating of siblings of "organic" children was higher than that of siblings of "nonorganic" children. The families with at least one psychotic parent exhibited inadequate functioning; the families rated highest in the interaction situations were those of the "organic" children, neither of whose parents had been adjudged psychotic.

Bonner (1950) compared case histories of 125 persons diagnosed as paranoid-schizophrenic with those of 125 with diagnoses of paranoia or paranoid condition. He divided family patterns into four categories: (1) neglectful, (2) suppressive and cruel, (3) dominating and critical, and (4) normal and permissive. Over half of the paranoid cases fell in the category "suppressive and cruel"; the paranoid schizophrenics split between the "neglectful" and the "dominating and critical." The sensitivity of schizophrenics to parental censure was investigated by Dunham (1959) in a study of normals and a group of schizophrenics with good and poor premorbid histories; the subjects were shown slides depicting scenes of censure by a mother figure and by a father figure, and neutral scenes. Schizophrenics with good premorbid histories were as accurate as the normals in their judgments, except for the scenes of father's censure. The poor premorbids, however, were inaccurate on scenes showing censure by the mother and the neutral scenes, but not on those showing censuring by the father. Baxter and associates (Baxter, Becker, and Hooks, 1963), in investigating defensive behavior in the families of schizophrenics and of neurotics, tested parents of good and poor premorbid schizophrenics and of neurotics by the Rorschach method in order to evaluate their relative levels of ego maturity. A rating schedule was devised whereby the subjects' defensive behavior was found to differ significantly as to maturity. Parents of poor premorbids exhibited immature defensive behavior more frequently than did parents of good premorbids, with parents of the neurotics falling intermediate between the two schizophrenic groups. The difference between parents of poor premorbids and of neurotics approached significance, while the difference found between parents of good premorbids and neurotics was clearly unreliable.

Recently, Nameche, Waring, and Ricks (1964) compared a population of children treated for emotional problems who subsequently were identified and hospitalized as schizophrenic, with children whose histories, though by no means free of disturbance, did not include hospitalization. After matching cases by socioeconomic and familial variables, they found that child-rearing and familial patterns typically regarded as disruptive typified the adolescent lives of children in the hospitalized group.

A number of studies of attitudes of parents of schizophrenics toward child rearing have been undertaken in which these parents were compared with parents of children manifesting other pathologies and of normals (Berger, 1959; Farahmand, 1961; Garmezy, Clark, and Stockner, 1958; Guertin, 1958; Heilbrun, 1960). While several of them used one instrument, the Parent Attitude Research Instrument, the findings are contradictory and no clear pattern of pathogenic parental attitudes emerges. Furthermore, even were the findings more consistent, it would be difficult to assess the degree to which attitudinal differences are indicative of behavioral variation among parents of the variously afflicted and nonafflicted offspring.

There is a considerable body of work of a more qualitative nature, based on the observations of parents and families of schizophrenics, many of whom were in some form of therapy with the investigators. Most of these studies contain no comparative data on other pathological groups or on normals. Further, they were carried on almost exclusively among upper-class families, the only ones who could afford treatment by the given investigators. This research focused on patterns of family interaction and on personal characteristics of the parents. Bateson and his group (Bateson, 1960; Bateson *et al.*, 1956; Haley, 1959, 1960; Weakland, 1960) concentrated on patterns of communication within the schizophrenic family, and developed the "double bind" hypothesis. The double bind is defined as a pattern of communication postulated to provoke behavior characteristic of the schizophrenic, particularly with reference to mother-child interaction. The premises of the double-bind hypothesis are that (1) the individual is involved in an intense relationship in which he feels it vitally important to comprehend accurately what sort of message is being communicated so that he may respond appropriately; (2) the other person in the relationship expresses two orders of message, one of which contradicts the other; and (3) the individual is unable to comment on the messages, that is, "he cannot make a communicative message." Such conditions have been observed between mothers of schizophrenics and their schizophrenic offspring, sometimes extended to three-party interaction to include fathers.

Lidz and others have made extensive study of the intrafamilial environment of schizophrenics (Fleck, 1960; Lidz *et al.*, 1958; Lidz and Fleck, 1959; Lidz, Parker, and Cornelison, 1956). Their material is derived from the study of 16 patients at the Yale Psychiatric Institute over a period of years. Only families in which the mother and at least one sibling were available for repeated interviews were selected, fathers being included in all but two cases. These writers conclude that the intrafamilial environment in which schizophrenic patients grow up is virtually always marked by serious parental strife or eccentricity, that is, "marital schism," where there is an open breach between the parents, and "marital skew," where one parent dominates and the other subtly undercuts (Lidz *et al.*, 1957a, 1957b).

Ryckoff, Day, and Wynne (1959) have reported that the interaction in families of schizophrenics is similar to that in institutions, because, as in other purposefully established organizations, the members tend to conceive of themselves and to function in strongly defined roles and not in terms of interaction and individual development. Bowen (Bowen, Dysinger, and Basamania, 1959) reported on cases of entire families hospitalized with the nominal patients on a given ward. The parents struggled with the marked emotional distance between them, maintained by combinations of covert, highly emotional disagreement and formal, controlled accord. Some families were at one extreme, some at the other; most were aware of differences but consciously avoided touchy points, remaining sufficiently impersonal to keep disagreements at a minimum. In therapy with these families, increasing self-assertion by the father heralded progress, marked by more overt mother-father conflict at first and then improvement of family relationships in general. Bowen concluded that families where disagreement was most open made the most therapeutic progress.

On balance, the evidence suggests that differences in family patterns do exist between families of the mentally ill and those of normals, and sometimes even among different diagnostic groups. The recurrent theme seems to be that of maternal dominance, paternal passivity, disharmony, and contradictory expectations. The emphasis on these characteristics, however, may simply reflect the investigators' interest in pursuing them to the exclusion of others. It also appears that the more carefully controlled the research, the less startling are the differences between groups.

The identification of differences between families of normals and those of the mentally ill is not in itself sufficient to provide an adequate causal explanation. The caution about *ex post facto* investigations must be repeated. It is difficult to refute the argument that the disruptive family conditions occur subsequent to the onset of illness or at least are exacerbated during episodes of active illness. In this regard it is unfortunate that there is not more work like that of Farina (1960). In addition to a normal comparison group, he also studied a group of families with physically ill offspring so that the impact of illness *per se* on family interaction might be evaluated.

Certainly investigations that fail to use any comparison group must be treated very cautiously, together with those studies where variables such as social class, with a demonstrated relevance, are not controlled. Apart from the issues involved in the evidence of special family patterns, the etiological significance of familial variables is weakened by the diffusion of explanations offered about these relationships. Some look upon these conditions as a result of the impact of devious outside forces on interpersonal relations and their consequent effects on the patient; to others, differences in socialization produce a defective psyche and disorganized ego controls; while still others see the explanation in the link between communication and the potential for making adjustments in behavior. Perhaps it is just this diffusion of interest in the family, with its appeal to investigators of different persuasions, that will continue to make the family the focus of much etiological research for a long time to come.

LABORATORY STUDIES

So great is the plethora of experimental work done by psychologists on mental illness that a complete review of it is not possible: the selection here is limited to studies of the type of psychological functioning immediately relevant to the social behavior of the individual, that is, perception, concept formation, and selected aspects of learning; or investigations calling for the manipulation of social-psychological variables, such as affective stimulus content and reward-punishment. Some inquiries may best be characterized as descriptive or explanatory of the nature of the disorder in schizophrenia, while others do bear directly upon cause and development. In many, comparisons between the mentally ill and the normal are explored not so much to test a theory of the differences between the well and the ill as to probe differences previously established between other identifiable aggregates, such as males and females.

But the major problem is the difficulty in attributing the differences identified to the illness or wellness of the population studied. In many, no background variables are controlled; in some, a heroic attempt is made to apply statistical controls but the sample's size has usually prevented the simultaneous partialing out of a series of variables. Further, there have been a paucity of replications—despite the continuity of their topics, few studies have sampled exactly the same populations and used the same test equipment and statistical techniques. Thus, the discontinuities in the research preclude almost any hard and fast generalization.

By far the largest number of investigators have been concerned with the perceptual processes. Disturbances in perceptual acumen in schizophrenia have been investigated through experimentation with basic perceptual tasks involving perception of size, shape, and time. Lovinger (1956) studied three groups, schizophrenics in good and in poor contact and normals, to determine constancy of size—the capacity to see the given object in different contexts and at different distances as identical in size, shape, and color. The subjects' perception was examined under three conditions of cues of distance: maximal, minimal, and no cue at all. Differences among groups were found only when minimal cues were offered; in this situation schizophrenics in poor contact achieved less constancy than the others. Those in good contact and the normals did not differ significantly from each other.

In an investigation of a similar type, Rausch (1956) had subjects select from a series of circles the one that most clearly approximated an overcoat button, an average scoop of ice cream, and a cross section of an average cigar. Schizophrenics gave disproportionately larger estimates of the ice cream and the cigar. Weckowicz (1957) found, in chronic schizophrenics with deteriorating personality and disordered thought, significantly reduced perceptual constancy in comparison with normals and nonpsychiatric patients. He also reported that schizophrenics showed poorer constancy of distance, and concluded that they live in a "flatter world" (Weckowicz, Sommer, and Hall, 1958). Weckowicz (1964) also studied constancy of shape among chronic and acute schizophrenics and normals, and found that the responses of the chronic schizophrenics varied more than those of the other groups. Further, a study of absolute judgment in constancy of size in chronic schizophrenics and normals under conditions of minimal cues of distance showed the schizophrenics to be prone to significant and consistent underestimation (Boardman *et al.*, 1964). The research workers concluded that schizophrenics in good contact show stable overconstancy, while the acutely disturbed undergo loss of perceptual stability.

Disturbances in the estimation of time have been found among schizophrenics. Dobson (1954), for one, reported that matched groups of neurotics, normals, and time-oriented and disoriented schizophrenics differed not in mean accuracy but in variability of sets of estimates, the disoriented being most variable. When Rabin (1957) asked schizophrenics and normals to estimate the time taken by an interview, he found the judgments of schizophrenics significantly poorer than those of non-psychotics, though precision and direction of error were stable in both groups during the testing period. Along the same lines, Weinstein, Gladstone, and Boardman (1958) found that schizophrenics were more likely to overestimate the duration of a clock second and to respond only to the pulling effect of immediate anchors than were normal college students. Wright, Goldstone, and Boardman (1962) also report that, while active schizophrenics' estimates of one second were significantly less than that of normals, the estimates of a group of schizophrenics in remission were significantly longer than those of the active group. Lanzkron and Wolfson (1958) found a group of long-hospitalized patients tended to retain the past as a frame of reference. Ehrentheil and Jenney (1960) asked a number of elderly schizophrenic patients, "How old are you?" and found that one-third of those who answered the question gave their age at the onset of illness.

These and other studies reveal in schizophrenics greater variability than in normals with regard to constancy of perception of size, shape, time, and so on. There is less consistency in findings, however, about the direction of error, that is, over- or underestimation; and, further, the schizophrenics vary among themselves.

McReynolds (1960) has postulated that perceptual material is assimilated most easily if it is congruent with one's attitudes, goals, and standards, but if it is sufficiently in opposition it cannot be assimilated; that this unassimilated perceptual material is cumulative; and that if in quantity, it underlies feelings of anxiety. Within this theoretical framework, symptomatic behavior functions to reduce unassimilated material and hence anxiety. For example, withdrawal reduces the input of material difficult to assimilate. Experiments to test this hypothesis indicated in very withdrawn schizophrenics a relatively greater tendency to seek familiar stimuli, whereas those less withdrawn showed a relatively greater preference for the novel (McReynolds, 1961). Related work confirms the conclusion that normals exhibit greater stimulus-seeking behavior (McReynolds, 1962).

Perceptual deficit has been thought to manifest itself in both the social and self-cognition of schizophrenics. Paranoid schizophrenics are reported to reveal less disparity between real and ideal self than do normals and other schizophrenics (Havener and Izard, 1962; Rogers, 1958). Achenbach and Zigler (1963) report that subjects of greater social competence show more real-ideal disparity than do those with less. Block and Thomas (1955) found a curvilinear relationship between adjustment and disparity between the ideal and the real self. Cleveland (1960) reports that schizophrenics gave significantly greater estimates of the size of parts of the body than did nonpsychiatric controls, though the groups did not differ in their estimates of size of a neutral object.

Distortion in the perception of others has been related to a deficit in role-taking ability among schizophrenics (Diamond, 1958; Milgram, 1961). Dinitz, Mangus, and Pasamanick (1959) found a significant difference between patients' conceptions of significant others and their self-conceptions. Gwaltney (1958) inquired what was the reference group of chronic and convalescent patients and found that the convalescents identified more with people outside the hospital than with chronic patients. Chronic patients identified themselves as much with people outside as with patients. The ideal self of both groups was more like that of employed men outside.

Schizophrenia was early identified with concrete thinking as contrasted with abstract thinking (Goldstein, 1946). Education, length of hospitalization, and differential diagnosis were found to affect the schizophrenic's performance of conceptual tasks (Becker, 1956; Cavanaugh, 1958; Flavell, 1956; Senf, Huston, and Cohen, 1956), and the question of whether the deficit is actually due to a failure in abstraction or to autistic communication has been raised (McGaughran and Moran, 1956, 1957).

A tendency of schizophrenics to be easily distracted has been postulated as contributory to their relatively poor performance, and as quantitatively rather than qualitatively different from that found in normals (Chapman, 1958). While deficit in concept formation does appear to be a concomitant of schizophrenia, the sources of variance are many and precision in scrutiny of the problem is limited. One reviewer (Winder, 1960) has observed that, despite a rather long history, this arena of research persists in a plethora of repeatedly used, inadequately refined tests and appealing but overly comprehensive concepts.

The differential effect on perception, concept formation, and learning obtained by varying the stimulus has been increasingly studied, as has the manipulation of such motivation as reward-punishment and success-failure. Though not to be reviewed here, this also is an area of continuing research in psychomotor behavior (Goodstein, Guertin, and Blackburn, 1961; Karras, 1962; Rosenbaum, Mackavey, and Grisell, 1957).

Studies of schizophrenics indicate that perceptual thresholds and estimation of size are dependent on the emotional concomitants of the visual stimuli ordinarily employed (Daston, 1956; Dunn, 1954; McGinnies and Adornetto, 1952; Zahn, 1959). Pearl and Berg (1963) found that schizophrenics exhibited relatively great distortion in estimating time when presented with stimuli relating to aggressive conflict. Moriarty and Kates (1962) investigated the effects of social approval and disapproval on concept attainment. Variation in difficulty in dealing with stimuli having human content was found in a study by Davis and Harrington (1957). In measuring conceptual ability, Webb (1955) found that an experimental group of schizophrenics who had received a report of failure after a session of testing did not improve in the second session, while the controls did.

Rodnick and Garmezy (1957) and their students have reported that schizophrenics show behavioral deficit following censure in experimental tasks involving stimulus generalization and concept formation. However, Olson (1958) reported that facilitation in a simple digit-symbol task followed both success and failure, but the successes were the more facilitating. Neiditch (1963) found that psychotics' preference for a neutral task was lessened when associated with failure.

Considerable work continues to be done on the relative effects of reward and punishment on learning in schizophrenics (Sherman, 1964). Findings are, in general, not consistent, and there is also a question of just what constitutes the "reward." In work primarily on stimulus generalization along the pitch continuum, Garmezy (1952) found no difference between schizophrenics and normals in the absence of stress conditions. However, under a mild stress-reward-punishment condition, schizophrenics made fewer correct responses and less effort to succeed. Bleke (1955), in a study of normals and good and poor premorbid schizophrenics who were set a learning task, found no differences in rate of learning under reward-punishment conditions; however, poor premorbids who had been punished during learning proved superior in retention.

Atkinson (1958), using verbal rewards and punishment in a learning task given schizophrenic and normal women, reported that the latter learned more efficiently when rewarded, while the schizophrenics learned more efficiently when punished. Robinson (1958) obtained similar results with a group of men. In Leventhal's study (1959), using verbal and nonverbal conditions, better performance was obtained from chronic schizophrenics when they were verbally rewarded and punished, while among normals one method sufficed as well as the other.

Many experimental studies not referred to here are noted in an extensive two-part review by Buss and Lang (1965), who, after considering five explanations of psychological deficit, rejected theories attributing differences in response to social censure, to specified stimuli, to insufficient modification, or to regression, in favor of a theory of interference. This interference theory assumes that, given a task that the schizophrenic cannot undertake properly or in a systematic manner, ongoing responses suffer interference from irrelevant external cues and from internal stimuli. The view of Buss and Lang is that the schizophrenic allows irrelevant stimuli to intrude or attempts to defend himself from distracting internal stimuli. They argue that, on the one hand, the schizophrenic may be overexclusive of distraction because he admits the intrusion of irrelevant external stimuli or attempts to defend himself against distracting internal stimuli; on the other hand, he may be underexclusive whenever he needs to shift to a new set—hence, probably, his greater responsiveness to punishment. It further follows, they claim, that some schizophrenics alternate between the two and thus either over- or underexclusiveness or vacillation between the two may be found when the individual is presented with conceptual tasks. They conclude that "the generality of interfering effects suggests a fundamental sensorimotor defect" (Lang and Buss, 1965). They advise that the centers involved, particularly those of sensory inhibition, should be given extensive study in schizophrenic patients; they take care, however, to point out that even this generalization is limited, since relationships which hold for men may not hold for women.

The key question, however, is whether such theories are to be properly regarded as etiological, whether certain of the differences between patients and normals are causative or simply another indicator of the illness. In many studies, patients with symptoms in remission are found to show no significant differences from normals, though the "sick ones" do. One must be pessimistic about the likelihood that such studies will reach a definitive statement of the etiology of mental disorders.

In reviewing the various types of etiological studies, we have made the same criticism several times: there is great difficulty in making causal inferences given the practical limitations of undertaking *a priori* investigations and the limited opportunities for longitudinal investigations of long duration and large sample size. Unlike many other fields in which epidemiological and *ex post facto* investigations can lead to experimental studies, the mental health field is pretty well without such opportunities, since ethical considerations, as well as practical, preclude basic experimentation with manipulation of variables on a random basis. The other alternative is that of testing, through treatment programs, relationships identified in research of a non-etiological character. As we shall see in the next section, the types of inputs in treatment programs that are of sufficient strength and duration to effect changes in phenomena such as social isolation, disrupted family relationships, and so on are difficult to induce. Thus, the many notions on etiology, though they often have substantive theoretical bases, remain relatively untested, given the criteria of rigor that hold for much of medical and social-psychological research. That this of necessity is the present course and that of the future is obvious. But this situation too, like the problems of definition, has resulted in considerable discouragement on the part of both investigators and practitioners.

TREATMENT

Mental illness, being at once a social and an economic problem, is a rallying point for spirited community "do-gooders"; the sensitivity of the public has reinforced the social psychologist's concern both with its extent and with its treatment. Along these lines, the importance of mental illness as a social problem must be recognized.

Attempts have been made to estimate its extent in various ways, for example, by means of community-wide assessments that are in line with the medical concepts of the illness (Leighton, 1959; Srole, 1962). Thus the "Midtown Manhattan study" sought to develop structured scales that would yield an estimate of the prevalence of illness in a community (Srole, 1962). Alas! Two problems have confronted those engaged in such endeavors. First, despite careful work, no one as yet has devised scales that correlate well with psychiatric judgment. Second, there is no agreement on what constitutes the appropriate cutting points, even among the scales conventionally used to make estimates of a community's illness. In the Midtown Manhattan study, for instance, of some 1660 adults studied, only 18.5 percent were regarded as "well" and over 50 percent were suffering from moderate symptom formation or even more severe incapacities. Congruence between structured measures and psychiatric judgments are found more often in studies of limited populations; for example, a correlation of 0.8 was found between an index of the mental health and the clinical ratings of automobile workers (Kornhauser, 1965).

However, regardless of the cutoff point, or whether scales or hospitalization rates are employed, differences are found between communities (Leighton, 1959), between aggregates within communities (Hollingshead, 1958; Jaco, 1960), and between groups defined by demographic characteristics (Malzberg, 1956a, 1956c).

By far the commonest method of assessing the extent of mental illness is through investigation of the numbers of individuals under treatment for it. Treatment takes place in several types of institutions: in hospitals, in "semi-institutions" such as day hospitals and night hospitals, in community clinics, and in private practitioners' offices. Treatment modalities may be classified as somatic (drug, shock, surgery), environmental (custodial and therapeutic milieu), and interpersonal (psychotherapy, group therapy, casework, counseling, psychoanalysis). Beyond the presentation of some rather gross figures, problems of definition make it impossible to estimate the extent of treatment; the number being treated does not equal the full number who are receiving the treatment. Individuals may receive therapy without considering themselves "mentally ill" or being so considered by others; obvious examples are pregnant women receiving tranquilizers and social workers undergoing psychoanalysis "for didactic reasons."

Though the populations of resident treatment centers have been reduced slightly from their peak in 1955, somewhere between 500,000 and 600,000 persons at any given time are part of the institutional population. The vast majority are in public hospitals, the greatest number being in state institutions. Though the number hospitalized at any time has declined over the past years and with it, in general, the length of stay, the number of admissions and, particularly, of readmissions is increasing. There is even at the present time a dispute about whether or not "mental illness" has increased, decreased, or remained the same throughout the history of civilized man or during the period of marked organization in the United States and other Western countries. A study discussed already contends that, if various ecological and social factors are taken into account, the overall rates of mental illness will be found not to have increased at all (Goldhamer and Marshall, 1953). No one has been able to demonstrate empirically an increase in mental illness, though the current belief in the association of mental illness with the stresses of urban life and technological change implies it (Duhl, 1963; Lindemann, 1960).

As to the cost, it is estimated that approximately three and one-half billion dollars are spent per year for the care and treatment of the mentally ill, and to this must be added the large expenditures for training of personnel and related expenditures. It is commonly assumed that these figures largely reflect mental illness as a medical phenomenon seen through the maze of the social structure at a given time. Certainly, regional differences in institutionalized populations, and differences in rates between social class and ethnic, age, and religious groups, cannot be accounted for solely on the basis of etiological differences within the nation's population (Belknap, 1956; Hollingshead and Redlich, 1958; Jaco, 1959). Rather, admission, release, length of stay, and type of treatment are clearly determined by the interaction of medical and social variables.

The types of available resources have shifted: outpatient psychiatric caseloads have increased markedly and so has the number of persons treated for psychiatric illness in general hospitals. The number of patients on the rolls of outpatient clinics is set at somewhere near three-quarters of a million (Blue Cross Association, 1964; Health Information Foundation, 1960).

The predominant mode of treatment by outpatient clinics and private practitioners is some form of interpersonal therapy, often supplemented by drugs. In hospitals, at least the large public hospitals, the predominant therapies are somatic—drugs and electric shock (Greenblatt, York, and Brown, 1955). In addition, therapy is often regarded as including the hospital milieu itself. Further, hospitals—on paper at least—offer a variety of ancillary treatments, such as therapies which may be occupational, industrial, or musical. Finally, a system of agencies is devoted specially to the social integration of released hospital patients, such as reemployment services, social clubs, foster homes, sheltered workshops, and the like (Grob, 1963).

The personnel engaged in the direct treatment of the mentally ill come predominantly from four professions: psychiatry, psychology, nursing, and social work. With the exception of nursing (though it is increasingly true of nurses, too), the goal of training of all four is to develop a cadre who can perform some kind of interpersonal therapy. However, in the case of patients in public mental hospitals, the largest proportion of the treated mentally ill, the congruence of such training with the realities of providing care is open to serious question (Schwartz and Schwartz, 1964). Not only existing patient-professional staff ratios, but also those recommended by the American Psychiatric Association preclude the rendering of interpersonal therapy to any fraction of the patients, simply on the basis of available time (Albee, 1959; American Psychiatric Association, 1956). As Clausen (1961) has pointed out, the picture is not very different in the outpatient clinics. In spite of the extremely high dropout rates in clinics, waiting lists are enormously long. This interferes with plans for providing immediate service to acute cases to prevent further deterioration.

While the great bulk of patients are in state mental hospitals, research about hospitals tends to be concentrated in private institutions. Private hospitals, particularly if associated with universities, are nicer places and more receptive to study. And while there are strong indications that the commonest form of treatment is "no treatment," most research tends to be on specific modes of therapy, regardless of how many patients actually receive them; thus the studies presented here overrepresent a small fraction of what is going on.

Given the problems concerning etiology already depicted, it is needless to say that there is neither consensus as to the proper treatment of mental disorders nor substantial testimony on the efficacy of a given treatment. The most definitive information is descriptive (what is being done to whom, by whom, and for how long) rather than evaluative (how effective the treatment is or even how it might be effective).

THE HOSPITAL

The distribution of characteristics in a population of first admissions to hospital is not the same as in the total resident population. For example, while psychoses account for less than 80 percent of first admissions, psychotics constitute over 90 percent of the resident hospital population. Similarly, schizophrenia is the diagnosis reported in 24 percent of first admissions but accounts for 46 percent of the resident population; though psychoneurotics represent five percent of first admissions, they constitute only one percent of the residential population (Health Information Foundation, 1960).

Duration of illness, as reflected in length of stay, is obviously not the same in all admissions. The differential characteristics of first-admission patients and long-term resident populations serve as prognostic indicators as well as descriptive variables, and this review of research is intended to serve both purposes. As already noted, lower socioeconomic status is associated with a higher incidence of mental disorder, particularly of schizophrenia. Two studies (Hardt and Feinhandler, 1959; Myers, Bean, and Pepper, 1964) conclude that social status is associated with prognosis, though there is some question whether this finding holds if the pool of patients in each class is taken into account as a determinant in calculating release rates (Freeman and Gartner, in press).

Data on first admissions to mental hospitals in selected areas of the United States indicate higher rates of all psychoses among men than among women, except of the affective disorders (Dayton, 1940; Lindemann, 1950; Rose and Stub, 1955). Lemkau and Crocetti (1958) report higher release rates among female schizophrenics, but according to Baker *et al.* (1957) their prognosis is poorer.

Landis and Page (1938) report, as do others (Wing, Denham, and Munro, 1959), that unmarried males are overrepresented among first admissions to state mental hospitals, less so than are unmarried women. These data may well indicate that sex is so confounded with other prognostic variables that generalizations cannot be made about its prognostic worth alone.

Among the functional psychoses, a diagnosis of schizophrenia is clearly the strongest indicator of poor prognosis. Therefore, considerable work has gone into refining the prognostic indicators of schizophrenia. Marital status has perhaps been the most thoroughly investigated of demographic variables (Adler, 1953; Farina, Garmezy, and Barry, 1963; Jenkins and Gurel, 1959; Lindemann *et al.*, 1959; Malamud and Render, 1939; Malzberg, 1936; Norris, 1956; Odegaard, 1946, 1953; Orr, 1955; Phillips, 1953; Simon and Wirt, 1961; Wing, Denham, and Munro, 1959; Wittman, 1944). In general, it can be stated that never having been married is associated with longer hospital stay among schizophrenics; having been married at some time, with a somewhat better prognosis; and being currently married, with the best. The association is somewhat stronger for men than for women.

The interpretation of this finding varies. On the one hand, it is viewed as a symptom of the disease itself, not marrying being part of the schizophrenic's general immaturity and isolation. On the other hand, marriage itself is seen as a screening device, schizophrenics not being regarded as desirable mates. Still a third interpretation is that the longer hospital stay of the unmarried schizophrenic is simply due to the fact he is less likely to have someone to take him home from the hospital (Freeman and Simmons, 1963).

Poor premorbid histories apparently are associated in schizophrenia with early impoverishment of social relationships, inadequate heterosexual adjustment, early onset of symptoms, and inferior social and economic achievement; good premorbid histories show greater adequacy in all these things, with an onset of symptoms that is often sudden and related to some observable stress (Becker, 1959; Chase and Silverman, 1941; Rodnick and Garmezy, 1957; Zubin, 1954).

Several methods have been developed to measure premorbid adjustment (Lorr, Wittman, and Schanberger, 1951; Phillips, 1953; Steffey and Becker, 1961; Ullmann and Giovannoni, 1964; Wittman, 1944), and they have proved useful in predicting remission and also in explaining some of the variety in outcome of psychological-experimental work with schizophrenics (Chapman, Day, and Burstein, 1961; Kantor and Winder, 1959, 1961; Wittman, 1944; Zimet and Fine, 1959).

Thus, while a diagnosis of schizophrenia points to a poor prognosis, there are differences in potential between individuals. Thus a further indicator of poor prognosis is the length of time a patient has been hospitalized. It is generally believed that, if a schizophrenic patient has been hospitalized for over two years, his chances of ever leaving the hospital substantially decline; Belknap (1956), basing his observation on the process of release in a Texas hospital, concluded that patients who left at all usually did so within a year. A review of biometric research on release rates of schizophrenics admitted between 1900 and 1951 (Brown, 1960) shows that, in spite of differences in levels of retention and release in 16 studies, the rates accelerate rapidly during the first year and then begin to flatten out and are relatively constant between the second and fifth postadmission years. Brown's survey included the studies of Warren State Hospital (Kramer *et al.*, 1955), Delaware State Hospital (Freyhan, 1958), and New York's state hospital system (Fuller, 1930; Malzberg, 1952). These studies set the expectation of release of schizophrenics who have been hospitalized continuously for two years at between six and seven percent.

While there is little to suggest that prospects for the release of the long-hospitalized patient are growing brighter, there is some justification for the notion that fewer patients are reaching such a state of chronicity. A reversal of the trend of over half a century occurred in 1956, the date up to which the populations of hospitals had annually increased (Kramer and Pollack, 1958). Reductions in hospital population were not accompanied by a decrease in the admission rate but by an acceleration in discharges (Freyhan, 1958; Kramer *et al.*, 1956). One experimental psychologist (McReynolds, 1962) has remarked that research on the chronic deteriorated schizophrenic may be disappearing for lack of subjects.

Chronicity and rates of discharge bring into focus the hospital itself, since the fate of the patient does not rest solely on his own characteristics. The rise in the rates of discharge cannot be attributed to a mutation in the disease itself; rather, as Klerman (1961) has pointed out, it was preceded by several historical trends, beginning with a shift of attention away from the organic to the functional psychoses in the 1930's.

Perhaps more than any other medical institution, the mental hospital has come under severe criticism for violating the medical dictum "do no harm," in particular, for its role in the development of chronicity as observed by both medical and nonmedical critics (Downing, 1958; Lehrman, 1961; Ullmann, 1958; Wing, 1961). Though one early observer (Devereux, 1944, 1949) found some good things to say, more recent commentators have damned hospitals, and not even with faint praise. Goffman (1961) described the essential characteristics of the large regimented hospital as those of a "total institution" which processes its inmates impersonally. Others have described how elements in the hospital's social system and in its staff's interaction can produce disturbance in patients (Caudill, 1958; Stanton and Schwartz, 1954).

Quantitatively, the mental hospital's characteristics have been more recently correlated with outcome, patient-centered prognostic indicators held constant. Studies comparing properties of several hospitals, such as size and staffing patterns, reveal these elements to be related to differentials in speed of release (Ullmann and Gurel, 1964). Also, Mabry (1962) reported that in "open" hospitals periods of stay were significantly briefer than in closed, though patients in the two did not differ appreciably in age and marital status; and Wing and Brown (1961), in a comparison of three hospitals, found that differences in the philosophy of care were related to the clinical condition of patients and also to their length of stay (Wing, Denham, and Munro, 1959).

So far as work devoted to a microscopic view of hospital life is concerned, one generalization is untenable: that the behavior of staff toward patients, even in making decisions about treatment, is entirely patient-centered. Various investigators have examined the process of decision in hospitals as to admission, intramural treatment, and release of patients (Freeman and Simmons, 1963; Mishler and Waxler, 1963; Pasamanick *et al.*, n.d.; Simmons, Davis, and Spencer, 1956). In all of these it was apparent that many circumstances extrinsic to the patient and his condition affect decisions; such are the structural characteristics of the organization, extraorganizational professional commitments, the social status of the patients, and the activity of their families.

Two studies scrutinize the effect of the hospital's status system on the behavior of personnel toward patients. Perucci (1963), after studying the status system of a psychiatric ward, reported that social distance is manipulated to protect position or to enhance status; Pearlin (1962), who surveyed the nursing force of a large hospital, concluded that the subordination of patients to staff occurred most frequently where the staff enjoyed comparatively high position, was subservient to superiors, and was blocked in its aspirations to mobility. In a study of resistance to change in hospitals, Pearlin (1962) also found the staff's attitudes toward change among personnel and whether their motives were patient-centered to be related to their status in the hierarchy.

In a rather rare study of the formal structure of a mental hospital, Henry (1954) focused on the ways in which bureaucratic arrangements adversely affect the performance of personnel. As Perrow (1964) has noted, however, the issue of the "good" and "bad" functioning of a bureaucracy should raise the question whether treatment settings can be nonbureaucratic at all.

In a thoroughgoing series of interlocking studies, parts of which have already been described here, the characteristics of ward attendants, who probably spend the most time with patients, were examined; it was demonstrated that there are interrelationships among their personalities, the institutional policies under which they operate, their conception of treatment, and their ideas and performance of their roles. Aides who were generally more humane were rated as the most effective with patients (Gilbert and Levinson, 1956, 1957; Pine and Levinson, 1957). Age, social class, and the attitudes of patients are associated with the forms of treatment they receive; younger patients, of higher social class, with a low authoritarianism score, most frequently receive psychotherapy, and those with the opposite characteristics undergo one of the somatic procedures (Gallagher, Levinson, and Ehrlich, 1957). Klerman and his associates (Klerman *et al.*, 1960), studying characteristics of resident psychiatrists, found authoritarianism, status, and assertiveness to be negatively related to their adherence to drugs as therapy. Pasamanick and his group, in a study already mentioned, report that not only were diagnostic practices idiosyncratic, but also the treatment given patients and their length of hospitalization were related to the diagnosis. From this they concluded that, despite practitioners' protestations that their focus is always the individual patient, they, in fact, respond to a variety of forces besides his condition, and these largely predetermine diagnosis and treatment (Pasamanick, Dinitz, and Lefton, 1959).

Finally, a study of influences on treatment that deserves mention is one by Sinnett and Hanford (1962), who note that patients' relationships with other patients and their popularity with them are associated with their selection for psychotherapy, the most unpopular and isolated being those least often chosen.

Schwartz and associates (Schwartz, Schwartz, and Stanton, 1951) found that significantly fewer of the requests of withdrawn patients, in comparison with those of the active, were heeded by the nursing staff. Dinitz and associates (1958) systematically observed the patients' behavior in a small hospital and related it to differential ward policies and practices. Contrary to the Schwartz study, differences in patient behavior were not found to be specific to the ward. They concluded that either the overall hospital structure or specific characteristics of the illness may be more important in the determination of the patients' behavior than unit substructures. The study by Strauss and associates (1964), however, points to both the total and the specific structures as important influences on the patients' behavior.

Several studies which examine social behavior of patients who varied in severity of illness and who were in different types of setting all report an association between severity of illness and social behavior (Hunter, Schooler, and Spohn, 1962; Murray and Cohen, 1959; O'Connor, Carstairs, and Rawnsley, 1957; Schooler and Spohn, 1960). It is difficult, however, to evaluate the differential effects of environmental structure and severity of illness on social behavior, since these are inevitably confounded (that is, "sicker" patients are put on similar wards, and thus both variables simultaneously influence social behavior).

There has been a growing disposition to focus not so much on the deleterious effects of the social milieu as on the positive force that the hospital environment might become in the recuperative process. Thus the concept of the hospital as a "therapeutic community" has taken form and achieved great popularity (Jones, 1953).

In practice, the notions of the therapeutic community have at times become oversimplified and confused with issues about open and closed doors, relaxation of restrictions, and the like. M. S. Schwartz (1957) has warned against these errors, outlining the basic elements of the therapeutic community as follows:

> An adequate concept must include consideration of organizational arrangements, informal aspects of social structure, patient participation and distribution, specific therapeutic activities, the physical setting and relations with the non-hospital world. It refers to these aspects individually and collectively—to their interrelation, organization and coordination as a whole.

With all its complexity, it is most difficult to know when, in fact, a "therapeutic community" has been established, let alone to try to analyze its effectiveness.

There have been several investigations of the effect of manipulation of social-psychological variables in the patient's environment. On the one hand, Faquin, Daniels, and Margolis (1962) report that staff-initiated activity resulted in greater interaction among patients, who regard it as more satisfactory than activity initiated either by patients or by patients and staff cooperatively. On the other hand, Lerner and Fairweather (1963) report that minimally supervised groups develop more cohesiveness than those with maximal supervision. Wing and Freudenburg (1961), who varied the supervision of a group of male schizophrenic patients in a hospital workshop, found a sharp increase in output whenever social incentives were introduced, and a sharp fall whenever passive supervision was resumed. Time sampling of workshop behavior showed that the increase in work under active conditions of supervision was accompanied by a significant decrease in various kinds of abnormal behavior.

In a cooking class, Rosengren (1959) observed socialization among a group of "acting-out" boys. He noted in the early sessions that deliberative behavior on the part of the leaders tended to call forth impulsive behavior on the part of the boys, but in the later sessions the leaders' deliberative behavior more frequently called forth similar conduct in the boys. Other experiments, particularly those with chronic schizophrenic patients, include one by Tourney *et al.* (1961), who initiated a therapeutic program involving increased patient-staff ratios, coed living arrangements, ward planning, meetings, and individual attention to patients. They report that the accessory symptoms of schizophrenia were in many cases reduced by this regimen, but that basic pathology remained unchanged; they also noted that the mixing of the sexes on the ward revealed a "potentiality for heterosexual object relations in schizophrenics, sometimes thought of as solely narcissistic or inhibited sexually."

King, Armitage, and Tilton (1960) used an operant-interpersonal therapy which involved a sequence of problem-solving tasks with social and concrete rewards, which increased in complexity and interpersonal involvement, with concomitant use of verbalization. In a group of chronic schizophrenics they found that treatment was associated with increased verbalization, motivation to leave the ward, and other clinical variables. The growing use of operant-conditioning methods in mental hospitals, with rather encouraging results, has recently been reported in a compendium by Ullmann and Krasner (1965).

The extent to which promising results achieved by any treatment have lasting rehabilitative effects is questionable. Fairweather and his associates (1964) found that efforts at establishing group cohesiveness among patients have favorable effects, but they point out that gains made during hospitalization are probably lost if the systems established in the group are not maintained in the community. Along this line, Rapoport's (1960) study of Maxwell Jones's institution suggests that, as evidenced by outcome variables (rehospitalization, social performance in the community, and so on), there is little to show the greater efficacy of the therapeutic community. It may well be that such a setting is more humane and even that patients "behave better" in it but, at least from a sociological standpoint, there is little indication so far that it will solve their long-term social problems.

The role of the family in the treatment and rehabilitation of the hospitalized mental patient has been receiving increasing attention. In the studies reported here, the family is seen as introducing intervening variables which may enhance or deter rehabilitative efforts on behalf of the individual who has already become ill.

Several studies have raised the question whether, in rehabilitation, there has been some family involvement or none, and if the former, what is the quality of involvement. It is generally agreed that, while the patient is in hospital, visits by relatives can be of considerable help (Brouwer and Brown, 1955; Cumming and Cumming, 1957; Kaplan and Wolf, 1954).

A careful investigation of relatives' visits which goes beyond the usual exhortation to personnel to "involve the family in treatment" is that by Groth and associates (1960). In a survey of the total population in a somewhat isolated mental hospital, they report that 41 percent of the patients had not had a visitor within the last year, and 16 percent had not had a visitor since admission. While the literature abounds in prescriptions about the relationship between patients and their relatives, not inconsequential is the total lack of relationship, at least face-to-face, between them.

The contact between patient's relatives and the hospital has been analyzed by Deasy and Quinn (1955) and by Myers and Roberts (1959), among others. Myers and Roberts reveal rather dramatically the rejecting and downright rude behavior that lower-class relatives are shown by hospital personnel. Deasy and Quinn, in their investigation of wives' expectations of, demands upon, and experiences with staff members of the hospital where their husbands were patients, found a significantly higher rate of rejection of requests of wives for changes in the course of hospitalization than of rejection of requests for help with personal problems or for simple information. When hospital psychiatrists also were asked to rate requests made by wives, they named questions about the nature of mental illness as most difficult to answer, and they further reported that, because of the pressure of work, they had to concentrate on the patient to the exclusion of the relative.

An intensive study of 17 families where the wife had been admitted to a state mental hospital for the first time has been undertaken by Sampson, Messinger, and Towne (1964). In their assessment of the entire experience, they note that hospitalization seems to provide a moratorium in an already disintegrating social engagement. When the wife was defined as "ill," the obligations of her role could be suspended without abrogation. Hospitalization provided an opportunity for a process of reintegration, but one totally unguided by the institution. The concept of the sick role has received much attention, though originally developed to explain somatic illness (Mechanic and Volkart, 1961; Parsons, 1951).

Follow-up studies of mental patients (Angrist *et al.*, 1961; Brown *et al.*, 1962; Freeman and Simmons, 1963; Morrow and Robins, 1961) have attempted to specify interpersonal and structural correlates of posthospital performance. These studies have faced squarely the various conceptions of mental illness. Certain structural factors, for example, marital status, are related, at least in some of these studies, to return to the hospital but, in general, social-psychological measures and expectations of relatives are much more strongly related to the patient's occupational and social performance while in the community than to lapses in health, that is, rehospitalization (Brown, 1959; Freeman and Simmons, 1963). Freeman and Simmons argue that psychiatric symptoms of illness, that is, bizarre behavior, are relatively independent of work and social performance, and that the determinants of each should, at least analytically, be separated. From these studies it is fair to state that general observations about the social functioning of persons in general apply equally to mental patients, but as a case study on work and mental illness suggests, there appears to be little evidence of the links between inadequate social functioning, interpersonal processes, and rehospitalization or illness in a medical sense (Simmons, 1965).

BEYOND THE HOSPITAL

The hospital is still the treatment center for the largest number of the mentally ill, and the center where the greatest expenditure of funds for therapy is made. Increasingly, all forms of treatment are being offered both in- and outpatients within the same institution. However, certain distinctions can be drawn between services ordinarily offered on an outpatient basis (that is, where the patient does not spend 24 hours a day in the same establishment) and the traditional hospital.

Today, there is an abundance of services to be discussed later under rehabilitation and prevention; however, psychotherapy was for long the principal method of outpatient treatment, and its social implications call for special mention.

In research on selection of outpatients, the notion is implicit that psychotherapy is the preferred method and that patients not given it are somehow being slighted. Certainly, it is the most expensive, yet there is little definitive evidence that it is more effective than any other form of treatment or than no treatment at all (Berelson and Steiner, 1964; Eysenck, 1961). While psychotherapeutic literature abounds in case studies claiming success, there is a marked paucity of rigorously controlled work to support psychotherapy's high reputation. An exhaustive review of studies of psychotherapy yielded less than 10 percent where a control group was used. Meanwhile, even if it is efficacious in the cases treated, its general applicability is questionable. Thus, it need not be concluded that the many people screened out of the psychotherapeutic process are necessarily being deprived.

The work by Hollingshead and Redlich (1958) and by Myers and Shaffer (1954) strongly supports the notion that psychotherapy is middle-class-oriented; not only were lower-class patients in their samples more frequently screened away from it but, when accepted, they were significantly less often declared improved. Other studies also indicate that patients in analysis are largely white, middle-class, professional people (Hunt, 1960; Siegel, 1962). Siegel and Fink (1962), in a study of an outpatient clinic, found its entire applicant population to have had the advantage of more education than the general population.

The risk that stigma attached to mental illness might induce some not to seek help was a hypothesis investigated by Phillips (1963) in an analysis of rejections in hypothetical situations. He concludes that to draw upon certain sources of help entails a reward in improved mental health but at the cost of rejection and a consequent negative self-image, and points out the need to assess the net balance of gains and losses.

There are two ecological studies. The first, by Raphael (1964), examined the ecological distribution of cases in a child guidance clinic and argued that it supports a hypothesis relating distribution to diffusion of psychological and psychiatric explanations of conduct: variations in rates between areas were observed to correspond to the community's acceptance of psychological and psychiatric interpretations. The second inquiry is by Jaco (1957), who investigated attitudes toward mental illness in census tracts of high and of low incidence, and discarded the notion that high incidence is associated with acceptance, though his explanation of the results supports it. It is unfortunate that neither work elaborated the possible influence of social class.

The behavioral scientist's involvement in treatment programs is often the sequel of his grave concern with the intolerable conditions found in large treatment institutions. To some extent, at least on the conceptual level, the social psychologists have attempted to inject into treatment practices a neo-Freudian theory of interpersonal processes together with a humanistic concern with the lot of the patient during treatment. But the question remains: Do treatment settings or experiences in them have any long-range impact on the course of the illness or on the patient's interpersonal performance after release or at the end of the "interpersonal therapies"?

REHABILITATION AND PREVENTION

Though practitioners in mental health at times use the concepts of prevention and rehabilitation interchangeably, the rehabilitation of the individual patient and the prevention of widespread mental disorder in the community must be distinguished (Sussman, 1965; Williams, 1953).

On the subject of prevention, at least two common views have been examined earlier here. One stems from a general emphasis on role theory and the insistence that mental health is a function of one's socialization into different roles and opportunities to learn the repertoire of expressive and instrumental expectations. A comprehensive view of these matters is developed by Foote and Cottrell (1955), who set forth a number of social-psychological characteristics of personality (for example, empathy, autonomy, and judgment) as important components of interpersonal competence.

The enhancement of such attributes has often been the focal point of therapy dominated by the idea of "group dynamics." Though the rationale is not always explicit, concepts underlying socialization into roles and appropriate expectations have found their way into many of the transitional programs such as halfway houses, former patient's clubs, and so on (Grob, 1963). Thus the concept of role performance and role socialization has a place in both prevention and rehabilitation.

A large number of work programs have been developed and studied. They start out with one of two viewpoints: one objective is to provide the patient with work settings in which there is a muting of normative community expectations and gradual building of confidence and an ability to cope with stress; the other is to socialize him to the standards of the community. But one study yields the finding that the "trainable" patient is least likely to participate in the programs—he typically goes out into the world and makes his own place (Meyer and Borgatta, 1958). Work and the inculcation of skills do occupy much of the rehabilitative activity in mental health, despite meager findings on their efficacy.

Certainly, however, many social psychiatrists and public health practitioners look toward role theory in developing community-wide programs aimed at prevention, and, if one may speculate, it is at the preventive rather than the rehabilitative level that the concept has the most significance.

Many theories of mental illness propose links between inadequate performance and uncertain and unclear expectations of role, stress, and psychiatric illness. Such notions are involved in the programs of prevention of community psychiatrists (Caplan, 1964), and have led to the view that gatekeepers and intermediaries, such as nurses and teachers, are proper consultants and that work with them provides an entry into the larger population.

The second theory emphasizes the social structure and the importance of modifying its impact in developing preventive and rehabilitative programs. Thus, such structural variables as socioeconomic status are associated with illness, usually, it is thought, through processes of stress and inadequate development of role. The middle 1960's have seen a surge of effort concentrated on the structural dimension, for example, in the nationwide programs for the poor (Freeman, 1965). The argument is that the greatest results will be obtained through modification of the social structure, an undertaking seriously engaging the energies of the federal government (Cloward and Ohlin, 1960).

With respect to rehabilitation, structural dimensions have not been neglected. The therapeutic community is inspired by the doctrine that a flexible, nonauthoritarian setting provides the most effective milieu in which the patient may develop a repertoire of roles conforming to social standards. The association is commonly made between structure, role, and pathology (Merton, 1949).

An offshoot, at least in part, is the concern with the general problems of deviance (Freidson, 1965; Lemert, 1951). At the preventive level, the agencies of health education have frequently sought to modify the community's conception of normal conduct (Cumming and Cumming, 1957). Moreover, opportunities are promoted for redefining deviant behavior in an effort to rescue individuals from the warping effect of forces emanating from the social structure or from inadequate socialization. And, to turn to rehabilitation, there has been considerable concern over the labeling of the individual as deviant and the effects of hostility and stigma, and measures have been directed at the patient himself and the general community—in particular, at specialized groups such as employers. Then, too, patients and sometimes members of their families are being helped by recommendations to reduce stigma and feelings of inferiority, including suggestions of alternatives to hospitalization such as treatment at home or in the emergency room (Carlton, 1965).

The connection is not complete between the theoretical positions discussed here and the actual empirical investigations. Over the years, however, there has been a serious attempt to develop evaluative research and research demonstration programs to assess specific programs of treatment and test their theoretical frameworks. But, in fact, very few studies are adequately conceived (Freeman and Sherwood, 1965). Nevertheless, there is an encouraging awareness of the need for a merging of theory and empirical research and for doing so by way of research demonstration programs.

CONCLUSIONS

We have tried here to examine mental health research and work bearing on it that could reasonably be defined as relevant to social psychology. That there is great activity in this area is obvious from the many investigations reported here, which constitute only a fraction of the total studies conducted.

One can fairly ask: Why so much work and so few definitive generalizations? To give a partial answer: The limited opportunities for experimental investigation, the tampering with ideal designs caused by the practitioner's concern for the patient or his suspicious attitude toward scientific inquiry in the field, and, finally, the public's insistence on immediate action—all serve as effective barriers to the systematic accumulation of knowledge.

To look, finally, at a basic question: If indeed the goal of all treatment is the maintenance or restoration of "mental health," how is the attainment of so diffuse and ill-defined a goal to be measured objectively? In all types of research, whether it be on etiology, on experimentation with treatment modalities, or on the evaluation of them, a constant problem is identification of the elusive parameters of "mental health."

Most important of all is the fact that all the inadequacies of social psychology and the limitations of theories and methods of studying social behavior beset the investigators of the social psychology of mental health. It is to be hoped, however, that as studies continue they will become increasingly relevant to the social behavior of *all* persons, and as social behavior becomes better understood, social psychologists occupied with the subtle, diverse, and very pressing phenomenon of mental health will be able to progress more rapidly.

REFERENCES

Achenbach, T., and E. Zigler (1963). Social competence and self-image disparity in psychiatric and nonpsychiatric patients. *J. abnorm. soc. Psychol., 67*, 197–205.

Adler, L. (1953). The relationship of marital status to incidence and recovery from mental disease. *Soc. Forces, 32*, 185–194.

Albee, G. W. (1959). *Mental health manpower trends.* New York: Basic Books.

American Psychiatric Association (1956). *Standards for hospitals and clinics.* Washington, D.C.: American Psychiatric Association.

Angrist, S., S. Dinitz, M. Lefton, and B. Pasamanick (1961). Social and psychological factors in the rehospitalization of female mental patients. *Arch. gen. Psychiat., 4*, 363–370.

Ash, P. (1949). The reliability of psychiatric diagnosis. *J. abnorm. soc. Psychol., 44*, 272–277.

Atkinson, R. (1958). Paired-associate learning by schizophrenic and normal subjects under conditions of verbal reward and verbal punishment. Ph.D. dissertation, Stanford University.

Baker, A., *et al.* (1957). Social status after five years in a mental hospital. *Brit. J. med. Psychol., 30*, 113–118.

Barton, W. (1958). Viewpoint of a clinician. In M. Jahoda (Ed.), *Current concepts of positive mental health.* New York: Basic Books. Pp. 111–120.

Bateson, G. (1960). Minimal requirements for a theory of schizophrenia. *Arch. gen. Psychiat., 2*, 477–491.

Bateson, G., D. D. Jackson, J. Haley, and J. Weakland (1956). Toward a theory of schizophrenia. *Behav. Sci., 1*, 251–264.

Baxter, J. C., J. Becker, and W. Hooks (1963). Defensive style in the families of schizophrenics and controls. *J. abnorm. soc. Psychol., 66*, 512–518.

Beck, S. J. (1960). Families of schizophrenic and of well children: methods, concepts, and some results. *Amer. J. Orthopsychiat., 30*, 247–275.

Becker, W. C. (1956). A genetic approach to the interpretation and evaluation of the process-reactive distinction in schizophrenia. *J. abnorm. soc. Psychol., 53*, 229–236.

—————— (1959). The process-reactive distinction: a key to the problem of schizophrenia. *J. nerv. ment. Dis., 129*, 442–449.

Belknap, I. (1956). *Human problems of a state mental hospital.* New York: McGraw-Hill.

Belknap, I., and H. J. Friedsam (1950). Age and sex categories as sociological variables in the mental disorders of later maturity. *Amer. sociol. Rev., 14*, 367–376.

Benedict, P. E., and I. Jacks (1954). Mental illness in primitive societies. *Psychiatry, 17*, 377–389.

Berelson, B., and G. A. Steiner (1964). *Human behavior: an inventory of scientific findings.* New York: Harcourt, Brace, and World. Pp. 287–289.

Berger, A. (1959). Inconsistency of attitudes in the formation of schizophrenia. Ph.D. dissertation, University of Missouri.

Bleke, R. (1955). Reward and punishment as determiners of reminiscence effects in schizophrenic and normal subjects. *J. Pers., 23*, 479–498.

Bleuler, E. (1950). *Dementia praecox and the group of schizophrenias* (transl. from German ed., 1911). New York: International Univ. Press.

Block, J., and H. Thomas (1955). Is satisfaction with self a measure of adjustment? *J. abnorm. soc. Psychol., 51*, 254–259.

Blue Cross Association (1964). New directions toward community mental health. *Blue Cross Reports*, No. 2.

Boardman, W. K., S. Goldstone, M. L. Reiner, and S. Himmel (1964). Constancy of absolute judgements of size by normals and schizophrenics. *J. abnorm. soc. Psychol., 68*, 346–348.

Bonner, H. (1950). Sociological aspects of paranoia. *Amer. J. Sociol., 56*, 255–262.

Borgatta, E. F., and L. S. Cottrell (1957). Directions for research in group behavior. *Amer. J. Sociol., 63*, 42–48.

Bowen, M., R. H. Dysinger, and B. Basamania (1959). The role of the father in families with schizophrenic patients. *Amer. J. Psychiat., 115*, 1017–1020.

Brouwer, J., and R. R. Brown (1955). The relatives conference in an 'isolated' neuro-psychiatric hospital. *J. psychiat. soc. Work, 24*, 215–219.

Brown, G. W. (1959). The experiences of discharged chronic schizophrenic patients in various types of living groups. *Milbank Mem. Fund Quart., 37*, 105–131.

—————— (1960). Length of hospital stay and schizophrenia: a review of statistical studies. *Acta psychiat. neurolog. Scand., 35*, 414–430.

Brown, G. W., E. M. Monck, G. M. Carstairs, and J. K. Wing (1962). Influence of family life on the course of schizophrenic illness. *Brit. J. prevent. soc. Med., 16*, 55–68.

Buss, H., and P. J. Lang (1965). Psychological deficit in schizophrenia: I. Affect, reinforcement, and concept attainment. *J. abnorm. soc. Psychol., 70*, 2–24.

Caplan, G. (1961). *An approach to community mental health.* New York: Grune and Stratton.

—————— (1964). *Principles of preventive psychiatry.* New York: Basic Books.

Caputo, D. V. (1961). Characteristics of the parents of schizophrenics. Ph.D. dissertation, University of Illinois.

Carlton, M. G. (1965). The pre-admission period and precare programs for the mentally ill: a review of the literature. *Comm. ment. Health J., 1*, 43–54.

Cattell, R. B. (1957). *Personality and motivation structure and measurement.* Yonkers, N.Y.: World.

Caudill, W. (1958). *The mental hospital as a small society.* Cambridge: Harvard Univ. Press.

Cavanaugh, D. K. (1958). Improvement in the performance of schizophrenics on concept formation tasks as a function of motivational change. *J. abnorm. soc. Psychol., 57*, 8–12.

Chapman, L. J. (1958). Intrusion of associative responses into schizophrenic conceptual performance. *J. abnorm. soc. Psychol., 56*, 374–379.

Chapman, L. J., D. Day, and A. Burstein (1961). The process-reactive distinction and prognosis in schizophrenia. *J. nerv. ment. Dis., 133,* 383–391.

Chase, L. S., and S. Silverman (1941). Prognostic criteria in schizophrenia. *Amer. J. Psychiat., 98,* 360–368.

Clark, R. E. (1948). Psychoses, income and occupational prestige. *Amer. J. Sociol., 13,* 325–330.

Clausen, J. A. (1961). Mental disorders. In R. Merton (Ed.), *Contemporary social problems.* New York: Harcourt, Brace, and World. Pp. 127–180.

Clausen, J. A., and M. L. Kohn (1954). The ecological approach in social psychiatry. *Amer. J. Sociol., 60,* 140–149.

―――― (1956). Parental authority behavior and schizophrenia. *Amer. J. Orthopsychiat., 26,* 297–313.

―――― (1959). Relation of schizophrenia to the social structure of a small city. In B. Pasamanick (Ed.), *Epidemiology of mental disorder.* Washington, D.C.: American Association for the Advancement of Science. Pp. 69–94.

Clausen, J. A., and M. R. Yarrow, Eds. (1955). The impact of mental illness on the family. *J. soc. Issues, 11,* 3–67.

Cleveland, S. E. (1960). Body image changes associated with personality reorganization. *J. consult. Psychol., 24,* 256–261.

Cloward, R. A., and L. E. Ohlin (1960). *Delinquency and opportunity.* New York: Free Press.

Cohen, J., and E. L. Struening (1962). Opinions about mental illness in the personnel of two large mental hospitals. *J. abnorm. soc. Psychol., 64,* 349–360.

Cottrell, L. S. (1942). The adjustment of the individual to his age and sex roles. *Amer. sociol. Rev., 7,* 617–620.

Cumming, E., and J. Cumming (1956). Affective symbolism, social norms and mental illness. *Psychiatry, 19,* 77–85.

―――― (1957). *Closed ranks.* Cambridge: Harvard Univ. Press.

Daston, P. G. (1956). Perception of homosexual words in paranoid schizophrenia. *Percept. mot. Skills, 6,* 45–55.

Davis, J. A., H. E. Freeman, and O. G. Simmons (1957). Rehospitalization and performance level among former mental patients. *Soc. Problems, 5,* 37–44.

Davis, R. H., and R. W. Harrington (1957). The effect of stimulus class on the problem solving behavior of schizophrenics and normals. *J. abnorm. soc. Psychol., 54,* 126–128.

Dawber, T. R., F. E. Moore, and V. Mann (1957). Coronary heart disease in the Framingham study. *Amer. J. publ. Health, 47,* 4–23.

Dayton, N. A. (1940). *New facts on mental disorders.* New York: Thomas.

Deasy, L. C., and O. W. Quinn (1955). The wife of the mental patient and the hospital psychiatrist. *J. soc. Issues, 11,* 49–60.

Devereux, G. (1944). The social structure of a schizophrenia ward and its therapeutic fitness. *J. clin. Psychopath., 6,* 231–265.

————— (1949). The social structure of the hospital as a factor in total therapy. *Amer. J. Orthopsychiat., 19,* 492–500.

Diamond, M. D. (1958). Role-taking ability and schizophrenia. *J. clin. Psychol., 14,* 321–324.

Dinitz, S., *et al.* (1958). The ward behavior of psychiatric patients. *Soc. Problems, 6,* 107–115.

Dinitz, S., A. R. Mangus, and B. Pasamanick (1959). Integration and conflict in self-other conceptions as factors in mental illness. *Sociometry, 22,* 44–55.

Dobson, W. R. (1954). An investigation of various factors involved in time perceptions as manifested by different nosological groups. *J. genet. Psychol., 50,* 277–298.

Doering, C. R. (1934). Reliability of observations of psychiatric and related characteristics. *Amer. J. Orthopsychiat., 4,* 249–257.

Dohrenwend, B. P., V. W. Bernard, and C. Kolb (1962). The orientations of leaders in an urban area toward problems of mental illness. *Amer. J. Psychiat., 118,* 683–691.

Downing, J. (1958). Chronic mental hospital dependency as a character defense. *Psychiat. Quart., 32,* 489–499.

Duhl, L. J., Ed. (1963). *The urban condition.* New York: Basic Books.

Dunham, H. W. (1947). Current status of ecological research in mental disorder. *Soc. Forces, 25,* 321–326.

————— (1953). Some persistent problems in the epidemiology of mental disorders. *Amer. J. Psychiat., 109,* 567–575.

Dunham, R. M. (1959). Sensitivity of schizophrenics to parental censure. Ph.D. dissertation, Duke University.

Dunn, W. L., Jr. (1954). Visual discrimination of schizophrenic subjects as a function of stimulus meaning. *J. Pers., 23,* 48–64.

Durkheim, E. (1951). *Suicide* (transl. G. Simpson). Glencoe, Ill.: Free Press.

Eaton, J. W., and R. J. Weil (1953). The mental health of the Hutterites. *Sci. Amer., 189,* 31–37.

————— (1955). *Culture and mental disorders.* New York: Free Press.

Ehrentheil, O. F., and P. B. Jenney (1960). Does time stand still for some psychotics? *Arch. gen. Psychiat., 3,* 1–3.

Eitinger, L. (1959). The incidence of mental disease among refugees in Norway. *J. ment. Sci., 105,* 326–338.

Elinson, J. (1963). Methods of socio-medical research. In H. E. Freeman, S. Levine, and L. G. Reeder (Eds.), *Handbook of medical sociology.* New Jersey: Prentice-Hall. Pp. 423–448.

Eliot, T. D. (1955). Interaction of psychiatric and social theory prior to 1940. In A. M. Rose (Ed.), *Mental health and mental disorder.* New York: Norton. Pp. 18–41.

Elkin, F. (1947). Specialists interpret the case of Harry Holzer. *J. abnorm. soc. Psychol., 42,* 99–111.

Eysenck, H. J. (1961). *Handbook of abnormal psychology, an experimental approach.* New York: Basic Books. Pp. 697–726.

Fairweather, G. W., Ed. (1964). *Social psychology in treating mental illness: an experimental approach.* New York: Wiley.

Faquin, D. R., R. S. Daniels, and P. M. Margolis (1962). The effect of staff leadership roles on patient participation in activity therapy. *Int. J. soc. Psychiat., 8,* 122–128.

Farahmand, S. S. (1961). Personality characteristics and child-rearing attitudes of fathers of schizophrenic patients. Ph.D. dissertation, Washington State University.

Farina, A. (1960). Patterns of role dominance and conflict in parents of schizophrenic patients. *J. abnorm. soc. Psychol., 61,* 31–38.

Farina, A., N. Garmezy, and H. Barry (1963). Relationship of marital status to incidence and prognosis of schizophrenia. *J. abnorm. soc. Psychol., 67,* 624–629.

Faris, R. E. L., and H. W. Dunham (1939). *Mental disorders in urban areas.* Chicago: Univ. of Chicago Press.

Fisher, S. T., B. E. Walker, and D. Sheer (1959). Parents of schizophrenics, neurotics and normals. *Arch. gen. Psychiat., 1,* 149–166.

Flavell, J. H. (1956). Abstract thinking and social behavior in schizophrenia. *J. abnorm. soc. Psychol., 52,* 208–211.

Fleck, S. (1960). Family dynamics and origin of schizophrenia. *Psychosom. Med., 22,* 333–344.

Foote, N. N., and L. S. Cottrell (1955). *Identity and interpersonal competence: a new direction in family research.* Chicago: Univ. of Chicago Press.

Foulds, G. (1955). The reliability of psychiatric and the validity of psychological diagnosis. *J. ment. Sci., 101,* 851–862.

Freeman, H. E. (1965). Social change and the organization of mental health care. *Amer. J. Orthopsychiat., 35,* 717–722.

Freeman, H. E., and R. Gartner (in press). The changing posture of the mental health consortium. *Amer. J. Orthopsychiat.*

Freeman, H. E., and G. G. Kassebaum (1960). The relationship of education and knowledge to opinions about mental illness. *Ment. Hyg., 44,* 42–47.

Freeman, H. E., and C. C. Sherwood (1965). Research in large-scale intervention programs. *J. soc. Issues, 21,* 11–28.

Freeman, H. E., and O. G. Simmons (1958). Mental patients in the community: family settings and performance levels. *Amer. sociol. Rev., 23,* 147–154.

—— (1961). Feelings of stigma among relatives of former mental patients. *Soc. Problems, 8,* 312–321.

—— (1963). *The mental patient comes home.* New York: Wiley.

Freidson, E. (1963). The organization of medical practice. In H. E. Freeman, S. Levine, and L. Reeder (Eds.), *Handbook of medical sociology.* Englewood Cliffs, N.J.: Prentice-Hall. Pp. 299–320.

—— (1965). The concept of deviance and changing concept of rehabilitation. Paper read at Vocational Rehabilitation Administration: Sociological Theory, Research, and Rehabilitation Conference, Carmel, Calif.

Freyhan, F. A. (1958). Eugene Bleuler's concept of the group of schizophrenias at midcentury. *Amer. J. Psychiat., 114,* 769–779.

Fried, M. (1963). Grieving for a lost home. In L. J. Duhl (Ed.), *The urban condition.* New York: Basic Books. Pp. 421–444.

—————— (1964). Transitional functions of working class communities: implications for forced relocation. In M. Kantor (Ed.), *Mobility and mental health.* Princeton: Van Nostrand. Pp. 123–166.

Frumkin, R. M. (1955). Occupation and major mental disorders. In A. M. Rose (Ed.), *Mental health and mental disorders.* New York: Norton. Pp. 136–160.

Fuller, R. G. (1930). Expectation of hospital life and outcome for mental patients on first admission. *Psychiat. Quart., 4,* 295–323.

Gallagher, E. B., D. J. Levinson, and I. Erlich (1957). Some sociopsychological characteristics of patients and their relevance for psychiatric treatment. In M. Greenblatt, D. J. Levinson, and R. H. Williams (Eds.), *The patient and the mental hospital.* New York: Free Press. Pp. 357–380.

Garmezy, N. (1952). Stimulus differentiation by schizophrenic and normal subjects under conditions of reward and punishment. *J. Pers., 21,* 253–276.

Garmezy, N. A., H. R. Clark and C. Stockney (1958). Child rearing attitudes of mothers and fathers as reported by schizophrenic and normal patients. *J. abnorm. soc. Psychol., 63,* 176–182.

Gelfand, S., and L. P. Ullmann (1961). Change in opinion about mental illness associated with psychiatric clerkship training. *Int. J. soc. Psychiat., 7,* 292–298.

Gerard, D. L., and L. G. Houston (1953). Family setting and the social ecology of schizophrenia. *Psychiat. Quart., 27,* 90–101.

Gerard, D. L., and J. Siegel (1950). The family background of schizophrenia. *Psychiat. Quart., 24,* 47–73.

Gergen, K. J., and E. E. Jones (1963). Mental illness, predictability and affective consequences as stimulus factors in person perception. *J. abnorm. soc. Psychol., 67,* 95–104.

Gilbert, D. C., and D. J. Levinson (1956). Ideology, personality and institutional policy in the mental hospital. *J. abnorm. soc. Psychol., 53,* 263–271.

—————— (1957). Role performance, ideology and personality in the mental hospital aides. In M. Greenblatt, D. J. Levinson, and R. H. Williams (Eds.), *The patient and the mental hospital.* New York: Free Press. Pp. 197–208.

Ginzberg, E., J. K. Anderson, S. W. Ginsburg, and J. L. Herma (1959). *The ineffective soldier: patterns of performance.* Vol. 3. New York: Columbia Univ. Press.

Giovannoni, J. M., and L. P. Ullmann (1963). Characteristics of schizophrenics associated with posthospital employment. Paper read at meeting of Western Psychological Association, Santa Monica.

—————— (1963). Conceptions of mental health held by psychiatric patients. *J. clin. Psychol., 19,* 398–400.

Goffman, E. (1961). *Asylums.* Garden City, N.Y.: Doubleday.

—————— (1963). *Stigma: notes on the management of spoiled identity.* Englewood Cliffs, N.J.: Prentice-Hall.

Goldhamer, H. (1959). Review of A. B. Hollingshead and F. C. Redlich, "Social Class and Mental Illness." *Amer. sociol. Rev., 24,* 579–581.

Goldhamer, H., and A. Marshall (1953). *Psychosis and civilization.* New York: Free Press.

Goldstein, K. (1946). Methodological approach to the study of schizophrenic thought disorder. In J. S. Kasanin (Ed.), *Language and thought in schizophrenia.* Berkeley: Univ. of California Press. Pp. 17–41.

Goodstein, L. D., W. M. Guertin, and H. L. Blackburn (1961). Effects of social motivational variables on choice reaction time of schizophrenics. *J. abnorm. soc. Psychol., 62,* 24–27.

Greenblatt, M., R. H. York, and E. L. Brown (1955). *From custodial to therapeutic patient care in mental hospitals.* New York: Russell Sage Foundation.

Grob, S., Ed. (1963). *The community social club and the returning mental patient.* Proceedings of a conference, Framingham, Mass.

Groth, C., H. Gordon, and F. Dietrich (1960). The problem of unvisited patients in a mental hospital. *Ment. Hyg., 44,* 710–717.

Gruenberg, E. M. (1954). The epidemiology of mental disease. *Sci. Amer., 190,* 38–42.

Guertin, W. H. (1958). Are differences in schizophrenic symptoms related to the mother's attitudes toward child-rearing? *J. abnorm. soc. Psychol., 63,* 440–442.

Gurel, L. (1964). Correlates of psychiatric hospital effectiveness. Paper read at 72nd annual convention of American Psychological Association, Los Angeles.

Gurin, G., J. Veroff, and S. Feld (1960). *Americans view their mental health.* New York: Basic Books.

Gwaltney, H. O. (1958). Reference group identification as a variable in convalescence and chronicity of mental hospital patients. Ph.D. dissertation, University of Missouri.

Haley, J. (1959). An interactional description of schizophrenia. *Psychiatry, 22,* 321–332.

———— (1960). Observation of the family of the schizophrenic. *Amer. J. Orthopsychiat., 30,* 460–467.

Hammer, M., and E. Leacock (1961). Source material on the epidemiology of mental illness. In J. Zubin (Ed.), *Field studies in the mental disorders.* New York: Grune and Stratton. Pp. 418–487.

Hardt, R. H., and S. J. Feinhandler (1959). Social class and mental hospitalization prognosis. *Amer. sociol. Rev., 24,* 815–822.

Hare, E. H. (1956). Family setting and the urban distribution of schizophrenia. *J. ment. Sci., 102,* 753–760.

Hare, E. H., and G. K. Shaw (1965). *Mental health on a new housing estate.* London: Oxford Univ. Press.

Havener, P. H., and C. E. Izard (1962). Unrealistic self enhancement in paranoid schizophrenics. *J. consult. Psychol., 26,* 65–68.

Health Information Foundation (1960). *Hospitalized mental illness in the United States.* Foundation Pamphlet Series, No. 9, pp. 1–8.

Heilbrun, A. B. (1960). Perception of maternal child rearing attitudes in schizophrenics. *J. consult. Psychol., 24,* 169–173.

Henry, J. (1954). The formal social structure of a psychiatric hospital. *Psychiatry,* *17,* 139–151.

Hicks, J. M., and F. E. Spaner (1962). Attitude change and mental hospital experience. *J. abnorm. soc. Psychol., 65,* 112–120.

Hollingshead, A. B., and F. C. Redlich (1958). *Social class and mental illness.* New York: Wiley.

Horner, R. F. (1961). A search for important stimulus variables in the early family relationships of schizophrenic patients. Ph.D. dissertation, University of Tennessee.

Hunt, R. G. (1960). Social class and mental illness: some implications for clinical theory and practice. *Amer. J. Psychiat., 116,* 1065–1069.

Hunter, M., C. Schooler, and H. E. Spohn (1962). The measurement of characteristic patterns of ward behavior in chronic schizophrenics. *J. consult. Psychol., 26,* 281–294.

Hyde, R. W., L. V. Kingsley, and R. M. Chisholm (1944). Studies in medical sociology. *New Eng. J. Med., 231,* 571–577.

Jaco, E. G. (1954). The social isolation hypothesis and schizophrenia. *Amer. sociol. Rev., 19,* 567–577.

———— (1957). Attitudes toward and incidence of mental disorder: a research note. *Southwest soc. Sci. Quart., 34,* 27–38.

———— (1959). Mental health of the Spanish-American in Texas. In M. K. Opler (Ed.), *Culture and mental health.* New York: Macmillan. Pp. 467–488.

———— (1960). *The social epidemiology of mental disorders.* New York: Russell Sage Foundation.

Jahoda, M. (1958). *Current concepts of positive mental health.* New York: Basic Books.

Jellinek, E. (1939). Some principles of psychiatric classification. *Psychiatry, 2,* 161–165.

Jenkins, R. L., and L. Gurel (1959). Predictive factors in early release. *Ment. Hosp., 10,* 11–14.

Jones, M. (1953). *The therapeutic community.* New York: Basic Books.

Kantor, R. E., and C. L. Winder (1959). The process-reactive continuum: theoretical proposal. *J. nerv. ment. Dis., 129,* 429–434.

———— (1961). Schizophrenia: correlates of life history. *J. nerv. ment. Dis., 132,* 221–226.

Kaplan, A., and L. Wolf (1954). The role of the family in relation to the institutionalized mental patient. *Ment. Hyg., 38,* 634–639.

Kaplan, B., R. B. Reed, and W. Richardson (1956). A comparison of the incidence of hospitalized and non-hospitalized cases of psychosis in two communities. *Amer. sociol. Rev., 21,* 472–479.

Karras, A. (1962). The effects of reinforcement and arousal on the psychomotor performance of chronic schizophrenics. *J. abnorm. soc. Psychol., 65,* 104–111.

King, G. F., S. G. Armitage, and J. R. Tilton (1960). A therapeutic approach to schizophrenics of extreme pathology: an operant interpersonal method. *J. abnorm. soc. Psychol., 61,* 276–286.

Klerman, G. (1961). Historical baselines for the evaluation of maintenance drug therapy of discharged psychiatric patients. In M. Greenblatt *et al.* (Eds.), *Mental patients in transition.* Springfield, Ill.: Charles C. Thomas. Pp. 287–301.

Klerman, G. L., M. R. Sharaf, M. Holzman, and D. J. Levinson (1960). Sociopsychological characteristics of resident psychiatrists and their use of drug therapy. *Amer. J. Psychiat., 117,* 111–117.

Kohn, M. S., and J. A. Clausen (1955). Social isolation and schizophrenia. *Amer. sociol. Rev., 20,* 265–273.

Kornhauser, A. (1965). *Mental health of the industrial worker.* New York: Wiley.

Kramer, M., H. Goldstein, R. H. Israel, and N. A. Johnson (1955). *A historical study of the disposition of first admissions to a state mental hospital.* Washington, D.C.: Government Printing Office. Public Health Monograph No. 32.

———— (1956). *Application of life table methodology to the study of mental hospital populations.* Washington, D.C.: American Psychiatric Association.

Kramer, M., and E. S. Pollack (1958). Problems in the interpretation of trends in the population movement of the public mental hospitals. *Amer. J. publ. Health, 48,* 1003–1019.

Kramer, M. E., E. S. Pollack, and R. W. Redick (1961). Studies of the incidence and prevalence of hospitalized mental disorders in the United States: current status and future goals. In P. H. Hoch and J. Zubin (Eds.), *Comparative epidemiology of the mental disorders.* New York: Grune and Stratton. Pp. 56–100.

Landis, E., and J. D. Page (1938). *Modern society and mental disease.* New York: Farrar and Rinehart.

Lane, R. C., and J. L. Singer (1959). Familial attitudes in paranoid schizophrenics and normals from two socioeconomic classes. *J. abnorm. soc. Psychol., 59,* 328–339.

Lang, P. J., and A. H. Buss (1965). Psychological deficit in schizophrenia: II. Interference and activation. *J. abnorm. soc. Psychol., 70,* 77–106.

Lanzkron, J., and W. Wolfson (1958). Prognostic value of perceptual distortion of temporal orientation in chronic schizophrenics. *Amer. J. Psychiat., 114,* 744–746.

LaPouse, R., M. A. Monk, and M. Terris (1956). The drift hypothesis and socioeconomic differentials in schizophrenia. *Amer. J. publ. Health, 46,* 978–986.

Leacock, E. (1957). Three social variables and the occurrence of mental disorder. In A. H. Leighton, J. A. Clausen, and R. N. Wilson (Eds.), *Explorations in social psychiatry.* New York: Basic Books. Pp. 308–340.

Lee, E. S. (1963). Socioeconomic and migration differentials in mental disease. *Milbank Mem. Fund Quart., 41,* 249–268.

Lehrman, N. S. (1961). Do our hospitals help make acute schizophrenics chronic? *Dis. nerv. Syst., 22,* 1–5.

Leighton, A. H. (1959). *My name is legion.* New York: Basic Books.

———— (1960). *An introduction to social psychiatry.* Springfield, Ill.: Charles C. Thomas.

Lemert, E. M. (1948). An exploratory study of mental disorders in a rural problem area. *Rural Sociol., 13,* 47–64.

———— (1951). *Social Pathology.* New York: McGraw-Hill.

_____ (1962). Paranoia and the dynamics of exclusion. *Sociometry, 25*, 2–20.

Lemkau, P. V., and G. M. Crocetti (1958). Vital statistics of schizophrenia. In L. Bellak (Ed.), *Schizophrenia: a review of the syndrome.* New York: Logas Press. Pp. 64–81.

_____ (1962). An urban population's opinion and knowledge about mental illness. *Amer. J. Psychiat., 118,* 692–700.

Lemkau, P. V., C. Tietze, and M. Cooper (1943). A survey of statistical studies on the prevalence and incidence of mental disorder in sample populations. *Publ. Health Reports, 58,* 1090–1127.

Lerner, M., and G. W. Fairweather (1963). Social behavior of chronic schizophrenics in supervised and unsupervised work groups. *J. abnorm. soc. Psychol., 67,* 219–225.

Leventhal, A. M. (1959). The effects of diagnostic category and reinforcer on learning without awareness. *J. abnorm. soc. Psychol., 59,* 162–166.

Lewis, A. J. (1942). Incidence of neurosis in England under war conditions. *Lancet,* 2, 175–181.

_____ (1953). Health as a social concept. *Brit. J. Sociol., 4,* 109–124.

Lidz, T., A. R. Cornelison, S. Fleck, and D. Terry (1957a). The environment of schizophrenic patients: II. Marital schism and marital skew. *Amer. J. Psychiat., 114,* 241–248.

_____ (1957b). The intrafamilial environment of the schizophrenic patient: I. The father. *Psychiatry, 20,* 329–342.

_____ (1958). The interfamilial environment of the schizophrenic patient. *Amer. J. Orthopsychiat., 28,* 764–777.

Lidz, T., and S. Fleck (1959). Schizophrenia, human integration and the role of the family. In D. Jackson (Ed.), *The etiology of schizophrenia.* New York: Basic Books. Pp. 323–344.

Lidz, T., B. Parker, and A. Cornelison (1956). The role of the father in the family environment of the schizophrenic patient. *Amer. J. Psychiat., 113,* 126–132.

Lindemann, E. (1944). Symptomatology and management of acute grief. *Amer. J. Psychiat., 101,* 141–148.

_____ (1950). *Minor disorders in epidemiology of mental disorders.* New York: Milbank Memorial Fund.

_____ (1960). Psycho-social factors as stressor agents. In J. M. Tanner (Ed.), *Stress and psychiatric disorder.* Oxford: Blackwell Scientific Publications.

Lindemann, J. E., G. W. Fairweather, G. B. Stone, R. S. Smith, and I. T. London (1959). The use of demographic characteristics in predicting length of neuropsychiatric hospital stay. *J. consult. Psychol., 23,* 482–491.

Locke, B. Z., M. Kramer, and B. Pasamanick (1960). Mental diseases in the senium at mid-century: first admissions to Ohio state public mental hospitals. *Amer. J. publ. Health, 50,* 998–1012.

Lorr, M., R. Wittman, and W. Shanberger (1951). An analysis of the Elgin prognostic scale. *J. clin. Psychol., 7,* 260–263.

Love, A. G., and C. B. Davenport (1920). Defects found in drafted men. Prepared for the War Department under the direction of the Surgeon General. Washington, D.C.

Lovinger, E. (1956). Perceptual contact with reality in schizophrenia. *J. abnorm. soc. Psychol., 52,* 87–91.

Lu, Yi-Chuang (1962). Contradictory parental expectations in schizophrenia. *Arch. gen. Psychiat., 6,* 219–234.

Mabry, J. H. (1962). Statistical notes on some British 'open' mental hospitals. *Int. J. soc. Psychiat., 8,* 19–31.

McGaughran, L. S., and L. J. Moran (1956). Conceptual level vs. conceptual area analysis of object-sorting behavior of schizophrenic and nonpsychiatric groups. *J. abnorm. soc. Psychol., 52,* 43–50.

———— (1957). Differences between schizophrenic and brain-damaged groups in conceptual aspects of object-sorting. *J. abnorm. soc. Psychol., 54,* 44–49.

McGinnies, E., and J. Adornetto (1952). Perceptual defense in normal and in schizophrenic observers. *J. abnorm. soc. Psychol., 47,* 833–837.

McKeown, J. E. (1950). The behavior of parents of schizophrenics, neurotics, and normal children. *Amer. J. Sociol., 56,* 175–179.

MacMahon, B., T. F. Pugh, and T. Ipsen (1960). *Epidemiologic method.* Boston: Little, Brown.

McReynolds, P. (1960). Anxiety, perception, and schizophrenia. In P. Jackson (Ed.), *The etiology of schizophrenia.* New York: Basic Books. Pp. 248–295.

———— (1961). Response duration to novel and familiar stimuli as related to degree of schizophrenic withdrawal. *Amer. Psychologist, 16,* 427.

———— (1962). What is schizophrenia?—some ideas and some data. Paper presented at meetings of California State Psychological Association, Los Angeles.

Malamud, W., and N. Render (1939). Course and prognosis in schizophrenia. *Amer. J. Psychiat., 95,* 1039–1057.

Malzberg, B. (1936). Marital status in relation to the prevalence of mental illness. *Psychiat. Quart., 10,* 245–261.

———— (1940). *Social and biological aspects of disease.* New York: State Hospital Press.

———— (1952). Rates of discharge and rates of mortality among first admissions to the New York civil state hospitals. *Ment. Hyg., 36,* 104–120.

———— (1955). Mental disease among the native and foreign-born populations of New York state, 1939, 1941. *Ment. Hyg., 39,* 545–563.

———— (1956a). Education and mental disease in New York state. *Ment. Hyg., 40,* 177–195.

———— (1956b). Mental disease among native and foreign-born Negroes in New York state. *J. Negro Educ., 25,* 175–181.

———— (1956c). Mental disease in relation to economic status. *J. nerv. ment. Dis., 123,* 257–261.

———— (1959). Mental disease among Negroes: an analysis of first admissions in New York state, 1949–1951. *Ment. Hyg., 43,* 422–459.

Malzberg, B., and E. S. Lee (1956). *Migration and mental disease.* New York: Social Science Research Council.

Manis, M., P. Houts, and J. Blake (1963). Beliefs about mental illness as a function of psychiatric status and psychiatric hospitalization. *J. abnorm. soc. Psychol.*, 67, 226–233.

Marks, J., J. Stouffacher, and C. Lyle (1963). Predicting outcome in schizophrenia. *J. abnorm. soc. Psychol.*, 3, 117–127.

Maslow, A. H. (1954). *Motivation and personality.* New York: Harper.

Mechanic, D., and E. H. Volkart (1961). Stress, illness behavior, and the sick role. *Amer. sociol. Rev.*, 26, 51–58.

Mehlman, B. (1952). The reliability of psychiatric diagnosis. *J. abnorm. soc. Psychol.*, 47, 577–578.

Merton, R. K. (1949). *Social theory and social structure.* Glencoe, Ill.: Free Press.

Merton, R. K., and A. S. Kitt (1957). Reference groups. In L. A. Coser and B. Rosenberg, (Eds.), *Sociological theory.* New York: Macmillan. Pp. 264–271.

Meyer, H. J., and E. F. Borgatta (1958). *An experiment in mental patient rehabilitation.* New York: Russell Sage Foundation.

Middleton, J. (1953). Prejudices and opinions of mental hospital employees regarding mental illness. *Amer. J. Psychiat.*, 110, 133–138.

Milgram, N. A. (1961). Role-taking in female schizophrenic patients. *J. clin. Psychol.*, 17, 409–411.

Miller, S. M., and E. G. Mishler (1959). Social class, mental illness and American psychiatry. *Milbank Mem. Fund Quart.*, 37, 174–199.

Mishler, E. G., and N. A. Scotch (1963). Sociocultural factors in the epidemiology of schizophrenia: a review. *Psychiatry*, 26, 315–351.

Mishler, E. G., and N. E. Waxler (1963). Decision process in psychiatric hospitalization. *Amer. sociol. Rev.*, 28, 576–587.

Moriarty, D., and S. L. Kates (1962). Concept attainment of schizophrenics on materials involving social approval and disapproval. *J. abnorm. soc. Psychol.*, 65, 355–364.

Morrow, W. R., and A. J. Robins (1961). Family relations and social recovery of psychotic mothers. *J. Health hum. Behav.*, 5, 14–24.

Moustakos, D. E. (1965). True experience and the self. In Moustakos (Ed.), *The self.* New York: Harper. Pp. 3–14.

Murray, E. J., and M. Cohen (1959). Mental illness and social organization in ward groups. *J. abnorm. soc. Psychol.*, 58, 48–55.

Myers, D., and M. Goldfarb (1962). Psychiatric appraisals of parents and siblings of schizophrenic children. *Amer. J. Psychiat.*, 118, 902–908.

Myers, J. K., L. L. Bean, and M. P. Pepper (1964). Social class and mental illness: a ten year follow up of psychiatric patients. *Conn. Med.*, 28, 355–362.

Myers, J. K., and B. H. Roberts (1959). *Family and class dynamics in mental illness.* New York: Wiley.

Myers, J. K., and L. Shaffer (1954). Social stratification and psychiatric practice. *Amer. sociol. Rev.*, 19, 206–219.

Nameche, G., M. Waring, and D. Ricks (1964). Early indicators of outcome in schizophrenia. *J. nerv. ment. Dis.*, 139, 232–240.

Neiditch, S. J. (1963). Differential response to failure in hospital and non-hospital groups. *J. abnorm. soc. Psychol., 66,* 449–453.

Nolan, W. J. (1917). Occupation and dementia praecox. *N.Y. State Hosp. Quart., 3,* 127–154.

Norris, V. A. (1956). A statistical study of the influence of marriage on the hospital care of the mentally sick. *J. ment. Sci., 102,* 467–486.

Nunnally, J. C. (1961). *Popular conceptions of mental health.* New York: Holt, Rinehart, and Winston.

O'Connor, N., G. M. Carstairs, and K. Rawnsley (1957). Communication in a mental hospital population. *Int. J. soc. Psychiat., 3,* 183–187.

Odegaard, O. (1932). Emigration and insanity: a study of mental disease among the Norwegian born population of Minnesota. *Acta psychiat. neurolog. Suppl., 4.*

_____ (1936). Emigration and mental health. *Ment. Hyg., 20,* 546–553.

_____ (1946). Marriage and mental disease: a study in social psycho-pathology. *J. ment. Sci., 92,* 35–39.

_____ (1953). New data on marriage and mental disease: the incidence of psychosis in the widowed and the divorced. *J. ment. Sci., 99,* 778–785.

_____ (1956). The incidence of psychoses in various occupations. *Int. J. soc. Psychiat., 2,* 85–104.

Olshansky, S., S. Grob, and I. T. Malamud (1958). Employer's attitudes and practices in the hiring of ex-mental patients. *Ment. Hyg., 42,* 391–401.

Olson, G. W. (1958). Failure and subsequent performance of schizophrenics. *J. abnorm. soc. Psychol., 57,* 310–314.

Orr, W. F., R. B. Anderson, M. P. Martin, and D. F. Philpot (1955). Factors influencing discharge of female patients from a state mental hospital. *Amer. J. Psychiat., 111,* 576–582.

Parsons, T. (1951). *The social system.* Glencoe, Ill.: Free Press.

Pasamanick, B. (1961). A survey of mental disease in urban population: IV. An approach to total prevalence rates. *Arch. gen. Psychiat., 5,* 151–155.

Pasamanick, B., S. Dinitz, and M. Lefton (1959). Psychiatric orientation and its relation to diagnosis and treatment in a mental hospital. *Amer. J. Psychiat., 116,* 127–132.

Pasamanick, B., M. Lefton, J. Simpson, and S. Dinitz (n.d.). Decision-making in a mental hospital: real, perceived, and ideal. (Mimeo)

Pasamanick, B., and L. Ristine (1961). Differential assessment of posthospital psychological functioning: evaluations by psychiatrist and relatives. *Amer. J. Psychiat., 117,* 40–46.

Pearl, D., and P. S. D. Berg (1963). Time perception and conflict arousal in schizophrenia. *J. abnorm. soc. Psychol., 66,* 332–338.

Pearlin, L. I. (1962). Sources of resistance to change in a mental hospital. *Amer. J. Sociol., 67,* 325–334.

Pearlin, L., and M. Rosenberg (1962). Nurse-patient social distance in a mental hospital. *Amer. sociol. Rev., 27,* 56–65.

Perrow, E. (1964). Hospitals: goals, structure, and technology. In J. G. March (Ed.), *Handbook of organizations.* Chicago: Rand McNally. Pp. 223–256.

Perrucci, R. (1963). Social distance and stratification on a psychiatric ward. *Amer. sociol. Rev., 28,* 951–962.

Phillips, D. L. (1953). Rejection: a possible consequence of seeking help for mental disorders. *Amer. sociol. Rev., 28,* 963–972.

———— (1964). Rejection of the mentally ill. *Amer. sociol. Rev., 29,* 679–687.

Phillips, L. (1953). Case history data and prognosis in schizophrenia. *J. nerv. ment. Dis., 117,* 515–525.

Phillips, L., and M. S. Rabinovitch (1958). Social role and patterns of symptomatic behaviors. *J. abnorm. soc. Psychol., 57,* 181–186.

Pine, F., and D. J. Levinson (1957). Two patterns of ideology, role conception, and personality among hospital aides. In M. Greenblatt, D. Levinson, and R. H. Williams (Eds.), *The patient and the mental hospital.* New York: Free Press. Pp. 209–218.

Pollack, H. M., and W. J. Nolan (1929). Mental disease in cities, villages, and rural districts of New York state, 1915–1920. *State Hosp. Quart., 7.*

Pugh, T. F., and B. MacMahon (1962). *Epidemiologic findings in United States mental hospital data.* Boston: Little, Brown.

Query, J. M. N. (1961). Premorbid adjustment and family structure: a comparison of selected rural and urban schizophrenic men. *J. nerv. ment. Dis., 133,* 333–338.

Rabin, A. I. (1957). Time estimation of schizophrenics and non-psychotics. *J. clin. Psychol., 13,* 88–90.

Raphael, E. E. (1964). Community structure and acceptance of psychiatric aid. *Amer. J. Sociol., 64,* 340–358.

Rapoport, R. (1963). Normal crises and family structure and mental health. *Family Proc., 2,* 68–80.

Rapoport, R. N. (1960). *Community as doctor.* London: Tavistock Publications.

Raush, H. L. (1952). Perceptual constancy in schizophrenia: I. Size constancy. *J. Pers., 21,* 176–187.

Rawnsley, K., and J. B. Loudon (1962). Factors influencing the referral of patients to psychiatrists by general practitioners. *Brit. J. prevent soc. Med., 16,* 174–182.

Rennie, T. A. C., and L. Srole (1956). Social class prevalence and distribution of psychosomatic conditions in an urban population. *Psychosom. Med., 18,* 449–456.

Robertson, J. W. (1903). Prevalence of insanity in California. *Amer. J. Insanity, 60,* 81–82.

Robinson, N. (1958). Paired-associate learning by schizophrenic subjects under conditions of personal and impersonal reward and punishment. Ph.D. dissertation, Stanford University.

Robinson, W. S. (1950). Ecological correlations and the behavior of individuals. *Amer. sociol. Rev., 15,* 351–357.

Rodnick, E. H., and N. Garmezy (1957). An experimental approach to the study of motivation in schizophrenia. In M. R. Jones (Ed.), *Nebraska symposium on motivation, 1957.* Lincoln: Univ. of Nebraska Press. Pp. 37–49.

Roe, A. (1949). Integration of personality theory and clinical practice. *J. abnorm. soc. Psychol., 44,* 36–41.

Rogers, A. (1958). The self concept in schizophrenia. *J. clin. Psychol., 14,* 365–366.

Rogler, L. H., and A. B. Hollingshead (1965). *Trapped: families and schizophrenia.* New York: Wiley.

Rose, A. M., and H. R. Stub (1955). Summary of studies on the incidence of mental disorders. In A. M. Rose (Ed.), *Mental health and mental disorder.* New York: Norton. Pp. 87–117.

Rosenbaum, G., W. R. Mackavey, and J. L. Grisell (1957). Effects of biological and social motivation on schizophrenic reaction time. *J. abnorm. soc. Psychol., 54,* 364–368.

Rosengren, W. R. (1959). Symptom manifestations as a function of situational press: a demonstration in socialization. *Sociometry, 22,* 113–123.

Ryckoff, I., J. Day, and L. C. Wynne (1959). Maintenance of stereotyped roles in the families of schizophrenics. *A. M. A. Arch. Psychiat., 1,* 93–98.

Sampson, H., S. L. Messinger, and R. D. Towne (1964). *Schizophrenic women: studies in marital crises.* New York: Atherton.

Schooler, C., and H. E. Spohn (1960). Social interaction on a ward of chronic schizophrenics. *Int. J. soc. Psychiat., 6,* 115–119.

Schroeder, C. W., and T. A. Beegle (1955). Suicide: an instance of high rural rates. In A. M. Rose (Ed.), *Mental health and mental disorder.* New York: Norton.

Schwartz, C. G., M. S. Schwartz, and A. H. Stanton (1951). A study of need-fulfillment on a mental hospital ward. *Psychiatry, 14,* 223–242.

Schwartz, C. G. (1957). Perspectives on deviance—wives' definitions of their husbands' mental illness. *Psychiatry, 20,* 275–291.

Schwartz, M. S. (1957). What is a therapeutic milieu? In M. Greenblatt, D. J. Levinson, and R. H. Williams (Eds.), *The patient and the mental hospital.* New York: Free Press. Pp. 130–144.

Schwartz, M. S., and C. G. Schwartz (1964). *Social approaches to mental patient care.* New York: Columbia Univ. Press.

―――― (1968). Mental health. In D. L. Sills (Ed.), *International encyclopedia of the social sciences.* Vol. 10. Crowell-Collier and Macmillan. Pp. 215–221.

Scott, J. F., and H. E. Freeman (1963). The one night stand in mental health education. *Soc. Problems, 10,* 277–284.

Scott, W. A. (1958a). Research definitions of mental health and mental illness. *Psychol. Bull., 55,* 29–45.

―――― (1958b). Social psychological correlates of mental illness and mental health. *Psychol. Bull., 55,* 65–87.

Senf, R., P. E. Huston, and B. D. Cohen (1956). The use of comic cartoons for the study of social comprehension in schizophrenia. *Amer. J. Psychiat., 113,* 45–51.

Sherman, M. (1964). The responsiveness of chronic schizophrenics to social reinforcement as a function of subject variables, situation, and performance criterion. Ph.D. dissertation, Stanford University.

Shoben, E. J. (1957). Toward a concept of the normal personality. *Amer. Psychologist, 12*, 183–189.

Siegel, N. H. (1962). Characteristics of patients in psychoanalysis. *J. nerv. ment. Dis., 135*, 155–158.

Siegel, N. H., and M. Fink (1962). The disposition of applications for psychotherapy in an outpatient clinic. *Soc. Casework,* 545–547.

Simmons, O. G. (1965). Work in mental illness. New York: Wiley.

Simmons, O. G., J. A. Davis, and K. Spencer (1956). Interpersonal strains in release from a mental hospital. *Soc. Problems, 4*, 21–28.

Simon, W., and R. D. Wirt (1961). Prognostic factors in schizophrenia. *Amer. J. Psychiat., 117*, 887–890.

Sinnett, E. R., and D. B. Hanford (1962). The effects of patients' relationships with peers and staff on their psychiatric treatment programs. *J. abnorm. soc. Psychol., 64*, 151–154.

Smith, M. B. (1959). Research strategies toward a conception of positive mental health. *Amer. Psychologist, 14*, 673–681.

――――― (1961). Mental health reconsidered: a special case of the problem of values in psychology. *Amer. Psychologist, 16*, 299–306.

Srole, L., *et al.* (1962). *Mental health in the metropolis.* New York: McGraw-Hill.

Stanton, A. H., and M. S. Schwartz (1954). *The mental hospital.* New York: Basic Books.

Star, S. (1955). The public's ideas about mental illness. Paper presented at annual meeting of National Association for Mental Health, Indianapolis.

Steffey, R. A., and W. C. Becker (1961). Measurement of the severity of disorder in schizophrenia by means of the Holzman inkblot test. *J. consult. Psychol., 25*, 555.

Stein, L. (1957). Social class gradient in schizophrenia. *Brit. J. prevent. soc. Med., 11*, 181–195.

Stouffer, S. A., A. A. Lumsdaine, M. H. Lumsdaine, R. M. Williams, Jr., M. B. Smith, I. L. Janis, S. A. Starr, and L. S. Cottrell, Jr. (1949). *The American soldier: conflict and its aftermath.* Princeton: Princeton Univ. Press.

Strauss, A., L. Schatzman, R. Bucher, D. Ehrlich, and M. Sabshen (1964). *Psychiatric ideologies and institutions.* London: Free Press.

Sussman, M. B. (1965). Rehabilitation occupations. Paper read at Vocational Rehabilitation Administration: Sociological Theory, Research, and Rehabilitation Conference, Carmel, Calif.

Szasz, T. S. (1961). The myth of mental illness: foundations of a theory of personal conduct. New York: Harper and Row.

Tietze, C., P. Lemkau, and M. Cooper (1941). Schizophrenia, manic-depressive psychosis and social-economic status. *Amer. J. Sociol., 47*, 167–175.

Tourney, G., R. Senf, H. W. Dunham, R. S. Glen, and J. S. Gottleib (1961). The effect of resocialization techniques on chronic schizophrenic patients. *Amer. J. Psychiat., 116*, 993–1000.

Ullmann, L. P. (1958). On the relationship between amount of hospitalization and self-assertion. Paper read at American Psychological Association, Washington, D.C.

Ullmann, L. P., and L. Gurel (1964). Size, staffing and psychiatric hospital effectiveness. *Arch. gen. Psychiat., 11*, 360–367.

Ullmann, L. P., and J. M. Giovannoni (1964). The development of a self-report measure of the process reactive continuum. *J. nerv. ment. Dis., 138*, 38–42.

Ullmann, L. P., and L. Krasner, Eds. (1965). *Case studies in behavior modification.* New York: Holt, Rinehart, and Winston.

Weakland, J. H. (1960). The 'double-bind' hypothesis of schizophrenia and three-party interaction. In D. D. Jackson (Ed.), *The etiology of schizophrenia.* New York: Basic Books. Pp. 373–388.

Webb, W. W. (1955). Conceptual ability of schizophrenics as a function of threat of failure. *J. abnorm. soc. Psychol., 50*, 221–224.

Weckowicz, T. E. (1957). Size constancy in schizophrenic patients. *J. ment. Sci., 103*, 475–486.

―――― (1964). Shape constancy in schizophrenic patients. *J. abnorm. soc. Psychol., 68*, 177–183.

Weckowicz, T. E., R. Sommer, and R. Hall (1958). Distance constancy in schizophrenic patients. *J. ment. Sci., 104*, 1174–1182.

Weinstein, A. D., S. Gladstone, and W. K. Boardman (1958). The effect of recent and remote frames of reference on the temporal judgements of schizophrenic patients. *J. abnorm. soc. Psychol., 57*, 241–244.

Whatley, C. D. (1959). Social attitudes toward discharged mental patients. *Soc. Problems, 6*, 313–320.

―――― (1963). Status, role and vocational continuity of discharged mental patients. *J. Health hum. Behav., 4*, 105–112.

Williams, R. H. (1953). Psychiatric rehabilitation in the community. *Publ. Health Reports, 68*, 1231–1236.

Wilner, D. M., R. P. Walkley, M. N. Glasser, and M. Tayback (1958). The effects of housing quality on morbidity. *Amer. J. publ. Health, 48*, 1607–1615.

Wilson, D. C., and E. M. Lantz (1957). The effects of culture change on the Negro race in Virginia as indicated by a study of state hospital admissions. *Amer. J. Psychiat., 114*, 25–32.

Winder, C. L. (1960). Some psychological studies of schizophrenia. In D. Jackson (Ed.), *The etiology of schizophrenia.* New York: Basic Books. Pp. 191–247.

Winder, C. L., and R. E. Kantor (1958). Rorschach maturity scores of the mothers of schizophrenics. *J. consult. Psychol., 22*, 438–440.

Wing, J. K. (1961). A simple and reliable subclassification of chronic schizophrenia. *J. ment. Sci., 107*, 862–875.

―――― (1962). Institutionalism in mental hospitals. *Brit. J. soc. clin. Psychol., 1*, 38–51.

Wing, J. K., and G. W. Brown (1961). Social treatment of chronic schizophrenia: a comparative survey of three mental hospitals. *J. ment. Sci., 107*, 847–861.

Wing, J. K., J. Denham, and A. B. Munro (1959). Duration of stay in hospital of patients suffering from schizophrenia. *Brit. J. prevent. soc. Med., 13,* 145–148.

Wing, J. K., and R. K. Freudenberg (1961). The responses of severely ill chronic schizophrenic patients to social stimulation. *Amer. J. Psychiat., 118,* 311–322.

Wittman, P. A. (1944). A scale for measuring prognosis in patients. *Elgin State Hosp. Papers, 4,* 20–33.

Woodward, J. L. (1951). Changing ideas on mental illness and its treatment. *Amer. sociol. Rev., 16,* 443–454.

Wright, D. J., S. Goldstone, and W. K. Boardman (1962). Time judgment and schizophrenia: step interval as a relevant contextual factor. *J. Psychol., 54,* 33–38.

Yap, P. M. (1951). Mental diseases peculiar to certain cultures: a survey of comparative psychiatry. *J. ment. Sci., 97,* 313–327.

Yarrow, M. R., C. G. Schwartz, H. S. Murphy, and L. C. Deasy (1955). The psychological meaning of mental illness in the family. *J. soc. Issues, 11,* 12–24.

Zahn, T. P. (1959). Acquired and symbolic affective value as determinants of size estimation in schizophrenic and normal subjects. *J. abnorm. soc. Psychol., 58,* 39–47.

Zigler, E., and L. Phillips (1961). Psychiatric diagnosis and symptomatology. *J. abnorm. soc. Psychol., 63,* 69–75.

Zimet, C. N., and H. J. Fine (1959). Perceptual differentiation and two dimensions of schizophrenia. *J. nerv. ment. Dis., 129,* 435–441.

Zubin, J., and C. Windle (1954). Psychological prognosis of outcome in the mental disorders. *J. abnorm. soc. Psychol., 49,* 272–281.

Zuckerman, M., M. Oltean, and I. Monashkin (1958). The parental attitudes of mothers of schizophrenics. *J. consult. Psychol., 22,* 307–310.

Author Index

Subject Index

mental illness and, 661–662, 670–671
middle-class, 383, 389
nonalignment, 585–586
normlessness, 202
partisanship, 438
political, 381, 384–385, 389, 405, 408, 413,
424, 432, 439
production, 224–227
conformity to, 224–226
direction of, 224–227
rational-independent, 439–440, 442
rationality, 5–6, 8, 12–13, 22
regional, 386
religion and, 638, 642, 644, 647–648
of restraint, 96
restriction of output, 226
shared, 586
voting, 342–344
in work groups, 209–210, 221, 223–227,
236
Novelty, religious drug use and, 646–647
Nuclear weapons and warfare, 540–552, 560,
572–573, 581, 584–585
Nurturance and imitation, 135

Obedience
modeling and, 137–138
prejudice and, 38–39
religious, 607, 609, 613, 638
Observation Schedule and Record (OScAR),
502
Occupation
mental illness and, 670, 678–679
political behavior, 331, 356, 398, 400–405,
411–412, 422
prestige, 404, 422
Occupational contact, interethnic, 51–54
Oedipus complex, religion and, 605, 643, 645
Oligopoly, 269, 294–297
"Omnicompetent" citizen, 324
"Open frontier," 586
Open-mindedness *vs.* closed-mindedness, 387,
389, 642–643
Operant-interpersonal therapy, 697
Operations research, 302
Opinion; *see also* Attitudes *and* Belief
climate of political, 386, 388–390, 398
formation and change, political, 332–333,
338–348, 359, 368–373, 396, 414–415,
428–429, 431, 439–440, 442–443; *see
also* Political behavior
long-term changes, 386
without information, 365

public, and international relations, 569, 573,
575–577, 580, 585
Optimality, Pareto, 296
Optimism
political behavior and, 423–424
religion and, 638–639, 643
"Optimization" solution, 279–280
Organism-environment interaction, 490
Organizational behavior, 289–291; *see also*
Industrial social psychology
Organizational theory, 289–291
size, 304–305
Orientation
action, 4, 22–23, 36, 47
candidate, 319–320, 419, 439
cognitive, 37
emotional, 9–10, 23, 36
ethnic, 17–21, 24, 26, 39, 51
evaluative, 19
fantasy, 121, 123, 136
ideological, 349
issue, 319–320
"policy," 4, 52
political, 378
reality, 121, 123
status, 38–39
value, 36
Originality, education and, 494
Orthodoxy, religious, 610–611, 614, 617–618,
620, 629, 631, 639–641
Otis Alpha test, 475
Outguessing, 296, 298
Overcompensation, 206, 218–220
Overexclusion *vs.* underexclusion, and mental
illness, 689
Overidealization of the President, 417–419,
432
Overprotection, 682–683
"Overreward," 206
"Own forces," 233, 236

Pacification, 583–584, 587
Pacifism, 571
unilateral, 538
Panic, 95
Paranoia, 684
international relations and, 547–548, 580
paranoid-schizophrenic, 684, 687–688
teaching and, 512–513
Parent
discipline and prejudice, 38–39
influence of, and ethnic relations, 27–28
norms, 27

Cumulative Author and Subject Indexes

for Volumes I through V

Kantor, M., V: 707

Kantor, R. E., V: 675, 683, 693, 709, 718

Kanungo, R., II: 458, 495, 517

Kanungo, R. N., III: 191, 293

Kanzer, M., II: 628, 647, 682

Kanzer, P., III: 500, 588

Kaplan, A., II: 403, 408, 425, 444, 532, 592, 597, 598, 601, 653, 657, 660, 667, 673, 682, 683. III: 196, 295. V: 697, 709

Kaplan, A. M., II: 632, 679

Kaplan, B., I: 297, 309, 313. III: 382, 386, 454, 564, 572, 863, 872, 913, 916. IV: 397, 402, 420, 423, 427, 444, 453, 454, 479, 493-495, 497, 499, 501, 504, 505. V: 679, 709

Kaplan, D., II: 608, 648, 658, 678, 679

Kaplan, H. B., III: 10, 11, 44

Kaplan, M., III: 827, 848

Kaplan, M. A., V: 584, 595

Kaplan, W. K., II: 581, 593

Kappauf, W. E., II: 198, 199

Karacan, I., III: 249, 275

Kardiner, A., I: 104, 168, 273, 279, 281, 282, 286, 294-297, 303, 313. III: 452, 453, 475, 477, 480, 572, 575. IV: 326, 344, 348, 349, 359, 384, 403, 419, 421, 424, 425, 427, 432, 436, 443, 449-451, 454, 457, 460, 461, 464-468, 478, 480, 490, 499. V: 556, 595

Karelitz, R., III: 572

Karelitz, S., III: 463, 572

Karlin, S., I: 239, 243. V: 312

Karp, S. A., III: 393, 463, 587, 665

Karpf, F. B., I: 4, 74, 290, 313

Karras, A., V: 688, 709

Karsten, A., I: 438, 483

Karsten, Anitra, V: 218, 260

Karwoski, T. F., III: 862, 913

Kasanin, J. S., V: 108

Kasl, S. V., II: 393, 395, 396, 444

Kassebaum, G. G., V: 706

Kastenbaum, R., III: 164, 293

Katagiri, A., V: 182, 187, 190

Katahn, M., III: 107, 127

Kates, S. L., III: 595, 656. V: 39, 67, 713

Katkovsky, W., II: 519. III: 544, 545, 553, 563, 572

Kato, H., V: 190

Katona, G., I: 12, 74, 303, 313. II: 528, 592. V: 281, 282, 284, 286, 287, 311

Katori, H., III: 327, 387

Katz, B., III: 327, 391

Katz, D., I: 63, 74, 81, 168, 607. II: 267, 444, 447, 551, 584, 592, 676, 743, 758, 772. III: 141, 155, 157, 158, 160, 185, 186, 196, 197, 201, 210, 247, 254, 256, 271, 293, 306, 309, 598, 656. IV: 216, 279. V: 7, 8, 12, 22, 23, 45, 67, 74, 214, 228, 240, 241, 260, 449

Katz, E., I: 607. III: 179, 229-231, 234, 281, 301, 618, 655. IV: 111, 174, 195. V: 85, 118, 123, 142-146, 149-151, 153, 154, 161-167, 172, 176, 180, 185, 189, 285, 305, 307, 312, 341, 348, 350, 450

Katz, E. W., II: 392, 396, 426, 427, 444, 450

Katz, F. E., V: 353, 424, 450

Katz, I., II: 772. III: 624, 656. IV: 22, 24, 94, 227, 228, 279. V: 488, 530

Katz, J. J., III: 671, 675, 690, 692-697, 716, 727, 742, 784, 786, 788, 794

Katz, L., II: 464, 470-474, 506, 515, 517.

III: 76, 88, 95, 127.

IV: 112, 113, 191, 195

Katz, P., III: 497, 499, 572

Katz, R., II: 387, 412, 445

Kauffman, P. E., II: 392, 450, 631, 682. III: 399, 447

Kaufman, H. J., V: 185

Kaufman, W. C., V: 38, 39, 67

Kaufmann, H., I: 159, 168, 607. V: 127-129, 185, 199, 209, 221, 260

Kauranne, U., III: 400, 442, 445

Kaustler, D. H., III: 107, 127. V: 222, 260

Kautsky, J. N., V: 552, 595

Kavolis, V., IV: 355, 403

Kay, E., V: 201, 237, 263, 280, 295, 310, 311, 314

Kayatani, M., IV: 47, 100

Kaye, D., III: 56, 127, 131, 185, 198, 201, 206, 292

Kaye, H., III: 34, 44

Kayser, J., II: 617, 655, 682

Kearl, B., II: 641, 682

Keats, J., III: 873

Kecskemeti, P., I: 293, 313

Keedy, T. C., V: 629, 654

Keen, R., III: 192, 309

Keene, J., V: 610-613, 627, 632, 641, 654

Skeels, D., IV: 355, 412
Skinner, B. F., I: 90-95, 101, 102, 123, 126, 128, 137, 139, 141, 150, 153, 154, 157, 165, 166, 175, 310, 338, 374, 407. II: 76, 480, 605, 624, 647, 689. III: 30, 48, 60, 68, 70, 133, 465, 466, 631, 663, 671, 710, 783, 792. IV: 36, 99, 296, 322
Skinner, G. W., V: 581, 599
Skinner, J., IV: 355, 412
Skipper, J. K., Jr., V: 343, 447
Skolnick, A., III: 582
Slack, C. W., III: 323, 325, 363, 364, 387, 392
Slater, C., I: 499, 506, 566
Slater, C. W., II: 577, 593. V: 265
Slater, G., III: 44
Slater, P. E., I: 558. IV: 160, 186
Sleator, M. D., III: 700, 788
Sliosberg, S., I: 438, 487. III: 824, 851
Slobin, D. I., III: 705, 712, 721, 722, 725, 755, 792, 793
Slotkin, J. S., IV: 387, 405, 412
Sluckin, W., IV: 617, 618, 642
Smedslund, J., I: 333, 407. III: 458, 582
Smelser, N., II: 506, 523
Smelser, N. J., I: 43, 78, 319, 609. III: 474-476, 582, 584. IV: 322, 422, 505, 507, 532, 538, 555-558, 560-562, 581, 590, 591, 609. V: 290, 313
Smelser, W. T., I: 319, 524, 525, 566. III: 474-476, 582, 584. IV: 28, 99, 220, 281, 422, 505
Smith, A., I: 11, 24, 25, 27, 78. V: 313
Smith, A. A., III: 8, 9, 45
Smith, A. G., III: 781
Smith, A. J., II: 507, 508, 523. III: 626, 663. IV: 39, 99, 225, 226, 281
Smith, B. B., II: 91, 201
Smith, B. L., II: 683
Smith, B. L. R., V: 580, 599
Smith, B. O., V: 503, 509, 535
Smith, C., III: 29, 48. V: 102, 153, 188
Smith, C. A. B., II: 161
Smith, C. H., V: 192
Smith, C. R., V: 36, 73
Smith, C. S., III: 684, 685, 793
Smith, E., III: 527, 567. V: 130, 183
Smith, E. C., Jr., IV: 26, 92
Smith, E. D., III: 812, 846
Smith, E. E., I: 387, 407, 503, 566. II: 370, 450. III: 192, 238, 308, 314. IV: 40, 99

Smith, F., III: 679, 712, 784, 789, 793
Smith, F. T., III: 253, 308. V: 50, 73
Smith, G. H., III: 392
Smith, H. L., III: 760, 793
Smith, H. L., Jr., III: 688, 793
Smith, H. P., V: 38, 39, 73
Smith, H. T., III: 539, 541, 582
Smith, J. G., IV: 342, 409
Smith, L., III: 304. V: 142, 191
Smith, L. H., II: 396, 407, 417, 424, 433, 434, 447
Smith, M., II: 503, 523. V: 5, 73, 646, 657
Smith, M. B., I: 204, 239. II: 371, 438, 564, 595. III: 94, 133, 141, 153, 155, 157, 158, 160, 184, 188, 189, 201, 202, 210, 241, 262, 263, 265, 271, 282, 308, 309. V: 4, 22, 35, 36, 73, 599, 642, 657, 660, 663, 664, 717
Smith, M. E., III: 723, 793
Smith, M. G., IV: 588, 609
Smith, M. S., II: 314, 349, 355, 665, 666, 667, 676, 677, 682, 685-687, 689, 690
Smith, M. W., III: 909. IV: 423, 441, 497, 499-502, 504
Smith, P., I: 306, 318
Smith, P. A., V: 455
Smith, P. B., II: 456, 485, 523
Smith, P. C., V: 198, 235, 261, 265
Smith, R. B., II: 298, 322, 332, 352
Smith, R. L., III: 18, 44
Smith, R. T., IV: 365, 412
Smith, R. S., V: 711
Smith, S., IV: 138
Smith, W., III: 22, 48
Smith, W. A. S., IV: 17, 93
Smith, W. D., II: 476, 523
Smith, W. I., II: 733, 773
Smith, W. L., IV: 529, 605
Smith, W. N., II: 198, 199
Smith, W. P., III: 419, 447
Smith, W. R., IV: 348, 412
Smith, W. S., III: 202, 308
Smock, C. D., III: 89, 90, 133
Smoke, K. L., III: 711, 793
Smoke, W. H., IV: 53, 54, 101
Smoker, P., V: 562, 599
Smucker, O., II: 465, 466, 523
Smythe, D. W., II: 599, 613, 618, 687, 689. V: 84, 116, 192
Snell, J. L., I: 181, 185, 230, 238, 241
Snider, M., III: 203, 308
Snodgrass, Q. C., II: 675

Subject Index

Abbreviation, as a duplicatory error, II: 429, 434

Abbreviation, psycholinguistic phenomenon of, III: 758-760

self-, III: 596, 601-602

Ability

mental or intellectual, V: 472-473, 482-484, 489, 496, 499-501, 504, 507, 510-512, 516-517

role-taking, V: 688

Abnormal-normal continuum, V: 664-665, 670

Absence rates, V: 200-202, 226, 253

"Absorbing situation" strategy, in observation, II: 375

Acceleration, in crowds, IV: 530

Acceptance

absolute, V: 604-648

of decisions, V: 233-237, 239

leadership and, IV: 239-240, 251

need for, IV: 438. V: 503

in organizations, V: 201, 211, 224

social, ethnic relations and, V: 15, 19-20, 50, 53-54

Acceptance behavior, specific vs. global, III: 626

Acceptance-rejection indices, II: 465

Accessibility, emotional, III: 637

Accessibility, of information in interviewing, II: 535-536, 539-543, 548, 559-563, 573-578

memory problems, II: 541-543, 548, 560-563

in question formulation, II: 559-563

"Accident" manipulations, II: 45, 59-60

Accident proneness, and sociometric status, II: 491

Accommodation, V: 490

developmental, III: 456

play and, III: 837-838

Accommodative strategies of coalition formation, IV: 135-136

Accomplices, use of, II: 378

Acculturation, IV: 325, 340, 357, 367, 369-375, 389, 486, 490-491

"controlled," V: 677

cultural stress and, IV: 383-391

Accuracy

interpersonal, III: 408, 415, 417, 428-429, 433

measurement of, III: 411-414

specificity vs. generality of, III: 412-414

stereotype vs. differential, III: 412-413, 433

Accuracy, of interview data, II: 542-549

Achievement, IV: 81, 125, 135, 220, 251, 367-369, 370, 436-437, 447, 456, 467, 473, 477

aggression and, III: 548

anxiety, V: 493

concepts, I: 416-417

Retention, selective, V: 89, 101, 161-162
Reticular formation, III: 104
Reticular system and learning, I: 88
Retreatism, IV: 300, 352, 369-370
Revenge
  masochistic, IV: 389
  suicide of, IV: 389-390
Reversal
  role, IV: 365
  status, IV: 365
Revisionism, I: 280-284, 291-292
Revitalistic movements, IV: 369, 372-374
Revolution, V: 55-56
Revolution and Development of International Relations (RADIR) studies, in content analysis, II: 598, 610, 612, 646-647, 664
Reward, II: 323, 328. IV: 48-49
  of aggression, IV: 328-329
  allocation, V: 205
  anxiety reduction as, II: 759
  coalition formation and, IV: 129, 132-134
  as a component of Dollard and Miller's social learning theory, I: 137-139
  contingent, V: 211, 213
  and cost theory of social interaction, I: 107-108
  differential, V: 205-206
  drive, and authoritarian leadership, IV: 258
  economic behavior and, V: 273, 276-279, 284-285, 289
  economic, and leadership, IV: 248, 251, 259
  education and, V: 483, 493-496
  externally mediated, and performance, V: 208-214, 216, 222
  function, V: 279
  and groups, IV: 116-118, 120-122, 124-125
  immediate vs. deferred, V: 122-123, 491
  insufficient reward, I: 370-376
  "intangible," V: 276-277
  internally mediated, and performance, V: 214-223
  international relations and, V: 542, 559, 586-587
  levels in organizations, V: 204-208, 221
  mental illness and, V: 686, 688-689, 697, 699
  monetary, V: 273, 276, 284-285

mutual fate control, I: 151
national character and, IV: 433, 435, 460, 470, 472-473
"overreward" and "underreward," V: 206
portrayed, and mass media, V: 100, 122-123, 126, 129, 136-138
power, IV: 166, 168, 174, 177, 180-184. V: 237
reciprocal, I: 132-133
relative vs. absolute, V: 206
religious, V: 609
reward-investment index, V: 205
reward power, I: 157
rewards and punishers, I: 154
satisfaction and, V: 199-201, 204-207
secondary, II: 757
self-persuasion and, I: 374-375
social organization and, IV: 618
social power and, IV: 162-165
structure, and mixed-motive groups, IV: 38-40
theory of biosocial rewards, II: 757
in work groups, V: 223, 237
Rewards, III: 54, 64, 71-72, 76-79, 100-101
  attitudes toward others and, III: 55-59
  cost and, III: 72, 77-80, 83-86, 632-635
  deprivation and, III: 60-61
  humor and, III: 806
  vs. incentive, III: 72
  minimal, and compliance, III: 237-239
  personality, and, III: 593-594
  play and, III: 818-819, 843
  power, III: 73
  socialization and, III: 468, 495, 500-501, 503, 507, 529-530, 532, 535, 541-542, 550-551, 553
  symbolic, III: 501
Rhetoric of risk vs. rhetoric of caution, IV: 82
Ricardian theory, V: 270-271
Ridicule, national character and, IV: 472-473
Right-wing radicalism, V: 394, 399-414
Rigidity, V: 38, 622, 640-643
  political, V: 387-388
Rigidity, and tension systems, I: 437
Ring structure, of crowds, IV: 518-521
Riot, IV: 509-510, 516-517, 522-523, 531, 535-539, 541, 547, 549, 551, 570-577, 601-602
  "outsider," IV: 552